The LaTeX Companion

Third Edition – Part II

Addison-Wesley Series on Tools and Techniques for Computer Typesetting

This series focuses on tools and techniques needed for computer typesetting and information processing with traditional and new media. Books in the series address the practical needs of both users and system developers. Initial titles comprise handy references for LaTeX users; forthcoming works will expand that core. Ultimately, the series will cover other typesetting and information processing systems, as well, especially insofar as those systems offer unique value to the scientific and technical community. The series goal is to enhance your ability to produce, maintain, manipulate, or reuse articles, papers, reports, proposals, books, and other documents with professional quality.

Ideas for this series should be directed to frank.mittelbach@latex-project.org. Send all other feedback to the publisher at informit.com/about/contact_us or via email to community@informit.com.

Series Editor

Frank Mittelbach
Technical Lead, LaTeX Project, Germany

Editorial Board

Jacques André
Irisa/Inria-Rennes, France (Ret.)

Barbara Beeton
Editor, TUGboat, USA

David Brailsford
University of Nottingham, UK

Peter Flynn
University College, Cork, Ireland (Ret.)

Matthew Hardy
Adobe, USA

Leslie Lamport
Microsoft, USA

Chris Rowley
Open University, UK (Ret.)

William Robertson
The University of Adelaide, Australia

Steven Simske
Colorado State University, USA

Series Titles

Guide to LaTeX, Fourth Edition by Helmut Kopka and Patrick W. Daly

The LaTeX Companion, Third Edition by Frank Mittelbach, with Ulrike Fischer and contributions by Javier Bezos, Johannes Braams, and Joseph Wright

The LaTeX Graphics Companion, Second Edition by Michel Goossens, Frank Mittelbach, Sebastian Rahtz, Denis Roegel, and Herbert Voß
Reprinted 2022 by Lehmanns Media, Berlin

The LaTeX Web Companion by Michel Goossens and Sebastian Rahtz

Also from Addison-Wesley and New Riders:

LaTeX: A Document Preparation System, Second Edition by Leslie Lamport

Computers & Typesetting, Volumes A–E by Donald E. Knuth

The Type Project Book: Typographic projects to sharpen your creative skills & diversify your portfolio by Nigel French and Hugh D'Andrade

The LaTeX Companion
Third Edition – Part II

Frank Mittelbach
LaTeX Project, Mainz, Germany

Ulrike Fischer
LaTeX Project, Bonn, Germany

With contributions by
Javier Bezos, Johannes Braams, and Joseph Wright

✦Addison-Wesley

Boston • Columbus • New York • San Francisco • Amsterdam • Cape Town
Dubai • London • Madrid • Milan • Munich • Paris • Montreal • Toronto • Delhi • Mexico City
São Paulo • Sydney • Hong Kong • Seoul • Singapore • Taipei • Tokyo

Cover illustration by Lonny Garris/Shutterstock
Photo of Sebastian Rahtz courtesy of Leonor Barroca
All other photos taken by the authors

Book design by Frank Mittelbach
Typeset with LaTeX in Lucida Bright at 8.47pt/11.72pt

For information about buying this title in bulk quantities, or for special sales opportunities, please contact our corporate sales department at corpsales@pearsoned.com or (800)382-3419.

For government sales inquiries, please contact governmentsales@pearsoned.com. For questions about sales outside the United States, please contact intlcs@pearson.com.

Visit us on the Web: informit.com/aw

Library of Congress Control Number: 2022921608

The examples can be downloaded from https://ctan.org/pkg/tlc3-examples.

Part I:	ISBN-13:	978-0-13-465894-0
	ISBN-10:	0-13-465894-9
Part II:	ISBN-13:	978-0-201-36300-5
	ISBN-10:	0-201-36300-3
Part I+II:	ISBN-13:	978-0-13-816648-9
(bundle)	ISBN-10:	0-13-816648-X

1 2023

Pearson's Commitment to Diversity, Equity, and Inclusion

Pearson is dedicated to creating bias-free content that reflects the diversity of all learners. We embrace the many dimensions of diversity, including but not limited to race, ethnicity, gender, socioeconomic status, ability, age, sexual orientation, and religious or political beliefs.

Education is a powerful force for equity and change in our world. It has the potential to deliver opportunities that improve lives and enable economic mobility. As we work with authors to create content for every product and service, we acknowledge our responsibility to demonstrate inclusivity and incorporate diverse scholarship so that everyone can achieve their potential through learning. As the world's leading learning company, we have a duty to help drive change and live up to our purpose to help more people create a better life for themselves and to create a better world.

Our ambition is to purposefully contribute to a world where:

- Everyone has an equitable and lifelong opportunity to succeed through learning.

- Our educational products and services are inclusive and represent the rich diversity of learners.

- Our educational content accurately reflects the histories and experiences of the learners we serve.

- Our educational content prompts deeper discussions with learners and motivates them to expand their own learning (and worldview).

While we work hard to present unbiased content, we want to hear from you about any concerns or needs with this Pearson product so that we can investigate and address them.

- Please contact us with concerns about any potential bias at https://www.pearson.com/report-bias.html.

This picture of Sebastian was taken 2007 in Cinque Terre.

I dedicate this edition to all my friends in the TeX world and in particular
to the memory of my good friend Sebastian Rahtz (1955–2016),
with whom I spent many happy hours discussing parenting, literature,
LaTeX, and other important aspects of life [78].

Contents

Part I

List of Figures

List of Tables

Foreword, Part II

I'm back! Readers who have already read the first part of this comprehensive third edition of *The LATEX Companion* may recall that I wrote the Foreword to that book. Those who have not seen that piece might want to start there to find my perspective on this unique resource, which I was proud to publish in its first two editions. You will also see there my praise for its authors: An incredible amount of work goes into these Companions, sorting and compiling for every LATEX user what is most useful to know, and what should be avoided, defining thereby the current state of the system. If you are serious about learning and using LATEX to format your writing, you could not be better advised than to keep both these new volumes close at hand.

One passing reference I made in my first Foreword, given the reaction to it in some quarters, bears immediate attention: digital rectal examinations. If you missed that reference, you probably are wondering how it could possibly relate to LATEX typesetting. Some of the people asked to review the Foreword were apparently equally puzzled. In context, I think that the example made a good point, but the reviewers, for whatever reason, seemed unable to get the procedure out of their mind. As a result, they missed my broader observation about the use of LATEX in surprisingly diverse fields, and in unusual places. If only those reviewers could have seen the initial draft, in which I described in greater detail — well, never mind; that is all behind us now!

I actually have very little more to say in this second Foreword beyond what I said in the first, except to emphasize that, especially if you are new, or relatively new, to LATEX, you probably should begin with the first of the two volumes that comprise this revision. Honestly, I think that the only reason Frank asked, or allowed, me to write it was to maintain a certain symmetry, each book thus having an apparent beginning and end, even if, logically, they're really one book in the guise of two. Given the growth in LATEX use, and the ongoing development of contributions to the system itself, I see future authors, likewise intent on being definitive, projecting a yet-unknown number of volumes.

With little otherwise to relate, you might at least be interested to know that I offered Frank cover ideas for the new books — too late, he informed me, and I think I heard a sigh of relief. One idea suggested a parody of Leda and the Swan. It pictured a bespectacled swan hunched over a computer trying to resolve some onetime typesetting issue, while an obviously bored, half-naked Leda lay nearby on a luxurious bed, hoping eventually to give birth to LaTeX (not sure how to fit Leslie into that story). I know, given the swan's divinity, why the need for help with typesetting — or any interest in writing, for that matter? I guess I recalled the large graffiti I saw years ago on a Metro station wall in Paris: "God is studying French, and having trouble with the subjunctive."

Anyway, I suspect Frank was concerned that potential users might think that LaTeX is hard to learn and use — which it is not. Rather, it is just so rich with tools and techniques, and so many are available, you simply need help in knowing which are the most valuable — the very purpose of this revision. Just flip through the pages to see what I am talking about! Perhaps Frank was also concerned that people would imagine that the swan had become a new LaTeX mascot. There have already been, what, lions, ducks, frogs — and do you remember the first Companion, known as the doggie book (proof that my cover ideas work)? Now we see there is a hummingbird.

So I proposed a second cover, a scene that might suggest the origins and nature of *The LaTeX Companion* as an indispensable aid to a successful and more pleasurable typesetting experience. Picture, then, another snowy Alpine scene (as first illustrated in the aforementioned doggie book), this time with an old lion and lioness, seen from the back, relaxing in adjacent bathtubs. A hummingbird is seen perched on a rescue keg lying in the snow, under the banner, "LaTeX IS HERE", or, like *Seinfeld* characters seeking serenity, "LaTeX NOW!". Receding pawprints add a nostalgic touch. As with the swan cover, of course, given the timing, I had to ask Frank to consider this second idea for the next edition — and this time, I am sure I heard a scream.

I had better end there and let you get into the content that truly makes the third edition a necessary addition to every LaTeX user's library. There is only so much that a mythical swan, revitalized lions, and, yes, digital rectal examinations can do for you — well, the swan and the lions, in any case.

Peter S. Gordon
Publishing Partner (Ret.)

Author note from Frank: I cannot believe I approved these Forewords! ☺

Preface, Part II

Divide each difficulty into as many parts
as is feasible and necessary to resolve it.
René Descartes (1595–1650)

Taking Descartes's advice to heart, we decided to split this edition of *The LaTeX Companion* into two parts of roughly a thousand pages each. Thus, we are now at the midpoint in describing the fascinating features of today's LaTeX and we start with a chapter on text and symbol fonts, which is completely new — ten years ago nearly none of these fonts could have been used with LaTeX at all. The same is true for Chapter 12 on math font setups, the discussions of mathtools, biblatex, upmendex, new developments in babel, the new features of the LaTeX format covered in Appendix A, and various other new packages discussed in the upcoming chapters.

Otherwise, given that this is really just the second part of "one book in the guise of two", as Peter put it in his Foreword, there is nothing new to reveal if you have read the Preface to the first part.

Thus, instead of repeating anything from there, all we are going to do is to repeat the section on conventions used in this book, because that is probably helpful to have close at hand if you have the second part open on your desk.

Frank Mittelbach

November 2022

Working with this book

Below we give an overview of the structure of this edition, the typographic conventions used, and ways to use the examples given. Because of its size, this edition is typeset as two separate physical volumes (Part I and Part II), which has some implications on the presentation.

Chapters are numbered consecutively across both volumes, but we restart the page numbers in Part II to keep the numbers readable. As a consequence, cross-references to pages come in two forms: if they are to a page in the same volume, they read "see page 127", but if they refer to a page in the other volume, they look like "see page →I 253" or similar.

The main index, which contains entries for the whole edition, is replicated at the end of each physical volume to improve its usability and make it easier to work with. To identify the volume each page number in an entry refers to, the start of each volume sequence is identified by →I and →II, respectively.

What's where

Following is a summary of the subject areas covered by each chapter and appendix. In principle, all chapters can be read independently because, when necessary, pointers are given to where necessary supplementary information can be found in other parts of the edition.

Part I—

Chapter 1 gives a short introduction to the LaTeX system and this book.

Chapter 2 discusses document structure markup, including sectioning commands and cross-references as well as document source management.

Chapter 3 describes LaTeX's basic typesetting commands for the paragraph level. It also contains a section on packages offering document development support.

Chapter 4 looks at the typesetting of larger structures, such as lists and code displays, and shows how to work with multiple columns.

Chapter 5 explains how to influence the visual layout of the pages in various ways.

Chapter 6 shows how to lay out material tables, on single and multiple pages.

Chapter 7 surveys floating material and caption formatting.

Chapter 8 covers image loading and manipulation and the generation of portable graphics. It also offers an extensive overview on the tcolorbox package and an introduction to the world of tikz.

Chapter 9 discusses in detail LaTeX's Font Selection Scheme and shows how to access new fonts in 8-bit and Unicode TeX engines.

Part II—

Chapter 10 gives a comprehensive list with examples of high-quality text and symbol fonts available out of the box to LaTeX users today.

Chapter 11 reviews mathematical typesetting, particularly the packages supported by the American Mathematical Society.

Chapter 12 describes aspects of font usage in math formulas and offers a comparison between available font setups with 8-bit and Unicode TeX engines.

Chapter 13 discusses the support for using LaTeX with multiple languages, particularly the babel system.

Chapter 14 discusses the preparation and typesetting of an index with a focus on the programs *MakeIndex* and upmendex.

Chapter 15 explains how to create and use bibliographical databases in conjunction with LaTeX, and how to generate typeset bibliographies according to publishers' or style guide expectations.

Chapter 16 describes LaTeX's support for the different citation systems for bibliographical references in common use and how to produce multiple bibliographies by chapter and topic.

Chapter 17 shows how to document LaTeX packages and classes and how to use such files provided by others. It also covers setting up a development and testing environment and working with version control, which is useful for essentially every project.

Appendix A reviews how to handle and manipulate the basic LaTeX programming structures and how to produce class and package files.

Appendix B discusses how to trace and resolve problems and explains common error and warning messages and their likely causes.

Appendix C shows where to go beyond this book if that is ever needed, e.g., how to obtain the packages and systems described, how to access help or take an online course, and much more.

Some of the material covered in the book may be considered "low-level" TeX that has no place in a book about LaTeX. However, to the authors' knowledge, much of this information has never been described in the "LaTeX" context even though it is important. Moreover, we do not think that it would be helpful simply to direct readers to books like *The TeXbook*, because most of the advice given in books about "plain TeX" either is not directly applicable to LaTeX or, worse, produces subtle errors if used with LaTeX. In some sections we have, therefore, tried to make the treatment as self-contained as possible by providing all the information about the underlying TeX engine that is relevant and useful within the LaTeX context.

Typographic conventions

It is essential that the presentation of the material immediately conveys its function in the framework of the text. Therefore, we present below the typographic conventions used in this book.

Commands, environments, packages, …   Throughout the text, LaTeX command and environment names are set in monospaced type (e.g., `\caption`, `enumerate`, `\begin{tabular}`), while names of packages, class files, and programs are in sans serif type (e.g., article). Commands to be typed by the user on a computer terminal are shown in monospaced type and are underlined, e.g., showing how to call the LaTeX development format on the command line:

> pdflatex-dev ⟨*file*⟩

Syntax descriptions   The syntax of the more complex LaTeX commands is presented inside a rectangular box. Command arguments are shown in italic type:

> ┌──┐
> │ `\titlespacing*{`*cmd*`}{`*left-sep*`}{`*before-sep*`}{`*after-sep*`}[`*right-sep*`]` │
> └──┘

In LaTeX, optional arguments are denoted with square brackets, and the star indicates a variant form (i.e., is also optional), so the above box means that the `\titlespacing` command can come in four different incarnations:

> `\titlespacing{`*cmd*`}{`*left-sep*`}{`*before-sep*`}{`*after-sep*`}`
> `\titlespacing{`*cmd*`}{`*left-sep*`}{`*before-sep*`}{`*after-sep*`}[`*right-sep*`]`
> `\titlespacing*{`*cmd*`}{`*left-sep*`}{`*before-sep*`}{`*after-sep*`}`
> `\titlespacing*{`*cmd*`}{`*left-sep*`}{`*before-sep*`}{`*after-sep*`}[`*right-sep*`]`

For some commands, not all combinations of optional arguments and/or star forms are valid. In that case the valid alternatives either are explained in the text or are explicitly shown together, as, for example, in the case of LaTeX's sectioning commands:

> ┌──┐
> │ `\section*{`*title*`}`   `\section[`*toc-entry*`]{`*title*`}` │
> └──┘

Here the optional *toc-entry* argument can be present only in the unstarred form; thus, we get the following valid possibilities:

> `\section{`*title*`}`   `\section*{`*title*`}`   `\section[`*toc-entry*`]{`*title*`}`

Code examples …   Lines containing examples with LaTeX commands are indented and are typeset in a monospaced type at a size somewhat smaller than that of the main text:

```
\addtocontents{lof}{\protect\addvspace{10pt}}
\addtocontents{lot}{\protect\addvspace{10pt}}
```

… with output …   However, in the majority of cases we provide complete examples together with the output they produce side by side:

```
\usepackage{ragged2e}
```

The right column shows the input text to be treated by LaTeX with preamble material shown in blue. In the left column one sees the result after typesetting.

```
The right column shows the input text to be treated
by \LaTeX{} with preamble material shown in blue.
In the left column one sees the result after
typesetting.
```

preface-I

Note that all preamble commands are always shown in blue in the example source.

In case several pages need to be shown to prove a particular point, (partial) "page spreads" are displayed and usually framed to indicate that we are showing material from several pages.

... with several pages ...

1 A TEST	1 A TEST
1 A test	page that might get reused over and over again.
Some text for our page that might get reused over and over again.	
Some text for our	
Page 6 of 7	Page 7 of 7

reface-II-2

```
\usepackage{fancyhdr,lastpage}
\pagestyle{fancy}
\fancyhf{} % --- clear all fields
\fancyhead[RO,LE]{\leftmark}
\fancyfoot[C]{Page \thepage\
               of \pageref{LastPage}}
% \sample defined as before

\section{A test}
\sample \par \sample
```

A number of points should be noted here:

- We usually arrange the examples to show pages 6 and 7 so that a double spread is displayed.

- We often use the command \sample to hold a short piece of text to keep the example code short: the definition for this command is either given as part of the example or, as indicated here, repeated from a previous example — which in this case is simply a lie because \sample was not defined earlier. In other examples we make use of lipsum or kantlipsum to generate sample text.

- The output may or may not show a header and footer. In the above case it shows both. Because the "pages" are very small but show the real output from the given input on the right, there are often deficiencies in line breaking, etc.

For large examples, where the input and output cannot be shown conveniently alongside each other, the following layout is used:

... with large output ...

```
\usepackage{ragged2e,kantlipsum}  \RaggedRight
This is a wide line, whose input commands and output result cannot
be shown nicely in two columns. \kant[1][1-3]
```

Depending on the example content, some additional explanation might appear between input and output (as in this case). Then the output is displayed:

eface-II-3

This is a wide line, whose input commands and output result cannot be shown nicely in two columns. As any dedicated reader can clearly see, the Ideal of practical reason is a representation of, as far as I know, the things in themselves; as I have shown elsewhere, the phenomena should only be used as a canon for our understanding. The paralogisms of practical reason are what first give rise to the architectonic of practical reason. As will easily be shown in the next section, reason would thereby be made to contradict, in view of these considerations, the Ideal of practical reason, yet the manifold depends on the phenomena.

... or with lines indicating the margins

Chapter 11 shows yet another example format, where the margins of the example are explicitly indicated with thin blue vertical rules. This is done to better show the precise placement of displayed formulas and their tags in relation to the text margins.

$$(1) \qquad (a+b)^2 = a^2 + 2ab + b^2$$

```
\usepackage[leqno]{amsmath}
\begin{equation} (a+b)^2 = a^2+2ab+b^2 \end{equation}
```

preface-I

Color usage in this book

Some examples make use of color commands, e.g., \color or \textcolor, but because the book is printed only with two colors, it is not possible to do them justice. The approach we took is that all colors appear as shades of gray except for blue, which we changed to produce the "lightblue" that is used as a second color in the book. Thus, all examples actually deploy the declarations as shown in the next example if they use color, but to save space none of them is shown elsewhere.

Black blue
red green
yellow blue
bluish

```
\usepackage{xcolor}
\definecolor{blue}{cmyk}{1,0.56,0,0}  % what we call 'blue' in this book
\definecolor{red}{gray}{.7}     \definecolor{green}{gray}{.8}
\definecolor{yellow}{gray}{.9}
Black \textcolor{blue}{blue} \textcolor{red}{red} {\color{green} green}
\textcolor{yellow}{yellow} \colorbox{black!30}{\color{blue} blue}
\fcolorbox{blue}{blue!8}{\color{blue}bluish}
```

preface-I

The notation blue!8 is a short form for writing blue!8!white. It is xcolor's way to specify simple color mixes and means that we mix 8% blue with 92% white.

All of these examples are "complete" if you mentally add a \documentclass line (with the article class[1] as an argument) and surround the body of the example with a document environment. In fact, this is how all of the examples in this book were produced. When processing the book, special LaTeX commands take the source lines for an example and write them to an external file, thereby automatically adding the \documentclass and the document environment lines. This turns each example into a small but complete LaTeX document. These documents are then externally processed (using a mechanism that runs each example as often as necessary, including the generation of a bibliography through BibTeX). The resulting PDF (Portable Document Format) is then cropped to the smallest size that shows all output, using the program pdfcrop and if necessary separated into individual pages using pdfseparate. The resulting graphic files are then loaded in the appropriate place the next time LaTeX is run on the whole book. More details on the actual implementation of this scheme can be found in Section 4.2.4 on page →I 315.

Watch out for these

Throughout the book, blue notes are sprinkled in the margin to help you easily find certain information that would otherwise be hard to locate. In a few cases these notes exhibit a warning sign, indicating that you should probably read this information even if you are otherwise only skimming through the particular section.

---

[1]Except for examples involving the \chapter command, which need the report or book class.

Most of the material presented in this book is applicable to all TeX engine flavors, e.g., pdfTeX, XeTeX, or LuaTeX. However, some aspects are applicable only to Unicode engines, and to help you identify this at a glance we have placed such information into boxes like this: *Information relevant only to Unicode TeX engines*

> **Unicode engines**
>
> This is information that applies only to Unicode engines, e.g., XeTeX or LuaTeX.

The only exceptions are Section 9.6 on fontspec and Section 12.4 on unicode-math, both of which would have ended up completely within such boxes — which would be rather hard to read.

A similar approach is used to highlight any differences between a workflow that uses BibTeX and traditional citation methods and one that uses the biblatex package and the biber program. As both methods have a large overlap, they are described together, and specific considerations are placed into boxes like this: *Information specific to biblatex/biber*

> **biber/biblatex**
>
> This is information specific to biblatex/biber and often gives tips how to ensure compatibility between the biber/biblatex and the BibTeX workflow.

This convention is used in Chapter 15.

Using the examples

Our aim when producing this book was to make it as useful as possible for our readers. For this reason the book contains more than 1 500 complete, self-contained examples of all aspects of typesetting covered in the book.

All examples are made available in source format on CTAN at `https://ctan.org/pkg/tlc3-examples`. The examples are numbered per section, and each number is shown in a small box in the inner margin (e.g., preface-II-6 on page xxxviii). These numbers are also used for the external file names by appending `.ltx` (single-page examples) or `.ltx2` (double-page examples).

To reuse any of the examples it is usually sufficient to copy the preamble code (typeset in blue) into the preamble of your document and, if necessary, adjust the document text as shown. In some cases it might be more convenient to place the preamble code into your own package (or class file), thus allowing you to load this package in multiple documents using `\usepackage`. If you want to do the latter, there are two points to observe:

- Any use of `\usepackage` in the preamble code needs to be replaced by a `\RequirePackage` declaration, which is the equivalent command for use in package and class files (see Section A.6.7).

- Any occurrence of `\makeatletter` and `\makeatother` *must* be removed from the preamble code. This is very important because the `\makeatother` would stop correct reading of such a file.

So let us assume you wish to reuse the code from the following example:

A line of text[1] with some[2] footnotes.

```
\makeatletter
\renewcommand\@makefntext[1]%
    {\noindent\makebox[0pt][r]{\@thefnmark.\,}#1}
\makeatother
A line of text\footnote{The first}
with some\footnote{The second} footnotes.
```

preface-I

---

1. The first
2. The second

You have two alternatives: you can copy the preamble code (i.e., the code colored blue) into your own document preamble or you can place that code — but without the \makeatletter and \makeatother — in a package file (e.g., lowfnnum.sty) and afterwards load this "package" in the preamble of your own documents with \usepackage{lowfnnum}.

Text and Symbol Fonts

When we wrote the first edition of the *LaTeX Companion* in 1994, the section on available text fonts for LaTeX was a few pages long and listed a handful of font families. Not because they were best in class, but because that was all that was available including those of a somewhat dubious quality. Basically when typesetting with TeX in those days, one could use any font as long as it was called Computer Modern.

A decade later the situation finally started to change, and it was in theory possible to use any font available in Type 1 format [1] — but only after somewhat extensive work preparing the necessary support files needed by TeX, in particular the font metric files (.tfm) and usually virtual font files (.vf) that reencoded the fonts to put the glyphs into the positions expected by the TeX engine. Providing these was not magic, especially after the appearance of the fontinst program[1] by Alan Jeffrey, Rowland

---

[1]This is actually a TeX file that, when processed and given the right configuration data, produced the necessary helper files in human-readable format. In a further step those had to be converted by external programs to the binary format used by TeX.

McDonnell, and Lars Hellström, but it took time and effort (even if necessary only once per font) and a good understanding of the underlying mechanisms. Thus, the number of available text fonts for use with TeX compared to other programs remained severely restricted. The second edition of the book again covered all that was freely available for LaTeX users, which amounted to fewer than two dozen font families. Of course, the CTAN archive already then contained some further support packages for a few commercial fonts. They were not included because the packages were useless unless you owned the particular family.

But with the third edition I faced a problem. With Unicode engines you can use essentially any freely or commercially available font by simply specifying it in the fontspec setup of your document. But also for the pdfTeX engine, font support exploded due to two factors: first the number of freely available fonts on the Web in either Type 1 [1], TrueType [6], or OpenType [69] format grew enormously, and second a few individuals like Marc Penninga, the author of autoinst, and Bob Tennent, Michael Sharpe, and a few others[1] took the time to prepare configuration files for Marc's autoinst program and with the necessary further adjustments and documentation produced packages that made a huge number of those freely usable fonts available to the LaTeX community at large.

My initial thought was to select only a few of the high-quality free fonts and largely ignore the rest — with just a mention that you find more possibilities in your TeX installation and on CTAN. But while working through all the font packages on CTAN to make a selection, I realized how difficult it is to hunt for them and that most likely any family not described in an overview remains unnoticed by the majority of users. Furthermore, while in the early days most free fonts were of a somewhat dubious quality, that too has now changed quite impressively for the better.

So in the end I decided to continue the tradition of offering a fairly comprehensive overview[2] about today's freely available fonts for LaTeX so that you can make an informed selection by just skimming this chapter and comparing the different possibilities and only then look further at the package documentation of the fonts you have chosen. You may also want to take a look at the online font catalogue maintained by Palle Jørgensen [38].

10.1 Overview

General font availability All fonts described in this chapter are freely available and with a few exceptions are included in the major TeX distributions such as TeX Live or MiKTeX so that you can start using them directly. We made two exceptions and also included the commercially available Cambria fonts as well as the Lucida font families that we use in this book. The Cambria fonts, while under a proprietary license, ship as part of Windows and

---

[1]All package authors are acknowledged next to their work and listed in the index. There are too many to enumerate here. However, Bob and Michael are the ones who produced the major part of the work, which I think deserves an explicit acknowledgment.

[2]For the first time restricted to only high-quality or otherwise (for some reason) interesting fonts. A heartfelt thanks to Adam Twardoch who helped me a lot with his knowledge and expertise to select the high-quality fonts from the huge number of freely available fonts today.

Office products and are therefore widely available without the need for buying an additional license. They offer excellent math support and for that alone are worth a closer look. The Lucida families are sold by the TEX Users Group (TUG) at a special price for members of TUG and several other user groups.[1]

In the open source world, "free" is a widely debated word, and some fonts are just not "free enough" to be included in free software distributions, because their license is somewhat restrictive, typically either forbidding modifications of the fonts (which is most likely not any issue for the readers of this book) or disallowing commercial usage. The latter refers to actions such as selling them or distributing them as part of a commercial system — none of the licenses of the fonts we cover prohibit the free use of the fonts even if the result, say, a book like this, is then sold. Thus, this should not pose a problem either, but of course, you should be aware that fonts you need to install "manually" have a special license, and you better check what it says if you intend to do anything with it other than simply typesetting your texts.

Omitting high-quality fonts because of license restrictions (even if very minor) is a sensible approach, as it means that the users of the distribution can rely on the fact that everything contained is covered by one of the major free licenses and that there are no restrictions on use and only well-known ones on modification; e.g., most LaTeX software uses the LaTeX Project Public License (LPPL), GNU Public License (GPL), or any other of the few major open source licenses.

But of course, it puts an additional burden on the user, as they have to manually install the fonts (besides checking the license requirements). Fortunately, there is an easy way to integrate such font packages into your installation. At the TEX Users Group website a script by Reinhard Kotucha is provided. It is a simple matter of downloading the install-getnonfreefonts installer from `https://www.tug.org/fonts/getnonfreefonts/` and processing it on the command line (in a Windows, macOS, or Linux terminal window) using

```
texlua install-getnonfreefonts
```

As this is a Lua program and texlua is part of the standard distributions, this works on any operating system, provided your user has write access to the distribution directories. After this you have the program getnonfreefonts available on your system, and you can invoke it with lines such as

```
getnonfreefonts --sys --help      # see the help info or
getnonfreefonts --sys --lsfonts   # list all available fonts or
getnonfreefonts --sys luximono    # (re)install a fonts package or
getnonfreefonts --sys --all       # (re)install all available fonts
```

The line first displays the program usage information and the available options; the second gives you an overview about the currently supported fonts and their

---

[1] The set includes matching serif, sans serif, and typewriter families; a full set of fonts for use in math; and several specialized fonts; see Table 10.11 on page 22 for an overview. They can be used with all TEX engines if both Type 1 and OpenType versions are ordered, which you can do at `https://tug.org/store/lucida/order.html`.

state on your installation; the third installs or reinstalls such a font (or more if you add additional font names); and the final one installs or updates all supported font packages (which are eleven in total at the moment). Instead of `--sys`, you can use `--user`, in which case the installation is done in the user's TeX tree instead of the system-wide one. However, except in a few special cases, this is *the wrong thing to do*, so please read `https://tug.org/texlive/scripts-sys-user.html` first if you are considering using `--user`, because of its possibly undesirable side effects.

10.1.1 Notes on the font samples

All font families in this chapter are exhibited using the same example text to allow for easy comparison and at the same time to show many details and possible limitations of the fonts. The standard setup uses the following text:

Palatino 10pt/12.4pt
(qp1) `TeX Gyre Pagella`

With a price of £148, **almost anything** can be found Floating In Fields. — ¿But aren't Kafka's Schloß & Æsop's Œuvres often *naïve* vis-à-vis the dæmonic *phœnix's official rôle* in fluffy soufflés?

In the margin we show the common name of the font (*Palatino*), the font size and the leading used (*10/12.4pt*), the NFSS family name to refer to it in parentheses (`qp1`), and finally with gray background the OpenType or TrueType name to use with Unicode engines (*TeX Gyre Pagella*). Depending on the length of the font names, this may be split differently over up to four lines.

The text is not typeset justified but slightly ragged right (still allowing hyphenation as one can see in a few of the later samples; e.g., on page 34). This is done so that the word spaces are not (or only minimally) altered from their default width. Most examples are set in 10/12pt, which is the default in most document classes, but sometimes we use a larger leading and/or a smaller or larger font size to account for the look and feel of the family.

The example text attempts to show different aspects of the font while still being concise (otherwise this chapter would be even longer). It contains some **bold** text, some **BOLD AND** NONBOLD SMALL CAPITALS, a *slanted word*, and a *few words in italics*. Above, these words are all typeset in blue. In the real samples they would be in black, unless the corresponding shape or series either is not available or is faked.

For instance, most families do not have both an italic and an oblique/slanted shape. Sometimes it is missing, but quite often the oblique shape is really just an alias for italics (or vice versa), which is fairly easy to see if you look at the shape of the "a" in "*naïve*" and "*official*" and compare it to "can" in the first line. Regardless of whether the slanted or italic shape is missing or aliased, it is shown in blue.

The bold text is normally shown in blue only if the series is missing altogether; the exception is the Concrete family where it is faked (by aliasing it to the bold typeface of a different font family, which is a somewhat questionable approach).

When the SMALL CAPS TEXT is shown in blue, half of the time it is because there is simply no such shape in the family and in the other half because the small capitals are faked using a scaled-down version of the uppercase letters. As explained on

Family	Series	Shapes	Typeface Examples
⟨*official font family name*⟩		⟨*font name (or names)*⟩	(*Encodings:* ⟨*list of supported font encodings*⟩)
⟨*NFSS family*⟩	⟨*series value(s)*⟩	⟨*shape value(s)*⟩	Font sample *with several* DIFFERENT SHAPES, **weights**, and/or **widths** (*but not all possibilities*)
⟨*official companion family name*⟩		⟨*font name (or names)*⟩	(*Encodings:* ⟨*list of supported font encodings*⟩)
⟨*NFSS family*⟩	⟨*series value(s)*⟩	⟨*shape value(s)*⟩	Font sample `with several` DIFFERENT SHAPES, `weights, and/or` widths

Supported figure styles for ⟨*font family*⟩ *are* ⟨*list of figure styles*⟩.
*Bold extended weights (*bx*) exist as an alias for bold medium (*b*) if not explicitly listed.*
The `font names` *with gray background are for use with the* fontspec *package in Unicode engines.*

Table 10.1: Structure of the font family classification tables

page →I 654 this approach gives inferior results — sometimes still acceptable, but usually not really. In other words, such fonts do not allow for using \textsc or only in an emergency.

But not only are different shapes shown in the example, the text also contains a number of diacritics, several special characters, and also most of the common f-ligatures such as ffi, fl, and ffl so you can see how they are typeset.

Finally, you should pay special attention to the number 148 in the first line. Whenever supported by the family, these digits are typeset as oldstyle numerals, and many fonts support this style (Palatino/Pagella above, for example, does not). Thus, if they are typeset as lining numbers, then the font does not support alternative number styles. If they are shown as oldstyle numbers, then this is usually adjustable through options to the support package or by changing the suffix of the family name if you use NFSS commands directly; see the next section.

10.1.2 Notes on the font family tables

In addition to the sample text, we show for each font family a table that contains the necessary information to select a font from that family in a document using the NFSS conventions. These tables are always identically structured; a sample table is shown as Table 10.1.

We show the ⟨*official font family name*⟩ followed by the ⟨*font name or names*⟩ that you need to use when accessing the family in a Unicode engine using fontspec. In the remainder of the line we then list the supported encodings, e.g., OT1, T1, etc. The next lines show the NFSS classification, i.e., the NFSS ⟨*family*⟩ and supported ⟨*series*⟩ and ⟨*shape*⟩ values, followed by a short text sample exhibiting some of the series/shape combinations (but usually not all).

If the font family consists of several distinctive designs, e.g., a serif, a sans serif, or a monospaced design, then this structure is repeated as often as necessary.

Series or shape values that are given in parentheses are faked in one way or the other. For example, (it) means the family has no real italics shape, and the oblique shape is used as a substitute, or vice versa if you see (sl). What we do not show in any table is (bx). The extended bold series is nearly always implemented as an alias to the medium bold series, but showing that in all tables takes up a lot of unnecessary space. In other words, in all tables you should mentally add (bx) next to every b series, unless the series list contains bx already, which means there is a real difference between bold medium (b) and bold extended (bx).

We do not list (bx) *in tables*

At the bottom of the table there may be some table notes. If the family supports several figure styles (e.g., oldstyle numbers or table numbers), we list them here. Any other pertinent information for this family is given there as well.

NFSS font family naming conventions

If the *NFSS family* name consists of a few apparently random letters (like qpl for Pagella), it is a clear indication that the LaTeX support files for this family got created a long time ago when packing a lot of information into a few bytes was essential and file names needed to conform to the 8+3 rule for DOS and Windows systems; see [13] for the description of that scheme.

However, these days the majority of *NFSS family* names are quite uniformly constructed from the *official font family name*[1] (typically in mixed case with spaces dropped), e.g., FiraSans or NotoSansMono followed by a suffix starting with a hyphen that indicates the figure style. This is nice because it is easy to remember, provides direct feedback, and allows one to quickly change a font from lining figures to oldstyle tabular figures, etc., when using NFSS commands directly.

-LF   This font uses lining figures, i.e., ones that all have the same height similar to capitals in the font. The glyph width may vary.

-TLF   This font has lining figures of identical width. This makes them suitable for tabulating numbers (which explains the name "table figures").

-OsF   This font has oldstyle figures of different heights and depths and possibly different widths.

-TOsF   This font has oldstyle figures with identical widths suitable for tables.

There are two further suffixes for fonts not intended for direct typesetting but as support for implementing the commands \textin and \textsu discussed below:

-Sup   This font contains superior digits, punctuations, and letters, often only an incomplete set, e.g., *abdeilmnorst* to support 1st, 2nd, etc. With the help of this special figure style, the command \textsu is implemented.

-Inf   This font contains inferior glyphs, usually only digits and some punctuations. With the help of this special figure style, the command \textin is implemented.

---

[1]Unfortunately, that is not always the case. Some of the freely available OpenType fonts have license restrictions that already require a name change when only the font format is changed to Type 1 (as needed by pdfTeX). You therefore sometimes find crippled names in the tables of this chapter; e.g., instead of Merriweather, we get Merriwthr-OsF as the NFSS family name — a pity, but it cannot be helped.

The *NFSS family* name in the table normally shows the −LF or −TLF suffix. If the family supports other figure styles, then they are mentioned in a table note.

> **Unicode engines**
>
> Most font tables list TU as one of the supported encodings. This means that the font family can be (easily) used with Unicode engines, such as X∃TEX or LuaTEX. If this encoding is missing, one should normally use that family only with pdfTEX.

Many tables also list the LY1 encoding, which is an alternative to LATEX's standard T1 encoding. It omits a few uncommon glyphs available with T1, which has the advantage that it therefore contains a few free slots. In some families these slots are then filled with additional ligatures available in the OpenType version of the font that would otherwise be unaccessible if the font is used with pdfTEX.

Extra ligatures when using LY1 encoding

10.1.3 Font support packages

As mentioned earlier, the bulk of the font support packages has been provided by a few individuals, and because of this, the majority of the packages are very similar in nature and provide identically named options for the same tasks in most circumstances. Thus, instead of adding a list of every option or command to the description of each of the more than 120 font packages, we give an overview here so that you know what to expect. For further details you then have to consult the package documentation, but in most cases this overview will hopefully suffice.

Please also note that many of the packages, in particular those by Bob Tennent, provide compatibility between the different processing engines; i.e., they successfully hide the differences between NFSS as used by pdfTEX and fontspec needed in the Unicode engines X∃TEX or LuaTEX.

Package naming conventions

Not so consistent are, unfortunately, the package names. While they usually have a clear relationship to the font family they support, you will find all sort of variants, from all lowercase with or without hyphens to mixed-case package names. Often this is due to the age of a package and to changes in how file names for support files got generated by fontinst or autoinst, and it is nothing that can easily be altered after the fact.

Figure style options

If font families support different figure style variants, then these are selectable in nearly all packages through the following set of options (each of which has a short name and a long name):

`lining` (`lf` or `nf`) or `oldstyle` (`osf`)	Select lining or oldstyle figures.
`proportional` (`pf`) or `tabular` (`tf`)	Select proportional or table figures.

They can (and may have to) be combined, e.g., `oldstyle,tabular` would internally request the font family with the −TOsF suffix in its name.

Support for different figure styles within the document

Packages for fonts that support more than one such figure style usually also implement commands to access different styles of numerals within the document. The commands are \textfigures (oldstyle), \liningfigures, \tabularfigures (identical width), and \proportionalfigures. They all expect one argument in which you can place the number to typeset. For example, if you have selected a family with the −OsF suffix (oldstyle numerals), then \liningfigures would switch temporarily to the font with the −LF suffix (if that exists as well).

Font scaling, weight, and width selection

Many packages also allow you to scale the fonts up or down by providing a scaling factor so that you can ensure that they become visually compatible with other fonts used. In most cases the option scaled or scale can be used, but sometimes only scale is provided.

The more modern packages often provide options to select the weight to be used as the default. Which option names are available then depends on what weights are offered by the family, but the names as such are usually a subset of the following list: thin, ultralight, extralight, light, regular, medium, semibold, bold, ultrabold, heavy, black, or extrablack. These option names reflect what has be used by the font designer as the weight name, so if the extra-bold weight is called heavy, then that is used as an option name. Sometimes packages also support short forms like sb for semibold, etc. For details you have to consult the individual package documentation.

Some families offer condensed versions, and in that case the support packages normally support the option condensed to select that variant as the default.

Changes to \rmdefault, \sfdefault, and friends

Packages supporting a single font family normally ensure that the family is automatically used. This is done by changing \rmdefault when it is a serif font, \sfdefault when it is a sans serif font, and \ttdefault if it is a monospaced design.

This means that a serif font automatically becomes the document default font, as that is determined by \familydefault, which, if unchanged, simply calls \rmdefault. However, some serif fonts are normally not intended to be used for a whole document. For example, Cinzel is suitable only for displays, because it contains only uppercase letters. Its support package therefore provides only commands such as \textcinzel for selecting the font but leaves \rmdefault untouched unless you give it the option default. For some reason this option is also needed with the gfsbodoni package even though the font is a perfectly reasonable document font and could have been set up automatically.

Since you may want to set up a sans serif font as the default font for your document, packages that load such families usually support the option sfdefault. If given, this option changes \familydefault to point to the sans serif family. A few packages call this option default instead.

So while there is some overall consistency, there are also a few packages that use the option names differently. Exceptions are explicitly listed with the packages.

Multifamily support

If a package sets up several font families in parallel, e.g., a sans serif and a monospaced family, then this can be very convenient, but it is not always appropriate. To support a selective setup, such packages usually offer the options rm, sf, or tt as appropriate so that one can request that only the roman (serif) and/or the sans serif and/or the typewriter family is set up instead.

Such packages may also prefix other option names with rm sf, or tt to denote that they should apply only to that particular family setup. For example, sfosf would state that the sans serif family should get oldstyle numbers, but this convention is not implemented very often.

Some packages have their own naming scheme for such options, so if the above names do not work with one of the packages discussed in Section 10.2, consult their documentation to see what they provide instead.

Commands defined by font packages

Some of the older font support packages provide only fairly limited features, e.g., changing \rmdefault or \sfdefault and maybe offering a scaled option. However, with more recently developed packages you usually also get a number of document commands defined. We give a short overview of what might be available; the details vary from package to package, and you have to read the relevant package documentation for this.

Many packages add commands to access the font family that they support, in addition to, or as an alternative to, making it available via \textrm or \textsf, etc. In most cases the command names use the following convention: \text⟨*pkg-name*⟩ with one argument and \⟨*pkg-name*⟩ for the declaration form that switches to the font. For example, the cinzel package offers \textcinzel and \cinzel.

Support for additional \text.. commands

Roughly fifty packages support superior figures and about twenty also support inferior figure styles. This is shown in the font tables by listing –Sup or –Inf as supported figure styles. If so, the commands to access these glyphs are normally \textsu and \textin or as declarations \sufigures and \infigures. If available, these command usually produce much better results than LaTeX's generic \textsuperscript and \textsubscript commands, as those commands simply take the current font, use it in a smaller size, and raise or lower the result. For comparison here is text in Alegreya (see page 11) showing both methods:

Support for superior and inferior glyphs

Catch₂₂ in Room¹³
Catch₂₂ in Room¹³

```
\usepackage{Alegreya}

Catch\textin{22}           in Room\textsu{13}           \par
Catch\textsubscript{22} in Room\textsuperscript{13}
```

10-1-1

The problem with both commands or the declarations is that they normally unconditionally switch to the package font, so if you load two packages that both define them, the last one loaded wins.

There are sometimes a number of other commands or options available with individual packages, but there is little consistency across the whole set. So once you have selected a particular set of font families for your document, it might be worth reading the documentation to see if there is anything else not covered here.

10.1.4 Direct use of the fonts (without a package)

Using a font support package is often convenient, but it is seldom really necessary, and in some cases it is actually counterproductive. For example, most font packages install the family as a default of some sort, e.g., as the document sans serif family (\sfdefault). But if you want to use that font for only a special effect, then you have to undo that kind of setup or make sure to load all support packages in the right order so that part of their configuration gets undone by the next package (if possible).

Fortunately, the font classification tables are enough to directly use any font exhibited in this chapter. All you have to do is to place the relevant data from the tables into the appropriate NFSS commands, e.g., \fontfamily, \fontseries, \fontshape, or \usefont, or use them for changing the document defaults, e.g., \rmdefault, \sfdefault, and so on.

In the next example we set up Fira Sans with lining figures (-LF) as the sans serif document font and then use Alegreya with oldstyle figures (-OsF) in ultra-bold at 42 points (without any leading) for a splashing headline (using \usefont). We then change the size to \tiny and the font to \sffamily. That means the text would still be in ultra-bold (which is available in Fira-Sans; see Table 10.5 on page 14), but we want a strong contrast, so we go for extra-light via \fontseries{el}. We can omit the \selectfont as that is implicitly done by \sffamily.

Alegreya-
Ultra 42

A tiny light Fira Sans 42

```
\renewcommand\sfdefault{FiraSans-LF}

\centering
\fontsize{42pt}{42pt}%                Select a size
\usefont{T1}{Alegreya-OsF}{ub}{n}%    Select a font
Alegreya-Ultra~42              %           Go

\tiny\fontseries{el}\sffamily  %        Change
A tiny light Fira Sans 42
```

10-1-2

Unicode engines

When typesetting using one of the Unicode engines, the procedure is slightly different, because with fontspec only the medium and bold series are set up automatically. Therefore, something like ultra-bold or extra-light is not available out of the box and thus cannot be requested in the way we did in the previous example without first doing some setup work using the FontFace key or the \newfontface command of fontspec. For example:

```
\setsansfont{Fira Sans}[FontFace={el}{n}{FiraSans-ExtraLight.otf}]
\newfontface\AlegreyaHeading{Alegreya-Black.otf}
```

How to find the correct font file names — starting with the data from the font classification tables in this chapter — is described at length in Section 9.6, starting on page →I 705.

Family	Series	Shapes	Typeface Examples
Alegreya	Alegreya (*Encodings:* T1, TS1, OT1, LGR, LY1, and TU)		
Alegreya-LF	m, sb, b, eb, ub	n, it, (sl), sc, scit, (scsl)	Alegreya *italic*, **bold**, and SMALL CAPS
Alegreya Sans	Alegreya Sans (*Encodings:* T1, TS1, OT1, LGR, LY1, and TU)		
AlegreyaSans-LF	el, l, m, sb, b, eb, ub	n, it, (sl), sc, scit, (scsl)	Alegreya Sans in **ultra-bold** and thin

Supported figure styles for Alegreya and Alegreya Sans are -LF, -OsF, -TLF, -TOsF, -Sup, *and* -Inf.

Table 10.2: Classification of the Alegreya font families

10.2 Samples of larger font families

We start by discussing the freely available bigger families in alphabetical order, i.e., those that offer matching serif, sans serif, and monospaced designs (or at least two of them). We already covered LaTeX's standard families Computer Modern and Latin Modern in Section 9.5.1 on page →I 684 in the previous chapter, so they are not repeated here. Samples for all of them (including CM and LM fonts) are later repeated in the sections devoted to serif, sans serif, and typewriter fonts, to allow for easy comparison to other fonts that have similar characteristics.

10.2.1 Alegreya

The Humanist typeface Alegreya, designed by Juan Pablo del Peral, is intended for body text but also works well in display sizes. One of its characteristic features is the widening of its stems towards the top. It is offered in five weights, upright, italics, and Small Caps, and has a matching sans serif Alegreya Sans.

LaTeX support for all engines is provided by the Alegreya and AlegreyaSans packages by Bob Tennent with the typical options such as scaled, oldstyle, etc.

> With a price of £148, **almost anything** can be found FLOATING IN FIELDS. — ¿But aren't Kafka's Schloß & Æsop's Œuvres often *naïve* vis-à-vis the dæmonic *phœnix's official rôle* in fluffy soufflés?

Alegreya 10pt/12pt
(Alegreya-OsF) Alegreya

Here is a sample of Alegreya Sans equally well equipped with weights and shapes. Just like its serifed counterpart it offers all standard font faces in even more weights, including small capitals in each of them. It also has true italics, though there is no oblique/slanted font face — for this italics are substituted as elsewhere:

> With a price of £148, **almost anything** can be found FLOATING IN FIELDS. — ¿But aren't Kafka's Schloß & Æsop's Œuvres often *naïve* vis-à-vis the dæmonic *phœnix's official rôle* in fluffy soufflés?

Alegreya Sans 10pt/12pt
(AlegreyaSans-OsF) Alegreya Sans

11

Family	Series	Shapes	Typeface Examples
CM Bright	—no OpenType—		(*Encodings:* OT1, T1, TS1)
cmbr	m, sb	n, (it), sl	CM Bright medium, *oblique*, and **semi-bold** *oblique*
	(b), bx	n	**CM Bright bold extended (upright only and limited size range)**
CM Bright Typewriter Light	—no OpenType—		(*Encodings:* OT1, T1, TS1)
cmtl	m	n, sl	CM Bright Typewriter Light and *oblique*

Table 10.3: Classification of the Computer Modern Bright font families

10.2.2 CM Bright—A design based on Computer Modern Sans

The Computer Modern Bright (CM Bright) fonts by Walter Schmidt (1960–2021) are based on the METAFONT sources of Computer Modern Sans. This family of sans serif fonts is designed to serve as a legible body font. It comes in three weights with matching typewriter and math fonts, including the AMS symbols. LATEX support for the pdfTEX engines is provided through the package cmbright. A sample page with mathematics is shown in Figure 12.42 on page 290.

> **Unicode engines**
>
> The fonts exist only as METAFONT sources and in Type 1 format (in T1 or OT1 encoding) and are therefore not really suitable for Unicode engines.

In the example below we show semi-bold (sb) instead of using the default bold extended series, as this is a good combination when typesetting in CM Bright.

CM Bright 10pt/12pt (cmbr)
—no OpenType—

With a price of £148, **almost anything** can be found Floating In Fields. — ¿But aren't Kafka's Schloß & Æsop's Œuvres often *naïve* vis-à-vis the dæmonic *phœnix's official rôle* in fluffy soufflés?

CM Bright Typewriter Light 10pt/12pt (cmtl)
—no OpenType—

With a price of £148, almost anything can be found Floating In Fields. - ¿But aren't Kafka's Schloß & Æsop's Œuvres often *naïve* vis-à-vis the dæmonic *phœnix's official rôle* in fluffy soufflés?

10.2.3 DejaVu—A fork of Bitstream Vera

Bitstream Vera is a freely available set of typefaces in TrueType format designed by Jim Lyles from Bitstream. It consists of slab serif, sans serif, and monospace fonts in two weights. The monospaced font is suitable for technical work with a clear distinction of often similar characters. The sans serif font is the default font used by Python's Matplotlib library for producing plots.

The Vera families were released with a license that permits changes, and as a result several projects used Vera as a basis. The DejaVu project was initiated by

Family	Series	Shapes	Typeface Examples
DejaVu Serif DejaVu Serif	*(Encodings:* T1, TS1, T2A, T2B, T2C, OT1, X2, LGR, and TU)		
DejaVuSerif-TLF	m, b	n, it, (sl)	DejaVu Serif regular, *italics,* and **bold**
DejaVu Serif Condensed	*(Encodings:* T1, TS1, T2A, T2B, T2C, OT1, X2, LGR, and TU)		
DejaVuSerifCondensed-TLF	m, b	n, it, (sl)	DejaVu Serif condensed, *italics,* and **bold**
DejaVu Sans DejaVu Sans	*(Encodings:* T1, TS1, T2A, T2B, T2C, OT1, X2, LGR, and TU)		
DejaVuSans-TLF	m, b	n, (it), sl	DejaVu Sans regular, *oblique,* and **bold**
DejaVu Sans Condensed	*(Encodings:* T1, TS1, T2A, T2B, T2C, OT1, X2, LGR, and TU)		
DejaVuSansCondensed-TLF	m, b	n, (it), sl	DejaVu Sans condensed, *oblique,* and **bold**
DejaVu Mono DejaVu Sans Mono	*(Encodings:* T1, TS1, T2A, T2B, T2C, OT1, X2, LGR, and TU)		
DejaVuSansMono-TLF	m, b	n, (it), sl	DejaVu Mono regular, *oblique,* and **bold**

Table 10.4: Classification of the DejaVu (Vera) font families

Štěpán Roh with the aim to provide a wider range of characters while maintaining the original look and feel through the process of collaborative development.

For LaTeX, there has been support for the original Vera fonts for a long time under the name Bera fonts, but this covered only the Latin character encoding T1. More recently Pavel Farář provided pdfTeX support for the DejaVu families (which offers additional shapes and also covers Greek and Cyrillic) through the packages DejaVuSerif, DejaVuSans, DejaVuSansCondensed, and DejaVuSansMono. All packages support the option scaled, which is helpful if the fonts are combined with other families. There also exists the package dejavu that simply calls all three packages in turn.

Unicode engines

For Unicode engines you can instead use the package dejavu-otf by Herbert Voß, which provides the necessary fontspec support and also sets up the matching math fonts developed in Poland by TeX Gyre. For available options refer to the package documentation. An example page with mathematics is shown in Figure 12.41 on page 289.

With a price of £148, **almost anything** can be found Floating In Fields. — ¿But aren't Kafka's Schloß & Æsop's Œuvres often *naïve* vis-à-vis the dæmonic *phœnix's official rôle* in fluffy soufflés?

DejaVu Serif 9pt/12.5pt
(DejaVuSerif-TLF)
DejaVu Serif

With a price of £148, **almost anything** can be found Floating In Fields. — ¿But aren't Kafka's Schloß & Æsop's Œuvres often *naïve* vis-à-vis the dæmonic *phœnix's official rôle* in fluffy soufflés?

DejaVu Sans 9pt/12.5pt
(DejaVuSans-TLF)
DejaVu Sans

Family	Series	Shapes	Typeface Examples
Fira Sans Fira Sans	(*Encodings:* T1, TS1, OT1, LGR, LY1, and TU)		
FiraSans-LF	ul, el, l, sl, m, sb, b, eb, ub	n, it, (sl), sc, scit, (scsl)	Fira Sans *italic*, SMALL CAPS, light, **bold**, **semi-bold**, and ***ultra-bold italic***
Fira Mono Fira Mono	(*Encodings:* T1, TS1, OT1, LGR, LY1, and TU)		
FiraMono-TLF	m, sb, b	n, (it), sl	Fira Mono, *oblique*, semi-bold, and **bold**

Supported figure styles for Fira Sans are -LF, -OsF, -TLF, -TOsF, *and* -Sup *and for Fira Mono* -TLF, -TOsF, *and* -Sup.

Table 10.5: Classification of the Fira font families

DejaVu Sans Mono
9pt/12.5pt
(DejaVuSansMono-TLF)
DejaVu Sans Mono

With a price of £148, **almost anything** can be found Floating In **Fields**. — ¿But aren't Kafka's Schloß & Æsop's Œuvres often *naïve* vis-à-vis the dæmonic *phœnix's official rôle* in fluffy soufflés?

Both the DejaVu Serif and Sans but not Mono also exist in condensed versions. These can be loaded with the packages DejaVuSerifCondensed and DejaVuSansCondensed.

DejaVu Serif Condensed
9pt/12.5pt
(DejaVuSerifCondensed-TLF)
DejaVu Serif Condensed

With a price of £148, **almost anything** can be found Floating In **Fields**. — ¿But aren't Kafka's Schloß & Æsop's Œuvres often *naïve* vis-à-vis the dæmonic *phœnix's official rôle* in fluffy soufflés?

DejaVu Sans Condensed
9pt/12.5pt
(DejaVuSansCondensed-TLF)
DejaVu Sans Condensed

With a price of £148, **almost anything** can be found Floating In **Fields**. — ¿But aren't Kafka's Schloß & Æsop's Œuvres often *naïve* vis-à-vis the dæmonic *phœnix's official rôle* in fluffy soufflés?

10.2.4 Fira fonts

The Fira fonts have been designed by Erik Spiekermann and Ralph du Carrois for the Firefox OS. The Humanist sans serif typeface Fira Sans is available in seventeen weights of which a suitable subset has been set up for use with LaTeX. The accompanying monospaced font Fira Mono is available in three weights, offers oblique (and faked italics), but does not offer Small Caps shapes.

LaTeX support for all engines is provided by the packages FiraSans and FiraMono by Bob Tennent with the typical options such as scaled, oldstyle, etc.

Fira Sans 10pt/12pt
(FiraSans-OsF) Fira Sans

With a price of £148, **almost anything** can be found FLOATING IN **FIELDS**. — ¿But aren't Kafka's Schloß & Æsop's Œuvres often *naïve* vis-à-vis the dæmonic *phœnix's official rôle* in fluffy soufflés?

Family	Series	Shapes	Typeface Examples
Gandhi Serif Gandhi Serif			(*Encodings:* T1, TS1, OT1, LY1, and TU)
GandhiSerif-LF	m, b	n, it, (sl), sc, scit, (scsl)	Gandhi Serif *italic*, **bold**, and Small Caps
Gandhi Sans Gandhi Sans			(*Encodings:* T1, TS1, OT1, LY1, and TU)
GandhiSans-LF	m, b	n, it, (sl), sc, scit, (scsl)	Gandhi Sans *italic,* **bold**, and Small Caps

Supported figure styles for Gandhi Serif and Gandhi Sans are -LF, -OsF, -TLF, *and* -TOsF.

Table 10.6: Classification of the Gandhi font families

With a price of £148, **almost anything** can be found Floating In **Fields**. — ¿But aren't Kafka's Schloß & Æsop's Œuvres often *naïve* vis-à-vis the dæmonic *phœnix's official rôle* in fluffy soufflés?

Fira Mono 10pt/12pt
(FiraMono-TOsF)
Fira Mono

Unicode engines

Xiangdong Zeng developed matching math fonts; see Figure 12.43 on page 291 for an example page.

10.2.5 Gandhi fonts

The Gandhi families are designed by Cristobal Henestrosa and Raul Plancarte in collaboration with David Kimura and Gabriela Varela for Librerias Gandhi, a bookstore chain in Mexico that makes them freely available.

LaTeX support for all engines is provided through the package gandhi by Bob Tennent offering the usual options such as scaled, sfdefault, oldstyle, etc. The fonts are not part of the standard distribution but can be installed with getnonfreefonts.

With a price of £148, **almost anything** can be found Floating In Fields. — ¿But aren't Kafka's Schloß & Æsop's Œuvres often *naïve* vis-à-vis the dæmonic *phœnix's official rôle* in fluffy soufflés?

Gandhi Serif 10pt/12pt
(GandhiSerif-OsF)
Gandhi Serif

With a price of £148, **almost anything** can be found Floating In **Fields**. — ¿But aren't Kafka's Schloß & Æsop's Œuvres often *naïve* vis-à-vis the dæmonic *phœnix's official rôle* in fluffy soufflés?

Gandhi Sans 10pt/12pt
(GandhiSans-OsF)
Gandhi Sans

10.2.6 Go fonts

Designed by Kris Holmes and Charles Bigelow for the Go project, the Go font families consist of a humanistic sans serif font in three weights and a matching monospaced, slap serif font available in two weights.

Family	Series	Shapes	Typeface Examples
Go Sans Go Sans		(*Encodings:* T1, TS1, OT1, LY1, and TU)	
Go-TLF	m	n, it, (sl), sc, scit, (scsl)	Go Sans regular, *italic, and* SMALL CAPS ITALICS
	sb, b	n, it, (sl)	Go Sans semi–bold ***and bold italic***
Go Mono Go Mono		(*Encodings:* T1, TS1, OT1, LY1, and TU)	
GoMono-TLF	m, b	n, it, (sl)	Go Mono regular ***and bold italic***

The supported figure style of the Go Sans and Go Mono fonts is -TLF.

Table 10.7: Classification of the Go font families

Both families have very distinctive forms for zero, capital O, lowercase l, digit one, and capital I, making them very suitable for displaying computer code without the danger of misinterpretations. LaTeX support for all engines is provided by the packages GoSans and GoMono by Bob Tennent.

Go Sans 10pt/12pt
(Go-TLF) Go Sans

With a price of £148, **almost anything** can be found FLOATING IN Fields. — ¿But aren't Kafka's Schloß & Æsop's Œuvres often *naïve* vis–à–vis the dæmonic *phœnix's official rôle* in fluffy soufflés?

Go Mono 9pt/11.5pt
(GoMono-TLF) Go Mono

With a price of £148, **almost anything** can be found Floating In **Fields**. — ¿But aren't Kafka's Schloß & Æsop's Œuvres often *naïve* vis–à–vis the dæmonic *phœnix's official rôle* in fluffy soufflés?

10.2.7 Inria fonts

The Inria families are free fonts designed by the Black foundry for the Inria research institute in France. Offered are a serif and sans serif design in three weights with matching italics. For \slshape the italics are substituted; Small Caps are not available. LaTeX support for the pdfTeX engine is provided by the packages InriaSerif and InriaSans by Nicolas Markey.

Unicode engines

For Unicode engines use the fontspec package to set up the fonts.

Inria Serif 10pt/12pt
(InriaSerif-OsF)
Inria Serif

With a price of £148, **almost anything** can be found Floating In Fields. — ¿But aren't Kafka's Schloß & Æsop's Œuvres often *naïve* vis–à–vis the dæmonic *phœnix's official rôle* in fluffy soufflés?

Inria Sans 10pt/12pt
(InriaSans-OsF)
Inria Sans

With a price of £148, **almost anything** can be found Floating In **Fields**. — ¿But aren't Kafka's Schloß & Æsop's Œuvres often *naïve* vis–à–vis the dæmonic *phœnix's official rôle* in fluffy soufflés?

Family	Series	Shapes	Typeface Examples
Inria Serif `Inria Serif`		(*Encodings:* T1, TS1, OT1, LY1, and TU)	
`InriaSerif-LF`	l, m, b	n, it, (sl)	Inria Serif regular *and bold italic*
	l, m, b	tl, tlit (tlsl)	Also some nonstandard Heavy Shapes
Inria Sans `Inria Sans`		(*Encodings:* T1, TS1, OT1, LY1, and TU)	
`InriaSans-LF`	l, m, b	n, it, (sl)	Inria Sans regular *and bold italic*
	l, m, b	tl, tlit (tlsl)	Also some nonstandard Heavy Shapes

Supported figure styles of the Inria Serif and Inria Sans fonts are –LF, –OsF, –TLF, –TOsF, and –Sup. Inria Code is offered with –TLF and –TOsF.

Table 10.8: Classification of the Inria font families

10.2.8 Kp (Johannes Kepler) fonts

The Kp family of typefaces has been designed by Christophe Caignaert in the first two decades of the 21st century. It was inspired by Hermann Zapf's (1918-2015) Palatino. Recently Daniel Flipo produced OpenType versions of the fonts, so now they can be used with all engines.

The fonts support both oldstyle and lining numbers. To get oldstyle numerals with pdfTEX, you need to append `osn` to the base family name shown in Table 10.9 on the next page; e.g., use `jkpxosn`. Alternatively, it is possible to select oldstyle numerals as well as two further glyph variations: a swash uppercase Q and rare (historical) ligatures. This is done by appending `os` instead, and it gives you output such as

Queer, faſt, ſtrange, and satisfying actions!

It is also possible to select a "very oldstyle" with `vos`, which is like `os` but additionally uses a long "ſ" instead of the normal "s" as well as a special "ſt" ligature by default. When you typeset with pdfTEX, you then get the "short s" through the ligature `s=`:

Queer, faſt, ſtrange, and ſatisfying actions!
(*written as* ...`satis=fying actions=!` *this time*)

A further differentiator is the support for either petite capitals (the default) or somewhat larger small capitals by appending `k` to the family name:

Petite Capitals   *compared to*   Larger Small Capitals

Finally, it is also possible to prevent the use of the usual f-ligatures by appending `f`, which then gives you

fi ffi ff ffl   *instead of the usual*   fi ffi ff ffl.

Family	Series	Shapes	Typeface Examples
Kp Roman KpRoman	*(Encodings:* T1, TS1, OT1, and TU)		
jkpx	l, m, sb, sbx, b, bx	n, it, sl, sc, scsl	Light, regular, *slanted*, *italic*, **semi bold**, **bold**, **bold extended** & Small Caps with lining numerals 123... (for oldstyle numerals see note)
jkpl	m, b, bx	n, it, sl, sc, scsl	Light, *slanted*, *italic*, **bold**, **bold extended** & Small Caps with lining numerals 123... (see note)
Kp Sans KpSans	*(Encodings:* T1, TS1, OT1, and TU)		
jkpss	m, b, bx	n, (it), sl, sc, scsl	Regular, *slanted*, **bold**, **bold extended** & Small Caps with lining numerals 123... (see note)
Kp Typewriter KpMono	*(Encodings:* T1, TS1, OT1, and TU)		
jkptt	m, b	n, (it), sl	Regular, *slanted* & **bold**

The NFSS family names shown above are base names. If used with pdfTEX, the fonts use different family names to distinguish oldstyle numerals from lining numerals and the use or absence of special ligatures. See the explanation in the text on how to select the appropriate family names.

Table 10.9: Classification of the Kp font families

The different suffixes can be combined in the following way:

⟨*base family name*⟩⟨k *or missing*⟩⟨f *or missing*⟩⟨osn, os, vos *or missing*⟩

For example, jkpxkos gives you larger small capitals as well as all ligatures and oldstyle numbers. There are a few restrictions, though: using f together with os or vos makes little sense, so that is not supported. The typewriter family never has f-ligatures and does not offer small caps, so neither f nor k is available with jkptt. Further explicit examples are shown in the text samples.

> **Unicode engines**
>
> Note that with Unicode engines you use the feature sets of fontspec instead of playing around with different NFSS family names.

Part of this meta family is a full set of matching math fonts that include all math symbols and alphabets from LATEX as well as those from the AMS fonts. Examples with mathematical content are shown in Figures 12.6 to 12.8 on pages 266–267 and for Kepler Sans in Figure 12.47 on page 293.

To use the Kp fonts for both text and math you can use the support package kpfonts (by Christophe Caignaert), when typesetting with pdfTEX, or the package kpfonts-otf (by Daniel Flipo), when using a Unicode engine.

Both packages offer a large number of options that let you select various font features, e.g., light, oldstylenums, oldstyle, largesmallcaps, and many more. You can also use it to only set up text fonts or some of the text fonts with nomath, onlyrm, nott, and a few more. How to make use of the Kp math fonts, and the support options for them, is covered in Chapter 12.

> With a price of £148, **almoſt anything** can be found FLOATING IN FIELDS. — ¿But aren't Kafka's Schloß & Æsop's Œuvres often *naïve* vis-à-vis the dæmonic *phœnix's official rôle* in fluffy soufflés?

Kp Roman in oldstyle 10pt/12pt
(jkpxos) `KpRoman`

The light face saves about 10% of toner. It prints fine but may be less suited if viewed mainly on screens. Metrically it is identical to the normal weight font (if you keep all other font features identical), so you should not experience different line or page breaks if you change your mind at some point. The only restriction is that unlike the jkpx family it offers only two weights and not four.

> With a price of £148, **almost anything** can be found FLOATING IN FIELDS, — ¿But aren't Kafka's Schloß & Æsop's Œuvres often *naïve* vis-à-vis the dæmonic *phœnix's official rôle* in fluffy soufflés?

Kp Roman light 10pt/12pt
(jkpl) `KpRoman`

The Sans family is shown below with the f-ligatures turned off. As with most sans typefaces, italics are really just oblique shapes with otherwise identical design.

> With a price of £148, **almost anything** can be found FLOATING IN FIELDS. — ¿But aren't Kafka's Schloß & Æsop's Œuvres often *naïve* vis-à-vis the dæmonic *phœnix's official rôle* in fluffy soufflés?

Kp Sans without f-ligatures but larger small capitals 10pt/12pt
(jkpsskf) `KpSans`

One of the interesting aspects of the Kp typewriter font is that you can have it with oldstyle numerals through the osn. Because typewriter fonts have no ligatures, using the os suffix gives you only the swash Q in addition (as a double-wide character), which is fairly pointless, and getting "long s" in a typewriter font is also questionable.

> ```
> With a price of £148, almost anything can be found
> Floating In Fields. -- ¿But aren't Kafka's Schloß & Æsop's
> Œuvres often naïve vis-à-vis the dæmonic phœnix's official
> rôle in fluffy soufflés?
> ```

Kp Typewriter with oldstyle numerals 10pt/12pt
(jkpttosn) `KpMono`

10.2.9 Libertinus — A fork of Linux Libertine and Biolinum

Linux Libertine, designed by Philipp H. Poll, is a transitional serif typeface inspired by 19th century book type and is intended as a replacement for the Times font family. It is available in three weights, each with italics and small capitals. Philipp also designed a complementary humanist sans serif face named Linux Biolinum and a matching monospaced font Linux Libertine Mono.

Work on the fonts ceased in 2003, and afterwards a number of forks appeared that continued the development under new names. Interesting from a LATEX perspective is Libertinus by Khaled Hosny, who also added supporting math fonts. Package support

Family	Series	Shapes	Typeface Examples
Libertinus Serif	Libertinus Serif	(*Encodings:* T1, TS1, T2A, T2B, T2C, OT1, LGR, LY1, and TU)	
LibertinusSerif-LF	m, sb, b	n, it, (sl), sc, scit, (scsl)	Regular, *italic*, **semi-bold**, **bold**, and SMALL CAPS *ITALIC*
Libertinus Serif Display	Libertinus Serif Display	(*Encodings:* T1, TS1, T2A, T2B, T2C, OT1, LGR, LY1, and TU)	
LibertinusSerifDisplay-LF	m	n	Only one weight and shape
Libertinus Sans	Libertinus Sans	(*Encodings:* T1, TS1, T2A, T2B, T2C, OT1, LGR, LY1, and TU)	
LibertinusSans-LF	m, sb, b	n, it, (sl), sc, scit, (scsl)	Regular, *italic*, **semi-bold**, **bold**, and SMALL CAPS *ITALIC*
Libertinus Mono	Libertinus Mono	(*Encodings:* T1, TS1, OT1, LY1, and TU)	
LibertinusMono-TLF	m, b	n, (it), sl	Regular, *oblique*, **bold**

Supported figure styles for Libertinus Serif, Serif Display, and Sans are -LF, -OsF, -TLF, -TOsF, *and* -Sup. *Libertinus Mono is offered with* -LTF *and* -Sup.

Table 10.10: Classification of the Libertinus font families

for this fork[1] is provided through the libertinus package by Bob Tennent and Herbert Voß. The package offers options to set up all families or individual ones, scale some of them, select oldstyle figures, etc.

> **Unicode engines**
>
> The Libertinus math fonts are currently supported only by Unicode engines; see Figure 12.23 on page 277 for a sample page. There is, however, also support through Michael Sharpe's newtxmath package, which offers a Libertine version in math, as shown in Figure 12.22 on page 277.

Libertinus Serif 10pt/12pt
(LibertinusSerif-OsF)
Libertinus Serif

With a price of £148, **almost anything** can be found FLOATING IN FIELDS. — ¿But aren't Kafka's Schloß & Æsop's Œuvres often *naïve* vis-à-vis the dæmonic *phœnix's official rôle* in fluffy soufflés?

Libertinus Sans 10pt/12pt
(LibertinusSans-OsF)
Libertinus Sans

With a price of £148, **almost anything** can be found FLOATING IN **FIELDS**. — ¿But aren't Kafka's Schloß & Æsop's Œuvres often *naïve* vis-à-vis the dæmonic *phœnix's official rôle* in fluffy soufflés?

Because the monospaced font often appears to be rather large, you may want to use it scaled down.

---

[1]The original fonts are also supported under LaTeX through the packages libertine and biolinum, but for new projects using libertinus is the better choice.

With a price of £148, **almost anything** can be found Floating In **Fields**. — ¿But aren't Kafka's Schloß & Æsop's Œuvres often *naïve* vis-à-vis the dæmonic *phœnix's official rôle* in fluffy soufflés?

Libertinus Mono 9pt/12pt
(LibertinusMono-TLF)
Libertinus Mono

There also exists a special version for use on title pages, etc.

Libertinus Display 123

Libertinus Serif Display
30pt/36pt
(LibertinusSerifDisplay-OsF)
Libertinus Serif Display

For comparison, here is the regular Serif at the same size, which appears compressed and much darker while at the same time running slightly wider:

Libertinus Display 123

Libertinus Serif 30pt/36pt
(LibertinusSerif-OsF)
Libertinus Serif

10.2.10 Lucida fonts

The Lucida extended family of typefaces has been designed by Charles Bigelow and Kris Holmes. Besides being popular choices in computer operating systems, because of their screen legibility, the fonts are also widely used for scientific and technical publishing. Lucida Bright, Lucida Sans, and Lucida Math are the main typeface families used for this book. They are commercial, so you have to buy them, but for a high-quality printout that requires full support for all of LaTeX's math capabilities, they are an attractive choice.[1] Table 10.11 on the next page lists all Lucida text[2] families that are sold as a set by TeX Users Group. As you will notice, there are some differences in coverage between Type 1 fonts for use with pdfTeX and Opentype fonts for use with the Unicode engines. Lucida Bright, Lucida Sans, Lucida Sans Typewriter, Lucida Blackletter, Lucida Casual, Lucida Calligraphy, and Lucida Handwriting are available for all engines (though the Opentype versions of the fonts have a far larger glyph coverage, because they are not restricted to 256 glyphs). However, there are also a number of typefaces that are available only in Type 1 for pdfTeX or only in OpenType format for XeTeX or LuaTeX.

All Lucida font families share common design principles and are intended to be mixed and matched in arbitrary (possibly surprising) ways. In particular, Lucida Bright, Lucida Sans, and Lucida Sans Typewriter are meant to be used in unison, and this is possible in all engines. For pdfTeX there is the package lucidabr that also sets up Lucida Math for you — sample pages with mathematics are shown in Figures 12.24 to 12.26 on pages 278–279. If you want only the text fonts, then altering \rmdefault,

---

[1]However, most freestanding math examples in this book are *deliberately not* set in Lucida Math but in Computer Modern Math, because that is what most people are used to seeing. The look and feel is noticeably different between the two, and I wanted the examples to resemble the typical TeX look with respect to formulas. For the same reason, Latin Modern Typewriter is used for typesetting command names and code.

[2]The math fonts, which are also part of the set, are covered in Chapter 12.

Family	Series	Shapes	Typeface Examples
			Serif, Sans & matching Typewriter families
Lucida Bright		Lucida Bright OT	(*Encodings:* T1, TS1, LY1, and TU)
hlh	m, b	n, it, sl, sc	Regular, *slanted*, *italic*, **bold** & Small Caps with lining numerals
Lucida Bright		Lucida Bright OT	(*Encodings:* T1, TS1, and TU)
hlhj	m	n, it, (sl), sc	Regular, *italic* & Small Caps with oldstyle numerals (12345)
	b	sc	**Bold, bold italic & Bold Small Caps (12345)**
Lucida Sans		Lucida Sans OT	(*Encodings:* T1, TS1, LY1, and TU)
hls	m, b, ub	n, it, (sl)	Regular, *italic*, **bold** & **ultra-bold**
Lucida Typewriter		—no OpenType—	(*Encodings:* T1, TS1, and LY1)
hlct	m, b	n, (it), sl	Regular, *slanted*, **bold** & ***bold slanted***
Lucida Sans Typewriter		Lucida Sans Typewriter OT	(*Encodings:* T1, TS1, LY1, and TU)
hlst	m, b	n, (it), sl	Regular, *slanted*, **bold** & ***bold slanted***
			Special font faces
Lucida Fax		—no OpenType—	(*Encodings:* T1, TS1, and LY1)
hlx	m, b	n, it, (sl)	Regular, *italic*, **bold** & ***bold italic***
Lucida Blackletter		Lucida Blackletter OT	(*Encodings:* T1, TS1, LY1, and TU)
hlcf	m	n	Only available in medium regular
Lucida Casual		—no OpenType—	(*Encodings:* T1, TS1, and LY1)
hlcn	m	n, it, (sl)	Only regular & *italic*
Lucida Calligraphy		Lucida Calligraphy OT	(*Encodings:* T1, TS1, and LY1)
hlce	m	it, (sl)	*Only available in medium italic*
Lucida Handwriting		Lucida Handwriting OT	(*Encodings:* T1, TS1, LY1, and TU)
hlcw	m	it, (sl)	*Only available in medium italic*
			OpenType-only Typewriter families
Lucida Console		Lucida Console DK	(*Encodings:* TU)
—	m, b	n, it, (sl)	—A monospaced design; see Example 10-2-3 on page 24
Lucida Grande Mono		Lucida Grande Mono DK	(*Encodings:* TU)
—	m, b	n, it, (sl)	—Another monospaced design; see Example 10-2-4

Oldstyle numerals as a default are implemented as a second, differently named font family in pdfTEX. If you use the hlh *family (with lining numerals), you can get them through* \oldstylenums.
Some of the font families are available only in Type 1 format (for pdfTEX); others are available only in OpenType format for Unicode engines (X$_{\text{E}}$TEX or LuaTEX).

Table 10.11: Classification of the Lucida font families

\sfdefault, or \ttdefault is all that is needed as long as you remember to also change the font encoding to T1 or LY1, because none of the fonts is available in OT1.

Unicode engines

In Unicode engines you have to set up the fonts yourself using fontspec and unicode-math; suitable .fontspec files are provided.

10-2-1

With a price of £148, **almost anything** can be found FLOATING IN FIELDS. — ¿But aren't Kafka's Schloß & Æsop's Œuvres often *naïve* vis-à-vis the dæmonic *phœnix's official rôle* in fluffy soufflés?

Lucida Bright 9pt/12pt
(hlh) Lucida Bright OT

If you prefer oldstyle numerals by default and you typeset with pdfTEX, use hlhj as the family name. With the Unicode engines apply Numbers=OldStyle in your fontspec declarations instead.

10-2-2

With a price of £148, **almost anything** can be found Floating In Fields. — ¿But aren't Kafka's Schloß & Æsop's Œuvres often *naïve* vis-à-vis the dæmonic *phœnix's official rôle* in fluffy soufflés?

Lucida Sans 9pt/12pt
(hls) Lucida Sans OT

With a price of £148, **almost anything** can be found Floating In **Fields**. -- ¿But aren't Kafka's Schloß & Æsop's Œuvres often *naïve* vis-à-vis the dæmonic *phœnix's official rôle* in fluffy soufflés?

Lucida Sans Typewriter
9pt/12pt (hlst)
Lucida Sans Typewriter OT

As you will have observed, the Lucida fonts appear to be rather large (even if set at 9pt, as we did in the above example), and it is important to give them enough leading so that they do not appear cramped. In the book we used an even smaller measure[1] of 8.5pt/11.7pt, which works fine; i.e., it is possible to scale them noticeably down while maintaining a balanced and pleasing look. With pdfTEX, the method to produce such downscaling is to define the command \DeclareLucidaFontShape — the documentation coming with the fonts explains how.

If you prefer a matching typewriter font with serifs, you can use Lucida Typewriter if you typeset with pdfTEX.

With a price of £148, **almost anything** can be found Floating In **Fields**. -- ¿But aren't Kafka's Schloß & Æsop's Œuvres often *naïve* vis-à-vis the dæmonic *phœnix's official rôle* in fluffy soufflés?

Lucida Typewriter 9pt/12pt
(hlct) —no OpenType—

Notice that Lucida Typewriter runs considerably wider than its sans serif counterpart. However, if you place both side by side, you see that their x-heights match. If

---

[1]This is the reason why these examples are not done in-line, but externally. If in-line as most other typeface examples, the fonts would have picked up the scale used for the body fonts of the book.

you use a Unicode engine, then Lucida Typewriter is not available, but there are two further sans serif typewriter alternatives: Lucida Console and Lucida Grande Mono.

Lucida Console 9pt/12pt
(— only OpenType —)
`Lucida Console DK`

```
With a price of £148, almost anything can be found
Floating In Fields. — ¿But aren't Kafka's Schloß
& Æsop's Œuvres often naïve vis-à-vis the dæmonic
phœnix's official rôle in fluffy soufflés?
```

10-2-3

Lucida Grande Mono
9pt/12pt
(— only OpenType —)
`Lucida Grande Mono DK`

```
With a price of £148, almost anything can be found
Floating In Fields. — ¿But aren't Kafka's Schloß
& Æsop's Œuvres often naïve vis-à-vis the dæmonic
phœnix's official rôle in fluffy soufflés?
```

10-2-4

On first glance you may not see any difference, given that both fonts have the same running length and are nearly identical in design. But if you look carefully, you can see that the uppercase letters of Lucida Grande Mono are noticeably taller than those of Lucida Console and that some characters have subtle differences, e.g., the bottoms of the "l" or the italic "i" are rounded in Lucida Grande Mono, while they are straight in Lucida Console.

The "DK" in their names stands for Donald Knuth, who, in a reply to [16], asked for an alternate "squarish" design for O and Q in Lucida Console [50] to make them easier distinguishable from the digit 0. Charles Bigelow acted on his request [17] and produced special versions of his fonts that are available only through TUG. They use Don's suggested letter forms by default, but also allow you to activate the default designs through the feature set `ss01` (which also changes to a slashed zero), and it is also possible to combine the squared O with the slashed zero as shown in the third line of the example. The alternate designs are available in both typefaces.

```
Q OIl 011    \usepackage{fontspec}
Q OIl 011      \LARGE
                \fontspec{Lucida Console DK}[]                       Q OIl 011 \par
Q OIl 011      \fontspec{Lucida Console DK}[RawFeature=ss01]         Q OIl 011 \par
                \fontspec{Lucida Console DK}[Numbers=SlashedZero] Q OIl 011
```

10-2-5

The set of Lucida fonts also contains a number of special font faces. Lucida Fax, as the name implies, was originally developed for use in fax transmissions and is very legible in bad reading conditions. This makes it a great choice for small print, e.g., in footnotes (as long as you do not need small capitals). Below we exhibit it in 7pt:

Lucida Fax 7pt/9pt
(hlx) *— no OpenType —*

With a price of £148, **almost anything** can be found Floating In Fields. — ¿But aren't Kafka's Schloß & Æsop's Œuvres often *naïve* vis-à-vis the dæmonic *phœnix's official rôle* in fluffy soufflés?

The other four fonts — Lucida Casual, Calligraphy, Handwriting, and Blackletter — all exist in only one weight and only one or two variants, upright and italics. They are

Family	Series	Shapes	Typeface Examples
Merriweather	Merriweather	(*Encodings:* T1, TS1, OT1, LY1, and TU)	
Merriwthr-OsF	l, m, b, ub	n, it, (sl)	Regular, light, *italic*, **bold**, and ultra-bold
Merriweather Sans	Merriweather Sans	(*Encodings:* T1, TS1, OT1, LY1, and TU)	
MerriwthrSans-OsF	l, m, b, eb	n, it, (sl)	Sans regular, light, *italic*, **bold**, and **extra-bold**

Figure styles are -OsF *and* -Sup.

Table 10.12: Classification of the Merriweather font families

thus useful only in special circumstances, but all of them can be freely mixed with other Lucida variants.

With a price of £148, almost anything can be found Floating In Fields. — ¿But aren't Kafka's Schloß & Æsop's Œuvres often *naïve* vis-à-vis the dæmonic *phœnix's official rôle* in fluffy soufflés?

Lucida Casual 9pt/12pt
(hlcn) —no OpenType—

Both Lucida Calligraphy and Lucida Handwriting appreciate extra leading:

With a price of £148, almost anything can be found Floating In Fields. — ¿But aren't Kafka's Schloß & Æsop's Œuvres often naïve vis-à-vis the dæmonic phœnix's official rôle in fluffy soufflés?

Lucida Calligraphy 9pt/13pt
(hlce)
Lucida Calligraphy OT

With a price of £148, almost anything can be found Floating In Fields. — ¿But aren't Kafka's Schloß & Æsop's Œuvres often naïve vis-à-vis the dæmonic phœnix's official rôle in fluffy soufflés?

Lucida Handwriting 9pt/13pt
(hlcw) —no OpenType—

With pdfTeX, Lucida Blackletter should be primarily used for individual letters in math. As a text typeface (while properly kerned) it is missing the "long s" in that engine, which is needed for setting historically correct type. However, when using one of the Unicode engines, it is available in its appropriate Unicode position U+017F.

With a price of £148, almost anything can be found floating In fields. — ¿But aren't Kafka's Schloß & Æsop's Œuvres often naïve vis-à-vis the dæmonic phœnix's official rôle in fluffy soufflés?

Lucida Blackletter 9pt/12pt
(hlcf)
Lucida Blackletter OT

10.2.11 Merriweather fonts

Designed by Eben Sorkin for Adobe, Merriweather features a large x-height and open letterforms, making it very readable at small sizes. The companion sans serif design Merriweather Sans is semi-condensed. Both families are offered in four weights with

Family	Series	Shapes	Typeface Examples
Droid Serif	Droid Serif	(*Encodings:* T1, TS1, T2A, T2B, T2C, OT1, LGR, and TU)	
droidserif	m, b	n, it, sl, ui	Serif regular, *slanted, italic,* **bold**, and upright italics
Droid Sans	Droid Sans	(*Encodings:* T1, TS1, T2A, T2B, T2C, OT1, LGR, and TU)	
droidsans	m, b	n, sl, (it)	Sans regular, *oblique,* **bold**, and ***bold oblique***
Droid Mono	Droid Sans Mono	(*Encodings:* T1, TS1, T2A, T2B, T2C, OT1, LGR, and TU)	
droidsansmono	m	n, sl, (it)	Mono regular and *oblique*

Table 10.13: Classification of the Google Droid font families

upright and italic shapes. Note that Merriweather has ultra-bold (ub), while the Sans has a somewhat lighter extra-bold (eb) series.

LaTeX support for all engines is provided through the package merriweather by Bob Tennent, which offers various options to set up different aspects of the fonts.

Merriweather 9pt/12pt
(Merriwthr-OsF)
Merriweather

With a price of £148, **almost anything** can be found FLOATING IN FIELDS. — ¿But aren't Kafka's Schloß & Æsop's Œuvres often *naïve* vis-à-vis the dæmonic *phœnix's official rôle* in fluffy soufflés?

Merriweather Sans 9pt/12pt
(MerriwthrSans-OsF)
MerriweatherSans

With a price of £148, **almost anything** can be found FLOATING IN FIELDS. — ¿But aren't Kafka's Schloß & Æsop's Œuvres often *naïve* vis-à-vis the dæmonic *phœnix's official rôle* in fluffy soufflés?

10.2.12 Google's Noto and Droid fonts

The Noto family of fonts are Google's attempt to eventually provide glyph coverage for all languages and scripts defined by the Unicode standard. Right now it consists of more than 100 individual fonts with a total of nearly 64000 characters covering most (though clearly not all, given that Unicode 14 has more than twice the number of defined characters) scripts in their entirety.[1] Besides the goal of full coverage, Noto is designed to provide visual harmony across multiple languages/scripts (e.g., compatible heights and stroke thicknesses) allowing the different Noto fonts to be easily used together.

Noto is normally preferable over Droid

The Latin, Greek, and Cyrillic glyphs in the Noto fonts are derived from the Droid family designed by Steve Matteson — an earlier commission by Google for the Android operating system. They are in fact the Droid fonts, but with additional weights, real small capitals, a greater glyph coverage (e.g., full polytonic Greek), and some errors corrected.

---

[1]When computer programs, such as browsers, cannot represent glyphs because they are missing in the current font, they often display a little rectangle. These rectangles got nicknamed "tofu" in some circles, and Noto aims to remove the tofu from the Web, hence the name **No to**fu.

To use Droid with the pdfTEX engine, the packages droid, droidmono, droidsans, and droidserif by Mohamed El Morabity are available. Except for droid, the packages accept the option `scaled` to specify a scale factor when loading individual fonts.

> **Unicode engines**
>
> For Unicode engines you have to set up Droid using the fontspec package. But if you use such an engine, then Noto is the better choice, as it simply offers more extensive glyph support and additional weights and shapes throughout.

LATEX support for Noto for all engines is provided through the packages noto, noto-mono, noto-sans, and noto-serif by Bob Tennent, which support the typical options such as `scaled` or `oldstyle` as well as some special ones to access the huge number of weights offered by the Noto families.[1] The condensed faces have their own support packages notocondensed (for Serif and Sans) and notocondensed-mono. Because of their size, the condensed fonts are not automatically included in the TEX Live distribution but need a simple manual installation. Follow the instructions at `https://contrib.texlive.info/` for that or download the package from CTAN.

Note that because of their size, the Noto condensed faces need a manual installation

The Droid fonts do not support `\scshape`, whereas Noto has real small capitals that look rather nice. This means that one should normally prefer Noto over Droid unless oblique shapes in addition to italics are needed as those are offered only by Droid. For comparison we show both Droid Serif and Noto Serif below so that you can study the differences:

With a price of £148, **almost anything** can be found Floating In Fields. — ¿But aren't Kafka's Schloß & Æsop's Œuvres often *naïve* vis-à-vis the dæmonic *phœnix's official rôle* in fluffy soufflés?

Droid Serif 10pt/12pt
(droidserif) Droid Serif

With a price of £148, **almost anything** can be found FLOATING IN FIELDS. — ¿But aren't Kafka's Schloß & Æsop's Œuvres often *naïve* vis-à-vis the dæmonic *phœnix's official rôle* in fluffy soufflés?

Noto Serif 10pt/12pt
(NotoSerif-OsF)
Noto Serif

The Noto families are available in four running lengths: besides a regular version, there exist three condensed versions that can easily be made the default by using the package notocondensed and passing the options `semicondensed`, `condensed`, or `extracondensed`. You can also request a condensed version for only Noto Serif or Sans through `rm` and `sf` or prevent that Noto Sans Mono is used with `nott`. As usual, several other options and commands exist for specialized requirements. Below are the condensed variants of the Serif family — notice how we gradually get more and more words into the lines:

With a price of £148, **almost anything** can be found FLOATING IN FIELDS. — ¿But aren't Kafka's Schloß & Æsop's Œuvres often *naïve* vis-à-vis the dæmonic *phœnix's official rôle* in fluffy soufflés?

Noto Serif (option semicondensed) *10pt/12pt*
(NotoSerif-OsF)
Noto Serif Semi Condensed

---

[1] Noto is one of the few families that supports a huge number of the NFSS series combinations, as it has weights from ultra-light to extra-bold and three compressed versions on top of the regular one; see Tables 10.14 and 10.15 on pages 28–29 for the full setup.

Family	Series	Shapes	Typeface Examples
Noto Serif	Noto Serif	*(Encodings:* T1, TS1, T2A, T2B, T2C, OT1, LGR, LY1, and TU)	
NotoSerif-LF	ul, el, sl, l, m, sb, b, eb, ub	n, it, (sl), sc, scit, (scsl)	Serif regular, *italic*, **bold**, and Small Caps
	Noto Serif Semi Condensed		
	ulsc, elsc, lsc, slsc, sc, sbsc, bsc, sbsc, ubsc	n, it, (sl), sc, scit, (scsl)	Serif semi-condensed, *italics*, **bold**, and Small Caps
	Noto Serif Condensed		
	ulc, elc, lc, slc, c, sbc, bc, ebc, ubc	n, it, (sl), sc, scit, (scsl)	Serif condensed, *italics*, **bold**, and Small Caps
	Noto Serif Extra Condensed		
	ulec, elec, lec, slec, ec, sbec, bec, sbec, ubec	n, it, (sl), sc, scit, (scsl)	Serif extra-condensed, *italics*, **bold**, and Small Caps
Noto Sans	Noto Sans	*(Encodings:* T1, TS1, T2A, T2B, T2C, OT1, LGR, LY1, and TU)	
NotoSans-LF	ul, el, l, sl, m, sb, b, eb, ub	n, it, (sl), sc, scit, (scsl)	Sans regular, *italics*, **bold**, and Small Caps
	Noto Sans Semi Condensed		
	ulsc, elsc, lsc, slsc, sc, sbsc, bsc, sbsc, ubsc	n, it, (sl), sc, scit, (scsl)	Sans semi-condensed, *italics*, **bold**, and Small Caps
	Noto Sans Condensed		
	ulc, elc, lc, slc, c, sbc, bc, ebc, ubc	n, it, (sl), sc, scit, (scsl)	Sans condensed, *italics*, **bold**, and Small Caps
	Noto Sans Extra Condensed		
	ulec, elec, lec, slec, ec, sbec, bec, sbec, ubec	n, it, (sl), sc, scit, (scsl)	Sans extra-condensed, *italics*, **bold**, and Small Caps

Supported figure styles of the Noto Serif and Sans fonts are -LF, -OsF, -TLF, -TOsF, *and* -Sup.

Table 10.14: Classification of the Google Noto font families

Noto Serif (option condensed*) 10pt/12pt* (NotoSerif-OsF) Noto Serif Condensed

With a price of £148, **almost anything** can be found Floating In Fields. — ¿But aren't Kafka's Schloß & Æsop's Œuvres often *naïve* vis-à-vis the dæmonic *phœnix's official rôle* in fluffy soufflés?

Noto Serif (option extracondensed*) 10pt/12pt* (NotoSerif-OsF) Noto Serif Extra Condensed

With a price of £148, **almost anything** can be found Floating In Fields. — ¿But aren't Kafka's Schloß & Æsop's Œuvres often *naïve* vis-à-vis the dæmonic *phœnix's official rôle* in fluffy soufflés?

Family	Series	Shapes	Typeface Examples
Noto Sans Mono	Noto Sans Mono	(*Encodings:* T1, TS1, T2A, T2B, T2C, OT1, LGR, LY1 and TU)	
NotoSansMono-TLF	ul, el, l, sl, m, sb, b, eb, ub	n, sc	Sans Mono regular, thin, **bold**, and **black**
	Noto Sans Mono Semi Condensed		
	ulsc, elsc, lsc, slsc, sc, sbsc, bsc, sbsc, ubsc	n, sc	Sans Mono semi-condensed, thin, **bold**, and **black**
	Noto Sans Mono Condensed		
	ulc, elc, lc, slc, c, sbc, bc, sbc, ubc	n, sc	Sans Mono condensed, thin, **bold**, and **black**
	Noto Sans Mono Extra Condensed		
	ulec, elec, lec, slec, ec, sbec, bec, sbec, ubec	n, sc	Sans Mono extra-condensed, thin, **bold**, and **black**

Supported figure styles of the SansMono are -TLF *and* -Sup.

Table 10.15: Classification of the Google Noto font families (cont.)

Here we exhibit all sans serif width variants with their different running lengths from regular down to extra-condensed.

With a price of £148, **almost anything** can be found FLOATING IN FIELDS. — ¿But aren't Kafka's Schloß & Æsop's Œuvres often *naïve* vis-à-vis the dæmonic *phœnix's official rôle* in fluffy soufflés?

Noto Sans 10pt/12pt (NotoSans-OsF) Noto Sans

With a price of £148, **almost anything** can be found FLOATING IN FIELDS. — ¿But aren't Kafka's Schloß & Æsop's Œuvres often *naïve* vis-à-vis the dæmonic *phœnix's official rôle* in fluffy soufflés?

Noto Sans (option semicondensed) 10pt/12pt (NotoSans-OsF) Noto Sans Semi Condensed

With a price of £148, **almost anything** can be found FLOATING IN FIELDS. — ¿But aren't Kafka's Schloß & Æsop's Œuvres often *naïve* vis-à-vis the dæmonic *phœnix's official rôle* in fluffy soufflés?

Noto Sans (option condensed) 10pt/12pt (NotoSans-OsF) Noto Sans Condensed

With a price of £148, **almost anything** can be found FLOATING IN FIELDS. — ¿But aren't Kafka's Schloß & Æsop's Œuvres often *naïve* vis-à-vis the dæmonic *phœnix's official rôle* in fluffy soufflés?

Noto Sans (option extracondensed) 10pt/12pt (NotoSans-OsF) Noto Sans Extra Condensed

The Noto Serif and Sans families both have matching math fonts, which are exhibited in Figure 12.38 on page 287 (Noto Serif) and Figure 12.50 on page 295 (Noto Sans). They have been prepared by Michael Sharpe.

Noto Sans Mono is also offered in four different running lengths, and if you want to use one of the condensed faces together with some other font families, use notocondensed-mono for setup. These condensed versions are a great choice if you have tight spacing requirements as even the extra-condensed version is very readable.

Noto Sans Mono 9pt/12pt
(NotoSansMono-TLF)
Noto Sans Mono

With a price of £148, **almost anything** can be found FLOATING IN FIELDS. — ¿But aren't Kafka's Schloß & Æsop's Œuvres often naïve vis-à-vis the dæmonic phœnix's official rôle in fluffy soufflés?

For comparison here is the extra-condensed version of Noto Sans Mono, which shows that you can save quite a lot of space when using it:

Noto Sans Mono (option
extracondensed) 9pt/12pt
(NotoSansMono-TLF)
Noto Sans Mono
Extra Condensed

With a price of £148, **almost anything** can be found FLOATING IN FIELDS. — ¿But aren't Kafka's Schloß & Æsop's Œuvres often naïve vis-à-vis the dæmonic phœnix's official rôle in fluffy soufflés?

However, Noto Sans Mono has neither italics nor oblique shapes, but it does offer different weights, which is perhaps more important. Droid Sans Mono on the other hand has no bold but offers italics. Thus, which to deploy depends on your use case.

Droid Mono 9pt/12pt
(droidsansmono)
Droid Sans Mono

With a price of £148, almost anything can be found Floating In Fields. — ¿But aren't Kafka's Schloß & Æsop's Œuvres often *naïve* vis-à-vis the dæmonic *phœnix's official rôle* in fluffy soufflés?

10.2.13 IBM Plex

The IBM Plex families have been developed by Mike Abbink at IBM in collaboration with Bold Monday and others with the intention to represent the IBM Brand spirit. Each family is offered in eight different weights with upright and italic shapes. Small capitals are not supported, and \slshape is aliased to italics.

IBM Plex Serif was inspired by Bodoni and Janson and incorporates oldstyle and Didone design aspects. IBM Plex Sans is a grotesque sans serif typeface with a design that was inspired by Franklin Gothic. It also exists in a condensed version offering all weights and shapes and can thus be used as a drop-in replacement for the regular sans serif. The letter forms of IBM Plex Mono upright are based on Plex Sans, while its italic shape was inspired by an italic typeface used on IBM's Selectric typewriter (one with a typeball).

LaTeX support for all engines is provided by the packages plex-serif, plex-sans, and plex-mono by Bob Tennent with the usual options for selecting the weights or a scaling factor (scaled).

Family	Series	Shapes	Typeface Examples
IBM Plex Serif	IBM Plex Serif (*Encodings:* T1, TS1, OT1, LY1, and TU)		
IBMPlexSerif-TLF	ul, el, l, m, sb, b	n, it, (sl)	IBM Plex Serif, *italic*, **bold**, and light
IBM Plex Sans	IBM Plex Sans, IBM Plex Sans Condensed (*Encodings:* T1, TS1, OT1, LY1, and TU)		
IBMPlexSans-TLF	ul, el, l, sl, m, sb, b ulc, elc, lc, slc, c, sbc, bc	n, it, (sl)	IBM Plex Sans, *italic*, **bold**, light, and thin Condensed Sans *italic*, **bold**, light, and thin
IBM Plex Mono	IBM Plex Mono (*Encodings:* T1, TS1, OT1, LY1, and TU)		
IBMPlexMono-TLF	ul, el, l, sl, m, sb, b	n, it, (sl)	IBM Plex Mono, *italic*, and **bold**

Supported figure styles of the IBM Plex fonts are -TLF *and* -Sup.

Table 10.16: Classification of the IBM Plex font families

With a price of £148, **almost anything** can be found Floating In Fields. — ¿But aren't Kafka's Schloß & Æsop's Œuvres often *naïve* vis-à-vis the dæmonic *phœnix's official rôle* in fluffy soufflés?

Plex Serif 10pt/12pt
(IBMPlexSerif-TLF)
IBM Plex Serif

With a price of £148, **almost anything** can be found Floating In Fields. — ¿But aren't Kafka's Schloß & Æsop's Œuvres often *naïve* vis-à-vis the dæmonic *phœnix's official rôle* in fluffy soufflés?

Plex Sans 10pt/12pt
(IBMPlexSans-TLF)
IBM Plex Sans

To use IBM Plex Sans Condensed as the default sans serif font in your document, you can pass the option condensed to the plex-sans package. Alternatively, you can select it individually through the c font series.

With a price of £148, **almost anything** can be found Floating In **Fields**. — ¿But aren't Kafka's Schloß & Æsop's Œuvres often *naïve* vis-à-vis the dæmonic *phœnix's official rôle* in fluffy soufflés?

Plex Sans (option condensed)
10pt/12pt
(IBMPlexSans-TLF)
IBM Plex Sans Condensed

With a price of £148, **almost anything** can be found Floating In **Fields**. — ¿But aren't Kafka's Schloß & Æsop's Œuvres often *naïve* vis-à-vis the dæmonic *phœnix's official rôle* in fluffy soufflés?

Plex Mono 9pt/12pt
(IBMPlexMono-TLF)
IBM Plex Mono

10.2.14 PT fonts

Paratype PT fonts have been designed by Alexandra Korolkova with assistance from Olga Umpeleva and Vladimir Yefimov. They consist of a humanistic sans serif, a serif, and a monospaced font all available in regular and bold weights. All fonts offer a wide glyph range and thus are capable of typesetting text in most Latin and Cyrillic languages.

Family	Series	Shapes	Typeface Examples
PT Serif	PT Serif	(*Encodings:* T1, TS1, T2A, T2B, T2C, OT1, and TU)	
PTSerif-TLF	m, b	n, it, sl	PT Serif regular, *slanted*, *italic*, **bold**, and ***bold italic***
PT Sans	PT Sans	(*Encodings:* T1, TS1, T2A, T2B, T2C, OT1, and TU)	
PTSans-TLF	m, b	n, it, (sl)	PT Sans regular, *italic*, **bold**, and ***bold italic***
	c, bc	n	PT Sans narrow **and narrow bold**
PT Sans Narrow	PT Sans Narrow	(*Encodings:* T1, TS1, T2A, T2B, T2C, OT1, and TU)	
PTSansNarrow-TLF	m, b	n, sl	PT Sans Narrow, *oblique*, **bold**, and ***bold oblique***
PT Serif Caption	PT Serif Caption	(*Encodings:* T1, TS1, T2A, T2B, T2C, OT1, and TU)	
PTSerifCaption-TLF	m	n, it, sl	PT Serif Caption, *italic*, *slanted*, bold, and bold italic
PT Sans Caption	PT Sans Caption	(*Encodings:* T1, TS1, T2A, T2B, T2C, OT1, and TU)	
PTSansCaption-TLF	m, b	n, sl	PT Sans Caption, *oblique*, **bold**, and ***bold oblique***
PT Mono	PT Mono	(*Encodings:* T1, TS1, T2A, T2B, T2C, OT1, and TU)	
PTMono-TLF	m, b	n, sl	PT Mono regular, *oblique/slanted*, **bold**, and ***bold oblique***

Table 10.17: Classification of the Paratype PT font families

Most of the slanted shapes are mechanically generated and are therefore of a somewhat lesser quality; however, when used only occasionally, they should work well enough.

Support for the pdfTeX engine is provided by Pavel Farář through the paratype bundle that contains the packages PTSerif, PTSerifCaption, PTSans, PTSansCaption, PTSansNarrow, and PTMono. All of them support the option scaled to specify a scale factor when loading individual fonts and set the corresponding family up as the default serif, sans serif, or typewriter font.

Unicode engines

For Unicode engines you have to set them up using the fontspec package.

PT Serif 10pt/12.6pt (PTSerif-TLF) PT Serif

With a price of £148, **almost anything** can be found Floating In Fields. — ¿But aren't Kafka's Schloß & Æsop's Œuvres often *naïve* vis-à-vis the dæmonic *phœnix's official rôle* in fluffy soufflés?

PT Sans 10pt/12.6pt (PTSans-TLF) PT Sans

With a price of £148, **almost anything** can be found Floating In **Fields**. — ¿But aren't Kafka's Schloß & Æsop's Œuvres often *naïve* vis-à-vis the dæmonic *phœnix's official rôle* in fluffy soufflés?

Family	Series	Shapes	Typeface Examples
Quattrocento	Quattrocento		*(Encodings:* T1, TS1, OT1, LY1, and TU*)*
Quattro-LF	m, b	n, (it), sl	Quattrocento regular, *oblique*, **bold**, and ***bold oblique***
Quattrocento Sans	Quattrocento Sans		*(Encodings:* T1, TS1, OT1, LY1, and TU*)*
QuattroSans-LF	m, b	n, (it), sl	Quattrocento Sans regular, *oblique*, **bold**, and ***bold oblique***

Supported figure styles for the Quattrocento families are –LF *and* –Sup.

Table 10.18: Classification of the Quattrocento font families

The monospaced family has oblique shapes but not italics nor any small capitals:

> With a price of £148, **almost anything** can be found Floating In **Fields**. – ¿But aren't Kafka's Schloß & Æsop's Œuvres often *naïve* vis-à-vis the dæmonic *phœnix's official rôle* in fluffy soufflés?
>
> *PT Mono 8pt/10pt*
> *(PTMono-TLF)* PT Mono

PT Sans also exists in a narrow version for documents that have tight spacing requirements. Note, however, that for this version no italic shape has been set up.

> With a price of £148, **almost anything** can be found Floating In **Fields**. – ¿But aren't Kafka's Schloß & Æsop's Œuvres often *naïve* vis-à-vis the dæmonic *phœnix's official rôle* in fluffy soufflés?
>
> *PT Sans Narrow 10pt/12.6pt*
> *(PTSansNarrow-TLF)*
> PT Sans Narrow

Finally, both PT Serif and PT Sans have a Caption variant for typesetting in small type, e.g., credentials or captions in small size, hence the name.

> With a price of £148, almost anything can be found Floating In Fields. – ¿But aren't Kafka's Schloß & Æsop's Œuvres often *naïve* vis-à-vis the dæmonic *phœnix's official rôle* in fluffy soufflés?
>
> *PT Serif Caption 7pt/10pt*
> *(PTSerifCaption-TLF)*
> PT Serif Caption

Note, however, that with PT Serif Caption there is no bold weight, and with PT Sans Caption you do not get any italics (\textsl works, though).

> With a price of £148, **almost anything** can be found Floating In **Fields**. – ¿But aren't Kafka's Schloß & Æsop's Œuvres often *naïve* vis-à-vis the dæmonic *phœnix's official rôle* in fluffy soufflés?
>
> *PT Sans Caption 7pt/10pt*
> *(PTSansCaption-TLF)*
> PT Sans Caption

10.2.15 Quattrocento

Quattrocento, designed by Pablo Impallari, is a typeface with wide and open letter-forms and a large x-height, making it very legible at small sizes. It is offered in two weights and upright and oblique shapes. Quattrocento Sans is the matching sans serif design.

LATEX support for all engines is provided through the quattrocento package by Bob Tennent, which sets up one or both families based on options.

Quattrocento 9pt/11pt
(Quattro-LF)
Quattrocento

With a price of £148, **almost anything** can be found Floating In Fields. — ¿But aren't Kafka's Schloß & Æsop's Œuvres often *naïve* vis-à-vis the dæmonic *phœnix's official rôle* in fluffy soufflés?

Quattrocento Sans 9pt/11pt
(QuattroSans-LF)
Quattrocento Sans

With a price of £148, **almost anything** can be found Floating In **Fields**. — ¿But aren't Kafka's Schloß & Æsop's Œuvres often *naïve* vis-à-vis the dæmonic *phœnix's official rôle* in fluffy soufflés?

10.2.16 Google Roboto families

Roboto, designed by Christian Robertson for Google, is a neo-grotesque sans serif typeface. It has been used as the operating system font for Android since 2011 (replacing Droid) and several of Google's web applications, which contributed to its growing popularity. The companion monospaced font is Roboto Mono. Roboto is offered in six weights and three condensed cuts and Roboto Mono in five weights each time with upright and oblique shapes. Roboto Slab is a slab serif font based on Roboto. It comes in four weights but only in upright shape.

LATEX support for all engines is provided by Bob Tennent through the packages roboto and roboto-mono supporting the usual options, such as scaled, various figure styles, and weight selections.

Roboto 10pt/12pt
(Roboto-OsF) Roboto

With a price of £148, **almost anything** can be found FLOATING IN **FIELDS**. — ¿But aren't Kafka's Schloß & Æsop's Œuvres often *naïve* vis-à-vis the dæmonic *phœnix's official rôle* in fluffy soufflés?

To use the Roboto Condensed font as the default sans serif font in your document you can pass the option condensed to the roboto package. Alternatively, you can select it individually through the c font series.

Roboto (option condensed)
10pt/12pt (Roboto-OsF)
Roboto Condensed

With a price of £148, **almost anything** can be found FLOATING IN **FIELDS**. — ¿But aren't Kafka's Schloß & Æsop's Œuvres often *naïve* vis-à-vis the dæmonic *phœnix's official rôle* in fluffy soufflés?

Note that the Small Caps in both Roboto Mono and Roboto Slab make no distinction between upper and lowercase as you can see below:

Roboto Mono 9pt/12pt
(RobotoMono-TLF)
Roboto Mono

With a price of £148, **almost anything** can be found FLOATING IN FIELDS. — ¿But aren't Kafka's Schloß & Æsop's Œuvres often *naïve* vis-à-vis the dæmonic *phœnix's official rôle* in fluffy soufflés?

Family	Series	Shapes	Typeface Examples
Roboto	Roboto, Roboto Condensed	*(Encodings:* T1, TS1, OT1, LGR, LY1, and TU)	
Roboto-LF	el, l, m, sb, b, eb	n, (it), sl, sc, (scit), scsl	Roboto regular, *oblique*, **bold**, and SMALL CAPS OBLIQUE
	lc, c, bc	n, (it), sl, sc, (scit), scsl	Condensed, *oblique*, **bold**, and light
Roboto Slab	Roboto Slab	*(Encodings:* T1, TS1, OT1, LGR, LY1, and TU)	
RobotoSlab-TLF	el, l, m, b	n	Roboto Slab regular, thin, and **bold**
Roboto Mono	Roboto Mono	*(Encodings:* T1, TS1, OT1, LGR, LY1, and TU)	
RobotoMono-TLF	el, l, m, sb, b	n, it, (sl), sc, scit, (scsl)	Roboto Mono *oblique*, SMALL CAPS, and **bold**

Supported figure styles for Roboto and Roboto Condensed are -LF, -OsF, -TLF, *and* -TOsF.
Roboto Mono and Roboto Slab offer only -TLF *figures.* LGR *is not fully provided: the families offer only monotonic Greek.*
Roboto Mono's italic shape is in reality oblique. Also note that in the sc *shape all letters have the same height.*

Table 10.19: Classification of the Roboto font families

With a price of £148, **almost anything** can be found FLOATING IN FIELDS. — ¿But aren't Kafka's Schloß & Æsop's Œuvres often naïve vis-à-vis the dæmonic phœnix's official rôle in fluffy soufflés?

Roboto Slab Serif (option rm*)*
10pt/13pt
(RobotoSlab-TLF)
Roboto Slab

To set up the Roboto Slab font as the default roman font, pass the option rm to the roboto package. It does not happen automatically as you may want to combine Roboto Sans with some other serif font.

10.2.17 Adobe Source Pro

Adobe's Source Serif Pro, designed by Frank Grießhammer, is a typeface inspired by the work of Pierre-Simon Fournier. The companion sans serif font Source Sans Pro and the monospaced Source Code Pro were designed by Paul D. Hunt. Source Sans Pro is inspired by typefaces by Morris Fuller Benton (1872-1948), such as Franklin Gothic, but with larger x-height and Humanist-influenced italics. The italics for Source Code Pro got added later by Teo Tuominen.

LATEX support for all engines is provided by Silke Hofstra through the three packages sourceserifpro, sourcesanspro, and sourcecodepro; for options see the package documentation.

With a price of £148, **almost anything** can be found FLOATING IN FIELDS. — ¿But aren't Kafka's Schloß & Æsop's Œuvres often *naïve* vis-à-vis the dæmonic *phœnix's official rôle* in fluffy soufflés?

Source Serif Pro 10pt/12pt
(SourceSerifPro-OsF)
Source Serif Pro

Family	Series	Shapes	Typeface Examples
Adobe Source Serif Pro	Source Serif Pro	(*Encodings:* T1, TS1, OT1, LY1, and TU)	
SourceSerifPro-LF	el, l, m, sb, b, k	n, it, (sl), sc	Source Serif Pro regular *and bold italic*
Adobe Source Sans Pro	Source Sans Pro	(*Encodings:* T1, TS1, OT1, LY1, and TU)	
SourceSansPro-LF	el, l, m, sb, b, k	n, it, (sl), sc	Source Sans Pro regular *and bold italic*
Adobe Source Code Pro	Source Code Pro	(*Encodings:* T1, TS1, T2A, T2B, T2C, OT1, LY1, and TU)	
SourceCodePro-TLF	el, l, m, mb, sb, b, k	n, it, (sl)	SourceCodePro *and bold italic*

Supported figure styles of the Source Serif Pro and Source Sans Pro fonts are -LF, -OsF, -TLF, -TOsF, *and* -Sup.
Source Code Pro supports only -TLF, -TOsF, *and* -Sup.
Source Code Pro supports the Cyrillic encodings only in upright shape and not in italics!

Table 10.20: Classification of the Adobe SourceCode font families

Source Sans Pro 10pt/12pt
(SourceSansPro-OsF)
Source Sans Pro

With a price of £148, **almost anything** can be found FLOATING IN **FIELDS**. — ¿But aren't Kafka's Schloß & Æsop's Œuvres often *naïve* vis-à-vis the dæmonic *phœnix's official rôle* in fluffy soufflés?

Source Code Pro 9pt/11pt
(SourceCodePro-TLF)
Source Code Pro

With a price of £148, **almost anything** can be found Floating In **Fields**. — ¿But aren't Kafka's Schloß & Æsop's Œuvres often *naïve* vis-à-vis the dæmonic *phœnix's official rôle* in fluffy soufflés?

10.3 Humanist (Oldstyle) serif fonts

Historically, Humanist or Renaissance typefaces are the earliest fonts following the Blackletter types used by Gutenberg and other early printers. They mimic Latin handwriting and started to appear in the middle of the 15th century in places like Venice and Florence. Primarily they are very calligraphic in nature, which shows in the strongly leftward axis most apparent in the bowls of characters and the lowercase o but often also in an angled e. Other defining characteristics include a small x-height and a fairly low contrast between thick and thin strokes.

Of course, Humanist typefaces do not need to come from that time period: modern designers also picked up the concepts and produced original designs in the Humanist spirit. Centaur, for example, was designed in 1916, and below we show the recent Coelacanth inspired by it.

Few fonts in that style are freely available, but the selection widens considerably if you also look at commercially sold ones. All commercial fonts can be used with Unicode engines with the help of the fontspec package, assuming that you buy the OpenType or TrueType versions. Using them with pdfTEX is less straightforward — you need to take a look at the autoinst program for that.

Family	Series	Shapes	Typeface Examples
Coelacanth	Coelacanth	(*Encodings:* T1, TS1, OT1, LY1, and TU)	
Coelacanth-LF	m	n, it, (sl), sc, scit, (scsl)	Coelacanth regular, *italic*, and Small Caps
	el, l, sb, b, eb	n, (it), sc	Thin, light, semi-bold, **bold**, and **heavy**

Supported figure styles for Coelacanth are −LF, −OsF, −TLF, and −TOsF. Italic shape is always medium weight!

Table 10.21: Classification of the Coelacanth font family

In the following sections we show three free high-quality typefaces that have been set up for use with LaTeX. None of them has oblique shapes (italics are substituted if you ask for them), but that is not surprising because slanted or oblique is a more recent invention and not really in spirit with such typefaces.

10.3.1 Alegreya

Alegreya has a matching sans serif design. Both families are described on page 11, and their NFSS classifications are in Table 10.2 on the same page.

With a price of £148, **almost anything** can be found Floating In **Fields**. — ¿But aren't Kafka's Schloß & Æsop's Œuvres often *naïve* vis-à-vis the dæmonic *phœnix's official rôle* in fluffy soufflés?

Alegreya 10pt/12pt
(Alegreya-OsF)
Alegreya Sans

10.3.2 Coelacanth

Designed by Ben Whitmore, Coelacanth is inspired by the classic Centaur Type design of Bruce Rogers (1870–1957). It is one of the few Humanist serif families freely available for use with LaTeX. The family provides six weights. However, the italics are available only in medium weight and are used unchanged in other weights as well in the LaTeX setup. Support for all engines is provided through the package coelacanth by Bob Tennent.

With a price of £148, **almost anything** can be found Floating In **Fields**. — ¿But aren't Kafka's Schloß & Æsop's Œuvres often *naïve* vis-à-vis the dæmonic *phœnix's official rôle* in fluffy soufflés?

Coelacanth 10pt/12pt
(Coelacanth-OsF)
Coelacanth

10.3.3 fbb — A version of Cardo

Cardo is a Humanist font by David J. Perry that is based on a Venetian type from the 15th century, which was also used as the basis for Monotype's commercial Bembo family. It was developed as part of the Medieval Unicode Font Initiative.

Family	Series	Shapes	Typeface Examples
Cardo	`fbb`, `Cardo`	(*Encodings:* T1, TS1, OT1, LY1, and TU)	
`fbb-LF`	m, b	n, it, (sl), sc, scit, (scsl)	Cardo regular, *italic*, **bold**, ***bold italic***, Small Caps, Small Caps Italic and Small Caps Italic Bold

Supported figure styles for fbb are `-LF`, `-OsF`, `-TLF`, `-TOsF`, `-Sup`, *and* `-Inf`.

Table 10.22: Classification of fbb (Cardo) font family

Unicode engines

The font is freely available on the Web in TrueType format (but not included in standard TeX distributions in that form). It contains more than 3000 glyphs and ligatures covering many modern, classical, and medieval languages. It also supports other rather specialized applications such as historical Greek music notation, phonetic alphabets, and much more. In this form it is available only for Unicode engines.

Starting from the Cardo font, Michael Sharpe produced a version under the name "fbb" but with many modifications, e.g., adding bold italic, Small Caps, and different figure styles. However, his fonts provide only a more restricted glyph set, but still a set of roughly 1000 characters each. Support for pdfTeX is provided through the package fbb, which accepts typical options such as `scaled` for a scale factor, `oldstyle`, `lining`, etc. You can also supply the option `altP` to use the historically correct open form of "P" instead of the more modern closed rendering "P" usually used — a tiny but interesting detail.

Unicode engines

For Unicode engines a `fontspec` configuration file is provided.

Cardo 10pt/12pt
(fbb-OsF) `fbb` With a price of £148, **almost anything** can be found Floating In Fields. — ¿But aren't Kafka's Schloß & Æsop's Œuvres often *naïve* vis-à-vis the dæmonic *phœnix's official rôle* in fluffy soufflés?

10.4 Garalde (Oldstyle) serif fonts

Named after two influential type designers from the period, Claude Garamond (1499-1561) and Aldus Manutius (1449-1515), Garalde fonts first appeared at the end of the 15th century. There is now less calligraphic influence because typesetting began to be viewed as different from writing. Still, we do have a tilted axis in many characters, but it is subtler and less obvious than in Humanist typefaces. The serifs become more carefully formed and on ascenders more wedge shaped. Characters are designed more proportionally, and there is now a greater contrast between thick and thin strokes.

Family	Series	Shapes	Typeface Examples
Accanthis Accanthis	(*Encodings:* T1, TS1, OT1, LY1, and TU)		
AccanthisADFStdNoThree-LF	m, b	n, it, (sl)	Accanthis regular, *italic*, **bold**, and ***bold italic***

The supported figure style for Accanthis is -LF*.*

Table 10.23: Classification of the Accanthis Font family

Generally speaking we start to see more refinement and details in the characters, in parts surely augmented by the improving skills of the punch cutters of that time. Another difference is the crossbar on the e, which is now fully straight while in Humanist typefaces it was typically sloped.

The number of free high-quality Garalde typefaces prepared for use with LaTeX is still fairly small; below we show most of them.

10.4.1 Accanthis

The Accanthis family by Hirwen Harendal, which also incorporates some aspects of Humanist fonts (e.g., the tilted e), is suitable as an alternative to fonts such as Garamond, Galliard, and similar Garalde designs. It is offered in two weights with upright and italic characters. LaTeX support for all engines is provided through the package accanthis by Bob Tennent. The option scaled lets you select a scaling factor.

With a price of £148, **almost anything** can be found Floating In Fields. — ¿But aren't Kafka's Schloß & Æsop's Œuvres often *naïve* vis-à-vis the dæmonic *phœnix's official rôle* in fluffy soufflés?

Accanthis 10pt/12pt
(AccanthisADFStdNoThree-LF)
Accanthis ADF Std No3

10.4.2 GFS Artemisia

GFS Artemisia is a slightly calligraphic general-purpose typeface designed by Takis Katsoulidis. LaTeX support for pdfTeX is provided through the package gfsartemisia, which sets the font up as \rmdefault and uses the txfonts[1] for formulas. Alternatively, with the package gfsartemisia-euler it uses the euler package instead. Besides Latin languages, the family fully supports polytonic Greek.

With a price of £148, **almost anything** can be found Floating In Fields. — ¿But aren't Kafka's Schloß & Æsop's Œuvres often *naïve* vis-à-vis the dæmonic *phœnix's official rôle* in fluffy soufflés?

GFS Artemisia 10pt/12pt
(artemisia)
GFS Artemisia

---

[1]Please note that the txfonts have spacing problems and cannot be really recommended; see Section 12.3.4 on page 243 for details. We therefore recommend to use either the gfsartemisia-euler package or set up the font manually and add suitable math fonts with the help of the newtxmath package.

39

Family	Series	Shapes	Typeface Examples
GFS Artemisia	GFS Artemisia	(*Encodings:* T1, OT1, LGR, and TU)	
artemisia	m, b	n, it, sl, sc, sco	Artemisia regular, **bold**, *italic*, oblique, and SMALL CAPS OBLIQUE

The supported figure style for GFS Artemisia is -TLF *(but not called this).*
Unfortunately, sco *is a nonstandard shape name for* scsl; *thus, low-level shape commands are needed to access it.*

Table 10.24: Classification of the GFS Artemisia font family

Family	Series	Shapes	Typeface Examples
Crimson Pro	Crimson Pro	(*Encodings:* T1, TS1, OT1, LY1, and TU)	
CrimsonPro-LF	el, l, sl, m, sb, b, eb, ub	n, it, (sl)	Crimson Pro regular, *italic*, **bold**, extra-light, **semi-bold**, and **ultra-bold**
Cochineal	Cochineal	(*Encodings:* T1, TS1, OT1, LGR, LY1, and TU)	
Cochineal-LF	m, b	n, it, (sl), sw, sc, scit, (scsl)	Cochineal regular, *italic*, **bold**, and SMALL CAPS ITALIC

Supported figure styles for Crimson Pro and Cochineal are -LF, -OsF, -TLF, -TOsF, -Sup, *and* -Inf.

Table 10.25: Classification of the Crimson Pro/Cochineal font families

10.4.3 Crimson, Crimson Pro, and Cochineal

The Crimson family of fonts has been designed by Sebastian Kosch in the tradition of beautiful Garalde oldstyle typefaces, such as Jan Tschichold's (1902–1974) Sabon or Robert Slimbach's Minion. Provided are upright and italic shapes in three weights. The family got extended by Jacques Le Bailly under the name Crimson Pro to cover a total of seven weights from thin to black; also oldstyle figures got added. Support for all TeX engines is provided by Bob Tennent through the package CrimsonPro.

Michael Sharpe also extended the Crimson fonts by providing roughly 1 500 additional glyphs (including polytonic Greek) so that all glyphs are available in all styles including bold Small Caps and different types of figures (the original Crimson had only lining tabular figures). This extension is distributed as Cochineal fonts, and the LaTeX support package is called cochineal. Thus, his package is the better choice if you want small capitals or need Greek. The family also has matching mathematical fonts exhibited in Figure 12.2 on page 263.

Cochineal 10pt/12pt
*(*Cochineal-OsF*)*
Cochineal

With a price of £148, **almost anything** can be found FLOATING IN FIELDS. — ¿But aren't Kafka's Schloß & Æsop's Œuvres often *naïve* vis-à-vis the dæmonic *phœnix's official rôle* in fluffy soufflés?

Family	Series	Shapes	Typeface Examples
Cormorant Garamond	Cormorant Garamond		(*Encodings:* T1, TS1, T2A, T2B, T2C, OT1, LY1, and TU)
CormorantGaramond-LF	l, m, sb, b	n, it, (sl), sc	CormorantGaramond regular, semi-bold, and *bold italic*

Supported figure styles for Cormorant Garamond are -LF, -OsF, -TLF, -TOsF, -Sup, *and* -Inf.

Table 10.26: Classification of the Cormorant Garamond font family

However, Cochineal does not provide the additional weights that Crimson Pro offers. The next sample shows the extra-light (el) series of Crimson Pro with \textbf using medium-bold (b). But note the missing Small Caps in that case.

With a price of £148, **almost anything** can be found Floating In **Fields** — ¿But aren't Kafka's Schloß & Æsop's Œuvres often *naïve* vis-à-vis the dæmonic *phœnix's official rôle* in fluffy soufflés?

Crimson Pro 10pt/12pt
(CrimsonPro-OsF)
Crimson Pro

10.4.4 Cormorant Garamond

Cormorant Garamond, designed by Christian Thalmann, is inspired by Claude Garamond's work but not explicitly based on a particular set of specimens. Its intended usage is that of a display typeface, which is quite visible if set in normal body size because it then appears to be extremely light. Here is an example of regular and light weights at 20 points:

Cormorant Garamond regular and light

Cormorant Garamond 20pt/24pt
(CormorantGaramond-OsF)
Cormorant Garamond

Compare this to the following example showing the regular weight at ten points. In this setting, it appears to be extremely light.

With a price of £148, **almost anything** can be found Floating In Fields. — ¿But aren't Kafka's Schloß & Æsop's Œuvres often *naïve* vis-à-vis the dæmonic *phœnix's official rôle* in fluffy soufflés?

Cormorant Garamond 10pt/12pt
(CormorantGaramond-OsF)
Cormorant Garamond

LaTeX support for all engines is available with the CormorantGaramond package by Bob Tennent providing the usual options such as scaled or oldstyle, etc.

10.4.5 EB Garamond

EB Garamond, designed by Georg Duffner and Octavio Pardo, is one of the revivals of the fonts designed by Claude Garamond (1499-1561). The source for the letterforms is a scan of a text known as the "Egenolff-Berner specimen", composed in the 16th century by Conrad Berner at the Egenolff print office, showing Garamond's roman

Family	Series	Shapes	Typeface Examples
EBGaramond	EBGaramond	(*Encodings:* T1, TS1, OT1, LY1, and TU)	
EBGaramond-LF	sl, m, sb, b, eb	n, it, (sl), sw, sc, scit, (scsl)	Roman, *italic*, SMALL CAPS (*ITALICS*), **bold**, **extra-bold**, and *Swash Letters*

Supported figure styles for EB Garamond are -LF, -OsF, -TLF, -TOsF, -Sup, and -Inf.

Table 10.27: Classification of the EBGaramond font family

and Robert Granjon's (1513-1589) italic types at different sizes[1] — hence the reason for the name of this project. LaTeX support for all engines is provided through the ebgaramond package by Bob Tennent. It also offers access to a few initials and swash letters provided with the fonts. Typesetting with matching mathematical fonts is shown in Figures 12.3 to 12.5 on pages 264-265.

EBGaramond 10pt/12pt
(EBGaramond-OsF)
EBGaramond

With a price of £148, **almost anything** can be found FLOATING IN **FIELDS**. — ¿But aren't Kafka's Schloß & Æsop's Œuvres often *naïve* vis-à-vis the dæmonic *phœnix's official rôle* in fluffy soufflés?

10.4.6 Garamond Libre

The Garamond Libre fonts are an extended fork by D. Benjamin Miller from fonts originally developed by George Douros. They are another Garamond revival with the roman face following Claude Garamond's (1499-1561) original design. The italics are from a 16th-century engraver too — not Garamond's (no specimens have survived) but that of Robert Granjon (1513-1589). The upright Greek that is included in the OpenType fonts follow a design by Firmin Didot (1764-1836), while the Greek italics are based on a design by Alexander Wilson (??-1784).

The fonts include support for Latin, Greek, and Cyrillic scripts, and if used with Unicode engines, you can also use the full IPA alphabet, Byzantine musical symbols, and various other glyphs that the limited font support with pdfTeX can not or only rudimentary provide.

LaTeX support for all engines is provided through the package garamondlibre by Bob Tennent. The package supports the usual options implemented by Bob; e.g., scaled lets you select a scaling factor, osf makes oldstyle numerals the default, etc.

Garamond Libre 10pt/12pt
(GaramondLibre-OsF)
Garamond Libre

With a price of £148, **almost anything** can be found FLOATING IN FIELDS. — ¿But aren't Kafka's Schloß & Æsop's Œuvres often *naïve* vis-à-vis the dæmonic *phœnix's official rôle* in fluffy soufflés?

Garamond Libre offers Swash glyphs[2]: the nw shape gives you Swash upright and

---

[1] https://image.linotype.com/files/pdf/specimen.pdf
[2] Not sure I would use them, at least not in upright shape — they do not seem to blend in well.

Family	Series	Shapes	Typeface Examples
Garamond Libre	`Garamond Libre`	(*Encodings:* T1, TS1, OT1, LY1, LGR, T2A, T2B, T2C, and TU)	
`GaramondLibre-LF`	`m, b`	`n, it, (sl), sc, scit, (scsl)`	Libre Garamond regular, *italic*, **bold** *& italic*
	`m, b`	`nw, sw`	Libre Garamond Swash upright *and Swash italics*

Supported figure styles for Garamond Libre are `-LF`, `-OsF`, `-Sup`, *and* `-Inf`.

Table 10.28: Classification of the Garamond Libre fonts

`sw` Swash italics; e.g., the next example is made by starting it with `\fontshape{nw}`
`\selectfont`. Note that there is no `scnw`, so we get normal small caps.

> With a price of £148, **almost anything** can be found FLOATING IN FIELDS. — *¿But aren't Kafka's Schloß & Æsop's Œuvres often* naïve *vis-à-vis the* dæmonic *phœnix's official rôle* in fluffy soufflés?

Garamond Libre Swash (shape nw) 10pt/12pt (GaramondLibre-OsF) `Garamond Libre`

`\fontshape{sw}\selectfont` gets you Swash italics, but for short phrases or individual letters or words you can alternatively use `\textsw` to access them.

> *With a price of £148, **almost anything** can be found FLOATING IN FIELDS. — ¿But aren't Kafka's Schloß & Æsop's Œuvres often* naïve *vis-à-vis the dæmonic phœnix's official rôle in fluffy soufflés?*

Garamond Libre Swash (shape sw) 10pt/12pt (GaramondLibre-OsF) `Garamond Libre`

If you know that you have an italic and upright Swash face (`sw` and `nw`) but no small caps Swash (`scsw`), consider adding the following rule to your document:

`\DeclareFontShapeChangeRule{sw}{sc}{scsw}{nw}`

This directs NFSS to switch to the upright Swash face if `scsw` is unavailable instead of switching to `sc`; see the discussion on page →I 735. If we apply that, then the first line of the example text changes to

> *With a price of £148, **almost anything** can be found* Floating In Fields. —

which is arguably better than getting straight small capitals without Swash.

10.4.7 URW Garamond No. 8

In the first quarter of the last century the Stempel Type Foundry released a Garamond adaption for hot-metal typesetting that has remained popular since. URW Garamond No. 8 is a freeware version based on this design and contributed by URW++ to the Ghostscript project under the AFP license. Because of this license, it is not automatically included in most TeX distributions but can be easily installed using the getnonfreefonts script. The design has relatively short descenders, allowing it to be used with little leading.

Family	Series	Shapes	Typeface Examples
URW Garamond No. 8 —no OpenType—			(*Encodings:* T1 and TS1)
ugm	m, b	n, it, (sl)	Roman, *italic*, **bold**, and ***bold italics***
Garamondx GaramondNo8		(*Encodings:* T1, TS1, LY1, and TU)	
zgmx	m, b	n, it, (sl), sc, scit, (scsl)	Roman, *italic*, **bold**, and Small Caps *Italics*
zgmj			ditto, but with 1234...9 oldstyle figures

URW Garamond No. 8 supports only lining figures in its original freeware release.
Garamondx supports lining and oldstyle figures (family name zgmj *).*

Table 10.29: Classification of the URW Garamond No. 8 font family

To use the font with pdfTEX simply set \rmdefault to ugm or select that family explicitly, but note that the LATEX support files are offered only for the T1 encoding.

URW Garamond No. 8
10pt/12pt (ugm)

With a price of £148, **almost anything** can be found Floating In Fields. — ¿But aren't Kafka's Schloß & Æsop's Œuvres often *naïve* vis-à-vis the dæmonic *phœnix's official rôle* in fluffy soufflés?

If you look closely, the fonts are missing some of the f-ligatures; e.g., you get "ffl" instead of "ffl". These ligatures are missing in the Stempel Garamond as well, so their absence is not surprising. However, that and the missing small capitals limit the usefulness of the otherwise nice font.

So in 2006 Gaël Varoquaux produced an updated version of the fonts that included oldstyle figures, a first attempt at providing small capitals, a swash Q, and some kerning improvements.

Michael Sharpe used that version as a starting point for his reworking of URW Garamond No. 8 fonts, completely redoing the Small Caps shapes and making further improvements. LATEX support for his version is provided through the package garamondx and because of the AFP license of the original fonts also has to be manually installed using getnonfreefonts. Besides scaled and osf, the package supports special options such as swashQ to make the swash Q the default. Alternatively, you can get individual swash Qs with the command \swashQ that we use in the example below. A typesetting sample with matching mathematical fonts is shown in Figure 12.4 on page 264.

URW Garamondx 10pt/12pt
(zgmj) GaramondNo8

With a price of £148, **almost anything** can be found Floating In Fields. — ¿But aren't Kafka's Schloß & Æsop's Œuvres often *naïve* vis-à-vis the dæmonic *phœnix's official rôle* in fluffy soufflés? Qui or *Qui?*

Unicode engines

The freeware version of URW Garamond No. 8 was originally released in Type 1 format only. To make it available for Unicode engines, it was later converted

Family	Series	Shapes	Typeface Examples
Gentium Plus	Gentium Plus	(*Encodings:* T1, TS1, T2A, T2B, T2C, T5, OT1, LGR, LY1, and TU)	
gentium	m, sb, b, eb	n, it, (sl), sc, scit	Gentium regular, *italic*, SMALL CAPS, and *SMALL CAPS ITALICS*
			Gentium bold, *italic*, SMALL CAPS, and *SMALL CAPS ITALICS*

Bold series and Small Caps shape are available only for Latin alphabets.

Table 10.30: Classification of the Gentium Plus font family

by Khaled Hosny to TrueType. In this format the family can, for example, be downloaded from `https://garamond.org/urw/` and set up using `fontspec`. The TrueType fonts also support small capitals, a full set of f-ligatures, and oldstyle figures.

10.4.8 Gentium Plus

Gentium is an award-winning design by Victor Gaultney with the aim to produce readable, high-quality publications. It supports a wide range of Latin- and Cyrillic-based alphabets as well as full support for polytonic and monotonic Greek.

LaTeX support for the pdfTeX is provided through the package `gentium` that makes the font the `\rmdefault` and also supports the option `scaled`.

Unicode engines

For Unicode engines you have to set up your own `fontspec` declaration.

With a price of £148, **almost anything** can be found FLOATING IN FIELDS. — ¿But aren't Kafka's Schloß & Æsop's Œuvres often *naïve* vis-à-vis the dæmonic *phœnix's official rôle* in fluffy soufflés?

Gentium Plus 10pt/12pt
(gentium) `Gentium Plus`

10.4.9 Kp (Johannes Kepler) Roman

Kp Roman is inspired by Palatino and has matching sans serif and monospaced designs and a full set of math fonts. When used with pdfTeX, certain features, such as special ligatures or oldstyle numerals (shown below), can be activated by altering the family name as described on page 17; you can find the description of all three families and their NFSS classifications in Table 10.9 on page 18. If used with Unicode engines, the features can be activated through the typical feature sets as supported by `fontspec`. Examples with mathematics are shown in Figures 12.6 to 12.8 on pages 266–267.

With a price of £148, **almost anything** can be found FLOATING IN FIELDS. — ¿But aren't Kafka's Schloß & Æsop's Œuvres often *naïve* vis-à-vis the dæmonic *phœnix's official rôle* in fluffy soufflés?

Kp Roman with oldstyle numerals 10pt/12pt
(jkposn) `KpSans`

45

Family	Series	Shapes	Typeface Examples
Palatino	TeX Gyre Pagella		(*Encodings:* T1, TS1, T5, OT1, LY1, and TU)
qpl	m, b	n, it, (sl), sc, scit, (scsl)	Palatino regular, *italic*, **bold**, and Small Caps

Table 10.31: Classification of the Pagella (Palatino) family from the TeX Gyre distribution

10.4.10 Palatino (TeX Gyre Pagella)

Palatino, designed by Hermann Zapf (1918–2015), is one of the most widely used typefaces today [20]. You can feel the brush that created it, which gives it a lot of elegance. Although originally designed as a display typeface, due to its legibility, Palatino soon gained popularity as a text face as well.

    TeX Gyre Pagella shown here is based on the URW Palladio L version of the font family (which is set up with the TeX Gyre tgpagella package). Typesetting samples with matching math fonts are shown in Figures 12.10 to 12.13 on pages 269–270.

Palatino 10pt/12.4pt
(qpl) TeX Gyre Pagella

With a price of £148, **almost anything** can be found Floating In Fields. — ¿But aren't Kafka's Schloß & Æsop's Œuvres often *naïve* vis-à-vis the dæmonic *phœnix's official rôle* in fluffy soufflés?

10.5 Transitional/Neoclassical serif fonts

The Humanist and Garalde fonts discussed above are also often collectively referred to as Oldstyle fonts, and the Didone designs that we show in the next section are also known as Modern. In-between we have fonts classified as Transitional or Neoclassical that first appeared in the late 17th century.

    There is no longer a calligraphic influence, and the letter axis is now nearly, if not completely, vertical. The weight difference between the thickest and thinnest points shows an even higher contrast compared to Garalde designs. The serifs are now (nearly) horizontal and less bracketed, and overall details become very refined. In this section we show roughly a dozen high-quality transitional designs, some of which are revivals of famous types of that period; others are new designs in the transitional style.

10.5.1 Antykwa Poltawskiego

The Antykwa Poltawskiego fonts (originally named "Antykwa Polska") were designed in the 1920s by typographer Adam Półtawski with special shapes for frequent letters in the Polish language. For a long time it has been the major text type for musical publications in Poland.

Unicode engines

For Unicode engines you need to set up the font using fontspec declarations.

Family	Series	Shapes	Typeface Examples
Antykwa Poltawskiego		Antykwa Poltawskiego	(*Encodings:* T1, TS1, T5, OT1, OT4, LY1, and TU)
`antp`	l, m, sb, b	n, it, (sl), sc, scit, (scsl)	Light, regular, semi-bold, **bold**, *italic*, and SMALL CAPS ITALICS
Antykwa Poltawskiego Light		Antykwa Poltawskiego Light	(*Encodings:* T1, TS1, T5, OT1, OT4, LY1, and TU)
`antpl`	m, sb, b, eb	n, it, (sl), sc, scit, (scsl)	Regular, semi-bold, **bold**, **extra-bold**, *italic*, and SMALL CAPS ITALICS

The series specifications in Antykwa Poltawskiego Light are shifted by one weight with respect to Antykwa Poltawskiego; e.g., m in Antykwa Poltawskiego becomes sb in Antykwa Poltawskiego Light.

Table 10.32: Classification of the Antykwa Poltawskiego font family

LaTeX support for pdfTeX is provided through the package antpolt by Janusz Marian Nowacki (1951–2020). The standard weight can be selected through the options `regular` (default) or `light`.

With a price of £148, **almost anything** can be found FLOATING IN FIELDS. — ¿But aren't Kafka's Schloß & Æsop's Œuvres often *naïve* vis-à-vis the dæmonic *phœnix's official rôle* in fluffy soufflés?

Antykwa Poltawskiego Light 10pt/12pt (`antpl`)
Antykwa Poltawskiego Light

With a price of £148, **almost anything** can be found FLOATING IN FIELDS. — ¿But aren't Kafka's Schloß & Æsop's Œuvres often *naïve* vis-à-vis the dæmonic *phœnix's official rôle* in fluffy soufflés?

Antykwa Poltawskiego 10pt/12pt (`antp`)
Antykwa Poltawskiego

10.5.2 BaskervilleF and Libre Baskerville

Libre Baskerville is a revival of John Baskerville's (1706–1775) typeface, designed by Pablo Impallari and Rodrigo Fuenzalida as a font family optimized for web usage. It is based on the American Type Founder's Baskerville from 1941, but with a taller x-height, wider counters, and somewhat less contrast, making it work well for reading on computer screens. LaTeX support for all engines is available with the librebaskerville package by Bob Tennent. There are matching math fonts by Michael Sharpe; see page 271.

With a price of £148, **almost anything** can be found Floating In Fields. — ¿But aren't Kafka's Schloß & Æsop's Œuvres often *naïve* vis-à-vis the dæmonic *phœnix's official rôle* in fluffy soufflés?

Libre Baskerville 9pt/12pt (`LibreBskvl-LF`)
Libre Baskerville

The web optimization of Libre Baskerville means that it is less suited for traditional printing. For this reason Michael Sharpe created a variant version under the name BaskervilleF mostly by hollowing out the interiors of the Libre Baskerville

Family	Series	Shapes	Typeface Examples
Libre Baskerville	Libre Baskerville	(*Encodings:* T1, TS1, OT1, LY1, and TU)	
LibreBskvl-LF	m, b	n, it, (sl)	Libre Baskerville regular, **bold**, and *italic* only
BaskervilleF	BaskervilleF	(*Encodings:* T1, TS1, OT1, LY1, and TU)	
BaskervilleF-LF	m, b	n, it, (sl), sw, sc	BaskervilleF regular, **bold**, and *italic* only

Supported figure styles for Libre Baskerville are -LF *and* -Sup*; BaskervilleF supports* -OsF, -TLF, -TOsF, *and* -Sup.

Table 10.33: Classification of the Libre Baskerville and BaskervilleF font families

glyphs to increase the contrast. His version also provides small capitals (though they are perhaps a bit too thin) and additional figure styles. LaTeX support for pdfTeX is through the package baskervillef. Typesetting with matching math fonts is exhibited in Figure 12.14 on page 271.

> **Unicode engines**
>
> For Unicode engines a fontspec specification file is provided.

BaskervilleF 10pt/12pt
(BaskervilleF-OsF)
BaskervilleF

With a price of £148, **almost anything** can be found Floating In Fields. — ¿But aren't Kafka's Schloß & Æsop's Œuvres often *naïve* vis-à-vis the dæmonic *phœnix's official rôle* in fluffy soufflés?

10.5.3 Baskervald (Baskervaldx)

Another font inspired by Baskerville is Baskervald designed by Hirwen Harendal. It was extended with additional accented glyphs and oldstyle figures by Michael Sharpe. His version, named Baskervaldx, is made available for the pdfTeX engine through the package Baskervaldx, providing typical options such as scaled or oldstyle. This family has matching math fonts too, which are shown in Figures 12.15 to 12.16 on page 272.

> **Unicode engines**
>
> For Unicode engines a fontspec specification file is provided.

Baskervaldx 10pt/12pt
(Baskervaldx-OsF)
ADFBaskerville

With a price of £148, **almost anything** can be found Floating In Fields. — ¿But aren't Kafka's Schloß & Æsop's Œuvres often *naïve* vis-à-vis the dæmonic *phœnix's official rôle* in fluffy soufflés?

10.5.4 ITC Bookman (TeX Gyre Bonum)

Bookman was originally designed in 1860 by Alexander Phemister (1829–1894) for the Miller & Richard foundry in Scotland (commercially available from Bitstream). The

Family		Series	Shapes	Typeface Examples
Baskervaldx	ADFBaskerville		*(Encodings:* T1, TS1, OT1, LY1, and TU)	
Baskervaldx-LF		m, b	n, it, (sl), sw, sc, scit, (scsl)	Regular, *italic*, **bold**, and SMALL CAPS

Supported figure styles for Baskervaldx are LF, -OsF, -lLF, -TOsF, *and* -Sup.

Table 10.34: Classification of the Baskervaldx font family

Family	Series	Shapes	Typeface Examples
Bookman TeX Gyre Bonum		*(Encodings:* T1, TS1, T5, OT1, LY1, and TU)	
qbk	m, b	n, it, (sl), sc, scit, (scsl)	Bookman, *italic*, **bold**, and SMALL CAPS

Table 10.35: Classification of the Bonum (Bookman) family from the TEX Gyre distribution

ITC revival by Ed Benguiat has a larger x-height and a moderate stroke contrast that is well suited for body text and display applications.

TEX Gyre Bonum shown here is based on the URW Bookman L version of the font family (which is set up with the TEX Gyre tgbonum package).

Unicode engines

Matching mathematical fonts are available for Unicode engines; see Figure 12.17 on page 273.

With a price of £148, **almost anything** can be found FLOATING IN FIELDS. — ¿But aren't Kafka's Schloß & Æsop's Œuvres often *naïve* vis-à-vis the dæmonic *phœnix's official rôle* in fluffy soufflés?

ITC Bookman 9.6pt/11.5pt (qbk) TeX Gyre Bonum

10.5.5 Cambria

Cambria is a commercial transitional serif typeface designed by Jelle Bosma with contributions from Steve Matteson and Robin Nicholas. It has even spacing and proportions, is intended to be used for body text, is especially suitable for small print, and displays well on low-resolution screens. This makes it, together with the fact that it offers extensive support for Latin, Greek, Cyrillic, Armenian, IPA symbols, and a full collection of math symbols, a very versatile solution for typesetting documents for consumption on screen as well as on paper.

Commissioned by Microsoft, it is shipped as part of the Windows operating system as well as in several Office products for different platforms. Thus, while the font requires a license for use, many users will have this license if they work on

Family	Series	Shapes	Typeface Examples
Cambria	Cambria	(*Encodings:* TU)	
—	m, b	n, it, (sl), sc, scit, (scsl)	*Only for Unicode engines; see Example 10-5-1 below.*

Supported figure styles are lining and oldstyle, selectable through fontspec*'s* Numbers *key.*

Table 10.36: Classification of the Cambria family

Windows or because they own a product that installs the font. Because of this and its excellent math capabilities, we decided to include it in the collection even though it is available only for Unicode engines and has the license restrictions.

> **Unicode engines**
>
> There is no support for pdfTeX, only for Unicode engines. Lining figures are the default figure style, but oldstyle figures are supported as well. Below we have selected them through the fontspec feature Numbers=OldStyle.
>
> A larger example of the mathematical typesetting capabilities is shown in Figure 12.18 on page 274.

Cambria 10pt/12pt
(—only TrueType—)
Cambria

With a price of £148, almost anything can be found FLOATING IN Fields. — ¿But aren't Kafka's Schloß & Æsop's Œuvres often *naïve* vis-à-vis the dæmonic *phœnix's official rôle* in fluffy soufflés?

10-5-1

10.5.6 Bitstream Charter

Bitstream Charter is an original design by Matthew Carter based on the characters of Pierre-Simon Fournier, intended to work well on low-resolution devices; hence, it contains squared serifs and avoids excessive use of curves and diagonals. It is useful for many applications, including books and manuals. Charter was contributed by Bitstream to the X consortium.

Basic LaTeX support for the pdfTeX engine is provided through the package charter, but these days it is much better to use the package XCharter by Michael Sharpe as it offers improved small capitals, oldstyle, superior figures, and the typical options of a modern font package. Mathematical typesetting with matching fonts is shown in Figure 12.19 on page 275.

> **Unicode engines**
>
> For Unicode engines, a fontspec configuration is provided.

Bitstream Charter
10pt/12.4pt
(XCharter-TOsF) XCharter

With a price of £148, **almost anything** can be found FLOATING IN FIELDS. — ¿But aren't Kafka's Schloß & Æsop's Œuvres often *naïve* vis-à-vis the dæmonic *phœnix's official rôle* in fluffy soufflés?

Family	Series	Shapes	Typeface Examples
Charter XCharter		*(Encodings:* T1, TS1, T2A, OT1, LY1, and TU)	
XCharter-TLF	m, b	n, it, sl, sc, scit, scsl	Charter Roman, *italic*, **bold**, *slanted*, and SMALL CAPS

Supported figure styles for XCharter -TLF, -TOsF, -Inf, *and* -Sup.

Table 10.37: Classification of the Charter family

Family	Series	Shapes	Typeface Examples
Charis SIL CharisSIL		*(Encodings:* T1, TS1, T2A, T2B, T2C, OT1, LY1, and TU)	
charssil-TLF	m, b	n, it, (sl), sc, scit, (scsl)	Charis SIL, **bold**, *italic*, and SMALL CAPS *ITALICS*

The supported figure style for Charis SIL is -TLF.

Table 10.38: Classification of the Charis SIL family

10.5.7   Charis SIL — A design based on Bitstream Charter

Charis SIL (developed by SIL International) is a transitional typeface that is closely based on the design of Bitstream Charter. However, its glyphs were completely redrawn with significant differences in serif structure, proportions, diacritics, and other characteristics, which can be easily seen if you compare the previous and the following sample. The font offers support for Latin and Cyrillic, and, if used with a Unicode engine, offers many additional glyphs including a full set of IPA symbols. LaTeX integration is provided through the CharisSIL package by Bob Tennent.

With a price of £148, **almost anything** can be found FLOATING IN **FIELDS**. — ¿But aren't Kafka's Schloß & Æsop's Œuvres often *naïve* vis-à-vis the dæmonic *phœnix's official rôle* in fluffy soufflés?

Charis SIL 10pt/12.4pt
(charssil-TLF)   CharisSIL

10.5.8   Caslon — Reinterpreted as Libre Caslon

The Libre Caslon fonts are designed by Pablo Impallari as a reinterpretation of the typeface by William Caslon (1692-1766) from the 17th century of which there are still many revivals in wide use today. LaTeX support for all engines is available with the librecaslon package by Bob Tennent.

With a price of £148, **almost anything** can be found Floating In Fields. — ¿But aren't Kafka's Schloß & Æsop's Œuvres often *naïve* vis-à-vis the dæmonic *phœnix's official rôle* in fluffy soufflés?

Libre Caslon 9pt/12pt
(LibreCsln-OsF)
Libre Caslon Text

Table 10.39 on the next page shows the NFSS for Libre Caslon. Note that this family

Family	Series	Shapes	Typeface Examples
Libre Caslon	Libre Caslon Text		(*Encodings:* T1, TS1, OT1, LY1, and TU)
LibreCsln-LF	m	n, it, (sl)	Libre Caslon regular *and italic typeface*
	b	n, (it), sl	**Libre Caslon bold** *and bold artificially slanted*

Supported figure styles for Libre Caslon are -LF, -OsF, -TLF, -Inf, *and* -Sup.

Table 10.39: Classification of the Libre Caslon font family

has no bold italic face. Instead, the bold type is artificially slanted and this is what you get if you ask for bold italics.

10.5.9 Gandhi Serif

The Gandhi Serif fonts have a matching sans serif design described on page 15. Table 10.6 with their NFSS classifications are there too.

Gandhi Serif 10pt/12pt
(GandhiSerif-OsF)
Gandhi Serif

With a price of £148, **almost anything** can be found FLOATING IN FIELDS. — ¿But aren't Kafka's Schloß & Æsop's Œuvres often *naïve* vis-à-vis the dæmonic *phœnix's official rôle* in fluffy soufflés?

10.5.10 Inria Serif

The Inria Serif family, designed for the French research institute Inria, has a matching sans serif design (but no monospaced variant). You can find the description of both families on page 16 and the NFSS classification in Table 10.8 on page 17.

Inria Serif 10pt/12pt
(InriaSerif-OsF)
Inria Serif

With a price of £148, **almost anything** can be found Floating In Fields. — ¿But aren't Kafka's Schloß & Æsop's Œuvres often *naïve* vis-à-vis the dæmonic *phœnix's official rôle* in fluffy soufflés?

10.5.11 Libertinus Serif

The Libertinus families consists of a serif, a sans serif, and a monospaced family. They are described together on page 19, and their NFSS classifications can be found in Table 10.10 on page 20.

Unicode engines

For Unicode engines matching math fonts are available; see Figure 12.23 on page 277 for a page sample.

Libertinus Serif 10pt/12pt
(LibertinusSerif-OsF)
Libertinus Serif

With a price of £148, **almost anything** can be found FLOATING IN FIELDS. — ¿But aren't Kafka's Schloß & Æsop's Œuvres often *naïve* vis-à-vis the dæmonic *phœnix's official rôle* in fluffy soufflés?

Family	Series	Shapes	Typeface Examples
Literaturnaya		—no OpenType—	(*Encodings:* T1, TS1, T2A, OT1)
tli	m, b	n, it, sl, sc, si	Literaturnaya, *italic, slanted,* **bold,** and *ITALIC SMALL CAPS*

The unusual si shape name selects Small Caps Italics (normally this is called scit*).*

Table 10.40: Classification of the Literaturnaya font family

10.5.12 Literaturnaya — A favorite in the days of the USSR

Based on a design by Hermann Berthold from 1899, Literaturnaya was designed around 1940 by Anatolii Shchukin. Towards the end of the last century a digital version was developed by Lyubov Kuznetsova. The family was predominately used in the USSR and other socialist countries and was the standard Cyrillic typeface there in the period between 1950 and 1990. After the cold war it got more and more displaced by the then popular Times New Roman and is nowadays rarely seen.

LaTeX support files are provided by Vladimir Volovich. To make the font the default roman typeface, load his literat package (no options). The fonts are not part of the standard distributions but can be installed with getnonfreefonts.

Unicode engines

TrueType versions of the family are freely available on the Web, but they are not distributed through CTAN, so you have to install them yourself and then use fontspec if you want to use the family with a Unicode engine.

With a price of £148, **almost anything** can be found FLOATING IN FIELDS. — ¿But aren't Kafka's Schloß & Æsop's Œuvres often *naïve* vis-à-vis the dæmonic *phœnix's official rôle* in fluffy soufflés?

Literaturnaya 10pt/12pt
(tli) —no OpenType—

10.5.13 Lucida Bright

Lucida Bright is a modern design, but according to its designer Charles Bigelow, "[...] its inner forms are based on writing styles of the Italian Renaissance, and its sophisticated detailing is reminiscent of printing types of the French Enlightenment. It can be classified as a 'Transitional' or 'Reale' style of typeface, like the 18th century designs of Baskerville or Fournier". They show, however, in my opinion aspects of Didone and even tend towards slap serif in parts — which just proves that classification in few categories is difficult.

The Lucida Bright fonts have matching sans and monospaced designs and a full set of math fonts. The families are described together in Section 10.2.10 on page 21, and the NFSS classification is given in Table 10.11 on page 22. They are the fonts we have used for this book, except that we have set them even smaller than the typeface

Family	Series	Shapes	Typeface Examples
New Century Schoolbook	`TeX Gyre Schola`		(*Encodings:* T1, TS1, T5, OT1, LY1, and TU)
qcs	m, b	n, it, (sl), sc, scit, (scsl)	New Century Schoolbook in *italic*, **bold**, and Small Caps

Table 10.41: Classification of the Schola (New Century Schoolbook) family from the TEX Gyre distribution

example here. Examples of typesetting mathematics (in all engines) are exhibited in Figures 12.24 to 12.26 on pages 278–279.

Lucida Bright 9pt/12pt
(hlh) Lucida Bright OT

With a price of £148, **almost anything** can be found Floating In Fields. — ¿But aren't Kafka's Schloß & Æsop's Œuvres often *naïve* vis-à-vis the dæmonic *phœnix's official rôle* in fluffy soufflés?

10-5-2

10.5.14 Lucida Fax

This is another typeface in the Lucida extended family of fonts that you obtain if you purchase the set from TUG. It is particularly useful if you need small sizes because it remains nicely readable. Its description and NFSS classification is given in Section 10.2.10 on page 21.

Lucida Fax 7pt/9pt
(hlx) — no OpenType —

With a price of £148, **almost anything** can be found Floating In Fields. — ¿But aren't Kafka's Schloß & Æsop's Œuvres often *naïve* vis-à-vis the dæmonic *phœnix's official rôle* in fluffy soufflés?

10.5.15 Merriweather

The Merriweather fonts have a matching sans serif described on page 25. The NFSS classifications are found in Table 10.2.11 on same page.

Merriweather 9pt/12pt
(Merriwthr-OsF)
Merriweather

With a price of £148, **almost anything** can be found Floating In Fields. — ¿But aren't Kafka's Schloß & Æsop's Œuvres often *naïve* vis-à-vis the dæmonic *phœnix's official rôle* in fluffy soufflés?

10.5.16 New Century Schoolbook (TEX Gyre Schola)

The New Century Schoolbook typeface was designed at the beginning of the 20th century by Morris Fuller Benton (1872–1948) of the American Type Founders. It was created in response to a publisher's commission that sought a typeface with maximum legibility for elementary schoolbooks. Italics were originally not part of the design; they were added in later revivals by Linotype and ITC.

TEX Gyre Schola shown here is based on the URW Century Schoolbook L version of the font family (which is set up with the TEX Gyre tgschola package).

Typesetting with matching mathematical fonts is available for all engines; see Figures 12.20 to 12.21 on page 276 for examples.

With a price of £148, **almost anything** can be found Floating In Fields. — ¿But aren't Kafka's Schloß & Æsop's Œuvres often *naïve* vis-à-vis the dæmonic *phœnix's official rôle* in fluffy soufflés?

New Century Schoolbook 9.6pt/12pt
(qcs) TeX Gyre Schola

10.5.17 Plex Serif

The IBM Plex families consist of a serif, sans serif, and monospaced family described on page 30. The NFSS classifications are found in Table 10.16 on page 31.

With a price of £148, **almost anything** can be found Floating In Fields. — ¿But aren't Kafka's Schloß & Æsop's Œuvres often *naïve* vis-à-vis the dæmonic *phœnix's official rôle* in fluffy soufflés?

Plex Serif 10pt/12pt
(IBMPlexSerif-TLF)
IBM Plex Serif

10.5.18 PT Serif

Paratype's PT fonts also consist of a serif, sans serif, and monospaced family. They are described on page 30, and the NFSS classifications are in Table 10.16 on page 31.

With a price of £148, **almost anything** can be found Floating In Fields. — ¿But aren't Kafka's Schloß & Æsop's Œuvres often *naïve* vis-à-vis the dæmonic *phœnix's official rôle* in fluffy soufflés?

PT Serif 10pt/12.6pt
(PTSerif-TLF) PT Serif

10.5.19 Quattrocento

The Quattrocento families consists of serif and sans serif fonts. They are described together on page 33, and their NFSS classifications can be found in Table 10.18 on page 33.

With a price of £148, **almost anything** can be found Floating In Fields. — ¿But aren't Kafka's Schloß & Æsop's Œuvres often *naïve* vis-à-vis the dæmonic *phœnix's official rôle* in fluffy soufflés?

Quattrocento 9pt/11pt
(Quattro-LF)
Quattrocento

10.5.20 Times Roman (TₑX Gyre Termes and Tempora)

Times Roman is Linotype's version of Monotype's Times New Roman, which was originally designed under the direction of Stanley Morison (1889-1967) for the *London Times* newspaper. The Adobe font that is built into many PostScript devices uses Linotype's 12-point design.

TₑX Gyre Termes shown here is based on the URW Roman No9 L version of the font family, which is set up with the TₑX Gyre tgtermes package.

Family	Series	Shapes	Typeface Examples
Times Roman	`TeX Gyre Termes`		(*Encodings:* T1, TS1, T5, OT1, LY1, and TU)
qtm	m, b	n, it, (sl), sc, scit, (scsl)	Times Roman, *italic*, **bold**, and SMALL CAPS

Table 10.42: Classification of the Termes (Times) family from the TEX Gyre distribution

Family	Series	Shapes	Typeface Examples
Times Roman	`TeXGyreTermesX`		(*Encodings:* T1, TS1, OT1, LY1, and TU)
ntxlf	m, b	n, it, (sl), sc, scit, (scsl)	Times Roman, *italic*, **bold**, and SMALL CAPS with 12345
ntxosf	m, b	n, it, (sl), sc, scit, (scsl)	Times Roman, *italic*, **bold**, and SMALL CAPS with 12345

The family offers normal and larger Small Caps, but a selection can be made only through the newtxtext *package, and not by changing the NFSS font family name.*

Table 10.43: Classification of the Termes (Times) family from the New TX distribution

Times Roman 10pt/12pt
(qtm) `TeX Gyre Termes`

With a price of £148, **almost anything** can be found FLOATING IN FIELDS. — ¿But aren't Kafka's Schloß & Æsop's Œuvres often *naïve* vis-à-vis the dæmonic *phœnix's official rôle* in fluffy soufflés?

Michael Sharpe developed a slight modification of the family under the name of TeXGyreTermesX that is used by his newtxtext package. It offers slightly enlarged small capitals (with the option `largesc`) and can set up oldstyle numerals (with the option `osf`). It also alters the positions of dots above i and j and makes other minor modifications.

Note that while it is possible to select oldstyle numbers by choosing the appropriate NFSS family name, the enlarged small capitals are available only when using the support package (which we did in the next sample behind the scenes).

Times Roman (with options
`largesc,osf`) *10pt/12pt*
(ntxosf)
`TeXGyreTermesX`

With a price of £148, **almost anything** can be found FLOATING IN FIELDS. — ¿But aren't Kafka's Schloß & Æsop's Œuvres often *naïve* vis-à-vis the dæmonic *phœnix's official rôle* in fluffy soufflés?

Matching math fonts for all engines are available; see Figures 12.27 and 12.28 on pages 280–281 to see them in action.

There has been another font based on URW Roman No9 L constructed by Alexey Kryukov. He extended it with Greek and Cyrillic glyphs, and Michael Sharpe added LATEX support for it in the form of the tempora package. This is useful for documents that

Family	Series	Shapes	Typeface Examples
Tempora Tempora		(*Encodings:* T1, TS1, OT1, LGR, and TU)	
Tempora-TLF	m, b	n, it, (sl)	Tempora regular *and italic typeface* **and bold** *and bold italic*

Supported figures style for Tempora are TLF, -TOsF, *and* -Sup.

Table 10.44: Classification of the Tempora font family

Family	Series	Shapes	Typeface Examples
Tinos Tinos		(*Encodings:* T1, TS1, OT1, LY1, and TU)	
Tinos-TLF	m, b	n, it, (sl)	Tinos regular *and italic typeface* **and bold** *and bold italic*

Supported figure style for Tinos is -TLF.

Table 10.45: Classification of the Tinos font family

need Latin as well as Greek or Cyrillic — for purely Latin-based documents, tgtermes or newtxtext are preferable as they support small capitals, which tempora does not:

> With a price of £148, **almost anything** can be found Floating In **Fields**. — ¿But aren't Kafka's Schloß & Æsop's Œuvres often *naïve* vis-à-vis the dæmonic *phœnix's official rôle* in fluffy soufflés?

Tempora 10pt/12pt (Tempora-TOsF) Tempora

10.5.21 Tinos

As an alternative to New Times Roman, the Tinos fonts by Steve Matteson have a very similar running length. They are, however, not offering a Small Caps shape.

LaTeX support for all engines is available with the tinos package by Bob Tennent.

> With a price of £148, **almost anything** can be found Floating In **Fields**. — ¿But aren't Kafka's Schloß & Æsop's Œuvres often *naïve* vis-à-vis the dæmonic *phœnix's official rôle* in fluffy soufflés?

Tinos 10pt/12pt (Tinos-TLF) Tinos

10.5.22 STIX 2

The Scientific and Technical Information Exchange (STIX) Fonts project, sponsored by several leading scientific and technical publishers, intends to provide a comprehensive font set of mathematical symbols and alphabets under a royalty-free license for electronic and print publications. STIX 2, the current version, is an original design by Ross Mills, John Hudson, and Paul Hanslow of Tiro Typeworks, loosely based on Times New Roman but with a larger x-height.

Family	Series	Shapes	Typeface Examples
STIX 2 STIX Two Text	(*Encodings:* T1, TS1, OT1, and TU)		
SticksTooText-LF	m, b	n, it, (sl), sc, scit, (scsl)	STIX 2 regular, *italic*, **bold**, and SMALL CAPS

Supported figure styles for STIX 2 fonts are -LF, -OsF, -TLF, -TOsF, -Sup, *and* -Inf.

Table 10.46: Classification of the STIX 2 font family

LATEX support for the pdfTEX engine is provided through the stickstootext[1] package by Michael Sharpe. It accepts the typical options such as scaled or osf but also others related to STIX's math support; see the package documentation for details. Typesetting examples involving mathematics are shown in Figure 12.30 on page 282 (pdfTEX) and Figure 12.31 on page 282 (Unicode engines).

Unicode engines

The STIX fonts also include text glyphs for Latin, Greek, and Cyrillic as well as IPA symbols, but these are available only with Unicode engines.

STIX 2 10pt/12pt
(SticksTooText-OsF)
STIX Two Text

With a price of £148, **almost anything** can be found FLOATING IN FIELDS. — ¿But aren't Kafka's Schloß & Æsop's Œuvres often *naïve* vis-à-vis the dæmonic *phœnix's official rôle* in fluffy soufflés?

10.5.23 Utopia (Heuristica, Erewhon, and Linguistics Pro)

Utopia, designed by Robert Slimbach, combines the vertical stress and pronounced stroke contrast of 18th century Transitional types with contemporary innovations in shape and stroke details.

Andrey V. Panov extended the Utopia font family under the name Heuristica by adding additional accented glyphs, additional figure styles, and small capitals for the regular weight. The LATEX support for pdfTEX is provided by Michael Sharpe through the package heuristica with options like scaled, osf, and others.

Unicode engines

For Unicode engines a fontspec specification file is provided.

Utopia 9.6pt/12pt
(Heuristica-TOsF)
Heuristica

With a price of £148, **almost anything** can be found FLOATING IN Fields. — ¿But aren't Kafka's Schloß & Æsop's Œuvres often *naïve* vis-à-vis the dæmonic *phœnix's official rôle* in fluffy soufflés?

Michael also extended the Heuristica family further by adding small capitals in all weights and real slanted shapes. He also changed the oldstyle design somewhat

---

[1] This is indeed the package name: there is also a stix2, but that offers only very basic support.

Family	Series	Shapes	Typeface Examples
Heuristica	Heuristica	(*Encodings:* T1, TS1, T2A, T2B, T2C, LY1, and TU)	
Heuristica-TLF	m	n, it, (sl), sc	Heuristica regular, *italic*, and Small Caps Shapes
	h	n, it, (ol)	**Heuristica bold and *bold italic* but no Small Caps**
Erewhon	Erewhon	(*Encodings:* T1, TS1, T2A, T2B, T2C, LY1, and TU)	
erewhon-LF	m, b	n, it, sl, sc	Erewhon regular, *italic*, *slanted*, **bold**, and Small Caps
Linguistics Pro	Linguistics Pro	(*Encodings:* T1, TS1, T2A, T2B, T2C, T3, TS3, OT1, LGR, LY1, and TU)	
LinguisticsPro-LF	m, b	n, it, (sl), sc	Linguistics Pro in *italic*, **bold**, and Small Caps

Supported figure styles for Heuristica are TLF, -TOsF, -Sup, *and* -Inf.
Supported figure styles for Erewhon are LF, -OsF, -TLF, -TOsF, -Sup, *and* -Inf.
Linguistics Pro is available only in -LF *and* -OsF.

Table 10.47: Classification of the Utopia family and its forks

and scaled down the fonts by 6% to match the original Utopia font sizes. His version is named Erewhon, and the support package is erewhon. Compare it to the previous example.

With a price of £148, **almost anything** can be found Floating In Fields. — ¿But aren't Kafka's Schloß & Æsop's Œuvres often *naïve* vis-à-vis the dæmonic *phœnix's official rôle* in fluffy soufflés?

Utopia 10pt/12pt
(erewhon-TOsF) erewhon

A different extension of the original Utopia is Linguistics Pro by Stefan Peev. It is of special interest if you need to combine Latin, polytonic Greek, and/or Cyrillic, as it offers modern Bulgarian letterforms and with Unicode engines also traditional forms for the Russian language (available through the OpenType Stylistic Set 01). Otherwise they are more or less identical to Heuristica with a slightly wider running length. It also offers IPA symbols.

LaTeX support for all engines is provided by Bob Tennent through the package linguisticspro, which accepts the option scaled.

With a price of £148, **almost anything** can be found Floating In Fields – ¿But aren't Kafka's Schloß & Æsop's Œuvres often *naïve* vis-à-vis the dæmonic *phœnix's official rôle* in fluffy soufflés?

Linguistics Pro 9.6pt/12pt
(LinguisticsPro-OsF)
LinguisticsPro

Michael Sharpe prepared matching math fonts that work well with all of the Utopia variants; see Figure 12.32 on page 283 for an example page. There is also the Fourier-GUT*enberg* bundle by Michel Bovani, which too is based on Adobe Utopia and offers full support for math, especially in the French style. For text, the fonts have a glyph coverage similar to Heuristica, which is why they are not covered here, but only briefly in Chapter 12 on math fonts.

10.6 Didone (Modern) serif fonts

Fonts classified as Didone or Modern (with Modern referring to a period starting in the second half of the 18th century) take the Transitional design ideas even further and introduce new aspects. The name is coined from the surnames of two very famous type designers of the period: Firmin Didot (1764–1836) and Giambattista Bodoni (1740–1813).

Stroke contrast now becomes even more pronounced, with heavy parts getting even heavier and light strokes being reduced to hairlines. The weight axis is now completely vertical. The counters (the partially enclosed, somewhat rounded space in characters such as a, c, e, f, s, etc.) often become very tight. Serifs are very abrupt, narrow, and unbracketed with a nearly constant stroke width. While we have seen in Transitional fonts that some character terminals start looking more like droplets, Didone fonts often show pronounced ball terminals, either full circles or heavier teardrops.

Below we show a handful of high-quality Didone designs that have been set up for use with pdfTEX and can be used as alternatives to LATEX's bread and butter family Computer Modern (which too is a Didone design). Most have equally good coverage in terms of different shapes (compared to CM) but often offer more weights — in the case of the Noto families this amounts to a truly impressive number of possible alternatives.

10.6.1 Computer Modern Roman / Latin Modern Roman

Donald Knuth's Computer Modern, the first fonts available for TEX, are classical Didone designs, and so are the derived Latin Modern fonts. Together with their matching sans serif and monospaced companions and the matching math fonts, they enable you to typeset any kind of document using a single consistent "design". For many years these have been the fonts that most people had to use and even nowadays usually still use (after all, they work out of the box) — so much that seeing COMPUTER MODERN TYPEFACES became a synonym for "was produced with LATEX" and vice versa.[1] You can find the description of these families in Section 9.5.1 and their NFSS classifications in Tables 9.5 and 9.6.

Latin Modern Roman
10pt/12pt (lmr)
`Latin Modern Roman`

With a price of £148, **almost anything** can be found FLOATING IN FIELDS. — ¿But aren't Kafka's Schloß & Æsop's Œuvres often *naïve* vis-à-vis the dæmonic *phœnix's official rôle* in fluffy soufflés?

Unicode engines

For Unicode engines only there is also the New Computer Modern OpenType family of fonts by Antonis Tsolomitis. Its aim is to augment Computer Modern and enable typesetting in many more scripts and languages. See Figure 12.36 on page 286 for an example of its math typesetting quality.

---

[1]I hope that this chapter proves that this is an unwarranted prejudice and that we are long past the stage that using LATEX means "you can use any font you like as long as it is called Computer Modern".

Family	Series	Shapes	Typeface Examples
GFS Bodoni	GFS Bodoni	(*Encodings:* T1, OT1, LGR, and TU)	
bodoni	m, b	n, it, sl, sc, sco	GFS Bodoni regular, **bold**, *italic*, slanted, and SMALL CAPS

The supported figure style for GFS Bodoni is -TLF.

Table 10.48: Classification of the GFS Bodoni font family

Family	Series	Shapes	Typeface Examples
Libre Bodoni	Libre Bodoni	(*Encodings:* T1, TS1, OT1, LY1, and TU)	
LibreBodoni-TLF	m, b	n, it, (sl)	Libre Bodoni regular, *italics*, **bold**, and ***bold italics***

Supported figure styles for Libre Bodoni are -TLF, -Sup, *and* -Inf.

Table 10.49: Classification of the Libre Bodoni font family

10.6.2 GFS Bodoni

GFS Bodoni was designed by Takis Katsoulidis based on the work of the famous 18th century Italian type cutter Giambattista Bodoni (1740–1813). LaTeX support is provided through the package gfsbodoni, which defines the command \textbodoni to access the font selectively. If loaded with the option default, GFS Bodoni is also made the roman default font. Besides Latin languages, the family fully supports polytonic Greek.

With a price of £148, **almost anything** can be found FLOATING IN Fields. — ¿But aren't Kafka's Schloß & Æsop's Œuvres often *naïve* vis-à-vis the dæmonic *phœnix's official rôle* in fluffy soufflés?

GFS Bodoni 10pt/12pt
(bodoni) GFS Bodoni

10.6.3 Libre Bodoni

Designed by Pablo Impallari and Rodrigo Fuenzalida, the Libre Bodoni fonts are based on the 19th century Morris Fuller Benton (1872–1948)'s Bodoni ATF design. Note that this family appears to be already quite dark in its medium weight. LaTeX support for all engines is available with the LibreBodoni package by Bob Tennent.

With a price of £148, **almost anything** can be found Floating In Fields. — ¿But aren't Kafka's Schloß & Æsop's Œuvres often *naïve* vis-à-vis the dæmonic *phœnix's official rôle* in fluffy soufflés?

Libre Bodoni 10pt/12pt
(LibreBodoni-TLF)
Libre Bodoni

Not that there is anything wrong with Computer or Latin Modern, but as you can see, there are many beautiful designs out there, and they are usually just a package load away.

Family	Series	Shapes	Typeface Examples
GFS Didot	GFS Didot	(*Encodings:* T1, TS1, OT1, LGR, and TU)	
udidot	m, b	n, it, sl, sc, sco	GFS Didot regular, **bold**, *italic*, *slanted*, and Small Caps Slanted

The supported figure style for GFS Didot is -TLF.

Table 10.50: Classification of the GFS Didot font family

10.6.4 GFS Didot

In 1805 the famous French type cutter Firmin Didot (1764–1836) designed a new Greek typeface influenced by the neoclassical ideals of that time that, after arriving in Greece, became widely popular and was used for all kinds of publications until the last decades of the 20th century.

GFS Didot is a new design from 1994 by Takis Katsoulidis based on Didot's original work. Unfortunately the Latin alphabet added into the font cannot be recommended because it contains very inconsistently designed characters, and the fact that it is partly inspired by Hermann Zapf's (1918-2015) Palatino does not help. It also means that it is no longer a pure Didone design but shows a mixture of oldstyle and modern aspects. Thus, while the font provides a valuable polytonic Greek alphabet, you should match it with a different font for typesetting in Latin; i.e., do not use the gfsdidot support package because that makes the Latin font the default. A much better alternative for classical texts is Theano Didot described in the next section.

GFS Didot 10pt/12pt
(udidot) GFS Didot

With a price of £148, **almost anything** can be found Floating In Fields. — ¿But aren't Kafka's Schloß & Æsop's Œuvres often naïve vis-à-vis the dæmonic *phœnix's official rôle* in fluffy soufflés?

10.6.5 Theano Didot

The Theano Didot font is one of several fonts designed by Alexey Kryukov from historic samples, in this case, the work of Firmin Didot (1764-1836). Originally meant to be polytonic Greek-only typefaces, Alexey supplemented them with stylistically matching Latin letters (and some of his fonts, though not Theano Didot, also with Cyrillic). This makes them very suitable for scholarly work reproducing the look of old classical text editions.

LaTeX support for all engines is provided through the package TheanoDidot by Bob Tennent offering the options scaled and oldstyle. Note that this font, though of high-quality, does not offer small capitals, italics, or an oblique shape and is therefore suitable only for more classical texts that do not require such shapes.

Theano Didot 10pt/12pt
(TheanoDidot-TOsF)
Theano Didot

With a price of £148, **almost anything** can be found Floating In Fields. — ¿But aren't Kafka's Schloß & Æsop's Œuvres often naïve vis-à-vis the dæmonic phœnix's official rôle in fluffy soufflés?

Family	Series	Shapes	Typeface Examples
Theano Didot Theano Didot		(*Encodings:* T1, TS1, OT1, LGR, LY1, and TU)	
TheanoDidot-TLF	m, b	n	Theano Didot regular **and bold** only

Supported figure styles for Theano Didot are -TLF *and* -TOsF.

Table 10.51: Classification of the Theano Didot font family

Family	Series	Shapes	Typeface Examples
Old Standard Old Standard		(*Encodings:* T1, TS1, T2A, T2B, T2C, OT1, LGR„ LY1, and TU)	
OldStandard-TLF	m, b	n, it, (sl), sc, scit, (scsl)	Old Standard, *italic*, **bold**, and Small Caps

Supported figure styles for Old Standard are -TLF *and* -Sup.

Table 10.52: Classification of the Old Standard font family

10.6.6 Noto Serif

The Noto Serif fonts (an extended version of Droid Serif with well-designed small capitals) have matching sans and monospaced designs. The families are described together on page 26, and the NFSS classification is given in Table 10.14 on page 28. A sample page with matching math fonts is shown in Figure 12.38 on page 287.

> With a price of £148, **almost anything** can be found Floating In **Fields**. — ¿But aren't Kafka's Schloß & Æsop's Œuvres often *naïve* vis-à-vis the dæmonic *phœnix's official rôle* in fluffy soufflés?

Noto Serif 10pt/12pt
(NotoSerif-OsF)
Noto Serif

10.6.7 Old Standard

Designed by Alexey Kryukov, Old Standard (revised in 2019 by Robert Alessi) reproduces the printing style of the early 20th century, reviving a specific type of Modern (classicist) style of serif typefaces. The glyph set provided by the font supports typesetting of Old and Middle English, Old Icelandic, Cyrillic (with historical characters, extensions for Old Slavonic and localized forms), Gothic transliterations, critical editions of Classical Greek, Latin, etc.

Unicode engines

However, some of the glyph variants are available only if a Unicode engine is used, because of limitations in the number of glyph slots in Type 1 fonts.

Family	Series	Shapes	Typeface Examples
Playfair Display	Playfair Display	(*Encodings:* T1, TS1, OT1, LY1, and TU)	
PlyfrDisplay-LF	m, b, eb	n, it, (sl), sc, scit, (scsl)	Playfair Display regular *italic*, SMALL CAPS, **bold**, and **extra-bold**

Supported figure styles for Playfair Display are -LF, -OsF, *and* -Sup.

Table 10.53: Classification of the Playfair Display font family

LATEX support for all engines is available with the OldStandard package by Bob Tennent.

Old Standard 10pt/12pt
(OldStandard-TLF)
Old Standard

With a price of £148, **almost anything** can be found FLOATING IN FIELDS. — ¿But aren't Kafka's Schloß & Æsop's Œuvres often *naïve* vis-à-vis the dæmonic *phœnix's official rôle* in fluffy soufflés?

10.6.8 Playfair Display

As the name indicates, Playfair Display, designed by Claus Eggers Sørensen, is well suited for titling and headlines, but less so for continuous body text. The font has a large x-height, while capitals and descenders are fairly short. The latter allows it to be set with little leading if space requirements are tight.

LATEX support for all engines is available with the PlayfairDisplay package by Bob Tennent supporting the usual options such as scaled or oldstyle.

Playfair Display 10pt/12pt
(PlyfrDisplay-OsF)
Playfair Display

With a price of £148, **almost anything** can be found FLOATING IN FIELDS. — ¿But aren't Kafka's Schloß & Æsop's Œuvres often *naïve* vis-à-vis the dæmonic *phœnix's official rôle* in fluffy soufflés?

This sample shows the black weight (eb) at a larger size. It works nicely in combination with one of the Baskerville revivals.

Playfair Display (option
black) 30pt/34pt
(PlyfrDisplay-OsF)
Playfair Display

Playfair Display 123

10.7 Slab serif (Egyptian) fonts

Slab serif fonts got introduced in the 19th century, and perhaps because anything Egyptian was quite popular after Napoleon's expedition of Egypt, they were popularized as Egyptian Hieroglyph Slab Serif and are these days still sometimes referred to as Egyptian fonts even though there is no real relationship to this country whatsoever.

Family	Series	Shapes	Typeface Examples
Bitter Bitter		*(Encodings:* T1, TS1, OT1, LY1, and TU)	
Bttr-TLF	m	n, it, (sl)	Regular and *italic shapes*
	b	n	**Bold has no italics**

Table 10.54: Classification of the Bitter font family

Slap serif fonts form a large and varied genre. What they have in common is a fairly heavy weight (especially in fonts for display usage), low contrast between thick and thin strokes, and very prominent unbracketed serifs. Otherwise, many different design concepts are employed by different families. There are geometric designs with minimal stroke differences (like a sans serif font with added serifs), while others are very similar to traditional serif designs but with more prominent serifs.

Slab serif designs intended especially for display usage are usually very bold with exaggerated serifs to get the reader's attention in posters, etc., by "shouting out loud". Fonts oriented towards use at body text size or smaller usually show less extreme characteristics and often use only slab serifs to increase legibility but are otherwise close to conventional book type fonts. This is certainly true for the families shown below that are all intended for continuous text.

You can find further slab serif designs in Section 10.9 on monospaced fonts. However, the fonts there are less suited for use in continuous text because all the characters show the same width. They have therefore got their own section.

10.7.1 Bitter

Designed by Sol Matas, Bitter is a contemporary slab serif typeface for text, specially for comfortably reading on computer displays. It has a large x-height and little variation in stroke width and is somewhat darker than the regular weight of most other fonts. LaTeX support for all engines is available through the bitter package by Bob Tennent, which supports the option scaled for specifying a scale factor.

With a price of £148, **almost anything** can be found Floating In **Fields.** — ¿But aren't Kafka's Schloß & Æsop's Œuvres often *naïve* vis-à-vis the dæmonic *phœnix's official rôle* in fluffy soufflés?

Bitter 10pt/13pt
(Bttr-TLF) Bitter

10.7.2 Concrete Roman

For the text of his book *Concrete Mathematics* [32], Donald Knuth designed a new typeface [46] to go with the Euler mathematics fonts designed by Hermann Zapf (1918-2015) [92]. This font family, called Concrete Roman, was created from the Computer Modern METAFONT sources by supplying different parameter settings.

Family	Series	Shapes	Typeface Examples
Concrete Roman		—no OpenType—	(*Encodings:* T1, TS1, OT1)
ccr	m	n, it, sl, sc	Concrete Roman medium in *italic, slanted,* and SMALL CAPS shapes
	c	sl	*Concrete Roman condensed slanted (only* OT1 *and 9pt font size)*

Table 10.55: Classification of the Concrete font family

LaTeX support for the pdfTeX engine is provided through the package ccfonts by Walter Schmidt (1960–2021). The package takes care of small but important typographical details, such as increasing the value of \baselineskip slightly because of the darker color of the font. The feature provided by the exscale package is available as the package option exscale; see Section 9.5.7 on page →I 704 for details. The exscale package itself cannot be used because it is set up to work with only Computer Modern math fonts.

Example pages of mathematical typesetting are shown in Figure 12.39 on page 288 (with Concrete Math) and in Figure 12.40 on page 289 (with Euler fonts).

> **Unicode engines**
>
> This family does not exist in OpenType format or TU encoding, which makes it nearly impossible to use successfully with Unicode engines.

Note that the font has no bold weight. Instead, the LaTeX support file uses Computer Modern bold by default as a substitute, which does not work very well if the fonts are mixed (though it gets emphasized due to the color change).

Concrete Roman 10pt/13pt (ccr) —no OpenType—

With a price of £148, almost anything can be found FLOATING IN FIELDS. — ¿But aren't Kafka's Schloß & Æsop's Œuvres often *naïve* vis-à-vis the dæmonic *phœnix's official rôle* in fluffy soufflés?

As an alternative for the missing bold typeface, the ccfonts package offers the option boldsans to use the semi-bold series of the Computer Modern Sans fonts as a replacement. This means that if used without any further adjustments, headings in standard classes are then typeset using this font series, which actually looks quite nice.

The condensed cut is of very limited use because it exists only as a slanted shape in OT1 encoding and 9pt font size. It was produced just for typesetting the marginal comments in Don's book and was never meant for general use. Still, if you have a similar use case, it might be handy. Below we deliberately asked for condensed slanted at 12pt: watch what happens:

Concrete Roman condensed slanted 12pt/14pt (ccr)

With a price of £148, almost anything can be found Floating In Fields. — ¿But aren't Kafka's Schloß & Æsop's Œuvres often naïve vis-à-vis the dæmonic phœnix's official rôle in fluffy soufflés?

10.7.3 DejaVu Serif

DejaVu Serif exists in a regular and a condensed cut and has a matching sans serif and monospaced design. You can find the description of all three families on page 12 and their NFSS classifications in Table 10.4 on page 13.

> Unicode engines
>
> For Unicode engines there are matching math fonts, shown in Figure 12.41 on page 289.

With a price of £148, **almost anything** can be found Floating In **Fields**. — ¿But aren't Kafka's Schloß & Æsop's Œuvres often *naïve* vis-à-vis the dæmonic *phœnix's official rôle* in fluffy soufflés?

DejaVu Serif 10pt/13pt
(DejaVuSerif-TLF)
DejaVu Serif

With a price of £148, **almost anything** can be found Floating In **Fields**. — ¿But aren't Kafka's Schloß & Æsop's Œuvres often *naïve* vis-à-vis the dæmonic *phœnix's official rôle* in fluffy soufflés?

DejaVu Serif Condensed 10pt/13pt
(DejaVuSerifCondensed-TLF)
DejaVu Serif Condensed

10.7.4 Roboto Slab Serif

Roboto Slab Serif has a sans serif companion and a matching monospaced font as well. All three families are described in more detail on page 34, and their NFSS classifications are found in Table 10.19 on page 35.

With a price of £148, **almost anything** can be found FLOATING IN FIELDS. — ¿But aren't Kafka's Schloß & Æsop's Œuvres often naïve vis-à-vis the dæmonic phœnix's official rôle in fluffy soufflés?

Roboto Slab Serif 10pt/13pt
(RobotoSlab-TLF)
Roboto Slab

10.7.5 Source Serif Pro

Yet another family with matching sans serif and monospaced families but by more than one designer is Source Serif Pro. The three families are described together on page 35, and their NFSS classifications are found in Table 10.20 on page 36.

With a price of £148, **almost anything** can be found FLOATING IN **FIELDS**. — ¿But aren't Kafka's Schloß & Æsop's Œuvres often *naïve* vis-à-vis the dæmonic *phœnix's official rôle* in fluffy soufflés?

Source Serif Pro 10pt/13pt
(SourceSerifPro-OsF)
Source Serif Pro

10.8 Sans serif fonts

In contrast to the serif font families, we present all sans serif font families in alphabetical order by name. There are, of course, also classification schemes for sans serif fonts, but the distinctions are much hazier and are less useful when trying to find suitable fonts.

Many books on typography discuss how to select a suitable sans serif font to a given serif one, but it depends so much on how the two are used together that we give only a few general rule of thumbs here.

If the sans font is used as part of the body text and is intermixed with the serif font within sentences (as in this book, where we use sans serif for denoting package names, etc.), then it is best if both families have the same flow, i.e., a similar width of individual characters and consequentially a similar running length. In most cases they should also have similar characteristics in x-height, capital height, slope of their italics, etc., so that they blend well with each other.

If you are typesetting using one of the few larger "meta"-families such as Latin Modern or IBM Plex, then this is automatically the case when selecting the corresponding sans serif font from the family.

For many fonts shown in the previous sections, you have to decide on a companion sans serif by yourself — by setting up some typical sample text and studying the results. Sometimes one or the other family needs scaling up or down to achieve a similar x-height; this is why most font packages offer you a `scaled` or `scale` option. For example, here we combine Palatino (TeX Gyre Pagella) with Quattrocento Sans scaled down to 96% to get matching x-heights.

The dazed brown fox quickly gave 123456789 jumps while counting backwards from 9 to 1. *Then he repeated the exercise!*

```
\usepackage{tgpagella}
\usepackage[sf,scaled=.96]{quattrocento}
The \textsf{dazed brown} fox quickly gave 123456789
jumps while \textsf{counting backwards} from 9 to 1.
\emph{Then he \textsf{repeated} the exercise}!
```

10-8-1

Below we show samples of roughly thirty sans serif designs. A few of them are suitable only for display, but many can be successfully used as the main document font or as a companion to a serif family, depending on your use case. Typically the support packages offer options to set the fonts up either way.

10.8.1 Alegreya Sans

The Alegreya Sans family has a matching serif design (but no monospaced variant). You can find the description of both families on page 11 and the NFSS classification in Table 10.2 on the same page.

Alegreya Sans 10pt/12pt
(AlegreyaSans-OsF)
Alegreya Sans

With a price of £148, **almost anything** can be found Floating In **Fields**. — ¿But aren't Kafka's Schloß & Æsop's Œuvres often *naïve* vis-à-vis the dæmonic *phœnix's official rôle* in fluffy soufflés?

10.8.2 Arimo

The Arimo family, designed by Steve Matteson, is a sans serif font that is metrically compatible with Arial. It contains the glyphs necessary for typesetting in many languages including Greek and Cyrillic. However, the non-Latin glyphs are accessible

Family	Series	Shapes	Typeface Examples
Arimo Arimo		(*Encodings:* T1, TS1, OT1, LY1, and TU)	
Arimo-TLF	m, b	n, it, (sl)	Arimo regular, *italic*, and **boldface**

Table 10.56: Classification of the Arimo family

Family	Series	Shapes	Typeface Examples
Avant Garde TeX Gyre Adventor		(*Encodings:* T1, TS1, OT1, LY1, and TU)	
qag	m	n, (it), sl, sc, (scit), scsl	Avant Garde regular, *oblique*, **bold**, and Small Caps

Table 10.57: Classification of the Adventor (Avant Garde) family from the TEX Gyre distribution

only in Unicode engines at the moment as the support files for pdfTEX cover only Latin languages. Basic LATEX support for all engines is provided through the package arimo by Bob Tennent, which sets up Arimo as \sfdefault and offers the usual options such as scaled or sfdefault.

> With a price of £148, **almost anything** can be found Floating In Fields. — ¿But aren't Kafka's Schloß & Æsop's Œuvres often *naïve* vis-à-vis the dæmonic *phœnix's official rôle* in fluffy soufflés?

Arimo 10pt/12pt
(Arimo-TLF) Arimo

10.8.3 ITC Avant Garde Gothic (TEX Gyre Adventor)

Avant Garde Gothic was designed by Herb Lubalin and Tom Carnase based on the distinctive logo designed for *Avant Garde* magazine. It is a geometric sans serif type with basic shapes built from circles and lines. It is effective for headlines and short texts, but it needs generous leading. A (commercially available) condensed version that better retains legibility in lengthier texts was designed by Ed Benguiat. The TEX Gyre Adventor version shown here is based on the URW Gothic L version of the font family.

> With a price of £148, **almost anything** can be found Floating In Fields. — ¿But aren't Kafka's Schloß & Æsop's Œuvres often *naïve* vis-à-vis the dæmonic *phœnix's official rôle* in fluffy soufflés?

ITC Avant Garde Gothic
9pt/13pt
(qag) TeX Gyre Adventor

The font family can be set up as the document sans serif font with the help of the TEX Gyre tgadventor package. Like all other TEX Gyre support packages it provides the options scale, matchlowercase, and matchuppercase, to allow matching font family to other fonts used in the document.

Family	Series	Shapes	Typeface Examples
Cabin	Cabin, CabinCondensed		*(Encodings:* T1, TS1, OT1, LY1, and TU)
Cabin-TLF	m, sb, b	n, it, (sl), sc	Regular, *italic*, **bold**, and Small Caps
	c, sbc, bc		Condensed regular and *semi-bold italic*

Supported figure styles for Cabin are –TLF *and* –Sup.

Table 10.58: Classification of the Cabin font family

10.8.4 Cabin

Cabin is a humanist sans serif family designed by Pablo Impallari. It offers four weights with italics and true small capitals. A compatible condensed family is also available. According to the designer, it was inspired by typefaces from Eric Gill (1882–1940) and Edward Johnston, with a touch of modernism.

LaTeX support for all engines is available through the package cabin by Bob Tennent providing the typical options such as condensed, sfdefault, medium, and others.

Cabin 10pt/12pt
(Cabin-TLF) Cabin

With a price of £148, **almost anything** can be found Floating In Fields. — ¿But aren't Kafka's Schloß & Æsop's Œuvres often *naïve* vis-à-vis the dæmonic *phœnix's official rôle* in fluffy soufflés?

If the package is loaded with the option condensed, you get the following output:

Cabin (option condensed*)*
10pt/12pt (Cabin-TLF)
Cabin Condensed

With a price of £148, **almost anything** can be found Floating In Fields. — ¿But aren't Kafka's Schloß & Æsop's Œuvres often *naïve* vis-à-vis the dæmonic *phœnix's official rôle* in fluffy soufflés?

10.8.5 Chivo

Chivo (Spanish for goat) is a Grotesque sans serif font family designed by Héctor Gatti. It offers upright and italic shapes in seven weights from thin (extra-light) to black (ultra-bold). The light and regular weights are usable for body texts, while the bold and black weights are meant for headlines. LaTeX support for all engines is provided through the package Chivo by Arash Esbati. With the options thin, light, or medium you can change the default sans serif body font, and with extrabold or black you can request that the black weight be used instead of bold.

Chivo 10pt/12pt
(Chivo-OsF) Chivo

With a price of £148, **almost anything** can be found Floating In Fields. — ¿But aren't Kafka's Schloß & Æsop's Œuvres often *naïve* vis-à-vis the dæmonic *phœnix's official rôle* in fluffy soufflés?

Family	Series	Shapes	Typeface Examples
Chivo Chivo	(*Encodings:* T1, TS1, OT1, LY1, and TU)		
Chivo-LF	el, l, m, sb, b, eb, ub	n, it, (sl)	Regular, light, *italic*, and ***bold italic shapes***

Supported figure styles for Chivo are -LF, -OsF, -TLF, -TOsF, -Sup, *and* -Inf.

Table 10.59: Classification of the Chivo font family

Here is a sample of Chivo Black produced with `\fontseries{ub}\selectfont`:

With a price of £148, almost anything can be found Floating In Fields. — ¿But aren't Kafka's Schloß & Æsop's Œuvres often *naïve* vis-à-vis the dæmonic *phœnix's official rôle* in fluffy soufflés?

Chivo 10pt/12pt
(Chivo-OsF) Chivo

10.8.6 Classico — A design based on Optima

Optima, designed by Hermann Zapf (1918–2015) in 1958, is a font family I personally like very much. It is very calligraphic in nature with varying stroke width in the letters and works well as a display face but equally well in body text size for whole documents. It is a bit like an Oldstyle serif design with only implied serifs. In 1998 Zapf in collaboration with Akira Kobayashi reworked its design, which was released under the name Optima Nova. As with many fonts by Hermann Zapf (1918–2015) Optima has many admirers and as a result unfortunately many pirate copies (usually of inferior quality) under different names.

If you are using a Macintosh, then Optima (but not Optima Nova) is one of the system fonts, which is lovely as it allows you to use this superb family in a Unicode TEX engine directly using its TrueType name Optima . But this does not work on other operating systems or for pdfTEX.

Fortunately, there is also the family URW Classico, which is a rework of the original Optima by its designer for the URW foundry. This family is freely usable (though you have to install it yourself via getnonfreefonts due to its license restrictions).

LATEX support for all engines is provided through the package classico by Bob Tennent providing the options `scaled` to specify a scale factor and `sfdefault` (which I often use) to make this family the default document family. Being a sans serif design the italics are more oblique than true italics, and the small capitals are faked — however, they do not come out too badly because the characters have a varied stroke width.

With a price of £148, **almost anything** can be found FLOATING IN FIELDS. — ¡But aren't Kafka's Schloß & Æsop's Œuvres often *naïve* vis-à-vis the dæmonic *phœnix's official rôle* in fluffy soufflés?

URW Classico 10pt/12pt
(URWClassico-LF)
URW Classico

71

Family	Series	Shapes	Typeface Examples
URW Classico	URW Classico	(*Encodings:* T1, TS1, OT1, LY1, and TU)	
URWClassico-LF	m, b	n, it, (sl), (sc)	Regular, **bold**, *italic*, FAKED SMALL CAPS and **FAKED BOLD SMALL CAPS**

The supported figure style for URW Classico is –LF.

Table 10.60: Classification of the URW Classico font family

Family	Series	Shapes	Typeface Examples
Clear Sans	Clear Sans, Clear Sans Light, Clear Sans Thin	(*Encodings:* T1, TS1, OT1, LY1, and TU)	
ClearSans-TLF	m, sb, b	n, it, (sl)	Clear Sans regular, *italic*, and **boldface**
	el, l	n	Clear Sans Light and extra-light (only upright)

Supported figure styles for Clear Sans are –LF *and* –TLF.

Table 10.61: Classification of the Clear Sans family

10.8.7 Clear Sans

Clear Sans is a design by Daniel Ratighan at Monotype. It was commissioned by Intel, and it is particularly suitable for user interfaces, because it has slightly narrow proportions and unambiguous glyphs; e.g., "I" (uppercase i) has serifs to distinguish it from "l" (lowercase l). Clear Sans is available in three weights with corresponding italics (regular, medium, and bold), plus thin and light upright (without italics).

Basic LaTeX support for all engines is provided through the package ClearSans by Bob Tennent, which sets up Clear Sans as \sfdefault and offers the usual options such as scaled, sfdefault, or medium. The light and thin weights are made available through \textsfl and \textsft, respectively.

Clear Sans 10pt/12pt
(ClearSans-TLF)
Clear Sans

With a price of £148, **almost anything** can be found Floating In Fields. — ¿But aren't Kafka's Schloß & Æsop's Œuvres often *naïve* vis-à-vis the dæmonic *phœnix's official rôle* in fluffy soufflés?

10.8.8 CM Bright

The CM Bright sans serif fonts have a matching monospaced design. The families are described on page 12, and the NFSS classification is given in Table 10.3.

The sample on the opposite page shows the words "almost anything" in bold extended. A (probably better) alternative is semi-bold as shown in the sample on

Family	Series	Shapes	Typeface Examples
Cuprum `Cuprum`	(*Encodings:* T1 and TU)		
cpr	m, b	n, it, (sl), (sc)	Regular, *italic*, **bold**, and ***boldface italic***

Table 10.62: Classification of the Cuprum font family

page 12. Matching math fonts are exhibited in Figure 12.42 on page 290.

With a price of £148, **almost anything** can be found Floating In Fields. — ¿But aren't Kafka's Schloß & Æsop's Œuvres often *naïve* vis-à-vis the dæmonic *phœnix's official rôle* in fluffy soufflés?

CM Bright 10pt/12pt (cmbr)
—no OpenType—

10.8.9 Cuprum

Cuprum, designed by Ivan Gladkikh (a.k.a. Jovanny Lemonad), is a narrow grotesque sans serif typeface inspired by the works of Miles Newlyn. It is offered in two weights and upright and italic shapes. LaTeX support for pdfTeX is provided through the package **cuprum** by Federico Roncaglia. Somewhat unconventionally, the missing Small Caps shape is aliased to boldface when pdfTeX is used.

Unicode engines

For Unicode engines you have to set up the font using fontspec.

With a price of £148, **almost anything** can be found Floating In Fields. — ¿But aren't Kafka's Schloß & Æsop's Œuvres often *naïve* vis-à-vis the dæmonic *phœnix's official rôle* in fluffy soufflés?

Cuprum 10pt/12pt
(cpr) `Cuprum`

10.8.10 Cyklop

The Cyklop typeface was designed roughly a hundred years ago in a workshop at a type foundry in Warsaw. This sans serif typeface has a highly modulated stroke with vertical stems that are much heavier than horizontal ones. Most characters have thin rectangles as additional counters, which give the unique shape of the characters. The font is available in only one weight — a request for the medium series gives you the same as `\bfseries`.

LaTeX support for pdfTeX is provided through the package **cyklop** by Janusz Marian Nowacki (1951–2020), but that just sets `\rmdefault`, which is not very helpful unless you really want the whole document in this typeface. As the font is mainly of interest for headings and other display material and not for body text, it is probably best to set it up manually as needed.

A Cyklop Heading

Cyklop 17pt/20pt
(cyklop) `Cyklop`

Family	Series	Shapes	Typeface Examples
Cyklop	Cyklop	*(Encodings:* T1, TS1, T5, OT1, OT4, LY1, and TU)	
cyklop	m (b)	n, it, sc, scit	**Regular, *italic*, and SMALL CAPS ITALICS**

Table 10.63: Classification of the Cyklop font family

10.8.11 DejaVu Sans

DejaVu Sans has a matching slab serif and a monospaced design. You can find the description of all three families on page 12 and their NFSS classifications in Table 10.4 on page 13.

DejaVu Sans 9pt/12.5pt
(DejaVuSans-TLF)
DejaVu Sans

With a price of £148, **almost anything** can be found Floating In Fields . — ¿But aren't Kafka's Schloß & Æsop's Œuvres often *naïve* vis-à-vis the dæmonic *phœnix's official rôle* in fluffy soufflés?

DejaVu Sans Condensed 9pt/12.5pt
(DejaVuSansCondensed-TLF)
DejaVu Sans Condensed

With a price of £148, **almost anything** can be found Floating In **Fields** . — ¿But aren't Kafka's Schloß & Æsop's Œuvres often *naïve* vis-à-vis the dæmonic *phœnix's official rôle* in fluffy soufflés?

10.8.12 Fira Sans

Erik Spiekermann's Fira Sans has a matching monospaced design. This Humanist Sans works great as a body text font with many different weights and also offers polytonic Greek if that is needed. Both families are described on page 14, and their NFSS classifications can be found in Table 10.5.

> **Unicode engines**
>
> Xiangdong Zeng provided matching math fonts; see Figure 12.43 on page 291.

Fira Sans 10pt/13pt
(FiraSans-OsF) Fira Sans

With a price of £148, **almost anything** can be found FLOATING IN FIELDS. — ¿But aren't Kafka's Schloß & Æsop's Œuvres often *naïve* vis-à-vis the dæmonic *phœnix's official rôle* in fluffy soufflés?

10.8.13 Gandhi Sans

The Gandhi Sans fonts have a matching serif family described on page 15. The NFSS classifications are found in Table 10.6.

Gandhi Sans 10pt/12pt
(GandhiSans-OsF)
Gandhi Sans

With a price of £148, **almost anything** can be found FLOATING IN FIELDS. — ¿But aren't Kafka's Schloß & Æsop's Œuvres often *naïve* vis-à-vis the dæmonic *phœnix's official rôle* in fluffy soufflés?

Family	Series	Shapes	Typeface Examples
GFS Neo-Hellenic	GFS Neo-Hellenic		(*Encodings:* T1, OT1, LGR, and TU)
neohellenic	m, b	n, it, sl, sc, sco	Regular, **bold**, *italic*, oblique, and SMALL CAPS OBLIQUE

The supported figure style for GFS Neo-Hellenic is -TLF.

Table 10.64: Classification of the GFS Neo-Hellenic font family

10.8.14 GFS Neo-Hellenic

In 1927 a Greek type called New Hellenic designed by Victor Scholderer (1880–1971) was cut by Lanston Monotype in Britain. GFS Neo-Hellenic is a digitalization based on this design. It offers both true italics and an oblique shape, although the differences are not easy to spot.

LaTeX support is provided through the package gfsneohellenic that defines the command \textneohellenic to access the font selectively. If loaded with the option default, GFS Neo-Hellenic is also made the roman default font. The family is well matched to mathematical fonts from CM Bright, which makes this an option when typesetting with pdfTeX. Besides Latin languages, it fully supports polytonic Greek.

With a price of £148, **almost anything** can be found FLOATING IN Fields. — ¿But aren't Kafka's Schloß & Æsop's Œuvres often *naïve* vis-à-vis the dæmonic *phœnix's official rôle* in fluffy soufflés?

GFS Neo-Hellenic 10pt/12pt (neohellenic)
GFS Neohellenic

Unicode engines

In 2018, GFS Neohellenic Math, a matching math font, was commissioned. This font exists only in OpenType format and thus can be used only with Unicode engines. It is made available through the package gfsneohellenicot. As a high-quality solution for sans serif text and math, this makes the package very attractive for situations such as presentations; see Figure 12.44 on page 291.

10.8.15 Gillius

The Gillius family of fonts designed by Hirwen Harendal was inspired by Eric Gill's (1882–1940) famous Gill Sans. It is available in medium and condensed width in all faces. LaTeX support for all engines is provided through the packages gillius and gillius2 by Bob Tennent. The option condensed lets you use the condensed faces for the whole document.

With a price of £148, **almost anything** can be found Floating In Fields. — ¿But aren't Kafka's Schloß & Æsop's Œuvres often *naïve* vis-à-vis the dæmonic *phœnix's official rôle* in fluffy soufflés?

Gillius 10pt/12pt (GilliusADF-LF)
Gillius ADF

75

Family	Series	Shapes	Typeface Examples
Gillius ADF	Gillius ADF		(*Encodings:* T1, TS1, OT1, LY1, and TU)
GilliusADF-LF	m, b	n, it, (sl)	Regular, *italic*, **bold**, and ***bold italic***
Gillius ADF Condensed	Gillius ADF Cond		(*Encodings:* T1, TS1, OT1, LY1, and TU)
GilliusADFCond-LF	m, b	n, it, (sl)	Condensed, *italic*, **bold**, and ***bold italic***
Gillius ADF No2	Gillius ADF No2		(*Encodings:* T1, TS1, OT1, LY1, and TU)
GilliusADFNoTwo-LF	m, b	n, it, (sl)	Regular, *italic*, **bold**, and ***bold italic***
Gillius ADF No2 Condensed	Gillius ADF No2 Cond		(*Encodings:* T1, TS1, OT1, LY1, and TU)
GilliusADFNoTwoCond-LF	m, b	n, it, (sl)	Condensed, *italic*, **bold**, and ***bold italic***

The supported figure style for Gillius and Gillius No2 is -LF.

Table 10.65: Classification of the Gillius and Gillius No2 font families

Gillius No2 has some slight redesigns in certain characters, e.g., the "a" vs. "a", and in general slightly less wide round shapes. As a result, it runs a little tighter, which can be seen in the last line of the sample:

Gillius No2 10pt/12pt
(GilliusADFNoTwo-LF)
Gillius ADF No2

With a price of £148, **almost anything** can be found Floating In Fields. — ¿But aren't Kafka's Schloß & Æsop's Œuvres often *naïve* vis-à-vis the dæmonic *phœnix's official rôle* in fluffy soufflés?

The condensed fonts are implemented as a separate family; thus, \textbf and \textit produce condensed shapes as well.

Gillius No2 Condensed
10pt/12pt
(GilliusADFNoTwoCond-LF)
Gillius ADF No2 Cond

With a price of £148, **almost anything** can be found Floating In Fields. — ¿But aren't Kafka's Schloß & Æsop's Œuvres often *naïve* vis-à-vis the dæmonic *phœnix's official rôle* in fluffy soufflés?

10.8.16 Helvetica (TEX Gyre Heros)

Helvetica was originally designed by Max Miedinger (1910–1980) for the Haas foundry of Switzerland, hence the name. It was later extended by the Stempel foundry, with further refinements being made by Mergenthaler Linotype in the United States. Helvetica is purported to be one of the most popular typefaces of all time.

TEX Gyre Heros shown here is based on the URW Nimbus Sans L version of the font family (which is set up with the TEX Gyre tgheros package):

Helvetica 10pt/13pt
(qhv) TeX Gyre Heros

With a price of £148, **almost anything** can be found Floating In Fields. — ¿But aren't Kafka's Schloß & Æsop's Œuvres often *naïve* vis-à-vis the dæmonic *phœnix's official rôle* in fluffy soufflés?

Family	Series	Shapes	Typeface Examples
Helvetica		TeX Gyre Heros (*Encodings:* T1, TS1, T5, OT1, LY1, and TU)	
qhv	m, c, b, bc	n, (it), sl, sc, (scit), scsl	Helvetica regular, *oblique*, **bold**, and Small Caps
Helvetica Condensed		TeX Gyre Heros Cn (*Encodings:* T1, TS1, T5, OT1, LY1, and TU)	
qhvc	m, x, b, bx	n, (it), sl, sc, (scit), scsl	Helvetica Narrow regular, *oblique*, **bold**, and Small Caps

Table 10.66: Classification of the Heros (Helvetica) family from the TₑX Gyre distribution

The TₑX Gyre Heros Condensed family implements a narrow version of Helvetica. It can be selected through the package option condensed or directly via the NFSS family name.

> With a price of £148, **almost anything** can be found Floating In Fields. — ¿But aren't Kafka's Schloß & Æsop's Œuvres often *naïve* vis-à-vis the dæmonic *phœnix's official rôle* in fluffy soufflés?

Helvetica Condensed 10pt/12pt (qhvc) TeX Gyre Heros Cn

10.8.17 Inria Sans

The Inria Sans family has a matching serif design. You can find the description of both families on page 16 and their NFSS classifications in Table 10.8 on page 17.

> With a price of £148, **almost anything** can be found Floating In Fields. — ¿But aren't Kafka's Schloß & Æsop's Œuvres often *naïve* vis-à-vis the dæmonic *phœnix's official rôle* in fluffy soufflés?

Inria Sans 10pt/12pt (InriaSans-OsF) Inria Sans

10.8.18 Iwona

Iwona was designed by Małgorzata Budyta for typesetting newspapers and similar periodicals as an alternative version of her Kurier fonts shown below. The difference lies in the absence of ink traps, which typify the Kurier family, e.g., "any" (Kurier) vs. "any" (Iwona). As a result, Iwona runs noticeably shorter even though it has a similar design. The family is offered in five weights and two widths and supports an extended character set including Latin and Cyrillic.

LATEX support for pdfTₑX is provided through the package iwona by Janusz Marian Nowacki (1951–2020). The default weight can be changed through light, and with condensed you can reduce the width. Note that the package installs the family as the document body font, i.e., as \rmdefault!

Matching math fonts are available too and can be activated with the option math. They cover the basic symbols but not those from amssymb, which would keep their shapes if used; see sample pages in Figures 12.45 to 12.46 on page 292.

Family	Series		Shapes	Typeface Examples
Iwona		Iwona	(*Encodings:* T1, TS1, T2A, T2B, T2C, OT1, OT2, OT4, LY1, and TU)	
iwona	l, m, sb, b, eb		n, it, sc, scit	Regular, **bold**, *italic*, and Sᴍᴀʟʟ Cᴀᴘꜱ Iᴛᴀʟɪᴄꜱ
	lc, c, sbc, bc, ebc			… and condensed, **bold**, *italic*, and Sᴍᴀʟʟ Cᴀᴘꜱ Iᴛᴀʟɪᴄꜱ
Iwona Light		Iwona Light	(*Encodings:* T1, TS1, T2A, T2B, T2C, OT1, OT2, OT4, LY1, and TU)	
iwonal	m, sb, b, eb, ub		n, it, sc, scit	Light regular, **bold**, *italic*, and Sᴍᴀʟʟ Cᴀᴘꜱ Iᴛᴀʟɪᴄꜱ
	c, sbc, bc, ebc, ubc			… and light condensed, **bold**, *italic*, and Sᴍᴀʟʟ Cᴀᴘꜱ Iᴛᴀʟɪᴄꜱ
Iwona Condensed		Iwona Cond	(*Encodings:* T1, TS1, T2A, T2B, T2C, OT1, OT2, OT4, LY1, and TU)	
iwonac	l, m, sb, b, eb		n, it, sc, scit	Condensed regular, **bold**, *italic*, and Sᴍᴀʟʟ Cᴀᴘꜱ Iᴛᴀʟɪᴄꜱ
	lx, mx, sbx, bx, ebx			… and expanded, **bold**, *italic*, and Sᴍᴀʟʟ Cᴀᴘꜱ Iᴛᴀʟɪᴄꜱ
Iwona Light Condensed		Iwona Light Cond	(*Encodings:* T1, TS1, T2A, T2B, T2C, OT1, OT2, OT4, LY1, and TU)	
iwonalc	m, sb, b, eb, ub		n, it, sc, scit	Regular, **bold**, *italic*, and Sᴍᴀʟʟ Cᴀᴘꜱ Iᴛᴀʟɪᴄꜱ
	mx, sbx, bx, ebx, ubx			… and expanded, **bold**, *italic*, and Sᴍᴀʟʟ Cᴀᴘꜱ Iᴛᴀʟɪᴄꜱ

The series specifications in Iwona Light are shifted by one weight with respect to Iwona; e.g., m in Iwona becomes sb in Iwona Light. Similarly, the expansion codes are shifted; e.g., bx in Iwona Condensed is the same as b in Iwona. The slanted shapes (sl, scsl) are accepted but generate a warning and are then replaced by italics (it, scit).

Table 10.67: Classification of the Iwona font family

Unicode engines

For Unicode engines you need to set up the font yourself using fontspec declarations.

Iwona 10pt/12pt
(iwona) Iwona

With a price of £148, **almost anything** can be found Fʟᴏᴀᴛɪɴɢ Iɴ Fɪᴇʟᴅꜱ. — ¿But aren't Kafka's Schloß & Æsop's Œuvres often *naïve* vis-à-vis the dæmonic *phœnix's official rôle* in fluffy soufflés?

Iwona Light 10pt/12pt
(iwonal) Iwona Light

With a price of £148, **almost anything** can be found Fʟᴏᴀᴛɪɴɢ Iɴ Fɪᴇʟᴅꜱ. — ¿But aren't Kafka's Schloß & Æsop's Œuvres often *naïve* vis-à-vis the dæmonic *phœnix's official rôle* in fluffy soufflés?

For comparison, here are the condensed versions for both regular and light:

Iwona Condensed 10pt/12pt
(iwonac) Iwona Cond

With a price of £148, **almost anything** can be found Fʟᴏᴀᴛɪɴɢ Iɴ Fɪᴇʟᴅꜱ. — ¿But aren't Kafka's Schloß & Æsop's Œuvres often *naïve* vis-à-vis the dæmonic *phœnix's official rôle* in fluffy soufflés?

Iwona Cond. Light 10pt/12pt
(iwonalc)
Iwona Light Cond

With a price of £148, **almost anything** can be found Fʟᴏᴀᴛɪɴɢ Iɴ Fɪᴇʟᴅꜱ. — ¿But aren't Kafka's Schloß & Æsop's Œuvres often *naïve* vis-à-vis the dæmonic *phœnix's official rôle* in fluffy soufflés?

10.8.19 Kp (Johannes Kepler) Sans

Kp Sans has both a matching serif and monospaced design. When used with pdfTeX, certain features, such as special ligatures or oldstyle numerals, can be activated by altering the family name as described on page 17; you can find the description of all three families and their NFSS classifications in Table 10.9 on page 18. If used with Unicode engines, the features can be activated through the typical feature sets as supported by fontspec. An example with mathematics is shown in Figures 12.47 on page 293.

With a price of £148, **almost anything** can be found FLOATING IN FIELDS. — ¿But aren't Kafka's Schloß & Æsop's Œuvres often *naïve* vis-à-vis the dæmonic *phœnix's official rôle* in fluffy soufflés?

Kp Sans 10pt/12pt
(jkpss) KpSans

10.8.20 Kurier

For her diploma in typeface design in 1975 at the Warsaw Academy of Fine Arts, Małgorzata Budyta designed the sans serif typeface Kurier with its characteristic ink traps. The family is offered in five weights and two widths and supports an extended character set including Latin and Cyrillic.

LaTeX support for pdfTeX is provided through the package kurier by Janusz Marian Nowacki (1951–2020). The default weight can be changed with the option `light`, and with `condensed` you can reduce the width. Note that the package installs the family as the document body font, i.e., as \rmdefault!

Matching math fonts can be activated with the option `math`. They cover the basic symbols but not those from `amssymb`, which would keep their shapes if used; see Example 12.48 on page 294.

Unicode engines

For Unicode engines you need to set up the font yourself using fontspec declarations.

Kurier is well suited as a display typeface; the example here shows the light version:

Kurier Light as heading font

Kurier Light 20pt/24pt
(kurierl) Kurier Light

For comparison, here are the `condensed` versions in body text size:

With a price of £148, **almost anything** can be found FLOATING IN FIELDS. — ¿But aren't Kafka's Schloß & Æsop's Œuvres often *naïve* vis-à-vis the dæmonic *phœnix's official rôle* in fluffy soufflés?

Kurier Condensed 10pt/12pt
(kurierc) Kurier Cond

With a price of £148, **almost anything** can be found FLOATING IN FIELDS. — ¿But aren't Kafka's Schloß & Æsop's Œuvres often *naïve* vis-à-vis the dæmonic *phœnix's official rôle* in fluffy soufflés?

Kurier Light Cond. 10pt/12pt
(kurierlc)
Kurier Light Cond

Family	Series	Shapes	Typeface Examples
Kurier		Kurier	(*Encodings:* T1, TS1, T2A, T2B, T2C, OT1, OT2, OT4, LY1, and TU)
kurier	l, m, sb, b, eb	n, it, sc, scit	Regular, **bold**, *italic* & Small Caps Italics
	lc, c, sbc, bc, ebc		… and condensed, **bold**, *italic* & Small Caps Italics
Kurier Light		Kurier Light	(*Encodings:* T1, TS1, T2A, T2B, T2C, OT1, OT2, OT4, LY1, and TU)
kurierl	m, sb, b, eb, ub	n, it, sc, scit	Light regular, **bold**, *italic* & Small Caps Italics
	c, sbc, bc, ebc, ubc		… and light condensed, **bold**, *italic* & Small Caps Italics
Kurier Condensed		Kurier Cond	(*Encodings:* T1, TS1, T2A, T2B, T2C, OT1, OT2, OT4, LY1, and TU)
kurierc	l, m, sb, b, eb	n, it, sc, scit	Condensed regular, **bold**, *italic* & Small Caps Italics
	lx, mx, sbx, bx, ebx		… and expanded, **bold**, *italic* & Small Caps Italics
Kurier Light Condensed		Kurier Light Cond	(*Encodings:* T1, TS1, T2A, T2B, T2C, OT1, OT2, OT4, LY1, and TU)
kurierlc	m, sb, b, eb, ub	n, it, sc, scit	Light condensed regular, **bold**, *italic* & Small Caps Italics
	mx, sbx, bx, ebx, ubx		… and expanded, **bold**, *italic* & Small Caps Italics

The series specifications in Kurier Light are shifted by one weight with respect to Kurier; e.g., m *in Kurier becomes* sb *in Kurier Light. Similarly, the expansion codes are shifted; e.g.,* bx *in Kurier Condensed is the same as* b *in Kurier. The slanted shapes (*sl, scsl*) are accepted but generate a warning and are then replaced by italics (*it, scit*).*

Table 10.68: Classification of the Kurier font family

10.8.21 Latin Modern Sans

You can find the description of the Latin Modern families in Section 9.5.1 and their NFSS classifications in Table 9.6 on page →I 687.

Just like its cousin Computer Modern Sans, this family has no small capitals, and a request to \textsc uses Latin Modern Roman instead — a questionable choice, but consistent with the way CM fonts have been set up for decades.

Latin Modern Sans 10pt/12pt
(lmss) Latin Modern Sans

With a price of £148, **almost anything** can be found Floating In **Fields**. — ¿But aren't Kafka's Schloß & Æsop's Œuvres often *naïve* vis-à-vis the dæmonic *phœnix's official rôle* in fluffy soufflés?

10.8.22 Lato

Lato is a geometric sans serif design by Łukasz Dziedzic. A few years ago, the family was greatly extended with the help of Adam Twardoch and Botio Nikoltchev to cover more than 3 000 glyphs and can now be used to typeset most Latin or Cyrillic-based languages, Greek, and IPA phonetics. It is offered in several weights from hairline to extra-heavy and has upright and italic shapes. \slshape is aliased to italics.

LATEX support for all engines is provided through the package lato by Mohamed El Morabity. To set up Lato as the default sans serif font, use defaultsans. To set

Family	Series	Shapes	Typeface Examples
Lato Lato	(*Encodings:* T1, TS1, T2A, T2B, T2C, LGR, OT1, and TU)		
lato-LF	ul, el, l, m, sb, b, eb, ub	n, it, (sl)	Regular, *italic*, **bold**, ***bold italics***, ultra-light, extra-light, light, **semi-bold**, **extra bold**, and **ultra-bold**

Table 10.69: Classification of the Lato font family

it up as the default document font, use the option `default` instead. Use `scaled` to provide a font scaling factor. For other options see the package documentation.

> With a price of £148, **almost anything** can be found Floating In **Fields**. — ¿But aren't Kafka's Schloß & Æsop's Œuvres often *naïve* vis-à-vis the dæmonic *phœnix's official rôle* in fluffy soufflés?   *Lato 10pt/12pt* (lato-OsF) Lato

For comparison, here is the text in extra-light with `\textbf` now producing medium:

> With a price of £148, **almost anything** can be found Floating In **Fields**. — ¿But aren't Kafka's Schloß & Æsop's Œuvres often *naïve* vis-à-vis the dæmonic *phœnix's official rôle* in fluffy soufflés?   *Lato 10pt/12pt* (lato-OsF) Lato

10.8.23 Libertinus Sans

Libertinus Sans has both a matching serif and monospaced design. The description of all three families is given on page 19 and their NFSS classifications in Table 10.10 on page 20.

> With a price of £148, **almost anything** can be found Floating In **Fields**. — ¿But aren't Kafka's Schloß & Æsop's Œuvres often *naïve* vis-à-vis the dæmonic *phœnix's official rôle* in fluffy soufflés?   *Libertinus Sans 10pt/12pt* (LibertinusSans-OsF) Libertinus Sans

10.8.24 Libre Franklin

Libre Franklin is an interpretation of Morris Fuller Benton (1872–1948)'s Franklin Gothic, designed by Pablo Impallari, Rodrigo Fuenzalida, and Nhung Nguyen. It offers upright and italics in nine weights from ultra-light to ultra-bold.

LaTeX support for all engines is provided through the package librefranklin by Bob Tennent with typical options such as `scaled`, `default`, `sfdefault`, etc.

> With a price of £148, **almost anything** can be found Floating In **Fields**. — ¿But aren't Kafka's Schloß & Æsop's Œuvres often *naïve* vis-à-vis the dæmonic *phœnix's official rôle* in fluffy soufflés?   *Libre Franklin 10pt/12pt* (LibreFranklin-TLF) Libre Franklin

Family	Series	Shapes	Typeface Examples
Libre Franklin Libre Franklin	(*Encodings:* T1, TS1, OT1, LY1, and TU)		
LibreFranklin-TLF	ul, el, l, sl, m, sb, b, eb, ub n, it, (sl)		Regular and *italics* from *thin* to **ultra**

Supported figure styles for Libre Franklin are -TLF *and* -Sup.

Table 10.70: Classification of the Libre Franklin font family

10.8.25 Lucida Sans

Lucida Sans comes with matching serif and monospaced designs, described together in Section 10.2.10 on page 21. Their NFSS classifications are given in Table 10.11 on page 22. This is the font family used in this book for package names and other items.

Lucida Sans 9pt/12pt
(hls) Lucida Sans OT

With a price of £148, **almost anything** can be found Floating In Fields. — ¿But aren't Kafka's Schloß & Æsop's Œuvres often *naïve* vis-à-vis the dæmonic *phœnix's official rôle* in fluffy soufflés?

10-8-2

10.8.26 Merriweather Sans

Merriweather Sans has a matching serif design. The description of both families is given on page 25 and their NFSS classifications in Table 10.12.

Merriweather Sans 9pt/12pt
(MerriwthrSans-TLF)
MerriweatherSans

With a price of £148, **almost anything** can be found FLOATING IN FIELDS. — ¿But aren't Kafka's Schloß & Æsop's Œuvres often *naïve* vis-à-vis the dæmonic *phœnix's official rôle* in fluffy soufflés?

10.8.27 Mint Spirit

The Mint Spirit family of fonts were originally designed by Hirwen Harendal for use as a system font on a Linux Mint system. The font combines aspects of Universalis, NeoGothis, and Gillius by the same designer and combines it with the appearance of the Ubuntu font family designed by Dalton Maag.

LaTeX support for all engines is provided through the packages mintspirit and mintspirit2 by Bob Tennent.

Mint Spirit 10pt/12pt
(MintSpirit-OsF)
Mint Spirit

With a price of £148, **almost anything** can be found Floating In **Fields**. — ¿But aren't Kafka's Schloß & Æsop's Œuvres often *naïve* vis-à-vis the dæmonic *phœnix's official rôle* in fluffy soufflés?

Mint Spirit No2 has some slight redesigns in certain characters, i.e., "AMNVWvwy" vs. "AMNVWvwy" (Mint Spirit), making them more conventional. The initial design certainly has its own charm (which I favor), but perhaps those of No2 blend better with the shapes of the other characters — the choice is yours.

Family	Series	Shapes	Typeface Examples
Mint Spirit	Mint Spirit	(*Encodings:* T1, TS1, OT1, LY1, and TU)	
MintSpirit-LF	m, b	n, it, (sl)	Regular, *italic*, **bold**, and ***bold italic***
Mint Spirit No2	Mint Spirit No2	(*Encodings:* T1, TS1, OT1, LY1, and TU)	
MintSpiritNoTwo-LF	m, b	n, it, (sl)	Regular, *italic*, **bold**, and ***bold italic***

Supported figure styles for Mint Spirit and Mint Spirit No2 are -LF, -OsF, -TLF, -TOsF, -Sup, *and* -Inf.

Table 10.71: Classification of the Mint Spirit and Mint Spirit No2 font families

Family	Series	Shapes	Typeface Examples
Montserrat	Montserrat	(*Encodings:* T1, TS1, OT1, LY1, and TU)	
Montserrat-LF	ul, el, l, sl, m, sb, b, eb, ub	n, it, (sl), scit, (scsl)	Medium, *italic* & SMALL CAPS Hairline to **black**
Montserrat Alternates	Montserrat Alternates	(*Encodings:* T1, TS1, OT1, LY1, and TU)	
MontserratAlternates-LF	ul, el, l, sl, m, sb, b, eb, ub	n, it, (sl), scit, (scsl)	Medium, *italic* & SMALL CAPS. Hairline to **black**

Supported figure styles for Montserrat and Montserrat Alternates are -LF, -OsF, -TLF, -TOsF, -Sup, *and* -Inf.

Table 10.72: Classification of the Montserrat font families

10.8.28 Montserrat

Montserrat is a geometric sans serif design by Julieta Ulanovsky inspired by street art from the historical Buenos Aires neighborhood of the same name. There is also a variant called Montserrat Alternates with a noticeably different design. Both fonts are offered in several weights from hairline to heavy and have upright, italic, and Small Caps shapes. \slshape is aliased to italics.

LaTeX support for pdfTeX is provided through the package montserrat by Michael Sharpe. It offers many options to adjust the font loading, e.g., alternates to use Montserrat Alternates or defaultfam to make the font the default document font. Use scaled to provide a font scaling factor and light, etc., to adjust the weight. For other options see the package documentation.

Unicode engines

For Unicode engines a suitable fontspec declarations file is provided.

For comparison we show a medium width and weight sample as well as a sample with the text in extra light and \textbf producing medium. This second sample runs noticeably shorter than the first, even though both are nominally medium width:

Montserrat 10pt/12pt
(Montserrat-OsF)
Montserrat

With a price of £148, **almost anything** can be found
FLOATING IN **FIELDS**. — ¿But aren't Kafka's Schloß & Æsop's
Œuvres often *naïve* vis-à-vis the dæmonic *phœnix's official
rôle* in fluffy soufflés?

Montserrat 10pt/12pt
(Montserrat-OsF)
Montserrat

With a price of £148, **almost anything** can be found FLOATING
IN FIELDS. — ¿But aren't Kafka's Schloß & Æsop's Œuvres often
naïve vis-à-vis the dæmonic *phœnix's official rôle* in fluffy
soufflés?

The variant Montserrat Alternates has a quite different appeal with its more
rounded shapes, a Humanist "e", and the unusual fl-ligature.

Montserrat Alternates
10pt/12pt
(MontserratAlternates-OsF)
Montserrat Alternates

With a price of £148, **almost anything** can be found
FLOATING IN **FIELDS**. — ¿But aren't Kafka's Schloß & Æsop's
Œuvres often *naïve* vis-à-vis the dæmonic *phœnix's official
rôle* in fluffy soufflés?

10.8.29 Noto Sans

The Noto Sans fonts (an extended version of Droid Sans with well-designed small
capitals) have matching serif and monospaced designs. The families are described
on page 26, and the NFSS classification is given in Table 10.14 on page 28. Michael
Sharpe prepared matching math fonts for use when the family is selected for body
text; an example page is shown in Figure 12.50 on page 295.

Noto Sans 10pt/12.6pt
(NotoSans-OsF) Noto Sans

With a price of £148, **almost anything** can be found FLOATING
IN **FIELDS**. — ¿But aren't Kafka's Schloß & Æsop's Œuvres often *naïve*
vis-à-vis the dæmonic *phœnix's official rôle* in fluffy soufflés?

10.8.30 Overlock

Overlock, designed by Dario Manuel Muhafara, is a rounded sans serif typeface
inspired by the Overlock sewing technique. It is offered in three weights with upright
and italic shapes. Small capitals are available only in medium weight. LaTeX support for
all engines is provided through the package **overlock** by Bob Tennent with the usual
options. The package adjusts \scshape so that it automatically changes families
behind the scenes to account for this somewhat unconventional font setup.

Overlock 10pt/12pt
(Ovrlck-OsF) Overlock

With a price of £148, **almost anything** can be found FLOATING IN Fields. —
¿But aren't Kafka's Schloß & Æsop's Œuvres often *naïve* vis-à-vis the dæmonic
phœnix's official rôle in fluffy soufflés?

Family	Series	Shapes	Typeface Examples
Overlock	Overlock	(*Encodings:* T1, TS1, OT1, LY1, and TU)	
Ovrlck-LF	m, b, eb	n, it, (sl)	Regular, *italic*, **bold**, ***bold italic***, and **extra-bold with *italics***
	m	sc	Only regular Small Caps

Supported figure styles for Overlock are -LF and -OsF.

Table 10.73: Classification of the Overlock font family

10.8.31 Plex Sans

The Plex Sans family has a matching serif and monospace design. The description of all three families is given on page 30, and their NFSS classifications are in Table 10.16 on page 31.

> With a price of £148, **almost anything** can be found Floating In Fields. — ¿But aren't Kafka's Schloß & Æsop's Œuvres often *naïve* vis-à-vis the dæmonic *phœnix's official rôle* in fluffy soufflés?

Plex Sans 10pt/12pt
(IBMPlexSans-TLF)
IBM Plex Sans

10.8.32 PT Sans

Paratype's PT Sans is also accompanied by a matching serif and monospace design. The descriptions are given on page 31 and the NFSS classifications in Table 10.17 on page 32. The sans family also exists in a narrow version, but that has no italic shape.

> With a price of £148, **almost anything** can be found Floating In **Fields**. — ¿But aren't Kafka's Schloß & Æsop's Œuvres often *naïve* vis-à-vis the dæmonic *phœnix's official rôle* in fluffy soufflés?

PT Sans 10pt/12.6pt
(PTSans-TLF) PT Sans

> With a price of £148, **almost anything** can be found Floating In **Fields**. — ¿But aren't Kafka's Schloß & Æsop's Œuvres often *naïve* vis-à-vis the dæmonic *phœnix's official rôle* in fluffy soufflés?

PT Sans Narrow 10pt/12.6pt
(PTSansNarrow-TLF)
PT Sans Narrow

10.8.33 Quattrocento Sans

Quattrocento Sans also has a companion serif design but no monospaced variant. The description of both families is given on page 33 and the NFSS classifications in Table 10.18.

> With a price of £148, **almost anything** can be found Floating In Fields. — ¿But aren't Kafka's Schloß & Æsop's Œuvres often *naïve* vis-à-vis the dæmonic *phœnix's official rôle* in fluffy soufflés?

Quattrocento Sans 9pt/11pt
(QuattroSans-LF)
Quattrocento Sans

Family	Series	Shapes	Typeface Examples
Raleway	Raleway	(*Encodings:* T1, TS1, OT1, LY1, and TU)	
Raleway-TLF	el, l, m, sb, b, eb	n, it, (sl), sc, scit, (scsl)	Regular, *italic,* and **BOLD SMALL CAPS**
	t, mb, k	n, it, (sl), sc, scit, (scsl)	Some nonstandard **widths**

Supported figure styles for Raleway are -TLF *and* -TOsF.

Table 10.74: Classification of the Raleway font family

10.8.34 Raleway

Raleway is a sans serif display typeface, designed by Matt McInerney. In 2012 it was extended by Pablo Impallari and Rodrigo Fuenzalida to cover nine weights with upright, italic, and Small Caps shapes. With Unicode engines it offers a number of stylistic alternates inspired by more geometric sans serif typefaces than its neo-grotesque-inspired default character set. LATEX support for all engines is provided through the package raleway by Silke Hofstra.

Raleway 10pt/12pt
(Raleway-TOsF) Raleway

With a price of £148, **almost anything** can be found FLOATING IN FIELDS. — ¿But aren't Kafka's Schloß & Æsop's Œuvres often *naïve* vis-à-vis the dæmonic *phœnix's official rôle* in fluffy soufflés?

10.8.35 Roboto Sans

Roboto Sans exists in two widths and has a matching monospaced font as well as a slab serif companion. All three families are described in more detail on page 34, and the NFSS classifications are found in Table 10.19 on page 35.

Roboto 10pt/12pt
(Roboto-OsF) Roboto

With a price of £148, **almost anything** can be found FLOATING IN FIELDS. — ¿But aren't Kafka's Schloß & Æsop's Œuvres often *naïve* vis-à-vis the dæmonic *phœnix's official rôle* in fluffy soufflés?

Roboto (option condensed*)*
10pt/12pt (Roboto-OsF)
Roboto Condensed

With a price of £148, **almost anything** can be found FLOATING IN FIELDS. — ¿But aren't Kafka's Schloß & Æsop's Œuvres often *naïve* vis-à-vis the dæmonic *phœnix's official rôle* in fluffy soufflés?

10.8.36 Rosario

Rosario is a Humanist sans serif designed by Héctor Gatti with classic proportions, subtle contrast, and weak endings. It comes in two weights with upright and italic shapes. As often, \slshape is aliased to the italics. LATEX support for all engines is provided through the package Rosario by Arash Esbati.

Family	Series	Shapes	Typeface Examples
Rosario	Rosario	(*Encodings:* T1, TS1, OT1, LY1, and TU)	
Rosario-LF	l, m, sb, b	n, it, (sl)	Regular, *italic*, **bold**, light, and *semi-bold italic shapes*

Supported figure styles for Rosario are -LF, -OsF, -TLF, -TOsF, -Sup, *and* -Inf.

Table 10.75: Classification of the Rosario font family

With a price of £148, **almost anything** can be found Floating In Fields. — ¿But aren't Kafka's Schloß & Æsop's Œuvres often *naïve* vis-à-vis the dæmonic *phœnix's official rôle* in fluffy soufflés?

Rosario 10pt/12pt
(Rosario-OsF) Rosario

10.8.37 Source Sans Pro

Source Sans Pro is yet another family with matching serif and monospaced families, but by more than one designer. They are described together on page 35, and the NFSS classifications are found in Table 10.20 on page 36.

With a price of £148, **almost anything** can be found FLOATING IN FIELDS. — ¿But aren't Kafka's Schloß & Æsop's Œuvres often *naïve* vis-à-vis the dæmonic *phœnix's official rôle* in fluffy soufflés?

Source Sans Pro 10pt/12pt
(SourceSansPro-OsF)
Source Sans Pro

10.8.38 Universalis

Universalis is a legible modern style font family designed by Hirwen Harendal suitable as an alternative to designs from Adrian Frutiger (1928–2015) such as Univers or Frutiger. It is available in two weights in upright and italics and also has condensed shapes.

LaTeX support for all engines is provided by Bob Tennent through the package universalis supporting options such as scaled, sfdefault, and condensed.

With a price of £148, **almost anything** can be found Floating In Fields. — ¿But aren't Kafka's Schloß & Æsop's Œuvres often *naïve* vis-à-vis the dæmonic *phœnix's official rôle* in fluffy soufflés?

Universalis 10pt/12pt
(UniversalisADFStd-LF)
Universalis ADF Std

The package offers the option condensed to use the condensed running width with all shapes.

With a price of £148, **almost anything** can be found Floating In Fields. — ¿But aren't Kafka's Schloß & Æsop's Œuvres often *naïve* vis-à-vis the dæmonic *phœnix's official rôle* in fluffy soufflés?

Universalis (option condensed) 10pt/12pt
(UniversalisADFStd-LF)
Universalis ADF Cond

Family	Series	Shapes	Typeface Examples
Universalis	Universalis ADF Std, Universalis ADF Std Cond		*(Encodings:* T1, TS1, OT1, LY1, and TU)
UniversalisADFStd-LF	m, b	n, it, (sl)	Regular, **bold**, *italic*, and ***bold italic***
	c, bc		Condensed, **bold**, *italic*, and **bold italic**

Supported figure style for Universalis is –LF.

Table 10.76: Classification of the Universalis font family

10.9 Monospaced (typewriter) fonts

The choice of monospaced (typewriter) fonts for use in program listings and other applications is not very wide though it has considerably increased in recent years. Of course, with the Computer or Latin Modern fonts a suitable typewriter family is included, but if the main document fonts are being replaced, freely available choices for typewriter fonts are still relatively few. While staying with Computer or Latin Modern Typewriter (which have an identical design) might be an option, the font may not blend well with the chosen document font.

We start with a few guidelines for selecting a suitable monospaced font and then show examples of roughly a dozen typewriter fonts to choose from.

Running length and x-height

If you use a monospaced font mixed with your main document font, then you typically want to make it comfortably fit in by not showing large deviations from the normal running length nor from the x-height of your body font. The following example compares LuxiMono (scaled down to 85% using the option `scaled`), Computer Modern Typewriter, and Adobe Courier (or more precisely TeX Gyre Cursor). Among those three, LuxiMono has the largest x-height (`\fontdimen5`) and, at the same time, the smallest width. Courier, running very wide, occupies the other end of the spectrum, with CM Typewriter being comfortably in between the two extremes.

```
LuxiMono:
The dazed brown fox quickly gave 12345-67890
jumps!  x-height=4.50502pt
CM Typewriter:
The dazed brown fox quickly gave 12345-67890
jumps!  x-height=4.3045pt
Adobe Courier:
The dazed brown fox quickly gave
12345-67890 jumps!  x-height=4.17pt
```

```
\usepackage[T1]{fontenc}
\usepackage[scaled=0.85]{luximono}
\newcommand\allletters{The dazed brown
  fox quickly gave 12345--67890 jumps!
  x-height=\the\fontdimen5\font\ }
\raggedright
\texttt{LuxiMono:\\ \allletters}
\par \renewcommand\ttdefault{cmtt}
\texttt{CM Typewriter:\\ \allletters}
\par \renewcommand\ttdefault{qcr}
\texttt{Adobe Courier:\\ \allletters}
```

10-9-1

Besides choosing a font with a suitable running length and x-height, it is often also important to use one that shows characteristics different designs in letters that are otherwise easily mistaken for another. Especially in code display this might

Family	Series	Shapes	Typeface Examples
Algol AlgolRevived	*(Encodings:* T1, TS1, OT1, LY1, and TU)		
AlgolRevived-TLF	m, sb, (b)	n, sl, (it)	Regular, *slanted*, and **semi bold**

Supported figure styles for AlgolRevived are -TLF, -Sup, *and* -Inf.

Table 10.77: Classification of the AlgolRevived font family

lead to confusion if they look similar or even identical. For this reason all the samples in this section show the text "OI1 or 011?" so that you can judge for yourself how well Capital O differs from 0 (zero) and Capital I is distinguishable from lowercase l as well as from the digit 1. Charles Bigelow has written an interesting article on the subject that discusses how font designers struggled through the centuries with this problem and shows their solutions [16].

 *Watch out for confusingly similar character shapes*

Another important aspect to check is whether or not the monospaced font contains ligatures that have been set up for use with TeX. While using ligatures is normally a sign of high typographical quality and it is great that TeX does this automatically, this is not wanted with monospace fonts; in fact in a line like

Beware of bad ligatures

> Often we *officially* find offers floating in far offline fjords.

the "fi" and "fl" ligatures look rather out of place, especially as the "ffi" and "ffl" ligatures are missing in this particular font. Unfortunately, in older font setups of some fonts, they have been incorrectly added. If that is the case, you have to obtain newer releases of the font support files, or disable the ligatures with the help of the microtype package; see Section 3.1.3 on page →I 135.

Finally, the different shapes of monospaced fonts do not always have the same running width; e.g., regular and bold may both be monospaced, but mixing them may mean that characters are no longer vertically aligned. If this is the case, the font may not be suitable at all[1] or only if you stick to a single (typically the regular) shape. This was the case with the Libertinus fonts in the past but is now corrected. It can also happen when you use the microtype package, and it does not realize that it is a monospaced font that should not be expanded or compressed. If typewriter material does not line up as expected, disable the package and see if that was the cause. If so, you need to explicitly instruct microtype how to handle your font.

Fonts may just claim to be fully monospaced

10.9.1 Algol

Algol is a font by Adrian Frutiger (1928-2015) that was designed for printing Algol code in manuals; i.e., it is not really meant to be a general-purpose text font. One

---

[1]This is, for example, the case with URW Letter Gothic, which is a nice sans serif monospaced font, except that it adds some kerning between a few letters in the version on CTAN, making it basically unsuitable for any purpose.

Family	Series	Shapes	Typeface Examples
Anonymous Pro	Anonymous Pro		(*Encodings:* T1, TS1, OT1, and TU)
AnonymousPro	m, b	n, sl, (it), (sc)	Regular, *italic*, **bold italic**, and BOLD SMALL CAPS

There is also a U encoding for a few symbols.

Table 10.78: Classification of the Anonymous Pro font family

interesting aspect of it is that it is actually not a monospaced font[1] — so use it only for typewriter if you do not require that all characters line up.

It was digitalized and prepared for use with LaTeX by Michael Sharpe under the name Algol Revived. Note that his algolrevived package sets up the font for use as the document font, unless you give it the option tt! With medium you select the medium bold series as the default, and with scaled you can supply a scale factor as usual. The package also defines a few additional text symbols; see its documentation for details.

Algol 10pt/12pt
(AlgolRevived-TLF)
AlgolRevived

With a price of £148, **almost anything** can be found Floating In Fields. — ¿But aren't Kafka's Schloß & Æsop's Œuvres often *naïve* vis-à-vis the dæmonic *phœnix's official rôle* in fluffy soufflés? OIl or 011?

10.9.2 Anonymous Pro

Anonymous Pro is a monospaced font family designed by Mark Simonson. Special care has been taken to make it suitable for code display by giving glyphs that could be mistaken for each other distinct shapes (such as zero and capital O, etc.).

LaTeX support for pdfTeX is provided through the package AnonymousPro by Arash Esbati. With the option scaled, you can specify a scale factor for the font. The package also defines a number of command names to access extra symbols, many of which represent Apple keyboard keys, such as ⏏ ⌘ ⇧, as well as a few others. Note that the small capitals are faked and appear much too thin.

Anonymous Pro 10pt/12pt
(AnonymousPro)
Anonymous Pro

With a price of £148, **almost anything** can be found FLOATING IN FIELDS. -- ¿But aren't Kafka's Schloß & Æsop's Œuvres often *naïve* vis-à-vis the dæmonic *phœnix's official rôle* in fluffy soufflés? OIl or 011?

10.9.3 CM Bright Typewriter Light

The CM Bright Typewriter Light fonts are designed to be combined with the sans serif family CM Bright. Both families are described together on page 12, and the NFSS

---

[1]We have included it in this section because it is mainly of interest to display code, which is usually done with monospaced fonts.

Family	Series	Shapes	Typeface Examples
Courier	`TeX Gyre Cursor`	*(Encodings:* T1, TS1, T5, OT1, LY1, and TU)	
qcr	m	n, (it), sl, sc, (scit), scsl	Courier and *oblique shape*
	b, (bx)	n, (it), sl, sc, (scit), scsl	**Courier bold in *OBLIQUE SMALL CAPS***

Table 10.79: Classification of the Cursor (Courier) family from the TₑX Gyre distribution

classification is given in Table 10.3. If you think of combining it with other families, consider using LM Typewriter instead, which also offers a light version, and additional shapes.

With a price of £148, almost anything can be found Floating In Fields. - ¿But aren't Kafka's Schloß & Æsop's Œuvres often *naïve* vis-à-vis the dæmonic *phœnix's official rôle* in fluffy soufflés? OI1 or 011?

CM Bright Typewriter Light
10pt/12pt (cmt1)
—no OpenType—

10.9.4 Courier

Courier is a wide-running, thin-stroked monospaced font. It was designed by Howard Kettler (1919–1999) of IBM and later redrawn by Adrian Frutiger (1928-2015). These days it is often used in combination with Times Roman, producing a striking contrast. One reason for the popularity of this combination is certainly its availability on any PostScript device.

TₑX Gyre Cursor shown here is based on the URW Nimbus Mono L version of the font family (which is set up with the TₑX Gyre tgcursor package).

With a price of £148, **almost anything** can be found FLOATING IN **FIELDS.** – ¿But aren't Kafka's Schloß & Æsop's Œuvres often *naïve* vis-à-vis the dæmonic *phœnix's official rôle* in fluffy soufflés? OI1 or 011?

Courier 10pt/12pt
(qcr) `TeX Gyre Cursor`

10.9.5 DejaVu Sans Mono

DejaVu Sans Mono is the monospaced font matching the serif and sans serif DejaVu designs. You can find the description of all three families on page 12 and their NFSS classifications in Table 10.4 on page 13.

With a price of £148, **almost anything** can be found Floating In **Fields.** — ¿But aren't Kafka's Schloß & Æsop's Œuvres often *naïve* vis-à-vis the dæmonic *phœnix's official rôle* in fluffy soufflés?

DejaVu Sans Mono
9pt/12.5pt
(DejaVuSansMono-TLF)
`DejaVu Sans Mono`

Family	Series	Shapes	Typeface Examples
Inconsolata	Inconsolatazi4, InconsolataN		(*Encodings:* T1, TS1, OT1, LY1, and TU)
zi4	m, b	n	Only upright shape in regular **and bold weight** available

Table 10.80: Classification of the Inconsolata font family

10.9.6 Fira Mono

This font by Erik Spiekermann is the companion to the Humanist sans serif Fira Sans. See page 14 for the font descriptions and Table 10.5 for the NFSS font classification and further details on the families.

Fira Mono 9pt/11pt
(FiraMono-TLF) Fira Mono

With a price of £148, **almost anything** can be found Floating In **Fields**. – ¿But aren't Kafka's Schloß & Æsop's Œuvres often *naïve* vis-à-vis the dæmonic *phœnix's official rôle* in fluffy soufflés? OIl or 011?

10.9.7 Go Mono

Designed by Charles Bigelow this monospaced font has Go Sans as the matching sans serif family. See page 15 for the font description and Table 10.7 on page 16 for the NFSS font classification and further details.

Go Mono 9pt/12pt
(GoMono-TLF) Go Mono

With a price of £148, **almost anything** can be found Floating In **Fields**. – ¿But aren't Kafka's Schloß & Æsop's Œuvres often *naïve* vis-à-vis the dæmonic *phœnix's official rôle* in fluffy soufflés? OIl or 011?

10.9.8 Inconsolata

Inconsolata is a monospaced sans serif font designed by Raph Levien. It is provided in regular and bold weights but offers only a single shape, e.g., no italics, etc. By default, word spaces are flexible; i.e., only the characters are monospaced and thus can be used justified.

LaTeX support for pdfTeX is provided through the package inconsolata by Michael Sharpe. It offers a bundle of options, e.g., scaled, narrow (for a somewhat condensed width), hyphenate (allow hyphenation), mono (make word spaces also mono-width), and several others. Support for a number of variant characters such as a nonslashed zero is also provided through options. See the package documentation for details.

Unicode engines

For Unicode engines some fontspec configuration files are provided.

With a price of £148, **almost anything** can be found Floating In Fields. – ¿But aren't Kafka's Schloß & Æsop's Œuvres often naïve vis-à-vis the dæmonic phœnix's official rôle in fluffy soufflés? OIl or 011?

Inconsolata 10pt/12pt
(zi4) `Inconsolatazi4`

10.9.9 Kp (Johannes Kepler) Typewriter

Kp Mono has both a matching serif and sans serif design. All three families are described on page 17 where you also find their NFSS classifications in Table 10.9 on page 18. An interesting aspect of the font is that it offers both lining and oldstyle numbers (as shown below). If you prefer lining numerals, use the family jkptt with pdfTeX; with Unicode engines use the feature set of fontspec.

With a price of £148, almost anything can be found Floating In Fields. -- ¿But aren't Kafka's Schloß & Æsop's Œuvres often *naïve* vis-à-vis the dæmonic *phœnix's official rôle* in fluffy soufflés? OIl or 011?

Kp Mono 10pt/12pt
(jkpttosn) `KpMono`

10.9.10 Latin Modern Typewriter

If you load the lmodern package, all fonts are going to be from the Latin Modern families. On the Unicode engines Latin Modern is already the default, so you do not even have to load a package.

In either case, this means that \texttt selects the regular monospaced version of the Latin Modern Typewriter font. You can find the description of the Latin Modern families in Section 9.5.1 and their NFSS classifications in Table 9.6 on page →I 687.

With a price of £148, almost anything can be found FLOATING IN Fields. – ¿But aren't Kafka's Schloß & Æsop's Œuvres often *naïve* vis-à-vis the dæmonic *phœnix's official rôle* in fluffy soufflés? OIl or 011?

LM Typewriter 10pt/12pt
(lmtt)
`Latin Modern Mono`

As we have seen in that section, this font actually has several weights, as well as a proportional variant, in addition to the monospaced one. To be able to easily provide access to these variants within a document, as well as setting up any of them as default just for the typewriter font, Michael Sharpe produced the package zlmtt that you can use instead or in addition to lmodern.

The package has a number of options, such as light or lightcondensed to choose the light weight as default, as well as med to use the medium weight when bold is requested. Furthermore, the option proportional requests the proportionally spaced version instead of the default monospaced one, and scaled applies a scale factor, which helps if you combine the font with other families.

The package also offers the commands \monott \proptt, and \lctt to unconditionally select the monospaced, proportionally, or light condensed version of the font regardless of the options chosen during package loading.

The example below shows the result of these commands in different circumstances. The default here is the light proportional version; thus, we see no change when we explicitly request proportional for the second sentence. \monott then forces monospaced glyphs. Then we switch explicitly to light condensed. As you see, that has italics, but the bold comes out in normal running length as there is not a bold condensed series. Finally, in the last line we use \texttt again, which switches back to the document default but still keeps the italic shape that was requested earlier.

The dazed brown fox *quickly* gave 12–3 **jumps!** (proportional)

The dazed brown fox *quickly* gave 12–3 **jumps!** (no change)

The dazed brown fox *quickly* gave 12-3 **jumps**! (monospaced)

The dazed brown fox *quickly* gave 12-3 **jumps**! (light cond.)

The dazed brown fox quickly gave 12-3 jumps! (+italic …)

The dazed brown fox quickly gave 12–3 jumps!

```
\usepackage{lmodern}
\usepackage[proportional,light]{zlmtt}
\newcommand\allletters{The dazed brown fox
 \textit{quickly} gave 12--3 \textbf{jumps}!}
\texttt{\allletters} (proportional)  \par
\proptt{\allletters} (no change)     \par
\monott{\allletters} (monospaced)    \par
\lctt  {\allletters} (light cond.)   \par
\itshape
\lctt  {\allletters} (+italic \dots) \par
\texttt{\allletters}                 \par
```
10-9-2

10.9.11 Libertinus Mono

For this font by Philipp H. Poll and Khaled Hosny there exists a matching serif and sans serif family. See page 19 for the font description and Table 10.10 on page 20 for the NFSS font classification and further details on the fonts. I would avoid the bold weight as it is far too dark and fuzzy for my taste.

Libertinus Mono 9pt/12pt
(LibertinusMono-TLF)
Libertinus Mono

With a price of £148, **almost anything** can be found Floating In **Fields**. — ¿But aren't Kafka's Schloß & Æsop's Œuvres often *naïve* vis-à-vis the dæmonic *phœnix's official rôle* in fluffy soufflés? OI1 or 011?

10.9.12 Lucida's monospaced families

There are several closely related monospaced Lucida designs intended to be used with matching Lucida serif and sans serif families. They are described together in Section 10.2.10 on page 21, and their NFSS classifications are given in Table 10.11 on page 22.

Lucida Typewriter is a serifed design running comparably wide, while the other three families are sans serif designs with a shorter running length.

Lucida Typewriter 9pt/12pt
(hlct) —no OpenType—

With a price of £148, **almost anything** can be found Floating In **Fields**. -- ¿But aren't Kafka's Schloß & Æsop's Œuvres often *naïve* vis-à-vis the dæmonic *phœnix's official rôle* in fluffy soufflés? OI1 or 011?

Family	Series	Shapes	Typeface Examples
LuxiMono	—no OpenType—		(*Encodings:* T1, TS1)
ul9	m, b	n, sl	LuxiMono and *LuxiMono oblique shapes*

Table 10.81: Classification of the LuxiMono font family

The differences between the sans serif designs are fairly subtle. Lucida Sans Typewriter has a slanted shape, while the other two have real italics. Lucida Console has noticeably shorter capitals, and there are small alterations in the design of some letter shapes in Lucida Grande Mono. Furthermore, the DK fonts use a slightly "squarish" O by default; see the discussion on page 24 for details.

With a price of £148, **almost anything** can be found Floating In **Fields**. -- ¿But aren't Kafka's Schloß & Æsop's Œuvres often *naïve* vis-à-vis the dæmonic *phœnix's official rôle* in fluffy soufflés? OI1 or 011?

> *Lucida Sans Typewriter 9pt/12pt* (hlst)
> Lucida Sans Typewriter OT

With a price of £148, **almost anything** can be found Floating In **Fields**. – ¿But aren't Kafka's Schloß & Æsop's Œuvres often *naïve* vis-à-vis the dæmonic *phœnix's official rôle* in fluffy soufflés? OI1 or 011?

> *Lucida Console 9pt/12pt* (—only OpenType—)
> Lucida Console DK

10-9-3

With a price of £148, **almost anything** can be found Floating In **Fields**. – ¿But aren't Kafka's Schloß & Æsop's Œuvres often *naïve* vis-à-vis the dæmonic *phœnix's official rôle* in fluffy soufflés? OI1 or 011?

> *Lucida Grande Mono 9pt/12pt* (— only OpenType—)
> Lucida Grande Mono DK

10-9-4

10.9.13 Luximono

The Luximono fonts are original designs by Kris Holmes and Charles Bigelow (Bigelow and Holmes, Inc.), for which hinting and kerning tables have been added by URW++ Design and Development GmbH. The family has two weights with upright and oblique shapes. In that respect, it differs from other monospaced fonts, which are often offered only in medium series and more rarely in italic or oblique shapes.

With a price of £148, **almost anything** can be found Floating In **Fields**. -- ¿But aren't Kafka's Schloß & Æsop's Œuvres often *naïve* vis-à-vis the dæmonic *phœnix's official rôle* in fluffy soufflés? OI1 or 011?

> *Luximono 9pt/12pt* (ul9) —no OpenType—

The LaTeX integration for pdfTeX is provided through the luximono package written by Walter Schmidt (1960–2021). If the option scaled is given without a value, the fonts are loaded at a running length approximately equal to that of Computer Modern Typewriter. Without scaling, LuxiMono has the same running length as Adobe Courier. The fonts are not included in all distributions but can be installed with getnonfreefonts.

10.9.14 Noto Sans Mono

The Noto Sans Mono fonts (and the earlier version Droid Sans Mono) have matching serif and sans serif designs. They are described on page 26, and the NFSS classification is given in Table 10.14 on page 28.

Noto Sans Mono 9pt/12pt
(NotoSansMono-TLF)
Noto Sans Mono

With a price of £148, **almost anything** can be found FLOATING IN **FIELDS**. – ¿But aren't Kafka's Schloß & Æsop's Œuvres often naïve vis-à-vis the dæmonic phœnix's official rôle in fluffy soufflés? OIl or 0Il?

This family is also offered in three narrow versions (semi-condensed, condensed, and extra-condensed), which is of great help if space requirements are tight. Here is an example of the condensed version:

Noto Sans Mono (option
condensed) 9pt/12pt
(NotoSansMono-TLF)
Noto Sans Mono Condensed

With a price of £148, **almost anything** can be found FLOATING IN **FIELDS**. – ¿But aren't Kafka's Schloß & Æsop's Œuvres often naïve vis-à-vis the dæmonic phœnix's official rôle in fluffy soufflés? OIl or 0Il?

10.9.15 Plex Mono

For the Plex Mono font by Mike Abbink there exists a matching serif and sans serif family. See page 30 for the font description and Table 10.16 on page 31 for the NFSS font classification.

Plex Mono 9pt/12pt
(IBMPlexMono-TLF)
IBM Plex Mono

With a price of £148, **almost anything** can be found Floating In **Fields**. – ¿But aren't Kafka's Schloß & Æsop's Œuvres often naïve vis-à-vis the dæmonic phœnix's official rôle in fluffy soufflés? OIl or 0Il?

10.9.16 PT Mono

Paratype's PT Mono is the monospaced font intended as a companion to PT Serif and PT Sans — all designed by Alexandra Korolkova. See page 31 for the family descriptions and Table 10.17 on page 32 for the NFSS font classification and further details.

PT Mono 9pt/11pt
(PTMono-TLF) PT Mono

With a price of £148, **almost anything** can be found Floating In **Fields**. – ¿But aren't Kafka's Schloß & Æsop's Œuvres often naïve vis-à-vis the dæmonic phœnix's official rôle in fluffy soufflés? OIl or 0Il?

10.9.17 Roboto Mono

Roboto Mono is the monospaced companion to Roboto Sans and slab serif font Roboto Slab. All three families are described in more detail on page 34, and the NFSS classifications are found in Table 10.19 on page 35.

> With a price of £148, **almost anything** can be found FLOATING IN **FIELDS**. – ¿But aren't Kafka's Schloß & Æsop's Œuvres often *naïve* vis-à-vis the dæmonic *phœnix's official rôle* in fluffy soufflés? OIl or 0Il?

Roboto Mono 9pt/11pt
(RobotoMono-TLF)
Roboto Mono

10.9.18 Source Code Pro

The monospaced font Source Code Pro is the companion to the families Source Serif Pro and Source Sans Pro. All three are described in more detail on page 35, and their NFSS classifications are found in Table 10.20 on page 36.

> With a price of £148, **almost anything** can be found Floating In **Fields**. – ¿But aren't Kafka's Schloß & Æsop's Œuvres often *naïve* vis-à-vis the dæmonic *phœnix's official rôle* in fluffy soufflés? OIl or 0Il?

Source Code Pro 9pt/11pt
(SourceCodePro-TLF)
Source Code Pro

10.10   Historical and other fonts

The fonts that we are going to showcase in this section are a mixed bunch that for one or another reason did not fit well into the classification that we used above. A few are historically before the periods covered, e.g., Cinzel and Marcellus that are based on 1st century roman inscriptions. The Blackletter shapes that we cover briefly at the end were the first fonts used as movable type and thus represent the period before the Humanist fonts took over. Because they are useful only in special circumstances, we cover them here.

On the other side of the spectrum are the Chancery and handwriting fonts that are in some sense the predecessors of what we nowadays call the italic shape because the glyph forms were originally developed in the Vatican in the 15th century based on the Humanist minuscule of that time.

Two of the families inspired by chancery handwriting, Almendra and Antykwa Toruńska, are explicitly intended for body text (though they work nicely in display sizes too). Due to their stronger personality, they are suitable only in a few scenarios, which is why they are also placed in this section.

The actual fonts that we exhibit here are — with one exception — all contemporary and have been designed in the last or even in this century. The exceptions are the Fell types, which are digitalized versions of the 17th century originals, charmingly showing all the imperfections of the original type.

Family	Series	Shapes	Typeface Examples
Cinzel	Cinzel	(*Encodings:* T1, TS1, OT1, LY1, and TU)	
Cinzel-LF	m, b, eb	n	SMALL CAPS IN **THREE DIFFERENT WEIGHTS**
Cinzel Decorative	Cinzel Decorative	(*Encodings:* T1, TS1, OT1, LY1, and TU)	
CinzelDecorative-LF	m, b, eb	n	DECORATIVE ALL CAPS ONLY **IN THREE WEIGHTS**

Table 10.82: Classification of the Cinzel font family

Family	Series	Shapes	Typeface Examples
Marcellus	Marcellus	(*Encodings:* T1, TS1, OT1, LY1, and TU)	
Mrcls-LF	m	n, sc	Regular and SMALL CAPS SHAPES only

Supported figure styles for Marcellus are -LF *and* -Sup.

Table 10.83: Classification of the Marcellus font family

10.10.1 Cinzel

The classical proportions of the Cinzel fonts are inspired by 1st century roman inscriptions. Designed by Natanael Gama, the fonts are available in three different weights (but naturally, without italics, which is an invention of the 15th century).

LaTeX support for all engines is provided through the package cinzel by Bob Tennent. If the option default is given, \rmdefault is changed to select the family. In any case, the font is made available through the commands \textcinzel and \textcinzelblack or the declarations \cinzel and \cinzelblack.

Cinzel 10pt/12pt
(Cinzel-LF) Cinzel

WITH A PRICE OF £148, **ALMOST ANYTHING** CAN BE FOUND FLOATING IN **FIELDS**. — ¿BUT AREN'T KAFKA'S SCHLOSS & ÆSOP'S ŒUVRES OFTEN NAÏVE VIS-À-VIS THE DÆMONIC PHŒNIX'S OFFICIAL RÔLE IN FLUFFY SOUFFLÉS?

Upper and lowercase letters in Cinzel Decorative have the same height, but only the uppercase glyphs have decorations; thus, when used with only some letters uppercased, it gives some interesting results.

Cinzel Decorative
10pt/13.6pt
(CinzelDecorative-LF)
Cinzel Decorative

ALL UPPERCASE: ABCDEFGHIJKLMNOPQRSTUVWXYZ
MIXED CASE: THE DAZED BROWN FOX QUICKLY GAVE 123 JUMPS!

If the cinzel package is used, then \textit or the declaration \itshape switches to the decorative font as long as you are currently typesetting in Cinzel.

Family	Series	Shapes	Typeface Examples
Fell Types IM FELL English			*(Encodings:* T1, TS1, OT1, LY1, and TU)
IMFELLEnglish-TLF	m	n, it, (sl), sc	Fell regular, *italic*, and SMALL CAPS shapes

The family has oldstyle numbers despite the fact the suffix -TLF.

Table 10.84: Classification of the Fell Types

10.10.2 Marcellus

Like Cinzel, the Marcellus fonts by Brian J. Bonislawsky are also inspired by classical roman inscriptions. The small capitals are well suited for display text, while the regular version lends itself to a wider range of usage having both capitals and lowercase letters. Note, though, that this family is offered only in regular weight and does not provide any italics.

LaTeX support for all engines is provided through the package marcellus by Bob Tennent with the option `scaled` providing a scale factor.

With a price of £148, almost anything can be found FLOATING IN Fields. — ¿But aren't Kafka's Schloß & Æsop's Œuvres often naïve vis-à-vis the dæmonic phœnix's official rôle in fluffy soufflés?

Marcellus 10pt/12pt (Mrcls-LF) Marcellus

10.10.3 The Fell Types

The so-called Fell Types, which are of Dutch origin, were in use in the 17th century at the Oxford University Press. They have been procured by Dr. John Fell, Bishop of Oxford and Dean of Christ Church, who also collected an impressive number of ornamental flower specimen. The fonts have been digitalized by Igino Marini,[1] and LaTeX support for all engines is available through the package imfellEnglish by Bob Tennent. The sample shows the fonts at their nominal font size of 13.5pt.

With a price of £148, almost anything can be found FLOATING IN Fields. — ¿But aren't Kafka's Schloß & Æsop's Œuvres often *naïve* vis-à-vis the dæmonic *phœnix's official rôle* in fluffy soufflés?

Fell 13.5pt/15pt (IMFELLEnglish-TLF) IM FELL English

Unicode engines

With Unicode engines it is also possible to access the ornamental flower designs collected by Dr. Fell, as shown in the next example. They are available from CTAN but normally not distributed. Thus, you have to download them first, either from there or from the designer's home page.

---

[1] See the `https://www.iginomarini.com` website.

Family	Series	Shapes	Typeface Examples
Almendra	Almendra	(*Encodings:* T1, TS1, OT1, LY1, and TU)	
Almndr-OsF	m, b	n, it, (sl), sc	Regular, *italic*, **bold**, and SMALL CAPS

Table 10.85: Classification of the Almendra font family

Dr. Fell collected a larger number of ornamental flower types, some of which are shown in this example.

Which letters produce which FLOWERS was found by looking at the fonts with the *unicodefonttable* package.

```
\usepackage{imfellEnglish}
\newfontfamily\Fellflower{IMFeFlow1.otf}
\newfontfamily\Fellflowerii{IMFeFlow2.otf}
\begin{center}\Fellflower
    KLM ACBCD OPQ          \end{center}
Dr.\ Fell collected a larger number of ornamental
flower types, some of which are shown in this example.
\begin{center}\Fellflowerii
    1 Aa 2                 \end{center}
Which letters produce which \textsc{Flowers} was
found by looking at the fonts with the
\emph{unicodefonttable} package.
\begin{center}\Fellflowerii
    N m O F o M n          \end{center}
```

10-10-1

10.10.4 Almendra

The Almendra family, designed by Ana Sanfelippo, is a typeface inspired by chancery and gothic handwriting. It was exhibited at the Bienal Iberoamericana de Diseño in 2010 and was part of the German editorial project Typodarium 2012. The font is intended for body text but also works nicely in display sizes. One of its unusual features is that its italics are upright.

LaTeX support for all engines is provided through the package almendra by Bob Tennent. With the option scaled you can provide a scale factor.

Almendra 10pt/12pt
(Almndr-OsF) Almendra

With a price of £148, **almost anything** can be found FLOATING IN **Fields**. — ¿But aren't Kafka's Schloß & Æsop's Œuvres often *naïve* vis-à-vis the dæmonic phœnix's official rôle in fluffy soufflés?

10.10.5 Antykwa Toruńska

Antykwa Toruńska, which means "Antiqua of Toruń", was designed by Zygfryd Gardzielewski, a typographer from the city of Toruń[1] (Thorn), Poland. Some of its characteristic features are the widening of its stems towards the top and the wave-like form of some of the horizontal and diagonal lines as well as the form of its serifs. It was first cut in metal in 1960 in Warsaw and digitalized in 2005 by Janusz Marian

---

[1] The birthplace of Nicolaus Copernicus (Mikołaj Kopernik).

Family	Series	Shapes	Typeface Examples
Antykwa Toruńska		Antykwa Torunska	(*Encodings:* T1, TS1, T5, OT1, OT4, LY1, and TU)
antt	l, m, sb, b	n, it, sc, scit	Regular **bold**, *italic*, and SMALL CAPS ITALICS
	lc, c, sbc, bc		Condensed **bold**, *italic*, and SMALL CAPS ITALICS
Antykwa Toruńska Light		Antykwa Torunska Light	(*Encodings:* T1, TS1, T5, OT1, OT4, LY1, and TU)
anttl	m, sb, b, eb	n, it, sc, scit	Regular, **bold**, *italic*, and SMALL CAPS ITALICS
	c, sbc, bc, ebc		Condensed regular, **bold**, *italic*, and SMALL CAPS ITALICS
Antykwa Toruńska Condensed		Antykwa Torunska Cond	(*Encodings:* T1, TS1, T5, OT1, OT4, LY1, and TU)
anttc	l, m, sb, b	n, it, sc, scit	Regular, **bold**, *italic*, and SMALL CAPS ITALICS
	lx, x, sbx, bx		Expanded regular, **bold**, *italic*, and SMALL CAPS ITALICS
Antykwa Toruńska Light Cond.		Antykwa Torunska Light Cond	(*Encodings:* T1, TS1, T5, OT1, OT4, LY1, TU)
anttlc	m, sb, b, eb	n, it, sc, scit	Regular, **bold**, *italic*, and SMALL CAPS ITALICS
	x, sbx, bx, ebx		Expanded, **bold expanded**, *italic*, and SMALL CAPS ITALICS & **extra-bold expanded**

The series specifications in Antykwa Toruńska Light are shifted by one weight with respect to Antykwa Toruńska; e.g., m in Antykwa Toruńska becomes sb in Antykwa Toruńska Light. Similarly, the expansion codes are shifted; e.g., bx in Antykwa Toruńska Condensed is the same as b in Antykwa Toruńska.

Table 10.86: Classification of the Antykwa Toruńska font family

Nowacki (1951–2020). It is offered in five weights and two widths. Note that there is no \slshape.

LATEX support for pdfTEX is provided through the package anttor by Janusz Marian Nowacki (1951–2020). The standard weight can be selected through the options regular (default) and light, and with condensed you can reduce the width.

Matching math fonts are available too and can be activated with the option math. They cover the basic symbols but not those from amssymb, which would keep their shapes if used; see Figures 12.51 to 12.52 on page 296.

Unicode engines

For Unicode engines you need to provide your own fontspec declaration.

With a price of £148, **almost anything** can be found FLOATING IN FIELDS. — ¿But aren't Kafka's Schloß & Æsop's Œuvres often *naïve* vis-à-vis the dæmonic *phœnix's official rôle* in fluffy soufflés?

Antykwa Toruńska Light
10pt/12pt (anttl)
Antykwa Torunska Light

With a price of £148, **almost anything** can be found FLOATING IN FIELDS. — ¿But aren't Kafka's Schloß & Æsop's Œuvres often *naïve* vis-à-vis the dæmonic *phœnix's official rôle* in fluffy soufflés?

Antykwa Toruńska
10pt/12pt
(antt) Antykwa Torunska

For comparison, here are the condensed versions:

With a price of £148, **almost anything** can be found FLOATING IN FIELDS. — ¿But aren't Kafka's Schloß & Æsop's Œuvres often *naïve* vis-à-vis the dæmonic *phœnix's official rôle* in fluffy soufflés?

With a price of £148, **almost anything** can be found FLOATING IN **FIELDS.** — ¿But aren't Kafka's Schloß & Æsop's Œuvres often *naïve* vis-à-vis the dæmonic *phœnix's official rôle* in fluffy soufflés?

10.10.6 Lucida Casual, Calligraphy, and Handwriting

In the Lucida set of fonts sold by TUG there are three typefaces that are inspired in varying degrees by handwriting. You can find their NFSS 10.11 on page 22 together with those of other Lucida families. Lucida Casual supports upright and italic shapes; the others only italics as is typical for handwritten fonts.

With a price of £148, almost anything can be found Floating In Fields. — ¿But aren't Kafka's Schloß & Æsop's Œuvres often *naïve* vis-à-vis the dæmonic *phœnix's official rôle* in fluffy soufflés?

With a price of £148, almost anything can be found Floating In Fields. — ¿But aren't Kafka's Schloß & Æsop's Œuvres often naïve vis-à-vis the dæmonic phœnix's official rôle in fluffy soufflés?

With a price of £148, almost anything can be found Floating In Fields. — ¿But aren't Kafka's Schloß & Æsop's Œuvres often naïve vis-à-vis the dæmonic phœnix's official rôle in fluffy soufflés?

10.10.7 Zapf Chancery (TEX Gyre Chorus)

Zapf Chancery is another and quite famous contemporary script based on chancery handwriting, as developed during the Italian Renaissance for use by the scribes in the papal offices. Highly legible, it can be usefully applied for short texts and applications like invitations and awards.

TEX Gyre Chorus shown here is based on the URW Chancery L Medium Italic version of the font (which is set up by the TEX Gyre tgchorus package). Note that this font is available only in an italic shape, which is why the sample text does not show any bold or small capitals.

With a price of £148, almost anything can be found Floating In Fields. — ¿But aren't Kafka's Schloß & Æsop's Œuvres often naïve vis-à-vis the dæmonic phœnix's official rôle in fluffy soufflés?

Family	Series	Shapes	Typeface Examples
Zapf Chancery		TeX Gyre Chorus	(*Encodings:* T1, TS1, OT1, T5, LY1, and TU)
qzc	m	it	*Zapf Chancery Medium Italic*

Table 10.87: Classification of the Chorus (Zapf Chancery) family from the TₑX Gyre distribution

Family	Series	Shapes	Typeface Examples
Miama Nueva		Miama Nueva	(*Encodings:* T1, T2A, T2B, T2C, T5, OT1, LGR, and TU)
fmm	m	n, (it), (sl), (sc)	*Miama Nueva handwriting*

Table 10.88: Classification of the Miama Nueva family

10.10.8 Miama Nueva

This typeface, designed by Linus Romer, also mimics handwriting and offers a large glyph set that supports the Latin, polytonic Greek, and Cyrillic scripts. The `miama` package for the pdfTₑX engine supports the option `scaled` to provide a scaling factor and offers the command `\miama` and the declaration `\fmmfamily` to select the font — document font defaults are not changed. Thus, if you want to typeset a whole document in this hand, use `\fmmfamily`, and if you cannot stop talking about TₑX or LATEX in your invitation letter, then `\fmmTeX` and `\fmmLaTeX` provide you with a way, as the standard commands do not work well in this font.

> **Unicode engines**
>
> With Unicode engines, use `fontspec` to set up the font.

With a price of £148, almost anything can be found Floating In Fields. — ¿But aren't Kafka's Schloß & Æsop's Œuvres often naïve vis-à-vis the dæmonic phœnix's official rôle in fluffy soufflés? Also supported: TₑX and LATEX instead of TₑX and LATEX

Miama Nova 9pt/20pt
(fmm) Miama Nueva

The font has roughly the same x-height as Computer Modern, but due to the long ascenders and descenders, you need to either scale it down or enlarge the leading to avoid that characters run into each other. In the above example, we therefore changed from the usual 9/11 pt to 9/20 pt.

10.10.9 Lucida Blackletter

The Lucida set of fonts as sold by TUG also contains a blackletter font, which is primarily meant to be used in math (at least when using pdfTeX) and not in text as we do here. See Section 10.2.10 on page 25 for a discussion of why.

Lucida Blackletter 9pt/12pt
(hlcf)
Lucida Blackletter OT

With a price of £148, almost anything can be found floating In fields. — ¡But aren't Kafka's Schloß & Æsop's Œuvres often naïve vis-à-vis the dæmonic phœnix's official rôle in fluffy soufflés?

10.10.10 Blackletter — Yannis Gothic, Schwabacher, and Fraktur

There exists a set of beautiful fonts for typesetting in Gothic, Schwabacher, and Fraktur designed in METAFONT after traditional typefaces by Yannis Haralambous [35]. The collection also contains a font with baroque initials. These days Type 1 versions of the fonts are available as well that are automatically used.

LaTeX support for all engines is provided through the yfonts package written by Walter Schmidt (1960–2021). This package internally defines some local encodings (i.e., even on Unicode engines it does not use fontenc) that reflect the special features found in the fonts and integrates them fully with LaTeX's font management.

The commands \gothfamily, \swabfamily, and \frakfamily switch to Gothic, Schwabacher, and Fraktur, respectively. The corresponding commands with one argument are \textgoth, \textswab, and \textfrak. If one wants to typeset a whole document in such a typeface, the corresponding command should be used directly *after* \begin{document}. Because of the nonstandard encodings of the fonts, redefining the document defaults (e.g., \familydefault) is not possible. In addition to the font switches, the usual \text.. commands for typesetting short fragments are provided.

The package provides Gotisch, also called Textur, Schwabacher, and Fraktur typefaces, also generally known as „gebrochene Schriften".

```
\usepackage{yfonts}\usepackage[document]{ragged2e}
The package provides \textgoth{Gotisch, also
called Textur}, \textswab{Schwabacher}, and
\textfrak{Fraktur} typefaces, also  generally
known as \textfrak{``ge\-bro\-che\-ne Schriften''}.
```

10-10-2

The fonts are available in the usual LaTeX sizes starting from 10pt so that size-changing commands (e.g., \normalsize and larger) work. There are, however, no further font series or shapes, so commands like \emph, \textit, and \textbf have no effect other than producing a warning. Following historical practice, you can use Schwabacher to emphasize something inside text typeset in Fraktur.

For accented characters one can use the standard LaTeX representations (e.g., either Unicode characters or \"a for ä, etc.). To facilitate easy input (long before Unicode became common), the fonts also contain ligatures that represent umlauts (e.g., "a). In Fraktur and Schwabacher there also exist alternate umlauts, which can be accessed with *a and similar ligatures. If the yfonts package is loaded with the option varumlaut, then the variant glyphs are selected automatically. All three fonts contain a glyph for the "short s", accessed through the ligature s:; and "sharp s", accessed by "ß", \ss, through the ligature sz, or through "s.

The next example shows the various ligatures, but except for the "short s", one would these days normally simply use the Unicode characters ÄÖÜäöü unless one needs both accent variants in one document.

```
\usepackage{yfonts}

\Large \frakfamily Fraktur: "a "e "u "o
\hfil *a *e *u *o \hfil sz \hfil s vs.\ s:
\par\swabfamily    Swab:    "a "e "u "o
\hfil *a *e *u *o \hfil sz \hfil s vs.\ s:
\par\gothfamily    Gothic:  "a "e "u "o
\hfil (unavail) \hfil sz \hfil s vs.\ s:
```

The font selected with `\gothfamily` is not a copy of Gutenberg's font used for his Bible (which had 288 glyphs altogether), but it follows Gutenberg's guidelines on lowercase characters and implements as many ligatures as can be fit into a 7-bit font (e.g., the "va" in the previous example). For this reason many standard ASCII symbols are unavailable in this font.

The two other fonts also implement only a subset of visible ASCII. Problematic are the semicolon (which is missing in Schwabacher) and the characters +, =, `, [,], /, *, @, &, and % (which either are missing or produce wrong or nonmatching shapes). Their omission is seldom a problem, because typically they are not needed in documents using such fonts. However, one needs to be aware that no warning or error message is issued if they are used — the only indication is missing or wrong glyphs in the printed output!

```
\usepackage{yfonts}
\newcommand\test{+  = ` [ ] / * \$ \% \& ; @}

Symbols: \ttfamily              \test \par
\frakfamily Fraktur problems:: \test \par
\swabfamily Swab    problems:: \test \par
\gothfamily Gothic  problems:: \test
```

The default line spacing of the standard classes is too large for the blackletter fonts. For this reason the package implements the `\fraklines` command, which selects a suitable `\baselineskip` for Fraktur or Schwabacher. It must be repeated after every size-changing command.

The font collection also contains a font with decorative initials, as shown in the next example. Note the use of Unicode characters and the option `varumlaut`:

```
\usepackage[german]{babel}   \usepackage{color}
\usepackage[varumlaut]{yfonts}

\frakfamily\fraklines
\yinipar{\color{blue}D}ies: ist ein Blindtext an dem
sich verschiedene Dinge ablesen lassen. Der Grauwert
der Schriftfläche wird sichtbar und man kann an ihm
prüfen, wie gut die Schrift zu lesen ist und wie sie
auf den Leser wirkt. Bei genauerem Hinsehen werden
die einzelnen Buchstaben und ihre Besonderheiten
erkennbar, \etc
```

The command `\yinipar` used in the previous example starts a new paragraph without indentation, producing a baroque dropped initial. For this command to work, a full paragraph (up to and including the next blank line or `\par`) must be typeset using `\fraklines`. Otherwise, the space left for the initial is either too large or too small.

As an alternative, you can access these initials with the `\textinit` command or the font switch `\initfamily`, in which case initials aligned at the baseline are produced. The example also used the command `\etc`, which produces a once-popular symbol for "etc."; it is available in Fraktur only.

The font collection contains a second Fraktur font that has slightly wider glyphs with, at the same time, slightly thinner stems. It can be selected by redefining `\frakdefault` as shown in the next example. When compared to Example 10-10-5, the difference in running length can be clearly observed, resulting in an overfull box on the third line.

```
\usepackage[german]{babel}    \usepackage{color}
\usepackage[varumlaut]{yfonts}
\renewcommand\frakdefault{ysmfrak}

\frakfamily\fraklines
\yinipar{\color{blue}D}ies: ist ein Blindtext an dem
sich verschiedene Dinge ablesen lassen. Der Grauwert
der Schriftfläche wird sichtbar und man kann an ihm
prüfen, wie gut die Schrift zu lesen ist und wie
sie auf den Leser wirkt. Bei genauerem Hinsehen \dots
```

Dies ist ein Blindtext an dem sich verschiedene Dinge ablesen lassen. Der Grauwert der Schriftfläche wird sichtbar und man kann an ihm prüfen, wie gut die Schrift zu lesen ist und wie sie auf den Leser wirkt. Bei genauerem Hinsehen ...

10-10-6

10.11 Fonts supporting Latin and polytonic Greek

The Greek Font Society, a nonprofit organization in Greece devoted to improving Greek digital typography, made a larger number of fonts with support for the Greek language publicly available. Antonis Tsolomitis and others adapted several of them for use with pdfTeX. Besides support for polytonic Greek, some of these fonts also contain a full set of Latin glyphs — those have been shown already in the previous sections. If you are primarily interested in typesetting in polytonic Greek, then a few more GFS fonts exist that support only the Greek language.[1]

Some of the fonts from the previous sections also offer polytonic Greek in addition to Latin, and for a quick comparison all of them are shown here once more with a short sample text exhibiting English and Greek together (and bold, italic, and small capitals if available). Small capitals are often not implemented for Greek letters (even if available for Latin), and in some cases only characters without diacritics are available.

The standard encoding for Greek is called LGR and listed in this way in the tables throughout this chapter, but note that not all fonts that claim to support this encoding offer polytonic Greek; some provide only basic glyphs without diacritics. Such fonts are not listed below.

---

[1] The relevant support packages are gfsbaskerville, gfscomplutum, gfsporson, and gfssolomos.

10.11.1 Serif designs

Alegreya is fairly complete so can serve as a sample for the different font faces.

Once said the great poet Constantin CAVAFY: Σὰ βγεῖς στὸν πηγαιμὸ γιὰ τὴν ᾿Ιθάκη, νὰ εὔχεσαι νἆναι μακρὺς ὁ δρόμος, γεμᾶτος περιπέτειες, γεμᾶτος ΓΝΩΣΕΙΣ (When you set out on the journey to **Ithaca**, pray that road be *long*, full of adventures, full of KNOWLEDGE). — See page 11 for font family details.

Alegreya 10pt/12pt
(Alegreya-OsF) Alegreya

Cambria is a commercial TrueType font that ships with Windows and Office products; thus, many people have them on their system. The Greek small capitals are not complete as you can observe in the sample.

Once said the great poet Constantin CAVAFY: Σὰ βγεῖς στὸν πηγαιμὸ γιὰ τὴν Ἰθάκη, νὰ εὔχεσαι νἆναι μακρὺς ὁ δρόμος, γεμᾶτος περιπέτειες, γεμᾶτος ΓΝΩΣΕΙΣ. — See page 49 for font family details.

Cambria 10pt/12pt
(— only TrueType —)
Cambria

Cochineal has issues with the "Iota with Psili"; the spacing is wrong. There is also no Small Caps shape with Greek — a restriction shared with many other font families.

Once said the great poet Constantin CAVAFY: Σὰ βγεῖς στὸν πηγαιμὸ γιὰ τὴν ᾿Ιθάκη, νὰ εὔχεσαι νἆναι μακρὺς ὁ δρόμος, γεμᾶτος περιπέτειες, γεμᾶτος γνώσεις. — See page 40 for font family details.

Cochineal 10pt/12pt
(Cochineal-OsF)
Cochineal

Once said the great poet Constantin Cavafy: Σὰ βγεῖς στὸν πηγαιμὸ γιὰ τὴν ᾿Ιθάκη, νὰ εὔχεσαι νἆναι μακρὺς ὁ δρόμος, γεμᾶτος περιπέτειες, γεμᾶτος γνώσεις. — See page 12 for font family details.

DejaVu Serif 9pt/12.5pt
(DejaVuSerif-TLF)
DejaVu Serif

Garamond Libre's upright Greek is based on Firmin Didot's (1764-1836) design (i.e., like GFS Didot), the Greek italics after a design by Alexander Wilson (??-1784).

Once said the great poet Constantin CAVAFY: Σὰ βγεῖς στὸν πηγαιμὸ γιὰ τὴν ᾿Ιθάκη, νὰ εὔχεσαι νἆναι μακρὺς ὁ δρόμος, γεμᾶτος περιπέτειες, γεμᾶτος ΓΝΩΣΕΙΣ. — See page 42 for font family details.

Garamond Libre 10pt/12pt
(GaramondLibre-LF)
Garamond Libre

Once said the great poet Constantin CAVAFY: Σὰ βγεῖς στὸν πηγαιμὸ γιὰ τὴν ᾿Ιθάκη, νὰ εὔχεσαι νἆναι μακρὺς ὁ δρόμος, γεμᾶτος περιπέτειες, γεμᾶτος γνώσεις. — See page 45 for font family details.

Gentium Plus 10pt/12pt
(gentium) Gentium Plus

Once said the great poet Constantin CAVAFY: Σὰ βγεῖς στὸν πηγαιμὸ γιὰ τὴν ᾿Ιθάκη, νὰ εὔχεσαι νἆναι μακρὺς ὁ δρόμος, γεμᾶτος περιπέτειες, γεμᾶτος ΓΝΩΣΕΙΣ. — See page 39 for font family details.

GFS Artemisia 10pt/12pt
(artemisia)
GFS Artemisia

Once said the great poet Constantin CAVAFY: Σὰ βγεῖς στὸν πηγαιμὸ γιὰ τὴν ᾿Ιθάκη, νὰ εὔχεσαι νἆναι μακρὺς ὁ δρόμος, γεμᾶτος περιπέτειες, γεμᾶτος ΓΝΩΣΕΙΣ. — See page 61 for font family details.

GFS Bodoni 10pt/12pt
(bodoni) GFS Bodoni

The GFS Didot, while offering Latin in addition to its good Greek alphabet, is really suited only to typeset Greek; just look at the "t" as an example.

GFS Didot 10pt/12pt
(udidot) `GFS Didot`

Once said the great poet Constantin Cavafy: Σὰ βγεῖς στὸν πηγαιμὸ γιὰ τὴν Ἰθάκη, νὰ εὔχεσαι νἆναι μακρὺς ὁ δρόμος, γεμάτος περιπέτειες, γεμάτος ΓΝΩΣΕΙΣ. — See page 62 for font family details.

Latin Modern's Greek has no diacritics on small capitals.

Latin Modern 10pt/12pt
(lmr) `Latin Modern`

Once said the great poet Constantin Cavafy: Σὰ βγεῖς στὸν πηγαιμὸ γιὰ τὴν Ἰθάκη, νὰ εὔχεσαι νἆναι μακρὺς ὁ δρόμος, γεμάτος περιπέτειες, γεμάτος ΓΝΩΣΕΙΣ. — See page ‑I 686 for font family details.

Libertinus Serif 10pt/12pt
(LibertinusSerif-OsF)
`Libertinus Serif`

Once said the great poet Constantin Cavafy: Σὰ βγεῖς στὸν πηγαιμὸ γιὰ τὴν Ἰθάκη, νὰ εὔχεσαι νἆναι μακρὺς ὁ δρόμος, γεμάτος περιπέτειες, γεμάτος γνώσεις. — See page 19 for font family details.

Be careful with Linguistics Pro, because it offers a complete set of diacritics only in its regular shape. In bold and italics you get missing characters as seen in the example:

Linguistics Pro 9.6pt/12pt
(LinguisticsPro-OsF)
`LinguisticsPro`

Once said the great poet Constantin Cavafy: Σὰ βγεῖς στὸν πηγαιμὸ γιὰ τὴν Ιθκη, νὰ εὔχεσαι νἆναι μακρς ὁ δρόμος, γεμάτος περιπέτειες, γεμάτος γνώσεις. – See page 59 for font family details.

Noto Serif 10pt/12.6pt
(NotoSerif-OsF)
`Noto Serif`

Once said the great poet Constantin Cavafy: Σὰ βγεῖς στὸν πηγαιμὸ γιὰ τὴν Ἰθάκη, νὰ εὔχεσαι νἆναι μακρὺς ὁ δρόμος, γεμάτος περιπέτειες, γεμάτος γνώσεις. — See page 26 for font family details.

Old Standard 10pt/12pt
(OldStandard-TLF)
`Old Standard`

Once said the great poet Constantin Cavafy: Σὰ βγεῖς στὸν πηγαιμὸ γιὰ τὴν Ἰθάκη, νὰ εὔχεσαι νἆναι μακρὺς ὁ δρόμος, γεμάτος περιπέτειες, γεμάτος ΓΝΏΣΕΙΣ. — See page 63 for font family details.

Tempora 10pt/12pt
(Tempora-TOsF) `Tempora`

Once said the great poet Constantin Cavafy: Σὰ βγεῖς στὸν πηγαιμὸ γιὰ τὴν Ἰθάκη, νὰ εὔχεσαι νἆναι μακρὺς ὁ δρόμος, γεμάτος περιπέτειες, γεμάτος γνώσεις. — See page 56 for font family details.

Theano Didot is a high-quality Didot revival with well-done stylistically matching Latin. The only limitation is that the family does not offer italics or small capitals.

Theano Didot 10pt/12pt
(TheanoDidot-TOsF)
`Theano Didot`

Once said the great poet Constantin Cavafy: Σὰ βγεῖς στὸν πηγαιμὸ γιὰ τὴν Ἰθάκη, νὰ εὔχεσαι νἆναι μακρὺς ὁ δρόμος, γεμάτος περιπέτειες, γεμάτος γνώσεις. — See page 62 for font family details.

10.11.2 Sans Serif designs

Once said the great poet Constantin CAVAFY: Σὰ βγεῖς στὸν πηγαιμὸ γιὰ τὴν Ἰθάκη, νὰ εὔχεσαι νἆναι *μακρὺς* ὁ δρόμος, γεμᾶτος περιπέτειες, γεμᾶτος ΓΝΏΣΕΙΣ. — See page 11 for font family details.

Alegreya Sans 10pt/12pt
(AlegreyaSans-OsF)
Alegreya Sans

Once said the great poet Constantin Cavafy: Σὰ βγεῖς στὸν πηγαιμὸ γιὰ τὴν Ἰθάκη, νὰ εὔχεσαι νἆναι *μακρὺς* ὁ δρόμος, γεμᾶτος περιπέτειες, γεμᾶτος γνώσεις. — See page 12 for font family details.

DejaVu Sans 9pt/12.5pt
(DejaVuSans-TLF)
DejaVu Sans

Once said the great poet Constantin CAVAFY: Σὰ βγεῖς στὸν πηγαιμὸ γιὰ τὴν Ἰθάκη, νὰ εὔχεσαι νἆναι *μακρὺς* ὁ δρόμος, γεμᾶτος περιπέτειες, γεμᾶτος ΓΝΏΣΕΙΣ. — See page 14 for font family details.

Fira Sans 10pt/12pt
(FiraSans-OsF) Fira Sans

Once said the great poet Constantin CAVAFY: Σὰ βγεῖς στὸν πηγαιμὸ γιὰ τὴν Ἰθάκη, νὰ εὔχεσαι νἆναι *μακρὺς* ὁ δρόμος, γεμᾶτος περιπέτειες, γεμᾶτος γνώσεις. — See page 75 for font family details.

GFS Neo-Hellenic 10pt/12pt
(neohellenic)
GFS Neohellenic

Once said the great poet Constantin CAVAFY: Σὰ βγεῖς στὸν πηγαιμὸ γιὰ τὴν Ἰθάκη, νὰ εὔχεσαι νἆναι *μακρὺς* ὁ δρόμος, γεμᾶτος περιπέτειες, γεμᾶτος ΓΝΏΣΕΙΣ. — See page ─I 686 for font family details.

Latin Modern Sans 10pt/12pt
(lmss) Latin Modern Sans

Once said the great poet Constantin Cavafy: Σὰ βγεῖς στὸν πηγαιμὸ γιὰ τὴν Ἰθάκη, νὰ εὔχεσαι νἆναι *μακρὺς* ὁ δρόμος, γεμᾶτος περιπέτειες, γεμᾶτος γνώσεις. — See page 80 for font family details.

Lato 10pt/12pt
(lato-OsF) Lato

Once said the great poet Constantin CAVAFY: Σὰ βγεῖς στὸν πηγαιμὸ γιὰ τὴν Ἰθάκη, νὰ εὔχεσαι νἆναι *μακρὺς* ὁ δρόμος, γεμᾶτος περιπέτειες, γεμᾶτος γνώσεις. — See page 19 for font family details.

Libertinus Sans 10pt/12pt
(LibertinusSans-OsF)
Libertinus Sans

Once said the great poet Constantin CAVAFY: Σὰ βγεῖς στὸν πηγαιμὸ γιὰ τὴν Ἰθάκη, νὰ εὔχεσαι νἆναι *μακρὺς* ὁ δρόμος, γεμᾶτος περιπέτειες, γεμᾶτος ΓΝΏΣΕΙΣ. — See page 26 for font family details.

Noto Sans 10pt/12.6pt
(NotoSans-OsF) Noto Sans

10.11.3 Monospaced fonts

Once said the great poet Constantin Cavafy: Σὰ βγεῖς στὸν πηγαιμὸ γιὰ τὴν Ἰθάκη, νὰ εὔχεσαι νἆναι *μακρὺς* ὁ δρόμος, γεμᾶτος περιπέτειες, γεμᾶτος γνώσεις. – See page 12.

DejaVu Sans Mono
9pt/12.5pt
(DejaVuSansMono-TLF)
DejaVu Sans Mono

Once said the great poet Constantin Cavafy: Σὰ βγεῖς στὸν πηγαιμὸ γιὰ τὴν Ἰθάκη, νὰ εὔχεσαι νἆναι *μακρὺς* ὁ δρόμος, γεμᾶτος περιπέτειες, γεμᾶτος γνώσεις. – See page 14.

Fira Mono 9pt/11pt
(FiraMono-TOsF)
Fira Mono

Latin Modern Typewriter
10pt/12pt (lmtt)
Latin Modern Mono

Once said the great poet Constantin CAVAFY: Σὰ βγεῖς στὸν πηγαιμὸ γιὰ τὴν Ἰθάκη, νὰ εὔχεσαι νἆναι μακρὺς ὁ δρόμος, γεμᾶτος περιπέτειες, γεμᾶτος ΓΝΩΣΕΙΣ. – See page ⤏ 686.

Noto Sans Mono 9pt/12.6pt
(NotoSansMono-TLF)
Noto Sans Mono

Once said the great poet Constantin CAVAFY: Σὰ βγεῖς στὸν πηγαιμὸ γιὰ τὴν **Ἰθάκη**, νὰ εὔχεσαι νἆναι μακρὺς ὁ δρόμος, γεμᾶτος περιπέτειες, γεμᾶτος γνώσεις. – See page 26.

10.11.4 Handwriting fonts

Miama Nova 9pt/13pt
(fmm) Miama Nueva

Once said the great poet Constantin Cavafy: Σὰ βγεῖς στὸν πηγαιμὸ γιὰ τὴν Ἰθάκη, νὰ εὔχεσαι νἆναι μακρὺς ὁ δρόμος, γεμᾶτος περιπέτειες, γεμᾶτος γνώσεις. — See page 103 for font family details.

10.12 Fonts supporting Latin and Cyrillic

In this section we exhibit fonts that support both Latin and Cyrillic alphabets. The sample text shows bold, italic, and small capitals when available. If not, it is highlighted as usual. Many of these fonts also support polytonic Greek shown in the previous section, but often there are some restrictions, either with the Cyrillic or with the Greek support with respect to available shapes.

10.12.1 Serif designs

Cambria is a commercial TrueType font that ships with Windows and Office products; thus, many people have them on their system.

Cambria 10pt/12pt
(— only TrueType —)
Cambria

The quote "Хороший композитор не подражает; он *ворует*" (A good composer does not imitate; he steals) is attributed to Igor Stravinsky (Игорь Стравинский). — See page 49.

10-12-1

Bitstream Charter
10pt/12.4pt
(XCharter-TOsF) XCharter

The quote "Хороший **композитор** не подражает; он *ворует*" is attributed to Igor Stravinsky (Игорь Стравинский). — See page 50.

Charis SIL 10pt/12.4pt
(charssil-TLF) CharisSIL

The quote "Хороший **композитор** не подражает; он *ворует*" is attributed to Igor Stravinsky (Игорь Стравинский). — See page 51.

Cormorant Garamond
10pt/12pt
(CormorantGaramond-OsF)
Cormorant Garamond

The quote "Хороший **композитор** не подражает; он *ворует*" is attributed to Igor Stravinsky (Игорь Стравинский). — See page 41.

In many fonts, the Small Caps shape is not available for Cyrillic letters, but you have to look closely to see it (i.e., the "a" and "p").

The quote "Хороший **композитор** не подражает; он *ворует*" is attributed to Igor Stravinsky (Игорь Стравинский). — See page 12.

DejaVu Serif 9pt/12.5pt
(DejaVuSerif-TLF)
DejaVu Serif

With Garamond Libre, bold and small caps are supported, but the bold is not easy to distinguish from the medium series.

The quote "Хороший **композитор** не подражает; он *ворует*" is attributed to Igor Stravinsky (Игорь Стравинский). — See page 42.

Garamond Libre 10pt/12pt
(GaramondLibre-LF)
Garamond Libre

Gentium offers no bold series for Cyrillic letters.

The quote "Хороший композитор не подражает; он *ворует*" is attributed to Igor Stravinsky (Игорь Стравинский). — See page 45.

Gentium Plus 10pt/12pt
(gentium) Gentium Plus

The quote "Хороший **композитор** не подражает; он *ворует*" is attributed to Igor Stravinsky (Игорь Стравинский). — See page 19.

Libertinus Serif 10pt/12pt
(LibertinusSerif-OsF)
Libertinus Serif

The quote "Хороший **композитор** не подражает; он *ворует*" is attributed to Igor Stravinsky (Игорь Стравинский). — See page 59.

Linguistics Pro 9.6pt/12pt
(LinguisticsPro-OsF)
LinguisticsPro

The quote "Хороший **композитор** не подражает; он *ворует*" is attributed to Igor Stravinsky (Игорь Стравинский). — See page 53.

Literaturnaya 10pt/12pt
(tli) —no OpenType—

The quote "Хороший **композитор** не подражает; он *ворует*" is attributed to Igor Stravinsky (Игорь Стравинский). — See page 26.

Noto Serif 10pt/12pt
(NotoSerif-OsF)
Noto Serif

The quote "Хороший **композитор** не подражает; он *ворует*" is attributed to Igor Stravinsky (Игорь Стравинский). — See page 63.

Old Standard 10pt/12pt
(OldStandard-TLF)
Old Standard

The quote "Хороший **композитор** не подражает; он *ворует*" is attributed to Igor Stravinsky (Игорь Стравинский). — See page 31.

PT Serif 10pt/12.6pt
(PTSerif-TLF) PT Serif

10.12.2 Sans Serif designs

None of the sans serif designs provide small capitals, but most of them offer an italic or oblique shape.

The quote "Хороший **композитор** не подражает; он *ворует*" is attributed to Igor Stravinsky (Игорь Стравинский). — See page 12.

DejaVu Sans 9pt/12.5pt
(DejaVuSans-TLF)
DejaVu Sans

The quote "Хороший **композитор** не подражает; он *ворует*" is attributed to Igor Stravinsky (Игорь Стравинский). — See page 77.

Iwona 10pt/12pt
(iwona) Iwona

The quote "Хороший **композитор** не подражает; он *ворует*" is attributed to Igor Stravinsky (Игорь Стравинский). — See page 79.

Kurier Light 10pt/12pt
(kurier1) Kurier Light

Lato 10pt/12pt
(lato-OsF) Lato

The quote "Хороший **композитор** не подражает; он *ворует*" is attributed to Igor Stravinsky (Игорь Стравинский). — See page 80.

Libertinus Sans 10pt/12pt
(LibertinusSans-OsF)
Libertinus Sans

The quote "Хороший **композитор** не подражает; он *ворует*" is attributed to Igor Stravinsky (Игорь Стравинский). — See page 19.

Noto Sans 9pt/12pt
(NotoSans-OsF) Noto Sans

The quote "Хороший **композитор** не подражает; он *ворует*" is attributed to Igor Stravinsky (Игорь Стравинский). — See page 26.

PT Sans 10pt/12.6pt
(PTSans-TLF) PT Sans

The quote "Хороший **композитор** не подражает; он *ворует*" is attributed to Igor Stravinsky (Игорь Стравинский). — See page 31.

10.12.3 Monospaced fonts

Like the sans serif designs none of the monospaced fonts offer small capitals and only half of them provide italics or oblique shapes.

DejaVu Sans Mono
9pt/12.5pt
(DejaVuSansMono-TLF)
DejaVu Sans Mono

The quote "Хороший **композитор** не подражает; он *ворует*" is attributed to Igor Stravinsky (Игорь Стравинский). — See page 12.

The Lucida font families are commercial and can be obtained through TUG.

Lucida Console 9pt/12pt
(— only OpenType —)
Lucida Console DK

The quote ``Хороший **композитор** не подражает; он *ворует*'' is attributed to Igor Stravinsky (Игорь Стравинский). — See pages 21--24.

10-12-2

Lucida Grande Mono
9pt/12pt
(— only OpenType —)
Lucida Grande Mono DK

The quote ``Хороший **композитор** не подражает; он *ворует*'' is attributed to Igor Stravinsky (Игорь Стравинский). — See pages 21--24.

10-12-3

Noto Sans Mono 9pt/12pt
(NotoSansMono-TLF)
Noto Sans Mono

The quote "Хороший **композитор** не подражает; он *ворует*" is attributed to Igor Stravinsky (Игорь Стравинский). — See page 26.

PT Mono 9pt/11pt
(PTMono-TLF) PT Mono

The quote "Хороший **композитор** не подражает; он *ворует*" is attributed to Igor Stravinsky (Игорь Стравинский). — See page 31.

Note that Source Code Pro does not have Cyrillic glyphs in its italic shape, so you get "missing characters"; e.g., the word ворует is missing.

Source Code Pro 9pt/11pt
(SourceCodePro-TLF)
Source Code Pro

The quote "Хороший **композитор** не подражает; он " is attributed to Igor Stravinsky (Игорь Стравинский). — See page 35.

10.12.4 Handwriting fonts

The quote "Хороший композитор не подражает; он ворует"
(A good composer does not imitate; he steals) is attributed to Igor
Stravinsky (Игорь Стравинский). — See page 103.

Miama Nova 9pt/20pt
(fmm) Miama Nueva

10.13 The LaTeX world of symbols

Shortly after TeX and METAFONT came into existence, people started to develop new symbol fonts for use with the system. Over time the set of available symbols grew to a considerable number. The *Comprehensive LaTeX Symbol List* by Scott Pakin [81] lists more than 18 000 symbols on 422 pages[1] and the corresponding LaTeX commands that produce them. For some symbols the necessary fonts and support packages may have to be obtained (e.g., from a CTAN host; see Appendix C.4.1) and installed by the user. They are usually accompanied by installation instructions and general documentation.

Obviously, the few fonts and packages described in this section form only a small subset of what is available. If you cannot find a symbol here, the 422 pages of [81] are a valuable resource for locating what you need.

There are also a few online resources that can be very helpful: you draw the symbol that you are looking for with your mouse and get back possible suggestions. Especially for LaTeX there is `https://detexify.kirelabs.org/classify.html`[2] by Daniel Kirsch that reports back the LaTeX command name (and any necessary package information), and if you want to hunt for some unusual Unicode character, then `http://shapecatcher.com/` is worth a try as it knows about a large number of shapes.

Online resources for finding LaTeX symbols

We start by looking at the pifont package that offers some generic support to symbol fonts that are offered in U encoding. This is followed by a small number of interesting symbol fonts, including two that contain ornaments for page borders and similar applications. The chapter concludes with an introduction to the TIPA system, which provides support for phonetic symbols.

All packages and fonts listed in this section and in [81] are freely available: in one or two cases you need to install the support files using getnonfreefonts.

10.13.1 pifont—Accessing Pi and Symbol fonts

Fonts containing collections of special symbols, which are normally not found in a text font, are called Pi fonts. One such font, the PostScript font Zapf Dingbats, is available if you use the pifont package originally written by Sebastian Rahtz (1955-2016).

The directly accessible characters of the PostScript Zapf Dingbats font are shown in Table 10.89 on the following page. A given character can be chosen via the `\ding`

Accessing glyphs from Zapf Dingbats

---

[1]Counted in 2022.
[2]For the Macintosh this also exists as a local App that does not need an Internet connection.

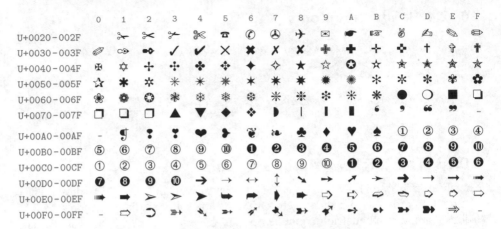

Table 10.89: Glyphs in the PostScript font Zapf Dingbats

command. The parameter for the \ding command is an integer that specifies the character to be typeset according to the table. It can also be specified as an octal value (preceding it with ') or very conveniently as a hexadecimal (preceding it with ") as this matches the way font tables are usually organized. For example, \ding{"A1} gives ¶, and you can find that number immediately when looking at the font table.

The dinglist environment is a variation of the itemize list. The argument specifies the number of the character to be used at the beginning of each item.

➤ The first item.

➤ The second item in the list.

➤ A final item.

```
\usepackage{pifont}
\begin{dinglist}{"E4}
  \item The first item.    \item The second
    item in the list.    \item A final item.
\end{dinglist}
```

10-13-1

The environment dingautolist allows you to build an enumerated list from a sequence of Zapf Dingbats characters. In this case, the argument specifies the number of the first character of the sequence. Subsequent items are numbered by incrementing this number by one. This makes some starting positions like "AC, "B6, "C0, and "CA (i.e., in hexadecimal notation) in Table 10.89 very attractive, as differently designed circled number sequences (1–10) start there.

① The first item in the list.

② The second item in the list.

③ The third item in the list.

References to list items work as expected: ①, ②, ③

```
\usepackage{pifont}
\begin{dingautolist}{"C0}
  \item The first item in the list.\label{lst:a}
  \item The second item in the list.\label{lst:b}
  \item The third item in the list.\label{lst:c}
\end{dingautolist}
References to list items work as expected:
\ref{lst:a}, \ref{lst:b}, \ref{lst:c}
```

10-13-2

	0	1	2	3	4	5	6	7	8	9	A	B	C	D	E	F
U+0000–000F	⌘	⌥	≈	⇤	♦	✓	▣	…	↪	▷	≥	♯	ħ	∞	↳	∫
U+0010–001F	≤	◇	≠	⌁	∂	∏	π	∏	⇧	⬆	Σ	σ	ς	Σ	⇥	↵
U+0020–002F	⌣	∧	⌘	⌧	↻	⎵	Δ	⌦	№	–	–	–	–	–	–	–

Table 10.90: Glyphs in the AnonymousPro Symbol font

You can fill a complete line (with a 0.5-inch space at left and right) with a given character using the command \dingline, where the argument indicates the slot of the desired character. For filling parts of a line, use the command \dingfill. This command works similar to LATEX's \dotfill command but uses the specified glyph instead of dots.

10-13-3

✂ ✂ ✂ ✂ ✂ ✂ ✂ ✂ ✂ ✂

⇨ ⇨ ⇨ some text ↩ ↩ some more ✖ ✖

```
\usepackage{pifont}
\dingline{"22}                          \par\medskip
\noindent\dingfill{"E9} some text
\dingfill{"EB} some more \dingfill{"36}
```

Besides providing direct support for the Zapf Dingbats font, the pifont package includes a general mechanism for coping with any Pi font that conforms to the NFSS classification U/*family*/m/n.

To access individual glyphs from such a Pi font, use the \Pisymbol command, which takes the *family* name as its first argument and the glyph position in the font as its second argument. For example, using this command one can readily access the Macintosh keyboard symbols from the Anonymous Pro Symbol font, shown in Table 10.90. All you need to know is the NFSS family name and the glyph position in the font. In fact, \ding (discussed earlier) is simply an abbreviation for \Pisymbol with the first argument set to pzd.

Accessing individual glyphs from a Pi font

You can also make itemized lists using Pilist or enumerated lists using the Piautolist environments as follows:

⌘ The Cmd key is ⌘.

⌘ The Alt key is ⌥.

✫ The first item.

✹ The second.

10-13-4

✹ The third.

```
\usepackage{pifont}
\begin{Pilist}{AnonymousPro}{1}
\item The Cmd key is \Pisymbol{AnonymousPro}{"22}.
\item The Alt key is \Pisymbol{AnonymousPro}{"13}.
\end{Pilist}
\begin{Piautolist}{pzd}{"4B}
   \item The first item. \item The second.
   \item The third.
\end{Piautolist}
```

The \dingline and \dingfill commands are also merely abbreviations for the more general commands \Piline and \Pifill, as shown below. The example reveals curious gaps in the last line. They are due to \Piline and \Pifill

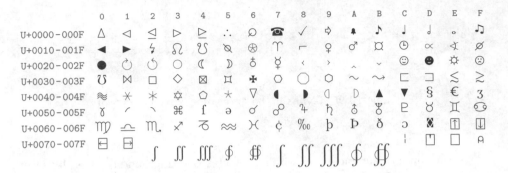

	0	1	2	3	4	5	6	7	8	9	A	B	C	D	E	F
U+0000-000F	△	◁	⊴	▷	⊵	∴	⌀	☎	✓	⇨	♠	♪	♩	𝅗𝅥	𝅝	♫
U+0010-001F	◀	▶	↯	☊	☋	☍	⊛	♈	⌐	♀	♂	¤	◷	∝	∢	⌀
U+0020-002F	●	↻	↺	○	☾	☽	♁	☿	‹	›	^	ˇ	☺	☻	☼	☹
U+0030-003F	℧	⋈	□	◇	⊠	⌑	✠	⬡	⯃	⬡	∼	⇝	⊏	⊐	≲	≳
U+0040-004F	≋	⋇	∗	✡	⬠	⋆	∇	◖	◗	◖	◗	▲	▼	§	€	ʒ
U+0050-005F	♉	◜	◝	⌘	ʃ	ə	☌	☍	♃	♄	⛢	⛢	♇	♉	♊	♋
U+0060-006F	♍	♎	♏	♐	♑	♒	♓	¢	‰	þ	Þ	ð	ɔ	⧗	⍐	⍗
U+0070-007F	⍇	⍈	∫	∬	∭	∮	∯	∫	∬	∭	∮	∯	¦	⍞	⎕	⍝

Table 10.91: Glyphs in Waldi's symbol font (wasy)

typesetting their symbols on an invisible grid so that symbols on different lines come out vertically aligned.

✎ ✎ ✎ text ✏ ✏ ✏ text ✐ ✐ ✐

```
\usepackage{pifont}
\Piline{AnonymousPro}{0}        \par\medskip
\noindent\Pifill{pzd}{"2E} text
\Pifill{pzd}{"2F} text \Pifill{pzd}{"30}
```

10-13-5

10.13.2 wasysym — Waldi's symbol font

Waldi's symbol font (wasy), designed by Roland Waldi, was one of the first Pi fonts that was developed especially for use with LaTeX. It offers a wide range of symbols from different areas, including astronomical and astrological symbols, APL, musical notes, circles, polygons, and stars, that were not available otherwise (see Table 10.91). These days several of those have found their way into amsmath or into the TS1 text companion encoding and are thus readily available without using the font. However, there are still many symbols that are not or that are of interest because of their design.

The wasysym package developed by Axel Kielhorn defines command names like \phone to access each glyph. Alternatively, if you want only a few glyphs from the font, you can use the pifont interface and access the symbols directly under its NFSS family name wasy.

☎ using wasysym
☎ using pifont

```
\usepackage{wasysym,pifont}
\phone\              using \texttt{wasysym} \par
\Pisymbol{wasy}{7} using \texttt{pifont}
```

10-13-6

It is important to note that the font also contains a set of upright integral signs, which (for historical reasons) are automatically used in math mode if the package is loaded without options. If that is not desired, load it with the option nointegrals. If,

	0	1	2	3	4	5	6	7	8	9	A	B	C	D	E	F
U+0020–002F																
U+0030–003F																
U+0040–004F																
U+0050–005F																
U+0060–006F																
U+0070–007F							FAX	FAX								
U+0080–008F																
U+0090–009F																
U+00A0–00AF																
U+00B0–00BF																
U+00C0–00CF																
U+00D0–00DF			95	95	60	60	50	40	40	40	30					
U+00E0–00EF																
U+00F0–00FF																

Table 10.92: Glyphs in the MarVoSym font (mvs)

however, you want the upright integrals, it is best to explicitly signal that intention by adding the option integrals because that allows the package to cooperate properly with amsmath or mathtools (see Section 11.4.6 on page 168).

10.13.3 marvosym — Interface to the MarVoSym font

The MarVoSym font designed by Martin Vogel is another Pi font containing symbols from various areas including quite uncommon ones, such as laundry signs (in case you are doing your own laundry lists ☺), astronomy and astrology symbols, and many others. In 2015 Martin wrote in his blog that he thinks the font is no longer needed as most characters are by now in Unicode fonts, but it is still quite popular in the LaTeX world, because the glyphs are well done and not easy to obtain otherwise.

The LaTeX support package marvosym was written by Thomas Henlich, who also converted the font from TrueType format to Type 1. His package defines command names for all symbols, some of which are listed in the next example; the full set is given in marvodoc.pdf accompanying the distribution.

```
\usepackage{marvosym}

\Large \AtForty\ \Bicycle\ \Cancer\ \Coffeecup\ \ComputerMouse\
\FEMALE\ \Faxmachine\ \Female\ \Fixedbearing\ \Football\
\ForwardToIndex\ \Frowny\ \IroningII\ \Keyboard\ \Lineload\
\Mobilefone\ \RewindToStart\ \Smiley\ \Virgo\ \Yingyang
```

10-13-7

As with other Pi fonts, one can also access the symbols directly by using the

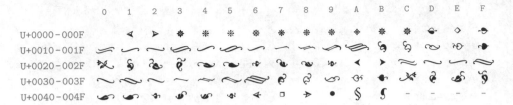

	0	1	2	3	4	5	6	7	8	9	A	B	C	D	E	F
U+0000–000F																
U+0010–001F																
U+0020–002F																
U+0030–003F																
U+0040–004F																

Table 10.93: Glyphs in the Ornements ADF font (`OrnementsADF`)

glyph chart in Table 10.92 on the preceding page and the pifont interface with the Pi font name being `mvs`.

```
\usepackage{pifont}
\Huge \Pisymbol{mvs}{"49} \Pisymbol{mvs}{"4A} \Pisymbol{mvs}{"66}
      \Pisymbol{mvs}{"68} \Pisymbol{mvs}{"6D} \Pisymbol{mvs}{"78}
      \Pisymbol{mvs}{"79} \Pisymbol{mvs}{"DE} \Pisymbol{mvs}{"DF}
```

10-13-8

10.13.4 adforn — Adding ornaments to your document

A more recent addition to the symbol fonts for use with LaTeX is the Ornements ADF font designed by Hirwen Harendal. The ornaments made available by this font are shown in Table 10.93. (Ornements is the French spelling in case you are wondering.)

LaTeX support is provided through the package adforn by Clea F. Rees, which defines the command \adforn to access symbols by *slot-number* (which is yet another application of \Pisymbol from the pifont package, this time using the family name OrnementsADF). In addition to the numerical interface each ornament is also available through an individual LaTeX command; e.g., \adfflowerleft and \adforn{"20} would both produce ✄. Clearly the longer command names have the advantage that you can easily guess what they represent, but you have to look them up in the package documentation, while the slot numbers are readily available from Table 10.93.

✄ In this example we start most paragraphs with an ornament instead of an indentation.

But we do not always use the same one—most of the time we use a solid leaf, shown next.

✄ Also note the fancy page number below, set up with the help of `fancyhdr`.

∽6∽

```
\usepackage{fancyhdr,adforn}
\pagestyle{fancy} \fancyhf{} \renewcommand\headrulewidth{0pt}
\fancyfoot[C]{\adfdoubleflourishleft\ \thepage\
                              \adfdoubleflourishright}
\newcommand\paraA{\par\noindent\adfhangingflatleafright\ }
\newcommand\paraB{\par\noindent\adfflatleafsolidright  \ }

\paraA In this example we start most paragraphs with an
ornament instead of an indentation.  \par   But we do not
always use the same one---most of the time we use a solid
leaf, shown next.  \paraB Also note the fancy page number
below, set up with the help of \texttt{fancyhdr}.
```

10-13-9

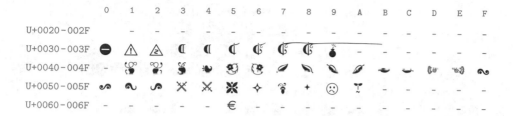

	0	1	2	3	4	5	6	7	8	9	A	B	C	D	E	F
U+0020 – 002F	-	-	-	-	-	-	-	-	-	-	-	-	-	-	-	-
U+0030 – 003F	⬤	⚠	⚠	ℂ	ℂ	ℂ	ℂ	ℂ	ℂ	💣	-	-	-	-	-	-
U+0040 – 004F	-	❦	❦	❦	❀	❦	❦	❧	❧	❦	❦	∾	∾	❦	❦	∾
U+0050 – 005F	∾	∾	∾	✕	✕	✖	✦	❦	✦	☹	⬎	-	-	-	-	-
U+0060 – 006F	-	-	-	-	-	-	€	-	-	-	-	-	-	-	-	-

Table 10.94: Glyphs in the Fourier Ornaments font (futs)

10.13.5 fourier-orns — GUTenberg-Fourier's ornaments

The Fourier Ornaments font, designed by Michel Bovani, is part of the Fourier-GUTenberg setup, but it is also available on its own through the fourier-orns package. The available glyphs are shown in Table 10.94. The package defines names, for each symbol, e.g., \grimace, \lefthand, or \aldine (☹, ☞, ❦), but of course, you can alternatively access them directly through the pifont package using the family name futs, as we show below.

The interesting pilcrow symbols in slots "33 to "38 are accessible through the commands \oldpilcrowone, \oldpilcrowtwo, ..., \oldpilcrowsix after loading the package; below we access them by slot number instead.[1] If you use them in your text, you have to make sure that you choose in each case the one with the appropriate length based on the position in the paragraph — the tail takes up no space and thus sticks into the margin if it gets too close.

ℂAll the world's a stage, and all the men and women merely players. ℂThey have their exits and their entrances; ℂAnd one man in his time plays many parts.

(As You Like It, Act 2, Scene 7)

```
\usepackage{color,pifont}
\newcommand\pilcrow[1]
    {\textcolor{blue}{\Pisymbol{futs}{"3#1}}\ignorespaces}
\noindent\pilcrow{5} All the world's a stage, and all the men
and women merely players. \pilcrow{7} They have their exits
and their entrances; \pilcrow{8} And one man in his time
plays many parts.\\ (\emph{As You Like It, Act 2, Scene 7})
```

10-13-10

10.13.6 Web-O-Mints — Another collection of ornaments and borders

The Web-O-Mints font, designed by George Ryan, provides a number of typographical decorations inspired by historical sources.[2] Basic LaTeX support in the form of mapping and font definition files has been provided by Maurizio Loreti. Due to the font license, the font and the LaTeX support files have to be manually installed using getnonfreefonts (at least with TeX Live).

---

[1] The slot positions differ in different versions of the font, so you may have to adjust the example.
[2] See page 99 on the historical Fell types that also provide historical ornaments.

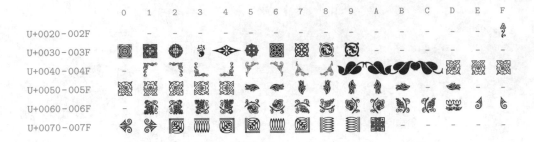

Table 10.95: Glyphs in the webomints font (`webo`)

The example below defines a few commands to access the font, which has the family name `webo`. The `\webosym` command expects slot numbers that we can read off Table 10.95, whereas the second argument of `\webo` expects ASCII characters and simply draws the glyphs that are in their slot position (you may have to guess those or look them up in a font table of a text font).

```
\newcommand\webofamily{\usefont{U}{webo}{m}{n}}
\newcommand\webo[2]{{\fontsize{#1}{#1}\webofamily #2}}
\newcommand\webosym[1]{{\webofamily\symbol{#1}}}
\webo{12pt}{IJLK}                                      \\[5pt]
\webo{3ex}{pq} \webo{20pt}{ced} \webo{3ex}{UnoV}       \\[5pt]
\webo{13pt}{rst} \webo{13pt}{RSTP} \webo{13pt}{uvw} \\[10pt]
Text \webosym{"32} mixed \webosym{"37} with
\webosym{"6D} ornaments \webosym{"7A}
```

Text ⬡ mixed ⬛ with 〜 ornaments ⬛

10-13-1

There is also a nonstandard NFSS series `xl` defined that produces 20% larger glyphs.

10.13.7 fontawesome5 — Accessing Font Awesome icons

Font Awesome in version 5 is a collection of more than 5 000 icons out of which roughly 1 500 are available under a free license.

The icons have been packaged for use with all LaTeX engines by Marcel Krüger. The support package is fontawesome5, which defines command names for every glyph. The naming convention is to take the glyph name,[1] convert it to CamelCase, and prefix it with `\fa`. For example, the icon `map-marker` would be accessed as `\faMapMarker`, generating ◉. Alternatively, you can use `\faIcon`, which expects the official icon names as its argument, i.e., `\faIcon{map-marker}` for the map marker symbol. A number of icons also have alternative versions (names that end in `-alt`). They can be accessed by using the star form of the base command; e.g., `\faMapMarker*` gives ◉.

---

[1]The names can be found on the Web (see https://www.fontawesome.com) or in the documentation of the fontawesome5 package.

Table 10.96: Glyphs in `fontawesomefree0` solid

Table 10.97: Glyphs in `fontawesomefree0` regular

All free icons are available in `solid` style, with a number of them also in `regular` (which is far less dark), for example, all the different smiley variants. The style can be changed by specifying it in an optional argument to the command; e.g., `\faAngry` gives 😠, while `\faAngry[regular]` gets you 😠. It is also possible to change the default style from `solid` to `regular` with the command `\faStyle{regular}`.

> **Unicode engines**
>
> If you own the commercial Pro version of the font (which works only with Unicode engines), then there is also a `light` style, which can be accessed in the same way. To enable the Pro font use the package option `pro`.

	0	1	2	3	4	5	6	7	8	9	A	B	C	D	E	F
U+0000–000F
U+0010–001F
U+0020–002F
U+0030–003F
U+0040–004F
U+0050–005F
U+0060–006F
U+0070–007F
U+0080–008F
U+0090–009F
U+00A0–00AF
U+00B0–00BF
U+00C0–00CF
U+00D0–00DF
U+00E0–00EF
U+00F0–00FF

Table 10.98: Glyphs in `fontawesomefree1` solid

	0	1	2	3	4	5	6	7	8	9	A	B	C	D	E	F
U+0000–000F
U+0010–001F
U+0020–002F
U+0030–003F
U+0040–004F
U+0050–005F
U+0060–006F
U+0070–007F
U+0080–008F
U+0090–009F
U+00A0–00AF
U+00B0–00BF
U+00C0–00CF
U+00D0–00DF
U+00E0–00EF
U+00F0–00FF

Table 10.99: Glyphs in `fontawesomefree1` regular

When using pdfTEX, the 1500 icons need to be distributed over different fonts (as each Type 1 font can contain only up to 256 glyphs). The family names are then `fontawesomefree0` to `..free3` for ordinary icons and `fontawesomebrands0` and `..brands1` for icons representing brands. The whole set is shown in Tables 10.96 to 10.103 on pages 121–124.

All brand icons are trademarks of their respective owners, and it is requested to use these brand logos only to represent the company, product, or service to which they refer but not for other purposes.

Most of the icons have roughly the same width, but this is not always the case. If you prefer to have them all occupying the same space, you can load the package

	0	1	2	3	4	5	6	7	8	9	A	B	C	D	E	F
U+0000-000F																
U+0010-001F																
U+0020-002F																
U+0030-003F																
U+0040-004F																
U+0050-005F																
U+0060-006F																
U+0070-007F																
U+0080-008F																
U+0090-009F																
U+00A0-00AF																
U+00B0-00BF																
U+00C0-00CF																
U+00D0-00DF																
U+00E0-00EF																
U+00F0-00FF																

Table 10.100: Glyphs in `fontawesomefree2` solid

	0	1	2	3	4	5	6	7	8	9	A	B	C	D	E	F
U+0000-000F	-	-	-	-	-					-	-		-	-	-	-
U+0010-001F			-	-	-		-	-	-	-	-	-	-	-	-	-
U+0020-002F	-	-	-	-	-	-	-		-	-	-	-	-	-	-	-
U+0030-003F	-	-	-	-	-	-	-				-	-	-	-	-	-
U+0040-004F	-	-	-	-	-	-		-	-	-	-		-	-	-	-
U+0050-005F	-		-	-	-	-	-	-	-	-	-			-	-	
U+0060-006F		-	-	-	-	-	-	-		-	-	-	-	-	-	-
U+0070-007F	-	-	-		-	-	-	-	-	-	-	-	-	-	-	-
U+0090-009F	-	-	-		-	-		-	-	-	-	-	-	-	-	-
U+00A0-00AF	-	-	-	-	-	-	-	-	-	-	-	-	-	-		-
U+00B0-00BF	-	-	-	-	-	-	-	-	-	-	-	-		-	-	-
U+00D0-00DF	-	-			-	-		-	-	-	-	-	-	-	-	-
U+00E0-00EF	-	-	-	-	-	-		-	-	-	-	-	-	-	-	-

Table 10.101: Glyphs in `fontawesomefree2` regular

with the option `fixed`, which basically places each icon centered into a box of width 1.5em.

10-13-12

```
\usepackage[fixed]{fontawesome5}
\fbox{\faExclamation} \fbox{\faFile} \fbox{\faFile*}
\fbox{\faFile[regular]} \fbox{\faFile*[regular]}
```

If you prefer not to load the support package (that defines 1500 commands of which you need one or two) but rather access the icons directly by font slot number, then this is easily possible too. The next example defines two commands that let you do this: \fasym expects the font number 0-3, the glyph slot number, and also accepts

Table 10.102: Glyphs in `fontawesomefree3` solid only

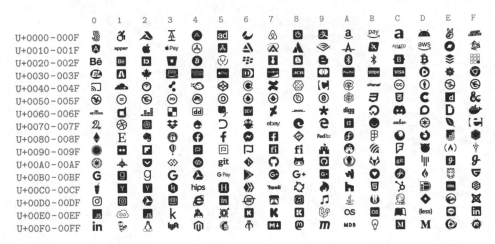

Table 10.103: Brand logos in `fontawesomebrands0`

the string `regular` as an optional argument. As the brands exist only in `solid` style, the `\fabrand` omits the optional argument.

```
\newcommand\fasym[3][solid]{{\usefont{U}{fontawesomefree#2}{#1}{n}\symbol{#3}}}
\newcommand\fabrand[2]{{\usefont{U}{fontawesomebrands#1}{solid}{n}\symbol{#2}}}
\fasym[regular]{0}{"DA}  \fasym{1}{"DD}  \fasym{2}{"D6}  \fasym[regular]{2}{"D6}
\fabrand{0}{"21}         \fabrand{0}{"71}     \fabrand{1}{"4A}  \fabrand{1}{"98}
```

10-13-1

This approach works with all engines by using the Type 1 fonts even in the Unicode engines.

Table 10.104: Brand logos in `fontawesomebrands1`

10.13.8 tipa — International Phonetic Alphabet symbols

The TIPA bundle [30] developed by FUKUI Rei consists of a set of fonts and a corresponding package to enable typesetting of phonetic symbols with LATEX. TIPA contains all the symbols, including diacritics, defined in the 1979, 1989, 1993, and 1996 versions of the International Phonetic Alphabet (IPA). Besides IPA symbols, TIPA contains symbols that are useful for other areas of phonetics and linguistics, e.g.:

- Symbols used in American phonetics, for example, œ, ɛ, ɷ, and ʎ;
- Symbols used in the historical study of Indo-European languages, such as þ, ƥ, ʮ, ɀ, ь, ъ, and accents such as á̄ and ë̆;
- Symbols used in the phonetic description of languages in East Asia, such as ʅ, ʮ, ɖ, ɳ, ȶ (needs option `extra`);
- Diacritics used in *extIPA Symbols for Disordered Speech* and *VoQS* (*Voice Quality Symbols*), for example, n̺̥, f̺, and m̋ (needs option `extra`).

The IPA symbols are encoded in the standard LATEX encoding T3, for which the package tipa provides additional support macros. The encoding is available for the font families Computer Modern Roman, Sans, and Typewriter (based on the METAFONT designs for Computer Modern by Donald Knuth), as well as for older implementations of Times Roman and Helvetica; see below.

Strictly speaking, T3 is not a proper LATEX text encoding, as it does not contain the visible ASCII characters in their standard positions. However, one can take the position that phonetic symbols form a language of their own, and for this language, the TIPA system provides a highly optimized input interface in which digits and uppercase letters serve as convenient shortcuts (see Table 10.105 on the next page) to input common phonetic symbols within the argument of \textipa or the environment IPA. All phonetic symbols are also available in long form; for example, to produce a ə one can use \textschwa. The following example shows the TIPA system in a Times and Helvetica environment. Unfortunately, tipa offers direct support only for the old font

input	:	;	"	|	0	1	2	3	4	5	6	7	8	9
TIPA	:	˙	ʼ	|	ʉ	ɨ	ʌ	ɜ	ɥ	ʁ	ɒ	ɣ	θ	ə

input	@	A	B	C	D	E	F	G	H	I	J	K	L	M
TIPA	ə	ɑ	β	ç	ð	ɛ	ɸ	ɣ	ɦ	ɪ	j	ʁ	ʎ	ŋ

input	N	O	P	Q	R	S	T	U	V	W	X	Y	Z
TIPA	ŋ	ɔ	ʔ	ʕ	ɾ	ʃ	θ	ʊ	ʋ	ɯ	χ	ʏ	ʒ

Table 10.105: TIPA shortcut characters

family names ptm and phv. Thus, to use it with the modern TEX Gyre fonts Termes and Heros, we have to explicitly substitute the old family names in T3 encoding.

In linguistics, fəʊˈnɛtɪk transcriptions are usually shown in square brackets, e.g., phonetics [fəʊˈnɛtɪks].

```
\usepackage{tgtermes,tgheros,tipa}
\DeclareFontFamilySubstitution{T3}{qtm}{ptm}
\DeclareFontFamilySubstitution{T3}{qhv}{phv}

In linguistics, f\textschwa\textupsilon\textprimstress
n\textepsilon t\i k transcriptions are usually shown in square
brackets, e.g., \textsf{phonetics \textipa{[f@U"nEtIks]}}.
```

10-13-1

TIPA defines *, \;, \:, \!, and \| as special macros with which to easily input phonetic symbols that do not have a shortcut input as explained above. In standard LATEX all five are already defined for use in math mode, so loading tipa highjacks them for use by linguists. If that is not desirable, the option safe prevents these redefinitions. The long forms then have to be used—for example, the command \textroundcap instead of \|c. The following lines show a few more complicated examples with the output in Computer Modern Roman, Sans, and Typewriter:

Redefined math commands

ŋŎo̧õ ŋŎâʔã

A) dɔg, B) kæt, C) maʊs

*k̃m̥tóm *bhrátēr

```
\usepackage{tipa}
\begin{IPA} \textrm{N\!o\'{\~*o}\~o \r*N\!o\^aP\~a} \par
    \textsf{\*A) dOg, \*B) k\ae{}t, \*C) maUs}        \par
    \texttt{*\|c{k}\r*mt\'om *bhr\'=at\=er}          \end{IPA}
```

10-13-1

If loaded with the option tone, TIPA provides a \tone command to produce "tone letters". The command takes one argument consisting of a string of numbers denoting pitch levels, 1 being the lowest and 5 the highest. Within this range, any combination is allowed, and there is no limit on the length of the combination, as exemplified in the last line of the next example, which otherwise shows the usage of \tone to display the four tones of Chinese.

˥ma (mother) ˨˩˦ma (horse)
˧˥ma (hemp) ˥˩ma (scold)
˧˥˧˧˨˥˦˩˧

```
\usepackage[tone]{tipa}
\tone{55}ma (mother) \tone{214}ma (horse) \par
\tone{35}ma (hemp)    \tone{51}ma (scold) \par \tone{153325413}
```

10-13-1

The above examples merely scrape the surface of the possibilities offered by TIPA. To explore it in detail consult the tipaman manual, which is part of the TIPA distribution.

Higher Mathematics

Basic LATEX offers excellent mathematical typesetting capabilities for straightforward documents. However, when complex displayed equations or more advanced mathematical constructs are heavily used, something more is needed. Although it is possible to define new commands or environments to ease the burden of typing in formulas, this is not the best solution. The American Mathematical Society (AMS) provides a major package, amsmath, which makes the preparation of mathematical documents much less time-consuming and more consistent.[1] It forms the core of a collection of packages known as $\mathcal{A}_{\mathcal{M}}\mathcal{S}$-LATEX [4] and is the major subject of this chapter. A useful book by George Grätzer [33] also covers these packages in detail.

This chapter describes briefly, and provides examples of, a substantial number of the many features of these packages as well as a few closely related packages; it also gives a few pointers to other relevant packages. In addition, it provides some essential background on mathematical typesetting with TEX. Thus, it covers some of standard LATEX's features for mathematical typesetting and layout and contains some general hints on how to typeset mathematical formulas, though these are not the main aims of this chapter. It is also definitely not a comprehensive manual of good practice for typesetting mathematics with LATEX. Indeed, many of the examples are

---

[1] This package has its foundations in the macro-level extensions to TEX known as $\mathcal{A}_{\mathcal{M}}\mathcal{S}$-TEX.

offered purely for illustration purposes and, therefore, present neither good design nor good mathematics nor necessarily good LaTeX coding.

Advice on how to typeset mathematics according to late 20th century U.S. practice can be found in Ellen Swanson's *Math into Type* [88]. Many details concerning how to implement this advice using TeX or, equally, standard LaTeX appear in Chapters 16–18 of Donald Knuth's *The TeXbook* [42].

To use the majority of the material described in this chapter, you need to load at least the amsmath or mathtools package in the preamble of your document. If other packages are needed, they are clearly marked in the examples. Detailed installation and usage documentation is included with the individual packages.

11.1 Introduction to amsmath **and** mathtools

The *AMS*-LaTeX project commenced in 1987, and three years later *AMS*-LaTeX version 1.0 was released. This was the original conversion to LaTeX of the mathematical capabilities in Michael Spivak's *AMS*-TeX by Frank Mittelbach and Rainer Schöpf, working as consultants to the American Mathematical Society, with assistance from Michael Downes (1958–2003) of the AMS technical staff. In 1994, further work was done with David Jones. This work was coordinated by Michael Downes, and the packages have throughout been supported and much enhanced under his direction and the patronage of the AMS.[1] Initially *AMS*-LaTeX was a separate format, which is the reason for the separate name, but at some point, when computers got faster and faster, the functionality was moved to the package amsmath, which could be loaded into standard LaTeX, and the support for a separate format was dropped. Thus, these days speaking of *AMS*-LaTeX simply refers to amsmath or the AMS document classes that evolved from that project.

In 2016 the AMS passed maintenance and control of amsmath and some of its accompanying packages back to the LaTeX Project Team, because its math capabilities are a core functionality of LaTeX.[2]

Thanks to a great guy! Michael Downes (1958–2003) would have been the author of this chapter when we wrote the second edition of this book had he not died in spring 2003. Much of the chapter is based on the documentation he prepared for *AMS*-LaTeX; thus, what you are reading is a particular and heartfelt tribute by its current author to the life and work of a dear friend and colleague with whom we shared many coding adventures in the uncharted backwaters of TeX.

Available package options A few options are recognized by the amsmath package. Most of these affect only detailed positioning of the "limits" on various types of mathematical operators (Section 11.4.4) or that of equation tags (Section 11.2.4).

---

[1]Some material in this chapter is reprinted from the documentation that was distributed with *AMS*-LaTeX (with permission from the American Mathematical Society).

[2]However, the American Mathematical Society retained maintenance and support of the AMS fonts and the document classes amsart, amsbook, and amsproc; thus, any issue or inquiries concerning these classes or font packages have to be taken up with their technical stuff and not the LaTeX Project Team.

The following three options are often supplied as global document options, set on the \documentclass command. They are, however, also recognized when the amsmath package is loaded with the \usepackage command.

reqno (**default**) Place equation numbers (tags) on the right.

leqno Place equation numbers (tags) on the left.[1]

fleqn Position equations at a fixed indent from the left margin rather than centered in the text column.

For historical reasons some components of the amsmath package exist as separate packages so that they can be loaded on their own — a feature that was essential when computer memory was tight and just loading a large package like amsmath was taking considerable time. These days the advice is to always load amsmath and not try to determine what is needed and what is not.

Available subpackages

amsopn Provides \DeclareMathOperator for defining new operator names such as \Ker and \esssup.

amstext Provides the \text command for typesetting a fragment of text in the correct type size.

The following packages, providing functionality additional to that in amsmath, must be loaded explicitly; they are listed here for completeness.

Extension packages

amscd Defines some commands for easing the generation of commutative diagrams by introducing the CD environment (see Section 11.3.5 on page 159). There is no support for diagonal arrows.

amsthm Provides a method to declare theorem-like structures and offers a proof environment. It is discussed in Section 4.1.4 on page →I 281.

amsxtra Provides certain odds and ends that are needed for historical compatibility, such as \fracwithdelims, \accentedsymbol, and commands for placing accents as superscripts.

upref Makes \ref print cross-reference numbers in an upright/roman font regardless of context.

The principal documentation for these packages is the *User's Guide for the* amsmath *Package (Version 2.1)* [4], which is part of the LaTeX distribution.

The amsmath package is very comprehensive and provides most of what is needed when attempting serious mathematical typesetting. It is, however, rather static; i.e., it has not seen a lot additions (or fixes) since its initial development in the nineties. Because of this, several smaller packages, some of which we discuss in this chapter, have been developed to add one or the other missing feature. In addition, there is

mathtools — *A drop-in replacement for* amsmath

---

[1]When using one of the AMS document classes, the default is leqno.

also the mathtools package by Morten Høgholm now maintained by Lars Madsen that has been explicitly developed to offer a replacement for amsmath. It provides all features of amsmath (including the support for all of its package options), augments it with several new features, and fixes a number of known bugs in amsmath. We give examples of its extended functionality in the appropriate places, and if you intend to use any of this, you should load mathtools in place of amsmath.

The $\mathcal{A}_{\mathcal{M}}$S-LATEX document classes

As already mentioned, the three document classes amsart, amsproc, and amsbook from the original $\mathcal{A}_{\mathcal{M}}$S-LATEX collection are still maintained by the American Mathematical Society. They correspond to LATEX's article, proc, and book, respectively, and are designed to be used in the preparation of manuscripts for submission to the AMS. However, given that they are part of every LATEX distribution, nothing prohibits their use for other purposes. In fact, they are often used as the base class for other journals instead of the standard LATEX classes.

With these class files the amsmath package is automatically loaded so that you can start your document simply with \documentclass{amsart}. These classes are not covered in this book because they provide an interface similar to that provided by the LATEX standard classes; refer to [3] for details of their use.

The AMSfonts collection

Some of the material in this chapter refers to another collection of packages from the American Mathematical Society, namely, the AMSfonts distribution. These packages, listed below, set up various fonts and commands for use in mathematical formulas.

amsfonts Defines the \mathfrak and \mathbb commands and sets up the fonts msam (extra math symbols A), msbm (extra math symbols B and blackboard bold), eufm (Euler Fraktur), extra sizes of cmmib (bold math italic and bold lowercase Greek), and cmbsy (bold math symbols and bold script) for use in mathematics.

amssymb Defines the names of the mathematical symbols available with the AMSfonts collection. These commands are discussed in Section 11.8. The package automatically loads the amsfonts package.

eufrak Sets up the fonts for the Euler Fraktur letters (\mathfrak), as discussed in Section 12.3.3. This alphabet is also available from the amsfonts package.

eucal Makes \mathcal use the Euler script instead of the usual Computer Modern script letters; see Section 12.3.3 for details.

The above packages and fonts are maintained by the American Mathematical Society, and the principal piece of documentation for both is the *User's Guide to AMSFonts Version 2.2d* [2]. However, the distribution is now in version 3, while the documentation

Documentation is somewhat dated, but still relevant

is still describing version 2.2d. Though most of it is still accurate and relevant, there is one area where the guide talks about METAFONT (bitmapped) versus Type 1 (outline) fonts that you need to ignore. These days only the Type 1 fonts are distributed, so this part is giving incorrect advice. In particular, the psamsfonts option described there should no longer be used, because it is no longer recognized by all of the packages and produces either a warning or an error.

A few important warnings

Many of the commands described in this chapter have been fragile in the past and needed to be \protected in moving arguments (see Appendix B.1 on page 715). Thus, when strange error messages appear, a missing \protect is a likely cause. A part of the maintenance work of the LATEX Project Team is to make all of them robust so that over time this issue should vanish.

Watch out for fragile commands

It is never a good idea to use shortcut codes for LATEX environments. With the amsmath display environments described in this chapter, such shortcuts are always disastrous — do not do it! For closely related reasons, you will also find that verbatim material cannot be used within these environments. Here are some examples of declarations for disaster:

Do not abbreviate environments

```
\newenvironment{mlt}{\begin{multline}}{\end{multline}}
\newcommand\bga{\begin{gather}}  \newcommand\ega{\end{gather}}
```

Both produce errors of the form "\begin{...} ended by ...". However, you can define synonyms and variant forms of these environments as follows:

```
\newenvironment{mlt}{\multline}{\endmultline}
\newenvironment{longgather}{\allowdisplaybreaks\gather}{\endgather}
```

Note that these must have the command form of an existing environment as the last command in the "begin-code", and the corresponding \end... command as the first thing in the "end-code". See also Section A.1.3 for more details.

11.2 Display and alignment structures for equations

The amsmath package defines several environments for creating displayed mathematics. These cover single- and multiple-line displays with single or multiple alignment points and various options for numbering equations within displays.

Throughout this section the term "equation" is used in a very particular way: to refer to a *logically* distinct part of a mathematical display that is frequently numbered for reference purposes and is also labeled (commonly by its number in parentheses). Such labels are often called *tags*.

11-2-1

(1) $(a + b)^2 = a^2 + 2ab + b^2$

   $\sin^2 \eta + \cos^2 \eta = 1$

```
\usepackage[leqno]{amsmath}

\begin{equation} (a+b)^2 = a^2+2ab+b^2 \end{equation}
\[ \sin^2\eta+\cos^2\eta = 1  \]
```

None of the math environments allow empty lines in their body. If you wish to structure your input source, use lines that are empty except for a %-sign at the beginning.

The complete list of all the display environments from amsmath and mathtools available for mathematical typesetting is given in Table 11.1 on the next page; the majority of these environments are covered in this section, along with examples of

Math Display Environments		*Effect*
equation	equation*	One line, one equation (equation* corresponds to \[...\])
multline	multline*	One unaligned multiple-line equation, one equation number
gather	gather*	Several equations without alignment
align	align*	Several equations with multiple alignments
flalign	flalign*	Several equations: horizontally spread form of align
split		A simple alignment within a multiple-line equation
gathered		A "mini-page" with unaligned equations
aligned		A "mini-page" with multiple alignments
Environments added by mathtools		
lgathered	rgathered	A "mini-page" with left or right equations
multlined		A "mini-page" with a multline inside

Table 11.1: Display environments in the amsmath/mathtools packages

their use. Where appropriate they have starred forms in which there is no numbering or tagging of the equations.

To position the mathematics at a fixed indent from the left margin, rather than centered in the text column, use the option fleqn. You then normally need to set the size of the indent in the preamble. It is the value of the rubber length \mathindent, which gets its default value from the indentation of a first-level list — which is probably not the value you want! Observe the differences between the next example and the previous example. In this particular case, use of the reqno option is redundant (as it is the default), but it forces the equation number to the right side regardless of what the document class specifies.

$$(a+b)^2 = a^2 + 2ab + b^2 \tag{1}$$

$$\sin^2 \eta + \cos^2 \eta = 1$$

```
\usepackage[fleqn,reqno]{amsmath}
\setlength\mathindent{1pc minus 1pc}

\begin{equation} (a+b)^2 = a^2+2ab+b^2 \end{equation}
\[  \sin^2\eta+\cos^2\eta = 1  \]
```

11-2-2

If you use a minus component in the value for \mathindent as we did in the previous example, very wide formulas can protrude into that indentation if they do not otherwise fit into the available space.

As later examples show, as in standard LaTeX, & and \\ are used for column and line separation within displayed alignments. The details of their usage change in the amsmath environments, however (see the next section).

11.2.1 Comparison of amsmath/mathtools with standard LaTeX

Some of the multiple-line display environments allow you to align parts of the formula. In contrast to the original LaTeX environments eqnarray and eqnarray*, the structures implemented by the amsmath package use a slightly different and more straightforward method for marking the alignment points. Standard LATEX's eqnarray* is similar to an array environment with {rcl} as the preamble and, therefore, requires two ampersand characters indicating the two alignment points. In the equivalent amsmath structures there is only a single alignment point (similar to a {rl} preamble), so only a single ampersand character should be used, placed to the left of the symbol (usually a relation) that should be aligned.

The amsmath structures give fixed spacing at the alignment points, whereas the eqnarray environment produces extra space depending on the parameter settings for array. The difference can be seen clearly in the next example, where the same equation is typeset using the equation, align, and eqnarray environments; the spaces in the eqnarray environment come out too wide for conventional standards of mathematical typesetting.

$$x^2 + y^2 = z^2 \tag{1}$$

$$x^2 + y^2 = z^2 \tag{2}$$
$$x^3 + y^3 < z^3 \tag{3}$$

$$x^2 + y^2 \;=\; z^2 \tag{4}$$
$$x^3 + y^3 \;<\; z^3 \tag{5}$$

11-2-3

```
\usepackage{amsmath}
\begin{equation}
   x^2 + y^2  =  z^2
\end{equation}
\begin{align}
   x^2 + y^2 &=  z^2 \\ x^3 + y^3 &<  z^3
\end{align}
\begin{eqnarray}
   x^2 + y^2 &=& z^2 \\ x^3 + y^3 &<& z^3
\end{eqnarray}
```

As in standard LATEX, lines in an amsmath display are marked with \\ (or the end of the environment). Because line breaking in a mathematical display usually requires a thorough understanding of the structure of the formula, it is commonly considered to be beyond today's software capabilities. However, one of the last bigger projects undertaken by Michael Downes (1958–2003) precisely tackled this problem; it resulted in the breqn package (see Section 11.2.12 on page 146 for an overview).

Unlike eqnarray, the amsmath environments do not, by default, allow page breaks between lines (see Section 11.2.10).

Another difference concerns the use of \\[*dimension*] or * within mathematical display environments. With amsmath, there must be no space between the \\ and the [or the *; otherwise, the optional argument or star will not be recognized. The reason is that brackets and stars are very common in mathematical formulas, so this restriction avoids the annoyance of having a genuine bracket belonging to the formula be mistaken for the start of the optional argument.

Space after \\ not ignored

11.2.2 A single equation on one line

The equation environment produces a single equation with an automatically generated number or tag placed on the extreme left or right according to the option in use (see Section 11.2.13); equation* does the same but omits a tag.[1]

---

[1] Standard LATEX also has equation, but not equation*, because the latter is similar to the standard displayed math environment.

Note that the presence of the tag does not affect the positioning of the contents. If there is not enough room for it on the one line, the tag is shifted up or down: to the previous line when equation numbers are on the left, and to the next line when numbers are on the right.

$$n^2 + m^2 = k^2$$

$$(1) \qquad n^p + m^p \neq k^p \qquad p > 2$$

```
\usepackage[leqno]{amsmath}
\begin{equation*}
  n^2 + m^2 = k^2
\end{equation*}
\begin{equation}
  n^p +m^p \neq k^p  \qquad p > 2
\end{equation}
```

11-2-4

11.2.3 A single equation on several lines: no alignment

The `multline` environment is a variation of the `equation` environment used only for equations that do not fit on a single line. In this environment \\ must be used to mark the line breaks, because they are not found automatically.

The first line of a `multline` is aligned on an indentation from the left margin and the last line on the same indentation from the right margin.[1] The size of this indentation is the value of the length \multlinegap; thus, it can be changed using LaTeX's \setlength and \addtolength commands.

If a `multline` contains more than two lines, each line other than the first and last is centered individually within the display width (unless the option `fleqn` is used). It is, however, possible to force a single line to the left or the right by adding either \shoveleft or \shoveright within that line.

A `multline` environment is a single (logical) equation and thus has only a single tag, the `multline*` having none; thus, none of the individual lines can be changed by the use of \tag or \notag. The tag, if present, is placed flush right on the last line with the default `reqno` option or flush left on the first line when the `leqno` option is used.

First line of a multline
$\qquad$ Centered Middle line
$\qquad\qquad$ A right Middle
$\qquad$ Another centered Middle
$\qquad$ Yet another centered Middle
A left Middle
$\qquad\qquad$ Last line of the multline $\quad$ (1)

```
\usepackage{amsmath}
\begin{multline}
  \text{First line of a multline}      \\
  \text{Centered Middle line}          \\
  \shoveright{\text{A right Middle}} \\
  \text{Another centered Middle}       \\
  \text{Yet another centered Middle} \\
  \shoveleft{\text{A left Middle}}    \\
  \text{Last line of the multline}
\end{multline}
```

11-2-5

The next example shows the effect of \multlinegap. In the first setting, the "dy"s line up and make it appear that a tag is missing from the first line of the equation.

---

[1] Never use `multline` for a single-line equation because the effect is unpredictable.

When the parameter is set to zero, the space on the left of the second line does not change because of the tag, while the first line is pushed over to the left margin, thus making it clear that this is only one equation.

$$\sum_{t\in\mathbf{T}} \int_a^t \left\{ \int_a^t f(t-x)^2\, g(y)^2\, dx \right\} dy$$
$$= \sum_{t\notin\mathbf{T}} \int_t^a \left\{ g(y)^2 \int_t^a f(x)^2\, dx \right\} dy \quad (2)$$

11-2-6

```
\usepackage{amsmath}
\begin{multline}  \tag{2}
  \sum_{t \in \mathbf{T}} \int_a^t
    \biggl\lbrace \int_a^t f(t - x)^2 \,
            g(y)^2 \,dx \biggr\rbrace \,dy \\
   = \sum_{t \notin \mathbf{T}} \int_t^a
      \biggl\lbrace g(y)^2 \int_t^a
        f(x)^2 \,dx \biggr\rbrace \,dy
\end{multline}
\setlength\multlinegap{0pt}
\begin{multline}  \tag{2}
  \sum_{t \in \mathbf{T}} \int_a^t
    \biggl\lbrace \int_a^t f(t - x)^2 \,
            g(y)^2 \,dx \biggr\rbrace \,dy \\
   = \sum_{t \notin \mathbf{T}} \int_t^a
      \biggl\lbrace g(y)^2 \int_t^a
        f(x)^2 \,dx \biggr\rbrace \,dy
\end{multline}
```

$$\sum_{t\in\mathbf{T}} \int_a^t \left\{ \int_a^t f(t-x)^2\, g(y)^2\, dx \right\} dy$$
$$= \sum_{t\notin\mathbf{T}} \int_t^a \left\{ g(y)^2 \int_t^a f(x)^2\, dx \right\} dy \quad (2)$$

11.2.4 A single equation on several lines: with alignment

When a simple alignment is needed within a single multiple-line equation, the split environment is almost always the best choice. It uses a single ampersand (&) on each line to mark the alignment point.

11-2-7

$$(a+b)^4 = (a+b)^2(a+b)^2$$
$$= (a^2 + 2ab + b^2)(a^2 + 2ab + b^2) \quad (1)$$
$$= a^4 + 4a^3b + 6a^2b^2 + 4ab^3 + b^4$$

```
\usepackage{amsmath}
\begin{equation}
  \begin{split}
   (a + b)^4
    &= (a + b)^2 (a + b)^2          \\
    &= (a^2 + 2ab + b^2)
       (a^2 + 2ab + b^2)            \\
    &= a^4 + 4a^3b + 6a^2b^2 + 4ab^3 + b^4
  \end{split}
\end{equation}
```

Because it is always used as the content of a single (logical) equation, a split does not itself produce any numbering tag, and hence there is no starred variant. If needed, the outer display environment provides any needed tags.

Apart from commands such as \label or \notag that produce no visible material, a split structure should normally constitute the entire body of the equation being split. It can consist of either a whole equation or equation* environment or one whole line of a gather or gather* environment; see Section 11.2.5.

When the `centertags` option is in effect (the default), the tag (and any other material in the equation outside the `split`) is centered vertically on the total height of the material from the `split` environment. When the `tbtags` option is specified, the tag is aligned with the last line of the split when the tag is on the right, and with the first line of the split when the tag is on the left.

$$
\begin{aligned}
(a+b)^3 &= (a+b)(a+b)^2 \\
&= (a+b)(a^2 + 2ab + b^2) \\
&= a^3 + 3a^2b + 3ab^2 + b^3 \qquad (1)
\end{aligned}
$$

```
\usepackage[tbtags]{amsmath}

\begin{equation}
  \begin{split}
    (a + b)^3 &= (a + b) (a + b)^2    \\
          &= (a + b)(a^2 + 2ab + b^2) \\
          &= a^3 + 3a^2b + 3ab^2 + b^3
  \end{split}
\end{equation}
```

11-2-8

In the next example the command `\phantom` is used to adjust the horizontal positioning. It is first used in the preamble to define an "invisible relation symbol" of width equal to that of its argument (in this case, $=$). Within the example it is used to align certain lines by starting them with a "phantom or invisible subformula" (see Section 11.7.2 on page 197).

Ensure that + is interpreted as a binary symbol   The empty pair of braces, {}, is equivalent to `\mathord{}` and provides an invisible zero-width "letter" that is needed to achieve the correct spacing of $+h$ (without the {} it would look like this: $+h$).

```
\usepackage{amsmath}
\newcommand\relphantom[1]{\mathrel{\phantom{#1}}}
\newcommand\ve{\varepsilon}   \newcommand\tve{t_{\varepsilon}}
\newcommand\vf{\varphi}       \newcommand\yvf{y_{\varphi}}
\newcommand\bfE{\mathbf{E}}

\begin{equation}
  \begin{split}
    f_{h, \ve}(x, y)
      &= \ve \bfE_{x, y} \int_0^{\tve} L_{x, \yvf(\ve u)} \vf(x) \,du  \\
      &= h \int L_{x, z} \vf(x) \rho_x(dz)                            \\
      &\relphantom{=} {} + h \biggl[
         \frac{1}{\tve}
         \biggl( \bfE_{y} \int_0^{\tve}  L_{x, y^x(s)} \vf(x) \,ds
                 - \tve \int L_{x, z} \vf(x) \rho_x(dz)         \biggr) + \\
      &\relphantom{=} \phantom{{} + h \biggl[ }
         \frac{1}{\tve}
         \biggl( \bfE_{y} \int_0^{\tve}  L_{x, y^x(s)} \vf(x) \,ds
                 - \bfE_{x, y} \int_0^{\tve} L_{x, \yvf(\ve s)}
                                \vf(x) \,ds     \biggr) \biggr]
  \end{split}
\end{equation}
```

Note that the equation number tag has been moved to the line below the displayed material. Although this does not seem to be a very wise decision, it is as far as the automated expertise built into the system at this stage can take us.

11-2-9

$$
\begin{aligned}
f_{h,\varepsilon}(x,y) &= \varepsilon \mathbf{E}_{x,y} \int_0^{t_\varepsilon} L_{x,y_\varphi(\varepsilon u)} \varphi(x)\, du \\
&= h \int L_{x,z} \varphi(x) \rho_x(dz) \\
&\quad + h \left[\frac{1}{t_\varepsilon} \left(\mathbf{E}_y \int_0^{t_\varepsilon} L_{x,y^x(s)} \varphi(x)\, ds - t_\varepsilon \int L_{x,z} \varphi(x) \rho_x(dz) \right) + \right. \\
&\qquad \left. \frac{1}{t_\varepsilon} \left(\mathbf{E}_y \int_0^{t_\varepsilon} L_{x,y^x(s)} \varphi(x)\, ds - \mathbf{E}_{x,y} \int_0^{t_\varepsilon} L_{x,y_\varphi(\varepsilon s)} \varphi(x)\, ds \right) \right]
\end{aligned}
$$
(1)

11.2.5 Equation groups without alignment

The gather environment is used to put two or more equations into a single display without alignment between the equations. Each equation is separately centered within the display width and has its individual number tag, if needed. Each line of a gather is a single (logical) equation.

11-2-10

$$
(a+b)^2 = a^2 + 2ab + b^2 \tag{1}
$$
$$
(a+b) \cdot (a-b) = a^2 - b^2 \tag{2}
$$

```
\usepackage{amsmath}
\begin{gather}
   (a + b)^2 = a^2 + 2ab + b^2        \\
   (a + b) \cdot (a - b) = a^2 - b^2
\end{gather}
```

Use \notag within the logical line to suppress the equation number for that line; or use gather* to suppress all equation numbers.

11-2-11

$$
D(a,r) \equiv \{ z \in \mathbf{C} : |z - a| < r \}
$$
$$
\mathrm{seg}(a,r) \equiv \{ z \in \mathbf{C} : \Im z < \Im a,\ |z - a| < r \} \tag{1}
$$
$$
C(E,\theta,r) \equiv \bigcup_{e \in E} c(e,\theta,r) \tag{2}
$$

```
\usepackage{amsmath}
\begin{gather}
   D(a,r) \equiv \{ z \in \mathbf{C}
      \colon |z - a| < r \}        \notag \\
   \operatorname{seg} (a, r) \equiv
      \{ z \in \mathbf{C} \colon
      \Im z < \Im a, \ |z - a| < r \}      \\
   C (E, \theta, r) \equiv
      \bigcup_{e \in E} c (e, \theta, r)
\end{gather}
```

11.2.6 Equation groups with simple alignment

The `align` environment should be used for two or more equations in a single display with vertical alignment. The simplest form uses a single ampersand (&) on each line to mark the alignment point (usually just before a Relation symbol).

$$(a+b)^3 = (a+b)(a+b)^2 \tag{1}$$
$$= (a+b)(a^2 + 2ab + b^2) \tag{2}$$
$$= a^3 + 3a^2b + 3ab^2 + b^3 \tag{3}$$

$$x^2 + y^2 = 1 \tag{4}$$
$$x = \sqrt{1 - y^2} \tag{5}$$

```
\usepackage{amsmath}
\begin{align}
  (a + b)^3  &= (a + b) (a + b)^2          \\
             &= (a + b)(a^2 + 2ab + b^2) \\
             &= a^3 + 3a^2b + 3ab^2 + b^3
\end{align}
\begin{align}
  x^2   + y^2 & = 1                         \\
  x           & = \sqrt{1-y^2}
\end{align}
```

11-2-12

11.2.7 Multiple alignments: `align` and `flalign`

An `align` environment can include more than one alignment point. The layout contains as many column-pairs as necessary and is similar to an `array` with a preamble of the form `{rlrl...}` except that it does not change the spacing around the alignment points. If it consists of n such `rl` column-pairs, then the number of ampersands per line is $2n - 1$: one ampersand for alignment within each column-pair giving n; and $n - 1$ ampersands to separate the column-pairs.

Within the `align` environment, the material is spread out evenly across the display width. All extra (or white) space within the line is distributed equally "between consecutive `rl` column-pairs" and the two display margins.

This example has two column-pairs.

$$\text{Compare } x^2 + y^2 = 1 \qquad x^3 + y^3 = 1 \tag{1}$$
$$x = \sqrt{1 - y^2} \qquad x = \sqrt[3]{1 - y^3} \tag{2}$$

This example has three column-pairs.

$$x = y \qquad X = Y \qquad a = b + c \tag{3}$$
$$x' = y' \qquad X' = Y' \qquad a' = b \tag{4}$$
$$x + x' = y + y' \quad X + X' = Y + Y' \quad a'b = c'b \tag{5}$$

```
\usepackage{amsmath}
This example has two column-pairs.
\begin{align}     \text{Compare }
  x^2 + y^2 &= 1                   &
  x^3 + y^3 &= 1                   \\
  x         &= \sqrt  {1-y^2} &
  x         &= \sqrt[3]{1-y^3}
\end{align}
This example has three column-pairs.
\begin{align}
  x     &= y      & X  &= Y  &
  a     &= b+c                    \\
  x'    &= y'     & X' &= Y' &
  a'    &= b                      \\
  x + x' &= y + y'                &
  X + X' &= Y + Y' & a'b &= c'b
\end{align}
```

11-2-13

In the variant `flalign` the layout is similar except that there is no space at the margins. As a result, in the next example, Equation (3) now fits on a single line (while in Equation (2) this was still not possible).

This example has two column-pairs.

Compare $x^2 + y^2 = 1$ $\qquad x^3 + y^3 = 1$ (1)

$$x = \sqrt{1 - y^2} \qquad\qquad x = \sqrt[3]{1 - y^3}$$ (2)

This example has three column-pairs.

$x = y$	$X = Y$	$a = b + c$ (3)
$x' = y'$	$X' = Y'$	$a' = b$ (4)
$x + x' = y + y'$	$X + X' = Y + Y'$	$a'b = c'b$ (5)

11-2-14

```
\usepackage{amsmath}
This example has two column-pairs.
\begin{flalign}  \text{Compare }
    x^2 + y^2 &= 1                        &
    x^3 + y^3 &= 1                        \\
    x         &= \sqrt    {1-y^2} &
    x         &= \sqrt[3]{1-y^3}
\end{flalign}
This example has three column-pairs.
\begin{flalign}
    x    &= y       & X   &= Y   &
    a    &= b+c                  \\
    x'   &= y'      & X'  &= Y'  &
    a'   &= b                    \\
    x + x' &= y + y'                      &
    X + X' &= Y + Y' & a'b &= c'b
\end{flalign}
```

In both cases the minimum space between column-pairs can be set by changing `\minalignsep`. Its default value is 10pt, but, misleadingly, it is *not* a length parameter. Thus, it must be changed by using `\renewcommand`. If we set it to zero for the first part of the example, Equation (2) gets squeezed onto a single line; if we set it to 15pt later, the label (3) gets forced onto a line by itself.

`\minalignsep`
is not a length

Unfortunately, there is no such simple parametric method for controlling the spacing at the margins.

This example has two column-pairs.

Compare $x^2 + y^2 = 1$ $\qquad x^3 + y^3 = 1$ (1)

$$x = \sqrt{1 - y^2} \qquad x = \sqrt[3]{1 - y^3}$$ (2)

This example has three column-pairs.

$x = y$	$X = Y$	$a = b + c$ (3)
$x' = y'$	$X' = Y'$	$a' = b$ (4)
$x + x' = y + y'$	$X + X' = Y + Y'$	$a'b = c'b$ (5)

11-2-15

```
\usepackage{amsmath}
This example has two column-pairs.
\renewcommand\minalignsep{0pt}
\begin{align}      \text{Compare }
    x^2 + y^2 &= 1                        &
    x^3 + y^3 &= 1                        \\
    x         &= \sqrt    {1-y^2} &
    x         &= \sqrt[3]{1-y^3}
\end{align}
This example has three column-pairs.
\renewcommand\minalignsep{15pt}
\begin{flalign}
    x    &= y       & X   &= Y   &
    a    &= b+c                  \\
    x'   &= y'      & X'  &= Y'  &
    a'   &= b                    \\
    x + x' &= y + y'                      &
    X + X' &= Y + Y' & a'b &= c'b
\end{flalign}
```

The next example illustrates a very common use for `align`. Note the use of `\text` to produce normal text within the mathematical material.

$$x = y \qquad \text{by hypothesis} \quad (1)$$
$$x' = y' \qquad \text{by definition} \quad (2)$$
$$x + x' = y + y' \qquad \text{by Axiom 1} \quad (3)$$

```
\usepackage{amsmath}
\renewcommand\minalignsep{30pt}
\begin{align}
   x      &= y      && \text{by hypothesis} \\
          x' &= y'       && \text{by definition} \\
   x + x' &= y + y' && \text{by Axiom 1}
\end{align}
\renewcommand\minalignsep{10pt}
```

11-2-16

11.2.8 Display environments as mini-pages

All the environments described so far produce material set to the full display width. A few of these environments have also been adapted to provide self-contained alignment structures, as if they were set as the only content of a `minipage` environment whose size, in both directions, is determined by its contents.

The environment names are changed only slightly: to `aligned` and `gathered`, and when using `mathtools`, there are also `lgathered`, `rgathered`, and `multlined`. *mathtools additions to amsmath* Note that an `aligned` environment avoids unnecessary space on the left and right; thus, it mostly resembles the `flalign` environment.

Like `minipage`, these environments take an optional argument that specifies the vertical positioning with respect to the material on either side. The default alignment of the box is centered (`[c]`). Of course, like `split`, they are used only within equations, and they never produce tags.

$$x^2 + y^2 = 1$$
$$x = \sqrt{1 - y^2}$$
$$\text{and also } y = \sqrt{1 - x^2}$$

$$(a + b)^2 = a^2 + 2ab + b^2$$
$$(a + b) \cdot (a - b) = a^2 - b^2 \qquad (1)$$

```
\usepackage{amsmath}
\begin{equation}
\begin{aligned}
   x^2 + y^2  &= 1                        \\
          x &= \sqrt{1-y^2}  \\
   \text{and also }
          y &= \sqrt{1-x^2}
\end{aligned}
\qquad
\begin{gathered}
  (a + b)^2 = a^2 + 2ab + b^2 \\
  (a + b) \cdot (a - b)
          = a^2 - b^2
\end{gathered}
\end{equation}
```

11-2-17

The same mathematics can also be typeset, albeit not very beautifully, using different vertical alignments for the environments.

$$x^2 + y^2 = 1$$

$$x = \sqrt{1 - y^2}$$

and also $y = \sqrt{1 - x^2}$ $(a+b)^2 = a^2 + 2ab + b^2$ (1)

$$(a+b) \cdot (a-b) = a^2 - b^2$$

11-2-18

```
\usepackage{amsmath}
\begin{equation}
\begin{aligned}[b]
   x^2 + y^2  &= 1                          \\
   x          &= \sqrt{1-y^2}               \\
   \text{and also }y &= \sqrt{1-x^2}
\end{aligned}
\begin{gathered}[t]                          \qquad
   (a + b)^2 = a^2 + 2ab + b^2    \\
   (a + b) \cdot (a - b) = a^2 - b^2
\end{gathered}
\end{equation}
```

They may be used in many ways — for example, to do some creative and useful grouping of famous equations. Incidentally, these mini-page display environments are among the very few from **amsmath** that are robust enough to be used inside other definitions, as in the following example:

11-2-19

$$\left. \begin{aligned} \boldsymbol{B}' &= -c\nabla \times \boldsymbol{E} \\ \boldsymbol{E}' &= c\nabla \times \boldsymbol{B} - 4\pi\boldsymbol{J} \end{aligned} \right\}$$ Maxwell's equations

```
\usepackage{amsmath,bm}
\newenvironment{rcases}
    {\left.\begin{aligned}}
    {\end{aligned}\right\rbrace}
\begin{equation*}
 \begin{rcases}
 \bm{B}' &=-c\nabla\times\bm{E}                \\
 \bm{E}' &=c\nabla\times\bm{B} - 4\pi\bm{J}\,,
 \end{rcases}
 \quad \text {Maxwell's equations}
\end{equation*}
```

You can also use the `\minalignsep` command to control the space between pairs of columns in an `aligned` environment, as shown in the next example:

11-2-20

$$V_j = v_j \qquad X_i = x_i - q_i x_j \qquad = u_j + \sum_{i \ne j} q_i$$ (1)

$$V_i = v_i - q_i v_j \quad X_j = x_j \qquad U_i = u_i$$

```
\usepackage{amsmath}
\renewcommand\minalignsep{5pt}
\begin{equation} \begin{aligned}
   V_j &= v_j                      &
   X_i &= x_i - q_i x_j            &
       &= u_j + \sum_{i\ne j} q_i \\
   V_i &= v_i - q_i v_j            &
   X_j &= x_j                      &
   U_i &= u_i
\end{aligned} \end{equation}
```

As mentioned earlier, mathtools adds three additional environments that box their content. In contrast to gathered that centers the display lines, lgathered aligns them on the left and rgathered on the right. Both environments are defined

mathtools additions to amsmath

141

with the help of a declaration `\newgathered`, through which you can define more complicated display environments that "gather and box" their content.

> `\newgathered{`*env-name*`}{`*line-start*`}{`*line-end*`}{`*after*`}`

This defines a new environment with the name *env-name*. It collects all display lines and prepends *line-start* to each line and *line-end* after it. Finally, when the display is finished, it executes the *after-code*, which can be used to do some housekeeping. Using this command, all that was necessary to provide the `lgathered` environment in the package was the following declaration:

```
\newgathered{lgathered}{}{\hfil}{}
```

Existing environments can be redefined using `\renewgathered` instead.

```
\usepackage{mathtools}                 \newcounter{xgnum}
\newcommand\xgnum{\stepcounter{xgnum}\textbf{\arabic{xgnum}*}}
\newgathered{xgathered}{\xgnum\qquad\hfil}{\hfil}{\setcounter{xgnum}{0}}
```

Using these definitions in the next example, we get the following result:

<table>
<tr><td>

1* $x_0 = 1, \quad x_1 = 2$

2* $x_3 = 3$

(1)

</td><td>

```
% xgathered as defined above
\begin{gather}
    \begin{xgathered} x_0=1,\quad x_1=2 \\
                      x_3=3            \end{xgathered}
\end{gather}
```

</td><td>

11-2-21

</td></tr>
</table>

The third environment is `multlined`, which is the boxed version of `multline` discussed on page 134. In contrast to the other boxed environments, it has two optional arguments: the first defines the vertical position of the result as usual and accepts the value b, t, or c (default), and with the second you can specify an explicit width for the resulting box. If the *width* argument is not given, then the box is made wide enough to ensure that all continuation lines are indented compared to the first and that the last line slightly sticks out to the right. To indicate the box size, we added vertical delimiters to the left and right in the next example.

<table>
<tr><td>

$$\left| \begin{aligned} (a+b)^2 &= \\ (a+b)(a+b) \\ &= a^2 + 2ab + b^2 \end{aligned} \right|$$

</td><td>

```
\usepackage{mathtools}
\[ \left|
  \begin{multlined}[c]
    (a+b)^2 = \\ (a+b)(a+b) \\ = a^2 + 2ab + b^2
  \end{multlined}
\right| \]
```

</td><td>

11-2-22

</td></tr>
</table>

The commands `\shoveleft` and `\shoveright` also work with `multlined`, but there are a number of limitations with the environment; see the package documentation if you run into problems.

11.2.9 Interrupting displays with short text

The \intertext command is used for a short passage of text (typically at most a few lines) that appears between the lines of a display alignment. Its importance stems from the fact that all the alignment properties are unaffected by the text, which itself is typeset as a normal paragraph set to the display width; this alignment would not be possible if you simply ended the display and then started a new display after the text. This command may appear only immediately after a \\ or * command.

Here the words "and finally" are outside the alignment, at the left margin, but all three equations are aligned.

11-2-23

$$A_1 = N_0(\lambda; \Omega') - \phi(\lambda; \Omega') \tag{1}$$
$$A_2 = \phi(\lambda; \Omega')\phi(\lambda; \Omega) \tag{2}$$

and finally

$$A_3 = \mathcal{N}(\lambda; \omega) \tag{3}$$

```
\usepackage{amsmath}
\begin{align}
  A_1 &= N_0 (\lambda ; \Omega') -
         \phi ( \lambda ; \Omega')   \\
  A_2 &= \phi (\lambda ; \Omega')
         \phi (\lambda ; \Omega)     \\
\intertext{and finally}
  A_3 &= \mathcal{N} (\lambda ; \omega)
\end{align}
```

In some situations, such as in the previous example where only short text is used, the vertical separation between the formula parts and the interruption appears to be too large, and for such cases mathtools offers \shortintertext as an alternative; see Example 11-4-25 on page 174.

mathtools addition to amsmath

11.2.10 Vertical space in and around displays

As is usual in LaTeX, the optional argument \\[*dimension*] gives extra vertical space between two lines in all amsmath display environments (there must be no space between the \\ and the [character delimiting the optional argument). The vertical spaces before and after each display environment are controlled by the following rubber lengths, where the values in parentheses are those for \normalsize with the (default) 10pt option in the standard LaTeX classes[1]:

Space within the display...

...and around the display

\abovedisplayskip, \belowdisplayskip   The normal vertical space added above and below a mathematical display (default 10pt plus 2pt minus 5pt).

\abovedisplayshortskip, \belowdisplayshortskip   The (usually smaller) vertical space added above and below a "short display" (0pt plus 3pt and 6pt plus 3pt minus 3pt, respectively). A *short display* is one that starts to the right of where the preceding text line ends.

If you look closely, you can observe the results of these space parameters in the following example. The second equation is surrounded by less space because the text

---

[1]These defaults are very much improved by the $\mathcal{A}_{\mathcal{M}}$S-LaTeX document classes.

in front of it does not overlap with the formula.

We now have the following:

$$X = a \qquad a = c$$

and thus we have

$$X = c \tag{1}$$

And now we do not get much space around the display!

```
\usepackage{amsmath}
We now have the following:
\[ X = a \qquad  a = c \]
and thus we have
\begin{equation}  X = c \end{equation}
And now we do not get much space
around the display!
```

11-2-24

Since the four parameters \abovedisplay.. and \belowdisplay.. depend on the current font size, they cannot be modified in the preamble of the document using \setlength. Instead, they must be changed by modifying \normalsize, \small, and similar commands—a job usually done in a document class. More precisely, they can be changed mid-document, but their change survives only until the next font sizing command. This also explains why a change in the preamble has no effect: at \begin{document} a call to \normalsize is executed.

Be wary of empty lines around displays

Many authors wisely use empty lines between major structures in the document source to make it more readable. In most cases, such as before and after a heading, these empty lines do no harm. This is not universally true, however. Especially around and within mathematical display environments, one has to be quite careful: a blank line in front of such an environment produces unexpected formatting because the empty line is in effect converted into a paragraph containing no text (and so containing just the invisible paragraph indentation box). The following display is consequently surrounded by spaces of size \..displayshortskip. Thus, the combined result is quite a lot of (possibly too much) space before the display (a whole empty line plus the \abovedisplayshortskip) and a very small amount of space after the display, as this example shows. To show the issue more clearly we have internally set both \abovedisplayshortskip and \belowdisplayshortskip to 0pt for the next two examples. As a result there is "just" the empty line above and no space below the two displays.

Empty line before display:

$$a \neq b$$

In both cases, too much space before! ...

$$a \neq b \tag{1}$$

... and not a lot of space after!

```
\usepackage{amsmath}
Empty line before display:

\[ a \neq b   \]

In both cases, too much space before! \ldots

\begin{equation} a \neq b \end{equation}

\ldots\ and not a lot of space after!
```

11-2-25

With the amsmath package loaded, this behavior is exhibited by all the display math environments. Strangely enough, with standard LaTeX the \[case comes out looking more or less right. The reason is that standard LaTeX pretends that an empty line in front of a \[...\] display (but only for that one) has no height but a large width. It therefore overlaps with the formula, and thus \abovedisplayskip and \belowdisplayskip are applied.

Empty line before display:	% The behavior without amsmath Empty line before display:
$$a \neq b$$	\[a \neq b \]
Enough space now, but do not rely on it!	Enough space now, but do not rely on it!
$$a \neq b \qquad (1)$$	\begin{equation} a \neq b \end{equation}
Less space after in this case!	Less space after in this case!

11-2-26

To summarize, do not use empty lines around display environments! If you want a visual separation in your source, use an empty line with a % inside instead.

Sometimes the lines in a display appear to be too close together and you want to set them slightly farther apart. For individual lines this can be done with the optional argument to \\, but if several lines are involved, it is more efficient to use the spreadlines environment offered by the mathtools package. It expects one argument and opens up all display lines in its scope by the specified amount.

mathtools addition to amsmath

A gather with normal spacing:	
$$A = \sum_{i=1}^{n} x_i \qquad (1)$$	\usepackage{mathtools} A \texttt{gather} with normal spacing:
$$B = x_1 + x_2 + x_3 \qquad (2)$$	\begin{gather} A=\sum_{i=1}^n x_i \\ B = x_1 + x_2 + x_3 \end{gather}
And now spread farther apart:	And now spread farther apart:
$$A = \sum_{i=1}^{n} x_i \qquad (3)$$	\begin{spreadlines}{15pt} \begin{gather}
$$B = x_1 + x_2 + x_3 \qquad (4)$$	A=\sum_{i=1}^n x_i \\ B = x_1 + x_2 + x_3 \end{gather} \end{spreadlines}

11-2-27

11.2.11 Page breaks in and around displays

Automatic page breaking before and after each display environment is controlled by the penalty parameters \predisplaypenalty (for breaking before a display; default 10000, i.e., no break allowed) and \postdisplaypenalty (for breaking after a display, default 0; i.e., break allowed). The defaults are already set in standard LaTeX and are not changed by amsmath.

Page breaks around the display...

...and within the display

Unlike standard LaTeX, the amsmath display environments do not, by default, allow page breaks between lines of the display. The reason for this behavior is that correct page breaks in such locations depend heavily on the structure of the display, so they often require individual attention from the author.

With amsmath such individual control of page breaks is best achieved via the `\displaybreak` command, but it should be used only when absolutely necessary to allow a page break within a display. The command must go before the `\\`, at which a break may be taken, and it applies only to that line and can be used only within an environment that produces a complete display. Somewhat like standard LaTeX's `\pagebreak` (see Section 6.2.2 in [56]), `\displaybreak` takes an optional integer as its argument, with a value ranging from zero to four, denoting the desirability of the page break: `\displaybreak[0]` means "it is permissible to break here" without encouraging a break; `\displaybreak` with no optional argument is the same as `\displaybreak[4]` and forces a break. This command cannot be used to discourage or prevent page breaks. Note that it makes no sense to break within a "mini-page display", as those environments should never be split over two pages.

This kind of adjustment is fine-tuning, like the insertion of line breaks and page breaks in text. It should therefore be left until your document is nearly finalized. Otherwise, you may end up redoing the fine-tuning several times to keep up with changing document content.

The command `\allowdisplaybreaks`, which obeys the usual LaTeX scoping rules, is equivalent to putting `\displaybreak[0]` before every line end in any display environment within its scope; i.e., it allows page breaks anywhere in the math displays. The command can take an optional argument for finer control: [1] means allow page breaks but avoid them as far as possible, while [2] to [4] allow breaks with increasing permissiveness. Within the scope of an `\allowdisplaybreaks` command, the `\\*` command can be used to prohibit a page break and individual `\displaybreak` commands override both the default and the effect of an `\allowdisplaybreaks`.

11.2.12 breqn — Automatic line breaking in math displays

Shortly before his early death, Michael Downes (1958–2003) started to develop a sophisticated package for automatic line breaking in display math equations. Morten Høgholm adopted this code and made it available to the general public. These days it is maintained by him and Will Robertson.

> `\begin{dmath}` [*key/value list*]   *formula*   `\end{dmath}`

The `dmath` environment corresponds to the `equation` environment with the difference that it automatically breaks the *formula* into different lines if necessary and aligns them at relation symbols or binary symbols (but then indented). There also exists a `dmath*` version that omits the equation number, i.e., it corresponds to amsmath's `equation*` environment. With the help of the optional *key/value list*, several aspects of the display can be adjusted.

As a teaser we repeat Example 11-2-9 from page 136 but now use `dmath` instead of `split`. As you can see, the source gets much simpler now (relatively speaking), because we do not have to define alignment points, line breaks, extra \phantoms, etc., to get the formula adequately broken across several lines. All that is done automatically behind the scenes by the package.

If you compare the output of the two examples, you see that they are almost identical. The most noticeable difference is the move of the + from the end of the second line to the third, but this is arguably even better than our manual layout in Example 11-2-9.

```
\usepackage{breqn}
\newcommand\ve{\varepsilon}    \newcommand\tve{t_{\varepsilon}}
\newcommand\vf{\varphi}        \newcommand\yvf{y_{\varphi}}
\newcommand\bfE{\mathbf{E}}
  \begin{dmath}
    f_{h, \ve}(x, y)
    = \ve \bfE_{x, y} \int_0^{\tve} L_{x, \yvf(\ve u)} \vf(x) \,du
    = h \int L_{x, z} \vf(x) \rho_x(dz) + h
    \biggl[ \frac{1}{\tve}
      \biggl( \bfE_{y} \int_0^{\tve}  L_{x, y^x(s)} \vf(x) \,ds
      - \tve \int L_{x, z} \vf(x) \rho_x(dz)        \biggr)
      + \frac{1}{\tve}
      \biggl( \bfE_{y} \int_0^{\tve}  L_{x, y^x(s)} \vf(x) \,ds
      - \bfE_{x, y} \int_0^{\tve} L_{x, \yvf(\ve s)}
      \vf(x) \,ds      \biggr) \biggr]
  \end{dmath}
```

11-2-28

$$f_{h,\varepsilon}(x,y) = \varepsilon \mathbf{E}_{x,y} \int_0^{t_\varepsilon} L_{x,y_\varphi(\varepsilon u)}\varphi(x)\,du$$

$$= h \int L_{x,z}\varphi(x)\rho_x(dz)$$

$$+ h\left[\frac{1}{t_\varepsilon}\left(\mathbf{E}_y \int_0^{t_\varepsilon} L_{x,y^x(s)}\varphi(x)\,ds - t_\varepsilon \int L_{x,z}\varphi(x)\rho_x(dz)\right)\right.$$

$$\left.+ \frac{1}{t_\varepsilon}\left(\mathbf{E}_y \int_0^{t_\varepsilon} L_{x,y^x(s)}\varphi(x)\,ds - \mathbf{E}_{x,y}\int_0^{t_\varepsilon} L_{x,y_\varphi(\varepsilon s)}\varphi(x)\,ds\right)\right]$$

(1)

By default `breqn` breaks and aligns the formula on the first relation symbol, which may not be the optimal choice if there are several relation symbols in quick succession as in the next example:

11-2-29

$$0 < x$$
$$= x_0 + x_1 + x_2 + x_3 + \cdots + x_{n-1} + x_n$$

(1)

```
\usepackage{breqn}
  \begin{dmath} 0 < x =
    x_0 + x_1 + x_2 + x_3 + \dots + x_{n-1} + x_n
  \end{dmath}
```

For this problem breqn offers two solutions. With \hiderel you can hide a relation symbol so that it is not considered as a potential break and alignment point. The result is shown in the next example:

$$0 < x = x_0 + x_1 + x_2 + x_3 \\ + \cdots + x_{n-1} + x_n \qquad (1)$$

```
\usepackage{breqn}

\begin{dmath}
    0 \hiderel{<} x =
    x_0 + x_1 + x_2 + x_3 + \dots + x_{n-1} + x_n
\end{dmath}
```

11-2-30

Alternatively, you can use the key `compact` that directs the environment to fill the lines as best as possible without attempting to align them at relation symbols. In the example we also used the key `spread` to ask for some extra line separation. There are several other keys available; see the package documentation [28] for details.

$$0 < x = x_0 + x_1 + x_2 + x_3 \\ + \cdots + x_{n-1} + x_n \qquad (1)$$

```
\usepackage{breqn}

\begin{dmath}[compact,spread=1pt]
    0 < x =
    x_0 + x_1 + x_2 + x_3 + \dots + x_{n-1} + x_n
\end{dmath}
```

11-2-31

Multiformula displays do not work

The `dmath` environment assumes that it contains only a single logical formula and therefore aligns all continuation lines to the right of the relation from the first line. This means that placing several independent formulas into it always comes out wrong, even if you try to add an explicit \\ to indicate the line break. In the latter case $(a - b)^2$ would end on a line by itself, vertically aligned with the equal signs above and below. Bottom line, for such multiformula displays you have to use the grouping environments discussed below and not what is shown in the next example:

A bad result:

$$(a + b)^2 = a^2 + 2ab + b^2 (a - b)^2 \\ = a^2 - 2ab + b^2 \qquad (1)$$

```
\usepackage{breqn}

A bad result:
\begin{dmath}
    (a+b)^2 = a^2 +2ab + b^2    % A \\ is not helping;
                                % see explanation above!
    (a-b)^2 = a^2 -2ab + b^2
\end{dmath}
```

11-2-32

The package offers a number of other environments and commands; we show two of them in the next example.

With the environment `dgroup*` you can group a number of `dmath` or `dmath*` environments; the result is comparable to amsmath's `align` environment with one alignment point. If instead you use `dgroup`, then the whole group uses one equation number with subnumbering applied, i.e., (1a), (1b), etc.

Also shown is \condition, which is similar to the \text command but automatically adds punctuation and extra spacing.

11-2-33

$$(a + b)^2 = a^2 + 2ab + b^2 \quad (1)$$
$$(a - b)^2 = a^2 - 2ab + b^2 \quad (2)$$
$$(a + b)(a - b) = a^2 - b^2$$

$$\frac{1}{x}, \quad \text{for } x \neq 0 \quad (3)$$

```
\usepackage{breqn}
\begin{dgroup*}
  \begin{dmath} (a+b)^2 = a^2+2ab+b^2 \end{dmath}
  \begin{dmath} (a-b)^2 = a^2-2ab+b^2 \end{dmath}
  \begin{dmath*} (a+b)(a-b) = a^2-b^2 \end{dmath*}
\end{dgroup*}
\begin{dmath}
  \frac{1}{x} \condition{for $x\ne 0$}
\end{dmath}
```

As you can imagine, the package has to change a lot of the internal code that defines characters for math mode in order to identify which symbols are relations and binary symbols and are therefore candidates for line breaks. This is done in a helper package flexysym that redefines \DeclareMathSymbol among other things. This way packages such as stmaryrd that define additional math symbols can do this in a way that allows them participate in the line-breaking effort of breqn as long as they are loaded after that package. For amssymb and core LaTeX symbols this is not necessary because the package knows about them and does the necessary adjustment regardless of the loading order. More detail is given in the package documentation.

Loading order of math font packages with respect to breqn

While on the whole the package produces impressive results, there are unfortunately a number of cases where it fails or has problems. If you intend to use it, you should read the package documentation [28] carefully to understand the current limitations and the situations where manual breaking of display formulas is simply the safer bet.

11.2.13 Equation numbering and tags

In LaTeX the tags for equations are typically generated automatically and contain a printed representation of the LaTeX counter equation. This involves three processes: setting (normally by incrementing) the value of the equation counter, formatting the tag, and printing it in the correct position.

In practice, the first two processes are nearly always linked. Thus, the value of the equation counter is increased only when a tag containing its representation is automatically printed. For example, when a mathematical display environment has both starred and unstarred forms, the unstarred form automatically tags each logical equation, while the starred form does not. Only in the unstarred form is the value of the equation counter changed.

Within the unstarred forms the setting of a tag (and the incrementing of the counter value) for any particular logical equation can be suppressed by putting \notag (or \nonumber[1]) *before* the \\. You can override the default automatic tag with one of your own design (or provide a new one) by using the command \tag

---

[1] The command \notag is interchangeable with \nonumber.

before the \\. The argument of this command can be arbitrary normal text that is typeset (within the normal parentheses) as the tag for that equation.

Note that the use of \tag suppresses the incrementing of the counter value. Thus, the default tag setting is only visually the same as \tag{\theequation}; they are not equivalent forms. The starred form, \tag*, causes the text in its argument to be typeset without the parentheses (and without any other material that might otherwise be added with a particular document class).

$$x^2 + y^2 = z^2 \qquad (1)$$
$$x^3 + y^3 = z^3$$
$$x^4 + y^4 = r^4 \qquad (*)$$
$$x^5 + y^5 = r^5 \qquad *$$
$$x^6 + y^6 = r^6 \qquad (1')$$

```
\usepackage{amsmath}

\begin{align}
  x^2+y^2 &= z^2 \label{eq:A}        \\
  x^3+y^3 &= z^3 \notag              \\
  x^4+y^4 &= r^4 \tag{$*$}           \\
  x^5+y^5 &= r^5 \tag*{$*$}          \\
  x^6+y^6 &= r^6 \tag{\ref{eq:A}$'$}
\end{align}
```

11-2-34

Notice this example's use of the \label and \ref commands to provide some kinds of "relative numbering" of equations. If you want to repeat the tag number from the previous line with some extra mark, it is, of course, simpler to use \theequation to retrieve it.

$$A_1 = N_0(\lambda; \Omega') - \phi(\lambda; \Omega') \qquad (1)$$
$$A_2 = \phi(\lambda; \Omega')\, \phi(\lambda; \Omega) \qquad \text{ALSO } (1)$$
$$A_3 = \mathcal{N}(\lambda; \omega) \qquad (2)$$

```
\usepackage{amsmath}

\begin{align}
    A_1 &= N_0 (\lambda ; \Omega')
          - \phi ( \lambda ; \Omega') \\
    A_2 &= \phi (\lambda ; \Omega')
           \, \phi (\lambda ; \Omega)
           \tag*{ALSO (\theequation)} \\
    A_3 &= \mathcal{N} (\lambda ; \omega)
\end{align}
```

11-2-35

Referencing equations

To facilitate the creation of cross-references to equations, the \eqref command (used in Example 11-2-40 on page 153) automatically adds the parentheses around the equation number, adding an italic correction if necessary. See also Section 2.4 on page →I 75 for more general solutions to managing references.

11.2.14 Fine-tuning tag placement

Optimal placement of equation number tags can be a rather complex problem in multiple-line displays. These display environments try hard to avoid overprinting an equation number on the equation contents; if necessary, the number tag is moved down or up, onto a separate line. The difficulty of accurately determining the layout of a display can occasionally result in a tag placement that needs further adjustment. Here is an example of the kind of thing that can happen and a strategy for fixing it. The automatic tag placement is clearly not very good.

```
\usepackage{amsmath}
\begin{equation}  \begin{split}
  \lvert I_2 \rvert   &=      \left\lvert \int_{0}^T \psi(t)
     \left\{  u(a, t) - \int_{\gamma(t)}^a \frac{d\theta}{k}
       (\theta, t) \int_{a}^\theta c (\xi) u_t (\xi, t) \,d\xi
     \right\} dt \right\rvert                                    \\
                        &\le  C_6  \Biggl\lvert
     \left\lvert f \int_\Omega \left\lvert
        \widetilde{S}^{-1,0}_{a,-} W_2(\Omega, \Gamma_1)
       \right\rvert \ \right\rvert
     \left\lvert \lvert u \rvert
       \overset{\circ}{\to} W_2^{\widetilde{A}} (\Omega; \Gamma_r,T)
     \right\rvert                 \Biggr\rvert
\end{split} \end{equation}
A line of text after the equation \ldots
```

11-2-36

$$\left| I_2 \right| = \left| \int_0^T \psi(t) \left\{ u(a,t) - \int_{\gamma(t)}^a \frac{d\theta}{k}(\theta,t) \int_a^\theta c(\xi) u_t(\xi,t)\,d\xi \right\} dt \right|$$

$$\le C_6 \left\| f \int_\Omega \left| \widetilde{S}_{a,-}^{-1,0} W_2(\Omega, \Gamma_l) \right| \right\| \left| |u| \overset{\circ}{\to} W_2^{\widetilde{A}}(\Omega; \Gamma_r, T) \right|$$

(1)

A line of text after the equation ...

A fairly easy way to improve the appearance of such an equation is to use an `align` environment instead together with a \notag on the first equation line:

```
\begin{align}
  \lvert I_2 \rvert &= \left\lvert \int_{0}^T \psi(t)
                                              ...       \notag \\
                    &\le  C_6  \Biggl\lvert     ...
\end{align}
```

This produces a good visual result, but note that it misuses logical markup — it assumes the equation numbers to be on the right! It also means that to the system your single equation is represented as two separate equations; i.e., any software that tries to interpret the markup (such as a screen reader) will therefore misunderstand it.

11-2-37

$$\left| I_2 \right| = \left| \int_0^T \psi(t) \left\{ u(a,t) - \int_{\gamma(t)}^a \frac{d\theta}{k}(\theta,t) \int_a^\theta c(\xi) u_t(\xi,t)\,d\xi \right\} dt \right|$$

$$\le C_6 \left\| f \int_\Omega \left| \widetilde{S}_{a,-}^{-1,0} W_2(\Omega, \Gamma_l) \right| \right\| \left| |u| \overset{\circ}{\to} W_2^{\widetilde{A}}(\Omega; \Gamma_r, T) \right| \quad (1)$$

A line of text after the equation ...

As a better alternative the `\raisetag` command is available that adjusts the vertical position of the current equation number but *only* when it has been automatically moved from its "normal position". For example, to move the tag in Example 11-2-36 upward we could have added `\raisetag{21pt}` and achieved the result below without using logically incorrect markup. Finding the appropriate value may need some trials, but once you used the command a couple of times, it is usually easy. Note that the text following will also get closer to the display if the tag is raised.

$$
\left| |I_2| = \left| \int_0^T \psi(t) \left\{ u(a,t) - \int_{\gamma(t)}^a \frac{d\theta}{k}(\theta,t) \int_a^\theta c(\xi) u_t(\xi,t)\, d\xi \right\} dt \right| \right.
$$

$$
\left. \le C_6 \left\| f \int_\Omega \left| \tilde{S}_{a,-}^{-1,0} W_2(\Omega,\Gamma_l) \right| \right\| \left\| |u| \overset{\circ}{\to} W_2^{\tilde{A}}(\Omega;\Gamma_r,T) \right\| \right| \tag{1}
$$

11-2-38

A line of text after the equation …

A different use is shown in the next example, where `\raisetag` with a negative argument is used to move the tag on the left down into the display.

(1)

The sign function: $\mathcal{S}(x) = \begin{cases} -1 & x < 0 \\ 0 & x = 0 \\ 1 & x > 0 \end{cases}$

```
\usepackage[leqno]{amsmath}

\begin{gather}    \raisetag{-10pt}
    \text{The sign function: \ }
        \mathcal{S}(x) =  \begin{cases}
                -1   &  x < 0 \\
                 0   &  x = 0 \\
                 1   &  x > 0
            \end{cases}    \end{gather}
```

11-2-39

Here we used a `gather` environment with a single line because the `equation` environment is (the only) one within which `\raisetag` unfortunately has no effect (it is coded using low-level TEX).

These kinds of adjustment constitute "fine-tuning", like line breaks and page breaks in text. They should therefore be left until your document is nearly finalized. Otherwise, you may end up redoing the fine-tuning several times to keep up with changing document content.

11.2.15 Subordinate numbering sequences

The amsmath package provides a `subequations` environment to support "equation subnumbering" with tags of the form (2a), (2b), (2c), and so on. All the tagged equations within it use this subnumbering scheme based on two normal LATEX counters: `parentequation` and `equation`.

The next example demonstrates that the tag can be redefined to some extent, but note that the redefinition for `\theequation` must appear within the `subequations` environment! (Appendix A.2.1 discusses counter manipulations.)

$$f - y \qquad \text{(1a)}$$
$$f' = g' \qquad \text{(1b)}$$
$$\mathcal{L}f = \mathcal{L}g \qquad \text{(1c)}$$

$$f = g \qquad \text{(2i)}$$
$$f' = g' \qquad \text{(2ii)}$$
$$\mathcal{L}f = \mathcal{L}g + K \qquad \text{(2iii)}$$

Note the relationship between (1) and (2): only 1c and 2iii differ.

```
\usepackage{amsmath}
\begin{subequations}  \label{eq:1}
\begin{align}  f  &= g              \label{eq:1A} \\
               f' &= g'             \label{eq:1B} \\
      \mathcal{L}f  &= \mathcal{L}g \label{eq:1C}
\end{align}
\end{subequations}
\begin{subequations}  \label{eq:2}
\renewcommand\theequation
          {\theparentequation\roman{equation}}
\begin{align}  f  &= g              \label{eq:2A} \\
               f' &= g'             \label{eq:2B} \\
      \mathcal{L}f  &= \mathcal{L}g + K  \label{eq:2C}
\end{align}
\end{subequations}
Note the relationship between~\eqref{eq:1}
and~\eqref{eq:2}: only~\ref{eq:1C} and~\ref{eq:2C} differ.
```

11-2-40

The `subequations` environment must appear *outside* the displays that it affects. Also, it should not be nested within itself. Each use of this environment advances the "main" equation counter by one. A `\label` command within the `subequations` environment but outside any individual (logical) equation produces a `\ref` to the parent number (e.g., to 2 rather than 2i).

11.2.16 Resetting the equation counter

It is a fairly common practice to have equations numbered within sections or chapters, using tags such as (1.1), (1.2), ..., (2.1), (2.2), ... These days this can be easily set up with standard LaTeX by using the declaration `\counterwithin`.[1]

For example, to get compound equation tags including the section number, with the equation counter being automatically reset for each section, put this declaration in the preamble: `\counterwithin{equation}{section}`.

Sometimes such a setup is already done by the document class you use, e.g., the report or book classes of standard LaTeX number equations per chapter. If you would like to undo such a setting, use `\counterwithout`.

11.3 Matrix-like environments

The amsmath package offers a number of matrix-like environments, all of which are similar to `array` in syntax and layout. Thinking of complex mathematical layouts in

---

[1]As the name implies, `\counterwithin` can be applied to any pair of counters, but the results may not be satisfactory in all cases because of potential complications. See the explanations in Appendix A.2.1 where these commands are further discussed.

this way is a useful exercise, as quite a wide variety of two-dimensional mathematical structures and table-like layouts can be described like this.

Three of these environments replace old commands that are kept well hidden in standard LATEX: matrix and pmatrix (discussed in the next section) and cases (discussed in the section after that). Because these old command forms use a totally different notation inherited from plain TEX, they are not truly part of LATEX, and they cannot be mixed with the environment forms described here. Indeed, amsmath produces an explanatory error message if one of the old commands is used (see page 735). If, contrariwise, you make the mistake of using the amsmath environment forms without loading that package, then you most probably get this error message: "Misplaced alignment tab character &".

Old "plain TEX" commands disabled

With delarray and bigdelim, two further packages are described that allow placing various delimiters around and within matrix-like structures. The section concludes with a discussion of two commutative diagram packages: amscd and tikz-cd.

11.3.1 amsmath, mathtools — The matrix environments

The matrix environments are similar to LATEX's array, except that they do not have an argument specifying the formats of the columns. Instead, a default format is provided: up to ten centered columns. Also, the spacing differs slightly from the default in array. The example below illustrates the matrix environments matrix, pmatrix, bmatrix, Bmatrix, vmatrix, and Vmatrix[1]:

$$\begin{matrix} 0 & 1 \\ 1 & 0 \end{matrix} \quad \begin{pmatrix} 0 & -i \\ i & 0 \end{pmatrix}$$

$$\begin{bmatrix} 0 & -1 \\ 1 & 0 \end{bmatrix} \quad \begin{Bmatrix} 1 & 0 \\ 0 & -1 \end{Bmatrix}$$

$$\begin{vmatrix} a & b \\ c & d \end{vmatrix} \quad \begin{Vmatrix} i & 0 \\ 0 & -i \end{Vmatrix}$$

```
\usepackage{amsmath}
\begin{gather*}
  \begin{matrix}  0 &  1 \\ 1 &  0 \end{matrix}  \quad
  \begin{pmatrix} 0 & -i \\ i &  0 \end{pmatrix}
\\[10pt]
  \begin{bmatrix} 0 & -1 \\ 1 &  0 \end{bmatrix} \quad
  \begin{Bmatrix} 1 &  0 \\ 0 & -1 \end{Bmatrix}
\\[10pt]
  \begin{vmatrix} a &  b \\ c &  d \end{vmatrix} \quad
  \begin{Vmatrix} i &  0 \\ 0 & -i \end{Vmatrix}
\end{gather*}
```

11-3-1

As in standard arrays, the amount of space between the columns is given by the value of \arraycolsep, but no space is added on either side of the array.

The maximum number of columns in a matrix environment is determined by the counter MaxMatrixCols, which you can change using LATEX's standard counter commands. With more columns LATEX has to work a little harder and needs slightly more resources. However, with today's typical TEX implementations, such limits are less important, so setting MaxMatrixCols to 20 or higher is possible without a noticeable change in processing speed.

---

[1] Note the warning above about possible problems when using matrix and pmatrix.

```
\usepackage{amsmath}
\setcounter{MaxMatrixCols}{20}
\[
\begin{Vmatrix}
 \,,a&b&c&d&e&f&g&h&i&j &\cdots\,{} \\
    &a&b&c&d&e&f&g&h&i &\cdots\,{} \\
    & &a&b&c&d&e&f&g&h &\cdots\,{} \\
    & & &a&b&c&d&e&f&g &\cdots\,{} \\
    & & & &\ddots&\ddots&\hdotsfor[2]{5}\,{}
\end{Vmatrix} \]
```

This example also demonstrates the use of the command \hdotsfor to produce a row of dots in a matrix, spanning a given number of columns (here 5). The spacing of the dots can be varied by using the optional parameter (here 2) to specify a multiplier for the default space between the dots; the default space between dots is 3 math units (see Appendix A.2.4). The thin space and the brace group {} at the end of each row simply make the layout look better; together they produce two thin spaces, about 6mu or 1/3em. (Spacing in formulas is discussed in more detail in Section 11.7.7 on page 204.)

The amsmath matrix environment always centers the cell contents. As this is not always appropriate, the mathtools package adds starred forms of the environments that enable you to alter that behavior on a case-by-case basis.

mathtools additions to amsmath

```
\begin{matrix*}[col-align]   content  \end{matrix*}
\begin{pmatrix*}[col-align]  content  \end{pmatrix*}
    ⋮
\begin{Vmatrix*}[col-align]  content  \end{Vmatrix*}
```

All the environments have an additional optional *col-align* argument that specifies the column alignment. Allowed values are l, r, or c (default; i.e., if the optional argument is omitted, the starred environments behave like their unstarred variants).

To produce a small matrix suitable for use in text, use the smallmatrix environment. Note that the text lines are not spread apart even though the line before the small matrix contains words with descenders.

To show the effect of the matrix on surrounding lines inside a paragraph, we put it here $\left(\begin{smallmatrix} -1 & 0 \\ 0 & -1 \end{smallmatrix}\right)$ and follow it with some more text on the next line.

```
\usepackage{amsmath}
To show the effect of the matrix on surrounding
lines inside a paragraph, we put it here
$\left(\begin{smallmatrix}
        -1 & 0 \\ 0 & -1 \end{smallmatrix}\right)$
and follow it with some more text on the next line.
```

Again, mathtools provides a corresponding starred environment smallmatrix* that allows altering the column alignments and also typesets the fencing delimiters automatically if you precede the environment name (starred or nonstarred form) with p (parentheses), b (brackets), B (braces), v (vertical bars), or V (double vertical

Another set of mathtools additions

bars). We repeat the previous example but use braces as delimiters and right-align the columns:

```
\usepackage{mathtools}
```

To show the effect of the matrix on surrounding lines inside a paragraph, we put it here $\left\{\begin{smallmatrix} -1 & 0 \\ 0 & -1 \end{smallmatrix}\right\}$ and follow it with some more text on the next line.

```
To show the effect of the matrix on surrounding
lines inside a paragraph, we put it here
$\begin{Bsmallmatrix*}[r]
    -1 & 0 \\ 0 & -1 \end{Bsmallmatrix*}$
and follow it with some more text on the next line.
```

11-3-4

11.3.2 amsmath, mathtools, cases — Some case environments

Constructions like the following, where a single equation has a few variants, are very common in mathematics. To handle these constructions, amsmath provides the cases environment. It produces a decorated array with two columns, both left aligned.

$$P_{r-j} = \begin{cases} 0 & \text{if } r - j \text{ is odd,} \\ r! \, (-1)^{(r-j)/2} & \text{if } r - j \text{ is even.} \end{cases} \tag{1}$$

```
\usepackage{amsmath}
\begin{equation}        P_{r - j} =
\begin{cases}
    0   & \text{if $r - j$ is odd,} \\
    r! \, (-1)^{(r - j)/2}
        & \text{if $r - j$ is even.}
\end{cases}             \end{equation}
```

11-3-5

Even though the right-most column usually contains explanatory text, it is processed in math mode. We therefore have to use \text with "embedded math mode" in the text strings as needed. The equation number is supplied by the outer environment: the individual cases are not labeled.

mathtools additions to amsmath

The lines of the cases environments are processed in \textstyle, which may not be appropriate, if they contain operators taking limits. For this reason the mathtools packages defines dcases that works like cases but uses \displaystyle throughout. It also offers rcases and drcases that place the brace to the right instead of the left.

Thus, instead of defining rcases manually with the help of the aligned environment as we did in Example 11-2-19 on page 141, we could have used the mathtools environment directly:

$$\left. \begin{aligned} \boldsymbol{B}' &= -c\nabla \times \boldsymbol{E} \\ \boldsymbol{E}' &= c\nabla \times \boldsymbol{B} - 4\pi\boldsymbol{J} \end{aligned} \right\} \text{ Maxwell}$$

```
\usepackage{mathtools,bm}
\begin{equation*} \begin{rcases}
    \bm{B}' = -c\nabla\times\bm{E}              \\
    \bm{E}' =  c\nabla\times\bm{B} - 4\pi\bm{J}\,,
\end{rcases} \enspace \text{Maxwell}
\end{equation*}
```

11-3-6

To support the common situation that the explanation column contains text rather than a formula, mathtools also defines starred versions of all four environments that typeset only their first column in math mode.

An alternative approach is provided by the small package cases by Donald Arseneau. It defines two environments, numcases and subnumcases, that allow you to number each case with an equation (or subequation) number. Since they produce equation numbers, they are standalone display environments similar to align, whereas cases is like aligned, i.e., needs an outer environment such as equation.

The approach taken by the cases package

The material to the left of the cases is specified as an argument to the environment: the body then holds the different case lines. In contrast to the cases environment from amsmath, the "explanation" column is treated as text. Thus, there is no need to add \text as we had to in the previous example. Of course, if most of your explanations are mathematically stated, then you have to supply $ signs each time.

If you want to omit an equation number on one line, you can use \nonumber before the \\. If the amsmath package is also loaded, then \notag works as well, and \tag can be used to manually specify a tag.

$$f(x) = \begin{cases} -1 & \text{if } x < 0, \\ 0 & \text{if } x = 0, \\ 1 & \text{if } x > 0. \end{cases}$$

(1a)
(∗)
(1b)

Reference to a subequation (1b) and to the overall equation (1) are possible.

```
\usepackage{amsmath,cases}
\begin{subnumcases}{f(x) = \label{L1}}
   -1  &  if $x<0$\,,                       \\
    0  &  if $x=0$\,,       \tag{$*$}       \\
    1  &  if $x>0$\,.       \label{L2}
\end{subnumcases}
Reference to a subequation \eqref{L2} and to
the overall equation \eqref{L1} are possible.
```

11-3-7

As seen in the previous example, referencing the individual case numbers is done by placing a \label on the appropriate line. In the case of subnumbering, you can also refer to the main equation number (even though it is not shown) by placing the \label into the argument of the environment. When referencing, you can use \ref or \pageref as usual: in the example we used \eqref from the amsmath package.

Besides handling equation numbers differently, there is also a noticeable difference in spacing: the left brace has more space around it, and the space between the two columns is noticeably larger. What looks better is certainly a matter of opinion; personally I prefer Donald's style over the more cramped amsmath one.

Given that one may want to use both subnumcases and cases in the same document, the cases package offers a number of options to bring both approaches closer together: amsstyle switches to the cramped spacing and treats the explanations as math, while casesstyle defines or redefines the cases environment in the style of the cases package, e.g., with more space and the explanations in text mode.

Altering the style

Finally, there is a subnum option that treats all numcases environments as subnumcases.

11.3.3 delarray — Delimiters surrounding an array

This section describes a useful general extension to the array package (see Section 6.2 on page →I 437) that allows the user to specify opening and closing extensible delimiters (see Section 11.5.6) to surround a mathematical array environment. The delarray package was written by David Carlisle, and its use is illustrated in the next, rather odd-looking, example (note that the delarray package is independent of amsmath, but it automatically loads the array package if necessary).

$$\left| Q = (\ X \quad Y \ ) \begin{bmatrix} A & B \\ C & D \end{bmatrix} \left(\begin{array}{c} L \\ M \end{array} \right) \right|$$

```
\usepackage{delarray}
\[ \mathcal{Q} =
\begin{array}[t] ( {cc} ) X & Y \end{array}
\begin{array}[t] [ {cc} ] A & B \\ C & D  \end{array}
\begin{array}[b] \lgroup{c}\rgroup L \\ M \end{array}
\]
```

11-3-8

The delimiters are placed on either side of the "preamble declaration" (here {cc}). They must be delimiters from Table 11.5 on page 190.

The most useful feature of this package is also illustrated in the preceding example: the use of the [t] and [b] optional arguments, which are not available with amsmath's matrix environments. These show that the use of the delarray syntax is not equivalent to surrounding the array environment with \left and \right, because the delimiters are raised as well as the array itself.

11.3.4 bigdelim — Delimiters around and inside arrays

A different way of adding braces or other delimiters to arrays (or tabular structures) is provided by Pieter van Oostrum with the bigdelim package, which is based on his multirow package. In contrast to delarray where the delimiters are specified as part of the overall array specification or the matrix environment from amsmath where the environment name defines the used delimiters, this package requires dedicated array cells to be reserved for receiving the delimiters. Thus, if you want to build a three-column matrix surrounded by parentheses, you need to specify a five-column array, in which the first and last columns are there just to receive the delimiters.

If you think this is more work than with the other approaches, then this is a correct observation. However, while slightly more work, it also offers you more freedom in placement; e.g., you can let the delimiter embrace only some of the rows or even put a delimiter right in the middle of your array. Furthermore, you can attach material at the outside of the delimiter centered on its height, which is sometimes useful.

\ldelim{*delim*}[*vmove*]{*rows*}{*width*}[*text*]
\rdelim{*delim*}[*vmove*]{*rows*}{*width*}[*text*]

The two commands provided by the package are \ldelim and \rdelim. Their first argument is the *delim*iter to be placed, which can be any delimiter from Table 11.5 on page 190 that can vertically grow to arbitrary sizes.

In *rows* you specify how many rows this delimiter should span. The delimiter is placed starting in the cell where the command is used and extending the specified number of *rows* downwards. If the *rows* value is negative, it extends upwards. This can be useful in conjunction with colored tables (e.g., when using the colortbl package) because the delimiter is then placed on top of the already colored rows. Otherwise, color in later rows would come on top of the delimiter and thus effectively hide it.

With the optional *vmove* argument you can fine-tune the vertical position. If your rows are unusually high, you may have to slightly enlarge the *row* value (which can take fractional values) above the nominal number of rows to span.

In *width* you specify the space the delimiter and any *text* (if present) can take up. If you make that too small, you get an overfull box warning, and the material sticks out to the right; if you make it larger than the needed space, you will effectively produce white space at the right side of the delimiter. In some cases, that can be useful, but usually it is best to simply put a * into this argument, which tells the command to use the natural width.[1] Finally, there is an optional *text* argument. If present, the *text* is placed vertically centered next to the delimiter, for \ldelim on the left and for \rdelim on the right.

In the next example we place two delimiters on the right, each covering only some of the rows. Note that we horizontally shifted one to the right so that they do not overprint each other. The brace on the left is printed starting from the last row to show how this is done. Also interesting is the array preamble where we used @{\,} between the data columns and the columns for the delimiters. This suppresses the usual separation between array rows and instead inserts only a tiny space.

11-3-9

$$\text{This is}\begin{cases}\begin{bmatrix}1 & 2 & 3 \\ 0 & 1 & 2 \\ 0 & 0 & 1 \\ 0 & 0 & 0 \\ & \Delta\end{bmatrix}\begin{matrix}\ \\ \left.\vphantom{\begin{matrix}1\\0\\0\end{matrix}}\right\}\text{quite}\\ \\ \left.\vphantom{\begin{matrix}1\\0\end{matrix}}\right\}\text{special}\\ \\ \end{matrix}\end{cases} \quad (1)$$

```
\usepackage{bigdelim}
\begin{equation}
  \begin{array}{r@{\,}ccc@{\,}l}
    & 1 & 2 & 3 & \hspace{2mm}\rdelim]{3}{*}[quite]  \\
    & 0 & 1 & 2 &                                    \\
    & 0 & 0 & 1 & \rdelim]{3}{*}[special]            \\
    & 0 & 0 & 0 &                                    \\
  \ldelim\{{-5}{*}[This is] & & \Delta     \end{array}
\end{equation}
```

11.3.5 Commutative diagrams with standard LaTeX

Simple commutative diagrams can in principle be produced by using an array environment and placing elements and arrows into appropriate cells. Of course, this allows only for horizontal and vertical connectors, and as you see in the next example, the results are only modestly satisfying, while the input is rather complex and difficult to read.

11-3-10

$$\begin{array}{ccc} S^{\mathcal{W}_\Lambda} \otimes T & \stackrel{j}{\longrightarrow} & T \\ \Big\downarrow & & \Big\downarrow \text{End } P \\ (S \otimes T)/I & = & (Z \otimes T)/J \end{array}$$

```
\[\begin{array}{ccc}
  S^{\mathcal{W}_\Lambda}\otimes T &
    \stackrel{j}{\longrightarrow}  &     T \\
  \Big\downarrow                   & &
  \Big\downarrow\vcenter{%
    \rlap{$\scriptstyle{\mathrm{End}}\,P$}}  \\
  (S\otimes T)/I                  & = & (Z\otimes T)/J
\end{array}\]
```

---

[1] This argument is inherited from \multirow where it makes much more sense to be able to specify a width. It would have made the usage simpler to hide it and internally always pass on *. But given that it is there, you can perhaps sometimes use it to your advantage.

The `picture` environment could in theory be used for more complex commutative diagrams, but in practice this is the wrong tool as any changes in the diagram would require extensive manual recalculations of coordinates.

Fortunately, there are a number of specialized packages for producing sophisticated and beautiful diagrams, among them Kristoffer Rose's (1965–2016) XY-pic system and its extension [7] by Michael Barr (see [31, Chapter 7]).

For this book we selected two packages. One is the `amscd` package for producing simple commutative diagrams like the one from the previous example. The other package that allows for arbitrarily complex diagrams is tikz-cd, discussed at the end of the section.

11.3.6 amscd — Commutative diagrams a là AMS

Being based on the `array` environment, the `amscd` package allows only for horizontal and vertical connectors. It provides some useful shorthand forms for specifying the decorated arrows and other connectors, which makes the input easier and the results nicer, but otherwise it does not offer new features compared to standard LaTeX.

In the CD environment the notations `@>>>`, `@<<<`, `@VVV`, and `@AAA` give right, left, down, and up arrows, respectively. The following examples also show the use of the command `\DeclareMathOperator` (see Section 11.6.2):

$$
\begin{array}{ccccc}
\mathrm{cov}(L) & \longrightarrow & \mathrm{non}(K) & \longrightarrow & \mathrm{cf}(K) \\
\downarrow & & \uparrow & & \uparrow \\
\mathrm{add}(L) & \longrightarrow & \mathrm{add}(K) & \longrightarrow & \mathrm{cov}(K)
\end{array}
$$

```
\usepackage{amsmath,amscd}
\DeclareMathOperator\add{add}
\DeclareMathOperator\cf {cf}
\DeclareMathOperator\cov{cov}
\DeclareMathOperator\non{non}
\[ \begin{CD}
    \cov (L) @>>> \non (K) @>>> \cf (K)  \\
    @VVV            @AAA           @AAA   \\
    \add (L) @>>> \add (K) @>>> \cov (K) \\
\end{CD} \]
```

11-3-11

Decorations on the arrows are specified as follows. For the horizontal arrows, material between the first and second > or < symbols is typeset as a superscript, and material between the second and third is typeset as a subscript. Similarly, material between the first and second, or second and third, As or Vs of vertical arrows is typeset as left or right "side-scripts"; this format is used in the next example to place the operator End P to the right of the arrow. The notations `@=` and `@|` give horizontal and vertical double lines. A "null arrow" (produced by `@.`) can be used instead of a visible arrow to fill out an array cell where needed.

$$
\begin{array}{ccc}
S^{W_\Lambda} \otimes T & \xrightarrow{j} & T \\
\downarrow & & \downarrow{\scriptstyle \mathrm{End}\,P} \\
(S \otimes T)/I & =\!\!=\!\!= & (Z \otimes T)/J
\end{array}
$$

```
\usepackage{amsmath,amscd} \DeclareMathOperator{\End}{End}
\[ \begin{CD}
    S^{W_\Lambda}\otimes T @>j>>        T         \\
    @VVV                        @VV{\End P}V \\
    (S \otimes T)/I            @=    (Z\otimes T)/J
\end{CD} \]
```

11-3-12

If you compare this to Example 11-3-10, it shows clearly how much better the results are with the amscd package: the notation is enormously easier and, for example, the package produces longer horizontal arrows and much improved spacing between elements of the diagram. The more specialized packages enable you to get even more beautiful results, as we see exemplified in the next section.

11.3.7 tikz-cd — Commutative diagrams based on tikz

The tikz-cd package by Augusto Stoffel is one of the more recent additions in the area of specialized packages for drawing and enables you to easily prepare arbitrarily complex commutative diagrams. It is based on the powerful tikz system for drawing[1] and is able to harness all of its powers if needed. Nevertheless, its input syntax is easy to learn, and the diagram sources are understandable, even without knowing the details of the package syntax as you will see below.

The package provides the environment tikzcd for producing diagrams. Inside, elements are laid out in a grid separated by &, and rows are separated by \\ as usual. For specifying "arrows" between different element there is the command \arrow or its short form \ar if you do not like typing long command names.

> \arrow[*options*]   or   \ar[*options*]

While the *options* argument is specified in brackets, it is not optional, because you need to specify at least the target direction through a combination of l, r, u, or d characters (for left, right, up, or down). For example, to have an arrow from the first element in the first row to the third element in the second row, you would specify rrd. Specifying labels for the arrows is done by surrounding their text with "⟨*math*⟩" (typeset in math mode), and if you require a special arrow form, there is a multitude of keywords to adjust the shape, etc.

These basic features are exhibited in the next example where we reimplement Example 11-3-10 once more.

11-3-13

$$S^{W_\Lambda} \otimes T \xrightarrow{\;\;j\;\;} T$$
$$\downarrow \qquad\qquad \downarrow {\scriptstyle \mathrm{End}\,P}$$
$$(S \otimes T)/I == (Z \otimes T)/J$$

```
\usepackage{amsmath,tikz-cd}
\DeclareMathOperator\End{End}
\begin{tikzcd}
  S^{W_\Lambda}\otimes T \arrow[r, "j"] \arrow[d] &
        T \arrow[d, "\End P"]    \\
  (S \otimes T)/I  \arrow[r, equal] & (Z\otimes T)/J
\end{tikzcd}
```

The tikzcd environment can be used inside or outside of math mode; e.g., if you need an equation number, place it into an equation environment. If used by its own, it does not add any vertical spacing and does not end the current paragraph, which explains the offset in the above example — the paragraph indentation. Thus, it is usually best to place it into \[...\] or equation to achieve a consistent look and feel. However, it is unfortunately not possible to use it in environments that process

Ⓢ *Restrictions with some math display environments*

---

[1]See Section 8.5 on page →I 631 for further information on the tikz package.

their content several times to determine the final layout. This includes some of the other math display environments such as `align` or `gather`.

The number of keywords that can be used is quite large, so here we show only a small but hopefully useful fraction of them. If you need more, consult the nice manual [87]. As a teaser we show two more examples exhibiting several options. They are modified examples taken from the manual to show you most common variants. New features in the first one are several keywords for specifying different arrow shapes[1], some useful label placement options such as `near␣start`, the ' syntax that moves a label to the "other" side of the arrow, and ways to make simple curved arrows with `bend␣left` or `bend␣right`.

The `description` key places the label on top of the arrow. Note that this key should act on the label so should follow the label without a comma.

Finally, the package understands basic color names (and more can be defined). Such colors can be applied to just the label (e.g., the y in the example) or to the whole arrow *and* its labels, (as done for the downward arrows). To just get an arrow colored but not its labels you need to undo the coloring inside the label, which is why we explicitly made F black again to show how this can be done.

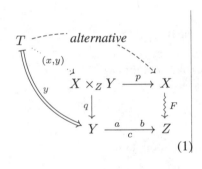

(1)

```
\usepackage{tikz-cd}
\usetikzlibrary{decorations.pathmorphing}

\begin{equation}
  \begin{tikzcd}
  T \arrow[drr, dashrightarrow, bend left,
          "\textit{alternative}" description]
    \arrow[ddr, Mapsto, bend right, "y" blue]
    \arrow[dr, dotted, "{(x,y)}" description] & &   \\
    & X \times_Z Y \arrow[r, "p"] \arrow[d, blue, "q"']
      & X \arrow[d, rightsquigarrow, blue, "F" black] \\
    & Y \arrow[r, "a" near start, "c"', "b" near end] & Z
  \end{tikzcd}
\end{equation}
```

11-3-14

The final example shows that it is possible to apply the full power of tikz in specifying arrows. If you use other tikz-based packages more regularly, you probably immediately recognize the features; otherwise, take them as something to explore further if needed, because you will probably seldom need strange paths in your commutative diagrams. However, looping arrows are more common; we show two variants below. The other possible keywords for loops are not surprisingly called `loop␣left` and `loop␣down`.

The `dash` key is an arrow shape without head or tail, i.e., a straight line; `dotted` is a modifier that uses dots on the stem. A `hook` modifies the tail, and if you append a ', the hook goes into the opposite direction. In a similar fashion, `two␣heads` modifies the head. Arrows can start at empty cells, but they need to end at a cell with content, which is why we had to place something invisible into the top-right corner.

---

[1]Using the `rightsquigarrow` shape requires you to load an additional tikz library, but if you forget, it tells you so.

```
\usepackage{tikz-cd}
\[ \begin{tikzcd}
  A \arrow[dr, hook', controls={+(1.5,0.5) and +(-1,0.8)}]
    \arrow[dr, dashed, to path=|- (\tikztotarget)]
    \arrow[loop above, Rightarrow] & \mbox{}                        \\
    \arrow[ur, dash, dotted]        & B \arrow[loop right, two heads]
\end{tikzcd} \]
```

11-3-15

11.4 Compound structures and decorations

This section presents some commands that produce a variety of medium-sized mathematical structures including decorated symbols and fraction-like objects. Many of
them are provided by the amsmath package, but in some cases further packages need
to be loaded.

11.4.1 amsmath, mathtools, extarrows — Decorated arrows

The amsmath commands \xleftarrow and \xrightarrow produce horizontal
relation arrows similar to those used for the commutative diagrams in Section 11.3.5;
they are intended to have textual decorations above and/or below the arrow, and the
length of the arrow is chosen automatically to accommodate the text. These arrows
are normally available in only one size. Thus, they will probably not be suited for use
in fractions, subscripts, or superscripts, for example.

The textual decorations below and above the arrows are specified in an optional
and a mandatory argument to the command.

11-4-1

$$0 \xleftarrow[\zeta]{} F \times \Delta(n-1) \xrightarrow{\partial_0 \alpha(b)} E^{\partial_0 b}$$

```
\usepackage{amsmath}
\[ 0 \xleftarrow[\zeta]{}  F \times \Delta (n - 1)
   \xrightarrow{\partial_0 \alpha(b)} E^{\partial_0 b} \]
```

Further extensible arrows with the same syntax for superscript and subscript
material are provided by the mathtools package. This includes three double line
arrows, two hook arrows, and various harpoons as shown in the next example. In the
case of the double line arrows, you may have to add some extra spacing inside the
arguments to avoid the material bumping into the arrowhead (as we did with \␣ in
the example); for the harpoons this is usually not necessary.

mathtools additions to amsmath

11-4-2

$$A \xLeftarrow{x} B \xRightarrow[y]{} C \xLeftrightarrow[y]{x} D \tag{1}$$
$$A \xhookleftarrow{x} B \xhookrightarrow[bbb]{a} C \tag{2}$$
$$\xleftharpoondown{} \xleftharpoonup{} \xleftrightharpoons{xxx} \xrightleftharpoons[yy]{} \xrightharpoondown{} \xrightharpoonup{} \tag{3}$$
$$\xmapsto{x>0} A \xleftrightarrow[\text{letters}]{} Z \tag{4}$$

```
\usepackage{mathtools}
\begin{gather}
  A \xLeftarrow{\ x} B \xRightarrow[y\ ]{}
                   C \xLeftrightarrow[y]{\ x\ } D       \\
  A \xhookleftarrow{x} B \xhookrightarrow[bbb]{a} C  \\
  \xleftharpoondown{} \xleftharpoonup{}
  \xleftrightharpoons{xxx} \xrightleftharpoons[yy]{}
  \xrightharpoondown{} \xrightharpoonup{}                 \\
  \xmapsto{x>0} A \xleftrightarrow[\text{letters}]{} Z
\end{gather}
```

Arrows of the extarrows package

Another arrow package is extarrows by Kỳ-Anh Huỳnh. Besides the commands `\xLeftrightarrow` ⇔ and `\xleftrightarrow` ↔ also offered by mathtools, it provides several extensible arrows whose names start with `\xlong....` These are `\xLongleftarrow` ⟸, `\xLongrightarrow` ⟹, `\xlongleftarrow` ⟵ , `\xlongleftrightarrow` ⟷, `\xlongrightarrow` ⟶, and `\xlongequal` =.

On its own the "long equal" looks like a normal equal sign, =, but if it has material above or below, then it grows appropriately. In contrast, the minimal length of the other "long" arrows is noticeable longer than that of their counterparts `\xrightarrow`, etc., as shown in the next example:

$$A \xlongequal{\substack{+12 \\ \text{characters}}} M \xLongrightarrow{\substack{\text{more} \\ \text{characters}}} Z \quad (1)$$

$$0 \xrightarrow{x} \epsilon \xrightarrow{x} 1 \quad (2)$$

$$\xLongleftarrow{} \xLongrightarrow{} \xlongleftarrow{} \xlongrightarrow{} \xlongleftrightarrow{} \quad (3)$$

```
\usepackage{mathtools,extarrows}
\begin{gather}
  A \xlongequal          [\text{characters}]{ +12 }
  M \xLongrightarrow [\text{characters}]{\text{more}} Z \\
  0 \xrightarrow{x} \epsilon  \xlongrightarrow{x} 1      \\
  \xLongleftarrow{1} \xLongrightarrow{2} \xlongleftarrow{3}
  \xlongrightarrow{4} \xlongleftrightarrow{5}
\end{gather}
```

11-4-3

11.4.2 Fractions and their generalizations

In addition to the `\frac` command from standard LaTeX, the amsmath package provides `\dfrac` and `\tfrac` as convenient abbreviations for `{\displaystyle \frac ...}` and `{\textstyle\frac ...}` (mathematical styles are discussed in more detail in Section 11.7.1 on page 195).

$$\frac{1}{k} \log_2 c(f) \quad \tfrac{1}{k} \log_2 c(f) \quad (1)$$

Text: $\sqrt{ \frac{1}{k} \log_2 c(f) } \quad \sqrt{ \dfrac{1}{k} \log_2 c(f) }.$

```
\usepackage{amsmath}
\begin{equation} \frac{1}{k} \log_2 c(f) \quad
                 \tfrac{1}{k} \log_2 c(f)
\end{equation}
Text: $ \sqrt{ \frac{1}{k} \log_2 c(f) } \quad
       \sqrt{ \dfrac{1}{k} \log_2 c(f) }\, $.
```

11-4-4

For binomial coefficients such as $\binom{n}{k}$, use the corresponding commands `\binom`, `\dbinom`, and `\tbinom`.

$$\binom{k}{2}2^{k-1} + \binom{k-1}{2}2^{k-2} \quad (1)$$

Text: $\binom{k}{2}2^{k-1} + \binom{k-1}{2}2^{k-2}.$

```
\usepackage{amsmath}
\begin{equation} \binom{k}{2} 2^{k - 1}
                 + \tbinom{k - 1}{2} 2^{k - 2}
\end{equation}
Text: $ \binom{k}{2} 2^{k - 1}
       + \dbinom{k - 1}{2} 2^{k - 2} $.
```

11-4-5

All of these `\binom` and `\frac` commands are special cases of the generalized fraction command `\genfrac`, which has six parameters.

Style	Default Thickness (approximately)
text/display	0.40 pt
script	0.34 pt
scriptscript	0.24 pt

Table 11.2: Default rule thickness in different math styles

`\genfrac{`*ldelim*`}{`*rdelim*`}{`*thick*`}{`*style*`}{`*num*`}{`*denom*`}`

The first two parameters, *ldelim* and *rdelim*, are the left and right delimiters, respectively. They must be either both empty or both nonempty; to place a single delimiter, use a period "." on the "empty" side. The third parameter, *thick*, is used to override the default thickness of the fraction rule; for instance, `\binom` uses 0pt for this argument so that the line is invisible. If it is left empty, the line thickness has the default value specified by the font setup in use for mathematical typesetting. The examples in this chapter use the defaults listed in Table 11.2 in the various styles (see also Section 11.7.1).

The fourth parameter, *style*, provides a "mathematical style override" for the layout and font sizes used. It can take integer values in the range 0–3 denoting `\displaystyle`, `\textstyle`, `\scriptstyle`, and `\scriptscriptstyle`, respectively. If this argument is left empty, then the style is selected according to the normal rules for fractions (described in Table 11.7 on page 195). The last two arguments are simply the numerator (*num*) and denominator (*denom*).

To illustrate, here is how `\frac`, `\tfrac`, and `\binom` might be defined:

```
\newcommand\frac [2]{\genfrac{}{}{}{}{#1}{#2}}
\newcommand\tfrac[2]{\genfrac{}{}{}{1}{#1}{#2}}
\newcommand\binom[2]{\genfrac{(}{)}{0pt}{}{#1}{#2}}
```

Of course, if you want to use a particular complex notation (such as one implemented with `\genfrac`) repeatedly throughout your document, then you can do yourself (and your editor) a favor if you define a meaningful command name with `\newcommand` as an abbreviation for that notation, as in the examples above.

The old generalized fraction commands `\over`, `\overwithdelims`, `\atop`, `\atopwithdelims`, `\above`, and `\abovewithdelims` (inherited in standard LaTeX from plain TeX) produce warning messages if they are used with the amsmath package.

Sometimes the numerator or the denominator is very large, and in such cases it would be nice to be able to split them over two lines. This is made possible by the following two commands offered by mathtools:

mathtools additions to amsmath

`\splitfrac{`*start*`}{`*continuation*`}`   `\splitdfrac{`*start*`}{`*continuation*`}`

Both commands typeset the two lines in `\textstyle` (despite the "d" in the name), but `\splitdfrac` spreads them wider apart. The difference is clearly visible in the next example. Nesting is possible, but you may have to add a \mathstrut to achieve even spacing in all lines.

```
\usepackage{mathtools}
\[ A =    \frac{\splitfrac{a + b + c + d}{ + e + f + \sum_i x_i}}{\alpha}
  \simeq \frac{\splitdfrac{a + b + c + d}{ + e + f + \sum_i x_i}}{\beta}
     <    \frac{\omega}{\splitfrac{z - y - x - w - v - u}
                    {\splitfrac{\mathstrut - t - s - r - q}
                     { - p - o - n - m}}}        \]
```

$$A = \frac{\splitfrac{a+b+c+d}{+e+f+\sum_i x_i}}{\alpha} \simeq \frac{\splitfrac{a+b+c+d}{+e+f+\sum_i x_i}}{\beta} < \frac{\omega}{\splitfrac{z-y-x-w-v-u}{\splitfrac{-t-s-r-q}{-p-o-n-m}}} \qquad \boxed{11\text{-}4\text{-}6}$$

11.4.3 Continued fractions

The \cfrac command produces fraction arrays known as "continued fractions". By default, each numerator formula is centered; left or right alignment of a numerator is achieved by adding the optional argument [l] or [r].

$$\cfrac{1}{\sqrt{2}+\cfrac{1}{\sqrt{3}+\cfrac{1}{\sqrt{4}+\cfrac{1}{\sqrt{5}+\cfrac{1}{\sqrt{6}+\cdots}}}}}$$

```
\usepackage{amsmath}
\begin{equation*}
\cfrac {1}{\sqrt{2} +
 \cfrac {1}{\sqrt{3} +
  \cfrac {1}{\sqrt{4} +
   \cfrac[r] {1}{\sqrt{5} +
    \cfrac[l] {1}{\sqrt{6} + \dotsb }
   }}}}
\end{equation*}
```

$\boxed{11\text{-}4\text{-}7}$

11.4.4 Limiting positions

Subscripts and superscripts on integrals, sums, or other operators can be placed either above and below the mathematical operator or in the normal sub/super positions on the right of the operator. They are said to "take limits" if the superscript and subscript material is placed (in the "limit positions") above and below the symbol or operator name. Typically, no limits are used in text (to avoid spreading lines apart); in a display, the placement depends on the operator used. The default placements in LATEX are illustrated in the following example:

$$\sum_{i=1}^n \qquad \int_0^\infty \qquad \lim_{n \to 0}$$

Text: $\sum_{i=1}^n$, $\int_0^\infty$, $\lim_{n\to0}$.

```
\[
    \sum_{i=1}^n \qquad \int_0^\infty \qquad \lim_{n \to 0}
\]
Text: $\sum_{i=1}^n$, $\int_0^\infty$, $\lim_{n \to 0}$.
```

$\boxed{11\text{-}4\text{-}8}$

The placement of subscripts and superscripts on integrals, sums, and other operators is often dictated by the house style of a journal. Recognizing this fact, amsmath offers a long list of options for controlling the positioning. In the following summary, *default* indicates what happens when the amsmath package is used with a standard LaTeX class but without any of these options.[1]

amsmath options to control subscript and superscript placements

intlimits, nointlimits In displayed equations only, place superscripts and subscripts of integration-type symbols above and below or at the side (default), respectively.

sumlimits, nosumlimits In displayed equations only, place superscripts and subscripts of summation-type symbols (also called "large operators") above and below (default) or at the side, respectively.

These optione also affect other big operators — $\prod$, $\coprod$, $\otimes$, $\oplus$, and so forth — but not integrals.

namelimits, nonamelimits Like sumlimits or nosumlimits but for certain "operator names", such as det, inf, lim, and max, min, that traditionally have subscripts placed underneath, at least when they occur in a displayed equation.

The positioning on individual symbols/names can be controlled directly by placing one of the following TeX primitive commands immediately after the symbol or operator name: \limits, \nolimits, or \displaylimits. This last command, which specifies that the operator "takes limits" only when the mathematical style is a display style, is the default whenever a symbol of class Operator[2] appears or a \mathop construction is used. If an operator is to "take limits" outside a display, then this must be declared individually using the \limits command. Compare the next example to Example 11-4-8, noting that some commands show no effect as they merely reinforce the default.

11-4-9

$$\sum_{i=1}^{n} \quad \int_0^\infty \quad \lim_{n\to 0}$$

Text: $\sum_{i=1}^{n}, \int_0^\infty, \lim_{n\to 0}$.

```
\[
    \sum\nolimits_{i=1}^n       \qquad
    \int\limits_0^\infty        \qquad
    \lim\displaylimits_{n \to 0}
\]
Text: $\sum\nolimits_{i=1}^n$, $\int\limits_0^\infty$,
$\lim\displaylimits_{n \to 0}$.
```

11.4.5 Stacking in subscripts and superscripts

The standard LaTeX \substack command is most commonly used to typeset several lines within a subscript or superscript, using \\ as the row delimiter.

A slightly more general structure is the subarray environment provided by the amsmath package, which allows you to specify that the lines should be left

---

[1] But not necessarily when using the $\mathcal{A}_{\mathcal{M}}S$-LaTeX document classes.
[2] See Section 11.8.1 on page 209 for a discussion of the various mathematical classes of symbols.

aligned instead of centered (no right alignment). Note that both structures need to be surrounded by braces when they appear as a subscript or superscript.

$$\sum_{\substack{0\le i\le m \\ 0<j<n}} P(i,j) \qquad (1)$$

$$\sum_{\substack{i\in\Lambda \\ 0\le i\le m \\ 0<j<n}} P(i,j) \qquad (2)$$

```
\usepackage{amsmath}
\begin{gather}
  \sum_{\substack{0 \le i \le m \\ 0 < j < n}} P(i, j) \\
  \sum_{\begin{subarray}{l}  i \in \Lambda    \\
                            0 \le i \le m    \\
                            0 < j < n
        \end{subarray}}  P(i, j)
\end{gather}
```

11-4-10

mathtools additions to amsmath

If your `subarray` or your `\substack` involves sub or superscripts, you should consider using the cramped versions offered by `mathtools`. Without it the superscripts are raised too much, and while the difference is small, it is noticeable. Compare the product on the left and the right with that in the middle in the next example:

$$\prod_{a^2<c} \quad \prod_{\substack{a^2<c \\ c<1}} \quad \prod_{\substack{a^2<c \\ c<1}}$$

```
\usepackage{mathtools}
\[ \prod_{a^2<c} \quad
   \prod_{\begin{subarray}{l} a^2<c\\c<1 \end{subarray}} \quad
   \prod_{\begin{crampedsubarray}{l} a^2<c\\c<1 \end{crampedsubarray}} \]
```

11-4-11

11.4.6 amsmath, esint, wasysym — Multiple integral signs

Using amsmath, the commands `\iint`, `\iiint`, and `\iiiint` give multiple integral signs with well-adjusted spaces between them, in both running text and displays. The command `\idotsint` gives two integral signs with ellipsis dots between them. These commands are all built up from single integrals placed side by side (with somewhat reduced spacing), whereas the esint package (described below) uses a separate symbol font with individual glyphs for each integral.

The following example also shows the use of `\limits` to override the default for integral constructions and place the limit V underneath the symbol; as an alternative, we could have used the package option `intlimits`.

$$\iint\limits_V \mu(v,w)\,du\,dv$$

$$\iiint\limits_V \mu(u,v,w)\,du\,dv\,dw$$

$$\iiiint\limits_V \mu(t,u,v,w)\,dt\,du\,dv\,dw$$

$$\int\limits_V \cdots \int \mu(z_1,\dots,z_k)\,\mathbf{dz}$$

```
\usepackage{amsmath}
\begin{gather*}
  \iint\limits_V     \mu(v,w)      \,du \,dv              \\
  \iiint\limits_V    \mu(u,v,w)    \,du \,dv \,dw         \\
  \iiiint\limits_V   \mu(t,u,v,w)  \,dt \,du \,dv \,dw    \\
  \idotsint\limits_V \mu(z_1, \dots, z_k) \,\mathbf{dz}
\end{gather*}
```

11-4-12

Do not try to apply superscripts to these integrals when setting them with
\limits; they come out in fairly strange places as the next example shows. This time
we used intlimits so that all integrals have limits by default.

```
\usepackage[intlimits]{amsmath}
\begin{gather*}
    \int_a^b \quad \iint_a^b \quad \iiint_a^b \quad
    \iiiint_a^b \quad \oint_a^b \quad \idotsint_a^b
\end{gather*}
```

11-4-13

If you think that the amsmath versions of the multiple integral signs are too
much spaced apart or if you need other integral signs that are not in that set, you
can load the esint package by Eddie Saudrais. Like amsmath it supports the options
intlimits and nointlimits (default). If both packages are used, amsmath has to
be loaded first; otherwise, it reinstalls its version of the integrals, and only the new
ones are available.

If you compare the first line of the next example with the previous one, you can
see that the individual integrals are much closer together and that with the esint
package version the upper limits, though not perfect, come out more or less right.
The second and third rows show the additionally defined integrals by the package,
in case you have a need for one or the other in that set. Again, we use the option
intlimits and override it a few times with an explicit \nolimits command.

```
\usepackage[intlimits]{amsmath,esint} % order is important!
\begin{gather*}
    \int_a^b        \quad   \iint_a^b                        \quad
    \iiint_a^b      \quad   \iiiint_a^b                      \quad
    \oint_a^b       \quad   \idotsint_a^b
\\[5pt]
    \oiint_a^b                      \quad \varoiint_a^b      \quad
    \sqint\nolimits_a^b     \quad   \sqiint_a^b              \quad
    \landupint_a^b \quad \landdownint\nolimits_a^b
\\[5pt]
    \ointclockwise_a^b                                       \quad
    \ointctrclockwise\nolimits_a^b                           \quad
    \varointclockwise\nolimits_a^b                          \quad
    \varointctrclockwise_a^b  \quad  \fint_a^b
\end{gather*}
```

11-4-14

As the package uses its own symbol font, it should be used only if you use
the default Computer Modern Math fonts or a set of math fonts that are visually
compatible with these integrals.

Some people prefer upright integral symbols instead of the default slanted
ones. This can be achieved using the package wasysym with the option integrals.
If amsmath is loaded too (order is irrelevant), then \iiiint and \idotsint are
also changed; otherwise, these two amsmath commands are not available. The other

*Upright integrals
with wasysym*

special integrals provided by the esint package are not available in this style. See Section 10.13.2 on page 116 for further information on the wasysym package.

$$\int\limits_a^b \quad \iint\limits_a^b \quad \iiint\limits_V \quad \iiiint\limits_V$$

$$\oint\limits_a^b \quad \oiint\limits_a^b \quad \int\limits_V \cdots \int$$

```
\usepackage[integrals]{wasysym}   \usepackage{amsmath}
\begin{gather*}
    \int\limits_a^b        \quad   \iint\limits_a^b       \quad
    \iiint\limits_V        \quad   \iiiint\limits_V       \\
    \oint\limits_a^b       \quad   \oiint\limits_a^b      \quad
    \idotsint\limits_V
\end{gather*}
```

11-4-15

11.4.7 diffcoeff — Handling derivatives of arbitrary order

If you often need ordinary, partial, and other derivatives, then take a look at the diffcoeff package by Andrew Parsloe, because it helps you to produce them in a consistent manner with the ability to adjust their style in various ways. By default, it implements the ISO 80000-2 recommendation, and with the help of a `def-file` option you can specify a file to hold your own conventions and adjustments for reuse in several documents.

> `\diff**[order]{differentiand}{variable of differentiation}[evaluated at]`

The command `\diff` produces an ordinary derivative, while `\diffp` is responsible for partial derivatives — the argument structure is the same for both commands. The differentiand is normally set as a numerator; the starred form appends it instead, and a second star also swaps the mandatory arguments — i.e., *variable* first, to retain the reading order. If you prefer a slashed style use `\difs` or `\difsp`, and for a very compact representation, use `\difc` or `\difcp` instead. The *order* of differentiation (default 1) is specified in the first optional argument, and a point of evaluation can be set in the second optional argument. Below we show a few examples:

$$\left(\frac{\mathrm{d}^2 \ln\sin x}{\mathrm{d}(\sin x)^2}\right)_\pi \qquad \frac{\partial^{n+1} F}{\partial x^{n+1}} \qquad \frac{\mathrm{d}}{\mathrm{d}x}(ax^2+bx+c)$$

```
\usepackage{diffcoeff}
\[ \diff[2]{\ln\sin x}{\sin x}[\pi]   \quad
   \diffp[n+1]{F}{x}                  \quad
   \diff*{(ax^2+bx+c)}{x}             \]
```

11-4-16

If you prefer to have fewer braces in your formula, you can leave them out around the mandatory arguments — but, of course, only if they are single tokens! We have done this in the next example, which uses slashed and compact style, because this usually works better in text. Otherwise, this repeats the previous example to allow for easy comparison.

$$(\mathrm{d}^2 \ln\sin x / \mathrm{d}(\sin x)^2)_\pi \text{ and } \partial^{n+1} F/\partial x^{n+1} \text{ and } (\mathrm{d}/\mathrm{d}x)(ax^2+bx+c)$$

$$\left(\mathrm{d}^2_{\sin x} \ln\sin x\right)_\pi \text{ and } \partial^{n+1}_x F \text{ and } \mathrm{d}_x(ax^2+bx+c)$$

```
\usepackage{diffcoeff}
$\difs[2]{\ln\sin x}{\sin x}[\pi]$ and
$\difsp[n+1] Fx$ and $\difs*{(ax^2+bx+c)}x$

$\difc[2]{\ln\sin x}{\sin x}[\pi]$ and
$\difcp[n+1] Fx$ and $\difc*{(ax^2+bx+c)}x$
```

11-4-17

Notations like dx or $\mathrm{d}x$ (ISO style) also appear in other places than derivatives, e.g., in integrals. If you switch between different styles (because the publishing journal has requirements to use or not use ISO style), you would want to see the expressions change throughout without the need to manually alter the source. To accomodate this, the package offers the small command \dl, which changes appearance based on the overall style you have selected. By default, the d's are written upright:

11-4-18

$$dP = \frac{\partial P}{\partial x}\,dx + \frac{\partial P}{\partial y}\,dy + \frac{\partial P}{\partial z}\,dz$$

```
\usepackage{diffcoeff}
\[ \dl P = \diffp Px \dl x + \diffp Py \dl y
          + \diffp Pz \dl z                    \]
```

The package offers many customization possibilities. You can, for example, produce derivatives with symbols such as D, δ, or Δ; adjust the spacing; define new variants; and much more. For reuse in different documents, the necessary declarations can be stored in a file with the extension .def and loaded with the option def-file =⟨file⟩. See the extensive package documentation for further details.

11.4.8 Modular relations

Standard LaTeX already provides the commands \bmod and \pmod. The amsmath package augments this set with \mod and \pod to deal with special spacing conventions of the "mod" notation for equivalence classes of integers. These extra commands are variants of \pmod that are preferred by some authors; \mod omits the parentheses, whereas \pod omits the "mod" and retains the parentheses. Furthermore, with amsmath the spacing of \pmod is decreased within an inline formula.

11-4-19

$$u \equiv v + 1 \quad \mathrm{mod}\ n^2$$
$$u \equiv v + 1\ \mathrm{mod}\ n^2$$
$$u = v + 1 \quad (\mathrm{mod}\ n^2)$$
$$u = v + 1 \quad (n^2)$$

The in-text layout: $u = v + 1 \pmod{n^2}$

$$k^2 = (m \bmod n)\,; \quad x \equiv y \quad (\mathrm{mod}\ b)\,;$$
$$x \equiv y \quad \mathrm{mod}\ c\,; \quad x \equiv y \quad (d)\,.$$

```
\usepackage{amsmath}
\begin{align*}
   u & \equiv v + 1 \mod{n^2}         \\
   u & \equiv v + 1 \bmod{n^2}        \\
   u &    =    v + 1 \pmod{n^2}       \\
   u &    =    v + 1 \pod{n^2}   \end{align*}
The in-text layout: $ u = v + 1 \pmod{n^2} $
\begin{align*}
   k^2 &= (m \bmod n)      \, ; &
   x &\equiv y \pmod b \, ;        \\
   x &\equiv y \mod c  \, ; &
   x &\equiv y \pod d  \, .    \end{align*}
```

11.4.9 mathtools, interval — **Properly spaced intervals**

Specifying intervals is usually done by using brackets as fences, e.g., "$[a, b]$". This is simple for closed intervals, but the natural input for open or half-open intervals fails rather miserably with respect to spacing as seen in the next example:

11-4-20

$$[a, e[= [a, b] +]b, c[+]c, d[-[d, e[$$

```
$  [a,e[ = [a,b] + ]b,c] + ]c,d[ - [d,e[ $
```

The reason for this spacing result is that "[" is considered by TeX as an opening and "]" as a closing symbol. However, if used as fences for half or fully open intervals, their interpretation should be reversed — something TeX cannot determine by itself. So it sees an opening symbol "[" followed by an "=" (relation), and that does not get any space added. With the help of explicit \mathopen and \mathclose commands (see Section 11.8.1 on page 209), this can be corrected; however, the resulting input becomes rather noncomprehensible at the same time:

$$[a, d[= [a, b] +]b, c] +]c, d[- [d, e[$$

```
$ [a,d\mathclose{[} = [a,b] + \mathopen{]}b,c] +
  \mathopen{]}c,d\mathclose{[} - [d,e\mathclose{[} $
```

11-4-21

mathtools addition to amsmath

To avoid such source code monsters, mathtools offers the possibility of defining new commands that automatically supply opening and closing delimiters around their argument.

> \DeclarePairedDelimiter{*cmd*}{*left-delimiter*}{*right-delimiter*}

This declaration defines a new command *cmd* with one mandatory argument that is typeset surrounded by the *left-delimiter* and *right-delimiter*. Also defined is a starred form that sets the delimiters using \left and \right, which is why you can use only real delimiters that are allowed after those commands, e.g., those from Table 11.5 on page 190 or Table 11.30 on page 224. Instead of the star, you can use an optional argument to specify the size explicitly using \big, \Big, \bigg, or \Bigg.

$$\begin{aligned}
&[a, d[= [a, b] +]b, c] + \cdots \\
&]\frac{a}{b}[\approx]\frac{a}{b}[\neq \left[x \right]
\end{aligned}$$

```
\usepackage{mathtools} \DeclarePairedDelimiter\closed{[}{]}
\DeclarePairedDelimiter\open{]}{[}\DeclarePairedDelimiter\ropen{[}{[}
\DeclarePairedDelimiter\lopen{]}{]}

\begin{gather*}
 \ropen{a,d}=\closed{a,b} + \lopen{b,c} + \dotsb \\[3pt]
 \open{\frac{a}{b}} \approx \open*{\frac{a}{b}}
                 \neq    \closed[\Bigg]{x}
\end{gather*}
```

11-4-22

The interval approach

An alternative specifically for intervals is provided by Lars Madsen with the package interval. It allows you to input intervals as logical constructs and takes care of the correct formatting in the background.

> \interval[*key/value-list*]{*left*}{*right*}

The two mandatory arguments are the *left* and *right* boundaries of the interval, and with the *key/value-list* you specify the type and possibly some formatting features. The \interval command then selects the appropriate fences, selects the separator symbol, and ensures appropriate spacing.

$$[a, d[= [a, b] +]b, c] +]c, e[- [d, e[$$

```
\usepackage{interval}
\[ \interval[open right]{a}{d} = \interval{a}{b} +
   \interval[open left]{b}{c} + \interval[open]{c}{e}
    - \interval[open right]{d}{e}                    \]
```

11-4-23

Beside the various `open...` keys shown above, you can use the key `scaled`, which scales the fences to automatically match the height of the content. It can alternatively be used with a value (such as `\Big`), in which case that determines the size of the fences. A (nonsense) example is shown in Example 11-4-24.

```
\ointerval [key/value-list] {left}{right}
\linterval [key/value-list] {left}{right}
\rinterval [key/value-list] {left}{right}
```

As the keywords are rather verbose, there are also three shorthands for the most common cases: open and half-open intervals. Scaling or other keys can still be set in the *key/value-list* argument. This is also shown in the next example.

```
\intervalconfig{key/value-list}
```

Some people prefer a semicolon or two periods as the separator between the boundaries instead of a comma. Also quite common is to use parentheses instead of brackets for the open fences (called *soft fences*). All this and more can be specified in the argument to `\intervalconfig` as exhibited below:

```
\usepackage{color,interval}
\intervalconfig{soft open fences,separator symbol=..,
                colorize=\color{blue}}
\[
   \rinterval{a}{d} = \interval{a}{b} +
   \linterval{b}{c} + \ointerval{c}{e}
                    - \rinterval[scaled=\Bigg]{d}{e}
\]
```

11-4-24

$$\left| [a..d) = [a..b] + (b..c] + (c..e) - \left[d..e \right) \right|$$

Colorizing all intervals is normally not useful, but it can help if you change an existing document to use the interval package. You can then easily check if all intervals have been properly converted to the new syntax.

11.4.10 braket — Dirac bra–ket and set notation

The bra–ket notation, also known as Dirac notation, was established by Paul Dirac around 1940. In quantum mechanics it is a common notation for describing quantum states. Donald Arseneau produced a small package, bracket, that offers a handful of commands to enter the notation consistently.

`\bra{formula}`	`\ket{formula}`	`\braket{formula}`	`\set{formula}`
`\Bra{formula}`	`\Ket{formula}`	`\Braket{formula}`	`\Set{formula}`

Commands starting with an uppercase letter grow vertically to enclose their content (using internally `\left` and `\right`), while the lowercase commands do not change sizes. You can use | in the argument to generate extensible vertical lines as needed, and with || or \| you get doubled lines. As sets have a similar structure involving vertical lines, they are also provided via \set and \Set.

$$|\psi\rangle\,\langle\phi| : |\xi\rangle \mapsto |\psi\rangle\,\langle\psi|\xi\rangle$$

$$\left\langle \phi \left| \frac{\partial^2}{\partial t^2} \right| \psi \right\rangle$$

Also:

$$\left\{ x \in \Re^2 \,\middle|\, 0 < |x| < 5 \right\}$$

```
\usepackage{mathtools,braket}

\begin{gather*}
\ket{\psi}\bra{\phi} : \ket{\xi}
        \mapsto    \ket{\psi} \braket{\psi|\xi}             \\
\Braket{ \phi | \frac{\partial^2}{\partial t^2} | \psi} \\
\shortintertext{Also:} \Set{ x\in \Re^2 | 0 < |x| < 5 }
\end{gather*}
```

11-4-25

11.4.11 amsmath, mathtools, empheq — Boxed formulas

The amsmath command \boxed puts a box around its argument; it works just like \fbox, except that the contents are in math mode.

$$\boxed{W_t - F \subseteq V(P_i) \subseteq W_t} \qquad (1)$$

```
\usepackage{amsmath}
\begin{equation}
    \boxed { W_t - F \subseteq V(P_i) \subseteq W_t }
\end{equation}
```

11-4-26

mathtools addition to amsmath

The mathtools package extends this approach with the command \Aboxed. This command can be used to produce a boxed formula across an alignment point (&) in math display environments such as align. Do not use it when there is no alignment point to cross, e.g., in the second equation in the example, because it would generate an error in that case.

$$\boxed{f(x) = \int h(x)\,dx} \qquad (1)$$

$$= \boxed{g(x)} \qquad (2)$$

```
\usepackage{mathtools}
\begin{align}
    \Aboxed{ f(x) & = \int h(x)\, dx} \\
                 & = \boxed{g(x)}
\end{align}
```

11-4-27

Annotating amsmath environments with empheq

A much more general approach is taken by the package empheq by Morten Høgholm and Lars Madsen. In essence it offers a wrapper environment for most of the amsmath environments so that you can specify special extra formatting, such as (colored) boxes or adding something to the left or right of the formula, regardless of whether or not there are equation numbers. The general syntax is the following:

```
\begin{empheq} [key/value list] {amsmath-env}
   ... contents of the amsmath environment ...
\end{empheq}
```

In the amsmath-env argument you specify the name of one of the amsmath display environments from Sections 11.2.2 to 11.2.7 on pages 133–138. Not supported are the "boxed" environments, i.e., aligned, gathered, etc.

If used without the optional *key/value list*, this should produce identical output compared to using the amsmath environment directly, though with a few restrictions. It is not possible to use \intertext or \displaybreak because the empheq environment puts the display into unbreakable boxes to attach extra material. For the same reason, the automatic movement of the equation tag if the display is too wide no longer works, and you have to make any necessary adjustments manually.

In the *key/value list* you can specify a number of keys to annotate your formula; the next example shows the most important ones, though normally you will not use all of them at the same time.

With box you specify a box command, e.g., \fbox, that is applied to the whole display formula excluding the equation tags but including any left or right annotation if also given. The innerbox key does the same but applies only to the formula itself. There is also a marginbox key (not shown) for special effects when equations are set flushed left (fleqn option in force).

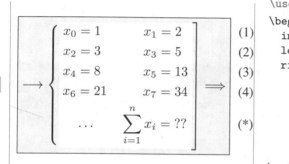

11-4-28

```
\usepackage{empheq,xcolor}
\begin{empheq}[box=\fcolorbox{black}{blue!10},
    innerbox=\colorbox{white},
    left=\longrightarrow \empheqlbrace,
    right=\empheqbigrbrack \Longrightarrow]{align}
    x_0&=1      &  x_1&=2      \\
    x_2&=3      &  x_3&=5      \\
    x_4&=8      &  x_5&=13     \\
    x_6&=21     &  x_7&=34     \\
        &\ldots & \sum_{i=1}^n x_i
                &=\mathord{??}  \tag{*}
\end{empheq}
```

The use of left and right keys in the previous example shows some package-specific commands: \empheqlbrace and \empheqbigrbrack. As one can see, they produce vertically extensible braces matching (or slightly exceeding) the innerbox height. If we had used \lbrace and \rbrace, we would have gotten nonextensible braces, but we could, of course, have used both \left and \right to scale them with a similar result to \empheqbig.. as we did. Several other delimiters are available by preceding their name with empheq or empheqbig, for example, \empheqlparen or \empheqrangle; the full list of supported delimiter names is angle "⟨", brace "{", brack "[", ceil "⌈", floor "⌊", paren "(", vert "|", and Vert "‖".

You might wonder why the *key/value list* is optional, given that there is no obvious reason to use the environment at all if that argument is not supplied. The reason is the package option overload: If you load the package with that option, then the amsmath environments are all redefined to use empheq internally; e.g., you can then write \begin{align}[box...]= instead of the code shown in Example 11-4-28.

The original environments are still available if needed, e.g., if you want to use \intertext or \displaybreak. All you have to do is to prefix the original name with AmS; thus, AmSalign will be amsmath's original align environment, etc.

11.4.12 amsmath, accents, mathdots — Various accents

TEX distinguishes sharply between accented characters in text and in math. To obtain "à" in text, you can use the Unicode character "à" or the command "\'a", both of which fail in math mode. Depending on the engine you might get a warning or error message, but the character may also be silently ignored with only an entry in the transcript file saying something like

```
Missing character: There is no à in font lmmi10!
```

Thus, to typeset accents over mathematical symbols you should always use special math accent commands, i.e., \grave in this case. The full set of math accents provided by standard LATEX is shown in the next example.

Note that most accents change with the math alphabet currently in use; e.g., all but \vec, \widehat, and \widetilde become bold when we place them inside \mathbf. This means you have a choice: if you use \hat or any other varying math accent within a math alphabet command, you get accents in the "style" of the alphabet; if you use them outside, you get ordinary ones. This is shown on the third line.

$$\dot{x}\;\ddot{x}\;\mathring{x}\;\acute{x}\;\grave{x}\;\hat{x}\;\check{x}\;\breve{x}\;\bar{x}\;\tilde{x}\quad \vec{x}\;\widehat{x}\;\widetilde{x}$$

$$\dot{y}\;\ddot{y}\;\mathring{y}\;\acute{y}\;\grave{y}\;\hat{y}\;\check{y}\;\breve{y}\;\bar{y}\;\tilde{y}\quad \vec{y}\;\widehat{y}\;\widetilde{y}$$

$$\hat{\mathbf{C}} \simeq \hat{\mathbf{C}}$$

```
\newcommand\accsample[1]{\dot{#1} \; \ddot{#1} \;
   \mathring{#1} \; \acute{#1} \; \grave{#1} \; \hat{#1}
   \; \check{#1} \; \breve{#1} \; \bar{#1} \; \tilde{#1}
   \quad \vec{#1} \; \widehat{#1} \; \widetilde{#1}}
\[ \accsample{x} \]      \[ \mathbf{\accsample{y}} \]
\[ \hat{\mathbf{C}} \simeq \mathbf{\hat{C}}  \]
```

11-4-29

Be careful with accents inside math alphabets

However, the fact that many math accents vary inside math alphabets has a downside: if they are lacking accents, then you get whatever is in the font at the position TEX believes the accent is stored. For example, the \mathcal alphabet is part of the standard symbol font, which contains no accents. Thus, using math accents that vary inside \mathcal gives you very strange results (without a warning).

As shown in the first line of the example, only the three nonchanging accents come out right here. The remedy in that case is to use \mathcal only for your base letter and the accent command outside to get the normal math accent, as shown in the second line.

```
% \accsample as previously defined
\[ \mathcal{\accsample{A}} \]
\[ \accsample{\mathcal{B}} \]
```

11-4-30

More dot accents with amsmath

The \dot and \ddot mathematical accents from standard LATEX are supplemented in amsmath by \dddot and \ddddot, giving triple and quadruple dot accents, respectively.

$$\dot{S} \quad \ddot{P} \quad \dddot{Q} \quad \ddddot{R}$$

```
\usepackage{amsmath}
$ \dot{S} \quad \ddot{P} \quad \dddot{Q} \quad \ddddot{R} $
```

11-4-31

… mathdots …

There are also refined versions provided by the mathdots package if loaded in addition to amsmath. They use slightly tighter spacing between the dots.

11-4-32

$$\dot{S} \quad \ddot{P} \quad \dddot{Q} \quad \ddddot{R}$$

```
\usepackage{amsmath,mathdots}
$ \dot{S} \quad \ddot{P} \quad \dddot{Q} \quad \ddddot{R} $
```

Even tighter spacing is used by the accents package: *... and* accents

11-4-33

$$\dot{S} \quad \ddot{P} \quad \dddot{Q} \quad \ddddot{R}$$

```
\usepackage{amsmath,accents}
$ \dot{S} \quad \ddot{P} \quad \dddot{Q} \quad \ddddot{R} $
```

If you want to set up your own mathematical accents, then you should probably use the accents package developed by Javier Bezos. It provides methods of defining "faked" accents (see \accentset in the example) and general under-accents (\underaccent, \undertilde), along with other features. It can be used together with amsmath as shown in the previous example but has to be loaded after it. We give two examples of its possibilities; for further details see [14]. *... and also many additional accents with* accents

11-4-34

$$\overset{*}{X} \quad \hat{\overset{\star}{\tilde h}} \quad \underaccent{\diamond}{\mathcal{M}} \quad \undertilde{C} \quad \undertilde{M} \quad \undertilde{ABC}$$

```
\usepackage{accents}
\[ \accentset{\ast}{X}                          \quad
   \hat{\accentset{\star}{\tilde h}}    \quad
   \underaccent{\diamond}{\mathcal{M}} \quad
   \undertilde{C}\quad\undertilde{M}\quad\undertilde{ABC} \]
```

The warning that not all accents work inside all math alphabets is equally true for the accents provided by the accents package. If that is the case, you have to ensure that the accent is outside of the math alphabet's scope.

11-4-35

$\hat{\overset{\star}{\tilde h}}$ (ok) but $\overset{A}{\mathcal{X}}$ (bad) $\hat{\overset{\star}{\tilde{\mathcal{X}}}}$ (ok again)

```
\usepackage{accents}
$\mathbf{\hat{\accentset{\star}{\tilde h}}}$ (ok) but
$\mathcal{\hat{\accentset{\star}{\tilde X}}}$ (bad)
$\hat{\accentset{\star}{\tilde{\mathcal{X}}}}$ (ok again)
```

When adding an accent to an i or j in mathematics, it is best to use the dotless variants \imath and \jmath; however, they always produce the same symbol. If you want them to vary based on the current math alphabet, use \dotlessi or \dotlessj provided by the dotlessi package written by Javier Bezos: *Accents over the characters i or j*

11-4-36

$\hat{\imath} \neq \hat{\imath} \neq \mathbf{\hat{\imath}}$

```
\usepackage{dotlessi,amsmath}
$ \hat\imath \neq \mathbf{\hat\imath} \neq \mathbf{\hat\dotlessi} $
```

A collection of simple commands for placing accents as superscripts to a subformula is available with the package amsxtra. This is not a very common layout, but it is occasionally used: *Accents as superscripts*

11-4-37

$$(xyz)^{\cdots} \quad (xyz)^{\cdot\cdot} \quad (xyz)^{\cdot}$$
$$(xyz)^{\smile} \quad (xyz)^{\vee}$$
$$(xyz)^{\wedge} \quad (xyz)^{\sim}$$

```
\usepackage{amsxtra}
$(xyz)\spdddot$ \quad $(xyz)\spddot$ \quad $(xyz)\spdot$ \\
$(xyz)\spbreve$ \quad $(xyz)\spcheck$ \\
$(xyz)\sphat$   \quad $(xyz)\sptilde$
```

Type	Command	Description	Output
Physical row vector	\aS [*accent*] {*symbol*}	*arrow-symbol*	$\vec{\boldsymbol{u}}$
Physical column vector	\Sa [*accent*] {*symbol*}	*symbol-arrow*	$\underset{\rightarrow}{\boldsymbol{v}}$
Physical tensor	\aSa [*accent*] {*symbol*}	*arrow-symbol-arrow*	$\vec{\underset{\rightarrow}{\boldsymbol{E}}}$
Column vector	\bS [*accent*] {*symbol*}	*bar-symbol*	$\overline{\boldsymbol{x}}$
Row vector	\Sb [*accent*] {*symbol*}	*symbol-bar*	$\underline{\boldsymbol{y}}$
Tensor	\bSb [*accent*] {*symbol*}	*bar-symbol-bar*	$\overline{\underline{\boldsymbol{R}}}$
Tensor (mixed base)	\aSb [*accent*] {*symbol*}	*arrow-symbol-bar*	$\vec{\underline{\boldsymbol{S}}}$
Tensor (mixed base)	\bSa [*accent*] {*symbol*}	*bar-symbol-arrow*	$\overline{\underset{\rightarrow}{\boldsymbol{T}}}$
Cross-produce tensor[a]	\aCSa [*accent*] {*symbol*}	*array-symbol-arrow*	$\vec{\underset{\rightarrow}{\tilde{\boldsymbol{z}}}}$
	\bCSb [*accent*] {*symbol*}	*bar-symbol-bar*	$\overline{\underline{\tilde{\boldsymbol{z}}}}$

[a] *In the cross-product tensors the tilde is automatically added to the symbol by the command.*

Table 11.3: List of matrix tensor input commands

11.4.13 mattens—Commands to typeset tensors

There exist quite a number of different notations for denoting vectors and tensors, and not surprisingly, there are a number of packages that implement an input syntax for them. For the book we selected the mattens package by Danie Els, because it offers a simple and very flexible interface, but if this does not appeal to you, then there are a handful of other packages on CTAN and probably in your distribution.

> \□S□*[*accent*]{*sym*}   \aCSa*[*accent*]{*sym*}   \bCSb*[*accent*]{*sym*}

The commands offered by the package all follow the naming scheme, where the placeholder □ stands for either a (arrow), b (bar), or nothing (no embellishment), which gives you a total of eight commands as shown in Table 11.3. All follow the same argument structure: mandatory *symbol* and an optional (math) *accent*. The starred forms typeset the symbol as an ordinary symbol, i.e., not boldened.

There are also two cross-product tensors: \aCSa and \bCSb. The example below exhibits some of the different combinations:

$$\underrightarrow{\underline{x}} \neq \vec{\underline{x}} \neq \hat{\vec{x}} \neq \overline{\underset{\rightarrow}{X}} \qquad (1)$$

$$\overline{\delta} \neq \vec{\delta} \neq \hat{\vec{\delta}} \qquad (2)$$

$$\overline{\underline{\tilde{a}}} \cdot \overline{c} = \overline{a} \times \overline{c} \qquad (3)$$

```
\usepackage{mattens}
\begin{gather}
  \aSb{x} \neq \aSb*{x} \neq \aSb[\hat]{x} \neq \bSa{X} \\
  \bS{\delta} \neq \bS*{\delta} \neq \bS[\hat]{\delta}   \\
  \bCSb{a} \cdot \bS{c} = \bS{a} \times \bS{c}
\end{gather}
```

11-4-38

178

As you can deduce from the previous example (because `gather` is available), the package implicitly loads `amsmath`. What you also see is that with Computer Modern fonts the arrows (being very large) touch the x — with Lucida Math (as shown in the table) this is not an issue. One way to solve that is to use the package option `mathstrut`, which adds a `\mathstrut` into each tensor thereby forcing upper and lower arrows and bars farther apart. You can alternatively define your own struts using, for example, `\SetSymbStrut{\vphantom{`*material*`}}` as explained in the package documentation.

Some people prefer to show tensors and vectors in a different font instead of boldening the symbols. The next example shows how to do this with the help of `\SetSymbFont`. Note that this acts only on symbols that are affected by math alphabets; e.g., the Greek letter is not altered. For the same reason you still see the ordinary x when the starred form is used, because that suppresses special formatting.

The Computer Modern fonts do not have a bold sans serif font shape, but the Latin Modern do, so we define a math alphabet for it and use that.

11-4-39

$$\vec{\boldsymbol{x}} \neq \vec{x} \neq \vec{\hat{\boldsymbol{x}}} \neq \overline{\boldsymbol{X}} \tag{1}$$
$$\overline{\delta} \neq \vec{\overline{\delta}} \neq \hat{\overline{\delta}} \tag{2}$$
$$\underline{\overline{\boldsymbol{a}}} \cdot \underline{\boldsymbol{c}} = \underline{\boldsymbol{a}} \times \underline{\boldsymbol{c}} \tag{3}$$

```
\usepackage[mathstrut]{mattens}  \SetSymbFont{\mathsfsl}
\DeclareMathAlphabet\mathsfsl{OT1}{lmss}{bx}{sl}
\begin{gather}
  \aSb{x} \neq \aSb*{x} \neq \aSb[\hat]{x} \neq \bSa{X} \\
  \bS{\delta} \neq \bS*{\delta} \neq \bS[\hat]{\delta}  \\
  \bCSb{a} \cdot \bS{c} = \bS{a} \times \bS{c}
\end{gather}
```

If you find yourself always using the starred forms, because you want to supply your own formatting, you can instead load the package with the option `noformat`, which suppresses the boldening or other automatic formatting of the symbols.

11.4.14 Extra decorations for symbols

Standard LaTeX provides `\stackrel` for placing a superscript above a Relation symbol.

A set of possibly more useful commands is provided by the `amsmath` package with the commands `\overset`, `\underset`, and `\overunderset`. They can be used to place material above and/or below any Ordinary symbol or Binary operator symbol, in addition to Relation symbols, and automatically determine the correct math type for the resulting compound symbol.

11-4-40

$$\overset{*}{X} \underset{*}{>} X \underset{\text{loc.}}{\overset{\text{def}}{\iff}} {\sideset{}{'}\sum_{a,b \in \mathbf{R^*}}} \overset{a}{\underset{b}{X}} = X$$

```
\usepackage{amsmath}
\[ \overset{*}{X} > \underset{*}{X}
   \overunderset{\mathsf{def}}{\mathsf{loc.}}{\iff}
   \sideset{}{'}\sum_{a,b \in \mathbf{R^*}}
      \overset{a}{\underset{b}{X}} = X \]
```

The command `\sideset` serves a special purpose, complementary to the others: it adds decorations additional to the "normal" limits (which are set above and below) to any Operator symbol such as $\sum$ or $\prod$. These are placed in the subscript and superscript positions, on both the left and right of the Operator.

This more complex example shows how to fully decorate a product symbol.

$$\prod_{\substack{i=1 \\ k>1}}^{n}{}_{j=2}^{m}\,\mathcal{T}_{i,j}^{k}$$

```
\usepackage{amsmath}
\[ \sideset{_{i = 1}^n}{_{j = 2}^m}\prod_{k > 1}
                        \mathcal{T}_{i, j}^k \]
```

11-4-41

mathtools addition to amsmath

If you want to attach subscripts or superscript to the left of an ordinary symbol, the standard approach is to fake this with an empty brace group. However, if both are present and of different width, they get left aligned rather than being attached to a following symbol. Michael Downes (1958–2003) suggested an alternative, which is implemented by \prescript in the mathtools package. It takes three arguments: *pre-superscript*, *pre-subscript*, and *base symbol* as shown in the example.

$${}_{2}^{14}\mathbf{C}_{2}^{5+} \quad {}_{2}^{14}\mathbf{C}_{2}^{5+} \quad {}^{14}\mathbf{C}_{2}^{5+}$$

```
\usepackage{mathtools}
\[      {}^{14}_{2} \mathbf{C} ^{5+}_{2} \quad
\prescript{14}{2}{\mathbf{C}}^{5+}_{2} \quad
\prescript{14}{} {\mathbf{C}}^{5+}_{2}        \]
```

11-4-42

11.5 Variable symbol commands

Many LATEX commands are often thought of as producing a particular symbol when, in fact, the exact form is not fixed (even when the font and size are fixed). Certain features of TEX's mathematical typesetting can even be used to produce structures that can, in principle, grow to whatever size is required.

Such context-dependent variability is very important in mathematical typesetting, and this section discusses some aspects of it. With a few clearly noted exceptions, the commands covered in this section are available in standard LATEX.

A well-known, but not very exciting, example of such variability entails the mathematical operator symbols, such as \sum and \prod, which typically come in just two sizes: a smaller size that is used in running text and a larger size that is used in displayed formulas. Such symbols appear in Table 11.27 on page 222.

11.5.1 Ellipsis and other kinds of ...

Standard LATEX provides several types of mathematical ellipsis dots: \ldots, \cdots, and so on. When using amsmath, however, such ellipsis dots within math mode should almost always be marked up using \dots,[1] and amsmath should decide what kind of dots are to be used.

The vertical position (on the baseline or centered) of the ellipsis, together with the space around it, are both automatically selected according to what kind of symbol follows \dots. For example, if the next symbol is a plus sign, the dots will be centered; if it is a comma, they are typeset on the baseline. In all cases, three dots are used, but

---

[1]The commands \dots and \ldots can also be used in text mode, where both always produce a normal text ellipsis.

the spacing varies. These defaults from the amsmath package can be changed in a class file when different conventions are in use.

11-5-1

A series $H_1, H_2, \ldots, H_n$, a sum $H_1 + H_2 + \cdots + H_n$, an orthogonal product $H_1 \times H_2 \times \cdots \times H_n$.

```
\usepackage{amsmath}
A series $H_1, H_2, \dots, H_n$, a sum
$H_1 + H_2 + \dots + H_n$, an orthogonal product
$H_1 \times H_2 \times \dots \times H_n$.
```

If the dots fall at the end of a mathematical formula, the next object will be something like \end or \] or $, which does not give any information about how to place the dots. In such a case, you must help by using \dotsc for "dots with commas", \dotsb for "dots with Binary operator/Relation symbols", \dotsm for "multiplication dots", \dotsi for "dots with integrals", or even \dotso for "none of the above". These commands should be used only in such special positions: otherwise you should just use \dots.

In this example, low dots are produced in the first instance and centered dots in the other cases, with the space around the dots being nicely adjusted.

11-5-2

A series $H_1, H_2, \ldots$, a sum $H_1 + H_2 + \cdots$, an orthogonal product $H_1 \times H_2 \times \cdots$, and an infinite integral:

$$\int_{H_1} \int_{H_2} \cdots -\Gamma \, d\Theta$$

```
\usepackage{amsmath}
A series $H_1, H_2, \dotsc\,$, a sum
$H_1 + H_2 + \dotsb\,$, an orthogonal product
$H_1 \times H_2 \times \dotsm\,$, and an infinite
integral:   \[ \int_{H_1} \int_{H_2} \dotsi \;
                {-\Gamma}\, d\Theta \]
```

You can customize the symbols and spacing produced by the \dots command in various contexts by redefining the commands \dotsc, \dotsb, \dotsm, and \dotsi; this would normally be done in a class file. Thus, for example, you could decide to use only two dots in some cases.

For vertical ellipsis, standard LaTeX already offers \vdots, but while this works well in situations such as inside matrices (with centered cells), it is rather suboptimal when indicating continuation in math displays. Here it is usually preferable if the vertical dots take the width of an equal sign or some other symbol so that they appear centered with respect to nearby relation symbols next to the alignment point.

mathtools additions to amsmath

This is provided by mathtools with the command \vdotswithin. It takes one argument (typically a relational ⟨*symbol*⟩ such as =), measures the width of the formula ${}⟨symbol⟩{}$, and then typesets the vertical dots centered in a box of that width.

11-5-3

$a = b + c \qquad a = b + c$
$\vdots \qquad\quad \vdots$
$x = y + z \quad x = y + z$.

```
\usepackage{mathtools}
\begin{align*} a &= b+c   &   a &= b+c            \\
               & \vdots   &     &\vdotswithin{=} \\
               x &= y+z   &   x &= y+z   \end{align*}
```

If vertical ellipsis are used in formulas, then there is often too much white space above and below, because of the usual line separation in display formulas. To allow for shortening that space in this and other scenarios, mathtools offers the two commands

\MTFlushSpaceAbove (to be used directly after \\) and \MTFlushSpaceBelow (to be used the line *instead* of \\). If we apply them, we get:

$$a = b + c \qquad a = b + c$$
$$\vdots \qquad\qquad \vdots$$
$$x = y + z \qquad x = y + z$$

```
\usepackage{mathtools}
\begin{align*} a &= b+c    & a &= b+c      \\ \MTFlushSpaceAbove
             & \vdotswithin{=} & &\vdotswithin{=} \MTFlushSpaceBelow
             x &= y+z    & x &= y+z    \end{align*}
```

11-5-4

For the most common case of vertical dots after an alignment point there is also \shortvdotswithin{⟨*symbol*⟩}, which is a shorthand for

\MTFlushSpaceAbove & \vdotswithin{⟨*symbol*⟩} \MTFlushSpaceBelow

and therefore has to follow a \\, and there cannot be anything else in that row — which is why we could not use it in the previous example. If you ever need it, there is also \shortvdotswithin*, which differs in that it typesets the \vdotswithin before and not after the alignment point.

The mathdots package extensions

Standard LATEX already offers \ddots for diagonal dots, but if you need them, in the other direction you can load the mathdots package by Dan Luecking, which offers \iddots for this purpose. Note, though, that this package also changes the definitions of \ddots, \vdots, and if amsmath is loaded, the two accents \dddot and \ddddot so that they are slightly better placed when used at different sizes, e.g., in exponents. Especially for the accents the latter feature can be quite interesting. Here is an example:

command	large	script	tiny
\ddots	$\ddots$	$\ddots$	$\ddots$
\iddots	$\iddots$	$\iddots$	$\iddots$
\vdots	$\vdots$	$\vdots$	$\vdots$
\dddot{Z}	$\dddot{Z}$	$\dddot{z}$	$\dddot{z}$
\ddddot{Z}	$\ddddot{Z}$	$\ddddot{z}$	$\ddddot{z}$

```
\usepackage{array,amsmath,mathdots}
\begin{tabular}{l@{}>{\large$}c<{$}>{\scriptsize$}c<{$}
                  >{\tiny$}c<{$}}
   command   &   \multicolumn{1}{c}{large}
         &    \multicolumn{1}{c}{script}
             &   \multicolumn{1}{c}{tiny}    \\[3pt]
\verb=\ddots=    & \ddots    & \ddots   & \ddots   \\
\verb=\iddots=   & \iddots   & \iddots  & \iddots  \\
\verb=\vdots=    & \vdots    & \vdots   & \vdots   \\
\verb=\dddot{Z}= & \dddot{Z} & \dddot{Z} & \dddot{Z}\\
\verb=\ddddot{Z}= & \ddddot{Z} & \ddddot{Z} & \ddddot{Z}
\end{tabular}
```

11-5-5

11.5.2 Horizontal extensions in standard LATEX

In principle, any mathematical accent command can be set up to produce the appropriate glyph from a range of widths whenever these are provided by the available fonts. However, in standard LATEX there are only two such commands: \widehat and \widetilde.

This section describes a few commands that produce constructions similar to these extensible accents. All, except \overbrace and \underbrace, produce compound symbols of mathematical class Ordinary (see Section 11.8.1 on page 209). They are illustrated in this example:

$$\widehat{\psi_\delta(t) E_t h} \neq \widetilde{\psi_\Delta(t) E_t h}$$

$$\overline{\psi_\delta(t) E_t h} \approx \underline{\psi_\Delta(t) E_t h}$$

$$\overrightarrow{\psi_\delta(t) E_t h} \cong \overleftarrow{\psi_\Delta(t) E_t h}$$

Combinations are possible too:

$$\overline{\overline{\psi_\delta(t) E_t h}} \leq \underline{\overrightarrow{\psi_\Delta(t) E_t h}}$$

Braces have extra possibilities as explained below.

$$\overbrace{\psi_\delta(t) E_t h} \doteq \underbrace{\psi_\Delta(t) E_t h}$$

```
\[ \widehat   {\psi_\delta(t) E_t h} \neq
   \widetilde {\psi_\Delta(t) E_t h}
\]
\[ \overline  {\psi_\delta(t) E_t h} \approx
   \underline {\psi_\Delta(t) E_t h}
\]
\[ \overrightarrow {\psi_\delta(t) E_t h} \cong
   \overleftarrow  {\psi_\Delta(t) E_t h}
\]
Combinations are possible too:
\[ \overline  {\overline {\psi_\delta(t) E_t h}}
   \leq
   \underline {\overrightarrow
                {\psi_\Delta(t) E_t h}}
\]
Braces have extra possibilities as explained below.
\[ \overbrace   {\psi_\delta(t) E_t h} \doteq
   \underbrace {\psi_\Delta(t) E_t h}
\]
```

The \overbrace and \underbrace commands are somewhat special in that they produce compound symbols of the Operator class and take \limits. This means that you can easily attach some explanatory text or other material to the brace. For this the \text command from amsmath can be very useful.

$$\overbrace{\psi_\delta(t) E_t h}^{\text{explanation}} = \underbrace{\psi_\Delta(t) E_t h}_{\iff x>0}$$

```
\usepackage{amsmath}  % for the \text command
\[
  \overbrace {\psi_\delta(t) E_t h}^{\text{explanation}} =
  \underbrace{\psi_\Delta(t) E_t h}_{\iff x > 0}
\]
```

Another horizontally extensible feature of LaTeX is the bar in a radical sign; it is described at the end of the next subsection.

11.5.3 Further horizontal extensions

To the basic set of horizontally extensible structures, amsmath adds a few more arrows and perhaps more importantly also reimplements \overrightarrow and \overleftarrow so that they change their mathematical style. This means that they look right when used, for example, in fractions or subscripts/superscripts (see Section 11.7.1 on page 195). In contrast, the arrowheads in standard LaTeX always stay at the same size so that the commands without amsmath are suitable for use only at the top level of displayed mathematics.

$$\overrightarrow{\psi_\delta(t)E_t h} \approx \overleftarrow{\psi_\Delta(t)E_t h} \quad \text{No style change}$$
$$\text{without amsmath}$$

$$\underrightarrow{\psi_\delta(t)E_t h} \simeq \underleftarrow{\psi_\Delta(t)E_t h} \quad \text{Needs amsmath}$$

$$\overleftrightarrow{\psi_\delta(t)E_t h} \sim \underleftrightarrow{\psi_\Delta(t)E_t h} \quad \text{Needs amsmath}$$

```
\usepackage{amsmath}
\begin{align*}
\overrightarrow {\psi_\delta(t) E_t h}
&\approx \overleftarrow {\psi_\Delta(t) E_t h}
& &    \text{No style change}              \\[-3pt]
& & & \text{without \textsf{amsmath}}       \\
\underrightarrow  {\psi_\delta(t) E_t h}
&\simeq \underleftarrow {\psi_\Delta(t) E_t h}
& & \text{Needs \textsf{amsmath}}            \\
\overleftrightarrow {\psi_\delta(t) E_t h}
&\sim \underleftrightarrow{\psi_\Delta(t) E_t h}
& & \text{Needs \textsf{amsmath}}
\end{align*}
```

11-5-8

mathtools additions to amsmath   The **mathtools** package offers two additional commands for producing over and under brackets.

\overbracket [*bracket thickness*] [*bracket height*] {*content*}
\underbracket [*bracket thickness*] [*bracket height*] {*content*}

Both command have one mandatory *content* argument for the material bracketed and two optional arguments to specify the *bracket thickness* and *bracket height*. The defaults are chosen to blend well with the size and thickness of \underbrace, but if you do not like them or need several different weights, use the optional arguments.

The next example shows a couple of variations. Note the use of \, and \! to make the brace and the innermost bracket slightly wider on the right without changing the spacing of the + signs.

$$\overbracket{a+\underbracket{b+\overbrace{c+d\,}}\!+e}+f$$

$$\overbracket{a+\underbracket{b+\overbracket{c+d\,}}\!+e}+f$$

```
\usepackage{mathtools}
\begin{gather*}
  \overbracket{a+\underbracket{b+\overbrace{c+d\,}}\!+e}+f} \\
    \overbracket[1.5pt][3pt]{a+
      \underbracket[3pt][4pt]{b+
        \overbracket[.7pt][2pt]{c+d\,}}\!+e}+f}
\end{gather*}
```

11-5-9

The **mathtools** package also corrects some spacing problems with \underbrace and \overbrace because the LaTeX versions are optimized for 10pt body font size and do not work that well with other sizes. With some math font families, such as Concrete Math, the original definitions are superior, though (because of a different brace design), and if that is the case, specify

\let\underbrace\LaTeXunderbrace   \let\overbrace\LaTeXoverbrace

in the preamble of your document to get the LaTeX definitions back.

pattern	Effect		pattern	Effect
1	⌣		A	Horizontal line (anchor) with the width of a D or U
L	⌐		0	Single empty fill (same width as 1)
r	⌣		1,…,9	Copies of regular fill ——
R	⌐		@{*material*}	Places *material* into brace
U	⌣		!{*length*}	Regular fill of specific *length*
D	⌣		*{*num*}{*material*}	Repeat *material* a total of *num* times
'	⌐ Bracket end up		'[*height*]	Bracket up with extra *height*
,	⌐ Bracket end down		,[*height*]	Bracket down with extra *height*

Table 11.4: Pattern elements to construct braces and brackets

11.5.4 abraces — Customizable over and under braces

If you have a need for more specialized over or under braces, e.g., with special tips, or the middle part of the brace not centered or dashes instead of straight horizontal parts, etc., then take a look at the abraces package by Werner Grundlingh.

This package offers a construction method (somewhat modeled after the preamble of a tabular) allowing for a huge number of variant extensible braces.

\aoverbrace [*pattern*] {*material*}   \aunderbrace [*pattern*] {*material*}

Without the optional argument the commands behave just like \overbrace and \underbrace, and if you load the package with the option overload, the standard LaTeX commands get the optional argument added so that you can continue to use the standard names.

The optional argument lets you construct specially formed braces by specifying a *pattern* out of the characters given in Table 11.4. For example, the standard over brace would have the specification of L1U1R where the two numbers represent the horizontal filler parts and their values define the ratio, i.e., "1:1" in that case. Thus, if you want to move the middle part to the left, you could use a ratio like "1:3" or "2:5", etc. Similarly, if you want to have several "middle" parts, place several U or D characters at the right point into the pattern. A few variants are shown in the following example:

11-5-10

$$\overbrace{a^3 + 3ab^2 + 3a^2b + b^3}$$

$$\overbrace{\text{Some text with a brace}}$$

$$\underbrace{x_1, x_2, x_3, \ldots, x_n}$$

$$\underbrace{(a+b)^2} = \underbrace{a^2 + 2ab + b^2}$$

```
\usepackage{abraces,amsmath}
\begin{gather*}
   \aoverbrace [L1U3R] {a^3 +3ab^2 + 3a^2b +b^3}            \\
   \aunderbrace[l1U1D1U1r] {\text{Some text with a brace}} \\
   \aunderbrace[l10@{\ldots}04r] {x_1,x_2,x_3,\dots,x_n}    \\
   \aunderbrace['1'] {\smash[b]{(a+b)}}\nolimits^2
       = \aunderbrace['1,[5pt]1'] {\smash[b]{\; a^2+2ab+b^2}}
\end{gather*}
```

Visual adjustments and other fine-tuning

The last line of the previous example is interesting on three accounts. For one, \aunderbrace takes limits to add material above or below the brace as discussed later, but here the ^2 is meant to apply to (a+b), so we need \nolimits to cancel this.[1] The second adjustment concerns the vertical position of the brackets. Given that the first one contains material with a parenthesis adding to the depth, the bracket would be placed lower than the second one. To correct this we use \smash to ignore the depth on both sides. This brings the bracket fairly close to the formula parts; an alternative there would have been to add a \mathstrut. Finally, we also add some extra space at the beginning of the formula part embraced by the second bracket to make it appear visually balanced. See Section 11.7 on page 194 for more examples of such fine-tuning.

Nesting the commands is equally possible as long as you do not need braces that overlap. In the latter case take look at the underoverlap package discussed in the next section. Both packages can be jointly used as shown in Example 11-5-18 on page 190.

$$x + \underbrace{y + z}_{} - a$$

```
\usepackage{abraces,amsmath}
\[ \aoverbrace[L1U6R]{x +
    \aunderbrace[16D1r]{ \aoverbrace[,1,]{y+z} - a} } \]
```

11-5-11

If you need a certain pattern repeatedly, you can save yourself some effort by defining an additional pattern character and assigning the pattern to it.

> \newbracespec{*char*}{*pattern-elements*}

This declaration is comparable to the \newcolumntype approach in the array package. Once given, the *char* can be used in any *pattern* representing the *pattern-elements*. Even though the declaration has "new" in its name, it is perfectly permissible to use it to overwrite a previously defined *char*, even one of the predefined ones — though that means its original functionality is lost and so seldom a good idea.

The approach is used in the next example, in which we define the pattern element s representing a brace with two tips and a few dots. Half of the brace is colored blue to show that coloring is possible too.

$$\underbrace{x_1, x_2, x_3, x_4, \ldots, x_n}$$

```
\usepackage{abraces,amsmath,color}
\newbracespec{s}{11D2@{\,\ldots}0@{\color{blue}\ldots\,}2D1r}
\[ \aunderbrace[s]{x_1,x_2,x_3,x_4,\dots,x_n} \]
```

11-5-12

As you can observe in the previous example, any color change (or in fact any other declaration) inside an @{..} pattern element is applied to the remaining part of the pattern (or until changed again). Thus, if you want only to color the dots in the example, another \color{black} or the use of \textcolor is needed.

Attaching super and subscripts

In many cases one does not only want to brace some part of a formula but also add some text or a formula above or below the brace. This can be easily achieved with

---

[1] Without it the ^2 would not be displayed at all, because the specified *pattern* does not contain any D elements to attach it to.

the help of ^ and _ after the mandatory argument. Normally you would use ^ with
\aoverbrace and _ with \aunderbrace, but it is possible to apply either or both.

The material is placed centered around the tip(s) of the brace. For this the *pattern*
is evaluated in the following way: material in ^{..} is placed above the first U or A
pattern element, while material in _{..} attaches below the first D or A element. If
you have several Us or Ds, you can attach material to each of them by using & to split
the material in several parts that are then applied from left to right.

In the next example we set up a brace pattern with three anchor points for ^{..}
(U, A, and another U). As shown in the example, you can attach superscript material
to any of them using the right number of & symbols. For a subscript there is only one
anchor point, because the pattern has no D so that the subscript made with _{..}
can attach only to the A element in the center.

If you split the super or subscript into more parts than you have anchors available,
you will get an error message, and the excess parts are dropped. This is what happens *Special cases*
in the last line of the next example where the word "dropped" is not in the output. *involving &*

If you need & as an ordinary character, just use \& as usual. However, if your
super or subscript material does contain an array, smallmatrix, or some other
environment that uses & in its syntax, you need to hide this use from abraces by
surrounding it with an extra brace group as shown below:

11-5-13

$$\overbrace{\text{a braced formula}}^{x\&y}$$
$$\overbrace{\text{a braced formula}}^{x\quad y}$$
$$\overbrace{\text{a braced formula}}^{x\quad z}$$
$$\overbrace{\text{a braced formula}}^{\;z}_{\substack{a\;b\\c\;d}}$$

```
\usepackage{abraces,amsmath}
\newbracespec{s}{L1U1A1U1R}
\begin{gather*}
  \aoverbrace[s]{\text{a braced formula}}^{x \& y}          \\
  \aoverbrace[s]{\text{a braced formula}}^{x & y}           \\
  \aoverbrace[s]{\text{a braced formula}}^{x & & z}         \\
  \aoverbrace[s]{\text{a braced formula}}^{ & & z}
    _{{\begin{smallmatrix}a&b\\c&d\end{smallmatrix}} & dropped}
\end{gather*}
```

Up to now all examples use a single *pattern* for constructing the brace as well
as placing any super or subscripts. In nearly all circumstances this is all you need *The extended syntax*
to get the results you are after. There are, however, a few cases where you want the
annotation placed in a way that is incompatible with the brace construction; e.g., you
want a normal brace above and also a centered annotation below the formula.

For these cases, both \aoverbrace and \aunderbrace offer a second optional
argument so the extended syntax (with *above* and *below* also both optional) is actually
as follows:

\aoverbrace [*brace-pattern*] {*material*} [*anchor-pattern*] ^{*above*}_{*below*}
\aunderbrace [*brace-pattern*] {*material*} [*anchor-pattern*] ^{*above*}_{*below*}

If the optional *anchor-pattern* argument is given, it is used instead of the *brace-pattern*
for determining the position of any super or subscript annotations. The fact that
there is only a single pattern is not a problem, even if both ^{..} and _{..} are

used, because you can guide the anchoring either by supplying the right number of & characters or by specifying a suitable combination of U (only for superscripts), D (only for subscripts), and A (anchor for both) in the *anchor-pattern*. In the example below we use 1A1 in the *anchor-pattern* to have one centered anchor for both super and subscripts:

with text above

a braced formula

and some below

```
\usepackage{abraces,amsmath}
\[
  \aoverbrace{\text{a braced formula}}[1A1]
           ^{\text{with text above}}
           _{\text{and some below}}
\]
```

11-5-14

The problem of trailing optional arguments

There is a potential problem with a syntax using trailing optional arguments: if no optional argument is wanted but the command is followed by a bracket group (even on the next line), then that group is parsed as an optional argument and not considered part of the formula. Fortunately, with the abraces commands it is easy to identify that this is a mistake: if there is neither a super nor a subscript, then such a bracket group is not an *anchor-pattern* argument (as that would be of no use) but must belong to the formula itself. The first line in the example shows such a case and the fact that it is correctly handled.

However, if what follows is an open bracket that does not have a matching closing bracket, then this no longer works because the parser scans for the closing symbol until it finds one (unlikely), or until it finds a \par, and then responds with a low-level error message. The solution for this scenario is therefore to explicitly tell LATEX to stop scanning earlier, for example, by adding \relax.

$(x + y + z)[a, b]$

$(x + y + z)[a, b)$

```
\usepackage{abraces,amsmath}
\begin{gather*}
  \aoverbrace [,1,]{(x+y+z)} [a,b]            \\
  \aunderbrace['1']{(x+y+z)} \relax [a,b)
\end{gather*}
```

11-5-15

Over or under braces split across several display lines

With all these tools at hand it is fairly simple to produce braces that are split across two lines in a display. To make it even simpler we define five new pattern characters: B or b (for begin brace), e or E (for end brace), and M (for any middle part with a tip). The uppercase letters produce a brace containing a middle part with a tip, while the lowercase ones do not. Thus, you would normally select one upper and one lowercase character (depending on where you want to place your annotations, if any). Also note the use of \enspace to run the brace a little wider at the open side to indicate that it is continuing.

In the example the M element is only indirectly used when defining B and E, but if you want to span three or more lines, you can use it for the middle one. If you need a continuation without any tip, then just use the pattern 1 on its own instead.

```
\usepackage{amsmath}  \usepackage[overload]{abraces}
\newbracespec{M}{1U1}     \newbracespec{B}{LM}      \newbracespec{e}{1R}
                          \newbracespec{b}{L1}      \newbracespec{E}{MR}
\begin{multline*}
  f(x)=a_0+a_1x+a_2x^2+
  \overbrace[B]{a_3x^3 + a_4x^4 + \dots + a_{i-1}x^{i-1} + \enspace}
              ^{\text{some explanation}}                                  \\
  \overbrace[e]{\enspace a_ix^i + a_{i+1}x^{i+1}} + \dots + a_{n-1}x^{n-1}
\end{multline*}
```

11-5-16

$$f(x) = a_0 + a_1x + a_2x^2 + \overbrace{a_3x^3 + a_4x^4 + \cdots + a_{i-1}x^{i-1} +}^{\text{some explanation}}$$
$$\overbrace{a_ix^i + a_{i+1}x^{i+1} + \cdots + a_{n-1}x^{n-1}}$$

11.5.5 underoverlap — Partly overlapping horizontal braces

While it is possible to nest \overbrace or \underbrace commands (or the equivalents from the abraces package), it is rather difficult with the standard tools to produce partly overlapping braces within a single formula. If this is needed, you can use the underoverlap package by Michiel Helvensteijn.[1] It offers by default four commands that can produce partly overlapping structures. Others can be added as needed.

> \UOLoverbrace{*private*} [*common*]   \UOLunderbrace{*private*} [*common*]

The brace spans both the *private* and the *common* parts, i.e., as if both parts are inside the argument of \overbrace. However, the optional *common part* is typeset only by the next \UOL... command, which therefore should follow immediately. If not, you get results as shown in the second and third formula of the next example.

By default \UOLoverline and \UOLunderline are also available, and all commands can be intermixed freely.

11-5-17

$$a + \overbrace{b + c + d}^{\text{both}} + f + g \qquad (1)$$
$$a + \overbrace{b +}^{\text{wrong!!}} + f + g \qquad (2)$$
$$a + \overbrace{b + + f}^{\text{clearly wrong}} \underbrace{c + d}_{\text{too!}} + g \qquad (3)$$

```
\usepackage{underoverlap,amsmath}
\begin{gather} a + \UOLoverbrace{b +}[c + d]^{\text{both}}
               \UOLunderline{+ f}_{\text{fine}} + g  \\
 a + \UOLoverline{b +}[c + d]^{\text{wrong!!}} + f + g  \\
 a + \UOLoverbrace{b +}[c + d]^{\text{clearly wrong}}
    + f \UOLunderbrace{+ g}_{\text{too!}}        \end{gather}
```

---

[1] An alternative based on an array-like syntax is the oubrace package by Donald Arseneau.

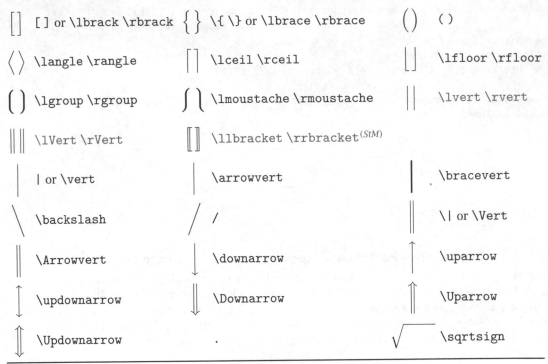

`[ ]` `[ ] or \lbrack \rbrack`	`{ }` `\{ \} or \lbrace \rbrace`	`( )` `( )`
`⟨ ⟩` `\langle \rangle`	`⌈ ⌉` `\lceil \rceil`	`⌊ ⌋` `\lfloor \rfloor`
`( )` `\lgroup \rgroup`	`∫ ∫` `\lmoustache \rmoustache`	`‖` `\lvert \rvert`
`‖‖` `\lVert \rVert`	`⟦ ⟧` `\llbracket \rrbracket`(StM)	
`|` `| or \vert`	`\arrowvert`	`\bracevert`
`\` `\backslash`	`/` `/`	`‖` `| or \Vert`
`\Arrowvert`	`↓` `\downarrow`	`↑` `\uparrow`
`↕` `\updownarrow`	`⇓` `\Downarrow`	`⇑` `\Uparrow`
`⇕` `\Updownarrow`	`.`	`√‾` `\sqrtsign`

Symbols in blue require either the amsmath package or, if additionally denoted with (StM), the stmaryrd package. A period (.) is not itself an extensible symbol, but it can be used to produce an "invisible" delimiter. The `\sqrtsign` symbol cannot be used with `\left`, `\right`, or `\middle`.

Table 11.5: Vertically extensible symbols

With the declaration `\newUOLdecorator` you can even define new `\UOL...`-like commands, and there is also the possibility of augmenting existing commands (like `\overline`) so that they behave as `\UOL...` commands.

The next example is not going to win us a design award, but it shows both features and also the fact that with a little care you can chain these commands. Note, however, that there are a number of restrictions that need to be taken into account. So if you intend to define your own variants, consult the package documentation.

$$\left| a + \overline{b + c + \overrightarrow{d} + e + \overleftarrow{f}} + g \right.$$

```
\usepackage{underoverlap,abraces}
\newUOLdecorator\rightunderbrace{\aunderbrace[14D1r]{#1}}
\UOLaugment\underline
\UOLaugment\overleftarrow \UOLaugment\overrightarrow
\[ \underline{a +}[b] \overrightarrow{+}[c + d]
    \rightunderbrace{+ e +}[f] \overleftarrow{+ g}
\]
```

11-5-18

11.5.6 Vertical extensions

While only a few symbols are horizontally extensible, there is a much larger range available with vertical extensions. The full list is given in Table 11.5. These symbols become extensible only in certain usages; they must all be based on a construction of the following form:

  \left⟨*ext-Open*⟩ … \middle⟨*ext-Middle*⟩ … \right⟨*ext-Close*⟩

The \middle⟨*ext-Middle*⟩ is optional, while \left and \right have to be present. The ⟨*ext-Open*⟩, ⟨*ext-Middle*⟩, and ⟨*ext-Close*⟩ can be any of the symbols (except \sqrtsign) listed in Table 11.5, or possibly others if additional packages are loaded. They must be symbols that have been set up to be extensible using the methods described in [60], which is part of every LATEX distribution; thus, a symbol must be available to represent the absence of an actual glyph. This symbol, which is sometimes called the *null delimiter*, is denoted by a period ".".

The sizes of the actual glyphs used to typeset the extensible symbols are chosen to fit with the vertical size (height and depth) of the typeset *subformula* that lies in between them; the exact details of how this is done, and of the parameters that affect the process, can be found in Chapter 17 and Appendix G (Rule 19) of *The TEXbook* [42]. One can also request specific sizes for such symbols as explained in Section 11.7.4 on page 199.

The TEX engine's way of scaling delimiters with the help of \left and \right has a problem: it may in some cases change the spacing with respect to the material before and after. This can be avoided by using \mleft and \mright from the mleftright package instead; see the discussion in Section 11.8.1 on page 211 for details.

Possible spacing issues with \left and \right

The radical sign \sqrtsign is even more amazing than the delimiters — it grows both vertically and horizontally to fit the size of its argument. In LATEX it is typically not used directly but accessed via the \sqrt command, which is discussed further in Section 11.7.5 on page 199.

11-5-19

$$\sqrt{1 + \sqrt{2 + \sqrt{3 + \sqrt{4 + \sqrt{5 + \sqrt{6 + \sqrt{7 + \sqrt{8 + x}}}}}}}}$$

```
\[
\sqrtsign{1 + \sqrtsign{2 +
  \sqrtsign{3 + \sqrtsign{4 +
    \sqrtsign{5 + \sqrtsign{6 +
      \sqrtsign{7 + \sqrtsign{8 + x}}}}}}}}
\]
```

11.6 Words in mathematics

Most of the time formulas consist only of symbols and individual letters denoting variables. However, sometimes ordinary text is made part of a formula, either to annotate some part of it or to continue the outer text with words like "and", etc. In addition, a number of common operators are typeset using words rather than symbols.

11.6.1 The \text command

Math font-changing commands such as \mathrm are not intended for putting normal text inside mathematics as the fonts used are fixed and may not bear any relation to the font used in the text surrounding the formula. To produce "text" fonts inside a formula in standard LaTeX you can use \textrm, \textsf, etc., or you can simply use \mbox if you want to typeset in the font used outside the current mathematical material. However, one problem with all these commands in standard LaTeX is that they always typeset their text in a fixed font size, regardless of the position in the formula.

The amsmath package improves[1] on this by additionally providing the command \text, which is similar to \mbox but is much better, ensuring that the text is set using the correct font size. It also modifies \textrm and friends to change the font size as necessary, as can be observed in the next example:

Some text outside the formula . . .

Also, if $\Delta_{\text{max up}} \geq \Delta_{\text{min down}} + \epsilon$
(for all ups and downs) then
$$\Delta_{\text{sum of ups}} > \Delta_{\text{sum of downs}}$$

```
\usepackage{amsmath}

Some text outside the formula \ldots
\begin{multline*}
    \text{Also, if } \Delta_{\text{max up}}
    \geq \Delta_{\text{min down}} + \epsilon \\
    \text{(for all ups and downs) then}        \\
    \Delta_\textsf{sum of ups}
                    > \Delta_{\textsf{sum of downs}}
\end{multline*}
```

11-6-1

11.6.2 Operator and function names

The names of many well-known mathematical functions (such as log and sin) and operators (such as max and lim) are traditionally typeset as words (or abbreviations) in roman type so as to visually distinguish them from shorter variable names that are set in "math italic". The most common function names have predefined commands to produce the correct typographical treatment; see Table 11.6 on the next page. Most functions are available in standard LaTeX; those listed in blue in the table require loading amsmath. The functions marked with (ℓ) may "take limits" in display formulas (see Section 11.4.4).

$$\lim_{x \to 0} \frac{\sin^2(x)}{x^2} = 1$$
$$\varliminf_{n \to \infty} |a_{n+1}| / |a_n| = 0$$
$$\varinjlim (m_i^\lambda \cdot M)^* \leq \varprojlim_{A/p \to \lambda(A)} A_p \leq 0$$

```
\usepackage{amsmath} \newcommand\abs[1]{\lvert#1\rvert}

\begin{gather*}
    \lim_{x \rightarrow 0} \frac{ \sin^2(x) }{ x^2 }=1 \\
    \varliminf_{n \rightarrow \infty}
            \abs{a_{n+1}} / \abs{a_n} = 0            \\
    \varinjlim (m_i^\lambda \cdot M)^* \le
            \varprojlim_{A/p\rightarrow\lambda(A)}A_p \le 0
\end{gather*}
```

11-6-2

---

[1] This particular improvement is also available separately in the package amstext.

arccos	\arccos	arcsin	\arcsin	arctan	\arctan
arg	\arg	cos	\cos	cosh	\cosh
cot	\cot	coth	\coth	csc	\csc
deg	\deg	det	\det$^{(\ell)}$	dim	\dim
exp	\exp	gcd	\gcd$^{(\ell)}$	hom	\hom
inf	\inf$^{(\ell)}$	inj lim	\injlim$^{(\ell)}$	ker	\ker
lg	\lg	lim	\lim$^{(\ell)}$	lim inf	\liminf$^{(\ell)}$
lim sup	\limsup$^{(\ell)}$	ln	\ln	log	\log
max	\max$^{(\ell)}$	min	\min$^{(\ell)}$	Pr	\Pr$^{(\ell)}$
proj lim	\projlim$^{(\ell)}$	sec	\sec	sin	\sin
sinh	\sinh	sup	\sup$^{(\ell)}$	tan	\tan
tanh	\tanh	$\varinjlim$	\varinjlim$^{(\ell)}$	$\varliminf$	\varliminf$^{(\ell)}$
$\varlimsup$	\varlimsup$^{(\ell)}$	$\varprojlim$	\varprojlim$^{(\ell)}$		

Blue functions require the amsmath *package.*　　(ℓ) *indicates that the operator takes limits in displays.*

Table 11.6: Predefined operators and functions

New functions of this type are needed frequently in mathematics, so the amsmath package provides a general mechanism for defining new "operator names".[1]

\DeclareMathOperator*{*cmd*}{*text*}　　\operatorname*{*text*}

\DeclareMathOperator defines *cmd* to produce *text* in the appropriate font for "textual operators". If the new function being named is an operator that should, when used in displays, "take limits" (so that any subscripts and superscripts are placed in the "limits" positions, above and below, as with, for example, lim, sup, or min), then use the starred form \DeclareMathOperator*. In addition to using the proper font, \DeclareMathOperator sets up good spacing on either side of the function name when necessary. For example, it gives $A \operatorname{meas} B$ instead of $A meas B$. The *text* argument is processed using a "pseudo-text mode" in which

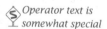
Operator text is somewhat special

- The hyphen character – prints as a text hyphen (and not as a minus sign); see \supminus in the next example.

- The asterisk character * prints as a raised text asterisk (not centered).

- Otherwise, the text is processed in math mode so that spaces are ignored and you can use subscripts, superscripts, and other elements.

The related command \operatorname (and its *-form) simply turns its argument into a function name, as in Example 11-2-11 on page 137. It is useful for "one-off" operators.

---
[1] This functionality is also separately available in the package amsopn.

The next example shows how to provide the command \meas for the new function name "meas" (short for measure) and the operator functions \esssup and \supminus, both of which take limits.

$$\|f\|_\infty = \operatorname{ess\,sup}_{x \in R^n} |f(x)|$$

$$\operatorname{meas}_1\{u \in R^1_+ : f^*(u) > \alpha\} =$$

$$\operatorname{ess\,sup}_{x \in R^i} \operatorname{meas}_i\{u \in R^n : |f(u)| \geq \alpha\}$$

$$(\forall \alpha \in \operatorname{sup-minus}^*_{f^*} R_{*+})$$

```
\usepackage{amsmath}
\DeclareMathOperator \meas    {meas}
\DeclareMathOperator*\esssup  {ess \, sup}
\DeclareMathOperator*\supminus{sup - minus*}
\newcommand\abs [1]{\lvert#1\rvert}
\newcommand\norm[1]{\lVert#1\rVert}
\begin{multline*}
  \norm{f}_\infty = \esssup_{x \in R^n} \abs{f(x)} \\
  \meas_1 \{ u \in R_+^1 \colon f^*(u)>\alpha \} = \\
  \esssup_{x \in R^i} \; \meas_i
    \{ u \in R^n \colon \abs{f(u)} \geq \alpha \}  \\
  (\forall \alpha \in \supminus_{f^*} R_{*+})
\end{multline*}
```

11-6-3

Unfortunately, such declarations must appear in the preamble, so it is not possible to change a declaration temporarily. In fact, \DeclareMathOperator works only for command names that have not been used previously, so it is not possible to overwrite an existing command directly. To do so, you must first remove the previous definition (in this case, of \csc) before redeclaring it; this removal is accomplished by using low-level TeX coding, as LaTeX provides no method for completing this task.

$$\varlimsup_{n\to\infty} \mathcal{Q}(u_n, u_n - u^{\#}) \geq \operatorname{cosec}(\mathcal{Q}'(u^{\#})) \qquad (1)$$

```
\usepackage{amsmath}
%% Low-level TeX needed here to cancel
%% the old definition of \csc:
\let \csc \relax
\DeclareMathOperator\csc{cosec}
\newcommand\calQ{\mathcal{Q}}
\begin{equation}
  \varlimsup_{n\to\infty}
            \calQ (u_n, u_n - u^{\#})
  \ge \csc (\calQ' (u^{\#}))
\end{equation}
```

11-6-4

11.7 Fine-tuning the mathematical layout

Although LaTeX generally does a good job of laying out the elements of a formula, it is sometimes necessary to fine-tune the positioning. This section describes how to achieve some of the many detailed adjustments to the layout that are used to produce mathematical typography that is just a little bit better. Most of this section applies to all LaTeX mathematical material, but a few features are available only with the amsmath or mathtools package; these are clearly labeled.

Style	Superscript	Subscript	Numerator	Denominator
D	S	S'	T	T'
D'	S'	S'	T'	T'
T	S	S'	S	S'
T'	S'	S'	S'	S'
S, SS	SS	SS'	SS	SS'
S', SS'	SS'	SS'	SS'	SS'

Table 11.7: Mathematical styles in subformulas

11.7.1 Controlling the automatic sizing and spacing

Letters and mathematical symbols normally get smaller, and are more tightly spaced, when they appear in fractions, superscripts, or subscripts. In total, TeX has eight different styles in which it can lay out formulas:

D, D'	\displaystyle	Displayed on lines by themselves
T, T'	\textstyle	Embedded in text
S, S'	\scriptstyle	In superscripts or subscripts
SS, SS'	\scriptscriptstyle	In all higher-order superscripts or subscripts

The prime versions (D', T', etc.) represent the so-called *cramped* styles, which are similar to the normal styles except that superscripts are not raised so much.

TeX uses only three type sizes for mathematics in these styles: text size (also used in \displaystyle), script size, and scriptscript size. The size of each part of a formula can be determined according to the following scheme:

A symbol in style	is typeset in	and produces
D, D', T, T'	text size	(text size)
S, S'	script size	(script size)
SS, SS'	scriptscript size	(scriptscript size)

In LaTeX, the top-level part of a formula set in running text (within a $ pair or between \(...\)) is typeset using text style (style T). A displayed formula (e.g., one between \[...\]) is typeset in display style (style D). The kind of style used in a subformula can then be determined from Table 11.7, where the last two columns describe the styles used in the numerator and the denominator of a fraction or similar construct, for example, produced with \frac or \binom. In particular, notice this difference between fractions in display and text style; in the latter case the numerator and denominator are typeset in script style, i.e., noticeably smaller.

195

The various styles can be seen in this example:

```
\normalsize                    %% Style:
\[ b                           %% D
    ^0                         %% S
    +                          %% D
    \frac{(k + p)              %% T
         _{j'}                 %% S'
    % \displaystyle  %% <-- possible modification
    \pm                        %% T      [D]  |
    \frac{(f + q)              %% S      [T]  |
         ^{(pk)                %% SS     [S]  V
         ^y                    %% SS
         _{j'}}}               %% SS'
         {(h + y)}}            %% S'     [T']
         {(1 + q)              %% T'
         ^{(pk)}}              %% S'
\]
```

$$b^0 + \frac{(k+p)_{j'} \pm \frac{(f+q)^{(pk)^y_{j'}}}{(h+y)}}{(l+q)^{(pk)}}$$

11-7-1

You can change the layout of this example by explicitly specifying the style to be used in each part. For example, if you remove the comment character in front of \displaystyle, then some of the styles will change to those shown in brackets. The result looks like this:

$$b^0 + \frac{(k+p)_{j'} \pm \frac{(f+q)^{(pk)^y_{j'}}}{(h+y)}}{(l+q)^{(pk)}}$$

11-7-2

mathtools additions to amsmath

In standard LaTeX or amsmath it is not possible to explicitly request that a formula should be typeset in cramped style. The only possibilities you have is requesting one of the uncramped styles and letting TeX decide the rest based on its logic described in Table 11.7 on the preceding page. However, with mathtools you have a command at your disposal that lets you ask for cramped style explicitly.

\cramped [*mathstyle*] {*subformula*}

The *subformula* is typeset in the cramped version of the current math style. In the op-tional *mathstyle* argument you can explicitly ask for a different cramped style by spec-ifying \displaystyle, \textstyle, \scriptstyle, or \scriptscriptstyle. To the outer formula the *subformula* looks like a single object of type Ordinary. If that is not appropriate, you need to additionally use \mathop, etc., to change its interpretation (see Section 11.8 on page 208).

In the next example a sum is typeset in a display formula. In cramped style the superscripts are noticeably lowered, and in cramped \textstyle the sum operator additionally takes no limits. See also page 204 for additional commands that provide subformulas in *cramped* style.

11-7-3

$$\sum_i x^{i^2} \neq \sum_i x^{i^2} \neq \sum_i x^{i^2}$$

```
\usepackage{mathtools}
\Large \[ \sum_i x^{i^2} \neq \cramped{\sum_i x^{i^2}}
          \neq \cramped[\textstyle]{\sum_i x^{i^2}} \]
```

11.7.2 Subformulas

Whereas in text a pair of braces can simply indicate a group to which the effects of some declaration should be confined, within mathematics they do more than this. They delimit a subformula, which is always typeset as a separate entity that is added to the outer formula. As a side effect, subformulas are always typeset at their natural width and do not stretch or shrink horizontally when TeX tries to fit a formula in a paragraph line during line breaking. As shown earlier, the subformula from a simple brace group is treated as if it was just a single symbol (of class Ordinary). An empty brace group, therefore, generates an invisible symbol that can affect the spacing. The exact details can be found in Chapters 17 and 18 and Appendix G of *The TeXbook* [42].

Subformulas are always typeset at their natural width

The contents of subscripts/superscripts and the arguments of many (but not all) commands, such as \frac and \mathrel, are also subformulas and get this same special treatment. Important examples of arguments that are not necessarily set as subformulas include those of \bm (see Section 12.2.1). If a group is needed only to limit the scope of a declaration (i.e., where a separately typeset subformula would be wrong), then \begingroup and \endgroup and not {...} should be used. Note that specialized mathematical declarations such as style changes apply until the end of the current subformula, irrespective of the presence of any other groups.

In the following artificial example you can see that the mathematical styles are restricted to the subformulas of the operator subscripts, but the \scriptstyle inside \bm is neither restricted to the argument nor does it end at the \endgroup. However, that group delimits the scope of the color declaration.

Scope of mathematical styles

11-7-4

$$\sum_i \prod_j X_{i_j} = A + B + C$$

```
\usepackage{color,bm}
\[ \sum_{\textstyle i} \prod_{\scriptscriptstyle j} X_{i_j} = A
   \begingroup\color{blue} + \bm{\scriptstyle B} + \endgroup C \]
```

11.7.3 Line breaking in inline formulas

LaTeX can break an inline formula (e.g., produced with $...$) over several lines if necessary, but it does this by default only after Relation or Binary symbols. The penalty for breaking at these positions is customizable through the TeX counters \relpenalty (default value 500) and \binoppenalty (default 700). This means that LaTeX discourages breaking a formula, but if necessary, it slightly prefers breaking after a Relation over breaking after a Binary symbol. If you want to discourage this further, you can set the parameter to even higher values, but it has to be done with low-level assignments, e.g.,

```
\binoppenalty = 10000   % never break after a Binary symbol
\relpenalty   = 0       % but do not penalize a break after a Relation
```

If you never want any automatic line breaking happening within a formula, you can set both to 10000 (TeX's number for ∞), but you might have to also alter the definitions of \pmod and \bmod because they use their own hardwired penalties — or handle them manually.

The penalty values used are the ones that are current *at the end* of the formula; thus, changing their values anywhere inside a formula affects all Relation and Binary symbols, not just a single one. For local adjustments, it is therefore better to place explicit penalties inside a formula that you want to affect, i.e., \nobreak for preventing a break after a specific symbol[1] or \allowbreak, \linebreak[*num*], or \nolinebreak[*num*] to allow, encourage, or discourage it at any point within the formula, which makes it possible to break anywhere.

In the next example LaTeX breaks after the + sign, which looks a bit odd with the b on its own at the beginning of the line. So we correct it by adding \nobreak, after which LaTeX uses the only remaining breakpoint after the = sign. This makes the line look a bit spaced out in the example (because it is so narrow), but in real life with a wider paragraph measure, this adjustment would be a clear improvement.

Some words of text before the formula $\sum x_i = a + b$ and after.

Some words of text before the formula $\sum x_i = a + b$ and after.

```
Some words of text before the formula
$ \sum x_i = a + b $ and after.
```

```
Some words of text before the formula
$ \sum x_i = a +\nobreak b $ and after.
```

11-7-5

Do not use \mbox or $\{...\}$ to prevent a line break in a formula

You sometimes see the advice that putting some material into an \mbox is a good way to prevent an unwanted line break. While this is a good solution for preventing hyphenation in a word, it is not really good to keep several words together nor to keep a formula from breaking across lines. The reason is that the spaces in the formula (or between words) are then always set at their natural width and no longer participate in shrinking or stretching to fill the line. This also happens if you turn your formula into a subformula: they too are always set at their natural width.

The next example clearly shows the problem. Assume that you wanted to prevent the short formula from being broken, so you make sure, but after a few rewrites, it is no longer anywhere near a line break. In the first two paragraphs the formula is now set at its natural width, resulting in the word "af-ter" being broken, and only in the third paragraph was LaTeX able to squeeze the formula slightly to make everything fit onto a single line.

---

[1] Normally TeX evaluates all penalties in sequence, which makes it impossible to disallow a break through \nobreak if there is already a penalty allowing it. However, in formulas an explicit penalty after a Relation or Binary symbol overwrites the default penalty, so here it works.

However, even if the line breaking comes out reasonably well, a line with some spaces set at their natural width, while all others are squeezed or expanded, looks bad and distracts from reading — you should therefore avoid that trap.

11-7-6

Words before $\sum x_i = a + b$ and after.

Words before $\sum x_i = a + b$ and after.

Words before $\sum x_i = a + b$ and after.

```
Words before \mbox{$ \sum x_i = a + b $}  and after.

Words before ${ \sum x_i = a + b }$         and after.

Words before $ \sum x_i =\nobreak a +\nobreak b $
                                            and after.
```

11.7.4 Big-g delimiters

To provide direct control of the sizes of extensible delimiters, LaTeX offers four commands: \big, \Big, \bigg, and \Bigg. These take a single parameter, which *must* be an extensible delimiter, and they produce ever-larger versions of the delimiter, from 1.2 to 3 times as big as the base size.

Three extra variants exist for each of the four commands, giving four sizes of Opening symbol (e.g., \bigl), four sizes of Relation symbol (e.g., \Bigm), and four sizes of Closing symbol (e.g., \Biggr).[1] All 16 of these commands can (and must) be used with any symbol that can come after either \left, \right, or \middle (see Table 11.5 on page 190).

In standard LaTeX the sizes of these delimiters are fixed. With the amsmath package, however, the sizes adapt to the size of the surrounding material, according to the type size and mathematical style in use, as shown in the next example. The same is true when you load the exscale package (see Section 9.5.7) or when you use a font package that implements the exscale functionality as an option (e.g., several of the packages discussed in Sections 12.3 and 12.5).

11-7-7

$$\left(\mathbf{E}_y \int_0^{t_\varepsilon} L_{x,y^x(s)} \varphi(x)\, ds \right)$$

$$\left(\mathbf{E}_y \int_0^{t_\varepsilon} L_{x,y^x(s)} \varphi(x)\, ds \right)$$

```
\usepackage{amsmath}
\[ \biggl( \mathbf{E}_{y} \int_0^{t_\varepsilon}
      L_{x, y^x(s)} \varphi(x)\, ds \biggr) \]
\bigskip\Large
\[ \biggl( \mathbf{E}_{y} \int_0^{t_\varepsilon}
      L_{x, y^x(s)} \varphi(x)\, ds \biggr) \]
```

11.7.5 Radical movements

In standard LaTeX, the placement of the index on a radical sign is sometimes not good. With amsmath, the commands \leftroot and \uproot can be used within the optional argument of the \sqrt command to adjust the positioning of this index.

---

[1] See Section 11.8.1 on page 209 for the various mathematical classes of symbols.

Positive integer arguments to these commands move the root index to the left and up, respectively, while negative arguments move it right and down. These arguments are given in terms of math units (see Section 11.7.7), which are quite small, so these commands are useful for fine adjustments.

$$\sqrt[\beta]{k} \qquad \sqrt[\beta]{k} \qquad \sqrt[\beta]{k}$$

```
\usepackage{amsmath}
\[ \sqrt[\beta]{k}                               \qquad
   \sqrt[\leftroot{2}\uproot{4} \beta]{k} \qquad
   \sqrt[\leftroot{1}\uproot{3} \beta]{k}        \]
```

11-7-8

11.7.6 Ghostbusters™

To get math spacing and alignment "just right", it is often best to make creative use of some of primitive TEX's unique and sophisticated typesetting abilities. These features are accessed by a collection of commands related to \phantom and \smash; and they can be used in both mathematical and other text.

For instance, the large alignment example (Example 11-2-9 on page 136) uses lots of phantoms to get the alignment just right. Each of these phantoms produces an invisible "white box" whose size (width and total height plus depth) is determined by typesetting the text in its argument and measuring its size.

Conversely, the command \smash typesets its contents (in an LR-box) but then ignores both their height and depth, behaving as if they were both zero. The standard LATEX command \hphantom is a combination of these, producing the equivalent of \smash{}: an invisible box with zero height and depth but the width of the phantom contents.

The \vphantom command makes the width of the phantom zero but preserves its total height plus depth. An example is the command \mathstrut, which is defined as "\vphantom(" so that it produces a zero-width box of height and depth equal to that of a parenthesis.

The amsmath package provides an optional argument for \smash, used as follows: \smash[t]{...} ignores the height of the box's contents but retains the depth, while [b] ignores the depth and keeps the height. Compare these four lines, in which only the handling of $\sqrt{y}$ varies:

$$\sqrt{x} + \sqrt{y} + \sqrt{z}$$
$$\sqrt{x} + \sqrt{y} + \sqrt{z}$$
$$\sqrt{x} + \sqrt{y} + \sqrt{z}$$
$$\sqrt{x} + \sqrt{y} + \sqrt{z}$$

```
\usepackage{amsmath}
$\sqrt{x} + \sqrt{y}                + \sqrt{z}$ \\
$\sqrt{x} + \sqrt{\mathstrut y} + \sqrt{z}$ \\
$\sqrt{x} + \sqrt{\smash{y}}        + \sqrt{z}$ \\
$\sqrt{x} + \sqrt{\smash[b]{y}} + \sqrt{z}$
```

11-7-9

To get the three radical signs looking pleasantly similar, it seems that the thing to do may be to give the y some extra height with a strut — but that makes things only worse! The best solution turns out to be to smash the bottom of the y (but not the whole of it!).

In the next example, the two case lines are spread too far apart due to the depth of the denominator in the first line and the superscript on the numerator of the large fraction in the second line.

11-7-10

$$f_p(x) = \begin{cases} \frac{1}{p} & x = p \\ \frac{(1-x)^{\frac{1}{2}}}{x - \sin(x-p)} \Big/ \sqrt{1-p}\,\cos(x-p) & x \neq p \end{cases}$$

```
\usepackage{amsmath}
\[ f_p (x) =
\begin{cases}
    \frac{1}{p}                              & x = p  \\
    \frac{\frac{(1 - x)^{\frac{1}{2}}}
              { x - \sin (x - p)}    }
         {\sqrt{1 - p} \, \cos (x - p)}      & x \neq p
\end{cases}  \]
```

As the lines do not overlap if we bring them closer together, we can ask LATEX to disregard the depth of the p in the denominator on the first line and the top of the large fraction in the second line using bottom and top \smash commands. We also have to add an empty brace group because of the unfortunate optimization of TEX to ignore the \smash if it is the only object in the fraction; see also page 203.

11-7-11

$$f_p(x) = \begin{cases} \frac{1}{p} & x = p \\ \frac{(1-x)^{\frac{1}{2}}}{x-\sin(x-p)} \Big/ \sqrt{1-p}\,\cos(x-p) & x \neq p \end{cases}$$

```
\usepackage{amsmath}
\[ f_p (x) =
\begin{cases}
    \frac{1}{\smash[b]{p}} & x = p \\    % smash added
    \frac{{}                             % and
          \smash[t]{\frac{(1 - x)^{\frac{1}{2}}}  % here
              { x - \sin (x - p)   } } }
         {\sqrt{1 - p} \, \cos (x - p)}  & x \neq p
\end{cases}  \]
```

This, of course, would bring the two lines in this example confusingly close together. For this reason we also add a \strut so that the numerator of the main fraction still appears to have a certain height (a \mathstrut, which has the dimensions of a parenthesis, would not produce enough extra space):

11-7-12

$$f_p(x) = \begin{cases} \frac{1}{p} & x = p \\ \frac{(1-x)^{\frac{1}{2}}}{x-\sin(x-p)} \Big/ \sqrt{1-p}\,\cos(x-p) & x \neq p \end{cases}$$

```
\usepackage{amsmath}
\[ f_p (x) =
\begin{cases}
    \frac{1}{\smash[b]{p}} & x = p  \\
    \frac{\strut                          % strut added
          \smash[t]{\frac{(1 - x)^{\frac{1}{2}}}
              { x - \sin (x - p)   } } }
         {\sqrt{1 - p} \, \cos (x - p)}  & x \neq p
\end{cases}  \]
```

As you probably realize, in this case a much simpler way to achieve the same effect is to request some negative vertical space between the case lines, e.g., using \\[-4pt]. Nevertheless, some moderate use of smashing is often of benefit to such unbalanced displays.

You may also think that this only partly solves the issue with this display and that it would look better if there is a bit more vertical space in the main fraction. In that case you could try adding a strut to both its numerator and denominator. A \mathstrut is too small and would have no effect, and a text \strut is too large. For such cases mathtools offers \xmathstrut.

\xmathstrut [*bottom-enlarge*] {*enlarge*}

This produces a strut of the height and depth of a parenthesis in the current math style, e.g., smaller in a script or scriptscript situation. The mandatory *enlarge* argument defines the factor by which it is enlarged at the top and by default also at the bottom. If the optional *bottom-enlarge* is also given, it is used for bottom instead. Thus, \xmathstrut[.1]{.2} makes a strut that is 30% larger than a normal \mathstrut with 20% being added above. Using a value of 0 in an argument means that this part of the strut is not altered at all, while using a negative value shortens the strut (usually useful only for the top part).

The behavior is best explained in an example. We show different \xmathstrut commands inside a \boxed command and highlight its height and depth by showing a vertical blue rule that extends through the full size of the box (using \vrule).

```
\usepackage{color,mathtools} \setlength\fboxrule{0pt}\setlength\fboxsep{0pt}
\newcommand\xx[2]{{\scriptscriptstyle #1}\boxed{#2\color{blue}\vrule}\,}
```

(a) ⎪₁⎪₂₃⎪₄₅₆⎪(z)

```
$ (a) \xx{1}{\mathstrut}            % normal strut (size of parentheses)
\xx{2}{\xmathstrut{0}}              % 0 gives normal strut
\xx{3}{\xmathstrut{0.5}}            % add 50% at top + bottom (= 100% bigger)
\xx{4}{\xmathstrut[0]{-0.2}}        % remove 20% from top, but keep bottom
\xx{5}{\xmathstrut[0.3]{-1}}        % bottom 30% larger, no height
\xx{6}{\xmathstrut{-0.5}} (z) $ %   -> see explanation below ...
```

11-7-13

The setting for \fboxrule and \fboxsep in the example was made to prevent the \boxed command from adding its own rules or spaces. The reason that −0.5 in the last line of the example does not remove the strut altogether is due to the fact that the top part of a strut is roughly 70% of the overall size. Thus, 20% remains, while in the bottom part −0.3 would already remove everything.

Using \xmathstrut, we can now easily open up the parts of the fractions a bit to make them more readable; we used it three times with slightly different values — finding the most appropriate values may need some experimentation.

$$f_p(x) = \begin{cases} \frac{1}{p} & x = p \\ \frac{(1-x)^{\frac{1}{2}}}{\frac{x-\sin(x-p)}{\sqrt{1-p}\,\cos(x-p)}} & x \neq p \end{cases}$$

```
\usepackage{mathtools}
\[ f_p (x) =
\begin{cases}
    \frac{1}{p}                            & x = p                 \\[-4pt]
    \frac{\frac{\xmathstrut{.1} (1 - x)^{\frac{1}{2}}}
              {\xmathstrut{.25} x - \sin (x - p)}    }
         {\xmathstrut{.3} \sqrt{1 - p} \, \cos (x - p)}
                                           & x \neq p
\end{cases} \]
```

11-7-14

Another collection of examples illustrates a very common application of smashing: using a partial `\smash` to give fine control over the height of surrounding delimiters. It also shows that smashing can lead to problems because the real height of the line needs to be known; this is restored by `\vphantom`. In the following code, `\Hmjd` is the compound symbol defined by

```
\newcommand\Hmjd{\widetilde{\mathcal{H}^2}_{MJD}(\chi)}
```

To show the resulting vertical space we added some rules:

Appearance	Code	Comment
$\overline{\left(\widetilde{\mathcal{H}^2}_{MJD}(\chi)\right)}$	`\left(` `{\Hmjd } \right)`	*Outer brackets too large*
$\overline{(\widetilde{\mathcal{H}^2}_{MJD}(\chi))}$	`\left(` `\smash{\Hmjd } \right)`	*Outer brackets too small and rules too close*
$\overline{(\widetilde{\mathcal{H}^2}_{MJD}(\chi))}$	`\left( \smash[t]{\Hmjd } \right) \vphantom{\Hmjd}`	*Just right!*
$\overline{(\widetilde{\mathcal{H}^2}_{MJD}(\chi))}$	`\left( \smash[t]{\Hmjd } \right)`	*Both vphantom and partial smash are needed*

A word of warning: in a few places, deficiencies in the very low-level TeX processing may cause errors in the fine details of typesetting. These possibilities are of particular concern in mathematical layouts where (1) a subformula (such as the numerator/denominator of a fraction or subscripts/superscripts) consists of exactly one LR-box, or a similarly constructed mathematical box, and also (2) that box does not have its natural size, as with the more complex forms of `\makebox`, smashes, and some phantoms. As an example, look at the following:

Smashes being ignored by TeX sometimes

11-7-15

$$\left| \sqrt{\frac{a+b}{x_j}} \quad \sqrt{\frac{a+b}{x_j}} \quad \sqrt{\frac{a+b}{x_j}} \quad \sqrt{\frac{a+b}{x_j+b}} \right|$$

```
\[
\sqrt{ \frac{a+b}{x_j} }                  \quad
\sqrt{ \frac{a+b}{\smash{x_j}} }          \quad
\sqrt{ \frac{a+b}{{}\smash{x_j}} }        \quad
\sqrt{ \frac{a+b}{\smash{x_j+b}} }
\]
```

To shorten the depth of the radical, a `\smash` was added in the second radical, but without any effect. With an empty brace group (third radical), it suddenly worked. On the other hand, no workaround was needed for the fourth radical.[1] For the same reason, the `\strut` or an empty brace group was actually necessary in Example 11-7-11 on page 201 to see any effects from the second `\smash` command there. In summary, whenever you find that a `\smash` does not work, try adding an empty math subformula (from {}) before the lonely box, to keep it from being mistreated.

---

[1] Technically this is due to the denominator being wider than the numerator in this case so that it was not reboxed by TeX.

mathtools
correction

A probably better solution, though, is to use mathtools instead of amsmath because it has code for \smash and similar constructs that works around this deficiency so that the second radical is also correct if mathtools is loaded.[1]

$$\left| \sqrt{\frac{a+b}{x_j}} \quad \sqrt{\frac{a+b}{x_j}} \quad \sqrt{\frac{a+b}{x_j}} \quad \sqrt{\frac{a+b}{x_j+b}} \right.$$

```
\usepackage{mathtools}
\[ \sqrt{ \frac{a+b}{x_j} }                  \quad
   \sqrt{ \frac{a+b}{\smash{x_j}} }          \quad
   \sqrt{ \frac{a+b}{{}\smash{x_j}} } \quad
   \sqrt{ \frac{a+b}{\smash{x_j+b}} }        \]
```

11-7-16

Standard LaTeX has inherited from plain TeX the commands \llap, \rlap, and added \clap that produce boxes of zero width with the text sticking out to the left, right, or both sides, respectively; e.g., \rlap is similar to the following convoluted code: \makebox[0pt][l]{*text*}.

When using \makebox in this way, you have to use l if the text should stick out to the right and r if it should stick out to the left, which is somewhat counterintuitive. There is, however, another difference between the two forms. Usually text-producing commands in LaTeX start a paragraph if necessary, but \llap, \rlap, and \clap do not, which is something to watch out for. But given that they have nice and short names, they can be quite useful if hiding the width of some material is needed.

mathtools *additions
to* amsmath

If used in math mode, the commands process their argument as *text*, which requires you to add $...$ inside and possibly specify the math style to get the size right. To make this easier, mathtools offers six companion commands.

```
\mathllap[mathstyle]{subformula} \mathclap...      \mathrlap...
\crampedllap...                  \crampedclap...\crampedrlap...
```

They also produce zero-sized boxes but process their mandatory argument in math mode using the current *mathstyle*. If necessary, you can explicitly set a different *mathstyle* in the optional argument.

The \cramped... variants use a *cramped* math style as discussed in Section 11.7.1 on page 195. They are useful, for example, when one wants to hide the width of the subscript below an operator. The difference between the second and the third sum with the cramped exponent is small but noticeable (the exponent a^2 is lowered):

$$\left| \sum_{i+j<a^2} x_{ij} \simeq \sum_{i+j<a^2} x_{ij} \approx \sum_{i+j<a^2} x_{ij} \right.$$

```
\usepackage{mathtools}
\Large \[ \sum_{i+j<a^2} x_{ij} \simeq
          \sum_{\mathclap{i+j<a^2}} x_{ij} \approx
          \sum_{\crampedclap{i+j<a^2}} x_{ij}    \]
```

11-7-17

11.7.7 Horizontal spaces

Even finer, and more difficult, tuning requires the explicit spacing commands shown in Table 11.8 on the next page. Both the full and short forms of these commands are

---

[1]This is not corrected in LaTeX core or amsmath for compatibility reasons, i.e., to avoid altering the large number of existing documents.

| Positive Spaces | | | Negative Spaces | | | Amount | |
Short	Space	Long	Short	Space	Long	Math	Text
\,	⊐⊢	\thinspace	\!	⊐⊢	\negthinspace	3 mu	0.1667 em
\:	⊐⊢	\medspace		⊐⊢	\negmedspace	4 mu plus 2 mu minus 4 mu	0.2222 em
\;	⊐⊢	\thickspace		⊐⊢	\negthickspace	5 mu plus 5 mu	0.2777 em
	⊐ ⊢	\enskip					0.5 em
	⊐ ⊢	\quad					1 em
	⊐ ⊢	\qquad					2 em

Note: The "Amount" columns are discussed in the text.

Table 11.8: Mathematical spacing commands

robust, and they can also be used outside math mode in normal text. They are related to the thin, medium, and thick spaces available on the machines used to typeset mathematics in the mid-20th century.

If used in text mode, the amount of space added by these \..space commands is based on fractions of 1 em as listed in the rightmost column of the table. However, if used in math mode, the amounts are, in fact, defined by the current values of the three parameters \thinmuskip, \medmuskip, and \thickmuskip; the table lists their default values with amsmath. These very low-level TeX parameters require values in "mu" (*math units*). They must therefore be set only via low-level TeX assignments (as shown in Example 11-8-2 on page 210) and not by \setlength or similar commands. Moreover, in normal circumstances their values should not be modified because they are used internally by TeX's mathematical typesetting (see Table 11.9 on page 210).

Do not change the muskip parameter values

One math unit (1 mu) is 1/18 of an em in the current mathematical font size (see also Table A.1 on page 652). Thus, the absolute value of a math unit varies with the mathematical style, giving consistent spacing whatever the style.

These math units can be used more generally to achieve even better control over space within mathematics. This is done via the amsmath command \mspace, which is like \hspace except that it can be used only within mathematics, and its length argument must be given in math units (e.g., \mspace{0.5mu}). Thus, while a \quad in a mathematical formula always produces the same space of 1 em based on the main mathematical font size, specifying \mspace{18mu} produces a space that is about two-thirds the space in a double subscript size. This is shown in the next example, where different em-based spaces are used in the first and second line and then corresponding mu-based spaces are used in the third line.

11-7-18

$$X\,a\quad b\quad c\qquad d \quad (1)$$
$$X_{y_{a\ b\ c\ d}} \quad (2)$$
$$X_{y_{a\ b\ c\ d}} \quad (3)$$

```
\usepackage[fleqn]{amsmath}
\begin{gather}
    X \,  a \enspace b \quad c \qquad d                              \\
    X_{y_{a \enspace b \quad c \qquad d}}                            \\
    X_{y_{a \mspace{9mu} b \mspace{18mu} c \mspace{36mu} d}}
\end{gather}
```

11.7.8 resizegather — **Downscaling an equation**

Sometimes a formula is just a tiny bit too large to fit the text width, as is the case with the next example, which is quite ugly looking:

$$a + b + c + d + e + f + g = X \tag{1}$$
$$a + b + c + d + e + f + g + h = Y \tag{2}$$

```
\usepackage{amsmath}

\begin{gather} a+b+c+d+e+f+g   = X \\
               a+b+c+d+e+f+g+h = Y \end{gather}
```

11-7-19

In such a case you have the option of manually breaking the formula over two lines, but usually that does not work well when the excess width is only small, because then both lines are fairly empty. As an alternative, Heiko Oberdiek developed the package resizegather that redefines gather, equation, and their starred forms (but not \[...\]) so that they scale down the formula in each line to fit into the available space.

Usually this is preferable to a split of the line, but only when the excess is small. Therefore, if it is larger than 5%, a warning is given, and you better visually verify that the result is acceptable. With the package option warningthreshold, you can alter the default. In the example we increase it to 10% to get only warnings for substantial resizing.

$$a + b + c + d + e + f + g = X \tag{1}$$
$$a + b + c + d + e + f + g + h = Y \tag{2}$$

```
\usepackage[warningthreshold=.1]{resizegather}

\begin{gather} a+b+c+d+e+f+g   = X \\
               a+b+c+d+e+f+g+h = Y \end{gather}
```

11-7-20

In the previous example the first line is fine (correcting Example 11-7-19), but the second line in direct comparison becomes too tiny, and you get the following warning on the terminal

```
Package resizegather Warning: Equation line 2 is too large by 20.54451pt
(resizegather)                in environment 'gather' on input line 25.
```

to alert you about this fact so that you can take manual actions.

11.7.9 subdepth — **Normalizing subscript positions**

Subscripts in formulas are not always placed at the same vertical position by the TEX engine. Instead, their placement depends on surrounding conditions: if there is also a superscript, then TEX lowers the subscript slightly in order to leave enough space between the two. If you compare the different subscripts in

$$X_a = Y_b \geq Z_c^2 \qquad C_2H_5^+$$

you see that the c is lower than a or b. This is usually fine and desirable, but there are applications, for example, when typesetting chemical formulas, where it is preferable if all subscripts are properly aligned; e.g., the 2 is in the same position as the 5.

To help with this task, Donald Arseneau wrote a short piece of code that later got packaged by Will Robertson as subdepth. All you have to do is to load this package in order to get all subscripts in *all* formulas aligned.

11-7-21

$$X_a = Y_b \geq Z_c^2 \qquad C_2H_5^+$$

```
\usepackage{subdepth}
\[    X_a = Y_b \ge Z^2_c          \qquad
      \mathrm{C}_2 \mathrm{H}_5^+                        \]
```

If you look carefully, you see that this not only aligns the subscripts but also slightly raises the superscripts in certain situations (e.g., in Z_c^2). If you do not like that aspect of the package behavior, load it with the package option low-sup.

11.7.10 Color in formulas

If you prepare educational material, but also in other situations, it is sometimes helpful if parts of a formula are highlighted, e.g., by using color. Even though color is not a concept natively available in TeX (and therefore needs to be handled by the backend, for example, in the Portable Document Format (PDF) generation), it is fairly easy to color parts of a formula without any negative side effects to spacing as long as you avoid a few traps.

To color a complete formula, all you need to do is to place the whole formula inside \textcolor. It is also possible to use \color inside the formula for this purpose, but this may color less than you intended if you place the command in a place with a restricted scope, e.g., between \left and \right or into one of the amsmath display environments, because in there the scope ends at the next & or the end of the line. In either case, the color is automatically reset when the scope ends.

11-7-22

What is $(a + b)(a - b)$?

$$(a + b)^2 = a^2 + 2ab + b^2$$
$$(a - b)^2 = a^2 - 2ab + b^2$$

```
\usepackage{amsmath,color}
What is \textcolor{blue}{$(a+b)(a-b)$}?
\begin{align*}
  \color{blue} (a+b)^2 &= a^2 + 2ab + b^2 \\
  (a-b)^2 &=  a^2 \color{blue}- 2ab + b^2 \end{align*}
```

While you can put whole formulas inside \textcolor, you should not use it inside a math formula, because this usually results in bad spacing as shown in the next example where the binary minus suddenly comes out as a unary minus — a defect that does not happen with \mathcolor that was designed for this.

Thus, if you want to color only parts of a formula, you have two options: either change the color back and forth using several \color commands (which is fairly cumbersome and on some occasions results in spacing problems or even errors) or, assuming you have a recent LaTeX release, use \mathcolor inside the formula.

Here is an example for comparison:

$$(a + b)^2 = a^2 + 2ab + b^2$$
$$(a - b)^2 = a^2 - 2ab + b^2$$

But don't do this:

$$(a - b)^2 = a^2{-}2ab + b^2$$

```
\usepackage{amsmath,color}
\begin{align*}
  (a+b)^2 &= a^2 \color{blue}+2ab\color{black} + b^2 \\
  (a-b)^2 &= a^2 \mathcolor{blue}{-2ab} + b^2          \\
\intertext{But don't do this:}
  (a-b)^2 &= a^2 \textcolor{blue}{-2ab}+ b^2 \end{align*}
```

11-7-23

As you see, using \mathcolor is much simpler than trying to alter the color with \color, and it is designed to work correctly even in far more complicated cases, e.g., when coloring just a large operator but not its limits[1] or coloring an opening or closing symbol made with \left or \right[2]. With \mathcolor all this is easy, so it should be the preferred choice.

It preserves the nature of the math symbols inside of its argument and allows them to interact correctly with their uncolored neighbors, which explains why the spacing around the equal sign in the next example, or the minus in the previous one, remains correct. It also understands about subscripts and superscripts and puts the color changes in appropriate places in order to not affect their placement.

$$\sum_{i=1}^{n} x_i = \left\{ \frac{1}{2} \right\}^{\alpha+\beta}$$

```
\usepackage{color}
\[ \mathcolor{blue}{\sum}_{i=1}^n x_i
   \mathcolor{blue}{ = \left\{} \frac{1}{2}
   \mathcolor{blue}{\right\}}^{\alpha+\beta}   \]
```

11-7-24

The \mathcolor commands can be nested as exhibited in the next example where the integral and its upper limit (but not its lower) are in black, while the rest of the formula, except for the \dotsb, is in blue.

$$a + b + \int_0^1 f(x)\,dx + \cdots$$

```
\usepackage{amsmath,color}
\[ \mathcolor{blue}{ a + b +
   \mathcolor{black}{\int^1}_0 f(x)\,dx + } \dotsb \]
```

11-7-25

What \mathcolor cannot do for you is to color across boundaries of LATEX's or amsmath's display environments; i.e., you cannot place an & or a \\ inside the argument of \mathcolor. Instead, you have to color each part of such display environments separately — unless you want to color the whole formula, in which case you can place it inside \textcolor.

11.8 Symbols in formulas

The tables at the end of this section advertise the large range of mathematical symbols provided by the $\mathcal{AMS}$ font packages, including the command to use for each symbol. They also include the supplementary symbols from the St. Mary Road Font, which

---

[1]This needs four \color commands and extra braces in the sub and superscripts — try it out.
[2]This is simply not possible with \color unless you color both — again a good exercise to try.

was designed by Alan Jeffrey and Jeremy Gibbons. This font extends the Computer Modern and $\mathcal{A}_{\mathcal{M}}\mathcal{S}$ symbol font collections; the corresponding stmaryrd package should normally be loaded in addition to amssymb, but always after it. It provides extra symbols for fields such as functional programming, process algebra, domain theory, linear logic, and many more. For a wealth of information about an even wider variety of symbols, see the *Comprehensive LATEX Symbol List* by Scott Pakin [81].

The tables indicate which extra packages need to be loaded to use each symbol command. They are organized as follows: symbols with command names in black are available in standard LATEX without loading further packages; symbols in blue require loading either amsmath, amssymb, or stmaryrd, as explained in the table notes. If necessary, further classification is given by markings: (StM) signals a symbol from stmaryrd when the table also contains symbols from other packages; (kernel) identifies symbols that are available in standard LATEX but only by combining two or more glyphs, whereas a single glyph exists in the indicated package; and (var) marks "Alphabetic characters/symbols" (of type \mathalpha; see Table 9.20 on page →I 751) that change appearance when used within the scope of a math alphabet identifier (see Section 9.4).

11.8.1 Mathematical symbol classes

The symbols are classified primarily by their "mathematical class", occasionally called their "math symbol type". This classification is related to their "meaning" in standard technical usage, but its importance for mathematical typography is that it influences the layout of a formula. For example, TEX's mathematical formatter adjusts the horizontal space on either side of each symbol according to its mathematical class. There are also some finer distinctions made, for example, between accents and simple symbols and in breaking up the enormous list of Relation symbols into several tables.

The setup for mathematics puts each symbol into one of these classes: Ordinary (Ord), Operator (Op), Binary (Bin), Relation (Rel), Opening (Open), Closing (Close), or Punctuation (Punct). This classification can be explicitly changed by using the commands \mathord, \mathop, \mathbin, \mathrel, \mathopen, \mathclose, and \mathpunct, thereby altering the surrounding spacing. In the next example, \# and \top (both Ord by default) are changed into a Rel and an Op:

11-8-1

$a \# \top^{\alpha}_{x} x^{\alpha}_{b}$

$a \mathrel{\#} \underset{x}{\top}{}^{\alpha} x^{\alpha}_{b}$

```
\usepackage[fleqn]{amsmath}
\[ a            \#            \top _x^\alpha x^\alpha_b \]
\[ a \mathrel{\#} \mathop{\top}_x^\alpha x^\alpha_b \]
```

A symbol can be declared to belong to one of the above classes using the mechanism described in Section 9.8.5. In addition, certain subformulas — most importantly fractions, and those produced by \left and \right — form a class called Inner; it is explicitly available through the \mathinner command.

In TEX, spacing within formulas is done simply by identifying the class of each object in a formula and then adding space between each pair of adjacent objects as

Right Object

	Ord	Op	Bin	Rel	Open	Close	Punct	Inner
Ord	0	1	(2)	(3)	0	0	0	(1)
Op	1	1	*	(3)	0	0	0	(1)
Bin	(2)	(2)	*	*	(2)	*	*	(2)
Rel	(3)	(3)	*	0	(3)	0	0	(3)
Open	0	0	*	0	0	0	0	0
Close	0	1	(2)	(3)	0	0	0	(1)
Punct	(1)	(1)	*	(1)	(1)	(1)	(1)	(1)
Inner	(1)	1	(2)	(3)	(1)	0	(1)	(1)

Left Object (label at left of rows Rel and Open)

*0 = no space,   1 = \thinmuskip,   2 = \medmuskip,   3 = \thickmuskip,   * = impossible*

Entries in (blue) are not added when in the mathematical "script styles" (see also Sections 11.7.1 and 11.7.7).

Table 11.9: Space between symbols

defined in Table 11.9; this table is unfortunately hardwired into TEX's mathematical typesetting routines and so cannot be changed by macro packages.[1] In this table 0, 1, 2, and 3 stand for no space, a thin space (\,), a medium space (\:), and a thick space (\;), respectively. The exact amounts of space used are listed in Section 11.7.7 on page 204.

A Binary symbol is turned into an Ordinary symbol whenever it is not preceded and followed by symbols of a nature compatible with a binary operation; for this reason, some entries in the table are marked with a star to indicate that they are not possible. For example, $+x$ gives $+x$ (a "unary plus") and not $+x$; the latter can be produced by ${}+x$.

Finally, an entry in (blue) in Table 11.9 indicates that the corresponding space is not inserted when the style is script or scriptscript.

As an example of applying these rules, consider the following formula (the default values are deliberately changed to show the added spaces more clearly):

$$|a \; - \; b \; = \; - \max\{x,\, y\}$$

```
\thinmuskip=10mu \medmuskip=17mu \thickmuskip=30mu
\[    a  -  b  =  -\max \{ x , y \}    \]
```

11-8-2

TEX identifies the objects as Ord, Bin, Ord, Rel, and so on, and then inserts spaces as follows:

```
    a        -        b        =        -   \max  \{   x    ,      y  \}
Ord \: Bin \: Ord \; Rel \; Ord \, Op  Open Ord Punct \, Ord Close
```

The minus in front of \max is turned into an Ordinary because a Binary cannot follow a Relation.

---

[1] Although a few of the entries in the table are questionable, on the whole it gives pleasing results.

Table 11.9 reveals a difference[1] between a "\left...\right" construction, in which the entire subformula delimited by the construction becomes a single object of class Inner (see Section 11.5.6 on page 191) and commands like \Bigl and \Bigr that produce individual symbols of the classes Opening and Closing, respectively. Although they may result in typesetting delimiters of equal vertical size, spacing differences can arise depending on adjacent objects in the formula. For example, Ordinary followed by Opening gets no space, whereas Ordinary followed by Inner is separated by a thin space. In the next example we again use larger spaces to highlight these differences:

Possible spacing issues with \left and \right

11-8-3

$$a\left(\sum x\right) \neq a\left(\sum x\right)$$
$$\sin(x^2),\ x \neq \sin\left(x^2\right),\ x$$

```
\thinmuskip=10mu \medmuskip=15mu \thickmuskip=20mu
\[ a \Bigl( \sum x \Bigr) \neq a \left( \sum x \right) \]
\[ \sin(x^2),x           \neq \sin\left(x^2\right),x   \]
```

The spaces inside the subformula within a "\left...\right" construction are as expected, beginning with an Opening symbol and ending with a Closing symbol. However, especially with the $\sin(x^2)$ example the extra spaces are not correct, and to avoid this problem, you can use the commands \mleft and \mright from the mleftright package (written by Heiko Oberdiek) in their place. Here we repeat the previous examples using these commands:

11-8-4

$$a\left(\sum x\right) = a\left(\sum x\right)$$
$$\sin(x^2),\ x \simeq \sin(x^2),\ x$$

```
\usepackage{mleftright}
\thinmuskip=10mu \medmuskip=15mu \thickmuskip=20mu
\[ a \Bigl( \sum x \Bigr) = a \mleft( \sum x \mright) \]
\[ \sin(x^2),x           \simeq \sin\mleft(x^2\mright),x   \]
```

In fact, you can even change the meanings of \left and \right to locally (or globally) act as Opening and Closing symbols by executing \mleftright and \mleftrightrestore to get the original TeX definitions back.

In summary, it is not enough to look up a symbol in the tables that follow; rather, it is also advisable to check that the symbol has the desired mathematical class to ensure that it is properly spaced when used. Example 11-8-5 on page 214 shows how to define new symbols that differ only in their mathematical class from existing symbols.

11.8.2 Letters, numerals, and other Ordinary symbols

The unaccented ASCII Latin letters and arabic numeral digits (see Table 11.10) are referred to as "Alphabetic symbols". The font used for them can vary: in mathematical formulas, the default font for Latin letters is italic, whereas for the arabic digits it is upright/roman. Alphabetical symbols are all of class Ordinary.

Unlike the Latin letters, the mathematical Greek letters are no longer closely related to the glyphs used for typesetting normal Greek text. Due to an interesting 18th

---

[1]Another important distinction is that the material within a "\left...\right" construction is processed separately as a subformula (see Section 11.7.2 on page 197).

$$A B C D E F G H I J K L M N O P Q R S T U V W X Y Z$$
$$a b c d e f g h i j k l m n o p q r s t u v w x y z$$
$$0 1 2 3 4 5 6 7 8 9$$

Table 11.10: Latin letters and arabic numerals

Δ	\Delta$^{(var)}$	Γ	\Gamma$^{(var)}$	Λ	\Lambda$^{(var)}$	Ω	\Omega$^{(var)}$	Φ	\Phi$^{(var)}$
Π	\Pi$^{(var)}$	Ψ	\Psi$^{(var)}$	Σ	\Sigma$^{(var)}$	Θ	\Theta$^{(var)}$	Υ	\Upsilon$^{(var)}$
Ξ	\Xi$^{(var)}$	α	\alpha	β	\beta	χ	\chi	δ	\delta
F	\digamma	ϵ	\epsilon	η	\eta	γ	\gamma	ι	\iota
κ	\kappa	λ	\lambda	μ	\mu	ν	\nu	ω	\omega
ϕ	\phi	π	\pi	ψ	\psi	ρ	\rho	σ	\sigma
τ	\tau	θ	\theta	υ	\upsilon	ε	\varepsilon	$\varkappa$	\varkappa
φ	\varphi	ϖ	\varpi	ϱ	\varrho	ς	\varsigma	ϑ	\vartheta
ξ	\xi	ζ	\zeta						

Symbols in blue require the amssymb *package.* $^{(var)}$ *indicates a variable Alphabetic symbol.*

Table 11.11: Symbols of class \mathord (Greek)

century happenstance, in the major European tradition of mathematical typography the default font for lowercase Greek letters in mathematical formulas is italic, whereas for uppercase Greek letters it is upright/roman. (In other fields, such as physics and chemistry, the typographical traditions are slightly different.)

The capital Greek letters in the first rows of Table 11.11 are also Alphabetic symbols whose font varies, with the default being upright/roman. Those capital Greek letters not present in this table are the letters that have the same appearance as some Latin letter (e.g., *A* and *Alpha*, *B* and *Beta*, *K* and *Kappa*, *O* and *Omicron*). Similarly, the list of lowercase Greek letters contains no omicron because it would be identical in appearance to the Latin *o*. Thus, in practice, the Greek letters that have Latin look-alikes are not used in mathematical formulas.

Table 11.12 on the facing page lists other letter-shaped symbols of class Ordinary. The first four are Hebrew letters. Table 11.13 lists the remaining symbols in the Ordinary class, including some common punctuation. These behave like letters and digits, so they never get any extra space around them.

A common mistake is to use the symbols from Table 11.13 directly as Binary operator or Relation symbols, without using a properly defined math symbol command for that type. Thus, if you use commands such as \#, \square, or \&, check carefully that you get the correct inter-symbol spaces or, even better, define your own symbol command, which can be done with \DeclareMathSymbol, which is explained in Section 9.8.5 on page →I 750.

ℵ	\aleph	ℶ	\beth	ℸ	\daleth	ℷ	\gimel
ℑ	\Im	ℜ	\Re	𝕜	\Bbbk	®	\circledR
Ⓢ	\circledS	∁	\complement	ℓ	\ell	ð	\eth
⅃	\Finv	⅁	\Game	ℏ	\hbar^(kernel)	ℏ	\hslash
ı	\imath	ȷ	\jmath	$	\mathdollar	¶	\mathparagraph
§	\mathsection	£	\mathsterling	℧	\mho	∂	\partial
℘	\wp	¥	\yen				

Symbols in blue require the amssymb *package.*

Synonyms: $ \mathdollar, \$ ¶ \mathparagraph, \P   § \mathsection, \S   £ \mathsterling, \pounds

The synonyms can be used in math and in ordinary text.

Table 11.12: Symbols of class \mathord (letter-shaped)

!	!	.	.	/	/	
?	?	@	@	|	| or \vert	
#	\#	%	\%	&	\&	
–	_	‖	\\| or \Vert	∠	\angle^(kernel)	
‖	\Arrowvert			\arrowvert	`	\backprime	
\	\backslash	★	\bigstar	♦	\blacklozenge	
■	\blacksquare	▲	\blacktriangle	▼	\blacktriangledown	
⊥	\bot			\bracevert	✓	\checkmark	
♣	\clubsuit	©	\copyright	╲	\diagdown	
/	\diagup	◇	\diamondsuit	∅	\emptyset	
∃	\exists	♭	\flat	∀	\forall	
♡	\heartsuit	∞	\infty	↯	\lightning^(StM)	
¬	\lnot or \neg	◊	\lozenge	✠	\maltese	
∡	\measuredangle	∇	\nabla	♮	\natural	
∄	\nexists	′	\prime	♯	\sharp	
♠	\spadesuit	◁	\sphericalangle	□	\square	
√	\surd	⊤	\top	△	\triangle	
▽	\triangledown	©	\varcopyright^(StM)	∅	\varnothing	

Symbols in blue require either the amssymb *package or, if flagged with* ^(StM)*, the* stmaryrd *package.*

Note that the exclamation mark, period, and question mark are not treated as punctuation in formulas.

Table 11.13: Symbols of class \mathord (miscellaneous)

To avoid this problem, we make use of the \DeclareMathSymbol declaration in Example 11-8-5 on the next page. Values for its arguments are most easily found by looking at the definitions in the file amssymb.sty or fontmath.ltx (for the core

$\acute{x}$	\acute{x}	$\bar{x}$	\bar{x}	$\breve{x}$	\breve{x}	$\check{x}$	\check{x}
$\ddddot{x}$	\ddddot{x}	$\dddot{x}$	\dddot{x}	$\ddot{x}$	\ddot{x}	$\dot{x}$	\dot{x}
$\grave{x}$	\grave{x}	$\hat{x}$	\hat{x}	$\mathring{x}$	\mathring{x}	$\tilde{x}$	\tilde{x}
$\vec{x}$	\vec{x}	$\widehat{xyz}$	\widehat{xyz}	$\widetilde{xyz}$	\widetilde{xyz}		

Accents in blue require the amsmath or accents package.

The last two accents are available in a range of widths, the largest suitable one being automatically used.

Table 11.14: Mathematical accents, giving subformulas of class \mathord

symbols). For example, we looked up \neg and \square, replaced the \mathord in each case, and finally gave the resulting symbol a new name. To better show the difference, we also enlarged the default spacing (not advisable for real documents).

Symbols of wrong class (ord):

$$a\neg b \qquad x\square y + z$$

Manual correction:

$$a \neg b \qquad x \;\square\; y + z$$

Symbols of correct class:

$$a \neg b \qquad x \;\square\; y + z$$

```
\usepackage[fleqn]{amsmath}   \usepackage{amssymb}
\DeclareMathSymbol\bneg   {\mathbin}{symbols}{"3A}
\DeclareMathSymbol\rsquare{\mathrel}{AMSa}{"03}
\thickmuskip=10mu plus 5mu
\noindent Symbols of wrong class (ord):
\[ a \neg b            \qquad  x \square         y + z \]
Manual correction:
\[ a \mathbin{\neg} b \qquad  x \mathrel{\square} y + z \]
Symbols of correct class:
\[ a \bneg         b \qquad  x \rsquare         y + z \]
```

11-8-5

11.8.3 Mathematical accents

The basic accent commands available for use in formulas are listed in Table 11.14. Most of them are already defined in standard LaTeX. See Section 11.4.12 for ways to define additional accent commands and ways to make compound accents and Section 11.5.2 for information about extensible accents. Adding a mathematical accent to a symbol always produces a symbol of class Ordinary. Thus, without additional help from \mathbin or \mathrel, one cannot use the accents to produce new Binary or Relation symbols.

$$a = b \text{ but } a\tilde{=}b \text{ which is not } a \stackrel{\sim}{=} b$$

```
\usepackage{amsmath}
\[  a = b  \text{ but }  a \tilde{=} b
    \text{ which is not } a \mathrel{\tilde{=}} b  \]
```

11-8-6

Other ways to place symbols over Relation symbols are shown in Section 11.4.14.

11.8.4 Binary operator symbols

There are more than 100 symbols of class Binary operator from which to choose. Most of these Binary symbols are shown in Table 11.15 on the next page. Some of

∗	`* or \ast`	+	`+`	−	`-`
∐	`\amalg`	⍉	`\baro`^(StM)	⊼	`\barwedge`
⑊	`\bbslash`^(StM)	▽	`\bigtriangledown`	△	`\bigtriangleup`
⋒	`\Cap or \doublecap`	∩	`\cap`	⋓	`\Cup or \doublecup`
∪	`\cup`	⋎	`\curlyvee`	⋏	`\curlywedge`
†	`\dag or \dagger`	‡	`\ddag or \ddagger`	⋄	`\diamond`
÷	`\div`	⊛	`\divideontimes`	∔	`\dotplus`
⍀	`\fatbslash`^(StM)	⨟	`\fatsemi`^(StM)	⫽	`\fatslash`^(StM)
⋗	`\gtrdot`	⊺	`\intercal`	⦀	`\interleave`^(StM)
∧	`\land or \wedge`	⟒	`\lbag`^(StM)	◁	`\leftslice`^(StM)
⋋	`\leftthreetimes`	⋖	`\lessdot`	∨	`\lor or \vee`
⋉	`\ltimes`	⋀	`\merge`^(StM)	⊖	`\minuso`^(StM)
⊻	`\moo`^(StM)	∓	`\mp`	⊞	`\nplus`^(StM)
±	`\pm`	⨏	`\rbag`^(StM)	▷	`\rightslice`^(StM)
⋌	`\rightthreetimes`	⋊	`\rtimes`	∖	`\setminus`
╲	`\smallsetminus`	⊓	`\sqcap`	⊔	`\sqcup`
⫻	`\sslash`^(StM)	⋆	`\star`	⫾	`\talloblong`^(StM)
×	`\times`	◁	`\triangleleft`	▷	`\triangleright`
⊎	`\uplus`	▽	`\varbigtriangledown`^(StM)	△	`\varbigtriangleup`^(StM)
⋎	`\varcurlyvee`^(StM)	⋈	`\vartimes`^(StM)	⊻	`\veebar`
∧	`\wedge`	≀	`\wr`	⅄	`\Ydown`^(StM)
⋋	`\Yleft`^(StM)	⋋	`\Yright`^(StM)	⋏	`\Yup`^(StM)

Symbols in *blue require either the* amssymb *package or, if flagged with* ^(StM), *the* stmaryrd *package.*

The left and right triangles are also available as Relation symbols.

The stmaryrd *package confusingly changes the Binary symbols* `\bigtriangleup` *and* `\bigtriangledown` *into Operators, leaving only the synonyms* `\varbigtriangleup` *and* `\varbigtriangledown` *for the Binary operator forms.*

Table 11.15: Symbols of class `\mathbin` (miscellaneous)

⊡	`\boxast`^(StM)	⊟	`\boxbar`^(StM)	⊡	`\boxbox`^(StM)	⧅	`\boxbslash`^(StM)
⊚	`\boxcircle`^(StM)	⊡	`\boxdot`	□	`\boxempty`^(StM)	⊟	`\boxminus`
⊞	`\boxplus`	⧄	`\boxslash`^(StM)	⊠	`\boxtimes`	□	`\oblong`^(StM)

All symbols require either the amssymb *package or, if flagged with* ^(StM), *the* stmaryrd *package.*

Table 11.16: Symbols of class `\mathbin` (boxes)

them are also available, under different names, as Relation symbols. The amssymb package offers a few box symbols for use as Binary operators; many more are added by stmaryrd. These are shown in Table 11.16.

215

○	\bigcirc	⊛	\oast$^{(StM)}$ or \circledast$^{(StM)}$	⦶	\obar$^{(StM)}$
○	\varbigcirc$^{(StM)}$	⊛	\varoast$^{(StM)}$	⦶	\varobar$^{(StM)}$
⊘	\obslash$^{(StM)}$	○	\ocircle$^{(StM)}$ or \circledcirc$^{(StM)}$	⊙	\odot
⊘	\varobslash$^{(StM)}$	◎	\varocircle$^{(StM)}$	⊙	\varodot$^{(StM)}$
⊜	\ogreaterthan$^{(StM)}$	⊘	\olessthan$^{(StM)}$	⊖	\ominus
⊜	\varogreaterthan$^{(StM)}$	⊘	\varolessthan$^{(StM)}$	⊖	\varominus$^{(StM)}$
⊕	\oplus	⊘	\oslash	⊗	\otimes
⊕	\varoplus$^{(StM)}$	⊘	\varoslash$^{(StM)}$	⊗	\varotimes$^{(StM)}$
ⓥ	\ovee$^{(StM)}$	⟁	\owedge$^{(StM)}$	ⓥ	\varovee$^{(StM)}$
⟁	\varowedge$^{(StM)}$	●	\bullet	·	\cdot
▪	\centerdot	○	\circ	⊝	\circleddash

Symbols in blue require either the amssymb *package or, if flagged with* $^{(StM)}$*, the* stmaryrd *package.*

Option heavycircles *of the* stmaryrd *package affects all commands starting with* \var *and their normal variants.*

Table 11.17: Symbols of class \mathbin (circles)

The stmaryrd package can be loaded with the option heavycircles. It causes each circle symbol command in Table 11.17 that starts with \var to swap its definition with the corresponding command without the "var"; for example, the symbol \varodot becomes \odot, and vice versa.

11.8.5 Relation symbols

The class of binary Relation symbols forms a collection even larger than that of the Binary operators. The lists start with symbols for equality and order (Table 11.18 on the next page). You can put a slash through any Relation symbol by preceding it with the \not command; this negated symbol represents the complement (or negation) of the relation.

$u \not< v$ or $a \notin \mathbf{A}$ `$ u \not< v$ or $a \not\in \mathbf{A} $`   11-8-7

Especially with larger symbols, this generic method of negating a Relation symbol does not always give good results because the slash will always be of the same size, position, and slope. Therefore, some specially designed "negated symbols" are also available (see Table 11.19 on the facing page). If a choice is available, the designed glyphs are usually preferable. To see why, compare the symbols in this example.

```
\usepackage{amssymb}
$ \not\leq \ \not\succeq \ \not\sim $   \par
$ \nleq    \ \nsucceq    \ \nsim    $
```
11-8-8

< `<`	= `=`	> `>`	≈ `\approx`
≊ `\approxeq`	≍ `\asymp`	∽ `\backsim`	⋍ `\backsimeq`
≎ `\Bumpeq`	≏ `\bumpeq`	≗ `\circeq`	≅ `\cong`
≼ `\curlyeqprec`	≽ `\curlyeqsucc`	≑ `\Doteq or\doteqdot`	≐ `\doteq`
≖ `\eqcirc`	≂ `\eqsim`	⪖ `\eqslantgtr`	⪕ `\eqslantless`
≡ `\equiv`	≒ `\fallingdotseq`	≥ `\ge or \geq`	≧ `\geqq`
⩾ `\geqslant`	≫ `\gg`	⋙ `\ggg or \gggtr`	⪆ `\gtrapprox`
⋛ `\gtreqless`	⪌ `\gtreqqless`	≷ `\gtrless`	≳ `\gtrsim`
≤ `\le or \leq`	⇔ `\leftrightarroweq`[(StM)]	≦ `\leqq`	⩽ `\leqslant`
⪅ `\lessapprox`	⋚ `\lesseqgtr`	⪋ `\lesseqqgtr`	≶ `\lessgtr`
≲ `\lesssim`	≪ `\ll`	⋘ `\lll or \llless`	≺ `\prec`
⪷ `\precapprox`	≼ `\preccurlyeq`	≼ `\preceq`	≾ `\precsim`
≓ `\risingdotseq`	∼ `\sim`	≃ `\simeq`	≻ `\succ`
⪸ `\succapprox`	≽ `\succcurlyeq`	≽ `\succeq`	≿ `\succsim`
≈ `\thickapprox`	∼ `\thicksim`	≜ `\triangleq`	

Symbols in blue require either the amssymb package or, if flagged with [(StM)], the stmaryrd package.

Table 11.18: Symbols of class \mathrel (equality and order)

⪦ `\gnapprox`	≩ `\gneq`	≩ `\gneqq`	⋧ `\gnsim`	⪈ `\gvertneqq`
⪥ `\lnapprox`	≨ `\lneq`	≨ `\lneqq`	⋦ `\lnsim`	⪇ `\lvertneqq`
≇ `\ncong`	≠ `\ne or \neq`	≱ `\ngeq`	≧̸ `\ngeqq`	⪖̸ `\ngeqslant`
≯ `\ngtr`	≰ `\nleq`	≦̸ `\nleqq`	⪕̸ `\nleqslant`	≮ `\nless`
⊀ `\nprec`	⋠ `\npreceq`	≁ `\nsim`	⊁ `\nsucc`	⋡ `\nsucceq`
⪹ `\precnapprox`	⪵ `\precneqq`	⋨ `\precnsim`	⪺ `\succnapprox`	⪶ `\succneqq`
⋩ `\succnsim`				

Symbols in blue require either the amssymb package.

Table 11.19: Symbols of class \mathrel (equality and order — negated)

In problematic cases for which no predefined symbol exists you can try the \centernot command defined in a package with the same name (written by Heiko Oberdiek). In contrast to \not, it always centers the negation slash based on the

◀ \blacktriangleleft	▶ \blacktriangleright	∈ \in
∉ \inplus⁽ˢᵗᴹ⁾	∋ \ni or \owns	∋̇ \niplus⁽ˢᵗᴹ⁾
⋬̸ \ntrianglelefteqslant⁽ˢᵗᴹ⁾	⋭̸ \ntrianglerighteqslant⁽ˢᵗᴹ⁾	⊏ \sqsubset
⊑ \sqsubseteq	⊐ \sqsupset	⊒ \sqsupseteq
⋐ \Subset	⊂ \subset	⊆ \subseteq
⊆ \subseteqq	⊂⁺ \subsetplus⁽ˢᵗᴹ⁾	⊆⁺ \subsetpluseq⁽ˢᵗᴹ⁾
⋑ \Supset	⊃ \supset	⊇ \supseteq
⊇ \supseteqq	⊃⁺ \supsetplus⁽ˢᵗᴹ⁾	⊇⁺ \supsetpluseq⁽ˢᵗᴹ⁾
⊴ \trianglelefteq	⊴ \trianglelefteqslant⁽ˢᵗᴹ⁾	⊵ \trianglerighteq
⊵ \trianglerighteqslant⁽ˢᵗᴹ⁾	△ \vartriangle	◁ \vartriangleleft
▷ \vartriangleright		

Symbols in blue require either the amssymb package or, if flagged with ⁽ˢᵗᴹ⁾, the stmaryrd package.

Table 11.20: Symbols of class \mathrel (sets and inclusion)

∉ \notin	⊈ \nsubseteq	⊈ \nsubseteqq
⊉ \nsupseteq	⊉ \nsupseteqq	⋪ \ntriangleleft
⋬ \ntrianglelefteq	⋫ \ntriangleright	⋭ \ntrianglerighteq
⊊ \subsetneq	⊊ \subsetneqq	⊋ \supsetneq
⊋ \supsetneqq	⊊ \varsubsetneq	⊊ \varsubsetneqq
⊋ \varsupsetneq	⊋ \varsupsetneqq	

Symbols in blue require the amssymb package.

Table 11.21: Symbols of class \mathrel (sets and inclusion — negated)

width of the next symbol. You can compare the results of the different algorithms in the following example:

```
\usepackage{centernot}
$ \not\parallel        \ \not\frown        \ \not\longmapsto $  \par
$ \centernot\parallel \ \centernot\frown \ \centernot\longmapsto    $
```

11-8-9

Next come the Relation symbols for sets and inclusions, and their negations (see Tables 11.20 and 11.21). They are followed by Relation symbols that are arrow-shaped (see Tables 11.22 and 11.23). Some extensible arrow constructions that produce compound Relation symbols are described in Section 11.5.2 on page 182.

↺ \circlearrowleft	↻ \circlearrowright	⅄ \curlyveedownarrow(StM)
⅄ \curlyveeuparrow(StM)	⋏ \curlywedgedownarrow(StM)	⋏ \curlywedgeuparrow(StM)
↶ \curvearrowleft	↷ \curvearrowright	--→ \dasharrow
←-- \dashleftarrow	--→ \dashrightarrow	⇓ \Downarrow
↓ \downarrow	⇊ \downdownarrows	⇂ \downharpoonright
← \gets	↩ \hookleftarrow	↪ \hookrightarrow
⇐ \Leftarrow	← \leftarrow or \gets	↢ \leftarrowtail
⇽ \leftarrowtriangle(StM)	↔ \leftrightarrowtriangle(StM)	↽ \leftharpoondown
↼ \leftharpoonup	⇇ \leftleftarrows	⇆ \Leftrightarrow
↔ \leftrightarrow	⇆ \leftrightarrows	⇋ \leftrightharpoons
↭ \leftrightsquigarrow	⇚ \Lleftarrow	⟸ \Longleftarrow
⟵ \longleftarrow	⟺ \Longleftrightarrow	⟷ \longleftrightarrow
⟽ \Longmapsfrom(StM)	⟵ \longmapsfrom(StM)	⟾ \Longmapsto(StM)
⟼ \longmapsto	⟹ \Longrightarrow	⟶ \longrightarrow
↫ \looparrowleft	↬ \looparrowright	↰ \Lsh
⇐ \Mapsfrom(StM)	↤ \mapsfrom(StM)	⇨ \Mapsto(StM)
↦ \mapsto	⊸ \multimap	↗ \nearrow
↗ \nnearrow(StM)	↖ \nnwarrow(StM)	↖ \nwarrow
↾ \restriction	⇒ \Rightarrow	→ \rightarrow or \to
↣ \rightarrowtail	⇾ \rightarrowtriangle(StM)	⇁ \rightharpoondown
⇀ \rightharpoonup	⇄ \rightleftarrows	⇌ \rightleftharpoons
⇉ \rightrightarrows	↝ \rightsquigarrow	⇛ \Rrightarrow
↱ \Rsh	↘ \searrow	↓ \shortdownarrow(StM)
← \shortleftarrow(StM)	→ \shortrightarrow(StM)	↑ \shortuparrow(StM)
↘ \ssearrow(StM)	↙ \sswarrow(StM)	↙ \swarrow
↞ \twoheadleftarrow	↠ \twoheadrightarrow	⇑ \Uparrow
↑ \uparrow	⇕ \Updownarrow	↕ \updownarrow
↿ \upharpoonleft	↾ \upharpoonright	⇈ \upuparrows

Symbols in blue require either the amssymb *package or, if flagged with* (StM)*, the* stmaryrd *package.*

Synonyms: --→ \dasharrow, \dashrightarrow   ⟺ \iff, \Longleftrightarrow *(with additional spacing)*

Table 11.22: Symbols of class \mathrel (arrows)

The standard arrow relational symbols are provided as part of the Computer Modern Math fonts by Donald Knuth, and further symbols are part of the American Mathematical Society math or St. Mary Road fonts—the arrowheads of the latter symbols all followed in the original design by Knuth. However, around 1992 Donald Knuth made a number of corrections to the Computer Modern fonts and as part of

The standard arrowhead design in Computer Modern fonts

| ⇍ | \nLeftarrow | ↚ | \nleftarrow | ⇎ | \nLeftrightarrow |
| ↮ | \nleftrightarrow | ⇏ | \nRightarrow | ↛ | \nrightarrow |

All symbols require the amssymb *package.*

Table 11.23: Symbols of class \mathrel (arrows — negated)

／	\Arrownot $^{(StM)}$	∕	\arrownot $^{(StM)}$	ᶜ	\lhook	／	\Longarrownot $^{(StM)}$
∕	\longarrownot $^{(StM)}$	∣	\Mapsfromchar $^{(StM)}$	∣	\mapsfromchar $^{(StM)}$	∣	\Mapstochar $^{(StM)}$
∣	\mapstochar	／	\not	ᵓ	\rhook		

Symbols in blue require the stmaryrd *package.*
These symbols are for combining, mostly with arrows; e.g., \longarrownot\longleftarrow *gives* ↚.
Use \joinrel *to "glue" relational symbols together, e.g.,* \lhook\joinrel\longrightarrow *gives* ↪.
The dimensions of these symbols make them unsuitable for other uses.

Table 11.24: Symbol parts of class \mathrel (negation and arrow extensions)

this also changed the design of the arrowheads, by making them noticeably larger and more visible.

This design change was not carried over to the American Mathematical Society fonts, and as a result there is some strange discrepancy if you look, for example, at \rightarrow → (Knuth 1992) and compare it with \rightarrowtail ↣ (American Mathematical Society) or \shortrightarrow → (St. Mary Road).[1]

If you want to use Computer Modern Math but prefer a homogeneous look and feel for all arrows, there is a way to get the original design back: just load the package old-arrows by Riccardo Dossena after amsmath or stmaryrd. Without any options it reverts the arrows to Donald Knuth's design before 1992. If loaded with the option new, you can even use both styles in parallel: in that case the old design is the default, and the newer design is available by prepending var to the symbol name as shown in the next example. If you use the option old instead, then the \var.. commands refer to the old design, and the new design is used by default.

```
\usepackage[new]{old-arrows}
```

← → ↓ ↘ ↪ ↙ ↕ ↦ $ \gets\   \to \   \downarrow\   \searrow\   \hookrightarrow\
                       \swarrow\   \updownarrow\   \longmapsto $ \\[6pt]
← → ↓ ↘ ↪ ↙ ↕ ↦ $\vargets\ \varto\   \vardownarrow\ \varsearrow\ \varhookrightarrow\
                       \varswarrow\   \varupdownarrow\ \varlongmapsto $
```

11-8-10

[1]This statement refers to Computer Modern-based math symbols: if you use other math font setups, as discussed in Chapter 12, there may be no such differences, because all symbols have been redrawn based on a single design.
```

:	\ratio	::	\coloncolon	≈:	\approxcolon
≈::	\approxcoloncolon	:≈	\colonapprox	::≈	\coloncolonapprox
=:	\equalscolon	=::	\equalscoloncolon	:=	\colonequals
::=	\coloncolonequals	−:	\minuscolon	−::	\minuscoloncolon
:−	\colonminus	::−	\coloncolonminus	∼:	\simcolon
∼::	\simcoloncolon	:∼	\colonsim	::∼	\coloncolonsim

All symbols require the colonequals *package.*

Table 11.25: Symbols of class \mathrel (various colons)

:	:	ꝫ	\backepsilon	∵	\because	𝟬	\between
⋈	\bowtie	⊣	\dashv	⌢	\frown	⋈	\Join
|	\mid	⊨	\models	∤	\nmid	∦	\nparallel
∤	\nshortmid	⫲	\nshortparallel	⊯	\nVDash	⊮	\nVdash
⊭	\nvDash	⊬	\nvdash	∥	\parallel	⊥	\perp
⋔	\pitchfork	∝	\propto	∣	\shortmid	∥	\shortparallel
⌢	\smallfrown	⌣	\smallsmile	⌣	\smile	∴	\therefore
∝	\varpropto	⊩	\Vdash	⊨	\vDash	⊢	\vdash
⊪	\Vvdash						

Relation symbols in blue *require the* amssymb *package.*

\therefore *is a Relation symbol, so its spacing may not be as expected in common uses.*

Table 11.26: Symbols of class \mathrel (miscellaneous)

In addition to \not, used to negate general Relation symbols, other building blocks have been especially designed to negate or extend arrow-like symbols; these are collected in Table 11.24.

<table>
<tr><td>11-8-11</td><td>↮   ↩̸</td><td>

```
\usepackage{stmaryrd}
$\Longarrownot\longleftrightarrow \qquad  \arrownot\hookleftarrow$
```
</td></tr>
</table>

Table 11.25 shows Relation symbols that involve one or two colons. They are provided if you load the package colonequals by Heiko Oberdiek. The symbols are constructed from other glyphs; e.g., \colonequals is made up from a colon and an equal sign with some negative space between the two and can therefore be used with different math font setups. To fine-tune the constructed symbols, the commands \colonsep and \doublecolonsep can be adjusted (with \renewcommand).

Finally, in Table 11.26 you will find a miscellaneous collection of Relation symbols provided by the kernel or amssymb.

∫∫	`\int`	∮∮	`\oint`	□□	`\bigbox`(StM)
∩∩	`\bigcap`	∪∪	`\bigcup`	⅄⅄	`\bigcurlyvee`(StM)
人人	`\bigcurlywedge`(StM)	‖‖	`\biginterleave`(StM)	⊞⊞	`\bignplus`(StM)
⊙⊙	`\bigodot`	⊕⊕	`\bigoplus`	⊗⊗	`\bigotimes`
‖‖	`\bigparallel`(StM)	⊓⊓	`\bigsqcap`(StM)	⊔⊔	`\bigsqcup`
▽▽	`\bigtriangledown`	△△	`\bigtriangleup`	⊎⊎	`\biguplus`
⋁⋁	`\bigvee`	⋀⋀	`\bigwedge`	∐∐	`\coprod`
∏∏	`\prod`	∫∫	`\smallint`	∑∑	`\sum`

Operator symbols in blue require the stmaryrd package.

The stmaryrd package confusingly changes the Binary symbols `\bigtriangleup` and `\bigtriangledown` into Operators, but there are alternative commands for the Binary operator forms.

Note that `\smallint` does not change size.

Further integral operators are provided by the esint package; see Section 11.4.6 on page 169.

Table 11.27: Symbols of class `\mathop`

11.8.6 Operator symbols

The Operator symbols typically come in two sizes, for text and display uses; most of them are related to similar Binary operator symbols. Whether an Operator symbol takes limits in displays depends on a variety of factors (see Section 11.4.4). The available collection is shown in Table 11.27.

11.8.7 Punctuation

The symbols of class Punctuation appear in Table 11.28, together with some other punctuation-like symbols. Note that some of the typical punctuation characters (i.e., ". ! ?") are not set up as mathematical punctuation but rather as symbols of class Ordinary. This can cause unexpected results for common uses of these symbols, especially in the cases of ! and ?. Some of the dots symbols listed here are of class Inner; Section 11.5.1 on page 180 provides information about using dots for mathematical ellipsis.

The : character produces a colon with class Relation — not a Punctuation symbol. As an alternative, standard LaTeX offers the command `\colon` as the Punctuation

| , | , | $\cdots$ | \cdots*(inner)* | ... | \hdots*(inner)* | ... | \ldots*(inner)* | ... | \mathellipsis*(inner)* |
| ; | ; | : | \colon | $\ddots$ | \ddots*(inner)* | $\vdots$ | \vdots*(ord)* | | |

Punctuation symbols in blue *require the* amsmath *package.*

The logical amsmath *commands normally used to access* \cdots *and* \ldots *are described in Section 11.5.1.*

The \colon *command is redefined in* amsmath, *making it unsuitable for use as a general punctuation character.*

Synonyms: ... \hdots, \ldots   ... \mathellipsis, \ldots

Table 11.28: Symbols of class \mathpunct, \mathinner, \mathord (punctuation)

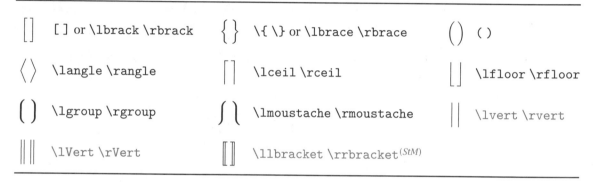

[]	[ ] or \lbrack \rbrack	{}	\{ \} or \lbrace \rbrace	()	( )
$\langle\rangle$	\langle \rangle	$\lceil\rceil$	\lceil \rceil	$\lfloor\rfloor$	\lfloor \rfloor
()	\lgroup \rgroup	∫∖	\lmoustache \rmoustache	‖	\lvert \rvert
‖‖	\lVert \rVert	[[ ]]	\llbracket \rrbracket*(StM)*		

Delimiters in blue *require either the* amsmath *package or, if flagged with* *(StM)*, *the* stmaryrd *package.*

Delimiters \lgroup, \rgroup, \lmoustache, *and* \rmoustache *are available only in sizes greater than* \big.

Table 11.29: Symbol pairs of class \mathopen and \mathclose (extensible)

symbol. However, the amsmath package makes unfortunate major changes to the spacing produced by the command \colon so that it is useful only for a particular layout in constructions such as f\colon A\to B where it produces $f\colon A \to B$. It is therefore wise to always use \mathpunct{:} for the simple punctuation colon in mathematics.

11.8.8 Opening and Closing symbols

The paired extensible delimiters, when used on their own (i.e., without a preceding \left, \right, or \middle), produce symbols of class Opening or Closing; these pairs are listed in Table 11.29. See Section 11.5.6 on page 191 for further information about the extensible symbols.

223

⌞⌟ \llcorner \lrcorner   ⌜⌝ \ulcorner \urcorner

⟦⟧ \llceil \rrceil[StM]   &⅋ \binampersand \bindnasrepma[StM]   ⟨⟩ \Lbag \Rbag[StM]

⟦⟧ \llfloor \rrfloor[StM]   ⟨⟩ \llparenthesis \rrparenthesis[StM]

Symbols on the first line require the amssymb *package; all others the* stmaryrd *package. They are not extensible.*

Table 11.30: Symbol pairs of class \mathopen and \mathclose (nonextensible)

To improve the flexibility of the vertical bar notation, amsmath defines some new pairs of paired extensible delimiter commands: \lvert, \rvert, \lVert, and \rVert. These commands are comparable to standard LATEX's \langle and \rangle commands.

Finally, there are a few nonextensible paired symbols of class Opening and Closing, as listed in Table 11.30. They should not be used after \left or \right.

CHAPTER 12

Fonts in formulas

For most symbols in a formula, the font used for a glyph cannot be changed by a font declaration as it can be in text. Indeed, there is no concept of, for example, an italic plus sign or a small capital less than sign.

One exception involves the letters of the Latin alphabet, whose appearance can be altered by the use of math alphabet identifier commands such as \mathcal. The commands provided by standard LaTeX for this purpose are discussed in Section 9.4; in the first section of this chapter we introduce a few more and discuss their use in some detail.

Another exception relates to the use of bold versions of arbitrary symbols to produce distinct symbols with new meanings. This potentially doubles the number of symbols available, as boldness can be a recognizable attribute of a glyph for nearly every shape: depending on the font family, even "<" is noticeably different from "<". Although there is a \mathbf command, the concept of a math alphabet identifier cannot be extended to cover bold symbols — better solutions are the topic of the second section.

To change the overall appearance of the mathematics in a document, the best approach is to replace all the fonts used to typeset formulas. This is usually done in the preamble of a document by loading a (set of) suitable packages, such as those discussed in Section 12.3 starting on page 238.

In the world of text fonts (Chapter 10) there is a clear separation between fonts suitable only for use with pdfTeX and fonts for exclusive use in Unicode engines. Fonts for pdfTeX are available as 8-bit fonts, encoded in OT1, T1, or some other 8-bit font encoding from Table 9.18 on page →I 737 and typically available as Type-1 or METAFONT fonts. In contrast, OpenType or TrueType fonts are usable only with XTEX or LuaTEX and are encoded in the TU font encoding.[1,2]

For symbol fonts this is not the case, at least in one direction: it is easily possible to use an 8-bit symbol font, e.g., MarVoSym, originally designed for use with pdfTEX, with one of the Unicode engines.

Given that formulas largely consist of fixed symbols together with a few alphabetical characters and that there have not been (many) Unicode fonts dedicated to mathematics (i.e., fonts that contain the mathematical symbols in their appropriate Unicode slots), it should come as no surprise that the Unicode engines have been designed to work with traditional TEX math fonts.

This has changed in recent years, and while developing OpenType Math fonts (compared to Text fonts) remains a niche market, there are now a number of fonts available that make it interesting to provide a LATEX math setup that directly uses such fonts. Such a setup is available with the **unicode-math** package by Will Robertson, and we will describe it in Section 12.4 on page 253.

In the final section of this chapter, starting at page 261, we showcase the effects of extensive changes to documents on a sample page of mathematics, made with just a few keystrokes. It uses the same input material typeset with both Computer Modern Math fonts (the default in LATEX) and nearly 50 other font family setups for text and mathematics. All of the fonts used are readily available and, except for Lucida fonts, provided free of charge.

12.1 The world of (Latin) math alphabets

It is easily possible to add additional new math alphabets for use in formulas. While this can be done using arbitrary command names, by convention \mathcal (a calligraphic alphabet), \mathscr (a script alphabet), \mathfrak (a fraktur alphabet), and \mathbb (a double-stroke also known as blackboard bold alphabet) are normally used as command names. Out of the box only \mathcal is available; for the others you have to add a suitable package (e.g., mathalpha) in the preamble or make a declaration manually using \DeclareMathAlphabet.

By loading the amsfonts (or the amssymb) package, both the Euler Fraktur alphabet by Hermann Zapf (\mathfrak) and a blackboard bold alphabet[3] (\mathbb) become available.

$$\forall n \in \mathbb{N} : \mathfrak{M}_n \leq \mathfrak{A}$$

```
\usepackage{amsfonts}
$ \forall n \in \mathbb{N} : \mathfrak{M}_n \leq \mathfrak{A} $
```

12-1-1

---

[1] While it is possible to load 8-bit text fonts in Unicode engines, this is not a good idea because correct hyphenation depends on using the appropriate font encoding, which means that words with diacritics come out wrong if a legacy font encoding such as T1 is used.

[2] If text fonts are usable with all engines (and many are), then this is because somebody generated Type-1 fonts from Unicode fonts (restricting them to 8-bit and the appropriate encoding) or that somebody built an OpenType font from existing 8-bit sources.

[3] Not much is known about the origin of this alphabet. Research in old archives (thanks to Nelson Beebe, Barbara Beeton, and Ulrik Vieth for digging) produced no conclusive results.

If you also want to use upright Euler Script, you can load the eucal package that is also part of the amsfonts distribution. Loaded without options, it replaces the default \mathcal, but if loaded with the option mathscr, as done below, it becomes accessible as \mathscr, and \mathcal remains free for a different alphabet:

The Euler Script font by Hermann Zapf

$$ \mathcal{ABCDEFGHIJKLMNOPQRSTUVWXYZ} $$
$$ \mathscr{ABCDEFGHIJKLMNOPQRSTUVWXYZ} $$

12-1-2

```
\usepackage[mathscr]{eucal}
\[ \mathcal{ABCDEFGHIJKLMNOPQRSTUVWXYZ} \]
\[ \mathscr{ABCDEFGHIJKLMNOPQRSTUVWXYZ} \]
```

If you prefer a geometric hollowed-out blackboard bold font in \mathbb, you can load, for example, the bboldx package that provides support for a font designed by Alan Jeffrey. One interesting aspect of this font is that it contains many more glyphs than the usual (Uppercase) alphabet?!, which even allows you to use it outside formulas by accessing it as \usefont{U}{bboldx}{m}{n} as we did here. Michael Sharpe added an additional thin and a bold face to the original font and made it available through the package bboldx.

A double-stroke font by Alan Jeffrey

$$ \mathbb{N} = \{0, 1, 2, 3, \dots\} $$
$$ ABCDEFGHIJKLMNOPQRSTUVWXYZ $$
$$ abcdefghijklmnopqrstuvwxyz $$

12-1-3

```
\usepackage[light]{bboldx}
\[ \mathbb{N}=\{\mathbfbb{0},1,2,3,\ldots\} \]
\[ \mathbb    {ABCDEFGHIJKLMNOPQRSTUVWXYZ}      \]
\[ \mathbfbb{abcdefghijklmnopqrstuvwxyz}      \]
```

By default the medium series is offered as \mathbb, while \mathbfbb selects the bold series. If you load the package with the option light, you get the thin and medium series with the two commands instead. Alternatively, you can use bfbb, which forces the package to use the bold series for \mathbf as if bold were the regular weight. You can also easily scale the alphabet slightly to make it fit with other glyphs in your formulas by using the option scale.

By default the other available characters in the font, such as the Greek letters or the special braces or brackets, are not available in math. If you want those in a formula, you can load the package with the option bbsymbols. However, note that using that option means that the font is declared as a symbol font, and as discussed in Section 9.4.1 on page →I 681, this means you are reducing your options to use other math fonts in your document. Therefore, do this only if you really intend to use any of the extra symbols.

$$ 0 \neq 1 \neq 1 $$

$$ G = [\![< \alpha, \beta, \gamma, \delta, \dots, \omega $$
$$ \Gamma, \Delta, \Theta, \Lambda, \dots, \Omega >]\!] < G $$

12-1-4

```
\usepackage[bbsymbols,scale=0.9]{bboldx} \usepackage{amsmath}
$ \mathbfbb{0} \neq \mathbb{1} \neq \mathbfbb{1} $
\begin{align*} \mathbb{G} = \bbLbrack \bbLparen \bbLangle
  & \bbalpha, \bbbeta, \bbgamma, \bbdelta, \dots,\bbomega  \\
  & \bbGamma, \bbDelta, \bbTheta, \bbLambda, \dots,\bbOmega
  \bbRangle \bbRparen \bbRbrack < \mathbfbb{G} \end{align*}
```

A serifed double stroke alphabet based on the Courier clone of URW in regular and bold is provided through the dsserif package by Michael Sharpe. It offers lower and uppercase Latin characters as well as digits and makes them available as \mathbb

A double-stroke font by Michael Sharpe

and \mathbfbb. As usual, scale can be used to adjust the font size to other letters in the formulas.

$$\mathbb{N} = \{\mathbf{0}, 1, 2, 3, \ldots\}$$

ABCDEFGHIJKLMNOPQRSTUVWXYZ

abcdefghijklmnopqrstuvwxyz

```
\usepackage{dsserif}
\[ \mathbb{N}=\{\mathbfbb{0},1,2,3,\ldots\} \]
\[ \mathbb   {ABCDEFGHIJKLMNOPQRSTUVWXYZ}      \]
\[ \mathbfbb{abcdefghijklmnopqrstuvwxyz}      \]
```

12-1-5

A double-stroke font by Olaf Kummer

The DS font designed by Olaf Kummer is a double stroke font that is based on the Computer Modern font shapes and thus works well in formulas done with Computer Modern or Latin Modern math fonts. Besides the usual uppercase alphabet, the font supports four additional characters: a variant form for the uppercase A (accessed by typing a lowercase a), lowercase h and k, and the digit 1. Trying anything else results in missing glyph warnings.

The package makes the alphabet available through the command \mathds and not through \mathbb. If you prefer the latter, you can alternatively set it up with the help of the mathalpha package or by using \DeclareCommandCopy.

ABCDEFGHIJKLMNOPQRSTUVWXYZ

A h k 1

```
\usepackage{dsfont}
\[ \mathds{ABCDEFGHIJKLMNOPQRSTUVWXYZ} \]
\[ \mathds{a \quad h \quad k \quad 1}  \]
```

12-1-6

A nice feature of the package is that it alternatively offers you a matching Sans double stroke font, which is useful if your formulas are typeset with sans serif fonts, e.g., when making slides.

ABCDEFGHIJKLMNOPQRSTUVWXYZ

A h k 1

```
\usepackage[sans]{dsfont}
\[ \mathds{ABCDEFGHIJKLMNOPQRSTUVWXYZ} \]
\[ \mathds{a \quad h \quad k \quad 1}  \]
```

12-1-7

Setting up math alphabets with \DeclareMathAlphabet

As an example of small-scale changes to the mathematical typesetting, those who prefer a visually distinct blackboard bold alphabet can load a different one, for example, the one contained in the PX fonts. The necessary declaration is done with \DeclareMathAlphabet, which is described in Section 9.4.1. In the example we first load the amsfonts package and then overwrite its definition of \mathbb.

$$\{n, m \in \mathbb{N} \mid \mathfrak{N}_{n,m}\}$$

```
\usepackage{amsfonts}  \DeclareMathAlphabet\mathbb{U}{px-ds}{m}{n}
$ \lbrace n,m \in \mathbb{N} \mid  \mathfrak{N}_{n,m} \rbrace $
```

12-1-8

The previous example shows how to include arbitrary alphabets from your LaTeX distribution as math alphabets, with the crucial part being the arguments of the \DeclareMathAlphabet declaration. Although getting these right may appear to be a tricky matter, it is not so difficult once you know where to look. Fonts suitable for inclusion need to have an .fd file of the form ⟨enc⟩⟨name⟩.fd, where the ⟨name⟩ is the font family name, often abbreviated — see the discussion on NFSS font family naming conventions on page 6. Chapter 10 covers more than one hundred high-quality font families and the necessary information to use them.

For example, Table 10.11 on page 22 shows the different Lucida fonts[1] including Lucida Handwriting, which has the name `hlcw` as documented there. Table 10.85 on page 100 exhibits the freely available Almendra family with the name `Almndr-OsF`. Both families are inspired by chancery handwriting. The tables also show which encodings and which shapes are supported. If you want to use a family not documented in this chapter, look into its `.fd` file to find the information for the remaining arguments for the `\DeclareMathAlphabet` declaration.

Both families are available in several encodings, but Lucida Handwriting exists only in series `m` and shape `it`, so there is no choice there. Almendra in contrast is offered in several shapes. In the example below we use this information to set up Lucida Handwriting as the `\mathcal` alphabet and the italic Almendra shape (which is fairly upright) as the `\mathscr` alphabet:

```
\DeclareMathAlphabet\mathcal{T1}{hlcw}{m}{it}
\DeclareMathAlphabet\mathscr{T1}{Almndr-OsF}{m}{it}
\[ A_B \neq \mathscr{A}_\mathscr{B}
                \neq \mathcal{A}_\mathcal{B}          \]
\[ \mathcal{ABCDEFGHI} \dots \mathscr{PQRSTUVWXYZ} \]
```

$$A_B \neq A_B \neq A_B$$

ABCDEFGHI ... *PQRSTUVWXYZ*

12-1-9

The above example clearly shows that you have to be careful which fonts you mix and match: the two alphabets used there show noticeable difference in the heights of the capitals. If this is the case, then using `\DeclareMathAlphabet` may not be a viable option because it does not offer you a way to customize the loading. For this you would need to alter the information in the `.fd` file and provide your own. While this is possible (see Section 9.8 on page →I 740), it is much simpler to use the `mathalpha` package if the font is supported by it, because that package allows you to load math alphabets scaled up or down as necessary; see Section 12.1.1 on the next page.

As mentioned, except for the Lucida fonts all font families documented in Chapter 10 are freely available, so you should be able to choose any of them and get it working without problems. Of course, in general the presence of an `.fd` file (such as `t1hlcw.fd`) on your system does not mean that you can use the font it describes successfully. Most modern LATEX installations contain such support files for various commercial font sets so that you can use these fonts the moment you buy them and add them to your system. Thus, the previous example will work for you only if you own the Lucida fonts.

In truth, you probably do not need to buy any fonts (though most are definitely worth the cost), because the freely available fonts already include a huge — and high-quality — choice as exhibited in Chapter 10. The `nfssfont.tex` or `unicodefont.tex` programs can provide valuable help in choosing a font, by producing glyph tables for the fonts available to your installation (see Sections 9.5.9 and 9.6.7).

As a final example for manual math alphabet setup we look at the RSFS script font by Ralph Smith, which was one of the first available alternatives to the calligraphic Computer Modern letters designed by Donald Knuth. Given that both alphabets are quite distinct, many people use the more formal RSFS script as `\mathscr` and retain

*Ralph Smith's
Formal Script
Symbol Font*

---

[1]This is one of the two commercial font families covered in the book; all others are freely available.

a second calligraphic alphabet in `\mathcal` as shown in the example. There also exists a small mathrsfs package in most distributions, but it sets up the font as a symbol font and so wastes one of the precious sixteen math family slots. We therefore recommend declaring it as shown below (or by using the mathalpha package):

```
\usepackage{amsmath}
\DeclareMathAlphabet\mathscr{U}{rsfs}{m}{n}
\begin{multline*} \mathscr{ABCDEFGHIJKLM} \\
    \mathscr{NOPQRSTUVWXYZ}   \end{multline*}
\[   \mathcal{ABCDEFGHIJKLMNOPQRSTUVWXYZ}   \]
```

12-1-10

If you prefer a more upright design, then you can try the RSFSO variant by Michael Sharpe shown below. It too can be set up using mathalpha if that is preferred.

```
\usepackage{amsmath}
\DeclareMathAlphabet\mathscr{U}{rsfso}{m}{n}
\begin{multline*} \mathscr{ABCDEFGHIJKLM} \\
    \mathscr{NOPQRSTUVWXYZ} \end{multline*}
```

12-1-11

12.1.1 mathalpha — Simplified setup for math alphabets

So far we have seen small packages for setting up additional math alphabets as well as the manual method through `\DeclareMathAlphabet`. In his mathalpha package, Michael Sharpe offers a much more convenient interface to this that allows you to set up `\mathcal`, `\mathscr`, `\mathbb`, and `\mathfrak` in one go by supplying suitable key/value pairs as package options. To give a practical example we assign different font families to the math alphabets by using the keys cal, scr, bb, and frak and as values the chosen fonts, e.g., zapfc stands for Hermann Zapf's Chancery italic script. Other font values are discussed below.

```
\usepackage[cal=zapfc,scr=boondoxo,bb=txof,frak=esstix]
    {mathalpha}
\newcommand\sample[1]{$#1{ABCDEFGHIJKLMNOP\dots}$ \par}
\sample\mathcal  \sample\mathscr
\sample\mathbb   \sample\mathfrak
```

12-1-12

Some fonts, for example dutchcal, have bold variants. If that is the case, then those are made accessible through further math alphabets named `\mathbfcal`, `\mathbfscr`, `\mathbfbb`, and `\mathbffrak` as shown below:

```
\usepackage[cal=dutchcal,frak=euler]{mathalpha}
\newcommand\sample[1]{$#1{ABCDEFGHIJKLMNOP\dots}$ \par}
\sample\mathcal  \sample\mathbfcal
\sample\mathfrak \sample\mathbffrak
```

12-1-13

If you want to use the bold variant as the default, you can use one or more of the options bfbb, bfcal, bffrak, or bfscr to arrange for this.

We already mentioned that alphabets sometimes need slight adjustments in size to comfortably fit with the rest of the math formula. To help you with this task, the package offers four keys that allow you to scale the alphabets up or down. They are named `bbscaled`, `calscaled`, `frakscaled`, and `scrscaled`, and if given, they expect a numerical value, such as `0.95`, to scale the respective alphabet down by 5%, etc.

The package knows about many font families that are useful candidates for math alphabets: several commercial fonts as well as many free ones. However, it is obviously impossible for the package to cover everything; e.g., if you want to use Almendra as we did in Example 12-1-9 on page 229, you have to use the method shown there, because Almendra is not in the list of supported font families. Once in a while Michael adds support for further math alphabets, and to give you a simple way to see what is currently available, there is the option `showoptions`. If you use it when loading the package, it replies by throwing an error message that lists all available option keys and their supported values; i.e., you get output like this:

```
Package mathalfa Error: Package Options:

  bb=ams, lucida, mathpi, mma, mt, mth, pazo, fourier, esstix, boondox,
     px, tx, txof, libus, dsserif, bboldxLight, bboldx, dsfontserif,
     dsfontsans, stixtwo, stix

  cal=cm, euler, rsfso, rsfs, lucida, mathpi, mma, mt, mtc, zapfc, esstix,
      boondox, boondoxo, dutchcal, pxtx, bickham, bickhams, stix, txupr,
      boondoxupr, kp, stixplain, stixfancy, stixtwoplain, stixtwofancy

  frak=euler, lucida, mathpi, mma, mt, esstix, boondox, pxtx, stixtwo

  scr=cm, euler, rsfso, rsfs, lucida, mathpi, mma, mt, mtc, zapfc, esstix,
      boondox, boondoxo, dutchcal, pxtx, bickham, bickhams, stix, txupr,
      boondoxupr, kp, stixplain, stixfancy, stixtwoplain, stixtwofancy

  bbscaled=1.0, calscaled=1.0, frakscaled=1.0, scrscaled=1.0

Bold versions may be forced by one of options bfbb, bfcal, bffrak, bfscr.
```

To help you with the selection, we show samples of different supported fonts sorted by type. The value to use is shown in the margin; if the font has a bold variant the indicator (*bold*) is added after the value. This means that `\mathbfcal`, `\mathbfscr`, `\mathbffrak`, or `\mathbfbb` is also set up when such a font is chosen as the value.

Selection of supported Calligraphic and Script math alphabets

We start with the calligraphic fonts that can be used with the keys `cal` or `scr`, grouped into "upright", "oblique restrained", and "oblique embellished". Initially, the list of allowed alphabets for `cal` and `scr` differed, but as shown above, they now accept the same set of values. For details on which alphabets are supported, see the output of the `showoptions` option.

The value `euler` refers to the Euler Script fonts, which we have already seen in Example 12-1-2 on page 227; `txupr` is an upright script that is based on the TX fonts, and `boondoxupr` is based on the STIX font designs.

euler	$\mathcal{A\ B\ C\ D\ E\ F\ G\ H\ I\ J\ K\ L\ M\ N\ O\ P\ Q\ R\ S\ T\ U\ V\ W\ X\ Y\ Z}$
euler *(bold)*	$\boldsymbol{\mathcal{A\ B\ C\ D\ E\ F\ G\ H\ I\ J\ K\ L\ M\ N\ O\ P\ Q\ R\ S\ T\ U\ V\ W\ X\ Y\ Z}}$
txupr	$\mathcal{A\ B\ C\ D\ E\ F\ G\ H\ I\ J\ K\ L\ M\ N\ O\ P\ Q\ R\ S\ T\ U\ V\ W\ X\ Y\ Z}$
boondoxupr	$\mathcal{A\ B\ C\ D\ E\ F\ G\ H\ I\ J\ K\ L\ M\ N\ O\ P\ Q\ R\ S\ T\ U\ V\ W\ X\ Y\ Z}$

In the second group we compare the slanted alphabets with relatively simple (restrained) glyph shapes. The value `cm` refers to the Computer Modern Calligraphic alphabet (which is the default for `\mathcal`), `lucida` refers to the Lucida calligraphic math alphabet (i.e., designed for use in math), `zapfc` is Hermann Zapf's chancery font (see Table 10.87 on page 103) but adjusted for math instead of text typesetting, and `pxtx` is the calligraphic math alphabet from the TX/PX fonts inspired by Palatino.

cm	$\mathcal{A\ B\ C\ D\ E\ F\ G\ H\ I\ J\ K\ L\ M\ N\ O\ P\ Q\ R\ S\ T\ U\ V\ W\ X\ Y\ Z}$
cm *(bold)*	$\boldsymbol{\mathcal{A\ B\ C\ D\ E\ F\ G\ H\ I\ J\ K\ L\ M\ N\ O\ P\ Q\ R\ S\ T\ U\ V\ W\ X\ Y\ Z}}$
lucida	$\mathcal{A\ B\ C\ D\ E\ F\ G\ H\ I\ J\ K\ L\ M\ N\ O\ P\ Q\ R\ S\ T\ U\ V\ W\ X\ Y\ Z}$
lucida *(bold)*	$\boldsymbol{\mathcal{A\ B\ C\ D\ E\ F\ G\ H\ I\ J\ K\ L\ M\ N\ O\ P\ Q\ R\ S\ T\ U\ V\ W\ X\ Y\ Z}}$
zapfc	$\mathcal{A\ B\ C\ D\ E\ F\ G\ H\ I\ J\ K\ L\ M\ N\ O\ P\ Q\ R\ S\ T\ U\ V\ W\ X\ Y\ Z}$
pxtx	$\mathcal{A\ B\ C\ D\ E\ F\ G\ H\ I\ J\ K\ L\ M\ N\ O\ P\ Q\ R\ S\ T\ U\ V\ W\ X\ Y\ Z}$
pxtx *(bold)*	$\boldsymbol{\mathcal{A\ B\ C\ D\ E\ F\ G\ H\ I\ J\ K\ L\ M\ N\ O\ P\ Q\ R\ S\ T\ U\ V\ W\ X\ Y\ Z}}$
stixplain	$\mathcal{A\ B\ C\ D\ E\ F\ G\ H\ I\ J\ K\ L\ M\ N\ O\ P\ Q\ R\ S\ T\ U\ V\ W\ X\ Y\ Z}$
stixplain *(bold)*	$\boldsymbol{\mathcal{A\ B\ C\ D\ E\ F\ G\ H\ I\ J\ K\ L\ M\ N\ O\ P\ Q\ R\ S\ T\ U\ V\ W\ X\ Y\ Z}}$
stixtwoplain	$\mathcal{A\ B\ C\ D\ E\ F\ G\ H\ I\ J\ K\ L\ M\ N\ O\ P\ Q\ R\ S\ T\ U\ V\ W\ X\ Y\ Z}$

The embellished scripts are much more expressive than the previous set. The value `dutchcal` refers to an adaptation by Michael Sharpe of a design from Elsevier Publishing later donated to the STIX project, `rsfs` is Ralph's Smith Formal Script as shown in Example 12-1-10 on page 230; `boondox` is the calligraphic math alphabet of the STIX fonts, slightly adjusted by Michael Sharpe; and the `kp` fonts represent the calligraphic alphabet from the Johannes Kepler fonts (a.k.a. KP fonts). There are also `rsfso` and `boondoxo`, both being less slanted variants of their originals. They have been also prepared by Michael Sharpe.

dutchcal	$\mathcal{A\ B\ C\ D\ E\ F\ G\ H\ I\ J\ K\ L\ M\ N\ O\ P\ Q\ R\ S\ T\ U\ V\ W\ X\ Y\ Z}$
dutchcal *(bold)*	$\boldsymbol{\mathcal{A\ B\ C\ D\ E\ F\ G\ H\ I\ J\ K\ L\ M\ N\ O\ P\ Q\ R\ S\ T\ U\ V\ W\ X\ Y\ Z}}$

$\mathscr{A\,B\,C\,D\,E\,F\,G\,H\,I\,J\,K\,L\,M\,N\,O\,P\,Q\,R\,S\,T\,U\,V\,W\,X\,Y\,Z}$	rsfso
$\mathscr{A\,B\,C\,D\,E\,F\,G\,H\,I\,J\,K\,L\,M\,N\,O\,P\,Q\,R\,S\,T\,U\,V\,W\,X\,Y\,Z}$	rsfs
$\mathscr{A\,B\,C\,D\,E\,F\,G\,H\,I\,J\,K\,L\,M\,N\,O\,P\,Q\,R\,S\,T\,U\,V\,W\,X\,Y\,Z}$	boondoxo
$\boldsymbol{\mathscr{A\,B\,C\,D\,E\,F\,G\,H\,I\,J\,K\,L\,M\,N\,O\,P\,Q\,R\,S\,T\,U\,V\,W\,X\,Y\,Z}}$	boondoxo (bold)
$\mathscr{A\,B\,C\,D\,E\,F\,G\,H\,I\,J\,K\,L\,M\,N\,O\,P\,Q\,R\,S\,T\,U\,V\,W\,X\,Y\,Z}$	boondox
$\boldsymbol{\mathscr{A\,B\,C\,D\,E\,F\,G\,H\,I\,J\,K\,L\,M\,N\,O\,P\,Q\,R\,S\,T\,U\,V\,W\,X\,Y\,Z}}$	boondox (bold)
$\mathscr{A\,B\,C\,D\,E\,F\,G\,H\,I\,J\,K\,L\,M\,N\,O\,P\,Q\,R\,S\,T\,U\,V\,W\,X\,Y\,Z}$	kp
$\boldsymbol{\mathscr{A\,B\,C\,D\,E\,F\,G\,H\,I\,J\,K\,L\,M\,N\,O\,P\,Q\,R\,S\,T\,U\,V\,W\,X\,Y\,Z}}$	kp (bold)
$\mathscr{A\,B\,C\,D\,E\,F\,G\,H\,I\,J\,K\,L\,M\,N\,O\,P\,Q\,R\,S\,T\,U\,V\,W\,X\,Y\,Z}$	stixfancy
$\boldsymbol{\mathscr{A\,B\,C\,D\,E\,F\,G\,H\,I\,J\,K\,L\,M\,N\,O\,P\,Q\,R\,S\,T\,U\,V\,W\,X\,Y\,Z}}$	stixfancy (bold)

Selection of supported Fraktur math alphabets

Most Fraktur alphabets follow a similar design, but with recognizable differences in several shapes. The only exception is the lucida blackletter alphabet, which offers various shapes that are noticeably different from historical models. pxtx and euler are designs by Hermann Zapf (1918–2015) (or rather inspired by in the case of pxtx) and esstix and boondox are adaptations of the Fraktur fonts from STIX, and one can easily see the close relationship.

$\mathfrak{A\,B\,C\,D\,E\,F\,G\,H\,I\,J\,K\,L\,M\,N\,O\,P\,Q\,R\,S\,T\,U\,V\,W\,X\,Y\,Z}$	pxtx
$\boldsymbol{\mathfrak{A\,B\,C\,D\,E\,F\,G\,H\,I\,J\,K\,L\,M\,N\,O\,P\,Q\,R\,S\,T\,U\,V\,W\,X\,Y\,Z}}$	pxtx (bold)
$\mathfrak{A\,B\,C\,D\,E\,F\,G\,H\,I\,J\,K\,L\,M\,N\,O\,P\,Q\,R\,S\,T\,U\,V\,W\,X\,Y\,Z}$	euler
$\boldsymbol{\mathfrak{A\,B\,C\,D\,E\,F\,G\,H\,I\,J\,K\,L\,M\,N\,O\,P\,Q\,R\,S\,T\,U\,V\,W\,X\,Y\,Z}}$	euler (bold)
$\mathfrak{A\,B\,C\,D\,E\,F\,G\,H\,I\,J\,K\,L\,M\,N\,O\,P\,Q\,R\,S\,T\,U\,V\,W\,X\,Y\,Z}$	esstix
$\mathfrak{A\,B\,C\,D\,E\,F\,G\,H\,I\,J\,K\,L\,M\,N\,O\,P\,Q\,R\,S\,T\,U\,V\,W\,X\,Y\,Z}$	boondox
$\boldsymbol{\mathfrak{A\,B\,C\,D\,E\,F\,G\,H\,I\,J\,K\,L\,M\,N\,O\,P\,Q\,R\,S\,T\,U\,V\,W\,X\,Y\,Z}}$	boondox (bold)
$\mathfrak{A\,B\,C\,D\,E\,F\,G\,H\,I\,J\,K\,L\,M\,N\,O\,P\,Q\,R\,S\,T\,U\,V\,W\,X\,Y\,Z}$	stixtwo
$\boldsymbol{\mathfrak{A\,B\,C\,D\,E\,F\,G\,H\,I\,J\,K\,L\,M\,N\,O\,P\,Q\,R\,S\,T\,U\,V\,W\,X\,Y\,Z}}$	stixtwo (bold)
$\mathfrak{A\,B\,C\,D\,E\,F\,G\,H\,I\,J\,K\,L\,M\,N\,O\,P\,Q\,R\,S\,T\,U\,V\,W\,X\,Y\,Z}$	lucida

Selection of supported Blackboard Bold math alphabets

Among the blackboard bold alphabets are two major styles: those that show hollowed-out shapes, i.e., where most parts of the glyphs show their contours, and the more geometric shapes where the usual character shape is augmented by a single extra vertical or diagonal line (the Lucida design is somewhere in between the two).

Hollowed-out shapes are those from the AMS fonts referred to as `ams`; the open-faced design from the TX fonts is accessed with `txof`, and `lucida` represents the more sans serif open-faced design of the Lucida math fonts.

ams	A B C D E F G H I J K L M N O P Q R S T U V W X Y Z
txof	A B C D E F G H I J K L M N O P Q R S T U V W X Y Z
txof *(bold)*	A B C D E F G H I J K L M N O P Q R S T U V W X Y Z
lucida	A B C D E F G H I J K L M N O P Q R S T U V W X Y Z

If you are looking for a more traditional[1] geometric-shaped blackboard bold typeface, then you have a choice between serifed designs, i.e., `pazo` from the Pazo Math fonts and `px` from the PX fonts, both of which are based on Palatino and nearly identical, and the `dsfontserif` math alphabet from the DS fonts.

pazo	A B C D E F G H I J K L M N O P Q R S T U V W X Y Z
px	A B C D E F G H I J K L M N O P Q R S T U V W X Y Z
px *(bold)*	A B C D E F G H I J K L M N O P Q R S T U V W X Y Z
dsfontserif	A B C D E F G H I J K L M N O P Q R S T U V W X Y Z

The DS fonts also offer a sans variant with `dsfontsans`. The other sans designs are nearly identical. Between `esstix` and `boondox` there are minor differences in stroke lengths of E and F and the `bbold` alphabet by Alan Jeffrey and its light and bold versions by Michael Sharpe have some stroke variations in some letters compared to the former two alphabets.

dsfontsans	A B C D E F G H I J K L M N O P Q R S T U V W X Y Z
esstix	A B C D E F G H I J K L M N O P Q R S T U V W X Y Z
boondox	A B C D E F G H I J K L M N O P Q R S T U V W X Y Z
bbold *(light)*	A B C D E F G H I J K L M N O P Q R S T U V W X Y Z
bbold	A B C D E F G H I J K L M N O P Q R S T U V W X Y Z
bbold *(bold)*	A B C D E F G H I J K L M N O P Q R S T U V W X Y Z

The list of supported designs is larger than the number of examples shown above; not included are the commercial fonts (except for Lucida) and a few that are virtually identical to others. Furthermore, the list might grow over time; thus, for the full list, use the `showoptions` key or refer to the package documentation.

---

[1] At least my math teachers used the approach of an extra stroke in this way on a blackboard.

12.2 Making it bold

For bold Latin letters only, you can use the command `\mathbf`; for everything else, there is the bm package. Although `amsmath` provides `\boldsymbol` and `\pmb`, the rules about when to use which command, and many of the restrictions on when they work, can now be avoided: just load the bm package and use `\bm` to make any formula as bold and beautiful as the available fonts allow.

12.2.1 bm — Making bold

The bm package by David Carlisle addresses the problem that it is rather difficult to bolden individual symbols in a math formula without altering the spacing or introducing other unwanted side effects.[1]

The example below shows many ways to use the `\bm` and `\mathbf` commands and a strategy for defining shorthand names for frequently occurring bold symbols, using both standard LaTeX's `\newcommand` and `\bmdefine`, which is provided by bm. Note that `\mathbf{xy}` is not identical to `\bm{xy}`: the former produces bold roman "**xy**", and the latter produces "$\boldsymbol{xy}$" (i.e., bold math italic).

```
\usepackage{amsmath,amssymb,bm}
\newcommand\bfB{\mathbf{B}}    \newcommand\bfx{\mathbf{x}}
\bmdefine\bpi{\pi}             \bmdefine\binfty{\infty}
\section{The bold equivalence
  $\sum_{j < B} \prod_\lambda : \bm{\sum_{x_j} \prod_\lambda}$}
\begin{gather}
  B_\infty + \pi B_1 \sim  \bfB_{\binfty} \bm{+}\bpi \bfB_{\bm{1}}
    \bm {\sim B_\infty + \pi B_1}                               \\
  B_\binfty + \bpi B_{\bm{1}} \bm{\in} \bm{\biggl\lbrace}
    (\bfB, \bfx) : \frac {\partial \bfB}{\partial \bfx}
    \bm{\lnapprox} \bm{1} \bm{\biggr\rbrace}
\end{gather}
```

1   The bold equivalence $\sum_{j<B} \prod_\lambda : \boldsymbol{\sum_{x_j} \prod_\lambda}$

$$B_\infty + \pi B_1 \sim \boldsymbol{B_\infty + \pi B_1} \sim \boldsymbol{B_\infty + \pi B_1} \tag{1}$$

$$\boldsymbol{B_\infty + \pi B_1} \in \left\{ (\mathbf{B}, \mathbf{x}) : \frac{\partial \mathbf{B}}{\partial \mathbf{x}} \lessgtr 1 \right\} \tag{2}$$

12-2-1

In the above example bm tries its best to fulfill the requests for bold versions of individual symbols and letters, but if you look closely, you will see that the results are not always optimal. For example, $\sum$, $\prod$, and $\lessgtr$ are all made bold by the use of a technique known as *poor man's bold*, in which the symbol is overprinted three times with slight offsets. Also, the { is not made bold in any way. Such deficiencies are

bm cannot do miracles if symbols are not available in a bold variant

---

[1]However, bm is unfortunately not usable with Unicode engines — this might change though.

unavoidable because for some symbols there is simply no bold variant available when using the Computer Modern math fonts.

The situation changes when other fonts are used; e.g., below we set up Times and Helvetica clones for text (newtxtext) and compatible math fonts (newtxmath) by changing the first line of the previous example to

```
\usepackage{amsmath,amssymb,
            newtxtext,newtxmath, % <- This changes the math setup;
            bm}                  %    bm should come afterwards!
```

This family of fonts contains bold variants for *all* symbols from standard LaTeX and amssymb. It produces the following output:

1   The bold equivalence $\sum_{j<B} \prod_\lambda : \sum_{x_j} \prod_\lambda$

$$B_\infty + \pi B_1 \sim \mathbf{B_\infty} + \pi\mathbf{B_1} \sim B_\infty + \pi B_1 \tag{1}$$

$$B_\infty + \pi B_1 \in \left\{ (\mathbf{B}, \mathbf{x}) : \frac{\partial \mathbf{B}}{\partial \mathbf{x}} \gtrless 1 \right\} \tag{2}$$

12-2-2

What are the precise rules used by \bm to produce bold forms of the symbols in its argument? In a nutshell, it makes use of the fact that LaTeX includes a **bold** math version (accessible via \boldmath) for typesetting a whole formula in bold (provided suitable bold fonts are available and set up).

Load the bm package after packages that change the existing math font setup!

For each symbol, the \bm command looks at this math version to see what would be done in that version. If the font selected for the symbol is different from the one selected in the normal math version, it then typesets the symbol in this bold font, obtaining a perfect result (assuming that the bold math version was set up properly). If the fonts in both versions are identical, it assumes that there is no bold variant available and applies its poor man's bold approach (see above).

With delimiters, such as \biggl\lbrace in the example, the situation is even more complex: a delimiter in TeX is typically typeset by a glyph chosen to match a requested height from a sequence of different sizes (see Section 11.5.6 on page 191). Moreover, these glyphs can live in different fonts, and a particular size may or may not have bold variants, making it impossible for \bm to reliably work out whether it needs to apply poor man's bold. It therefore essentially typesets the delimiter using whatever fonts the bold math version offers. With the Computer Modern math fonts, only the smallest delimiter size is available in bold; all other sizes come from fonts that have no bold variants.

```
\usepackage{bm}
$\bm{\Biggl\lbrace\biggl\lbrace\Bigl\lbrace\bigl\lbrace \lbrace
      \mathcal{Q}
      \rangle \bigr\rangle\Bigr\rangle\biggr\rangle\Biggr\rangle}$
```

12-2-3

This situation can be improved by use of the newtxmath package (as in Example 12-2-2) or use of another font set with full bold variants, such as the newpxmath shown here:

$$\left\{\Bigg\lbrace\bigg\lbrace\Big\lbrace\big\lbrace\lbrace\mathcal{Q}\rangle\big\rangle\Big\rangle\bigg\rangle\Bigg\rangle\right\}$$

```
\usepackage{newpxmath,bm}
$\bm{\Biggl\lbrace\biggl\lbrace\Bigl\lbrace\bigl\lbrace \lbrace
     \mathcal{Q}
     \rangle \bigr\rangle\Bigr\rangle\biggr\rangle\Biggr\rangle}$
```

12-2-4

Normally, \bm requires that if a command that itself takes arguments is within its argument, then that command must be fully included (i.e., both the command and its arguments must appear) in the argument of \bm; as a result, all parts of the typeset material are typeset in bold. If you really need the output of a command with arguments to be only partially bold, then you have to work harder. You should place the symbol(s) that should not be bold in an \mbox and explicitly reset the math version within the box contents using \unboldmath. TeX considers an \mbox to be a symbol of class Ordinary (see Section 11.8.1); hence, to get the spacing right, you may have to surround it by a \mathbin, \mathrel, or \mathop.

$\sqrt[2]{x \times \alpha}$ but $\sqrt[2]{x \times \alpha}$ or the similar $\sqrt{x \times \alpha}$

```
\usepackage{amsmath,bm}
$ \bm{\sqrt[2]{x \times \alpha}} $  but
$ \bm{\sqrt[2]{x \mathbin{\mbox{\unboldmath$\times$}}
                        \alpha}} $
   or the similar
$ \bm{\sqrtsign}{\bm{x} \times \bm{\alpha}} $
```

12-2-5

Fortunately, such gymnastics are seldom needed. In most cases involving commands with arguments, only parts of the arguments need to be made bold, which can be achieved by using \bm inside those arguments. As with \sqrtsign in the example above, for the common case of bold accents \bm is specially programmed to allow the accent's argument to be outside its own argument. However, if you need such accents regularly, it is wise to define your own abbreviation using \bmdefine, as in the next example:

$\hat a \neq \hat{a} \neq \hat{a} = \hat{a} \neq \widehat{a}$

```
\usepackage{bm}   \bmdefine\bhat{\hat}
$\hat a \neq \bm{\hat a} \neq \bm\hat a = \bhat a
                    \neq \bm\widehat a $
```

12-2-6

This example also shows that the variable-width accents (e.g., \widehat) share a deficiency with the delimiters: in the Computer Modern math setup they come from a font for which no bold variant is available.

Although \bmdefine\blambda{\lambda} appears to be simply a shorthand for \newcommand\blambda{\bm{\lambda}}, in fact almost the opposite is true: \bm defines a new hidden temporary command using \bmdefine and then immediately uses this temporary command to produce the bold symbol. In other words,

Speeding up the processing

\bmdefine does all the hard work! If you frequently use, for example, something that is defined via \bm{\alpha}, then a new \bmdefine is executed at every use. If you set things up by doing \bmdefine\balpha{\alpha}, then \bmdefine does its time-consuming work only once, however many times \balpha is used.

Dealing with strange errors

The bm package tries very hard to produce the correct spacing between symbols (both inside and outside the argument of \bm). For this effort to work, \bm has to "investigate" the definitions of the commands in its argument to determine the correct mathematical class to which each of the resulting symbols belongs (see Section 11.8.1 on page 209). It is possible that some complicated constructions could confuse this investigation. If this happens, then LATEX will almost certainly stop with a strange error. Ideally, this problem should not arise with constructs from standard LATEX or amsmath, but proper parsing in TEX is extremely difficult, and the odd overlooked case might still be present.[1]

If some command does produce an error when used inside \bm, you can always surround it *and all its arguments* with an extra level of braces — for example, writing \bm{..{\cmd..}..} rather than simply \bm{..\cmd..}. The \bm command does not attempt to parse material surrounded by braces but uses the \boldmath version to typeset the whole of the formula within the braces. The resulting bold subformula is then inserted as if it were a "symbol" of class Ordinary. Thus, to obtain the right spacing around it, you may have to explicitly set its class; for instance, for a relation you would use \bm{..\mathrel{\cmd..}..} (see Section 11.8.1 on page 209).

12.3 Traditional math font setup through packages

Implementing a setup for math in LATEX is a rather complicated undertaking and not something you do in a preamble of your document. There you might add a few declarations for math alphabets with \DeclareMathAlphabet or through the packages discussed in Section 12.1 or define your own notations as we have done in several examples throughout the book.

However, if you want to replace all glyphs used in formulas with new ones that have a different design, you typically simply call one or more packages that do the hard work for you behind the scenes. In this section we discuss a number of them. As mentioned earlier, most of them can be used with every TEX engine even if they are based on 8-bit fonts.[2] Setting up math using Unicode fonts (and thus usable only with Unicode engines) is the subject of Section 12.4.

12.3.1 ccfonts — The Concrete fonts for text and math

Starting from the work done for the EC fonts, it was relatively easy to create Concrete Roman fonts in T1 and TS1 encodings (original work by Frank Mittelbach; current version by Walter Schmidt (1960–2021)). Ulrik Vieth used the construction method

---

[1] For instance, the author got trapped when writing this section by the fact that \bm was trying to process the argument of \hspace instead of producing the desired space (now fixed).

[2] As long as they do not also set up text fonts, that is.

outlined by Knuth [46] to develop a companion set of Concrete Math fonts including the full range of AMS symbols (as provided by the amssymb or amsfonts package).

The first package that provided access to these font families for normal text was beton (by Frank Jensen). A more recent development that also provides the use of Concrete fonts for math and supports the T1 and TS1 encodings is the ccfonts package by Walter Schmidt; see page 65 for details.

Because the Concrete fonts have no boldface series, the ccfonts package offers the option boldsans to use the semibold series of the Computer Modern Sans fonts as a replacement. As a result, without any further adjustments, headings in standard classes are typeset using this font series. A larger sample page is shown in Figure 12.39 on page 288.

1   Testing headings

An example showing a trigonometric function:

$$\sin \frac{\alpha}{2} = \pm \sqrt{\frac{1 - \cos \alpha}{2}}$$

The script looks like this: $\mathcal{ABC}$.

Text symbols: $ ₠ ⋆ ∞ † …

```
\usepackage[boldsans]{ccfonts}

\section{Testing headings}
An example showing a trigonometric function:
\[ \sin \frac{\alpha}{2} =
    \pm \sqrt{\frac{1-\cos\alpha}{2}}       \]
The script looks like this: $\mathcal{ABC}$.    \\
Text symbols: \textdollaroldstyle\ \texteuro\
\textborn\ \textmarried\ \textdied\ \ldots
```

12-3-1

Because the Concrete fonts are of considerably heavier weight than, say, Computer Modern, it is advisable to use them with a larger leading than most document classes provide by default. For this reason the package automatically enlarges the leading to 10/13 and similar ratios for other document sizes. If this adjustment is undesirable for some reason, it can be canceled with the option standard-baselineskips.

The feature provided by the exscale package is available as the package option exscale; see Section 9.5.7 on page →I 704 for details. The exscale package itself cannot be used because it is set up to work with only Computer Modern math fonts.

If the amssymb or amsfonts package is loaded, the ccfonts package automatically arranges to use the Concrete variants of the AMS symbol fonts.

Finally, the package offers the option slantedGreek to make uppercase Greek letters slanted instead of being upright (default). The two extra commands \upDelta and \upOmega always typeset an upright Δ and Ω, respectively.

12.3.2 cmbright — The Computer Modern Bright fonts

Another font family whose design is based on the METAFONT sources of the CM fonts are the Computer Modern Bright (CM Bright) fonts by Walter Schmidt (1960–2021), shown in Table 10.3 on page 12. This family of sans serif fonts is designed to serve as a legible body font. It comes with matching typewriter and math fonts, including the American Mathematical Society symbols.

Loading the cmbright package in the preamble ensures that these families are selected throughout the document. It is recommended that you combine this package with fontenc, as shown in the next example, to achieve proper hyphenation with languages other than English. All CM Bright fonts have fully implemented T1 and TS1 encoding support.

1 A CM Bright document

The CM Bright family contains typewriter fonts and matching fonts for math formulas, e.g.,

$$\sum_{0 \leq k < n} k = \frac{n(n-1)}{2}$$

```
\usepackage[T1]{fontenc}
 \usepackage{cmbright}

\section{A CM Bright document}
The CM Bright family contains
\texttt{typewriter} fonts and matching fonts
for math formulas, e.g.,
\[ \sum_{0\leq k<n} k = \frac{n(n-1)}{2} \]
```

12-3-2

By default, the package selects a slightly larger leading than the default classes to account for the use of sans serif fonts; this can be canceled by specifying the package option standard-baselineskips. Also in other respects, this package works similarly to other works by Walter: the option slantedGreek produces slanted uppercase Greek letters, with \upDelta and \upOmega typesetting an upright Δ and Ω, respectively. When the amssymb or amsfonts package is loaded, the cmbright package automatically arranges to use the CM Bright variants of the AMS symbol fonts.

The METAFONT implementation of the fonts is freely available from CTAN archives; Type 1 format versions have been commercially sold by MicroPress. In 2002, a freely available Type 1 (although without manual hinting) was made available by Harald Harders under the name hfbright. Moreover, as mentioned in Section 9.5.1, the freely available CM-Super Type 1 fonts also cover parts of the CM Bright fonts.

12.3.3 euler, eulervm — Accessing Zapf's Euler fonts

As mentioned earlier, Hermann Zapf (1918–2015) designed a beautiful set of fonts for typesetting mathematics — upright characters with a handwritten flavor — named after the famous mathematician Leonhard Euler [52]. These fonts can be accessed as (math) alphabets of their own, or you can generally modify the math font setup, thus making LaTeX use Euler math fonts (rather than Computer Modern) by default.

The Euler fonts contain three math alphabets: $\mathcal{SCRIPT}$, $\mathfrak{Euler\ Fraktur}$, and Euler Roman.[1] The script and the fraktur alphabets can be easily set up with the mathalpha package, but for historical reasons there also exist individual packages to set them up. For the script alphabet you can alternatively use the eucal package, which makes this math alphabet available under the name \mathcal. If the package is loaded with the mathscr option, the alphabet becomes available through the command \mathscr, with \mathcal retaining its original definition. The package for Euler Fraktur is eufrak, which defines the math alphabet \mathfrak. There is no particular package to access the Euler Roman alphabet separately.

---

[1] None of these alphabets is suitable for typesetting text because the individual glyphs have side-bearings specially tailored for use in math formulas.

The next example shows Computer Modern Calligraphic, Euler Script, and Euler Fraktur side by side. We use the `mathalpha` approach but also show the equivalent older way using the packages `eucal` and `eufrak`:

12-3-3

$$\mathcal{A} \neq \sum_{k<n} \mathscr{A}_k \neq \mathfrak{A}$$

```
%\usepackage[mathscr]{eucal} \usepackage{eufrak} % old way
\usepackage[scr=euler,frak=euler]{mathalpha}
\[ \mathcal{A} \neq \sum_{k<n} \mathscr{A}_k \neq \mathfrak{A} \]
```

Unfortunately, the Euler fonts use font encodings that differ from all other encoding schemes for mathematics. For this reason, the fonts are all assigned the encoding U (unknown) in NFSS classification.

These nonstandard encodings make it difficult to simply substitute the Euler alphabets and symbols for the default CM math fonts. Yet the euler package, written by Frank Jensen, went exactly this way, redeclaring most of LaTeX's math font setup. In conjunction with the package `beton`, which sets up Concrete as the default text font family, it simulates the typography of Knuth's book *Concrete Mathematics* [32], as shown below:

Concrete Roman blends well with Euler Math,
as can be seen with

12-3-4

$$\sum_{0 \leq k < n} k = \frac{n(n-1)}{2}$$

```
\usepackage{beton,euler}
Concrete Roman blends well with Euler Math,
as can be seen with
\[ \sum_{0\leq k<n} k = \frac{n(n-1)}{2} \]
```

One of the problems with extensive reencoding in macro packages, as done by the euler package, is that it is likely to break other packages that assume certain symbols in slot positions, as defined by the established standard font encodings. The `eulervm` package developed by Walter Schmidt (1960–2021) attempts to avoid this problem by providing reencoded virtual fonts that follow as much as possible the standard math encodings OML, OMS, and OMX.

Virtual Euler fonts

The `eulervm` package sets up a `\mathnormal` alphabet, which is based mainly on Euler Roman, and a `\mathcal` alphabet, which is based on Euler Script. It does not provide immediate support for the Euler Fraktur alphabet — to access this math alphabet one needs to additionally load the `eufrak` or `mathalpha` package. Also, the math symbols are taken from the Euler fonts, with a few exceptions coming from the Computer Modern math fonts. Compare the next example to Example 12-3-3 and you see that `\mathcal` has changed and that `\sum` and the indices are different, because they are now taken from the Euler fonts.

12-3-5

$$\mathcal{A} \neq \sum_{k<n} A_k \neq \mathfrak{A}$$

```
\usepackage{eulervm,eufrak}
\[ \mathcal{A} \neq \sum_{k<n} A_k \neq \mathfrak{A} \]
```

In typical font setups the same digits are used in text and math formulas. The Euler fonts contain a set of digits that have a distinctive look and thus make digits in text and math look noticeably different.

By default, the digits of the main document font are used in formulas as well. To switch to the digits from Euler Roman, one has to explicitly request them by specifying the option `euler-digits`. It then becomes very important to distinguish between a number in a mathematical or a textual context. For example, one must watch out for omitted $ signs, as in the first line of the next example:

The value can be 1, 2, or −1 (wrong!)
The value can be 1, 2, or −1 (right!)

```
\usepackage{ccfonts}
\usepackage[euler-digits]{eulervm}
The value can be 1, 2, or $-1$      (wrong!)\par
The value can be $1$, $2$, or $-1$ (right!)
```

12-3-6

A full sample page with this setup is shown in Figure 12.40 on page 289.

The option `small` causes eulervm to load all Euler fonts at 95% of their normal size, thereby enabling them to blend better with some document fonts (e.g., Adobe Minion). This option also affects the Euler Fraktur fonts if they are loaded with **eufrak** and the AMS symbol fonts.

The functionality provided by the `exscale` package is automatically available. See Section 9.5.7 on page →I 704 for details.

Some peculiarities of the Euler fonts

Neither the standard `\hbar` command nor `\hslash` (from the amssymb package) is really usable with the Euler fonts if it is used without modification (i.e., with euler), because `\hslash` uses a Computer Modern style "h" and `\hbar` gets the slash in a strange position.

This issue restricts the usage of the euler package somewhat for physics and related fields. The eulervm package resolves this problem (partially) by providing a properly slashed "h" glyph built using the possibilities offered by the virtual font mechanism ([45] explains the concepts). It does, however, provide only a slashed version (`\hslash`); if `\hbar` is used, a warning is issued, and the slashed glyph is used nevertheless.

```
\usepackage{amssymb,euler}
\[ \hslash \neq \hbar \]
```

$$\hslash \neq \hbar$$

12-3-7

```
\usepackage{eulervm}
\[ \hslash \neq \hbar \]
```

$$\hslash \neq \hbar$$

Normally, the math accent `\hat` is taken from the main document font, which might not be a good choice when text and math fonts are noticeably different. With the option `euler-hat-accent`, an alternative version from the Euler fonts is used instead. In the example we mimic that option and define the alternate accent under the name `\varhat` manually to enable comparison of the two (neither looks really perfect).

$$\hat{x} \neq \hat{x} \text{ and } \hat{\mathfrak{K}} \neq \hat{\mathfrak{K}}$$

```
\usepackage{tgpagella,eulervm,eufrak}
\DeclareMathAccent\varhat{\mathalpha}{symbols}{222}
\Large $ \hat x \neq \varhat x $ and
$ \hat \mathfrak{K} \neq \varhat \mathfrak{K} $
```

12-3-9

If \mathbf is used in an eulervm setup, it uses the bold text font, e.g., Concrete Bold in the next example (as the ccfonts package is used for text). To get bold Euler letters instead, you can use \mathbold provided by eulervm for this purpose.

```
\usepackage{ccfonts,eulervm}
```

12-3-10

Compare: $a + b \neq a + b \neq a + b$

```
Compare: $ a + b \neq \mathbf{a} + \mathbf{b}
             \neq \mathbold{a} + \mathbold{b}$
```

Because eulervm defines the math alphabets (\mathbf, \mathsf, etc.) by evaluating the document's default information current at the time of loading, it is usually best to load the package after all the document fonts have been defined. In the previous and the next examples the loading order is in fact absolutely essential because the ccfonts package also tries to set up the math fonts, and thus the one that comes last wins.

In the book *Concrete Mathematics* [32], where Euler and Concrete fonts were first used together, one can see that slanted $\leqslant$ and $\geqslant$ signs were once part of the Euler Math fonts. Somewhere along the way these two symbols got lost, though traces of their existence can be found in [46] and in macros that Donald Knuth developed for producing the book. With the help of the virtual font mechanism, Walter Schmidt brought them back in the eulervm package; compare the next example to Example 12-3-4 on page 241, which shows the straight $\leq$ sign.

Concrete Roman blends well with Euler Math, as can be seen with

$$\sum_{0 \leqslant k < n} k = \frac{n(n-1)}{2}$$

```
\usepackage{ccfonts,amssymb}
\usepackage[euler-digits]{eulervm}
Concrete Roman blends well with Euler Math,
as can be seen with
\[ \sum_{0\leq k<n} k = \frac{n(n-1)}{2} \]
```

12-3-11

12.3.4 newtxmath — A Swiss[1] knife for math font support

In 2000, Young Ryu released a set of virtual fonts together with accompanying Type 1 fonts to provide math support for documents using Times Roman as the document font. LaTeX support was implemented through the package txfonts.

This implementation was fairly comprehensive in offering a large glyph set including all symbols from the American Mathematical Society fonts, but unfortunately it had some serious problems in that the glyph side-bearings in math were extremely tight, up to the point that characters actually touched if used in subscripts or superscripts. Compare the next two examples: the first is using the original TX fonts, while the second is using similar fonts prepared by Michael Sharpe.

A problematic example:

$$t[u_1, \ldots, u_n] = \sum_{k=1}^{n} \binom{n-1}{k-1} (1-t)^{n-k} t^{k-1} u_k$$

```
\usepackage{amsmath,txfonts}
A problematic example:
\[ t[u_1, \dots, u_n] = \sum_{k=1}^n
     \binom{n-1}{k-1} (1-t)^{n-k}t^{k-1}u_k \]
```

12-3-12

---

[1] Or rather an Australian/California knife.

Here is the same text but using newtxtext (Times as text font) and newtxmath (Times as math font). The latter package automatically loads amsmath, so strictly speaking we could have dropped that from the \usepackage call.

A better result:

$$t[u_1, \dots, u_n] = \sum_{k=1}^{n} \binom{n-1}{k-1} (1-t)^{n-k} t^{k-1} u_k$$

```
\usepackage{amsmath,newtxtext,newtxmath}
A better result:
\[ t[u_1, \dots, u_n] = \sum_{k=1}^n
   \binom{n-1}{k-1} (1-t)^{n-k}t^{k-1}u_k \]
```
12-3-13

The differences may seems tiny, but they drastically improve readability, so instead of txfonts, you should always use the newer implementation by loading newtxmath. For the text font there are several possibilities, which is why Michael provided independent packages for text and math. You could can use his package or one of the Times fonts from Chapter 10 or any other text font that blends reasonably well with math based on Times.

Options for the newtxtext package

If you intend to use a Times family as your document font, newtxtext may be a good option because it offers you a number of interesting package options to customize the text appearance. Despite the package name, it is no longer based on the TX fonts but uses TEX Gyre Termes underneath with a few twists; e.g., trueslanted offers you true slanted characters (not italics), osf gives you oldstyle numerals, and p makes them additionally proportional. While TEX Gyre Termes normally has petite small capitals, you can also ask for larger ones, by specifying the option largesc. With the options tighter or looser you alter the default behavior of interword spacing, and if you want even more granular control, you can explicitly set its stretch and shrink to any desired value. By default the package uses real superscript characters for footnote markers, but this too can be changed using the option defaultsups. In addition, the package adds a number of document commands, e.g., for producing different figure styles (proportional, tabular, lining, oldstyle), text fractions, etc. For details take a look at its documentation.

The package pairs Times with Helvetica (or rather TEX Gyre Termes and Heros) appropriately scaled to match, and used together with newtxmath, the math fonts are perfectly sized as well.

Support for Times math

In contrast to newtxtext, the newtxmath package continues to use the TX math fonts by Young Ryu, albeit heavily edited and corrected in their side-bearings as shown in the earlier example. Michael Sharpe's package offers several options to adjust the math typesetting. The default for integrals is slanted, but with upint you can change this to upright.

```
\usepackage[upint]{newtxmath}
\[ \int \iint \iiint \iiiint       \quad
   \oint \oiint \oiiint            \quad
   \varointclockwise \ointctrclockwise \quad
   \fint \sumint \sqint                 \]
```
12-3-14

In fact, you can have both types in a single document by appending `up` or `sl` to the normal command names; which you need depends on your chosen default.

```
\usepackage{newtxmath}
\[ \intsl \iintup \iiintsl \iiiintup      \enspace
   \ointsl \oiintup \oiiintsl             \enspace
   \varointclockwiseup \ointctrclockwisesl\enspace
   \fintup \sumintsl \sqintup                     \]
```

12-3-15

The full set of the integral commands is also available as tiny symbols by prepending `small` to the names for upright and sloped integrals, e.g., `\smalliintsl`. These small versions may help in inline formulas when it is important to keep line registration and not open up the line with large symbols. The example below has the same input as Example 12-3-14, but with `small` prefixed to all command names, and the second set by additionally appending `sl`:

12-3-16

With the option `smallerops` you can reduce the size of all operators that can take `\limits`, e.g., those from Table 11.27 on page 222, about 20%. Integrals are not affected by this option.

The package also defines a few additional commands for use in math: `\smallsum`, `\smallprod`, and `\smallcoprod` are small versions of the operators and may sometimes be useful (for comparison, the normal size in running text is shown as well). There are also a number of "wide accents" that span the whole of their argument. They are shown in the display formulas of the example.

In running text: $\sum \Sigma_{i=1}^{n} \prod \Pi_x^y \coprod_z !$

$$\overline{AB} \quad \overrightarrow{CDEF} \quad \overleftrightarrow{\ldots LMN \ldots} \quad \overset{\circ}{XYZ}$$

$$\underline{abc} \quad \underrightarrow{de} \quad \underleftarrow{\ldots xyz}$$

```
\usepackage{newtxtext,newtxmath}
In running text: $ \sum \smallsum_{i=1}^n  \prod
                  \smallprod_x^y \smallcoprod\limits_z $!
\[ \overgroup{AB} \enspace \overgroupra{CDEF} \enspace
   \overgroupla{\ldots LMN\ldots} \enspace \widering{XYZ}
\]
\[ \undergroup{abc} \enspace \undergroupra{de} \enspace
   \undergroupla{\ldots xyz}
\]
```

12-3-17

It is customary in Anglo-American mathematical typesetting to use upright Greek uppercase letters and italic Greek lowercase together with all Latin characters in italics. ISO also suggests using slanted uppercase Greek. This can be controlled through the options `uprightGreek` (default) and `slantedGreek`. In any case all commands to access Greek letters (upper or lowercase) have a variant to explicitly access the upright form by prepending `up` to the command name, e.g., `\upDelta`, `\upOmega`, `\upalpha`, `\upbeta`, etc.

With the option `frenchmath` you set the default style in math mode for rendering uppercase Latin and all Greek letters to upright. Latin lowercase remains italic. You can still get the italic uppercase Latin glyphs by using `\mathnormal`.

```
\usepackage{newtxtext}
\usepackage{newtxmath}
\[ \mathrm{A} = \alpha + \beta
              < A_k          \]
```

$$A = \alpha + \beta < A_k$$

12-3-18

```
\usepackage{newtxtext}
\usepackage[frenchmath]{newtxmath}
\[ A = \alpha + \beta
             < \mathnormal{A}_k \]
```

$$\mathrm{A} = \alpha + \beta < \mathrm{A}_k$$

12-3-19

The math italic v and the Greek `\nu` are often fairly similar as shown in Example 12-3-20. For that reason the `newtxmath` package offers the option `varvw` to give both v and w a different shape, or the option `varg` that changes the shapes of v, w, g, and y. If you compare the two example, you can observe the differences. Unfortunately, the options make w now look closer to `\omega`, so you have to pick and choose what works better for you.

```
\usepackage{newtxmath}
\[ v w \neq \nu \omega \quad (gy)  \]
```

$$vw \neq \nu\omega \quad (gy)$$

12-3-20

```
\usepackage[varg]{newtxmath}
\[ v w \neq \nu \omega \quad (gy)  \]
```

$$vw \neq \nu\omega \quad (gy)$$

12-3-21

With many heavily sloped math fonts there is a problem that the side-bearings of individual characters would need to change based on their usage, e.g., whether they appear as a variable in a formula or as a subscript character. This is not automatically possible for TeX when sticking glyphs together, and the package attempts to solve this by some clever programming. To enable it, specify the option `subscriptcorrection`. If activated, an external file (default `newtx-subs.tex`) is read that specifies corrective actions for individual characters that are carried out whenever the glyph appears as the first character in a subscript (and only there). Compare the subscript placements in the next two examples:

```
\usepackage{newtxmath}
\[ xjfA \to  x_j \neq y_f
            \neq z_A  \]
```

$$xjfA \to x_j \neq y_f \neq z_A$$

12-3-22

```
\usepackage[subscriptcorrection]{newtxmath}
\[ xjfA \to  x_j \neq y_f
            \neq z_A  \]
```

$$xjfA \to x_j \neq y_f \neq z_A$$

12-3-23

Which characters are affected depend on the math fonts used (as we see below, you are not confined to Times), and it is customizable. How to do this is explained in the package documentation in case you feel you need to make further adjustments.

The original TX fonts offered two blackboard bold alphabets; the `newtxmath` packages adds yet another one (taking it from the STIX2 fonts). The alphabets are available through \mathbb, \vmathbb, and \vvmathbb. Given that you probably want only one within your document, you can make a selection via an option (varbb or vvarbb), in which case \mathbb is made equal to one of the other ones.

```
\usepackage{newtxtext}
\usepackage{newtxmath}
\[ \mathbb{AN} \textrm{\ (default)}
   < \vmathbb{AN} < \vvmathbb{AN} \]
```

```
\usepackage{newtxtext}
\usepackage[vvarbb]{newtxmath}
\[ \mathbb{AN} \textrm{\ (default)}
   < \vmathbb{AN} < \vvmathbb{AN} \]
```

12-3-24

AN (default) < **AN** < AN

12-3-25

AN (default) < **AN** < AN

A sample page using Times for text and math by loading the packages newtxtext and newtxmath is shown in Figure 12.27 on page 280.

Support for other math font families

Michael's package started out as a reimplementation for the TX fonts, but over time support for more and more math font families got added. They can be accessed by adding an appropriate option when loading the package. The options change the math italics and bold math italics being loaded. If the new base family offers Greek glyphs (i.e., Cochineal, EB Garamond, Garamondx, Libertine, Minion, STIX 2, or XCharter), then these are used as well.

The other symbols remain the same, which is a compromise that is not necessarily perfect with all combinations compared to a design that was made to go together from the outset.

When one of these font options is selected, the options varg and varvw are both ignored (if given). Instead, there are a few extra options to cater for peculiarities of some of the font families, as explained below:

baskervaldx This loads math italics based on the glyphs from Baskervaldx; see Figure 12.15 on page 272 for a sample page. In Figure 12.16 there is also an example of Baskervaldx text combined with Times math.

baskerville **or** baskervillef This provides math italics based on BaskervilleF instead. An example is given in Figure 12.14 on page 271; compare it with Figure 12.15.

charter **or** xcharter In this case the math italics are based on the XCharter design. When this option is chosen, you can also use alty to get an alternative glyph for "y" and noxchvw to have the original "v" and "w" from Charter italics. This makes them harder to distinguish from \nu, but that is a problem only if you use that Greek character. A sample page is shown in Figure 12.19 on page 275.

cochineal Figure 12.2 on page 263 shows the usage. With this option the italics from Cochineal are used as the basis for the math italics. It can be combined with the options cochf and cochrho to use a longer italic "f" and \rho, respectively.

ebgaramond   Use math italics based on EB Garamond; see Figure 12.3 on page 264 for an example.

garamondx   This uses Garamondx instead of EB Garamond as math italics. There is also an example page showing the OpenType font version. Compare Figures 12.3 to 12.5 on pages 264–265.

libertine   This option uses math italics based on Libertine fonts. With the option libaltvw you can alter the look of "v" and "w", and with liby that of "y" of the family. Figure 12.22 on page 277 shows an example. Compare this with Figure 12.23, which exhibits the Libertinus math fonts that are available only for Unicode engines.

minion   This option bases the math italics on the commercial MinionPro fonts, which requires that you own a recent version of this family, and it requires manual installation because some components are not part of the TEX Live distribution.

nc or ncf   Both options use math italics based on New Century Schoolbook, the difference between the two options is that the ncf option uses Greek math from the Fourier fonts, while nc retains the glyphs from the TX fonts. An example is given in Figure 12.20 on page 276.

noto or notosans   Use Noto Serif or Noto Sans as the basis for the math italics. If you also want to use the Noto fonts as your text fonts, then it is better to use the notomath described in Section 12.3.7 on page 252.

stix2   This option bases the math italics on the STIX 2 fonts. An example is given in Figure 12.30 on page 282. Compare this to Figure 12.31, which shows the OpenType STIX 2 fonts, and to Figure 12.29 (based on OpenType STIX 1), both usable only in Unicode TEX engines.

utopia or erewhon   The Utopia clone Erewhon is used as the basis for the math italics; an example page is shown in Figure 12.32 on page 283.

There are a few more options related to reducing the number of allocated math alphabets. However, with the more recent addition of localmathalphabets to the LaTeX kernel, this is less of an issue. See Section 9.4.1 on page →I 681 for details.

12.3.5 newpxmath — Using the PX fonts for math

Besides support for Times in math, Young Ryu also developed a set of math fonts to work together with Palatino-like font families. These PX fonts were based on a Palatino Italic clone, together with all necessary symbols to cover all of the standard LaTeX and amsmath symbols. Unfortunately, just as with his TX fonts the PX fonts have metrics that are overly tight.

For this reason Michael Sharpe produced a new version, made a few glyph additions, and completely reworked the metrics. His fonts (New PX) are made available through the newpxmath package. Below are both fonts set side by side for comparison:

```
\usepackage{amsmath,pxfonts}
A problematic example:
\[ t[u_1, \dots, u_n] = \sum_{k=1}^n
   \binom{n-1}{k-1} (1-t)^{n-k}t^{k-1}u_k \]
```

```
\usepackage{amsmath,newpxtext,newpxmath}
A better result:
\[ t[u_1, \dots, u_n] = \sum_{k=1}^n
   \binom{n-1}{k-1} (1-t)^{n-k}t^{k-1}u_k \]
```

A problematic example:

A better result:

$$t[u_1,\ldots,u_n] = \sum_{k=1}^{n}\binom{n-1}{k-1}(1-t)^{n-k}t^{k-1}u_k$$

12-3-26

$$t[u_1,\ldots,u_n] = \sum_{k=1}^{n}\binom{n-1}{k-1}(1-t)^{n-k}t^{k-1}u_k$$

12-3-27

Michael's package alters only the math setup, so you are free to combine it with any text font to which you think it fits with. Above we have combined it with his companion package for text, called newpxtext. This uses an augmented version of TEX Gyre Pagella (Palatino clone) with superior figures and an additional set of larger small capitals added. You can activate them in your document by adding the option largesc. The package also sets up TEX Gyre Heros (Helvetica clone) appropriately scaled as the sans serif family; this can be prevented through the option nohelv. Figure 12.10 on page 269 shows the combination of newpxtext and newpxmath on a sample page.

Most of the general functionality seen with the newtxmath package is also available with newpxmath, so we rehash it here only with a few examples. There is the same extended set of integrals available both in slanted form (default) or upright when using the option upint. You can explicitly select either form by appending up or sl to the command names.

12-3-28

```
\usepackage[upint]{newpxmath}
\[ \int \iint \iiint \iiiint \oint \oiint \oiiint
   \varointclockwise \ointctrclockwise
                              \fint \sumint \sqint \]
\[ \intsl \iintup \iiintsl \iiiintup
   \ointsl \oiintup   \ldots   \sumintsl \sqintup \]
```

As with newtxmath the package supports the full set of integrals upright and slanted in tiny size by prepending small to the integral command name.

12-3-29

The option smallerops forces all big operators to render about 20% smaller with the result that many display formulas occupy noticeably less vertical space.

Also supported are additional small operators and wide accents as exhibited here:

In running text: $\sum \sum_{i=1}^{n} \prod \Pi_x^y \amalg!$

```
\usepackage{newpxtext,newpxmath}
In running text: $ \sum \smallsum_{i=1}^n \prod
                \smallprod_x^y \smallcoprod\limits_z $!
```

$\overline{AB} \quad \overrightarrow{CDEF} \quad \overrightarrow{\ldots LMN \ldots} \quad \overset{\circ}{\overline{XYZ}}$

$\underline{abc} \quad \underrightarrow{de} \quad \underleftarrow{\ldots xyz}$

```
\[ \overgroup{AB} \enspace \overgroupra{CDEF} \enspace
\overgroupla{\ldots LMN\ldots} \enspace \widering{XYZ} \]
\[ \undergroup{abc} \enspace \undergroupra{de} \enspace
                \undergroupla{\ldots xyz}\]
```
12-3-30

With the option `frenchmath` you set the default style in math mode for rendering uppercase Latin and all Greek letters to upright. Latin lowercase glyphs remain italic. You can still get the italic uppercase Latin glyphs by using `\mathnormal`.

```
\usepackage{newpxtext}
\usepackage{newpxmath}
\[ \mathrm{A} = \alpha + \beta < A_k \]
```

$A = \alpha + \beta < A_k$ 12-3-31

```
\usepackage{newpxtext}
\usepackage[frenchmath]{newpxmath}
\[ A = \alpha + \beta < \mathnormal{A}_k \]
```

$A = \alpha + \beta < A_k$ 12-3-32

If you want to follow the ISO style recommendations, you can set all uppercase Greek letters slanted by using the option `slantedGreek`. In any case, all commands to access Greek letters (upper or lowercase) have a variant to explicitly access the upright form by prepending up to the command name, e.g., `\upDelta`, `\upOmega`, `\upalpha`, `\upbeta`, etc.

The `newpxmath` package offers the same selection of blackboard bold math alphabets as `newtxmath` including the options `varbb` and `vvarbb` for a preselection and the commands `\vmathbb` and `\vvmathbb`.

```
\usepackage{newpxtext}
\usepackage{newpxmath}
\[ \mathbb{AN} \textrm{\ (default)}
   < \vmathbb{AN} < \vvmathbb{AN} \]
```

$\mathbb{AN}$ (default) $< \mathbb{AN} < \mathbb{AN}$ 12-3-33

```
\usepackage{newpxtext}
\usepackage[vvarbb]{newpxmath}
\[ \mathbb{AN} \textrm{\ (default)}
   < \vmathbb{AN} < \vvmathbb{AN} \]
```

$\mathbb{AN}$ (default) $< \mathbb{AN} < \mathbb{AN}$ 12-3-34

The subscript correction code is also available with the `newpxmath` when you specify `subscriptcorrection`. The default adjustments are more subtle compared to those made for other fonts, but still visible.

```
\usepackage{newpxmath}
\[  xjfA \to  x_j \neq y_f \neq z_A\]
```

$xjfA \to x_j \neq y_f \neq z_A$ 12-3-35

```
\usepackage[subscriptcorrection]{newpxmath}
\[ xjfA \to  x_j \neq y_f \neq z_A\]
```

$xjfA \to x_j \neq y_f \neq z_A$ 12-3-36

Michael offers only one alternative glyph in his version of the PX fonts: you can have either a math italic g (default) or, by specifying the option `varg`, this g shape.

12.3.6 mathpazo — Another Palatino-based approach for math

A package named mathpple supporting Adobe Palatino with matching math fonts was originally developed by Walter Schmidt (1960–2021) based on earlier work by Aloysius Helminck. It was built on the virtual font mechanism, combining symbols from Palatino, Symbol, Euler, and CM Math. Because these fonts only partly match the style of Palatino, Diego Puga developed a set of Type 1 fonts (Pazo Math) intended to repair the defects apparent in the initial mathpple solution.

The Pazo Math fonts contain glyphs that are unavailable in Palatino and for which Computer Modern or glyphs from Symbol look odd when combined with Palatino. These include a number of math glyphs, the uppercase Greek alphabet (upright and slanted), a blackboard bold alphabet, as well as several other glyphs (such as the euro symbol) in regular and bold weights and upright and slanted shapes.

The fonts are accessible with the mathpazo package developed by Diego Puga and Walter Schmidt as part of the PSNFSS collection. It makes Palatino the document text font and provides a math setup that works by using virtual fonts accessing Palatino Italic, the Pazo Math fonts, and CM fonts (for the remaining symbols).

An example showing a trigonometric function:

$$\sin \frac{\alpha}{2} = \pm\sqrt{\frac{1-\cos\alpha}{2}}$$

Scripts: $A \neq \mathcal{A} \neq \mathbb{A}$.

```
\usepackage{mathpazo}
An example showing a trigonometric function:
\[ \sin \frac{\alpha}{2} =
        \pm \sqrt{\frac{1-\cos\alpha}{2}}  \]
Scripts: $ A \neq \mathcal{A}
             \neq \mathbb{A} $.
```

12-3-37

The package supports the option slantedGreek to make uppercase Greek letters slanted instead of upright (the default). In either case the two extra commands \upDelta and \upOmega print an upright Δ and Ω, respectively. The package also provides the functionality of the exscale package.

Pazo Math has bold font variants, but in contrast to the PX fonts, it does not offer dedicated fonts replacing the American Mathematical Society symbol fonts. Thus, the latter are unavailable (unless you additionally load amssymb), and they do not change their weight in a bold context if that package is loaded.

Bold is easy to achieve: $\alpha \neq A$. It also blends in well: $A \neq \mathbf{A} = \alpha - \gamma$.

```
\usepackage{mathpazo,bm}
Bold is easy to achieve: {\boldmath$\alpha
 \neq A$}. It also blends in well:
$A \neq \mathbf{A} = \bm\alpha - \bm\gamma$.
```

12-3-38

As mentioned above, the Pazo Math fonts contain a blackboard bold alphabet, which can be accessed through the math alphabet identifier \mathbb. The font contains the uppercase Latin letters and the digit "1". Be careful, however: all other digits are silently ignored!

$$\mathbb{ABCDEFGHIJK}\ 1$$

```
\usepackage{mathpazo}
$\mathbb{ABCDEFGHIJK}$ $\mathbb{0123}$
```

12-3-39

If \mathbb should select a different alphabet, provided by some other package, it is best to suppress the Pazo Math one by using the option noBBppl when loading it.

Commercial Palatino fonts The package also offers two additional options that deal with the use of commercially available Palatino fonts[1] for the text font: sc selects Palatino with true small capitals (font family name pplx), and osf selects Palatino with small caps and oldstyle numerals (font family name pplj) instead of basic Palatino (ppl).

12.3.7 notomath — Setting up Noto fonts for math and text

The Noto fonts is a huge collection of text fonts in Serif, Sans, and Mono designs available as OpenType fonts for many languages and scripts across the world. There are also Type 1 versions in T1 and other encodings (see Table 10.14 on page 28), and these are supported by Bob Tennent's noto package.

As part of newtxmath (with the option noto or notosans) Michael Sharpe provides math support for the Noto families; thus, in principle, his package, together with Bob's, would be sufficient to set a whole document in Noto Serif or Noto Sans. There are, however, a few wrinkles that make combining them nicely a bit awkward. Michael, therefore, offers notomath as a simple frontend package that does all necessary work for you behind the scenes.

If you want a document in Noto Serif, all you have to do is to load the package without options. This sets up Noto Serif for the body text and Noto Sans for \textsf. Both families are slightly scaled down to better fit with the mathematical symbols.

If instead you want Noto Sans as your main document font, add the option sfdefault. This changes the \familydefault but leaves the \rmdefault untouched; thus, \textrm still produces Noto Serif.

An example showing a trigonometric function:

$$\sin \frac{\alpha}{2} = \pm \sqrt{\frac{1 - \cos \alpha}{2}}$$

Scripts: $\mathcal{A} \neq \mathscr{A} \neq \mathfrak{A} \neq \mathbb{A}$.

```
\usepackage[sfdefault]{notomath}
An example showing a trigonometric function:
\[ \sin \frac{\alpha}{2} =
        \pm \sqrt{\frac{1-\cos\alpha}{2}}  \]
Scripts: $\mathcal{A} \neq \mathscr{A}
\neq \mathfrak{A} \neq \mathbb{A} $.
```

12-3-40

Note that the typewriter family is not set up — the package uses whatever has already been set up when it is loaded. Thus, to be able to use the typewriter font in text also with math (via \mathtt), you should do the typewriter setup first. However, if you want to use Noto Mono as the typewriter font, you can simply specify the option mono. This then loads and scales down the family appropriately.

Package options that are relevant to the noto package can be given to notomath, which passes them on, e.g., oldstyle or proportional to alter the figure style. Similarly, the general options for newtxmath can all be given to notomath too, e.g., varbb or upint, but not those that change the math italic glyphs, e.g., stix2.

Figure 12.38 on page 287 shows a sample page using a Noto Serif setup, and in Figure 12.50 on page 295 you can study the same sample using Noto Sans instead.

---

[1] These fonts are commercially available and are *not* part of the Base 35 fonts.

12.4 unicode-math — Using Unicode math fonts

The original motivation for developing TeX engines that understand Unicode and accept UTF-8 input was the desire to use text fonts with more than 256 addressable glyphs. While the engines also supported such bigger fonts for use in formulas, this was of little relevance, simply because TeX requires special attributes for fonts used in math, and no fonts, other than a few 8-bit fonts tailored for use with TeX, offered this.

Furthermore, Unicode itself did not explicitly encode math symbols, except for very common ones also found in typical text fonts or that were a carry-over of 8-bit input encodings — i.e., keyboard layouts used across the world. Consequently, there was little incentive for devising a set of extended font encodings for mathematics; after all, there was no standard to follow, and any change would involve a huge effort. Thus, for a long time, all engines followed the traditional 8-bit font setup for typesetting as originally devised by Donald Knuth and only marginally changed since the eighties.[1]

This started to change when mathematical symbols finally got embraced by the Unicode Consortium and code points for all standard symbols in use with TeX and many more got defined. Once that had happened, the door of opportunity opened, and the first Unicode-encoded math fonts appeared not long after. Even though the TeX world was the driving force in this adoption into Unicode, the focus of the first such fonts was by no means TeX (but commercial systems such as Word); in fact, the new fonts initially missed crucial font parameters to make them usable with TeX. However, that changed too over time, and now there a dozen or more free and commercial Unicode Math fonts that you can use for typesetting with TeX.

If you have read Chapter 9, then you know that it is not enough to have fonts for math and TeX engines that can access them. You also need hundreds of definitions that make commands (such as \sum or \alpha) fetch the right glyph from the correct slot in the appropriate font and apply the TeX magic to make it become a binary, relational, or whatever math symbol. Obviously, in Unicode fonts the glyphs are stored in completely different places than in the 8-bit fonts to which the LaTeX math commands are tailored to, so nothing would work if you load such a font.

To say it differently: in the past making a new symbol font available for use with TeX meant (re)encoding the font so that it used the same slots as Computer Modern Symbol (cmsy), and then all LaTeX math commands automatically selected the right glyphs. This is what the packages provide that we discussed in the previous section.

Now, with Unicode-encoded fonts, the LaTeX commands have to change instead to make everything work with the new font setup, and this is what unicode-math by Will Robertson is undertaking for you, and which is the subject of this section.

> **Unicode engines**
>
> To use the unicode-math package, you need a Unicode engine, e.g., LuaTeX or XeTeX. Thus, the remainder of this section should be inside a box like this —

---

[1] The fact that Don's fonts are really 7-bit fonts (leaving half of the available slots unused) was of some considerable concern, but the attempt to develop a set of real 8-bit encodings for math never got beyond the theoretical work [93] and a single prototype implementation using virtual fonts — the obstacles in introducing this and getting it embraced and used everywhere proved to be too large. But this work was not in vain, because it helped with the Unicode adoption later.

> which is not done to avoid straining your eyes.

As a first simple example: all you need in order to typeset using Unicode Math fonts is to load the package and use a Unicode engine. Without further adjustments this typesets your document in Latin Modern Math OpenType fonts.

An example showing a trigonometric function:

$$\sin\frac{\alpha}{2} = \pm\sqrt{\frac{1-\cos\alpha}{2}}$$

Scripts: $\mathcal{A} \equiv \mathscr{A} \neq \mathfrak{A} \neq \mathbb{A}$.

```
\usepackage{unicode-math}
An example showing a trigonometric function:
\[ \sin \frac{\alpha}{2} =
    \pm \sqrt{\frac{1-\cos\alpha}{2}} \]
Scripts: $\mathcal{A} \equiv \mathscr{A}
\neq \mathfrak{A} \neq \mathbb{A} $.
```

12-4-1

So what do you gain by loading the package (after all, Latin Modern is the default font for LaTeX when using a Unicode engine)? The answer is that without making further adjustments (e.g., loading a different Unicode Math font), there is not much gain that it is immediately visible. You see that \mathbb, \mathscr, and \mathfrak are available without loading an extra package, but that is about all.[1]

But there are already now invisible but important differences between the output of the above example and that of the similar ones from the previous section. These become noticeable if you take the PDF of the examples and copy and paste parts of the formula into a different application (or into a new document). If you use Example 12-4-1, then the α, for example, copies as the Unicode character U+1D6FC (*Mathematical Italic Small Alpha*), $\neq$ copies as U+2260 (*Not Equal To*), and the three different "A" characters copy as U+1D49C (*Mathematical Script Capital A*), U+1D504 (*Mathematical Fraktur Capital A*), and U+1D538 (*Mathematical Double-Struck Capital A*), respectively. That is, they all carry their mathematical meaning as part of their Unicode character information with them.

If on the other hand you started from Example 12-3-37, then the α is pasted as a *Greek Small Alpha* (a text character) or even as an "a", the $\neq$ as $/=$ or worse, and the different capital A's as simple identical ASCII A's; i.e., the material becomes unusable for further processing. For the question of accessible PDFs, this makes quite a difference.

12.4.1 Math alphabets revisited

Math alphabets as used in LaTeX were introduced in Section 9.4.1 on page →I 677 and further discussed in Section 12.1 in this chapter. In a nutshell, each is related to a font that has in its ASCII slot positions for A to Z (and sometimes a to z) glyphs that are suitable as special alphabetic letters in formulas, e.g., a calligraphic alphabet such as $\mathcal{ABC}$.... These alphabets fall into two distinct groups. There are those where each glyph is always intended to be used by its own, i.e., \mathbb, \mathcal, \mathfrak, \mathnormal, and \mathscr. The side-bearing of each glyph is specially adjusted to give them enough room when used as a single symbol in a formula, and that makes

---

[1]As you see, \mathscr is in fact by default nothing more than a different name for \mathcal.

them often unsuitable and uneven looking, if you try to form words with them; e.g, while you could use \mathcal to typeset $\mathcal{CALLIGRAPHY}$, it is clearly not what this alphabet was intended for.

The second group are those math alphabets that have a dual purpose. They can be used to typeset a single alphabetic character, e.g., $\forall g \in G$, but alternatively can also be used to properly typeset words or word fragments within a formula, e.g., V_{min}. In this group we have \mathbf, \mathit, \mathrm, \mathsf, and \mathtt, and they all point to text fonts, which means that they provide proper kerning and ligatures if their argument consists of more than one character. The difference to the corresponding \text... commands (which can also be used in formulas) is that they do not change fonts based on surrounding conditions. For example, \mathrm is usually used to build the textual operators, such as \lim or \max, and it always produces the same roman letters in all formulas no matter what.

When the Unicode Consortium extended its support for mathematics, this dual rôle of some of the \math... alphabet commands in LaTeX turned out to be somewhat of a problem. In the Unicode block "Mathematical Alphanumeric Symbols" U+1D400 to U+1D7FF, Unicode places Latin and Greek letters as separate mathematical alphabets. The description in the Unicode standard for this block reads:

Mathematical Alphanumeric Symbols

To be used for mathematical variables where style variations are important semantically. For general text, use standard Latin and Greek letters with markup.

Thus, the use of \mathsf{G} should produce U+1D5A6 (*Mathematical Sans-Serif Capital G*) in the PDF output, whereas \mathsf{min} should produce ordinary Latin letters, i.e., U+006D, U+0069, and U+006E.

To cater for this additional complexity, unicode-math introduced \symsf and similarly named commands that take one argument and expect it to contain a single Latin character from the ranges A...Z, a...z, or 0...9. These commands then output the corresponding character from the "Mathematical Alphanumeric Symbols" block of Unicode. Where applicable, e.g., for \symbf, they also accept commands such as \alpha or \Omega to produce Greek mathematical letters from this block. Table 12.1 shows the supported set of characters for the different \sym... commands—as you can see, Unicode is unfortunately somewhat selective in what is offered.

\symrm{*char*}	\symbf{*char*}	\symsf{*char*}	\symtt{*char*}

These four commands select an appropriate symbol for a given *char* from the mathematical alphanumeric symbols block of Unicode. \symrm and \symtt are always set upright; for the other two the result is either upright or italic depending on the chosen style selected through the package keys bold-style and sans-style; see Section 12.4.2 on page 257. There is also \symnormal, but this is essentially the same as just typesetting *char*.

```
\symup{char}    \symsfup{char}    \symbfup{char}    \symbfsfup{char}
\symit{char}    \symsfit{char}    \symbfit{char}    \symbfsfit{char}
```

If you want to explicitly set the style for a *char* regardless of the document setup, you can do so with one of these eight commands; e.g., \symsfit{\delta} generates a sans serif italic Greek delta, even if the sans-style is set to upright. In a similar fashion you can overwrite the package's bold-style setting and request a *char* in one of the above bold styles. Note that not all imaginable combinations are supported, but only those encoded by Unicode.

```
\symbb{char}    \symbbit{char}     \symfrak{char}    \symbffrak{char}
\symcal{char}   \symbfcal{char}    \symscr{char}     \symbfscr{char}
```

The traditional math alphabets offer fewer variations than those associated with text fonts, and in many font setups they support only uppercase letters. Note that the blackboard bold italic (\symbbit) is supported only for the letters D, d, e, i, and j in Unicode, so it is of comparably little use. Also important to know is that by default \symcal and \symbfcal are only synonyms for \symscr and \symbfscr.

In the next example, most of the commands discussed above are used, and the characters are dancing horribly in front of your eyes. Still, it is worth looking at the example from line to line and observing what changes and why.

$a, b, X, Y, Z, \pi, \Gamma$

$a, \mathbf{b}, Y, X, Z, \pi, \Gamma$

$\boldsymbol{a}, \mathbf{b}, X, \mathbf{Y}, \mathbf{Z}, \pi, \boldsymbol{\Gamma}$

$\mathfrak{a}, \mathbf{b}, \mathbb{X}, \mathscr{Y}, \mathscr{Z}, \pi, \boldsymbol{\Gamma}$

$\mathbb{0}, \mathbb{1}, \mathbb{2}, \mathbb{3}, \dots, \mathbf{7}, \mathbf{8}, \mathbf{9}$

```
\usepackage{amsmath,unicode-math}
\begin{gather*}          a,b,X,Y,Z,\pi,\Gamma \\ % default
 \symrm{a},\symbf{b},\symsf{Y},X,\symtt{Z},\symrm{\pi},\symit{\Gamma} \\
 \symbfsfit{a},\symbfit{b},X,\symbfsfit{Y},\symbfsfup{Z},
                         \symbfup{\pi},\symbfit{\Gamma} \\
 \symfrak{a},\symbffrak{b},\symbb{X},\symscr{Y},\symbfscr{Z},
                         \symbfit{\pi},\symbfsf{\Gamma} \\
 \symbb{0},\symbb{1},\symbb{2},\symbb{3},\dots,
         \symbfsfup{7},\symbfsfup{8},\symbfsfup{9}  \end{gather*}
```

12-4-2

If the default set of math alphabet, i.e., bb, bf, cal, frak, sf, and tt, are not sufficient, you can declare additional ones for 8-bit fonts for which you know the NFSS values with \DeclareMathAlphabet; see Section 9.4.1 on page →I 677. For Unicode fonts use \setmathfontface instead.

```
\setmathfontface{cmd}{font name}[font features]
```

The *cmd* can be any command name, though something like \math... or \mathtext... would be customary and fit well with other math alphabets.[1] The *font name* and *font features* are describing the Unicode (text) font and are passed to the fontspec package for loading; see Section 9.6 on page →I 705. In the following example we define \mathhw and assign the handwriting font Miama Nueva to it. Because of

---

[1]There is a good chance that LaTeX adopts both \sym... and \mathtext... as the new standard for all engines during the next years — this is currently under discussion to bridge the gap between 8-bit and Unicode engines.

Command	Math alphabet			Affected characters		
	family	*series*	*shape*	*Latin*	*Greek*	*Numeral*
\symnormal	serif	medium	(a)	•	•	(•)
\symbf		bold	(b)	•	•	•
\symrm(c)		medium	upright	•		•
\symsf	sans serif	medium	(d)	•		•
\symtt	typewriter	medium	upright	•		•
\symup	serif	medium	upright	•	•	•
\symit			italic	•	•	(•)
\symbfup		bold	upright	•	•	•
\symbfit			italic	•	•	(•)
\symsfup	sans serif	medium	upright	•		•
\symsfit			italic	•		(•)
\symbfsfup		bold	upright	•	•	•
\symbfsfit			italic	•	•	(•)
\symbb	blackboard	medium	upright	•		•
\symbbit		medium	italic	•(e)		
\symscr	script/cal(f)	medium	upright	•		
\symbfscr		bold	upright	•		
\symfrak	fraktur	medium	upright	•		
\symbffrak		bold	upright	•		

A (•) indicates that numerals are always set upright.

(a) *The shape depends on the setting for* math-style *and may differ for different characters.*

(b) *The shape depends on the setting for* bold-style *and may differ for different characters.*

(c) *This is just a synonym for* \symup.

(d) *The shape depends on the setting for* sans-style *and may be upright or italic throughout.*

(e) *There is only support for the characters D, d, e, i, and j in Unicode.*

(f) *By default* \symcal *and* \symbfcal *just are synonyms for* \symscr *and* \symbfscr.

Table 12.1: Behavior and argument scope of \sym... commands

its large design size we have to rigorously scale it down to match the size of Latin Modern used for the rest of the glyphs.

$$ABCDEFG \neq ABCDEFG$$
$$X^{Hand}_{writing} \napprox X^{Formal}_{writing}$$

12-4-3

```
\usepackage{amsmath,unicode-math}
\setmathfontface\mathhw{Miama Nueva}[Scale=.75]
\begin{align*} \mathhw{ABCDEFG} &\neq \mathcal{ABCDEFG} \\
        X^\mathhw{Hand}_\mathhw{writing} &\not\approx
        X^\mathrm{Formal}_\mathit{writing}    \end{align*}
```

Note that for alphabets defined in this way, there are no dedicated Unicode ranges, so they are all placed as ordinary Latin characters into the PDF.

12.4.2 Adjusting the formula style

By default formulas typeset with TEX use an italic alphabet for variables denoted by Latin characters. Lowercase Greek letters are also in italic, but uppercase Greek is set upright. While this is a widely accepted style, it is by no means the only one in use. ISO recommends the use of italics throughout (i.e., uppercase Greek in italics

A choice of italic or upright Greek and Latin letters

math-style		*Latin*	*Greek*
TeX	$\rightarrow$	a, b, X, Y	$\alpha, \beta, \Gamma, \Omega$
ISO	$\rightarrow$	a, b, X, Y	$\alpha, \beta, \Gamma, \Omega$
french	$\rightarrow$	a, b, X, Y	$\alpha, \beta, \Gamma, \Omega$
upright	$\rightarrow$	$\mathrm{a, b, X, Y}$	$\alpha, \beta, \Gamma, \Omega$

bold-style		*Latin*	*Greek*
TeX	$\rightarrow$	$\mathbf{a, b, X, Y}$	$\boldsymbol{\alpha, \beta, \Gamma, \Omega}$
ISO	$\rightarrow$	$\boldsymbol{a, b, X, Y}$	$\boldsymbol{\alpha, \beta, \Gamma, \Omega}$
upright	$\rightarrow$	$\mathbf{a, b, X, Y}$	$\mathbf{\alpha, \beta, \Gamma, \Omega}$

12-4-4

There also exists the value `literal`, which means use the style of the input characters.

Table 12.2: Effects of `math-style` and `bold-style`

too), and some people prefer to use upright for everything — the Euler fonts are a prominent example for this style; see Figure 12.40 on page 289. Finally, there is the French tradition to set everything upright except for lowercase Latin letters. The different styles can be set with the package key `math-style` as shown in Table 12.2; the default style is `TeX`.

Setting the style applies to the whole document. It is, however, still possible to set individual Greek letters explicitly upright or slanted by prefixing their command names with `up` or `it`, respectively, e.g., `\upbeta`, `\itDelta`, etc. Also possible is to use the command `\symup` or `\symit` to explicitly set a single Latin or Greek letter upright or italic, e.g., `\symup{A}`, `\symit{\Delta}`, and so forth.

How to typeset bold Greek and Latin letters

Using bold letters shows a similar diversity in conventions. TeX by default sets all but lowercase Greek in upright bold style. ISO, as before, suggests using bold italics throughout, and if you want, you can have upright bold for both alphabets. Specifying the style is done through the package key `bold-style` also shown in Table 12.2. This then alters the behavior of `\symbf` used to bolden individual letters. There are no variant commands for Greek letters, but if necessary, you can explicitly select the style for a letter of either alphabet by applying `\symbfit` or `\symbfup` instead.

Note that these `\symbf..` commands apply only to upper and lowercase letters of the Latin and Greek alphabet and not to other symbols, such as accents, binary operators, relational symbols, etc., and you cannot use the bm package in Unicode engines — however, this may change in the future.

How to typeset sans serif and bold sans serif Latin letters

The use of sans serif letters in formulas is less common, but they appear often enough to warrant proper support. You typeset an individual letter with `\symsf`, which applies the style set up by the package key `sans-style` (either `upright`, which is the default, or `italic`). To individually set the style on a single letter, `\symsfit` and `\symsfup` are available, and for bold sans serif letters there is `\symbfsf` and `\symbfsfit` or `\symbfsfup` with the same semantics.

Adjusting the style for nabla and partial symbols

There are a few symbols whose style is often independently chosen. The most important ones are ∇ (`\nabla`) and ∂ (`\partial`). For them you can individually decide if it should be typeset upright or in italics by using the package keys `nabla` and `partial` and using either `upright` (default for ∇) or `italic` (default for ∂).

There is also the package option `colon` that can be used to adjust the behavior of the `\colon` command, and there is `slash-delimiter` with which you can specify which of the various Unicode slashes is stretchable, e.g., can appear after `\left` or `\right`. For details on these rather special areas, see the package documentation.

All five package keys also support the special value `literal`, which means that *Forcing literal input*
unicode-math does not undertake any input normalization (e.g., typeset Latin letters *style*
in italic) but uses the style given by the source character; e.g., if it is a *Latin Small X*
(U+0078), it typesets an upright x, but if it is *Mathematical Italic Small X* (U+1D465),
it typesets it as x in the formula; see the package documentation when this might be
useful. You can also force "literal" style through `\symliteral`, which undoes the
effect of `\symnormal`.

12.4.3 Setting up Unicode math fonts

Up until now we have loaded unicode-math, which gives us the features and commands *Changing the main*
described, but our documents are still typeset using Latin Modern, because that is *font for math*
LaTeX's default in Unicode engines. If we want to use a different Unicode math font, we *formulas*
need to tell the package about it.

> `\setmathfont{`*family*`}` [*feature-list*]

This declaration sets up the math font *family* to be used (which needs to be a specially
prepared font). The command is modeled after the declarations provided by the
fontspec package, e.g., `\setmainfont`, and you may want to review Section 9.6.1 on
page →I 706 to familiarize yourself with the different ways to find and specify the
family name and the various features that you can put into the *feature-list*.

There are a few keys that are specific to setting up math fonts, and those are
discussed below. However, it is often enough to just give the right *family* name, as
shown in the next example where we use Fira Sans and Fira Math for typesetting.

An example showing a trigonometric
function:

$$\sin \frac{\alpha}{2} = \pm\sqrt{\frac{1-\cos\alpha}{2}}$$

Scripts: $A \neq \mathsf{A}$; no other math alphabets
are available in Fira Sans.

```
\usepackage{fontspec}        \setmainfont{Fira Sans}
\usepackage{unicode-math} \setmathfont{Fira Math}
An example showing a trigonometric function:
\[ \sin \frac{\alpha}{2} =
        \pm \sqrt{\frac{1-\cos\alpha}{2}} \]
Scripts: $A \neq \symbb{A} $; no other math
alphabets are available in Fira Sans.
```

12-4-5

Well-known mathematical functions (such as $\sin \alpha$ and $\cos \beta$) are usually type- *Adjusting the*
set in a font distinct from surrounding letters denoting variables in a formula. In *"operator" font*
LaTeX such functions are declared with `\DeclareMathOperator`; see Section 11.6.2
on page 192. They all use the same fixed font, typically upright roman (e.g.,
`\mathrm`). With `\setoperatorfont{`*alphabet*`}` the unicode-math package offers
a simple way to choose a different math alphabet for this task. For example, after
`\setoperatorfont{\mathsf}` you get $\sin \alpha$ and $\cos \beta$ in your formulas.

Adjusting parts of the font setup

Simply adding a single `\setmathfont` declaration works fine if the Unicode math *Making adjustments*
font that you use implements all the math glyphs that you are interested in. However, *for a range of*
this may not be the case. You may find that individual characters or whole alphabets *characters*

are missing, in which case you need to provide some additional declarations. For example, the Fira Math fonts used above do not offer a script or a fraktur math alphabet, and many examples in Section 12.5 miss individual symbols that need to be provided from elsewhere. For this you can use the `range` key.

In the next example we repeat the setup from above but add a second declaration that loads the STIX 2 math font. By specifying a `range`, we tell the loader that it should be replacing only the ranges `frak` and `scr` and leave the rest of the math setup alone. As a result we can now typeset in all three math alphabets (though our choice of using the STIX font alphabets is not that great).

```
\usepackage{fontspec}      \setmainfont{Fira Sans}          % text setup
\usepackage{unicode-math} \setmathfont{Fira Math}          % math setup
\setmathfont{STIX Two Math Regular}[range={frak,scr}] % replacement
```

Scripts: $A \neq \mathcal{A} \neq \mathbb{A} \neq \mathfrak{A}$ Scripts: `$A \neq \symscr{A} \neq \symbb{A} \neq \symfrak{A}$`   12-4-6

The previous example showed "named" ranges as the value for the `range` key. The supported names are `bb`, `bbit`, `bfcal`, `bffrak`, `bfit`, `bfscr`, `bfsfit`, `bfsfup`, `bfup`, `cal`, `frak`, `it`, `scr`, `sfit`, `sfup`, `tt`, and `up` — hopefully all self-explanatory.

Replacing individual characters or adding missing ones

They are useful if you want to include a whole alphabet from a different font, but perhaps you need to add only a few missing characters. In that case the syntax is a comma-separated list of hexadecimal slot numbers, e.g., `range={"2A04,"2A0C}`, which we need in Figure 12.26 on page 279 to make the example work. Note that you need braces around the value if it contains commas.

If you want to load a consecutive range (one that is not matching any of the named ones), you can simplify the input, by giving the start and end hexadecimal codes separated by a hyphen instead of a comma, e.g., `"27D0-"27EB`. There are further (less often needed) syntax variations: see the package documentation if the above does not seem sufficient.

Script and scriptscript fonts and features

Characters in formulas come in three sizes, e.g., a^{a^a} (text, script, and second-order script size). In many situations, TeX simply loads the same font at three different sizes, but this is not always the case. Some font families, such as Computer or Latin Modern, have separate optically adjusted fonts for different sizes and thus for different sizes different fonts are loaded (see Figure 9.6 on page →I 657 for an example). With OpenType fonts, such optical adjustments may all be bundled in a single font and selected through font features — for example, with Cambria Math.

To cater for both approaches (or a combination thereof), unicode-math offers the keys `script-font` and `sscript-font` to select alternate fonts for the index sizes and `script-features` and `sscript-features` to apply individual feature lists for them. The keys are preset with `Style=MathScript` and `Style=MathScriptScript`, respectively, which are the correct settings in most cases.

Providing several math versions

In standard LaTeX you can switch "math versions" (different setups for formulas) using `\mathversion{version}`. By default, two *versions* are provided, `normal` and `bold`, and with the mechanisms described on Section 9.8.5 on page →I 753 you can define further versions, if necessary. This concept of versions is also supported for Unicode fonts, but because these fonts are loaded differently, the declaration mechanism differs too. To indicate that a Unicode font is for a specific *version*, use

```
\setmathfont{family}[version=version,... other features...]
```

12.5 A visual comparison of different math setups

In this section we repeatedly show the same sample text, typeset with different font setups for math and text. It assumes amsmath and with pdfTeX also the bm package.

We start by briefly discussing the input used, highlighting points to look at in the examples with blue color. At the beginning of the example file, we define \ibinom, which is used later. This is followed by the section title, which differs in each example, denoted here with three dots:

```
\newcommand\ibinom[2]{\genfrac\lbrace\rbrace{0pt}{}{#1}{#2}}
\section*{...}
```

In the first paragraph we use a \smash around the first inline formula in order to avoid it pushing the baseline apart. One point to keep track of in the output is the different math alphabets (always used with the letter Q), and compare we should their results — here we use the calligraphic one. Also noteworthy are the different integrals: in some examples they are shown upright.

```
First some large operators both in text:
\smash{$ \iiint\limits_{\mathcal{Q}} f(x,y,z)\,dx\,dy\,dz $} and
$ \prod_{\gamma\in\Gamma_{\widetilde{C}}}
          \partial(\widetilde{X}_\gamma) $; and also on display:
```

The first line of the split equation is deliberately long so as to show differences in widths in different font setups; it is a little wider than the space needed with Computer Modern fonts. \iiiint is marked blue, because it is missing in some OpenType fonts. The output line also shows two further "Q"s, both bold, but one produced with \mathbf, and the other with \bm from the bm package.[1]

```
\begin{equation} \begin{split}
   \iiiint\limits_{\mathbf{Q}} f(w,x,y,z) dwdxdydz
 & \leq \oint_{\bm{\partial Q}} f' \left( \max \left\lbrace
           \frac{\lVert w \rVert}{\lvert w^2 + x^2 \rvert} ;
           \frac{\lVert z \rVert}{\lvert y^2 + z^2 \rvert} ;
           \frac{\lVert w \oplus z \rVert}{\lVert x \oplus y \rVert}
                     \right\rbrace \right)                 \\
```

The three symbols ⊎ (from core LaTeX) and ≾ and ⋐ (from the American Mathematical Society symbol set) are all problematical (i.e., missing) in one or the other Open-Type font and there are some further "Q"s. This time we have two blackboard bold (\mathbb) and another ordinary bold one. Further down we have marked \nu and v blue, as an example of glyphs that may be hard to distinguish in some font families.

```
 & \precapprox \biguplus_{\mathbb{Q} \Subset \bar{\mathbf{Q}}}
           \left[ f^{\ast} \left(
              \frac{\left\lmoustache\mathbb{Q}(t)\right\rmoustache}
                  {\sqrt {1 - t^2}}
             \right) \right]_{t=\alpha}^{t=\vartheta} - ( \Delta + \nu - v )^3
  \end{split}  \end{equation}
```

---

[1] In the Unicode font examples \symbf is used instead of \bm.

The next paragraph gives you an indication for the running length of the text and math fonts if you take a look at where the two words in blue show up:

```
For $x$ in the open interval $ \left] -1, 1 \right[ $ the infinite
sum in Equation~\eqref{eq:binom1} is convergent; however, this does
not hold throughout the closed interval $ \left[ -1, 1 \right] $.
```

In the last equation we have two places where there may be spacing issues with superscripts and another blackboard alphabet character, this time "N".

```
\begin{equation}
   (1 - x)^{-k} = 1 + \sum_{j=1}^{\infty} (-1)^j \ibinom{k}{j} x^j
   \text{\quad for $k \in \mathbb{N}$; $k \neq 0$.}  \label{eq:binom1}
\end{equation}
```

Figure 12.1 shows the sample text typeset in Computer Modern text and math fonts — the default font setup in LaTeX. We reuse this input throughout the remainder of this section to exhibit different font setups and allow you to compare them with each other. The only thing that changes is the section title.

The remaining examples (Figures 12.2 to 12.51) in this section follow the classification we introduced in Chapter 10. The fonts in some groups, e.g., Humanist serif, have no matching math support at all, in which case we bypass them, but otherwise

---

Mathematical typesetting with Computer Modern

First some large operators both in text: $\iiint f(x, y, z)\, dx\, dy\, dz$ and $\prod_{\gamma \in \Gamma_{\tilde{C}}} \partial(\tilde{X}_\gamma)$; and also on display:

$$\iiiint_Q f(w, x, y, z)\, dw\, dx\, dy\, dz \leq \oint_{\partial Q} f'\left(\max\left\{\frac{\|w\|}{|w^2 + x^2|}; \frac{\|z\|}{|y^2 + z^2|}; \frac{\|w \oplus z\|}{\|x \oplus y\|}\right\}\right)$$

$$\gtrsim \biguplus_{Q \in \bar{Q}} \left[f^*\left(\frac{\int Q(t)}{\sqrt{1 - t^2}}\right)\right]_{t=\alpha}^{t=\vartheta} - (\Delta + \nu - v)^3 \tag{1}$$

For x in the open interval $]{-1}, 1[$ the infinite sum in Equation (2) is convergent; however, this does not hold throughout the closed interval $[-1, 1]$.

$$(1 - x)^{-k} = 1 + \sum_{j=1}^{\infty} (-1)^j \left\{ {k \atop j} \right\} x^j \quad \text{for } k \in \mathbb{N};\ k \neq 0. \tag{2}$$

Figure 12.1: Sample page typeset with Computer Modern text + math fonts

the order is preserved so that you can easily hunt for similar text fonts to go with a certain math setup or vice versa.

Each setup is explained in the accompanying text, e.g., on some occasions we use special package options or have to substitute a few glyphs, because they are missing in the font.[1]

Many font setups can be used both with pdfTEX or Unicode engines — in this case we show the pdfTEX version in the book. With fonts that are not usable with pdfTEX, the sample has been processed with LuaTEX. This is explained in the text, but also visually indicated by displaying the figure caption with a gray background, e.g., Figure 12.5.

12.5.1 Garalde (Oldstyle) serif fonts with math support

Math support for the Crimson family of fonts designed by Sebastian Kosch is provided by Michael Sharpe through his `newtxmath` package by passing it the option `cochineal`. To set up matching text fonts you can use either CrimsonPro or cochineal; see Section 10.4.3 on page 40 for the differences. For Figure 12.2 we used the following simple setup:

Crimson, Crimson Pro, and Cochineal

```
\usepackage{cochineal}    \usepackage[cochineal]{newtxmath}
```

---

[1]Especially with OpenType fonts that can happen rather easily. It is therefore quite important to use \tracinglostchars=3 in your document preamble to receive an error message in such a case.

Mathematical typesetting with Cochineal

First some large operators both in text: $\iiint_Q f(x,y,z)\,dx\,dy\,dz$ and $\prod_{\gamma \in \Gamma_{\widetilde{C}}} \partial(\widetilde{X}_\gamma)$; and also on display:

$$\iiiint_Q f(w,x,y,z)\,dw\,dx\,dy\,dz \leq \oint_{\partial Q} f'\left(\max\left\{\frac{\|w\|}{|w^2+x^2|}; \frac{\|z\|}{|y^2+z^2|}; \frac{\|w \oplus z\|}{\|x \oplus y\|}\right\}\right)$$

$$\gtrapprox \biguplus_{Q \in \bar{Q}}\left[f^*\left(\frac{\int Q(t)\rangle}{\sqrt{1-t^2}}\right)\right]_{t=\alpha}^{t=\vartheta} - (\Delta + \nu - \upsilon)^3 \tag{1}$$

For x in the open interval $]-1,1[$ the infinite sum in Equation (2) is convergent; however, this does not hold throughout the closed interval $[-1,1]$.

$$(1-x)^{-k} = 1 + \sum_{j=1}^{\infty}(-1)^j\left\{{k \atop j}\right\}x^j \quad \text{for } k \in \mathbb{N}; k \neq 0. \tag{2}$$

12-2-fig

Figure 12.2: Sample page typeset with Cochineal text + math fonts

Mathematical typesetting with EB Garamond

First some large operators both in text: $\iiint_Q f(x, y, z)\, dx\, dy\, dz$ and $\prod_{\gamma \in \Gamma_{\widetilde{C}}} \partial(\widetilde{X}_\gamma)$; and also on display:

$$\iiiint_Q f(w, x, y, z)\, dw\, dx\, dy\, dz \le \oint_{\partial Q} f'\left(\max\left\{\frac{\|w\|}{|w^2 + x^2|}; \frac{\|z\|}{|y^2 + z^2|}; \frac{\|w \oplus z\|}{\|x \oplus y\|}\right\}\right)$$

$$\gtrapprox \biguplus_{Q \in \bar{Q}} \left[f^*\left(\frac{\int Q(t)}{\sqrt{1 - t^2}}\right)\right]_{t=\alpha}^{t=\vartheta} - (\Delta + \nu - v)^3$$

(1)

For x in the open interval $]-1, 1[$ the infinite sum in Equation (2) is convergent; however, this does not hold throughout the closed interval $[-1, 1]$.

$$(1 - x)^{-k} = 1 + \sum_{j=1}^{\infty} (-1)^j \begin{Bmatrix} k \\ j \end{Bmatrix} x^j \quad \text{for } k \in \mathbb{N}; k \ne 0.$$

(2)

12-3-fig

Figure 12.3: Sample page typeset with EB Garamond text + math fonts

Mathematical typesetting with Garamondx

First some large operators both in text: $\iiint_Q f(x, y, z)\, dx\, dy\, dz$ and $\prod_{\gamma \in \Gamma_{\widetilde{C}}} \partial(\widetilde{X}_\gamma)$; and also on display:

$$\iiiint_Q f(w, x, y, z)\, dw\, dx\, dy\, dz \le \oint_{\partial Q} f'\left(\max\left\{\frac{\|w\|}{|w^2 + x^2|}; \frac{\|z\|}{|y^2 + z^2|}; \frac{\|w \oplus z\|}{\|x \oplus y\|}\right\}\right)$$

$$\gtrapprox \biguplus_{Q \in \bar{Q}} \left[f^*\left(\frac{\int Q(t)}{\sqrt{1 - t^2}}\right)\right]_{t=\alpha}^{t=\vartheta} - (\Delta + \nu - v)^3$$

(1)

For x in the open interval $]-1, 1[$ the infinite sum in Equation (2) is convergent; however, this does not hold throughout the closed interval $[-1, 1]$.

$$(1 - x)^{-k} = 1 + \sum_{j=1}^{\infty} (-1)^j \begin{Bmatrix} k \\ j \end{Bmatrix} x^j \quad \text{for } k \in \mathbb{N}; k \ne 0.$$

(2)

12-4-fig

Figure 12.4: Sample page typeset with Garamondx text + math fonts

Mathematical typesetting with Garamond Math

First some large operators both in text: $\iiint_Q f(x,y,z)\,dx\,dy\,dz$ and $\prod_{\gamma\in\Gamma_{\widetilde{C}}}\partial(\widetilde{X}_\gamma)$; and also on display:

$$\iiiint_Q f(w,x,y,z)\,dw\,dx\,dy\,dz \leq \oint_{\partial \mathbf{Q}} f'\left(\max\left\{\frac{\|w\|}{|w^2+x^2|};\frac{\|z\|}{|y^2+z^2|};\frac{\|w\oplus z\|}{\|x\oplus y\|}\right\}\right)$$

$$\gtrapprox \biguplus_{Q\in\bar{\mathbf{Q}}}\left[f^*\left(\frac{Q(t)}{\sqrt{1-t^2}}\right)\right]_{t=\alpha}^{t=\vartheta} - (\Delta+\nu-v)^3 \tag{1}$$

For x in the open interval $]-1,1[$ the infinite sum in Equation (2) is convergent; however, this does not hold throughout the closed interval $[-1,1]$.

$$(1-x)^{-k} = 1 + \sum_{j=1}^{\infty}(-1)^j\begin{Bmatrix}k\\j\end{Bmatrix}x^j \quad \text{for } k\in\mathbb{N}; k\neq 0. \tag{2}$$

12-5-fig

Unicode engines

Figure 12.5: Sample page typeset with Garamond Libre + Garamond Math fonts

There are many revivals of the fonts designed by Claude Garamond, and a number of them have been made freely available for use with TeX; see Sections 10.4.4 to 10.4.7. *A number of setups based on Garamond*

We show three combinations: EB Garamond designed by Georg Duffner and Octavio Pardoin for math and text (Figure 12.3); Garamondx, a reworking of URW's Garamond by Michael Sharpe, in math and text (Figure 12.4); and a combination of Garamond Libre by D. Benjamin Miller for text and Garamond Math by Yuansheng Zhao and Xiangdong Zeng (Figure 12.5). The setup used for EB Garamond was:

```
\usepackage[lining,semibold,scaled=1.05]{ebgaramond}
\usepackage[ebgaramond,varbb,subscriptcorrection]{newtxmath}
```

and somewhat simpler for Garamondx:

```
\usepackage{garamondx}    \usepackage[garamondx]{newtxmath}
```

Compared to Garamondx, EB Garamond runs slightly shorter (which can be seen in the second paragraph) even though it is scaled up a bit. Otherwise, the differences are small with some differences in individual letter forms, such as the v and the different blackboard bold alphabet.

The OpenType Garamond Math font (which offers some stylistic sets, not used) is available only for Unicode engines, and the setup that we used looks as follows:

```
\usepackage{fontspec}     \setmainfont{Garamond Libre}
\usepackage{unicode-math}  \setmathfont{Garamond Math}
\setmathfont{Asana Math}[range="2AB7,Scale=.84]
```

The last line shows a substitution because a character was missing — note the scaling.

Mathematical typesetting with Kp Roman Light

First some large operators both in text: $\iiint_Q f(x,y,z)\,dx\,dy\,dz$ and $\prod_{\gamma\in\Gamma_{\widetilde{C}}}\partial(\widetilde{X}_\gamma)$; and also on display:

$$\iiiint_Q f(w,x,y,z)\,dw\,dx\,dy\,dz \leq \oint_{\partial Q} f'\left(\max\left\{\frac{\|w\|}{|w^2+x^2|};\frac{\|z\|}{|y^2+z^2|};\frac{\|w\oplus z\|}{\|x\oplus y\|}\right\}\right)$$

$$\gtrapprox \biguplus_{Q\in\bar{Q}}\left[f^*\left(\frac{\int Q(t)}{\sqrt{1-t^2}}\right)\right]_{t=\alpha}^{t=\vartheta} - (\Delta+\nu-\nu)^3$$

(1)

For x in the open interval $]-1,1[$ the infinite sum in Equation (2) is convergent; however, this does not hold throughout the closed interval $[-1,1]$.

$$(1-x)^{-k} = 1 + \sum_{j=1}^{\infty}(-1)^j\begin{Bmatrix}k\\j\end{Bmatrix}x^j \quad \text{for } k\in\mathbb{N};\ k\neq 0.$$

(2)

12-6-fig

Figure 12.6: Sample page typeset with Kp Roman Light text + math fonts

Mathematical typesetting with Kp Roman

First some large operators both in text: $\iiint_Q f(x,y,z)\,dx\,dy\,dz$ and $\prod_{\gamma\in\Gamma_{\widetilde{C}}}\partial(\widetilde{X}_\gamma)$; and also on display:

$$\iiiint_Q f(w,x,y,z)\,dw\,dx\,dy\,dz \leq \oint_{\partial Q} f'\left(\max\left\{\frac{\|w\|}{|w^2+x^2|};\frac{\|z\|}{|y^2+z^2|};\frac{\|w\oplus z\|}{\|x\oplus y\|}\right\}\right)$$

$$\gtrapprox \biguplus_{Q\in\bar{Q}}\left[f^*\left(\frac{\int Q(t)}{\sqrt{1-t^2}}\right)\right]_{t=\alpha}^{t=\vartheta} - (\Delta+\nu-\nu)^3$$

(1)

For x in the open interval $]-1,1[$ the infinite sum in Equation (2) is convergent; however, this does not hold throughout the closed interval $[-1,1]$.

$$(1-x)^{-k} = 1 + \sum_{j=1}^{\infty}(-1)^j\begin{Bmatrix}k\\j\end{Bmatrix}x^j \quad \text{for } k\in\mathbb{N};\ k\neq 0.$$

(2)

12-7-fig

Figure 12.7: Sample page typeset with Kp Roman text + math fonts

Mathematical typesetting with Kp Roman

First some large operators both in text: $\iiint_{\mathcal{Q}} f(x,y,z)\,dx\,dy\,dz$ and $\prod_{\gamma \in \Gamma_{\hat{C}}} \partial(\tilde{X}_\gamma)$; and also on display:

$$\iiint_Q f(w,x,y,z)\,dw\,dx\,dy\,dz \le \oint_{\partial Q} f'\left(\max\left\{\frac{\|w\|}{|w^2+x^2|}; \frac{\|z\|}{|y^2+z^2|}; \frac{\|w \oplus z\|}{\|x \oplus y\|}\right\}\right) \tag{1}$$

$$\gtrapprox \biguplus_{Q \in \bar{Q}} \left[f^*\left(\frac{\int Q(t)\int}{\sqrt{1-t^2}}\right)\right]_{t=\alpha}^{t=\vartheta} - (\Delta + \nu - \upsilon)^3$$

For x in the open interval $]-1, 1[$ the infinite sum in Equation (2) is convergent; however, this does not hold throughout the closed interval $[-1, 1]$.

$$(1-x)^{-k} = 1 + \sum_{j=1}^{\infty} (-1)^j \left\{{k \atop j}\right\} x^j \quad \text{for } k \in \mathbb{N}; k \ne 0. \tag{2}$$

Figure 12.8: Sample page typeset with KpRoman + Kp Math fonts

The Kp family of fonts by Christophe Caignaert is based on the Palatino design and offers full math support in all engines. On this page we show three variations. The first two use kpfonts for pdfTeX, which comes with a huge number of options for customization, out of which we have chosen seven. The setup for Figure 12.6 was this:

The Kp (Johannes Kepler) fonts

```
\usepackage[light,lighttext,narrowiints,frenchstyle]{kpfonts}
```

This applies lighter fonts, both for text and math, and brings multiple integrals closer together. Finally, `frenchstyle` typesets all math letters — except for lowercase Latin letters — upright (Q, γ, C, X in the first line). Figure 12.7 then used this setup:

```
\usepackage[oldstyle,oldstylenumsmath,sfmathbb]{kpfonts}
```

Here, the `oldstyle` option is responsible for the extra ligatures, e.g., in "First", and for the oldstyle numerals in text; `oldstylenumsmath` requests them also in math; and `sfmathbb` changes the blackboard bold alphabet to sans serif.

The final example exhibits the OpenType versions of the family, as provided by Daniel Flipo. He also offers the package kpfonts-otf to set them up, but for Figure 12.8 we have used fontspec and unicode-math instead, because that also shows how to combine the math fonts with other text families.

```
\usepackage{fontspec}                    \setmainfont{KpRoman}
\usepackage[math-style=ISO]{unicode-math} \setmathfont{Kp Math}[StylisticSet=3]
```

The feature `StylisticSet=3` sets the integral closer; for a full set of features see the font documentation or the kpfonts-otf package documentation.

267

Mathematical typesetting with Math Pazo

First some large operators both in text: $\iiint_Q f(x,y,z)\,dx\,dy\,dz$ and $\prod_{\gamma \in \Gamma_{\widetilde{C}}} \partial(\widetilde{X}_\gamma)$; and also on display:

$$\iiiint_Q f(w,x,y,z)\,dw\,dx\,dy\,dz \leq \oint_{\partial Q} f'\left(\max\left\{\frac{\|w\|}{|w^2+x^2|}; \frac{\|z\|}{|y^2+z^2|}; \frac{\|w \oplus z\|}{\|x \oplus y\|}\right\}\right)$$

$$\gtrapprox \biguplus_{Q \in \bar{Q}} \left[f^*\left(\frac{\int Q(t)}{\sqrt{1-t^2}}\right)\right]_{t=\alpha}^{t=\vartheta} - (\Delta + \nu - v)^3 \tag{1}$$

For x in the open interval $]-1,1[$ the infinite sum in Equation (2) is convergent; however, this does not hold throughout the closed interval $[-1,1]$.

$$(1-x)^{-k} = 1 + \sum_{j=1}^{\infty}(-1)^j\begin{Bmatrix}k\\j\end{Bmatrix}x^j \quad \text{for } k \in \mathbb{N}; k \neq 0. \tag{2}$$

12-9-fig

Figure 12.9: Sample page typeset with Palatino text + Pazo Math fonts

Different math setups for use with Palatino

The typeface Palatino was designed by Hermann Zapf (1918–2015) for the Stempel foundry in 1948 based on lettering from the Italian Renaissance. Since then it has become one of the most widely used typefaces, and probably the most popular Old Style revival in existence [20]. A number of math font setups are available for use with Palatino as the text font.

Figure 12.9 shows the freely available Pazo Math fonts (designed by Diego Puga), which can be activated with \usepackage{mathpazo}. It offers boldface symbols and a matching blackboard bold alphabet but does not contain specially designed shapes for the AMS symbol set; see also Section 12.3.6.

In contrast, the free PX fonts (designed by Young Ryu) comprise the complete symbol set. Shown in Figure 12.10 is the version of the fonts that was reworked by Michael Sharpe; see also Section 12.3.5 on page 248. The setup used for the example was the following simple line:

```
\usepackage{newpxtext,newpxmath}
```

For comparison Figure 12.11 combines Pagella with the Kp fonts for math using the following setup:

```
\usepackage{newpxtext}  \usepackage[notext]{kpfonts}
```

The notext option for kpfonts tells the package to only set up math font support but leave the text fonts untouched.

Mathematical typesetting with Pagella/New PX

First some large operators both in text: $\iiint_Q f(x,y,z)\,dx\,dy\,dz$ and $\prod_{\gamma \in \Gamma_{\widetilde{C}}} \partial(\widetilde{X}_\gamma)$; and also on display:

$$\iiiint_Q f(w,x,y,z)\,dw\,dx\,dy\,dz \le \oint_{\partial Q} f'\left(\max\left\{\frac{\|w\|}{|w^2+x^2|}; \frac{\|z\|}{|y^2+z^2|}; \frac{\|w \oplus z\|}{\|x \oplus y\|}\right\}\right)$$

$$\gtrapprox \biguplus_{Q \in \bar{Q}} \left[f^*\left(\frac{\int Q(t)}{\sqrt{1-t^2}}\right)\right]_{t=\alpha}^{t=\vartheta} - (\Delta + \nu - \upsilon)^3 \tag{1}$$

For x in the open interval $]-1,1[$ the infinite sum in Equation (2) is convergent; however, this does not hold throughout the closed interval $[-1,1]$.

$$(1-x)^{-k} = 1 + \sum_{j=1}^{\infty} (-1)^j \begin{Bmatrix} k \\ j \end{Bmatrix} x^j \quad \text{for } k \in \mathbb{N}; k \ne 0. \tag{2}$$

12-10-fig

Figure 12.10: Sample page typeset with Pagella text + New PX math fonts

Mathematical typesetting with Pagella/Kp

First some large operators both in text: $\iiint_Q f(x,y,z)\,dx\,dy\,dz$ and $\prod_{\gamma \in \Gamma_{\widetilde{C}}} \partial(\widetilde{X}_\gamma)$; and also on display:

$$\iiiint_Q f(w,x,y,z)\,dw\,dx\,dy\,dz \le \oint_{\partial Q} f'\left(\max\left\{\frac{\|w\|}{|w^2+x^2|}; \frac{\|z\|}{|y^2+z^2|}; \frac{\|w \oplus z\|}{\|x \oplus y\|}\right\}\right) \tag{1}$$

$$\gtrapprox \biguplus_{Q \in \bar{Q}} \left[f^*\left(\frac{\int Q(t)}{\sqrt{1-t^2}}\right)\right]_{t=\alpha}^{t=\vartheta} - (\Delta + \nu - \upsilon)^3$$

For x in the open interval $]-1,1[$ the infinite sum in Equation (2) is convergent; however, this does not hold throughout the closed interval $[-1,1]$.

$$(1-x)^{-k} = 1 + \sum_{j=1}^{\infty} (-1)^j \begin{Bmatrix} k \\ j \end{Bmatrix} x^j \quad \text{for } k \in \mathbb{N}; k \ne 0. \tag{2}$$

12-11-fig

Figure 12.11: Sample page typeset with Pagella text + Kp math fonts

Mathematical typesetting with Pagella

First some large operators both in text: $\iiint_Q f(x,y,z)\,dx\,dy\,dz$ and $\prod_{\gamma \in \Gamma_{\widetilde{C}}} \partial(\widetilde{X}_\gamma)$; and also on display:

$$\iiiint_Q f(w,x,y,z)\,dw\,dx\,dy\,dz \leq \oint_{\partial Q} f'\left(\max\left\{\frac{\|w\|}{|w^2+x^2|}; \frac{\|z\|}{|y^2+z^2|}; \frac{\|w \oplus z\|}{\|x \oplus y\|}\right\}\right)$$

$$\gtrapprox \biguplus_{Q \in \bar{Q}}\left[f^*\left(\frac{Q(t)}{\sqrt{1-t^2}}\right)\right]_{t=\alpha}^{t=\vartheta} - (\Delta + \nu - v)^3 \tag{1}$$

For x in the open interval $]-1,1[$ the infinite sum in Equation (2) is convergent; however, this does not hold throughout the closed interval $[-1,1]$.

$$(1-x)^{-k} = 1 + \sum_{j=1}^{\infty}(-1)^j\left\{{k \atop j}\right\}x^j \quad \text{for } k \in \mathbb{N}; k \neq 0. \tag{2}$$

12-12-fig

Unicode engines

Figure 12.12: Sample page typeset with Pagella + Pagella Math fonts

Mathematical typesetting with Pagella/Asana

First some large operators both in text: $\iiint_{\mathscr{C}} f(x,y,z)\,dx\,dy\,dz$ and $\prod_{\gamma \in \Gamma_{\widetilde{C}}} \partial(\widetilde{X}_\gamma)$; and also on display:

$$\iiiint_Q f(w,x,y,z)\,dw\,dx\,dy\,dz \leq \oint_{\partial Q} f'\left(\max\left\{\frac{\|w\|}{|w^2+x^2|}; \frac{\|z\|}{|y^2+z^2|}; \frac{\|w \oplus z\|}{\|x \oplus y\|}\right\}\right)$$

$$\gtrapprox \biguplus_{Q \in \bar{Q}}\left[f^*\left(\frac{Q(t)}{\sqrt{1-t^2}}\right)\right]_{t=\alpha}^{t=\vartheta} - (\Delta + \nu - v)^3 \tag{1}$$

For x in the open interval $]-1,1[$ the infinite sum in Equation (2) is convergent; however, this does not hold throughout the closed interval $[-1,1]$.

$$(1-x)^{-k} = 1 + \sum_{j=1}^{\infty}(-1)^j\left\{{k \atop j}\right\}x^j \quad \text{for } k \in \mathbb{N}; k \neq 0. \tag{2}$$

12-13-fig

Unicode engines

Figure 12.13: Sample page typeset with Pagella + Asana Math fonts

When it comes to Unicode engines, there are a few additional alternatives available. The TeX Gyre foundry (Bogusław Jackowski, Piotr Pianowski, Piotr Strzelczyk) developed a set of OpenType math fonts to accompany their text fonts, one of which is Pagella Math. The sample in Figure 12.12 was produced with the following setup:

```
\usepackage{fontspec}    \setmainfont{TeX Gyre Pagella}
\usepackage{unicode-math} \setmathfont{TeX Gyre Pagella Math}
\setmathfont{Asana Math}[range="2AB7,Scale=1.1]
```

Again, we have to fix a missing character by using a scaled version from Asana Math, but this time we have to enlarge it to get the correct size.

In the final example involving Palatino, we pair it with Asana Math by Apostolos Syropoulos. This font has no missing glyphs, so we simply load it with the help of unicode-math: the result is shown in Figure 12.13 on the facing page.

```
\usepackage{fontspec}    \setmainfont{TeX Gyre Pagella}
\usepackage{unicode-math} \setmathfont{Asana Math}
```

12.5.2 Transitional serif fonts with math support

Among the transitional serif typefaces there are many with matching math support. As always, we progress in alphabetical order starting with versions of Baskerville. Figure 12.14 exhibits BaskervilleF, and Figures 12.15 and 12.16 on the next page show Baskervaldx. In all cases the math support was developed by Michael Sharpe.

Mathematical typesetting with BaskervilleF

First some large operators both in text: $\iiint_Q f(x, y, z)\, dx\, dy\, dz$ and $\prod_{\gamma \in \Gamma_{\widetilde{C}}} \partial(\widetilde{X}_\gamma)$; and also on display:

$$\iiiint_{\mathbf{Q}} f(w, x, y, z)\, dw\, dx\, dy\, dz \leq \oint_{\partial \mathbf{Q}} f'\left(\max\left\{\frac{\|w\|}{|w^2 + x^2|}; \frac{\|z\|}{|y^2 + z^2|}; \frac{\|w \oplus z\|}{\|x \oplus y\|}\right\}\right)$$

$$\gtrless \biguplus_{\mathbf{Q} \in \bar{\mathbf{Q}}} \left[f^*\left(\frac{\lfloor \mathbb{Q}(t)\rfloor}{\sqrt{1 - t^2}}\right)\right]_{t=\alpha}^{t=\vartheta} - (\Delta + \nu - \upsilon)^3 \tag{1}$$

For x in the open interval $]-1, 1[$ the infinite sum in Equation (2) is convergent; however, this does not hold throughout the closed interval $[-1, 1]$.

$$(1 - x)^{-k} = 1 + \sum_{j=1}^{\infty} (-1)^j \begin{Bmatrix} k \\ j \end{Bmatrix} x^j \quad \text{for } k \in \mathbb{N}; \, k \neq 0. \tag{2}$$

12-14-fig

Figure 12.14: Sample page typeset with BaskervilleF text + math fonts

Mathematical typesetting with Baskervaldx

First some large operators both in text: $\iiint_Q f(x,y,z)\,dx\,dy\,dz$ and $\prod_{\gamma \in \Gamma_{\widetilde{C}}} \partial(\widetilde{X}_\gamma)$; and also on display:

$$\iiiint_Q f(w,x,y,z)\,dw\,dx\,dy\,dz \leq \oint_{\partial Q} f' \left(\max \left\{ \frac{\|w\|}{|w^2+x^2|}; \frac{\|z\|}{|y^2+z^2|}; \frac{\|w \oplus z\|}{\|x \oplus y\|} \right\} \right)$$

$$\gtrapprox \biguplus_{Q \in \bar{Q}} \left[f^* \left(\frac{\int Q(t)}{\sqrt{1-t^2}} \right) \right]_{t=\alpha}^{t=\vartheta} - (\Delta + \nu - \upsilon)^3$$

$$(1)$$

For x in the open interval $]-1,1[$ the infinite sum in Equation (2) is convergent; however, this does not hold throughout the closed interval $[-1,1]$.

$$(1-x)^{-k} = 1 + \sum_{j=1}^{\infty} (-1)^j \left\{ {k \atop j} \right\} x^j \quad \text{for } k \in \mathbb{N};\ k \neq 0. \tag{2}$$

12-15-fig

Figure 12.15: Sample page typeset with Baskervaldx text + math fonts

Mathematical typesetting with Baskervaldx and Times

First some large operators both in text: $\iiint_Q f(x, y, z)\,dx\,dy\,dz$ and $\prod_{\gamma \in \Gamma_{\widetilde{C}}} \partial(\widetilde{X}_\gamma)$; and also on display:

$$\iiiint_Q f(w,x,y,z)\,dw\,dx\,dy\,dz \leq \oint_{\partial Q} f' \left(\max \left\{ \frac{\|w\|}{|w^2+x^2|}; \frac{\|z\|}{|y^2+z^2|}; \frac{\|w \oplus z\|}{\|x \oplus y\|} \right\} \right)$$

$$\gtrapprox \biguplus_{Q \in \bar{Q}} \left[f^* \left(\frac{\int Q(t)}{\sqrt{1-t^2}} \right) \right]_{t=\alpha}^{t=\vartheta} - (\Delta + \nu - \upsilon)^3$$

$$(1)$$

For x in the open interval $]-1, 1[$ the infinite sum in Equation (2) is convergent; however, this does not hold throughout the closed interval $[-1, 1]$.

$$(1-x)^{-k} = 1 + \sum_{j=1}^{\infty} (-1)^j \left\{ {k \atop j} \right\} x^j \quad \text{for } k \in \mathbb{N};\ k \neq 0. \tag{2}$$

12-16-fig

Figure 12.16: Sample page typeset with Baskervaldx text + Times math fonts

Mathematical typesetting with Bonum

First some large operators both in text: $\iiint_Q f(x, y, z)\, dx\, dy\, dz$ and $\prod_{\gamma \in \Gamma_{\widetilde{C}}} \partial(\widetilde{X}_\gamma)$; and also on display:

$$\iiiint_{\mathsf{g}} f(w, x, y, z)\, dw\, dx\, dy\, dz \leq \oint_{\partial\mathsf{g}} f'\left(\max\left\{\frac{\|w\|}{|w^2 + x^2|}; \frac{\|z\|}{|y^2 + z^2|}; \frac{\|w \oplus z\|}{\|x \oplus y\|}\right\}\right)$$

$$\gtrapprox \biguplus_{Q \in \bar{\mathsf{g}}} \left[f^*\left(\frac{Q(t)}{\sqrt{1 - t^2}}\right)\right]_{t=a}^{t=\vartheta} - (\Delta + \upsilon - \upsilon)^3 \tag{1}$$

For x in the open interval $]-1, 1[$ the infinite sum in Equation (2) is convergent; however, this does not hold throughout the closed interval $[-1, 1]$.

$$(1 - x)^{-k} = 1 + \sum_{j=1}^{\infty} (-1)^j \begin{Bmatrix} k \\ j \end{Bmatrix} x^j \quad \text{for } k \in \mathbb{N}; \ k \neq 0. \tag{2}$$

12-17-fig

Unicode engines

Figure 12.17: Sample page typeset with Bonum + Bonum Math fonts

Math setups for Baskerville

Figure 12.14 on page 271 was produced by loading BaskervilleF's support package with an option to get oldstyle numerals in text, and the math was set up using Michael's workhorse newtxmath with an appropriate option.

```
\usepackage[osf]{baskervillef} \usepackage[baskervillef]{newtxmath}
```

The showcases for Baskervaldx on the opposite page were produced in a similar fashion, except that we used a few more options and also deployed a different calligraphic math alphabet with the help of the mathalpha package:

```
\usepackage[osf]{Baskervaldx}   \usepackage[baskervaldx,vvarbb]{newtxmath}
\usepackage[cal=boondoxo]{mathalfa} % \mathcal from STIX, slightly slanted
```

The setup for the combination of Baskervaldx with Times in Figure 12.16 is again simpler: \usepackage{Baskervaldx,newtxmath}.

Bookman math support with Unicode engines

The Bookman (Bonum) fonts have a matching math font for Unicode engines produced by the TEX Gyre foundry. Again, we have to fix a missing glyph.

```
\usepackage{fontspec}       \setmainfont{TeX Gyre Bonum}
\usepackage{unicode-math} \setmathfont{TeX Gyre Bonum Math}
\setmathfont{KpMath}[range="2AB7,Scale=1.2] % difficult to find a good match
```

Mathematical typesetting with Cambria

First some large operators both in text: $\iiint_Q f(x, y, z)\, dx\, dy\, dz$ and $\prod_{\gamma \in \Gamma_{\widetilde{c}}} \partial(\widetilde{X}_\gamma)$; and also on display:

$$\iiiint_Q f(w, x, y, z)\, dw\, dx\, dy\, dz \leq \oint_{\partial Q} f' \left(\max \left\{ \frac{\|w\|}{|w^2 + x^2|}; \frac{\|z\|}{|y^2 + z^2|}; \frac{\|w \oplus z\|}{\|x \oplus y\|} \right\} \right)$$

$$\gtrapprox \biguplus_{Q \in \bar{Q}} \left[f^* \left(\frac{\int \mathbb{Q}(t)\, \rbrace}{\sqrt{1 - t^2}} \right) \right]_{t=\alpha}^{t=\vartheta} - (\Delta + \nu - v)^3$$

$$(1)$$

For x in the open interval $]{-}1, 1[$ the infinite sum in Equation (2) is convergent; however, this does not hold throughout the closed interval $[-1, 1]$.

$$(1 - x)^{-k} = 1 + \sum_{j=1}^{\infty} (-1)^j \left\{ \begin{matrix} k \\ j \end{matrix} \right\} x^j \quad \text{for } k \in \mathbb{N}; k \neq 0. \qquad (2)$$

12-18-fig

Unicode engines

Figure 12.18: Sample page typeset with Cambria text and math fonts

Cambria math support with Unicode engines Cambria is a font family commissioned by Microsoft. It is one of the two commercial font families described in this book, because of its excellent math support and because of the fact that, despite its commercial nature, it is available to most users because it is shipped as part of the Windows operating system and several office products on different platforms. The sample shown in Figure 12.18 was produced with the following setup:

```
\usepackage{fontspec}       \setmainfont{Cambria}
\usepackage{unicode-math} \setmathfont{Cambria Math}
```

Cambria math works well with many other transitional font families that do not have dedicated math support.

Bitstream Charter math support The Bitstream Charter fonts are best accessed through the XCharter package by Michael Sharpe, and matching math support is provided by the same author as part of his newtxmath package. For the sample in Figure 12.19 on the opposite page we used both, each with a number of options. The text fonts are slightly scaled down and use oldstyle figures, and we have slightly increased leading with \linespread.

For the math we scale the fonts slightly up, request an alternative to Charter's normal italic y, and use upright integrals and one of the alternative blackboard bold alphabets offered by the newtxmath package. This makes the setup look as follows:

```
\usepackage[scaled=.98,osf]{XCharter}     \linespread{1.04}
\usepackage[charter,scaled=1.05,alty,upint,vvarbb]{newtxmath}
```

Mathematical typesetting with Bitstream Charter

First some large operators both in text: $\iiint_Q f(x, y, z)\, dx\, dy\, dz$ and $\prod_{\gamma \in \Gamma_{\widetilde{C}}} \partial(\widetilde{X}_\gamma)$; and also on display:

$$\iiiint_Q f(w, x, y, z)\, dw\, dx\, dy\, dz \leq \oint_{\partial Q} f'\left(\max\left\{\frac{\|w\|}{|w^2 + x^2|}; \frac{\|z\|}{|y^2 + z^2|}; \frac{\|w \oplus z\|}{\|x \oplus y\|}\right\}\right)$$

$$\gtrsim \biguplus_{Q \in \bar{Q}}\left[f^*\left(\frac{\int Q(t) \backslash}{\sqrt{1 - t^2}}\right)\right]_{t=\alpha}^{t=\vartheta} - (\Delta + \nu - \upsilon)^3$$

(1)

For x in the open interval $]{-}1, 1[$ the infinite sum in Equation (2) is convergent; however, this does not hold throughout the closed interval $[-1, 1]$.

$$(1 - x)^{-k} = 1 + \sum_{j=1}^{\infty} (-1)^j \begin{Bmatrix} k \\ j \end{Bmatrix} x^j \quad \text{for } k \in \mathbb{N}; \, k \neq 0.$$

(2)

12-19-fig

Figure 12.19: Sample page typeset with XCharter text + math fonts

New Century Schoolbook has two notably different sets of matching math fonts. Figure 12.20 on the next page shows the version by Michael Sharpe, generated with the following setup: \usepackage{tgschola} \usepackage[ncf]{newtxmath}. The newtxmath package can also be used with Unicode engines. However, you need to load the text font through fontspec, as shown below: *New Century Schoolbook math support*

The second setup, exhibited in Figure 12.21, is again a work of the TEX Gyre foundry; this is how the sample was produced:

```
\usepackage{fontspec}      \setmainfont{TeX Gyre Schola}
\usepackage{unicode-math} \setmathfont{TeX Gyre Schola Math}
\setmathfont{KpMath}[range="2AB7,Scale=1.2] % difficult to find a good match
```

Page 277 shows examples of Libertine (Libertinus) by Philipp H. Poll and the math support available for it. Figure 12.22 exhibits the math fonts by Michael Sharpe; we used the following setup to produce it: *Libertinus math support*

```
\usepackage{libertinus}   \usepackage[libertine,upint]{newtxmath}
```

There is also an OpenType font to accompany Libertinus designed by Khaled Hosny. This time we used the New Computer Modern Book font (which is slightly bold) and scaled it down by 10% to replace the missing glyphs.

```
\usepackage{fontspec}      \setmainfont{Libertinus Serif}
\usepackage{unicode-math} \setmathfont{Libertinus Math}
\setmathfont {NewCMMath-Book}[range={"22D0,"2AB7},Scale=.9]
```

New Century Schoolbook text & math

First some large operators both in text: $\iiint_Q f(x,y,z)\,dx\,dy\,dz$ and $\prod_{\gamma\in\Gamma_{\widetilde{C}}}\partial(\widetilde{X}_\gamma)$; and also on display:

$$\iiiint_Q f(w,x,y,z)\,dw\,dx\,dy\,dz \le \oint_{\partial Q} f'\left(\max\left\{\frac{\|w\|}{|w^2+x^2|}; \frac{\|z\|}{|y^2+z^2|}; \frac{\|w\oplus z\|}{\|x\oplus y\|}\right\}\right)$$

$$\gtrsim \biguplus_{Q\in\bar{Q}}\left[f^*\left(\frac{\int Q(t)}{\sqrt{1-t^2}}\right)\right]_{t=a}^{t=\vartheta} - (\Delta+\nu-v)^3 \tag{1}$$

For x in the open interval $\,]{-}1,1[\,$ the infinite sum in Equation (2) is convergent; however, this does not hold throughout the closed interval $[-1,1]$.

$$(1-x)^{-k} = 1 + \sum_{j=1}^{\infty}(-1)^j\left\{{k\atop j}\right\}x^j \quad \text{for } k\in\mathbb{N};\ k\neq 0. \tag{2}$$

12-20-fig

Figure 12.20: Sample page typeset with New Century Schoolbook text + math fonts

Mathematical typesetting with Schola

First some large operators both in text: $\iiint_Q f(x,y,z)\,dx\,dy\,dz$ and $\prod_{\gamma\in\Gamma_{\widetilde{C}}}\partial(\widetilde{X}_\gamma)$; and also on display:

$$\iiiint_Q f(w,x,y,z)\,dw\,dx\,dy\,dz \le \oint_{\partial\mathbf{Q}} f'\left(\max\left\{\frac{\|w\|}{|w^2+x^2|}; \frac{\|z\|}{|y^2+z^2|}; \frac{\|w\oplus z\|}{\|x\oplus y\|}\right\}\right)$$

$$\gtrsim \biguplus_{Q\in\bar{\mathbf{Q}}}\left[f^*\left(\frac{Q(t)}{\sqrt{1-t^2}}\right)\right]_{t=a}^{t=\vartheta} - (\Delta+\nu-v)^3 \tag{1}$$

For x in the open interval $\,]{-}1,1[\,$ the infinite sum in Equation (2) is convergent; however, this does not hold throughout the closed interval $[-1,1]$.

$$(1-x)^{-k} = 1 + \sum_{j=1}^{\infty}(-1)^j\left\{{k\atop j}\right\}x^j \quad \text{for } k\in\mathbb{N};\ k\neq 0. \tag{2}$$

12-21-fig

Unicode engines

Figure 12.21: Sample page typeset with Schola + Schola Math fonts

---

Mathematical typesetting with Libertine

First some large operators both in text: $\iiint_Q f(x,y,z)\,dx\,dy\,dz$ and $\prod_{\gamma \in \Gamma_{\widehat{C}}} \partial(\widetilde{X}_\gamma)$; and also on display:

$$\iiiint_Q f(w,x,y,z)\,dw\,dx\,dy\,dz \le \oint_{\partial Q} f' \left(\max\left\{ \frac{\|w\|}{|w^2 + x^2|}; \frac{\|z\|}{|y^2 + z^2|}; \frac{\|w \oplus z\|}{\|x \oplus y\|} \right\} \right)$$

$$\gtrapprox \biguplus_{Q \in \bar{Q}} \left[f^* \left(\frac{\int Q(t)\,\ell}{\sqrt{1 - t^2}} \right) \right]_{t=\alpha}^{t=\vartheta} - (\Delta + \nu - \upsilon)^3$$

(1)

For x in the open interval $]{-1},1[$ the infinite sum in Equation (2) is convergent; however, this does not hold throughout the closed interval $[-1,1]$.

$$(1 - x)^{-k} = 1 + \sum_{j=1}^{\infty} (-1)^j \begin{Bmatrix} k \\ j \end{Bmatrix} x^j \quad \text{for } k \in \mathbb{N};\, k \ne 0.$$

(2)

Figure 12.22: Sample page typeset with Libertinus text + Libertine math fonts

---

Mathematical typesetting with Libertinus

First some large operators both in text: $\iiint_Q f(x,y,z)\,dx\,dy\,dz$ and $\prod_{\gamma \in \Gamma_{\widehat{C}}} \partial(\widetilde{X}_\gamma)$; and also on display:

$$\iiiint_Q f(w,x,y,z)\,dw\,dx\,dy\,dz \le \oint_{\partial Q} f' \left(\max\left\{ \frac{\|w\|}{|w^2 + x^2|}; \frac{\|z\|}{|y^2 + z^2|}; \frac{\|w \oplus z\|}{\|x \oplus y\|} \right\} \right)$$

$$\gtrapprox \biguplus_{Q \in \bar{Q}} \left[f^* \left(\frac{\int Q(t)\,\ell}{\sqrt{1 - t^2}} \right) \right]_{t=\alpha}^{t=\vartheta} - (\Delta + \nu - \upsilon)^3$$

(1)

For x in the open interval $]{-1},1[$ the infinite sum in Equation (2) is convergent; however, this does not hold throughout the closed interval $[-1,1]$.

$$(1 - x)^{-k} = 1 + \sum_{j=1}^{\infty} (-1)^j \begin{Bmatrix} k \\ j \end{Bmatrix} x^j \quad \text{for } k \in \mathbb{N};\, k \ne 0.$$

(2)

Unicode engines

Figure 12.23: Sample page typeset with Libertinus + Libertinus Math fonts

Mathematical typesetting with Lucida Bright

First some large operators both in text: $\iiint_{Q} f(x, y, z)\, dx\, dy\, dz$ and $\prod_{y \in \Gamma_{\tilde{c}}} \partial(\tilde{X}_y)$; and also on display:

$$\iiiint_{Q} f(w, x, y, z)\, dw\, dx\, dy\, dz \leq \oint_{\partial Q} f' \left(\max \left\{ \frac{\|w\|}{|w^2 + x^2|}; \frac{\|z\|}{|y^2 + z^2|}; \frac{\|w \oplus z\|}{\|x \oplus y\|} \right\} \right)$$

$$\gtrapprox \biguplus_{Q \in \bar{Q}} \left[f^* \left(\frac{\int Q(t)}{\sqrt{1 - t^2}} \right) \right]_{t=\alpha}^{t=\vartheta} - (\Delta + v - v)^3 \tag{1}$$

For x in the open interval $]-1, 1[$ the infinite sum in Equation (2) is convergent; however, this does not hold throughout the closed interval $[-1, 1]$.

$$(1 - x)^{-k} = 1 + \sum_{j=1}^{\infty} (-1)^j \begin{Bmatrix} k \\ j \end{Bmatrix} x^j \quad \text{for } k \in \mathbb{N}; \ k \neq 0. \tag{2}$$

12-24-fig

Figure 12.24: Sample page typeset with Lucida Bright text + Lucida Math fonts

Lucida Bright math support
Three examples of Lucida Bright and Lucida New Math fonts are exhibited on this double spread. This set of commercial text and math fonts has been designed by Charles Bigelow and Kris Holmes and can be obtained from the TeX Users Group at a reduced price for members. The font bundle covers all standard mathematical symbols including AMS additions. It can be used with all engines, but there are some differences in scope and design of individual glyphs between Type 1 and OpenType fonts.

As you will notice, the formulas run very wide, which enhances legibility at the cost of space. In this book the body font is Lucida Bright; however, for the examples we usually used Computer Modern to make them come out as in standard LaTeX.

In pdfTeX, all that you need to do to set text and math in Lucida Bright is to load the package lucidabr (with options expert and T1) — this is what we did for Figure 12.24. For ways to use only some of its text fonts, see Section 10.2.10 on page 21. By default, lucidabr scales the fonts down, and if you use the OpenType versions directly, you probably want to do that too. So here is the setup for Figure 12.25:

```
\usepackage{fontspec}     \setmainfont{Lucida Bright OT}[Scale=.95]
\usepackage{unicode-math}\setmathfont{Lucida Bright Math OT}[Scale=.95]
```

The Lucida families also contain a full demibold series, albeit only in OpenType format. These are shown for comparison in Figure 12.26. However, the demibold faces are incomplete, and again we had to substitute two characters — can you spot them?

```
\usepackage{fontspec}\setmainfont{Lucida Bright OT Demibold}[Scale=.95]
\usepackage{unicode-math}
\setmathfont{Lucida Bright Math OT Demibold}[Scale=.95]
\setmathfont{Lucida Bright Math OT}[range={"2A04,"2A0C},Scale=.95]
```

Mathematical typesetting with Lucida Bright

First some large operators both in text: $\iiint f(x,y,z)\,dx\,dy\,dz$ and $\prod_{y\in\Gamma_{\tilde{c}}}\partial(\tilde{X}_y)$; and also on display:

$$\iiiint_Q f(w,x,y,z)\,dw\,dx\,dy\,dz \leq \oint_{\partial Q} f'\left(\max\left\{\frac{\|w\|}{|w^2+x^2|};\frac{\|z\|}{|y^2+z^2|};\frac{\|w\oplus z\|}{\|x\oplus y\|}\right\}\right)$$

$$\gtrsim \biguplus_{Q\in\bar{Q}}\left[f^*\left(\frac{\mathbb{Q}(t)}{\sqrt{1-t^2}}\right)\right]_{t=\alpha}^{t=\vartheta} - (\Delta+v-v)^3$$

$$(1)$$

For x in the open interval $]-1,1[$ the infinite sum in Equation (2) is convergent; however, this does not hold throughout the closed interval $[-1,1]$.

$$(1-x)^{-k} = 1 + \sum_{j=1}^{\infty}(-1)^j\left\{{k\atop j}\right\}x^j \quad\text{for } k\in\mathbb{N}; k\neq 0. \qquad (2)$$

Unicode engines

Figure 12.25: Sample page typeset with Lucida Bright + Math fonts

Mathematics with Lucida Bright Demibold

First some large operators both in text: $\iiint f(x,y,z)\,dx\,dy\,dz$ and $\prod_{y\in\Gamma_{\tilde{c}}}\partial(\tilde{X}_y)$; and also on display:

$$\iiiint_Q f(w,x,y,z)\,dw\,dx\,dy\,dz \leq \oint_{\partial Q} f'\left(\max\left\{\frac{\|w\|}{|w^2+x^2|};\frac{\|z\|}{|y^2+z^2|};\frac{\|w\oplus z\|}{\|x\oplus y\|}\right\}\right)$$

$$\gtrsim \biguplus_{Q\in\bar{Q}}\left[f^*\left(\frac{\mathbb{Q}(t)}{\sqrt{1-t^2}}\right)\right]_{t=\alpha}^{t=\vartheta} - (\Delta+v-v)^3$$

$$(1)$$

For x in the open interval $]-1,1[$ the infinite sum in Equation (2) is convergent; however, this does not hold throughout the closed interval $[-1,1]$.

$$(1-x)^{-k} = 1 + \sum_{j=1}^{\infty}(-1)^j\left\{{k\atop j}\right\}x^j \quad\text{for } k\in\mathbb{N}; k\neq 0. \qquad (2)$$

Unicode engines

Figure 12.26: Sample page typeset with Lucida Bright Demibold + Math fonts

---

Mathematical typesetting with Times (TX)

First some large operators both in text: $\iiint_Q f(x, y, z)\, dx\, dy\, dz$ and $\prod_{\gamma \in \Gamma_{\widetilde{C}}} \partial(\widetilde{X}_\gamma)$; and also on display:

$$\iiiint_Q f(w, x, y, z)\, dw\, dx\, dy\, dz \leq \oint_{\partial Q} f' \left(\max \left\{ \frac{\|w\|}{|w^2 + x^2|}; \frac{\|z\|}{|y^2 + z^2|}; \frac{\|w \oplus z\|}{\|x \oplus y\|} \right\} \right) \tag{1}$$

$$\gtrapprox \biguplus_{Q \in \bar{Q}} \left[f^* \left(\frac{\int Q(t)}{\sqrt{1 - t^2}} \right) \right]_{t=\alpha}^{t=\vartheta} - (\Delta + \nu - v)^3$$

For x in the open interval $]-1, 1[$ the infinite sum in Equation (2) is convergent; however, this does not hold throughout the closed interval $[-1, 1]$.

$$(1 - x)^{-k} = 1 + \sum_{j=1}^{\infty} (-1)^j \begin{Bmatrix} k \\ j \end{Bmatrix} x^j \quad \text{for } k \in \mathbb{N};\ k \neq 0. \tag{2}$$

12-27-fig

Figure 12.27: Sample page typeset with Times text (Termes) + TX math fonts

Times Roman math support

    With Times Roman being one of the predominant fonts in use today, several solutions have been developed to provide support for it. This page spread and the next show five math font setups for use with Times Roman or a similar design as a body font. Figure 12.27 exhibits the TX fonts reworked by Michael Sharpe; see also Section 12.3.4 on page 243. The setup is as follows:

```
\usepackage{newtxtext} \usepackage[upint,subscriptcorrection]{newtxmath}
```

    In Figure 12.28 the TeX Gyre foundry solution is presented. One can argue that the *j* is set too tight. Here is the setup:

```
\usepackage{fontspec}      \setmainfont{TeX Gyre Termes}
\usepackage{unicode-math} \setmathfont{TeX Gyre Termes Math}
\setmathfont{KpMath}[range="2AB7]    % ok without scaling this time
```

    Figure 12.29 shows fonts by Khaled Hosny based on STIX version 1 with smaller running length compared to STIX 2. All fonts based on STIX implement the full range of mathematical symbols including boldface variants, so no substitutions are needed.

```
\usepackage{fontspec}      \setmainfont{XITS}
\usepackage{unicode-math} \setmathfont{XITS Math}
```

In Figure 12.30 on page 282 we have Michael Sharpe's setup for the STIX 2 fonts:

```
\usepackage[p,osf]{stickstootext} \usepackage[stix2,vvarbb]{newtxmath}
```

and Figure 12.31 shows the OpenType version of the fonts:

```
\usepackage{fontspec}      \setmainfont{STIX Two Text}
\usepackage{unicode-math} \setmathfont{STIX Two Math Regular}
```

Mathematical typesetting with Termes

First some large operators both in text: $\iiint_Q f(x, y, z) \, dx \, dy \, dz$ and $\prod_{\gamma \in \Gamma_{\tilde{C}}} \partial(\tilde{X}_\gamma)$; and also on display:

$$\iiiint_Q f(w, x, y, z) \, dw \, dx \, dy \, dz \le \oint_{\partial Q} f' \left(\max \left\{ \frac{\|w\|}{|w^2 + x^2|}; \frac{\|z\|}{|y^2 + z^2|}; \frac{\|w \oplus z\|}{\|x \oplus y\|} \right\} \right)$$

$$\gtrsim \biguplus_{Q \in \bar{Q}} \left[f^* \left(\frac{Q(t)}{\sqrt{1 - t^2}} \right) \right]_{t=\alpha}^{t=\vartheta} - (\Delta + \nu - v)^3$$

(1)

For x in the open interval $]-1, 1[$ the infinite sum in Equation (2) is convergent; however, this does not hold throughout the closed interval $[-1, 1]$.

$$(1 - x)^{-k} = 1 + \sum_{j=1}^{\infty} (-1)^j \left\{ {k \atop j} \right\} x^j \quad \text{for } k \in \mathbb{N}; \; k \ne 0.$$

(2)

12-28-fig

Unicode engines

Figure 12.28: Sample page typeset with Termes + Termes Math fonts

Mathematical typesetting with XITS

First some large operators both in text: $\iiint_Q f(x, y, z) \, dx \, dy \, dz$ and $\prod_{\gamma \in \Gamma_{\tilde{C}}} \partial(\tilde{X}_\gamma)$; and also on display:

$$\iiiint_Q f(w, x, y, z) \, dw \, dx \, dy \, dz \le \oint_{\partial Q} f' \left(\max \left\{ \frac{\|w\|}{|w^2 + x^2|}; \frac{\|z\|}{|y^2 + z^2|}; \frac{\|w \oplus z\|}{\|x \oplus y\|} \right\} \right)$$

$$\gtrsim \biguplus_{Q \in \bar{Q}} \left[f^* \left(\frac{\lceil Q(t) \rceil}{\sqrt{1 - t^2}} \right) \right]_{t=\alpha}^{t=\vartheta} - (\Delta + \nu - v)^3$$

(1)

For x in the open interval $]-1, 1[$ the infinite sum in Equation (2) is convergent; however, this does not hold throughout the closed interval $[-1, 1]$.

$$(1 - x)^{-k} = 1 + \sum_{j=1}^{\infty} (-1)^j \left\{ {k \atop j} \right\} x^j \quad \text{for } k \in \mathbb{N}; \; k \ne 0.$$

(2)

12-29-fig

Unicode engines

Figure 12.29: Sample page typeset with XITS + XITS Math fonts

Mathematical typesetting with STIX 2

First some large operators both in text: $\iiint_Q f(x,y,z)\,dx\,dy\,dz$ and $\prod_{\gamma\in\Gamma_{\tilde{C}}}\partial(\widetilde{X}_\gamma)$; and also on display:

$$\iiiint_Q f(w,x,y,z)\,dw\,dx\,dy\,dz \le \oint_{\partial Q} f'\left(\max\left\{\frac{\|w\|}{|w^2+x^2|};\frac{\|z\|}{|y^2+z^2|};\frac{\|w\oplus z\|}{\|x\oplus y\|}\right\}\right)$$

$$\gtrapprox \biguplus_{Q\in\bar{Q}}\left[f^*\left(\frac{\int Q(t)}{\sqrt{1-t^2}}\right)\right]_{t=\alpha}^{t=\vartheta} - (\Delta+\nu-\upsilon)^3 \tag{1}$$

For x in the open interval $]-1,1[$ the infinite sum in Equation (2) is convergent; however, this does not hold throughout the closed interval $[-1,1]$.

$$(1-x)^{-k} = 1 + \sum_{j=1}^{\infty}(-1)^j\begin{Bmatrix}k\\j\end{Bmatrix}x^j \quad \text{for } k\in\mathbb{N}; k\ne 0. \tag{2}$$

12-30-fig

Figure 12.30: Sample page typeset with STIX 2 using package stickstootext

Mathematical typesetting with STIX 2

First some large operators both in text: $\iiint_Q f(x,y,z)\,dx\,dy\,dz$ and $\prod_{\gamma\in\Gamma_{\tilde{C}}}\partial(\widetilde{X}_\gamma)$; and also on display:

$$\iiiint_Q f(w,x,y,z)\,dw\,dx\,dy\,dz \le \oint_{\partial Q} f'\left(\max\left\{\frac{\|w\|}{|w^2+x^2|};\frac{\|z\|}{|y^2+z^2|};\frac{\|w\oplus z\|}{\|x\oplus y\|}\right\}\right)$$

$$\gtrapprox \biguplus_{Q\in\bar{Q}}\left[f^*\left(\frac{\int Q(t)}{\sqrt{1-t^2}}\right)\right]_{t=\alpha}^{t=\vartheta} - (\Delta+\nu-\upsilon)^3 \tag{1}$$

For x in the open interval $]-1,1[$ the infinite sum in Equation (2) is convergent; however, this does not hold throughout the closed interval $[-1,1]$.

$$(1-x)^{-k} = 1 + \sum_{j=1}^{\infty}(-1)^j\begin{Bmatrix}k\\j\end{Bmatrix}x^j \quad \text{for } k\in\mathbb{N}; k\ne 0. \tag{2}$$

12-31-fig

Unicode engines

Figure 12.31: Sample page typeset with STIX 2 text + math fonts

Mathematical typesetting with Utopia (Erewhon)

First some large operators both in text: $\iiint_Q f(x, y, z)\, dx\, dy\, dz$ and $\prod_{\gamma \in \Gamma_{\widetilde{C}}} \partial(\widetilde{X}_\gamma)$; and also on display:

$$\iiiint_Q f(w, x, y, z)\, dw\, dx\, dy\, dz \leq \oint_{\partial Q} f'\left(\max\left\{\frac{\|w\|}{|w^2 + x^2|}; \frac{\|z\|}{|y^2 + z^2|}; \frac{\|w \oplus z\|}{\|x \oplus y\|}\right\}\right)$$

$$\gtrless \biguplus_{Q \in \bar{Q}}\left[f^*\left(\frac{\int Q(t)}{\sqrt{1 - t^2}}\right)\right]_{t=\alpha}^{t=\vartheta} - (\Delta + \nu - \upsilon)^3 \tag{1}$$

For x in the open interval $]-1, 1[$ the infinite sum in Equation (2) is convergent; however, this does not hold throughout the closed interval $[-1, 1]$.

$$(1 - x)^{-k} = 1 + \sum_{j=1}^{\infty} (-1)^j \left\{\begin{matrix} k \\ j \end{matrix}\right\} x^j \quad \text{for } k \in \mathbb{N}; k \neq 0. \tag{2}$$

12-32-fig

Figure 12.32: Sample page typeset with Erewhon text + math fonts

Adobe Utopia, originally designed by Robert Slimbach, due to its open source license, has been extended by several people; see Section 10.5.23 on page 58. Math support for these fonts, as often, is available through Michael Sharpe's newtxmath package. It works equally well with the different versions of Utopia, e.g., Heuristica or Linguistics Pro. For Figure 12.32 we have used the following setup deploying Erewhon as the text font:

Utopia math support

```
\usepackage[osf]{erewhon}
\usepackage[utopia,vvarbb]{newtxmath}
```

If you want to use the math setup with other fonts, you may need to scale the text fonts a bit down or the math fonts up to get a perfect fit, e.g., for Heuristica:

```
\usepackage[osf,scaled=.92]{heuristica}
\usepackage[utopia,vvarbb]{newtxmath}
```

There is also the Fourier-GUT*enberg* bundle by Michel Bovani, which is also based on Adobe Utopia. It sets up both text and math fonts and is intended as a self-contained solution (automatically loading amsmath and other packages); in particular it offers "french-style" mathematics if loaded with the option upright, e.g.,

```
\usepackage[upright]{fourier}
```

12.5.3 Didone serif fonts with math support

The majority of LaTeX documents are typeset using Didone fonts simply because LaTeX's standard fonts, Computer Modern, are Didone designs and because not so long ago these were the only fonts that could be used, if decent math support was needed — the current chapter shows that those days are history.

Computer Modern — LaTeX's math default

Figure 12.33 shows our example page using LaTeX's default setup when using pdfTeX. This is a repeat of Figure 12.1 from the beginning of the section to make it easier to compare it to other fonts in this section.

> **Unicode engines**
>
> When you use a Unicode engine without loading any math support package, then LaTeX keeps the math setup (i.e., Computer Modern), but it changes the text fonts to Latin Modern.

Latin Modern math support

To use Latin Modern Math, designed by Bogusław Jackowski and Janusz Marian Nowacki (1951–2020), in pdfTeX, the following setup is sufficient:

```
\usepackage{lmodern}
```

The result is shown in Figure 12.34 (and is, not surprisingly, very similar to Computer Modern). Figure 12.35 then exhibits the OpenType fonts of LM:

```
\usepackage{fontspec}      \setmainfont{Latin Modern Roman}
\usepackage{unicode-math}  \setmathfont{Latin Modern Math}
\setmathfont{NewCMMath-Regular}[range="2AB7]
```

Mathematical typesetting with Computer Modern

First some large operators both in text: $\iiint_Q f(x,y,z)\,dx\,dy\,dz$ and $\prod_{\gamma \in \Gamma_{\tilde{C}}} \partial(\widetilde{X}_\gamma)$; and also on display:

$$\iiiint_Q f(w,x,y,z)\,dw\,dx\,dy\,dz \leq \oint_{\partial Q} f'\left(\max\left\{\frac{\|w\|}{|w^2+x^2|};\frac{\|z\|}{|y^2+z^2|};\frac{\|w \oplus z\|}{\|x \oplus y\|}\right\}\right)$$

$$\precapprox \biguplus_{Q \in \bar{Q}} \left[f^*\left(\frac{\int Q(t)}{\sqrt{1-t^2}}\right)\right]_{t=\alpha}^{t=\vartheta} - (\Delta + \nu - v)^3 \tag{1}$$

For x in the open interval $]-1,1[$ the infinite sum in Equation (2) is convergent; however, this does not hold throughout the closed interval $[-1,1]$.

$$(1-x)^{-k} = 1 + \sum_{j=1}^{\infty}(-1)^j\begin{Bmatrix}k\\j\end{Bmatrix}x^j \quad \text{for } k \in \mathbb{N};\ k \neq 0. \tag{2}$$

12-33-fig

Figure 12.33: Sample page typeset with Computer Modern text + math fonts

---

Mathematical typesetting with Latin Modern

First some large operators both in text: $\iiint_Q f(x, y, z)\, dx\, dy\, dz$ and $\prod_{\gamma \in \Gamma_{\widetilde{C}}} \partial(\widetilde{X}_\gamma)$; and also on display:

$$\iiiint_Q f(w, x, y, z)\, dw\, dx\, dy\, dz \leq \oint_{\partial Q} f' \left(\max \left\{ \frac{\|w\|}{|w^2 + x^2|}; \frac{\|z\|}{|y^2 + z^2|}; \frac{\|w \oplus z\|}{\|x \oplus y\|} \right\} \right)$$

$$\gtrapprox \biguplus_{Q \in \bar{Q}} \left[f^* \left(\frac{\int Q(t)}{\sqrt{1 - t^2}} \right) \right]_{t=\alpha}^{t=\vartheta} - (\Delta + \nu - v)^3$$

$$(1)$$

For x in the open interval $]-1, 1[$ the infinite sum in Equation (2) is convergent; however, this does not hold throughout the closed interval $[-1, 1]$.

$$(1 - x)^{-k} = 1 + \sum_{j=1}^{\infty} (-1)^j \left\{ {k \atop j} \right\} x^j \quad \text{for } k \in \mathbb{N};\ k \neq 0. \tag{2}$$

12-34-fig

Figure 12.34: Sample page typeset with Latin Modern text + math fonts

---

Mathematical typesetting with Latin Modern

First some large operators both in text: $\iiint_Q f(x, y, z)\, dx\, dy\, dz$ and $\prod_{\gamma \in \Gamma_{\widetilde{C}}} \partial(\widetilde{X}_\gamma)$; and also on display:

$$\iiiint_Q f(w, x, y, z)\, dw\, dx\, dy\, dz \leq \oint_{\partial Q} f' \left(\max \left\{ \frac{\|w\|}{|w^2 + x^2|}; \frac{\|z\|}{|y^2 + z^2|}; \frac{\|w \oplus z\|}{\|x \oplus y\|} \right\} \right)$$

$$\gtrapprox \biguplus_{Q \in \bar{Q}} \left[f^* \left(\frac{Q(t)}{\sqrt{1 - t^2}} \right) \right]_{t=\alpha}^{t=\vartheta} - (\Delta + \nu - v)^3$$

$$(1)$$

For x in the open interval $]-1, 1[$ the infinite sum in Equation (2) is convergent; however, this does not hold throughout the closed interval $[-1, 1]$.

$$(1 - x)^{-k} = 1 + \sum_{j=1}^{\infty} (-1)^j \left\{ {k \atop j} \right\} x^j \quad \text{for } k \in \mathbb{N};\ k \neq 0. \tag{2}$$

12-35-fig

Unicode engines

Figure 12.35: Sample page typeset with Latin Modern + Latin Modern Math fonts

Mathematical typesetting with NewComputerModern

First some large operators both in text: $\iiint_Q f(x,y,z)\,dx\,dy\,dz$ and $\prod_{\gamma\in\Gamma_{\widetilde{C}}}\partial(\widetilde{X}_\gamma)$; and also on display:

$$\iiiint_Q f(w,x,y,z)\,dw\,dx\,dy\,dz \leq \oint_{\partial\mathbf{Q}} f'\left(\max\left\{\frac{\|w\|}{|w^2+x^2|};\frac{\|z\|}{|y^2+z^2|};\frac{\|w\oplus z\|}{\|x\oplus y\|}\right\}\right)$$

$$\gtrsim \biguplus_{Q\in\bar{\mathbf{Q}}}\left[f^*\left(\frac{\int Q(t)\wr}{\sqrt{1-t^2}}\right)\right]_{t=\alpha}^{t=\vartheta} - (\Delta+\nu-v)^3 \tag{1}$$

For x in the open interval $]-1,1[$ the infinite sum in Equation (2) is convergent; however, this does not hold throughout the closed interval $[-1,1]$.

$$(1-x)^{-k} = 1 + \sum_{j=1}^{\infty}(-1)^j\left\{{k\atop j}\right\}x^j \quad \text{for } k\in\mathbb{N};\ k\neq 0. \tag{2}$$

12-36-fig

Unicode engines

Figure 12.36: Sample page typeset with NewComputerModern + Math fonts

Mathematical typesetting with NewComputerModern

First some large operators both in text: $\iiint_Q f(x,y,z)\,dx\,dy\,dz$ and $\prod_{\gamma\in\Gamma_{\widetilde{C}}}\partial(\widetilde{X}_\gamma)$; and also on display:

$$\iiiint_Q f(w,x,y,z)\,dw\,dx\,dy\,dz \leq \oint_{\partial\mathbf{Q}} f'\left(\max\left\{\frac{\|w\|}{|w^2+x^2|};\frac{\|z\|}{|y^2+z^2|};\frac{\|w\oplus z\|}{\|x\oplus y\|}\right\}\right)$$

$$\gtrsim \biguplus_{Q\in\bar{\mathbf{Q}}}\left[f^*\left(\frac{\int Q(t)\wr}{\sqrt{1-t^2}}\right)\right]_{t=\alpha}^{t=\vartheta} - (\Delta+\nu-v)^3 \tag{1}$$

For x in the open interval $]-1,1[$ the infinite sum in Equation (2) is convergent; however, this does not hold throughout the closed interval $[-1,1]$.

$$(1-x)^{-k} = 1 + \sum_{j=1}^{\infty}(-1)^j\left\{{k\atop j}\right\}x^j \quad \text{for } k\in\mathbb{N};\ k\neq 0. \tag{2}$$

12-37-fig

Unicode engines

Figure 12.37: Sample page typeset with NewComputerModern Book + Math fonts

---

Mathematical typesetting with Noto Serif

First some large operators both in text: $\iiint_Q f(x, y, z)\, dx\, dy\, dz$ and $\prod_{y \in \Gamma_{\tilde{c}}} \partial(\widetilde{X}_y)$; and also on display:

$$\iiiint_Q f(w, x, y, z)\, dw\, dx\, dy\, dz \leq \oint_{\partial Q} f' \left(\max \left\{ \frac{\|w\|}{|w^2 + x^2|}; \frac{\|z\|}{|y^2 + z^2|}; \frac{\|w \oplus z\|}{\|x \oplus y\|} \right\} \right)$$

$$\gtrapprox \biguplus_{Q \in \bar{Q}} \left[f^* \left(\frac{\int Q(t)}{\sqrt{1 - t^2}} \right) \right]_{t=\alpha}^{t=\vartheta} - (\Delta + \nu - \nu)^3 \tag{1}$$

For x in the open interval $]-1, 1[$ the infinite sum in Equation (2) is convergent; however, this does not hold throughout the closed interval $[-1, 1]$.

$$(1 - x)^{-k} = 1 + \sum_{j=1}^{\infty} (-1)^j \begin{Bmatrix} k \\ j \end{Bmatrix} x^j \quad \text{for } k \in \mathbb{N}; k \neq 0. \tag{2}$$

Figure 12.38: Sample page typeset with Noto text + math fonts

The New Computer Modern OpenType family by Antonis Tsolomitis is the new kid on the block when it comes to designs that are based on or mimic Donald Knuth's Computer Modern family. Antonis is working very hard on making his family usable across various disciplines by adding more and more glyphs to support various scripts and languages. At the time of writing the Roman font contained 3171 glyphs and the math support font a whopping 6938 and I would not be surprised if there are many more by the time you hold this book in your hands — check it by using `unicodefont.tex`, but make sure to set `range-end` to FFFFF to get to all characters.

Math setup for New Computer Modern

Figure 12.36 on the facing page has been produced by this input:

```
\usepackage{fontspec}      \setmainfont{NewCM10-Regular}
\usepackage{unicode-math} \setmathfont{NewCMMath-Regular}
```

The slightly darker Book version in Figure 12.37 was generated with:

```
\usepackage{fontspec}      \setmainfont{NewCM10-Book}
\usepackage{unicode-math} \setmathfont{NewCMMath-Book}
```

The last Didone family we exhibit in Figure 12.38 is Noto Serif. The math support is again courtesy of Michael Sharpe, this time through his notomath package; see Section 12.3.7 on page 252. We used the following setup:

Not Serif math support

```
\usepackage[vvarbb,upint]{notomath}
```

12.5.4 Slab serif fonts with math support

Math support for Concrete Roman

The Concrete Roman text fonts were designed by Donald Knuth, and matching math fonts were designed by Ulrik Vieth; see Section 12.3.1. They are shown in Figure 12.39, which was produced by adding `\usepackage[boldsans]{ccfonts}` to the preamble of the sample document.

Figure 12.40 combines Concrete Roman with Euler Math, designed by Hermann Zapf (1918–2015). This combination was produced with

```
\usepackage{ccfonts}     \usepackage[euler-digits]{eulervm}
```

See also Section 12.3.3. You probably want to design different headings: because the Concrete fonts have no bold series, the heading in the example shows a larger size of the medium series, though substitution.

Math support for DejaVu

The other Slab serif family with math support is DejaVu, again provided by the TeX Gyre foundry. The design size is rather large, so we scaled everything down for Figure 12.41. Given that the font is fairly black we used a bold symbol from the Kp math font to supply the missing glyph. Not perfect, but …

```
\usepackage{fontspec}    \setmainfont{DejaVu Serif}[Scale=.9]
\usepackage{unicode-math} \setmathfont{TeX Gyre DejaVu Math}[Scale=.95]
\setmathfont{KpMath-Bold}[range="2AB7,Scale=.97]        % more or less ok
```

Mathematical typesetting with Concrete

First some large operators both in text: $\iiint_Q f(x,y,z)\,dx\,dy\,dz$ and $\prod_{\gamma\in\Gamma_{\underset{\sim}{C}}}\partial(\widetilde{X}_\gamma)$; and also on display:

$$\iiiint_Q f(w,x,y,z)\,dw\,dx\,dy\,dz \leq \oint_{\partial Q} f'\left(\max\left\{\frac{\|w\|}{|w^2+x^2|}; \frac{\|z\|}{|y^2+z^2|}; \frac{\|w\oplus z\|}{\|x\oplus y\|}\right\}\right)$$

$$\gtrsim \biguplus_{Q\in\bar{Q}}\left[f^*\left(\frac{\int Q(t)}{\sqrt{1-t^2}}\right)\right]_{t=\alpha}^{t=\vartheta} - (\Delta+\nu-v)^3 \tag{1}$$

For x in the open interval $]-1,1[$ the infinite sum in Equation (2) is convergent; however, this does not hold throughout the closed interval $[-1,1]$.

$$(1-x)^{-k} = 1 + \sum_{j=1}^{\infty}(-1)^j\begin{Bmatrix}k\\j\end{Bmatrix}x^j \quad\text{for } k\in\mathbb{N};\ k\neq 0. \tag{2}$$

12-39-fig

Figure 12.39: Sample page typeset with Concrete text + math fonts

Mathematical typesetting with Concrete and Euler

First some large operators both in text: $\iiint_Q f(x,y,z)\,dx\,dy\,dz$ and $\prod_{\gamma\in\Gamma_{\widetilde{C}}}\partial(\widetilde{X}_\gamma)$; and also on display:

$$\iiiint_Q f(w,x,y,z)\,dw\,dx\,dy\,dz \leqslant \oint_{\partial Q} f'\left(\max\left\{\frac{\|w\|}{|w^2+x^2|};\frac{\|z\|}{|y^2+z^2|};\frac{\|w\oplus z\|}{\|x\oplus y\|}\right\}\right)$$

$$\precsim \biguplus_{Q\in\bar{Q}}\left[f^*\left(\frac{\int Q(t)}{\sqrt{1-t^2}}\right)\right]_{t=\alpha}^{t=\vartheta}-(\Delta+\nu-\upsilon)^3 \tag{1}$$

For x in the open interval $]{-}1,1[$ the infinite sum in Equation (2) is convergent; however, this does not hold throughout the closed interval $[-1,1]$.

$$(1-x)^{-k}=1+\sum_{j=1}^{\infty}(-1)^j\left\{{k\atop j}\right\}x^j \quad \text{for } k\in\mathbb{N};\ k\neq 0. \tag{2}$$

Figure 12.40: Sample page typeset with Concrete text + Euler math fonts

Mathematical typesetting with DejaVu

First some large operators both in text: $\iiint_{\bar{Q}} f(x,y,z)\,dx\,dy\,dz$ and $\prod_{\gamma\in\Gamma_{\widetilde{C}}}\partial(\widetilde{X}_\gamma)$; and also on display:

$$\iiiint_Q f(w,x,y,z)\,dw\,dx\,dy\,dz \leq \oint_{\partial Q} f'\left(\max\left\{\frac{\|w\|}{|w^2+x^2|};\frac{\|z\|}{|y^2+z^2|};\frac{\|w\oplus z\|}{\|x\oplus y\|}\right\}\right)$$

$$\precsim \biguplus_{Q\in\bar{Q}}\left[f^*\left(\frac{Q(t)}{\sqrt{1-t^2}}\right)\right]_{t=\alpha}^{t=\vartheta}-(\Delta+\nu-\upsilon)^3 \tag{1}$$

For x in the open interval $]{-}1,1[$ the infinite sum in Equation (2) is convergent; however, this does not hold throughout the closed interval $[-1,1]$.

$$(1-x)^{-k}=1+\sum_{j=1}^{\infty}(-1)^j\left\{{k\atop j}\right\}x^j \quad \text{for } k\in\mathbb{N};\ k\neq 0. \tag{2}$$

Unicode engines

Figure 12.41: Sample page typeset with DejaVu + DejaVu Math fonts

12.5.5 Sans serif fonts with math support

Math support for Computer Modern Bright

Figure 12.42 shows the Computer Modern Bright set of fonts (designed by Walter Schmidt (1960–2021)), which is based on the Computer Modern font design. The solution offers the full range of math symbols in normal and bold weights and is activated by loading the cmbright package; see Section 12.3.2.

Math support for Fira Sans

Xiangdong Zeng developed a Fira Math font based on FiraSans and FiraGo. As with many of the OpenType Math fonts there are some glyphs missing, and finding a suitable substitute font proved to be difficult. In Figure 12.43, I used bold Kp Math scaled down by 30% for \precapprox and 10% for \biguplus and \Subset.

```
\usepackage{fontspec}      \setmainfont{Fira Sans}
\usepackage{unicode-math} \setmathfont{Fira Math}
\setmathfont{KpMath-Bold}[range="2AB7,Scale=.75]   % not a good match
\setmathfont{KpMath-Bold}[range={"2A04,"22D0},Scale=.9]
```

This clearly shows limitations of the approach: \precapprox is still too wide and at the same time too thin. Thus, if you cannot find a suitable substitute and you need the symbols, it is probably better to use a different font setup.

Math support for GFS Neo-Hellenic

The GFS Neo-Hellenic, designed in 1927 by Victor Scholderer (see Section 10.8.14 on page 75), has a matching OpenType math font, which was commissioned in 2018, but there is no support for math in pdfTeX. To use the OpenType fonts, all you have to do is to load a support package, which does the necessary setup for you, i.e.,

```
\usepackage{gfsneohellenicot}
```

Mathematical typesetting with CM Bright

First some large operators both in text: $\iiint_{\mathcal{Q}} f(x, y, z)\, dx\, dy\, dz$ and $\prod_{\gamma \in \Gamma_{\tilde{c}}} \partial(\widetilde{X}_\gamma)$; and also on display:

$$\iiiint_Q f(w, x, y, z)\, dw\, dx\, dy\, dz \leq \oint_{\partial Q} f'\left(\max\left\{\frac{\|w\|}{|w^2 + x^2|}; \frac{\|z\|}{|y^2 + z^2|}; \frac{\|w \oplus z\|}{\|x \oplus y\|}\right\}\right)$$

$$\gtrapprox \biguplus_{Q \in \bar{Q}} \left[f^*\left(\frac{\int \mathbb{Q}(t)}{\sqrt{1 - t^2}}\right)\right]_{t=\alpha}^{t=\vartheta} - (\Delta + \nu - v)^3 \tag{1}$$

For x in the open interval $]-1, 1[$ the infinite sum in Equation (2) is convergent; however, this does not hold throughout the closed interval $[-1, 1]$.

$$(1 - x)^{-k} = 1 + \sum_{j=1}^{\infty} (-1)^j \left\{ \begin{matrix} k \\ j \end{matrix} \right\} x^j \quad \text{for } k \in \mathbb{N};\ k \neq 0. \tag{2}$$

12-42-fi

Figure 12.42: Sample page typeset with CM Bright text + math fonts

Mathematical typesetting with Fira Sans

First some large operators both in text: $\iiint_Q f(x,y,z)\,dx\,dy\,dz$ and $\prod_{\gamma \in \Gamma_{\tilde{c}}} \partial(\tilde{X}_\gamma)$; and also on display:

$$\iiiint_Q f(w,x,y,z)\,dw\,dx\,dy\,dz \le \oint_{\partial Q} f'\left(\max\left\{\frac{\|w\|}{|w^2+x^2|}; \frac{\|z\|}{|y^2+z^2|}; \frac{\|w \oplus z\|}{\|x \oplus y\|}\right\}\right)$$

$$\gtrapprox \biguplus_{Q \in \tilde{Q}}\left[f^*\left(\frac{Q(t)}{\sqrt{1-t^2}}\right)\right]_{t=\alpha}^{t=\vartheta} - (\Delta + v - v)^3$$

(1)

For x in the open interval $]{-}1,1[$ the infinite sum in Equation (2) is convergent; however, this does not hold throughout the closed interval $[-1,1]$.

$$(1-x)^{-k} = 1 + \sum_{j=1}^{\infty}(-1)^j\begin{Bmatrix}k\\j\end{Bmatrix}x^j \quad \text{for } k \in \mathbb{N};\ k \ne 0.$$

(2)

12-43-fig

Figure 12.43: Sample page typeset with Fira Sans + Fira Math fonts

Mathematical typesetting with **GFS Neo-Hellenic**

First some large operators both in text: $\iiint_Q f(x,y,z)\,dx\,dy\,dz$ and $\prod_{\gamma \in \Gamma_{\tilde{c}}} \partial(\tilde{X}_\gamma)$; and also on display:

$$\iiiint_Q f(w,x,y,z)\,dw\,dx\,dy\,dz \le \oint_{\partial Q} f'\left(\max\left\{\frac{\|w\|}{|w^2+x^2|}; \frac{\|z\|}{|y^2+z^2|}; \frac{\|w \oplus z\|}{\|x \oplus y\|}\right\}\right)$$

$$\gtrapprox \biguplus_{Q \in \mathbf{Q}}\left[f^*\left(\frac{Q(t)}{\sqrt{1-t^2}}\right)\right]_{t=\alpha}^{t=\vartheta} - (\Delta + \nu - v)^3$$

(1)

For x in the open interval $]{-}1,1[$ the infinite sum in Equation (2) is convergent; however, this does not hold throughout the closed interval $[-1,1]$.

$$(1-x)^{-k} = 1 + \sum_{j=1}^{\infty}(-1)^j\begin{Bmatrix}k\\j\end{Bmatrix}x^j \quad \text{for } k \in \mathbb{N};\ k \ne 0.$$

(2)

12-44-fig

Figure 12.44: Sample page typeset with GFS Neo-Hellenic text + math fonts

Mathematical typesetting with Iwona

First some large operators both in text: $\iiint_Q f(x,y,z)\,dx\,dy\,dz$ and $\prod_{\gamma\in\Gamma_{\tilde{c}}}\partial(\tilde{X}_\gamma)$; and also on display:

$$\iiiint_Q f(w,x,y,z)\,dw\,dx\,dy\,dz \le \oint_{\partial Q} f'\left(\max\left\{\frac{\|w\|}{|w^2+x^2|};\frac{\|z\|}{|y^2+z^2|};\frac{\|w\oplus z\|}{\|x\oplus y\|}\right\}\right)$$

$$\gtrapprox \biguplus_{Q\in\tilde{Q}}\left[f^*\left(\frac{\int Q(t)}{\sqrt{1-t^2}}\right)\right]_{t=\alpha}^{t=\vartheta} - (\Delta+v-v)^3$$

$$(1)$$

For x in the open interval $]{-}1,1[$ the infinite sum in Equation (2) is convergent; however, this does not hold throughout the closed interval $[-1,1]$.

$$(1-x)^{-k} = 1 + \sum_{j=1}^{\infty}(-1)^j\left\{{k\atop j}\right\}x^j \quad \text{for } k\in\mathbb{N};\ k\neq 0. \tag{2}$$

12-45-fig

Figure 12.45: Sample page typeset with Iwona text + math fonts

Mathematical typesetting with Iwona Light Condensed

First some large operators both in text: $\iiint_Q f(x,y,z)\,dx\,dy\,dz$ and $\prod_{\gamma\in\Gamma_{\tilde{c}}}\partial(\tilde{X}_\gamma)$; and also on display:

$$\iiiint_Q f(w,x,y,z)\,dw\,dx\,dy\,dz \le \oint_{\partial Q} f'\left(\max\left\{\frac{\|w\|}{|w^2+x^2|};\frac{\|z\|}{|y^2+z^2|};\frac{\|w\oplus z\|}{\|x\oplus y\|}\right\}\right)$$

$$\gtrapprox \biguplus_{Q\in\tilde{Q}}\left[f^*\left(\frac{\int Q(t)}{\sqrt{1-t^2}}\right)\right]_{t=\alpha}^{t=\vartheta} - (\Delta+v-v)^3$$

$$(1)$$

For x in the open interval $]{-}1,1[$ the infinite sum in Equation (2) is convergent; however, this does not hold throughout the closed interval $[-1,1]$.

$$(1-x)^{-k} = 1 + \sum_{j=1}^{\infty}(-1)^j\left\{{k\atop j}\right\}x^j \quad \text{for } k\in\mathbb{N};\ k\neq 0. \tag{2}$$

12-46-fig

Figure 12.46: Sample page typeset with Iwona text + math fonts

Mathematical typesetting with Kp Sans

First some large operators both in text: $\iiint_Q f(x,y,z)\,dx\,dy\,dz$ and $\prod_{\gamma \in \Gamma_{\widetilde{C}}} \partial(\widetilde{X}_\gamma)$; and also on display:

$$\iiiint_Q f(w,x,y,z)\,dw\,dx\,dy\,dz \le \oint_{\partial Q} f'\left(\max\left\{\frac{\|w\|}{|w^2+x^2|}; \frac{\|z\|}{|y^2+z^2|}; \frac{\|w \oplus z\|}{\|x \oplus y\|}\right\}\right)$$

$$\gtrapprox \biguplus_{Q \in \bar{Q}}\left[f^*\left(\frac{\int Q(t)}{\sqrt{1-t^2}}\right)\right]_{t=\alpha}^{t=\vartheta} - (\Delta + \nu - v)^3$$

(1)

For x in the open interval $]{-}1,1[$ the infinite sum in Equation (2) is convergent; however, this does not hold throughout the closed interval $[-1,1]$.

$$(1-x)^{-k} = 1 + \sum_{j=1}^{\infty} (-1)^j \begin{Bmatrix} k \\ j \end{Bmatrix} x^j \quad \text{for } k \in \mathbb{N};\ k \ne 0.$$

(2)

12-47-fig

Figure 12.47: Sample page typeset with Kp Sans text + math fonts

The Iwona fonts, designed by Janusz Marian Nowacki (1951–2020), are provided in several font series (see Section 10.8.18 on page 77), and for all them there is matching math support if you add the option `math` when loading the iwona support package. For example, Figure 12.46 used

Math support for Iwona

```
\usepackage[math,light,condensed]{iwona}
```

to produce the light condensed setup. Unfortunately, all fonts miss the smallest glyph of the extensible delimiters \lVert and \rVert (normally slot "6B in the `symbols` math font), most likely a simple oversight by the author. Thus, to make our sample documents work, we also had to provide it from a different source and update the delimiter declarations as follows:

```
\DeclareSymbolFont{symbols2}{OMS}{cmsy}{m}{n}
\SetSymbolFont{symbols2}    {bold}{OMS}{cmsy}{b}{n}
\DeclareMathDelimiter{\lVert}{\mathopen} {symbols2}{"6B}{largesymbols}{"0D}
\DeclareMathDelimiter{\rVert}{\mathclose}{symbols2}{"6B}{largesymbols}{"0D}
```

For details on the above declarations see Section 9.8.5 on page →I 749.

Using Kp Sans as the body font to produce Figure 12.47 is as simple as loading the package kpfonts with the option `sfmath`, or, if you want to use OpenType fonts in Unicode engines, the package kpfonts-otf. There are many more package options available to adjust the setup; see Section 10.2.8 on page 17 for more details.

Math support for Kp Sans

Mathematical typesetting with Kurier

First some large operators both in text: $\iiint_Q f(x, y, z)\, dx\, dy\, dz$ and $\prod_{\gamma \in \Gamma_{\tilde{c}}} \partial(\tilde{X}_\gamma)$; and also on display:

$$\iiiint_Q f(w, x, y, z)\, dw\, dx\, dy\, dz \leq \oint_{\partial Q} f' \left(\max \left\{ \frac{\|w\|}{|w^2 + x^2|}; \frac{\|z\|}{|y^2 + z^2|}; \frac{\|w \oplus z\|}{\|x \oplus y\|} \right\} \right)$$

$$\approx \biguplus_{Q \in \tilde{Q}} \left[f^* \left(\frac{\int Q(t)}{\sqrt{1 - t^2}} \right) \right]_{t=\alpha}^{t=\vartheta} - (\Delta + v - v)^3$$

(1)

For x in the open interval $]-1, 1[$ the infinite sum in Equation (2) is convergent; however, this does not hold throughout the closed interval $[-1, 1]$.

$$(1 - x)^{-k} = 1 + \sum_{j=1}^{\infty} (-1)^j \left\{ {k \atop j} \right\} x^j \quad \text{for } k \in \mathbb{N};\ k \neq 0.$$

(2)

12-48-fig

Figure 12.48: Sample page typeset with Kurier text + math fonts

Mathematical typesetting with Kurier Light

First some large operators both in text: $\iiint_Q f(x, y, z)\, dx\, dy\, dz$ and $\prod_{\gamma \in \Gamma_{\tilde{c}}} \partial(\tilde{X}_\gamma)$; and also on display:

$$\iiiint_Q f(w, x, y, z)\, dw\, dx\, dy\, dz \leq \oint_{\partial Q} f' \left(\max \left\{ \frac{\|w\|}{|w^2 + x^2|}; \frac{\|z\|}{|y^2 + z^2|}; \frac{\|w \oplus z\|}{\|x \oplus y\|} \right\} \right)$$

$$\approx \biguplus_{Q \in \tilde{Q}} \left[f^* \left(\frac{\int Q(t)}{\sqrt{1 - t^2}} \right) \right]_{t=\alpha}^{t=\vartheta} - (\Delta + v - v)^3$$

(1)

For x in the open interval $]-1, 1[$ the infinite sum in Equation (2) is convergent; however, this does not hold throughout the closed interval $[-1, 1]$.

$$(1 - x)^{-k} = 1 + \sum_{j=1}^{\infty} (-1)^j \left\{ {k \atop j} \right\} x^j \quad \text{for } k \in \mathbb{N};\ k \neq 0.$$

(2)

12-49-fig

Figure 12.49: Sample page typeset with Kurier text + math fonts (light)

Mathematical typesetting with Noto Sans

First some large operators both in text: $\iiint_Q f(x,y,z)\,dx\,dy\,dz$ and $\prod_{\gamma\in\Gamma_{\bar{C}}}\partial(\widetilde{X}_\gamma)$; and also on display:

$$\iiiint_Q f(w,x,y,z)\,dw\,dx\,dy\,dz \leq \oint_{\partial Q} f'\left(\max\left\{\frac{\|w\|}{|w^2+x^2|};\frac{\|z\|}{|y^2+z^2|};\frac{\|w\oplus z\|}{\|x\oplus y\|}\right\}\right)$$

$$\gtrapprox \biguplus_{Q\in\bar{Q}}\left[f^*\left(\frac{\int Q(t)}{\sqrt{1-t^2}}\right)\right]_{t=\alpha}^{t=\vartheta} - (\Delta+v-v)^3$$

$$(1)$$

For x in the open interval $\,]-1,1[\,$ the infinite sum in Equation (2) is convergent; however, this does not hold throughout the closed interval $[-1,1]$.

$$(1-x)^{-k} = 1 + \sum_{j=1}^{\infty}(-1)^j\begin{Bmatrix}k\\j\end{Bmatrix}x^j \quad \text{for } k\in\mathbb{N};\, k\neq 0. \tag{2}$$

12-50-fig

Figure 12.50: Sample page typeset with Noto Sans text + math fonts

Just like his Iwona fonts, Kurier by Janusz Marian Nowacki (1951–2020) offers several different series values, all with full math support. The options of the support package kurier are also the same (but unfortunately also the lapse with respect to \lVert and \rVert). Thus, the setup for Figures 12.48 and 12.49 looks like this:

Math support for Kurier

```
\usepackage[math]{kurier}
\DeclareSymbolFont{symbols2}{OMS}{cmsy}{m}{n}
\SetSymbolFont{symbols2}    {bold}{OMS}{cmsy}{b}{n}
\DeclareMathDelimiter{\lVert}{\mathopen}{symbols2}{"06B}{largesymbols}{"0D}
\DeclareMathDelimiter{\rVert}{\mathclose}{symbols2}{"6B}{largesymbols}{"0D}
```

except that in the second example we additionally added the option light.

Matching math fonts for Noto Sans are provided by Michael Sharpe with a dedicated support package (see Section 12.3.7). The setup we used in Figure 12.50 was the following:

Math support for Noto Sans

```
\usepackage[vvarbb,upint,sfdefault]{notomath}
```

12.5.6 Historical fonts with math support

Out of the historical fonts covered in this book only Antykwa Toruńska comes with dedicated math fonts. Figures 12.51 and 12.52 on the next page have been both set up using the package anttor: the first with option math and the second additionally with options light and condensed.

Math support for Antykwa Toruńska

Mathematical typesetting with Antykwa Toruńska

First some large operators both in text: $\iiint\limits_Q f(x,y,z)\,dx\,dy\,dz$ and $\prod_{\gamma\in\Gamma_{\tilde{c}}} \partial(\widetilde{X}_\gamma)$; and also on display:

$$\iiiint\limits_Q f(w,x,y,z)\,dw\,dx\,dy\,dz \le \oint_{\partial Q} f'\left(\max\left\{\frac{\|w\|}{|w^2+x^2|};\frac{\|z\|}{|y^2+z^2|};\frac{\|w\oplus z\|}{\|x\oplus y\|}\right\}\right)$$

$$\underset{Q\in\bar{Q}}{\approx}\biguplus\left[f^*\left(\frac{\int Q(t)\,\lfloor}{\sqrt{1-t^2}}\right)\right]_{t=\alpha}^{t=\vartheta} - (\Delta + v - v)^3 \tag{1}$$

For x in the open interval $]{-}1,1[$ the infinite sum in Equation (2) is convergent; however, this does not hold throughout the closed interval $[-1,1]$.

$$(1-x)^{-k} = 1 + \sum_{j=1}^{\infty}(-1)^j\left\{{k\atop j}\right\}x^j \quad\text{for } k\in\mathbb{N};\ k\ne 0. \tag{2}$$

12-51-fig

Figure 12.51: Sample page typeset with Antykwa Toruńska text + math fonts

Mathematical typesetting with Antykwa Toruńska Light Condensed

First some large operators both in text: $\iiint\limits_Q f(x,y,z)\,dx\,dy\,dz$ and $\prod_{\gamma\in\Gamma_{\tilde{c}}} \partial(\widetilde{X}_\gamma)$; and also on display:

$$\iiiint\limits_Q f(w,x,y,z)\,dw\,dx\,dy\,dz \le \oint_{\partial Q} f'\left(\max\left\{\frac{\|w\|}{|w^2+x^2|};\frac{\|z\|}{|y^2+z^2|};\frac{\|w\oplus z\|}{\|x\oplus y\|}\right\}\right)$$

$$\underset{Q\in\bar{Q}}{\approx}\biguplus\left[f^*\left(\frac{\int Q(t)\,\lfloor}{\sqrt{1-t^2}}\right)\right]_{t=\alpha}^{t=\vartheta} - (\Delta + v - v)^3 \tag{1}$$

For x in the open interval $]{-}1,1[$ the infinite sum in Equation (2) is convergent; however, this does not hold throughout the closed interval $[-1,1]$.

$$(1-x)^{-k} = 1 + \sum_{j=1}^{\infty}(-1)^j\left\{{k\atop j}\right\}x^j \quad\text{for } k\in\mathbb{N};\ k\ne 0. \tag{2}$$

12-52-fig

Figure 12.52: Sample page typeset with Antykwa Toruńska text + math fonts (light, condensed)

Localizing documents

This chapter starts with a short introduction to the technical problems that must be solved if you want to use LATEX with a non-English language. Most of the remaining part of the chapter discusses the babel system, which provides a convenient way to generate documents in different languages. We look in particular at how we can typeset documents in French, Russian, and Greek, as the typesetting of those languages illustrates various aspects of the things one has to deal with in a non-English environment. We also say a few words about how to handle other languages, such as Arabic, Japanese, or Hindi, which are written with the so-called "complex scripts". Section 13.6 explains how to tailor the language styles to fit your needs in some common cases.

13.1 TEX and non-English languages

Due to its popularity in the academic world, TEX spread rapidly throughout the world and is now used not only with the languages based on the Latin alphabet, but also with languages using non-Latin alphabetic scripts, such as Russian, Greek, Arabic, Persian, Hebrew, Thai, Vietnamese, Malayalam, or Marathi. Implementations also exist for Chinese and Japanese (which use Kanji-based ideographic scripts) and Korean (which uses syllable blocks).

With the introduction of 8-bit TeX and METAFONT, which were officially released by Donald Knuth in March 1990, the problems of multilingual support could be more easily addressed for the first time. Nevertheless, by themselves, these versions did not solve all the problems associated with providing a convenient environment for using LaTeX with multiple and/or non–English languages, which were eventually addressed with the advent of Unicode engines like X_ETeX and LuaTeX.

To achieve this goal, TeX and its companion programs should be made truly international, and the following points should be addressed:

1. Adjust all programs to the particular language(s):

   - Handle properly fonts containing national symbols, which includes setting up the so-called Unicode fonts where necessary and appropriate [36],
   - Define line breaking and justification rules, which in Western languages means generating patterns for the hyphenation algorithm,
   - Support typesetting in different directions.

2. Provide a translation for the language-dependent strings, create national layouts for the standard documents, and provide TeX or Lua code to treat the language-dependent typesetting rules automatically [70].

3. Support processing of multilingual documents (more than one language in the same document) and work in international environments (one language per document, but a choice between several possibilities). For instance, the sorting of indexes and bibliographic references should be performed in accordance with a given language's alphabet and collating sequence; see the discussion on upmendex in Section 14.3 and biber in Section 15.2.2.

At the same time, you should be able to conveniently edit, view, and print your documents using any given character set, and LaTeX should be able to successfully process files created in this way. Encoding problems were ultimately solved with Unicode, which can encode not only the alphabetic languages but also ideographic scripts like Chinese or Japanese.

LaTeX uses by default the encoding known as UTF-8, which has been universally adopted in the computing and publishing worlds. There still exist other character encoding schemes, but their use is declining, because with them it is difficult for documents to be reproducible in different environments, issues of standardization become important, and it is necessary to know the encoding in which a document was produced if not UTF-8. For such legacy encodings LaTeX offers the inputenc package, described in Section 9.9.3 on page →I 758, but it is recommended to avoid it and use the default (UTF-8) for new documents.[1]

To adapt LaTeX to different languages, several approaches have been followed. The first to appear was to use dedicated packages, which very often were incompatible,

---

[1] A few packages, including some babel languages, have not been yet updated for the current default encoding and may display a warning like "No input encoding specified" or similar. It can be usually ignored.

thus making a multilingual document almost impossible. A second step was the introduction of babel, which eased the standardization and development of TₑX-related software adapted to different languages. The aim was to produce for each language or group of languages a package that would facilitate typesetting, with details about fonts, input conventions, hyphenation patterns, a LaTeX option file compatible with the babel concept (see Section 13.1.3), possibly a preprocessor, and, of course, documentation in English and the target language. Still, because each language takes its own solutions, interoperation remains problematic, and a new approach, based on a core providing the basic behavior with descriptive .ini files, is being developed at the time of this writing, although it has reached a very advanced stage.

In some languages, particularly East Asian ones, there is another approach, namely, extending the TₑX program to suit the needs of a particular family of languages. For example, upTₑX adds features for vertical writing and deals with other facets of typesetting Japanese.

Besides XₑTₑX and LuaTₑX, there have been other extensions to the TₑX program attempting to improve the TₑX multilingual support, like mlTₑX, EncTₑX, or Omega. The latter, by Yannis Haralambous and John Plaice, incorporated a sophisticated bidi algorithm, which has become part of LuaTₑX, and provided a mechanism to perform text transformations, which has inspired what in babel are called *transforms* (transliterations is an example).

13.1.1 Language-related aspects of typesetting

When thinking about supporting typesetting documents in languages other than English, a number of aspects that need to be dealt with come to mind.

First and foremost is the fact that other languages have different rules for line breaking, something that TₑX accommodates in Western languages through its support for multiple hyphenation patterns. In some languages, however, certain letter combinations change when they appear at a hyphenation point.

> **Unicode engines**
>
> TₑX does not support this capability "out of the box", but LuaTₑX can be extended to apply nonstandard hyphenation rules — a feature exploited by babel when using this engine. Scripts like Thai, Japanese, or Amharic follow some specific rules, which require XₑTₑX and LuaTₑX.

Some languages need different sets of characters to be properly typeset. This issue can vary from the need for additional "accented letters" (as is the case with many European languages) to the need for a completely different alphabet (as is the case with languages using the Cyrillic or Greek alphabet).

> **Unicode engines**
>
> When non-European languages need to be supported, the typesetting direction might be different as well (such as right to left for Arabic and Hebrew texts), or so many characters might be needed (as is the case with the Kanji script, for instance) that traditional TₑX's standard mechanisms cannot deal with them — in that case XₑTₑX or LuaTₑX is required.

A more "subtle" problem turns up when we look at the standard document classes that each LaTeX distribution supplies, because they were designed for the Anglo-American situation. A specific example where this preference interferes with supporting other languages is the start of a chapter. For some languages it is not enough to just translate the word "Chapter"; the order of the word and the denomination of the chapter needs to be changed as well, solely on the basis of grammatical rules. Where the English reader expects to see "Chapter 1", the Hungarian reader expects to see "1. fejezet".

13.1.2 Culture-related aspects of typesetting

An even thornier problem when faced with the need to support typesetting of many languages is the fact that typesetting rules differ, even between countries that use the same language. For instance, hyphenation rules differ between British English and American English. Translations of English words might vary between countries, just as they do for the German spoken in Germany and the German spoken (and written) in Austria.

Typographic rules may differ between countries, too. No worldwide standard tells us how nested lists should be typeset; on the contrary, their appearance may differ for different languages or countries or even printing houses. With these aspects we enter the somewhat fuzzy area comprising the boundary between the language aspects of typesetting and the cultural aspects of typesetting. It is not clear where that boundary lies. When implementing support for typesetting documents written in a specific language, this difference needs to be taken into account. The language-related aspects can be supported on a general level, but the cultural aspects are more often than not better (or more easily) handled by creating specific document classes.

13.1.3 babel — LaTeX speaks multiple languages

The LaTeX distribution contains a few standard document classes that are used by most users. These classes (article, report, book, and letter) have a certain American look and feel, which not everyone likes. Moreover, the language-dependent strings, such as "Chapter" and "Table of Contents" (see Table 13.2 on page 305 for a list of commands holding language-dependent strings), come out in English by default.

The babel package, originally developed by Johannes Braams [19] and now maintained and developed further by Javier Bezos [15], provides a set of options that allows the user to choose the language or language(s) in which the document is typeset. It has the following basic characteristics:

- Multiple languages can be used simultaneously.

- The list of hyphenation patterns to be loaded when the LaTeX format is generated can be defined via an external file.

- Translations for the language-dependent strings and commands for facilitating text input are provided for more than 60 languages (a selection of them is listed in Table 13.1 on the facing page).

afrikaans	esperanto	italian	russian
albanian	estonian	kurmanji	samin
azerbaijani	finnish	latin	scottish
basque	french	latvian	serbian
belarusian	friulan	lithuanian	serbianc
bosnian	galician	lowersorbian	slovak
breton	german, ngerman,	macedonian	slovene
bulgarian	austrian,	malay	spanish
catalan	naustrian	magyar	swedish
croatian	greek,	norsk, nynorsk	turkish
czech	polutonikogreek	occitan	turkmen
danish	hebrew	polish	ukrainian
dutch	icelandic	portuguese,	uppersorbian
english, USenglish,	indonesian	brazilian	vietnamese
UKenglish,	interlingua	romanian	welsh
australian	irish	romansh	

Alternatives for a language typically differ in hyphenation rules, date handling, or language-dependent strings. The option english *combines American hyphenation patterns with a British date format.*

Table 13.1: Selective list of language options supported by the babel system

In the next section we describe the user interface of the babel system. We then discuss the additional commands for various languages and describe the support for typesetting languages using non–Latin alphabets. Finally, we discuss ways to tailor babel to your needs. Throughout the sections, examples illustrate the use of various languages supported by babel.

13.2 The babel user interface

Languages that you use in your document should be declared as options when loading the babel package. Alternatively, because the languages in which a document is written constitute a global characteristic of the document, the languages can be indicated as *global options* on the \documentclass command. This strategy makes them available to any package that changes behavior depending on the language settings of the document. Most languages are identified by their English names (see Table 13.1 for the recommended names in many languages), although there are a few exceptions. For example, the following declaration prepares for typesetting in the languages German (option ngerman for new orthography) and Italian (option italian):

```
\usepackage[ngerman,italian]{babel}
```

The last language appearing on the `\usepackage` command line becomes the default language used at the beginning of the document. In the above example, the language-dependent strings, the hyphenation patterns (if they were loaded for the given language when the LaTeX format was generated; see the discussion on page 337), and possibly the interpretation of certain language-dependent commands (such as the date) will be for Italian from the beginning of the document up to the point where you choose a different language.

If one decides to make `ngerman` and `italian` global options, then other packages can also detect their presence. For example, the following code lets the package varioref (described in Section 2.4.1 on page →I 79) detect and use the options specified on the `\documentclass` command:

```
\documentclass[ngerman,italian]{article}
\usepackage{babel}
\usepackage{varioref}
```

If you use more than one language in your document and you want to define your own language-dependent strings for the varioref commands, you should use the methods described in Section 2.4.1.

Very often, a document is written entirely in a single language with a few words or phrases in other languages. In such a case and if the main font is appropriate for the latter, there is no need to declare those extra languages explicitly if all you need is to get them properly hyphenated, because they can be loaded by babel on the fly, with some basic features, when selected with one of the macros described in the following section.

13.2.1 Setting or getting the current language

Within a document it is possible to change the current language in several ways. For example, you can change all language-related settings including translations for strings like "Chapter", the typesetting conventions, and the setup for shorthand commands. Alternatively, you can keep the translations unchanged but modify everything else (e.g., when typesetting short texts in a foreign language within the main text). Finally, you can change only the hyphenation rules.

The two basic commands are `\selectlanguage`, for large blocks of text like paragraphs, and `\foreignlanguage`, for changes inside paragraphs. These are the preferred ways to switch a language, but in some cases the environment versions can be useful.

`\selectlanguage{`*language*`}`   `\begin{otherlanguage}{`*language*`}`

A change to all language-related settings is implemented via the `\selectlanguage` command. For instance, if you want to switch to German, you would use the command `\selectlanguage{german}`. The process is similar for switching to other languages. The `\selectlanguage` command calls the macros defined in the language definition file (see Section 13.6) and activates the special definitions for the language in question. It also updates the setting of TeX's \language primitive used for hyphenation or, in the case of languages like Thai and Chinese with X⅁LATEX and LuaLATEX, activates the line-breaking rules.

The environment otherlanguage provides the same functionality as the \selectlanguage declaration, except that the language change is local to the environment. The argument *language* is the language you want to switch to.

\foreignlanguage[*key list*]{*language*}{*phrase*}
\begin{otherlanguage*}[*key list*]{*language*}

The command \foreignlanguage typesets *phrase* according to the rules of *language*. It switches only the extra definitions and the line-breaking rules for the language, but not the names and dates, unless you specify captions or date in the *key list* argument. Its environment equivalent is otherlanguage*.

The expansion of fixed document element names depends on the language; e.g., in English we have "References" or "Chapter".
Auf Deutsch ergibt sich „Literatur" oder „Kapitel".
Voici en français : « Références » ou « Chapitre ».
However, in short phrases "Références" does not change by default!

```
\usepackage[german,french,english]{babel}
\raggedright

The expansion of fixed document element names
depends on the language; e.g., in English
we have ''\refname'' or ''\chaptername''.  \par
\selectlanguage{german} Auf Deutsch ergibt sich
"\refname" oder "\chaptername".          \par
\begin{otherlanguage}{french} Voici en français:
 \og\refname\fg{} ou \og\chaptername\fg.
 \par\foreignlanguage{english}{However, in short
 phrases ''\refname'' does not change by default!}
\end{otherlanguage}
```

13-2-1

\begin{hyphenrules}{*language*}

Inside the environment hyphenrules, *only* the hyphenation rules are switched to those of the specified *language*; \languagename and all other settings remain unchanged. When no hyphenation rules for *language* are loaded into the format, the environment has no effect.

As a special application, this environment can be used to prevent hyphenation altogether, provided that in language.dat the "language" nohyphenation is defined (by loading zerohyph.tex, as explained in Section 13.6.2 on page 337). This is, actually, the only recommended use for this environment.

This text shows the effect of hyphenation.
This text shows the effect of hyphenation turned off.

```
\usepackage[english]{babel}

This text shows the effect of hyphenation.\par
\begin{hyphenrules}{nohyphenation}
This text shows the effect of hyphenation turned off.
\end{hyphenrules}
```

13-2-2

Note that this approach works even if the "language" nohyphenation is not specified as an option to the babel package.

If more than one language is used, it might be necessary to know which language is active at a specific point in the document. This can be checked with a call to \iflanguage.

> \iflanguage{*language*}{*true-clause*}{*false-clause*}

The first argument in this syntax, *language*, is the name of a language, which is first checked to see whether it corresponds to a language declared to babel. If the *language* is known, the command compares its *hyphenation rules* with those for the current language. If they are the same, the commands specified in the *true-clause* are executed; otherwise, the commands specified in the third argument, *false-clause*, are executed.

The name of this macro is somewhat misleading, because it does not compare actual babel languages but the hyphenation patterns used, as the following example illustrates. If you need to check for the current language, you are better off resorting to the iflang package by Heiko Oberdiek.

The current language is naustrian, i.e., Austrian, and its hyphenation rules are the same as for German. English has different patterns.

```
\usepackage[english,ngerman,naustrian]{babel}
The current language is \texttt{naustrian},
i.e., Austrian, and its hyphenation rules
\iflanguage{ngerman}{are}{are not} the same as
for German. English has \iflanguage{english}{the
same}{different} patterns.
```
13-2-3

> \languagename

The control sequence \languagename contains the name of the current language.

(1) The language is english.
(2) The language is german.
(3) The language is french.
(4) The language is english.
(5) Pas en français.
(6) The language is german.

```
\usepackage[german,french,english]{babel}
\par(1) The language is \languagename.
\par(2) \selectlanguage{german} The language is \languagename.
\par(3) \begin{otherlanguage}{french}
        The language is \languagename.  \end{otherlanguage}
\par(4) \foreignlanguage{english}{The language is \languagename.}
\par(5) \iflanguage{french}{En français.}{Pas en français.}
\par(6) The language is \languagename.
```
13-2-4

Language-dependent strings Most document classes available in a LATEX installation define a number of commands that are used to store the various language-dependent strings. Table 13.2 on the facing page presents an overview of these commands, together with their default text strings.

13.2.2 Handling shorthands

A "shorthand" is a one- or two-character sequence, the first character of which introduces the shorthand and is called the "shorthand character". For a two-character shorthand, the second character specifies the behavior of the shorthand. This mechanism

Command	English String	Command	English String
\abstractname	Abstract	\indexname	Index
\alsoname	see also	\listfigurename	List of Figures
\appendixname	Appendix	\listtablename	List of Tables
\bibname	Bibliography	\pagename	Page
\ccname	cc	\partname	Part
\chaptername	Chapter	\prefacename	Preface
\contentsname	Contents	\proofname	Proof
\enclname	encl	\refname	References
\figurename	Figure	\seename	see
\glossaryname	Glossary	\tablename	Table
\headtoname	To (letter class)		

Table 13.2: Language-dependent strings in babel (English defaults)

was originally devised for authors who write in languages other than English, because it was sometimes awkward to type the input needed to produce the letters of their languages in the final document.

LaTeX now understands UTF-8 input (which is its default since 2018); thus, most characters can be directly entered from the keyboard, which means that for many European languages shorthands are not as necessary as in the past. Given that they require a lot of extra processing, you can nowadays tell babel not to define them with the package option shorthands=off. However, they can be still useful in some cases:

- Several kinds of discretionaries and breaks can be inserted easily with "-, "=, and others.

- Shorthands such as ! are used to insert the right amount of white space.

- In some languages, shorthands such as "a are defined to allow word hyphenation if the font encoding is OT1 (a better solution in most European languages is to use T1 instead, though).

- Finally, minority languages and some kinds of text can still require characters not easily available on the keyboards (and sometimes not even available as separated or precomposed Unicode characters).

The most important shorthands of these kinds are exhibited in later sections.

Babel knows about four shorthand levels — those defined by "the system", "the language", "the user", and "the user for a specific language". The purpose of this mechanism is to allow users to adapt easily its behavior to their needs. Shorthands can then act like a sort of customizable language-dependent markup.

Document-level commands for shorthands

This section describes the shorthand commands that can be used in the document and various aspects of the shorthand concept. Language-level or system-level shorthands are declared in language definition files; see Section 13.6 on page 332.

`\useshorthands*{`*char*`}`

The command `\useshorthands` initiates the definition of user-defined shorthand sequences. The argument *char* is the character that starts these shorthands.

Because languages may turn shorthands on and off, the starred variant makes sure user shorthands are always active.

`\defineshorthand{`*charseq*`}{`*expansion*`}`

The command `\defineshorthand` defines a shorthand. Its first argument, *charseq*, is a one- or two-character sequence; the second argument, *expansion*, is the code to which the shorthand should expand.

`\languageshorthands{`*language*`}`

The command `\languageshorthands` is used to switch between shorthands for the *language* specified as an argument. The *language* must have been declared to babel for the current document. When switching languages, the language definition files usually issue this command for the language in question. For example, the file `frenchb.ldf` contains the following command:

```
\languageshorthands{french}
```

Sometimes it is necessary to temporarily switch off the shorthand action of a given character because it needs to be used in a different way.

`\shorthandon{`*chars*`}`   `\shorthandoff{`*chars*`}`

The command `\shorthandoff` sets the `\catcode` for each of the characters in its argument *chars* to "other" (12). Conversely, the command `\shorthandon` sets the `\catcode` to "active" (13) for its argument *chars*. Both commands act only on "known" shorthand characters. If a character is not known to be a shorthand character, its category code is left unchanged.

For example, the language definition file for French (`frenchb.ldf`) makes the "double" punctuation characters "?", "!", ":", and ";" active. One can eliminate this behavior by specifying each as an argument to a `\shorthandoff` command. This step is necessary with certain packages, where the same characters have a special meaning.

The next example loads the xy package, where the use of ";" and "?" as shorthand characters is turned off inside xy's xy environment [31, Chapter 7], because these characters have a functional meaning there.

Voici un exemple avec *xypic* :

●——————→ *x*

Quelle belle flèche !

```
\usepackage{xy}
\usepackage[french]{babel}
Voici un exemple avec \emph{xypic}:
\[ \shorthandoff{;?}
\begin{xy}  (0,0)*{\bullet}, (0,0) ; (10,0),
   **\dir {-} ?>* \dir {>}, (12,0)*{x},  \end{xy}
\]
Quelle belle flèche !
```

On the other hand, tikz provides a library to overcome these issues.

13.2.3 Language attributes

Sometimes the support for language-dependent typesetting needs to be tailored for different situations. In such a case it is possible to define attributes for the particular language. Two examples of the use of attributes can be found in the support for typesetting of Latin texts. When the attribute usej is selected, certain document element names are spelled differently (for example, "Junii" instead of "Iunni"). The attribute withprosodicmarks can be used when typesetting grammars, dictionaries, teaching texts, and the like, where prosodic marks are important for providing complete information on the words or the verses.

\languageattribute{*language*}{*langattrs*}

The command \languageattribute declares which attributes are to be used for a given language. It must be used in the preamble of the document following the command \usepackage[...]{babel} that loads the babel package. The command takes two arguments: *language* is the name of a language, and *langattrs* is a comma-separated list of attributes to be used for that language. The command checks whether the *language* is known in the current document and whether the attributes are known for this language.

For instance, babel has two variants for the Greek language: monotoniko (one-accent), the default, and polutoniko (multi-accent). To select the polutoniko variant, one must specify it in the document preamble, using the \languageattribute command. The following two examples illustrate the difference:

The Greek word for 'Index' is Ευρετήριο.

```
\usepackage[greek,english]{babel}  \usepackage{lmodern}
The Greek word for 'Index' is \selectlanguage{greek}\indexname.
```

With the polutoniko attribute we get a different result:

The Greek word for 'Index' is Εὑρετήριο.

```
\usepackage[greek,english]{babel}  \usepackage{lmodern}
\languageattribute{greek}{polutoniko}
The Greek word for 'Index' is \selectlanguage{greek}\indexname.
```

Besides Greek, there are several language styles defining attributes, like Belarusian, Czech, Estonian, Japanese, and Latin, among others. For further information, refer to the corresponding manuals, which can be found on CTAN (`https://www.ctan.org/tex-archive/macros/latex/contrib/babel-contrib`).

13.2.4 BCP 47 tags

It has become customary in many environments to identify languages with the help of conventional labels. There are several sets of them, but the most popular by far are those defined following BCP 47, a standard published by IETF [84]. Languages are identified with two- or three-letter codes, which can be followed, in its most basic form, by a four-letter code for the script. Sometimes, a two-letter code for the region is added, too, like `de-AT`, which is the German language as spoken in Austria.

Requesting and selecting languages with the BPD 47 tags is usually cumbersome, and it is not the recommended practice, but they are often the preferred way to identify locales in documents generated by external tools, like bibliography managers. The `babel` package is able to select languages with them, if desired, and because the main document may not know which languages are required, the most basic settings can be loaded on the fly. Thus, a bibliographic reference with containing `\foreignlanguage{ru}{Some Russian title}` selects a Cyrillic font (which should be defined elsewhere) and the Russian hyphenation patterns, even if not explicitly declared as a class or package option.

This feature is primarily meant for special tasks, like the one just explained, and for this reason it must be activated explicitly, either by the user or by a package requiring it, in the following way:

```
\babeladjust{ autoload.bcp47 = on,
              autoload.bcp47.options = import }
```

`\babeladjust` is a multipurpose macro to configure the `babel` behavior (details on in can be found in the `babel` manual). In this case, it tells `babel` to allow BCP 47 tags in addition to language names and to import the data provided in a set of `.ini` files containing miscellaneous data for about 250 languages.

13.3 User commands provided by language options

This section gives a general overview of the features typically offered by the various language options. It includes translations of language-dependent strings and a survey of typical shorthands intended to ease language-specific document content or to solve language-specific typesetting requirements. Some language options define additional commands to produce special date formats or numbers in a certain style. Also discussed are layout modifications as undertaken for French as well as the interfaces for dealing with different scripts (e.g., Latin and Cyrillic) in the same document.

Command	French	Greek	Polish	Russian
\abstractname	Résumé	Περίληψη	Streszczenie	Аннотация
\alsoname	voir aussi	βλέπε επίσης	zob. także	см. также
\appendixname	Annexe	Παράρτημα	Dodatek	Приложение
\bibname	Bibliographie	Βιβλιογραφία	Bibliografia	Литература
\ccname	Copie à	Κοινοποίηση	Do wiadomości	исх.
\chaptername	Chapitre	Κεφάλαιο	Rozdział	Глава
\contentsname	Table des matières	Περιεχόμενα	Spis treści	Содержание
\enclname	P. J.	Συνημμένα	Załączniki	вкл.
\figurename	Figure	Σχήμα	Rysunek	Рис.
\glossaryname	Glossaire	Γλωσσάρι	Słowniczek	Словарь терминов
\headtoname		Προς	Do	вх.
\indexname	Index	Ευρετήριο	Skorowidz	Предметный указатель
\listfigurename	Table des figures	Κατάλογος Σχημάτων	Spis rysunków	Список иллюстраций
\listtablename	Liste des tableaux	Κατάλογος Πινάκων	Spis tabel	Список таблиц
\pagename	page	Σελίδα	Strona	с.
\partname	Deuxième partie	Μέρος	Część	Часть
\prefacename	Préface	Πρόλογος	Przedmowa	Предисловие
\proofname	Démonstration	Απόδειξη	Dowód	Доказательство
\refname	Références	Αναφορές	Literatura	Список литературы
\seename	voir	βλέπε	zob.	см.
\tablename	Table	Πίνακας	Tabela	Таблица

13-3-1 *In French \partname also generates the part number as a word, e.g., "Première, Deuxième, ... "*

Table 13.3: Language-dependent strings in babel (French, Greek, Polish, and Russian)

13.3.1 Translations of fixed texts

As discussed earlier, babel provides translations for document element names that LaTeX uses in its document classes. The English versions of these strings are shown in Table 13.2 on page 305. Table 13.3 on page 309 shows the translations for a number of languages, with some of them not using the Latin script.

Apart from the translated strings in Table 13.3, the language definition files supply alternative versions of the command \today, as shown in the following example. We explicitly load the T2A encoding to typeset Cyrillic. To have \today translated, we supply the option date in the optional argument to \foreignlanguage:

In England the date is '2nd February 2020', while in Bulgaria it is '2 февруари 2020 г.'. Catalonians write '2 de febrer de 2020'.

```
\usepackage[T2A,T1]{fontenc}   \usepackage{gentium}
\usepackage[catalan,bulgarian,british]{babel}
In England the date is '\today', while in Bulgaria
it is '\foreignlanguage[date]{bulgarian}{\today}'.
Catalonians write
'\foreignlanguage[date]{catalan}{\today}'.
```

13-3-2

13.3.2 Available shorthands

Many of the language definition files provide shorthands. Some are meant to ease typing, whereas others provide quite extensive trickery to achieve special effects. You might not be aware of it, but LaTeX itself defines a shorthand (although it is not called by that name) that you probably use quite often: the character tilde (~), which is used to enter a "nonbreakable" space.

As explained in Section 13.2.2, the default UTF-8 encoding makes shorthands for entering accented letters mostly unnecessary, so this section focuses on typographical tools and some special characters.

> **Unicode engines**
>
> With LuaLaTeX, many of the special effects can be achieved without explicit markup by means of what babel calls *transforms*. They are based on Lua's pattern matching mechanism and can be defined by the user, although there are some predefined ones, explained in the babel manual.

The double quote

The most popular character to be used as a shorthand character is the double quote character ("), which should not replace, let us remember, the so-called typographical quotes ("") when typing text. It is used in shorthands for Basque, Bulgarian, Catalan, Danish, Dutch, Estonian, Finnish, Galician, German, Icelandic, Italian, Latin, Norwegian, Polish, Portuguese, Russian, Serbian, Slovenian, Spanish, Swedish, Ukrainian, and Upper Sorbian, among others. Describing all uses of the double quote character as a shorthand character would be going too far. Instead, it is recommended that you check the documentation that comes with each language if you want to know the details. What can be said here is that its uses fall into a number of categories, each of which deserves a description and a few examples.

Insert accented letters For a number of languages, shorthands were created to facilitate typing accented characters. This mechanism was devised for the old 7-bit input and output encodings, and now this usage has become obsolete, but this is not true for all cases. For the Dutch language, for instance, an accent needs to be removed when the hyphenation point is next to the accented letter (although with LuaLaTeX there are tools to set nonstandard hyphenation rules like this without explicit markup).

Den Koning van Hispaniën heb ik altijd geeerd! Den Koning van Hispaniën heb ik altijd geëerd!

```
\usepackage[dutch]{babel}
Den Koning van Hispani"en heb ik altijd ge"eerd!
Den Koning van Hispani"en heb ik altijd ge"eerd!
```

13-3-3

Insert special characters In the Catalan language a special glyph, the "geminated l", is needed for proper typesetting [91].

```
\usepackage[catalan,english]{babel}
The ``geminated~l'' appears in words such as
\foreignlanguage{catalan}{inte"lig\`encia} and
\foreignlanguage{catalan}{i"lusió}.
```

The "geminated l" appears in words such as intel·ligència and il·lusió.

13-3-4

This character can also be typeset by using the commands \lgem and \Lgem or through the combinations "\l." and "\L." once catalan is selected.

Insert special quoting characters By default, LaTeX supports single and double quotes: 'quoted text' and "quoted text". This support is not desirable in European languages. Many have their own conventions and more often than not require different characters for this purpose. For example, in traditional Dutch typesetting, the opening quote should be placed on the baseline, in German typesetting the closing quote is reversed, and French typesetting requires guillemets. For Icelandic typesetting the guillemets are used as well, but the other way around — that is, pointing "inward" instead of "outward" (a convention also sometimes used in German typography).

English "quoted text" has quotes different from Dutch „quoted text" or German „quoted text" or French «quoted text».

```
\usepackage[dutch,ngerman,french,english]{babel}
English ''quoted text'' has quotes different from
\selectlanguage{dutch}Dutch "'quoted text"' or
\selectlanguage{ngerman}German "'quoted text"' or
\selectlanguage{french}French \og quoted text\fg.
```

13-3-5

The T1 font encoding provides the guillemets (see Table 9.22 on page →I 763), but its support for French typesetting relies on the commands \og and \fg. These commands not only produce the guillemets but also provide proper spacing between them and the text they surround. Note that the csquotes package, discussed in Section 3.4.2 on page →I 179, provides convenient methods to automatically generate the right quotes based on language context and configuration setup.

Insert special hyphenation rules A number of languages have specific rules about what happens to characters at a line break. For instance, in older German spelling ..ck.. is hyphenated as ..k-k.., and a triple f in a compound word is normally typeset as ff — except when hyphenated, in which case the third f reappears as shown in the example.

Brote bak-ken	Farbstoff-fabrik

```
\usepackage[german]{babel}
\fbox{\parbox[t]{1,5cm}{Brote ba"cken}}    \quad
\fbox{\parbox[t]{1,5cm}{Farbsto"ffabrik}}
```

13-3-6

Insert special hyphenation indications A number of shorthands are used to inform LaTeX about special situations with regard to hyphenation. For instance, in a number of languages it is sometimes necessary to prevent LaTeX from typesetting a ligature — for example, in a compound word. This goal can be achieved by inserting a small kern between the two letters that would normally form a ligature. The shorthand "| is available for this purpose in many language definitions.

Das deutsche Wort „Auflage" sollte nicht so, sondern als »Auflage« gesetzt werden.

```
\usepackage[german]{babel}
Das deutsche Wort "'Auflage"' sollte nicht so,
sondern als ">Auf"|lage"< gesetzt werden.
```

13-3-7

Another popular shorthand is `"-`, which indicates a soft or hard hyphen without suppressing hyphenation in the remainder of the word. Sadly, this has not been done consistently, because in Dutch, Portuguese, Catalan, or Danish, it is a hard hyphen, while in German, Spanish, Norwegian, Slovak, or Russian, it is a soft hyphen.

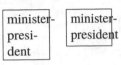 

```
\usepackage[dutch]{babel}
\fbox{\parbox[t]{1cm}{minister"-president}} \quad
\fbox{\parbox[t]{1cm}{minister\-president}} \quad
\fbox{\parbox[t]{1cm}{ministerpresident}}
```

13-3-8

There is also `""` (similar to `"-`, but does not print the -), `"=` (whose meaning, again, depends on the language), and `"~` (which usually inserts an explicit hyphen without a breakpoint). The following example shows the effects of these shorthands in German, using the same word:

1.	Gutenberg-Universität	Gutenberg-Universität
2.	GutenbergUniversität	Gutenberg-Universität
3.	GutenbergUniversität	Gutenberg Universität
4.	Gutenberg-Universi-tät	Gutenberg-Universität
5.	Gutenberg-Universität	Gutenberg-Universität

```
\usepackage[german]{babel}
\newcommand\present[1]{%
    \fbox{\parbox[t]{31mm}{#1}}
    \fbox{\parbox[t]{16mm}{#1}}
  \par}
1. \present{Gutenberg-Universität}
2. \present{Gutenberg"-Universität}
3. \present{Gutenberg""Universität}
4. \present{Gutenberg"=Universität}
5. \present{Gutenberg"~Universität}
```

13-3-9

The tilde

For the languages Basque, Galician, and Spanish, the construction `~~` (as well as `~--` and `~---`) produces a dash that disallows a line break after it. When the tilde is followed by any other character (or the empty group `{}`), it retains its original function as an "unbreakable space". That is why the first two lines of the example are very loosely typeset.

En español, la raya que abre incisos —como este— no debe quedar al final de una línea.

```
\usepackage[spanish,activeacute]{babel}
En español, la raya que abre incisos ~---como
este--- no debe quedar al final de~una línea.
```

13-3-10

The colon, semicolon, exclamation mark, and question mark

For the languages Breton, French, Russian, and Ukrainian, these four characters are used as shorthands to facilitate the use of correct typographic conventions. For Turkish typography, this ability is needed for the colon and semicolon only, while in French it is extended to the guillemets when so requested with `\frenchsetup`. The convention is that a little white space should precede (or follow) these characters.

En français on doit mettre un « petit espace » devant la ponctuation double : comme cela ! For English this is not done: as shown here!

```
\usepackage[english,french]{babel}
\frenchsetup{og=«, fg=»}
En français on doit mettre un «petit espace»
devant la ponctuation double: comme cela!
\selectlanguage{english}
For English this is not done: as shown here!
```

13-3-11

This white space is added automatically by default, but this setting can be changed in a configuration file. The use of the colon as a shorthand character can lead to problems with other packages or when including PostScript files in a document. In such cases it may be necessary to disable this shorthand (temporarily) by using \shorthandoff, as explained in Example 13-2-5 on page 307.

The grave accent

The support for the languages Catalan and Hungarian makes it possible to use the grave accent (') as a shorthand character. The purpose of this shorthand for Catalan is just to facilitate the entering of accented characters, and one has to specify the option activegrave when loading babel. For Hungarian this shorthand also adds some characters to invoke the correct behavior at hyphenation points.

```
\usepackage[hungarian]{babel}
\newcommand\present[1]
    {\fbox{\parbox[t]{20mm}{#1}}
     \fbox{\parbox[t]{8,5mm}{#1}}\par}
\present{lo'ccsan}
\present{e'ddzünk}
\present{po'ggyász}
\present{Kodá'llya}
\present{me'nnyei}
\present{vi'ssza}
\present{po'ttyan}
\present{ri'zzsel}
```

13-3-12

The equal sign

The support for the languages Latin and Turkish makes it possible to use the equal sign (=) as a shorthand character.

- When a Latin text is being typeset, the equal sign is defined to be a shorthand for adding a macron accent to the lowercase vowels (except, in pdfTeX, the medieval ligatures æ and œ). Because this shorthand may interfere with other packages, it must be explicitly requested when the package is loaded and additionally turned on with \ProsodicMarksOn.

13-3-13

ā ē ī ō ū

```
\usepackage[latin.withprosodicmarks]{babel}
\ProsodicMarksOn =a =e =i =o =u
```

- When Turkish typesetting rules are to be followed, the equal sign needs to be preceded by a little white space. This is achieved automatically by turning the equal sign into a shorthand that replaces a preceding space character with a tiny amount of white space.

a =b
a=b

```
\usepackage[english,turkish]{babel}
\selectlanguage{english} a =b \par \selectlanguage{turkish} a =b
```

13-3-14

The disadvantage of having the equal sign turn into a space character is that it may cause many other packages to fail, including the usage of PostScript files for graphics inclusions. Make sure that the shorthand is turned off with `\shorthandoff`.

The greater than and less than signs

The support for the Spanish language makes it possible to use the "greater than" and "less than" signs (< and >) as shorthand characters for inserting a special quoting environment. This environment inserts different quoting characters when it is nested within itself. It supports a maximum of three levels of nested quotations. It also automatically inserts the closing quote signs when a new paragraph is started *within* a quote, as seen in front of "Las comillas ...":

La regla es: «dentro de las comillas latinas se usan las "inglesas y dentro de éstas las 'sencillas'".
»Las comillas de seguir son como las de cerrar.»

```
\usepackage[spanish]{babel}
La regla es: <<dentro de las comillas latinas se usan
las <<inglesas y dentro de éstas las <<sencillas>>>>.

Las comillas de seguir son como las de cerrar.>>
```

13-3-15

Note that when characters are turned into shorthands, the ligature mechanism in the fonts no longer works for them. In the T1 font encoding, for instance, a ligature is defined for two consecutive "less than" signs that normally results in typesetting guillemets. In the example above, the nested quote shows clearly that this does not happen. To deactivate the Spanish quoting style, just pass `es-noquoting` as a package option.

The period

The support for the Spanish language also allows the use of the period (.) as a shorthand character in math mode. Its purpose is to control whether decimal numbers are written with the comma (`\decimalcomma`) or the period (`\decimalpoint`) as the decimal character.

1000,10
1000.10

```
\usepackage[spanish]{babel}
\decimalcomma $1000.10$ \par \decimalpoint $1000.10$
```

13-3-16

Thanks to this feature, documents may be adapted easily to either convention, depending on the country (for example, dot in Mexico, comma in Spain). To deactivate this feature, pass `es-nodecimaldot` as a package option.

13.3.3 Language-specific commands

Apart from the translations and shorthands discussed above, some language definition files provide extra commands. Some of them are meant to facilitate the production of documents that conform to the appropriate typesetting rules. Others provide extra functionality not available by default in LaTeX. A number of these commands are described in this section.

Formatting dates

For some languages more than one format is used for representing dates in the Gregorian calendar, which is the only one supported out of the box by LaTeX. In these cases extra commands are provided to produce a date in different formats, although you can resort alternatively to the package datetime2 by Nicola Talbot, which provides more sophisticated formatting options. The date in the next four examples is artificially set to a very important date in LaTeX's history;[1] see page →17 for the story behind this date.

In the Bulgarian tradition, months are indicated using uppercase roman numerals; for such dates the command \todayRoman is available.

13-3-17

2 февруари 2020 г.
2. II. 2020 г.

```
\usepackage[bulgarian]{babel}
\usepackage{XCharter}
\today  \par \todayRoman
```

When writing in the Esperanto language two slightly different ways of representing the date are provided by the commands \hodiau and \hodiaun.

13-3-18

2–a de februaro, 2020
la 2–a de februaro, 2020
la 2–an de februaro, 2020

```
\usepackage[esperanto]{babel}
\today \par \hodiau \par \hodiaun
```

When producing a document in the Greek language the date can also be represented with Greek numerals instead of arabic numerals. For this purpose the command \Grtoday is made available.

13-3-19

2 Φεβρουαρίου 2020
Β΄ Φεβρουαρίου ͵ΒΚ΄

```
\usepackage[greek]{babel}
\usepackage{Alegreya}
\today \par \Grtoday
```

The support for the Hungarian language provides the command \ontoday to produce a date format used in expressions such as "on February 10th".

For the Upper and Lower Sorbian languages two different sets of month names are employed. By default, the support for these languages produces "new-style" dates, but "old-style" dates can be produced as well. The "old-style" date format for the Lower Sorbian language can be selected with the command \olddatelsorbian;

---

[1] This is the day when the L3 programming layer was integrated in the LaTeX format.

`\newdatelsorbian` switches (back) to the modern form. For Upper Sorbian similar commands are available, as shown in the example:

```
\usepackage[usorbian,lsorbian]{babel}
```

2. februara 2020	`\newdatelsorbian \today \par`
2. małego rožka 2020	`\olddatelsorbian \today \par`
2. februara 2020	`\newdateusorbian \today \par`
2. małeho róžka 2020	`\olddateusorbian \today`

13-3-20

In Swedish documents it is customary to represent dates with just numbers. Such dates can occur in two forms: YYYY-MM-DD and DD/MM YYYY. The command `\datesymd` changes the definition of the command `\today` to produce dates in the first numerical form; the command `\datesdmy` changes the definition of the command `\today` to produce dates in the second numerical format.[1]

```
\usepackage[swedish]{babel}
```

Default date format: 30 februari 1712   `Default date format: \today\\`
`\datesymd` gives: 1712-02-30   `\verb|\datesymd| gives: \datesymd \today \\`
`\datesdmy` gives: 30/2 1712   `\verb|\datesdmy| gives: \datesdmy \today`

13-3-21

Numbering

Counting is a natural and basic activity of the human thought, and many cultures have developed their own particular, and sometimes unique, ways to do it. Although the Indo-Arabic numeral system is widespread, there are many other ways to represent quantities, and even the decimal system has some differences across countries (for example, the decimal mark can be either a dot or a comma).

Letters in their alphabetic order are customary in enumerations, and each script requires its own characters. Even in a single script, letters can be selected in different ways. For example, in Spanish the *ñ* is inserted after the *n*, and in Italian some letters are discarded in some types of documents. It is worth noting that there is not always a unique "alphabet" even in a single language and that stylistic decisions are relevant.

Alphabetic counting has been available in LaTeX since its beginnings with the commands `\alph` and `\Alph`, which assumes the bicameral system (lowercase and uppercase) in most Western languages.

The support for certain languages provides additional commands for representing numbers by letters. For the Esperanto language the commands `\esper` and `\Esper` are provided. The support for the Greek language changes the definition of `\alph` and `\Alph` to produce Greek letters, while the support for the Bulgarian language changes them to produce Cyrillic letters. The support for the Russian and Belarusian languages provides the commands `\asbuk` and `\Asbuk` as alternatives to the LaTeX commands. Table 13.4 on the facing page compares the results of the different commands and their redefinitions for certain languages.

---

[1] Fun fact: the date in the example was real — but only in Sweden.

value	default \alph\Alph		Esperanto \esper\Esper		Greek \alph\Alph		Russian \asbuk\Asbuk		Bulgarian \alph\Alph	
1	a	A	a	A	α′	Α′	а	А	а	А
2	b	B	b	B	β′	Β′	б	Б	б	Б
3	c	C	c	C	γ′	Γ′	в	В	в	В
4	d	D	ĉ	Ĉ	δ′	Δ′	г	Γ	г	Γ
5	e	E	d	D	ε′	Ε′	д	Д	д	Д
6	f	F	e	E	ϛ′	Ϛ′	е	Е	е	Е
7	g	G	f	F	ζ′	Ζ′	ж	Ж	ж	Ж
8	h	H	g	G	η′	Η′	з	З	з	З
9	i	I	ĝ	Ĝ	θ′	Θ′	и	И	и	И
10	j	J	h	H	ι′	Ι′	к	К	к	К
11	k	K	ĥ	Ĥ	ια′	ΙΑ′	л	Л	л	Л
12	l	L	i	I	ιβ′	ΙΒ′	м	М	м	М
13	m	M	j	J	ιγ′	ΙΓ′	н	Н	н	Н
14	n	N	ĵ	Ĵ	ιδ′	ΙΔ′	о	О	о	О
15	o	O	k	K	ιε′	ΙΕ′	п	П	п	П
16	p	P	l	L	ιϛ′	ΙϚ′	р	Р	р	Р
17	q	Q	m	M	ιζ′	ΙΖ′	с	С	с	С
18	r	R	n	N	ιη′	ΙΗ′	т	Т	т	Т
19	s	S	o	O	ιθ′	ΙΘ′	у	У	у	У
20	t	T	p	P	κ′	Κ′	ф	Ф	ф	Ф
21	u	U	r	R	κα′	ΚΑ′	х	Х	х	Х
22	v	V	s	S	κβ′	ΚΒ′	ц	Ц	ц	Ц
23	w	W	ŝ	Ŝ	κγ′	ΚΓ′	ч	Ч	ч	Ч
24	x	X	t	T	κδ′	ΚΔ′	ш	Ш	ш	Ш
25	y	Y	u	U	κε′	ΚΕ′	щ	Щ	щ	Щ
26	z	Z	ŭ	Ŭ	κϛ′	ΚϚ′	э	Э	ю	Ю
27	-	-	v	V	κζ′	ΚΖ′	ю	Ю	я	Я
28	-	-	z	Z	κη′	ΚΗ′	я	Я	-	-
29	-	-	-	-	κθ′	ΚΘ′	-	-	-	-
30	-	-	-	-	λ′	Λ′	-	-	-	-
40	-	-	-	-	μ′	Μ′	-	-	-	-
50	-	-	-	-	ν′	Ν′	-	-	-	-
100	-	-	-	-	ρ′	Ρ′	-	-	-	-
250	-	-	-	-	σν′	ΣΝ′	-	-	-	-
500	-	-	-	-	φ′	Φ′	-	-	-	-

Table 13.4: Different methods for representing numbers by letters

In some languages an alternative way of writing numbers exists, often named "additive" and based on assigning a letter or a combination of them to denote the numbers 1 to 9, 10 to 90, 100 to 900, and so on. An archetypal case is Greek, with a system that was used in official publications at the end of the 19th century and the beginning of the 20th century. At present most Greeks use it for small numbers.

The knowledge of how to write numbers larger than 20 or 30 is not very widespread, being primarily used by the Eastern Orthodox Church and scholars. They employ this approach to denote numbers up to 999999. This system works as follows:

- Only numbers greater than 0 can be expressed.

- For the units 1 through 9 (inclusive), the letters alpha, beta, gamma, delta, epsilon, stigma, zeta, eta, and theta are used, followed by a mark similar to the mathematical symbol "prime", called the "numeric mark". Because the letter stigma is not always part of the available font, it is often replaced by the first two letters of its name as an alternative. In the babel implementation the letter stigma is produced, rather than the digraph sigma tau.

- For the tens 10 through 90 (inclusive), the letters iota, kappa, lambda, mu, nu, xi, omikron, pi, and qoppa are used, again followed by the numeric mark. The qoppa that appears in Greek numerals has a distinct zig-zag form that is quite different from the normal qoppa, which resembles the Latin "q".

- For the hundreds 100 through 900 (inclusive), the letters rho, sigma, tau, upsilon, phi, chi, psi, omega, and sampi are used, also followed by the numeric mark.

- Using these rules, any number between 1 and 999 can be expressed by a group of letters denoting the hundreds, tens, and units, followed by *one* numeric mark.

- For the number range 1000 through 999000 (inclusive), the digits denoting multiples of a thousand are expressed by the same letters as above, this time with a numeric mark in front of this letter group. This mark is rotated 180 degrees and placed *under* the baseline. As can be seen in the example below, when two letter groups are combined, *both* numeric marks are used:

123456 in Greek notation: ͵ρ͵κ͵γυνϛ′

987654 in Greek notation: ͵Δ͵Π͵ΖΧΝΔ′

```
\usepackage{garamondlibre} \linespread{1.1}
\usepackage[english,greek]{babel}
\newcommand\eng[1]{\foreignlanguage{english}{#1}}

123456 \eng{in Greek notation:} \greeknumeral{123456} \par
987654 \eng{in Greek notation:} \Greeknumeral{987654}
```

13-3-23

In ancient Greece yet another numbering system was used, which closely resembles the roman one in that it employs letters to denote important numbers. Multiple occurrences of a letter denote a multiple of the "important" number; for example, the letter I denotes 1, so III denotes 3. Here are the basic digits used in the Athenian numbering system:

- I denotes the number one (1).

- Π denotes the number five (5).

- Δ denotes the number ten (10).

- H denotes the number one hundred (100).

- X denotes the number one thousand (1000).

- M denotes the number ten thousand (10000).

Moreover, the letters Δ, H, X, and M, when placed under the letter Π, denote five times their original value; for example, the symbol ⊠ denotes the number 5000, and the symbol △ denotes the number 50. Note that the numbering system does not provide negative numerals or a symbol for zero.

The Athenian numbering system, among others, is described *A History of Mathematical Notations* [22, pp. 21–29]. This numbering system is supported by the package athnum, which comes with the babel system and implements the command \athnum. Note that only a few font families besides Computer and Latin Modern provide the required characters, among them Kerkis and Garamond Libre.

13-3-24

6284 in Athenian notation:
ⴲXHHⴲ△△△IIII

```
\usepackage[english,greek]{babel}
\usepackage{garamondlibre,athnum}
\newcommand\eng[1]{\foreignlanguage{english}{#1}}
6284 \eng{in Athenian notation:} \\ \athnum{6284}
```

In Icelandic documents, numbers require special formatting to be typeset correctly. For this purpose the command \tala is provided. It takes an optional argument, which can be used to replace the decimal separator used, such as for use with the dcolumn package.

The dcolumn package formats numbers in math mode, which explains the different fonts in the two parts of the example (this book does not change the default math setup, so the digits inside the box are taken from Computer Modern):

3 141,592 653
3,141.592,653

13-3-25

| 3,14 |
| 123,456 7 |
| 9 876,543 |

```
\usepackage[english,icelandic]{babel}
  \usepackage{dcolumn} \newcolumntype{d}{D{,}{\decimalsep}{-1}}
\tala{3141,592653}                              \par
\foreignlanguage{english}{\tala{3141,592653}}\par \bigskip
\begin{tabular}{|d|}  \hline
             3,14      \\
  \tala[,]{123,4567}  \\ \tala[,]{9876,543}   \\ \hline
\end{tabular}
```

Miscellaneous extras

In French typesetting it is customary to print family names in small capitals, *without* hyphenating a name. For this purpose the command \bsc (boxed small capitals) is provided. Abbreviations of the French word "numéro" should be typeset according to specific rules; these have been implemented in the commands \no and \No. Finally, for certain enumerated lists the commands \primo, \secundo, \tertio, and \quarto are available when typesetting in French.

… for French

13-3-26

Leslie LAMPORT   Nº 9 1º 3º

```
\usepackage[french]{babel}
Leslie~\bsc{Lamport} \quad \No9 \ \primo \ \tertio
```

In some languages, e.g., Italian, it is customary to write together the article and the following noun — for example, "nell'altezza". To carry out the hyphenation of such constructs the character ' is made to behave as a normal letter.

… for Catalan, French, and Italian

... for Hungarian

In the Hungarian language the definite article can be either "a" or "az", depending on the context. Especially with references and citations, it is not always known beforehand which form should be used. The support for the Hungarian language contains commands that know the rules dictating when a "z" should be added to the article. These commands all take an argument that determines which form of the definite article should be typeset together with that argument.

```
\az{text}   \Az{text}
```

These commands produce the article and the argument. The argument can be a star (as in \az*), in which case just the article is typeset. The form \Az is intended for the start of a sentence.

```
\aref{text}   \Aref{text}      \apageref{text}   \Apageref{text}
```

The first two commands should be used instead of a(z)~\ref{*label*}. When an equation is being referenced, the argument may be enclosed in parentheses instead of braces. For page references use \apageref (or \Apageref) to allow LATEX to automatically produce the correct definite article.

```
\acite{text} \Acite{text}
```

For citations the command \acite should be used. Its argument may be a list of citations, in which case the first element of the list determines which form of the article should be typeset.

... specials for math

In Eastern Europe a number of mathematical operators have a different appearance in equations than they do in "the Western world". Table 13.5 on the next page shows the relevant commands, which can be used irrespective of the current language. The Russian commands are also valid for Bulgarian and Ukrainian language support. The package grmath, which comes as part of the Greek style, changes the definitions of these operators to produce abbreviations of their local names. The package can be used only in conjunction with the greek option of babel.

13.3.4 Layout considerations

Some of the language support files in the babel package provide commands for automatically changing the layout of the document. Some simply change the way LATEX handles spaces after punctuation characters or ensure that the first paragraph that follows a section heading is indented. Others go much further.

Spaces after punctuation characters

In *The TEXbook* [42, pp. 72–74], the concept of extra white space after punctuation characters is discussed. Good typesetting practice mandated that inter-sentence spaces behave a little differently than interword spaces with respect to shrinkage and expansion (during justification). However, this practice is not considered desirable in all cases — even in English it seems to be falling into disfavor, so for a number of languages (for example, Breton, Bulgarian, Czech, Danish, Estonian, Finnish, French,

LaTeX		Serbian		Russian		
\tan	tan	\tg	tg	\tg	tg	
\cot	cot	\ctg	ctg	\ctg	ctg	
\sinh	sinh	\sh	sh	\sh	sh	
\cosh	cosh	\ch	ch	\ch	ch	
\tanh	tanh	\th	th	\th	arctg	
\coth	coth	\cth	cth	\cth	cth	
\csc	csc			\cosec	cosec	
\arcsin	arcsin	\arsh	arsh			
\arccos	arccos	\arch	arch			
\arctan	arctan	\arctg	arctg	\arctg	arctg	
		\arcctg	arcctg	\arcctg	arcctg	*(extra)*

13-3-27

Note that the redefinition of \th conflicts with its standard use as an LICR command for
þ (thorn); therefore, babel restricts this redefinition to math mode in Cyrillic texts.

Table 13.5: Alternative mathematical operators for Eastern European languages

German, Norwegian, Russian, Spanish, Turkish, and Ukrainian) this feature is switched
off with a command called \frenchspacing (even though it is *not* used for French).

Another layout concept that is built into most LaTeX classes is the suppression of
the paragraph indentation for the first paragraph that follows a section heading. Again,
for some languages this behavior is wrong; the support for French, Serbo-Croatian,
and Spanish changes it to have *all* paragraphs indented. In fact, you can request this
behavior for any document by loading the package indentfirst.

Paragraph indention after heading

The support for French takes this somewhat further to accommodate the typesetting rules used in France. If this language has been set as the main one, it changes
the general way lists are typeset by LaTeX by reducing the amount of vertical white
space in them; this change is applied globally to preserve the consistency in the
document appearance. For the itemize environment, it removes all vertical white
space between the items and changes the appearance of the items by replacing "•"
with a dash.

Layout of lists

Some text with a list.
— item 1
— item 2
And some text following.

```
\usepackage[french]{babel}

Some text with a list.
\begin{itemize}
  \item item 1 \item item 2
\end{itemize}
And some text following.
```

13-3-28

\frenchsetup{*options*}

For documents that are typeset in more than one language, the support for French
provides a way to customize how several layout elements should be adapted. Different
results can be achieved by using key-value options in \frenchsetup in the preamble
of the document. An example is StandardLayout=true, which forces babel not to

interfere with lists, first paragraphs indentation, or footnotes. There are many options for fine-tuning the typographical conventions.

Layout of footnotes

For instance, in the French typesetting tradition, footnotes are handled differently than they are in the Anglo-American tradition. In the running text, a little white space should be added before the number or symbol that calls the footnote. This behavior is optional and can be selected by using the `AutoSpaceFootnotes` key in `\frenchsetup`.

The text of the footnote can also be typeset according to French typesetting rules; this result is achieved by using the key `FrenchFootnotes`, but the commands `\StandardFootnotes` and `\FrenchFootnotes` are also available for local changes (`\StandardFootnotes` in minipages, for instance, because the counter is `\alph`).

```
\usepackage[french,english]{babel}
\frenchsetup{AutoSpaceFootnotes,FrenchFootnotes}
\begin{minipage}{70pt} Some text\footnote{with a footnote}.
\end{minipage}
\selectlanguage{french}\StandardFootnotes
\begin{minipage}{70pt} Some text\footnote{with a footnote}.
\end{minipage}
```

Some text^a. Some text^a.

---

a. with a footnote ^awith a footnote

13-3-29

Layout of captions

Another change performed by the babel support for the French language is that the colon in captions for tables and figures is replaced with an en-dash when one of the document classes of standard LATEX is used.

Internal commands redefined for `magyar`

The support for typesetting Hungarian documents goes even further: it redefines a number of internal LATEX commands to produce correct captions for figures and tables. Using the same means, it changes the layout of section headings. The definition of the `theorem` environment is changed as well. As explained above, such changes may lead to unexpected and even unwanted behavior, so be careful.

Right to left typesetting

To support typesetting Hebrew or Arabic documents, even more drastic changes are needed; they are treated in Section 13.5 on page 332.

13.3.5 Languages and font encoding

As shown in some of the earlier examples, some languages cannot be supported by, for instance, simply translating some texts and providing extra support for special hyphenation needs. Many languages require characters that are not present in LATEX's T1 encoding. For some, just a few characters are missing and can be constructed from the available glyphs; other languages are not normally written using the Latin script. Some of these are supported by the babel system.

Extensions to the T1 encodings

For some languages just a few characters are missing in the T1 encoding, and they might not even be directly accessible on the keyboard. When the missing characters can be constructed from the available glyphs, it is relatively easy to rectify this situation. Such is the case for the Old Icelandic language. It needs a number of characters that can be represented by adding the "ogonek" to available glyphs. To access them, you can use the shorthands in the next example, which are activated explicitly in the package options:

13-3-30

ǫ Ǫ ǿ Ǿ ę Ę é Ę́

```
\usepackage[icelandic.utf8old]{babel}
"o "O "ó "Ó "e "E "é "É
```

Basic support for switching script-related features

Because scripts, writing directions, and so on, are strongly linked to each language, the babel core provides no user interface to set them. Instead, they are adjusted as needed when a language is selected. This high-level interface guarantees all the required features are set and applied consistently.[1]

As to writing directions, the model to deal with them in 8-bit engines like pdfTeX has many issues and requires a lot of manual intervention, which has been provided in different ways, depending on the language. See the manual for the language styles requiring bidi writing, particularly Arabic (which is supported with the arabi package, by Youssef Jabri) and Hebrew. Something similar can be said of XƎTEX, whose bidirectional model is basically the same as that of pdfTeX.

On the other hand, with LuaTeX, a more modern approach, based on the Unicode algorithm, can be applied so that the writing direction is switched automatically. See Section 13.5 on "Complex scripts" for further details, but here this macro is worth mentioning.

`\babelsublr{text}`

There are cases in which the Unicode algorithm fails and makes the wrong guess. An example is the string "2.5", which must be shown in this order when it refers to a real number, but also, and depending on the language, "5.2" when it refers to a section with a subsection. With LuaTeX the latter can be entered as `\babelsublr{2}.\babelsublr{5}`, which isolates the numbers from the dot. See the babel manual for the option `layout=counters`, which does this for you in some typical cases.

`\ensureascii{text}`

A few encodings used for text, notably LGR or X2, are not LICR-savvy, and the ASCII range contains non–Latin letters (for example, the slot for the letter "a" is replaced in the former by the Greek letter alpha). This command attempts to typeset its argument in a font encoding respecting the ASCII encoding, typically T1 or OT1, and can be used in the scope of those problematical encodings so that ASCII text is correctly typeset.

---

[1]A few macros to deal with those changes have been available for many years (for example, `\cyrillicencoding`), but they are deprecated, because even the Latin script may require several encodings.

13.4 Support for Cyrillic and Greek

The Greek and Cyrillic scripts are closely related to the Latin one, and it is not surprising that among the first non-Latin scripts to be supported by LaTeX were the former. Although currently they are usually best typeset with the Unicode engines, pdfTeX is still widely used, and this section is devoted to this engine.

Unicode engines

> In XeTeX and LuaTeX, you can resort, in addition, to the mechanism described below in "Complex scripts" (Section 13.5), which supports not only Monotonic and Polytonic Greek, but also Ancient Greek.

13.4.1 The Cyrillic alphabet

The Cyrillic alphabet is used by several of the Slavic languages in Eastern Europe, as well as for writing tens of languages used in the territory encompassed by the former Soviet Union. Vladimir Volovich and Werner Lemberg, together with the LaTeX Project Team, have integrated basic support for the Cyrillic language into LaTeX. This section addresses the issues of Cyrillic fonts, the encoding interface, and their integration with babel.

Historically, support for Russian in TeX has been available from the American Mathematical Society [10]. The AMS system uses the wncyr fonts and is based on a transliteration table originally designed for Russian journal names and article titles in the journal *Mathematical Reviews*. In this journal the AMS prefers that the same character sequence in the electronic files produce either the Russian text with Russian characters or its transliteration with English characters, without any ambiguities.

However, with the spread of TeX in Russia, proper support for typesetting Russian (and later other languages written in the Cyrillic alphabet) became necessary. Over the years several 7- and 8-bit input encodings were developed, as well as many font encodings. The Cyrillic system is designed to work for any 8-bit input encoding and is able to map all of them onto a few Cyrillic font encodings, each supporting a number of languages.

Font encodings

For compatibility reasons, only the upper 128 characters in an 8-bit TeX font are available for new glyphs. Because the number of glyphs in use in Cyrillic-based languages during the 20th century far exceeds 128, four "Cyrillic font encodings" have been defined [11]. Three of them — T2A, T2B, and T2C — satisfy the basic structural requirements of LaTeX's T* encodings and, therefore, can be used in multilingual documents with other languages being based on standard font encodings.[1]

The work on the T2* encodings was performed by Alexander Berdnikov in collaboration with Mikhail Kolodin and Andrew Janishevsky. Vladimir Volovich provided the integration with LaTeX. Table 13.6 shows the layout of the T2A encoding.

---

[1] The fourth Cyrillic encoding, X2, contains Cyrillic glyphs spread over the 256 character positions and is thus suitable only for specific, Cyrillic-only applications. It is not discussed here.

	´0	´1	´2	´3	´4	´5	´6	´7	
´00x	`	´	^	~	¨	˝	°	ˇ	″0x
´01x	˘	–	·	̦	̧	I	⟨	⟩	
´02x	"	"	^	˜	̆	–	—		″1x
´03x	0	1	J	ff	fi	fl	ffi	ffl	
´04x	␣	!	"	#	$	%	&	'	″2x
´05x	(	)	*	+	,	-	.	/	
´06x	0	1	2	3	4	5	6	7	″3x
´07x	8	9	:	;	<	=	>	?	
´10x	@	A	B	C	D	E	F	G	″4x
´11x	H	I	J	K	L	M	N	O	
´12x	P	Q	R	S	T	U	V	W	″5x
´13x	X	Y	Z	[	\	]	^	_	
´14x	`	a	b	c	d	e	f	g	″6x
´15x	h	i	j	k	l	m	n	o	
´16x	p	q	r	s	t	u	v	w	″7x
´17x	x	y	z	{	|	}	~	-	
´20x	Ѓ	Ғ	Ђ	Ћ	ҍ	Җ	Ӡ	Љ	″8x
´21x	Ї	Қ	Ҟ	К̡	Æ	Ң	Ҥ	Ѕ	
´22x	Ѳ	Ҫ	Ў	Ү	Ұ	Х̧	Ц	Ч	″9x
´23x	Ҷ	Є	Ә	Њ	Ё	№	¤	§	
´24x	ѓ	ғ	ђ	ħ	h	җ	ӡ	љ	″Ax
´25x	ї	қ	ҟ	к̡	æ	ң	ҥ	ѕ	
´26x	ѳ	ҫ	ў	ү	ұ	х̧	ц	ч	″Bx
´27x	ҷ	є	ә	њ	ё	„	«	»	
´30x	А	Б	В	Г	Д	Е	Ж	З	″Cx
´31x	И	Й	К	Л	М	Н	О	П	
´32x	Р	С	Т	У	Ф	Х	Ц	Ч	″Dx
´33x	Ш	Щ	Ъ	Ы	Ь	Э	Ю	Я	
´34x	а	б	в	г	д	е	ж	з	″Ex
´35x	и	й	к	л	м	н	о	п	
´36x	р	с	т	у	ф	х	ц	ч	″Fx
´37x	ш	щ	ъ	ы	ь	э	ю	я	
	″8	″9	″A	″B	″C	″D	″E	″F	

Characters marked in blue need to be present (in their specified positions) in every text encoding, as they are transparently passed through TEX.

Table 13.6: Glyph chart for a T2A-encoded font (larm1000)

Two other LaTeX Cyrillic font encodings exist, although they are best avoided: the 7-bit OT2 encoding developed by the American Mathematical Society, and the 8-bit LCY encoding, which are incompatible with the LaTeX's T* encodings and, therefore, unsuitable for typesetting multilingual documents. The OT2 encoding was designed in such a way that a transliterated source could be used to produce the text in that form and in the Cyrillic alphabet.

The basic LaTeX distribution come with all the encoding and font definition files for handling Cyrillic. The babel package includes support for Bulgarian, Russian, Belarusian, and Ukrainian, among others. Together with the font files, LaTeX can use this package to provide complete support for typesetting languages based on the Cyrillic alphabet. The Cyrillic font encodings support the languages listed in the document `cyrguide.pdf`. Note that some languages, such as Bulgarian and Russian, can be properly typeset with more than one of those encodings.

There are hyphenation patterns for several languages based on the T2A encoding in the `hyph-utf8` bundle, which is the default in current TeX distributions. A collection of hyphenation patterns for the Russian language that supports the T2* encodings, as well as other popular font encodings used for Russian typesetting, is available in the `ruhyphen` distribution on CTAN (`language/hyphenation/ruhyphen`).

Fonts

The default font family with LaTeX is Knuth's Computer Modern, in its 8-bit (T1-encoded EC fonts) incarnation. Olga Lapko and Andrey Khodulev developed the LH fonts, which provide glyph designs compatible with the Computer Modern font family and covering all Cyrillic font encodings. They provide the same font shapes and sizes as those available for its Latin equivalent, the EC family, and are now part of the CM-Super fonts package.

Other fonts can also be used, provided that their TeX font encoding is compatible with the T2* encodings, as several examples in this chapter show. More can be found in Section 10.12.

Using Cyrillic in your documents

Support for Cyrillic fonts in pdfTeX is based on the standard fontenc package and assumes by default that UTF-8 is used as the input encoding. If your files are stored in one of the legacy 8-bit input encodings, then inputenc is also needed. For instance, one can write the following in the preamble of the document:

```
\usepackage[T2A]{fontenc}     \usepackage[koi8-r]{inputenc}
\usepackage[russian]{babel}
```

The input encoding `koi8-r` (KOI8 optimized for Russian) is just one of the many alternatives to UTF-8 available for Cyrillic texts:

cp855 Standard MS-DOS Cyrillic code page.

cp866 Standard MS-DOS Russian code page. Several variants, distinguished by differences in the code positions 242–254, exist: cp866av (Cyrillic Alternative), cp866mav (Modified Alternative Variant), cp866nav (New Alternative Variant), and cp866tat (for Tatar).

cp1251 Standard MS Windows Cyrillic code page.

koi8-r Standard Cyrillic code page that is widely used on UN*X-like systems for Russian language support. Variants for Ukrainian are koi8-u and koi8-ru. An ECMA variant (ISO-IR 111 ECMA) is isoir111.

iso88595 ISO standard ISO 8859-5 (also called ISO-IR 144).

maccyr Apple Macintosh Cyrillic code page (also known as Microsoft cp10007) and macukr, the Apple Macintosh Ukrainian code page.

ctt, dbk, mnk, mos, ncc Mongolian code pages.

Not all of these code pages are part of the standard inputenc distribution, so some may have to be obtained separately.

When more than one input encoding is used within a document, you can use the \inputencoding command to switch between them. To define the case of text, two standard LATEX commands, \MakeUppercase and \MakeLowercase, can produce uppercase or lowercase, respectively. The low-level TEX \uppercase and \lowercase should never be used in LATEX and will not work for Cyrillic.

In the previous example of a preamble, the font encoding to be used was explicitly declared. For multilingual documents *all* encodings needed should be enumerated via the \usepackage[...]{fontenc} command. Changing from one font encoding to another can be accomplished by using the \fontencoding command, but it is advisable that such changes be performed by a higher-level interface such as the \selectlanguage command. In particular, when using babel, you can simply write

```
\usepackage[russian]{babel}
```

where babel will automatically choose (and load) the default font encoding for Russian, which is T2A, when it is available.

Indexes and bibliographies

There are a few tools to deal with indexes and bibliographies based on the default UTF-8 encoding. For indexes, upmendex is an alternative for *MakeIndex* supporting Unicode and many languages, even with pdfTEX. It is described in Chapter 14, so here we limit ourselves to the steps required to compose an index with Russian terms. In the document, set the index up in the preamble in the same way as with *MakeIndex*. An example is:

```
\documentclass{article}
\usepackage[T2A]{fontenc}    \usepackage[russian]{babel}
\usepackage{makeidx}         \makeindex
\begin{document}
один\index{один} два\index{два}
\printindex
\end{document}
```

Although the default collator does not do a bad job (for example, "ë" is correctly sorted under "e"), it is advisable to set the locale as explained in Section 14.3.2, where the reader can find further information on customizing upmendex. Just create a file containing the line:

```
icu_locale "ru"
```

and then include it in the list of styles. Thus, if you name the file ru_locale.ist, you have to run upmendex -s ru_locale ⟨filename⟩.idx to use it.

For bibliographic references, biblatex and biber provide a convenient replacement for BIBTEX. The package and program are Unicode aware and work smoothly with the three main engines. They are described in detail in Chapters 15 and 16.

13.4.2 The Greek alphabet

Greek support in babel comes in two variants: the one-accent monotoniko (the default), which is used in most cases in everyday communications in Greece today, and the multi-accent polutoniko, which has to be specified as an attribute, as explained in Section 13.2.3. These variants are mutually exclusive, and they cannot be combined in a single document. This limitation does not exist with the interface explained in the next section, but it requires XƎTEX or LuaTEX.

The first family of Greek fonts for TEX was created during the mid-1980s by Silvio Levy [66]. Other developers improved or extended these fonts or developed their own Greek fonts.

In babel the Greek language support is maintained by Günter Milde, based on the original work of Claudio Beccari in collaboration with Apostolos Syropoulos, who developed the Greek cb font family [8]. In their paper these authors discuss in some detail previous efforts[1] to support the Greek language with TEX.

It relies on the LGR encoding, whose layout is shown in Table 13.7 on the next page. Although it is automatically loaded with the greek option of babel, it is advisable to request it explicitly with fontenc, as any other encoding. The cb fonts were originally devised as a companion to the default Computer Modern family supporting this encoding, but, as shown in Section 10.11 on page 106, there are currently more fonts in the LGR encoding to choose from.

It should be stressed that this encoding does not conform to the LICR conventions because it has no ASCII glyphs at all. This can lead to potential conflicts in multilingual documents, which in many cases can be dealt with by using the command \ensureascii, but not always. This is one of the reasons why you should consider XƎTEX or LuaTEX instead of pdfTEX for Greek.

It is possible to use Latin alphabetic characters for inputting Greek according to the transliteration scheme shown in Table 13.8 on page 330. This table shows that the Latin "v" character has no direct equivalent in the Greek transcription. In fact, it is used to indicate that one *does not* want a final sigma. For example, "sv" generates a median form sigma although it occurs in a final position.

---

[1] A more recent overview about 25 years of Greek typesetting with TEX is given in [25].

	′0	′1	′2	′3	′4	′5	′6	′7	
′00x	–	ˆ	⊿	Ħ	X̄	M̄	ϛ	ϟ	″0x
′01x	ɪ	A_I	H_I	Ω_I	A	Ϋ	α	ü	
′02x	,	`	ʮ	ϙ	˘	ϙ	Ϭ	ƛ	″1x
′03x	€	‰	ə	ƛ	'	'	˘	–	
′04x	˜	!	'	ˌ	ˏ	%	·	'	″2x
′05x	(	)	*	+	,	-	.	/	
′06x	0	1	2	3	4	5	6	7	″3x
′07x	8	9	:	·	<	=	>	;	
′10x	˘	A	B	˓	Δ	E	Φ	Γ	″4x
′11x	H	I	Θ	K	Λ	M	N	O	
′12x	Π	X	P	Σ	T	Υ	˘	Ω	″5x
′13x	Ξ	Ψ	Z	[	˜	]	˅	˞	
′14x	`	α	β	ς	δ	ε	φ	γ	″6x
′15x	η	ι	ϑ	κ	λ	μ	ν	ο	
′16x	π	χ	ρ	ς	τ	υ		ω	″7x
′17x	ξ	ψ	ζ	«	,	»	~	—	
′20x	ὰ	ά	ᾶ	ᾰ	ᾳ	ᾁ	ᾲ	ᾷ	″8x
′21x	ἀ	ἄ	ἂ	ᾇ	ᾴ	ᾅ	ᾃ	ᾀ	
′22x	ᾶ	ᾱ	ᾰ	Ϝ	ᾷ	ᾅ	ᾆ	˘	″9x
′23x	ὴ	ή	ῆ		ὴ	ή	ῆ		
′24x	ή	ἤ	ἢ	ᾗ	ή	ἥ	ἣ	ᾐ	″Ax
′25x	ῆ	ῄ	ῂ	ῇ	ῆ	ῄ	ῂ	ῇ	
′26x	ὼ	ώ	ῶ	ᾧ	ῳ	ᾡ	ᾢ	ᾗ	″Bx
′27x	ὼ	ὤ	ὢ	ᾧ	ῴ	ᾥ	ᾣ	ᾠ	
′30x	ῶ	ῶ	ῶ	Ϝ	ῷ	ᾥ	ᾦ		″Cx
′31x	ὶ	ί	ῖ	ῗ	ὺ	ύ	ῦ	ῧ	
′32x	ἰ	ἴ	ἲ	ῗ	ὐ	ὔ	ὒ	ῧ	″Dx
′33x	ῖ	ῑ	ῐ	Ϊ	ῦ	ῡ	ῠ	Ϋ	
′34x	ὲ	έ	ὲ	ê	ὸ	ό	ὸ	ő	″Ex
′35x	έ	ἔ	ἒ	ᾔ	ό	ὄ	ὂ	ő	
′36x	ϊ	ί	ΐ	ῗ	ϋ	ύ	ΰ	ῧ	″Fx
′37x	ᾳ	η	ϡ	ῤ	ῥ		'	ˏ	
	″8	″9	″A	″B	″C	″D	″E	″F	

Characters marked in blue should be ASCII characters in every LATEX text encoding (compare Table 13.6 on page 325), as they are transparently passed through TEX. In LGR this is not the case for A–Z and a–z, which can produce problems in multilingual documents.

Table 13.7: Glyph chart for an LGR-encoded font (grmn1000)

Input	a	b	c	d	e	f	g	h	i	j	k	l	m	n	o	p	q	r	s	t	u	v	w	x	y	z
	α	β	ς	δ	ε	φ	γ	η	ι	ϑ	κ	λ	μ	ν	ο	π	χ	ρ	ς	τ	υ		ω	ξ	ψ	ζ
Input	A	B	C	D	E	F	G	H	I	J	K	L	M	N	O	P	Q	R	S	T	U	V	W	X	Y	Z
	Α	Β	ʽ	Δ	Ε	Φ	Γ	Η	Ι	Θ	Κ	Λ	Μ	Ν	Ο	Π	Χ	Ρ	Σ	Τ	Υ		Ω	Ξ	Ψ	Ζ

13-4-1

Table 13.8: Greek transliteration with Latin letters for the LGR encoding

	Input			Result	Example	
Acute	’a ’e ’h ’i ’o	’u ’w		ά έ ή ί ό ύ ώ	g’ata	γάτα
Diaeresis	"i "u "I "U			ϊ ϋ Ϊ Ϋ	qa"ide’uh|c	χαϊδεύῃς
Rough breathing	<a <e <h <i <o <r <u <w			ἁ ἑ ἡ ἱ ὁ ῥ ὑ ὡ	<’otan	ὅταν
Smooth breathing	>a >e >h >i >o >r >u >w			ἀ ἐ ἠ ἰ ὀ ῤ ὐ ὠ	>’aneu	ἄνευ
Grave	‘a ‘e ‘h ‘i ‘o	‘u ‘w		ὰ ὲ ὴ ὶ ὸ ὺ ὼ	dad‘i	δαδὶ
Circumflex	~a ~h ~i ~u ~w			ᾶ ῆ ῖ ῦ ῶ	ful~hc	φυλῆς
Diacritic below	a| h| w|			ᾳ ῃ ῳ		
	‘w| ’w| >‘w| >’w| <‘w| <’w|			ᾥ ᾣ ᾧ ᾥ ᾦ ᾤ		

13-4-2

Table 13.9: LGR ligatures producing single-accented glyphs

By default, the greek option of babel uses monotoniko Greek. Multi-accented mode is requested by specifying the language attribute polutoniko for the greek option:

`\usepackage[greek]{babel}   \languageattribute{greek}{polutoniko}`

For both modes, some seldom-used characters have been defined to behave like letters (`\catcode` 11). For monotoniko Greek, this is the case for the characters ’ and ". In the polutoniko variant, the characters <, >, ~, ‘, and | also behave like letters. The reason for this behavior is that the LGR encoding contains many ligatures with these characters to produce the right glyphs; see Table 13.9. Table 13.10 shows the available composite accent and spiritus combinations.

13.5 Complex scripts

Typesetting documents in the so-called complex scripts has been always a nuisance with "traditional" TEX. With the advent of XƎTEX and LuaTEX, it is now possible to write in any language of the world, provided you have a suitable font at hand, so babel has been extended to deal with those scripts and their needs for line breaking, layout, bidirectional behavior, etc.

Input	Result	Input	Result
'"i '"i '"u '"u	ΐΐΰΰ		
>'a >'e >'h >'i >'o >'u >'w	ἄἔἤἴὄὔῴ	>'A >'E >'H >'I >'O >'U >'W	Ἄ Ἔ Ἤ Ἴ Ὄ Ὕ Ὤ
>`a >`e >`h >`i >`o >`u >`w	ἂἒἢἲὂὒῲ	>`A >`E >`H >`I >`O >`U >`W	Ἂ Ἒ Ἢ Ἲ Ὂ Ὓ Ὢ
<'a <'e <'h <'i <'o <'u <'w	ἅἕἥἵὅὕῴ	<'A <'E <'H <'I <'O <'U <'W	Ἅ Ἕ Ἥ Ἵ Ὅ Ὕ Ὥ
<`a <`e <`h <`i <`o <`u <`w	ἃἓἣἳὃὓῲ	<`A <`E <`H <`I <`O <`U <`W	Ἃ Ἓ Ἣ Ἳ Ὃ Ὓ Ὣ
>~a >~h >~i >~u >~w	ἆἦἶὖῶ	>~A >~H >~I >~U >~W	Ἆ Ἦ Ἶ Ὗ Ὦ
<~a <~h <~i <~u <~w	ἇἧἷὗῷ	<~A <~H <~I <~U <~W	Ἇ Ἧ Ἷ Ὗ Ὧ

Table 13.10: Available composite spiritus and accent combinations

In many of these languages, an alternative way to define them is required, activated with the package option `provide=*`, as shown in the examples below. It resorts in turn to a specific macro named `\babelprovide`, described in the babel manual in full detail.

Because the default font families cover only the Latin script, you may need to set up different ones with `\babelfont`, which provides a high-level interface to fontspec. It defines not only the corresponding font for the family given in its first argument, but also passes the information required to render it correctly, according to the peculiarities of each script. The fonts used here are available in TEX Live, and they should work out of the box in this distribution. For Greek and Cyrillic, refer to Chapter 10, because these scripts are included in many fonts.

Chinese + Japanese + Korean, a.k.a. CJK

Given that Chinese and Japanese are written without spaces (and often Korean, too) and line breaking is possible between many characters (but not all), babel applies some basic rules based on the Unicode ones for this purpose.

義は険しい山よりも重く、死
は大鳥の羽よりも軽い。

```
\usepackage[japanese, provide=*]{babel}
\babelfont{rm}{IPAexMincho}
```
義は険しい山よりも重く、死は大鳥の羽よりも軽い。

In languages of this group, lines are written often top to bottom, which are in turn written right to left, but for a complete solution you must resort to dedicated packages like CJK, kotex, luatexja, or CTeX, because babel is restricted to horizontal writing. Some of these packages rely on upTEX, an extension to the TEX program that addresses this typographic need.

Indic scripts

Indic scripts may contain what are named clusters, combinations of consonants with a special graphical representation. In addition, letters are visually reordered so that a vowel may precede the corresponding consonant. Currently, the best option in most cases is to resort to Unicode engines, because the script complexities are handled by the fonts. With LuaTeX, the `Harfbuzz` renderer (instead of the default one) is usually to be preferred; see the `fontspec` manual for further details on the available font renderers.

```
\usepackage[hindi, provide=*]{babel}
\babelfont{rm}[Renderer=Harfbuzz]{FreeSerif}
```

जिस की लाठी उस की भैंस.　　　　जिस की लाठी उस की भैंस.　　　　13-5-2

Line breaking is often done without a hyphen, like in Thai. This language is, in addition, written without word spaces, so a special line-breaking algorithm is applied in both Unicode engines to insert flexible spaces at appropriate places in order to justify the text.

Bi-directional (bidi) scripts

Arabic, Hebrew, and Syriac among others require bidi writing, which must be explicitly activated with a package option. In the case of LuaTeX, which is the recommended engine in those languages, the option is `bidi=basic`. With it, left-to-write characters, including numerals, are automatically set in the correct direction. In the case of Arabic and Syriac, the letter shapes change according to their positions in a word.

```
\usepackage[bidi=basic, arabic, provide=*]{babel}
\babelfont{rm}{Amiri}
```

اجتنب مصاحبة الكذاب فإن اضطررت إليه فلا تصدقه.　　اجتنب مصاحبة الكذاب فإن اضطررت إليه فلا تصدقه.　　13-5-3

Arabic documents also have right-to-left layouts, which means margins, lists, footnotes, tables, and other elements must be readjusted. This can be done in LuaTeX in the most typical cases with minimal internal changes in the LaTeX code, because it has built-in primitives to set the origin of pages, boxes, and the like, so babel attempts to do it, but XeTeX requires patching a good deal of LaTeX macros and packages, and an external package is used (bidi, by Vafa Khalighi). Text justification with *kashida* (short horizontal extenders) can be accomplished in LuaTeX with user-definable rules.

13.6 Tailoring babel

As explained earlier, typographic rules are not always set in stone and may differ even among publishing houses. Therefore, users should be able to tailor easily the language styles, or even to create new ones from scratch for them to be adapted to their own needs. In most cases, this is best done with the help of dedicated packages, but in some cases all you need is either to readjust the decisions taken by babel or to make changes that are language or culture dependent.

This section starts with some tips about how to customize the styles and then describes briefly how to create `.ldf` files or, alternatively, descriptive `.ini` files based on key/value pairs. Some of these changes are based on the command `\babelprovide`.

13.6.1 User level

We start with describing the kind of changes that you may want to do in the preamble of an individual document, if you are not satisfied with the defaults offered by babel or by a language support package. Obviously the same commands are also used in class or package files to provide you with the initial configurations.

Modify caption strings

Although there are more or less traditional ways to name chapters, tables, and so on, they are not always unique, and the default values may need changes. For example, in Spanish *Table* has been traditionally named *Cuadro*, but *Tabla* is also frequent.

Redefining directly the macro (in this case \tablename) in the preamble or inside \AtBeginDocument may not work because the original definition is restored at every language selection. You must make sure the new definition correctly replaces the original one, and the best way in most cases is with \setlocalecaption, as shown:

```
\setlocalecaption{spanish}{table}{Tabla}
```

In this particular example, the macro name to be set is built from the second argument by adding name. These definitions should contain only the string and perhaps some basic formatting, but not, say, counters or labels.

Hyphenation rules

Some languages may follow several criteria to hyphenate words, as the well-known case of British vs. American English demonstrates. Furthermore, some disciplines like chemistry may require their own rules. On the other hand, if there are no hyphenation patterns for a language, you may want to apply those for a similar language. This can be done in your documents with \babelprovide in the following way, provided language.dat (described in Section 13.6.2) has been configured to load a set of patterns with the given name:

```
\babelprovide[hyphenrules=ngerman-x-2019-04-04]{german}
```

Another set of hyphenation parameters you may want to modify are the language-specific values for \lefthyphenmin (minimum number of characters on the left before the first hyphen point) and \righthyphenmin (minimum numbers on the right), which are stored in \⟨*language*⟩hyphenmins.

\providehyphenmins{*lang*}{*hyphenmins*}　　　\⟨*language*⟩hyphenmins

---

The command \providehyphenmins provides a *default* setting for these hyphenation parameters by defining \⟨*language*⟩hyphenmins unless it is already defined for some reason. The babel package detects whether the hyphenation file explicitly sets \lefthyphenmin and \righthyphenmin and automatically defines

\⟨*language*⟩hyphenmins, in which case the \providehyphenmins declaration has no effect.

The syntax inside babel is storage optimized, dating back to the days when every token counted. Thus, the argument *hyphenmins* contains the values for both parameters simply as two digits, making the assumption that you never want a minimum larger than 9. If this assumption is wrong, you must surround the values with braces within *hyphenmins*. For example,

```
\providehyphenmins{german}{{10}{5}}
```

would request leaving at least ten characters before a hyphen and at least five characters after it (thus essentially never hyphenate — except monsters such as Donaudampfschifffahrtkapitänsmütze).

If you want to explicitly overwrite the settings regardless of any existing specification, you can do so by providing a value for \⟨*language*⟩hyphenmins yourself. For instance,

```
\renewcommand*\germanhyphenmins{{4}{3}}
```

never considers hyphenation points with fewer than four letters before and three letters after the hyphen. Thus, LaTeX will never hyphenate a word with less than seven characters in that language.

Hyphenation patterns are built with a certain setting of these parameters in mind. Setting their values lower than the values used in the pattern generation may merely result in incorrect hyphenation. It is possible, however, to use higher values in which case the potential hyphenation points are simply reduced.

Counters and labels

Decimal numerals have different shapes in different scripts and are best entered directly in the final form, but sometimes and for practical reasons a conversion from the Western forms can be useful, particularly with automatically generated numbers. In languages loaded with the procedure described in "Complex scripts", you can map the \arabic counter to the local forms by setting the option maparabic in the optional argument of \babelprovide.

Babel provides a simple tool to create your own numeral systems, including additive ones, in case those provided by default do not met your requirements. Some .ini files provide them, but even so there might be the need to define more. This can be done with \babelprovide as shown in the following example, which defines two variants for the masculine ordinal:

```
\usepackage[spanish]{babel}
\babelprovide[counters/masc = 1\sptext{o} 2\sptext{o} 3\sptext{o},
              counters/masc.short = 1\sptext{er} 2\sptext{o} 3\sptext{er}]
             {spanish}
\localnumeral{masc.short}{3} \quad
\localnumeral{masc}{3}
```

3.ᵉʳ   3.º

13-6-1

The command `\localenumeral` prints the corresponding representation for a number. There is a companion named `\localecounter` whose second argument is a counter name, like `page` or `section`.

Executing some code when languages are selected

When a language is selected and unselected, babel executes several macros that set its behavior. Two of them are particularly important because they are responsible for most of the work, and therefore you need to know them in order to understand how to configure the language.

> `\extras`⟨*language*⟩

The macro `\extras`⟨*language*⟩ contains all extra definitions needed for the language ⟨*language*⟩ being defined in an `.ldf` file. Such extras can be commands to turn shorthands on or off, to make certain characters active, to initiate French spacing, to position umlauts, and so on.

> `\noextras`⟨*language*⟩

To allow switching between any two languages, it is necessary to return to a known state for the TeX engine — in particular, with respect to the definitions initiated by the command `\extras`⟨*language*⟩. The macro `\noextras`⟨*language*⟩ must contain code to revert all such definitions so as to bring TeX back to a known state.

> `\AddBabelHook`[*language*]{*label*}{*hook*}{*code*}

With this command, code can be injected at several places, like before and after `\extras`⟨*language*⟩. For example, if you want French spacing for every language, just say:

```
\AddBabelHook{nonfrench}{afterextras}{\frenchspacing}
```

Here `nonfrench` is just a label to identify the hook, and `afterextras` is the place where the piece of code in the following argument is executed and whose meaning in this case is self-explanatory. When the optional argument for the language is omitted, as in this case, it applies for all languages.

With the optional argument, the ⟨*code*⟩ is executed only with the specified ⟨*language*⟩. The following line in a document with `english` and `ngerman` makes accessible in the former language some shorthands defined in the latter:

```
\AddBabelHook[english]{en-de-shorthands}{afterextras}
  {\languageshorthands{ngerman}}
```

You may also need to activate them as user shorthands in the preamble with, for example, `\useshorthands` or `\useshorthands*`, described in Section 13.2.2 on page 304.

It is worth remembering here the hook mechanism provided by LaTeX itself and described in detail in Appendix A.4 on page 671. Although with some limitations in a few cases, the hooks available in \AddBabelHook can also be used as the first argument of \AddToHook. As explained in the appendix, one advantage of this approach is that you can configure babel even before the package has been actually loaded.

`\addto\`*cmd*`{`*code*`}`

This command is a tool provided by babel allowing you to extend the definition of the control sequence *cmd* with the TeX code specified in *code*. The control sequence *cmd* does not have to have been defined previously. The customary way to extend a language for years has been to modify directly \extras⟨*language*⟩ and \noextras⟨*language*⟩ with the help of this macro, but the more modern and robust interfaces based on hooks are preferable in most cases.

Language-specific tools

Some languages, like French, Spanish, or Hungarian, provide their own tools to tailor the style for specific needs, as an alternative to the use of \languageattribute commands. French and Hungarian understand a collection of key/value pairs, which are set with \frenchsetup, described in Section 13.3.4, and with the macro \magyarOptions, respectively. Spanish takes still another approach, using package options starting with the prefix es-.

13.6.2 Package level

This section is mainly for those who want to develop a language style or to better understand how babel works internally and explains briefly the basic concepts to define a language style.

Language definition files (file extension .ldf) have to conform to a number of conventions, because they complement the common shared code of babel provided in the file babel.def for producing language-dependent text strings. Similarly, to allow for language switching like the capability built into babel, certain rules apply. The basic working assumptions follow:

- Each language definition file ⟨*language*⟩.ldf must define five macros, which are subsequently used to activate and deactivate the language-specific definitions. These macros are \⟨*language*⟩hyphenmins, \captions⟨*language*⟩, \date⟨*language*⟩, \extras⟨*language*⟩, and \noextras⟨*language*⟩, where ⟨*language*⟩ is either the name of the language definition file or the name of a babel package option. Some of these macros and their functions were discussed above.

- When a language definition file is loaded, it can define \l@⟨*language*⟩ to be a variant (*dialect*) of \language0 when \l@⟨*language*⟩ is undefined.

- The language definition files must be written in a way that they can be read not just in the preamble of the document but also in the middle of document processing.

Hyphenating in several languages

Since TeX version 3.0, hyphenation patterns for multiple languages can be used together. These patterns have to be managed somehow. In particular, the plainTeX user has to know for which languages patterns have been loaded and to what values of the command sequence \language they correspond. The babel package abstracts from this low-level interface and manages this information by using an external file, language.dat, in which one records which languages have hyphenation patterns *and* in which files these patterns are stored. This configuration file is then processed[1] when the LaTeX format is built, except with LuaLaTeX, which loads it when the document is typeset. An example of such a file is shown here:

```
%%% Filename    : language.dat
%%% Description : Instructions which pattern files to load.

english        ushyph.tex                    % American English should be first
=usenglish
=USenglish
=american
dumylang       dumyhyph.tex                  % For testing a new language
nohyphenation  zerohyph.tex                  % Language with no patterns
ukenglish loadhyph-en-gb.tex                 % British English
=british
=UKenglish
german loadhyph-de-1901.tex                  % German language patterns
ngerman loadhyph-de-1996.tex
swissgerman loadhyph-de-ch-1901.tex
french loadhyph-fr.tex                       % French
=patois
=francais
spanish loadhyph-es.tex                      % Spanish
=espanol

... many more languages ...
```

In most TeX distributions this file is generated automatically[2] based on the available hyphenation patterns, which are coordinated by Arthur Reutenauer and Mojca

---

[1] Make sure that you do not have several such files in your TeX installation, because it is not always clear which of them is examined during the format generation. The author nearly got bitten during the book production when INITEX picked up the system configuration file and not the specially prepared one containing all the patterns for the examples.

[2] This means that changing it directly is often not a good idea, because it might get overwritten on the next update. See your distribution documentation on how to do it safely; e.g., there might be a special file that is used instead (if it is present) or some other mechanism.

Miklavec as a separate package named hyph-utf8. Despite its name, it also provides versions for 8-bit font encodings.

Users should not be usually concerned with this configuration file, because the default settings are fine in most situations, but a short explanation on how it works follows in case you need to customize it. It can contain empty lines and comments, as well as lines that start with an equal (=) sign. Such a line instructs LATEX that the hyphenation patterns just processed should be made known under an alternative name. The first element on each line specifies the name of the language; it is followed by the name of the file containing the hyphenation patterns. An optional third entry can specify a hyphenation exception file in case the exceptions are stored in a separate file (e.g., frhyphx.tex in the previous example).

For each language in language.dat, the command \l@⟨language⟩ is defined in the LATEX format (i.e., \l@english and so on). When the document is processed with such a format, babel checks for each language whether the command \l@⟨language⟩ is defined and, if so, loads the corresponding hyphenation patterns; otherwise, it loads the patterns for the default language 0 (the one loaded first); for compatibility reasons this language should contain US-English hyphenation patterns.

```
initex latex.ltx
This is pdfTeX, Version 3.141592653-2.6-1.40.23 (TeX Live 2022/dev) (INITEX)
   ....
(/Library/texmf/tex/latex/base/latex.ltx
   ....
1141 hyphenation exceptions
Hyphenation trie of length 419877 has 8811 ops out of 35111
   143 for language 86
   110 for language 85
   138 for language 84
   7 for language 83
   12 for language 82
   53 for language 81
   ....
   137 for language 5
   424 for language 4
   432 for language 3
   2 for language 1
   181 for language 0
No pages of output.
```

The above output shows what initex loads into the format on the machine of the author: patterns for 87 different languages. The language with the number 2 corresponds to nohyphenation and is missing from the output because it contains no patterns. Babel uses these text strings (or their equivalents, specified preceded by an = sign in language.dat) to identify a language; with the package option showlanguages, a list of the hyphenation patterns loaded, with their numbers and names, is printed to the .log file.

A couple of tools for shorthands

Although mainly intended for shorthands, they can be useful in other contexts, too.

`\TextOrMath{`*text-code*`}{`*math-code*`}`

Recognizing that some shorthands declared in the language definition files have to be usable in both text and math modes, this macro allows you to specify the code to execute when in text mode (*text-code*) or when in math mode (*math-code*). Providing commands for use in text and math can have unwanted side effects, so this macro should be used with great care.

The `\TextOrMath` command is already provided by the LaTeX format. The babel package offers the same functionality under the name `\textormath`, but if you want your text or commands to be processable with and without babel loaded, it is preferable to use the CamelCase command from the LaTeX format.

`\allowhyphens`   `\bbl@allowhyphens`

When LaTeX cannot hyphenate a word properly by itself — for instance, because it is a compound word or because the word contains accented letters constructed using the `\accent` primitive, particularly when the pdfTeX is used — it needs a little help. This help involves making LaTeX think it is dealing with two words, which appear as one word on the page. For this purpose babel provides the command `\allowhyphens`, which inserts an invisible horizontal skip, unless the current font encoding is T1.[1] In some cases one wants to insert this "help" unconditionally; for these cases `\bbl@allowhyphens` is available. This invisible skip has the effect of making LaTeX think it is dealing with two words that can be hyphenated separately.

13.6.3 The package file

Instead of just retouching existing language styles in your documents or styles, you can opt for a more radical approach, namely, creating a completely new one. This is the way to go, of course, if there is no style at all for a certain language.

There are two ways to create a new style. The old good one is based on `.ldf` files, and the best way to define them, at least the basic structure, is with a graphical user interface, based on HTML and JavaScript, named "Language incubator". This GUI is available on the babel GitHub repository (`https://github.com/latex3/babel`), under `tools`.

Note that many `.ldf` files use the concept of "dialect", which is somewhat of a historical misnomer, because *lang* and *variant* are at the same level as far as babel is concerned, without any connotation indicating whether one or the other is the main language. The "dialect" paradigm comes in handy if you want to share hyphenation patterns between various languages. Moreover, if no hyphenation patterns are

---

[1]In contrast to the OT1 encoding, the T1 encoding contains most accented characters as real glyphs so that the `\accent` primitive is almost never used.

preloaded in the format for the language *lang*, babel's default behavior is to define this language as a "dialect" of the default language (\language0).

Defining multiple languages or dialects in a single file is strongly discouraged. Although in the early days of babel this was a customary practice for optimization reasons, each language, dialect, or variant should be a language on its own, to follow the current trends for the handling of locales.

A more modern way to create languages is by means of .ini files, which has the advantage that the data are provided in a descriptive way. For example, the file for German (babel-de.ini) contains data such as:

```
[identification]
...
name.local = Deutsch
name.english = German
name.babel = german
name.polyglossia = german
tag.bcp47 = de
language.tag.bcp47 = de
tag.bcp47.likely = de-Latn-DE
tag.opentype = DEU
script.name = Latin
script.tag.bcp47 = Latn
script.tag.opentype = latn
encodings = T1 OT1 LY1
...
[captions]
preface = Vorwort
ref = Literatur
abstract = Zusammenfassung
bib = Literaturverzeichnis
...
[date.gregorian]
date.long = [d].[ ][MMMM] [y]
date.short = [dd].[MM].[yy]
months.wide.1 = Januar
months.wide.2 = Februar
...
[typography]
frenchspacing = yes
hyphenrules = ngerman
lefthyphenmin = 2
righthyphenmin = 2
...
```

This declarative approach helps to solve what is very likely one of the most common problems when creating a language style based on TeX code, namely, that linguistic communities often have no TeXnician among them to give a helping hand in developing such TeX code. There are .ini templates for about 500 languages in the babel GitHub repository (under locale-templates), which can be used as a starting point.

Note that .ini files enforce the paradigm of separate locales for variants.

13.7 Other approaches

In general, the babel package does a good job of translating document element names and making text input somewhat more convenient. However, for several languages, individuals or local user groups have developed packages and versions of TeX that cope with a given language on a deeper level — in particular, by better integrating the typographic traditions of the target language.

An example of such a package is frenchle [37], which was originally developed by Bernard Gaulle (1946–2007). Special customized versions of (LA)TeX exist (e.g., Polish and Czech, distributed by the TeX user groups GUST and C_STUG, respectively).

Unicode engines

There are also some packages taking advantage of the features of X‑TeX and LuaTeX. Besides those cited in Section 13.5, among others we have xgreek by Apostolos Syropoulos (CTAN: `macros/xetex/latex/xgreek`) and arabluatex by Robert Alessi (CTAN: `macros/luatex/latex/arabluatex`).

13.7.1 Complex languages with 8-bit engines

As explained above, the most convenient way to typeset languages with complex scripts is with X‑LATeX and LuaLATeX. In the case that you still need to resort to 8-bit engines, here are some alternatives.

Several systems to handle Hebrew are available on CTAN in the directory `hebrew`.[1] In particular, babel offers an interface for Hebrew written by Boris Lavva, although fonts are not included, and you must download and install them separately. For Arabic there is the ArabTeX system [54], developed by Klaus Lagally. This package extends the capabilities of (LA)TeX to generate Arabic writing using an ASCII transliteration (CTAN: `arabic/arabtex`). For a truly Arabic style, Youssef Jabri has developed arabi (CTAN: `arabic/arabi`).

Serguei Dachian, Arnak Dalalyan, and Vardan Hakobian provide Armenian support (CTAN: `armenian/armtex`).

For the languages of the Indian subcontinent, most of the support is based on the work of Frans Velthuis. In particular, Anshuman Pandey developed packages for Bengali (bengali package and associated fonts on CTAN: `bengali/pandey`), Sanskrit (Anshuman Pandey's devnag package on CTAN: `devanagari/velthuis`), and Gurmukhi (CTAN: `gurmukhi/pandey`).

Oliver Corff and Dorjpalam Dorj's montex package can be used for typesetting languages using the Manju (Mongolian) scripts (CTAN: `mongolian/montex`).

Ethiopian language support, compatible with babel, is available through Berhanu Beyene, Manfred Kudlek, Olaf Kummer, and Jochen Metzinger's ethiop package and fonts (CTAN: `ethiopia/ethiop`).

For Chinese, Japanese, and Korean (the so-called CJK scripts), one can use Werner Lemberg's CJK package [65], which contains fonts and utilities (CTAN: `chinese/CJK`).

---

[1] Preprend `https://www.ctan.org/tex-archive/language` in this and further references to obtain the full CTAN link, e.g., `https://www.ctan.org/tex-archive/language/hebrew`.

Another option for Chinese is CTEX, by Liam Huang, Qing Lee, Leo Liu, and several other contributors (CTAN: `chinese/ctex`).

13.7.2 Polyglossia

This package was originally developed as an alternative to babel for X$_\exists$TEX at a time when the former worked only with traditional TEX. Although babel currently supports all languages polyglossia does, the latter might be preferable for a few languages, e.g., Korean, particularly when using X$_\exists$LATEX. In some other cases, there are some differences in the way a language is supported. However, the development of babel continues, and the situation should improve over time in the few languages where the use of polyglossia together with X$_\exists$TEX might be currently still preferable.

If you intend to move a document from polyglossia to babel or vice versa, bear in mind that even if the basic macros in polyglossia have the same names as in babel, their syntax and behavior slightly differs. For example, some languages are gathered under a single name, and you may need to select the *variant* you want. For this purpose, `\foreignlanguage` supports an optional argument in polyglossia. This concept does not exist in babel, where all locales are treated on an equal footing.

Furthermore, class options are not recognized, and languages are not loaded by means of package options, but with of couple of macros (`\setmainlanguage` and `\setotherlanguages`).

Unless you are in a special situation where a language or script is notably better supported by polyglossia, the recommendation is to use babel with all engines.

Index Generation

To find a topic of interest in a large document, book, or reference work, you usually turn to the table of contents or, more often, to the index. Therefore, an index is a very important part of a document, and most users' entry point to a source of information is precisely through a pointer in the index. You should, therefore, plan an index and develop it along with the main text [24]. For reasons of consistency, it is beneficial, with the technique discussed below, to use special commands in the text to always print a given keyword in the same way in the text and the index throughout the whole document.

This chapter first reviews the basic indexing commands provided by standard LATEX and explains which tools are available to help you build a well-thought-out index. The *LATEX Manual* does not contain a lot of information about the syntax of the \index entries. However, several articles in *TUGboat* deal with the question of generating an index with TEX or LATEX. The syntax described in Section 14.1 is the one recognized by *MakeIndex* [23, 55] and the other indexing programs we discuss: upmendex, xindy, and xindex.

Section 14.2 describes how the *MakeIndex* processor is used. The interpretation of the input file and the format of the output file are controlled by style parameters. Section 14.2.4 lists these parameters and gives several simple examples to show how changing them influences the typeset result.

Section 14.3 presents upmendex, an Unicode-aware extension to *MakeIndex*. It is preferable to use this program whenever you have non-English documents or other special demands, such as the production of technical indexes.

① A raw index (.idx file) is generated by running LaTeX.

② The raw index, together with some optional style information (.ist file in the case of *MakeIndex* or upmendex), is used as input to the index processor, which creates an alphabetized index (.ind file) and a transcript (.ilg file).

③ The index (.ind file) is read by LaTeX to give the final typeset result.

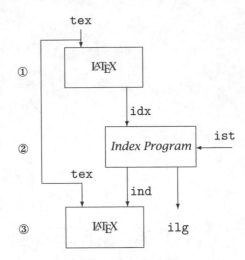

Figure 14.1: The sequential flow of index processing and the various auxiliary files used by LaTeX and an external index processor, e.g., *MakeIndex*

In Section 14.4 we briefly discuss two further alternatives that you may come across. The final section describes several LaTeX packages to enhance the index and to create multiple indexes such as those in the book you are reading.

*   *   *

The process of generating an index is shown schematically in Figure 14.1. The steps for generating an index with LaTeX and *MakeIndex* are illustrated in this figure. The same flow is used with other index processors; only the configuration of the processors is done differently in some cases, i.e., not with .ist style files.

Figure 14.2 on the next page shows, with an example, the various steps involved in transforming an input file into a typeset index. It also shows, in somewhat more detail, which files are involved in the index-generating process. Figure 14.2(a) shows some occurrences of index commands (\index) in the document source, with corresponding pages listed on the left. Figure 14.2(b) shows a raw index .idx file generated by LaTeX. File extensions may differ when using multiple indexes or glossaries. After running the .idx file through the index processor, it becomes an alphabetized index .ind file with LaTeX commands specifying a particular output format [Figure 14.2(c)]. The typeset result after formatting with LaTeX is shown in Figure 14.2(d).

LaTeX and *MakeIndex* (or upmendex or xindex), when employed together, use several markup conventions to help you control the precise format of the output. The xindy program has a *MakeIndex* compatibility mode that supports the same format. In Section 14.1, which describes the format of the \index command, we always use the default settings.

```
Page vi:    \index{animal}
Page 5:     \index{animal}
Page 6:     \index{animal}
Page 7:     \index{animal}
Page 11:    \index{animalism|see{animal}}
Page 17:    \index{animal@\emph{animal}}
            \index{mammal|textbf}
Page 26:    \index{animal!mammal!cat}
Page 32:    \index{animal!insect}
```

(a) The input file

```
\indexentry{animal}{vi}
\indexentry{animal}{5}
\indexentry{animal}{6}
\indexentry{animal}{7}
\indexentry{animalism|see{animal}}{11}
\indexentry{animal@\emph{animal}}{17}
\indexentry{mammal|textbf}{17}
\indexentry{animal!mammal!cat}{26}
\indexentry{animal!insect}{32}
```

(b) The `.idx` *file*

```
\begin{theindex}
  \item animal, vi, 5-7
    \subitem insect, 32
    \subitem mammal
      \subsubitem cat, 26
  \item \emph{animal}, 17
  \item animalism, \see{animal}{11}
  \indexspace
  \item mammal, \textbf{17}
\end{theindex}
```

(c) The `.ind` *file*

animal, vi, 5–7
    insect, 32
    mammal
      cat, 26
animal, 17
animalism, *see* animal

mammal, **17**

(d) The typeset output

Figure 14.2: Stepwise development of index processing

14.1 Syntax of the index entries

This section describes the default syntax used to generate index entries with LaTeX and either *MakeIndex* or one of the other programs described in this chapter. Different levels of complexity are introduced progressively, showing, for each case, the input file and the generated typeset output.

Figures 14.3 and 14.4 on page 353 show the input and generated output of a small LaTeX document, where various simple possibilities of the \index command are shown, together with the result of including the showidx package (see Section 14.5.2). To make the index entries consistent in these figures (see Section 14.1.7), the commands \Com and \Prog were defined and used. The index-generating environment theindex has been redefined to get the output on one page (Section 14.5.1 explains how this can be done).

After introducing the necessary \index commands in the document, we want to generate the index to be included once again in the LaTeX document on a subsequent run. If the main file of a document is main.tex, for example, then the following changes should be made to that file:

Generating the raw index

- Include the makeidx package with a \usepackage command.

- Put a \makeindex command in the document preamble.

- Put a `\printindex` command where the index is to appear — usually at the end, right before the `\end{document}` command.

You then run LATEX on the entire document, causing it to generate the file `main.idx`, which we shall call the `.idx` file.

14.1.1 Simple index entries

Each `\index` command causes LATEX to write an entry in the `.idx` file. The following example shows some simple `\index` commands, together with the index entries that they produce. The page number refers to the page containing the text where the `\index` command appears. As shown in the example below, duplicate commands on the same page (such as `\index{stylistic}` on page 23) produce only one "23" in the index.

style, 14	Page iii: `\index{style}`
style , 16	Page xi: `\index{Stylist}`
style, iii, 12	Page 12: `\index{style}`
style , 15	`\index{styles}`
style file, 34	Page 14: `\index{ style}`
styles, 12	Page 15: `\index{style }`
Stylist, xi	Page 16: `\index{ style }`
stylist, 34	Page 23: `\index{stylistic}`
stylistic, 23	`\index{stylistic}`
	Page 34: `\index{style file}`
	`\index{stylist}`

Spaces can be harmful Pay particular attention to the way spaces are handled in this example. Spaces inside `\index` commands are written literally to the output `.idx` file and, by default, are treated as ordinary characters by *MakeIndex*, which places them in front of all letters. In the example above, look at the `style` entries on pages 14 and 16. The leading spaces are placed at the beginning of the index and on two different lines because the trailing blank on page 16 lengthens the string by one character. We end up with four different entries for the same term, an effect that was probably not desired.

It is therefore important to eliminate such spurious spaces from the `\index` commands when you use *MakeIndex*. Alternatively, you can specify the `-c` option when running the index processor. This option suppresses the effect of leading and trailing blanks (see Sections 14.2.2 and 14.3.1). We recommend always using this option; it should really have been the default.

Inconsistent spelling Another frequently encountered error occurs when the same English word is spelled inconsistently with initial lowercase and uppercase letters (as with `Stylist` on page xi in the preceding example), leading to two different index entries.

Of course, this behavior is wanted in languages like German, where "Arm" (arm) and "arm" (poor) are really two completely different words.[1] In English, such spurious double entries should normally be eliminated.

---

[1] As the joke goes: "Besser arm dran als Arm ab" (better poor than without an arm).

14.1.2 Generating subentries

A maximum of three levels of index entries (main, sub, and subsub entries) are available. To produce such entries, the argument of the \index command should contain both the main entries and subentries, separated by a ! character. This character can be redefined in a style file (see Table 14.1 on page 357) if *MakeIndex* or upmendex is used as the index program.

box, 21
    dimensions of, 33
    parameters, 5
dimensions
    figure, 12
    rule
      height, 12
      width, 3
    table, 9

Page 3:   `\index{dimensions!rule!width}`
Page 5:   `\index{box!parameters}`
Page 9:   `\index{dimensions!table}`
Page 12: `\index{dimensions!rule!height}`
            `\index{dimensions!figure}`
Page 21: `\index{box}`
Page 33: `\index{box!dimensions of}`

14.1.3 Page ranges and cross-references

You can specify a page range by putting the command `\index{...|(}` at the beginning of the range and the command `\index{...|)}` at the end of the range. Page ranges should span a homogeneous numbering scheme (e.g., roman and arabic page numbers cannot fall within the same range). Note that *MakeIndex* and upmendex do the right thing when both ends of a page range fall on the same page or when another (individual) entry falls inside an active range.

You can also generate cross-reference index entries without page numbers by using the see encapsulator. Because the "see" entry does not print any page number, the commands `\index{...|see{...}}` can be placed anywhere in the input file *after* the `\begin{document}` command. For practical reasons, it is convenient to group all such cross-referencing commands in one place.

fonts
    Computer Modern, 13–25
    math, *see* math, fonts
    OpenType, 5
table, ii–xi, 14

Page ii: `\index{table|(}`
Page xi: `\index{table|)}`
Page 5:   `\index{fonts!OpenType|(}`
            `\index{fonts!OpenType|)}` `% same page`
Page 13: `\index{fonts!Computer Modern|(}`
Page 14: `\index{table}`
Page 17: `\index{fonts!math|see{math, fonts}}`
Page 21: `\index{fonts!Computer Modern}` `% within range`
Page 25: `\index{fonts!Computer Modern|)}`

14.1.4 Controlling the presentation form

Sometimes you may want to sort an entry according to a key, while using a different visual representation for the typesetting, such as Greek letters, mathematical symbols, or specific typographic forms. This function is available with the syntax *key@visual*, where *key* determines the alphabetical position and the string *visual* produces the typeset text of the entry.

delta, 14	Page 5: `\index{ninety-five}`
δ, 23	Page 14: `\index{delta}`
delta wing, 16	Page 16: `\index{delta wing}`
flower, 19	Page 19: `\index{flower@\textbf{flower}}`
ninety, 26	Page 23: `\index{delta@$\delta$}`
xc, 28	`\index{tabular@\texttt{tabular} environment}`
ninety-five, 5	Page 26: `\index{ninety}`
tabular environment, 23	Page 28: `\index{ninety@xc}`

For some indexes, certain page numbers should be formatted specially. For example, an italic page number might indicate a primary reference, or an *n* after a page number might denote that the item appears in a footnote on that page. *MakeIndex* allows you to format an individual page number in any way you want by using the encapsulator syntax specified by the | character. What follows the | sign "encapsulates" or encloses the page number associated with the index entry. For instance, the command `\index{keyword|xxx}` produces a page number of the form `\xxx{n}`, where *n* is the page number in question. Similarly, the commands `\index{keyword|(xxx}` and `\index{keyword|)xxx}` generate a page range of the form `\xxx{n-m}`.

Preexisting commands with one argument (like `\textit` in the example below) or user commands can be used to encapsulate the page numbers. As an example, a document containing the command definition

```
\newcommand\nn[1]{#1n}
```

would yield something like this:

tabular, **ii**, *21*, 22n	Page ii: `\index{tabular|textbf}`
tabbing, 7, *34–37*	Page 7: `\index{tabbing}`
	Page 21: `\index{tabular|textit}`
	Page 22: `\index{tabular|nn}`
	Page 34: `\index{tabbing|(textit}`
	Page 37: `\index{tabbing|)textit}`

The see encapsulator is a special case of this facility, where the `\see` command is predefined by the makeidx package.

14.1.5 Printing special characters

To typeset one of the characters having a special meaning to *MakeIndex* or the other indexing programs (i.e., !, ", @, or |)[1] in the index, precede it with a " character. More precisely, any character is said to be quoted if it follows an unquoted " that is not part of a \" command. The latter case allows for umlaut characters. Quoted !, @, "

---

[1] As noted earlier, in *MakeIndex* and upmendex other characters can be substituted for the default ones and carry a special meaning. This behavior is explained on page 359.

, and | characters are treated like ordinary characters, losing their special meaning. The " preceding a quoted character is deleted before the entries are alphabetized.

@ sign, 2		`\index{bar@\texttt{\idxvert }|see{vertical bar}}`
|, *see* vertical bar	Page 1:	`\index{quote (\verb+""+)}`
exclamation (!), 4		`\index{quote@\texttt{""} sign}`
Ah!, 5	Page 2:	`\index{atsign@\texttt{"@} sign}`
Mädchen, 3	Page 3:	`\index{maedchen@M\"{a}dchen}`
quote ("), 1	Page 4:	`\index{exclamation ("!)}`
" sign, 1	Page 5:	`\index{exclamation ("!)!Ah"!}`

14.1.6 Creating a glossary

LaTeX also has a `\glossary` command for making a glossary. The `\makeglossary` command produces a file with an extension of .glo, which is similar to the .idx file for the `\index` commands. LaTeX transforms the `\glossary` commands into `\glossaryentry` entries, just as it translates any `\index` commands into `\indexentry` entries.

MakeIndex can also handle these glossary commands, but you must change the value for some of the style file keywords, as shown in the style file `myglossary.ist`.

```
% MakeIndex style file myglossary.ist
keyword    "\\glossaryentry"       % keyword for glossary entry
preamble   "\n \\begin{theglossary}\n" % Begin glossary entries
postamble  "\n\n \\end{theglossary}\n" % End   glossary entries
```

In addition, you have to define a suitable `theglossary` environment.

14.1.7 Defining your own index commands

As was pointed out in the introduction, it is very important to use the same visual representation for identical names or commands throughout a complete document, including the index. You therefore can define user commands that always introduce similar constructs in the same way into the text and the index.

For example, you can define the command `\Index`, whose argument is entered at the same time in the text and in the index.

```
\newcommand\Index[1]{#1\index{#1}}
```

As explained in more detail below, you must be careful that the argument of such a command does not contain expandable material (typically control sequences) or spurious blanks. In general, for simple terms like single words, there is no problem, and this technique can be used. You can even go one step further and give a certain visual representation to the entry — for instance, typesetting it in a typewriter font.

```
\newcommand\indextt[1]{\texttt{#1}\index{#1@\texttt{#1}}}
```

349

Finally, you can group certain terms by defining commands that have a generic meaning. For instance, LATEX commands and program names could be treated with special commands, as in the following examples:

```
\newcommand\bs{\symbol{'134}} % print backslash in typewriter OT1/T1
\newcommand\Com[1]{\texttt{\bs#1}\index{#1@\texttt{\bs#1}}}
\newcommand\Prog[1]{\texttt{#1}\index{#1@\texttt{#1} program}}
```

The `\Com` command adds a backslash to the command's name in both text and index, simplifying the work of the typist. The `\bs` command definition is necessary, because `\textbackslash` would be substituted in an OT1 font encoding context,[1] as explained in Section 9.3.6 on page →I 670. At the same time, commands are ordered in the index by their names, with the "\" character being ignored during sorting. Similarly, the `\Prog` command provides a sort key not including the `\texttt` command, because otherwise the generated entry would be sorted into the wrong place in the index.

14.1.8 Special considerations

When an `\index` command is used directly in the text, its argument is expanded only when the index is typeset, not when the `.idx` file is written. However, when the `\index` command is contained in the argument of another command, characters with a special meaning to TEX, such as \, must be properly protected against expansion. This problem is likely to arise when indexing items in a footnote or when using commands that put their argument in the text and enter it at the same time in the index (see the discussion in Section 14.1.7). Even in this case, robust commands can be placed in the "@" part of an entry, as in `\index{rose@\textit{rose}}`, but fragile commands must be protected with the `\protect` command.

As with every argument of a command, you need to have a matching number of braces. However, because `\index` allows special characters like % or \ in its argument, if the command is used in the main text, the brace matching has an anomaly: braces in the commands `\{` and `\}` take part in the matching. Thus, you cannot write `\index{\{}` or something similar.

14.2 *MakeIndex* — A program to sort and format indexes

In the previous section we showed examples where we ran the *MakeIndex* program using its default settings. In this section we first take a closer look at the *MakeIndex* program and then discuss ways of changing its behavior. Nearly everything discussed in this section also applies to the **upmendex** program. The few places where there are differences between the two programs are explicitly marked.

---

[1] In Unicode engines one needs to use `\textbackslash`, though.

14.2.1 Generating the formatted index

To generate the formatted index, you should run the *MakeIndex* program by typing the following command (where `main` is the name of the input file):

```
makeindex main.idx
```

This produces the file `main.ind`, which is called the `.ind` file here. If *MakeIndex* generated no error messages, you can now rerun LATEX on the document, and the index appears. (You can then remove the `\makeindex` command if you do not want to regenerate the index.) Page 355 describes what happens at this point if there are error messages.

In reading the index, you may discover additional mistakes. These should be corrected by changing the appropriate `\index` commands in the document and regenerating the `.ind` file (rerunning LATEX *before* and *after* the last step).

An example of running *MakeIndex* is shown below. The `.idx` file, `main.idx`, is generated by a first LATEX run on the input shown in Figure 14.3 on the next page. You can clearly see that two files are written—namely, the ordered `.ind` index file for use with LATEX, called `main.ind`, and the index `.ilg` log file, called `main.ilg`, which (in this case) contains the same text as the output on the terminal. If errors are encountered, then the latter file contains the line number and error message for each error in the input stream. Figure 14.4 on page 353 shows the result of the subsequent LATEX run. The example uses the showidx package for controlling the index (see Section 14.5.2).

```
makeindex main
This is makeindex, version 2.15 [TeX Live 2021] (kpathsea + Thai support).
Scanning input file main.idx....done (8 entries accepted, 0 rejected).
Sorting entries....done (24 comparisons).
Generating output file main.ind....done (19 lines written, 0 warnings).
Output written in main.ind.
Transcript written in main.ilg.
```

14.2.2 Detailed options of the *MakeIndex* program

The syntax of the options of the *MakeIndex* program are described below. Most options are also available for upmendex, a Unicode-aware extension of the program, discussed in Section 14.3 on page 364. If an option applies only to *MakeIndex*, then this is explicitly noted.

```
makeindex [-ciglqrLT]  [-o ind]  [-p no]  [-s sty]  [-t log]  [idx0 idx1 ...]
```

−c   Enable blank compression. By default, every blank counts in the index key. The −c option ignores leading and trailing blanks and tabs and compresses intermediate ones to a single space. We recommend always using this option.

```
\documentclass{article}
\usepackage{makeidx,showidx,multicol,microtype}

\newcommand\bs{\symbol{'134}}    % print backslash in either OT1 or T1
\newcommand\Com[1]{\texttt{\bs#1}\index{#1@\texttt{\bs#1}}}
\newcommand\Prog[1]{\texttt{#1}\index{#1@\texttt{#1} program}}

\renewenvironment{theindex}
   {\begin{multicols}{2}[\section*{\indexname}][5\baselineskip]%
    \addcontentsline{toc}{section}{\indexname}%
    \setlength\parindent{0pt}\pagestyle{plain}%
    \ExpandArgs{Nc}\RenewCommandCopy{\item}{@idxitem}}%
   {\end{multicols}}

\makeindex
\begin{document}
\section{Generating an Index}
Using the \textsf{showidx} package, users can see where they define
index entries.

Entries are entered into the index by the \Com{index} command. More
precisely, the argument of the \Com{index} command is written
literally into the auxiliary file \texttt{idx}. Note, however, that
information is actually written into that file only when the
\Com{makeindex} command was given in the document preamble.

\section{Preparing the Index}
In order to prepare the index for printing, the \texttt{idx} file has
to be transformed by an external program, like \MakeIndex{}.  This
program writes the \texttt{ind} file.
\begin{verbatim}
makeindex filename
\end{verbatim}

\section{Printing the Index}\index{Final production run}
During the final production run of a document, the index can be
\index{include index}included by putting a \Com{printindex} command at
the position in the text where you want the index to appear (normally
at the end).This command will input the \texttt{ind} file prepared by
\MakeIndex{}, and \LaTeX{} will typeset the information.
\printindex
\end{document}
```

Figure 14.3: Example of \index commands and the showidx package

This file is run through LaTeX once; then the index processor is executed, and LaTeX is run a second time. The redefinition of the theindex environment is discussed in Section 14.5.1 on page 371.

1   Generating an Index

Using the showidx package, users can see where they define index entries.

Entries are entered into the index by the \index command. More precisely, the argument of the \index command is written literally into the auxiliary file idx. Note, however, that information is actually written into that file only when the \makeindex command was given in the document preamble.

2   Preparing the Index

In order to prepare the index for printing, the idx file has to be transformed by an external program, like makeindex. This program writes the ind file.

```
makeindex filename
```

3   Printing the Index

During the final production run of a document, the index can be included by putting a \printindex command at the position in the text where you want the index to appear (normally at the end). This command will input the ind file prepared by makeindex, and LaTeX will typeset the information.

Index

1

Figure 14.4: Printing the index and the output of the showidx option

This figure shows the index generated from the example input in Figure 14.3. All index entries are shown in the margin, so it is easy to check for errors or duplications.

-i   Use standard input (`stdin`) as the input file. When this option is specified and `-o` is not, output is written to standard output (`stdout`, the default output stream).

-g   Employ German word ordering in the index, following the rules given in German standard DIN 5007. In this case the normal precedence rule of *MakeIndex* for word ordering (symbols, numbers, uppercase letters, lowercase letters) is replaced by the German word ordering (symbols, lowercase letters, uppercase letters, numbers). Additionally, this option enables *MakeIndex* to recognize the German TEX commands "a, "o, "u, and "s as ae, oe, ue, and ss, respectively, for sorting purposes. The quote character must be redefined in a style file (see page 359); otherwise, you get an error message, and *MakeIndex* aborts. Note that not all versions of *MakeIndex* recognize this option.

     Note that this option has a different use in `upmendex`, which has a different way to enable German sorting rules.

-l   Use letter ordering. The default is word ordering. In word ordering, a space comes before any letter in the alphabet. In letter ordering, spaces are ignored. For example, the index terms "point in space" and "pointing" are alphabetized differently in letter and word ordering.

-o *ind*   Take *ind* as the output index file. By default, the file name base of the first input file *idx0* concatenated with the extension `.ind` is used as the output file name.

-p *no*   Set the starting page number of the output index file to *no*. This option is useful when the index file is to be formatted separately. Other than pure numbers, three special cases are allowed for *no*: any, odd, and even. In these special cases, the starting page number is determined by retrieving the last page number from the `.log` file of the last LaTeX run. The `.log` file name is determined by concatenating the file name base of the first raw index file (*idx0*) with the extension `.log`. The last source page is obtained by searching backward in the log file for the first instance of a number included in square brackets. If a page number is missing or if the `.log` file is not found, no attempt is made to set the starting page number. The meaning of each of the three special cases follows:

     `any`   The starting page is the last source page number plus one.

     `odd`   The starting page is the first odd page following the last source page number.

     `even`   The starting page is the first even page following the last source page number.

-q   Operate in quiet mode. No messages are sent to the error output stream (`stderr`). By default, progress and error messages are sent to `stderr` as well as the transcript file. The `-q` option disables the `stderr` messages.

-r   Disable implicit page range formation. By default, three or more successive pages are automatically abbreviated as a range (e.g., 1–5). The −r option disables this default, making explicit range operators the only way to create page ranges.

-s *sty*   Take *sty* as the style file. There is no default for the style file name. The environment variable INDEXSTYLE defines where the style file resides.

-t *log*   Take *log* as the transcript file. By default, the file name base of the first input file *idx0* concatenated with the extension .ilg is used as the transcript file name.

-L   Sort the index based on the current locale settings of the computer. This option is not available in all versions of *MakeIndex* and not available with upmendex, which uses style keywords to define the sorting behavior.

-T   Special support for Thai documents. This option is not available in all versions of *MakeIndex* and not offered by upmendex.

14.2.3 Error and warning messages

MakeIndex displays on the terminal how many lines were read and written and how many errors were found. Messages that identify errors are written in the transcript file, which, by default, has the extension .ilg. *MakeIndex* can produce error messages when it is reading the .idx file or when it is writing the .ind file. Each error message identifies the nature of the error and the number of the line where the error occurred in the file. In the reading phase, the line numbers in the error messages refer to the positions in the .idx file being read.

Errors in the reading phase

Extra '!' at position ...
> The \index command's argument has more than two unquoted ! characters. Perhaps some of them should be quoted.

Extra '@' at position ...
> The \index command argument has two or more unquoted @ characters with no intervening ! . Perhaps one of the @ characters should be quoted.

Extra '|' at position ...
> The \index command's argument has more than one unquoted | character. Perhaps the extras should be quoted.

Illegal null field
> The \index command argument does not make sense because some string is null that should not be. The command \index{!funny} produces this error, because it specifies a subentry "funny" with no entry. Similarly, the command \index{@funny} is incorrect, because it specifies a null string for sorting.

Argument ... too long (max 1024)
> The document contained an \index command with a very long argument. You probably forgot the right brace that should delimit the argument.

Errors in the writing phase In the writing phase, line numbers in the error messages refer to the positions in the `.ind` file being written.

`Unmatched range opening operator`
> An `\index{...|(}` command has no matching `\index{...|)}` command following it. The "`...`" in the two commands must be completely identical.

`Unmatched range closing operator`
> An `\index{...|)}` command has no matching `\index{...|(}` command preceding it.

`Extra range opening operator`
> Two `\index{...|(}` commands appear in the document with no intervening command `\index{...|)}`.

`Inconsistent page encapsulator ... within range`
> *MakeIndex* has been instructed to include a page range for an entry, and a single page number within that range is formatted differently — for example, by having an `\index{cat|see{animals}}` command between an `\index{cat|(}` command and an `\index{cat|)}` command.

`Conflicting entries`
> *MakeIndex* thinks it has been instructed to print the same page number twice in two different ways. For example, the command sequences `\index{lion|see{...}}` and `\index{lion}` appear on the same page.

MakeIndex can produce a variety of other error messages indicating that something is seriously wrong with the `.idx` file. If you get such an error, it probably means that the `.idx` file was corrupted in some way. If LaTeX did not generate any errors when it created the `.idx` file, then it is highly unlikely to have produced a bad `.idx` file. If, nevertheless, this does happen, you should examine the `.idx` file to establish what went wrong.

In some cases the program produces warnings instead of error messages, e.g., when it encounters data in the style file that it does not recognize. This may or may not be an issue; for example, at some point in the past a few keywords got renamed, and to cater for this some style files supply both versions, and thus one then generates such a warning. But it may also indicate that you misspelled a keyword. Thus, if the behavior is not as you expect, check the `.ilg` file for such warnings.

14.2.4 Customizing the index

MakeIndex ensures that the formats of the input and output files do not have to be fixed, but they can be adapted to the needs of a specific application. To achieve this format independence, the *MakeIndex* program is driven by a style file, usually characterized with a file extension of `.ist` (see also Figure 14.1 on page 344). This file consists of a series of keyword/value pairs. These keywords can be divided into input and output style parameters. Table 14.1 on the facing page describes the various keywords and their default values for the programming of the input file. This table shows, for instance, how to modify the index-level separator (`level`, with `!` as the

Keyword	Default Value	Description
keyword [s]	"\\indexentry"	Command telling *MakeIndex* that its argument is an index entry.
arg_open [c]	'{'	Argument opening delimiter.
arg_close [c]	'}'	Argument closing delimiter.
range_open [c]	'('	Opening delimiter indicating the beginning of an explicit page range.
range_close [c]	')'	Closing delimiter indicating the end of an explicit page range.
level [c]	'!'	Delimiter denoting a new level of subitem.
actual [c]	'@'	Symbol separating the sort key from the "actual" representation in the index file.
encap [c]	'|'	Symbol indicating that the rest of the argument list is to be used as an encapsulating command for the page number.
quote [c]	'"'	Symbol that escapes the character following it.
escape [c]	'\\'	Symbol without any special meaning unless it is followed by the quote character, in which case that character loses its special function and both characters are printed. This is included because \" is the umlaut accent in TeX. The two symbols quote and escape must be distinct.
page_compositor [s]	"-"	Composite page delimiter.

[s] *Attribute of type* string; [c] *attribute of type* char *(enclose in double or single quotes, respectively)*

Table 14.1: Input style parameters for *MakeIndex* and upmendex

default character value). Table 14.2 on the next page describes the various keywords and their default values for steering the translation of the input information into LaTeX commands. This table explains how to define the way the various levels are formatted (using the item series of keywords). Examples show in more detail how these input and output keywords can be used in practice. *MakeIndex* style files use Unix string syntax, so you must enter \\ to get a single \ in the output.

In the following sections we show how, by making just a few changes to the values of the default settings of the parameters controlling the index, you can customize the index.

A stand-alone index

The example style mybook.ist (shown below) defines a stand-alone index for a book, where "stand-alone" means that it can be formatted independently of the main source. Such a stand-alone index can be useful if the input text of the book is frozen (the page numbers do no longer change) and you want only to reformat the index.

```
% MakeIndex style file mybook.ist
preamble    "\\documentclass[12pt]{book} \n\n \\begin{document} \n
            \\begin{theindex}\n"
postamble   "\n\n\\end{theindex} \n \\end{document}\n"
```

Keyword	Default Value	Description
Context		
preamble [s]	"\\begin{theindex}\n"	Preamble command preceding the index.
postamble [s]	"\n\n\\end{theindex}\n"	Postamble command following the index.
Starting Page		
setpage_prefix [s]	"\n\\setcounter{page}{"	Prefix for the command setting the page.
setpage_suffix [s]	"}\n"	Suffix for the command setting the page.
New Group		
group_skip [s]	"\n\n\\indexspace\n"	Vertical space inserted before a new group.
Entry Separators		
item_0 [s]	"\n\\item "	Command to be inserted in front of a level 0 entry.
item_1 [s]	"\n \\subitem "	Ditto for a level 1 entry starting at level ≥ 1.
item_2 [s]	"\n \\subsubitem "	Ditto for a level 2 entry starting at level ≥ 2.
item_01 [s]	"\n \\subitem "	Command before a level 1 entry starting at level 0.
item_12 [s]	"\n \\subsubitem "	Ditto for a level 2 entry starting at level 1.
item_x1 [s]	"\n \\subitem "	Command to be inserted in front of a level 1 entry when the parent level has no page numbers.
item_x2 [s]	"\n \\subsubitem "	Ditto for a level 2 entry.
Page Delimiters		
delim_0 [s]	", "	Delimiter between entry and page number(s) at level 0.
delim_1 [s]	", "	Ditto at level 1.
delim_2 [s]	", "	Ditto at level 2.
delim_n [s]	", "	Delimiter between different page numbers.
delim_r [s]	"--"	Designator for a page range.
delim_t [s]	""	Terminator of the page number list.
suffix_2p [s]	*not set by default*	Suffix as replacement for a two-page range, e.g., "f.".
suffix_3p [s]	*not set by default*	Suffix as replacement for a three-page range, e.g., "ff.".
suffix_mp [s]	*not set by default*	Ditto for a multi-page range (three or more pages).
Page Encapsulators		
encap_prefix [s]	"\\"	Prefix to be used in front of a page encapsulator.
encap_infix [s]	"{"	Infix to be used for a page encapsulator.
encap_suffix [s]	"}"	Suffix to be used for a page encapsulator.
Page Number Precedence		
page_precedence [s] "rnaRA"		a, A are lower-, uppercase alphabetic; n is numeric; r and R are lower- and uppercase roman.
Line Wrapping		
line_max [n]	72	Maximum length of an output line.
indent_space [s]	"\t\t"	Indentation commands for wrapped lines.
indent_length [n]	16	Length of indentation for wrapped lines.

"\n" and "\t" are a new line and a tab;   [s] attribute of type string;   [n] attribute of type number

Table 14.2: Output style parameters for *MakeIndex* and upmendex

Keyword	Default Value	Description
Group headings — Control & Presentation		
headings_flag [(n)]	0	Controls all group headings: if zero, nothing is inserted before each group. Otherwise, a value >0 (<0) includes an uppercase (lowercase) instance of the symbol characterizing the new letter group, prefixed with heading_prefix and appending heading_suffix. For numbers and symbols special headings are inserted.
heading_prefix [(s)]	" "	Prefix for a new group heading.
heading_suffix [(s)]	" "	Suffix for a new group heading.
Group headings — Symbols		
symhead_positive [(s)]	"Symbols"	Heading for symbols, inserted if headings_flag is positive.
symhead_negative [(s)]	"symbols"	Heading for symbols, inserted if headings_flag is negative.
Group headings — Numbers (restrictions[(*)] with upmendex)		
numhead_positive [(s)]	"Numbers"	Heading for numbers, inserted if headings_flag is positive.
numhead_negative [(s)]	"numbers"	Heading for numbers, inserted if headings_flag is negative.

[(s)] *Attribute of type* string;   [(n)] *attribute of type* number

[(*)] *In* upmendex *both keys are ignored by default; see Table 14.4 on page 367 for how to enable them*

Table 14.3: Group headings style parameters for *MakeIndex* and upmendex

Assuming that the raw index commands are in the file mybook.idx, then you can call *MakeIndex* specifying the style file's name:

```
makeindex -s mybook.ist -o mybookindex.tex mybook
```

We have used a nondefault output file name to avoid clobbering the source output (presumably mybook.pdf). If the index is in file mybook.ind, then its typeset output also ends up in mybook.pdf, thus overwriting the .pdf file for the main document.

Moreover, if you want the page numbers for the index to come out correctly, then you can specify the page number where the index has to start (e.g., 181 in the example below):

```
makeindex -s mybook.ist  -o mybookindex.tex -p 181  mybook
```

MakeIndex can also read the LATEX log file mybook.log to find the page number to be used for the index (see the -p option described on page 354).

Changing the "special characters"

The next example shows how you can change the interpretation of special characters in the input file. To do so, you must specify the new special characters in a style file (for instance, myinchar.ist shown below). Using Table 14.1 on page 357, in the following example we change the @ character (see page 347) to =, the sublevel indicator ! (see page 347) to >, and the quotation character " (see page 348) to ! (the default sublevel indicator):

```
% MakeIndex style file myinchar.ist
actual '='        % = instead of default @
quote '!'         % !                          "
level '>'         % >                          !
```

The next example makes use of these declarations and shows some index entries and the resulting output. It also assumes the ngerman option of the babel package; i.e., the double quote character (") is used as a shortcut for the umlaut construct \".

This shows another feature of the ordering algorithm used by *MakeIndex*; namely, the constructs " and \" are considered to be different entries (Br"ucke and Br\"ucke, M"adchen and M\"adchen, although in the latter case the key entry was identical, Maedchen). Therefore, it is important to use the same input convention throughout a complete document.

" sign, 1	Page 1: \index{\texttt{"} sign}
= sign, 2	Page 2: \index{\texttt{@} sign}
@ sign, 2	Page 2: \index{\texttt{!=} sign}
Brücke, 5	Page 3: \index{Maedchen=M\"{a}dchen}
Brücke, V	Page c: \index{Maedchen=M"adchen}
Brücke, v	Page v: \index{Bruecke=Br"ucke}
dimensions	Page 5: \index{Br"ucke}
rule	Page V: \index{Br\"ucke}
width, 3	Page 3: \index{dimensions>rule>width}
exclamation (!), 4	Page 4: \index{exclamation (!!)}
Ah!, 5	Page 5: \index{exclamation (!!)>Ah!!}
Mädchen, c	
Mädchen, 3	

Note, however, that for languages such as German it is much nicer to be able to enter the index entries as UTF-8 strings; e.g., Brücke and Mädchen. This is possible if you use upmendex instead of *MakeIndex*.

Changing the output format of the index

You can also personalize the output format of the index. The first thing that we could try is to build an index with a nice, big letter between each letter group. This is achieved with the style myhead.ist, as shown below (see Table 14.3 on the previous page for more details on the various keywords available for headings):

```
% MakeIndex style file myhead.ist
headings_flag        1                        % Turn on headings (uppercase)
heading_prefix "{\\bfseries\\hfil "           % Insert in front of letter
heading_suffix "\\hfil}\\nopagebreak\n"       % Append after letter
```

This then gives a result such as the following:

Symbols	Page 2: `\index{\texttt{"@} sign}`
@ sign, 2	Page 3: `\index{dimensions!rule!width}`
B	Page 5: `\index{box!parameters}`
box, 21	Page 9: `\index{dimensions!table}`
dimensions of, 33	Page 12: `\index{dimensions!rule!height}`
parameters, 5	Page 17: `\index{dimensions!figure}`
D	Page 21: `\index{box}`
dimensions	Page 33: `\index{box!dimensions of}`
figure, 17	`\index{rule!depth}`
rule	Page 41: `\index{rule!width}`
height, 12	Page 48: `\index{rule!depth}`
width, 3	
table, 9	
R	
rule	
depth, 33, 48	
width, 41	

You could go a bit further and right-adjust the page numbers, putting in dots between the entry and the page number to guide the eye. This effect can be achieved by adding the following declarations:

```
% MakeIndex style file myright.ist
delim_0   "\\dotfill "
delim_1   "\\dotfill "
delim_2   "\\dotfill "
```

The result for the same input would then be this:

@ sign 2	Page 2: `\index{\texttt{"@} sign}`
box 21	Page 3: `\index{dimensions!rule!width}`
dimensions of 33	Page 5: `\index{box!parameters}`
parameters 5	Page 9: `\index{dimensions!table}`
dimensions	Page 12: `\index{dimensions!rule!height}`
figure 17	Page 17: `\index{dimensions!figure}`
rule	Page 21: `\index{box}`
height 12	Page 33: `\index{box!dimensions of}`
width 3	`\index{rule!depth}`
table 9	Page 41: `\index{rule!width}`
rule	Page 48: `\index{rule!depth}`
depth 33, 48	
width 41	

The LaTeX command `\dotfill` can be replaced by fancier commands, but the underlying principle remains the same.

Treating funny page numbers

As described earlier, *MakeIndex* accepts five basic kinds of page numbers: digits, uppercase and lowercase alphabetic, and uppercase and lowercase roman numerals. You can also build composed page numbers. The separator character for composed page numbers is controlled by the *MakeIndex* keyword `page_compositor`; the default is the hyphen character (-), as noted in Table 14.1 on page 357. The precedence of ordering for the various kinds of page numbers is given by the keyword `page_precedence`; the default is `rRnaA`, as noted in Table 14.2 on page 358.

Problems with letters as page numbers

Let us start with an example involving simple page numbers. Assume the pages with numbers `ii`, `iv`, `1`, `2`, `5`, `a`, `c`, `A`, `C`, `II`, and `IV` contain an `\index` command with the word `style`. With the default `page_precedence` of `rRnaA` this would be typeset in the index as shown below. The `c` and `C` entries are considered to be roman numerals, rather than alphabetic characters, so we get:

style, ii, iv, c, II, IV, C, 1, 2, 5, a, A

This order can be changed by using the `page_precedence` keyword to `"rnAaR"`. Running *MakeIndex* on the same index entries now yields:

style, ii, iv, c, 1, 2, 5, A, a, II, IV, C

As you see, the letters like `C` are still interpreted as roman numerals. Thus, as long as *MakeIndex* offers no possibility to modify this behavior, it is ill adapted for pages numbered by letters — either one accepts a potentially incorrect order in the page references or one has to manually correct the final index.

Composed page numbers

The situation looks somewhat different if composed page numbers are used, e.g., page numbers like "B-3" (where "B" is the appendix number and "3" the page number within this appendix). In this case `C` is interpreted as a letter, but `I` is still considered a roman numeral. Thus, in this setting you can have up to eight appendices before you run into trouble.

Suppose that the unsorted index entries show the page numbers `C--3`, `1--1`, `D--1--1`, `B--7`, `F--3--5`, `2--2`, `D--2--3`, `A--1`, `B--5`, and `A--2`. If this raw index is processed with *MakeIndex*, it results in an empty formatted index and a lot of error messages, because the default page separator is a single hyphen. However, by setting the `page_compositor` keyword to `"--"`, you can process this raw index successfully and get the following result:

style, 1-1, 2-2, A-1, A-2, B-5, B-7, C-3, D-1-1, D-2-3, F-3-5

Because *MakeIndex* supports only a single page separator, more complex page numbering schemes involving several different page separators (such as `A-4.1`) cannot be processed by the program.

14.2.5 Pitfalls to watch out for

The `\index` command tries to write its argument unmodified to the `.idx` file whenever possible. This behavior has a number of consequences, because LaTeX's way of dealing with the problem of preventing expansion is not always successful.

If the index text contains commands, as in \index{\Prog}, the entry is likely wrongly sorted, because if used in the main text this entry is sorted under the sort key \Prog (with the special character \ as the starting sort character) regardless of the definition of the \Prog command. On the other hand, if it is used in some argument of another command, \Prog expands before it is written to the .idx file; the placement in the index then depends on the expansion of \Prog. The same thing happens when you use \index inside your own definitions. That is, all commands inside the index argument are expanded (except when they are robust or preceded by \protect).[1]

For sorting, *MakeIndex* assumes that pages numbered with lowercase roman numerals precede those numbered with arabic numerals, which in turn precede those numbered with the lowercase alphabet, uppercase roman numerals, and finally the uppercase alphabet. This precedence order can be changed (see the entry page_precedence in Table 14.2 on page 358).

MakeIndex places symbols (i.e., patterns starting with a nonalphanumeric character) before numbers and before alphabetic entries in the output. Symbols are sorted according to their ASCII values. For word sorting, uppercase and lowercase are considered the same, but for identical words, the uppercase variant precedes the lowercase one. Numbers are sorted in numeric order. The upmendex program offers you some customization possibilities to alter the sort order of scripts and symbols.

Spaces are treated as ordinary characters when alphabetizing the entries and when deciding whether two entries are the same (see also the example on page 346). Thus, if "␣" denotes a space character, the commands \index{cat}, \index{␣cat}, and \index{cat␣} produce three separate entries. All three entries look similar when printed. Likewise, \index{a␣space} and \index{a␣␣space} produce two different entries that look exactly the same in the output. For this reason it is important to check for spurious spaces by being careful when splitting the argument of an \index command across lines in the input file. The *MakeIndex* option -c turns off that behavior and trims leading and trailing white space, compressing all white space within to one blank. We recommend that you use it all the time.

Consider always using the -c option

MakeIndex assumes that the input data in the .idx files contains only ASCII data. These days TeX writes UTF-8 files by default. This is fine because ASCII is a subset of UTF-8, but if the data contains UTF-8 characters outside of ASCII, they will be incorrectly read and processed by *MakeIndex* on a byte-by-byte basis resulting in incorrect sorting or worse — this is where the program upmendex comes into play.

Use MakeIndex only with ASCII input

The upmendex program, on the other hand, expects its input data to be encoded in UTF-8 and not in any legacy 8-bit encoding. The only indexing program that can handle such legacy file encodings successfully is xindy.

Use upmendex only with UTF-8 input

The programs *MakeIndex* and upmendex have similar but not identical options. Thus, if you change your workflow from one to the other, make sure that everything behaves as it should. Some options in upmendex have extended semantics, which is usually fine, but -g, for example, has a totally different meaning in both programs.

Program options are not exactly identical

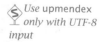

---

[1] The index package (see Section 14.5.3) uses a different approach that prevents expansion in *all* cases, which is arguably the better approach.

14.3 upmendex — A Unicode-aware indexing program

The program **upmendex** by TAKUJI Tanaka is an index processor that is Unicode-aware. It is fully compatible with *MakeIndex*'s input syntax and supports, except for a few minor differences, all configuration options described in the previous sections — any differences are explicitly discussed below.

The program was originally developed under the name **mendex** to offer a *MakeIndex* variant with tailored support for the Japanese language. For this, a number of new configuration options got added. The **upmendex** program extends this further, and by delegating the sorting to the International Components for Unicode (ICU) library, many different sorting schemes, based on languages or use case requirements, can be realized. For these features additional style keywords are available.

Because most of what was discussed for *MakeIndex* in the previous sections also applies to **upmendex**, we describe only the differences and extensions made by the program in detail below and otherwise refer to the *MakeIndex* documentation.

14.3.1 Options, warnings, and errors of the program

The **upmendex** program is called in the same way as *MakeIndex* and offers a comparable set of options.

```
upmendex [-cigflqr] [-d dic] [-o ind] [-p no] [-s sty] [-t log] [idx ...]
```

Unsupported MakeIndex options

Options shared with *MakeIndex* are only briefly listed here; more details on them are found in Section 14.2.2 on page 351. The *MakeIndex* options −L and −T are not supported by **upmendex**, and the option −g has a new meaning that is discussed below.

Options shared with MakeIndex

−c   Enable blank compression.

−i   Use standard input (`stdin`) as the input file.

−l   Use letter instead of word ordering.

−o *ind* Take *ind* as the output index file.

−p *no* Set the starting page number of the output index file to *no*.

−q   Operate in quiet mode.

−r   Disable implicit page range formation.

−s *sty* Take *sty* as the style file.

−t *log* Take *log* as the transcript file.

All other options are available only with **upmendex** and are needed if your index contains Japanese words that need sorting. However, as explained later, −d and −f are also useful with other scripts.

-d *dic* Employ *dic* as a dictionary file. Japanese Kanjis have one or more "reading", and in order to sort them, the reading to be used for sorting needs to be specified. This is done in dictionary files containing lines of the form

> ⟨*index entry*⟩ ⟨*key*⟩

Options specific to upmendex

which allows you to write \index{⟨*index entry*⟩} to achieve the same effect as when writing \index{⟨*key*⟩@⟨*index entry*⟩}. For correct sorting in Japanese the *key* should be written in Hiragana or Katakana script. The dictionary is consulted only if the *index entry* cannot be sorted automatically; i.e., you cannot use it to make arbitrary substitutions.

-f Force upmendex to output characters unchanged if it cannot determine a sort key and cannot find a dictionary entry. For example, indexing a "€" character would normally result in an error stopping the processing, because upmendex would not know how to sort it. This option would allow it to continue.

-g By default Japanese index entries are grouped by their component phonemes. This ordering is called a gojūon (lit. fifty sounds) table and consists of 48 kana because the table is not fully filled. When using the -g option, the entries are grouped into only five groups (the columns of the gojūon table corresponding to the vowels a, i, u, e, and o, in that order).
    In *MakeIndex* this option is used to implement German language sorting instead.

Like *MakeIndex*, the upmendex program displays information on the terminal and writes error and warnings in the transcript file. See Section 14.2.3 on page 355 for details on the error messages that are largely identical in both programs.

A number of messages are specific to upmendex, e.g., messages related to reading dictionary files (option -d), and there are a few new additional errors and warnings related to the extensions made for processing the full range of Unicode characters and the sorting with the ICU library. We describe here only those that one is more likely to encounter when generating an index for languages other than Japanese and that are not obvious from their message text.

Error: ⟨*entry*⟩ is no entry in dictionary file in ...
   upmendex does not know how to make a sort key for the index ⟨*entry*⟩, and it has not found an dictionary entry for it either. This is a hard error, and processing stops. Either you have to provide a dictionary file containing an appropriate entry line or you have to use the option -f to force the program to continue despite this error. This happens, for example, if the index entry contains symbols, such as † or €, unless you tell upmendex explicitly how to handle them.

Warning: [ICU] U_USING_DEFAULT_WARNING for locale ⟨*locale*⟩
   The ⟨*locale*⟩ specified in icu_locale in the style file has no effect because it is already covered by the default ICU sorting rules. For example, specifying de (for German) would have this effect. It can be safely ignored, but it means that the

specification was not necessary, in contrast to requesting, say, German phonebook ordering, which would be done with `de@collation=phonebook`.

Warning: Illegal input for icu_attributes (⟨*key*⟩:⟨*value*⟩)

The ⟨*key*⟩ and/or ⟨*value*⟩ specified for an ICU attribute in `icu_attributes` is not recognized. Check if there is a misspelling.

Warning: Sort key "⟨*key₁*⟩" is different from previous key "⟨*key₂*⟩" for same index "⟨*entry*⟩" in ...

There have been two or more index entries for ⟨*entry*⟩, using different sort keys, e.g., "abc@FOO" and "xyz@FOO". This is most likely a mistake in the input source, because it results in "FOO" appearing in two different places in the index. This issue is checked for only by `upmendex`, but not detected by *MakeIndex*.

14.3.2 Customizing the index with upmendex

Just like *MakeIndex*, the input and output behavior of the `upmendex` program can be customized through a style file (in fact with `upmendex` you can even supply several style files by repeatedly using the `-s` option).

The input style parameters are the same as for *MakeIndex* and are listed in Table 14.1 on page 357. The output style parameters listed in Tables 14.2 and 14.3 on pages 358–359 are also available. Consequently, all customization possibilities discussed in Section 14.2.4 on page 356 are also applicable for `upmendex`.

However, `upmendex` extends this set in several directions; the additional output parameters are shown in Table 14.4 on the next page. Below we discuss features that are available only when these parameters are used.

Adjusting the sorting to rules of a specific language or script

When it comes to sorting, different languages often have their own conventions, for example, whether to sort characters with diacritics under the base character or treat them as separate characters, etc. This makes the production of a properly sorted index challenging.

One of the main advantages of `upmendex` is therefore its ability to use the ICU services for sorting, which means that in many cases you have to specify only which "locale" should be used for sorting and let the ICU library worry about the rest. This locale is specified in the style file with the keyword `icu_locale`.

For example, if you have index entries for the words "Amme", "Apfel", "Äpfel", and "Axel", then the default sorting for English, German, and several other languages would be the following:

Amme, 1	Page 1:	`\index{Amme}`
Apfel, 2	Page 2:	`\index{Apfel}`
Äpfel, 2	Page 2:	`\index{Äpfel}`
Axel, 3	Page 3:	`\index{Axel}`

That is, the "Ä" is directly sorted after "A" within the letter group for A.

Keyword	Default Value	Description
Sorting		
icu_locale *(s)*	" "	The locale defining the basic sorting order for the index. Supported values are given in Table 14.5 on page 369.
icu_attributes *(s)*	" "	ICU attributes to further tailor the sorting. Supported values are given in Table 14.6 on page 369.
icu_rules *(s)*	" "	ICU rules to alter individual character sorting order.
Character/Script order		
character_order *(s)*	"SNLGCJKHDT"	The output order of scripts and symbols. The letters represent **Symbols**, **Numbers**, **Latin**, **Greek**, **Cyrillic**, **Japanese Kana**, **Korean Hangul**, **Hanja**, **Devanagari**, and **Thai** script.
Japanese specifics		
letter_head *(n)*	1	Use Katakana (default) or Hiragana (2) for Japanese Kana heading letters.
priority *(n)*	0	If nonzero, add one space between Japanese and non–Japanese text in an index entry while sorting.
Script heading characters		
devangari_head, hangul_head, hanzi_head, kana_head, thai_head, ...		Strings holding characters to be used as individual heading characters (one after the other) in front of entry groups within the script. For details, see the program documentation.
Group heading for Symbols and Numbers		
symbol_flag *(n)*	0	By Japanese conventions, symbols and numbers are sorted as a single group. If symbol_flag has the value 0, then symhead_positive or symhead_negative is used for the heading text of the group consisting of both symbols and numbers. If it is 1, then the value of symbol is used instead, and if it is set to 2, the program behaves like *MakeIndex*, and symbols and numbers get their own groups.
symbol *(s)*	" "	Heading text when symbol_flag is set to 1.

(s)Attribute of type string; *(n) attribute of type* number

Table 14.4: Additional output style parameters for upmendex

However, if you apply the Swedish locale (icu_locale␣"sv") in the style file, you get a different result because now "Ä" forms its own letter group.

Amme, 1	Page 1:	\index{Amme}
Apfel, 2	Page 2:	\index{Apfel}
Axel, 3	Page 2:	\index{Äpfel}
Äpfel, 2	Page 3:	\index{Axel}

Even within a language, sorting rules may differ based on the application; e.g., in Germany, sorting in phonebooks usually interprets the Umlaut "Ä" as "Ae".

This can in some cases be catered for by embellishing the locale information, i.e., `icu_locale␣"de@collation=phonebook"` after which the output shows "Äpfel" as the first entry, because it is sorted as "Aepfel":

Äpfel, 2	Page 1: `\index{Amme}`
Amme, 1	Page 2: `\index{Apfel}`
Apfel, 2	Page 2: `\index{Äpfel}`
Axel, 3	Page 3: `\index{Axel}`

Many languages are supported without the need for explicitly setting a locale

It is important to note that the locale used by `upmendex` is independent of the locale set on your operating system — only the value in `icu_locale` matters, and if not set, the ICU "root" order default applies. The latter is adequate for a large number of languages, among them Dutch, English, French, German, Italian, Portugese, etc. The list of supported locales that have special requirements is already quite large, but it is expected to grow even further. Table 14.5 on the facing page lists languages that need special locale settings as well as those that have supported variants for sorting; e.g., for German you do not need a locale setting unless you want phonebook sorting, so only the latter is listed in the table.

Tailoring the sorting with attributes

Besides setting the locale to influence the sorting, it is possible to tailor it by applying ICU attributes. These attributes can alter broader aspects, for example, whether lowercase characters should be sorted before or after uppercase characters. Supported attributes and their values are listed in Table 14.6 on the next page. You apply them by combining the attribute name with its value and assign this to `icu_attributes` in the style file. To set more than one attribute, separate them with a blank. Below we give a few examples of changes you may want to apply; for more details study the ICU documentation [90].

Sort numbers numerically

Digits in index entries are normally sorted as strings such that "V128" is placed before "V64". However, you may want to see them sorted by their numeric value, which can be achieved with

    `icu_attributes`   `"numeric-ordering:on"`

after which "V64" comes first, because 64 is numerically smaller than 128.

Lowercase first!

If entries differ only in the case of their characters, the uppercase entries are usually placed first. You can alter that by using

    `icu_attributes`   `"case-first:lower-first"`

French collation rules

In most languages, sorting is based on comparing strings from start to end, and if words differ only in some diacritics, then the first such difference determines the order. However, in some French dictionary traditions it is the last diacritics that are used for the ordering. For example, normally the words "cote", "coté", "côte", and "côté" would be sorted in exactly this order, but after specifying

    `icu_attributes`   `"french-collation:on"`

two words change their places, so we end up with "cotc", "côte", "coté", "côté".

language	locale(s)	language	locale(s)
Latin scripts			
Albanian	sq	Norwegian	nb, nn, no
Azerbaijan	az	Polish	pl
Catalan	ca	Romanian	ro
Croatian	hr, hr@collation=search	Serbian	sr-Latn,
Czech	cs, cs@collation=search		sr-Latn@collation=search
Danish	da	Slovak	sk, sk@collation=search
Esperanto	eo	Slovenian	sl
Finnish	fi	Spanish	es, es@collation=traditional,
Galician	gl		es@collation=search
German	de@collation=phonebook	Swedish	sv
Hungarian	hu	Turkish	tr
Lithuanian	lt	Vietnamese	vi
Greek script			
Greek	el		
Cyrillic scripts			
Belarusian	be	Serbian	sr
Bulgarian	bg	Ukraine	uk
Russian	ru		
CJK scripts			
Japanese	ja, ja@collation=unihan	Chinese	zh, zh@collation=unihan,
Korean	ko, ko@collation=search,		zh@collation=stroke,
	ko@collation=unihan		zh@collation=zhuyin

Many languages are directly supported by the default root sort order and therefore do not need an explicit setting. If you specify any of them, e.g., de (German), you get a warning that the default is used.

Table 14.5: Supported ICU locale settings for `icu_locale`

Attribute	Values	Attribute	Values
alternate	:shifted, :non-ignorable	normalization-mode	:on, :off
case-first	:off, :upper-first, :lower first	numeric-ordering	:on, :off
case-level	:on, :off	french-collation	:on, :off
strength	:primary. :secondary, :tertiary, :quaternary, :identical		

Table 14.6: ICU attributes supported by upmendex

Ignore punctuations while sorting

Perhaps a little less peculiar is the question of whether punctuation characters should play a rôle in sorting; e.g., how do you sort "high-level" and "higher"? By default "high-level" would come first because "-" gets compared to "e". If you want to ignore punctuation characters while sorting, you can specify

```
icu_attributes        "strength:tertiary alternate:shifted"
```

after which "higher" comes first, because now "e" is compared to "l".

Ignore diacritics while sorting

The `strength` attribute used above determines to what level of detail the sorting algorithm considers characters as being different; for example, the following

```
icu_attributes        "strength:primary"
```

would ignore diacritics.

There is also the possibility of specifying granular rules for individual character combinations that overwrite default sorting rules given through the locale. Such rules are then specified with the `icu_rules` keyword in the style file. The syntax and specification are rather technical and complicated and not something a user would normally undertake, so they are is not described here. See the documentation on the Internet [90] if you are curious.

Order of different scripts in the index

Given that `upmendex` supports different scripts and an index may contain several of them in parallel, there is the question how these should be ordered relative to each other; e.g., should Latin entries come before or after Cyrillic ones, etc. To adjust this order, you can use the keyword `character_order` in the style file. It expects a string of letters where each letter stands for a particular script or group of characters. For example, `"SNLCG"` would output first symbols and numbers, then Latin entries, then Cyrillic ones, and finally Greek entries. Note that you can separate symbol and number groups only if you additionally set `symbol_flag` to 2.

14.4 xindy, xindex — Two other indexing programs

There are other indexing programs, and in passing we like to mention two of them here. The first one is xindy by Roger Kehr and Joachim Schrod, which has been one of the early contenders as a replacement for *MakeIndex*. It avoids several of *MakeIndex*'s limits, especially for generating indexes in non–English languages. Being available for more than two decades, it was adapted to support many languages and scripts. However, most of this support was developed prior to the widespread use of Unicode, and while the program can handle Unicode to some extent, many aspects of it show that its original design assumes 8-bit codepages. The program and its support files are distributed as part of most TeX distributions, so there is no issue with continuing usage in existing projects, if the program's capabilities are sufficient for them. However, for new projects we recommend using upmendex or (with some caveats) xindex.

The program xindex is a recent development by Herbert Voß. It is a Unicode-aware index processor written in Lua that is compatible with the default syntax of *MakeIndex*.

However, it does not yet support the customization possibilities of *MakeIndex* and its
.ist style files. Similar to upmendex, it can be directed to use the ICU algorithms
and (some of) their tailoring features but uses a different syntax to enable this. At
the moment the feature and script support is still somewhat limited, but because it is
actively being developed, we might see further features in the future.

14.5 Enhancing the index with LaTeX features

This section describes LaTeX's support for index creation. It presents possibilities to
modify the index layout and to produce multiple indexes.

14.5.1 Modifying the layout

You can redefine the environment theindex, which by default is used to print the
index. The layout of the theindex environment and the definition of the \item,
\subitem, and \subsubitem commands are defined in the class files article, book,
and report. In the book class you can find the following definitions:

```
\newenvironment{theindex}
   {\@restonecoltrue\if@twocolumn\@restonecolfalse\fi
    \columnseprule \z@  \columnsep 35\p@
    \twocolumn[\@makeschapterhead{\indexname}]%
    \@mkboth{\MakeUppercase\indexname}{\MakeUppercase\indexname}%
    \thispagestyle{plain}\parindent\z@  \parskip\z@ \@plus .3\p@\relax
    \let\item\@idxitem}
   {\if@restonecol\onecolumn\else\clearpage\fi}
\newcommand\@idxitem  {\par\hangindent 40\p@}
\newcommand\subitem   {\par\hangindent 40\p@ \hspace*{20\p@}}
\newcommand\subsubitem{\par\hangindent 40\p@ \hspace*{30\p@}}
```

Although this is programmed in a fairly low-level internal language, you can probably
decipher what it sets up. First it tests for two-column mode and saves the result.
Then it sets some spacing parameters, resets the page style to plain, and calls
\twocolumn. Finally, it changes \item to execute \@idxitem, which produces a
paragraph with a hanging indentation of 40 points. A higher-level reimplementation
(using ifthen) might perhaps look as follows:

```
\renewenvironment{theindex}
   {\ifthenelse{\boolean{@twocolumn}}{\setboolean{@restonecol}{false}}%
                                     {\setboolean{@restonecol}{true}}%
    \setlength\columnseprule{0pt}\setlength\columnsep{35pt}%
    \twocolumn[\chapter*{\indexname}]%
    \markboth{\MakeUppercase\indexname}{\MakeUppercase\indexname}%
    \setlength\parindent{0pt}\setlength\parskip{0pt plus 0.3pt}%
    \thispagestyle{plain}\ExpandArgs{Nc}\RenewCommandCopy\item{@idxitem}}
   {\ifthenelse{\boolean{@restonecol}}{\onecolumn}{\clearpage}}
```

Adjusting this definition allows you to make smaller modifications, such as changing the page style or the column separation.

You can also make an index in three rather than two columns. To do so, you can use the multicol package and the `multicols` environment:

```
\renewenvironment{theindex}{%
    \begin{multicols}{3}[\chapter*{\indexname}][10\baselineskip]%
    \addcontentsline{toc}{chapter}{\indexname}%
    \setlength\parindent{0pt}\pagestyle{plain}%
    \ExpandArgs{Nc}\RenewCommandCopy{\item}{@idxitem}}%
    {\end{multicols}}
```

We require at least ten lines of free space on the current page; otherwise, we want the index to start on a new page. In addition to generating a title at the top, we enter the heading as a "Chapter" in the table of contents (`.toc`) and change the page style to `plain`. Then the `\item` command is redefined to cope with index entries (see above), and the entries themselves are typeset in three columns using the `multicols` environment.

14.5.2 showidx, repeatindex, tocbibind, indxcite — **Little helpers**

Several useful little LaTeX packages exist to support index creation. A selection is listed in this section, but by browsing through the Internet resources discussed in Section C.4 on page 789, you can probably find additional ones.

Show index entries in margin

The package `showidx` (by Leslie Lamport) can help you improve the entries in the index and locate possible problems. It shows all `\index` commands in the margin of the printed page. Figure 14.4 on page 353 shows the result of including the `showidx` package.

Handle page breaks gracefully

The package `repeatindex` (by Harald Harders) repeats the main item of an index if a page or column break occurs within a list of subitems. This helps the reader correctly identify to which main item a subitem belongs.

Table of contents support

The package `tocbibind` (by Peter Wilson) can be used to add the table of contents itself, the bibliography, and the index to the *Table of Contents* listing. See page →I 56 for more information on this package.

Automatic author index

The package `indxcite` (by James Ashton) automatically generates an author index based on citations made using BibTeX. This type of functionality is also available with the bibliography packages `natbib`, `jurabib`, and `biblatex`, all of which are described in detail in Chapter 16.

14.5.3 index — **Producing multiple indexes**

The `index` package (written by David Jones) augments LaTeX's indexing mechanism in several areas:

- Multiple indexes are supported.

- A two-stage process is used for creating the raw index files (such as the default `.idx` file) similar to that used to create the `.toc` file. First the index entries are written to the .aux file, and then they are copied to the .idx file at the end of the run. With this approach, if you have a large document consisting of several included files (using the \include command), you no longer lose the index if you format only part of the document with \includeonly. Note, however, that this makes the creation of a chapter index more difficult.

- A starred form of the \index command is introduced. In addition to entering its argument in the index, it typesets the argument in the running text.

- To simplify typing, the \shortindexingon command activates a short-hand notation. Now you can type ^{foo} for \index{foo} and _{foo} for \index*{foo}. These shorthand notations are turned off with the \shortindexingoff command. Because the underscore and circumflex characters have special meanings inside math mode, this shorthand notation is unavailable there.

- The package includes the functionality of the showidx package. The command \proofmodetrue enables the printing of index entries in the margins. You can customize the size and style of the font used in the margin with the \indexproofstyle command, which takes a font definition as its argument (e.g., \indexproofstyle{\footnotesize\itshape}).

- The argument of \index is never expanded when the index package is used. In standard LaTeX, using \index{\command} sometimes writes the expansion of \command to the .idx file (see Section 14.2.5 on page 362). With the index package, \command itself is always written to the .idx file. While this is helpful in most cases, macro authors can be bitten by this behavior. In Section 14.1.7, we recommended that you define commands that automatically add index entries. Such commands often expect that \index expands its parameter, and they may not work when you use the index package. Be careful and check the results of the automatic indexing — this is best practice anyway.

You can declare new indexes with the \newindex command. The command \renewindex, which has an identical syntax, is used to redefine existing indexes.

\newindex{*tag*}{*raw-ext*}{*proc-ext*}{*indextitle*}

The first argument, *tag*, is a short identifier used to refer to the index. In particular, the commands \index and \printindex are redefined to take an optional argument — namely, the tag of the index to which you are referring. If this optional argument is absent, the index with the tag "default" is used, which corresponds to the usual index. The second argument, *raw-ext*, is the extension of the raw index file to which LaTeX should write the unprocessed entries for this index (for the default index it is .idx). The third argument, *proc-ext*, is the extension of the index file in which LaTeX expects to find the processed index (for the default index it is .ind). The fourth argument, *indextitle*, is the title that LaTeX prints at the beginning of the index.

As an example we show the setup used to produce this book. The preamble included the following setting:

```
\RequirePackage{index}
\proofmodetrue                    % while proofing the index entries
\newindex{xauthor}{adx}{and}{People}
\newindex{xcmds}{cdx}{cnd}{Index of Commands and Concepts}
```

In the back matter, printing of the index was done with the following lines:

```
\printindex[xcmds] \printindex[xauthor]
```

For each generated raw index file (e.g., `tlc3.adx` for the list of authors) we ran *MakeIndex* to produce the corresponding formatted index file for LaTeX:

```
makeindex -o tlc3.and -t tlc3.alg tlc3.adx
```

While all of these tools help to get the correct page numbers in the index, the real difficulty persists: choosing useful index entries for your readers. This problem you still have to solve (if you are lucky, with help).

In fact, the index for the second edition of this book [77], as well as the indexes for the *LaTeX Graphics Companion* [31], was created by a professional indexer, Richard Evans of Infodex Indexing Services in Raleigh, North Carolina. Dick worked closely with me to produce comprehensive indexes that help you, the reader, find not only the names of things (packages, programs, commands, and so on) but also the tasks, concepts, and ideas described in the books. Let him tell you (from his FAQ):

Question: Why do I need an indexer? Can't the computer create an index?

Answer: To exactly the same degree that a word processor can write the book. Indexes are creative works, requiring human intellect and analysis.

LaTeX can process the indexing markup, but only a human indexer can decide what needs to be marked up. My sincere thanks to Dick for his excellent work and the teaching he delivered while working with him.

*   *   *

Unfortunately, Dick was unable to help me with this edition, as was initially planned. However, I learned a lot during our joint work on the other books, and with this knowledge and the good basis of terms selected for the previous edition, I am fairly confident that we have been able to deliver a useful result to you.

In this process I received invaluable help from Keith Harrison, who went through all pages of the book, identified new concepts worth indexing, and verified existing entries — a big thank you to him.

Bibliography Generation

While a table of contents (see Section 2.3) and an index (discussed in Chapter 14) make it easier to navigate through a book, the presence of bibliographic references should allow you to verify the sources and to probe further subjects you consider interesting. To make this possible, the references should be precise and lead to the relevant work with a minimum of effort.

There exist many ways to format bibliographies, and different fields of scholarly activities have developed very precise rules in this area. An interesting overview of Anglo-Saxon practices can be found in the chapter on bibliographies in *The Chicago Manual of Style* [24]. Normally, authors must follow the rules laid out by their publisher. Therefore, one of the more important tasks when submitting a book or an article for publication is to generate the bibliographic reference list according to those rules.

Traditional ways of composing such lists by hand, without the systematic help of computers, are plagued with the following problems:

- Citations and references, particularly in a document with contributions from many authors, are hard to make consistent. Difficulties arise, such as variations in the use of full forenames versus abbreviations (with or without periods); italicization or quoting of titles; spelling "ed.", "Ed.", or "Editor"; and the various forms of journal volume number.

- A bibliography laid out in one style (e.g., alphabetic by author and year) is extremely hard to convert to another (e.g., numeric citation order) if requested by a publisher.

- It is difficult to maintain one large database of bibliographic references that can be reused in different documents.

In the present chapter we concentrate on the formatting of reference lists and bibliographies, and we discuss possibilities for managing collections of bibliographic references in databases. The chapter is heavily based on the BibTEX program, written by Oren Patashnik, and the biber program written by François Charette and now maintained by Philip Kime, which both integrate well with LATEX. In Chapter 16 we are then mainly concerned with the citation of sources within the text.

We start by showing how a bibliography can be created manually in LATEX. Because the standard environment is also used in the output of most BibTEX styles, this prepares the ground for the BibTEX workflow. We then introduce the two programs. This is followed by a detailed introduction to the database format[1] used to specify bibliographical data in a suitable form for processing with BibTEX or biber. We continue with a description of how to produce bibliographic input files for LATEX from these databases.

Instead of collecting your own bibliographical data, there is also the possibility of drawing information from various online sources that offer such data in BibTEX format. Some of them are introduced in Section 15.5.

Having collected data for BibTEX databases, the next natural step is to look for tools that help in managing such databases. Section 15.6 offers tools of various flavors for this task, ranging from command-line utilities to GUI-based programs for various platforms.

Finally, in Section 15.7 we return to the task of typesetting a bibliography and discuss how different BibTEX and biblatex styles can be used to produce different bibliography layouts from the same input. Because there may not be a suitable style for a particular set of layout requirements available, Section 15.7.2 discusses how to generate customized styles using the custom-bib package without the need for any BibTEX style programming. How to create or adapt styles for biblatex is discussed in Chapter 16 where we review that package in detail.

15.1 The standard LATEX bibliography environment

The standard LATEX environment for generating a list of references or a bibliography is called thebibliography. It is not defined by LATEX itself but by the document class, so the layout can vary. In its default implementation in the standard classes, it automatically generates an appropriate heading and implements a vertical list structure in which every publication is represented as a separate item. It also creates

---

[1]Due to its origin, the format is commonly referred to as the BibTEX database format, even if used with biber. Thus, if you read "BibTEX database format" in the remainder of this chapter, it refers to the format usable by either of the programs.

for every item a label to allow referencing it in the document. The `thebibliography` environment can be created manually, but it is also used in the output of most BIBTEX styles. It is not used by the `biblatex` package, which typesets bibliographies with its own command, `\printbibliography`.

The different traditions regarding how such sources are then referred to in a document and how to produce such citations with LATEX is the topic of Chapter 16; here citation commands are mentioned only as far as necessary to understand how they affect the bibliography.

```
\begin{thebibliography}{widest-label}
\bibitem[label1]{cite-key1}  bibliographic information
\bibitem[label2]{cite-key2}  bibliographic information
     . . .
\end{thebibliography}
```

The *widest-label* argument is used to determine the right amount of indentation for individual items. If the works are numbered sequentially, for example, it should contain the number of items.

Individual publications are introduced with a `\bibitem` command. Its mandatory argument is a unique cross-reference *cite-key* that is used to refer to this publication in the text of the document. For this purpose LATEX offers the `\cite` command, which takes such a *cite-key* as its argument. Its precise syntax is described in Section 16.2.1 on page 475.

The optional argument defines the textual representation that is used in the citation and as the *label* in the list. If this argument is not specified, the publications are numbered with arabic numerals by default. Within a bibliographic entry the command `\newblock` may be used to separate major blocks of information. Depending on the layout produced by the document class, it may result in a normal space, may result in some extra space, or might start a new line.

The text of the heading is produced — depending on the class — by either the command `\bibname` or `\refname`. A language package, such as babel, localizes such commands and changes to them should be done by using the methods described in Chapter 13.

[1], [GOO97]

References

[1] Goossens, M., S. Rahtz, and F. Mittelbach (1997). *The LATEX Graphics Companion: Illustrating Documents with TEX and PostScript.* Reading, MA, USA: Addison-Wesley Longman.

[GOO97] Goossens, M., B. User, J. Doe (1997). Ambiguous citations.

```
\cite{LGC97}, \cite{GUD97}
\begin{thebibliography}{2}
\bibitem{LGC97}  Goossens, M., S.~Rahtz,
   and F.~Mittelbach (1997).
  \newblock \emph{The \LaTeX{} Graphics Companion:
  Illustrating Documents with \TeX{} and
  PostScript}. \newblock Reading, MA, USA:
  Ad\-di\-son-Wes\-ley Longman.
\bibitem[GOO97]{GUD97} Goossens, M., B.~User,
   J.~Doe (1997). \newblock Ambiguous citations.
\end{thebibliography}
```

Producing a large bibliography manually in this way is clearly a tedious and difficult task, and the result is normally not reusable, because nearly all journals and publishers have their own house styles with different formatting requirements. For this reason it is generally better to use programs, such as BibTeX or biber, that generate ready-to-use LaTeX input from a database of bibliographical information. This is discussed in the next section.

Order by first citation done manually

Note that the references are typeset and numbered in the order in which they appear in the bibliography. Thus, if you produce the bibliography manually, numbering and sorting the entries into the correct order becomes your task, which is especially difficult if they should be ordered by first reference in the text instead of alphabetically. In contrast, when using BibTeX or biber, either order can be achieved automatically.

Handling the requirement to use a thebibliography environment explicitly

Some journals provide templates in which you are required to provide the reference list as explicit \bibitems in a thebibliography environment. When generating the bibliography with BibTeX, this can be easily achieved by copying the final .bbl content into your document before submitting. However, when using biblatex/biber, this is not possible. In this case, the biblatex2bibitem package by Nikolai Avdeev can be of some help. Its usage is simple: load the package and issue \printbibitembibliography at the end of the document. This then typesets at this point a source representation of the thebibliography environment, which can be copied and pasted from the PDF into the source file intended for the journal. However, please note that when using the engine pdfTeX, you need to ensure that your document uses \usepackage[T1]{fontenc} so that you get real accented characters into the output — with the default OT1 encoding, cut and paste goes horribly wrong otherwise.

Copying from a PDF is not fool-proof even then, and the result should be checked for faulty characters and missing spaces. But it can save you from having to manually retype a possibly lengthy reference list.

15.2 The biber and BibTeX programs

The BibTeX program was designed by Oren Patashnik to provide a flexible solution to the problem of automatically generating bibliography lists conforming to different layout styles. It automatically detects the citation requests in a LaTeX document (by scanning its .aux file or files), selects the needed bibliographical information from one or more specified databases, and formats it according to a specified layout style. Its output is a file containing the bibliography listing as LaTeX code that is automatically loaded and used by LaTeX on the following run. Section 15.4 on page 409 discusses the interface between the two programs in some detail.

At the time of this book's writing BibTeX was available as version 0.99d, but if you look into the second edition of this book (a decade back), you find that it already talks about version 0.99c. Version 0.99a probably dates back to 1986. In other words, the program has been kept stable for a very long period of time. As a consequence, the BibTeX database format is very well established in the LaTeX world (and in fact even far beyond), with many people having numerous citation entries collected over the years. Thus, it comes as no surprise that all development that happened in the last decades is based on that format as a standard.

Due to its age and origins BibTeX is 7-bit, ASCII based. Although it is able to handle foreign characters, its functionality in this respect is rather limited. It can sort only ASCII characters and has trouble generating initials for non–ASCII characters. For this reason non–ASCII characters usually have to be input with macros as described on page 398. Most BibTeX styles then purify the sort key by converting some special control sequences like \oe to letters while ignoring all others and then removing all nonalphanumeric characters. This means that "Ælk" is sorted as aelk, but "Ålk", "Älk", and "Alk" all sort as alk.

This lack of support for Unicode and the sorting rules of languages different from English has led to the development of alternatives. In the rest of this section we briefly survey a variant of BibTeX and introduce the relatively new biber program.

15.2.1 bibtex8 — An 8-bit reimplementation of BibTeX

The BibTeX8 program written by Niel Kempson and Alejandro Aguilar-Sierra is an 8-bit reimplementation of BibTeX with the ability to specify sorting order information. This allows you to store your BibTeX database entries in an 8-bit code page and to use the inputenc package in your LaTeX document (see Sections 9.5.4 and 9.9.3).

While this is an improvement over BibTeX, the restriction to an 8-bit code page and therefore the missing support of the de facto standard encoding UTF-8 makes it nowadays useful only in isolated cases.

The BibTeX8 program offers command-line options that allow you to enlarge its internal tables. In 1995, when the first release of the program was written, standard BibTeX had only small, hardwired internal tables, making it impossible to typeset, say, a bibliography listing with several hundred citations. These days most installations use higher customizable defaults (e.g., 20000 citations in TeX Live) so that the flexibility of BibTeX8 in this respect is seldom needed. But in case a particular job hits one of the limits and emits a message like "Sorry -- you've exceeded BibTeX's...", you can use BibTeX8 with a suitable command-line setting to get around the problem or with BibTeX edit the texmf.cnf configuration file to alter the default setting.

There are other extensions of the original BibTeX program, but we found none that works reliably, which is why we suggest using biber and biblatex if the basic capabilities of BibTeX or BibTeX8 are not sufficient for your needs.

15.2.2 biber — A Unicode-aware bibliography processor

In 2009 François Charette released the first version of a successor for BibTeX called biber, whose development was driven by the increasing demand of tools that support out-of-the-box Unicode, UTF-8, and various languages and scripts. In the following years biber was improved in parallel to the package biblatex, and both are now closely coupled. Using biber requires using biblatex as the bibliography package in LaTeX, and while biblatex still can be used with BibTeX, this is not recommended as many of its new and sophisticated features work only with biber. All biblatex examples of this book have been processed with biber as the backend processor.

biber is written in perl, i.e., in a far more powerful programming language than the language used in the .bst style files of BibTeX. Among other features, biber deals with the full range of UTF-8 and sorts in a completely customizable manner using, when available, Unicode Common Locale Data Repository (CLDR) collation tailoring.

The biber program can be used in two modes: standard and tool mode. In the standard mode, which is used when you create bibliographic input for LaTeX, it expects as its main argument a .bcf control file — the extension can be omitted. The output is then a file with the same basename and the extension .bbl. In tool mode, which is triggered by the option --tool, the argument is a .bib file, and the result is a new .bib file with _bibertool appended to the basename. In both modes, the name of the output file can be changed with the option --output-file. biber accepts a large number of command-line options to adjust the output, which you can inspect if you call biber with the --help option or by consulting the documentation [39]. So, for example, the following converts all field names in a .bib file to lowercase:

```
biber --tool --output-fieldcase=lower ⟨file⟩.bib
```

The next command replaces the field name journaltitle with journal:

```
biber --tool --output-field-replace=journaltitle:journal ⟨file⟩.bib
```

Finally, the following can be used to nicely align the fields in the .bib file:

```
biber --tool --output-align ⟨file⟩.bib
```

Adaption of the editor needed — Most modern editors and TeX-workflows contain scripts, buttons, or menus to call the bibliography processor. Their settings must be changed if biber should be used instead of BibTeX. Instructions for various cases can be found on the Internet or, if the editor is already biber-aware, in the documentation of the editor. The settings can be checked by looking in the .blg file after a compilation. It contains messages of the bibliography processor, and biber announces itself in the first line:

```
[0] Config.pm:311> INFO - This is Biber 2.17
```

15.3 The BibTeX database format

As remarked on before, the bibliographic database format used by all programs was originally designed for BibTeX and is therefore commonly referred to as the "BibTeX database format". Such a BibTeX database is a plain-text file with the extension .bib that contains bibliographical entries internally structured as key/value pairs. Two database files are shown in Figures 15.1 and 15.2 on pages 382–383 and 391. The first shows a number of typical, real-world entries, while the second has been designed to demonstrate special points in the examples. In this section we study the allowed syntax of database entries in some detail; see also [82].

When using the 7-bit application BibTeX, the file should normally be a pure ASCII file; BibTeX8 as described in Section 15.2.1 can handle also 8-bit code pages. In contrast, biber supports all file encodings — using it with the now de facto standard UTF-8 is highly recommended.

The different requirements regarding the file encoding show that the format of the BibTeX database is quite flexible. This made it possible to adapt and extend the format over time to support modern needs like new fields to store a Uniform Resource Locator (URL) and references to digital archives, but it also means that it can depend on the post-processor, on the BibTeX style, and even on document settings if a field is used and which values it expects. Most notably there are a number of differences between a database meant for a BibTeX workflow and a database meant for biblatex and biber that stem from the much more powerful abilities of the latter to handle, e.g., dates, cross references, annotated data, new fields, and Unicode. Such differences are shown in small boxes, which will also often contain tips on how to stay compatible with a BibTeX workflow in such cases.

Explaining BibTeX/biber differences

> biber/biblatex
>
> The text in boxes such as this explain features specific to the biber/biblatex workflow and may give advice on what to do (or what not to use) when compatibility with the BibTeX workflow is required.

Each entry in a BibTeX database consists of three main parts: a *type* specifier, followed by a *key*, and finally the *data* for the entry itself. The *type* describes the general nature of the entry (e.g., whether it is an article, book, or some other publication). The *key* is used in the interface to LaTeX; it is the string that you have to place in the argument of a \cite command when referencing that particular entry. The *data* part consists of a series of *field entries* (depending on the *type*), which can have one of two forms as seen in the following generic format and example:

```
@type_specifier{key_identifier,        @book{lamport86,
   field_name_1 = "field_text_1",         author = "Leslie Lamport",
   field_name_2 = {field_text_2},         title  = "{\LaTeX{}} A Document
                                                    Preparation system",
       .   .   .                          publisher = {Addison-Wesley},
   field_name_n = {field_text_n}          year   = 1986                  }
}
```

The comma is the field separator. Spaces surrounding the equal sign or the comma are ignored. Inside the text part of a field (enclosed in a pair of double quotes or a pair of braces) you can have any string of characters, but braces must be matched. The quotes or braces can be omitted for text consisting entirely of numbers (like the year field in the example above).

Note that LaTeX's comment character % is not a comment character inside .bib database files and even leads to parsing errors if used inside of an entry. Instead, anything outside an entry is considered a comment as long as it does not contain an @ sign (which would be misinterpreted as the start of a new entry). Thus, to comment a field in an entry, change the name of the field to an ignored name or place it outside the entry. To exclude a full entry, remove the starting @ sign.

Comments in the .bib file

```
@String{ttct      = "Tools and Techniques for Computer
                     Typesetting"  }

@Book{TLC94,
   author =        "Michel Goossens and Frank Mittelbach
                    and Alexander Samarin",
   title =         "The {\LaTeX} Companion",
   publisher =     "Ad{\-d}i{\-s}on-Wes{\-l}ey Longman",
   address =       "Reading, MA, USA",
   pages =         "xxi + 528",
   year =          "1994",
   ISBN =          "0-201-54199-8",
   series =        ttct
}


@Book{LGC97,
   author =        "Michel Goossens and Sebastian Rahtz
                    and Frank Mittelbach",
   title =         "The {\LaTeX} Graphics Companion:
                    Illustrating Documents with {\TeX}
                    and {PostScript}",
   publisher =     "Ad{\-d}i{\-s}on-Wes{\-l}ey Longman",
   address =       "Reading, MA, USA",
   pages =         "xxi + 554",
   year =          "1997",
   ISBN =          "0-201-85469-4",
   series =        ttct
}


@Book{LWC99,
   author =        "Michel Goossens and Sebastian Rahtz",
   title =         "The {\LaTeX} {Web} companion:
                    integrating {\TeX}, {HTML},
                    and {XML}",
   publisher =     "Ad{\-d}i{\-s}on-Wes{\-l}ey Longman",
   address =       "Reading, MA, USA",
   pages =         "xxii + 522",
   year =          "1999",
   ISBN =          "0-201-43311-7",
   note =          "With Eitan M. Gurari and Ross Moore
                    and Robert S. Sutor",
   series =        ttct
}

@Book{Knuth-CT-a,
   Author    =     "Donald E. Knuth",
   Title     =     "The {\TeX}book",
   Publisher =     "Ad{\-d}i{\-s}on-Wes{\-l}ey",
   Address   =     "Reading, MA, USA",
   Volume    =     "A",
   Series    =     "Computers and Typesetting",
   pages     =     "ix + 483",
   year      =     1986,
   isbn      =     "0-201-13447-0",
}
```

```
@Article{Knuth:TB10-1-31,
   Author   =      "Donald E. Knuth",
   Title    =      "{Typesetting  Concrete
                    Mathematics}",
   Journal  =      "TUGboat",
   Volume   =      "10",
   Number   =      "1",
   Pages    =      "31--36",
   year     =      1989,
   month    =      apr,
   issn     =      "0896-3207"
}

@Book{vLeunen:92,
   author    =     "Mary-Claire van Leunen",
   gender    =     "sf",
   title     =     "A handbook for scholars",
   publisher =     "Oxford University Press",
   address   =     "Walton Street, Oxford OX2 6DP, UK",
   pages     =     "xi + 348",
   year      =     "1992"
}

@manual{GNUMake,      key = {make},
 title = {{GNU Make}, A Program for Directing
 Recompilation},  organization= "Free
 Software Foundation",address = "Boston,
 Massachusetts",ISBN={1-882114-80-9},year = 2000}

@book{G-G,
   TITLE     =     {{Gutenberg Jahrbuch}},
   EDITOR    =     {Hans-Joachim Koppitz},
   PUBLISHER =     {Gutenberg-Gesellschaft, Internationale
                    Vereinigung f\"ur Geschichte und
                    Gegenwart der Druckkunst e.V.},
   ADDRESS   =     {Mainz, Germany},
   NOTE      =     {Contains results on the past and present
                    history of the art of printing. Founded
                    by Aloys Ruppel. Published since 1926.}
}

@periodical{jcg,
   title      =    {Computers and Graphics},
   year       =    2011,
   issuetitle =    {Semantic {3D} Media and Content},
   volume     =    35,
   number     =    4,
   issn       =    {0097-8493},
   annotation =    {This is a \texttt{periodical} entry
                    with an \texttt{issn} field.}}
```

Figure 15.1: Sample BibTeX database (`tlc.bib`)

This database (continued one the next page) is used in many examples of the book. It exhibits different conventions in individual entries (e.g., lower-, upper-, or mixed-case field names, different indentations, etc.) to show some features and problems in later examples. By applying one of the tools from Section 15.6 it could be normalized.

```
@InProceedings{MR-PQ,
  author    = "Frank Mittelbach and Chris Rowley",
  title     = "The Pursuit of Quality: How can
               Automated Typesetting achieve the
               Highest Standards of Craft
               Typography?",
  pages     = "261--273",
  crossref  = "EP92"}

@InProceedings{Southall,
  Author    = "Richard Southall",
  Title     = "Presentation Rules and Rules of
               Composition in the Formatting of
               Complex Text",
  Pages     = "275--290",
  crossref  = "EP92"}

@Proceedings{EP92,
  title     = "{EP92}---Proceedings of Electronic
               Publishing, '92",
  shorttitle = "{EP92}",
  editor    = "Christine Vanoirbeek and Giovanni Coray",
  publisher = "Cambridge University Press",
  address   = "Cambridge",
  year      = 1992,
  booktitle = "{EP92}---Proceedings of Electronic
               Publishing, '92"
}

@article{angenendt,
  author      = {Angenendt, Arnold},
  title       = {In Honore Salvatoris--- Vom Sinn und
                 Unsinn der Patrozinienkunde},
  journaltitle = {Revue d'Histoire Ecclésiastique},
  date        = 2002,
  volume      = 97,
  pages       = {431--456, 791--823},
  langid      = {german},
  indextitle  = {In Honore Salvatoris},
  shorttitle  = {In Honore Salvatoris}}

@book{cicero,
  author      = {Cicero, Marcus Tullius},
  title       = {De natura deorum.
                 Über das Wesen der Götter},
  date        = 1995,
  editor      = {Blank-Sangmeister, Ursula},
  translator  = {Blank-Sangmeister, Ursula},
  afterword   = {Thraede, Klaus},
  language    = {langlatin and langgerman},
  publisher   = {Reclam},
  location    = {Stuttgart},
  langid      = {german},
  indextitle  = {De natura deorum},
  shorttitle  = {De natura deorum}}

@inbook{kant:kpv,
  title       = {Kritik der praktischen Vernunft},
  date        = 1968,
  author      = {Kant, Immanuel},
  booktitle   = {Kritik der praktischen Vernunft.
                 Kritik der Urtheilskraft},
  bookauthor  = {Kant, Immanuel},
  maintitle   = {Kants Werke. Akademie Textausgabe},
```

```
  volume      = 5,
  publisher   = {Walter de Gruyter},
  location    = {Berlin},
  pages       = {1-163},
  shorthand   = {KpV},
  langid      = {german},
  shorttitle  = {Kritik der praktischen Vernunft}}

@commentary{palandt,
  author      = {Palandt, Otto},
  location    = {München},
  publisher   = {C.H. Beck},
  edition     = {79},
  isbn        = {978-3-406-73800-5},
  pagination  = {paragraph},
  shorthand   = {Palandt},
  title       = {Bürgerliches Gesetzbuch
                 mit Nebengesetzen},
  year        = {2019}}

@BOOK{zpo,
  author      = {Adolf Baumbach and Wolfgang Lauterbach
                 and Jan Albers and Peter Hartmann},
  title       = {Zivilproze\ss ordnung mit
                 Gerichtsverfassungsgesetz und anderen
                 Nebengesetzen},
  shorttitle  = {ZPO},
  language    = {ngerman},
  edition     = {59. neubearb.},
  year        = 2002,
  address     = {M\"unchen}}

@BOOK{aschur,
  author      = {Hans Brox and Wolf-Dietrich Walker},
  title       = {Allgemeines Schuldrecht},
  language    = {ngerman},
  edition     = {29.},
  year        = 2003,
  address     = {M\"unchen}}

@BOOK{bschur,
  author      = {Hans Brox and Wolf-Dietrich Walker},
  title       = {Besonderes Schuldrecht},
  shorttitle  = {BSchuR},
  language    = {ngerman},
  edition     = {27.},
  year        = 2002,
  address     = {M\"unchen}}

@BOOK{bgb,
  author      = {Otto Palandt},
  shortauthor = {Otto Palandt},
  title       = {B\"urgerliches Gesetzbuch},
  shorttitle  = {BGB},
  language    = {ngerman},
  edition     = {62.},
  year        = 2003,
  publisher   = {Beck Juristischer Verlag},
  address     = {M\"unchen}}
```

biber/biblatex

> biber recognizes LaTeX's comment character %, and it is possible to exclude entries with it. Like BibTeX it ignores text in the `.bib` file, which does not belong to an entry, but it reports such text as junk characters in the `.blg` file (the log file of BibTeX and biber) unless the lines start like in a TeX file with a percent char.

The `key_identifier` can be freely chosen but should use only ASCII characters and should not contain a space or any one of the characters " # % , = { } ~ \.

BibTeX *ignores* the case of the letters for the entry type, key, and field names. You must, however, be careful with the key. LaTeX honors the case of the keys specified as the argument of a `\cite` command, so the key for a given bibliographic entry must match the one specified in the LaTeX file (see Section 16.2.1).

biber/biblatex

> With biber the key of the entry should not contain a space or any one of the characters " # % , = { } ' ( ) ~ \. Most important, that means that a key `author(1998)`, which is allowed with BibTeX, is not recognized correctly with biber. Keys can contain non–ASCII chars, so `Sträßer.2010` is allowed, but it should be used only if compatibility with BibTeX is not needed and if the `.tex` and `.bib` files use matching file encodings — at best UTF-8.

Various schemes exist for conveniently associating bibliography keywords with their entries in a database. A popular one is the so-called Harvard system, where you take the author's surname (converted to lowercase) and the year of publication and combine them using a colon (e.g., `smith:1987`).

15.3.1 Entry types and fields

As discussed above, you must describe each bibliographic entry as belonging to a certain type, with the information itself tagged by certain fields.

The first thing you have to decide is what type of entry you are dealing with. Although no fixed classification scheme can be complete, with a little creativity you can make BibTeX cope reasonably well with even the more bizarre types of publications. For nonstandard types, it is probably wise not to attach too much importance to BibTeX's or biber's warning messages (see below).

Most BibTeX styles have at least the 13 standard entry types, which are shown in Table 15.1 on page 386.

These different types of publications demand different kinds of information; a reference to a journal article might include the volume and number of the journal, which is usually not meaningful for a book. Therefore, different database types have different fields. In fact, for each type of entry, the fields are divided into three classes:

Required   Omission of the field produces a warning message and, possibly, a badly formatted bibliography entry. If the required information is not meaningful, you are most likely using the wrong entry type. If it is meaningful but, say, already included in some other field, ignore the warning, but check that the typeset entry is not mangled.

Optional The field's information is used if present, but you can omit it without causing formatting problems. Include the optional field if it can help the reader.

Ignored The field is ignored. BibTeX ignores any field that is not required or optional, so you can include any fields in a `.bib` file entry. It is a good idea to put all relevant information about a reference in its `.bib` file entry, even information that may never appear in the bibliography. For example, the abstract of a paper can be entered into an `abstract` field in its `.bib` file entry. The `.bib` file is probably as good a place as any for the abstract, and there exist bibliography styles for printing selected abstracts (see the `abstract` bibliography style mentioned in Table 15.7 on page 420).

> biber/biblatex
>
> With biber the `abstract` field is not ignored. This can lead to errors in the LaTeX compilation if this field has been used in the past to record data that were not expected to be typeset, e.g, contains hashes, #, or a percent characters, %.
>
> Either such special characters should be correctly escaped or the processing of the field should be suppressed with a source map as described in Example 15-3-5 on page 408.

Table 15.1 on the following page describes the standard entry types, along with their required and optional fields, as used by the standard bibliography styles. The fields within each class (required or optional) are listed in the typical order of occurrence in the output. A few entry types, however, may perturb the alphabetic ordering slightly, depending on which fields are missing. The meaning of the individual fields is explained in Tables 15.3/4 on pages 388–389. Nonstandard bibliography styles may ignore some optional fields or use additional ones like `isbn` when creating the reference (see also the examples starting on page 419). Remember that, when used in a `.bib` file, the entry-type name is preceded by an @ character.

> biber/biblatex
>
> Table 15.2 on page 387 shows which additional standard entry types are supported by biblatex along with their required fields. The list of optional fields supported by each type is not shown because it is much longer than in a typical BibTeX style: all entry types for example support fields for various electronic identifiers, fields to change sorting, date fields, and generic fields. So only some important new fields are described below, but for the full list the biblatex documentation should be consulted. The file `blx-dm.def`, which is part of the biblatex package, contains the declaration of the default entry types, the fields they support, and the constraints on these fields and so can be consulted for details.

article	An article from a journal or magazine. *Required*: author, title, journal, year. *Optional*: volume, number, pages, month, note.
book	A book with an explicit publisher. *Required*: author or editor, title, publisher, year. *Optional*: volume or number, series, address, edition, month, note.
booklet	A work that is printed and bound, but without a named publisher or sponsoring institution. *Required*: title. *Optional*: author, howpublished, address, month, year, note.
inbook	A part of a book, e.g., a chapter, section, or whatever and/or a range of pages. [biber/biblatex difference: Use the type only for a self-contained part with its own title.] *Required*: author or editor, title, chapter and/or pages, publisher, year. *Optional*: volume or number, series, type, address, edition, month, note.
incollection	A part of a book having its own title. *Required*: author, title, booktitle, publisher, year. *Optional*: editor, volume or number, series, type, chapter, pages, address, edition, month, note.
inproceedings	An article in a conference proceedings. *Required*: author, title, booktitle, year. *Optional*: editor, volume or number, series, pages, address, month, organization, publisher, note.
manual	Technical documentation. *Required*: title. *Optional*: author, organization, address, edition, month, year, note.
mastersthesis	A master's thesis. [biber/biblatex difference: The type is provided as an alias of the new type thesis.] *Required*: author, title, school, year. *Optional*: type, address, month, note.
misc	Use this type when nothing else fits. A warning is issued if all optional fields are empty (i.e., the entire entry is empty or has only ignored fields). *Required*: none. *Optional*: author, title, howpublished, month, year, note.
phdthesis	A Ph.D. thesis. [biber/biblatex difference: The type is provided as an alias of the new type thesis.] *Required*: author, title, school, year. *Optional*: type, address, month, note.
proceedings	Conference proceedings. *Required*: title, year. *Optional*: editor, volume or number, series, address, publisher, note, month, organization.
techreport	A report published by a school or other institution, usually numbered within a series. [biber/biblatex difference: The type is provided as an alias of the new type report.] *Required*: author, title, institution, year. *Optional*: type, number, address, month, note.
unpublished	A document having an author and title, but not formally published. *Required*: author, title, note. *Optional*: month, year.

Table 15.1: BibTeX's entry types as defined in most styles

bookinbook	This type is similar to inbook but intended for works originally published as a stand-alone book. A typical example is a book reprinted in the collected works of an author.
collection	A single-volume collection with multiple, self-contained contributions by distinct authors that have their own title. *Required*: editor, title, year/date.
dataset	A data set or a similar collection of (mostly) raw data. *Required*: author/editor, title, year/date.
mvbook mvcollection mvproceedings mvreference	Multivolume variants of the entry types.
online	This entry type is intended for sources such as websites, which are intrinsically online resources. *Required*: doi/eprint/url, year/date/urldate.
patent	A patent or patent request. *Required*: author, title, number, year/date.
periodical	A complete issue of a periodical, such as a special issue of a journal. *Required*: editor, title, year/date.
reference	A single-volume work of reference such as an encyclopedia or a dictionary, handled quite similar to collection.
report	A technical report, research report, or white paper published by a university. *Required*: author, title, type, institution, year/date.
set	An "entry set". This is a group of entries that are cited as a single reference and listed as a single item in the bibliography.
software	Computer software. The standard styles treat this entry type as an alias for @misc.
suppbook suppcollection suppperiodical	Supplemental material like a preface.
thesis	A thesis written for an educational institution to satisfy the requirements for a degree. *Required*: author, title, type, institution, year/date.
xdata	This entry type is special. xdata entries hold data that may be inherited by other entries using the xdata field.

Table 15.2: Additional standard entry types provided by biblatex

Most BibTeX style files sort the bibliographical entries. This is done by internally generating a sort key from the author's/editor's name, the date of the publication, the title, and other information. Entries with identical sort keys appear in citation order.

Sorting of entries

The author information is usually the author field, but some styles use the editor or organization field. In addition to the fields listed in Table 15.1, each entry type has an optional key field, used in some styles for alphabetizing, for cross-referencing, or for forming a \bibitem label. You should therefore include a key

address	Usually the address of the `publisher` or other institution. For major publishing houses, just give the city. For small publishers, specifying the complete address might help the reader. [biber/biblatex difference: `location` should be used instead, but `address` is provided as an alias.]
annote	An annotation. Not used by the standard bibliography styles, but used by others that produce an annotated bibliography (e.g., `annote`). The field starts a new sentence, and hence the first word should be capitalized. [biber/biblatex difference: `annotation` should be used instead, but `annote` is provided as an alias.]
author	The name(s) of the author(s), in BibTeX name format (Section 15.3.3).
booktitle	Title of a book, part of which is being cited (Section 15.3.3). For book entries use the `title` field.
chapter	A chapter (or section or whatever) number.
crossref	The database key of the entry being cross-referenced (Section 15.3.7).
edition	The edition of a book (e.g., "Second"). This should be an ordinal and should have the first letter capitalized, as shown above; the standard styles convert to lowercase when necessary. [biber/biblatex difference: This must be a number, not an ordinal.]
editor	Name(s) of editor(s), in BibTeX name format. If there is also an `author` field, then the `editor` field gives the editor of the book or collection in which the reference appears.
howpublished	How something strange has been published.
institution	Institution sponsoring a technical report.
journal	Journal name. Abbreviations are provided for many journals (Section 15.3.4). [biber/biblatex difference: `journaltitle` should be used instead, but `journal` is provided as an alias.]
key	Used for alphabetizing and creating a label when the `author` and `editor` information is missing. This field should not be confused with the key that appears in the `\cite` command and at the beginning of the database entry. [biber/biblatex difference: `sortkey` should be used instead, but `key` is provided as an alias. biblatex offers additional fields like `sortname` and `sorttitle` for finer control.]

Table 15.3: BibTeX's standard entry fields (A–K)

field for any entry whose author information is missing. Depending on the style, the key field can also be used to overwrite the automatically generated internal key for sorting.[1] A situation where a key field is useful is the following:

```
organization = "The Association for Computing Machinery",
key = "ACM"
```

Without the key field, the `alpha` style would construct a label from the first three letters of the information in the `organization` field. Although the style file strips off the article "The", you would still get a rather uninformative label like "[Ass86]".

---

[1] Some BibTeX styles (e.g., `jurabib`) use the `sortkey` field instead.

month	The month in which the work was published or, for an unpublished work, in which it was written. For reasons of consistency the standard three-letter abbreviations (`jan`, `feb`, `mar`, etc.) should be used (Section 15.3.4). [biber/biblatex difference: This must be a number. It is also recommended to use the `date` field instead.]
note	Any additional information that can help the reader.
number	The number of a journal, magazine, technical report, or work in a series. An issue of a journal or magazine is usually identified by its volume and number; a technical report normally has a number; and sometimes books in a named series carry numbers.
organization	The organization that sponsors a conference or that publishes a `manual`.
pages	One or more page numbers or range of numbers (e.g., 42--111 or 7,41,73--97 or 43+, where the '+' indicates pages that do not form a simple range). [biber/biblatex difference: The 42+ syntax is not known.]
publisher	The publisher's name.
school	The name of the school where the thesis was written.
series	The name of a series or set of books. When citing an entire book, the `title` field gives its title, and an optional `series` field gives the name of a series or multivolume set in which the book is published.
title	The work's title, typed as explained in Section 15.3.3.
type	The type of a technical report (e.g., "Research Note"). This name is used instead of the default "Technical Report". For the entry type `phdthesis` you could use the term "Ph.D. dissertation" by specifying `type = "{Ph.D.} dissertation"`. Similarly, for the `inbook` and `incollection` entry types you can get "section 1.2" instead of the default "chapter 1.2" with `chapter = "1.2"` and `type = "Section"`.
volume	The volume of a journal or multivolume book.
year	The year of publication or, for an unpublished work, the year it was written. Generally, it should consist of four numerals, such as 1984, although the standard styles can handle any `year` whose last four nonpunctuation characters are numerals, such as "about 1984". [biber/biblatex difference: This must be a number; using the `date` field instead is recommended.]

Table 15.4: BibTeX's standard entry fields (L–Z)

Using the `key` field yields a more acceptable "[ACM86]".

> biber/biblatex
>
> The "main" sort key is called `sortkey`, and the alias key is available too. It is complemented by the fields `sortname`, `sortyear`, `sorttitle`, and `sortshorthand`, which give finer control over the sorting process.
>
> Different from BibTeX, `sortkey` and its alias key are never used as a fallback to create a label. Depending on the use case, one of the fields `shortauthor`, `shorteditor`, or `label` should be used for this purpose.

We now turn our attention to the fields recognized by the standard bibliography styles. These "standard" fields are shown in Tables 15.3/4 on pages 388–389. Other fields, like `abstract`, can be required if you use one of the extended nonstandard styles shown in Tables 15.7-10 on pages 420-424. Because unknown fields are ignored by the BɪʙTᴇX styles, you can use this feature to include "comments" inside an entry: it is enough to put the information to be ignored inside braces following a field name (and = sign) that is not recognized by the BɪʙTᴇX style.

As with the names of the entry types in Table 15.1 on page 386, the names of the fields should be interpreted in their widest sense to make them applicable in a maximum number of situations. And you should never forget that a judicious use of the `note` field can solve even the more complicated cases.

15.3.2 Additional fields

A number of fields are not supported by the standard BɪʙTᴇX styles but are of such general use that it is typically recommended to add them to the `.bib` file and if possible to use a BɪʙTᴇX style that knows these fields.

URL and other electronic identifiers

BɪʙTᴇX and its standard styles predates the Internet and so do not support fields for URL, DOI, eprint, and similar data. When using these styles, such data have to be entered in the `note` or `howpublished` field. While this was a workable solution fifteen years ago when one could still write that references to electronic resources have become "more and more common", it is in today's world often not compatible with modern journal styles that expect that dedicated fields are used. It is therefore normally preferable to use the `url`, `doi`, and `eprint` fields for such data. Variants of the standard styles supporting these fields are for example provided by the package urlbst from Norman Gray or by babelbib from Harald Harders. Styles with an `url` field can also be created with custom-bib.

If the URL should be used for a clickable link, it should be correctly percent encoded. References pointing to an online resource typically should also contain the date when this resource was accessed. The predominant field names for this are `urldate` and `lastchecked`.

biber/biblatex

biber and biblatex provide a full set of fields in this area: `doi`, `eid`, `eprint`, `eprintclass`, `eprinttype`, `isan`, `isbn`, `ismn`, `isrn`, `issn`, `iswc`, `url`, and `urldate`.

The `eprint`, `eprintclass`, and `eprinttype` fields, for example, can be used to replace longish URLs in a bibliography for a large number of known resources like arXiv, jstor, or pubmed:

```
eprint      = {cs/0011047v1},
eprintclass = {cs.DS},
eprinttype  = {arxiv}
```

This typesets "arXiv: cs/0011047v1 [cs.DS]", and — if hyperref is loaded — hyperlinks it to `https://arxiv.org/abs/cs/0011047v1`.

It is possible to store URLs with non–ASCII characters and spaces. biber converts such URLs into the percent-encoded representation needed for a

```
@misc{smith, author = {Smith, Joe}, year = {2020}}
@misc{kirk1, author = {Kirk, Joe},  year = {2020}}
@misc{kirk2, author = {Kirk, Betty},year = {2020}}
@misc{pyne1, author = {Pyne, Joe},  year = {2020}}
@misc{pyne2, author = {Pyne, Jill}, year = {2020}}
@misc{doe1,  author = {Doe, Joe},   year = {2020}}
@misc{doe2,  author = {Doe, Betty}, year = {2019}}
@misc{webb1, author = {Webb, Max},  year = {2020}}
@misc{webb2, author = {Webb, Max},  year = {2020}}

@misc{list0, author = {Smith, Joe and Webb, Maria},
        year   = {2020}}
@misc{list1, author = {Pyne, Henry and Doe, Maria},
    year   = {2020}}
@misc{list2, author = {Pyne, Joe and Kirk, Maria},
    year   = {2020}}
@misc{list3, author = {Pyne, Joe and Webb, Maria},
    year   = {2020}}
@misc{list4, author = {Pyne, Joe and Webb, Maria},
    year   = {2020}}
@misc{list5, author = {Kirk, Jill and Webb, Maria},
    year   = {2020}}

@article{article1, author = {Doe, Jill},
    journaltitle = {Journal A}, title = {An article},
    year         = {2015}}
@article{article2, author = {Pyne, Mike},
    journaltitle = {Journal B},
    keywords     = {important,research},
    title        = {An important article}, year = {2020}}
@article{article3, author = {Webb, Henry},
    journaltitle = {Journal C}, title = {An article},
    year         = {2010}}

@book{book1, author = {Pyne, Mike},
    title  = {A book}, year   = {2020}}
@book{book2, author = {Kirk, Maria},
    keywords = {important}, title = {An important book},
    year     = {2020}}

@book{smith2020-2, author = {Smith, Maria},
    title = {A book}, year = {2020}}
@book{smith2020-1, author = {Smith, Maria},
    title = {Another book}, year = {2020}}

@book{jane-1, author = {Doe, Jane}, gender = {sf},
    title = {A book}, year = {2020}}
@book{jane-2, author = {Doe, Jane}, gender = {sf},
    title = {An second book}, year = {2020}}

@book{max-1, author = {Pyne, Max}, gender = {sm},
    title = {A book}, year = {2020}}
@book{max-2, author = {Pyne, Max}, gender = {sm},
    title = {A second book}, year = {2020}}

@misc{prefix-biber,
    author = {family=Cruz,given=Maria,prefix=De La},
    title  = {Uppercase prefixes (extended biber syntax)},
    year   = {2020}}
@misc{apostroph-biber, author = {d' Ormesson, Jean},
    title  = {Apostroph (only biber)}, year = {2020}}
```

```
@misc{label-biber,
    author = {de la Cierva y Codorníu, Juan},
    label = {CC}, title = {Forcing a label (only biber)},
    year   = {2020}}
@misc{prefix-both, author = {{D}e {L}a Cruz, Maria},
    label = {Cru}, title  = {Uppercase prefixes},
    year   = {2010}}
@misc{apostroph-both,
    author = {d'\relax Ormesson, Jean},
    title  = {Apostroph}, year = {2010}}
@misc{label-bibtex,
    author = {de la {Cierva y} Codorníu, Juan},
    title  = {Forcing a label (only {\BibTeX})},
    year   = {2010}}

@online{url:a,
    author   = {White, Maria and Green, Julia},
    language = {french}, url = {https://some.url},
    urldate  = {2021-09-01}}
@online{url:b,
    author   = {White, Maria and Green, Julia},
    language = {english}, url = {https://some.url},
    urldate  = {2021-09-01}}
@online{url:c,
    author   = {Joe Smith and Henry Webb},
    language = {french and spanish}, langid ={french},
    url      = {https://some.url}, urldate = {2021-09-01}}
@online{url:d,
    author   = {Joe Smith and Henry Webb},
    language = {spanish with some translations},
    langid   = {spanish},
    url      = {https://some.url}, urldate = {2021-09-01}}
@online{url:e,
    author   = {Joe Smith and Henry Webb},
    language = {english}, langid = {english},
    url      = {https://some.url}, urldate = {2021-09-01}}


@unpublished{test97,
    author = {Goossens, Michel and User, Ben
                and Doe, Joe and others},
    note   = {Submitted to the IBM J.~Res.~Dev.},
    title  = {Ambiguous citations}, year   = {1997}}
@misc{oddity,
    howpublished = {Quarterly published.},
    title = {{{{TUGboat} The Communications
                of the {\TeX} User Group}},
    year  = {1980ff}}
@misc{pagination,
    pagination = {section},
    title      = {test pagination}}
@article{sourcemap-test,
    author-biblatex = {Smith,Betty},
    author          = {Doe,Charles},
    abstract        = {About % and # chars}}
@book{location-list,
    author   = {Webb, Maria},
    title    = {Sämtliche Werke},
    date     = 1988,
    location = {München and Berlin and New York}}
```

Figure 15.2: A second sample BibTeX database (`tlc-ex.bib`)

This database contains various short, fictitious entries to produce concise examples.

correct link. If the URL is already percent encoded, it is left unchanged, so normally there should be no conflict with input meant for BibTeX.

biber requires that the date in `urldate` is in ISO 8601-2 format. If this is not possible, the ISO-date can be put in another field, and when using biblatex, a source map can be used to map this field to `urldate`:

```
\DeclareSourcemap{
  \maps{\map[overwrite]{\step[fieldsource=urlisodate,
                               fieldtarget=urldate,final]}}}
```

More details about entering dates in such fields are given on page 400.

Language support　A second type of field is related to the language of an entry. The styles from the babelbib package, for example, offer here the field `language`. If set to a name known by babel, it adapts generated text of an entry to that language. The following example shows the output of two entries of `tlc-ex.bib` from Figure 15.2 that differ only in the `language` setting: the first uses `french` and the second `english`.

Références

[1] White, Maria et Julia Green. `https://some.url`, visité le 2021-09-01.

[2] White, Maria and Julia Green. `https://some.url`, visited on 2021-09-01.

```
\usepackage[english,french]{babel}
\usepackage{babelbib}
\usepackage{hyperref}

\bibliographystyle{babplain}
\nocite{url:a,url:b}
\bibliography{tlc-ex}
```

15-3-1

biber/biblatex

biblatex declares the fields `langid` and `language`:

`langid`　This field declares the language rules to use when typesetting the entry in the bibliography. Depending on the setting of the package option `autolang` (which takes the values `none`, `hyphen`, `other`, and `other*`), it does nothing, changes only the hyphenation, or switches to the language by using the corresponding babel environments. It has a comparable purpose to the `language` field of babelbib, and a source map should be used to map `language` to `langid` if needed.

`language`　This field takes a list of languages separated by the and delimiter describing the languages of the work. The languages can be given literally or as a "localization key" — strings that represent a term, which can be translated with the localization commands of biblatex.

Example 15-3-2 shows for three entries how biblatex handles the `language` and `langid` settings. It uses again entries that differ only in these fields:

```
language = {french and spanish},          langid ={french}  %url:c
```

```
language = {spanish with some translations},langid ={spanish} %url:d
language = {english},  langid ={english} %url:e
```

Note in the example how the value `other` for the `autolang` option triggered the translation of various words in the Spanish and French entries and that the French entry uses French typographical rules like the space before the colon. The text "spanish with some translations" in the second entry is not translated and not capitalized as it is not a known localization key. Note also that the English entry does not show the language because it is identical to the main language of the document.

References

[1] Joe SMITH et Henry WEBB. Français et espagnol. URL : https: //some.url (visité le 01/09/2021).

[2] Joe Smith y Henry Webb. spanish with some translations. URL: https://some.url (visitado 01-09-2021).

[3] Joe Smith and Henry Webb. URL: https://some.url (visited on 09/01/2021).

```
\usepackage[french,spanish,
            english]{babel}
\usepackage[autolang=other]
           {biblatex}
\addbibresource{tlc-ex.bib}
\usepackage{hyperref}
\nocite{url:c,url:d,url:e}
\printbibliography
```

15-3-2

15.3.3 The text part of a field explained

The text part of a field in a BibTeX entry is enclosed in a pair of double quotes or braces. Part of the text itself is said to be *enclosed in braces* if it lies inside a matching pair of braces other than the ones enclosing the entire entry.

The field types have quite varied requirements regarding the parsing of the text, but for BibTeX no formal description of the data types exists. Most rules are given only implicitly through the existing BibTeX styles and the functions they implement.

---

biber/biblatex

With biber this is different: all fields have a declared and documented data type. There are three main data types:

Name lists are split up into individual items at the "and" delimiter. Each item in the list is then dissected into the name part components. Examples of name list fields are the author or the editor field. Most rules for the formatting and the parsing of names have been inherited from BibTeX. More details are given below.

Literal lists are also split up at the "and" delimiter but unlike names not dissected further. Examples are the `location`, the `publisher`, and the `language` field. The splitting of these texts into list elements allows localization of parts as has been shown above for languages, but it allows also localization and formatting of conjunctions: `New York and London` can be converted to "New York & London" or "New York et London" or ...

Fields are usually printed as a whole. There are several subtypes like integers, dates, or URLs.

The structure of a name

The `author` and `editor` fields contain a list of names. The exact format in which these names are typeset is decided by the bibliography style. The entry in the database tells BibTeX what the name is. You should always type names exactly as they appear in the cited work, even when they have slightly different forms in two works. For example:

```
author = "Donald E. Knuth"          author = "D. E. Knuth"
```

If you are sure that both authors are the same person, then you could list both in the form that the author prefers (say, Donald E. Knuth), but you should always indicate (e.g., in our second case) that the original publication had a different form.

```
author = "D[onald] E. Knuth"
```

BibTeX alphabetizes this as if the brackets were not there so that no ambiguity arises as to the identity of the author.

---

biber/biblatex

biber does not automatically ignore brackets, but it can be instructed to do so (and other character in names) either in a configuration file in XML notation

```
<nonamestring>
  <option name="author" value="[[]]"/>
</nonamestring>
```

or in the document with the `\DeclareNonamestring` command:

```
\DeclareNonamestring{%
  % strip square brackets
  \nonamestring{author}{\regexp{[\[\]]}}}
```

The interface supports Perl regular expressions[1] in various places; for details see the biber documentation.

Most names can be entered in the following two equivalent forms:

```
"John Chris Smith"           "Smith, John Chris"
"Thomas von Neumann"         "von Neumann, Thomas"
```

The second form, with a comma, should always be used for people who have multiple last names that are capitalized. For example,

```
"Parra Benavides, Miguel"
```

If you enter `"Miguel Parra Benavides"`, BibTeX interprets `Parra` as the middle name, which is wrong in this case. When the other parts are not capitalized, no such problem occurs (e.g., `"Johann von Bergen"` or `"Pierre de la Porte"`).

---

[1] See, for example, `https://perldoc.perl.org/perlre`.

If several words of a name have to be grouped, they should be enclosed in braces. BibTeX treats everything inside braces as a single name, as shown below:

```
"{Boss and Friends, Inc.} and {Snoozy and Boys, Ltd.}"
```

In this case, `Inc.` and `Ltd.` are not mistakenly considered as first names.

In general, BibTeX names can have four distinct parts, denoted as *First*, *von*, *Last*, and *Jr*. Each part consists of a list of name tokens, and any list but *Last* can be empty. Thus, the two entries below are different:

```
"von der Schmidt, Alex"        "{von der Schmidt}, Alex"
```

The first has *von*, *Last*, and *First* parts, while the second has only *First* and *Last* parts (`von der Schmidt`), resulting possibly in a different sorting order.

A "Junior" part can pose a special problem. Most people with "Jr." in their name precede it with a comma, thus entering it as follows:

```
"Smith, Jr., Robert"
```

Certain people do not use the comma, and these cases are handled by considering the "Jr." as part of the last name:

```
"{Lincoln Jr.}, John P."        "John P. {Lincoln Jr.}"
```

Recall that in the case of "Miguel Parra Benavides", you should specify

```
"Parra Benavides, Miguel"
```

The *First* part of his name has the single token "Miguel"; the *Last* part has two tokens, "Parra" and "Benavides"; and the *von* and *Jr* parts are empty.

A complex example is

```
"Johannes Martinus Albertus van de Groene Heide"
```

This name has three tokens in the *First* part, two in the *von* part, and two in the *Last* part. BibTeX knows where one part ends and the other begins because the tokens in the *von* part begin with lowercase letters (`van de` in this example).

In general, *von* tokens have the first letter at brace-level 0 in lowercase. Technically speaking, everything in a "special character" is at brace-level 0 (see page 398), so you can decide how BibTeX treats a token by inserting a dummy special character whose first letter past the TeX control sequence is in the desired case, upper or lower. For example, in

```
Maria {\MakeUppercase{d}e La} Cruz
```

BibTeX takes the uppercase "De La" as the *von* part, because the first character following the control sequence is lowercase. With the `abbrv` style you get the correct abbreviation M. De La Cruz, instead of the incorrect M. D. L. Cruz if you did not use this trick.

B<small>IB</small>T<small>E</small>X handles hyphenated names correctly. For example, an entry like

```
author = "Maria-Victoria Delgrande",
```

with the abbrv style results in "M.-V. Delgrande".

When multiple authors are present, their names should be separated with the word "and", where the "and" must not be enclosed in braces.

```
author = "Frank Mittelbach and Rowley, Chris"
editor = "{Lion and Noble, Ltd.}"
```

There are two authors, Frank Mittelbach and Chris Rowley, but only one editor, because the "and" is enclosed in braces. If the number of authors or editors is too large to be typed *in extenso*, then the list of names can be ended with the string "and␣others", which is converted by the standard styles into the familiar *"et al."*

To summarize, you can specify names in B<small>IB</small>T<small>E</small>X using three possible forms (the double quotes and braces can be used in all cases):

```
"First von Last"            e.g., {Johan van der Winden}
"von Last, First"           e.g., "von der Schmidt, Alexander"
"von Last, Jr, First"       e.g., {de la Porte, Fils, {\'Emile}}
```

The first form can almost always be used. It is, however, not suitable when there is a *Jr* part or when the *Last* part has multiple tokens and there is no *von* part.

---

biber/biblatex

The name parts *First*, *von*, *Last*, and *Jr* are called *given*, *prefix*, *family*, and *suffix* both in templates and command names. Initials are indicated by attaching an i, e.g., *given-i* or \namepartgiveni.

biber can process names given in key/value syntax. In this syntax the name Maria De La Cruz can be entered without the \MakeUpperCase trick:

```
author={family=Cruz,given=Maria,prefix=De La}
```

It is possible to declare keys for additional name parts and special name templates and to print names using other rules than Western names. The file 93-nameparts.tex in the example suite of biblatex contains the details; here we show only two name types that can be used with this system once it has been properly set up. The cjk template ensures that the name of the first author is typeset as Li Wei or Li, while the ethiopian template prints the second author as Kebede Daniel or — if needed to make the name unique — as Kebede Daniel Demeke.

```
author = {family=Li, given=Wei, nametemplates=cjk},
author = {given=Kebede, patronymic=Daniel, papponymic=Demeke,
          nametemplates=ethiopian},
```

Names not using the extended syntax are parsed by biber quite similarly to BibTeX. However, some tricks described in *Tame the BeaST* [68] to get longer initials, to improve labels in alphabetic styles, and to handle special prefixes and name parts can be problematic. As an example, to get a initial consisting of two letters you can with BibTeX use

```
author={Loe,{\relax Ch}arles}
```

This does not work with biber — the extended syntax is required instead:

```
author={family=Loe,given=Charles,given-i={Ch}}
```

Other tricks do not harm but are unnecessary. As a rule of thumb, names with unusual initials or prefixes are input at best with the extended name syntax. Special labels for alphabetic styles can be set with the `label` field.

The next two examples use again some bibliography entries from the sample database in Figure 15.2 on page 391 to demonstrate different input options. The first shows the result when using the BibTeX workflow. As you can see, BibTeX is unable to handle any of the biber-specific input conventions correctly and produces strange labels (third list entry) or badly formatted output (entries five and six):

```
\nocite{prefix-both,
    label-bibtex,apostroph-both}
```

References

[DLC10] Maria De La Cruz. Uppercase prefixes, 2010.
[dlCC10] Juan de la Cierva y Codorníu. Forcing a label (only BibTeX), 2010.
[dlCyC20] Juan de la Cierva y Codorníu. Forcing a label (only biber), 2020.
[dO10] Jean d'Ormesson. Apostroph, 2010.
[dO20] Jean d' Ormesson. Apostroph (only biber), 2010.
[fam20] prefix=De La family=Cruz, given=Maria. Uppercase prefixes (extended biber syntax), 2020.

```
% bad output (entries 3,5 & 6)
\nocite{prefix-biber,
    label-biber,apostroph-biber}
\bibliographystyle{alpha}
\footnotesize
\bibliography{tlc-ex}
```

15-3-3

In contrast biber and biblatex do a good job on all syntax variants as shown in the second example. Note that the BibTeX style `alpha` creates labels that use the *von* part, while biblatex ignores it by default, resulting in more readable labels:

```
\usepackage[style=alphabetic]
    {biblatex}
\addbibresource{tlc-ex.bib}
\nocite{prefix-both,
    label-bibtex,apostroph-both}
\nocite{prefix-biber,
    label-biber,apostroph-biber}
\AtNextBibliography
        {\footnotesize}
\printbibliography
```

References

[CC20] Juan de la Cierva y Codorníu. *Forcing a label (only biber)*. 2020.
[Cie10] Juan de la Cierva y Codorníu. *Forcing a label (only BibTeX)*. 2010.
[Cru10] Maria De La Cruz. *Uppercase prefixes*. 2010.
[Cru20] Maria De La Cruz. *Uppercase prefixes (extended biber syntax)*. 2020.
[Orm10] Jean d'Ormesson. *Apostroph*. 2010.
[Orm20] Jean d'Ormesson. *Apostroph (only biber)*. 2010.

15-3-4

The format of the title

The bibliography style decides whether a title is capitalized. Usually, titles of books are capitalized, but those for articles are not. A title should always be typed as it appears in the original work. For example:

```
TITLE = "A Manual of Style"
TITLE = "Hyphenation patterns for ancient Greek and Latin"
```

Different languages and styles have their own capitalization rules. If you want to override the decisions of the bibliography style, then you should enclose the parts that should remain unchanged inside braces. Note that this is not sufficient when the first character after the left brace is a backslash (see below). It is usually best to enclose whole words in braces, because otherwise LaTeX may lose kerning or ligatures when typesetting the word. In the following example, the first version is preferable over the second:

```
TITLE = "The Towns and Villages of {Belgium}"
TITLE = "The Towns and Villages of {B}elgium"
```

biber/biblatex

Capitalization or "sentence casing" is not done by the biber preprocessor, but during the LaTeX compilation, and will be discussed in more detail when we describe the biblatex package in Chapter 16.

As with BibTeX, words can be excluded from sentence casing by enclosing them in braces. Arguments of commands are protected too. To *undo* this protection to enable sentence casing in arguments or parts thereof, you have to use another pair of braces, e.g.,

```
title={a Story of \emph{Green} and {\emph{Blue}} {Ducks}}
```

Here "Green" and "Ducks" are protected from sentence casing, while the protection for "Blue" has been undone. The output if sentence casing is applied will be "A story of *Green* and *blue* Ducks".

Accented and special characters

BibTeX accepts accented characters. If you have an entry with two fields

```
author = "Kurt G{\"o}del", year = 1931,
```

then the `alpha` bibliography style yields the label [Göd31], which is probably what you want. As shown in the example above, the entire accented character must be placed in braces; in this case either `{\"o}` or `{\"{o}}` will work. These braces must not themselves be enclosed in braces (other than the ones that might delimit the entire field or the entire entry); also, a backslash must be the very first character inside the braces. Thus, neither `{G{\"{o}}del}` nor `{G\"{o}del}` works here.

This feature handles accented characters and foreign symbols used with LaTeX. It also allows user-defined "accents". For the purposes of counting letters in labels, BibTeX considers everything inside the braces to be a single letter. To BibTeX, an accented character is a special case of a "special character", which consists of everything from a left brace at the topmost level, immediately followed by a backslash, up through the matching right brace. For example, the field

```
author = "\OE{le} {\'{E}mile} {Ren\'{e}} van R{\i\j}den"
```

has two special characters: "{\'{E}mile}" and "{\i\j}".

In general, BibTeX does not process TeX or LaTeX control sequences inside a special character, but it processes other characters. Thus, a style that converts all titles to lowercase transforms

```
"The {\TeX BOOK\NOOP} Saga" into "The {\TeX book\NOOP} saga"
```

The article "The" remains capitalized because it is the first word in the title.

The special character scheme has its uses for handling accented characters, although the introduction of additional braces may upset the generation of ligatures and kerns, and — as has been mentioned at the begin of Section 15.2 — the capabilities of BibTeX to sort names with such accents are quite restricted. It may help to make BibTeX's alphabetizing do what you want, but again with some caveats; see the discussion of the \SortNoop command on page 405. Also, because BibTeX counts an entire special character as just one letter, you can force extra characters inside labels.

---

biber/biblatex

biber can handle UTF-8 and 8-bit encoded .bib files. Accented chars can be input directly, but it is also possible to use accent commands. Unlike BibTeX, biber does not ignore these commands when sorting; instead, it tries to convert them into their respective Unicode code points. For most standard accent commands this works fine, but a small number of odd inputs can give errors. Well known is the problem with {\'\i} (í) that is converted by biber into a dotless ı (U+0131) followed by the combining accent U+0301. pdflatex cannot handle this combination and errors. The best advice here is to replace such commands with the correct UTF-8 input í or to use {\'{i}}.

The biber program can also convert a .bib file with accented characters back to a pure ASCII:

```
biber --tool --output-safechars ⟨file⟩.bib
```

This creates *file*_bibertool.bib in which a line such as

```
author={Œle Émile René van Rıjden},
```

is replaced by

```
AUTHOR = {van R\i{}\j{}den, \OE{}le \'{E}mile Ren\'{e}},
```

The encoding of the input file can be set with the option --input-encoding. As the default, UTF-8 is assumed.

Description	Date input	Exemplary output
year	1850	1850
before Christ/common era	−0876	877 BC / 877 BCE
start year	1997/	1997–
stop year	/1997	–1997
year range	1988/1992	1988–1992
decade	201X	2010/2019
century	19XX	1900/1999
circa year	1723~	circa 1723
uncertain year	1723?	1723?
circa and uncertain year	1723%	circa 1723?
year and month	1967-02	02/1967
range with month	2002-01/2002-02	01/2002–02/2002
full year range	1999-XX	1999-01/1999-12
year with season[a]	2004-22	2004 (summer)
exact date	2009-01-31	31/01/2009
exact date range	1995-03-30/1995-04-05	30/03/1995–05/04/1995
full month range	1999-01-XX	1999-01-01/1999-01-31
full year range	2020-XX-XX	2020-01-01/2020-12-31
date with time	2004-04-05T14:34:00	05/04/2004 2:34 PM

[a] *The extended date format follows ISO 8601-2. Seasons have the "month" numbers 21–24 in this norm.*

Table 15.5: Examples of biblatex date inputs

Dates

All BibTeX styles support the `year` and `month` fields. Normally they should contain integers, but text like `year={n.D.}` is possible too. Months can also be given as three-letter abbreviations *without* quotes or braces as in `month=jan`; see Section 15.3.4. Newer BibTeX styles often also know the `urldate` field. Dates are normally not localized. You need to find a suitable style if, e.g., the month name should be output in another language.

biber/biblatex

The fields `year` and `month` can be used but should contain only integers. For compatibility with standard BibTeX, the three-letter strings for months are supported, but content like `year={n.D.}` or `month={January}` should be avoided; you do not get errors, but biber warns you that the sorting can be wrong.

    biblatex provides four dedicated date fields: `date` for the publication date (it should be preferred over `year` and `month`), `urldate` for the access date of an URL, `eventdate` for the date of a conference or some other event in a proceedings entry, and `origdate` for the publication date of the original edition of a reprinted work. All dates are fully localized and can be output in various formats. The fields can be used for sorting and comparison, and it is possible to access parts of a date like the month or the year. The date fields support ranges, time, BC dates, seasons, circa, and uncertain dates. To enable these features a date must be input in ISO 8601-2 format.

Table 15.5 shows some example input and possible formatting of the dates. These extended dates are not supported by BibTeX, so using them makes the `.bib` file incompatible with the BibTeX workflow, but to stay compatible with both workflows one can provide all three fields of the publication entry:

```
year  = 2020,
month = apr,
date  = {2020-04-01}
```

biber and biblatex then overwrite (with a warning) the `year` and `month` fields with values taken from the `date` field, while with BibTeX date is ignored.

15.3.4 Abbreviations in BibTeX

You can declare shorthands for BibTeX text field input for repeated use. Such an abbreviation is labeled with a string of ASCII characters starting with a letter and not containing a space or any of the following ten characters:

```
"  #  %  '  (  )  ,  =  {  }
```

Define your own abbreviations with the `@string` command in a `.bib` file, as shown below:

```
@string{AW        = "Addison--Wesley Publishing Company"}
@STRING{cacm      = "Communications of the ACM"}
@String{pub-AW    = {{Ad\-di\-son-Wes\-ley}}}
@String{pub-AW:adr = "Reading, MA, USA"}
@String{TUG       = "\TeX{} Users Group"}
@String{TUG:adr   = {Providence, RI, USA}}
```

Abbreviations can be used in the text part of BibTeX fields, but they should not be enclosed in braces or quotation marks. With the above string definitions, the following two ways of specifying the `journal` field are equivalent:

```
journal = "Communications of the ACM"
journal = cacm
```

The case of the name for an abbreviation is not important, so CACM and `cacm` are considered identical, but BibTeX produces a warning if you mix different cases. Also, the `@string` command itself can be spelled as all lowercase, all uppercase, or a mixture of the two cases.

@string commands can appear anywhere in the .bib file, but an abbreviation must be defined before it is used. It is good practice to group all @string commands at the beginning of a .bib file or to place them in a dedicated .bib file containing only a list of abbreviations. The @string commands defined in the .bib file take precedence over any definition made in the style file. If an abbreviation is defined more than once, the most recent definition before the entry is used.

You can concatenate several strings (or @string definitions) using the concatenation operator, #. Given the definition

```
@STRING{TUB = {TUGboat }}
```

you can easily construct nearly identical journal fields for different entries:

```
@article{tub-98,   journal = TUB # 1998,   ...
@article{tub-99,   journal = TUB # 1999,   ...
@article{tub-00,   journal = TUB # 2000,   ...
```

Most bibliography styles contain a series of predefined abbreviations. As a convention, there should always be three-letter abbreviations for the months: jan, feb, mar, and so forth. In your BibTeX database files you should always use these three-letter abbreviations for the months, rather than spelling them explicitly. This assures consistency inside your bibliography.

Information about the day of the month is usually best included in the month field if you are using BibTeX. You might, for example, make use of the possibility of concatenation:

```
month = apr # "~1",
```

> biber/biblatex
>
> However, note that the month field should contain only the month if you are planning to use the database with biber and biblatex. A day should be included through the date field in that case.

Names of popular journals in a given application field are also made available as abbreviations in most styles. To identify them you should consult the documentation associated with the bibliographic style in question. The set of journals listed in Table 15.6 on the next page should be available in all BibTeX styles.

> biber/biblatex
>
> The journal abbreviations are not predefined in biblatex styles. Suitable @string or xdata entries must therefore be added explicitly.

You can easily define your own set of journal abbreviations by putting them in @string commands in their own database file and listing this database file as an argument to LaTeX's \bibliography command or to biblatex's \addbibresource.

acmcs	ACM Computing Surveys	jcss	Journal of Computer and System Sciences
acta	Acta Informatica	scp	Science of Computer Programming
cacm	Communications of the ACM	sicomp	SIAM Journal on Computing
ibmjrd	IBM Journal of Research and Development	tocs	ACM Transactions on Computer Systems
ibmsj	IBM Systems Journal	tods	ACM Transactions on Database Systems
ieeese	IEEE Transactions on Software Engineering	tog	ACM Transactions on Graphics
ieeetc	IEEE Transactions on Computers	toms	ACM Transactions on Mathematical Software
ieeetcad	IEEE Transactions on Computer-Aided Design of Integrated Circuits	toois	ACM Transactions on Office Information Systems
ipl	Information Processing Letters	toplas	ACM Transactions on Programming Languages and Systems
jacm	Journal of the ACM	tcs	Theoretical Computer Science

Table 15.6: Predefined journal strings in BibTeX styles

15.3.5 Extended data references with biber: the xdata entry type

biber/biblatex

biber supports the @string command but offers also a more general solution to reuse data: the xdata entry type serves as a data container holding one or more fields. Data in xdata entries may be referenced and used by other entries. An xdata entry looks like other entries in the .bib file and can contain all known fields. The key of the xdata can be freely chosen but should not contain an equal symbol or a hyphen.

```
@xdata{hup,
publisher = {Harvard University Press},
location = {Cambridge, Mass.}}

@xdata{macmillan:name,
publisher = {Macmillan}}

@xdata{macmillan:place,
location = {New York and London}}

@xdata{somenames,
author = {Maria Fisher and Julia Green},
editor = {John Smith and Brian Brown}}
```

An xdata container can also reference other xdata entries through the xdata

403

field, which accepts a comma-separated list of `xdata` keys:

```
@xdata{macmillan,
    xdata = {macmillan:name,macmillan:place}}
```

The data can then be used as a whole with the `xdata` field:

```
@book{somebook:a,
  author = {Jane Doe},
  xdata  = {macmillan}}
```

This adds the publisher "Macmillan" and the location "New York and London" to the entry. As you can see, it is important to use a good naming structure for your `xdata` key names, because otherwise your database will be difficult to manage.

It is also possible to reference only individual fields and even parts of fields from an `xdata` entry.

```
@book{somebook:b,
  author    = {xdata=somenames-editor-1 and Maria Webb},
  editor    = {xdata=somenames-author-2},
  publisher = {xdata=hup-publisher},
  location  = {xdata=macmillan:place-location}}
```

This gives an entry that is equivalent to the following:

```
@book{somebook:b,
  author    = {Smith, John and Webb, Maria},
  editor    = {Green, Julia},
  publisher = {Harvard University Press},
  location  = {New York and London}}
```

There are a few important points to note here:

- The syntax of a reference to a part of an `xdata` field has the special form `xdata=`*key*−*field*−*index*, e.g., `xdata=somenames-editor-1`. The equal sign should not lead you to mistake this as a key/value input or a field setting: the reference is a special value, and there should be no spaces around the equal sign. The *index* is optional and allows you to select only one element from a list. If no index is given, the full list is returned.

- A field can pull only data from an `xdata` field of the same type. A field with names like `author` can retrieve data from another name field, e.g., the `editor` field, but not from a literal list like `location` or a simple field like `title`; see Section 15.3.3 for a description of the data types. biber issues a warning if the type of the reference is wrong.

BibTeX does not know the xdata entry type. If a .bib file using xdata should be used with BibTeX, all such references must be resolved. This can be done with biber in tool mode and the option --output-resolve, i.e.,

```
biber --tool --output-resolve ⟨file⟩.bib
```

which creates the file *file*_bibertool.bib and converts entries with xdata fields or values, such as

```
@book{somebook:a,
author = {Jane Doe and xdata=smithbrown-author-2},
xdata  = {macmillan}
}
```

to the form

```
@BOOK{somebook:a,
  AUTHOR = {Doe, Jane and Brown, Brian},
  LOCATION = {New York and London},
  PUBLISHER = {Macmillan},
}
```

15.3.6 The BibTeX database preamble command

Both BibTeX and biber offer a @preamble command with a syntax similar to that of the @string command except that there is no name or equals sign, just the string. For example:

```
@preamble{ "\providecommand\url[1]{\texttt{#1}}" #
           "\providecommand\SortNoop[1]{}"      }
@preamble{ "\providecommand\enquote[1]{``#1''}"}
```

You can see that the different command definitions inside the @preamble can be given as separate strings that are then concatenated using the # symbol. It is also possible to use @preamble more than once. Both are useful for readability if you have many definitions. The standard styles output the argument of the @preamble literally to the .bbl file so that the command definitions are available when LaTeX reads the file. If you add LaTeX commands in this way, you must ensure that they are added using \providecommand and not \newcommand. There are two reasons for this requirement. First, you should not deprive yourself of the ability to change the definition in the document (e.g., the bibliography might add a simple definition for the command \url that you may want to replace by the definition from the url package). Second, sometimes the bibliography is read in several times (e.g., with the chapterbib package), an operation that would fail if \newcommand were used.

The other example command used above (\SortNoop) was suggested by Oren Patashnik to guide BibTeX's sorting algorithm in difficult cases. This algorithm normally does an acceptable job, but sometimes you might want to override BibTeX's decision by specifying your own sorting key. This trick can be used with foreign languages, which have sorting rules different from those of English, or when you want to order the various volumes of a book in a way given by their original date of publication and independently of their re-edition dates.

Suppose that the first volume of a book was originally published in 1986, with a second edition appearing in 1991, and the second volume was published in 1990. Then you could write

```
@book{ ...  volume=1,  year = "{\SortNoop{86}}1991"  ...
@book{ ...  volume=2,  year = "{\SortNoop{90}}1990"  ...
```

According to the definition of \SortNoop, LaTeX throws away its argument and ends up printing only the true year for these fields. For BibTeX \SortNoop appears to be an "accent"; thus, it sorts the works according to the numbers 861991 and 901990, placing volume 1 before volume 2, just as you want.

Be aware that the above trick may not function with newer BibTeX styles (for example, those generated with custom-bib) and that some styles have added a `sortkey` field that solves such problems in a far cleaner fashion.

> biber/biblatex
>
> Tricks like the \SortNoop command are normally not needed because there are enough sort keys to handle a variety of use cases.

15.3.7 Cross-referencing entries

BibTeX entries can be cross-referenced. Suppose you specify \cite{Wood:color} in your document, and you have the following two entries in the database file:

```
@Inbook{Wood:color, author = {Pat Wood}, crossref={Roth:postscript},
      title = {PostScript Color Separation}, pages={201--225}}
@Book{Roth:postscript, editor = {Stephen E. Roth}, title =
      {{Real World PostScript}}, booktitle = {{Real World PostScript}},
      publisher=AW, address=AW:adr, year=1988, ISBN={0-201-06663-7}}
```

The special `crossref` field tells BibTeX that the Wood:color entry should inherit missing fields from the entry it cross-references — Roth:postscript. BibTeX automatically puts the Roth:postscript entry into the reference list if it is cross-referenced by a certain number of entries (default 2) on a \cite or \nocite command, even if the Roth:postscript entry itself is never the argument of a \cite or \nocite command. Thus, with the default settings, Roth:postscript automatically appears on the reference list if one other entry besides Wood:color cross-references it.

The default is compiled into the BibTeX program, but it can be changed on the command line[1] by specifying `--min-crossrefs` together with the desired value. For instance, the article by Mittelbach & Rowley [80] is part of a published proceedings book, and because it is the only article referenced from this book, all information — such as the editor and the book title — is included as part of it. If we had used

```
bibtex --min-crossrefs=1 tlc3
```

we would have gotten two entries, with [80] becoming much shorter and referencing a separate proceedings entry instead. An example of such cross-referencing in the bibliography of this book is [43], which is cross-referenced by eight articles, from [44] to [52]. Using such cross-references in case there are several entries saves space, and is especially useful if all entries are close together, which is true here, because all of them are publications by Donald Knuth.

On the other hand, if you want to avoid separate entries for whole books or proceedings, regardless of the number of entries referencing them (because they involve different authors and are therefore on different pages in the bibliography), set the `--min-crossrefs` option to a suitably large value (e.g., 500), and then each entry contains all the relevant data.

biber/biblatex

> The threshold can be set with the biblatex package option `mincrossrefs` or with the biber option `--mincrossrefs`.

A cross-referenced entry must occur later in the database files than every entry that cross-references it. Thus, all cross-referenced entries could be put at the end of the database. Cross-referenced entries cannot themselves cross-reference another entry.

biber/biblatex

> These restrictions do not exist when using biber.

You can also use LaTeX's `\cite` command inside the fields of your BibTeX entries. This can be useful if you want to reference some other relevant material inside a note field:

```
note = "See Eijkhout \cite{Eijkhout:1991} for more details"
```

However, such usage may mean that you need additional LaTeX and BibTeX runs to compile your document properly. This happens if the citation put into the `.bbl` file by BibTeX refers to a key that was not used in a citation in the main document. Thus, LaTeX will be unable to resolve this reference in the following run and needs an additional BibTeX and two additional LaTeX runs thereafter.

---

[1] In BibTeX8 this option is named `--min_crossrefs` or `-M`.

15.3.8 Managing the BibTeX and biber differences

In the previous sections a number of differences between `.bib` files for BibTeX and biblatex/biber have been discussed. While it is a rather long list, the effort is usually manageable — in many cases the needed changes are limited to correcting a number of date fields and moving some URLs.

It is, however, a fact that the formats of the entries can be incompatible, not only because biber has different parsing rules but also because many biblatex/biber features and specialities have no counterpart in BibTeX styles.

If one wishes to stay compatible with the BibTeX workflow, there are a number of options: a clean and simple way is to use two `.bib` files, one "BibTeX only", one *Two separate .bib* "biblatex only" for the diverging entries. The advantages are that the files can have *files* a clear format and that all biblatex options and commands can be used without problems. The disadvantage is that it requires more maintenance effort.

If using two `.bib` files is not possible or wanted, follow these guidelines:

- Avoid using, in fields also processed by BibTeX, features that it does not understand, such as the extended name syntax or UTF-8 input.

- Use `@preamble` to provide fallback definitions for biblatex commands, e.g.,

  ```
  @preamble{"\providecommand\nbhyphen{-}"}
  ```

- If it is unavoidable to have fields with different content, you can make use of the ability of biber to change and replace fields on the fly by declaring a "source map". Such a source map is a set of instructions for biber to change some fields. A source map can be given in a document but also in a configuration file.

Example 15-3-5 below shows a simple source map that tells biber to replace the `author` field with the `author-biblatex` field if it exists. Entries without this special field stay unchanged. The sample source map also removes the `abstract` field and so avoids errors due to special characters. The entry used for the example from Figure 15.2 on page 391 contains two different author names and a problematic abstract field that contains a hash, `#`, and a percent, `%`. With biblatex and its source map this gives the following output:

```
\usepackage[style=authoryear, uniquename=allfull]{biblatex}
\addbibresource{tlc-ex.bib}
\DeclareSourcemap{
 \maps{
  \map[overwrite]{
   \step[fieldsource=author-biblatex,fieldtarget=author]
   \step[fieldset=abstract,null]%suppress abstract
     }}}
```

The author is Betty Smith   `The author is \citename{sourcemap-test}[given-family]{author}`   15-3-5

If the same `.bib` file is used with BibTeX, it would use "Charles Doe" as the author name.

15.4 Using BibTeX or biber to produce the bibliography

In this section we outline how to create an input, usable by LaTeX, from .bib databases, discussed in the previous section. A document typically contains only a subset of the entries stored in such databases, and the bibliography should conform to a certain style with respect to the formatting and the sorting of the entries. Thus, the programs BibTeX and biber have to gather the entries from the keys specified in the document and use the style and sorting options and the database resources as directed by the document.

To enable BibTeX to access these data, the necessary information is written in a previous LaTeX run to the .aux file. BibTeX then reads the .aux file (or files if \include is involved) and searches through the specified bibliographic database(s) for the keys,[1] extracts all required entries, and formats them. Formatting these entries is controlled by an associated bibliography style (the .bst file) that contains a set of instructions written in a stack-based language. The latter is interpreted by the BibTeX program.

biber does not use the .aux file to communicate with LaTeX; instead, it reads a dedicated control file with the extension .bcf. This is an XML file that is generated by the package biblatex. This control file contains all the formatting instructions needed by biber, so no .bst file is used either.

BibTeX and biber know which fields are required, optional, and ignored for any given entry type (see Table 15.1 on page 386). They issue warnings on the terminal and in the .blg file, such as "author name required", if something is missing. Their style files can control the typesetting of both the citation string in the main text and the actual bibliography entry.

The procedure for running LaTeX and BibTeX or biber is shown schematically in Figure 15.3 on the next page. With BibTeX at least three LaTeX runs are necessary — first to produce data for BibTeX, then to load the result from the BibTeX run, and finally to resolve the cross-references to the bibliographical list added by the previous run. With biber and biblatex two LaTeX runs are often enough.

As can be seen in the figure, both programs create as main output a file with the extension .bbl that is then read in by LaTeX. Depending on the style, this file can have varying content.

With the standard styles and various other styles, BibTeX writes into the .bbl file a standard thebibliography environment as described in Section 15.1. It is possible to include the content of such a .bbl file in your document, if your LaTeX document has to be self-contained. It is also a simple matter to manually edit this output from BibTeX to cope with special cases.

Standard LaTeX bibliography environment

With other styles, BibTeX writes a thebibliography environment that contains special commands that require the loading of a supporting package to process and typeset the bibliography. The styles from the jurabib package are a prominent example (but not the only one) that create highly structured .bbl files with a large number of jurabib commands that allow adjusting the formatting of the bibliography and the citations with package options. Other examples are shown in Chapter 16, when we discuss packages supporting special citation conventions.

Bibliography environments with special commands

---

[1] If the keys are not unique across the databases, the first match wins with a warning.

① Run LaTeX, which generates from the \cite commands a number of \citation references in its auxiliary file, .aux, or—when using biblatex—instructions for biber in the biber control file, .bcf.

② Run BibTeX or biber, which reads the auxiliary file or the control file, looks up the references in a database (one or more .bib files), and then writes a file (the .bbl file) containing either the formatted references according to the format specified in the style file (the .bst file) or the commands needed by biblatex to format the bibliography. Warning and error messages are written to the log file (the .blg file). Note that neither BibTeX nor biber ever reads the original LaTeX source file.

③ Run LaTeX again, which now reads the .bbl file containing the bibliographic information.

④ Run LaTeX a third time, resolving all references—may not be necessary with biblatex.

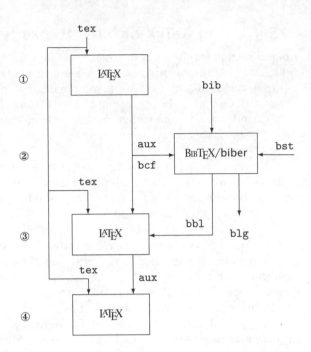

Figure 15.3: Data flow when running BibTeX or biber and LaTeX

.bbl files with only bibliography data

If you use biblatex, then the .bbl file no longer contains a thebibliography environment or any typesetting instructions at all, but only a structured, preprocessed, and sorted representation of the bibliography data. These .bbl files are no longer loaded at the place where the bibliography is printed, but at the start of the document, which explains why often only two LaTeX runs are needed to resolve all citations. The task to format and typeset the data is delegated fully to LaTeX and the biblatex package.

We now show in more detail the commands needed in the LaTeX document to pass the data to the bibliography processors.

$\boxed{\texttt{\textbackslash bibliography\{}\textit{file-list}\texttt{\}}}$

How to select the BibTeX databases

To inform BibTeX which databases are to be searched to resolve citations, you should specify their names, separated by commas (and *without* the extension .bib), as the argument to the command \bibliography. This command should be placed at the point where the bibliography should finally appear as the command is also used to typeset the bibliography. This coupling makes it a bit challenging to print more than one bibliography in a document—we discuss this in Section 16.8.

It is, of course, important that all cite keys used in the bibliography databases are unique, because it is otherwise not possible to reliably resolve the citation references when the document is processed.

biber/biblatex

> `\addbibresource[`*options*`]{`*file*`.bib}`
>
> With biblatex the databases should be declared in the preamble of the document with the command `\addbibresource`. The mandatory argument is the name of one database *with* the extension `.bib`. If you have more than one `.bib` file, use one `\addbibresource` for each. biber can use URLs to access remote files and is able to resolve patterns. Check the documentation for details.

`\bibliographystyle{`*style*`}`

With this command you tell BibTeX which style to use for the bibliography. The style refers to a `.bst` file, and the name must be given without the extension. There is no default style, so issuing the command is required; it can be placed in the document or in the preamble. Section 15.7 presents examples produced by a number of standard and nonstandard styles.

How to select the BibTeX style

   The style defines also the sorting of the entries. A "nonsorting" BibTeX style by order of first citation as required by the house styles of many publishers is, for example, `unsrt`.

Order by first citation produced with BibTeX

biber/biblatex

> biblatex does not make use of `\bibliographystyle` and errors if it detects it. The default biblatex style is a numeric style with alphabetic sorting; other styles and sortings are set through various package options and commands. Some of these options are passed to biber through the control file and affect its processing of the data; others are relevant only for the LaTeX compilation.
>
>   The package option that most closely matches the concept of a `.bst` style is the key `style`, which takes as a value a bibliography style name like `apa` or `authoryear`. The sorting is typically defined by such a style but can also be changed individually with the option `sorting`. This is described in more detail in Section 16.7.

   To select entries from the databases, they need to be cited in the document. Citation commands and their arguments are discussed in more detail in the next chapter, for now it is enough to know that in standard LaTeX you can use `\cite` or `\nocite` — with further citation commands provided by loading additional packages.

How to select entries from the database

   `\cite` also typesets the citations, while the sole purpose of `\nocite` is to write the keys in its argument into the `.aux` or `.bcf` file so that the associated bibliography information appears in the bibliography even if the publication is otherwise not referred to. Both commands can be used as often as necessary. As a special case, `\nocite{*}` includes all entries of the chosen BibTeX database(s) in the list of references.

> biber/biblatex
>
> The biblatex package offers a larger set of citation commands, and their syntax has been extended to accept two optional arguments. They are discussed in Section 16.7.3.

Putting everything together, a sample document for a standard BibTeX workflow would look like this:

```
\documentclass{article}
\begin{document}
  \nocite{MR-PQ}  ...  \cite{LGC97}  ...  \cite{Knuth-CT-a}

  \bibliographystyle{unsrt} \bibliography{tlc}
\end{document}
```

The .aux file would then contain:

```
\citation{MR-PQ}
\citation{LGC97}
\citation{Knuth-CT-a}
\bibstyle{unsrt}
\bibdata{tlc}
```

Do not use \bibdata *by mistake*

Do not confuse these commands with those intended for use in documents. They exist solely to facilitate the internal communication between LaTeX and BibTeX. If you mistakenly use \bibdata instead of \bibliography, then LaTeX processes your document without failure, but BibTeX complains that it does not find any database information in the .aux file.

> biber/biblatex
>
> A comparable document using the biber workflow together with the biblatex package would then be:
>
> ```
> \documentclass{article}
> \usepackage[sorting=none]{biblatex}
> \addbibresource{tlc.bib}
> \begin{document}
>   \nocite{MR-PQ}  ...  \cite{LGC97}  ...  \cite{Knuth-CT-a}
>
>   \printbibliography
> \end{document}
> ```
>
> Note that in contrast to the standard BibTeX workflow, a dedicated command like \printbibliography is needed (but not required) in order to print the full bibliography or parts of it. The available commands and their options are described in Section 16.7.8.

It is important to remember that BɪʙTEX or biber is not required for managing citations (except for packages such as biblatex and jurabib and those intended for producing multiple bibliographies). You can produce a bibliography without BɪʙTEX by providing the bibliographic entries yourself using the syntax described in Section 15.1.

15.5 On-line bibliographies

If you search the Internet, you find a large number of bibliography entries for both primary and secondary publications in free as well as commercial databases. In this section we mention a few free resources on scientific publications that offer bibliographic data in BɪʙTEX and some other formats.

Nelson Beebe maintains more than 1400 BɪʙTEX databases related to scientific journals and particular scientific topics.[1] These range from "Acta Informatica" and "Ada User Journal" to "X Journal" and "X Resource [journal]". All are available as .bib source files as well as listings in .html, .pdf, and .ps format.

Nelson Beebe's most interesting .bib databases, as far as TEX is concerned, are the files texbook1.bib, texbook2.bib, and texbook3.bib (articles and books about TEX, METAFONT, and friends), type.bib (a list of articles and books about typography), gut.bib (the contents of the French *Cahiers Gutenberg* journal), komoedie.bib (the contents of the German *Die TEXnische Komödie* journal), texgraph.bib (sources explaining how to make TEX and graphics work together), texjourn.bib (a list of journals accepting TEX as input), tugboat.bib (all the articles in *TUGboat*), and standard.bib (software standards). The web resources provided by Nelson Beebe also include a series of BɪʙTEX styles and many command-line tools for manipulating bibliography data (discussed in Section 15.6.3).

The Collection of Computer Science Bibliographies by Alf-Christian Achilles, containing more than 1.2 million references, can be found at https://liinwww. ira.uka.de/bibliography/index.html and at several mirror sites. The data included come from external bibliographical collections like those created by Nelson Beebe. One added-value feature is the search functionality, which allows you to research authors, particular subjects, topics, and other categories. Nearly all of the reference data are available in BɪʙTEX format.

Another interesting source is CiteSeer, Scientific Literature Digital Library, developed by Steve Lawrence, which can be found at https://citeseerx.ist.psu.edu. Helpful features include extensive search possibilities, context information on publications (e.g., related publications), citations to the document from other publications, statistical information about citations to a citation, and much more.

These examples represent merely a small selection of the vast amount of material found on the Internet. They might prove useful if you are interested in research papers on mathematics, computer science, and similar subjects.

---

[1] The bibliographic databases and support programs for maintaining and manipulating them can be found at https://www.math.utah.edu/pub/bibnet/ and https://www.math.utah.edu/pub/tex/bib/.

15.6 Bibliography database management tools

Because BIBTEX databases are plain-text files, they can be generated and manipulated with any editor that is able to write ASCII and UTF-8 files. However, with large collections of BIBTEX entries, this method can get quite cumbersome, and finding information becomes more and more difficult. For this reason people developed tools to help with these tasks.

An overview of programs with a graphical user interface for general database maintenance can be found at https://en.wikipedia.org/wiki/Comparison_ of_reference_management_software.

A selection of command-line tools for specific tasks is described in this section. Many of them can be found at https://ctan.org/tex-archive/biblio/ bibtex/utils/, but do not take Nelson Beebe's tools from there — CTAN has only old versions for some reason.

New products of both types are emerging, so it is probably worthwhile to check out available Internet resources (e.g., https://wiki.openoffice.org/ wiki/Bibliographic_Software_and_Standards_Information).

15.6.1 checkcites — Which citations are used, unused, or missing?

It can sometimes be useful to check if all references of a .bib file have been cited. For this the small tool **checkcites** from Paulo Cereda and Enrico Gregorio can be used. Its usage is simple. Compile your document as usual and then use

checkcites ⟨file⟩   or   checkcites --backend biber ⟨file⟩

The second call is meant for a document that uses biblatex and biber.

For a document using the tlc.bib file and citing the entries bschur and doody, this then reports on the terminal unused and unknown references:

```
------------------------------------------------------------------------
Report of unused references in your TeX document (that is, references
present in bibliography files, but not cited in the TeX source file)
------------------------------------------------------------------------

Unused references in your TeX document: 18
=> LGC97
=> LWC99
=> Knuth-CT-a
=> Knuth:TB10-1-31
...


------------------------------------------------------------------------
Report of undefined references in your TeX document (that is, references
cited in the TeX source file, but not present in the bibliography files)
------------------------------------------------------------------------

Undefined references in your TeX document: 1
=> doody
```

15.6.2 biblist — Printing BibTeX database files

A sorted listing of all entries in a BibTeX database is often useful for easy reference. Various tools, with more or less the same functionality, are available, and choosing one or the other is mostly a question of taste. In this section we discuss one representative tool, the biblist package written by Joachim Schrod. It can create a typeset listing of (possibly large) BibTeX databases. Later sections show some more possibilities.

To use biblist you must prepare a LaTeX document using the article class. Options and packages like twoside, ngerman, or geometry can be added. Given that entries are never broken across columns, it may not be advisable to typeset them in several columns using multicol, however.

The argument of the \bibliography command must contain the names of all BibTeX databases you want to print. With a \bibliographystyle command you can choose a specific bibliography style. By default, all bibliography entries in the database are typeset. However, if you issue explicit \nocite commands (as we did in the example), only the selected entries from the databases are printed. Internal cross-references via the crossref field or explicit \cite commands are marked using boxes around the *key* instead of resolving the latter.

(December 28, 2022)   `tlc.bib`

References

MR-PQ ....

    Frank Mittelbach and Chris Rowley.
    The pursuit of quality: How can automated typesetting achieve the highest standards of craft typography?
    In Vanoirbeek and Coray ⟨EP92⟩, pages 261–273.

EP92 ....

    Christine Vanoirbeek and Giovanni Coray, editors.
    EP92—Proceedings of Electronic Publishing, '92, Cambridge, 1992. Cambridge University Press.

```
\usepackage{biblist}
\bibliographystyle{alpha}

\nocite{MR-PQ}
\footnotesize
\bibliography{tlc}
```

15-6-1

You must run LaTeX, BibTeX, and LaTeX. No additional LaTeX run is necessary, because the cross-references are not resolved to conserve space. For this reason you will always see warnings about unresolved citations in such a case.

15.6.3 bibclean, etc. — A set of command-line tools

A set of tools to handle even very huge BibTeX databases was developed by Nelson Beebe. The tools can be obtained from `https://ftp.math.utah.edu/pub/bibtools.html` if they are not already on your system.[1] We give a brief description of each of them.

bibclean   This C program is a pretty-printer, syntax checker, and lexical analyzer for BibTeX bibliography database files [9]. The program, which runs on Unix, Vax/VMS,

---

[1]You may have to compile them yourself in that case.

and Windows platforms (with `cygwin`), has many options, but in general you can just type

> `bibclean` ⟨*bibfile(s)*⟩   or   `bibclean` < ⟨*infile*⟩ > ⟨*outfile*⟩   (useful in pipes)

For example, when used on the database file `tlc-ex.bib`, the `bibclean` program reports the following possible problem:

```
%% "EX/tlc-ex.bib", line 108: Unexpected value in
                            \enquote{year = "1980ff"}.
```

bibextract This program extracts from a list of BibTeX files those bibliography entries that match a pair of specified regular expressions, sending them to *stdout*, together with all `@preamble` and `@string` declarations. Two regular expressions must be specified: the first to select `keyword` values (if this string is empty, then all fields of an entry are examined), and the second to further select from the value part of the fields which bibliography entries must be output. Regular expressions should contain only lowercase strings.

For example, the following command extracts all entries containing the word "PostScript" (or some other capitalization) in any of the fields:

> `bibextract "" "postscript"` ⟨*bibfile(s)*⟩ > ⟨*new-bibfile*⟩

The next command extracts only those entries containing the string `Adobe` in the `author` or `organization` field:

> `bibextract "author|organization" "adobe"` ⟨*bibfile(s)*⟩ > ⟨*new-bibfile*⟩

Note that one might have to clean the `.bib` files using `bibclean` before `bibextract` finds correct entries. For example, the entry with "TUGboat" in the title is found with

> `bibclean tlc-ex.bib | bibextract "title" "tugboat"`

Using `bibextract` alone would fail because of the entry containing the line `year={1980ff}`.

citefind and citetags Sometimes you have to extract the entries effectively referenced in your publication from several large BibTeX databases. The Bourne shell scripts `citefind` and `citetags` use the `awk` and `sed` tools to accomplish that task.

First, `citetags` extracts the BibTeX citation keys from the LaTeX source or `.aux` files and sends them to the standard output *stdout*. There, `citefind` picks them up and tries to find the given keys in the `.bib` files specified. It then writes the resulting new bibliography file to *stdout*. For instance,

> `citetags *.aux | citefind -` ⟨*bibfile(s)*⟩ > ⟨*outfile*⟩

Nelson Beebe also developed the showtags package, which adds the citation key to a bibliography listing. In other words, it does a similar job to biblist as shown in Example 15-6-1 on page 415.

References

MR-PQ

```
\usepackage{showtags}
\bibliographystyle
    {is-alpha}
```

[MR92]   Frank Mittelbach and Chris Rowley.   The pursuit of quality: How can automated typesetting achieve the highest standards of craft typography?   In Vanoirbeek and Coray [VC92], pages 261–273.

EP92

```
\nocite{MR-PQ}
\footnotesize
\bibliography{tlc}
```

15-6-2

[VC92]   Christine Vanoirbeek and Giovanni Coray, editors.   *EP92—Proceedings of Electronic Publishing, '92.* Cambridge University Press, Cambridge, 1992.

15.6.4 Using biber as a tool

biber not only can be used to prepare a bibliography for a document, but it can also replace various of the tools described above.

Extracting entries used by a document

The scripts citefind and citetags described above extract the references used by a document from the .aux file and so target the BibTeX workflow. To get the references from the .bcf control file created for biber, biber can be used with the option --output-format to get a .bib file instead of a .bbl.

```
biber --output-format=bibtex ⟨file⟩
```

This creates a file *file*_biber.bib that contains only the entries needed for the document *file*.tex, which created *file*.bcf. Entries required to resolve cross-references are included too.

By using a source map in the document, this can also be used to filter the entries with regular expressions or other conditions. The following document for example suppresses all entries whose key does not contain Knuth or kant:

```
\documentclass{article}
\usepackage{biblatex}
\addbibresource{tlc.bib}
  \DeclareSourcemap{
     \maps⌊datatype=bibtex]{
        \map{%
           \step[fieldsource=entrykey,notmatch=\regexp{Knuth|kant},final]%
           \step[entrynull]}}}%
\nocite{*}
\begin{document}  \printbibliography  \end{document}
```

417

Validation

By using the option `--validate-datamodel` it is possible to validate one or more `.bib` files:

```
biber --tool --validate-datamodel tlc.bib tlc-ex.bib
```

This then reports on the terminal beside other information:

```
WARN - Datamodel: Entry 'G-G' (tlc.bib): Missing mandatory field 'author'
WARN - Datamodel: Entry 'oddity' (tlc-ex.bib): Invalid value of field 'year'
       must be datatype 'datepart' - ignoring field
```

Normalization and rewriting of entries

biber can also be used to clean up and normalize the entries of a `.bib` file, e.g.,

```
biber --tool --output-align tlc.bib
```

This creates a `tlc_bibertool.bib` file in which surrounding quotes are converted to braces, all field names are uppercased, their order is unified, and their values are aligned. biber also changes field names like `journal` to `journaltitle` and moves `year` and `month` to `date`. So, for example, the entry Knuth:TB10-1-31 will then have this format:

```
@ARTICLE{Knuth:TB10-1-31,
    AUTHOR       = {Knuth, Donald E.},
    DATE         = {1989-04},
    ISSN         = {0896-3207},
    JOURNALTITLE = {TUGboat},
    NUMBER       = {1},
    PAGES        = {31--36},
    TITLE        = {{Typesetting Concrete Mathematics}},
    VOLUME       = {10},
}
```

15.7 Formatting the bibliography with styles

Now that we know how to produce BibTeX database entries and manipulate them using various management tools, it is time to discuss the main purpose of the BibTeX and biber programs: to generate a bibliography containing the entries referenced in a document in a format conforming to a set of conventions.

We first discuss the use of existing BibTeX styles and present example results produced by a number of standard and nonstandard styles. We then show how the custom-bib package makes it possible to produce customized BibTeX styles for nearly every requirement with ease. We continue by discussing how styles are set when using the biblatex package, present an overview of existing biblatex styles, and finish with a number of examples. The customization of biblatex styles are discussed in Section 16.7.

15.7.1 A collection of BibTeX style files

Various organizations and individuals have developed style files for BibTeX that correspond to the house style of particular journals or editing houses. Nelson Beebe has collected a large number of such BibTeX styles. For each style he provides an example file, which allows you to see the effect of using the given style.[1] Some of the BibTeX styles — for instance, authordate⟨i⟩, jmb, and named — must be used in conjunction with their accompanying LaTeX packages (as indicated in Tables 15.7 to 15.9 on pages 420–423) to obtain the desired effect.

You can also customize a bibliography style, by making small changes to one of those in the table. Alternatively, you can generate your own style by using the custom-bib program (as explained in Section 15.7.2 on page 426).

In theory, it is possible to change the appearance of a bibliography by simply using another BibTeX style. In practice, there are a few restrictions because the BibTeX style interface was augmented by some authors so that their styles need additional support from within LaTeX. You are going to see several such examples in Chapter 16. For instance, all the author-date styles need a special LaTeX package such as natbib or harvard to function, and the BibTeX styles for jurabib work only if that package is loaded.

On the whole, the scheme works quite well, and we prove it in this section by showing the results of applying different BibTeX styles (plus their support packages if necessary) without otherwise altering the sample document. For this we use the familiar database from Figure 15.1 on page 382 and cite five publications from it: an article and a book by Donald Knuth, which shows us how different publications by the same author are handled; the manual from the Free Software Foundation, which is an entry without an author name; the unpublished entry with many authors and the special BibTeX string "and others"; and a publication that is part of a proceedings so that BibTeX has to include additional data from a different entry.

In our first example we use the standard plain BibTeX style, which means we use the following input:

```
\bibliographystyle{plain}
\nocite{Knuth:TB10-1-31,GNUMake,MR-PQ,Knuth-CT-a,test97}
\bibliography{tlc,tlc-ex}
```

To produce the final document, the example LaTeX file has to be run through LaTeX once to get the citation references written to the .aux file. Next, BibTeX processes the generated .aux file and reads the relevant entries from the BibTeX databases tlc.bib and tlc-ex.bib. The name of the bibliography style to use for formatting and sorting is specified with the command \bibliographystyle in the LaTeX source and picked up by BibTeX via the .aux file. The results are then placed into a .bbl file for further processing by LaTeX. Finally, LaTeX is run twice more — first to load the .bbl file and again to resolve all references.[2] A detailed explanation of this procedure was given in Section 15.4 on page 409, where you also find a graphical representation of the data flow (Figure 15.3).

---

[1] See Appendix C to find out how you can obtain these files from one of the TeX archives if they are not already on your system.

[2] In fact, for this example only one run is necessary — there are no cross-references to resolve because we used \nocite throughout.

Style Name	Description
abbrv.bst	Standard BibTeX style
abbrvnat.bst	natbib variant of abbrv style
abstract.bst	Modified alpha style with abstract keyword
acm.bst	Association for Computing Machinery BibTeX style
agsm.bst	Australian government publications BibTeX style; needs the harvard or natbib package
agu.bst	American Geophysical Union BibTeX style
alpha.bst	Standard BibTeX style
amsalpha.bst	alpha-like BibTeX style for $\mathcal{A}_{\mathcal{M}}S$-TeX
amsplain.bst	plain-like BibTeX style for $\mathcal{A}_{\mathcal{M}}S$-TeX (numeric labels)
annotate.bst	Modified alpha BibTeX style with annote keyword
annotation.bst	Modified plain BibTeX style with annote keyword
apa.bst	American Psychology Association BibTeX style
apalike.bst	Variant of apa BibTeX style; needs the apalike support package
apalike2.bst	Variant of apalike BibTeX style
astron.bst	*Astronomy* BibTeX style
authordate$i$.bst	i =[1,4]; series of BibTeX styles producing author-date reference list; all of them need the authordate1-4 support package
bbs.bst	*Behavioral and Brain Sciences* BibTeX style

Table 15.7: Selected BibTeX style files (A–B)

The plain style has numeric labels (in brackets), and the entries are alphabetically sorted by author, year, and title. In the case of the GNU manual the organization was used for sorting. This gives the following output:

References (plain style)

[1] Free Software Foundation, Boston, Massachusetts. *GNU Make, A Program for Directing Recompilation*, 2000.

[2] Michel Goossens, Ben User, Joe Doe, et al. Ambiguous citations. Submitted to the IBM J. Res. Dev., 1997.

[3] Donald E. Knuth. *The TeXbook*, volume A of *Computers and Typesetting*. Addison-Wesley, Reading, MA, USA, 1986.

[4] Donald E. Knuth. Typesetting Concrete Mathematics. *TUGboat*, 10(1):31–36, April 1989.

[5] Frank Mittelbach and Chris Rowley. The pursuit of quality: How can automated typesetting achieve the highest standards of craft typography? In Christine Vanoirbeek and Giovanni Coray, editors, *EP92—Proceedings of Electronic Publishing, '92*, pages 261–273, Cambridge, 1992. Cambridge University Press.

15-7-1

Style Name	Description
cbe.bst	Council of Biology Editors BibTeX style (includes such journals as *American Naturalist* and *Evolution*)
cell.bst	Small modifications to jmb BibTeX style
humanbio.bst	*Human Biology* BibTeX style
humannat.bst	*Human Nature* and *American Anthropologist* journals
ieeetr.bst	*Transactions of the Institute of Electrical and Electronic Engineers* BibTeX style
is-abbrv.bst	abbrv BibTeX style with ISSN and ISBN keyword added
is-alpha.bst	alpha BibTeX style with ISSN and ISBN keyword added
is-plain.bst	plain BibTeX style with ISSN and ISBN keyword added
is-unsrt.bst	unsrt BibTeX style with ISSN and ISBN keyword added
jmb.bst	*Journal of Molecular Biology* BibTeX style; this style requires the use of the jmb support package
jox.bst	Style for use with jurabib (Oxford style)
jtb.bst	*Journal of Theoretical Biology* BibTeX style
jurabib.bst	Style for use with jurabib
jureco.bst	Style for use with jurabib (compact)
jurunsrt.bst	Style for use with jurabib (unsorted)

Table 15.8: Selected BibTeX style files (C–J)

By replacing `plain` with `abbrv` we get a similar result. Now, however, the entries are more compact, because first names, months, and predefined journal names (Table 15.6 on page 403) are abbreviated. For instance, `ibmjrd` in the second reference now gives "IBM J. Res. Dev." instead of "IBM Journal of Research and Development".

References (abbrv style)

[1] Free Software Foundation, Boston, Massachusetts. *GNU Make, A Program for Directing Recompilation*, 2000.

[2] M. Goossens, B. User, J. Doe, et al. Ambiguous citations. Submitted to the IBM J. Res. Dev., 1997.

[3] D. E. Knuth. *The TeXbook*, volume A of *Computers and Typesetting*. Addison-Wesley, Reading, MA, USA, 1986.

[4] D. E. Knuth. Typesetting Concrete Mathematics. *TUGboat*, 10(1):31–36, Apr. 1989.

[5] F. Mittelbach and C. Rowley. The pursuit of quality: How can automated typesetting achieve the highest standards of craft typography? In C. Vanoirbeek and G. Coray, editors, *EP92—Proceedings of Electronic Publishing, '92*, pages 261–273, Cambridge, 1992. Cambridge University Press.

15-7-2

421

With the standard BIBTEX style `unsrt` we get the same result as with the `plain` style, except that the entries are printed in order of first citation, rather than being sorted.[1] The standard sets of styles do not contain a combination of `unsrt` and `abbrv`, but if necessary, it would be easy to integrate the differences between `plain` and `abbrv` into `unsrt` to form a new style.

[1] Donald E. Knuth. Typesetting Concrete Mathematics. *TUGboat*, 10(1):31–36, April 1989.

[2] Free Software Foundation, Boston, Massachusetts. *GNU Make, A Program for Directing Recompilation*, 2000.

[3] Frank Mittelbach and Chris Rowley. The pursuit of quality: How can automated typesetting achieve the highest standards of craft typography? In Christine Vanoirbeek and Giovanni Coray, editors, *EP92—Proceedings of Electronic Publishing, '92*, pages 261–273, Cambridge, 1992. Cambridge University Press.

[4] Donald E. Knuth. *The TEXbook*, volume A of *Computers and Typesetting*. Addison-Wesley, Reading, MA, USA, 1986.

[5] Michel Goossens, Ben User, Joe Doe, et al. Ambiguous citations. Submitted to the IBM J. Res. Dev., 1997.

15-7-3

The standard style `alpha` is again similar to `plain`, but the labels of the entries are formed from the authors' names and the year of publication. The slightly strange label for the GNU manual is because the entry contains a `key` field from which the first three letters are used to form part of the label. Also note the interesting label produced for the reference with more than three authors. The publications are sorted, with the label being used as a sort key, so that now the GNU manual moves to fourth place.

[GUD⁺97] Michel Goossens, Ben User, Joe Doe, et al. Ambiguous citations. Submitted to the IBM J. Res. Dev., 1997.

[Knu86] Donald E. Knuth. *The TEXbook*, volume A of *Computers and Typesetting*. Addison-Wesley, Reading, MA, USA, 1986.

[Knu89] Donald E. Knuth. Typesetting Concrete Mathematics. *TUGboat*, 10(1):31–36, April 1989.

[mak00] Free Software Foundation, Boston, Massachusetts. *GNU Make, A Program for Directing Recompilation*, 2000.

[MR92] Frank Mittelbach and Chris Rowley. The pursuit of quality: How can automated typesetting achieve the highest standards of craft typography? In Christine Vanoirbeek and Giovanni Coray, editors, *EP92—Proceedings of Electronic Publishing, '92*, pages 261–273, Cambridge, 1992. Cambridge University Press.

15-7-4

---

[1]In this and all following bibliography examples we suppress the heading that is normally placed in front of entries to save some space.

Style Name	Description
kluwer.bst	Kluwer Academic Publishers BⁱᵇTEX style
named.bst	BⁱᵇTEX style with [author(s), year] type of citation; requires the named support package
namunsrt.bst	Named variant of unsrt BⁱᵇTEX style
nar.bst	*Nucleic Acid Research* BⁱᵇTEX style; this style needs the nar support package
nature.bst	*Nature* BⁱᵇTEX style; this style requires the nature support package
newapa.bst	Modification of apalike.bst; needs the newapa support package
newcastle.bst	Newcastle University BⁱᵇTEX style; to be used with natbib
noTeX.bst	Style to generate HTML output instead of TEX input

Table 15.9: Selected BⁱᵇTEX style files (K–N)

Many BⁱᵇTEX styles implement smaller or larger variations of the layouts produced by the standard styles. For example, the phaip style for American Institute of Physics journals implements an unsorted layout (i.e., by order of first citation) but omits article titles, uses abbreviated author names, and uses a different structure for denoting editors in proceedings. Note that the entry with more than three authors has now been collapsed, showing only the first one.

[1] D. E. Knuth, TUGboat **10**, 31 (1989).

[2] Free Software Foundation, Boston, Massachusetts, *GNU Make, A Program for Directing Recompilation*, 2000.

[3] F. Mittelbach and C. Rowley, The pursuit of quality: How can automated typesetting achieve the highest standards of craft typography?, in *EP92—Proceedings of Electronic Publishing, '92*, edited by C. Vanoirbeek and G. Coray, pages 261–273, Cambridge, 1992, Cambridge University Press.

[4] D. E. Knuth, *The TEXbook*, volume A of *Computers and Typesetting*, Addison-Wesley, Reading, MA, USA, 1986.

[5] M. Goossens et al., Ambiguous citations, Submitted to the IBM J. Res. Dev., 1997.

15-7-5

Many of the journal and publisher styles, such as phaip used above, are not part of the standard LATEX distributions but available only from the journal or publisher websites. They may also be stored on CTAN but often not in their latest version. Thus, if you intend to publish in a specific journal, check out the website of the publisher to make sure you use their current BⁱᵇTEX style file and not an obsolete version.

If we turn to styles implementing an author-date scheme, the layout usually changes more drastically. For instance, numeric labels are normally suppressed (after

Style Name	Description
phaip.bst	*American Institute of Physics* journals BIBTEX style
phapalik.bst	American Psychology Association BIBTEX style
phcpc.bst	*Computer Physics Communications* BIBTEX style
phiaea.bst	Conferences of the International Atomic Energy Agency BIBTEX style
phjcp.bst	*Journal of Computational Physics* BIBTEX style
phnf.bst	*Nuclear Fusion* BIBTEX style
phnflet.bst	*Nuclear Fusion Letters* BIBTEX style
phpf.bst	*Physics of Fluids* BIBTEX style
phppcf.bst	Physics version of apalike BIBTEX style
phreport.bst	Internal physics reports BIBTEX style
phrmp.bst	*Reviews of Modern Physics* BIBTEX style
plain.bst	Standard BIBTEX style
plainnat.bst	natbib variant of plain style
plainyr.bst	plain BIBTEX style with primary sort by year
siam.bst	Society of Industrial and Applied Mathematics BIBTEX style
unsrt.bst	Standard BIBTEX style
unsrtnat.bst	natbib variant of unsrt style

Table 15.10: Selected BIBTEX style files (P–U)

all, the lookup process is by author). The chicago style, for example, displays the author name or names in abbreviated form (first name reversed), followed by the date in parentheses. In addition, we see yet another way to handle the editors in proceedings, and instead of the word "pages", we get "pp." For this example we loaded the natbib package to enable author-date support.

Free Software Foundation (2000). *GNU Make, A Program for Directing Recompilation*. Boston, Massachusetts: Free Software Foundation.

Goossens, M., B. User, J. Doe, et al. (1997). Ambiguous citations. Submitted to the IBM J. Res. Dev.

Knuth, D. E. (1986). *The TEXbook*, Volume A of *Computers and Typesetting*. Reading, MA, USA: Addison-Wesley.

Knuth, D. E. (1989, April). Typesetting Concrete Mathematics. *TUGboat 10*(1), 31–36.

Mittelbach, F. and C. Rowley (1992). The pursuit of quality: How can automated typesetting achieve the highest standards of craft typography? In C. Vanoirbeek and G. Coray (Eds.), *EP92—Proceedings of Electronic Publishing, '92*, Cambridge, pp. 261–273. Cambridge University Press.

15-7-6

As a final example we present another type of layout that is implemented with the help of the jurabib package. Because more customizing is necessary, we show the input used once more. The trick used to suppress the heading is *not* suitable for use in real documents because the space around the heading would be retained!

```
\usepackage[bibformat=ibidem]{jurabib}
\bibliographystyle{jurabib}   \jbuseidemhrule   % use default rule
\renewcommand\refname{}                % suppress heading for the example
\nocite{Knuth:TB10-1-31,GNUMake,MR-PQ,Knuth-CT-a,test97,LGC97}
\bibliography{tlc,tlc-ex}
```

This produces a layout in which the author name is replaced by a rule if it has been listed previously. In the case of multiple authors, the complete list has to be identical (see the first two entries). Also, for the first time, the International Standard Book Number (ISBN) and International Standard Serial Number (ISSN) are shown when present in the entry. If you look closely, you see many other smaller and larger differences. For example, this is the first style that does not convert titles of articles and proceeding entries to lowercase but rather keeps them as specified in the database.

Because the original application field for jurabib was law citations, it is one of the few BIBTEX styles that do not provide default strings for the journals listed in Table 15.6 on page 403; if you need any of them, you have to provide them yourself. BIBTEX warns you about the missing string in this case. You can then provide a definition for it in the database file or, if you prefer, in a separate database file that is loaded only if necessary.

Goossens, Michel/Rahtz, Sebastian/Mittelbach, Frank: The LATEX Graphics Companion: Illustrating Documents with TEX and PostScript. Reading, MA, USA: Addison-Wesley Longman, 1997, Tools and Techniques for Computer Typesetting, xxi + 554, ISBN 0–201-85469–4

Goossens, Michel et al.: Ambiguous citations. 1997, Submitted to the IBM J. Res. Dev.

Knuth, Donald E.: The TEXbook. Volume A, Computers and Typesetting. Reading, MA, USA: Addison-Wesley, 1986, ix + 483, ISBN 0–201–13447–0

——— Typesetting Concrete Mathematics. TUGboat, 10 April 1989, Nr. 1, 31–36, ISSN 0896–3207

Free Software Foundation: GNU Make, A Program for Directing Recompilation. 2000

Mittelbach, Frank/Rowley, Chris: The Pursuit of Quality: How can Automated Typesetting achieve the Highest Standards of Craft Typography? In **Vanoirbeek, Christine/Coray, Giovanni, editors:** EP92—Proceedings of Electronic Publishing, '92. Cambridge: Cambridge University Press, 1992, 261–273

15-7-7

If you wonder about the strange placement of the GNU Make manual entry, recall that this entry has no author but has a key specified, which is the reason for this placement when using the jurabib style.

Requirement	Example
Full name surname last	Donald Ervin Knuth/Michael Frederick Plass
Full name surname first	Knuth, Donald Ervin/Plass, Michael Frederick
Initials and surname	D. E. Knuth/M. F. Plass
Surname and initials	Knuth, D. E./Plass, M. F.
Surname and dotless initials	Knuth D E/Plass M F
Surname and concatenated initials	Knuth DE/Plass MF
Surname and spaceless initials	Knuth D.E./Plass M.F.
Only first author reversed with initials	Knuth, D. E./M. F. Plass
Only first author reversed with full names	Knuth, Donald Ervin/Michael Frederick Plass

Table 15.11: Requirements for formatting names

15.7.2 custom-bib — Generate BibTeX styles with ease

So far, we have discussed how to influence the layout of the bibliography by using different bibliography styles. If a particular BibTeX style is recommended for the journal or publisher you are writing for, then that is all that is necessary. However, a more likely scenario is that you have been equipped with a detailed set of instructions, which tells you how references should be formatted, but without pointing you to any specific BibTeX style — a program that may not even be known at the publishing house.

Of course, hunting for an existing style that fits the bill or can be adjusted slightly to do so is an option, but given that there are usually several variations in use for each typographical detail, the possibilities are enormous, and thus the chances of finding a suitable style are remote.

Consider, for example, the nine common requirements for presenting author names in Table 15.11. Combining these with a specification for the separation symbol to use (e.g., comma, semicolon, slash), the fonts to use for author names (i.e., roman, bold, small capitals, italic, other), and perhaps a requirement for different fonts for surname and first names, you end up with more than 500 different styles — just for presenting author names in the bibliography. Clearly, this combinatorial explosion cannot be managed by providing predefined styles for every combination.

Faced with this problem, Patrick Daly, the author of natbib, started in 1993 to develop a system that is capable of providing customized BibTeX styles by collecting answers to questions like the above (more than 70!) and then building a customized .bst file corresponding to the answers.

The system works in two phases: (1) a collection phase in which questions are interactively asked and (2) a generation phase in which the answers are used to build the BibTeX style. Both phases are entirely done by using LaTeX and thus can be carried out on any platform without requiring any additional helper program.

The collection is started by running the program makebst.tex through LaTeX and answering the questions posed to you. Most of the questions are presented in

the form of menus that offer several answers. The default answer is marked with a
* and can be selected by simply pressing ⟨return⟩. Other choices can be selected by
typing the letter in parentheses in front of the option. Selecting a letter not present
produces the default choice.

Initializing the system

We now walk you through the first questions, which are somewhat special because
they are used to initialize the system. Each time we indicate the suggested answer.

```
Do you want a description of the usage? (NO)
```

Replying with y produces a description of the procedure (as explained above); otherwise, the question has no effect.

```
Enter the name of the MASTER file (default=merlin.mbs)
```

Here the correct answer is ⟨return⟩. The default merlin.mbs is currently the only
production master file available, though this might change one day.

```
Name of the final OUTPUT .bst file? (default extension=bst)
```

Specify the name for your new BIBTEX style file, without an extension — for example,
ttct (Tools and Techniques for Computer Typesetting series). As a result of completing the first phase, you then receive a file called ttct.dbj from which the BIBTEX
style file ttct.bst is produced in the second phase.

```
Give a comment line to include in the style file.
Something like for which journals it is applicable.
```

Enter any free-form text you like, but note that a ⟨return⟩ ends the comment. It is
carried over into the resulting files and can help you at a later stage to identify the
purpose of this BIBTEX style.

```
Do you want verbose comments? (NO)
```

If you enter y to this question, the context of later questions is shown in the following
form:

```
<<STYLE OF CITATIONS:
    . . .
>>STYLE OF CITATIONS:
```

Whether this provides any additional help is something you have to decide for yourself.
The default is not to provide this extra information.

```
Name of language definition file (default=merlin.mbs)
```

If you are generating a BibTeX style for a language other than English, you can enter the name of the language here. Table 15.12 on the opposite page lists currently supported languages. Otherwise, reply with ⟨*return*⟩.

```
Include file(s) for extra journal names? (NO)
```

By answering y you can load predefined journal names for certain disciplines into the BibTeX style. You are then asked to specify the files containing these predefined names (with suitable defaults given).

This concludes the first set of questions for initializing the system. What follows are many questions that offer choices concerning layout and functional details. These can be classified into three categories:

Citation scheme The choice made here influences later questions. If you choose author-date support, for example, you get different questions than if you choose a numerical scheme.

Extensions These questions are related to extending the set of supported BibTeX fields, such as whether to include a `url` field.

Typographical details You are asked to make choices about how to format specific parts of the bibliographical entries. Several of the choices depend on the citation scheme used.

While it is possible to change your selections in the second phase of the processing (or to start all over again), it is best to have a clear idea about which citation scheme and which extensions are desired before beginning the interactive session. The typographical details can be adjusted far more easily in the second phase if that becomes necessary. We therefore discuss these main choices in some detail.

Selecting the citation scheme

The citation scheme is selected by answering the following question:

```
STYLE OF CITATIONS:
(*) Numerical as in standard LaTeX
(a) Author-year with some non-standard interface
(b) Alpha style, Jon90 or JWB90 for single or multiple authors
(o) Alpha style, Jon90 even for multiple authors
(f) Alpha style, Jones90 (full name of first author)
(c) Cite key (special for listing contents of bib file)
```

The default choice is "numerical". If you want to produce a style for the author-date scheme, select a (and disregard the mentioning of "nonstandard interface"). For alpha-style citations, use either b, o, or f depending on the label style you prefer. Choice c is of interest only if you want to produce a style for displaying BibTeX databases, so do not select it for production styles.

`catalan`	Language support for Catalan	`italian`	Language support for Italian
`dansk`	Language support for Danish	`norsk`	Language support for Norwegian
`dutch`	Language support for Dutch	`polski`	Language support for Polish
`esperant`	Language support for Esperanto	`portuges`	Language support for Portuguese
`finnish`	Language support for Finnish	`slovene`	Language support for Slovene
`french`	Language support for French	`spanish`	Language support for Spanish
`german`	Language support for German		

Table 15.12: Language support in `custom-bib`

If the default (i.e., a numerical citation scheme) was selected, the follow-up question reads:

```
HTML OUTPUT (if non author-year citations)
(*) Normal LaTeX output
(h) Hypertext output, in HTML code, in paragraphs
(n) Hypertext list with sequence numbers
(k) Hypertext with keys for viewing databases
```

Select the default. All other choices generate BibTeX styles that produce some sort of HTML output (which needs further manipulation before it can be viewed in browsers). This feature is considered experimental.

If you have selected an author-date citation scheme (i.e., a), you are rewarded with a follow-up question for deciding on the support interface from within LaTeX:

```
AUTHOR--YEAR SUPPORT SYSTEM (if author-year citations)
(*) Natbib for use with natbib v5.3 or later
(o) Older Natbib without full authors citations
(l) Apalike for use with apalike.sty
(h) Harvard system with harvard.sty
(a) Astronomy system with astron.sty
(c) Chicago system with chicago.sty
(n) Named system with named.sty
(d) Author-date system with authordate1-4.sty
```

The default choice, natbib, is usually the best, offering all the possibilities described in Sections 16.3.2 and 16.4.1. The option o should *not* be selected. If you have documents using citation commands from, say, the harvard package (see Example 16-3-4 on page 490), the option h would be suitable. For the same reason, the other options might be the right choice in certain circumstances. However, for document portability, natbib should be the preferred choice. Note in particular that some of the other packages mentioned in the options are no longer distributed in the mainstream LaTeX installation.

Determining the extensions supported

Besides supporting the standard BibTeX entry types (Table 15.1 on page 386) and fields (Tables 15.3/4 on pages 388–389), `makebst.tex` can be directed to support additional fields as optional fields in the databases so that they are used if present. Some of these extensions are turned off by default, even though it makes sense to include them in nearly every BibTeX style file.

```
LANGUAGE FIELD
(*) No language field
(1) Add language field to switch hyphenation patterns temporarily
```

Replying with 1 greatly helps in presenting foreign titles properly. If you additionally specify a nonstandard `language` key in your `.bib` files in all entries that have foreign titles or notes, then such entries temporarily switch to the specified language, using Babel's `\selectlanguage` command. If you use the `.bib` file with a different style that does not know about `language`, the key is ignored as usual. Thus, a deviation from the default is suggested.

```
ANNOTATIONS:
(*) No annotations will be recognized
(a) Annotations in annote field or in .tex file of citekey name
```

Choosing a integrates support for an `annote` field in the `.bst` file as well as support for including annotations stored in files of the form ⟨*citekey*⟩`.tex`. However, in contrast to jurabib, which also offers this feature, the inclusion cannot be suppressed or activated using a package option. Given that you quite likely want this feature turned on and off depending on the document, you might be best served by using two separate BibTeX styles differing only in this respect.

The nonstandard field `eid` (electronic identifier) is automatically supported by all generated styles. The fields `doi`, `isbn`, and `issn` are included by default but can be deselected. Especially for supporting the REVTeX package from the American Physical Society, a number of other fields can be added.

Finally, support for URLs can be added by answering the following question with something different from the default:

```
URL ADDRESS: (without REVTeX fields)
(*) No URL for electronic (Internet) documents
(u) Include URL as regular item block
(n) URL as note
(1) URL on new line after rest of reference
```

We suggest including support for URLs because references to electronic resources are common now. In the bibliography the URL is tagged with `\urlprefix\url{`*field-value*`}`, with default definitions for both commands. By loading the url package, better line breaking can be achieved.

As one of the last questions you are offered the following choice:

```
COMPATIBILITY WITH PLAIN TEX:
(*) Use LaTeX commands which may not work with Plain TeX
(t) Use only Plain TeX commands for fonts and testing
```

We strongly recommend retaining the default! LaTeX 2_ε is more than three decades old, and NFSS should have found its way into every living room. Besides, the plain TeX commands (\rm, \bf, and so on) are no longer officially part of LaTeX. They may be defined by a document class (for compatibility reasons with LaTeX 2.09) — but then they may not. Thus, choosing the obsolete syntax may result in the BibTeX style not functioning properly in all circumstances.

Always choose the default option here: the other may not work reliably!

Note that the questions about the extensions are mixed with those about typographical details and do not necessarily appear in the order presented here.

Specifying the typographical details

The remaining questions (of which there are plenty) concern typographical details, such as formatting author names, presenting journal information, and many more topics. As an example we show the question block that deals with the formatting of article titles:

```
TITLE OF ARTICLE:
(*) Title plain with no special font
(i) Title italic (\em)
(q) Title and punctuation in single quotes ('Title,' ..)
(d) Title and punctuation in double quotes (\enquote{Title,} ..)
(g) Title and punctuation in guillemets (<<Title,>> ..)
(x) Title in single quotes ('Title', ..)
(y) Title in double quotes (\enquote{Title}, ..)
(z) Title in guillemets (<<Title>>, ..)
```

If you make the wrong choice with any of them, do not despair. You can correct your mistake in the second phase of the processing as explained below.

Generating the BibTeX style from the collected answers

The result of running makebst.tex through LaTeX and answering all these questions is a new file with the extension .dbj. It contains all your selections in a special form suitable to be processed by DOCSTRIP, which in turn produces the final BibTeX style (see Section 17.2 for a description of the DOCSTRIP program). Technically speaking, a BibTeX bibliographic style file master (merlin.mbs by default) contains alternative coding that depends on DOCSTRIP options. By choosing entries from the interactive menus discussed above, some of this code is activated, thereby providing the necessary customization.

If you specified ttct in response to the question for the new .bst file, for example, you would now have a file ttct.dbj at your disposal. Hence, all that is necessary to generate the final BIBTEX style `ttct.bst` is to run

```
latex ttct.dbj
```

The content of the `.dbj` files generated from the first phase is well documented and presented in a form that makes further adjustments quite simple. Suppose you have answered `y` in response to the question about the title of articles on the previous page (i.e., use double quotes around the title), but you really should have replied with `d` (use double quotes around title and punctuation). Then all you have to do is open the `.dbj` file with a text editor and search for the block that deals with article titles:

```
%--------------------
%TITLE OF ARTICLE:
%    %: (def) Title plain
% tit-it,%: Title italic
% tit-qq,qt-s,%: Title and punctuation in single quotes
% tit-qq,%: Title and punctuation in double quotes
% tit-qq,qt-g,%: Title and punctuation in guillemets
% tit-qq,qt-s,qx,%: Title in single quotes
  tit-qq,qx,%: Title in double quotes
% tit-qq,qt-g,qx,%: Title in guillemets
%-------------------
```

Changing the behavior then entails nothing more than uncommenting the line you want and commenting out the line currently selected:

```
%--------------------
%TITLE OF ARTICLE:
%    %: (def) Title plain
% tit-it,%: Title italic
% tit-qq,qt-s,%: Title and punctuation in single quotes
  tit-qq,%: Title and punctuation in double quotes
% tit-qq,qt-g,%: Title and punctuation in guillemets
% tit-qq,qt-s,qx,%: Title in single quotes
% tit-qq,qx,%: Title in double quotes
% tit-qq,qt-g,qx,%: Title in guillemets
%-------------------
```

After that, rerun the file through LATEX to obtain an updated BIBTEX style.

15.7.3 An overview of biblatex styles

In the final section of this chapter we present a fairly comprehensive overview of biblatex styles in the form of short examples to help you find a style that fits your requirements, or at least one that is close and requires only minor customizations. We start with a short description of how styles are implemented and how the styles have been classified.

The main package option is the key `style`, which takes a *name* as its value. If given, biblatex loads the file *name*`.bbx`, which contains the settings for the formatting of the bibliography, and the file *name*`.cbx`, which contains the settings for the formatting of the citations. Both files must exist. If present, *name*`.dbx` is loaded too: this file can contain settings that extend the data model and, for example, declare new entry types or fields. Alternatively, you can set styles for citations and the bibliography independently, using the keys `citestyle` and `bibstyle`; then only a `.cbx` or `.bbx` is loaded. By default biblatex loads the `numeric` style.

Loading a style

The style files contain LaTeX code and definitions that are used during the LaTeX compilation. Various aspects can be adjusted through options, configuration commands, or with redefinitions, both in documents or when creating a new style based on an existing style. This makes them much more flexible than BibTeX styles.

The following two examples demonstrate this. They are both based on the style `authoryear`, but the second has a number of changes made for illustration purposes — not necessarily for the better! First the default version:

References

Knuth, Donald E. (1986). *The TeXbook*. Vol. A. Computers and Typesetting. Reading, MA, USA: Addison-Wesley, pp. ix + 483. ISBN: 0-201-13447-0.

– (Apr. 1989). "Typesetting Concrete Mathematics". In: *TUGboat* 10.1, pp. 31–36. ISSN: 0896-3207.

```
\usepackage[style=authoryear]{biblatex}
\addbibresource{tlc.bib}

\nocite{Knuth:TB10-1-31,Knuth-CT-a}
\printbibliography
```

15-7-8

In the second example we suppress the dashes and the ISBN, use initials instead of full author names, alter the format of dates, change the sorting, and adapt the title and the punctuation. We also declare that the overall document language is German (through the call to babel) — this affects not only the heading but also the prefix of the page numbers. Note that making such changes may require you to rerun biber. In other words, some take effect only if the `.bbl` file is regenerated, e.g., changing the sorting typically requires a reprocessing of the bibliography input.

```
\usepackage[ngerman]{babel}
\usepackage{csquotes}
\usepackage[style=authoryear,
   date=iso,dashed=false,isbn=false,
   sorting=none,giveninits]{biblatex}
\DeclareFieldFormat{title}{\mkbibbold{#1}}
\renewcommand\newunitpunct{%
   \addsemicolon\addspace}
\addbibresource{tlc.bib}

\nocite{Knuth:TB10-1-31,Knuth-CT-a}
\printbibliography
```

Literatur

Knuth, D. E. (1989-04); „Typesetting Concrete Mathematics"; in: *TUGboat* 10.1, S. 31–36.

Knuth, D. E. (1986); **The TeXbook**; Bd. A; Computers and Typesetting; Reading, MA, USA; Addison-Wesley, S. ix + 483.

15-7-9

This flexibility can make it difficult to choose a suitable style as starting point, because it is not always clear which parts are easy to adapt and which not. A rule of thumb: changing the order of fields is more difficult than adapting fonts and punctuation.

How to choose a style

Classification of
styles
We now present various packages that offer one or more biblatex styles. The list is restricted to packages available on CTAN — more can be found on the Internet or in local installations. The packages have been roughly classified into the following six categories:

Collections of generic styles (*starting on page 435*) Bundles that provide flexible styles with various options and interfaces to adapt them to local requirements.

Implementation of style guides (*starting on page 439*) Bundles that implement a style as promoted by style manuals like the *Publication Manual of the American Psychological Association* (*APA*) [5] or *The Chicago Manual of Style* [24].

University styles (*starting on page 445*) Bundles that implement the requirements of some university or faculty.

Journal styles (*starting on page 455*) Bundles implementing the style requirements of some journal.

Extensions (*starting on page 461*) Bundles whose main purpose is to extend the data model and to add new field or entry types.

Other styles (*starting on page 464*) These are bundles not fitting in one of the other categories.

Notes
on the following
biblatex samples
For every bundle we start with a short description and a rough classification of the citation systems it supports. We then list the names of the styles it offers: typically both a citation and the bibliography style is provided, and the names can be used with the `style` key, but in some cases only a citation or bibliography style exists, which can be set only with `citestyle` or `bibstyle` — these are listed separately. If `.bbx` and `.cbx` files contain only internal code (for example, `standard.bbx`), then they are not listed, because they are not meant to be used directly in a document.

This is then followed by sample output of a representative selection of the bundle styles (but not necessarily from *all* styles of the bundle). With a few exceptions — as noted in the bundle descriptions — the examples all use the same preamble, i.e.,

```
\usepackage[style=⟨style⟩]{biblatex}
\addbibresource{tlc-biblatex-special.bib}
```

The entries in the `tlc-biblatex-special.bib` file are based on existing entries from `biblatex-examples.bib`,[1] but names, titles, and annotations have been shortened to save space.

The document body contains four citations: the first is to an article with two authors, then we reference the same book twice to show how the style handles such repetitions, and finally we cite another work of the same author to exhibit how this is formatted in the bibliography — some styles use dashes, others abbreviations like "ders." (short for the German word "derselbe") or "idem", yet others simply repeat

---

[1] This is a sample `.bib` file provided by the biblatex package.

the author name. We use \cite for the first reference (to show what that command does) and \textcite for the remaining ones, because this command typically gives footnotes with verbose styles and so gives a better impression of the styles.[1]

The text is wrapped in a \textcolor command so that it appears in blue, which helps in distinguishing main text from bibliography list output, given that we suppress the list header. After the citations the bibliography is printed (without a heading to save space). Thus, the body for each example looks as follows:

```
\textcolor{See \cite{zar2099}        % Show what \cite does compared to
        and \textcite[4-8]{cole1983}  % \textcite for the other references
        and again                     % Check how a repeat and the same
        \textcite{cole1983,cole1995}} % author with a different work are handled
\printbibliography[heading=none]
```

15.7.4 Generic styles

The bundles in this category provide a large variety of standard style types with various options and interfaces to adapt them to local requirements. Two prominent examples are the biblatex bundle itself and the biblatex-ext bundle. The styles are kept up-to-date and are good starting points if you want to create your own style or want to learn what is needed to create a style. They are loaded and then modified by many other styles.

biblatex   *Philip Kime, Philipp Lehman*   The biblatex package comes with a large number of easy-to-customize styles. There is a matching bibliography style for every citation style, but note that many bibliography styles are only small wrappers around a base style. For example, the bibliography style authortitle-comp loads the authortitle style. So these styles differ only in the formatting of the citation.

Citation systems: various

Styles: alphabetic, alphabetic-verb, authortitle, authortitle-comp, authortitle-ibid, authortitle-icomp, authortitle-tcomp, authortitle-terse, authortitle-ticomp, authoryear, authoryear-comp, authoryear-ibid, authoryear-icomp, debug, draft, numeric, numeric-comp, numeric-verb, reading, verbose, verbose-ibid, verbose-inote, verbose-note, verbose-trad1, verbose-trad2, verbose-trad3

Style samples:

See [ZL99] and Cole [Col83, pp. 4–8] and again Cole [Col83; Col95]

[Col83]   Sam Ted Cole. *The cool works of Sam Ted Cole.* Vol. 7.2: *Life story, or Biographical sketches.* Ed. by Kate Cob, Jon Eng, and W. Jack Bate. Boll Series 75. London: Rout and Paul, 1983.

[Col95]   Sam Ted Cole. *Remake of Life story.* 1995.

[ZL99]   Zoë C. Zar and Adam D. Lau. "Algebra". Version 3. In: *Theory* 12 (2099), pp. 423–491. arXiv: math/9901.4711v13.

alphabetic

15-7-10

---

[1] The various citation commands are described in more detail in Section 16.7.3.

authortitle

See Zar and Lau, "Algebra" and Cole (*Life story*, pp. 4–8) and again Cole (*Life story*) and Cole (*Remake*)

Cole, Sam Ted. *The cool works of Sam Ted Cole*. Vol. 7.2: *Life story, or Biographical sketches*. Ed. by Kate Cob, Jon Eng, and W. Jack Bate. Boll Series 75. London: Rout and Paul, 1983.

– *Remake of Life story*. 1995.

Zar, Zoë C. and Adam D. Lau. "Algebra". Version 3. In: *Theory* 12 (2099), pp. 423–491. arXiv: `math/9901.4711v13`.

15-7-11

authoryear

See Zar and Lau 2099 and Cole (1983, pp. 4–8) and again Cole (1983) and Cole (1995)

Cole, Sam Ted (1983). *The cool works of Sam Ted Cole*. Vol. 7.2: *Life story, or Biographical sketches*. Ed. by Kate Cob, Jon Eng, and W. Jack Bate. Boll Series 75. London: Rout and Paul.

– (1995). *Remake of Life story*.

Zar, Zoë C. and Adam D. Lau (2099). "Algebra". Version 3. In: *Theory* 12, pp. 423–491. arXiv: `math/9901.4711v13`.

15-7-12

draft

See **zar2099** and Cole (**cole1983**, pp. 4–8) and again Cole (**cole1983**); Cole (**cole1995**)

cole1983 Sam Ted Cole. *The cool works of Sam Ted Cole*. Vol. 7.2: *Life story, or Biographical sketches*. Ed. by Kate Cob, Jon Eng, and W. Jack Bate. Boll Series 75. London: Rout and Paul, 1983.

cole1995 Sam Ted Cole. *Remake of Life story*. 1995.

zar2099 Zoë C. Zar and Adam D. Lau. "Algebra". Version 3. In: *Theory* 12 (2099), pp. 423–491. arXiv: `math/9901.4711v13`.

15-7-1

numeric

See [3] and Cole [1, pp. 4–8] and again Cole [1, 2]

[1] Sam Ted Cole. *The cool works of Sam Ted Cole*. Vol. 7.2: *Life story, or Biographical sketches*. Ed. by Kate Cob, Jon Eng, and W. Jack Bate. Boll Series 75. London: Rout and Paul, 1983.

[2] Sam Ted Cole. *Remake of Life story*. 1995.

[3] Zoë C. Zar and Adam D. Lau. "Algebra". Version 3. In: *Theory* 12 (2099), pp. 423–491. arXiv: `math/9901.4711v13`.

15-7-1

The following style is the first example of a reading style. Such styles are designed for personal reading lists and annotated bibliographies.

reading

See Zar and Lau, "Algebra" and Cole (*Life story*, pp. 4–8) and again Cole (*Life story*) and Cole (*Remake*)

Cole: Life story cole1983

Sam Ted Cole. *The cool works of Sam Ted Cole*. Vol. 7.2: *Life story, or Biographical sketches*. Ed. by Kate Cob, Jon Eng, and W. Jack Bate. Boll Series 75. London: Rout and Paul, 1983.

Annotations: One (partial) volume of a multivolume book.

Cole: Remake cole1995

Sam Ted Cole. *Remake of Life story*. 1995.

Zar et al.: Algebra zar2099

Zoë C. Zar and Adam D. Lau. "Algebra". Version 3. In: *Theory* 12 (2099), pp. 423–491. arXiv: `math/9901.4711v13`.

Annotations: An `article` with `eprint` and `eprinttype` fields.

15-7-

The next style is the first example of a verbose style where a full reference is given the first time a work is cited, normally in a footnote. Note the difference between the \cite and the \textcite behavior.

See Zoë C. Zar and Adam D. Lau. "Algebra". Version 3. In: *Theory* 12 (2099), pp. 423–491. arXiv: math/9901.4711v13 and Cole[1] and again Cole[2]

Cole, Sam Ted. *The cool works of Sam Ted Cole*. Vol. 7.2: *Life story, or Biographical sketches*. Ed. by Kate Cob, Jon Eng, and W. Jack Bate. Boll Series 75. London: Rout and Paul, 1983.
– *Remake of Life story*. 1995.
Zar, Zoë C. and Adam D. Lau. "Algebra". Version 3. In: *Theory* 12 (2099), pp. 423–491. arXiv: math/9901.4711v13.

verbose

----

[1]Sam Ted Cole. *The cool works of Sam Ted Cole*. Vol. 7.2: *Life story, or Biographical sketches*. Ed. by Kate Cob, Jon Eng, and W. Jack Bate. Boll Series 75. London: Rout and Paul, 1983, pp. 4–8.
[2]Cole, *Life story*; Sam Ted Cole. *Remake of Life story*. 1995.

15-7-16

biblatex-ext   *Moritz Wemheuer*   Extended and improved versions of the standard styles that ship with biblatex. There is a matching bibliography style for every citation style. Most bibliography styles are only small wrappers around the base styles shown in the samples.

Citation systems: various

Styles: ext-alphabetic, ext-alphabetic-verb, ext-authortitle, ext-authortitle-comp, ext-authortitle-ibid, ext-authortitle-icomp, ext-authortitle-tcomp, ext-authortitle-terse, ext-authortitle-ticomp, ext-authoryear, ext-authoryear-comp, ext-authoryear-ecomp, ext-authoryear-ibid, ext-authoryear-icomp, ext-authoryear-iecomp, ext-authoryear-tcomp, ext-authoryear-tecomp, ext-authoryear-terse, ext-authoryear-ticomp, ext-authoryear-tiecomp, ext-numeric, ext-numeric-comp, ext-numeric-verb, ext-verbose, ext-verbose-ibid, ext-verbose-inote, ext-verbose-note, ext-verbose-trad1, ext-verbose-trad2, ext-verbose-trad3

Bib styles: ext-authornumber, ext-authornumber-comp, ext-authornumber-ecomp, ext-authornumber-icomp, ext-authornumber-tcomp, ext-authornumber-tecomp, ext-authornumber-terse

Style samples:

See [ZL99] and Cole [Col83, pp. 4–8] and again Cole [Col83; Col95]

[Col83]   Sam Ted Cole. *The cool works of Sam Ted Cole*. Vol. 7.2: *Life story, or Biographical sketches*. Ed. by Kate Cob, Jon Eng, and W. Jack Bate. Boll Series 75. London: Rout and Paul, 1983.

[Col95]   Sam Ted Cole. *Remake of Life story*. 1995.

[ZL99]   Zoë C. Zar and Adam D. Lau. "Algebra". Version 3. In: *Theory* 12 (2099), pp. 423–491. arXiv: math/9901.4711v13.

ext-alphabetic

15-7-17

ext-authornumber

See Zar and Lau [1] and Cole [1, pp. 4–8] and again Cole [1] and Cole [2]

Cole, Sam Ted [1]. *The cool works of Sam Ted Cole*. Vol. 7.2: *Life story, or Biographical sketches*. Ed. by Kate Cob, Jon Eng, and W. Jack Bate. Boll Series 75. London: Rout and Paul, 1983.
– [2]. *Remake of Life story*. 1995.
Zar, Zoë C. and Adam D. Lau [1]. "Algebra". Version 3. In: *Theory* 12 (2099), pp. 423–491. arXiv: `math/9901.4711v13`.

15-7-18

ext-authortitle

See Zar and Lau, "Algebra" and Cole (*Life story*, pp. 4–8) and again Cole (*Life story*) and Cole (*Remake*)

Cole, Sam Ted. *The cool works of Sam Ted Cole*. Vol. 7.2: *Life story, or Biographical sketches*. Ed. by Kate Cob, Jon Eng, and W. Jack Bate. Boll Series 75. London: Rout and Paul, 1983.
– *Remake of Life story*. 1995.
Zar, Zoë C. and Adam D. Lau. "Algebra". Version 3. In: *Theory* 12 (2099), pp. 423–491. arXiv: `math/9901.4711v13`.

15-7-19

ext-authoryear

See Zar and Lau 2099 and Cole (1983, pp. 4–8) and again Cole (1983) and Cole (1995)

Cole, Sam Ted (1983). *The cool works of Sam Ted Cole*. Vol. 7.2: *Life story, or Biographical sketches*. Ed. by Kate Cob, Jon Eng, and W. Jack Bate. Boll Series 75. London: Rout and Paul.
– (1995). *Remake of Life story*.
Zar, Zoë C. and Adam D. Lau (2099). "Algebra". Version 3. In: *Theory* 12, pp. 423–491. arXiv: `math/9901.4711v13`.

15-7-2

ext-numeric

See [3] and Cole [1, pp. 4–8] and again Cole [1, 2]

[1] Sam Ted Cole. *The cool works of Sam Ted Cole*. Vol. 7.2: *Life story, or Biographical sketches*. Ed. by Kate Cob, Jon Eng, and W. Jack Bate. Boll Series 75. London: Rout and Paul, 1983.

[2] Sam Ted Cole. *Remake of Life story*. 1995.

[3] Zoë C. Zar and Adam D. Lau. "Algebra". Version 3. In: *Theory* 12 (2099), pp. 423–491. arXiv: `math/9901.4711v13`.

15-7-2

ext-verbose

See Zoë C. Zar and Adam D. Lau. "Algebra". Version 3. In: *Theory* 12 (2099), pp. 423–491. arXiv: `math/9901.4711v13` and Cole[1] and again Cole[2]

Cole, Sam Ted. *The cool works of Sam Ted Cole*. Vol. 7.2: *Life story, or Biographical sketches*. Ed. by Kate Cob, Jon Eng, and W. Jack Bate. Boll Series 75. London: Rout and Paul, 1983.
– *Remake of Life story*. 1995.
Zar, Zoë C. and Adam D. Lau. "Algebra". Version 3. In: *Theory* 12 (2099), pp. 423–491. arXiv: `math/9901.4711v13`.

---

[1]Sam Ted Cole. *The cool works of Sam Ted Cole*. Vol. 7.2: *Life story, or Biographical sketches*. Ed. by Kate Cob, Jon Eng, and W. Jack Bate. Boll Series 75. London: Rout and Paul, 1983, pp. 4–8.
[2]Cole, *Life story*; Sam Ted Cole. *Remake of Life story*. 1995.

15-7-

biblatex-trad *Moritz Wemheuer* Styles reimplementing some of the traditional BᴵʙTₑX styles (`abbrv`, `alpha`, `plain`, and `unsrt`).

Citation systems: various

Styles: `trad-abbrv`, `trad-alpha`, `trad-plain`, `trad-unsrt`

Style samples:

See [3] and Cole [1, pages 4–8] and again Cole [1, 2]

[1]   S. T. Cole. *The cool works of Sam Ted Cole*. Volume 7.2: *Life story, or Biographical sketches*. K. Cob, J. Eng, and W. J. Bate, editors, number 75 in *Boll Series*. Rout and Paul, London, 1983.

[2]   S. T. Cole. *Remake of Life story*. 1995.

[3]   Z. C. Zar and A. D. Lau. Algebra. Version 3. *Theory*, 12:423–491, 2099. arXiv: `math/9901.4711v13`.

trad-abbrv

`15-7-23`

See [ZL99] and Cole [Col83, pages 4–8] and again Cole [Col83; Col95]

[Col83]   Sam Ted Cole. *The cool works of Sam Ted Cole*. Volume 7.2: *Life story, or Biographical sketches*. Kate Cob, Jon Eng, and W. Jack Bate, editors, number 75 in *Boll Series*. Rout and Paul, London, 1983.

[Col95]   Sam Ted Cole. *Remake of Life story*. 1995.

[ZL99]   Zoë C. Zar and Adam D. Lau. Algebra. Version 3. *Theory*, 12:423–491, 2099. arXiv: `math/9901.4711v13`.

trad-alpha

`15-7-24`

See [3] and Cole [1, pages 4–8] and again Cole [1, 2]

[1]   Sam Ted Cole. *The cool works of Sam Ted Cole*. Volume 7.2: *Life story, or Biographical sketches*. Kate Cob, Jon Eng, and W. Jack Bate, editors, number 75 in *Boll Series*. Rout and Paul, London, 1983.

[2]   Sam Ted Cole. *Remake of Life story*. 1995.

[3]   Zoë C. Zar and Adam D. Lau. Algebra. Version 3. *Theory*, 12:423–491, 2099. arXiv: `math/9901.4711v13`.

trad-plain

`15-7-25`

See [1] and Cole [2, pages 4–8] and again Cole [2, 3]

[1]   Zoë C. Zar and Adam D. Lau. Algebra. Version 3. *Theory*, 12:423–491, 2099. arXiv: `math/9901.4711v13`.

[2]   Sam Ted Cole. *The cool works of Sam Ted Cole*. Volume 7.2: *Life story, or Biographical sketches*. Kate Cob, Jon Eng, and W. Jack Bate, editors, number 75 in *Boll Series*. Rout and Paul, London, 1983.

[3]   Sam Ted Cole. *Remake of Life story*. 1995.

trad-unsrt

`15-7-26`

15.7.5 Implementations of style guides

The bundles in this category implement styles promoted by important style manuals. They often contain quite complex styles with fixed settings, implemented with low-level coding. Some of them require special loading or nonstandard settings in the document, so the documentation should be consulted before use. They are good styles if used as is, but changing them can be difficult and requires some programming skills.

biblatex-apa   *Philip Kime*   Style implementing the APA (American Psychological Association) style.

Citation system: author-date   *Style:* `apa`

Style sample:

See Zar and Lau, 2099 and Cole (1983, pp. 4–8) and again Cole (1983, 1995)

apa

Cole, S. T. (1983). *The cool works of Sam Ted Cole. Vol. 72. Life story, or Biographical sketches* (K. Cob, J. Eng, & W. J. Bate, Eds.; *Vol. 7*). Rout and Paul.
    One (partial) volume of a multivolume book.

Cole, S. T. (1995). *Remake of life story.*

Zar, Z. C., & Lau, A. D. (2099). Algebra. *Theory, 12*, 423–491.
    An `article` with `eprint` and `eprinttype` fields.

15-7-27

biblatex-chicago   *David Fussner*   Styles implementing the specifications of *The Chicago Manual of Style*; see windycity for an alternative. To load the styles use the biblatex-chicago package and its options `authordate`, `authordate-trad`, or `notes`, e.g.,

```
\usepackage[authordate]{biblatex-chicago}
```

Citation systems: author-date, verbose

Styles: `chicago-authordate, chicago-authordate-trad, chicago-notes`

Style samples:

See Zar and Lau 2099 and Cole (1983, 4–8) and again Cole (1983, 1995)

chicago-authordate

Cole, Sam Ted. 1983. *Life story, or Biographical sketches.* Vol. 7, bk. 2 of *The cool works of Sam Ted Cole,* edited by Kate Cob, Jon Eng, and W. Jack Bate. Boll Series 75. London: Rout and Paul.

———. 1995. *Remake of Life story.*

Zar, Zoë C., and Adam D. Lau. 2099. "Algebra." *Theory* 12:423–491. arXiv: math/9901.4711v13.

15-7-2

See Zar and Lau 2099 and Cole (1983, 4–8) and again Cole (1983, 1995)

chicago-authordate-trad

Cole, Sam Ted. 1983. *Life story, or Biographical sketches.* Vol. 7, bk. 2 of *The cool works of Sam Ted Cole,* edited by Kate Cob, Jon Eng, and W. Jack Bate. Boll Series 75. London: Rout and Paul.

———. 1995. *Remake of life story.*

Zar, Zoë C., and Adam D. Lau. 2099. Algebra. *Theory* 12:423–491. arXiv: math/9901.4711v13.

15-7-:

See Zoë C. Zar and Adam D. Lau, "Algebra," *Theory* 12 (2099): 423–491, arXiv: math/9901.4711v13 and Cole[1] and again Cole[2]

Cole, Sam Ted. *Life story, or Biographical sketches.* Vol. 7, bk. 2 of *The cool works of Sam Ted Cole,* edited by Kate Cob, Jon Eng, and W. Jack Bate. Boll Series 75. London: Rout and Paul, 1983.

———. *Remake of Life story.* 1995.

chicago-notes

Zar, Zoë C., and Adam D. Lau. "Algebra." *Theory* 12 (2099): 423–491. arXiv: math/9901.4711v13.

---

1. Sam Ted Cole, *Life story, or Biographical sketches*, vol. 7, bk. 2 of *The cool works of Sam Ted Cole*, ed. Kate Cob, Jon Eng, and W. Jack Bate, Boll Series 75 (London: Rout and Paul, 1983), 4–8.
2. Cole, *Life story*; Sam Ted Cole, *Remake of Life story* (1995).

15-7-

biblatex-gb7714-2015   *Hu Zhenzhen*   Styles implementing the Chinese GBT7714-2015 bibliography style. The styles need the ctex package, a Unicode engine, and suitable fonts.

Citation system: various

Styles: chinese-erj, gb7714-1987, gb7714-1987ay, gb7714-2005, gb7714-2005ay, gb7714-2015, gb7714-2015ay, gb7714-2015ms, gb7714-2015mx

Bib styles: gb7714-CCNU, gb7714-NWAFU, gb7714-SEU

Style sample: — none shown —

biblatex-gost   *Oleg Domanov*   Styles implementing the Russian bibliography style GOST.

Citation systems: various

Styles: gost-alphabetic, gost-alphabetic-min, gost-authoryear, gost-authoryear-min, gost-footnote, gost-footnote-min, gost-inline, gost-inline-min, gost-numeric, gost-numeric-min

Style samples:

See [ZL99] and Cole [Col83, p. 4–8] and again Cole [Col83; Col95]

[Col83]	*Cole S. T.* The cool works of Sam Ted Cole. Vol. 7. Part 2. Life story, or Biographical sketches / ed. by K. Cob, J. Eng, W. J. Bate. — London : Rout and Paul, 1983. — (Boll Series ; 75).
[Col95]	*Cole S. T.* Remake of Life story. — 1995.
[ZL99]	*Zar Z. C., Lau A. D.* Algebra // Theory. — 2099. — Vol. 12. — P. 423–491.

gost-alphabetic

15-7-31

See [ZL99] and Cole [Col83, p. 4–8] and again Cole [Col83; Col95]

[Col83]	*Cole S. T.* The cool works of Sam Ted Cole. Vol. 7. Part 2. Life story, or Biographical sketches. — London : Rout and Paul, 1983.
[Col95]	*Cole S. T.* Remake of Life story. — 1995.
[ZL99]	*Zar Z. C., Lau A. D.* Algebra // Theory. — 2099. — Vol. 12. — P. 423–491.

gost-alphabetic-min

15-7-32

See Zar, Lau, 2099 and Cole (1983, p. 4–8) and again Cole (1983; 1995)

Cole S. T. The cool works of Sam Ted Cole. Vol. 7. Part 2. Life story, or Biographical sketches / ed. by K. Cob, J. Eng, W. J. Bate. — London : Rout and Paul, 1983. — (Boll Series ; 75).
Cole S. T. Remake of Life story. — 1995.
Zar Z. C., Lau A. D. Algebra // Theory. — 2099. — Vol. 12. — P. 423–491. — arXiv: math/9901.4711v13.

gost-authoryear

15-7-33

See Zar, Lau, 2099 and Cole (1983, p. 4–8) and again Cole (1983; 1995)

Cole S. T. The cool works of Sam Ted Cole. Vol. 7. Part 2. Life story, or Biographical sketches. — London : Rout and Paul, 1983.
Cole S. T. Remake of Life story. — 1995.
Zar Z. C., Lau A. D. Algebra // Theory. — 2099. — Vol. 12. — P. 423–491.

gost-authoryear-min

15-7-34

gost-footnote

See *Zar Z. C.*, *Lau A. D.* Algebra // Theory. 2099. Vol. 12. P. 423–491 and *Cole S. T.*[1] and again *Cole S. T.*[2]

Cole S. T. Remake of Life story. — 1995.

Cole S. T. The cool works of Sam Ted Cole. Vol. 7. Part 2. Life story, or Biographical sketches / ed. by K. Cob, J. Eng, W. J. Bate. — London : Rout and Paul, 1983. — (Boll Series ; 75).

Zar Z. C., *Lau A. D.* Algebra // Theory. — 2099. — Vol. 12. — P. 423–491. — arXiv: `math/9901.4711v13`.

---

[1]*Cole S. T.* The cool works of Sam Ted Cole. Vol. 7. Part 2. Life story, or Biographical sketches / ed. by K. Cob, J. Eng, W. J. Bate. London : Rout and Paul, 1983. (Boll Series ; 75). P. 4–8.

[2]*Cole S. T.* Life story. Vol. 7, part 2 ; *Cole S. T.* Remake of Life story. 1995.

15-7-3

gost-footnote-min

See *Zar Z. C.*, *Lau A. D.* Algebra // Theory. 2099. Vol. 12. P. 423–491 and *Cole S. T.*[1] and again *Cole S. T.*[2]

Cole S. T. Remake of Life story. — 1995.

Cole S. T. The cool works of Sam Ted Cole. Vol. 7. Part 2. Life story, or Biographical sketches. — London : Rout and Paul, 1983.

Zar Z. C., *Lau A. D.* Algebra // Theory. — 2099. — Vol. 12. — P. 423–491.

---

[1]*Cole S. T.* The cool works of Sam Ted Cole. Vol. 7. Part 2. Life story, or Biographical sketches. London : Rout and Paul, 1983. P. 4–8.

[2]*Cole S. T.* Life story. Vol. 7, part 2 ; *Cole S. T.* Remake of Life story. 1995.

15-7-3

The styles `gost-inline` and `gost-inline-min` are only minimally different from the previous two styles and would show the same results with our sample data.

gost-numeric

See [3] and Cole [2, p. 4–8] and again Cole [1; 2]

1. *Cole S. T.* Remake of Life story. — 1995.

2. *Cole S. T.* The cool works of Sam Ted Cole. Vol. 7. Part 2. Life story, or Biographical sketches / ed. by K. Cob, J. Eng, W. J. Bate. — London : Rout and Paul, 1983. — (Boll Series ; 75).

3. *Zar Z. C.*, *Lau A. D.* Algebra // Theory. — 2099. — Vol. 12. — P. 423–491. — arXiv: `math/9901.4711v13`.

15-7-

gost-numeric-min

See [3] and Cole [2, p. 4–8] and again Cole [1; 2]

1. *Cole S. T.* Remake of Life story. — 1995.

2. *Cole S. T.* The cool works of Sam Ted Cole. Vol. 7. Part 2. Life story, or Biographical sketches. — London : Rout and Paul, 1983.

3. *Zar Z. C.*, *Lau A. D.* Algebra // Theory. — 2099. — Vol. 12. — P. 423–491.

15-7-

biblatex-iso690 *Michal Hoftich* Styles that conform to the latest revision of the international standard ISO 690:2010.

Citation systems: various

Styles: `iso-alphabetic`, `iso-authortitle`, `iso-authoryear`, `iso-numeric`

Citation style: `iso-fullcite`

Style samples:

See [ZL99] and Cole [Col83, pp. 4–8] and again Cole [Col83; Col95]

[Col83]   COLE, Sam Ted. *The cool works of Sam Ted Cole*. Vol. 7.2, Life story, or Biographical sketches. Ed. by COB, Kate; ENG, Jon; BATE, W. Jack. London: Rout and Paul, 1983. Boll Series, no. 75.

[Col95]   COLE, Sam Ted. *Remake of Life story*. 1995.

[ZL99]   ZAR, Zoë C.; LAU, Adam D. Algebra. *Theory*. 2099, vol. 12, pp. 423–491. Available from arXiv: `math/9901.4711v13`.

`iso-alphabetic`

15-7-39

See Zar et al., "Algebra" and Cole (*Life story*, pp. 4–8) and again Cole (*Life story*) and Cole (*Remake*)

COLE, Sam Ted. *The cool works of Sam Ted Cole*. Vol. 7.2, Life story, or Biographical sketches. Ed. by COB, Kate; ENG, Jon; BATE, W. Jack. London: Rout and Paul, 1983. Boll Series, no. 75.

COLE, Sam Ted. *Remake of Life story*. 1995.

ZAR, Zoë C.; LAU, Adam D. Algebra. *Theory*. 2099, vol. 12, pp. 423–491. Available from arXiv: `math/9901.4711v13`.

`iso-authortitle`

15-7-40

See Zar et al., 2099 and Cole (1983, pp. 4–8) and again Cole (1983) and Cole (1995)

COLE, Sam Ted, 1983. *The cool works of Sam Ted Cole*. Vol. 7.2, Life story, or Biographical sketches. Ed. by COB, Kate; ENG, Jon; BATE, W. Jack. London: Rout and Paul. Boll Series, no. 75.

COLE, Sam Ted, 1995. *Remake of Life story*.

ZAR, Zoë C.; LAU, Adam D., 2099. Algebra. *Theory*. Vol. 12, pp. 423–491. Available from arXiv: `math/9901.4711v13`.

`iso-authoryear`

15-7-41

See [1] and Cole [2, pp. 4–8] and again Cole [2, 3]

1.   ZAR, Zoë C.; LAU, Adam D. Algebra. *Theory*. 2099, vol. 12, pp. 423–491. Available from arXiv: `math/9901.4711v13`.

2.   COLE, Sam Ted. *The cool works of Sam Ted Cole*. Vol. 7.2, Life story, or Biographical sketches. Ed. by COB, Kate; ENG, Jon; BATE, W. Jack. London: Rout and Paul, 1983. Boll Series, no. 75.

3.   COLE, Sam Ted. *Remake of Life story*. 1995.

`iso-numeric`

15-7-42

biblatex-mla *James Clawson*   Style implementing the specifications of the MLA handbook. The style recommends using `\autocite` as standard citation command.

Citation system: author-title

Styles: `mla, mla-strict, mla7`

Citation style: `mla-footnotes`

Style sample:

See Zar and Lau and Cole, *Life story* 4-8 and again *Life story*; *Remake*

Cole, Sam Ted. *Life story, or Biographical sketches*. Edited by Kate Cob et al., Rout and Paul, 1983. Boll Series 75. Vol. 7 of *The cool works of Sam Ted Cole*.
———. *Remake of Life story*. 1995.
Zar, Zoë C., and Adam D. Lau. "Algebra". *Theory*, vol. 12, 2099, pp. 423–91. *arXiv*, arxiv.org/abs/math/9901.4711v13.

`mla`

15-7-43

The style `mla` makes a few text transformation, e.g., shortening URLs or turning

"University Press" into "UP". These can be prevented by using `mla-strict` instead, Otherwise the two styles are identical. The style `mla7` implements an earlier version of the style guide, but right now it is not working correctly (maybe it does again by the time you have this book in your hands).

biblatex-oxref   *Alex Ball*   Implementations of the *2014 New Hart's Rules* and the *2002 Oxford Guide to Style.*

Citation systems: various

Styles: `oxalph`, `oxnotes`, `oxnum`, `oxyear`

Citation style: `oxnotes-ibid`, `oxnotes-inote`, `oxnotes-note`, `oxnotes-trad1`, `oxnotes-trad2`, `oxnotes-trad3`

Style samples:

oxalph

See [ZL99] and Cole [Col83: 4–8] and again Cole [Col83; Col95]

[Col83]   Cole, S. T. [Anon, M.] (1983), *Life story, or Biographical sketches*, ed. K. Cob, J. Eng, and W. J. Bate, [vol. vii.2 of *The cool works of Sam Ted Cole*] (Boll Series, 75; London: Rout and Paul).

[Col95]   Cole, S. T. (1995), *Remake of Life story*.

[ZL99]   Zar, Z. C. [Foo, P.] and Lau, A. D. [Zack, M.] (2099), "Algebra", version 3, *Theory*, 12: 423–91, arXiv: `math/9901.4711v13`.

15-7-4

oxnotes

See Zoë C. Zar [Pam Foo] and Adam D. Lau [Maria Zack], "Algebra", version 3, *Theory*, 12 (2099), 423–91, arXiv: `math/9901.4711v13` and Cole[1] and again Cole[2]

Cole, Sam Ted [Matt Anon], *Life story, or Biographical sketches*, ed. Kate Cob, Jon Eng, and W. Jack Bate, [vol. vii.2 of *The cool works of Sam Ted Cole*] (Boll Series, 75; London: Rout and Paul, 1983).

Cole, Sam Ted, *Remake of Life story* (1995).

---

[1]Sam Ted Cole [Matt Anon], *Life story, or Biographical sketches*, ed. Kate Cob, Jon Eng, and W. Jack Bate, [vol. vii.2 of *The cool works of Sam Ted Cole*] (Boll Series, 75; London: Rout and Paul, 1983), 4–8.

[2]Cole, *Life story*; Sam Ted Cole, *Remake of Life story* (1995).

15-7-4

oxnum

See [3] and Cole [1: 4–8] and again Cole [1; 2]

[1]   Cole, Sam Ted [Matt Anon], *Life story, or Biographical sketches*, ed. Kate Cob, Jon Eng, and W. Jack Bate, [vol. vii.2 of *The cool works of Sam Ted Cole*] (Boll Series, 75; London: Rout and Paul, 1983).

[2]   Cole, Sam Ted, *Remake of Life story* (1995).

[3]   Zar, Zoë C. [Pam Foo] and Lau, Adam D. [Maria Zack], "Algebra", version 3, *Theory*, 12 (2099), 423–91, arXiv: `math/9901.4711v13`.

15-7-

oxyear

See Zar and Lau 2099 and Cole (1983: 4–8) and again Cole (1983; 1995)

Cole, S. T. [Anon, M.] (1983), *Life story, or Biographical sketches*, ed. K. Cob, J. Eng, and W. J. Bate, [vol. vii.2 of *The cool works of Sam Ted Cole*] (Boll Series, 75; London: Rout and Paul).

Cole, S. T. (1995), *Remake of Life story*.

Zar, Z. C. [Foo, P.] and Lau, A. D. [Zack, M.] (2099), "Algebra", version 3, *Theory*, 12: 423–91, arXiv: `math/9901.4711v13`.

15-7-

biblatex-sbl *David Purton* Style implementing the recommendations of the Society of Biblical Literature (SBL) Handbook of Style.

Citation system: verbose   *Style:* `sbl`

Style sample:

See Zoë C. Zar and Adam D. Lau, "Algebra," version 3, *Theory* 12 (2099): 423–91, arXiv: math/9901 .4711v13 and Cole[1] and again Cole[2]

Cole, Sam Ted. *Life story, or Biographical sketches*. Vol. 7, part 2 of *The cool works of Sam Ted Cole*. Edited by Kate Cob, Jon Eng, and W. Jack Bate. Boll Series 75. London: Rout and Paul, 1983.

————. *Remake of Life story*. 1995.

Zar, Zoë C., and Adam D. Lau. "Algebra." Version 3. *Theory* 12 (2099): 423–91. arXiv: math/9901 .4711v13.

1. Sam Ted Cole, *Life story, or Biographical sketches*, in *The cool works of Sam Ted Cole*, ed. Kate Cob, Jon Eng, and W. Jack Bate, Boll Series 75 (London: Rout and Paul, 1983), 7.2:4–8.
2. Cole, *Life story*; Cole, *Remake of Life story* (1995).

sbl

15-7-48

biblatex-vancouver *Agnibho Mondal* Vancouver reference style.

Citation system: numeric   *Style:* `vancouver`

Style sample:

See [1] and Cole [2, pp. 4–8] and again Cole [2, 3]

1. Zar ZC and Lau AD. Algebra. Version 3. Theory. 2099; 12:423–91. arXiv: `math/9901.4711v13`
2. Cole ST. *The cool works of Sam Ted Cole*. Vol. 7.2: Life story, or Biographical sketches. Ed. by Cob K, Eng J, and Bate WJ. Boll Series 75. London: Rout and Paul, 1983
3. Cole ST. Remake of Life story. 1995

vancouver

15-7-49

windycity *Brian Chase* Style following *The Chicago Manual of Style* recommendations; see biblatex-chicago for an alternative.

Citation system: author-title (by default verbose)   *Style:* `windycity`

Style sample:

See Zoë C. Zar and Adam D. Lau, "Algebra," *Theory* 12 (2099): 423–491, 3, arXiv: `math/9901. 4711v13`. and Sam Ted Cole, *Life story, or Biographical sketches*, ed. Kate Cob, Jon Eng, and W. Jack Bate, Boll Series, vol. 7, no. 75, pt. 2, of *The cool works of Sam Ted Cole* (London: Rout and Paul, 1983), 4-8 and again Cole, *Life story*; Sam Ted Cole, *Remake of Life story*, 1995

Cole, Sam Ted. *Life story, or Biographical sketches*. Edited by Kate Cob, Jon Eng, and W. Jack Bate. Boll Series, vol. 7, no. 75, pt. 2, of *The cool works of Sam Ted Cole*. London: Rout and Paul, 1983.

————. *Remake of Life story*. 1995.

Zar, Zoë C., and Adam D. Lau. "Algebra." *Theory* 12 (2099): 423–491. 3. arXiv: `math/9901.4711v13`.

windycity

15-7-50

15.7.6 Implementations of university and institution styles

The set of bundles in this category available on CTAN is certainly not representative: many more are likely to be available directly from institution websites or from your friendly fellow student. The styles normally implement a rather inflexible layout without many options, often handle only a subset of all entry types, and sometimes support only a subset of the citation command's syntax. For example, some numeric styles in the current section do not properly handle page numbers in the optional argument, making it impossible to distinguish them from an entry reference.

However, they are less complex than style guide implementations, and so adapting them is usually possible. Typically, they load one of the generic styles and modify it, so they can also serve as examples on how to write a new style. Before using such a style, it is a good idea to check how old it is, if it is still maintained, and whether the rules it implements are actually still promoted by the institution.

archaeologie   *Lukas C. Bossert*   Style for the German Archaeological Institute (DAI).

Citation system: author-date   *Style:*   `archaeologie`

Style sample:

> See Zar – Lau 2099 and Cole (1983, 4–8) and again Cole (1983) and Cole (1995)
>
> Cole 1983   S. T. Cole, The cool works of Sam Ted Cole VII 2. Life story, or Biographical sketches, Boll Series 75, ed. by K. Cob – J. Eng – W. J. Bate (London 1983)
>
> Cole 1995   S. T. Cole, Remake of Life story (1995)
>
> Zar – Lau 2099
> > Z. C. Zar – A. D. Lau, Algebra, Theory 12, 2099, 423–491, arXiv: `math/9901.4711v13`

archaeologie

15-7-5

biblatex-archaeology   *Ingram Braun*   Styles for Romano-Germanic Commission and the Department of Prehistory of the German Archaeological Institute (Deutsches Archäologisches Institut).

Citation systems: various

Styles: `aefkw, afwl, amit, archa, authoryear-archaeology, authoryear-comp-archaeology, authoryear-ibid-archaeology, authoryear-icomp-archaeology, dguf, dguf-alt, dguf-apa, eaz, eaz-alt, foe, jb-halle, jb-kreis-neuss, karl, kunde, maja, mpk, mpkoeaw, niedersachsen, nnu, numeric-comp-archaeology, offa, rgk-inline, rgk-numeric, rgk-verbose, rgzm-inline, rgzm-numeric, rgzm-verbose, ufg-muenster-inline, ufg-muenster-numeric, ufg-muenster-verbose, verbose-archaeology, verbose-ibid-archaeology, verbose-trad2note-archaeology, volkskunde, zaak, zaes`

Style samples:

> See Z. C. Zar/A. D. Lau, Algebra, Version 3, *Theory* 12, 2099, 423–491 and Cole[1] and again Cole[2]
>
> Cole, S. T., *The cool works of Sam Ted Cole* VII.2: *Life story, or Biographical sketches* (1983). ders., *Remake of Life story* (1995).

aefkw

> [1] S. T. Cole, *The cool works of Sam Ted Cole* VII.2: *Life story, or Biographical sketches* (1983), 4–8.
> [2] Cole, Life story – S. T. Cole, *Remake of Life story* (1995).

15-7-

See ZAR/LAU 2099 and COLE (1983, 4–8) and again COLE (1983; 1995)

COLE 1983
Sam Ted Cole, The cool works of Sam Ted Cole 7.2: Life story, or Biographical sketches. Ed. by Kate Cob, Jon Eng and W. Jack Bate. Boll Series 75 (London 1983).

COLE 1995
Sam Ted Cole, Remake of Life story ([n. p.] 1995).

afwl

ZAR/LAU 2099
Zoë C. Zar/Adam D. Lau, Algebra. Version 3. Theory 12, 2099, 423–491.

15-7-53

See Zar/Lau 2099 and Cole (1983, 4–8) and again Cole (1983) and Cole (1995)

Colc 1983
    S. T. Cole, The cool works of Sam Ted Cole 7.2: Life story, or Biographical sketches. Ed. by K. Cob, J. Eng and W. J. Bate. Boll Series 75 (London 1983).
Cole 1995
    S. T. Cole, Remake of Life story (n. p. 1995).
Zar/Lau 2099
    Z. C. Zar/A. D. Lau, Algebra. Version 3. Theory 12, 2099, 423–491.

amit

15-7-54

See ZAR, LAU 2099 and COLE (1983, 4–8) and again COLE (1983) and COLE (1995)

COLE 1983
S. T. COLE, The cool works of Sam Ted Cole 7.2: Life story, or Biographical sketches. Ed. by K. COB, J. ENG and W. J. BATE, Boll Series 75 London 1983.
COLE 1995
S. T. COLE, Remake of Life story n. p. 1995.
ZAR, LAU 2099
Z. C. ZAR, A. D. LAU, Algebra, version 3, Theory 12, 2099, 423–491.

archa

15-7-55

See ZAR, LAU 2099 and COLE (1983, 4–8) and again COLE (1983) and COLE (1995)

COLE, Sam Ted: The cool works of Sam Ted Cole 7.2: Life story, or Biographical sketches. Ed. by Kate Cob, Jon Eng and W. Jack Bate. Boll Series 75 (London 1983).

COLE, Sam Ted: Remake of Life story (n. p. 1995).

dguf

ZAR, Zoë C., LAU, Adam D.: Algebra. Version 3. Theory 12, 2099, 423–491.

15-7-56

See ZAR et al. 2099 and COLE (1983, 4–8) and again COLE (1983) and COLE (1995)

COLE, S. T. (1983) The cool works of Sam Ted Cole 7.2: Life story, or Biographical sketches. Ed. by K. Cob et al. *Boll Series 75*. London 1983.

COLE, S. T. (1995) Remake of Life story. n. p. 1995.

dguf-alt

ZAR, Z. C. & A. D. LAU (2099) Algebra. Version 3. *Theory 12, 2099, 423–491.*

15-7-57

dguf-apa

See ZAR & LAU, 2099 and COLE (1983, 4–8) and again COLE (1983) and COLE (1995)

Cole, S. T. (1983). *The cool works of Sam Ted Cole* (7th volume).2: *Life story, or Biographical sketches* (Boll Series 75). London: Rout and Paul.

Cole, S. T. (1995). *Remake of Life story.* n. p.

Zar, Z. C. & Lau, A. D. (2099). Algebra. Version 3. *Theory, 12,* 423–491.

15-7-5

eaz

See Zar/Lau 2099 and Cole (1983, 4–8) and again Cole (1983) and Cole (1995)

Cole 1983: S. T. Cole, The cool works of Sam Ted Cole 7.2: Life story, or Biographical sketches. Ed. by K. Cob, J. Eng and W. J. Bate. Boll Series 75. London: Rout and Paul 1983.

Cole 1995: idem, Remake of Life story. n. p. 1995.

Zar/Lau 2099: Z. C. Zar/A. D. Lau, Algebra. Version 3. Theory 12, 2099, 423–491.

15-7-5

eaz-alt

See ZAR, LAU 2099 and COLE (1983, 4–8) and again COLE (1983; 1995)

COLE, S. T. 1983: The cool works of Sam Ted Cole 7.2: Life story, or Biographical sketches. Ed. by K. COB, J. ENG and W. J. BATE. (Boll Series 75.) London.
   – 1995: Remake of Life story. n. p.
ZAR, Z. C., & A. D. LAU 2099: Algebra. Version 3. In: Theory 12, 423–491.

15-7-6

foe

See ZAR and LAU 2099 and COLE (1983, 4–8) and again COLE (1983) and COLE (1995)

COLE 1983: SAM TED COLE, *The cool works of Sam Ted Cole* 7.2: *Life story, or Biographical sketches.* Ed. by KATE COB, JON ENG and W. JACK BATE, Boll Series 75, London 1983.

COLE 1995: SAM TED COLE, Remake of Life story, n. p. 1995.

ZAR and LAU 2099: ZOË C. ZAR and ADAM D. LAU, *Algebra,* version 3, Theory 12, 2099, 423–491.

15-7-6

jb-halle

See Zar/Lau 2099 and Cole (1983, 4–8) and again Cole (1983) and Cole (1995)

Cole 1983
   S. T. Cole, The cool works of Sam Ted Cole 7.2: Life story, or Biographical sketches. Ed. by K. Cob, J. Eng and W. J. Bate. Boll Series 75 (London 1983).
Cole 1995
   S. T. Cole, Remake of Life story ([n. p.] 1995).
Zar/Lau 2099
   Z. C. Zar/A. D. Lau, Algebra. Version 3. Theory 12, 2099, 423–491.

15-7-

jb-kreis-neuss

See Zar, Zoë C./ Lau, Adam D.: Algebra, version 3, in: Theory 12 (2099), pp. 423–491 and Cole[1] and again Cole[2]

Cole, Sam Ted: The cool works of Sam Ted Cole volume 7.2: Life story, or Biographical sketches ed. by Kate Cob, Jon Eng and W. Jack Bate, (= Boll Series, volume 75), London 1983.
– Remake of Life story, n. p. 1995.
Zar, Zoë C./ Adam D. Lau: Algebra, version 3, in: Theory 12 (2099), pp. 423–491.

---

[1]Cole, Sam Ted: The cool works of Sam Ted Cole volume 7.2: Life story, or Biographical sketches ed. by Kate Cob, Jon Eng and W. Jack Bate, (= Boll Series, volume 75), London 1983, pp. 4–8.
[2]Cole, Life story; Cole, Sam Ted: Remake of Life story, n. p. 1995.

15-7

See Zoë C. Zar and Adam D. Lau: Algebra, version 3, in: *Theory* vol. 12, 2099, pp. 423–491 and Cole[1] and again Cole[2]

Cole, Sam Ted: *The cool works of Sam Ted Cole* vol. 7.2: *Life story, or Biographical sketches*, ed. by Kate Cob, Jon Eng and W. Jack Bate. London 1983.
Cole, Sam Ted: *Remake of Life story*. n. p. 1995.
Zar, Zoë C. and Lau, Adam D.: Algebra, version 3, in: *Theory* vol. 12, 2099, pp. 423–491.

karl

---

[1]Sam Ted Cole: *The cool works of Sam Ted Cole* vol. 7.2: *Life story, or Biographical sketches*, ed. by Kate Cob et al. London 1983, pp. 4–8.
[2]Cole (see n. 1); Sam Ted Cole: *Remake of Life story*. n. p. 1995.

15-7-64

See Zar/Lau 2099 and Cole (1983, 4–8) and again Cole (1983; 1995)

Cole, Sam Ted 1983: The cool works of Sam Ted Cole 7.2: Life story, or Biographical sketches. Ed. by Kate Cob, Jon Eng and W. Jack Bate. Boll Series 75. London 1983.
Cole, Sam Ted 1995: Remake of Life story. n. p. 1995.
Zar, Zoë C./Lau, Adam D. 2099: Algebra. Version 3. Theory 12, 2099, 423–491.

kunde

15-7-65

See Z. C. Zar / A. D. Lau, Algebra, version 3, in: Theory 12 (2099), 423–491 and Cole[1] and again Cole[2]

Cole, S. T., The cool works of Sam Ted Cole 7.2: Life story, or Biographical sketches, Boll Series 75, London 1983.
Cole, S. T., Remake of Life story n. p. 1995.
Zar, Z. C. / Lau, A. D., Algebra, version 3, in: Theory 12 (2099), 423–491.

maja

---

[1]S. T. Cole, The cool works of Sam Ted Cole 7.2: Life story, or Biographical sketches, Boll Series 75, London 1983, 4–8.
[2]Cole, Life story – S. T. Cole, Remake of Life story n. p. 1995.

15-7-66

See Zar, Lau 2099 and Cole (1983, 4–8) and again Cole (1983. – Idem 1995)

Cole 1983
S. T. Cole, The cool works of Sam Ted Cole 7.2: Life story, or Biographical sketches. Ed. by K. Cob, J. Eng and W. J. Bate, Boll Series 75, London 1983.
Cole 1995
S. T. Cole, Remake of Life story, n. p. 1995.
Zar, Lau 2099
Z. C. Zar, A. D. Lau, Algebra, version 3, Theory 12, 2099, 423–491.

mpk

15-7-67

See Zar, Lau 2099 and Cole (1983, 4–8) and again Cole (1983) and Cole (1995)

Cole 1983
S. T. Cole, The cool works of Sam Ted Cole 7.2: Life story, or Biographical sketches. Ed. by K. Cob, J. Eng and W. J. Bate. Boll Series 75. London 1983.

Cole 1995
S. T. Cole, Remake of Life story. n. p. 1995.

mpkoeaw

Zar, Lau 2099
Z. C. Zar, A. D. Lau, Algebra, version 3. Theory 12/2099, 423–491.

15-7-68

niedersachsen

See Zar, Lau 2099 and Cole (1983, 4–8) and again Cole (1983; 1995)

Cole, S. T. 1983: The cool works of Sam Ted Cole 7.2: Life story, or Biographical sketches. Ed. by K. Cob, J. Eng and W. J. Bate. Boll Series 75. London 1983.

Cole, S. T. 1995: Remake of Life story. n. p. 1995.

Zar, Z. C., Lau, A. D. 2099: Algebra. Version 3. Theory 12, 2099, 423–491.

15-7-6

nnu

See Zar/Lau 2099 and Cole (1983, 4–8) and again Cole (1983; 1995)

Cole 1983
    S. T. Cole, The cool works of Sam Ted Cole 7.2: Life story, or Biographical sketches. Ed. by K. Cob, J. Eng and W. J. Bate. Boll Series 75 (London 1983).
Cole 1995
    S. T. Cole, Remake of Life story ([n. p.] 1995).
Zar/Lau 2099
    Z. C. Zar/A. D. Lau, Algebra. Version 3. Theory 12, 2099, 423–491.

15-7-7

offa

See Zar/Lau 2099 and Cole (1983, 4–8) and again Cole (1983; 1995)

Cole 1983: S. T. Cole, The cool works of Sam Ted Cole 7.2: Life story, or Biographical sketches. Ed. by K. Cob, J. Eng and W. J. Bate. Boll Series 75 (London 1983).
Cole 1995: S. T. Cole, Remake of Life story (n.p. 1995).
Zar/Lau 2099: Z. C. Zar/A. D. Lau, Algebra. Version 3. Theory 12, 2099, 423–491.

15-7-7

rgk-inline

See Zar / Lau 2099 and Cole (1983, 4–8) and again Cole (1983) and Cole (1995)

Cole 1983
    S. T. Cole, The cool works of Sam Ted Cole 7.2: Life story, or Biographical sketches. Ed. by K. Cob, J. Eng and W. J. Bate. Boll Series 75 (London 1983).

Cole 1995
    idem, Remake of Life story ([n. p.] 1995).

Zar / Lau 2099
    Z. C. Zar / A. D. Lau, Algebra. Version 3. Theory 12, 2099, 423–491.

15-7-

rgk-numeric

See [3] and Cole [1, 4–8] and again Cole [1, 2]

[1]   S. T. Cole, The cool works of Sam Ted Cole 7.2: Life story, or Biographical sketches. Ed. by K. Cob, J. Eng and W. J. Bate. Boll Series 75 (London 1983).

[2]   S. T. Cole, Remake of Life story ([n. p.] 1995).

[3]   Z. C. Zar / A. D. Lau, Algebra. Version 3. Theory 12, 2099, 423–491.

15-7-

rgk-verbose

See Z. C. Zar / A. D. Lau, Algebra. Version 3. Theory 12, 2099, 423–491 and Cole[1] and again Cole[2]

S. T. Cole, The cool works of Sam Ted Cole 7.2: Life story, or Biographical sketches. Ed. by K. Cob, J. Eng and W. J. Bate. Boll Series 75 (London 1983).
– Remake of Life story ([n. p.] 1995).
Z. C. Zar / A. D. Lau, Algebra. Version 3. Theory 12, 2099, 423–491.

---

[1]S. T. Cole, The cool works of Sam Ted Cole 7.2: Life story, or Biographical sketches. Ed. by K. Cob et al. Boll Series 75 (London 1983) 4–8.
[2]Cole (see n. 1); S. T. Cole, Remake of Life story ([n. p.] 1995).

15-7

See Zar/ Lau 2099 and Cole (1983, 4–8) and again Cole (1983; 1995)

Cole 1983: S. T. Cole, The cool works of Sam Ted Cole 7.2: Life story, or Biographical sketches. Ed. by K. Cob, J. Eng and W. J. Bate. Boll Series 75 (London 1983).

1995: S. T. Cole, Remake of Life story (n. p. 1995).

rgzm-inline

15-7-75 | Zar/ Lau 2099: Z. C. Zar/ A. D. Lau, Algebra. Version 3. Theory 12, 2099, 423–491.

See [3] and COLE [1, 4–8] and again COLE [1, 2]

[1]   S. T. Cole, The cool works of Sam Ted Cole 7.2: Life story, or Biographical sketches. Ed. by K. Cob, J. Eng and W. J. Bate. Boll Series 75 (London 1983).

[2]   S. T. Cole, Remake of Life story (n. p. 1995).

rgzm-numeric

15-7-76 | [3]   Z. C. Zar/ A. D. Lau, Algebra. Version 3. Theory 12, 2099, 423–491.

See Z. C. Zar/ A. D. Lau, Algebra. Version 3. Theory 12, 2099, 423–491 and Cole[1] and again Cole[2]

S. T. Cole, The cool works of Sam Ted Cole 7.2: Life story, or Biographical sketches. Ed. by K. Cob, J. Eng and W. J. Bate. Boll Series 75 (London 1983).
S. T. Cole, Remake of Life story (n. p. 1995).
Z. C. Zar/ A. D. Lau, Algebra. Version 3. Theory 12, 2099, 423–491.

rgzm-verbose

---

[1]S. T. Cole, The cool works of Sam Ted Cole 7.2: Life story, or Biographical sketches. Ed. by K. Cob, J. Eng and W. J. Bate. Boll Series 75 (London 1983), 4–8.

15-7-77 | [2]Cole, Life story; S. T. Cole, Remake of Life story (n. p. 1995).

See ZAR/LAU 2099 and COLE (1983, 4–8) and again COLE (1983) and COLE (1995)

S. T. Cole, The cool works of Sam Ted Cole 7.2: Life story, or Biographical sketches. Ed. by K. Cob, J. Eng and W. J. Bate. Boll Series 75 (London 1983).

S. T. Cole, Remake of Life story ([n. p.] 1995).

ufg-muenster-inline

15-7-78 | Z. C. Zar/A. D. Lau, Algebra. Version 3. Theory 12, 2099, pp. 423–491.

See [3] and COLE [1, 4–8] and again COLE [1, 2]

[1]   S. T. Cole, The cool works of Sam Ted Cole 7.2: Life story, or Biographical sketches. Ed. by K. Cob, J. Eng and W. J. Bate. Boll Series 75 (London 1983).

[2]   S. T. Cole, Remake of Life story ([n. p.] 1995).

ufg-muenster-numeric

15-7-79 | [3]   Z. C. Zar/A. D. Lau, Algebra. Version 3. Theory 12, 2099, pp. 423–491.

See Z. C. Zar/A. D. Lau, Algebra. Version 3. Theory 12, 2099, pp. 423–491 and COLE[1] and again COLE[2]

S. T. Cole, The cool works of Sam Ted Cole 7.2: Life story, or Biographical sketches. Ed. by K. Cob, J. Eng and W. J. Bate. Boll Series 75 (London 1983).
– Remake of Life story ([n. p.] 1995).
Z. C. Zar/A. D. Lau, Algebra. Version 3. Theory 12, 2099, pp. 423–491.

ufg-muenster-verbose

---

[1]S. T. Cole, The cool works of Sam Ted Cole 7.2: Life story, or Biographical sketches. Ed. by K. Cob et al. Boll Series 75 (London 1983), 4–8.

15-7-80 | [2]COLE see n. 1; S. T. Cole, Remake of Life story ([n. p.] 1995).

volkskunde

See Zar, Lau 2099 and Cole (1983: 4–8) and again Cole (1983) and Cole (1995)

Cole, Sam Ted (1983): The cool works of Sam Ted Cole 7.2: Life story, or Biographical sketches ed. by Kate Cob et al. (Boll Series, 75). London.
idem (1995): Remake of Life story. n. p.
Zar, Zoë C. et al. (2099): Algebra. Version 3. In: Theory 12, pp. 423–491.

15-7-8?

zaak

See Zar/ Lau 2099 and Cole (1983, pp. 4–8) and again Cole (1983) and Cole (1995)

Cole, Sam Ted
1983   The cool works of Sam Ted Cole vol. 7.2: Life story, or Biographical sketches (=Boll Series 75). London.

Cole, Sam Ted
1995   Remake of Life story. n. p.

Zar, Zoë C./ Lau, Adam D.
2099   Algebra. Version 3. In: Theory 12: pp. 423–491. n. p.

15-7-8

zaes

See Zar, Lau 2099 and Cole (1983, 4–8) and again Cole (1983) and Cole (1995)

Cole, S. T., 1983, The cool works of Sam Ted Cole 7.2: Life story, or Biographical sketches, ed. by K. Cob, J. Eng and W. J. Bate, Boll Series 75.
Cole, S. T., 1995, Remake of Life story, n. p.
Zar, Z. C., Lau, A. D., 2099, Algebra, version 3, Theory 12, 423–491.

15-7-8

biblatex-arthistory-bonn   *Lukas C. Bossert, Thorsten Kemper*   Style for the Kunsthistorisches Institut der Universität Bonn.

Citation system: author-date   *Style:* `arthistory-bonn`

Style sample:

arthistory-bonn

See Zar / Lau (2099) and Cole (1983, 4-8) and again Cole (1983) and Cole (1995)

Cole 1983	Cole, Sam Ted: The cool works of Sam Ted Cole, vol. 7.2: Life story, or Biographical sketches, ed. by Kate Cob / Jon Eng / W. Jack Bate (Boll Series, 75), London 1983
Cole 1995	Cole, Sam Ted: Remake of Life story, 1995
Zar / Lau (2099)	Zar, Zoë C. / Lau, Adam D.: Algebra, version 3, in: Theory 12 (2099), 423–491, arXiv: math/9901.4711v13

15-7-

biblatex-bath   *Alex Ball*   Style for the University of Bath Library.

Citation system: author-date   *Style:* `bath`

Style sample:

bath

See Zar and Lau, 2099 and Cole (1983, pp.4–8) and again Cole (1983; 1995)

Cole, S.T., 1983. *The cool works of Sam Ted Cole*. Vol. 7.2: *Life story, or Biographical sketches*. Ed. by K. Cob, J. Eng, and W.J. Bate, Boll series, 75. London: Rout and Paul.

Cole, S.T., 1995. *Remake of life story*.

Zar, Z.C. and Lau, A.D., 2099. Algebra (v.3). *Theory*, 12, pp.423–491. arXiv: `math/9901.4711v13`.

15-7-

biblatex-bwl *Herbert Voß* Style for the Business Administration Department of the Free University of Berlin.

Citation system: author-date *Style:* `bwl-FU`

Style sample:

See Zar and Lau (2099) and Cole (1983:pp. 4–8) and again Cole (1983) and Cole (1995)

Cole, Sam Ted (1983). *The cool works of Sam Ted Cole*. Vol. 7.2: *Life story, or Biographical sketches*. Ed. by Kate Cob, Jon Eng, and W. Jack Bate. Boll Series 75. Rout and Paul: London.

Cole, Sam Ted (1995). *Remake of Life story*.

Zar, Zoë C. and Adam D. Lau (2099). "Algebra". Version 3. In: *Theory* 12, pp. 423–491. arXiv: `math/9901.4711v13`.

15-7-86   bwl-FU

biblatex-enc *Jean-Baptiste Camps* Style for historical and philological works at the École nationale des chartes (Paris). The command `\autocite` cannot be used.

Citation system: verbose *Style:* `enc`

Style sample:

See Zᴀʀ (Zoë C.) and Lᴀᴜ (Adam D.), "Algebra", *Theory*, 12 (2099), pp. 423–491, arXiv: `math/9901.4711v13` and Sam Ted Cole, *The cool works of Sam Ted Cole*, vol. 7.2: *Life story, or Biographical sketches*, ed. by Kate Cob, Jon Eng, and W. Jack Bate, London, 1983 (Boll Series, 75), 4-8 and again ibid.; idem, *Remake of Life story*, 1995

Cᴏʟᴇ (Sam Ted), *The cool works of Sam Ted Cole*, vol. 7.2: *Life story, or Biographical sketches*, ed. by Kate Cob, Jon Eng, and W. Jack Bate, London, 1983 (Boll Series, 75).

– *Remake of Life story*, 1995.

Zᴀʀ (Zoë C.) and Lᴀᴜ (Adam D.), "Algebra", *Theory*, 12 (2099), pp. 423–491, arXiv: `math/9901.4711v13`.

15-7-87   enc

biblatex-musuos *Tobias Weh* Style for the Institut für Musik und Musikwissenschaft der Universität Osnabrück.

Citation system: verbose *Style:* `musuos`

Style sample:

See Zoë C. Zar and Adam D. Lau: *Algebra*. Version 3. In: *Theory* 12 (2099), pp. 423–491. arXiv: `math/9901.4711v13` and Cole[1] and again Cole[2]

Cole, Sam Ted: *The cool works of Sam Ted Cole*. Vol. 7.2: *Life story, or Biographical sketches*. Ed. by Kate Cob, Jon Eng, and W. Jack Bate. Boll Series 75. London: Rout and Paul, 1983.

Cole, Sam Ted: *Remake of Life story*. 1995.

musuos

[1] Sam Ted Cole: *The cool works of Sam Ted Cole*. Vol. 7.2: *Life story, or Biographical sketches*. Ed. by Kate Cob, Jon Eng, and W. Jack Bate. Boll Series 75. London: Rout and Paul, 1983, pp. 4–8.

15-7-88   [2] Ibid.; Sam Ted Cole: *Remake of Life story*. 1995.

biblatex-nottsclassic *Lukas C. Bossert* Style for the University of Nottingham.

Citation system: author-date *Style:* `nottsclassic`

Style sample:

nottsclassic

> See Zar and Lau (2099) and Cole (1983) 4-8 and again Cole (1983); Cole (1995)
>
> Cole, S. T. (1983), *The cool works of Sam Ted Cole*, vol. 7.2: *Life story, or Biographical sketches* (Cob, K., Eng, J., and Bate, W. J., eds.), Boll Series 75, London: Rout and Paul.
> ———— (1995), *Remake of Life story*.
> Zar, Z. C. and Lau, A. D. (2099), 'Algebra', version 3, *Theory* 12: 423–491, arXiv: math/9901.4711v13.

15-7-8

biblatex-socialscienceshuberlin *Lukas C. Bossert* Style for social sciences at the Humboldt-Universität zu Berlin. It has an option to color the author names.

Citation system: author-date   *Style:* `socialscienceshuberlin`

Style sample:

socialsciences-
huberlin

> See Zar and Lau 2099 and Cole (1983: 4–8) and again Cole (1983) and Cole (1995)
>
> Cole, Sam Ted 1983: *The cool works of Sam Ted Cole*. Vol. 7.2: *Life story, or Biographical sketches*. Ed. by Kate Cob, Jon Eng, and W. Jack Bate. Boll Series 75. London: Rout and Paul.
> – 1995: *Remake of Life story*.
> Zar, Zoë C. and Lau, Adam D. 2099: Algebra. Version 3. In: *Theory* 12, 423–491. arXiv: math/9901. 4711v13.

15-7-9

thuthesis *Tsinghua University TUNA Association, Ruini Xue* Styles for the Tsinghua University. They are part of a template and should be used together with the `thuthesis.cls` class.

Citation systems: various

Styles: `thuthesis-author-year`, `thuthesis-bachelor`, `thuthesis-numeric`

Citation style: `thuthesis-inline`

Style samples:

thuthesis-
author-year

> See (Zar et al., 2099) and Cole (1983, pp. 4-8) and again Cole (1983, 1995)
>
> Cole S T, 1983. The cool works of Sam Ted Cole. Vol. 7.2: Life story, or Biographical sketches: vol. 7 [M]. Ed. by Cob K, Eng J, Bate W J. London: Rout and Paul.
> Cole S T, 1995. Remake of Life story[M].
> Zar Z C, Lau A D, 2099. Algebra[J]. Theory, 12: 423-491. arXiv: math/9901.4711v13.

15-7-9

The two numeric styles in this bundle handle page numbers in a way that they cannot be distinguished from citation references and are therefore best avoided if the styles are used. Here is one example:

thuthesis-
bachelor

> See[1] and Cole [2, 4-8] and again Cole [2-3]
>
> [1]   ZAR Z C, LAU A D. Algebra[J]. Theory, 2099, 12: 423-491. arXiv: math/9901.4711v13.
> [2]   COLE S T. The cool works of Sam Ted Cole. Vol. 7.2: Life story, or Biographical sketches: vol. 7[M]. Ed. by COB K, ENG J, BATE W J. London: Rout and Paul, 1983.
> [3]   COLE S T. Remake of Life story[M]. 1995.

15-7-

uni-wtal-ger *Carsten Ace Dahlmann* Style for literary studies in the Faculty of Humanities at the Bergische Universität Wuppertal.

Citation system: author-title *Style:* `uni-wtal-ger`

Style sample:

See Zoë C. Zar / Adam D. Lau: "Algebra". Version 3. In: *Theory* 12 (2099). Pp. 423–491 and Cole (Kate Cob et al. [eds.]: *The cool works of Sam Ted Cole*. Vol. 7.2: *Life story, or Biographical sketches* [Boll Series 75]. London 1983, pp. 4–8) and again Cole (Life story); Cole (*Remake of Life story*. 1995)

Cole, Sam Ted: *The cool works of Sam Ted Cole*. Vol. 7.2: *Life story, or Biographical sketches*. Ed. by Kate Cob et al. (Boll Series 75). London 1983.

– *Remake of Life story*. 1995.

15-7-93   Zar, Zoë C. / Lau, Adam D.: "Algebra". Version 3. In: *Theory* 12 (2099). Pp. 423–491.

uni-wtal-ger

uni-wtal-lin *Carsten Ace Dahlmann* Style for the Institute of Linguistics at the Bergische Universität Wuppertal.

Citation system: author-date *Style:* `uni-wtal-lin`

Style sample:

See Zar/Lau 2099 and Cole (1983: 4-8) and again Cole (1983) & Cole (1995)

Cole, Sam Ted (1983). *The cool works of Sam Ted Cole*. Vol. 7.2: *Life story, or Biographical sketches*. Kate Cob/Jon Eng/W. Jack Bate (eds.). London: Rout and Paul. (= Boll Series 75)

Cole, Sam Ted (1995). *Remake of Life story*.

uni-wtal-lin

15-7-94   Zar, Zoë C./Adam D. Lau (2009). Algebra. Version 3. *Theory* 12, 423–491. arXiv: `math / 9901 . 4711v13`.

univie-ling *Jürgen Spitzmüller* Style for (Applied) Linguistics at the University of Vienna.

Citation system: author-date *Style:* `univie-ling`

Style sample:

See Zar & Lau 2099 and Cole (1983: 4–8) and again Cole (1983, 1995)

Cole, Sam Ted. 1983. *The cool works of Sam Ted Cole*. Vol. 7.2: *Life story, or Biographical sketches*. Kate Cob, Jon Eng & W. Jack Bate (eds.) (Boll Series 75). London: Rout and Paul.

Cole, Sam Ted. 1995. *Remake of life story*. N. L.

univie-ling

15-7-95   Zar, Zoë C. & Adam D. Lau. 2099. Algebra. Version 3. *Theory* 12. 423–491.

15.7.7 Implementations of journal styles

In most cases the bundle description just shows the name of the journal supported by the style(s). The remarks made for the "university" type are applicable here too.

acmart *Boris Veytsman* Association for Computing Machinery. The two styles in the bundle should be used in conjunction with the acmart class.

Citation systems: author-date, numeric

Styles: `acmauthoryear, acmnumeric`

Style samples:

acmauthoryear

See [Zar and Lau 2099] and Cole [1983, pp. 4–8] and again Cole [1983, 1995]

Sam Ted Cole. 1983. *The cool works of Sam Ted Cole*. Vol. 7.2: *Life story, or Biographical sketches*. Ed. by Kate Cob, Jon Eng, and W. Jack Bate. Boll Series 75. Rout and Paul, London.

Sam Ted Cole. 1995. *Remake of Life story*.

Zoë C. Zar and Adam D. Lau. 2099. "Algebra." Version 3. *Theory*, 12, 423–491. arXiv: `math/9901.4` `711v13`.

> 15-7-96

acmnumeric

See [3] and Cole [1, pp. 4–8] and again Cole [1, 2]

[1] Sam Ted Cole. 1983. *The cool works of Sam Ted Cole*. Vol. 7.2: *Life story, or Biographical sketches*. Kate Cob, Jon Eng, and W. Jack Bate, (Eds.) Number 75 in *Boll Series*. Rout and Paul, London.

[2] Sam Ted Cole. 1995. *Remake of Life story*.

[3] Zoë C. Zar and Adam D. Lau. 2099. Algebra. Version 3. *Theory*, 12, 423–491. arXiv: `math/990` `1.4711v13`.

> 15-7-97

biblatex-ajc2020unofficial *Nikolai Avdeev* Australasian Journal of Combinatorics.

Citation system: numeric *Style:* `ajc2020unofficial`

Style sample:

ajc2020unofficial

See [3] and Cole [1, pp. 4–8] and again Cole [1, 2]

[1] S. T. Cole, *The cool works of Sam Ted Cole*, vol. 7.2: Life story, or Biographical sketches, ed. by K. Cob, J. Eng, and W. J. Bate, Boll Series **75**, London: Rout and Paul, 1983.

[2] S. T. Cole, Remake of Life story, 1995.

[3] Z. C. Zar and A. D. Lau, Algebra, version 3, *Theory* 12 (2099), 423–491, arXiv: `math/9901.` `4711v13`.

> 15-7-9

biblatex-chem *Joseph Wright* A set of implementations of chemistry-related styles. The bundle comprises styles based on the conventions of the Royal Society of Chemistry, American Chemical Society, and Angewandte Chemie. It therefore covers styles of various common chemistry journals.

Citation system: numeric

Styles: `chem-acs, chem-angew, chem-biochem, chem-rsc`

Style samples:

chem-acs

See [1] and Cole [2, pp 4–8] and again Cole [2, 3]

(1) Zar, Z. C.; Lau, A. D., version 3 *Theory* **2099**, *12*, 423–491.

(2) Cole, S. T. *The cool works of Sam Ted Cole, Life story, or Biographical sketches*; Cob, K., Eng, J., Bate, W. J., Eds.; Boll Series 75, Vol. 7; Rout and Paul: London, 1983.

(3) Cole, S. T., *Remake of Life story*, 1995.

> 15-7-9

See [1] and Cole [2, pp. 4–8] and again Cole [2, 3]

[1]   Z. C. Zar, A. D. Lau, version 3, *Theory 2099*, *12*, 423–491.

[2]   S. T. Cole, *The cool works of Sam Ted Cole*, *Life story, or Biographical sketches*, (Eds.: K. Cob, J. Eng, W. J. Bate), Rout and Paul, London, **1983**.

[3]   S. T. Cole, *Remake of Life story*, **1995**.

15-7-100

chem-angew

See (*1*) and Cole (*2, pp 4–8*) and again Cole (*2, 3*)

(*1*)   Zar, Z. C., and Lau, A. D. (2099). Algebra. version 3 *Theory 12*, 423–491.

(*2*)   Cole, S. T. *The cool works of Sam Ted Cole*, *Life story, or Biographical sketches*; Cob, K., Eng, J., and Bate, W. J., Eds.; Boll Series 75, Vol. 7; Rout and Paul: London, 1983.

(*3*)   Cole, S. T., *Remake of Life story*, 1995.

15-7-101

chem-biochem

See [1] and Cole [2, pp. 4–8] and again Cole [2, 3]

(1)   Z. C. Zar and A. D. Lau, version 3, *Theory*, 2099, **12**, 423–491.

(2)   S. T. Cole, *The cool works of Sam Ted Cole*, *Life story, or Biographical sketches*, ed. K. Cob, J. Eng and W. J. Bate, Rout and Paul, London, 1983, vol. 7.

(3)   S. T. Cole, *Remake of Life story*, 1995.

15-7-102

chem-rsc

biblatex-ieee   *Joseph Wright*   IEEE (Institute of Electrical and Electronics Engineers).

Citation systems: numeric, alphabetic

Styles: `ieee`, `ieee-alphabetic`

Style samples:

See [1] and Cole [2, pp. 4–8] and again Cole [2], [3]

[1]   Z. C. Zar and A. D. Lau, "Algebra," version 3, *Theory*, vol. 12, pp. 423–491, 2099. arXiv: `math/9901.4711v13`.

[2]   S. T. Cole, *The cool works of Sam Ted Cole*, *Life story, or Biographical sketches* (Boll Series 75), K. Cob, J. Eng, and W. J. Bate, Eds. London: Rout and Paul, 1983, vol. 7.2.

[3]   S. T. Cole, *Remake of Life story*. 1995.

15-7-103

ieee

See [ZL99] and Cole [Col83, pp. 4–8] and again Cole [Col83; Col95]

[Col83]   S. T. Cole, *The cool works of Sam Ted Cole*, *Life story, or Biographical sketches* (Boll Series 75), K. Cob, J. Eng, and W. J. Bate, Eds. London: Rout and Paul, 1983, vol. 7.2.

[Col95]   S. T. Cole, *Remake of Life story*. 1995.

[ZL99]   Z. C. Zar and A. D. Lau, "Algebra," version 3, *Theory*, vol. 12, pp. 423–491, 2099. arXiv: `math/9901.4711v13`

15-7-104

ieee-alphabetic

biblatex-ijsra   *Lukas C. Bossert*   International Journal of Student Research in Archaeology.

Citation system: author-date   *Style:*   `ijsra`

457

Style sample:

ijsra

See Zar and Lau, 2099 and Cole (1983:4-8) and again Cole (1983) and Cole (1995)

Cole, Sam Ted (1983): *The cool works of Sam Ted Cole*. Vol. 7.2: *Life story, or Biographical sketches*. Ed. by Cob, Kate, Eng, Jon, and Bate, W. Jack. Boll Series 75. London: Rout and Paul.
– (1995): *Remake of Life story*.
Zar, Zoë C. and Lau, Adam D. (2099): Algebra. Version 3. *Theory* 12: 423–491. arXiv: `math/9901.4711v13`.

`15-7-10`

biblatex-lncs   *Merlin Göttlinger*   Springer Lecture Notes in Computer Science (LNCS).

Citation system: numeric   *Style:* `lncs`

Style sample:

lncs

See [3] and Cole [1, pp. 4–8] and again Cole [1, 2]

1. Cole, S.T.: Life story, or Biographical sketches. Rout and Paul, London (1983)
2. Cole, S.T.: Remake of Life story (1995)
3. Zar, Z.C., and Lau, A.D.: Algebra. Theory 12, 423–491 (2099)

`15-7-10`

biblatex-lni   *Oliver Kopp*   Lecture Notes in Informatics.

Citation system: alphabetic   *Style:* `LNI`

Style sample:

LNI

See [ZL99] and Cole [Co83, pp. 4–8] and again Cole [Co83; Co95]

[Co83]   Cole, S. T.: Life story, or Biographical sketches. Rout and Paul, London, 1983.
[Co95]   Cole, S. T.: Remake of Life story. 1995.
[ZL99]   Zar, Z. C.; Lau, A. D.: Algebra. Version 3, Theory 12/, pp. 423–491, 2099, arXiv: `math/9901.4711v13`.

`15-7-1`

biblatex-nature   *Joseph Wright*   Nature.

Citation system: numeric   *Style:* `nature`

Style sample:

nature

See [1] and Cole [2, pp. 4–8] and again Cole [2, 3]

1. Zar, Z. C. & Lau, A. D. Algebra. Version 3. *Theory* **12,** 423–491. arXiv: `math/9901.4711v13` (2099).
2. Cole, S. T. *The cool works of Sam Ted Cole*. 7.2: *Life story, or Biographical sketches* (eds Cob, K., Eng, J. & Bate, W. J.) *Boll Series* **75** (Rout and Paul, London, 1983).
3. Cole, S. T. *Remake of Life story* (1995).

`15-7-1`

biblatex-nejm   *Dilum Aluthge, Marco Daniel*   New England Journal of Medicine (NEJM).

Citation system: numeric   *Style:* `nejm`

Style sample:

See 1 and Cole [2, pp. 4–8] and again Cole [2, 3]

1. Zar ZC and Lau AD. Algebra. Version 3. Theory 2099;12:423–91.
2. Cole ST. *The cool works of Sam Ted Cole*. Vol. 7.2: Life story, or Biographical sketches. Ed. by Cob K, Eng J, and Bate WJ. Boll Series 75. London: Rout and Paul, 1983.
3. Cole ST. Remake of Life story. 1995.

nejm

15-7-109

biblatex-phys *Joseph Wright* American Institute of Physics, American Physical Society.

Citation system: numeric *Style:* `phys`

Style sample:

See [1] and Cole [2, pp. 4–8] and again Cole [2, 3]

[1]Z. C. Zar and A. D. Lau, "Algebra", version 3, Theory **12**, 423–491 (2099).

[2]S. T. Cole, *The cool works of Sam Ted Cole*, Vol. 7.2: *Life story, or Biographical sketches*, edited by K. Cob, J. Eng, and W. J. Bate, Boll Series 75 (Rout and Paul, London, 1983).

[3]S. T. Cole, *Remake of life story* (1995).

phys

15-7-110

biblatex-science *Joseph Wright* Science.

Citation system: numeric *Style:* `science`

Style sample:

See (*1*) and Cole (*2*, pp. 4–8) and again Cole (*2, 3*)

1. Z. C. Zar, A. D. Lau, version 3, *Theory* **12**, 423–491, arXiv: `math/9901.4711v13` (2099).
2. S. T. Cole, *The cool works of Sam Ted Cole*, vol. 7.2: *Life story, or Biographical sketches*, ed. by K. Cob, J. Eng, W. J. Bate (Rout and Paul, London, 1983), vol. 7.
3. S. T. Cole, *Remake of Life story*.

science

15-7-111

biblatex-spbasic *Herbert Voß* Springer's journals.

Citation system: author-date *Style:* `biblatex-spbasic`

Style sample:

See Zar, Lau 2099 and Cole (1983, 4–8) and again Cole (1983) and Cole (1995)

Cole ST (1983) *The cool works of Sam Ted Cole* vol. 7.2: *Life story, or Biographical sketches*. ed. by K Cob, J Eng, WJ Bate Boll Series 75 Rout and Paul, London
– (1995) *Remake of Life story*.
Zar ZC, Lau AD (2009) Algebra. version 3 *Theory* 12: 423–491 arXiv: `math/9901.4711v13`

biblatex-spbasic

15-7-112

biblatex-unified *Kai von Fintel* Implementation of the Unified Stylesheet for Linguistics Journals, used by Semantics and Pragmatics. The style requires the package hyperref.

Citation system: author-date *Style:* `unified`

Style sample:

> See Zar & Lau 2099 and Cole (1983: pp. 4–8) and again Cole (1983, 1995)
>
> Cole, Sam Ted. 1983. *The cool works of Sam Ted Cole*. Vol. 7.2: *Life story, or Biographical sketches*. Kate Cob, Jon Eng & W. Jack Bate (eds.) (Boll Series 75). London: Rout and Paul.
> Cole, Sam Ted. 1995. *Remake of life story*.
> Zar, Zoë C. & Adam D. Lau. 2099. Algebra. Version 3. *Theory* 12. 423–491.

unified

15-7-11

dtk   *Rolf Niepraschk, Herbert Voß*   Die TeXnische Komödie — the communications of the German TeX Users Group DANTE e.V.

Citation system: **numeric**   *Style:* `dtk`

Style sample:

> See [3] and Cole [1, pp. 4–8] and again Cole [1, 2]
>
> [1]   Sam Ted Cole: *The cool works of Sam Ted Cole*, Life story, or Biographical sketches, (Eds.: Kate Cob, Jon Eng, W. Jack Bate), Boll Series 75, Rout and Paul, London, 1983.
>
> [2]   — Remake of Life story, 1995.
>
> [3]   Zoë C. Zar, Adam D. Lau: "Algebra", version 3, *Theory*, *12* (2099), 423–491, arXiv: `math/ 9901.4711v13`.

dtk

15-7-1

emisa   *Martin Sievers, Stefan Strecker*   EMISA (Enterprise Modelling and Information Systems Architectures).

Citation system: **author-date**   *Style:* `emisa`

Style sample:

> See Zar. and Lau 2099 and Cole (1983, pp. 4–8) and again Cole (1983, 1995)
>
> Cole S. T. (1983) The cool works of Sam Ted Cole Vol. 7.2: Life story, or Biographical sketches Cob K., Eng J., Bate W. J. (eds.). Boll Series 75. Rout and Paul, London
>
> — (1995) Remake of Life story
>
> Zar Z. C., Lau A. D. (2099) Algebra Version 3. In: Theory 12, pp. 423–491 arXiv: math/9901.4711v13

emisa

15-7-1

historische-zeitschrift   *Dominik Waßenhoven*   Historische Zeitschrift, a German historical journal.

Citation system: **verbose**   *Style:* `historische-zeitschrift`

Style sample:

> See *Zoë C. Zar/Adam D. Lau*, Algebra, in: Theory 12, 2099. 423–491 and *Sam Ted Cole*, The cool works of Sam Ted Cole. Vol. 7.2: Life story, or Biographical sketches. Ed. by Kate Cob/Jon Eng/ W. Jack Bate. (Boll Series, vol. 75.) London 1983, 4-8 and again *Sam Ted Cole*, The cool works of Sam Ted Cole. Vol. 7.2: Life story, or Biographical sketches. Ed. by Kate Cob/Jon Eng/W. Jack Bate. (Boll Series, vol. 75.) London 1983; *Sam Ted Cole*, Remake of Life story. 1995
>
> *Sam Ted Cole*, The cool works of Sam Ted Cole. Vol. 7.2: Life story, or Biographical sketches. Ed. by Kate Cob/Jon Eng/W. Jack Bate. (Boll Series, vol. 75.) London 1983.
>
> – Remake of Life story. 1995.
>
> *Zoë C. Zar/Adam D. Lau*, Algebra, in: Theory 12, 2099. 423–491.

historische-
zeitschrift

15-7-

langsci   *Sebastian Nordhoff*   Language Science Press.

Citation system: author-date   *Style:* `langsci-unified`

Style sample:

> See Zar & Lau 2099 and Cole (1983: 4-8) and again Cole (1983, 1995)
>
> Cole, Sam Ted. 1983. *The cool works of Sam Ted Cole.* Vol. 7.2: *Life story, or Biographical sketches.* Kate Cob, Jon Eng & W. Jack Bate (eds.) (Boll Series 75). London: Rout and Paul.
> Cole, Sam Ted. 1995. *Remake of life story.*
> Zar, Zoë C. & Adam D. Lau. 2099. Algebra. Version 3. *Theory* 12. 423–491.

langsci-unified

15-7-117

nwejm   *Denis Bitouzé*   North-Western European Journal of Mathematics.

Citation system: numeric   *Style:* `nwejm`

Style sample:

> See Zar and Lau 2099 and Cole (1983, pp. 4–8) and again Cole (1983, 1995)
>
> Cole, S. T. (1983). *The cool works of Sam Ted Cole.* **7.2**: *Life story, or Biographical sketches.* Ed. by K. Cob, J. Eng, and W. J. Bate. Boll Series 75. London: Rout and Paul.
> – (1995). *Remake of Life story.*
> Zar, Z. C. and A. D. Lau (2099). "Algebra". Version 3. *Theory* **12**, pp. 423–491. arXiv: `math/9901.4711v13`.

nwejm

15-7-118

15.7.8 Styles that extend the data model

The following bundles provide styles that add new field or entry types. To give at least a small impression of their purpose, the samples show special entries, often based on examples found in the documentation of the bundle.

biblatex-bookinother   *Maïeul Rouquette*   The style adds new entry types and fields for books edited in other types, such as `bookinarticle`. It offers only a bib style that is based on the standard `verbose` and should be used together with a verbose or author-title citation style.

Citation system: —

Bib style: `bookinother`

Style sample:

> See Van Deun[1] and Cole[2]
>
> Cole, Sam Ted. *The cool works of Sam Ted Cole.* Vol. 7.2: *Life story, or Biographical sketches.* Ed. by Kate Cob, Jon Eng, and W. Jack Bate. Boll Series 75. London: Rout and Paul, 1983.
> *Mémoire sur le saint apôtre Barnabé.* Ed. by Peter Van Deun. In: Van Deun, Peter. "Un mémoire anonyme sur saint Barnabé (BHG 226e). Édition et traduction". In: *Analecta Bollandiana* 108 (1990), pp. 326–335.
>
> ─────────────
>
> [1]*Mémoire sur le saint apôtre Barnabé.* Ed. by Peter Van Deun. In: Peter Van Deun. "Un mémoire anonyme sur saint Barnabé (BHG 226e). Édition et traduction". In: *Analecta Bollandiana* 108 (1990), pp. 326–335.
> [2]Sam Ted Cole. *The cool works of Sam Ted Cole.* Vol. 7.2: *Life story, or Biographical sketches.* Ed. by Kate Cob, Jon Eng, and W. Jack Bate. Boll Series 75. London: Rout and Paul, 1983.

bookinother

15-7-119

biblatex-claves   *Maïeul Rouquette*   A special style for antic and medieval literature to handle many different texts published with the same title, or the same text published with different titles. It offers only a bib style: the example combines it with an author-title citation style.

Citation system: —

Bib style: `claves`

Style sample:

claves

See Bonnet (*Acta Barnabae*).

Acta Barnabae (BHG 225; CANT 285). In: *Acta Apostolorum Apocrypha*. Ed. by Maximilien Bonnet. Vol. 2.2. Leipzig: Hermann Mendelsohn, 1903, pp. 292–302.

15-7-1?

biblatex-cv   *Daniel E. Shub*   The package implements entry types useful for an (American) academic curriculum vitae. It requires a special loading: check the documentation for details.

Citation system: —   *Style:* `biblatex-cv`

Style sample:

cv

2019–2021 ($100,000,000, ongoing, PI): Funding Agency, Research Grant (123-456-abc). *A Grant Title.*
2010–2019 (£1,000,000, completed, CI): A Different Funding Agency, Fellowship (abc-def-123). *A Different Grant Title.*

By Smith, Alice and Bob Jones (Jan. 1, 2019). "An Internal Talk Abstract." In: *Journal of Talk Abstracts.* [Talk presented by Alice Smith and Bob Jones].

15-7-1

biblatex-manuscripts-philology   *Maïeul Rouquette*   The style adds a new entry type `manuscript` to manage manuscripts in classical philology. It offers only a bibliography style that is based on `verbose`. The sample shows an example manuscript, the used citation style is `verbose`, and the citation command is `\textcite`.

Citation system: —

Bib styles: `manuscripts, manuscripts-noautoshorthand`

Style samples:

manuscripts

See[1] and again[2]

Cambridge: University Library, *Additional greek manuscript 4489*. Perch. viii-ix^e c., 16 ff. (1 col.): ff. 11r–11v (inf. lay.).

---

[1]Cambridge: University Library, *Additional greek manuscript 4489*. Perch. viii-ix^e c., 16 ff. (1 col.): ff. 11r–11v (inf. lay.) (henceforth cited as C).
[2]C.

15-7-

See[1] and again[2]

Cambridge: University Library, *Additional greek manuscript 4489*. Perch. VIII-IXe c., 16 ff. (1 col.): ff. 11r–11v (inf. lay.).

---

[1]Cambridge: University Library, *Additional greek manuscript 4489*. Perch. VIII-IXe c., 16 ff. (1 col.): ff. 11r–11v (inf. lay.).

[2]Cambridge: University Library, *Additional greek manuscript 4489*.

15-7-123

manuscripts-noautoshorthand

biblatex-morenames   *Maïeul Rouquette*   The style adds new fields of "name" type, for example, more editor fields for books that are part of a collection. It is based on a verbose style.

Citation system: —

Bib style: `morenames`

Style sample:

See Maraval[1]

Maraval, Pierre. "La réception de Chalcédoine dans l'empire d'Orient". In: *Histoire du christianisme. des origines à nos jours.* Ed. by Charles Pietri et al. Vol. 3: *Les Églises d'Orient et d'Occident.* Ed. by Luce Pietri. 20 vols. Paris: Desclée, 1998, pp. 107–145.

morenames

---

[1]Pierre Maraval. "La réception de Chalcédoine dans l'empire d'Orient". In: *Histoire du christianisme. des origines à nos jours.* Ed. by Charles Pietri et al. Vol. 3: *Les Églises d'Orient et d'Occident.* Ed. by Luce Pietri. 20 vols. Paris: Desclée, 1998, pp. 107–145.

15-7-124

biblatex-realauthor   *Maïeul Rouquette*   The style adds a new field `realauthor`.

Citation system: —

Bib style: `realauthor`

Style sample:

See Zoë C. Zar and Adam D. Lau [= Pam Foo][= and Maria Zack]. "Algebra". Version 3. In: *Theory* 12 (2099), pp. 423–491. arXiv: `math/9901.4711v13` and Cole[1] and again Cole[2]

Cole, Sam Ted [= Matt Anon]. *The cool works of Sam Ted Cole.* Vol. 7.2: *Life story, or Biographical sketches.* Ed. by Kate Cob, Jon Eng, and W. Jack Bate. Boll Series 75. London: Rout and Paul, 1983.
– *Remake of Life story.* 1995.

Zar, Zoë C. and Adam D. Lau [= Pam Foo][= and Maria Zack]. "Algebra". Version 3. In: *Theory* 12 (2099), pp. 423–491. arXiv: `math/9901.4711v13`.

realauthor

---

[1]Sam Ted Cole [= Matt Anon]. *The cool works of Sam Ted Cole.* Vol. 7.2: *Life story, or Biographical sketches.* Ed. by Kate Cob, Jon Eng, and W. Jack Bate. Boll Series 75. London: Rout and Paul, 1983, pp. 4–8.

[2]Cole, *Life story*; Sam Ted Cole. *Remake of Life story.* 1995.

15-7-125

biblatex-software   *Roberto Di Cosmo*   The package implements software entry types in the form of a bibliography style extension. It requires a special loading: check the documentation for details.

Citation system: —

Bib style: `software`

Style sample:

<table>
<tr><td>software</td><td>

Delebecque et al. 1994

[SW Rel.] Delebecque, François et al., *Scilab* version 1.1, Jan. 1994. Inria. LIC: Scilab license. HAL: ⟨`hal-02090402v1`⟩, URL: `https://www.scilab.org/`, VCS: `https://github.com/scilab /scilab`, SWHID: ⟨`swh:1:dir:1ba0b67b5d0c8f10961d878d91ae9d6e499d746a;`⟩.

</td><td>15-7-12</td></tr>
</table>

biblatex-subseries   *Maïeul Rouquette*   Style that can handle book series with subseries. It offers only a bibliography style that is based on a verbose style.

Citation system: —

Bib style: `subseries`

Style sample:

<table>
<tr><td>subseries</td><td>

See *Encomiastica from the Pierpont Morgan Library*[1] and Cole[2]

Cole, Sam Ted. *The cool works of Sam Ted Cole*. Vol. 7.2: *Life story, or Biographical sketches*. Ed. by Kate Cob, Jon Eng, and W. Jack Bate. Boll Series 75. London: Rout and Paul, 1983.
Encomiastica from the Pierpont Morgan Library. Corpus Scriptorum Christianorum Orientalium 545 — Scriptores Coptici 48.

---

[1]*Encomiastica from the Pierpont Morgan Library*. Corpus Scriptorum Christianorum Orientalium 545 — Scriptores Coptici 48.
[2]Sam Ted Cole. *The cool works of Sam Ted Cole*. Vol. 7.2: *Life story, or Biographical sketches*. Ed. by Kate Cob, Jon Eng, and W. Jack Bate. Boll Series 75. London: Rout and Paul, 1983.

</td><td>15-7-1:</td></tr>
</table>

15.7.9 Styles not fitting in the other categories

The following bundles offer styles made for a specific field, such as philosophy, law, or film studies. Their complexity varies: some, like oscola, are quite complex and should be used unchanged; others can be configured, if necessary.

biblatex-dw   *Dominik Waßenhoven*   Styles for citations in the humanities.

Citation systems: author-title, verbose

Styles: `authortitle-dw, footnote-dw`

Style samples:

<table>
<tr><td>authortitle-dw</td><td>

See Zar/Lau: Algebra and Cole (Life story, pp. 4–8) and again Cole (Life story); Cole (Remake)

Cole, Sam Ted: The cool works of Sam Ted Cole, vol. 7.2: Life story, or Biographical sketches, ed. by Kate Cob, Jon Eng, and W. Jack Bate (Boll Series 75), London 1983.
Idem: Remake of Life story, 1995.
Zar, Zoë C. and Adam D. Lau: Algebra, version 3, in: Theory 12 (2099), pp. 423–491.

</td><td>15-7-1</td></tr>
</table>

See[1] and Cole[2] and again Cole/Cole[3]

Cole, Sam Ted: The cool works of Sam Ted Cole, vol. 7.2: Life story, or Biographical sketches, ed. by Kate Cob, Jon Eng, and W. Jack Bate (Boll Series 75), London 1983.
Idem: Remake of Life story, 1995.
Zar, Zoë C. and Adam D. Lau: Algebra, version 3, in: Theory 12 (2009), pp. 423–491.

<hr>

[1]Zoë C. Zar/Adam D. Lau: Algebra, version 3, in: Theory 12 (2009), pp. 423–491.
[2]Sam Ted Cole: The cool works of Sam Ted Cole, vol. 7.2: Life story, or Biographical sketches, ed. by Kate Cob/Jon Eng/W. Jack Bate (Boll Series 75), London 1983, pp. 4–8.
[3]Idem: The cool works of Sam Ted Cole, vol. 7.2: Life story, or Biographical sketches, ed. by Kate Cob/Jon Eng/W. Jack Bate (Boll Series 75), London 1983; idem: Remake of Life story, 1995.

footnote-dw

15-7-129

biblatex-fiwi *Simon Spiegel* Styles for citations in German Humanities, especially film studies.

Citation system: author-date

Styles: `fiwi, fiwi2`

Style samples:

See Zar/Lau 2099 and Cole (1983: 4-8) and again Cole (1983), Cole (1995)

Cole, Sam Ted: *The cool works of Sam Ted Cole*. Vol. 7.2: *Life story, or Biographical sketches*. Ed. by Kate Cob, Jon Eng and W. Jack Bate. London 1983.
Cole, Sam Ted: *Remake of Life story*. 1995.
Zar, Zoë C./Lau, Adam D.: "Algebra". In: *Theory*, vol. 12, 2099, 423–491. arXiv: `math / 9901 . 4711v13`.

fiwi

15-7-130

See Zar/Lau 2099 and Cole (1983: 4-8) and again Cole (1983), Cole (1995)

Cole, Sam Ted (1983): *The cool works of Sam Ted Cole*. Vol. 7.2: *Life story, or Biographical sketches*. Ed. by Kate Cob, Jon Eng and W. Jack Bate. London.
Cole, Sam Ted (1995): *Remake of Life story*.
Zar, Zoë C./Lau, Adam D. (2099): "Algebra". In: *Theory*, vol. 12, 423–491. arXiv: `math / 9901 . 4711v13`.

fiwi2

15-7-131

biblatex-german-legal *Dominik Brodowski* Styles for German legal texts.

Citation system: author-title   *Style:* `german-legal-book`

Style sample:

See *Zar/Lau*, Theory 2099, 423 and *Cole* (Life story, pp. 4–8) and again *Cole* (Life story) and *Cole* (Remake)

Cole, Sam Ted, The cool works of Sam Ted Cole, vol. 7.2: Life story, or Biographical sketches Cob, Kate / Eng, Jon / Bate, W. Jack (eds.), Boll Series 75, London 1983.
– Remake of Life story, 1995.
Zar, Zoë C. / Lau, Adam D., Algebra, version 3, Theory 12 (2099), 423–491, arXiv: `math / 9901 . 4711v13`.

german-legal-book

15-7-132

465

biblatex-jura2   *Christoph*   Style for German legal texts.

Citation system: author-title   *Style:* jura2

Style sample:

jura2

See *Zar/Lau*, Theory 12 (2099), 423 and *Cole* (Life story, pp. 4–8) and again *Cole* (Life story) and *Cole* (Remake)

Cole, *Sam Ted*: Remake of Life story. 1995.
– *The cool works of Sam Ted Cole*. Vol. 7.2: Life story, or Biographical sketches. Ed. by *Kate Cob/Jon Eng/W. Jack Bate*. Boll Series 75. London 1983.
Zar, Zoë C./Lau, Adam D.: Algebra. Version 3. In: Theory 12 (2099), 423–491. arXiv: `math/9901.4711v13`.

15-7-13

biblatex-juradiss   *Herbert Voß, Tobias Schwan*   Style for a German law thesis.

Citation system: author-title   *Style:* `biblatex-juradiss`

Style sample:

biblatex-juradiss

See *Zar/Lau*, Theory 2099, 423 and *Cole* (Life story, pp. 4–8) and again *Cole* (Life story); *Cole* (Remake)

Cole, *Sam Ted*, The cool works of Sam Ted Cole, vol. 7.2: Life story, or Biographical sketches (Boll Series 75), London 1983, *zitiert als*: *Cole*, Life story.
Idem, Remake of Life story, 1995, *zitiert als*: *Cole*, Remake.
Zar, *Zoë C.* / Lau, *Adam D.*, Algebra, Theory 2099, p. 423–491.

15-7-13

biblatex-philosophy *Ivan Valbusa*   The package provides two author-date styles (`philosophy-classic` and `philosophy-modern`) and a verbose style (`philosophy-verbose`).

Citation systems: author-date, verbose

Styles: `philosophy-classic, philosophy-modern, philosophy-verbose`

Style samples:

philosophy-classic

See Zar and Lau 2099 and Cole (1983, pp. 4-8) and again Cole (1983, 1995)

Cole, Sam Ted (1983), *The cool works of Sam Ted Cole*, vol. 7.2: *Life story, or Biographical sketches*, ed. by Kate Cob, Jon Eng, and W. Jack Bate, Boll Series, 75, Rout and Paul, London.
– (1995), *Remake of Life story*.
Zar, Zoë C. and Adam D. Lau (2099), "Algebra", version 3, *Theory*, 12, pp. 423-491, arXiv: `math/9901.4711v13`.

15-7-1

philosophy-modern

See Zar and Lau 2099 and Cole (1983, pp. 4-8) and again Cole (1983, 1995)

Cole, Sam Ted

1983   *The cool works of Sam Ted Cole*, vol. 7.2: *Life story, or Biographical sketches*, ed. by Kate Cob, Jon Eng, and W. Jack Bate, Boll Series, 75, Rout and Paul, London.

1995   *Remake of Life story*.

Zar, Zoë C. and Adam D. Lau

2099   "Algebra", version 3, *Theory*, 12, pp. 423-491, arXiv: `math/9901.4711v13`.

15-7-1

See Zoë C. Zar and Adam D. Lau, "Algebra", version 3, *Theory*, 12 (2099), pp. 423-491, arXiv: `math/9901.4711v13` and Cole[1] and again Cole[2]

Cole, Sam Ted, *The cool works of Sam Ted Cole*, vol. 7.2: *Life story, or Biographical sketches*, ed. by Kate Cob, Jon Eng, and W. Jack Bate, Boll Series, 75, Rout and Paul, London 1983.
– *Remake of Life story*, 1995.
Zar, Zoë C. and Adam D. Lau, "Algebra", version 3, *Theory*, 12 (2099), pp. 423-491, arXiv: `math/9901.4711v13`.

philosophy-verbose

---

[1] Sam Ted Cole, *The cool works of Sam Ted Cole*, vol. 7.2: *Life story, or Biographical sketches*, ed. by Kate Cob et al., Boll Series, 75, Rout and Paul, London 1983, pp. 4-8.
[2] Cole, *Life story* cit.; Sam Ted Cole, *Remake of Life story*, 1995.

15-7-137

biblatex-publist *Jürgen Spitzmüller* Style for publication lists. It allows omitting or highlighting the author's own name: in the sample this is demonstrated for Lau.

Citation system: numeric   *Style:* `publist`

Style sample:

See [1] and Cole [3, pp. 4–8] and again Cole [3, 2]

[1] Zar, Zoë C. and **Lau, Adam D. 2099**. "Algebra". Version 3. In: *Theory* 12, pp. 423–491. arXiv: `math/9901.4711v13`.
[2] Cole, Sam Ted. **1995**. *Remake of Life story*.
[3] Cole, Sam Ted. **1983**. *The cool works of Sam Ted Cole*. Vol. 7.2: *Life story, or Biographical sketches*. Ed. by Kate Cob, Jon Eng, and W. Jack Bate. Boll Series 75. London: Rout and Paul.

publist

15-7-138

cnltx *Clemens Niederberger* The style is part of a documentation bundle and defines the entry types `package`, `class`, and `bundle` to specify LaTeX packages in bib files.

Citation system: alphabetic   *Style:* `cnltx`

Style sample:

See [ZL99] and Cole [Col83, pp. 4–8] and again Cole [Col83; Col95]

[Col83] Sam Ted Cole. *The cool works of Sam Ted Cole*.
Vol. 7.2: *Life story, or Biographical sketches*.
Ed. by Kate Cob, Jon Eng, and W. Jack Bate. Boll Series 75.
London: Rout and Paul, 1983.

[Col95] Sam Ted Cole. *Remake of Life story*. 1995.

[ZL99] Zoë C. Zar and Adam D. Lau. "Algebra". Version 3. In: *Theory* 12 (2099), pp. 423–491. arXiv: `math/9901.4711v13`.

cnltx

15-7-139

oscola *Paul Stanley* Style implementing the OSCOLA style of legal citation (4th edition).

Citation system: verbose   *Style:* `oscola`

Style sample:

See Zoë C Zar and Adam D Lau, "Algebra" version 3 (2099) 12 Theory 423 and Cole[1] and again Cole[2]; Cole[3]

Cole ST, *The cool works of Sam Ted Cole*, vol 7.2, *Life story, or Biographical sketches* (Cob K, Eng J, and Bate WJ eds, Boll Series 75, Rout and Paul 1983).
– *Remake of Life story* (1995).
Zar ZC and Lau AD, "Algebra" version 3 (2099) 12 Theory 423.

oscola

----

[1] Sam Ted Cole, *The cool works of Sam Ted Cole*, vol 7.2, *Life story, or Biographical sketches* (Kate Cob, Jon Eng, and WJack Bate eds, Boll Series 75, Rout and Paul 1983) 4-8.
[2] n 1.
[3] Sam Ted Cole, *Remake of Life story* (1995).

15-7-14

savetrees   *Scott Pakin*   The goal of the savetrees package is to pack as much text as possible onto each page of a LATEX document.

Citation system: numeric   *Style:* `savetrees`

Style sample:

See [3] and Cole [1, pp. 4–8] and again Cole [1, 2]

[1]   S. T. Cole. *The cool works of Sam Ted Cole*. Vol. 7.2: *Life story, or Biographical sketches*. Ed. by K. Cob, J. Eng, et al. Boll Series 75. London: Rout and Paul, 1983.

savetrees

[2]   S. T. Cole. *Remake of Life story*. 1995.

[3]   Z. C. Zar and A. D. Lau. "Algebra". Version 3. In: *Theory* 12 (2099), pp. 423–491.

15-7-1

Managing Citations

16.1 Introduction

Citations are cross-references to bibliographical information outside the current document, such as to publications containing further information on a subject and source information about used quotations. It is certainly not necessary to back everything by a reference, but background information for controversial statements, acknowledgments of other work, and source information for used material should always be given.

The previous chapter showed numerous ways to compile bibliographies and reference lists. They can be prepared manually, if necessary, but usually they are automatically generated from a database containing bibliographic information. This chapter now introduces the many presentation forms of bibliographical sources, and it reviews different traditions regarding how such sources are referred to in a document.

We start the chapter with a short introduction to the major citation schemes in common use. Armed with this knowledge we then plunge into a detailed discussion of how LaTeX supports the different citation schemes. At the time we wrote the first edition of this book, LaTeX basically supported only the "number-only" system. Nearly three decades later, the situation has changed radically. Today, all major citation schemes are well supported by extension packages.

We end this chapter by discussing packages that can deal with multiple bibliographies in one document. This is not difficult if the reference lists are prepared manually or if biblatex together with biber is used, but it poses some challenges if you want to interact with BibTEX, as well.

16.1.1 Bibliographical reference schemes

There are five common methods of referring to sources: the "number-only", "author-date" (or "author-year"), "author-number", "author-title", and "verbose" systems. The last two of these are often used in books on humanities and jurisdiction; the second appears mainly in science and social science works. The other two are less often used, although the first is quite common within the LATEX world, because it has been actively promoted by Leslie Lamport and originally was the only form of citation supported by LATEX. Outside the LATEX world, a variation of it, called "numeric by first citation", is quite popular as well.

The number-only system In the number-only system, publications are sequentially numbered in the bibliography. Citations in the text refer to these numbers, which are usually surrounded by brackets or parentheses. Sometimes raised numbers are used instead.

One argument against this system — put forward, for example, in *The Chicago Manual of Style* [24] — is that it raises the costs of publication, because a late addition or deletion of a reference may require renumbering and consequently costly (and error-prone) changes to many pages throughout the manuscript. With automatic cross-referencing facilities as provided by LATEX, this argument no longer holds true. In fact, the number-only system is the default system provided with LATEX.

In a slight variation, known as "alpha" style, citations comprise the author's name and the year of the publication. Thus, the bibliographic label and the citation may look like "[Knu86]". This is still fairly compact compared with an author-date or author-title style and has the advantage that one can often deduce the reference from the context.

Numerical by first citation A fairly popular form of the number-only system numbers the publications sequentially by their first citation in the text (and presents them in that order in the bibliography). This is fairly easy to provide with either standard LATEX or biblatex. However, in that case it is important to avoid that references in the table of contents mess up the expected order; see Section 16.2.3 for advice on this.

The author-date system In the author-date system (often referred to as the Harvard system after one of its better known typographical variants), references to sources are also given directly in the text. They show the author's name (or names) and the year of the publication. The full citation is given in a list of references or a bibliography. If the author published more than one work in a given year, that year is suffixed with lowercase letters (e.g., 2001a, 2001b).

There have been many attempts over the years to provide author-date citation support for LATEX. With the natbib package (discussed in Section 16.3.2), the jurabib package (discussed in Section 16.5.1) and the biblatex package (discussed in Section 16.7 and 16.3.3), there are now three very flexible and general solutions available.

It should be possible for a reader to look up a cited reference in the bibliography lists. In all citation schemes that use author or editor names, the bibliography list therefore should normally be sorted alphabetically by these names. This can require special care if some of the names contain accented chars or are written in a non–Latin script; see Section 15.3.3 for some advice. The sorting should follow the rules of the main language of the document. This is easy to achieve with biblatex, because biber contains the necessary Unicode libraries, but with BⁱᵇTₑX it can be necessary to add sort keys to some entries to guide the sorting.

Care must also be taken to get unique citation "labels", which allow identifying the reference without ambiguity. For example, a work by three or more authors is usually referred to by using the name of the first author followed by *et al.* Especially with the author-date system, this may lead to ambiguous citations if different groups of authors with the same main author published in the same year. This problem can be seen in the following example:

Watch out for ambiguous citations

```
\usepackage{chicago} \bibliographystyle{chicago}
Entries with multiple authors can be problematical, e.g., \shortcite{TLC94},
\shortcite{LGC97} and \shortcite{test97} or worse \shortcite{TLC94,LGC97,test97}.

\bibliography{tlc,tlc-ex}
```

Entries with multiple authors can be problematical, e.g., (Goossens et al. 1994), (Goossens et al. 1997) and (Goossens et al. 1997) or worse (Goossens et al. 1994; Goossens et al. 1997; Goossens et al. 1997).

References

Goossens, M., F. Mittelbach, and A. Samarin (1994). *The LATEX Companion.* Tools and Techniques for Computer Typesetting. Reading, MA, USA: Addison-Wesley Longman.

Goossens, M., S. Rahtz, and F. Mittelbach (1997). *The LATEX Graphics Companion: Illustrating Documents with TEX and PostScript.* Tools and Techniques for Computer Typesetting. Reading, MA, USA: Addison-Wesley Longman.

Goossens, M., B. User, J. Doe, et al. (1997). Ambiguous citations. Submitted to the IBM J. Res. Dev.

16-1-1

In the above example the bibliography is produced from the sample BⁱᵇTₑX databases `tlc.bib` and `tlc-ex.bib` that we introduced in the previous chapter in Figure 15.1 on pages 382–383 and Figure 15.2 on page 391. Those databases are also used in most examples throughout this chapter. Above we applied the BⁱᵇTₑX style `chicago` and its accompanying support package to it, a style that aims to implement a bibliography and reference layout as suggested by *The Chicago Manual of Style* [24].

One way to resolve such ambiguous citations is to use more or all author names in such a case, although that approach can lead to lengthy citations and is not feasible if the number of identical authors exceeds a certain limit. Another solution is to append a, b, and so on, to the year, even though the citations are actually for different author groups. This strategy is, for example, advocated in [21]. If the bibliography is compiled manually, as outlined in Section 15.1, this result can be easily achieved.

When using BıBTEX, you have to use a BıBTEX style file that recognizes these cases and provides the right data automatically. For example, the style chicago cannot be used in this case, but all BıBTEX styles produced with custom-bib (see Section 15.7.2) offer this feature:

Entries with multiple authors might be problematical, e.g., Goossens et al. [1997a] and Goossens et al. [1997b] or even Goossens et al. [1997a,b]. But then they might not.

References

M. Goossens, S. Rahtz, and F. Mittelbach. *The LATEX Graphics Companion: Illustrating Documents with TEX and PostScript*. Tools and Techniques for Computer Typesetting. Addison-Wesley Longman, Reading, MA, USA, 1997a. ISBN 0-201-85469-4.

M. Goossens, B. User, J. Doe, et al. Ambiguous citations. Submitted to the IBM J. Res. Dev., 1997b.

```
\usepackage{natbib}
\bibliographystyle
              {abbrvnat}

Entries with multiple
authors might
be problematical,
e.g., \cite{LGC97} and
\cite{test97} or even
\cite{LGC97,test97}.
But then they might not.

\bibliography{tlc,tlc-ex}
```

16-1-2

When using biblatex with biber, the citations are almost[1] always unambiguous from the start. The package adds, if needed, initials, given names, more authors, or an extra year marker. The behavior can be fine-tuned with the options uniquelist, uniquename, maxnames, maxcitenames, and maxbibnames. The settings in the next example force short author lists and automatically append letters to the year if needed. Details on the customization possibilities of the biblatex package are covered in Section 16.7 starting on page 541.

```
\usepackage[style=authoryear,
   uniquelist=false,maxnames=1]{biblatex}
\addbibresource{tlc.bib}
\addbibresource{tlc-ex.bib}
```

Entries with multiple authors might be problematical, e.g., Goossens et al. 1997b and Goossens et al. 1997a or even Goossens et al. 1997b; Goossens et al. 1997a. But then they might not.

```
Entries with multiple authors might be
problematical, e.g., \cite{LGC97} and
\cite{test97} or even \cite{LGC97,test97}.
But then they might not.
```

16-1-3

With just `\usepackage[style=authoryear]{biblatex}` it would have produced the far lengthier result instead:

Entries with multiple authors might be problematical, e.g., Goossens, Rahtz, and Mittelbach 1997 and Goossens, User, Doe, et al. 1997 or even Goossens, Rahtz, and Mittelbach 1997; Goossens, User, Doe, et al. 1997. But then they might not.

16-1-4

---

[1]It can fail if two references have identical authors *and* title and an author-title style is used.

In the author-number system, the references to the sources are given in the form of the author's name (or names) followed by a number, usually in parentheses or brackets, indicating which publication of the author is cited. In the corresponding bibliography all publications are numbered on a per-author (or author group) basis. In the LaTeX world this system is fairly uncommon because it is difficult to produce manually. As far as we know, there is currently no BibTeX support available for it, but for biblatex suitable styles exist in the biblatex-ext bundle; see Section 16.4.2 on page 506.

The author-number system

In the author-title system, the reference to a source is also given directly in the text, either inline or as a footnote, this time using the author or editor names and the title often in the form "Hart, *Hart's Rules*, p. 52". In the context of the publication, if abbreviations for the title are established, the form "Goossens et al., *LGC*" may appear as an alternative. Many variations exist. For instance, the first time a work is cited it might be presented with a long title; later references might then use a shorter form — citing only the author's name and a short title or the year. In the case of repeated citations to the same work in direct succession, you might find *Ibid.* instead of a repeated reference.

The author-title system

An implementation of the author-title system, based on a BibTeX workflow, is provided by the jurabib [12] package discussed Section 16.5.1 on page 507 followed by an overview of the possibilities offered by biblatex in Section 16.5.2 on page 534.

Finally, in the verbose system a full reference is given the first time a work is cited — usually done in a footnote. Later references then use a shorter version. If this style is used, a list of references or a bibliography that contains all cited works in a single place is not strictly necessary and can be omitted. Typically verbose systems use some combination of the author's name and the title for the shorter reference and can be viewed as a variant of the author-title system. It is therefore not surprising that the two packages that support the author-title system (i.e., biblatex and jurabib) handle that format too. The bibentry package also offers some partial support.

The verbose system

Table 16.1 on the following page shows a broad comparison of the features of major citation packages. A check mark means that the package has sufficient support, if in parentheses there is only partial support. In general, biblatex has the most comprehensive coverage.

Comparison of bibliography packages

16.2 The number-only system

As mentioned earlier in this chapter, the number-only system is the default citation method directly supported by standard LaTeX. That is, without loading any additional packages, it is the only method supported by the provided markup commands. We start this section by describing those commands. We then cover the cite package that offers enhanced sorting and formatting of the citation numbers. This is followed by a brief look at the notoccite package that solves a small problem with citations in headings and captions. Then we explain how natbib handles number-only citations and at last present biblatex's approach to the number-only system.

Package features		cite	natbib	jurabib	biblatex
Citation systems	Numeric citations	✓	✓		✓
	Author-date citations		✓	✓	✓
	Author-title citations			✓	✓
	Verbose citations			✓	✓
	Author-number by author				✓[a]
	Author-number by document		✓		✓
Citation commands	References as superscripts	✓	✓		✓
	References as footnotes			✓	✓
	References as endnotes			✓	✓
	Full citation in text		(✓)	✓	✓
	Full citation in text (1st time)			✓	✓
	Full list of authors		✓[b]	✓	✓
	Full list of authors (1st time)		✓[b]	✓	✓
	Forced abbreviated authors list		✓[b]	✓	✓
	Short and long title			✓	✓
	Shorthand/"cited as"			✓	✓
	Support for ibidem, idem			✓	✓
	Support for gender			✓	✓
	Capitalize first letter		✓		✓
	Sort/compress	✓	✓		✓
	Prenote/postnote		✓	✓	✓
	Annotator			✓	✓[a]
Customization	Customize text in citation		✓	✓	✓
	Customize enclosing characters	✓	✓	✓	✓
	Customize punctuation in citation	✓	✓	✓	✓
Other features	Active links with hyperref	✓	✓	✓	✓
	Cross-references			✓	✓
	Index citations		✓	✓	✓
	Customize bibliography			✓	✓
	Backreferences in bibliography		✓	✓	✓
	Language support (babel)			✓	✓
	Locale support when sorting				✓
	Filtered bibliography				✓
	Multiple bibliographies	(✓)[c]	(✓)[c]	(✓)[c]	✓

[a] *Supported through styles from external packages.*   [b] *If the BibTeX style supports it.*
[c] *With external packages, see Section 16.8.*

Table 16.1: Comparison of different bibliographical support packages

16.2.1 Standard LaTeX — Reference by number

Bibliographic citations inside the text of a LaTeX document are produced with the command \cite.

```
\cite[post-note]{key_1, key_2,...}
```

The \cite command associates each key in the list in its mandatory argument with the argument of a \bibitem command from the thebibliography environment described in Section 15.1 to produce the citation reference. As with other LaTeX identifiers, these keys are case-sensitive.

The citation numbers generated are defined by the order in which the keys appear on the \bibitem commands inside the thebibliography environment or, if an optional argument is used with \bibitem, by the data provided in that argument.

The optional parameter *post-note* is an additional note, which is printed together with the text generated by the \cite command as shown in the following example. For comparison we have used an unbreakable space (~) in the first citation and a small space (\,) in the second. Of course, such typographical details should be handled uniformly throughout a publication.

The exact format of the citation in the text depends on the chosen bibliographic style and possible customizations made in the document class or in the preamble.

Color support for LaTeX is described in [2, chap. 9] and the hyperref package in [1, pp. 35–67].

16-2-1

```
\bibliographystyle{plain}
Color support for \LaTeX{} is described in
\cite[chap.~9]{LGC97} and the \texttt{hyperref}
package in \cite[pp.\,35--67]{LWC99}.
```

To save space, examples in this chapter based on BibTeX often omit the bibliography list. They are generated by placing \bibliography{tlc} at the end of the example document when automatically generating the example output for the book. Thus, you should read examples such as 16-2-1 as follows: the result is produced by generating the bibliography with BibTeX, applying the style plain (shown), and using the database tlc.bib (not shown; see Figure 15.1). Thus, the actual document that produced the example contained \newpage\bibliography{tlc} at the end, ending up on a page of its own. Examples using biblatex and biber do not need a bibliography list to show citations, so nothing is omitted in their source display.

A note on BibTeX-based examples in this chapter

```
\nocite{key_1, key_2,...}
```

In conjunction with BibTeX and biblatex, you can use the \nocite variant of the \cite command. Its sole purpose is to write the keys in its argument into the .aux or the .bcf file so that the associated bibliography information appears in the bibliography even if the publication is otherwise not cited (thus, this is useful only if you do not prepare the reference list manually). It can be used as often as necessary. As a special case, \nocite{*} includes all entries of the chosen BibTeX databases in the list of references.

Customizing citation references and the bibliography in standard LATEX

Unfortunately, standard LATEX is not equipped with an easily customizable interface through which you can adjust the formatting of the citation references. Thus, even to just change the default brackets around the numbers into parentheses, we need to redefine the internal LATEX command \@cite.

Even worse, the user-level \cite command uses an internal temporary switch (@tempswa) to indicate whether an optional argument was present. Thus, if we want to handle that optional argument, we need to evaluate the value of that switch. The \@cite command receives two arguments: the list of obtained references and the note (if present). In the following example we typeset (#1 and, if @tempswa is true, follow it by a comma and ␣#2. This is then followed by the closing parenthesis. The \nolinebreak[3] ensures that a break after the comma is taken only reluctantly.

Color support for LATEX is described in (2) and the hyperref package in (1, pp. 35–67).

```
\bibliographystyle{plain}  \usepackage{ifthen}
\makeatletter
\renewcommand\@cite[2]{(({#1\ifthenelse
    {\boolean{@tempswa}}{,\nolinebreak[3] #2}{}}))}
\makeatother
Color support for \LaTeX{} is described in \cite{LGC97} and
the \textttt{hyperref} package in \cite[pp.\,35--67]{LWC99}.
```
16-2-2

The redefinition of \@cite for purposes like the above can be avoided by loading the cite package; see Section 16.2.2.

For the thebibliography environment, which holds the list of the actual references, the situation is unfortunately not much better — the default implementation in the standard document classes offers few customization possibilities. To modify the layout of the labels in front of each publication (e.g., to omit the brackets), you have to change the internal LATEX command \@biblabel.

References

1. D. E. Knuth. *The TEXbook*, volume A of *Computers and Typesetting*. Addison-Wesley, Reading, MA, USA, 1986.

2. D. E. Knuth. Typesetting Concrete Mathematics. *TUGboat*, 10(1):31–36, Apr. 1989.

```
\bibliographystyle{abbrv}
\makeatletter
    \renewcommand\@biblabel[1]{#1.}
\makeatother
\nocite{Knuth-CT-a,Knuth:TB10-1-31}
\bibliography{tlc}
```
16-2-3

Packages that implement a variation of the author-date system (e.g., the apalike, chicago, or natbib package), typically unconditionally redefine \@biblabel to simply swallow its argument and typeset nothing. After all, such a bibliography is used by looking up the author name, so a label is unnecessary. The natbib package is somewhat more careful: if it detects that \@biblabel was changed, then it honors the redefinition.

As mentioned earlier, different blocks of information, such as the authors or the title, are separated inside one \bibitem in the bibliography by \newblock commands, which are also automatically inserted by most BIBTEX styles. Normally, bibliographic entries are typeset together in one paragraph. If, however, you want your bibliography to be "open", with each block starting on a new line with succeeding lines inside a block indented by a length \bibindent (default 1.5 em), then the class option openbib should be specified. This option is supported by all standard classes. The result is shown in the next example; we also redefine \@biblabel to produce raised labels.

References

[1] M. Goossens and S. Rahtz.
The LaTeX Web companion: integrating TEX, HTML, and XML.
Tools and Techniques for Computer Typesetting. Addison-Wesley Longman, Reading, MA, USA, 1999.
With Eitan M. Gurari and Ross Moore and Robert S. Sutor.

[2] D. E. Knuth.
Typesetting Concrete Mathematics.
TUGboat, 10(1):31–36, Apr. 1989.

16-2-4

```
\documentclass[openbib]{article}
\bibliographystyle{abbrv}
\setlength\bibindent{24pt}

\makeatletter
\renewcommand\@biblabel[1]
                {\textsuperscript{#1}}
\makeatother
\nocite{LWC99,Knuth:TB10-1-31}
\bibliography{tlc}
```

Customizing citation references and the bibliography with biblatex

With biblatex such customizations do not require the redefinitions of internal commands because the package provides various powerful interfaces to adapt the output. These are described in more detail in Section 16.7, but for comparison we repeat the adaptions made for standard LaTeX.

The next example uses \DeclareCiteCommand provided by biblatex to redefine the citation command. The \mkbibparens command used in the optional argument replaces \mkbibbrackets used in the default definition and adds parentheses instead of brackets around the citation. Note that with biblatex the page numbers are given as a simple range in the optional argument of the \cite command. biblatex converts the hyphen to an en-dash and adds the "pp." automatically.

```
\usepackage[style=numeric]{biblatex}
\addbibresource{tlc.bib}
\DeclareCiteCommand{\cite}[\mkbibparens]
  {\usebibmacro{prenote}}
  {\usebibmacro{citeindex}\usebibmacro{cite}}
  {\multicitedelim}
  {\usebibmacro{postnote}}
```

Color support for LaTeX is described in (2) and the hyperref package in (1, pp. 35–67).

See also (3, 4).

16-2-5

```
Color support for \LaTeX{} is described in \cite{LGC97}
and the \texttt{hyperref} package in \cite[35-67]{LWC99}.

See also \cite{MR-PQ,Southall}.
```

Such redefinitions of citation commands are always possible, but biblatex styles may also offer additional commands and options to ease such customizations. The next example demonstrates this with the command \DeclareOuterCiteDelims offered by the style `ext-numeric` — a generic, easy-to-customize style from the biblatex-ext package — to switch to parentheses like in Example 16-2-5.

Color support for LaTeX is described in (2) and the hyperref package in (1, pp. 35–67).

See also (3, 4).

```
\usepackage[style=ext-numeric]{biblatex}
\addbibresource{tlc.bib}
\DeclareOuterCiteDelims{cite}{\bibopenparen}{\bibcloseparen}
Color support for \LaTeX{} is described in \cite{LGC97} and
the \textttt{hyperref} package in \cite[35-67]{LWC99}.  \par
See also \cite{MR-PQ,Southall}.
```
16-2-6

To change the label in the bibliography to use only a period as in Example 16-2-3 you can use the `\DeclareFieldFormat` command. The example uses the style `trad-abbrv` from the biblatex-trad bundle — a reimplementation of the standard abbrv style.

References

1. D. E. Knuth. *The TeXbook*, volume A of *Computers and Typesetting*. Addison-Wesley, Reading, MA, USA, 1986, pages ix + 483. ISBN: 0-201-13447-0.

```
\usepackage[style=trad-abbrv]{biblatex}
\addbibresource{tlc.bib}
\DeclareFieldFormat{labelnumberwidth}{#1\adddot}
\nocite{Knuth-CT-a}
\printbibliography
```
16-2-7

The class option `openbib` used in Example 16-2-4 is also honored by `biblatex`; in addition, it offers a package option `block=par` to the same effect.

16.2.2 cite — Enhanced references by number

One shortcoming that becomes readily apparent when you use LaTeX's default method of citing publications is the fact that it faithfully keeps the order of citations as given in the *key-list* argument of the `\cite` command. The following example therefore shows a very strangely ordered list of numbers (the unresolved reference was added deliberately):

Good information about TeX and LaTeX can be found in [2, 1, 3, ?, 4].

```
\bibliographystyle{plain}
Good information about \TeX{} and \LaTeX{} can be found in
\cite{LGC97,LWC99,Knuth-CT-a,Knuth:ct-b,Knuth:TB10-1-31}.
```
16-2-8

For bibliographies produced with BibTeX the situation can be easily improved by simply loading the cite package (by Donald Arseneau), as in the following example:

Good information about TeX and LaTeX can be found in [?,1–4].

```
\usepackage{cite}    \bibliographystyle{plain}
Good information about \TeX{} and \LaTeX{} can be found in
\cite{LGC97,LWC99,Knuth-CT-a,Knuth:ct-b,Knuth:TB10-1-31}.
```
16-2-9

By default, the cite package sorts citation numbers into ascending order, representing three or more consecutive numbers as a number range. Any nonnumeric label is moved to the front (in the above example the "?" generated by the unresolved reference). If sorting is not desired, you can globally prevent it by loading the package with the option `nosort`. Suppressing range compression can be achieved by using the option `nocompress`.

To customize the typeset reference the `cite` package offers a number of commands. For example, `\citeleft` and `\citeright` determine the material placed on the left and right sides of the citation string, respectively. These commands can be used to typeset parentheses instead of brackets as seen in the following example, which should be compared to Example 16-2-2 on page 476. We can also redefine `\citemid`, the separation between citation and optional note, to produce a semicolon and a space.

Customizing the citation layout

Color support for LaTeX is described in (2) and the `hyperref` package in (1; pp. 35–67).

16-2-10

```
\usepackage{cite}      \bibliographystyle{plain}
\renewcommand\citeleft{(} \renewcommand\citeright{)}
\renewcommand\citemid{;\nolinebreak[3] }

Color support for \LaTeX{} is described in \cite{LGC97} and
the \texttt{hyperref} package in \cite[pp.\,35--67]{LWC99}.
```

Another important aspect of citation management is controlling the behavior near the end of a line. Consider the string "see [2–3,7,13]". Besides not allowing any kind of line break within this string, one could allow breaking after the "see", after the commas, or after the en-dash in a range.

Customizing breaks within citations

By default, the `cite` package discourages line breaks before the citation with `\nolinebreak[3]`, discourages line breaks after a comma separating the optional note with `\nolinebreak[2]`, and very strongly discourages line breaks after en-dashes in a range and after commas separating individual citation numbers. You can control the last three cases by redefining `\citemid`, `\citedash`, and `\citepunct`. For example, to prevent breaks after the en-dashes while allowing breaks after commas without much penalty, you could specify

```
\renewcommand\citedash{\mbox{--}\nolinebreak}
\renewcommand\citemid{,\nolinebreak[1] }
\renewcommand\citepunct{,\nolinebreak[1]\hspace{.13em plus .1em minus .1em}}
```

There are several interesting points to note here. All three definitions are responsible not only for controlling any line breaks but also for adding the necessary punctuation: a dash for the range, a comma and a full blank before the optional note, or a comma and a tiny space between individual citations. For instance, if you want no space at all between citations, you can redefine `\citepunct` to contain only a comma. The other important and probably surprising aspect is the `\mbox` surrounding the en dash. This box is absolutely necessary if you want to control LaTeX's ability to break at this point. TeX automatically adds a breakpoint after an explicit hyphen or dash, so without hiding it in a box, the `\nolinebreak` command would never have any effect — the internally added breakpoint would still allow a line break at this point. Finally, the `\hspace` command allows for some stretching or shrinking; if you prefer a fixed space instead, remove the `plus` and `minus` components.

A penalty of `\nolinebreak[3]` that is added before a citation is hardwired in the code. It is, however, inserted only if you have not explicitly specified a penalty in your document. For instance, "see~\cite{..}" is honored, and no break happens between "see" and the citation.

Customizing citation numbers
One more customization command, \citeform, allows you to manipulate the individual reference numbers. By default, it does nothing, so the labels are typeset unchanged. In the following example we colored them. Other kinds of manipulation are possible, too (e.g., adding parentheses as in Example 16-2-12 below).

Color support for LᴬTEX is described in [2] and the hyperref package in [1, pp. 35–67].

```
\usepackage{cite,color}  \bibliographystyle{plain}
\renewcommand\citeform[1]{\textcolor{blue}{#1}}
Color support for \LaTeX{} is described in \cite{LGC97} and
the \textttt{hyperref} package in \cite[pp.\,35--67]{LWC99}.
```
16-2-11

```
\citen{key₁,key₂,...}
```

The package offers an additional command, \citen (its aliases are \citenum and \citeonline), that can be used to get a list of numbers without the surrounding \citeleft and \citeright (e.g., the default brackets). Other formatting is still done. In the next example we surround individual references to citations with parentheses to prove that point, something that admittedly looks a little strange when used together with the default bracketing of the whole citation. Also note how undefined references (i.e., test97) are handled by that command: you get a bold question mark on its own.

```
\usepackage[nospace]{cite}  \bibliographystyle{plain}
\renewcommand\citeform[1]{(#1)}
```
?,(1),(2),(4) but [(3), §5]   `\citen{LGC97,LWC99,test97,vLeunen:92} but \cite[\S5]{Knuth-CT-a}`   16-2-12

Package options

The package offers a number of options to handle standard configuration requests or to influence the package behavior in other ways. Some of them have already been discussed, but here is the full list:

adjust/noadjust   Enables (default) or disables "smart" handling of space before a \cite or \citen command. By default, spaces before such commands are normalized to an interword space. If you write see\cite{..}, a space is inserted automatically.

compress/nocompress   Enables (default) or disables compression of consecutive numbers into ranges.

nobreak   Remove any default breakpoint from the citation reference so that it always appears on a single line, regardless of its length, preventing output such as in Example 16-2-8 on page 478. May result in bad line breaks in which case one needs to manually add line-break possibilities with \linebreak.

nospace Eliminates the spaces after commas in the list of numbers, but retains the space after the comma separating the optional note. The result of this option is shown in Example 16-2-12 on the preceding page. It is not the opposite of the space option!

space A full interword space is used after commas, and breaking at this point is not actively discouraged. The default (option not specified) is to use a small space and to discourage, but allow, breaking.

sort/nosort Enables (default) or prevents sorting of the numbers.

superscript or super Typeset citation references as superscript numbers (like footnotes). When this option is selected, there are a number of further options that can be useful. See the discussions below.

> ref Support option when using superscript numbers as citation references. Typesets Ref: in certain situations.
>
> move/nomove Support option when using superscript numbers as citation references. Moves (default) or does not move punctuation following a reference in front of it.
>
> biblabel Alter the label produced by \bibitem to produce the same output as the reference in the text. Mainly meant to get superscript labels when references use superscripts.

verbose By default, cite warns only once per reference for undefined citations. When this option is specified, the warning is repeated each time an undefined reference is cited.

Citations with superscript numbers

The cite package can also display citation references as superscript numbers if the package is loaded with the option superscript (or super). If the \cite command is used with an optional argument, then the whole list of citations is typeset as though the cite package was loaded without the superscript option.

With the superscript or super option in effect, the customization commands \citeleft, \citeright, and \citemid affect only citations with an optional argument, while \citedash, \citepunct, and \citeform affect all citations. For details of their use, see the discussion on pages 479–480.

```
\usepackage[superscript]{cite}
\bibliographystyle{plain}
\usepackage{color}
\renewcommand\citeform[1]{\textcolor{blue}{#1}}
\renewcommand\citeleft{(} \renewcommand\citeright{)}
```

Good information about TEX and LATEX can be found in.[?, 1-4] For hyperref see (1, pp. 35–67).

```
Good information about \TeX{} and \LaTeX{} can be found in
\cite{LGC97,LWC99,Knuth-CT-a,Knuth:ct-b,Knuth:TB10-1-31}.
For \texttt{hyperref} see \cite[pp.\,35--67]{LWC99}.
```

16-2-13

You can normally use the same input convention, regardless of whether the superscript option is used. In particular, a space before the citation command is ignored if the citations are raised. This means that you can add this option without having to adjust your document sources, provided your writing style does not use the numerical citation as part of the sentence structure, as we did in the previous example — producing a rather questionable result.

However, raised citations numbers can easily be confused with footnote markers, so using both together in a document is not recommended, unless you switch to symbols or alphabetic letters for footnote markers.

Good information[1] can be found in.[1,2]

---
[1]Confusing footnote!

```
\usepackage[superscript]{cite}
\bibliographystyle{plain}

Good information\footnote{Confusing footnote!}
can be found in \cite{LGC97,LWC99}.
```
16-2-14

If superscript numbers are used for citation labels, special care is needed when punctuation characters surround the citation. By default, the cite package automatically moves a punctuation character following a citation in front of the superscript. Punctuation characters that migrate in this way are stored in the command \CiteMoveChars, with ".,;:" being the default (! and ? are not included, but can be added). A problem that can result from this process is the doubling of periods. This case is usually detected by the package, and one punctuation character is suppressed; see the second citation in the next example.

... book;[2] see also Goossens et al.[1]

```
\usepackage[superscript]{cite}
\bibliographystyle{plain}

\ldots\ book~\cite{Knuth-CT-a}; see also
Goossens et al.~\cite{LGC97}.
```
16-2-15

Unfortunately, with capitalized abbreviations or the use of \@ *after* a period, the suppression of double periods fails. Possible workarounds are shown in the next example. Note, however, that the solution with U.S.A\@. works only together with the cite package, but it gives the wrong spacing if the citation is not raised (you are effectively claiming that the sentence ends after the abbreviation)!

et al..[1]
U.S.A..[?]

et al.[1]
U.S.A.[?]

```
\usepackage[super]{cite}
\bibliographystyle{plain}
et al.\@ \cite{LGC97}.   \hfil    et al.\ \cite{LGC97}.

U.S.A. \cite{unknown}.   \hfil    U.S.A\@. \cite{unknown}.
```
16-2-16

There is yet another pitfall that you may encounter: the final punctuation character does not migrate inside a preceding quotation — a style, for example, advocated by *The Chicago Manual of Style* [24]. In this case you may have to rewrite part of your source text accordingly.

<table>
<tr><td></td><td>

```
\usepackage[super]{cite}     \bibliographystyle{plain}
```
</td></tr>
<tr><td>

For details see "The TEXbook".[1] But wanted is "The TEXbook."[1]
</td><td>

```
For details see ''The \TeX book'' \cite{Knuth-CT-a}.
But wanted is ''The \TeX book.'' \cite{Knuth-CT-a}
```
</td></tr>
</table>

16-2-17

Three more options related to raising the reference numbers exist. With the option `nomove` specified, punctuation characters are not migrated before the superscript citation. With the option `ref` specified, citations with an optional argument have the word "Ref." prepended. This is internally implemented by changing `\citeleft`, so if you want a different string or want to change from brackets to, say, parentheses, you have to redefine the customization commands instead of using this option.

```
\usepackage[super,ref]{cite}
\bibliographystyle{plain}
```

Color support is described in "LGC"[2] and the hyperref package in "LWC" [Ref. 1, pp. 35–67].

```
Color support is described in ''LGC'' \cite{LGC97}
and the \texttt{hyperref} package in ''LWC''
\cite[pp.\,35--67]{LWC99}.
```

16-2-18

Finally, the `biblabel` option raises the labels in the bibliography. By default, their default layout is retained regardless of whether you use the option `superscript` or its alias `super`.

16.2.3 notoccite — Solving a problem with unsorted citations

If you want the publications in the bibliography to appear in exactly the order in which they are cited in the document, then you should use unsorted citation styles (e.g., the BibTEX style `unsrt`). This approach does not work, however, if citations are present inside headings or float captions. In that case, these citations also appear in the table of contents or list of figures, and so on. As a result they are moved to the beginning of the bibliography even though they appear much later in the text.

You can avoid this problem by providing an optional argument to `\caption`, `\section`, or similar commands not containing the citation so that no citations are written into such lists. If you have to use citations in these places, then a "manual" solution is to first delete any auxiliary files left over from previous LATEX runs, then run LATEX once, and then run BibTEX. In that case BibTEX picks up only citations from the main document. Clearly, this approach is prone to error, and you may find that your citation order got mangled after all when you finally see your article in print.

Donald Arseneau developed the small package `notoccite` to take care of this problem by redefining the internal command `\@starttoc` in such a way that citations do not generate `\citation` commands for BibTEX within the table of contents and similar lists. Simply loading that package takes care of the problem in all cases — provided you have not used some other package that redefines `\@starttoc` (for example, `notoccite` cannot be combined with the AMS document classes).

notoccite not needed with biblatex; see Section 16.2.5

16.2.4 natbib's approach to number-only references

Although originally designed to support the author-date system, natbib is also capable of producing number-only references. The natbib package *automatically* switches to numerical mode if any one of the \bibitem entries fails to conform to the possible author-date formats. In such cases the commands \cite and \citep are usable, but \citet issues a warning about the missing author and prints a bold "author?":

[1], [1], **(author?)** [1]

References

[1] Donald E. Knuth. Typesetting Concrete Mathematics. *TUGboat*, 10(1):31–36, April 1989.

```
\usepackage{natbib}
\bibliographystyle{plain}
\cite{Knuth:TB10-1-31},
\citep{Knuth:TB10-1-31},
\citet{Knuth:TB10-1-31}
\bibliography{tlc}
```

16-2-19

To force the numeric mode even if the bibliography style would allow an author-date system, load natbib with the numbers option or choose the citation style with \setcitestyle{numbers}.

(1), (1), Knuth (1)

References

[1] Donald E. Knuth. Typesetting Concrete Mathematics. *TUGboat*, 10(1):31–36, April 1989. ISSN 0896-3207.

```
\usepackage{natbib} \setcitestyle{numbers}
\bibliographystyle{plainnat}
\cite{Knuth:TB10-1-31},
\citep{Knuth:TB10-1-31},
\citet{Knuth:TB10-1-31}
\bibliography{tlc}
```

16-2-20

This creates a variant of the author-number system — details and examples are given in Section 16.4.1 on page 503 where we discuss this system.

16.2.5 biblatex's approach to number-only references

We describe the biblatex package in more detail in Section 16.7 but give also for every citation system an overview of the main points of its implementation.

The biblatex package ships with three numeric styles, numeric, numeric-comp, and numeric-verb. The "alpha" citation style is supported with alphabetic and alphabetic-verb — the latter being more verbose. More styles are provided by external packages as shown in the overview of styles in Section 15.7.3. Those styles are loaded in the package options with the style key, but because the initial value of the style key is numeric, simply loading the biblatex package is enough to select a number-only citation system.

Compatibility with natbib

Besides the \cite command, the biblatex package offers a large variety of other citation commands; as with natbib all commands have two optional arguments. The \textcite command gives an author-number citation — similar to the \citet command of natbib, while \parencite and \cite[1] are comparable to \citep. The package option natbib enables emulations of the natbib commands; this simplifies

---

[1] The difference between both is apparent only in author-based citation systems.

converting existing documents but does not cover all syntax differences: recall from Example 16-2-5 that the pages in the optional argument of biblatex's citation commands are given without a prefix and that the range uses a simple hyphen; thus, some syntax adaptions are needed.

The following example sets with the keys `maxnames` and `minnames` the length of the author list to demonstrate the difference between `\citet` and `\citet*`.

Knuth [2]
[see also 1, pp. 2–4]
Goossens, Rahtz, et al. [1]
Goossens, Rahtz, and Mittelbach [1]
[see 1, pp. 35–44]
Goossens, Rahtz, et al.
Goossens, Rahtz, and Mittelbach

```
\usepackage[natbib,minnames=2,maxnames=2]{biblatex}
\addbibresource{tlc.bib}

\textcite{Knuth:TB10-1-31}          \\
\parencite[see also][2-4]{LGC97} \\
\citet{LGC97}                       \\
\citet*{LGC97}                      \\
\citep[see][35-44]{LGC97}           \\
\citeauthor{LGC97}                  \\
\citeauthor*{LGC97}
```

16-2-21

Some starred citation commands are defined by both packages but behave differently. If the natbib emulation is enabled, the biblatex package redefines those commands to match the natbib behavior. Most importantly the `\citeauthor*` command shows with natbib and the natbib emulation *all* authors, while with biblatex it *truncates* the name list. If you want all authors for one citation, you can set the `maxnames` counter inside `\AtNextCite` as shown or define a citation command to this effect. The counter is automatically reset by biblatex afterwards.

natbib emulation changes starred commands

Goossens, Rahtz, et al.
Goossens et al.
Goossens, Rahtz, and Mittelbach
Goossens, Rahtz, et al.

```
\usepackage[minnames=2,maxnames=2]{biblatex}
\addbibresource{tlc.bib}

\citeauthor{LGC97}  \\
\citeauthor*{LGC97} \\
\AtNextCite{\setcounter{maxnames}{99}}%
\citeauthor{LGC97}  \\
\citeauthor{LGC97}  % maxnames automatically reset
```

16-2-22

Donald Arseneau's cite package is incompatible with biblatex, which addresses citation sorting differently. The functionality of notoccite is built into biblatex: citations in the table of contents and similar lists are printed but otherwise ignored and so do not affect the numbering. However, in contrast to the incompatibility between cite and biblatex, there is no conflict if notoccite is loaded too — it is simply not necessary.

For the purpose of fully adapting the format of citation commands, biblatex offers the command `\DeclareCiteCommand` that we describe in Section 16.7.16, but various typical layouts can be achieved either with existing package options or by switching to another citation style. The option `sortcites` sorts list of citations as they are sorted in the bibliography and also suppresses duplicates. Compare the output of the next two examples:

[2, 1, KpV]
[2, KpV, 2, 1]

```
\usepackage{biblatex}
\cite{cicero,angenendt,kant:kpv}\\
\cite{cicero,kant:kpv,cicero,angenendt}
```

16-2-23

In the previous example the reference to `cicero` appeared twice; now all references are sorted and duplicates are suppressed:

[1, 2, KpV]
[1, 2, KpV]

```
\usepackage[sortcites]{biblatex}
\cite{cicero,angenendt,kant:kpv}\\
\cite{cicero,kant:kpv,cicero,angenendt}
```
16-2-24

Compressed and sorted citations can be produced, for example, by using a style such as `numeric-comp`. Note that unresolved citations are not marked with a question mark but show the citation key in bold. Redoing Example 16-2-9 from page 478 thus gives:

Good information about TeX and LaTeX can be found in [**Knuth:ct-b**, 1–4].

```
\usepackage[style=numeric-comp]{biblatex}
\addbibresource{tlc.bib}
Good information about \TeX{} and \LaTeX{} can be found in
\cite{LGC97,LWC99,Knuth-CT-a,Knuth:ct-b,Knuth:TB10-1-31}.
```
16-2-25

How to use parentheses instead of brackets has already been demonstrated in Example 16-2-6 on page 478. We now extend this example and also change the punctuation before the *post-note* and the punctuation between two citations by redefining two standard biblatex commands:

Color support for LaTeX is described in (2) and the `hyperref` package in (1; pp. 35–67).
See also (3; 4).

```
\usepackage[style=ext-numeric-comp]{biblatex}
\addbibresource{tlc.bib} \DeclareOuterCiteDelims{cite}{(}{)}
\renewcommand\postnotedelim{\addsemicolon\addspace}
\renewcommand\multicitedelim{\addsemicolon\addspace}
Color support for \LaTeX{} is described in \cite{LGC97}
and the \texttt{hyperref} package in \cite[35-67]{LWC99}.
\par See also \cite{MR-PQ,Southall}.
```
16-2-26

Citations can be displayed as superscripts in selected bibliography styles (e.g., the numeric styles of `biblatex` and `biblatex-ext`) with the command `\supercite`. If the document uses `\autocite` as a citation command, the package option `autocite=superscript` switches to superscripts too. Citations typeset as superscripts ignore the *pre-note* and *post-note* arguments with a warning — you can use a normal `\cite` to get an unraised citation with notes. Below we repeat Example 16-2-13 on page 481 altered to use `biblatex` including the change to use parentheses, because that was also changed in the earlier example.

Good information about TeX and LaTeX can be found in[**Knuth:ct-b**, 1–4]. For hyperref see (1, pp. 35–67).

```
\usepackage[style=ext-numeric-comp,maxcitenames=1]{biblatex}
\addbibresource{tlc.bib} \DeclareOuterCiteDelims{cite}{(}{)}
Good information about \TeX{} and \LaTeX{} can be found
in \supercite{LGC97,LWC99,Knuth-CT-a,Knuth:ct-b,%
          Knuth:TB10-1-31}.
For \texttt{hyperref} see \cite[35-67]{LWC99}.
```
16-2-27

Similar to \cite in the cite package, \autocite tries to move punctuation before the citation if it is used with autocite=superscript. It does not suppress a double period created, for example, from an abbreviation. You have to rewrite your text in such cases.

```
\usepackage[maxcitenames=1,style=numeric-comp,
            autocite=superscript]{biblatex}
\addbibresource{tlc.bib}
See \citeauthor{Knuth-CT-a}~\autocite{Knuth-CT-a},
\citeauthor[see also][]{LGC97}~\autocite{LGC97}.
```

See Knuth,[2] see also Goossens et al..[1]

16-2-28

Above, we retrieved the author names with \citeauthor and forced the use of "et al." after the first author with the option maxcitenames=1.

In summary, the big difference between cite and biblatex with respect to superscript citations is that the latter expects you to use different commands for the citations in your document, i.e., \supercite, instead of getting an altered behavior of the standard \cite command. If this is not to your liking, you can copy the (quite short) definition of \supercite from numeric.cbx and use it to redefine \cite.

Finally, we show a short example for an "alpha" style that can be produced with, for example, the alphabetic style. In this style the label is built from the initials of some of the authors and a part of the year; additional authors are indicated by a plus symbol. In the following example we restrict the number of authors to two (the default is three) with maxalphanames:

The "alpha" style

```
\usepackage[style=alphabetic,minalphanames=2,
            maxalphanames=2]{biblatex}
\addbibresource{tlc.bib}
\textcite{Knuth-CT-a}, \textcite{Knuth:TB10-1-31} \\
\textcite{LGC97}    \\  \textcite{LWC99}
```

Knuth [Knu86], Knuth [Knu89]
Goossens, Rahtz, and Mittelbach [GR+97]
Goossens and Rahtz [GR99]

16-2-29

With the command \DeclareLabelalphaTemplate, the template for the label can be redefined; in its argument various instructions for how to construct the label can be given. The following example creates short labels based only on the names. Note how the two Knuth citations are distinguished with additional letters.

```
\usepackage[style=alphabetic,minalphanames=2,
            maxalphanames=2]{biblatex}
\DeclareLabelalphaTemplate
        {\labelelement{\field[varwidth]{labelname}}}
\addbibresource{tlc.bib}
\textcite{Knuth-CT-a}, \textcite{Knuth:TB10-1-31} \\
\textcite{LGC97}    \\  \textcite{LWC99}
```

Knuth [Ka], Knuth [Kb]
Goossens, Rahtz, and Mittelbach [GR+]
Goossens and Rahtz [GR]

16-2-30

16.3 The author-date system

Depending on the structure of the sentence, the author-date system normally uses one of two different forms for references: if the author's name appears naturally in the sentence, it is not repeated within the parentheses or brackets; otherwise, both the author's name and the year of publication are used. This style poses an unsolvable problem when LaTeX's standard syntax is used, because only one command (\cite) is available.

Consequently, anyone developing support for the author-date system has had to extend the LaTeX syntax for citing publications. The following example shows the two forms and their implementation (with two new commands) as provided by the natbib system.

Knuth (1989) shows ... This is explained in the authoritative manual on TeX (Knuth, 1986).

```
\usepackage{natbib}
\citet{Knuth:TB10-1-31} shows \ldots\ This is explained
in the authoritative manual on \TeX{}~\citep{Knuth-CT-a}.
```

16-3-1

Extending the LaTeX syntax for citing publications does not solve the problem completely. In order to produce the different forms of citation references needed in the author-date system, structured information must be provided by the bibliography. Without a special structure it is impossible to pick up the data needed for the textual references (e.g., producing just the year in parentheses). That is, a bibliographical entry like

```
\bibitem[Donald~E. Knuth 1986]{Knuth-CT-a}    Donald~E. Knuth.
    \newblock \emph{The {\TeX}book}, volume~A of \emph{Computers and
        Typesetting}. \newblock Addison-Wesley, Reading, MA, USA, 1986.
```

allows the \cite command to produce "(Donald E. Knuth 1986)" but not "Donald E. Knuth (1986)" or just "Knuth" or just "1986" as well. You also have to ensure that \bibitem does not display the label, but that outcome can be fairly easily arranged.

The solution used by all implementations for author-date support before the advent of the biblatex package was to introduce a special syntax within the optional argument of \bibitem. In some implementations this structure is fairly simple. For instance, chicago requires only

```
\bibitem[\protect\citeauthoryear{Goossens, Rahtz, and Mittelbach}
                {Goossens et~al.}{1997}]{LGC97}
```

This information can still be produced manually, if needed. Other packages go much further and encode a lot of information explicitly. For example, jurabib asks for the following kind of argument structure (same publication):

```
\bibitem[{Goossens\jbbfsasep Rahtz\jbbstasep Mittelbach\jbdy {1997}}%
    {}{{0}{}{book}{1997}{}{}{}{xxi + 554}{Reading, MA, USA\bpubaddr {}
    Ad{\-d}i{\-s}on-Wes{\-l}ey Longman\bibbdsep {} 1997}}{{The {\LaTeX}
    Graphics Companion: Illustrating Documents with {\TeX} and {PostScript}}%
    {}{}{}{}{}{}{}}]{LGC97}
```

This approach gives a lot of flexibility when referring to the publication, but it is clear that no one wants to produce a bibliography environment with such a structure manually. The same is true when biblatex is used, only in this case the .bbl file no longer contains \bibitem commands with structured arguments, but just the structured data in a special format; see the introduction to Section 16.7 on page 541. While that format may be easier to understand than the one produced, for example, for jurabib, it is not realistic to generate it manually either. Hence, the only usable solution in these cases is to use an external tool, i.e., biber or BibTeX (together with special style files) to generate the entries automatically.

16.3.1 Early attempts

Over the years several independent add-on packages have been developed to support the author-date system. Unfortunately, each one introduced a different set of user-level commands. Typically, the add-ons consist of a LaTeX package providing the user commands and one or more BibTeX styles to generate the thebibliography environment with a matching syntax in the optional argument of the \bibitem command.

For example, the chicago package, which aimed to implement the recommendations of *The Chicago Manual of Style* [24], offers the following list of commands (plus variants all ending in NP to omit the parentheses — for example, \citeNP):

(Goossens, Rahtz, and Mittelbach 1997)
(Goossens, Rahtz, and Mittelbach)
Goossens, Rahtz, and Mittelbach (1997)
(Goossens and Rahtz 1999)
(Goossens and Rahtz)
Goossens and Rahtz (1999)
(1999), 1999

```
\usepackage{chicago}
\bibliographystyle{chicago}

\cite{LGC97}                            \\
\citeA{LGC97}                           \\
\citeN{LGC97}                           \\
\shortcite{LWC99}                       \\
\shortciteA{LWC99}                      \\
\shortciteN{LWC99}                      \\
\citeyear{LWC99}, \citeyearNP{LWC99}
```

16-3-2

Several BibTeX styles (chicago, chicagoa, jas99, named, and newapa) are compatible with the chicago package. All of them are still in use, but the package itself is now rarely included in LaTeX documents (natbib can be used instead to provide the user-level syntax).

In contrast, only two commands are provided by David Rhead's authordate1-4 package, the original support package for the BibTeX styles authordate1 to authordate4. It implements recommendations by the Cambridge and Oxford University Presses and various British standards.

10-3-3

(Goossens *et al.*, 1997) or (1997)

```
\usepackage{authordate1-4}
\bibliographystyle{authordate2}

\cite{LGC97}   or  \shortcite{LGC97}
```

For a final example we take a brief look at the harvard package by Peter Williams and Thorsten Schnier. In contrast to the two previously described packages, harvard has been further developed and updated for LaTeX2ε. It implements a number of interesting features. For example, a first citation gives a full author list, whereas a later citation uses an abbreviated list (unless explicitly requested otherwise). The user-level commands are shown in the next example:[1]

(Goossens, Rahtz & Mittelbach 1997)
(Goossens et al. 1997)   second citation
(Goossens, Rahtz & Mittelbach 1997)   long names forced
Goossens et al. (1997)
(e.g., Goossens et al. 1997)
Goossens et al.
Knuth's (1986)

```
\usepackage{harvard}
\bibliographystyle{agsm}

\cite{LGC97}                                      \\
\cite{LGC97} \hfill second citation   \\
\cite*{LGC97}\hfill long names forced\\
\citeasnoun{LGC97}                         \\
\citeaffixed{LGC97}{e.g.,}              \\
\citename{LGC97}                             \\
\possessivecite{Knuth-CT-a}
```

16-3-4

The harvard package requires a specially prepared bibliography environment in which \bibitem is replaced by \harvarditem, a command with a special syntax used to carry the information needed for author-date citations. A few BibTeX styles (including agsm, dcu, kluwer, and nederlands) implement this special syntax.

Many of these packages support the author-date system quite well. Nevertheless, with different packages using their own syntax and supporting only half a dozen BibTeX styles each, the situation stayed unsatisfactory for a long time. Matters changed for the better when Patrick Daly published his natbib support package, described in the next section.

16.3.2 natbib—Customizable author-date references

Although most publishers indicate which bibliographic style they prefer, it is not always evident how to change from one system to the other if one has to prepare source texts adhering to multiple styles.

To solve the problem of incompatible syntaxes described in the previous section, Patrick Daly developed the natbib package (for "NATural sciences BIBliography"). This package can accept several \bibitem variants (including \harvarditem) as produced by the different BibTeX styles. Thus, for the first time, (nearly) all of the author-date BibTeX styles could be used with a single user-level syntax for the citation commands.

The natbib package is compatible with packages like babel, chapterbib, hyperref, index, and showkeys, and with various document classes including the standard LaTeX classes, amsbook and amsart, classes from the KOMA-Script bundle, and memoir. It cannot be used together with the cite package but provides similar sorting and compressing functions via options.

The natbib package therefore acts as a single, flexible interface for most of the available bibliographic styles for BibTeX when the author-date system is required. It can also be used to produce numerical references; see Sections 16.2.4 and 16.4.1.

---

[1]The small har2nat package allows using those commands also with natbib.

The basic syntax

The two central commands of natbib are \citet (for textual citation) and \citep (for parenthetical citation).[1]

```
\citet[post-note]{key1,key2,...}    \citet[pre-note][post-note]{key1,...}
\citep[post-note]{key1,key2,...}    \citep[pre-note][post-note]{key1,...}
```

Both commands take one mandatory argument (a *key-list* that refers to one or more publications) and one or two optional arguments to add text before and after the citation. LaTeX's standard \cite command can take only a single optional argument denoting a *post-note*. For this reason the commands implement the following syntax: with only one optional argument specified, this argument denotes the *post-note* (i.e., a note placed after the citation); with two optional arguments specified, the first denotes a *pre-note* and the second a *post-note*. To get only a *pre-note* you have to add an empty second argument, as seen in the last lines of the next two examples. Also note that natbib redefines \cite to act like \citet.[2]

Different \citet variants:

Goossens et al. (1997)

Goossens et al. (1997, chap. 2)

Goossens et al. (see 1997, chap. 2)

16-3-5   pre-note only: Goossens et al. (see 1997)

```
\usepackage{natbib}
Different \verb=\citet= variants:    \\[2pt]
\citet{LGC97}                        \\
\citet[chap.~2]{LGC97}               \\
\citet[see][chap.~2]{LGC97}          \\
pre-note only: \citet[see][]{LGC97}
```

Different \citep variants:

(Goossens et al., 1997)

(Goossens et al., 1997, chap. 2)

(see Goossens et al., 1997, chap. 2)

16-3-6   pre-note only: (see Goossens et al., 1997)

```
\usepackage{natbib}
Different \verb=\citep= variants:    \\[2pt]
\citep{LGC97}                        \\
\citep[chap.~2]{LGC97}               \\
\citep[see][chap.~2]{LGC97}          \\
pre-note only: \citep[see][]{LGC97}
```

Both commands have starred versions, \citet* and \citep* (with otherwise identical syntax), that typeset the full list of authors if it is known.[3] These variants work only if this feature is supported by the used BibTeX style file. In other words, the information must be made available through the optional argument of \bibitem; if it is missing, the abbreviated list is always printed.

Compare Goossens et al. (1997) with

Goossens, Rahtz, and Mittelbach (1997)

16-3-7   (see Goossens, Rahtz, and Mittelbach, 1997)

```
\usepackage{natbib}
Compare \citet{LGC97} with    \\
\citet*{LGC97}                \\
\citep*[see][]{LGC97}
```

---

[1] The commands exhibit the same behavior in most bibliographic styles, which is why we do not show a \bibliographystyle line in many of the upcoming examples.

[2] To be precise, \cite is redefined to act like \citet if natbib is used in author-date mode as discussed in this section. If used in author-number mode (see Section 16.4.1), it works like \citep.

[3] If you plan to also use the jurabib package (see Section 16.5.1), then avoid the starred forms because they are not supported by that package.

Two other variant forms exist: `\citealt` works like `\citet` but does not generate parentheses, and `\citealp` is `\citep` without parentheses. Evidently, some of the typeset results come out almost identically.

Goossens et al. 1997
Goossens et al., 1997
Goossens, Rahtz, and Mittelbach 1997
Goossens, Rahtz, and Mittelbach, 1997
Goossens and Rahtz, 1999, p. 236 etc.

```
\usepackage{natbib}
\citealt{LGC97}            \\
\citealp{LGC97}            \\
\citealt*{LGC97}           \\
\citealp*{LGC97}           \\
\citealp[p.~236]{LWC99} etc.
```

16-3-8

When using the author-date system, it is sometimes desirable to just cite the author(s) or the year. For this purpose natbib provides the following additional commands (`\citeauthor*` is the same as `\citeauthor` when the full author information is unavailable):

Goossens et al.
Goossens, Rahtz, and Mittelbach
1997 or (1997)

```
\usepackage{natbib}
\citeauthor{LGC97}          \\
\citeauthor*{LGC97}         \\
\citeyear{LGC97}  or  \citeyearpar{LGC97}
```

16-3-9

Even more complex mixtures of text and citation information can be handled with the command `\citetext`. It takes one mandatory argument and surrounds it with the parentheses or brackets used by other citation commands. By combining this command with `\citealp` or other commands that do not produce parentheses, all sorts of combinations become possible.

(see Goossens et al., 1997 or Knuth, 1986)

```
\usepackage{natbib}
\citetext{see \citealp{LGC97} or \citealp{Knuth-CT-a}}
```

16-3-10

Forcing names to uppercase Sometimes a sentence starts with a citation, but the (first) author of the cited publication has a name that starts with a lowercase letter. In that case, the commands discussed so far cannot be used. The natbib package solves this problem by providing for all commands variants that capitalize the first letter. They are easy to remember: just capitalize the first letter of the corresponding original command. For example, instead of `\citet*`, use `\Citet*`. Here are some additional examples:

Normal citation: van Leunen (1992)
Van Leunen (1992) or Van Leunen 1992
(Van Leunen, 1992) or Van Leunen, 1992
Van Leunen

```
\usepackage{natbib}
Normal citation: \citet{vLeunen:92}            \\
\Citet{vLeunen:92} or \Citealt{vLeunen:92}  \\
\Citep{vLeunen:92} or \Citealp{vLeunen:92}  \\
\Citeauthor{vLeunen:92}
```

16-3-11

As a final goody, natbib lets you define alternative text for a citation that can be used instead of the usual author-date combination. For the definition use

\defcitealias (usually in the preamble), and for the retrieval use \citetalias or \citepalias.

Goossens et al. (1997) = Dogbook II
(Goossens et al., 1997) = (Dogbook II)
Alias changed: (see Dogbook II 2ed)

```
\usepackage{natbib}
\defcitealias{LGC97}{Dogbook~II}
\citet{LGC97} = \citetalias{LGC97}   \\
\citep{LGC97} = \citepalias{LGC97}   \par
\defcitealias{LGC97}{Dogbook~II~2ed}
Alias changed: \citepalias[see][]{LGC97}
```

16-3-12

With the commands introduced in this section, natbib provides more features than the earlier attempts to support the author-date system (e.g., the packages described in Section 16.3.1). In the few cases where natbib does not offer directly equivalent commands, they can be easily built manually.

For example, harvard's \possessivecite command (shown in Example 16-3-4) can be emulated with \citeauthor and \citeyearpar, as is done in the first line of the next example:

Knuth's (1986)
Knuth's (1986)

```
\usepackage{natbib}
\bibliographystyle{agsm}
\newcommand\possessivecite[1]{\citeauthor{#1}'s \citeyearpar{#1}}
\citeauthor{Knuth-CT-a}'s \citeyearpar{Knuth-CT-a} \\
\possessivecite{Knuth-CT-a}
```

16-3-13

Multiple citations

In standard LaTeX, multiple citations can be made by including more than one citation *key-list* argument to the \cite command. The same is possible for the citation commands \citet and \citep (as well as their variant forms). The natbib package then automatically checks whether adjacent citations in the *key-list* have the same author designation. If so, it prints the author names only once. Unfortunately, it checks only the surnames; e.g., "Don Knuth" and "Jill Knuth" would be considered the same author and lumped together.

Careful with different authors with identical surnames

Goossens et al. (1997); Goossens and Rahtz (1999)
(Goossens et al., 1997; Goossens and Rahtz, 1999)
(Knuth, 1989, 1986)

```
\usepackage{natbib}
\citet{LGC97,LWC99}     \\
\citep{LGC97,LWC99}     \\
\citep{Knuth:TB10-1-31,Knuth-CT-a}
```

16-3-14

The last line in the previous example exhibits a potential problem when using several keys in one citation command: the references are typeset in the order of the *key-list*. If you specify the option sort, then the citations are sorted into the order in which they appear in the bibliography, usually alphabetical by author and then by year.

(Knuth, 1986, 1989)

```
\usepackage[sort]{natbib}
\citep{Knuth:TB10-1-31,Knuth-CT-a}
```

16-3-15

While all the citation commands support *key-lists* with more than one citation key, they are best confined to \citep; already \citet gives questionable results. The situation gets worse when you use optional arguments: with \citet any *pre-note* is added before each year (which could be considered a defect in the package). More generally, it is not at all clear what these notes are supposed to refer to. Hence, if you want to add notes, it is better to separate your citations.

```
\usepackage{natbib}
```

(see van Leunen, 1992; Knuth, 1986, p. 55)   `\citep[see][p.~55]{vLeunen:92,Knuth-CT-a}  \\`
(see Knuth, 1986, 1989, p. 55)   `\citep[see][p.~55]{Knuth-CT-a,Knuth:TB10-1-31} \\`
van Leunen (see 1992); Knuth (see 1986, p. 55)   `\citet[see][p.~55]{vLeunen:92,Knuth-CT-a}  \\`
Knuth (see 1986, 1989, p. 55)   `\citet[see][p.~55]{Knuth-CT-a,Knuth:TB10-1-31}`

16-3-16

Full author list only with the first citation

The harvard package automatically typesets the first citation of a publication with the full list of authors and subsequent citations with an abbreviated list. This style of citation is quite popular in some disciplines, and natbib supports it if you load it with the option longnamesfirst. Compare the next example to Example 16-3-4 on page 490:

```
\usepackage[longnamesfirst]{natbib}
\bibliographystyle{agsm}
```

(Goossens, Rahtz & Mittelbach 1997)   first citation   `\citep{LGC97} \hfill first citation  \\`
(Goossens et al. 1997)   second   `\citep{LGC97} \hfill        second \\`
(Goossens, Rahtz & Mittelbach 1997) names forced   `\citep*{LGC97}\hfill   names forced \\`
Goossens et al. (1997)   `\citet{LGC97}                 \\`
(e.g., Goossens et al. 1997)   `\citep[e.g.,][]{LGC97}           \\`
Goossens et al.   `\citeauthor{LGC97}`

16-3-17

Some B\textsc{ib}T\textsc{e}X style files are quite cleverly programmed. For example, when the agsm B\textsc{ib}T\textsc{e}X style, used in Example 16-3-17, detects that shortening a list of authors leads to ambiguous citations, it refuses to produce an abbreviated list. Thus, after adding the test97 citation to the example, all citations suddenly come out in long form.[1] B\textsc{ib}T\textsc{e}X styles produced with custom-bib avoid such ambiguous citations by adding a suffix to the year, but other B\textsc{ib}T\textsc{e}X styles (e.g., chicago) happily produce them; see Example 16-3-19 on the facing page and page 471.

```
\usepackage[longnamesfirst]{natbib}
\bibliographystyle{agsm}
```

(Goossens, Rahtz & Mittelbach 1997)   first citation   `\citep{LGC97} \hfill  first citation \\`
(Goossens, Rahtz & Mittelbach 1997)   second   `\citep{LGC97} \hfill        second \\`
(Goossens, User, Doe et al. 1997)   first citation   `\citep{test97}\hfill  first citation \\`
(Goossens, User, Doe et al. 1997)   second citation   `\citep{test97}\hfill second citation`

16-3-18

---

[1]Something that puzzled the author when he first encountered it while preparing the examples.

Some publications have so many authors that you may want to always cite them using their abbreviated name list, even the first time. You can achieve this effect by listing their keys, separated by commas, in the argument of a \shortcites declaration made in the preamble. The example also shows that use of the chicago style can lead to ambiguous citations (lines 1 and 2 versus line 5).

```
\usepackage[longnamesfirst]{natbib}
\bibliographystyle{chicago}
\shortcites{LGC97}
```

(Goossens et al., 1997)	first citation	`\citep{LGC97} \hfill   first citation \\`
(Goossens et al., 1997)	second citation	`\citep{LGC97} \hfill second citation \\`
(Goossens, Rahtz, and Mittelbach, 1997)	forced	`\citep*{LGC97}\hfill            forced \\`
(Goossens, User, Doe, et al., 1997)	first citation	`\citep{test97}\hfill   first citation \\`
(Goossens et al., 1997)	second citation	`\citep{test97}\hfill second citation`

16-3-19

Customizing the citation reference layout

So far, all of the examples have shown parentheses around the citations, but this is by no means the only possibility offered by natbib. The package internally knows about more than 20 BibTeX styles. If any such style is chosen with a \bibliographystyle command, then a layout appropriate for this style is selected as well. For example, when using the agu (American Geophysical Union) style, we get:

Goossens et al. [1997]	`\usepackage{natbib} \bibliographystyle{agu}`
[*Knuth*, 1986; *Goossens and Rahtz*, 1999]	`\citet{LGC97}  \\  \citep{Knuth-CT-a,LWC99} \\`
[see *Knuth*, 1986, chap. 2]	`\citep[see][chap.~2]{Knuth-CT-a}`

16-3-20

By default, the citation layout is determined by the chosen BibTeX style (or natbib's defaults if a given style is unknown to natbib). By including a \citestyle declaration you can request use of the citation style associated with a BibTeX style that is different from the one used to format the bibliography. In the next example we use the agsm style for the citations while the overall style remains agu. If you compare this example to Example 16-3-20, you see that the textual formatting is unchanged (e.g., italic for author names), but the parentheses and the separation between authors and year have both changed.

Goossens et al. (1997)	`\usepackage{natbib} \bibliographystyle{agu}`
(*Knuth* 1986, *Goossens and Rahtz* 1999)	`\citestyle{agsm}`
(see *Knuth* 1986, chap. 2)	`\citet{LGC97}  \\  \citep{Knuth-CT-a,LWC99} \\`
	`\citep[see][chap.~2]{Knuth-CT-a}`

16-3-21

It is also possible to influence the layout by supplying options: round (default for most styles), square, curly, or angle change the type of parentheses used, while colon[1] (default for most styles) and comma alter the separation between multiple

---

[1]Despite its name this option produces a ";" semicolon.

citations. In the next example, we overwrite the defaults set by the agu style, by
loading natbib with two options.

Goossens et al. {1997}
{*Knuth*, 1986, *Goossens and Rahtz*, 1999}
{see *Knuth*, 1986, chap. 2}

```
\usepackage[curly,comma]{natbib}
\bibliographystyle{agu}
\citet{LGC97}  \\  \citep{Knuth-CT-a,LWC99} \\
\citep[see][chap.~2]{Knuth-CT-a}
```

16-3-22

Yet another method to customize the layout is mainly intended for package
and/or class file writers: the \bibpunct declaration. It takes seven arguments (the
first optional) that define various aspects of the citation format. It is typically used to
define the default citation format for a particular BibTeX style. For example, the natbib
package contains many definitions like this:

```
\newcommand\bibstyle@chicago{\bibpunct{(}{)}{;}{a}{,}{,}}
```

That definition is selected when you choose chicago as your BibTeX style or when
you specify it as the argument to \citestyle. Similar declarations can be added for
BibTeX styles that natbib does not directly support. This effect is most readily realized
by grouping such declarations in the local configuration file natbib.cfg. For details
on the meanings of the arguments, see the documentation accompanying the natbib
package.

If there are conflicting specifications, then the following rules apply: the lowest
priority is given to internal \bibstyle@⟨name⟩ declarations, followed by the options specified in the \usepackage declarations. Both are overwritten by an explicit
\bibpunct or \citestyle declaration in the document preamble.

*Forcing all author
names on a single
line*

Normally, natbib does not prevent a line break within the author list of a citation.
By specifying the option nonamebreak, you can ensure that all author names in one
citation are kept on a single line. In normal circumstances this is seldom a good idea
because it is likely to cause overfull hboxes.

Customizing the bibliography layout

The thebibliography environment, as implemented by natbib, automatically adds
a heading before the list of publications. By default, natbib selects an unnumbered
heading of the highest level, such as \chapter* for a book type class or \section*
for the article class or a variant thereof. The actual heading inserted is stored in the
command \bibsection. Thus, to modify the default, you have to change its definition. For instance, you can suppress the heading altogether or choose a numbered
heading.

For one particular situation natbib offers direct support: if you specify the option sectionbib, you instruct the package to use \section*, even if the highest
sectional unit is \chapter. This option is useful if natbib and chapterbib are used
together (see Section 16.8.1).

Between \bibsection and the start of the list, natbib executes the hook
\bibpreamble. It allows you to place some text between the heading and the start

of the actual reference list. It is also possible to influence the font used for the bibliography by redefining the command `\bibfont`. This hook can also be used to influence the list in other ways, such as setting it unjustified by adding `\raggedright`. Note that `\bibpreamble` and `\bibfont` are defined by default (to do nothing) and thus require redefining with `\renewcommand`.

Finally, two length parameters are available for customization. The first line in each reference is set flush left, and all following lines are indented by the value stored in `\bibhang` (default `1em`). The vertical space between the references is stored in the rubber length `\bibsep` (the default value is usually equal to `\itemsep` as defined in other lists).

To show the various possibilities available we repeat Example 16-1-2 on page 472 but apply all kinds of customization features (not necessarily for the better!). Note the presence of `\par` at the end of `\bibpreamble`. Without it the settings in `\bibfont` would affect the inserted text!

Entries with multiple authors might be problematical, e.g., Goossens et al. [1997a] and Goossens et al. [1997b] or even Goossens et al. [1997a,b]. But then they might not.

1 References

Some material inserted between heading and list.

M. Goossens, S. Rahtz, and F. Mittelbach. *The LaTeX Graphics Companion: Illustrating Documents with TeX and PostScript*. Tools and Techniques for Computer Typesetting. Addison-Wesley Longman, Reading, MA, USA, 1997a. ISBN 0-201-85469-4.

M. Goossens, B. User, J. Doe, et al. Ambiguous citations. Submitted to the IBM J. Res. Dev., 1997b.

```
\usepackage{natbib}
\bibliographystyle{abbrvnat}
\renewcommand\bibsection{\section{\refname}}
\renewcommand\bibpreamble{Some material
     inserted between heading and list.\par}
\renewcommand\bibfont
              {\footnotesize\raggedright}
\setlength\bibhang{30pt}
\setlength\bibsep{1pt plus 1pt}

Entries with multiple authors might be
problematical, e.g., \cite{LGC97} and
\cite{test97} or even \cite{LGC97,test97}.
But then they might not.
\bibliography{tlc,tlc-ex}
```

16-3-23

Publications without author or year information

To use the author-date citation system, the entries in your list of publications need to contain the necessary information. If some information is missing, citations with `\citet` or its variants may produce strange results.

If the publication has no author but an editor, then most BibTeX styles use the latter. However, if both are missing, the solutions implemented differ greatly. BibTeX files in "Harvard" style (e.g., `agsm`) use the first three letters from the key field if present; otherwise, they use the first three letters from the organization field (omitting "The ," if necessary); and if that field is not available, they use the full title. If an entry has no year, then "n.d." is used. This results in usable entries except in the case where part of the key field is selected:

Koppitz (n.d.) / *TUGboat The Communications of the TeX User Group* (1980ff) / mak (2000)

```
\usepackage{natbib} \bibliographystyle{agsm}
\citet{G-G} / \citet{oddity} / \citet{GNUMake}
```

16-3-24

With the same entries, BIBTEX styles produced with custom-bib (e.g., `unsrtnat`) use the following strategy: if a key field is present, the whole field is used as an "author"; otherwise, if an organization field is specified, its first three letters are used (omitting "The␣" if necessary); and if the entry does not have such a field, the first three letters of the citation label are used. A missing year is completely omitted. In the case of textual citations, this means that only the author name is printed. In that situation, or when the key field is used, it is probably best to avoid `\citet` and always use `\citep` to make it clear to the reader that you are actually referring to a publication and not just mentioning some person in passing.

Koppitz / odd [1980ff] / make
[Koppitz] / [odd, 1980ff] / [make]

```
\usepackage{natbib} \bibliographystyle{unsrtnat}
\citet{G-G} / \citet{oddity} / \citet{GNUMake} \\
\citep{G-G} / \citep{oddity} / \citep{GNUMake}
```

16-3-25

As a final example we show the results when using the chicago BIBTEX style. Here the GNU manual comes out fine (the full organization name is used), but the entry with the date missing looks odd.

Koppitz (Koppitz) / odd (80ff) / Free Software Foundation (2000)
(Koppitz, Koppitz) / (odd, 80ff) / (Free Software Foundation, 2000)

```
\usepackage{natbib} \bibliographystyle{chicago}
\citet{G-G} / \citet{oddity} / \citet{GNUMake} \\
\citep{G-G} / \citep{oddity} / \citep{GNUMake}
```

16-3-26

Indexing citations automatically

Citations can be entered in the index by inserting a `\citeindextrue` command at any point in the document. From that point onward, and until the end of the current group or the next `\citeindexfalse` is encountered, all variants of the `\citet` and `\citep` commands generate entries in the index file (if one is written). With `\citeindextrue` in effect, the `\bibitem` commands in the `thebibliography` environment also generate index entries. If this result is not desired, issue a `\citeindexfalse` command before entering the environment (e.g., before calling `\bibliography`).

The format of the generated index entries is controlled by the internal command `\NAT@idxtxt`. It has the following default definition:

```
\newcommand\NAT@idxtxt{\NAT@name\ \NAT@open\NAT@date\NAT@close}
```

Thus, it produces entries like "Knuth (1986)" or "Knuth [1986]". For citations without author or year information, the results will most likely come out strangely. If enabled, the citations in Example 16-3-25 would generate the following entries:

```
\indexentry{{Koppitz}\ []}{6}
\indexentry{{odd}\ [1980ff]}{6}
\indexentry{{make}\ []}{6}
```

Sadly, the index entries generated in this way are not quite correct: as you can see above, \NAT@name contains braces around the name, which makes such index entries sort under "Symbols" and not under their alphabetic letter.

This might be corrected in the future, but in all likelihood you want to alter the outcome anyway and put only the author's name into the index. This can be done with the following declaration in the preamble (it also removes the disturbing braces around the names):

```
\makeatletter
\AtBeginDocument{\renewcommand\NAT@idxtxt{%
  \expandafter\@firstofone\NAT@name{}% drops the braces
% \ \NAT@open\NAT@date\NAT@close    % uncomment, if you also want the date
  }}
\makeatother
```

The \makeatletter and \makeatother are needed because internal commands are involved, and \AtBeginDocument is needed because the redefinition is otherwise overwritten again at \begin{document}.

It is also possible to produce a separate index of citations by using David Jones's index package (see Section 14.5.3). It allows you to generate multiple index lists using the \newindex command. For this to work you must first declare the list and then associate automatic citation indexing with this list in the preamble:

```
\usepackage{index}
\newindex{default}{idx}{ind}{Index}                % the main index
\newindex{cite}{cdx}{cnd}{Index of Citations}
\renewcommand\citeindextype{cite}
```

Later, use \printindex[cite] to indicate where the citation index should appear in the document.

BibTEX styles for natbib

As mentioned in the introduction, natbib was developed to work with various BibTEX styles that implement some form of author-date scheme. In addition to those third-party styles, natbib works with all styles that can be produced with the custom-bib bundle (see Section 15.7.2 on page 426). It is distributed with three styles — abbrvnat, plainnat, and unsrtnat — that are extensions of the corresponding standard styles. They have been adapted to work better with natbib, allowing you to use some of its features that would be otherwise unavailable. These styles also implement a number of extra fields useful in the days of electronic publications.

doi For use with electronic journals and related material. The Digital Object Identifier (DOI) is a system for identifying and exchanging intellectual property in the digital environment and is supposedly more robust than Uniform Resource Locators (URLs); see www.doi.org for details. The field is optional.

eid Because electronic journals usually have no page numbers, they use a sequence identifier (EID) to locate the article within the journal. The field is optional and is used in place of the page number if present.

isbn The International Standard Book Number (ISBN), a 13-digit (formerly 10) unique identification number (see `https://www.isbn.org`). The ISBN is defined in ISO Standard 2108 and has been in use for more than 50 years. The field is optional.

issn The International Standard Serial Number (ISSN), an 8-digit number that identifies periodical publications (see `https://www.issn.org`). The field is optional.

url The Uniform Resource Locator (URL) for identifying resources on the web. The field is optional. Because URL addresses are typically quite long and are set in a typewriter font, line-breaking problems may occur. They are therefore automatically surrounded with a `\url` command, which is given a simple default definition if undefined. Thus, by using the url package (see Section 3.4.7), you can drastically improve the line-breaking situation because then URLs can be broken at punctuation marks.

16.3.3 biblatex's approach to author-date references

The biblatex package ships with the styles `authoryear`, `authoryear-comp`, `authoryear-ibid`, and `authoryear-icomp`, and many additional author-date styles are provided by external packages as shown in the overview of styles in Section 15.7.3. With the exception of the styles from the biblatex-chicago package, all can be loaded in the package options with the key `style`.

Besides `\cite`, the biblatex package offers a large variety of citation commands including variants to access only parts of the citation; and as with natbib all commands have two optional arguments for the pre- and post-note. We demonstrate a few variants in the following example. Note that differently than natbib, the starred command `\citeauthor*` shows the shortened author list.

The `\textcite` variants:

Goossens, Rahtz, and Mittelbach (1997, chap. 2)
Goossens, Rahtz, and Mittelbach (see 1997, chap. 2)
Goossens, Rahtz, and Mittelbach (see 1997)

Other commands:

(see Goossens, Rahtz, and Mittelbach 1997, chap. 2)
see Goossens, Rahtz, and Mittelbach 1997, chap. 2
see 1997, chap. 2
Goossens, Rahtz, and Mittelbach
Goossens et al.
1997

```
\usepackage[style=authoryear]{biblatex}
\addbibresource{tlc.bib}

The \verb=\textcite= variants: \\[2pt]
\textcite[chap.~2]{LGC97}          \\
\textcite[see][chap.~2]{LGC97}     \\
\textcite[see][]{LGC97}            \\[12pt]
Other commands:                    \\[2pt]
\parencite[see][chap.~2]{LGC97}\\
\cite[see][chap.~2]{LGC97}         \\
\cite*[see][chap.~2]{LGC97}        \\
\citeauthor{LGC97}                 \\
\citeauthor*{LGC97}                \\
\citeyear{LGC97}
```

16-3-27

500

The `authoryear-comp` style sorts and compresses citation lists, while the style `authoryear-ibid` uses "ibidem" for repeated citations. The `authoryear-icomp` style combines both approaches:

§ The biblatex approach to the cite package

Goossens and Rahtz (1999), Goossens, Rahtz, and Mittelbach (1997), and Knuth (1986, 1989)
Knuth (see 1986)
Knuth (see ibid.)

16-3-28

```
\usepackage[style=authoryear-icomp]{biblatex}
\addbibresource{tlc.bib}
\textcite{LGC97,Knuth-CT-a,LWC99,Knuth:TB10-1-31}\\
\textcite[see][]{Knuth-CT-a} \\
\textcite[see][]{Knuth-CT-a} \\
```

The package provides citation commands that capitalize the first letter of a citation. As with natbib they are easy to remember: just capitalize the first letter of the corresponding original command. By default biblatex prints author names without a prefix in a citation; we change this with the option `useprefix` to show the effect.

§ Forcing names to uppercase

Normal citation: van Leunen (1992)
Van Leunen (1992)
(Van Leunen 1992)
Van Leunen

16-3-29

```
\usepackage[style=authoryear,useprefix]{biblatex}
\addbibresource{tlc.bib}
Normal citation: \textcite{vLeunen:92}\\
\Textcite{vLeunen:92} \\
\Parencite{vLeunen:92} \\
\Citeauthor{vLeunen:92}
```

The number of authors shown in citations can be globally adjusted with the options `maxcitenames` and `mincitenames`. In the document you can alter the setup for individual citations, e.g., to show more authors in one citation. There, it is done by setting the counters `maxnames` and `minnames` to suitable values. These counters are reset by biblatex at the start of every citation command, which means that setting them on the top level has no effect. Instead, you need to do this inside `\AtNextCite`, as shown below:

Goossens et al. (1997)
Goossens, Rahtz, et al. (1997)
Goossens et al. (1997)
Goossens, Rahtz, and Mittelbach (1997)

16-3-30

```
\usepackage[style=authoryear,
            maxcitenames=1]{biblatex}
\addbibresource{tlc.bib}
\textcite{LGC97}                                        \\
\AtNextCite{\setcounter{minnames}{2}%
            \setcounter{maxnames}{2}}\textcite{LGC97} \\
\textcite{LGC97}                                        \\
\AtNextCite{\setcounter{maxnames}{99}}\textcite{LGC97}
```

Remember that the author names and the year build a label that should allow the reader to find the entry in the bibliography. biblatex tries hard to ensure that this label is unique and if needed increases the number of authors or adds initials. Check the `uniquename` and `uniquelist` options shown in the introduction of this chapter in Example 16-1-3 and discussed in more detail in Section 16.7.7 if biblatex seems to ignore your maxnames setting.

The biblatex package offers various "multicite" commands — typically ending with a plural "s" — which allow adding an individual *pre-note* and *post-note* to all citations of a list. The following example shows a few variants. Similar to the natbib

Multiple citations

commands, the biblatex commands \textcite and \textcites add the *pre-note* before the year, and the output is rather questionable.

```
\usepackage[style=authoryear-comp]{biblatex}
\addbibresource{tlc.bib}
```

1: see Knuth 1986, p. 55; also Knuth 1989, p. 35
2: Knuth 1989, p. 35, 1986, p. 55
3: (see Knuth 1986, p. 55; also Knuth 1989, p. 35)
4: (Knuth 1989, p. 35, 1986, p. 55)
5: Leunen (see 1992, p. 55) and Knuth (also 1986, p. 43)
5: Knuth (see 1986, p. 55) and Knuth (also 1989, p. 43)

```
1: \cites[see][55]{Knuth-CT-a}
        [also][35]{Knuth:TB10-1-31}\\
2: \cites[35]{Knuth:TB10-1-31}[55]{Knuth-CT-a}      \\
3: \parencites[see][55]{Knuth-CT-a}
              [also][35]{Knuth:TB10-1-31}           \\
4: \parencites[35]{Knuth:TB10-1-31}[55]{Knuth-CT-a}\\
5: \textcites  [see][55]{vLeunen:92}
               [also][43]{Knuth-CT-a}               \\
5: \textcites  [see][55]{Knuth-CT-a}
               [also][43]{Knuth:TB10-1-31}
```

16-3-31

Full author list only with the first citation

The biblatex package has no built-in package option to get the full author list only with the first citation, but a similar effect can be achieved by activating the option citetracker and then checking at every cite key with the command \ifciteseen if a cite has already been seen:

```
\usepackage[style=authoryear,
    citetracker=true,maxnames=2]{biblatex}
\addbibresource{tlc.bib}
\AtEveryCitekey{%
    \ifciteseen{}{\setcounter{maxnames}{99}}}
\textcite{LGC97} \\ \textcite{LGC97}
```

Goossens, Rahtz, and Mittelbach (1997)
Goossens et al. (1997)

16-3-32

Publications without author or year information

If the publication has no author but an editor, the authoryear styles of biblatex uses the latter; if both are missing, the title is used. The field key is not used; thus, in the following example, which repeats Example 16-3-24, both entries without authors and editors use the title. If an entry has no year, then "n.d." is used. The string is localized and so uses the german "o.D." (for "ohne Datum") in the next example.

1: Koppitz (o. D.)
2: *TUGboat The Communications of the T_EX User Group* (1980ff)
3: *GNU Make, A Program for Directing Recompilation* (2000)

```
\usepackage[style=authoryear]{biblatex}
\usepackage[ngerman]{babel}
\addbibresource{tlc.bib} \addbibresource{tlc-ex.bib}
1: \textcite{G-G}       \\ 2: \textcite{oddity} \\
3: \textcite{GNUMake}
```

16-3-33

16.4 The author-number system

As mentioned in the introduction, no BIBT_EX style file to our knowledge exists that implements the author-number system for documents in which the publications should be numbered individually for each author; for this you have to turn to a biblatex style presented at the end of the section. If, however, the publications are numbered sequentially throughout the whole bibliography, then ample support is provided by BibTeX and by the natbib package already encountered in conjunction with the author-date system.

16.4.1 natbib — Revisited

Although originally designed to support the author-date system, natbib is also capable of producing author-number and number-only references. Both types of references are provided with the help of BibTeX styles specially designed for numbered bibliographies, similar to the BibTeX styles normally used for the author-date style of citations.

By default, natbib produces author-date citations. If you are primarily interested in citing references according to the number-only or author-number system, load natbib with the numbers option.

For comparison, we repeat Example 16-3-5 on page 491 with the numbers option loaded. This option automatically implies the options square and comma; thus, if you prefer parentheses, use the option round and overwrite the default choice.

```
Goossens et al. [1]                          \usepackage[numbers]{natbib}
Goossens et al. [1, chap. 2]                 \citet{LGC97}                      \\
Goossens et al. [see 1, chap. 2]             \citet[chap.~2]{LGC97}             \\
pre-note only: Goossens et al. [see 1]       \citet[see][chap.~2]{LGC97}        \\
                                             pre-note only: \citet[see][]{LGC97}  \\[5pt]
[1]                                          \citep{LGC97}                      \\
[1, chap. 2]                                 \citep[chap.~2]{LGC97}             \\
[see 1, chap. 2]                             \citep[see][chap.~2]{LGC97}        \\
pre-note only: [see 1]                       pre-note only: \citep[see][]{LGC97}
```

16-4-1

As you can see, the \citet command now generates citations according to the author-number system, while \citep produces number-only citations. In fact, if natbib is set up to produce numerical citations, LaTeX's \cite command behaves like \citep. In author-date mode, natbib makes this command act as the short form for the command \citet.

All variant forms of \citet and \citep, as discussed in Section 16.3.2, are also available in numerical mode, though only a few make sense. For example, \citep* gives the same output as \citep, because there are no authors inside the parentheses.

```
                                             \usepackage[numbers]{natbib}
Goossens, Rahtz, and Mittelbach [1]          \citet*{LGC97}                     \\
Goossens et al.                              \citeauthor{LGC97}                 \\
Goossens, Rahtz, and Mittelbach              \citeauthor*{LGC97}                \\
1997 or [1997]                               \citeyear{LGC97}  or  \citeyearpar{LGC97}
```

16-4-2

The commands \citealt and \citealt* should probably not be used, because without the parentheses the citation number is likely to be misinterpreted. However, in certain situations \citealp might be useful to obtain that number on its own and then perhaps use it together with \citetext.

```
                                      \usepackage[numbers]{natbib}
Goossens et al. 1                     \citealt{LGC97}                    \\
Goossens, Rahtz, and Mittelbach 1     \citealt*{LGC97}                   \\
1                                     \citealp{LGC97}                    \\
1, p. 236 etc.                        \citealp[p.~236]{LGC97} etc.
```
16-4-3

Some journals use numerical citations with the numbers raised as superscripts. If loaded with the option super, the natbib package supports this type of citation. In that case our standard example (compare with Example 16-4-1) gives this:

```
                                         \usepackage[super]{natbib}
Goossens et al.[1]                       \citet{LGC97}                          \\
Goossens et al.[1], chap. 2              \citet[chap.~2]{LGC97}                 \\
Goossens et al. see[1], chap. 2          \citet[see][chap.~2]{LGC97}            \\
pre-note only: Goossens et al. see[1]    pre-note only: \citet[see][]{LGC97}    \\[5pt]
[1]                                      \citep{LGC97}                          \\
[1] chap. 2                              \citep[chap.~2]{LGC97}                 \\
see[1] chap. 2                           \citep[see][chap.~2]{LGC97}            \\
pre-note only: see[1]                    pre-note only: \citep[see][]{LGC97}
```
16-4-4

As you will observe, the use of the optional arguments produces somewhat questionable results; in the case of \citep the *pre-note* does not appear at all. Thus, with this style of citation, it is usually best to stick to the basic forms of any such commands.

For superscript citations natbib removes possible spaces in front of the citation commands so as to attach the number to the preceding word. However, in contrast to the results produced with the cite package, punctuation characters do not migrate in front of the citation, nor is there any check for double periods. To illustrate this we repeat Example 16-2-15 from page 482.

```
                                 \usepackage[super]{natbib}
...Knuth's book[2]; see also     \ldots Knuth's book~\citep{Knuth-CT-a}; see also \citet{LGC97}.
Goossens et al.[1].              \par %%% Manually corrected in two places:
...Knuth's book;[2] see also     \ldots Knuth's book;\citep{Knuth-CT-a}  see also \citet{LGC97}
Goossens et al.[1]
```
16-4-5

The packages natbib and cite are unfortunately incompatible (both modify LaTeX's internal citation mechanism), so in cases like Example 16-4-5 you have to change the input if natbib is to be used.

Sorting and compressing numerical citations

As seen in Section 16.2.2 the cite package sorts multiple citations and optionally compresses them into ranges. This feature is also implemented by natbib and can be activated through the options sort and sort&compress.

We have already encountered `sort` in connection with author-date citations. With numerical citations (i.e., the options `numbers` and `super`), the numbers are sorted. To show the effect we repeat Example 16-2-8 from page 478, except that we omit the undefined citation.

Good information about TEX and LATEX can be found in [1, 2, 3, 4].

```
\usepackage[sort]{natbib} \bibliographystyle{plain}
Good information about \TeX{} and \LaTeX{} can be found in
\citep{LGC97,LWC99,Knuth-CT-a,Knuth:TB10-1-31}.
```

16-4-6

With the option `sort&compress`, the numbers are not only sorted but also compressed into ranges if possible. In author-date citation mode, this option has the same effect as `sort`.

Good information about TEX and LATEX can be found in [1–4].

```
\usepackage[sort&compress]{natbib}\bibliographystyle{plain}
Good information about \TeX{} and \LaTeX{} can be found in
\citep{LGC97,LWC99,Knuth-CT-a,Knuth:TB10-1-31}.
```

16-4-7

The rules for selecting numerical mode

As mentioned previously, natbib, by default, works in author-date mode. However, for the previous two examples, natbib selected numerical mode without being explicitly told to do so (via the `numbers` or `super` option). This result occurs because the `plain` BIBTEX style does not carry author-date information in the `\bibitem` commands it generates. Whenever there is a single `\bibitem` without the relevant information, natbib automatically switches to numerical mode. Even specifying the option `authoryear` does not work in that case.

If a BIBTEX style supports author-date mode, then switching to numerical mode can be achieved by one of the following methods, which are listed here in increasing order of priority:

1. By selecting a `\bibliographystyle` with a predefined numerical citation style (e.g., defined in a local configuration file or in a class or package file).

2. By specifying the option `numbers` or `super`, as shown in most examples in this section.

3. By explicitly using `\bibpunct` with the fourth mandatory argument set to n or s (for details, see the package documentation).

4. By explicitly using `\citestyle` with the name of a predefined numerical bibliography style.

Customizing natbib in numerical mode

The majority of options and parameters to customize natbib have already been discussed on pages 495–497, but in numerical mode there are two more commands available to modify the produced layout. By default, citation numbers are typeset in the main body font. However, if you redefine `\citenumfont` (a command with one argument), it formats the citation number according to its specification.

Similarly, you can manipulate the format of the number as typeset within the bibliography by redefining \bibnumfmt. The default definition for this command usually produces square brackets around the number.

Images are discussed elsewhere, see (**1, 2**).

References

1. M. Goossens, S. Rahtz, and F. Mittelbach. *The LaTeX Graphics Companion: Illustrating Documents with TeX and PostScript*. Tools and Techniques for Computer Typesetting. Addison-Wesley Longman, Reading, MA, USA, 1997. ISBN 0-201-85469-4.

2. D. E. Knuth. *The TeXbook*, volume A of *Computers and Typesetting*. Addison-Wesley, Reading, MA, USA, 1986. ISBN 0-201-13447-0.

```
\usepackage[numbers,round]{natbib}
\bibliographystyle{abbrvnat}
\renewcommand\bibfont{\small\raggedright}
\setlength\bibhang{30pt}          % ignored!
\setlength\bibsep{1pt plus 1pt}
\renewcommand\citenumfont[1]{\textbf{#1}}
\renewcommand\bibnumfmt[1]{\textbf{#1.}}

Images are discussed elsewhere,
see \citep{LGC97,Knuth-CT-a}.

\bibliography{tlc}
```

16-4-8

While \bibsection, \bibpreamble, \bibfont, and \bibsep work as before, the parameter \bibhang has no effect, because in a numbered bibliography the indentation is defined by the width of the largest number.

16.4.2 biblatex's approach to author-number references

Nothing special is needed to get references with author names and numbers similar to the natbib output. Because biblatex always has access to the author names, you need only to use a numeric style and a citation command, which shows also the author like \textcite (or the emulated natbib commands if you have activated them with the natbib option). How many authors are shown can be set with the options maxcitenames and mincitenames. More examples and information about the numeric styles can be found in Section 16.2.5.

```
\usepackage[maxcitenames=1]{biblatex}
\addbibresource{tlc.bib}
```

Knuth [2]
Goossens et al. [1]
Goossens et al. [see 1, chap. 2]
Goossens et al. [see 1]

```
\textcite{Knuth-CT-a}                    \\
\textcite{LGC97}                         \\
\textcite[see][chap.~2]{LGC97}           \\
\textcite[see][]{LGC97}                  \\
```

16-4-9

Numbering by author   A style to number not throughout the bibliography but on a per-author (or author group) basis is provided by the biblatex-ext package. It makes use of a special field extraname that is generated by biber[1] if an author is cited with more than one work and allows one to differentiate them. We show the style in action in the next example. It also changes the delimiter between the author name and the number to a newline,

---

[1] The style does not work with the BibTeX backend.

changes the period after the number to a space, and removes the dash normally inserted when a author is repeated.

Knuth [2]; Leunen [1]; Knuth [1]

References

Knuth, Donald E.
  [1] *The TEXbook*. Vol. A. Computers and Typesetting. Reading, MA, USA: Addison-Wesley, 1986, pp. ix + 483.
  [2] "Typesetting Concrete Mathematics". In: *TUGboat* 10.1 (Apr. 1989), pp. 31–36.
Leunen, Mary-Claire van
  [1] *A handbook for scholars*. Walton Street, Oxford OX2 6DP, UK: Oxford University Press, 1992, pp. xi + 348.

16-4-10

```
\usepackage[style=ext-authornumber,
            isbn=false]{biblatex}
\addbibresource{tlc.bib}
\DeclareDelimFormat[bib]
   {namenumberdelim}{\\*}
\DeclareDelimFormat[bib]
   {nametitledelim}{\addspace}
\renewcommand\bibnamedash
   {\hspace*{\leftmargin}}

\cite{Knuth:TB10-1-31,%
   vLeunen:92,Knuth-CT-a}
\printbibliography
```

16.5 The author-title system

We now turn to the author-title system, sometimes also called the short-title system. A reference containing the author names and the title allows easy identification of the work while reading but generates longer citations than an author-date or numeric style. Styles therefore often use in subsequent citations abbreviations such as shorter titles, special shorthands, or words like "ibidem" to reference a repeated citation. Due to those additional requirements, the system is supported neither in standard LaTeX nor with the natbib package.

We start this section with a description of the jurabib package. As the name implies, the package has various options to tweak the output to conform to the citation rules in (German) jurisdiction, but it can also be used in other fields. This is then followed with a description of biblatex's approach to the author-title system.

16.5.1 jurabib — Customizable short-title references

Classifying the jurabib package developed by Jens Berger as a package implementing the short-title system is not really doing it justice (no pun intended), because in fact it actually supports other citation systems as well.

Besides short-title citations, it offers support for author-date citations (by providing the natbib command interface), various options to handle specific requirements from the humanities, and special support for citing juridical works such as commentaries (hence the name jurabib).

The package uses an extended option concept where options are specified with a key/value syntax. It supports more than 30 options, each of which may be set to a number of values, covering various aspects of presenting the citation layout in the text and the references in the bibliography. In this book we can show only a small selection of these possibilities. For further information refer to the package documentation, which is available in English and German.

The defaults used for all examples in this section! It is inconvenient to handle so many options as part of the \usepackage decla-ration, so jurabib offers the \jurabibsetup command as an alternative. It can be used in the preamble or in the package configuration file jurabib.cfg (to set the defaults for all documents). Settings established when loading the package or via \jurabibsetup in the preamble overwrite such global defaults. For the examples in this section we use the following defaults

```
\jurabibsetup{titleformat=colonsep,commabeforerest=true}
```

and extend or overwrite them as necessary. The titleformat setting puts a colon be-tween authors and title (see Example 16-5-7 on page 511) and the commabeforerest places a comma before the *post-note*, if present (e.g., in Example 16-5-1 on the next page and many others in this section).

In contrast to natbib, the jurabib package requires the use of specially designed BibTeX style files. It expects a \bibitem command with a highly structured optional argument to pass all kinds of information back to the user-level citation commands (see page 488). These BibTeX styles also implement a number of additional fields useful in conjunction with jurabib.

To show the particular features of jurabib, we again use our main sample database (Figure 15.1 on pages 382–383). If not explicitly documented otherwise, all examples in this section have the line

```
\newpage\bibliography{tlc}
```

implicitly appended at the end when processed.

The basic syntax

Like the natbib package, the jurabib package extends the standard LaTeX citation command \cite with a second optional argument.

```
\cite[post-note]{key₁,key₂,...}
\cite[annotator][post-note]{key₁,...}
```

If two optional arguments are present, then the *post-note* argument moves to the second position, the same behavior found with the natbib syntax. In the default setup there is a big difference in that we do not have a *pre-note* argument but rather an *annotator* argument provided for a citation method used in legal works.[1] In that discipline, works often have an original author (under which the work is listed in the bibliography) as well as annotators who provide commentaries in the particular edition. These annotators are mentioned in the citation but not in the bibliography. Without further adjustments a citation lists only the author surnames (separated by slashes if there are several authors), followed by the *annotator* if present, followed

---

[1]See page 512 if you want it to be a *pre-note* instead.

by a possible *post-note*. If the BibTeX entry contains a `shortauthor` field, then it is used instead of the surnames. If you only want to specify an *annotator*, use an empty *post-note*. By default, a title or short title is shown only if the author is cited with different works in the same document.

Brox/Walker
Brox/Walker, § 123
Otto Palandt/Heinrichs
Otto Palandt/Heinrichs, § 26

```
\usepackage{jurabib} \bibliographystyle{jurabib}
\cite{aschur}                      \\
\cite[\S\,123]{aschur}             \\
\cite[Heinrichs][]{bgb}            \\
\cite[Heinrichs][\S\,26]{bgb}
```

16-5-1

As you see, there is no way to determine from the typeset result that "Walker" is a coauthor but "Heinrichs" is an annotator. To make this distinction immediately visible, jurabib offers a number of options implementing common citation styles. You can, for example, change the font used for the annotator or change the separator between author and annotator. Both of these changes have been specified in the first part of the next example. You can also move the annotator before the author, a solution shown in two variants in the second part of the example.

Brox/Walker
Otto Palandt–*Heinrichs*, § 26
Heinrichs, Otto Palandt, § 26
Heinrichs in: Otto Palandt, § 26

```
\usepackage{jurabib} \bibliographystyle{jurabib}
\jurabibsetup{annotatorformat=italic,
              annotatorlastsep=divis}
\cite{aschur}  \\ \cite[Heinrichs][\S\,26]{bgb} \\
\jurabibsetup{annotatorfirstsep=comma}
\cite[Heinrichs][\S\,26]{bgb} \\
\jurabibsetup{annotatorfirstsep=in,annotatorformat=normal}
\cite[Heinrichs][\S\,26]{bgb}
```

16-5-2

Another way to clearly distinguish authors and annotators is to use the option `authorformat` with the value `and` (which replaces slashes with commas and "and"), the value `dynamic` (in which case different fonts are used depending on whether an *annotator* is present), or the value `year` (which moves the publication year directly after the author). The `authorformat` option can also be used to influence other aspects of the formatting of author names. Some examples are shown below. A complete list of allowed values is given in the package documentation. Note that if you use several values together (as done below), you need an additional set of braces to indicate to jurabib where the value list ends and the next option starts.

Brox and Walker
Otto Palandt/Heinrichs, § 26

```
\usepackage{jurabib} \bibliographystyle{jurabib}
\jurabibsetup{authorformat={and,smallcaps}}
\cite{aschur}  \\ \cite[Heinrichs][\S\,26]{bgb} \par
```

16-5-3

If the value `dynamic` is used, the annotator's name is set in italics, while the original author's name is set in the body font.[1] For works without an annotator, author

---

[1]The fonts used can be customized by redefining the commands `\jbactualauthorfont` and `\jbactualauthorfontifannotator`.

names are set in italics. One can think of this style as labeling those people who have actually worked on the particular edition.

Brox/*Walker*
Otto Palandt/*Heinrichs*, § 26

```
\usepackage{jurabib} \bibliographystyle{jurabib}
\jurabibsetup{authorformat=dynamic}
\cite{aschur}  \\ \cite[Heinrichs][\S\,26]{bgb} \par
```
16-5-4

The values and, dynamic, and year can be combined, while smallcaps and italic override each other with the last specification winning:

Brox and *Walker* (2003)
Otto Palandt (2003)/*Heinrichs*, § 26

```
\usepackage{jurabib} \bibliographystyle{jurabib}
\jurabibsetup{authorformat={and,smallcaps,year,italic}}
\cite{aschur}  \\ \cite[Heinrichs][\S\,26]{bgb} \par
```
16-5-5

The information passed back by BibTeX is very detailed and structured into individual fields whose contents can be accessed using the \citefield command.

```
\citefield[post-note]{field}{key₁,key₂,...}
```

The *field* argument is one of the following fields from the BibTeX database entry referenced by the *key* argument: author, shortauthor, title, shorttitle, url, or year. It can also be apy (address-publisher-year combination).

Whether more than a single *key* is useful is questionable for most fields. Indeed, even with \cite multiple keys are seldom useful unless no optional arguments are present.

BROX, HANS/WALKER, WOLF-DIETRICH
BSchuR, § 53
Reading, MA, USA: Addison-Wesley Longman, 1997
Allgemeines Schuldrecht; Besonderes Schuldrecht

```
\usepackage{jurabib} \bibliographystyle{jurabib}
\jurabibsetup{authorformat=smallcaps}
\citefield{author}{aschur}                    \\
\citefield[\S\,53]{shorttitle}{bschur} \\
\citefield{apy}{LGC97}                         \\
\citefield{title}{aschur,bschur}
```
16-5-6

If you are familiar with the German language, you will have noticed that the hyphenation of "Schul-drecht" is incorrect: it should have been "Schuld-recht". How to achieve this hyphenation automatically is explained on page 524.

Citations with short and full titles

As mentioned earlier, by default jurabib does not include a title in the citation text. The exception occurs when there are several works cited by the same author so that a title is necessary to distinguish between them. This behavior can be changed in several ways, but first we have a look at the "title" that will be used in such cases.

If you compare the first two lines of the next example with the BibTeX database file listed in Figure 15.1 on pages 382–383, you see that the shorttitle field was used if available; otherwise, the title field was used. In fact, you get a warning from jurabib for this adjustment: "shorttitle for aschur is missing – replacing with title". A different approach is taken for entries of type `article` or `periodical`; there, a missing `shorttitle` is replaced by the journal name, volume number, and year of publication, which is why we got "TUGboat 10 [1989]".

Brox/Walker: Allgemeines Schuldrecht
Brox/Walker: BSchuR
Knuth: The TEXbook
Knuth: TUGboat 10 [1989]

16-5-7

```
\usepackage{jurabib} \bibliographystyle{jurabib}
\cite{aschur}      \\  \cite{bschur}      \\[2pt]
\cite{Knuth-CT-a} \\  \cite{Knuth:TB10-1-31}
```

The colon after the author names above is due to the `commabeforerest` default that we have applied to all examples in this section; see page 508.

```
\citetitle[post-note]{key1,key2,...} \citetitle[annotator][post-note]{key1,...}
\cite*[post-note]{key1,key2,...}        \cite*[annotator][post-note]{key1,...}
```

To force the production of a title in the citation, you can use `\citetitle` instead of `\cite`. To leave out the title, you can use `\cite*`. You should, however, be aware that the latter command can easily lead to ambiguous citations, as shown in the next example:

Baumbach et al.: ZPO, Brox/Walker, and Brox/ Walker are three different books, or not?

16-5-8

```
\usepackage{jurabib} \bibliographystyle{jurabib}
\citetitle{zpo}, \cite*{aschur}, and
\cite*{bschur} are three different books, or not?
```

Also note that this meaning of `\cite*` is quite different from its use in natbib (where it denotes using a full list of authors). If you switch between both packages depending on the circumstances, it might be better to avoid it altogether.

```
\citetitleonly[post-note]{key}
```

It is also possible to refer to only the title, including a *post-note* if desired.

16-5-9

ZPO, § 13

```
\usepackage{jurabib} \bibliographystyle{jurabib}
\citetitleonly[\S\,13]{zpo}
```

To generate short-title citations by default, specify the option `titleformat` with the value `all`. Like `authorformat`, this option can take several values. We already know about `colonsep`, which we used as a default setting for all the examples. In the next example we overwrite it with `commasep` and print the titles in `italic`.

Getting short-title citations automatically

Brox/Walker, *Allgemeines Schuldrecht*, § 123
Brox/Walker, *BSchuR*
Otto Palandt/Heinrichs, *BGB*
Knuth, *TUGboat 10 [1989]*

16-5-10

```
\usepackage{jurabib} \bibliographystyle{jurabib}
\jurabibsetup{titleformat={all,commasep,italic}}
\cite[\S\,123]{aschur}  \\ \cite{bschur}  \\
\cite[Heinrichs][]{bgb} \\ \cite{Knuth:TB10-1-31}
```

> `\citetitlefortype{`*BIBTEX-type-list*`}` `\citenotitlefortype{`*BIBTEX-type-list*`}`

Instead of citing all works with titles, you can select short-title citations based on a particular BIBTEX type. For example,

```
\citetitlefortype{article,book,manual}
```

would reference these three types with the title and all other publication types without it, unless the author is cited with several works. Because such a list can grow quite large, you can alternatively select automatic title citations for all works (with `titleformat`) and then specify those types that should have no titles when referenced. This is done in the next example for the type book. Nevertheless, the book by Knuth is cited with its title, because we also cite an article by him.

Brox/Walker	`\usepackage{jurabib}` `\bibliographystyle{jurabib}`
Goossens/Rahtz	`\jurabibsetup{titleformat=all}` `\citenotitlefortype{book}`
Knuth: The TEXbook	`\cite{bschur}` `\\` `\cite{LWC99}` `\\`
Knuth: TUGboat 10 [1989]	`\cite{Knuth-CT-a}` `\\` `\cite{Knuth:TB10-1-31}`

16-5-11

Indexing citations automatically

The author names in citations can be entered in the index by using the option `authorformat` with the value `indexed`. By default, this is done only for citations inside the text; authors referred to only in the bibliography are not listed. This behavior can be changed by setting `\jbindexbib` in the preamble or in a configuration file. For formatting the index entries, `\jbauthorindexfont` is available. For example,

```
\renewcommand\jbauthorindexfont[1]{\textit{#1}}
```

means that the author names appear in italic in the index.

Instead of placing the author names in the main index, you can produce a separate author index by loading the index package (see Section 14.5.3) and then using a construction like

```
\usepackage{index}
\newindex{default}{idx}{ind}{Index}            % the main index
\newindex{authors}{adx}{and}{Index of Authors}
\renewcommand\jbindextype{authors}
```

in the preamble, and later `\printindex[authors]` to indicate where the author index should appear in the document.

No support is available for more elaborate indexes as required for some types of law books (e.g., "Table of Cases" or "Table of Statutes"). If this is required, you have to generate the index by different means.

Using natbib citation semantics

The optional *annotator* argument is useful only in legal studies. In other disciplines, it is more common to require a *pre-note* (e.g., "compare...”). To account for this, the meanings of the optional arguments can be modified by loading the package with the option see.

\cite[*pre-note*] [*post-note*] {*key₁*, *key₂*, ... }   (with option see)

The see option replaces the default *annotator* optional argument with a *pre-note* argument in the case that two optional arguments are used. The \cite command then has the same syntax and semantics as it does with the natbib package.

(Goossens/Rahtz/Mittelbach)
(Goossens/Rahtz/Mittelbach, chap. 2)

(compare Goossens/Rahtz/Mittelbach)
(see Goossens/Rahtz/Mittelbach, chap. 2)

```
\usepackage[see,round]{jurabib}
\bibliographystyle{jurabib}
\cite{LGC97}              \\ \cite[chap.~2]{LGC97} \\[3pt]
\cite[compare][]{LGC97}\\ \cite[see][chap.~2]{LGC97}
```

16-5-12

This work was cited as ...

When using a short-title system for citations (e.g., by setting titleformat to all), it can be helpful to present the reader with a mapping between the full entry and the short title. This is commonly done by displaying the short title in parentheses at the end of the corresponding entry in the bibliography. The jurabib package supports this convention with the option howcited. It can take a number of values that configure the mechanism in slightly different ways. For example, the value all instructs the package to add "how cited" information to all entries in the bibliography. Thus, if we add to Example 16-5-10 on page 511 the line \jurabibsetup{howcited=all}, then we get the following bibliography listing. Note that the short title is formatted in exactly the same way as it appears in the citation.

Brox, Hans/Walker, Wolf-Dietrich: Besonderes Schuldrecht. 27th edition. München, 2002 (cited: Brox/Walker, *BSchuR*)

Brox, Hans/Walker, Wolf-Dietrich: Allgemeines Schuldrecht. 29th edition. München, 2003 (cited: Brox/Walker, *Allgemeines Schuldrecht*)

Knuth, Donald E.: Typesetting Concrete Mathematics. TUGboat, 10 April 1989, Nr. 1, 31–36, ISSN 0896–3207 (cited: Knuth, *TUGboat 10 [1989]*)

Palandt, Otto: Bürgerliches Gesetzbuch. 62th edition. München: Beck Juristischer Verlag, 2003 (cited: Otto Palandt, *BGB*)

16-5-13

However, it is usually not necessary to display for all entries how they are cited. For articles, the short-title citation is always "author name, journal, volume, and year". If a work is cited with its full title (i.e., if there is no shorttitle field) or if only a single publication is cited for a certain author, then the reader will generally be able to identify the corresponding entry without any further help. To allow for such a restricted type of "back-references", jurabib offers the values compare, multiple, and normal.

If you use compare, then a back-reference is created only if the entry contains a shorttitle field and the title and shorttitle fields differ. With respect to

Example 16-5-13 this means that only the first and last entries would show the back-references.

If you use `multiple` instead, then back-references are generated whenever an author is cited with several works except for citations of articles. In the above example, the first two entries would get back-references. If we also had a citation to `Knuth-CT-a`, then it would also show a back-reference, while Knuth's article in *TUGboat* would be still without one.

Both values can be used together. In that case back-references are added to entries for authors with several publications as well as to entries whose short titles differ from their main titles.

Finally, there is the value `normal` (it is also used if you specify the option without a value). This value works slightly differently from the others in that it needs support to be present in the BibTeX database. If it is used, an entry gets a back-reference if and only if the BibTeX field `howcited` is present. The field can have two kinds of values. If it has a value of "1", the back-reference lists exactly what is shown in the citation in text. With any other value, the actual contents of the `howcited` field are used for the back-reference, including any formatting directives contained therein.

The text surrounding the back-reference can be customized by redefining the commands `\howcitedprefix` and `\howcitedsuffix`. In addition, you can specify what should happen with entries that have been added via `\nocite` by changing `\bibnotcited` (empty by default). Because these commands may contain text that should differ depending on the main language of the document, they are redefined using a special mechanism (`\AddTo`) that is explained on page 524.

... Brox/Walker: BSchuR ... Knuth ...

References

Brox, Hans/Walker, Wolf-Dietrich: Besonderes Schuldrecht. 27th edition. München, 2002 (cited as Brox/Walker: BSchuR).

Brox, Hans/Walker, Wolf-Dietrich: Allgemeines Schuldrecht. 29th edition. München, 2003 (not cited).

Knuth, Donald E.: Typesetting Concrete Mathematics. TUGboat, 10 April 1989, Nr. 1, 31–36, ISSN 0896–3207 (cited as Knuth).

```
\usepackage{jurabib}
\bibliographystyle{jurabib}
\jurabibsetup{howcited=all}
\AddTo\bibsall{%
    \renewcommand\howcitedprefix
                    { (cited as }%
    \renewcommand\howcitedsuffix{).}%
    \renewcommand\bibnotcited
                    { (not cited).}}
\nocite{aschur}
\ldots \cite{bschur} \ldots
\cite{Knuth:TB10-1-31} \ldots
\bibliography{tlc}
```

16-5-14

Full citations inside the text

While producing full ("verbose") citations inside the text with natbib requires a separate package and some initial preparation, this citation method is fully integrated in jurabib. The complete entry can be shown for one or more individual citations, for all citations, or automatically for only the first citation of a work. This citation method is most often used in footnotes; see page 518 for information on how to automatically arrange footnote citations.

```
\fullcite[post-note]{key1,key2,...}
\fullcite[annotator][post-note]{key1,key2,...}
```

This command works like \cite but displays the full bibliographical data. The *annotator*, if present, is placed in front of the citation in the same way as if annotatorfirstsep=in had been specified.

Compare the next example with Example 16-6-1 from page 538. The value citationreversed arranges for the author name to appear with surname last (in the bibliography the surname comes first). Related values are allreversed (surname last in text and bibliography) and firstnotreversed (surname first for first author, last for all others in multiple-author works).

For details see Donald E. Knuth: Typesetting Concrete Mathematics. TUGboat, 10 April 1989, Nr. 1, ISSN 0896–3207. General information can be found in Donald E. Knuth: The TEXbook. Volume A, Computers and Typesetting. Reading, MA, USA: Addison-Wesley, 1986, ISBN 0–201–13447–0.

As shown by Knuth (1989) ...

16-5-15

```
\usepackage{jurabib}
\bibliographystyle{jurabib}
\jurabibsetup{authorformat=citationreversed}

\raggedright \setlength\parindent{12pt}
For details see \fullcite{Knuth:TB10-1-31}.
General information can be found in
\fullcite{Knuth-CT-a}.

As shown by \citet{Knuth:TB10-1-31} \ldots
```

The \cite command automatically generates full citations if the citefull option is specified together with one of the following values: all (all references are full citations), first (first citation is full, subsequent ones are abbreviated), chapter (same as first but restarts with each chapter), and section (like chapter but restarts at the \section level). All settings imply annotatorfirstsep=in, as can be seen in the second citation in the example. If one of the above settings has been included in the configuration file and you want to turn it off for the current document, use the value false.

Getting full citations automatically

See Baumbach, Adolf et al.: Zivilprozeßordnung mit Gerichtsverfassungsgesetz und anderen Nebengesetzen. 59th edition. München, 2002 ...

As shown by Heinrichs in: Baumbach et al., § 216 the interpretation

16-5-16

```
\usepackage{jurabib}
\bibliographystyle{jurabib}
\jurabibsetup{citefull=first}
See \cite{zpo} \ldots

As shown by \cite[Heinrichs][\S\,216]{zpo}
the interpretation \ldots
```

```
\citefullfirstfortype{BIBTEX-type-list}
```

Further control is possible by specifying the BIBTEX entry types for which a full citation should be generated on the first occurrence. In the example below (otherwise similar to Example 16-5-15), we request that only entries of type `article` should be subject to this process.

For details see Knuth, Donald E.: Typesetting Concrete Mathematics. TUGboat, 10 April 1989, Nr. 1, ISSN 0896–3207. General information can be found in Knuth: The TEXbook.
As shown by Knuth: TUGboat 10 [1989]

```
\usepackage{jurabib} \bibliographystyle{jurabib}
\jurabibsetup{citefull=first}
\citefullfirstfortype{article}

For details see \cite{Knuth:TB10-1-31}. General
information can be found in \cite{Knuth-CT-a}.

As shown by \cite{Knuth:TB10-1-31}
```

16-5-17

```
\nextciteshort{key1,key2,...} \nextcitefull{key1,key2,...}
\nextcitereset{key1,key2,...} \nextcitenotitle{key1,key2,...}
```

Sometimes it is not correct to make the first citation to a work be the full entry, such as in an abstract or preface. On the other hand, you may want to have a certain citation show the full entry again, even though it appeared earlier. For this purpose four commands are available that modify how individual citations are presented from the given point onward.[1]

If you use `\nextciteshort`, all citations specified in the *key-list* are typeset as short-title citations from then on (e.g., lines A, B, D in the example). If you use `\nextcitereset`, the citations are (again) typeset in the normal way; thus, the next citation will be a full citation if there has not been one yet (lines C and F), and otherwise citations are set as short-title citations (line E). With `\nextcitefull`, you force full entries from then on (line G). With `\nextcitenotitle`, you get only the author name(s), even if it results in ambiguous citations.

A) Knuth: The TEXbook
B) Knuth: TUGboat 10 [1989]
C) Knuth, Donald E.: The TEXbook. Volume A, Computers and Typesetting. Reading, MA, USA: Addison-Wesley, 1986, ISBN 0–201–13447–0
D) Knuth: TUGboat 10 [1989]
E) Knuth: The TEXbook
F) Knuth, Donald E.: Typesetting Concrete Mathematics. TUGboat, 10 April 1989, Nr. 1, ISSN 0896–3207
G) Knuth, Donald E.: The TEXbook. Volume A, Computers and Typesetting. Reading, MA, USA: Addison-Wesley, 1986, ISBN 0–201–13447–0
H) Knuth

```
\usepackage[citefull=first]{jurabib}
\bibliographystyle{jurabib}
\nextciteshort{Knuth-CT-a,Knuth:TB10-1-31}
A) \cite{Knuth-CT-a}                    \\
B) \cite{Knuth:TB10-1-31}               \\
\nextcitereset{Knuth-CT-a}
C) \cite{Knuth-CT-a}                    \\
D) \cite{Knuth:TB10-1-31}               \\
\nextcitereset{Knuth-CT-a,Knuth:TB10-1-31}
E) \cite{Knuth-CT-a}                    \\
F) \cite{Knuth:TB10-1-31}               \\
\nextcitefull{Knuth-CT-a}
\nextcitenotitle{Knuth:TB10-1-31}
G) \cite{Knuth-CT-a}                    \\
H) \cite{Knuth:TB10-1-31}
```

16-5-18

If full citations are used within the main document, it is not absolutely necessary to assemble them in a bibliography or reference list. You may, for example, have

---

[1] The command names seem to indicate that they change the "next" citation, but in fact they change all further citations until they are overwritten.

all citations inline and use a bibliography for suggested further reading or other secondary material.

\citeswithoutentry{*key-list*}

This declaration lists those keys that should not appear in the bibliography even though they are cited in the text. The *key-list* is a list of comma-separated keys without any white space. You can repeat this command as often as necessary. Think of it as the opposite of \nocite. Both commands are used in the next example:

This is explained in Brox, Hans/Walker, Wolf-Dietrich: Allgemeines Schuldrecht. 29th edition. München, 2003. As shown in Brox/Walker...

Selected further reading

Baumbach, Adolf et al.: Zivilprozeßordnung mit Gerichtsverfassungsgesetz und anderen Nebengesetzen. 59th edition. München, 2002

```
\usepackage{jurabib}
\renewcommand\refname
        {Selected further reading}
\bibliographystyle{jurabib}
\citeswithoutentry{aschur}
\jurabibsetup{citefull=first}
This is explained in \cite{aschur}.
\par As shown in \cite{aschur}\ldots
\nocite{zpo}
\bibliography{tlc}
```

16-5-19

While \citeswithoutentry prevents individual works from appearing in the bibliography, it is not possible to use it to suppress all entries, because you would get an empty list consisting of just the heading. If you want to omit the bibliography altogether, use \nobibliography in place of the usual \bibliography command. This command reads the .bbl file produced by BibTeX to enable citation references, but without producing a typeset result. You still need to specify jurabib as the BibTeX style and run BibTeX in the normal way.

Suppressing the bibliography altogether

Citations as footnotes or endnotes

All citation commands introduced so far have variants that generate footnote citations or, when used together with the endnotes package, generate endnotes. Simply prepend foot to the command name (e.g., \footcite instead of \cite, \footcitetitle instead of \citetitle, and so forth). This allows you to mix footnote and other citations freely, if needed.

The footnote citations produced by jurabib are ordinary footnotes, so you can influence their layout by loading the footmisc package, if desired.

...to use LaTeX on the web.* Also discussed by Goossens/Rahtz is generating PDF and HTML.

```
\usepackage[ragged,symbol]{footmisc}
\usepackage{jurabib}
\bibliographystyle{jurabib}

\ldots to use \LaTeX{} on the
web.\footfullcite{LWC99}
Also discussed by \cite{LWC99}
is generating PDF and HTML.
```

---

*Goossens, Michel/Rahtz, Sebastian: The LaTeX Web companion: integrating TeX, HTML, and XML. Reading, MA, USA: Addison-Wesley Longman, 1999, Tools and Techniques for Computer Typesetting, ISBN 0–201–43311–7.

16-5-20

517

*Getting footnote
citations
automatically* If all your citations should be automatically typeset as footnotes, use the `super` option. In that case jurabib automatically chooses the `\foot..` variants, so `\cite` produces `\footcite`, and so forth. This is shown in the next example. There we also use `citefull=first` so that the first footnote looks like the one in the previous example (to save space we show only the second page, where due to the ridiculously small height of the example page the last line of that footnote is carried over). The other two citations are then automatically shortened, with the third being shortened even further because of the `ibidem` option (explained on the next page).

We also use the option `lookat`, which is responsible for the back-reference to the earlier note containing the full citation. This option is allowed only if you simultaneously use the `citefull` option and have all your initial citations in footnotes, because it requires a "number" to refer to.

You have to be careful to use a footnote style that produces unique numbers. If footnotes are numbered by chapter or by page, for example, then such references are ambiguous. This problem can be solved by loading the varioref package, in which case these back-references also show page numbers. If varioref is loaded for other reasons and you do not want page references in this place, use `\jbignorevarioref` to suppress them. If footnotes are numbered by chapter, then an alternative solution is to use the `\labelformat` declaration to indicate to which chapter the footnote belongs:

```
\labelformat{footnote}{\thechapter--#1}
```

The `lookat` option is particularly useful in combination with the command `\nobibliography` so that all your bibliographical information is placed in footnotes without a summary bibliography.

Also discussed is generating PDF[2] and HTML.[3]

43311–7.

   [2]Goossens/Rahtz (as in n. 1), chap. 2.
   [3]Ibid., chap. 3–4.

```
\usepackage{jurabib} \bibliographystyle{jurabib}
\jurabibsetup{super,citefull=first,ibidem,lookat}

\ldots to use \LaTeX{} on the web.\cite{LWC99}
    \newpage % Next page shown on the left:
Also discussed is generating PDF\cite[chap.~2]
{LWC99} and HTML.\cite[chap.~3--4]{LWC99}
```

16-5-21

It is possible to customize the appearance of the back-references by using the commands `\lookatprefix` and `\lookatsuffix`. Both are language dependent, which is the reason for using the `\AddTo` declaration (see page 524). The example sets up a style commonly seen in law citations [18].

```
\usepackage{jurabib} \bibliographystyle{jurabib}
\jurabibsetup{super,citefull=first,lookat}
\AddTo\bibsall{\renewcommand\lookatprefix
    {, \emph{supra} note }
    \renewcommand\lookatsuffix{}}

\ldots to use \LaTeX{} on the web.\cite{LWC99}
    \newpage % Next page shown on the left:
Also discussed is generating PDF\cite[chap.~2]
{LWC99} and HTML.\cite[chap.~3--4]{LWC99}
```

16-5-22

Also discussed is generating PDF[2] and HTML.[3]

43311–7.

   [2]Goossens/Rahtz, *supra* note 1, chap. 2.
   [3]Goossens/Rahtz, *supra* note 1, chap. 3–4.

By loading the `endnotes` package in a setup similar to the one from the previous example, you can turn all your citations into endnotes.[1] As you can see, the endnotes do not have a final period added by default. If you prefer a period, add the option `dotafter` with the value `endnote`.

...to typeset with graphics.[1] Also discussed is typesetting music[2] and games.[3]

```
\usepackage{jurabib,endnotes}
\bibliographystyle{jurabib}
\jurabibsetup{citefull=first,
  super,lookat}
```

Notes

[1]Goossens, Michel/Rahtz, Sebastian/Mittelbach, Frank: The LaTeX Graphics Companion: Illustrating Documents with TeX and PostScript. Reading, MA, USA: Addison-Wesley Longman, 1997, Tools and Techniques for Computer Typesetting, ISBN 0–201–85469–4

[2]Goossens/Rahtz/Mittelbach (as in n. 1), chap. 7

[3]Goossens/Rahtz/Mittelbach (as in n. 1), chap. 8

```
\ldots to typeset with
graphics.\cite{LGC97} Also
discussed is typesetting
music\cite[chap.~7]{LGC97} and
games.\cite[chap.~8]{LGC97}
\theendnotes
```

16-5-23

Ibidem — In the same place

In some disciplines it is customary to use the Latin word "ibidem" (abbreviated as "ibid." or "ib.") if you repeat a reference to the immediately preceding citation. The `jurabib` package supports this convention in several variants if the option `ibidem` is specified. This option must be used with footnote-style citations (e.g., when using `\footcite` or with the option `super` activated).

If `ibidem` is used without a value (which is the same as using it with the value `strict`), then the following happens: if a citation refers to the same publication as the immediately preceding citation on the *current* page, then it is replaced by "Ibid.", if necessary keeping a *post-note*. You can see this situation in the next example: the first citation is a short-title citation; the second citation is identical, so we get "Ibid." with the *post-note* dropped; and the third and fourth citations refer to different parts of the same publication, so we get the *post-note* as well. The fifth citation refers to a different publication by the same authors, so another short-title citation is produced. The sixth citation refers to the same publication, but the short-title citation is repeated because it is on a new page. The seventh and eighth citations are again to the other publication, so we get first a short-title citation and then "Ibid." with a *post-note*.

A[1] legal[2,3] text.[4,5]

Some[6,7] more[8] text.

---

[1] Brox/Walker: BSchuR, § 7.
[2] Ibid.
[3] Ibid., § 16.
[4] Ibid., § 7.
[5] Brox/Walker: Allgemeines Schuldrecht.

[6] Brox/Walker: Allgemeines Schuldrecht, § 3.
[7] Brox/Walker: BSchuR.
[8] Ibid., § 15.

```
\usepackage[marginal,multiple]{footmisc}
\usepackage[super,ibidem]{jurabib}
\bibliographystyle{jurabib}
A \cite[\S\,7]{bschur}
legal \cite[\S\,7]{bschur}
    \cite[\S\,16]{bschur}
text \cite[\S\,7]{bschur} \cite{aschur}
\newpage   % <---
Some \cite[\S\,3]{aschur} \cite{bschur}
more \cite[\S\,15]{bschur} text.
```

16-5-24

---

[1]jurabib is currently not compatible with the newer enotez.

If you typeset your document with the class option `twoside`, then you can use the value `strictdoublepage`. It means that "Ibid." is also used across page boundaries as long as the preceding citation is still visible (i.e., on the same spread). Repeating Example 16-5-24 with this setting changes the sixth citation to "Ibid., §3".

The `ibidem` option usually generates a lot of very short footnotes, so it might be economical to use it together with the `para` option of `footmisc`. We also add the `perpage` option so that the footnote numbers remain small. Note, however, that this makes it impossible to use the `lookat` option because the footnote numbers are no longer unique.

Some[1] legal[2,3] text[4,5] with commentaries.	And[1,2] several more.[3]	`\usepackage[para,multiple,perpage]{footmisc}`

```
\usepackage[para,multiple,perpage]{footmisc}
\usepackage{jurabib}
\bibliographystyle{jurabib}
\jurabibsetup{super,ibidem=strictdoublepage}
Some \cite[\S\,7]{bschur} legal
\cite[\S\,7]{bschur} \cite[\S\,16]{bschur}
text \cite[\S\,7]{bschur} \cite{aschur}
with commentaries.
\newpage
And \cite[\S\,3]{aschur} \cite{bschur}
several more. \cite[\S\,15]{bschur}
```

[1] Brox/Walker: BSchuR, §7. [2] Ibid. [3] Ibid., §16. [4] Ibid., §7. [5] Brox/Walker: Allgemeines Schuldrecht.

[1] Ibid., §3. [2] Brox/Walker: BSchuR. [3] Ibid., §15.

16-5-25

It is even possible to ignore all page boundaries by using the `nostrict` value. The reader might find it difficult to decipher the references, however, because "Ibid." and the citation to which it refers may be moved arbitrarily far apart. If necessary, you can disable the `ibidem` mechanism for the next citation by preceding it with `\noibidem`.

A page without a citation.	This page has references.[2] Maybe better like this?[3]

```
\usepackage{jurabib} \bibliographystyle{jurabib}
\jurabibsetup{super,ibidem=nostrict}
   \ldots \fullcite{bschur} \ldots
\newpage % page above not shown on the left
            A page without a citation.
\newpage This page has references.\cite{bschur}
   Maybe better like this? \noibidem\cite{bschur}
```

[2] Ibid. [3] Brox/Walker.

16-5-26

The use of "Ibid." without any further qualification allows you to reference just the immediately preceding citation. Thus, if citations are frequently mixed, the mechanism inserts short-title references most of the time. This situation changes if you use the `ibidem` option with the value `name` (which automatically implies `citefull=first`). In that case "Ibid." is used with the full name of the author, thus allowing a reference to an earlier — not directly preceding — citation. If only the surnames of the authors are required, add the `authorformat` option with the value `reducedifibidem`. Its effect is seen in the next example, where citations to bschur and zpo alternate. A variant is to always use the name and short title except for the first citation of a publication; this format can be requested with the value `name&title`.

If the same author is cited with more than one publication, then using the `ibidem` option with the `name` value is likely to produce ambiguous references. For those citations the `jurabib` package automatically switches to the `name&title&auto` method described below.

A[1] legal[2,3] text[4,5] with[6] commentaries.

---

[1] Brox, Hans/Walker, Wolf-Dietrich: Besonderes Schuldrecht. 27th edition. München, 2002, § 7.
[2] Brox/Walker, ibid., § 8.
[3] Baumbach, Adolf et al.: Zivilprozeßordnung mit Gerichtsverfassungsgesetz und anderen Nebengesetzen. 59th edition. München, 2002, § 16.
[4] Brox/Walker, ibid., § 7.
[5] Baumbach et al., ibid.
[6] Baumbach et al., ibid., § 3.

16-5-27

```
\usepackage[marginal,ragged,multiple]{footmisc}
\usepackage{jurabib}
\bibliographystyle{jurabib}
\jurabibsetup{super,ibidem=name,
              authorformat=reducedifibidem}
A \cite[\S\,7]{bschur} legal
\cite[\S\,8]{bschur} \cite[\S\,16]{zpo}
text \cite[\S\,7]{bschur} \cite{zpo}
with \cite[\S\,3]{zpo} commentaries.
```

If `name&title&auto` was selected (either implicitly or explicitly), then the following happens: the first citation of a publication automatically displays the full entry (citation 5 in the next example). In the case of repeated citations to unambiguous works only the names of the authors are shown (citation 8). For ambiguous citations this is done only for immediately following citations (citation 4). However, if there are intervening citations, then the names and short titles are shown (citations 3, 6, and 7).

A[3] different[4,5] legal[6,7] text.[8]

---

[3] Brox, Hans/Walker, Wolf-Dietrich: Allgemeines Schuldrecht, ibid., § 7.
[4] Brox, Hans/Walker, Wolf-Dietrich, ibid., § 8.
[5] Baumbach, Adolf et al.: Zivilprozeßordnung mit Gerichtsverfassungsgesetz und anderen Nebengesetzen. 59th edition. München, 2002, § 16.
[6] Brox, Hans/Walker, Wolf-Dietrich: BSchuR, ibid., § 7.
[7] Brox, Hans/Walker, Wolf-Dietrich: Allgemeines Schuldrecht, ibid.
[8] Baumbach, Adolf et al., ibid., § 3.

16-5-28

```
\usepackage[marginal,ragged,multiple]{footmisc}
\usepackage{jurabib}
\bibliographystyle{jurabib}
\jurabibsetup{super,ibidem=name&title&auto}
  Full citations for \cite{aschur} and
  \cite{bschur} are put on an earlier
  page and therefore not displayed
  on the left!
\newpage
A \cite[\S\,7]{aschur} different
\cite[\S\,8]{aschur} \cite[\S\,16]{zpo}
legal \cite[\S\,7]{bschur} \cite{aschur}
text. \cite[\S\,3]{zpo}
```

Another convention in certain disciplines is to replace the author's name with the Latin word "Idem" (meaning "the same") if the author of successive citations is identical. This is catered for by the option `idem`, which accepts the values `strict`, `strictdoublepage`, and `nostrict` with the same semantics as used with the `ibidem` option. Both options can be combined as shown in Example 16-5-29 on the following page. Due to the values used, we get different citations: some use "Idem, ibid."; after the page break "Idem" is suppressed, because of the option `strict`; and in the last three citations it is used again (even with the full citation) because they all refer to different publications of Donald Knuth.

...some[1] text[2] and[3,4]...

---
[1] Knuth, Donald E.: The TeXbook. Volume A, Computers and Typesetting. Reading, MA, USA: Addison-Wesley, 1986, ISBN 0–201–13447–0.
[2] Idem, ibid., p. 22.
[3] Leunen, Mary-Claire van: A handbook for scholars. Walton Street, Oxford OX2 6DP, UK: Oxford University Press, 1992.
[4] Idem, ibid.

...a[5] bit[6] more[7] text[8,9]...

---
[5] Leunen, Mary-Claire van, ibid.
[6] Idem, ibid., p. 16.
[7] Knuth, Donald E.: The TeXbook, ibid., p. 308.
[8] Idem: Typesetting Concrete Mathematics. TUGboat, 10 April 1989, Nr. 1, ISSN 0896–3207.
[9] Idem: The TeXbook, ibid., p. 80.

```
\usepackage[flushmargin,%
            multiple]{footmisc}
\usepackage[super,idem=strict,%
            ibidem=name]{jurabib}
\bibliographystyle{jurabib}

\ldots some \cite{Knuth-CT-a}
text \cite[p.~22]{Knuth-CT-a}
and \cite{vLeunen:92}
\cite{vLeunen:92}\ldots
\newpage % <--
\ldots a \cite{vLeunen:92}
bit \cite[p.~16]{vLeunen:92}
more \cite[p.~308]{Knuth-CT-a}
text \cite{Knuth:TB10-1-31}
\cite[p.~80]{Knuth-CT-a}\ldots
```
16-5-29

You have to ask yourself whether this type of citation is actually helpful to your readers. Butcher [21], for example, argues against it. Of course, you may not have a choice in the matter — it might be required. You should, however, note that two citations in the previous example are actually wrong: van Leunen is a female author, so the correct Latin form would be "Eadem" and not "Idem" (though some style manuals do not make that distinction). If necessary, jurabib offers possibilities for adjusting your citations even on that level of detail; see page 525.

There is another convention related to recurring citations, though it is becoming less common: to signal that a citation refers to an earlier reference, it is flagged with *op. cit.* (*opere citato*, "in the work cited"). This practice is supported with the option `opcit`. The citation should be "close by" so that the reader has a chance to find it. For this reason jurabib offers the values `chapter` and `section` in analogy to the `citefull` option.

...some[1] text[2] and[3] some more text[4,5]

---
[1] Knuth, Donald E.: The TeXbook. Volume A, Computers and Typesetting. Reading, MA, USA: Addison-Wesley, 1986, ISBN 0–201–13447–0.
[2] Idem, *op. cit.*, p. 22.
[3] Free Software Foundation: GNU Make, A Program for Directing Recompilation. 2000.
[4] Knuth, *op. cit.*
[5] Free Software Foundation, *op. cit.*

```
\usepackage[multiple]{footmisc}
\usepackage[super,idem=strict,%
   citefull=first,opcit]{jurabib}
\bibliographystyle{jurabib}

\ldots some \cite{Knuth-CT-a} text
\cite[p.~22]{Knuth-CT-a} and
\cite{GNUMake} some more text
\cite{Knuth-CT-a}\cite{GNUMake}
```
16-5-30

In law citations [18], it is common to use the word "*supra*" to indicate a reference to a previous citation. This can be accomplished by changing the \opcit command, which holds the generated string, as follows:

```
\renewcommand\opcit{\textit{supra}}
```

Alternatively, you can use the method shown in Example 16-5-22 on page 518.

Cross-referencing citations

BIBTEX supports the notion of cross-references between bibliographical entries via the `crossref` field. For example, an entry of type `inproceedings` can reference the proceedings issue in which it appears. Depending on the number of references to such an issue, BIBTEX then decides whether to produce a separate entry for the issue or to include information about it in each `inproceedings` entry. See Section 15.3.7 for details.

If BIBTEX decides to produce separate entries for the cross-referenced citations, a question arises about what should happen if they are referenced in a `\fullcite` or `\footfullcite` command in the text. To handle this situation jurabib offers three values applicable to the `crossref` option: with the value `normal` (the default), cross-references are typeset as an `author/editor`, `title` combination (or `shortauthor`, `shorttitle` if available); with the value `short`, only the `author` or `editor` is used as long as there are no ambiguities; and with the value `long`, cross-references are listed in full. The default behavior is shown below (where the editors and the short title were selected by jurabib).

> Mittelbach, Frank/Rowley, Chris: The Pursuit of Quality: How can Automated Typesetting achieve the Highest Standards of Craft Typography? In Vanoirbeek/Coray: EP92
>
> Southall, Richard: Presentation Rules and Rules of Composition in the Formatting of Complex Text. In Vanoirbeek/Coray: EP92
>
> Mittelbach/Rowley

```
\usepackage{jurabib}
\jurabibsetup{citefull=first,
            crossref=normal}
\bibliographystyle{jurabib}

\cite{MR-PQ}      \par
\cite{Southall}   \par
\cite{MR-PQ}
```

`16-5-31`

You can combine any of the three values with the value `dynamic`, in which case a cross-reference is given in a longer form when cited the first time and in the shorter form on all later occasions. Here we combine it with the value `long` so that we get a full citation to Vanoirbeek/Coray in the first citation and a short title citation in the second.

> Frank Mittelbach/Chris Rowley: The Pursuit of Quality: How can Automated Typesetting achieve the Highest Standards of Craft Typography? In Christine Vanoirbeek/Giovanni Coray, editors: EP92—Proceedings of Electronic Publishing, '92. Cambridge: Cambridge University Press, 1992
>
> Richard Southall: Presentation Rules and Rules of Composition in the Formatting of Complex Text. In Vanoirbeek/Coray: EP92

```
\usepackage{jurabib}
\jurabibsetup{citefull=first,
    authorformat=
        citationreversed,
    crossref={dynamic,long}}
\bibliographystyle{jurabib}

\cite{MR-PQ}      \par
\cite{Southall}
```

`16-5-32`

Author-date citation support

As mentioned earlier, jurabib supports the commands `\citet` and `\citep` as introduced by natbib. It also offers `\citealt`, `\citealp`, `\citeauthor`, `\citeyear`, and `\citeyearpar`. Those forms for which it makes sense are also available as footnote citations by prefixing the command name with foot (e.g., \footcitet). Not provided are the starred forms available with natbib.

Goossens/Rahtz (1999)	```\usepackage{jurabib}```
Goossens/Rahtz (1999, chap. 2)	```\bibliographystyle{jurabib}```
see Goossens/Rahtz (1999, chap. 2)	```\citet{LWC99} \\```
pre-note only: see Goossens/Rahtz (1999)	```\citet[chap.~2]{LWC99} \\```
	```\citet[see][chap.~2]{LWC99} \\```
(Goossens/Rahtz, 1999)	```pre-note only: \citet[see][]{LWC99} \\[5pt]```
(Goossens/Rahtz, 1999, chap. 2)	```\citep{LWC99} \\```
(see Goossens/Rahtz, 1999, chap. 2)	```\citep[chap.~2]{LWC99} \\```
pre-note only: (see Goossens/Rahtz, 1999)	```\citep[see][chap.~2]{LWC99} \\```
	```pre-note only: \citep[see][]{LWC99} \\[5pt]```
Knuth, 1986	```\citealp{Knuth-CT-a} \\```
Knuth	```\citeauthor{Knuth-CT-a} \\```
(1986)	```\citeyearpar{Knuth-CT-a}```

16-5-33

A combination of author-date and short-title citations is achieved by setting authorformat=year, as already introduced in Example 16-5-5. The formatting of the year can be influenced with \jbcitationyearformat, and the position of the date can be moved after the title (if present) by specifying \jbyearaftertitle.

	```\usepackage{jurabib} \bibliographystyle{jurabib}```
	```\jurabibsetup{authorformat=year,annotatorformat=italic,```
Otto Palandt/*Heinrichs*: BGB 2003,	``` titleformat={all,colonsep}}```
§ 26	```\renewcommand\jbcitationyearformat[1]{\oldstylenums{#1}}```
Brox/Walker: Allgemeines Schuld-	```\jbyearaftertitle```
recht 2003	```\cite[Heinrichs][\S\,26]{bgb} \\ \cite{aschur}```

16-5-34

Language support

Most strings that are generated automatically in a bibliography entry or as part of a full citation are language dependent; they depend on the main language of the document. The jurabib package supports this by collaborating with the babel package. Depending on the main language of the document (determined by the last option to the babel package), jurabib loads a special language definition file (extension .ldf) that contains definitions for all kinds of commands that produce textual material within citations and bibliography entries. At the moment approximately 10 languages are supported. These language files (e.g., enjbbib.ldf for English) are a good source for finding out details about customization possibilities. To modify such a command from such files for a particular language (or for all languages), jurabib offers the \AddTo declaration.

```\AddTo\bibsall{code}   \AddTo\bibs⟨language⟩{code}```

The declaration \AddTo takes two arguments: a command name that holds all language-related definitions for one language and the *code* that should be added to this storage place.[1] The first argument is either \bibsall, in which case *code* is used for all languages, or \bibs⟨*language*⟩ (e.g., \bibsgerman), in which case *code* is applied for that particular *language*.[2] In Example 16-5-14 on page 514 and Example 16-5-22 on page 518 we used \AddTo to change the presentation of back-references for all languages, by adding the redefinitions to \bibsall. Below we shorten the "Ibid." string when typesetting in the English language. The default for other languages is left unchanged in this case.

Some text[1] and[2] some[3] more text.[4]

---

[1] van Leunen: A handbook for scholars.

[2] Ib.

[3] Knuth, Donald E.: The TEXbook. Volume A, Computers and Typesetting. Reading, MA, USA: Addison-Wesley, 1986, ISBN 0–201–13447–0.

[4] Knuth, Donald E., ib.

```
\usepackage[super,ibidem,titleformat=all]{jurabib}
\AddTo\bibsenglish{\renewcommand\ibidemname{Ib.}%
                   \renewcommand\ibidemmidname{ib.}}
\bibliographystyle{jurabib}

Some text\cite{vLeunen:92} and\cite{vLeunen:92}
\jurabibsetup{ibidem=name} % <-- change convention
some\cite{Knuth-CT-a} more text.\cite{Knuth-CT-a}
```

16-5-35

While certain strings — calling an editor (\editorname) "(Hrsg.)", for example — should clearly be consistent throughout the whole bibliography, certain other aspects — most importantly, hyphenation — depend on the language used in the actual entry. For instance, a book with a German title should be hyphenated with German hyphenation patterns, regardless of the main language of the document. This is supported by jurabib through an extra field (language) in the BIBTEX database file. If that field is specified in a given entry, then jurabib assumes that the title should be set in that particular language. Thus, if hyphenation patterns for that language are available (i.e., loaded in the format), they are applied. For instance, if we repeat the last part of Example 16-5-6 from page 510 with babel loaded, we get the correct hyphenation as shown below:

Allgemeines Schuldrecht; Besonderes Schuld-recht

```
\usepackage[ngerman,english]{babel}
\usepackage{jurabib} \bibliographystyle{jurabib}
\citefield{title}{aschur,bschur}
```

16-5-36

Distinguishing the author's gender

Earlier, we mentioned that the female form of "Idem" is "Eadem". In the German language, we have "Derselbe" (male), "Dieselbe" (female), "Dasselbe" (neuter), and "Dieselben" (plural). To be able to distinguish the gender of the author, jurabib offers the BIBTEX field gender, which takes a two-letter abbreviation for the gender as its value.

Possible values and the commands that contain the "Idem" strings, if specified, are given in Table 16.2 on the following page. The commands with an uppercase letter in

---

[1] The babel package uses a similar mechanism with the \addto declaration.

[2] Unfortunately, jurabib does not use exactly the same concept as babel. If you specify ngerman with babel to get German with new hyphenation patterns, then this is mapped to german, so you have to update \bibsgerman. If you use any of the dialects (e.g., austrian), then jurabib does not recognize those and uses english after issuing a warning. In that case use \bibsall for changing definitions.

gender	Meaning	In Citation	In Bibliography
sf	single female	\idemSfname, \idemsfname	\bibidemSfname, \bibidemsfname
sm	single male	\idemSmname, \idemsmname	\bibidemSmname, \bibidemsmname
pf	plural female	\idemPfname, \idempfname	\bibidemPfname, \bibidempfname
pm	plural male	\idemPmname, \idempmname	\bibidemPmname, \bibidempmname
sn	single neuter	\idemSnname, \idemsnname	\bibidemSnname, \bibidemsnname
pn	plural neuter	\idemPnname, \idempnname	\bibidemPnname, \bibidempnname

Table 16.2: Gender specification in jurabib

their name are used at the beginning of a sentence, the others in mid-sentence. Those starting with \bibidem.. are used in the bibliography if the option bibformat with the value ibidem is specified. Given that the feature is computing intensive, it is not activated by default but has to be requested explicitly. Thus, to change to "Eadem" in the case of female authors, we have to specify values for \idemSfname and \idemsfname and use the option lookforgender.

Some text[1] and[2] some[3] more text.[4]

---

[1] van Leunen: A handbook for scholars.
[2] Eadem: A handbook for scholars.
[3] Knuth: The TEXbook.
[4] Idem: The TEXbook.

```
\usepackage[super,idem=strict,titleformat=all,
            lookforgender=true]{jurabib}
\AddTo\bibsenglish{\renewcommand\idemSfname{Eadem}%
                   \renewcommand\idemsfname{eadem}}
\bibliographystyle{jurabib}
Some text\cite{vLeunen:92} and\cite{vLeunen:92}
some\cite{Knuth-CT-a} more text.\cite{Knuth-CT-a}
```

16-5-37

Customizing the in-text citation layout further

Most of the author and title formatting is handled by the options authorformat and titleformat, which were discussed earlier. There also exist a few more options and commands that we have not mentioned so far.

If the whole citation should be surrounded by parentheses, simply specify the option round or square.

To place information about the edition as a superscript after the short title, specify the option superscriptedition. With a value of all this is applied to all short-title citations, with the value commented applying only to publications of type commented, and with the value multiple applying only to publications that are cited with several different editions. The last two options are primarily intended for juridical works.

[Baumbach et al.: ZPO[59]]
[Brox/Walker[27], § 3]
[Otto Palandt/Heinrichs[62]]

```
\usepackage{jurabib} \bibliographystyle{jurabib}
\jurabibsetup{square,superscriptedition={all}}
\citetitle{zpo}\\ \cite[\S\,3]{bschur}\\ \cite[Heinrichs][]{bgb}
```

16-5-38

Alternatively, you can explicitly specify in the BibTeX database for each entry whether the edition should be shown as a superscript by setting the special field `ssedition` to the value 1 and by using the option `superscriptedition` with the value `switch`.

By specifying `authorformat=and` you get author names separated by commas and "and" (actually by `\andname`, a command that has different values in different languages). You cannot have the second and third author names separated by ", and" in this way. For adjustments on such a fine level, you can redefine `\jbbtasep` (**between** two authors **sep**aration), `\jbbfsasep` (**between** first and second authors **sep**aration), and `\jbbstasep` (**between** second and third authors **sep**aration).[1]

(Brox and Walker)
(Goossens, Rahtz, and Mittelbach)

16-5-39

```
\usepackage[round]{jurabib}
\renewcommand\jbbtasep{ and }   \renewcommand\jbbfsasep{, }
\renewcommand\jbbstasep{, and } \bibliographystyle{jurabib}
\cite{aschur} \\ \cite{LGC97}
```

You may also want to manually specify the fonts used for the author names and the short title, instead of relying on the possibilities offered by the supplied options. For this you have `\jbauthorfont`, `\jbannotatorfont`, `\jbactualauthorfont`, `\jbauthorfontifannotator`, and `\jbtitlefont` at your disposal, all of which are commands with one argument.

Customizing the bibliography layout

The formatting of the bibliography in standard LaTeX or with natbib is largely controlled by the used BibTeX style file or, if the bibliography entries are manually produced, by the formatting directives entered by the user. For example, a citation to the entry `Knuth-CT-a` from our sample database would be formatted by natbib's `plainnat` as follows:

```
Donald~E. Knuth.
\newblock {\em The {\TeX}book}, volume~A of {\em Computers and Typesetting}.
\newblock Ad{\-d}i{\-s}on-Wes{\-l}ey, Reading, MA, USA, 1986.
```

This means that formatting decisions, such as using emphasis for the title of the book and the series, and the presentation of the "volume" field, have all been made by the BibTeX style file.

In contrast, the BibTeX styles that come with the jurabib package use a drastically different approach: their output is highly structured, consisting of a large number of LaTeX commands, so that the final formatting (as well as the order of elements to some extent) can still be tweaked on the LaTeX level. In fact, they have to be adjusted on that level if you are not satisfied with the formatting produced from their default

---

[1] No other possibilities are needed, because jurabib always uses "et al." whenever there are four or more authors.

definitions. For example, the same citation as above processed with the `jurabib`
B<small>IB</small>T<small>E</small>X style results in the following entry:

```
\jbbibargs {\bibnf {Knuth} {Donald~E.} {D.~E.} {} {}} {Donald~E. Knuth} {au}
{\bibtfont {The {\TeX}book}\bibatsep\ \volumeformat {A} Computers and
Typesetting\bibatsep\  \apyformat {Reading, MA, USA\bpubaddr {}
Ad{\-d}i{\-s}on-Wes{\-l}ey\bibbdsep {} 1986} \jbPages{ix + 483}\jbisbn
{0--201--13447--0}} {\bibhowcited} \jbdoitem \bibAnnoteFile {Knuth-CT-a}
```

Most of the above commands are further structured. The `\bibnf` command takes
five arguments (the different parts of the author's name) and, depending on which are
nonempty, passes them on to commands like `\jbnfIndNoVonNoJr` (name without
"von" and "Junior" parts) for further processing. Consequently, it is possible to interact
with this process at many levels so that all kinds of requirements can be catered for,
although this somewhat complicates the customization of the layout. For this reason
we restrict ourselves to showing just the most important customization possibilities.
For further control strategies, consult the package documentation.

In the default setup, the formatting of the bibliography is fairly independent of
that used for the citations. If you specify `authorformat=italic`, author names are
typeset in italics in the text, but there is no change in the bibliography. The easiest
way to change that is to use the option `biblikecite`; then formatting decisions for
the citations are also used in the bibliography as far as possible. If that is not desired
or not sufficient, explicit formatting directives are available; they are discussed below.

The fonts used in a bibliographical entry are controlled by the following set of
commands: `\biblnfont` and `\bibfnfont` for formatting the last and first names of
the author, and `\bibelnfont` and `\bibefnfont` for the last and first names of the
editor, if present. The command `\bibtfont` is used for titles of books, `\bibbtfont`
for titles of essays (i.e., entries involving a B<small>IB</small>T<small>E</small>X `booktitle` field), and `\bibjtfont`
for titles, or rather names, of journals. The font for article titles within such a journal
is customized with `\bibapifont`. The commands all receive the text they act upon
as an argument, so any redefinition must also use an argument or `\text..` font
commands as shown in the next example (picking the argument up implicitly):

KNUTH, D<small>ONALD</small> E.: The T<small>E</small>Xbook. Volume A,
Computers and Typesetting. Reading, MA,
USA: Addison-Wesley, 1986, ix + 483, ISBN
0–201–13447–0

KNUTH, D<small>ONALD</small> E.: *"Typesetting Concrete Mathe-*
matics". TUGboat, 10 April 1989, Nr. 1, 31–
36, ISSN 0896–3207

```
\usepackage{jurabib}
\bibliographystyle{jurabib}
\renewcommand\biblnfont{\MakeUppercase}
\renewcommand\bibfnfont{\textsc}
\renewcommand\bibtfont {\textsf}
\renewcommand\bibapifont[1]{\textit{''#1''}}
\nocite{Knuth-CT-a,Knuth:TB10-1-31}
\bibliography{tlc}
```

16-5-40

The punctuation separating different parts in the entry can be customized by
another set of commands: `\bibansep` sets the punctuation and space after the author
name, `\bibeansep` does the same after the editor name, `\bibatsep` produces
punctuation after the title (the space is already supplied!), and `\bibbdsep` is the

punctuation *before* the date. With `\bibjtsep` the journal title separation is set. There are similar commands for adjusting other parts.[1] In the next example we use these commands to remove the default colon after the author's name and then typeset a semicolon after the title, no comma before the year, and the word "in" before the journal name. We also use the `dotafter` option with the value `bibentry` to add a final period after each entry.

Knuth, Donald E. Typesetting Concrete Mathematics; in TUGboat, 10 April 1989, Nr. 1, 31–36, ISSN 0896–3207.

Mittelbach, Frank/Rowley, Chris The Pursuit of Quality: How can Automated Typesetting achieve the Highest Standards of Craft Typography? In **Vanoirbeek/Coray** EP92, 261–273.

Vanoirbeek, Christine/Coray, Giovanni, editors EP92—Proceedings of Electronic Publishing, '92; Cambridge: Cambridge University Press 1992.

```
\usepackage[dotafter=bibentry]
          {jurabib}
\bibliographystyle{jurabib}
\renewcommand\bibjtsep{in }
\renewcommand\bibansep{ }
\renewcommand\bibatsep{;}
\renewcommand\bibbdsep{}
\nocite{Knuth:TB10-1-31,MR-PQ}
\bibliography{tlc}
```

16-5-41

We already saw that the separation between different author names in a citation can be adjusted by means of the `authorformat` option and various values. However, except for the value `allreversed`, this has no effect on the entries in the bibliography. To modify the formatting there, you have to redefine the commands `\bibbtasep`, `\bibbfsasep`, and `\bibbstasep`. The naming convention is the same as for the corresponding citation commands. A similar set of commands, `\bibbtesep`, `\bibbfsesep`, and `\bibbstesep`, is available to specify the separation between editor names in an entry.

Hans Brox and **Wolf-Dietrich Walker:** Allgemeines Schuldrecht. 29th edition. München, 2003

Michel Goossens, **Sebastian Rahtz**, and **Frank Mittelbach:** The LaTeX Graphics Companion: Illustrating Documents with TeX and PostScript. Reading, MA, USA: Addison-Wesley Longman, 1997, Tools and Techniques for Computer Typesetting, xxi + 554, ISBN 0–201–85469–4

```
\usepackage[authorformat=allreversed]
          {jurabib}
\bibliographystyle{jurabib}
\renewcommand\bibbtasep{ and }
\renewcommand\bibbfsasep{, }
\renewcommand\bibbstasep{, and }
\nocite{aschur,LGC97}
\bibliography{tlc}
```

16-5-42

The main option for influencing the general layout of the bibliography list is `bibformat`, which can take a number of values as its value. If you specify the value `nohang`, then the default indentation (of `2.5em`) for the second and subsequent lines of a bibliographical entry is suppressed. Alternatively, you can explicitly set the indentation by changing the dimension parameter `\jbbibhang`, as in the next example. There we also use the values `compress` (using less space around entries) and `raggedright` (typesetting entries unjustified). For improved quality, especially when typesetting to a small measure, you may want to load the package `ragged2e`.

Adjusting the general layout of the bibliography

---

[1] This area of jurabib is somewhat inconsistent in its naming conventions and command behavior.

Note the use of the `newcommands` option to overload the standard `\raggedright` (as used by jurabib) with `\RaggedRight`.

Brox, Hans/Walker, Wolf-Dietrich: Allgemeines Schuldrecht. 29th edition. München, 2003	
Baumbach, Adolf et al.: Zivilprozeßordnung mit Gerichtsverfassungsgesetz und anderen Nebengesetzen. 59th edition. München, 2002	
Brox, Hans/Walker, Wolf-Dietrich: Besonderes Schuldrecht. 27th edition. München, 2002	

```
\usepackage[newcommands]{ragged2e}
\usepackage[bibformat={compress,%
                       raggedright}]
          {jurabib}
\bibliographystyle{jurunsrt}
\setlength\jbbibhang{1pc}
\nocite{aschur,zpo,bschur}
\bibliography{tlc}
```

16-5-43

If you use the value `tabular`, then the bibliography is set in a two-column table with the left column containing the author(s) and the right column the remainder of the entry. By default, the first column is one-third of `\textwidth`, and both columns are set ragged. The defaults can be changed by redefining a number of commands, as shown in the next example. The width of the right column is specified by

```
\renewcommand\bibrightcolumn{\textwidth-\bibleftcolumn-\bibcolumnsep}
```

Normally it is enough to change `\bibleftcolumn` and/or `\bibcolumnsep`. The calc package is automatically loaded by jurabib, so we can make use of it when specifying dimensions.

Brox, Hans/ Walker, Wolf-Dietrich	Allgemeines Schuldrecht. 29th edition. München, 2003
Knuth, Donald E.	Typesetting Concrete Mathematics. TUGboat, 10 April 1989, Nr. 1, 31–36, ISSN 0896–3207
Free Software Foundation	GNU Make, A Program for Directing Recompilation. 2000

```
\usepackage[bibformat=tabular]{jurabib}
\bibliographystyle{jurabib}
\renewcommand\bibleftcolumn{6.5pc}
\renewcommand\bibcolumnsep{1pc}
\renewcommand\bibleftcolumnadjust
                    {\raggedright}
\renewcommand\bibrightcolumnadjust{}
\nocite{aschur,Knuth:TB10-1-31}
\nocite{GNUmake}
\bibliography{tlc}
```

16-5-44

If you use the value `numbered`, the bibliography is numbered even though the actual citations in the text use the author-date or short-title scheme. Currently, it is impossible to refer to those numbers.

Some publishers' house styles omit the author's name (or replace it by a dash or other character) if that author is cited with several works. This is supported through the value `ibidem`, which by default generates "Idem" or, more precisely, the result from executing `\bibidemSmname`. To get a (predefined) rule instead, use `\jbuseidemhrule`. If you want something else, redefine `\bibauthormultiple`. Both possibilities are shown in the next example. The jurabib package automatically detects if an entry appears on the top of a page and uses the author name in that case.

Because of this mechanism, it may take several (extra) LaTeX runs before the document compiles without "Rerun to get..."

Brox, Hans/Walker, Wolf-Dietrich: Besonderes Schuldrecht. 27th edition. München, 2002

—— Allgemeines Schuldrecht. 29th edition. München, 2003

Knuth, Donald E.: The TeXbook. Volume A, Computers and Typesetting. Reading, MA, USA: Addison-Wesley, 1986, ix + 483, ISBN 0–201–13447–0

—— Typesetting Concrete Mathematics. TUGboat, 10 April 1989, Nr. 1, 31–36, ISSN 0896–3207

```
\usepackage[bibformat=ibidem]
                {jurabib}
\bibliographystyle{jurabib}
\jbuseidemhrule  % use default rule
% Alternative generic redefinition
% instead of the default rule:
%\renewcommand\bibauthormultiple
%           {[same name symbol]}
\nocite{aschur,bschur}
\nocite{Knuth-CT-a,Knuth:TB10-1-31}
\bibliography{tlc}
```

16-5-45

A variant bibliography layout collecting works under the author names is available through the value `ibidemalt`. This value automatically implies the value `compress`.

Baumbach, Adolf et al.:
  ▷ Zivilprozeßordnung mit Gerichtsverfassungsgesetz und anderen Nebengesetzen. 59th edition. München, 2002

Brox, Hans/Walker, Wolf-Dietrich:
  ▷ Besonderes Schuldrecht. 27th edition. München, 2002
  ▷ Allgemeines Schuldrecht. 29th edition. München, 2003

Palandt, Otto:
  ▷ Bürgerliches Gesetzbuch. 62th edition. München: Beck Juristischer Verlag, 2003

```
\usepackage{jurabib}
\jurabibsetup{bibformat=ibidemalt}
\bibliographystyle{jurabib}
\nocite{aschur,bschur,zpo,bgb}
\bibliography{tlc}
```

16-5-46

If you want to produce an annotated bibliography, use the option `annote`. If the current BibTeX entry has an `annote` field, it is typeset after the entry using `\jbannoteformat` to format it (the default is to typeset it in `\small`). If there is no `annote` field, then jurabib searches for a file with the extension `.tex` and the key of the entry as its base name. If this file exists, its contents are used as the annotation text.

Annotated bibliographies

Knuth, Donald E.: The TeXbook. Volume A, Computers and Typesetting. Reading, MA, USA: Addison Wesley, 1986, ix + 483, ISBN 0–201–13447–0

> The authoritative user manual on the program TeX by its creator.

```
\begin{filecontents}{Knuth-CT-a.tex}
  The authoritative user manual on the program \TeX{}
  by its creator.
\end{filecontents}
\usepackage[annote]{jurabib}\bibliographystyle{jurabib}
\renewcommand\jbannoteformat[1]
  {{\footnotesize\begin{quote}#1\end{quote}}}
\nocite{Knuth-CT-a}
\bibliography{tlc}
```

16-5-47

Because it is a nuisance to have many files (one for each annotation) cluttering your current directory, jurabib offers a search path declaration in analogy to the `\graphicspath` command provided by the graphics package. Thus, after

```
\bibAnnotePath{{./books}{./articles}}
```

annotation files are searched for in the subdirectories `books` and `articles` of the current directory.

Using external configuration files

Customization of jurabib is possible on two levels: by specifying options or, for finer control, by redefining certain declarations or executing commands. In the previous sections we have already encountered a number of package options together with the values they accept, but they represented less than a third of what is available. In the default configuration file `jurabib.cfg`, you find a `\jurabibsetup` declaration listing *all* options together with all their values — nearly 100 possibilities in total. They are all commented out so that you can produce your own configuration file by copying the default one and uncommenting those options that you want to execute normally. If you save this configuration in a file with extension `.cfg`, you can load it instead of the default configuration by using the `config` option. For example,

```
\usepackage[config=law]{jurabib}
```

loads the option file `law.cfg`, which should contain a `\jurabibsetup` declaration and possibly some additional customization commands. For example, such a file might contain

```
\jurabibsetup{lookat,opcit,commabeforerest,titleformat=colonsep}
\renewcommand\opcit{\textit{supra}}
```

and perhaps some other initializations to implement citations for juridical publications. As mentioned earlier, such defaults stored in a file can be overwritten by using additional options during loading or with a `\jurabibsetup` declaration in the preamble.

BibTeX styles for jurabib

The jurabib package is distributed together with four BibTeX style files: `jurabib`, `jureco`, `jurunsrt`, and `jox`. They differ only in minor details: `jureco` produces a slightly more compact bibliography, leaving out some data, while `jurunsrt` is the same as `jurabib` without sorting so that the references appear in order of their citation in the document. The `jox` style produces references in "Oxford style". Because jurabib requires very specially formatted `\bibitem` commands, the above styles are currently the only ones that can be used together with the package.

All four styles provide several BibTeX entries as well as a number of additional fields for existing entries. Having additional fields in a BibTeX database is usually not a problem, because BibTeX ignores any field it does not know about. Thus, such a database can be used with other BibTeX styles that do not provide these fields. Additional entries are slightly different, because using them means that you have to load jurabib to be able to refer to them.

The additional entries are `www` for citing a URL, `periodical` for periodicals that are not cited by year but by volume number, and `commented` for commentaries in juridical works. *Additional BibTeX types*

The standard BibTeX fields are described in Tables 15.3/4 on pages 388–389. The following additional fields are available when using one of the jurabib BibTeX styles: *Additional BibTeX fields*

`annote`   An annotation that is typeset if jurabib is used with the option `annote`; see page 531 for details.

`booktitleaddon`   Extra information to be typeset after a `booktitle` text of a collection.

`dissyear`   Year of a dissertation, habilitation, or other source if that work is also being published as a book (perhaps with a different year).

`editortype`   Position of the person mentioned in the `editor` field (if not really an "editor").

`flanguage`   Foreign language, in the case of a translated work.

`founder`   In juridical works, the original founder of a publication (in contrast to the editor). The name is shown followed by the replacement text of `\foundername`, which defaults to "␣(Begr.)".

`gender`   Gender of the author or authors. The jurabib package uses this information to select the right kind of words for "Idem" in the current language; see page 525.

`howcited`   Text to use for back-reference information, or 1 to indicate that a normal back-reference should be generated. This field is evaluated by the option `howcited` if used together with the value `normal`; see page 513.

`oaddress/opublisher/oyear`   Information about the first edition of a work.

`shortauthor`   Text to use as the author information in a short-title citation. By default, jurabib automatically selects the last name (or names) from the author or editor field.

`shorttitle`   Text to use as the title information in a short-title citation. If it is not specified, the whole `title` is used.

`sortkey`   String to be used for sorting in unusual situations. To sort "von Bismarck, Otto" under B, you can use `sortkey="Bismarck, Otto von"`.

`ssedition`   Flag to indicate that this entry should be typeset with the edition shown as a superscript. It requires the use of the `superscriptedition` option together with the value `switch`; see page 526.

`titleaddon`   Extra information to be placed after a title but not used, for example, when generating a short title.

totalpages Total number of pages in a publication. If present, it is shown followed by the replacement text of the command `\bibtotalpagesname`, which is language dependent.

translator Translator of the publication.

updated Date of the last update in a loose-leaf edition or a similar work. The field is available only for the BibTeX type `commented`. By default, "last update *date*" is generated. This can be customized through the commands `\updatename` and `\updatesep`.

urldate Date when a URL was known to be current. By default, jurabib produces the string "visited on *date*" when this field is used. It can be changed by redefining the command `\urldatecomment`.

url A URL related to the current publication. In the case of the entry type `www`, it is required; otherwise, it is optional.

volumetitle A volume title that follows the volume number in the presentation. This field is available for the types `book`, `commented`, `incollection`, and `inbook`.

16.5.2 biblatex's approach to author-title references

The `biblatex` package ships with various author-title styles. The documentation includes examples showing the output and documenting style-specific options. More styles are provided by external packages. Remember that styles are loaded with the package option `style` and that commands of the `natbib` package are emulated if you use the option `natbib`.

In this section we discuss styles that are meant to be used together with a bibliography; the special case of verbose citations follows in the next section.

The styles provided together with the `biblatex` package mainly differ in the way they compress citation lists and handle recurrent authors, titles, and page numbers in repeated citations. The next example exhibits the `authortitle` style. It does not try to save space and repeats author and title in follow-up citations. In the EP92 entry it uses the `shorttitle` over the `title` field if it exists and falls back to the editor because no author exists.

Vanoirbeek and Coray (*EP92*)
Knuth ("Typesetting Concrete Mathematics"),
Leunen (*A handbook for scholars*), and Knuth
(*The TeXbook*)
(Knuth, "Typesetting Concrete Mathematics";
Knuth, *The TeXbook*)
Knuth (*The TeXbook*)... Knuth (*The TeXbook*)

```
\usepackage[style=authortitle]{biblatex}
\addbibresource{tlc.bib}
\textcite{EP92}\\
\textcite{Knuth:TB10-1-31,vLeunen:92,Knuth-CT-a}\\
\parencite{Knuth:TB10-1-31,Knuth-CT-a}\\
\textcite{Knuth-CT-a}\ldots \textcite{Knuth-CT-a}
```

16-5-48

Compare this with the output of the style `authortitle-ticomp`: this style activates the three features "terse", "ibid", and "compress": "terse" prints the title only if the bibliography contains more than one work by the respective author/editor;

"ibid" replaces repeated citations by the abbreviation "ibidem" unless the citation is the first one on the current page, and "compress" sorts and compresses the list of citations that share the same author. By choosing the style `authortitle-terse` or `authortitle-icomp` instead, it is possible to activate only a subset of the features.

Vanoirbeek and Coray
Knuth (*The TEXbook*, "Typesetting Concrete Mathematics") and Leunen
(Knuth, *The TEXbook*, "Typesetting Concrete Mathematics")
16-5-49   Knuth (*The TEXbook*)... Knuth (ibid.)

```
\usepackage[style=authortitle-ticomp]{biblatex}
\addbibresource{tlc.bib}
\textcite{EP92}\\
\textcite{Knuth:TB10-1-31,vLeunen:92,Knuth-CT-a}\\
\parencite{Knuth:TB10-1-31,Knuth-CT-a}\\
\textcite{Knuth-CT-a}\ldots \textcite{Knuth-CT-a}
```

When a reference contains a `shorthand` field, it is used instead of the title. A list of shorthands can then be printed with the `\printbiblist` command. We use the `csquotes` package to format the quotation:

"Handle so, daß die Maxime deines Willens jederzeit zugleich als Prinzip einer allgemeinen Gesetzgebung gelten könne." (KpV)

```
\usepackage[style=authortitle]{biblatex}
\usepackage{csquotes}
\SetCiteCommand{\parencite}
\addbibresource{tlc.bib}
\hyphenation{Ur-theils-kraft}
\textcquote{kant:kpv}[.]{Handle so, daß
  die Maxime deines Willens jederzeit
  zugleich als Prinzip einer allgemeinen
  Gesetzgebung gelten könne}
\printbiblist{shorthand}
```

Abbreviations

KpV   Immanuel Kant. "Kritik der praktischen Vernunft". In: *Kants Werke. Akademie Textausgabe*. Vol. 5: *Kritik der praktischen Vernunft. Kritik der Urtheilskraft.* Berlin: Walter de Gruyter, 1968, pp. 1–163.

16-5-50

It is possible to print only the author with the command `\citeauthor` (strictly speaking, `\citeauthor` prints the "labelname list", which may be the author, editor, or translator). `\citetitle` prints the `title` or the `shorttitle` (but not a `shorthand`). `\cite*` prints the nonauthor part of the citation.[1] Note that this meaning of `\cite*` is quite different from its use in natbib (where it denotes using a full list of authors) and jurabib (where it denotes leaving out the title).

To get the content of a specific field, you can use the `\citefield` command. It issues a warning and prints nothing if the field does not exist in the entry.

Vanoirbeek and Coray ... *EP92*
Vanoirbeek and Coray, *EP92*
EP92—Proceedings of Electronic Publishing, '92
Kant, "Kritik der praktischen Vernunft"
KpV
16-5-51   KpV

```
\usepackage[style=authortitle-ibid]{biblatex}
\addbibresource{tlc.bib}
\citeauthor{EP92}\ \ldots\ \citetitle{EP92}\\
\cite{EP92}                                  \\
\citefield{EP92}{title}                      \\
\citeauthor{kant:kpv}, \citetitle{kant:kpv}\\
\cite*{kant:kpv} \\
\citefield{kant:kpv}{shorthand}
```

---

[1]This can also be "ibid" — use `\mancite` to avoid this.

Handling annotators   As was noted in Section 16.5.1 the jurabib package interprets the first optional argument of the citation commands as the name of an annotator and formats it in a special way. There is no direct support for this citation format in the generic styles provided by biblatex, so you have to turn to an external package here.

However, even then the entries that we used in the jurabib examples are unsuitable for biblatex: the two packages we present below expect entries with annotators to be of the entry type commentary. In addition, the edition field should be a number, and the language should be given in the langid field. Hence, our sample database also contains the entry palandt that is structured according to these conventions. It also sets the pagination field to enable biblatex to format the "page" numbers automatically.

Unfortunately, the two packages also use incompatible conventions for specifying the annotator: when using the jura2 style, you must add an annotator in parentheses to the *post-note* argument, while the biblatex-juradiss style expects just the name in the *pre-note* argument. In short you have to choose up front, because changing from one to the other style (or to jurabib) involves extensive changes.

The "zit. als" (German for "cited as") in the bibliography of the next example is triggered by the howcited key. The style uses three localization strings, zitiertals, kommentarin, and bearbeiter, currently set up only for the German language.

siehe in Palandt/*Ellenberger*, Abs. 119
... (Palandt/*Heinrichs*, Abs. 50)

Literatur

Palandt, *Otto*: Bürgerliches Gesetzbuch mit Nebengesetzen. 79. Aufl., München 2019 (zit. als Palandt/*Bearbeiter*).

```
\usepackage[ngerman]{babel}
\usepackage[style=jura2,
            howcited=true]{biblatex}
\addbibresource{tlc.bib}
\cite[siehe][(Ellenberger)119]{palandt}\\
\ldots\ \parencite[(Heinrichs)50]{palandt}

\printbibliography
```

16-5-52

The biblatex-juradiss package by Tobias Schwan and Herbert Voß offers the style biblatex-juradiss. It is based on the authortitle-dw style from the biblatex-dw bundle by Dominik Waßenhoven. In this style the annotator should be given directly in the *pre-note* argument, i.e, using the jurabib convention. The style shows the edition as a superscript. It works properly only in German, because various strings are hard-coded and cannot be localized.

... *Ellenberger*, in: *Palandt*[79], Abs. 119
... (*Heinrichs*, ebd., Abs. 50)

Literatur

Palandt, *Otto*, Bürgerliches Gesetzbuch mit Nebengesetzen, 79. Aufl., München 2019, *zitiert als: Bearbeiter*, in: *Palandt*[79].

```
\usepackage[ngerman]{babel}
\usepackage[style=biblatex-juradiss]
            {biblatex}
\addbibresource{tlc.bib}
\ldots\ \cite[Ellenberger][119]{palandt}\\
\ldots\ \parencite[Heinrichs][50]{palandt}

\printbibliography
```

16-5-53

The rather special syntax for the annotators makes it difficult to switch to another style without changing the input. We demonstrate this by repeating the previous example with the style `oscola` — the output is definitively rather weird:

... Ellenberger Bürgerliches Gesetzbuch mit Nebengesetzen (Palandt) Abs. 119
... (Heinrichs Palandt, Abs. 50)

Literatur

Bürgerliches Gesetzbuch mit Nebengesetzen.

16-5-54

```
\usepackage[ngerman]{babel}
\usepackage[style=oscola]{biblatex}
\addbibresource{tlc.bib}

\ldots\ \cite[Ellenberger][119]{palandt}\\
\ldots\ \parencite[Heinrichs][50]{palandt}

\printbibliography
```

16.6 The verbose system

A verbose citation system is a variant of the author-title format with the unique property that the first time — or the first time in a sectioning unit — a work is cited, then a full, *verbose* reference is given, usually in a footnote. Later references then use a shorter version that is built from the author names and the title, a shorter title, or a special shorthand — sometimes introduced in the first reference with "*cited as ...*". Repeated citations typically make use of scholarly abbreviations like *ibidem* or *loc. cit.*

A dedicated bibliography list is not strictly needed in such a system, but if given, it can show additional information such as a DOI. The verbose citation system is not supported by standard LATEX; it requires the jurabib[1] or biblatex package.

We start this section with the description of the bibentry package, a first attempt for basic support of verbose citations when using a BIBTEX workflow. It allows insertion of a full citation in the running text but has no automatic test for the first citation or repeated citations, and shorter citations are mostly in the author-date format (or even only a number if natbib is used in numeric mode). We then continue with a description of biblatex's approach to verbose citations.

16.6.1 bibentry — **Full bibliographic entries in running text**

As mentioned in the introduction of this section, instead of grouping all cited publications in a bibliography, it is sometimes required to directly typeset the full information the first time a publication is referenced. To help with this task Patrick Daly developed the bibentry package as a companion to the natbib package.

```
\nobibliography{BIBTEX-database-list}     \bibentry{key}
```

These commands work as follows: instead of the usual `\bibliography` command, which loads the `.bbl` file written by BIBTEX and typesets the bibliography, you use `\nobibliography` with the same list of BIBTEX database files. It reads the `.bbl` and

---

[1]Refer to Section 16.5.1 for an overview of jurabib's handling of verbose citations in conjunction with its support for author-title citations.

processes the information so that references to entries can be made elsewhere in the document. To typeset a citation with the full bibliographical information, use `\bibentry`. The usual author-date citation can be produced with any of the natbib commands. Here is an example:

For details see Knuth, D. E., Typesetting Concrete Mathematics, *TUGboat*, *10*(1), 31–36, 1989. General information can be found in Knuth, D. E., *The TEXbook*, *Computers and Typesetting*, vol. A, ix + 483 pp., Addison-Wesley, Reading, MA, USA, 1986 and in *Goossens et al.* [1994, 1997].

As shown by *Knuth* [1989] ...

```
\usepackage{bibentry,natbib}
\bibliographystyle{agu}
\AtBeginDocument{\nobibliography{tlc}}
For details see \bibentry{Knuth:TB10-1-31}.
General information can be found in
\bibentry{Knuth-CT-a} and in
\citet{TLC94,LGC97}.

As shown by \citet{Knuth:TB10-1-31} \ldots
```

16-6-1

Potential pitfalls   There are a number of points to be noted here: the `\nobibliography` command must be placed inside the body of the document but before the first use of a `\bibentry` command. In the preamble a `\nobibliography` is silently ignored, and any `\bibentry` command used before it produces no output. Such a command is therefore best placed directly after `\begin{document}` or, if you prefer it in the preamble, by placing it inside `\AtBeginDocument` as we did above.

Another potential problem relates to the choice of BIBTEX style. The bibentry package requires the entries in the .bbl file to be of a certain form: they must be separated by a blank line, and the `\bibitem` command must be separated from the actual entry text by either a space or a newline character. This format is automatically enforced for BIBTEX styles produced with custom-bib, but other BIBTEX styles may fail, including some that work with natbib by its own.

Watch out for punctuations within the entry   The `\bibentry` command automatically removes a final period in the entry so that the reference can be used in mid-sentence. However, if the entry contains other punctuation, such as a period as part of a note field, the resulting text might still read strangely. In that case the only remedy might be to use an adjusted BIBTEX database entry.

One can simultaneously have a bibliography and use the `\bibentry` command to produce full citations in the text. In that case, place the `\bibliography` command to produce the bibliography list at the point where it should appear. Directly following `\begin{document}`, add the command `\nobibliography*`. This variant takes no argument, because the BIBTEX database files are already specified on the `\bibliography` command. As a consequence, all publications cited with `\bibentry` also automatically appear in the bibliography, because a single .bbl file is used.

16.6.2 biblatex's approach to verbose citations

Typesetting the full information of a publication is supported by biblatex twofolds. On the one hand you can typeset full citations with any style with the `\fullcite` command. It prints a citation in the same format as in the bibliography. Similar to the

\bibentry command, there is no final period in the entry so that the reference can be used in mid-sentence.

For details see Donald E. Knuth. "Typesetting Concrete Mathematics". In: *TUGboat* 10.1 (Apr. 1989), pp. 31–36. ISSN: 0896-3207 and also Goossens, Rahtz, and Mittelbach [1].

```
\usepackage{biblatex}
\addbibresource{tlc.bib}

For details see \fullcite{Knuth:TB10-1-31}
and also \textcite{LGC97}.
```

16-6-2

On the other hand, a suitable style can be loaded to use the verbose citation system in a document. With such a style the \textcite typesets the author name and creates a footnote with the reference, while \autocite or \footcite creates only a footnote. If an inline citation is wanted, \cite and \parencite can be used. The styles make use of various trackers to identify the first reference and repeated citations.

The biblatex package ships with a number of styles supporting this convention, i.e., verbose, verbose-ibid, verbose-note, verbose-inote, and verbose-trad1 to verbose-trad3. They mainly differ in the way they handle recurrent authors, titles, and page numbers in repeated citations. More styles are provided by various external packages; see Section 15.7.3 on page 432.

In the next example we show the style verbose-trad1. Note how repeated citations are handled in the example: for the Knuth citation "ibid." is used to repeat the immediately preceding citation, while the author name and "op. cit." are used for a farther away citation of the same work. Compare this with the handling of the Kant citation. Its entry has a shorthand field in the .bib-file, and the citation style adds "henceforth cited as KpV" to the first citation and uses the shorthand in subsequent citations.

... Knuth[1]   see[2]   Knuth[3]   Knuth[4]   see[5] ...

---

[1]see Donald E. Knuth. "Typesetting Concrete Mathematics". In: *TUGboat* 10.1 (Apr. 1989), pp. 31–36, p. 33.
[2]see Immanuel Kant. "Kritik der praktischen Vernunft". In: *Kants Werke. Akademie Textausgabe.* Vol. 5: *Kritik der praktischen Vernunft. Kritik der Urtheilskraft.* Berlin: Walter de Gruyter, 1968, pp. 1–163 (henceforth cited as KpV), p. 33.
[3]see Knuth, op. cit., p. 32.
[4]see ibid., p. 32.
[5]see KpV, p. 33.

```
\usepackage[style=verbose-trad1,
            isbn=false]{biblatex}
\addbibresource{tlc.bib}

\ldots\
\textcite[see][33]{Knuth:TB10-1-31}\quad
see\autocite[see][33]{kant:kpv}     \quad
\textcite[see][32]{Knuth:TB10-1-31}\quad
\textcite[see][32]{Knuth:TB10-1-31}\quad
see\autocite[see][33]{kant:kpv} \ldots
```

16-6-3

The style uses only *ibidem* if the citations are in the same or in consecutive footnotes to avoid potentially ambiguous citations:

... citation[1] and[2] footnote[3] mixup[4] ...

---

[1]Donald E. Knuth. "Typesetting Concrete Mathematics". In: *TUGboat* 10.1 (Apr. 1989), pp. 31–36.
[2]Ibid.
[3]Don't use footnotes, Don!
[4]Knuth, op. cit.

```
\usepackage[style=verbose-trad1,
   isbn=false]{biblatex}
\addbibresource{tlc.bib}

\ldots\ citation\autocite{Knuth:TB10-1-31}
and\autocite{Knuth:TB10-1-31}
footnote\footnote{Don't use footnotes, Don!}
mixup\autocite{Knuth:TB10-1-31} \ldots
```

16-6-4

In Example 16-6-3 you have observed that when a reference contains a `pages` field and has a post-note that we end up with two page specifications in the reference, e.g., "pp. 31–36, p. 33", and this may be confusing to the reader. The option `citepages`[1] controls how to deal with those fields in this case. The default value `permit` allows the duplication, `suppress` unconditionally suppresses the `pages` field, `omit` suppresses it only if there is a clashing post-note, and `separate` inserts the text "esp.":

... Knuth[1] ...

---
[1]see Donald E. Knuth. "Typesetting Concrete Mathematics". In: *TUGboat* 10.1 (Apr. 1989), pp. 31–36, esp. p. 33.

```
\usepackage[style=verbose-trad1,isbn=false,
            citepages=separate]{biblatex}
\addbibresource{tlc.bib}
\ldots\ \textcite[see][33]{Knuth:TB10-1-31} \ldots
```
16-6-5

With the option `ibidpage` you can control how references to the same page in repeated citations are handled. When set to true, the post-note is suppressed in an ibidem citation if the last citation was to the same page range. The next example demonstrates this in the second footnote:

... Knuth[1]   Knuth[2]   Knuth[3] ...

---
[1]see Knuth, "Typesetting Concrete Mathematics", p. 33.
[2]see ibid.
[3]see ibid., p. 32.

```
\usepackage[style=verbose-trad1,isbn=false,
            ibidpage=true]{biblatex}
\addbibresource{tlc.bib}
\ldots\ \textcite[see][33]{Knuth:TB10-1-31}\quad
\textcite[see][33]{Knuth:TB10-1-31}\quad
\textcite[see][32]{Knuth:TB10-1-31} \ldots
```
16-6-6

The `verbose-note` and `verbose-inote` styles add a back-reference to the earlier note containing the full citation similar to the `lookat` option from jurabib described on page 518. Below we repeat Example 16-5-21 using `verbose-inote` this time. The "i" in the style name indicates that it uses "ibidem". Note that "ibidem" is not used for the first citation on the page.

Also discussed is generating PDF[2] and HTML.[3]

---
[2]Goossens and Rahtz, see n. 1, chap. 2.
[3]Ibid., chap. 3–4.

```
\usepackage[style=verbose-inote]{biblatex}
\addbibresource{tlc.bib}
\ldots to use \LaTeX{} on the web.\autocite{LWC99}
    \newpage % Next page shown on the left:
Also discussed is generating PDF\autocite[chap.~2]
{LWC99} and HTML.\autocite[chap.~3--4]{LWC99}
```
16-6-7

If you want terms such as "ibidem" to be printed in italics, you may redefine `\mkibid`. We do this in the next example (a repeat of 16-6-3) but set also the language to German and use `\bibstrings` to demonstrate how terms are localized.

The term `see` then becomes "Siehe" and the term `confer` (Latin for "compare") changes from "Cf." to "Vgl." — the German abbreviation for "Vergleiche".

---
[1]If using a verbose style from an external package, consult its documentation to find out if similar options are available.

Knuth[1] auch[2] Knuth,[3] Knuth[4] und[5]

---

[1]Vgl. Donald E. Knuth. „Typesetting Concrete Mathematics". In: *TUGboat* 10.1 (Apr. 1989), S. 31–36, hier S. 33.

[2]Siehe Immanuel Kant. „Kritik der praktischen Vernunft". In: *Kants Werke. Akademie Textausgabe*. Bd. 5: *Kritik der praktischen Vernunft. Kritik der Urtheilskraft*. Berlin: Walter de Gruyter, 1968, S. 1–163 (im Folgenden zit. als KpV), hier S. 101.

[3]Siehe Knuth, *a. a. O.*, S. 16.

[4]Siehe *ebd.*, S. 17.

[5]Siehe KpV, S. 49.

16-6-8

```
\usepackage[ngerman]{babel} \usepackage{csquotes}
\usepackage[style=verbose-trad1,isbn=false,
  citepages=separate]{biblatex}
\renewcommand*{\mkibid}{\emph}
\addbibresource{tlc.bib}

\textcite[\bibstring{confer}][33]{Knuth:TB10-1-31}
auch\autocite[\bibstring{see}][101]{kant:kpv}
\textcite[\bibstring{see}][16]{Knuth:TB10-1-31},
\textcite[\bibstring{see}][17]{Knuth:TB10-1-31}
und\autocite[\bibstring{see}][49]{kant:kpv}
```

16.7 biblatex — One ring to rule them all

We now turn to a more in-depth discussion of the biblatex package [40]. As could be seen in the previous sections, biblatex supports in a consistent way all citation styles and various citation commands either directly or through external supporting packages.

It achieves this through a change of the rôle of the .bbl file. All other packages reviewed up to this point use a .bbl file that contains a standard thebibliography environment to typeset the bibliography. The \bibitem commands in there also pass the data needed to format the citations back to LaTeX: in standard LaTeX only a number or a label; with natbib and other packages the author and the date information. The jurabib package increases the amount of structured data passed back drastically — an example was given in the introduction to the author-date format on page 488. However, in all implementations the main purpose of the .bbl file remains the production of the *printed* representation of the bibliography and therefore ends up containing a mix of typesetting and data commands.

This changed radically in 2006 with the initial release of the biblatex package by Philipp Lehman. With biblatex the .bbl file no longer contains a thebibliography environment and several \bibitem commands. It does not contain any typesetting instructions at all, but only a structured, preprocessed, and sorted representation of the bibliography data. The (shortened and redacted) data of a publication looks, for example, like this:

```
\entry{LGC97}{book}{}
  \name{author}{3}{}{%
    {{un=0,uniquepart=base,hash=0743efb276e9219ee664a9b3dbd60619}{%
       family={Goossens},
       familyi={G\bibinitperiod},
       given={Michel},
       giveni={M\bibinitperiod},
       givenun=0}}%
  ... more names ...
  }
  \list{location}{1}{%
```

```
    {Reading, MA, USA}%
  }
  \list{publisher}{1}{%
    {Ad{\-d}i{\-s}on-Wes{\-l}ey Longman}%
  }
  \strng{namehash}{e0fe5244f7bd4501ecba8372b6fdd95b}
  ... more hashes ...
  \field{sortinit}{G}
  \field{extradatescope}{labelyear}
  \field{labeldatesource}{year}
  \field{labelnamesource}{author}
  \field{labeltitlesource}{title}
  \field{isbn}{0-201-85469-4}
  \field{series}{Tools and Techniques for Computer Typesetting}
  \field{title}{The {\LaTeX} Graphics Companion: ...}
  \field{year}{1997}
  \field{pages}{xxi + 554}
  \range{pages}{-1}
\endentry
```

As can be seen, biber passes more than the content from the .bib file. It also creates initials and metadata like hashes, and it records which field should be used as the source for the label name — a work without the author field will here perhaps use the editor field instead. As with the jurabib approach, such a representation of the bibliography data cannot be created manually without much work and so requires an external tool such as biber.

The shift to such a structured .bbl — made possible by the increasing memory[1] and speed available in the TEX-engines, which allows you to store and process more commands during the compilation — has several advantages:

- Every field of an entry can be used in citations, and thus a large variety of styles can be defined and used. biblatex is not confined to a subset of citation systems — it supports them all.

- Because the .bbl file is not used for printing, it can be loaded at the beginning — this can reduce the number of compilations needed to resolve the references.

- The data provided in the .bbl file can be reused as often as needed. This makes it easy to typeset more than one bibliography with various filter conditions.

- Changes to the format of the citations or the bibliography and even the creation of a complete new style can be done fully with LaTeX commands.

biber is recommended, but BIBTEX is possible too   In early biblatex versions the .bbl file was created with BIBTEX and a special .bst style. To stay compatible with this workflow it is still possible to choose BIBTEX as the processor through the package option backend=bibtex. However, it is highly recommended to use biber (see Section 15.2.2), because not every feature offered

---

[1] Very large bibliographies can still exhaust the available memory.

by biblatex can be faithfully backported to BibTEX, and this can lead to hard to spot output differences.

Recall that due to the differences between biblatex/biber and standard workflows with BibTEX, some changes to the .bib files are required or recommended; see Section 15.3.

16.7.1 Basic biblatex setup

The workflow and how to set up a basic document for biblatex has already been described in Section 15.4. The following example therefore repeats only the core commands: the `style` key to set up the main style (here an author-title format), the preamble-only command `\addbibresource` to declare which .bib files should be used as resources, a citation command to select the entry—we use here `\textcite`, which is similar to `\citet` of natbib—and `\printbibliography` to print the bibliography.

Knuth (*The TEXbook*)

References

Knuth, Donald E. *The TEXbook*. Vol. A. Computers and Typesetting. Reading, MA, USA: Addison-Wesley, 1986, pp. ix + 483. ISBN: 0-201-13447-0.

16-7-1

```
\usepackage[style=authortitle]{biblatex}
\addbibresource{tlc.bib}

\textcite{Knuth-CT-a}
\printbibliography
```

16.7.2 Package options

The package options of biblatex use a key/value syntax. A small number of the keys must be given as package options at load time:

Load-time options

backend   The option allows setting the bibliography processor. The (recommended) default is `biber`; other options are `bibtex` and `bibtex8`.

style, citestyle, bibstyle   These keys load the main style definitions for the citations and the bibliography. Style files have the extension .cbx (for `citestyle`) or .bbx (for `bibstyle`), and the value of the keys is the name of such a file without the extension. biblatex comes with a large number of styles — several have been presented in the previous sections — and more are provided by external packages (see Section 15.7.3 for an overview). Typically the style for the citations and the bibliography should be set simultaneously with the `style` key. They can be set to different styles with the keys `citestyle` and `bibstyle`, but not every combination is sensible: a numeric citation style, for example, is useless if the chosen bibiography style does not show any numbers.

natbib, mcite   These options load compatibility modules for the packages natbib and mcite/mciteplus. They provide implementation of the commands of these packages, which are very similar (but not identical) in syntax and function to the original commands and can make the transition of existing documents to biblatex easier.

Besides these load-time options, biblatex knows a large number of other keys. These keys can be set as package options or alternatively in the configuration file `biblatex.cfg` or in the preamble with

> `\ExecuteBibliographyOptions[`*entrytype*`,...]{`*key=value*`,...}`

The optional argument *entrytype* allows one to restrict some options to specific types such as `article` or `inproceedings`.

16.7.3 Citing with biblatex

The biblatex package defines a large set of citation commands for a variety of use cases, including citations in the text (`\textcite`), in parentheses (`\parencite`), as footnotes (`\footcite`), or — in some styles — as superscript (`\supercite`). Other commands capitalize the name (e.g., `\Textcite`). In addition, commands like `\citeauthor` or `\citefield` allow you to refer to a specific name or field of an entry.

There are flexible commands like `\smartcite` and `\autocite` that can change their behavior depending on the context or package options.

If the package option `natbib` is used, reimplementations of the citation commands of the `natbib` package are available too. The package also provides tools to create more citation commands if needed.

The argument structure for the different citation commands is identical. It is exemplified here with the `\cite` command:

> `\cite{`*key₁*`,`*key₂*`,...}`   `\cite[`*post-note*`]{`*key₁*`,`*key₂*`,...}`
> `\cite[`*pre-note*`][`*post-note*`]{`*key₁*`,`*key₂*`,...}`

Similar to the citation commands of natbib all citation commands in biblatex have one mandatory argument, which takes a comma-separated list of keys, and two optional arguments for the *pre-note* and the *post-note*. If only one optional argument is used, it is taken to be the *post-note*. If only a *pre-note* is wanted, an empty argument for the *post-note* must be added.

The *post-note* usually contains page numbers or page ranges. biblatex parses this argument and if it matches a simple pattern of page numbers and ranges, it formats the data as required by the style and the language. Page numbers should therefore be entered as arabic or roman numerals, ranges should be denoted by a single hyphen, and suffixes for "page sequences" should be added with the commands `\psq` and `\psqq`. biblatex converts the hyphen into an en-dash and adds localized and configurable prefixes like "p.", "S.", or "§" automatically — to suppress an automatic page prefix use the command `\nopp`. The "pagination scheme" can be changed or suppressed on a per-entry basis by setting the `pagination` field in the `.bib` file.

If the page numbers have some unusual format or if there is some additional text in the *post-note* argument, then page numbers must be formatted manually. In such cases prefixes can be added with the commands `\pno` and `\ppno`, and numbers can be formatted with `\pnfmt`.

Example 16-7-2 demonstrates the various commands. Note that in French 'p.' is used even for multiple pages and that the range is typeset with a shorter hyphen. The last line of the example demonstrates the effect of the pagination field: it has been set to 'section' for this entry and so § is used as page prefix.

```
\usepackage[ngerman,french,english]{babel}
\usepackage{biblatex}
\addbibresource{tlc.bib} \addbibresource{tlc-ex.bib}
```

[1, p. 1] [1, pp. 1–4] [1, pp. 1, 3, 5]
[1, p. IV] [1, pp. 5 sq.] [1, 25]
[1, p. 27a] [1, especially pp. 27–34]

```
\cite[1]{G-G} \cite[1-4]{G-G} \cite[1,3,5]{G-G}\\
\cite[IV]{G-G} \cite[5\psq]{G-G} \cite[\nopp 25]{G-G}\\
\cite[\pno~27a]{G-G} \cite[especially \pnfmt{27-34}]{G-G}
```

[1, p. 1]
[1, p. 1-4]

```
\bigskip\selectlanguage{french}        % French typography
\cite[1]{G-G}\\ \cite[1-4]{G-G}        % rules
```

[1, S. 1–4]
[1, S. 5 f.]

```
\bigskip\selectlanguage{ngerman}       % German typography
\cite[1-4]{G-G}\\ \cite[5\psq]{G-G}    % rules
```

[2, § 33]
[2, besonders §§ 27–34]

```
\bigskip
\cite[33]{pagination}\\
\cite[besonders \pnfmt{27-34}]{pagination}
```

16-7-2

The following two examples show the output of the most frequently used predefined citation commands in the two currently dominant citation systems: numeric and author-date. The \autocite command allows switching the citation command with a package option — first we use inline, which changes it to \parencite, and in the second example footnote, which gives as expected \footcite. This allows, for example, switching the citation style from author-date to numeric without having to adapt the source to avoid forlorn and odd-looking numbers in a footnote. There is no difference between \cite and \parencite in a numeric style, but the later command should be preferred if a citation in parentheses is wanted after a switch to an author-based style. All citation commands including \footcite and \autocite can be input with a space before them, because biblatex, if necessary, removes that space. This is important for \autocite, because it gives the right output also when its output is an inline citation. With useprefix, the examples force the name to start with "von" to show the effect of the capitalizing citation variants.

[see 1, p. 5]
[see 1, p. 5]
van Leunen [see 1, p. 5]
Van Leunen [see 1, p. 5]
footcite[1]
autocite [1]

```
\usepackage[autocite=inline,
            useprefix=true]{biblatex}
\addbibresource{tlc.bib}
\cite[see][5]{vLeunen:92}           \\
\parencite[see][5]{vLeunen:92}  \\
\textcite[see][5]{vLeunen:92}   \\
\Textcite[see][5]{vLeunen:92}   \\
footcite \footcite{vLeunen:92} \\
autocite \autocite{vLeunen:92}
```

16-7-3

---
[1]1.

Once more, but now with author-date style and `\autocite` set to `footnote`:

see van Leunen 1992, p. 5	`\usepackage[style=authoryear,autocite=footnote,`
(see van Leunen 1992, p. 5)	`                 useprefix=true]{biblatex}`
Van Leunen (see 1992, p. 5)	`\addbibresource{tlc.bib}`
van Leunen (see 1992, p. 5)	`\cite[see][5]{vLeunen:92}        \\`
footcite[1]	`\parencite[see][5]{vLeunen:92} \\`
autocite[2]	`\Textcite[see][5]{vLeunen:92}  \\`
	`\textcite[see][5]{vLeunen:92}  \\`
_____	`footcite \footcite{vLeunen:92} \\`
[1] Van Leunen 1992.	`autocite \autocite{vLeunen:92}`
[2] Van Leunen 1992.	

16-7-4

Lost punctuation after a citation ⚲

The biblatex package provides elaborate facilities designed to manage and track punctuation and spacing. The commands provided are mainly meant for style authors: they help prevent unwanted double punctuation marks if fields are missing or contain their own punctuation. In some cases the working of the punctuation tracker can also bite users because it can have an at first surprising effect that a punctuation symbol in the post-note "eats up" a following punctuation symbol in the text.

Example 16-7-5 demonstrates this for a semicolon: after a period it is suppressed, while it stays after an exclamation mark.

It is possible to overrule the behavior locally: `\bibsentence` marks the beginning of a sentence and so also hides all preceding punctuation marks. The counterpart is `\nopunct`, which suppresses the following punctuation:

```
\usepackage[style=authoryear]{biblatex}
\addbibresource{tlc.bib}
```

see Knuth 1986, for the details.	`\cite[see][for the details.]{Knuth-CT-a}; \\`
see Knuth 1986, for the details!;	`\cite[see][for the details!]{Knuth-CT-a};`
see Knuth 1986, for the details.;	`\cite[see][for the details.\bibsentence]{Knuth-CT-a}; \\`
see Knuth 1986, for the details!	`\cite[see][for the details!\nopunct]    {Knuth-CT-a};`

16-7-5

16.7.4 Indexing citations automatically

Indexing can be activated with the package option `indexing`. It takes the values `true`, `false`, `cite`, or `bib`. The last two values restrict indexing either to citations or to bibliographies. By default biblatex adds the author names and the title to the index. In the next example we demonstrate how to redefine the relevant bibliography macro `citeindex` so that only the name is indexed.

Index	`\usepackage{makeidx}   \makeindex`
Goossens, Michel, 6	`\usepackage[indexing=cite]{biblatex} \addbibresource{tlc.bib}`
Knuth, Donald E., 6	`\renewbibmacro{citeindex}{\ifciteindex{\indexnames{labelname}}{}}`
Mittelbach, Frank, 6	`\textcite{LGC97}, \textcite{Knuth-CT-a} % p.6 (not shown)`
Rahtz, Sebastian, 6	`\newpage \printindex              % p.7 (shown on the left)`

16-7-6

16.7.5 Back references and links

Sometimes it is useful to have a list of pages where a work has been cited in the bibliography. Such back references are fully supported by biblatex, and they are enabled with the option backref. The option backrefstyle allows you to set how consecutive pages are handled; by default a sequence of three or more pages is compressed to a range.

biblatex works well together with hyperref. If hyperref is loaded, citations, back references, and URLs are turned into active links. The following example shows such links in blue:

Smith and Webb (2021)

References

Smith, Joe and Henry Webb (2021). URL: https://some.url (visited on 09/01/2021) (cit. on pp. 6, 7).

16-7-7

```
\usepackage[backref,style=authoryear]{biblatex}
\addbibresource{tlc-ex.bib}
\usepackage{hyperref}
\hypersetup{colorlinks,allcolors=blue}
\textcite{url:e}  % p.6 (not shown)
\newpage          % p.7 (shown on the left)
\textcite{url:e}
\raggedright \printbibliography
```

16.7.6 Bibliography entries with multiple authors

Longer lists of names (authors, editors, publishers, etc.) are often truncated after a defined number of names (with *et al.* or something similar added at the end). With biblatex this can be controlled independently for the citations in the document, the entries in the bibliography, and, if necessary, for sorting within the bibliography.

For citations there are maxcitenames (default 3) and mincitenames (default 1). If the number of names in a citation exceeds maxcitenames, the list is truncated and only mincitenames names are shown; otherwise, all names are displayed. You can alter both values according to your needs but mincitenames should always be lower than or equal to maxcitenames. This means, assuming the defaults are used, that a citation with four or more authors is shown with only one author name followed by "et al.", while a citation with two or three authors displays all author names.

Baumbach et al. (2002)
Goossens, Rahtz, and Mittelbach (1997)
Goossens and Rahtz (1999)

16-7-8

```
\usepackage[style=authoryear]{biblatex}
\addbibresource{tlc.bib}
\textcite{zpo}    \\                        % 4 authors
\textcite{LGC97} \\ \textcite{LWC99} % 2-3 authors
```

If you always want to enforce a certain setting for an entry, you can add an options line into your .bib file, e.g., in the zpo entry:

```
options = {maxcitenames=4,maxbibnames=4},
```

To control name lists in the bibligraphy the same functionality is offered through the keys maxbibnames and minbibnames. This allows you to show more (or fewer) names in the bibliography compared to what is shown in a citation within the document. For example, you might always want the bibliography to display up to four names, with or without truncation, while you might only want to show one name in citations. In this case, the correct setting would be the following:

```
maxcitenames=1,minbibnames=4,maxbibnames=4
```

If the bibliography is sorted, then by default the sorting algorithm uses the name lists truncated according to the `maxbibnames` and `minbibnames` key settings. If this is not appropriate, you can use the keys `maxsortnames` and `minsortnames` to overwrite that default.[1] For example,

```
minbibnames=3,maxbibnames=3,minsortnames=1,maxsortnames=1
```

would show up to three names per entry in the bibliography but would disregard all authors except the first when sorting the bibliography.

However, most of the time identical settings are wanted for the minimum and maximum values. Therefore, biblatex also offers the two convenience keys `maxnames` and `minnames` to set all of the three `max...names` and `min...names` keys in one go.

All eight keys can only be set as options to the package or in the preamble.

16.7.7 Unambiguous citations

Citations must be unambiguous: they are labels pointing to the bibliography, and a reader must be able to identify the corresponding entry. For a numeric system a unique label merely requires increasing a counter. Author-based styles have to cater for the case that different authors and author lists might share the same names. As already described in the introduction of this chapter, author-based styles avoid ambiguities by adding initials (or even the full given name), by adding an extra year marker, or by showing more authors.

By default biblatex prefers to make the names unique by adding initials or the full given name. Thus, in the following example the two *Kirk* and *Doe* authors are differentiated by their initials, *Pyne* by the full given names, and *Webb* by extra year markers. The *Doe* authors get initials despite the fact that the year would already make their label unique because that makes it easier for humans to identify the correct publication.

Smith 2020; J. Kirk 2020; B. Kirk 2020
Joe Pyne 2020; Jill Pyne 2020
J. Doe 2020; B. Doe 2019
Webb 2020a; Webb 2020b

```
\usepackage[style=authoryear]{biblatex}
\addbibresource{tlc-ex.bib}

\cite{smith,kirk1,kirk2} \\
\cite{pyne1,pyne2}       \\
\cite{doe1,doe2}         \\
\cite{webb1,webb2}
```

16-7-9

This default behavior with its mix of names with and without initials and given names is not to everyone's liking, but it has the huge advantage of creating quite short citations that nevertheless allow the reader to identify almost all authors directly in the text without having to interrupt the reading and check the entry in the bibliography.

---

[1] If both `..bibnames` and `..sortnames` are specified they have to be in that order to take effect.

The output can be changed with the option `uniquename`. For example, with the setting `uniquename=init`, only initials are used and only for entries where initials are of no use in making the names unique, e.g., because they are identical, as in the two "Pyne" entries, an extra year marker is added instead.[1]

Smith 2020; J. Kirk 2020; B. Kirk 2020
Pyne 2020b; Pyne 2020a
J. Doe 2020; B. Doe 2019
Webb 2020a; Webb 2020b

16-7-10

```
\usepackage[style=authoryear,uniquename=init]{biblatex}
\addbibresource{tlc-ex.bib}

\cite{smith,kirk1,kirk2}\\ \cite{pyne1,pyne2}\\
\cite{doe1,doe2}\\         \cite{webb1,webb2}
```

The given names can be suppressed altogether with `uniquename=false`:

Smith 2020; Kirk 2020b; Kirk 2020a
Pyne 2020b; Pyne 2020a
Doe 2020; Doe 2019
Webb 2020a; Webb 2020b

16-7-11

```
\usepackage[style=authoryear,uniquename=false]{biblatex}
\addbibresource{tlc-ex.bib}

\cite{smith,kirk1,kirk2}\\ \cite{pyne1,pyne2}\\
\cite{doe1,doe2}\\         \cite{webb1,webb2}
```

To make citations with more than one author unique, biblatex again adds initials, given names and extra year markers, and if needed shows more authors. Similar to the handling of single authors, it also tries to make the authors identifiable. For example, the last citation *J. Kirk* has an initial to distinguish the author from *M. Kirk* in the third citation.

Unambiguous author lists

Smith et al. 2020
H. Pyne et al. 2020
J. Pyne and M. Kirk 2020
J. Pyne and Webb 2020a
J. Pyne and Webb 2020b
J. Kirk et al. 2020

16-7-12

```
\usepackage[style=authoryear,maxcitenames=1]{biblatex}
\addbibresource{tlc-ex.bib}


\cite{list0}\\ \cite{list1}\\
\cite{list2}\\ \cite{list3}\\
\cite{list4}\\ \cite{list5}
```

The list handling can be configured with the option `uniquelist`. The following example shows the same set of citations but with `uniquelist=false`, which restricts the list length to the `maxcitenames` value. *Kirk* is now shown without the initials because the author *M. Kirk* is no longer visible. This makes the citations quite concise at the cost of readability, because it is more difficult to identify the correct work without checking in the bibliography.

Smith et al. 2020
H. Pyne et al. 2020
J. Pyne et al. 2020a
J. Pyne et al. 2020b
J. Pyne et al. 2020c
Kirk et al. 2020

16-7-13

```
\usepackage[style=authoryear,maxcitenames=1,
            uniquelist=false]{biblatex}
\addbibresource{tlc-ex.bib}
\cite{list0}\\ \cite{list1}\\
\cite{list2}\\ \cite{list3}\\
\cite{list4}\\ \cite{list5}
```

---

[1]Initials can be forced, even in that case, by redefining the `labelname` format.

*Ambiguous
author-title
entries in rare cases* In an author-title style, identical citations pointing to different references are possible if the author and title are identical. The existing author-title style implementations do not try to avoid that rare case. For styles or documents that want better control here, biblatex offers the options `labeltitle` and `labeltitleyear`. They cause biber to check the author and title (and also the year) for uniqueness and to add data fields that can be queried in tests by style authors.

16.7.8 Printing the bibliography

We now describe in detail the main command to print, filter, and format the reference list with the `biblatex` package.

`\printbibliography[`*key/value options*`]`

To typeset a bibliography add `\printbibliography` at the place where it should appear. It can be used as often as wanted. If the list is empty, e.g., if the document does not contain any citation commands or if `biber` has not been called yet, nothing is printed, and a warning is added to the `.log` file:

```
LaTeX Warning: Empty bibliography on input line 57.
```

The `\printbibliography` command adds a heading before the reference list. By default it is formatted as an unnumbered top-level sectioning command of the class using `\refname` or `\bibname` as content.

*Changing the
heading*
The heading can be adapted with two keys: `title` sets the text of the heading, and `heading` allows you to change the formatting of the heading. For example, the value `subbibliography` switches a level down in the sectioning hierarchy, the value `bibintoc` adds the bibliography to the table of contents, and with `bibnumbered` a numbered sectioning command is used. To suppress the heading altogether, the value `none` is provided. More options can be found in the documentation. It also describes how to define new heading types with `\defbibheading`.

`\printbibheading[`*key/value options*`]`

It is sometimes necessary to add only a heading for example as a common title for subdivided bibliographies. This can be done with the standard sectioning commands of the class but also with `\printbibheading`. It also knows about the keys `heading` and `title`.

`\defbibnote{`*name*`}{`*text*`}`

To add arbitrary text to the bibliography two keys can be used in the optional argument of `\printbibliography`: `prenote` for text between the heading and the actual bibliography and `postnote` for text after the list. The value of both keys is a *name* referring to a text declared before with the `\defbibnote` command.

1   My References

Some text before the bibliography.

[1]   Donald E. Knuth. *The T_EXbook*. Vol. A. Computers and Typesetting. Reading, MA, USA: Addison-Wesley, 1986, pp. ix + 483.

[2]   Donald E. Knuth. "Typesetting Concrete Mathematics". In: *TUGboat* 10.1 (Apr. 1989), pp. 31–36.

```
\usepackage[isbn=false]{biblatex}
\addbibresource{tlc.bib}
\defbibnote{prebib}
  {Some text before the bibliography.}

\nocite{Knuth-CT-a,Knuth:TB10-1-31}
\printbibliography
  [heading=bibnumbered,prenote=prebib,
    title=My References]
```

16-7-14

A powerful feature of `\printbibliography` is the ability to apply filters to print only a subset of the entries of a bibliography, for example only articles, entries with a specific keyword, or entries cited in a specific part of the document and so to split the references into sublists by topic or location. Various common filters can be set directly with key/value options, and biblatex also provides interfaces to define more specialized filters.

Filtering entries

For some common selections of field values of the references biblatex offers predefined keys: `type`, `nottype`, `subtype`, `notsubtype`, `keyword`, and `notkeyword`. They expect as a value a type, like `article` or `book`, or a keyword and can be used multiple times to build up lists. Example 16-7-15 demonstrates some of these keys. Be aware that splitting a bibliography in many parts can make it difficult to find a reference. It is not obvious if one should search in the books or somewhere else for "Pyne (2020a)". Thus, such splits should normally not replace but accompany a full bibliography.

Common selections of field values

Doe (2015), Pyne (2020b), Pyne (2020a), Kirk (2020)

Books

Kirk, Maria (2020). *An important book.*
Pyne, Mike (2020a). *A book.*

Not Books

Doe, Jill (2015). "An article". In: *Journal A.*
Pyne, Mike (2020b). "An important article". In: *Journal B.*

Important

Kirk, Maria (2020). *An important book.*
Pyne, Mike (2020b). "An important article". In: *Journal B.*

```
\usepackage[style=authoryear]{biblatex}
\addbibresource{tlc-ex.bib}
\textcite{article1}, \textcite{article2},
\textcite{book1}, \textcite{book2}

\printbibliography
  [type=book,title=Books]

\printbibliography
  [nottype=book,title=Not Books]

\printbibliography
  [keyword=important,title=Important]
```

16-7-15

The following example demonstrates another problem with split bibliographies. By default the labels used are the ones from the full, alphabetically sorted bibliography, and this means entries in subsets are numbered in a rather wild way. To keep this and later examples small, we reduced the spacing between the entries by setting `\bibitemsep` to zero.

```
\usepackage{biblatex}
\addbibresource{tlc-ex.bib}
\setlength\bibitemsep{0pt}
```

Doe [1], Pyne [4], Pyne [3], Kirk [2]

Books

[2]   Maria Kirk. *An important book*. 2020.

[3]   Mike Pyne. *A book*. 2020.

Other

[1]   Jill Doe. "An article". In: *Journal A* (2015).

[4]   Mike Pyne. "An important article". In: *Journal B* (2020).

```
\textcite{article1},
\textcite{article2},
\textcite{book1},
\textcite{book2}
\printbibliography
   [type=book,title=Books]

\printbibliography
   [nottype=book,title=Other]
```

16-7-16

biblatex has a number of options to handle this problem. The most important one is the package option `defernumbers`. With it numbers are assigned in the order that the entries appear in a bibliography. This improves our example greatly, but note that this works satisfactorily only with disjoint bibliographies.

```
\usepackage[defernumbers]
            {biblatex}
\addbibresource{tlc-ex.bib}
\setlength\bibitemsep{0pt}
```

Doe [3], Pyne [4], Pyne [2], Kirk [1]

Books

[1]   Maria Kirk. *An important book*. 2020.

[2]   Mike Pyne. *A book*. 2020.

Not Books

[3]   Jill Doe. "An article". In: *Journal A* (2015).

[4]   Mike Pyne. "An important article". In: *Journal B* (2020).

```
\textcite{article1},
\textcite{article2},
\textcite{book1},
\textcite{book2}
\printbibliography
   [type=book,title=Books]

\printbibliography
   [nottype=book,title=Not Books]
```

16-7-17

Selection by cite location

To select the entries cited in a specific part of the document like a chapter, the keys `section` and `segment` are provided. They expect as a value the number of a reference section or a reference segment. How to define and use such sections and segments is described in Section 16.7.10 on page 556.

```
\DeclareBibliographyCategory{category}
\addtocategory{category}{key}
```

Selection by category

Categories allow splitting bibliographies into topics assigned to the entries on the fly in the document. With `\DeclareBibliographyCategory` you declare a category, where the value is an arbitrary name. With `\addtocategory` a *key* can be assigned to a *category*. To filter the bibliography by one or more categories the keys `category` and `notcategory` are provided. A typical use case for categories is to differentiate between cited works and works for further reading added with the `\nocite` command. This is shown in the following example. It makes use of the hook `\AtEveryCitekey` that is executed for every key in a citation command. With the `\thefield` command we retrieve the current key of the entry and add it to the category `cited`.

Knuth (1986)

References

Knuth, Donald E. (1986). *The TEXbook*. Vol. A. Computers and Typesetting. Reading, MA, USA: Addison-Wesley, pp. ix + 483. ISBN: 0-201-13447-0.

Further reading

Leunen, Mary-Claire van (1992). *A handbook for scholars.* Walton Street, Oxford OX2 6DP, UK: Oxford University Press, pp. xi + 348.

16-7-18

```
\usepackage[style=authoryear]{biblatex}
\addbibresource{tlc.bib}
\DeclareBibliographyCategory{cited}
\AtEveryCitekey{\addtocategory{cited}%
                {\thefield{entrykey}}}
\textcite{Knuth-CT-a}
\nocite{vLeunen:92}

\printbibliography[category=cited]
\printbibliography[notcategory=cited,
    title=Further reading]
```

By default the various filters are applied in an additive way, so all conditions must be met by an entry:

```
type=article,keyword=important,keyword=research,category=cited
```

This would select only articles that have both keywords in their `keywords` field and have been cited in the document — in our examples so far only `article2` would be printed if cited.

In the case that the standard selection keys are not sufficient, a more complicated filter can be defined and then used in the options of `\printbibliography` with `filter=`*filter name* or `check=`*check name*.

`\defbibfilter{`*filter name*`}{`*expression*`}`

The command `\defbibfilter` expects as its second argument a boolean expression based on the logical operators `and`, `or`, and `not` and some of the atomic tests discussed earlier. Parentheses surrounded by spaces can be used to specify the precedence of operators. However, there should be no spaces around the equal sign.

```
\defbibfilter{cited-or-important}{
    category=cited or
  ( keyword=important and not keyword=research )
  }
\printbibliography[filter=cited-or-important]
```

This prints all entries that have been cited or that contain the keyword `important` but not the keyword `research`, so it would exclude `article2` if not cited.

> \defbibcheck{*check name*}{*code*}

The \defbibcheck declaration is more low-level: its *code* argument can be arbitrary code using any test from the biblatex and the etoolbox package, and it can use all bibliography data of the current entry. The result of such a check is considered to be false (suppressing the printing of an entry) if the code leads to the execution of \skipentry. In the following example we print only entries published before the year 1988. The check first tests if the year actually contains a number — a tiny detail, but one that avoids strange errors if you use the check with arbitrary input data.

Kant, Immanuel (1968). "Kritik der praktischen Vernunft". In: *Kants Werke. Akademie Textausgabe.* Vol. 5: *Kritik der praktischen Vernunft. Kritik der Urtheilskraft.* Berlin: Walter de Gruyter, pp. 1–163.

Knuth, Donald E. (1986). *The TEXbook.* Vol. A. Computers and Typesetting. Reading, MA, USA: Addison-Wesley, pp. ix + 483. ISBN: 0-201-13447-0.

```
\usepackage[style=authoryear]{biblatex}
\addbibresource{tlc.bib}
\defbibcheck{before1988}{%
 \iffieldint{year}{%
   \ifnumless{\thefield{year}}{1988}%
     {}{\skipentry}}%
   {\skipentry}}
\nocite{*}
\printbibliography[heading=none,
              check=before1988]
```

16-7-19

16.7.9 The sorting of the bibliography

The sorting of the bibliography can be set with the package option sorting. Values are for example none (unsorted), nyt ("name year title"), or ydnt ("year descending name title"). More sorting schemes can be defined with \DeclareSortingTemplate. Typically the sorting scheme is set by the style, and overriding it should be done with care — for example, sorting=none together with an author-based style would make the bibliography unusable if you think about it.

It is possible to print multiple differently sorted bibliographies in a document, for example, one sorted by author and one sorted by year, by starting a so-called "new reference context" that changes the way the citation labels are built and sorted in the bibliography.

> \DeclareRefcontext{*name*}{*key/value options*}
> \newrefcontext[*key/value options*]{*name*}

\DeclareRefcontext declares a named reference context with a number of key/value settings. \newrefcontext starts a new reference context referring back to the declared context. The *name* argument is, despite the braces surrounding it, actually optional — this slightly odd syntax is a result of providing backward compatibility — an unnamed context, e.g., \newrefcontext{sorting=ynt,labelprefix=A}, could be used too. However, using a name simplifies assigning a reference context to citations and allows you to keep your settings together in the preamble.

The following example shows how this can be used to add a second bibliography with a different sorting. We additionally use a filter and print only articles in the second bibliography.

[3, A2, A1, 2]

References

[1]   Jill Doe. "An article". In: *Journal A* (2015).

[2]   Maria Kirk. *An important book*. 2020.

[3]   Mike Pyne. *A book*. 2020.

[4]   Henry Webb. "An article". In: *Journal C* (2010).

Articles by year

[A1]   Henry Webb. "An article". In: *Journal C* (2010).

[A2]   Jill Doe. "An article". In: *Journal A* (2015).

```
\usepackage[defernumbers]{biblatex}
\addbibresource{tlc-ex.bib}
\DeclareRefcontext{byyear}
        {sorting=ynt,labelprefix=A}

\cite{book1,article1,article3,book2}
\printbibliography[title=References]

\newrefcontext{byyear}
\printbibliography[type=article,
        title=Articles by year]
```

16-7-20

When printing multiple bibliographies like this, a work can have more than one label — in the example a number or a number with the prefix "A" added by specifying a `labelprefix`. The same can happen in a less obvious way also with author-date or author-title labels. In such cases one has to decide which label should be used for the citations. By default `biblatex` uses the label from the last bibliography in which the citation was printed.[1]

Because in the example the books are not shown in the second bibliography, the labels of the first bibliography are used for them, and we get as citations a — probably unwanted — mix of numbers with and without a prefix. This can be avoided by assigning the affected entry types or citation keys to a specific reference context to determine their labels. In the following example we assign all citations the labels of the first bibliography — for more complicated cases the documentation should be consulted.

[3, 1, 4, 2]

References

[1]   Jill Doe. "An article". In: *Journal A* (2015).

[2]   Maria Kirk. *An important book*. 2020.

[3]   Mike Pyne. *A book*. 2020.

[4]   Henry Webb. "An article". In: *Journal C* (2010).

Articles by year

[A1]   Henry Webb. "An article". In: *Journal C* (2010).

[A2]   Jill Doe. "An article". In: *Journal A* (2015).

```
\usepackage[defernumbers]{biblatex}
\addbibresource{tlc-ex.bib}
\DeclareRefcontext{byyear}
        {sorting=ynt,labelprefix=A}
\assignrefcontextentries[name=default]{*}
\cite{book1,article1,article3,book2}
\printbibliography[title=References]

\newrefcontext{byyear}
\printbibliography[type=article,
        title=Articles by year]
```

16-7-21

---

[1]This behavior has changed over time.

16.7.10 Document divisions

The biblatex package offers two concepts for document division: *reference sections* and *reference segments*. They can be started in various ways: with commands (\newrefsection and \newrefsegment), with environments (refsection and refsegment), or automatically at various sectioning units through package options like refsection=chapter. After a division has been created, it is possible to restrict a bibliography to the entries cited in this division with the keys segment and section; they take as the value the number of the division — in the current division you can access this number with \therefsection and \therefsegment.

Reference sections for independent bibliographies

A reference section encapsulates citations and bibliographies as if they were in a document of their own. Within such a reference section, all cited works are assigned labels that are local to the division: cross references and cite trackers are local too. Reference sections can also use resources (.bib files) specific to the division. Therefore, reference sections are useful if you want separate, *independent* bibliographies and bibliography lists. The typical use cases are articles in a journal where every article has its own specific bibliography. Reference sections can also be used for chapter bibliographies if the chapters build independent units, but it is important to realize that the same work may get assigned a different label in each reference section and so combining all entries in a global bibliography is not really possible.

Reference segments are filters

Reference segments in contrast divide the document into parts that can be used as filters. They are useful if you want to show a selected view by chapter or section but want also a global bibliography because labels are unique across the segment boundaries. Reference segments can be used inside reference sections but not the other way round.

The next two examples demonstrate both division types. Note the extra year marker in "Smith, 2020a" and "Smith, 2020b", which make the labels unique when the document is divided with reference segments and compare it with the "Smith, 2020" used for both works if reference sections are used instead.

```
\usepackage[style=authoryear,
            dashed=false]{biblatex}
\addbibresource{tlc-ex.bib}
```

… Smith 2020b …

References of refsegment 1

Smith, Maria (2020b). *Another book.*

```
\newrefsegment
\ldots\ \cite{smith2020-1} \ldots
```

```
\printbibliography
  [title=References of refsegment 1, segment=1]
```

… Smith 2020a …

References of refsegment 2

Smith, Maria (2020a). *A book.*

```
\newrefsegment
\ldots\ \cite{smith2020-2} \ldots
```

```
\printbibliography
  [title=References of refsegment 2, segment=2]
```

Global bibliography

Smith, Maria (2020a). *A book.*
Smith, Maria (2020b). *Another book.*

```
\printbibliography[title=Global bibliography]
```

16-7-22

When using reference selections, we do not need to select them explicitly if the bibliography is printed inside the reference section because the \printbibliography outputs only the works of the current reference section by default.

... Smith 2020 ...

References of refsection 1

Smith, Maria (2020). *Another book.*

... Smith 2020 ...

References of refsection 2

Smith, Maria (2020). *A book.*

```
\usepackage[style=authoryear]{biblatex}
\addbibresource{tlc-ex.bib}

\newrefsection
\ldots\ \cite{smith2020-1} \ldots
\printbibliography[title=References of refsection 1]

\newrefsection
\ldots\ \cite{smith2020-2} \ldots
\printbibliography[title=References of refsection 2]
```

16-7-23

If you wish to group all the bibliographies together (for example, at the end of the document), you can use the following commands:

> \bibbysection[*key/value options*]   \bibbysegment[*key/value options*]

They print the bibliographies of all reference sections or segments encountered so far. The title of such bibliographies should typically contain some number or reference to the chapter or section they refer to. For this purpose biblatex sets a label when starting a reference section. We demonstrate this in the next example by advancing the section counter and defining a heading that then references the label.

1   Article

... Smith 2020 ...

2   Another article

... Smith 2020 ...

References

References for Article 1

Smith, Maria (2020). *Another book.*

References for Article 2

Smith, Maria (2020). *A book.*

```
\usepackage[style=authoryear]{biblatex}
\addbibresource{tlc-ex.bib}
\defbibheading{subbibliography}{%
   \subsection*{References for Article
                  \ref{refsection:\therefsection}}}

\section{Article}          \newrefsection
\ldots\ \cite{smith2020-1} \ldots

\section{Another article}  \newrefsection
\ldots\ \cite{smith2020-2} \ldots

\printbibheading
\bibbysection[heading=subbibliography]
```

16-7-24

16.7.11 Annotated bibliographies

If you want to generate an annotated bibliography, you can use the reading style. The annotation should be in the field annotation (or in the alias annote provided for jurabib compatibility).

The style produces entries like the following:

Computers and Graphics   **jcg**

Computers and Graphics 35.4 (2011): *Semantic 3D Media and Content*.
ISSN: 0097-8493.

Annotations: This is a `periodical` entry with an `issn` field.

16-7-25

The `annotation` field can also be added to the bibliography made with styles that normally ignore this field. For example, you can insert the instruction to print the `annotation` field in the bibliography macro `finentry`, which is executed at the end of every entry.

Computers and Graphics (2011) 35.4:
Semantic 3D Media and Content.
ISSN: 0097-8493.
Annotation: This is a periodical
entry with an `issn` field.

```
\usepackage[style=authoryear]{biblatex}
\addbibresource{tlc.bib}
\DeclareFieldFormat{annotation}
   {\par\textsf{Annotation: #1}}
\renewbibmacro{finentry}{\setunit{\finentrypunct}%
   \printfield{annotation}\finentry}
\nocite{jcg}
\raggedright \printbibliography[heading=none]
```

16-7-26

16.7.12 Bibliography lists

In some fields it is common to use shorthands or short titles in the citation and to provide lists to look up such abbreviations.

`\printbiblist`[*key/value options*]{*biblistname*}

This command, which was already used in Example 16-5-50 on page 535, allows one to print lists of abbreviations, shorthands, and similar material. If differs from a normal bibliography in that it formats all entries in the same way (with the same "bibliography driver" given in the *biblistname* argument); i.e., it does not differentiate by entry type as `\printbibliography` does. biblatex provides automatic support for such lists for various fields that are short versions of other fields. They are marked as "label field" in the package documentation.

Angenendt (2002) schrieb in „In Honore Salvatoris" ...

Liste der Kurztitel

In Honore Salvatoris   Angenendt, Arnold (2002). „In Honore Salvatoris – Vom Sinn und Un-
sinn der Patrozinienkunde".

```
\usepackage[ngerman]{babel}
\usepackage{csquotes}
\usepackage[style=authoryear]{biblatex}
\addbibresource{tlc.bib}

\textcite{angenendt} schrieb in
\citetitle{angenendt} \ldots
\printbiblist[title=Liste der
   Kurztitel]{shorttitle}
```

16-7-27

16.7.13 Language support

The biblatex package collaborates with the babel package. For all declared languages biblatex loads special language definition files (extension .lbx) that contain definitions for all kinds of bibliography strings to produce textual material within citations and bibliography entries. At the moment more than 50 languages are supported.

Cicero, Marcus Tullius (1995). *De natura deorum. Über das Wesen der Götter*. Latin and German. Ed. and trans. by Ursula Blank-Sangmeister. With an afterw. by Klaus Thraede. Stuttgart: Reclam.

```
\usepackage[french,english]{babel}
\usepackage{csquotes}
\usepackage[style=authoryear]{biblatex}
\addbibresource{tlc.bib}
```

Cicero, Marcus Tullius (1995). *De natura deorum. Über das Wesen der Götter*. Latin et allemand. Éd. établie et trad. par Ursula Blank-Sangmeister. Avec une postf. de Klaus Thraede. Stuttgart : Reclam.

```
\nocite{cicero}
\printbibliography[heading=none]
\selectlanguage{french}
\printbibliography[heading=none]
```

16-7-28

The language support is not restricted to the main language of the document: biblatex also reacts to language changes inside the document as shown above or when typesetting citation references.

When biblatex detects that babel (or polyglossia) is loaded, it checks if csquotes is loaded as well and if not issues a warning that this is recommended. The reason is that bibliography entries often use quotes around titles, etc. — these should preferably be typeset according to the conventions of the document language, and biblatex delegates that to the csquotes package. See Example 16-7-27 above.[1]

Management of quotes

Many of the localized strings can take two forms: a long and an abbreviated variant. To switch between both, the key abbreviate can be used:

Cicero, Marcus Tullius (1995). *De natura deorum. Über das Wesen der Götter*. Latin and German. Edited and translated by Ursula Blank-Sangmeister. With an afterword by Klaus Thraede. Stuttgart: Reclam.

```
\usepackage[english]{babel}
\usepackage[style=authoryear,
   abbreviate=false]{biblatex}
\addbibresource{tlc.bib}
\nocite{cicero}
\printbibliography[heading=none]
```

16-7-29

Languages and countries often have their own conventions how to sort words containing accented letters, digraphs, ligatures, or spaces. More than one set of rules can exist for a language; for example, "Ä" can in German be sorted like "Ae" (this is called the phonebook rule) or always after "A". biber contains the relevant Unicode libraries, and by default biblatex uses the sorting rules from the main document language as set with babel. To select another sorting rule use the key sortlocale; allowed values are babel language names or standard identifiers for

---

[1]We have not done this in every example to conserve space; thus, if you rerun some of the examples using both babel and biblatex, but not csquotes, you are going to see a warning.

the locale. For example, `sortlocale=de_DE_phonebook` switches to the German phonebook sorting rule. The following example shows on the left the sorting with the Swedish locale and on the right the same entries if English is the main language.[1]

```
\usepackage[swedish,english]
                {babel}
\usepackage[style=authoryear]
                {biblatex}
\addbibresource{locale.bib}
\AtBeginBibliography{\small}
% declaration for swe-nyt not shown
\nocite{*}
\printbibliography
   [title=English Sorting]
\newpage
\newrefcontext[sorting=swe-nyt]
\printbibliography
   [title=Swedish Sorting]
```

16-7-30

English Sorting

Aachen, Georgina (n.d.). *Title AA.*
Ånten, Georgina (n.d.). *Title Å.*
Änten, Georgina (n.d.). *Title Ä.*
Önten, Georgina (n.d.). *Title Ö.*
Vn, A (n.d.). *Title VN.*
Vr, A (n.d.). *Title VR.*
Wolf, Ceasar (n.d.). *Title B.*

Swedish Sorting

Aachen, Georgina (n.d.). *Title AA.*
Vn, A (n.d.). *Title VN.*
Wolf, Ceasar (n.d.). *Title B.*
Vr, A (n.d.). *Title VR.*
Ånten, Georgina (n.d.). *Title Å.*
Änten, Georgina (n.d.). *Title Ä.*
Önten, Georgina (n.d.). *Title Ö.*

Recall from the discussion of additional bibliography fields (page 392, Section 15.3.2) that the language can also be set in the `.bib` file for individual references using the `langid` field and that the package option `autolang` governs how such entries are set if their language differs from the main language.

16.7.14 Distinguishing the author's gender

Just like jurabib, the biblatex package offers the BIBTEX field `gender`, which takes the two-letter abbreviation shown in Table 16.2 on page 526 and additionally also the value pp for a plural and mixed-gender list. It depends on the style and also on the language, if and how the `gender` field is actually used. In the following example the female form "Eadem" is used for the first author because she was labeled with `gender=sf` in the `tlc-ex.bib` file. The example also shows that biblatex's `\autocite` and `\footcite` commands work nicely together with the footmisc package.

Some[1] text referencing works[2] by Jane[3] and works[4] by Max.[5,6]

---

[1] Jane Doe. *A book*. 2020.
[2] Jane Doe. *An second book*. 2020.
[3] Eadem, *A book*.
[4] Max Pyne. *A book*. 2020.
[5] Max Pyne. *A second book*. 2020.
[6] Idem, *A book*.

```
\usepackage[multiple]{footmisc}
\usepackage[style=verbose-trad1]{biblatex}
\addbibresource{tlc-ex.bib}

Some\autocite{jane-1} text referencing
works\autocite{jane-2} by Jane\autocite{jane-1}
and works\footcite{max-1} by
Max.\footcite{max-2}\footcite{max-1}
```

16-7-31

---

[1] Not all code for the example is shown, because it is normally not supported to use different sorting rules in one and the same document. Therefore, swe-nyt was explicitly declared as a second sorting template. If you are interested, look at the full example source.

16.7.15 Sentence casing

As already mentioned in Section 15.3.3, sentence casing with biblatex, i.e., turning all words except the first to lowercase, is not done by the bibliography processor but with LaTeX code. This is a common practice in Anglo-Saxon bibliographies, typically used for titles of articles (but not books), but it would be wrong in many other languages, e.g., in German where nouns have to start with an uppercase letter.

For this, biblatex provides the command \MakeSentenceCase that can be used in formatting directives but also in other places. Its starred form is language aware and changes the case only if the language in the field langid or—if missing—the current language matches one of languages stored in a special list. By default this list contains only various English variants, but if necessary, more languages can be appended with \DeclareCaseLangs*.

Arguments of commands and words in braces are protected from sentence casing. To *override* this protection you have to use another pair of braces as done in the next example for the word *Blue*. Note that the second sentence is not altered because the current language at this point is German, and that language is for good reasons not in this special list; however, the third is (unconditionally), and that is wrong for German.[1]

A story of *Green* and *blue* Ducks.

Eine Geschichte *grüner* und *blauer* Enten.

Aber „Eine geschichte ..." ist falsch!

16-7-32

```
\usepackage[ngerman,english]{babel} \usepackage{biblatex}
\usepackage[autostyle]{csquotes}

\MakeSentenceCase*{a Story of \emph{Green} and {\emph{Blue}} {Ducks}.}

\selectlanguage{ngerman}
\MakeSentenceCase*{Eine Geschichte \emph{grüner} und {\emph{blauer}}
                {Enten}.}
Aber \enquote{\MakeSentenceCase{eine Geschichte \ldots}} ist falsch!
```

The standard biblatex styles do not use the command; if needed, it has to be added explicitly to a format directive. Format directives are discussed in the next section—as a teaser we show how they can be used to add sentence casing to inproceedings entries in an author-title format.

... Southall (*Presentation rules and rules of composition in the formatting of complex text*) ...

But when we switch to German, the citation changes and is no longer altered:

... Southall (*Presentation Rules and Rules of Composition in the Formatting of Complex Text*)

16-7-33

```
\usepackage[ngerman,english]{babel}
\usepackage[style=authortitle]{biblatex}
\addbibresource{tlc.bib}
\DeclareFieldFormat[inproceedings]{citetitle}
   {\mkbibemph{\MakeSentenceCase*{#1}}}

\ldots\ \textcite{Southall} \ldots\\[3pt]
But when we switch to German, the citation changes
and is no longer altered:\\[3pt]
\selectlanguage{ngerman}\ldots\ \textcite{Southall}
```

---

[1] With BibTeX this is a serious problem, because the styles change *all* entries if they implement sentence casing. Due to the language-awareness, biblatex does a better job as long as you have langid fields in your database entries set up.

16.7.16 Customizing

Customizing citations and bibliographies is not always a trivial task. Besides some LaTeX skills, you often also need some knowledge of the underlying traditions and rules of the citation system. For example, the title of an article is often formatted differently compared to that of a book, and if the editor and translator of a work are the same person, they should appear only once. Without some understanding of the reasoning behind such settings and how they affect the coding, customization is likely to fail or may not catch all cases correctly.

Before undertaking the endeavor to adapt the code with the tools provided by biblatex, you should therefore check if you can achieve your aims with package or style options, by switching to another style,[1] or even by sending the style author a feature request.

The biblatex package offers a rather large variety of customizing commands for style authors and users:

- commands to create new citation commands or even a complete style,

- commands to declare new entry types and fields,

- commands to communicate with biber and for example change the sorting or the formatting of labels,

- commands to adjust the formatting of fields, punctuation, and more.

It is out of scope of this introduction to describe all of them; we therefore concentrate on a few often needed methods in user documents. If you need more, e.g., when you want to design a completely new style from scratch, consult the extensive package documentation [40].

Core configuration files and commands

We start with a short overview of the files and the main commands relevant in a style definition. Customization quite often requires you to consult or copy code from these files.

Data models in `blx-dm.def` *and* `.dbx` *files*
The default data model of biblatex is defined in the file `blx-dm.def`. The files declare the standard entry types, fields, and their data type and various constraints. Style authors and users can add extensions to the data model through files with the extension `.dbx`. As an example we show the declarations needed for a simple contact list: a new entry type `address` with a name field `name` and two literal fields `street` and `town`.

```
\DeclareDatamodelEntrytypes{address}
\DeclareDatamodelFields[type=list, datatype=name] {name}
\DeclareDatamodelFields[type=field, datatype=literal]{street,town}
\DeclareDatamodelEntryfields[address]{name,street,town}
```

---

[1]For example, the biblatex-ext package provides variants of the standard biblatex styles with additional configuration options.

After these declarations, it is then possible to produce .bib files with entries such as

```
@address{beutlin-bilbo,
  name    = {Bilbo Beutlin},
  street  = {1 Bagshot Row},
  town    = {Hobbiton}
}
```

Citing such entries with the standard citation commands is probably of little use with this particular entry type—you also need to declare new citation commands for this. Consult the extensive package documentation [40] for the details.

The file biblatex.def is an important source if you want to customize a style, because it contains many default format instructions and various definitions loaded *Standard definitions* by all styles. The file is quite long, but skimming it can serve to understand the default *in* biblatex.def behavior and to find examples for own definitions.

Bibliography style files with the extension .bbx contain the definitions of bibliog- *Bibliography* raphy drivers and the definition of bibliography environments. The core command in *definitions in* .bbx such files is \DeclareBibliographyDriver. *files*

\DeclareBibliographyDriver{*entry type*}{*code*}

The first argument corresponds to the *entry type* used in .bib files, specified in lowercase letters. Alternatively, the argument may contain an asterisk, in which case a fallback for unknown entry types is defined. The second argument contains the *code* to typeset all bibliography entries of the type *entry type*. A .bbx file can load other .bbx files—all biblatex styles, for example, load the file standard.bbx that contains code common to all styles.

Citation style files with the extension .cbx contain definitions for citation com- *Citation definitions* mands; the main command in such files is \DeclareCiteCommand. *in* .cbx *files*

\DeclareCiteCommand{*cmd*}[*wrapper*]{*pre*}{*loop*}{*sep*}{*post*}

This declaration takes—besides the name of the citation command—four mandatory arguments. The *pre*-code handles the data from the pre-note argument of the citation command. The *loop*-code is executed for each key in the mandatory key-list argument of the citation command. This is the core code that prints the citation labels or any other data. The *sep*-code is executed between iterations of the *loop*-code and usually inserts some kind of separator, such as a comma or a semicolon. Finally, the *post*-code handles the post-note argument of the citation command. If the optional *wrapper* argument is given, then the entire citation is passed to it as an argument. Typical examples of wrapper commands are commands that add parentheses or put the citation into a footnote—the next example uses a font command for demonstration.

BEFORE *article1* SEP *article2* SEP *article3* AFTER

```
\DeclareCiteCommand{\citetesting}[\textit]
  {BEFORE }{\textbf{\thefield{entrykey}}}{ SEP }{ AFTER}
\citetesting{article1,article2,article3}
```

16-7-34

Localization definitions in .lbx files

Localization modules are files with the extension `.lbx`, typically the base name of the file refers to the language it supports. They contain all language-related settings, like translations for key terms in various languages, special date formats, or adaptions to punctuation.

`\DeclareBibliographyStrings{`*key/value list*`}`

This is the main command in such a localization module. The *key/value list* assigns to every key term two texts, a short and a long version. Such bibliography strings can also be used with the `\bibstring` command in the pre- and postnote of citations; e.g., `\bibstring{seealso}` prints "see also" or the equivalent in another language.

`\newbibmacro{`*name*`}[`*narg*`] [`*default*`] {`*bib macro definition*`}`
`\usebibmacro{`*name*`}` ... *arguments*...

"bibmacros"

These two commands can be found in many places in the biblatex files. The first defines a macro to be executed via `\usebibmacro` later. The syntax is very similar to `\newcommand` except that *name* may contain characters such as numbers and punctuation marks and does not start with a backslash. It can have up to nine *arguments*, and the first can be declared as being optional (if a *default* is given in the `\newbibmacro` declaration).

The underlying commands of "bibmacro" live in their own name space and do not clash with commands of other packages, and the use of non-letters has the advantage to allow more readable names; e.g., `\usebibmacro{doi+eprint+url}` quite obviously handles the doi, eprint, and url fields.

`\printdate`
`\printfield[`*format*`]{`*field*`}`
`\printlist  [`*format*`] [`*range*`] {`*literal list*`}`
`\printnames[`*format*`] [`*range*`] {`*name list*`}`
`\printtext  [`*format*`]{`*text*`}`

Print commands

These are some of the commands used to typeset fields and text inside citations and bibliography entries.[1] Their purpose is twofold: first, they interact with the punctuation tracker and help to avoid that missing fields lead to duplicated punctuation symbols. Second, with the exception of `\printdate`, they all apply a customizable *format* directive.

The print commands are specific to the field types as described in Section 15.3.3 on page 393 because every type has it own parsing rules that need different format definitions. If the optional *format* argument is given, it is used as the format directive.

---

[1] There are several other `\print...` commands, but these are the important ones.

Otherwise, a directive named like the field or list in the second argument is tried; e.g., `\printnames{editor}` tries to apply the format directive named `editor` while the declaration `\printnames[myformat]{editor}` tries to apply the format directive `myformat`. If the directive `myformat` is not declared, the optional argument is ignored, and the default format directive `editor` is tried instead. If that does not exist either, no format is applied, and the field content is printed as is.

Adapting localization strings

biblatex offers a dedicated command to customize the language-dependent bibliography strings in a document:

```
\DefineBibliographyStrings{language}{definitions}
```

Do not confuse this command with the `\DeclareBibliographyStrings` command used in the `.lbx` files. `\DefineBibliographyStrings` has an additional argument *language*, and the *definitions* are key/value pairs that assign text to one or more identifiers but do not distinguish between a long and an abbreviated form.

The main challenge when customizing such strings is to find the identifier name(s). You can search in the `.lbx` file, but what also often works is to temporarily set the language to `nil`. biblatex then issues a warning about missing translations and prints the identifiers in bold. However, note that this fails sometimes. The strings `langlatin` and `langgerman` inside the `language` field are not detected, and the following example shows `byeditor` and `bytranslator` instead of `byeditortr` that is used because the editor and translator are the same person in the `cicero` entry.

References

Cicero, Marcus Tullius (1995). *De natura deorum. Über das Wesen der Götter*. langlatin **and** langgerman. **byeditor**Ursula Blank-Sangmeister. **bytranslator**Ursula Blank-Sangmeister. **withafterword**Klaus Thraede. Stuttgart: Reclam.

16-7-35

```
\usepackage[nil]{babel}
\usepackage[style=authoryear]{biblatex}
\addbibresource{tlc.bib}
\AtBeginBibliography{\raggedright\small}
\nocite{cicero}
\printbibliography
```

In the next example we change some of the strings (not necessarily for the better). The new text should be without formatting instructions and — with exception of the language names — can be given in lowercase; it is capitalized by biblatex in places where that is needed.

References

Cicero, Marcus Tullius (1995). *De natura deorum. Über das Wesen der Götter*. Latin / Teutonic. Revised and adapted by Ursula Blank-Sangmeister. Addendum by Klaus Thraede. Stuttgart: Reclam.

16-7-36

```
\usepackage[english]{babel}
\usepackage[style=authoryear]{biblatex}
\addbibresource{tlc.bib}
\DefineBibliographyStrings{english}{ and = /,
  byeditortr     = revised and adapted by,
  langgerman     = Teutonic,
  withafterword  = addendum by}
\nocite{cicero}   \printbibliography
```

Customizing punctuation

In the standard styles, punctuation is typically inserted with one of two methods: as a named delimiter or as a command.

```
\setunit{\printdelim{nameyeardelim}}
\setunit{\bibpagerefpunct}
```

The command `\bibpagerefpunct` is inserted before back references: its default definition (which can be found in `biblatex.def`) is a space. It can be changed with `\renewcommand`.

The named delimiter `nameyeardelim` is — as the name implies — inserted in various places between a name and a year. Because it is inserted with the `\printdelim` command, it is context sensitive. Here "context" means things like "inside a text citation" or "inside a bibliography item". To adapt it, a special command is provided.

`\DeclareDelimFormat [`*context₁,context₂,...*`] {`*name*`}{`*code*`}`

The first mandatory argument holds the *name* of the delimiter format being declared, the *code* argument the typeset result. With the optional argument you can restrict the applicability to certain *contexts*. These are strings such as `bib`, `biblist`, or names of citation commands without the backslash, e.g., `textcite`.

There is no easy way to distinguish which customization method is suitable for a concrete punctuation delimiter — you have to check the documentation of the style or the code to find out. In the following example we give `nameyeardelim` three different definitions and also change `\bibpagerefpunct` to produce ↩.

---

textcite: Knuth ↦ (1986)
parencite: (Knuth ... 1986)

References

Knuth, Donald E. : (1986). *The TEXbook.*
Vol. A. Computers and Typesetting.
Reading, MA, USA: Addison-Wesley, pp. ix + 483. ISBN: 0-201-13447-0 ↩ (cit. on p. 6).

```
\usepackage[style=authoryear,backref]{biblatex}
\addbibresource{tlc.bib}
\renewcommand\bibpagerefpunct{ $\hookleftarrow$ }
\DeclareDelimFormat[bib]{nameyeardelim}{\,\addcolon\ }
\DeclareDelimFormat[parencite]{nameyeardelim}{\,\ldots}
\DeclareDelimFormat[textcite]{nameyeardelim}{ $\mapsto$ }
textcite: \textcite{Knuth-CT-a}\\
parencite: \parencite{Knuth-CT-a}
\printbibliography
```

16-7-37

Changing format directives

As discussed on page 564, the commands that are used by biblatex styles to print fields apply format directives. Such directives can be (re)defined with the following commands:

`\DeclareFieldFormat [`*entry type₁,entry type₂,...*`] {`*format*`}{`*code*`}`
`\DeclareListFormat  [`*entry type₁,entry type₂,...*`] {`*format*`}{`*code*`}`
`\DeclareNameFormat  [`*entry type₁,entry type₂,...*`] {`*format*`}{`*code*`}`

There are three separate commands to declare *format* directives for fields, lists, and names. The optional argument allows you to restrict the declaration to specific *entry types* in the `.bib` file. The *code* can refer to the current field or list item with #1; for names (which are substructured) a different method is available as discussed below.

```
\citefield [pre-note] [post-note] {key} [format] {field}
\citelist  [pre-note] [post-note] {key} [format] {literal}
\citename  [pre-note] [post-note] {key} [format] {name list}
```

These citation commands grant access to all lists and fields at a lower level. The optional *format* argument allows you to apply a format directive manually. This is useful to test and demonstrate formats and so we use them in the examples below.

A format directive defined with `\DeclareFieldFormat` is meant for use with `\printfield`, `\printtext`, or `\citefield`. In the *code* argument you can refer to the content of the field with #1 and to the name of the field with the command `\currentfield`.

Field formatting

In the following example we define a format directive for fields with a special formatting for articles and then apply it to some entries with the help of `\citefield`. Note that the LGC97 book entry has no `volume` information; thus, we get a missing field warning, and the field name is printed in bold.

book/volume/A
[volume/10]
book/year/1997
volume

16-7-38

```
\usepackage{biblatex} \addbibresource{tlc.bib}
\DeclareFieldFormat{myfieldformat}{\thefield{entrytype}/\currentfield/#1}
\DeclareFieldFormat[article]{myfieldformat}{[\currentfield/#1]}
\citefield{Knuth-CT-a}[myfieldformat]{volume}      \\ % a book
\citefield{Knuth:TB10-1-31}[myfieldformat]{volume} \\ % an article
\citefield{LGC97}[myfieldformat]{year}             \\
\citefield{LGC97}[myfieldformat]{volume}   % a book without volume info
```

A format directive defined with `\DeclareListFormat` is meant for use with `\printlist` or `\citelist`. They loop over the list items, and the current item is passed to *code* as argument #1. The item index number is available through the counter `listcount`, and the total number of items is stored in the counter `liststop`. Inside *code* you can access the name of the list with the command `\currentlist`.

List formatting

In the example we declare a new list directive and apply it to an entry with a location field with three items. Additionally, we format it with the default list directive to show the difference.

Location 1/3: München,
Location 2/3: Berlin,
Location 3/3: New York!

München, Berlin, and New
York

16-7-39

```
\usepackage{biblatex}  \addbibresource{tlc-ex.bib}
\DeclareListFormat{mylistformat}
  {Location \theliststcount/\theliststop: #1%
    \ifnumgreater{\value{listcount}}{\value{liststop}-1}%
      {!}%       -- list end reached
      {,\\}%     -- in list
  }
\citelist{location-list}[mylistformat]{location}
  \\[3pt]
\citelist{location-list}{location} % default directive
```

Name formatting A format directive defined with `\DeclareNameFormat` is meant for use with `\printnames` or `\citename`. Unlike the previous declarations, it should not make use of #1; instead, the individual parts of a name are made available in automatically created macros. For example, the family name is provided as `\namepartfamily`, and the initials of the given name as `\namepartgiveni`.

Below we define a new name format directive and apply it to the `author` and `editor` fields of two entries from our sample database:

1/3: M. Goossens (G.)
2/3: S. Rahtz (R.)
3/3: F. Mittelbach (M.)
1/2: C. Vanoirbeek (V.)
2/2: G. Coray (C.)

```
\usepackage{biblatex}
\addbibresource{tlc.bib}
\DeclareNameFormat{mynameformat}
  {\thelistcount/\theliststop:
   \namepartgiveni~\namepartfamily~(\namepartfamilyi)%
   \ifnumgreater{\value{listcount}}{\value{liststop}-1}%
            {}{\\}%        add a linebreak between names
  }
\citename{LGC97}[mynameformat]{author} \\[3pt]
\citename{EP92}[mynameformat]{editor}
```

16-7-40

Real format directives for names are typically much more complex than field and list format directives, because they have to test for missing name parts, etc. Fortunately, there exist various predefined formats that can be used by defining alias names. This is demonstrated in the next example where we define the name format directive `mynameformat` as an alias for the predefined format `family-given`. We also apply a second predefined directive (`family-given/given-family`) directly. Compare the order of the author names in both cases.

Goossens, M., Rahtz, S., and Mittelbach, F.
Goossens, M., S. Rahtz, and F. Mittelbach

```
\usepackage[giveninits]{biblatex}
\addbibresource{tlc.bib}
\DeclareNameAlias{mynameformat}{family-given}
\citename{LGC97}[mynameformat]{author}                \\
\citename{LGC97}[family-given/given-family]{author}
```

16-7-41

Common pitfalls A common error when declaring format directives is to use the wrong format name. For example, `journal` is wrong because the field is mapped to `journaltitle`. The title in an author-title citation uses the `citetitle` format directive, and the authors in the bibliography in an author-date style use the directive `sortname`. Another source of error is that some default format directives are entry type specific: to overwrite them one has to declare them for the specific type. For example, in Example 16-7-33 on page 561 we had to change the format specifically for `inproceedings` to overwrite the biblatex default. The same would be the case for the title of an article.

As a final example we change the default order of the author names in the bibliography by adapting the `sortname` format. We also show how to change the font of the names to small caps by redefining the wrapper commands like `\mkbibnamefamily` and `\mkbibnamegiven` used by biblatex around the name parts. We place everything into the hook `\AtBeginBibliography` to restrict the font changes to the bibliography and not affect the names in citation references.

Goossens, Rahtz, and Mittelbach (1997)

References

Goossens, Michel, Rahtz, Sebastian, and Mittelbach, Frank (1997). *The LATEX Graphics Companion: Illustrating Documents with TEX and PostScript*. Tools and Techniques for Computer Typesetting. Reading, MA, USA: Addison-Wesley Longman, pp. xxi + 554. ISBN: 0-201-85469-4.

16-7-42

```
\usepackage[style=authoryear]{biblatex}
\addbibresource{tlc.bib}
\DeclareNameAlias{sortname}{family-given}
\AtBeginBibliography{%
  \renewcommand\mkbibnamefamily[1]{\textsc{#1}}%
  \renewcommand\mkbibnamegiven [1]{\textsc{#1}}%
  \renewcommand\mkbibnameprefix[1]{\textsc{#1}}%
  \renewcommand\mkbibnamesuffix[1]{\textsc{#1}}}
\textcite{LGC97}
\printbibliography
```

16.8 Multiple bibliographies in one document

In large documents that contain several independent sections, such as conference proceedings with many different articles, or in a book with separate parts written by different authors, it is sometimes necessary to have separate bibliographies for each of the units. In such a scenario citations are confined to a certain part of the document, the one to which the bibliography list belongs.

A complementary request is to have several bibliographies in parallel, such as one for primary sources and one for secondary literature. In that case one has to be able to reference works in different bibliographies from any point in the document.

Both requests can be easily resolved when using the biblatex package. It has extended capabilities to print multiple bibliographies filtered and sorted by various conditions or to restrict their scope to parts of a document. This is described in Sections 16.7.8 to 16.7.10.

If using biblatex is not an option, both requests can also be automatically resolved if none of the bibliographies contains the same publication[1] and you are prepared to produce the bibliographies manually by means of several thebibliography environments without using BibTEX. In that case the \bibitem commands within the environment provide the right cross-referencing information for the \cite commands (or their variants) to pick up from anywhere in the document. Having the same publication in several bibliographies (or more exactly the same reference key) is not possible, because that would lead to a "multiply defined labels" warning (see page 761) and to incorrect references. Of course, this could be manually corrected by choosing a different key for such problematical citations.

Being deprived of using BibTEX or biblatex/biber has a number of consequences. First, it is more difficult to impose a uniform format on the bibliographical entries (something that the bibliography processors automatically handles for you). Second,

---

[1]This could happen, for example, if you compile the proceedings of a conference and each article therein has its own bibliography.

	Bibliographies per Unit				
	chapterbib	bibunits	bibtopic	biblatex	multibib
Bibliography per chapter	✓	✓	✓	✓	n/a
Bibliography per other unit	Restrictions	✓	✓	✓	n/a
Deal with escaping citations	✓	Restrictions	Error	✓	n/a
Additional global bibliography	Labor	✓	No	✓	n/a
Group bibliographies together	✓	No	No	✓	n/a
Multiple global bibliographies	No	No	✓	✓	✓
Multiple bibliographies per unit	No	No	✓	✓	No
cite compatible	✓	✓	✓	n/a	✓
jurabib compatible	✓	✓	Restrictions	n/a	✓
natbib compatible	✓	✓	✓	n/a	✓
Support for unsorted (BibTeX) styles	✓	✓	No	✓	✓
Works with standard .bib files	✓	✓	No	✓	✓
active links with hyperref	✓[a]	✓[b]	✓	✓	✓[c]
	chapterbib	bibunits	bibtopic	biblatex	multibib
					Per Topic

Blue entries indicate features (or missing features) that may force a selection.

[a] Only if \include is used. The option duplicate gives warnings about duplicate destinations; the links go from the citation to the first bibliography.   [b] Active links only when natbib is used too. Entries present in more than one bibliography give warnings about duplicate destinations; the links go to the first bibliography. [c] \newcites should be issued after \usepackage{hyperref}.

Table 16.3: Comparison of packages for multiple bibliographies

using an author-date or short-title citation scheme is difficult (because natbib requires a special structure within the optional argument of \bibitem) to downright impossible (because the structure required by jurabib or biblatex is not suitable for manual production); see Section 16.3 and 16.7 for a discussion of the required \bibitem or .bbl structures in those cases.

To be able to use BibTeX for this task people had to find a way to generate several .bbl files from one source document. As discussed in Section 15.4, the interaction with BibTeX normally works as follows: each citation command (e.g., \cite) writes its *key-list* as a \citation command into the .aux file. Similarly, \bibliography and \bibliographystyle commands simply copy their arguments to the .aux file. BibTeX then reads the master .aux file (and, if necessary, those from \included files) searching for occurrences of the above commands. From the provided information it produces a single .bbl file. To make BibTeX work for the above scenarios, four problems have to be solved:

1. Generate one .aux file for every bibliography in the document that can be used as input for BibTeX.

2. Ensure that each citation command writes its information to the correct `.aux` file so that BibTeX, when it processes a given `.aux` file, adds the corresponding bibliographical data in the `.bbl` file but not in the others.

3. Ensure that the resulting `.bbl` files are read back into LaTeX at the right place.

4. Handle the problem of escaping citations due to their placement in sectioning or `\caption` commands. A citation in such a place would later appear in the table of contents or list of figures, and there (in a different context) LaTeX would have problems in resolving it.

The packages chapterbib, bibunits, bibtopic, and multibib, which are described in this section, solve the above problems in different ways. They all have their own advantages and disadvantages. A short comparison of these packages appears in Table 16.3 on the preceding page, where blue entries indicate features (or missing features) that may force a selection when one is looking for a solution for bibliographies per unit or with bibliographies per topic, or a combination of both.

16.8.1 chapterbib — Bibliographies per included file

The chapterbib package (developed by Donald Arseneau based on original work by Niel Kempson) allows multiple bibliographies in a LaTeX document, including the same cited items occurring in more than one bibliography.

It solves the problem of producing several `.aux` files for BibTeX, by relying on the `\include` mechanism of LaTeX; you can have one bibliography per `\include`d file. This package can be used, for example, to produce a document with bibliographies per chapter (hence the name), where each chapter is stored in a separate file that is included with the `\include` command. This approach has the following restrictions:

- Each `\include` file needs to have its own `\bibliography` command. The database files that are listed in the argument can, of course, be different in each file. What is less obvious is that each file must contain a `\bibliographystyle` command, though for reasons of uniformity *preferably with the same style argument* (Example 16-8-1 on the following page shows that different styles can be applied).

- The `.aux` files of each `\include` file are processed individually by BibTeX. This means that *independent* bibliographies and labels are generated for each unit and that the same work can have differing labels in the units or two different works can have the same label; see also the discussion about the "reference sections" from the biblatex package in Section 16.7.10 on page 556.

- An `\include` file not containing a `\bibliography` command cannot contain citation commands, because they would not get resolved.

- Citation commands outside of `\include` files (with the exception of those appearing in the table of contents; see below) are not resolved, unless you include a `thebibliography` environment on that level. Without special precautions, this environment has to be entered manually. If you use BibTeX on the document's .aux file, you will encounter errors, because B<small>IB</small>T_EX sees multiple \bibdata and \bibstyle commands (when processing the included .aux files). In addition, you get *all* citations from *all* \include files added, and that is perhaps not desirable. If you do want a cohesive bibliography for the whole document, there is a rootbib option to help with this task. However, it requires adding and removing the option at different stages in the process; see the package documentation for details.

- Units containing a local bibliography always start a new page (because of the \include command). For cases where this is not appropriate, chapterbib offers some support through a \cbinput command and cbunit environment[1]; see the package documentation for details. Unless you need the gather option, it might be better to use the bibunits package in such situations.

By default, the thebibliography environment generates a numberless heading corresponding to the highest sectioning level available in the document class (e.g., \chapter* with the book class). However, if bibliographies are to be generated for individual parts of the document, this may not be the right level. In that case you can use the option sectionbib[2] to enforce \section* headings for the bibliographies.

In the following example, we present the \include files article-1.tex and article-2.tex in filecontents environments, which allows us to process this example automatically for the book. In real life these would be different files on your computer file system. We also use \stepcounter to change the chapter counter rather than using \chapter to avoid getting huge chapter headings in the example. Note that both included files refer to a publication with the key Knuth-CT-a. These are actually treated as different keys in the sense that one refers to the publication from article-1.bbl and the other refers to that from article-2.bbl.

... see [Knu86] ...	...see [2] and [1] ...	

Bibliography

[Knu86] Donald E. Knuth. *The T_EXbook*, volume A of *Computers and Typesetting*. Addison-Wesley, Reading, MA, USA, 1986.

Bibliography

[1] Hans Brox and Wolf-Dietrich Walker. *Besonderes Schuldrecht*. München, 27. edition, 2002.

[2] Donald E. Knuth. *The T_EXbook*, volume A of *Computers and Typesetting*. Addison-Wesley, Reading, MA, USA, 1986.

```
\begin{filecontents}{article-1.tex}
\stepcounter{chapter}
\ldots\ see \cite{Knuth-CT-a} \ldots
\bibliographystyle{alpha}
\bibliography{tlc}
\end{filecontents}
\begin{filecontents}{article-2.tex}
\stepcounter{chapter}
\ldots see \cite{Knuth-CT-a}
  and \cite{bschur} \ldots
\bibliographystyle{plain}
\bibliography{tlc}
\end{filecontents}
\usepackage[sectionbib]{chapterbib}
\include{article-1}
\include{article-2}
```

16-8-1

---

[1] cbunit can be used only together with manual thebibliography environments.
[2] If both chapterbib and natbib are used, use the sectionbib option of natbib instead!

If you wish to group all the bibliographies together (for example, at the end of the document), use the option gather and place a \bibliography command at the point where the combined bibliography should appear.[1] The argument of that command can be left empty because it is not used to communicate with BibTeX.

Instead of gather, you may want to use the option duplicate. It produces "chapter bibliographies", plus the combined listing. Both options work with the default settings only in document classes that have a \chapter command. The headings for each subbibliography generated by either option can be customized by redefining the command \FinalBibTitles. As you can see, you can make use of commands inside its definition, e.g., \thechapter and \chaptitle in the example. By altering their values (either implicitly or explicitly) before including the articles, different sub-bibliographies get different headings as shown below:

```
% Included files as in  previous example
    \usepackage [gather,sectionbib]{chapterbib}
    \newcommand\FinalBibTitles{References for Article~\thechapter
                              ~\mbox{---}~\chaptitle}
\newcommand\chaptitle{Intro}        \include{article-1}
\renewcommand\chaptitle{Summary}  \include{article-2}  \bibliography{}
```

Bibliography

References for Article 1 — Intro

[Knu86] Donald E. Knuth. *The TeXbook*, volume A of *Computers and Typesetting*. Addison-Wesley, Reading, MA, USA, 1986.

References for Article 2 — Summary

[1] Hans Brox and Wolf-Dietrich Walker. *Besonderes Schuldrecht*. München, 27. edition, 2002.

[2] Donald E. Knuth. *The TeXbook*, volume A of *Computers and Typesetting*. Addison-Wesley, Reading, MA, USA, 1986.

16-8-2

If the highest heading unit in your document is \section, you can redefine \StartFinalBibs. This gives you more control, but is a bit more complicated to set up: you can then use \refname in the main sectioning but should also redefine \bibname to \@auto@bibname for the headings of the subbibliographies; for details refer to the package documentation. In the following example we include slightly changed files that step the section counter instead of the chapter counter.

Using documents with \section as highest level

```
% Included files as before (i.e., from Example 16-8-1), but
% this time we are stepping the section counter.
    \usepackage [gather]{chapterbib}
    \sectionbib{\subsection*}{subsection}
```

---

[1]It should be placed after all units whose bibliography it should show.

```
\newcommand\FinalBibTitles{References for Article \thesection}
\renewcommand\StartFinalBibs{\section*{\refname}%
  \begingroup
    \setcounter{secnumdepth}{-1}%
    \addcontentsline{toc}{section}{\refname}%
    \sectionmark{\refname}%
  \endgroup
  \renewcommand\bibname{\UseName{@auto@bibname}}}

\include{article-1}   \include{article-2}   \bibliography{}
```

References

References for Article 1

[Knu86] Donald E. Knuth. *The TEXbook*, volume A of *Computers and Typesetting*. Addison-Wesley, Reading, MA, USA, 1986.

References for Article 2

[1] Hans Brox and Wolf-Dietrich Walker. *Besonderes Schuldrecht*. München, 27. edition, 2002.

[2] Donald E. Knuth. *The TEXbook*, volume A of *Computers and Typesetting*. Addison-Wesley, Reading, MA, USA, 1986.

16-8-3

If citations are placed into sectioning or \caption commands, they appear eventually in some table of contents list (i.e., at the top level). Nevertheless, chapterbib properly resolves them, by inserting extra code into .toc, .lof, and .lot files so that a \cite command is able to determine to which local bibliography it belongs. If you have additional table of contents lists set up, as explained in Section 2.3.4, you have to be careful to avoid citations that may end up in these new contents lists, because chapterbib is unaware of them.

Command already defined error

Some BIBTEX styles unfortunately use \newcommand declarations instead of \providecommand in the generated .bbl files, which makes such files unsuitable for repeated loading. If you get "Command ⟨*name*⟩ already defined" errors for this reason, surround the \bibliography commands and their arguments in braces. For example, write

```
{\bibliography{tlc}}
```

The chapterbib package is compatible with most other packages, including the citation packages discussed earlier in this chapter. If you plan to use it together with babel, load the chapterbib package first.

16.8.2 bibunits — **Bibliographies for arbitrary units**

The bibunits package developed by Thorsten Hansen (from original work by José Alberto Fernández) generates separate bibliographies for different units (parts) of the text (chapters, sections, or bibunit environments). The package separates the citations of each unit of text into a separate file to be processed by B\textsc{ib}T\textsc{e}X. A global bibliography can also appear in the document, and citations can be placed in both at the same time.

`\begin{bibunit}`[*style*] ... `\putbib`[*file-list*] ... `\end{bibunit}`

One way to denote the units that should have a separate bibliography is by enclosing them in a `bibunit` environment. The optional parameter *style* specifies a style for the bibliography different from a default that may have been set up (see below). Instead of `\bibliography`, you use a `\putbib` command to place the bibliography. It can appear anywhere within the unit as proven by the example. The optional argument *file-list* specifies a comma-separated list of B\textsc{ib}T\textsc{e}X database files; again a default can be set up. A default B\textsc{ib}T\textsc{e}X style can be set with `\defaultbibliographystyle`; without it, `plain` is used as the default. Similarly, `\defaultbibliography` can be used to define a default list of B\textsc{ib}T\textsc{e}X databases. In its absence `\jobname.bib` is tried. The example below uses both methods (explicit and defaults).

Setting up defaults

1 First one

[1] was used to produce [2].

References

[1] Free Software Foundation, Boston, Massachusetts. *GNU Make, A Program for Directing Recompilation*, 2000.

[2] Donald E. Knuth. Typesetting Concrete Mathemat-

ics. *TUGboat*, 10(1):31–36, April 1989.

2 Another one

As described by [Pyn20] ...

References

[Pyn20] Mike Pyne. *A book.* 2020.

```
\usepackage{bibunits}
\defaultbibliographystyle{alpha}
\defaultbibliography{tlc-ex}
\section{First one}
\begin{bibunit}[plain]
 \cite{GNUMake} was used to
 produce \cite{Knuth:TB10-1-31}.
 \putbib[tlc]
\end{bibunit}
\section{Another one}
\begin{bibunit}% default used
 As described by \cite{book1}
 \ldots
 \putbib        % default used
\end{bibunit}
```

16-8-4

For each unit bibunits writes the `\citation` commands (used to communicate with B\textsc{ib}T\textsc{e}X) into the file bu⟨*num*⟩.aux, where ⟨*num*⟩ is an integer starting with 1. Thus, to generate the necessary bibliographies, you have to run B\textsc{ib}T\textsc{e}X on the files bu1, bu2, and so forth. As a consequence, with the default settings you cannot process more than one document that uses bibunits in the same directory, because the auxiliary files would be overwritten.[1] After generating the bibliographies, you have to rerun L\textsc{a}T\textsc{e}X at least twice to resolve the new cross-references.

A global bibliography, in addition to the bibliographies for the individual units, can be generated by using `\bibliography` and `\bibliographystyle` as usual. Outside of a `bibunit` environment, the standard commands should be used to generate a citation for the global bibliography. Inside `bibunit`, use `\cite*` and `\nocite*` instead of `\cite` and `\nocite` to generate a citation for both the local

---

[1] If necessary, you can direct the package to use different names; see the package documentation.

and the global bibliography. There are, however, a number of restrictions. If the natbib package is also loaded, then \cite* has the meaning defined by natbib and cannot be used for generating a global citation (use \nocite outside the unit in that case). In addition, refrain from using numerical citation labels, because they are likely to produce ambiguous labels in the global bibliography, as shown in the next example. A better choice would be a BibTeX style such as alpha.

1   First one

[1] was used to produce [2].

References

[1] Free Software Foundation, Boston, Massachusetts. *GNU Make, A Program for Directing Recompilation*, 2000.

[2] Donald E. Knuth. Typesetting Concrete Mathematics. *TUGboat*, 10(1):31–36, April 1989.

2   Another one

As described by [1] …

References

[1] Donald E. Knuth. Typesetting Concrete Mathematics. *TUGboat*, 10(1):31–36, April 1989.

Global References

[1] Donald E. Knuth. Typesetting Concrete Mathematics. *TUGboat*, 10(1):31–36, April 1989.

```
\usepackage{bibunits}
\section{First one}
\begin{bibunit}[plain]
 \cite{GNUMake} was used to
 produce \cite*{Knuth:TB10-1-31}.
 \putbib[tlc]
\end{bibunit}
\section{Another one}
\begin{bibunit}[plain]
 As described by
 \cite*{Knuth:TB10-1-31}
 \ldots   \putbib[tlc]
\end{bibunit}
\renewcommand\refname
     {Global References}
\bibliographystyle{plain}
\bibliography{tlc}
```

16-8-5

Rather than using \cite* everywhere in your document, you can specify the package option globalcitecopy. All local citations are then automatically copied to the global bibliography as well.

`\bibliographyunit[`*unit*`]`

Instead of specifying the bibliography units with bibunit environments explicitly, you can specify the sectioning unit for which bibliography units should be generated automatically. The \bibliographyunit command defines with its optional argument for which document *unit* references must be generated, e.g., \chapter (for each chapter) or \section (for each section). If the optional argument is not given, the command deactivates further bibliography units. When \bibliographyunit is active, the \bibliographystyle and \bibliography commands specify the BibTeX files and the style to be used by default for a global bibliography, as well as in the local units. If you wish to specify information for local bibliographies only, use \bibliography* and \bibliographystyle* instead. These declarations *cannot* be used in the preamble but must be placed after \begin{document}.

Getting unresolved references   There is, however, a catch with the approach: the normal definition of the thebibliography environment, which surrounds the reference lists, generates a heading of the highest sectioning level. Hence, if you use \chapter units in a report, the heading generated by that environment prematurely ends the unit, and consequently you end up with undefined references, as shown in the example (using `\section` units in an article class).

---

1 First one

[?] was used to produce [?].

References

[1] Free Software Foundation, Boston, Massachusetts. *GNU Make, A Program for Directing Recompilation*, 2000.

[2] Donald E. Knuth. Typesetting Concrete Mathemat-

ics. *TUGboat*, 10(1):31–36, April 1989.

2 Another one

As described by [?] …

References

[1] Hans Brox and Wolf-Dietrich Walker. *Allgemeines Schuldrecht*.

```
\usepackage{bibunits}
\bibliographyunit[\section]
\bibliographystyle*{plain}
\bibliography*{tlc}
\section{First one}
  \cite{GNUMake} was
  used to produce
  \cite{Knuth:TB10-1-31}.
  \putbib
\section{Another one}
  As described by
  \cite{aschur} \ldots
  \putbib
```

16-8-6

To resolve this problem, you can provide your own `thebibliography` environment definition so that it uses a different sectioning level than the one specified on the `\bibliographyunit` declaration. Alternatively, you can use the option `sectionbib` (use `\section*` as a heading in `thebibliography`) or `subsectionbib` (use `\subsection*`) to change the `thebibliography` environment for you.

---

1 First one

[1] was used to produce [2].

References

[1] Free Software Foundation, Boston, Massachusetts. *GNU Make, A Program for Directing Recompilation*, 2000.

[2] Donald E. Knuth. Typesetting Concrete Mathemat-

ics. *TUGboat*, 10(1):31–36, April 1989.

2 Another one

As described by [1] …

References

[1] Hans Brox and Wolf-Dietrich Walker. *Allgemeines Schuldrecht*. München, 29. edition, 2003.

```
\usepackage[subsectionbib]
          {bibunits}
\bibliographyunit[\section]
\bibliographystyle*{plain}
\bibliography*{tlc}
\section{First one}
  \cite{GNUMake} was
  used to produce
  \cite{Knuth:TB10-1-31}.
  \putbib
\section{Another one}
  As described by
  \cite{aschur} \ldots
  \putbib
```

16-8-7

Note that the unit specified on the `\bibliographyunit` command has to be different from the one referred to in the option. In the above example the unit was `\section`, so we used the `subsectionbib` option.

To resolve the problem of escaping citations (see page 571), the package offers the option `labelstoglobalaux`. However, this has the side effects that such citations appear in the global bibliography and that numerical reference schemes are likely to produce incorrect labels; see the package documentation for details.

16.8.3 bibtopic — **Combining references by topic**

In contrast to chapterbib and bibunits, which collect citations for individual units of a document, the package bibtopic written by Stefan Ulrich (based on earlier work by Pierre Basso) combines reference listings by topic. You can, for example, provide a primary reference listing separate from a reference list for further reading or put all references to books separate from those to articles.

Within the document all citations are produced with \cite, \nocite, or variants thereof (if natbib or similar packages are also loaded). Thus, separation into topics is handled at a later stage. To produce separate bibliographies by topic you have to group the bibliographical entries that belong to one topic in a separate BibTeX database file (e.g., one for primary sources and one for secondary literature). The bibliographies are then generated by using several btSect environments. Ways to generate separate database files are described in Section 15.6: e.g., reference managers and also biber can be used to extract entries. Another option to extract reference entries according to some criteria from larger BibTeX database collections is the program bibtool developed by Gerd Neugebauer. It is distributed as a C source file, though you may find precompiled binaries — for example, in the Debian and FreeBSD distribution families.

> \begin{btSect} [*style*] {*file-list*}

The btSect environment generates a bibliography for all citations from the whole document that have entries in the BibTeX database files listed in the comma-separated *file-list* argument. If the optional *style* argument is present, it specifies the BibTeX style to use for the current bibliography. Otherwise, the style specified by a previous \bibliographystyle declaration is used. If no such declaration was given, the BibTeX style plain is used as a default.

Unless the package was loaded with the option printheadings, the environment produces no heading. Normally, you have to provide your own heading using \section* or a similar command.

> \btPrintCited   \btPrintNotCited   \btPrintAll

Within a btSect environment one of the above commands can be used to define which bibliographical entries are included among those from the specified *file-list* databases. The \btPrintCited command prints all references from *file-list* that have been somewhere cited in the document, \btPrintNotCited prints those that have not been cited, and \btPrintAll prints all entries in the BibTeX database files.

The following example shows the basic concepts using two topics: "TeX related" and "juridical" literature; it uses the databases tlc-tex.bib and tlc-jura.bib in which we copied some entries from our standard database. The first bibliography uses the default plain style; for the second bibliography we explicitly specified the BibTeX style abbrv (this is meant as an illustration — mixing styles is usually a bad idea). As you can see, if you specify numerical BibTeX styles, bibtopic automatically uses consecutive numbers throughout all bibliographies to ensure that the references in the document are unique.

We saw the citations [3], [2], and [1].

Juridical literature

[1] Hans Brox and Wolf-Dietrich Walker. *Besonderes Schuldrecht*. München, 27. edition, 2002.

[2] Hans Brox and Wolf-Dietrich Walker. *Allgemeines Schuldrecht*. München, 29. edition, 2003.

T_EX literature

[3] D. E. Knuth. *The T_EXbook*, volume A of *Computers and Typesetting*. Addison-Wesley, Reading, MA, USA, 1986.

16-8-8

```
\usepackage{bibtopic}
We saw the citations \cite{Knuth-CT-a},
\cite{aschur}, and \cite{bschur}.
\begin{btSect}{tlc-jura}
  \section*{Juridical literature}
  \btPrintCited
\end{btSect}
\begin{btSect}[abbrv]{tlc-tex}
  \section*{\TeX{} literature}
  \btPrintCited
\end{btSect}
```

For every `btSect` environment, the bibtopic package generates a separate `.aux` file that by default is constructed from the base name of the source document (`\jobname`) and a sequence number. You can change this naming scheme by redefining `\thebtauxfile` using the counter `btauxfile` to automatically obtain a sequence number. For the book examples we used the following redefinition:

```
\renewcommand\thebtauxfile{\jobname+\arabic{btauxfile}}
```

The bibtopic package is incompatible with chapterbib and bibunits. However, it provides the environment `btUnit` to confine the citations to logical units. Within such units the `btSect` environment can be used in the normal way, allowing for topic bibliographies by chapter or other unit. In that case *all* citations have to appear within such units (escaping citations, discussed on page 571, are not handled, so you have to ensure that they do not happen). By default, numerical styles restart their numbering per unit (e.g., per article in a proceedings issue). If you want continuous numbering, use the option `unitcntnoreset`.

Bibliographic topics per logical unit

While bibtopic works with most B_{IB}T_EX styles, there are some exceptions. The most important one is that it does not work as expected with "unsorted" styles (e.g., `unsrt`). If such a style is used, then the order in the bibliography is determined by the order in the B_{IB}T_EX database file and *not* by the order of citation in the document. If the latter order is required, you should use the multibib package described in the next section.

Problem with nonsorting B_{IB}T_EX styles

The bibtopic package is compatible with most other packages that provide extensions to the citation mechanism, including cite, natbib, and jurabib. There are, however, some restrictions with respect to the production of the bibliography lists. For example, hooks to influence the layout as provided by natbib or jurabib may not be functional. Details are given in the package documentation.

Here is a repeat of Example 16-8-8 but using jurabib this time:

We saw the citations Knuth The TEXbook, Brox/Walker Allgemeines Schuldrecht, and Brox/Walker BSchuR.

Juridical literature

Brox, Hans/Walker, Wolf-Dietrich: Besonderes Schuldrecht. 27th edition. München, 2002

Brox, Hans/Walker, Wolf-Dietrich: Allgemeines Schuldrecht. 29th edition. München, 2003

TEX literature

Knuth, Donald E.: The TEXbook. Volume A, Computers and Typesetting. Reading, MA, USA: Addison-Wesley, 1986, ix + 483, ISBN 0–201–13447–0

```
\usepackage{bibtopic,jurabib}
\bibliographystyle{jurabib}
We saw the citations \cite{Knuth-CT-a},
\cite{aschur}, and \cite{bschur}.
\begin{btSect}{tlc-jura}
  \section*{Juridical literature}
  \btPrintCited
\end{btSect}
\begin{btSect}{tlc-tex}
  \section*{\TeX{} literature}
  \btPrintCited
\end{btSect}
```

16-8-9

16.8.4 multibib — Separate global bibliographies

Like bibtopic, the multibib package written by Thorsten Hansen provides separate global bibliographies. While the former package separates the bibliographies by using separate BIBTEX database files, multibib works by providing separate citation commands to distinguish citations in different bibliographies.

There are advantages and disadvantages with either method. With multibib, different types of citations are clearly marked already in the source document. As a consequence, however, moving a citation from one bibliography to a different one in a consistent manner requires changes to the document in various places. In contrast, with bibtopic it merely requires moving the corresponding database entry from one file to another. On the other hand, bibtopic often requires tailored .bib files for each new document, while with multibib one can use generally available collections of BIBTEX database files.

The multibib package is compatible with most other packages that provide extensions to the cite mechanisms, including cite, jurabib, and natbib. Moreover, the package provides a general interface, which allows adding arbitrary extensions of cite commands to be recognized by multibib.

```
\newcites{type}{title}
```

The \newcites declaration defines an additional set of citation commands for a new *type* of citations. The heading for the additional bibliography listing is *title*. Once this declaration is given, the four additional commands are available for use. The command \cite⟨*type*⟩, like \cite, generates a citation within the text, and its corresponding reference appears in the bibliography listing for the new *type*. Similarly, \nocite⟨*type*⟩ adds a citation to the *type* bibliography without appearing in the text. The corresponding bibliography appears at the point where the \bibliography⟨*type*⟩ command is given, and the BIBTEX style used for this bibliography is defined with \bibliographystyle⟨*type*⟩. An example is shown below.

A book on graphics in LATEX is [1]; suggestions on citations can be found in [vL92].

```
\usepackage{multibib}
\newcites{latex}
          {\LaTeX{} references}

A book on graphics in \LaTeX{} is
\citelatex{LGC97}; suggestions on
citations can be found in
\cite{vLeunen:92}.

\bibliographystylelatex{plain}
\bibliographylatex{tlc}

\renewcommand\refname
          {General references}
\bibliographystyle{alpha}
\bibliography{tlc}
```

LATEX references

[1] Michel Goossens, Sebastian Rahtz, and Frank Mittelbach. *The LATEX Graphics Companion: Illustrating Documents with TEX and PostScript.* Tools and Techniques for Computer Typesetting. Addison-Wesley Longman, Reading, MA, USA, 1997.

General references

[vL92] Mary-Claire van Leunen. *A handbook for scholars.* Oxford University Press, Walton Street, Oxford OX2 6DP, UK, 1992.

16-8-10

The \newcites declaration can be used several times, thereby creating additional citation types. It is limited only by the number of output files that can be used simultaneously by TEX. The .aux file written for communication with BIBTEX has the name ⟨*type*⟩.aux. For this reason one has to be a bit careful when selecting the *type* in the first argument to \newcites, to avoid overwriting other .aux files.

For numerical citation styles the references are by default numbered sequentially over all bibliographies to avoid ambiguous references. When using the option resetlabels, each bibliography restarts the numbering.

LATEX offers an interface to include graphics.[1] LATEX's default citation scheme is number-only.[2]

```
\usepackage[super]{cite}
\usepackage{multibib}
\newcites{latex}{\LaTeX{} references}

\LaTeX{} offers an interface to include
graphics \citelatex{LGC97}. \LaTeX's
default citation scheme is
number-only \cite{vLeunen:92}.

\bibliographystylelatex{plain}
\bibliographylatex{tlc}

\renewcommand\refname
          {General references}
\bibliographystyle{plain}
\bibliography{tlc}
```

LATEX references

[1] Michel Goossens, Sebastian Rahtz, and Frank Mittelbach. *The LATEX Graphics Companion: Illustrating Documents with TEX and PostScript.* Tools and Techniques for Computer Typesetting. Addison-Wesley Longman, Reading, MA, USA, 1997.

General references

[2] Mary-Claire van Leunen. *A handbook for scholars.* Oxford University Press, Walton Street, Oxford OX2 6DP, UK, 1992.

16-8-11

LaTeX Package Documentation Tools

In this chapter we describe the doc system, a method to document LaTeX macros and environments. A large proportion of the LaTeX code available is documented using its conventions and support tools. The underlying principle is that LaTeX code and comments are mixed in the same file and that the documentation or the stripped package file or files are obtained from the latter in a standard way. In this chapter we explain the structure that these files should have and show how, together with the program DOCSTRIP, you can build self-installing procedures for distributing your LaTeX packages and generating the associated documentation. The chapter also helps you understand the code written by others, install it with ease, and produce the documentation for it (not necessarily in that order).

The third section then introduces the l3build program, which offers a flexible development environment. It supports a package developer in all important steps: code and documentation development, testing, and all aspects of the release management including upload to CTAN. It is the workflow environment used by the LaTeX Project Team for the code that they manage.

We end the chapter with a section on version control systems and explain how to extract and use their information with LaTeX. Applying version control methods is definitely useful for any larger documentation project, but in fact is advisable for any document that goes through a number of "revisions".

17.1 doc — Documenting LATEX and other code

The idea of integrated documentation was first employed by Donald Knuth when he developed the TEX program using the WEB system, which combines Pascal-like meta source code and documentation. Thanks to his approach, it was particularly easy to port TEX and its companion programs to practically any computer platform in the world.

Subsequently, authors of LATEX packages started to realize the importance of documenting their LATEX code. Many now distribute their LATEX macros using the framework defined with the **doc** package (by Frank Mittelbach) and its associated DOCSTRIP utility (originally by Frank Mittelbach with later contributions by Johannes Braams, Denys Duchier, Marcin Woliński, and Mark Wooding).

The **doc** package was written roughly 30 years ago (version 1 appeared in 1988, predating LATEX 2_ε). Since then it has been extensively used to document the LATEX kernel and most of the packages that are available on today's LATEX distributions. The core code of version 2 has existed since 1998, and that version was distributed with LATEX until 2022. At the TUG conference in Rio 2018 the author sketched out plans for a version 3 to improve it in several respects, but given it is so widely used, any change would need to be very light-weight, basically adding hyperlink support and adding a way to provide additional **doc** elements (not just macros and environments), with full compatibility to support all the existing uses.[1]

Both systems together allow LATEX code and documentation to be held in the same TEX source file. The obvious advantage is that a sequence of complex TEX instructions becomes easier to understand with the help of comments inside the file. In addition, updates are more straightforward because only a single source file needs to be changed.

The **doc** package provides a set of commands and establishes some conventions that allow specially prepared source files to contain both code and its documentation intermixed with each other. This is discussed in Sections 17.1.1 to 17.1.3.

To produce the documentation you need a driver (file) that loads the **doc** package and then interprets the source file. In its simplest form the driver for the documentation is an external file. However, the driver is more commonly made part of the source file so that all you have to do to produce the documentation is to run the source file through LATEX. The possibilities are discussed in detail in Section 17.1.4.

To produce a ready-to-run version of your code you need to first process the source package with DOCSTRIP (see Section 17.2). This step is usually implicitly done by providing an `.ins` file that is run through LATEX. The most important commands and concepts are discussed in the next sections. Tables 17.1 to 17.5 on pages 595–597 provide an overview of all **doc** user commands. Further details on any of them can be found in the documented source `doc.dtx` of the **doc** package, which can also serve as a prime (though somewhat aged) example of the **doc** system.

---

[1]If I restarted from scratch, I would do a lot of things differently now, and in fact several other people have tried to come up with better solutions. However, as the saying goes, a bad standard is better than none, so doc has prevailed, and changing it now in incompatible ways would be a nonstarter. Some of the ideas for the extensions have been borrowed from Didier Verna's DoX package, even though I did not use the document-level interfaces.

17.1.1 General conventions for the source file

A LATEX file to be used with the doc system consists of *documentation parts* intermixed with *code parts*. Every line of a documentation part starts with a percent sign (%) in the first column. It can contain arbitrary TEX or LATEX commands, but the % character cannot be used as a comment character. User comments are created by using the ^^A character or, if you prefer, the ^^X character instead. Longer text blocks can be turned into comments by surrounding them with %\iffalse ... %\fi. All other parts of the file are called code parts. They contain the code described in the documentation parts.

Depending on how the code parts are structured, it is possible to use such a file directly with LATEX, although these days this is seldom done. Instead, DOCSTRIP is typically used to produce the production files. If the former approach is taken, LATEX bypasses the documentation parts at high speed and pastes the macro definitions together, even if they are split into several code parts.

On the other hand, if you want to produce the documentation of the macros, then the code parts should be typeset verbatim. This is achieved by surrounding these parts by the `macrocode` environment.

```
%␣␣␣␣\begin{macrocode}
    ⟨one or more lines of code⟩
%␣␣␣␣\end{macrocode}
```

It is mandatory that you put *exactly* four spaces between the % character and \end{macrocode} and no space between \end and its argument. The reason is that when LATEX is processing the `macrocode` environment, it is actually looking for that particular string and not for the command \end with the argument `macrocode`.

Inside a code part all TEX commands are allowed. Even the percent sign can be used to suppress unwanted spaces at the ends of lines.

If you prefer, you can use the `macrocode*` instead of the `macrocode` environment. It produces the same results except that spaces are displayed as ␣ characters when the documentation is printed.

17.1.2 Describing new macros and environments

Most packages contain commands and environments to be employed by users in their documents. To provide a short manual describing their features, a number of constructs are offered by the doc package.

```
\DescribeMacro[keys]{\cmd₁,...}   \Describe⟨element⟩[keys]{entry₁,...}
```

The \DescribeMacro command takes one argument containing a comma-separated list of command names, which are shown in the margin, and for which special (usage) index entries are generated, for example,

```
% \DescribeMacro{\DocInput,\IndexInput}
% Finally the \meta{input commands} part ...
```

In the optional argument you can specify either `noindex` or `noprint` to suppress indexing or printing for that particular instance. Using both would be possible too, but pointless because then the command would do nothing.

A similar command, `\DescribeEnv`, can be used to indicate that at this point one or more LᴬTEX environments are being explained, and if you declare additional doc elements, e.g., ⟨element⟩, then `\Describe⟨element⟩` becomes available too.

`\begin{macro}[keys]{\cmd₁,...,\cmdₙ}`
`\begin{environment}[keys]{env₁,...,envₙ}`

To describe the definition of one or more commands, you use the `macro` environment. It takes one mandatory argument: a comma-separated list of the new commands. This argument is also used to print the names in the margin and to produce appropriate index entries. The index entries for usage (produced by `\Describe...`) and for definition are different, which allows for easy reference. Here is an example taken from the sources of the doc package itself:

```
% \begin{macro}{\check@angle}
%    Before looking ahead for the |<| the |%| is gobbled by the
%    argument here.
%    \begin{macrocode}
\def\check@angle#1{\futurelet\next\ch@angle}
%    \end{macrocode}
% \end{macro}
```

The optional *keys* argument lets you suppress indexing or printing of the command names in the margin, through specifying either `noindex` or `noprint` for that particular instance. If any such setting is made on the environment level, it overwrites whatever default was given when the doc element was defined or when the package was loaded.

By default the commands listed in the mandatory argument of the `macro` environment are not allowed to be declared with `\outer` (which is a plain TEX concept not officially supported by LᴬTEX). However, should you really want to document such a command, you can do so by specifying the key `outer` in the optional *keys* argument.

Another environment, with the unimaginative name `environment`, documents the code of environments. It works like the `macro` environment but expects the name or names of environments as its argument.

These two (`macro` and `environment`) are the doc elements supported out of the box by the package. How to define further elements is covered in Section 17.1.6 on page 592.

`\MakeShortVerb{\c}`   `\MakeShortVerb*{\c}`   `\DeleteShortVerb{\c}`

When you have to quote a lot of material verbatim, such as command names, it is awkward to always have to type `\verb+...+`. Therefore, the doc package provides an abbreviation mechanism that allows you to pick a character *c*, which you plan to use

only very rarely inside your document, to delimit your verbatim text—the character "
is often chosen, but if that character is already used for another purpose, such as
for shorthands in babel, then you may prefer | or some other character. Then, after
including the command \MakeShortVerb{\c}, the sequence *c*text*c* becomes the
equivalent of \verb*c*text*c*.

The variant form \MakeShortVerb* does the same but uses \verb*. If you
later want to use *c* with its original meaning, just type \DeleteShortVerb {\c}.
You can repeat this sequence using *c* as a shorthand for \verb and reverting to its
original meaning as many times as needed.[1] Note that such short forms for \verb,
just like \verb itself, cannot appear in the argument of another command, but the
characters may be used freely inside verbatim and macrocode environments.

You can divide your documented package file into two parts, the first typically
containing a general description and the second giving a detailed description of the
implementation of the macros. When generating the document, you can suppress this
latter part if you place the command \MaybeStop at the division point between the
two parts.[2]

\MaybeStop{*final text*}   \Finale

The \MaybeStop macro takes one argument in which you put all the information
that you want to see printed if the user decides to stop typesetting the document
at that point (for example, a bibliography, which is usually printed at the end of the
document). When the driver file contains an \OnlyDescription declaration, LaTeX
processes the argument of \MaybeStop and then stops reading the file. Otherwise, the
\MaybeStop macro saves its argument in a macro called \Finale, which can later be
used to get things back (usually at the very end). This scheme makes changes in two
places unnecessary. The default is to typeset the whole document. This default can
also be explicitly set by using the \AlsoImplementation command in the preamble.

A simple scheme to provide both user documentation and full documentation
including the code part is to provide a driver as part of the package .dtx file with
an \OnlyDescription in its preamble and then offer a second file with the name
⟨*package*⟩-code.tex that just contains the lines such as:

```
\AtBeginDocument{\AlsoImplementation}    % force full documentation
\input{doc.dtx}                          % load the package .dtx
```

You could alternatively use two such files, i.e., ⟨*package*⟩-code.tex for the code documentation and ⟨*package*⟩-doc.tex for the user interface, which is also often done.

---

[1]This feature has also been made available as a stand-alone package, shortvrb; it was discussed in
Section 4.2. See Example 4-2-3 on page →I 298.

[2]For a long time this command was called \StopEventually (still supported because it is used
all over the place in older documentation). The slightly strange command name was due to a "false
friend": the German word for 'perhaps' is 'eventuell', and when the author found out it was not saying
what he thought it was, it had been in use for years without anybody telling him.

> \changes{*version*}{*date*}{*text*}

To document the change history, the \changes command can be placed within the description part of the changed code. The information in the \changes command may be used to produce an auxiliary file (L^AT_EX's \glossary mechanism is used for this purpose), which can be printed after suitable formatting. To cause the change information to be written, include \RecordChanges in the driver file. To read and print the sorted change history, put the \PrintChanges command at a suitable point, typically after the \PrintIndex command in the driver.

To generate the sorted file containing the changes, you should run the raw glossary file through *MakeIndex* using an adequate style (like gglo.ist, supplied with the doc distribution; see Section 14.1.6 on page 349 for more information about how *MakeIndex* treats glossaries).

17.1.3 Cross-referencing all macros used

Inside a macrocode or macrocode* environment, index entries are produced for every command name that starts with a backslash. In this way you can easily find out where a specific macro is used. Since T_EX works considerably more slowly when it has to produce such an array of index entries, you can turn off this feature by using \DisableCrossrefs in the driver file. To turn it on again, use \EnableCrossrefs.

Finer control is provided with the \DoNotIndex command, which takes one argument containing a comma-separated list of commands that are *not* to be entered in the index. More than one \DoNotIndex command can be present, in which case their contents are combined. A frequent use of this macro is to exclude native L^AT_EX commands from the index.

\DisableCrossrefs, \EnableCrossrefs, and \DoNotIndex can be used in the document body. They obey the current grouping, which allows you, for example, to turn off indexing within a specific macro environment without the need to explicitly restart it afterwards.

The overall production (or not) of index entries is controlled by using or omitting the following declarations in the driver file preamble (if no declaration is provided, no index is produced). Using \PageIndex makes all index entries refer to their page number. With \CodelineIndex, index entries produced by \DescribeMacro and \DescribeEnv refer to the relevant page numbers, but those produced by the macro, environment, and macrocode environments refer to the code lines, which are numbered automatically. If you have defined your own environments with \NewDocElement, then they exhibit the same behavior.

If index entries are produced, they have to be sorted by an external program, such as *MakeIndex* (see Chapter 14). The doc package uses special conventions for the index entries, so you need to run *MakeIndex* with the −s switch (see Section 14.2.4 on page 356) to specify a suitable style — for example, gind.ist, which is distributed with the doc system.

To read and print the sorted index, you must put the \PrintIndex command near the end of your driver file, possibly preceded by bibliography commands, as needed for your citations. If you do not want to produce an index but you want the code lines numbered nevertheless, you can use the declaration \CodelineNumbered in the preamble.

17.1.4 The documentation driver

To get the documentation for a set of macros with the **doc** system, you have to prepare a driver (file) with the following characteristics:

```
\documentclass[⟨class options⟩]{⟨document-class⟩}
\usepackage[⟨package options⟩]{doc}
⟨preamble⟩
\begin{document}
    ⟨input-commands⟩
\end{document}
```

The ⟨document-class⟩ may be any legal class, such as article or ltxdoc (described in Section 17.1.9); in the latter case the **doc** package is already loaded by the class. In the ⟨preamble⟩, you should place declarations that manipulate the behavior of the **doc** system, such as \DisableCrossrefs, \OnlyDescription, and \CodelineIndex. Finally, the ⟨input-commands⟩ part should contain one or more \DocInput and/or \IndexInput commands.

\DocInput{*file name*}   \IndexInput{*file name*}

The \DocInput command is used for files prepared for the **doc** system, whereas \IndexInput can be used for macro files that do not obey the conventions of the **doc** system. The latter command takes a file name as its argument and produces a verbatim listing of the file, indexing every command as it goes along. This functionality can be handy if you want to learn something about macros without enough documentation.

It is also possible to use the \PrintIndex and \PrintChanges (if the changes are recorded by \RecordChanges) commands. Some people put them directly into the source file, but it is better practice to place them into the driver. You can then combine several packages in one document and produce a combined index.

As mentioned in the introduction, most often the driver is included directly in the source file instead of being a separate file of its own. How this works is explained in the next section.

Package options

Starting with version 3 the **doc** package now offers a small number of package options to modify its overall behavior. These are:

hyperref, nohyperref   Boolean (default `true`). Load the hyperref package and make index references to code lines, pages, and other items clickable links. nohyperref is the complementary key.

multicol, nomulticol Boolean (default `true`). Load the multicol package for use in typesetting the index and the list of changes. nomulticol is the complementary key.

debugshow Boolean (default `false`). Provide various tracing information at the terminal and in the transcript file. In particular, this shows which elements are indexed.

noindex Boolean (default `false`). If set, all automatic indexing is suppressed. This option can also be used on individual elements.

noprint Boolean (default `false`). If set, then printing of element names in the margin is suppressed. This option can also be used on individual elements as described below.

reportchangedates Boolean (default `false`). If set, the changes in the change log are listed with headings of the form "⟨*version*⟩ – ⟨*date*⟩" instead of just displaying the version.

Instead of providing options to the doc package you can call `\SetupDoc{`*key/value list*`}` in the ⟨*preamble*⟩ and provide them there. This allows, for example, changing default values in case doc was already loaded earlier.

17.1.5 Conditional code in the source

The features discussed so far can be used to produce a LᴬTEX source in literate programming style that can be directly used by loading it as a package (where TEX bypasses the comments) or printed by processing it with a driver file as explained in the previous section. This requires the structure of such a file to be linear; in other words, LᴬTEX sees *all* extracted code exactly in the order in which it is present in the file.

Experiences with the doc system soon suggested that it would be a valuable extension to be able to conditionally produce the ready-to-run files — by building them from several source files or extracting them from parts of one or more source files, for example. For this reason, the doc system was extended in two directions:

- A syntax was developed to label parts of the code so that the components could be referred to separately.

- The DOCSTRIP program (see Section 17.2), which was originally used only to strip the comments from doc files, was extended to offer a scripting language in which it became possible to specify how a ready-to-run file is generated from labeled code parts of one or more source files.

Of course, a source file containing such conditional code can usually no longer be used directly and requires the DOCSTRIP program before it can be turned into a ready-to-run file. However, the additional possibilities offered by this approach outweigh the inconvenience of an extra production step during installation so much that nearly all usages of doc now take advantage of it.

Code fragments for conditional inclusion are marked in the source file with "tags". The simplest format is a <*name> and </name> pair surrounding some part of the code. This enables us to include or exclude that part by referring to its *name* in a DOCSTRIP script. The tags must be placed at the beginning of the line preceded by a %. For example:

```
%<*style>
      some lines of code
%</style>
```

It is possible to attach more than one tag to a part by combining several *names* with the Boolean operators | for logical "or", & for logical "and", and ! for negation (using lazy evaluation from the left). For example,

```
%<*Aname|Bname&!Cname>
      some lines of code
%</Aname|Bname&!Cname>
```

means that this block should be included when either `Aname` is asked for or `Bname` is requested but `Cname` is not.

There are two other forms of directives for including or excluding single lines of code. A line starting with %<+*name*> or just %<*name*> is included (without its tag) if *name* is requested. A line starting with %<−*name*> is included if *name* is *not* requested in a DOCSTRIP run.

The above directives can be nested in each other. If this is done, the inner tags are evaluated only if the outer tags are true (i.e., if the whole block is requested for inclusion).

```
%<*Aname>
             code line 1
%<+Bname>    code line 2
%<-Bname>    code line 3
             code line 4
%</Aname>
```

Here nothing is included if `Aname` is not requested. If it is requested, we get code lines 1, 2, and 4 if `Bname` is also asked for, and lines 1, 3, and 4 otherwise.

You may have wondered how the conditional coding allows us to include the driver in the main source file. For this you have to place the code for the driver as the first code block and surround it by some tag (e.g., `driver`). If the user now runs the source file through LaTeX, the driver code is the first code that is not behind % signs, so it is executed. Because it ends in \end{document}, the LaTeX run will not execute any later code in the file. Thus, the documentation is typeset assuming that the driver loads the whole file using \DocInput. To generate the actual package file(s), you use a DOCSTRIP script (see Section 17.2 on page 599) that ignores the driver code by not requesting code from a block tagged `driver`.

17.1.6 Providing additional documentation elements

Out of the box the doc package offers the above commands and environments to document macros and environments. With version 3 this has now been extended in a generic fashion so that you can easily provide your own items, such as counters, length register, options, etc.

> \NewDocElement [*key/value list*] {*name*}{*env*}

By convention the *name* has the first letter uppercased as in Env or Macro. Such a declaration will define for you a few commands and one environment:

- The command \Describe⟨*name*⟩ with the same syntax as \DescribeMacro and \DescribeEnv.

- The environment env, which has the same syntax as macro or environment.

- The display command \PrintDescribe⟨*name*⟩, which has the same syntax as \PrintDescribeMacro or \PrintDescribeEnv.

- The \Print⟨*name*⟩Name display command that is used by the environment when displaying the element name in the margin, i.e., like \PrintMacroName or \PrintEnvName.

If any of the commands or the environment is already defined (which especially with a badly chosen *env* is a danger), then you receive an error telling you so.

If you want to modify an existing doc element, use \RenewDocElement instead. For example, the already provided "Env" doc element could have been defined simply by making the declaration \NewDocElement{Env}{environment} though that's not quite what has been done, as we see later.

The optional *key/value list* defines further details on how that doc element should behave. The following keys are supported:

macrolike   Boolean (default false). Does this doc element start with a backslash?

envlike   Boolean. Complementary key to macrolike.

toplevel   Boolean (default true). Should a top-level index entry be made? If set to false, then either no index entries are produced or only grouped index entries are generated (see idxgroup for details).

notoplevel Boolean. Complementary option to toplevel.

idxtype   String (default *env*). What to put (in parentheses if nonempty) at the end of a top-level index entry.

printtype   String (default *env*). What to put (in parentheses if nonempty) after an element name in the margin.

idxgroup   String (default *env*s). Name of the top-level index entry if entries are grouped. They are grouped only if this option is nonempty.

noindex   Boolean (default `false`). If set, this suppresses indexing for elements of this type. This setting overwrites any global setting of `noindex`.

noprint   Boolean (default `false`). If set, this suppresses printing the element name in the margin. This setting overwrites any global setting of `noprint`.

As usual, using a Boolean key without a value sets it to `true`.

In the syntax of `\NewDocElement` the two elements `Macro` and `Env`, provided by doc out of the box, are defined as follows:

```
\NewDocElement[macrolike, idxtype=, idxgroup=, printtype=]
            {Macro}{macro}
\NewDocElement[envlike, idxtype=env., idxgroup=environments,
            printtype=\textit{env.}] {Env}{environment}
```

This means that index entries for environments show the string "env." after the name in the index, and they appear both on the top level as well as grouped under the heading "environments". If typeset in the margin, they show "*env.*" after the environment name. If you prefer a different convention, use `\RenewDocElement` on these two elements.

For example, to set up a more structured index, all that you have to do is to define a few more doc elements and use them when documenting your code. For example, by using `notoplevel` and defining appropriate types to distinguish things like lengths, counters, public interface commands, etc., you can always group the commands by type, which might help your readers to find information easier.

```
\NewDocElement[macrolike, notoplevel, idxtype=, printtype=,
            idxgroup=Package interfaces] {Interface}{interface}
\NewDocElement[macrolike, notoplevel, idxtype=skip,
            idxgroup=LaTeX length\actualchar \LaTeX\ length (skip),
            printtype=\textit{skip}] {LaTeXSkip}{lskip}
\NewDocElement ...
```

Then use those doc elements instead or in addition to the commands and environments already offered by doc whenever appropriate. The package documentation of doc is an example of how this could look.

17.1.7 Producing the actual index entries

Several of the aforementioned macros produce one or more index entry. These entries have to be sorted by an external program — the current implementation assumes that the *MakeIndex* (or upmendex) program is used; see Chapter 14.

This is not built in: one has to redefine only some of the following commands to be able to use any other index program. All macros that are installation dependent are defined in such a way that they do not overwrite a previous definition. Therefore, it is safe to put the changed versions in a package file that might be read in before the doc package.

To allow the user to change the specific characters recognized by the index program, all characters that have special meaning in the *MakeIndex* program are given symbolic names.

The `\actualchar` is used to separate the "sort key" from the actual index entry. The `\quotechar` has to be used before a special index program character to suppress its special meaning. The `\encapchar` separates the indexing information from a letter string, which *MakeIndex* turns into a TEX command to format the page number associated with a special entry. It is used in this package to apply the `\main` and the `\usage` commands. Additionally, `\levelchar` is used to separate "item", "subitem", and "subsubitem" entries.

It is a good idea to stick to these symbolic names even if you know which index program is used. In this way your files remain portable. For example, you could make a manual index entry like this:

```
\newcommand\ltxconcept[1]{\index{LaTeX concepts\actualchar \LaTeX\
                            concepts\levelchar #1\encapchar main}}
\ltxconcept{level character '\quotechar\levelchar' in index}
```

With the default settings of **doc** this would produce the following line in the `.idx` file:

```
\indexentry{LaTeX concepts=\LaTeX  \ concepts>level character '!>'
                            in index|main}{1}
```

i.e., the various commands got replaced by the appropriate characters. Note that this works only because we have used `\index` inside a command definition: if `\index` is used directly in the document, the argument is written fully verbatim, which is not what is wanted here.

The page or code line numbers for main index entries are encapsulated by the `\main` macro (underlining its argument), and the numbers denoting the description are encapsulated by the `\usage` macro (which by default produces *italics*). Finally, `\code` encapsulates page or code line numbers in entries generated by parsing the code inside `macrocode` environments. As usual these commands are user definable.

As an example we modify the index output to better indicate that some numbers mean line numbers by prefixing them with the letter ℓ:

```
\CodelineIndex
\renewcommand\code[1]{\mbox{$\ell$-#1}}
\renewcommand\main[1]{\underline{\mbox{$\ell$-#1}}}
```

17.1.8 Overview about all doc commands

We conclude this section with a few tables that briefly list all interfaces provided by the **doc** package, including some that we have not talked about before, e.g., parameters for altering the layout. If you need more information on any of them, take a look at the package documentation where all of them are discussed in further detail.

\AlsoImplementation	Typeset the complete file marked up according to **doc** conventions, including code part (default).
\CheckModules	Format module directives of DOCSTRIP specially (default).
\CodelineIndex	Index commands using code line numbers.
\CodelineNumbered	Number code lines but do not index commands.
\DisableCrossrefs	Do not produce index entries for commands within the code.
\DocInput{*file*}	Read in *file* assuming **doc** conventions.
\DontCheckModules	Do not format module directives of DOCSTRIP specially.
\EnableCrossrefs	Produce index entries for commands within the code.
\IndexInput{*file*}	Read in *file*, print it verbatim, and produce a command cross-reference index.
\NewDocElement [*key/values*]{*XX*}{*env*}	Declare a new **doc** element of type *XX* with the characteristics *key/values* using the environment *env*.
\OnlyDescription	Do not format code; stop at \MaybeStop.
\PageIndex	Index commands using page numbers.
\PrintChanges	Print the history listing here.
\PrintIndex	Print the index listing here.
\RecordChanges	Produce a history listing.
\RenewDocElement [*key/values*]{*XX*}{*env*}	Redeclare an existing **doc** element of type *XX* with the characteristics *key/values* using the environment *env*.

Table 17.1: doc — *Preamble and input commands*

\bslash	Print a backslash (\). Only useful in typewriter fonts!
\cs{*cmd*}	Print the argument as a command by using a typewriter font and prefixing it with a backslash.
\DeleteShortVerb{\c}	Undo use of \MakeShortVerb or \MakeShortVerb* for character *c*.
\DescribeEnv{*env$_1$*,...}	Flag point in text where environment(s) *env$_1$* to *env$_n$* are described.
\DescribeMacro{*cmd$_1$*,...}	Flag point in text where the command(s) are described.
\Describe⟨*XX*⟩{*entry$_1$*,...}	Generalization of the above declared through \NewDocElement.
\begin{environment} {*env$_1$*,...}	Environment surrounding the definition of the environment(s) *env$_1$* to *env$_n$*.
\Finale	Command executed at very end of document (see also \MaybeStop).
\begin{macro}{*cmd$_1$*,...}	Environment surrounding the definition of the command(s) listed in the argument.
\begin{macrocode}	Environment surrounding the TEX code.
\begin{macrocode*}	Same as the macrocode environment, but spaces are printed as ␣ characters.
\MakeShortVerb{\c}	Define abbreviation character *c* for \verb.
\MakeShortVerb*{\c}	Define abbreviation character *c* for \verb*.
\MaybeStop{*cmds*}	In the argument *cmds*, specify the commands that should be executed at the end of the document (they are stored in \Finale).
\meta{*arg*}	Print the argument as a meta sentence (default ⟨*arg*⟩).
\SpecialEscapechar{\c}	Specify new single escape character *c* to be used instead of the default backslash character to identify the start of a command in code of the next macrocode or macrocode* environment.
\begin{verbatim}	Slightly altered version of LATEX's standard verbatim environment to surround verbatim text ignoring percent characters in column 1.
\begin{verbatim*}	Same as the verbatim environment, but spaces are printed as ␣ characters.

Table 17.2: doc — Document structure commands

`\*`	Symbol used in index entries to refer to a higher-level entry (default ~).
`\actualchar`	Character used to separate "key" and actual index in an index entry (default =).
`\DoNotIndex{cmd₁,...}`	Names of commands that should not show up in the index. This can be used several times.
`\code{number}`	The formatting style for code line or page numbers of index entries generated while parsing the code lines in `macrocode` environments. By default the *number* is used unchanged without special formatting.
`\encapchar`	Character used to separate the actual index and the command to format the page number in an index entry (default |).
`\IndexMin`	Length parameter (default 80pt) defining the minimal amount of space that should be left on a page to start an index.
`\IndexParms`	Macro controlling the formatting of the index columns.
`\IndexPrologue{text}`	Specify (overwrite) the text placed on top of the index.
`\levelchar`	Character used to separate different index levels in an index entry (default >).
`\main{number}`	The formatting style for page numbers or code line numbers of index entries for major references (default underlined digits).
`\quotechar`	Character used to suppress the special meaning of the following character in an index entry (default !).
`\SortIndex{key}{entry}`	Produce an index entry for *entry*, sorting it by *key*.
`\Special⟨XX⟩Index{entry}`	Produce a usage index entry for *entry*, which is a doc element of type ⟨*XX*⟩ (i.e., Macro or Env by default or one defined by `\NewDocElement`) using a `\usage` page encapsulator.
`\SpecialMain⟨XX⟩Index` `{entry}`	Produce a main index entry for *entry*, which is a doc element of type ⟨*XX*⟩ (`\main` page encapsulator).
`\SpecialIndex{\cmd}`	Produce a command index (printing the argument verbatim in the index). If the command is of a special type for which there is a doc element declared, it is automatically recognized.
`\SpecialShortIndex{\c}`	Produce a command index for a single character command \c. Some of them do not sort correctly if `\SpecialIndex` would be used, e.g., \{; therefore, doc uses a special (slow) command for them.
`\usage{number}`	The formatting style for page numbers of index entries for usage descriptions (default italic digits).
`\verbatimchar`	Character used to delimit `\verb` constructs within an index entry (default +).

Table 17.3: doc — Index commands

`\changes{version}{date}` `{reason}`	Record *reason* for *version* written on *date* as history information for use in a history listing. Use YYYY/MM/DD or YYYY–MM–DD for *date*.
`\GlossaryMin`	Length parameter (default 80pt) defining the minimal amount of space that should be left on a page to start the change history.
`\GlossaryParms`	Macro controlling the formatting of the change history columns.
`\GlossaryPrologue{text}`	Replace (overwrite) the default text placed on top of the history listing.

Table 17.4: doc — History information

`\@idxitem`	Macro specifying how index items should be typeset (by default, they are set as a paragraph with a hanging indentation of 30pt for items requiring more than one line).
`\AltMacroFont`	Font used to typeset DOCSTRIP module code (default `\small\ttfamily\slshape`).
`\DocstyleParms`	Macro controlling the formatting of the TeX code.
`\generalname`	String placed before change entries on the top level.
`\MacrocodeTopsep`	Vertical space above and below each `macrocode` environment.
`\MacroFont`	Font used to typeset the main part of the code (default `\small\ttfamily`).
`\MacroIndent`	Width of the indentation for every code line.
`\MacroTopsep`	Vertical space above and below each `macro` environment.
`\MakePercentComment`	Activate "%" as TeX's comment initiator character.
`\MakePercentIgnore`	Deactivate "%" as TeX's comment initiator character.
`\MakePrivateLetters`	Macro specifying symbols to be considered as letters (default `@`).
`\Module`	Macro with one argument defining the formatting of DOCSTRIP module directives.
`\PrintDescribe⟨XX⟩{entry}`	Command with one argument defining the formatting of `\Describe⟨XX⟩`.
`\Print⟨XX⟩Name{entry}`	Like `\PrintDescribe⟨XX⟩` but for the argument of the environment surrounding the definition.
`StandardModuleDepth`	Counter holding the highest level of DOCSTRIP directives, which are still formatted using `\MacroFont`. Deeper-nested directives are formatted using `\AltMacroFont`.
`\theCodelineNo`	Control the typesetting of line numbers (default script-size arabic numerals).

Table 17.5: doc — Layout and typesetting parameters

17.1.9 ltxdoc — A simple LaTeX documentation class

The ltxdoc class was designed for documenting the core LaTeX source files, which are used to build the LaTeX format and all packages distributed as part of the core distribution. This class is built on the article class, loads the doc package, but extends it slightly with a few commands that we found helpful for documenting LaTeX kernel code. It also includes some layout settings specially tailored to accommodate the typical requirements of a source file in doc style (e.g., a line width to hold 72 characters in typewriter fonts and a wider left margin to allow for long macro names to be placed into it).[1]

A special feature is that the class can be used to produce a single document from a larger number of source files in doc style. This has the advantage that one can produce a full index of macro usage across all source files. For example, the driver file `source2e.tex` generates the documented source listing of the close to 60 files that make up the LaTeX kernel. It generates a document with more than 1200 pages including an index and a change history (reaching back to the early 1990s).

---

[1] These days we often use l3doc for LaTeX Project documentation. However, this class is far from being finalized, and there are plans to alter it drastically — we therefore do not recommend using it, unless you are prepared to update your sources when it changes!

Extensions provided by ltxdoc

As extensions, the class offers a small set of commands to describe LᴬTEX commands and their arguments. These commands really should have been in the doc package, but due to some historical accident have never been added there.

```
\cmd{\name}  |...|   \marg{arg}  \oarg{arg}  \parg{arg}
```

The command `\cmd` prints a command *name* in typewriter font; for example, writing `\cmd{\foo}` typesets `\foo`. In contrast to `\verb+\foo+` (which is otherwise similar), it can be used anywhere — even in the arguments of other commands. The command `\cs`, which is already part of the doc package, offers the same functionality for those who prefer the syntax without the backslash. In fact, it is slightly more powerful because it can also typeset commands that are made `\outer` — a plain TEX concept normally not used in LᴬTEX. Furthermore, ltxdoc makes "|" an abbreviation for `\verb` so that you can type `|\foo|` in the documentation. If this is not desired for some reason, you have to cancel it in the source (after `\begin{document}`) via `\DeleteShortVerb{\|}`.

The commands `\marg`, `\oarg`, and `\parg` produce the LᴬTEX syntax for mandatory, optional, and picture arguments, respectively. Thus, writing

```
\cs{makebox}\parg{x-dimen,y-dimen}\oarg{pos}\marg{text}
```

produces the (probably less-known) syntax diagram for `\makebox` in picture environments: `\makebox((⟨x-dimen,y-dimen⟩))[⟨pos⟩]{⟨text⟩}`.

```
\DocInclude{file}
```

The `\DocInclude` command is similar to `\include` except that it uses `\DocInput` on *file* (with the implicit extension `.dtx` or `.fdd`) instead of using `\input` on a *file* (with the implicit extension `.tex`). This command is used in `source2e.tex` to "include" all `.dtx` files that form the LᴬTEX kernel.

Customizing the output of documents that use ltxdoc

To customize documents using the ltxdoc class you can create a configuration file (`ltxdoc.cfg`). This configuration file is read whenever the ltxdoc class is used, so it can be used to customize the typesetting of all the source files, without having to edit lots of small driver files, which would be the manual alternative.

If `ltxdoc.cfg` is installed in a directory always searched by LᴬTEX, it is applied to all documentation files using the ltxdoc class. If it is placed in the current directory, it applies only to documents processed in this directory.

The simplest form of customization is to pass one or more options to the article class upon which ltxdoc is based. For instance, if you wish all your documentation to be formatted for A4 paper, add the line

```
\PassOptionsToClass{a4paper}{article}
```

to `ltxdoc.cfg` and install it in a place searched by LᴬTEX.

As discussed in Section 17.1.2, the \MaybeStop command separates the source files into a "user" documentation and an "implementation" part. To be able to produce only the user manual, the doc package provides the command \OnlyDescription, which suppresses the implementation part. This command may also be used in the configuration file, but as the doc package is loaded after the configuration file is read, you must delay the execution of \OnlyDescription. The simplest way is to use \AtBeginDocument as follows:

```
\AtBeginDocument{\OnlyDescription}
```

For example, the documented source of the array package, the file array.dtx, generates 35 pages of documented code listings if you run

```
pdflatex array.dtx
```

without a configuration file. However, most people are not interested in *how* commands are implemented in this package, but rather what interfaces the package provides and how to use them. With the above configuration line the output is reduced to an 8-page user manual, listing only the interfaces together with a few examples.

Whencreating automatically the driver source2e.tex for the kernel documentation is processed, an index and a change history are produced by default; however, indexes are not normally produced for individual files. If you are really interested in the source listings in detail, you probably want to have an index as well. Again, the index commands provided by the doc package may be used, and again their execution must be delayed. Thus, the addition to the configuration file could look as follows:

```
\AtBeginDocument{\AlsoImplementation  % force processing everything
                 \CodelineIndex       % select index per code line
                 \EnableCrossrefs }   % enable it
\AtEndDocument{\PrintIndex}
```

Similar lines would be necessary if you want to produce a change history listing. Recall that the doc package generates .idx and .glo files with a special syntax that requires adequate style files for processing with *MakeIndex* (see Section 17.1.3 on page 588).

17.2 docstrip.tex — **Producing ready-to-run code**

When doc was originally written in the late 1980s, the intention was to provide a "literate programming" environment [41] for LATEX, in which LATEX code and documentation were intermixed in the same source file. As it soon turned out, making TEX parse (and then ignore) all the documentation when reading a file added a heavy time penalty.[1] To avoid this problem the author looked for ways to automatically strip all comments from files written for the doc system.

---

[1]In those days producing a single page with TEX could easily take half a minute or longer.

The problem with any external program developed for such a purpose is that it may or may not be available for the user's operating system and even if available may not be installed. But one program is always available on a system that can run LaTeX: the TeX program itself. To achieve the widest portability, the DOCSTRIP program was therefore written in low-level TeX language. Since those early days, the program has undergone many revisions that changed its purpose from being a simple stripping device to serving as a fully customizable installation tool — one that is even able to distribute files to the right directories on a target machine. Johannes Braams, Denys Duchier, Marcin Woliński, Mark Wooding, David Carlisle, and others contributed to this metamorphosis; details of the program's evolution can be found in the documented source (which uses literate programming, of course). Here are today's main applications of the DOCSTRIP program:

- Strip a literate programming source of most of its documentation (i.e., the lines that start with a single % sign in the first column).
- Build ready-to-run code files by using code from one or more source files and including parts of it according to options specified.

It is also possible with DOCSTRIP to automatically install the produced files in the right directories on the target machine if desired, which was initially important for a smooth update process. However, today this is better handled through l3build (see Section 17.3), so this is not covered in the book.

Will Robertson has produced a nice gallery [85] of sample .dtx files that exhibit various techniques using DOCSTRIP. Take a look at this after having read the current section.

17.2.1 Invocation of the docstrip utility

From its first days of existence DOCSTRIP could be run interactively by processing docstrip.tex with LaTeX:

```
latex docstrip.tex
```

LaTeX then asks a few questions about how to process a given file. When the user has answered these questions, DOCSTRIP does its job and strips the comments from the source.

However, this method of processing was intended to do nothing more than stripping off comments. With today's sources, which contain conditional code and are intended to be combined to form the final "executable", it is usually no longer appropriate. Instead, the developers of packages typically provide an installation file (by convention having the extension .ins) that is used to invoke DOCSTRIP behind the scenes. In this case the user simply says

```
latex ⟨name⟩.ins
```

This results in the generation of all "executables" from the source distribution and optionally installs them in the right places. All standard LaTeX distributions (e.g., `base`, `graphics`, and `tools`) are distributed in this form and so are most contributed packages that are described in this book. In the next section we discuss how to construct your own installation scripts for DOCSTRIP.

17.2.2 docstrip script commands

A DOCSTRIP installation script has the following general form:

```
\input docstrip
⟨other DOCSTRIP commands⟩
\endbatchfile
```

It starts by loading the DOCSTRIP code using the TeX primitive `\input` (typically without braces[1] around the file name).

This is followed by the DOCSTRIP commands that actually do the work of building new files, communicating with the user, and carrying out other necessary tasks. At the very end, the script contains `\endbatchfile`. Without that statement, DOCSTRIP would display a * prompt while waiting for further input from the user.

Generating new files

The main reason for constructing a DOCSTRIP script is to describe which files should be generated, from which sources, and which optional (tagged) chunks of code should be included. This is done by using `\generate` declarations.

```
\generate{\file{result-file₁}{\from{source-file₁}{tag-list₁}
                             \from{source-file₂}{tag-list₂}
                             . . .
                             \from{source-fileₙ}{tag-listₙ}}
          . . .
          \file{result-fileₙ}{...}
         }
```

Within the argument to `\generate` you specify the *result-file*s you want to produce by using `\file` declarations. The second argument to `\file` contains one or more `\from` commands listing the *source-files* that should be used to build one *result-file*. With each `\from` declaration the second argument specifies the *tag-list* to use with the particular *source-file*. Then only the code chunks tagged with the appropriate tags and all the untagged source lines from that file are included (see Section 17.1.5 on page 590 for a description how to tag code).

The *source-files* are used in the order specified: first the code from *source-file₁* is included (according to the tag specification), then the code from *source-file₂*, and so on. The *tag-lists* in each `\from` command are comma-separated lists and indicate that code with these tags should be included.

---

[1] This is actually no longer necessary because nowadays `\input` always accepts a braced argument.

With the syntax specification for \generate as given above, you can produce a single *result-file* from one or more *source-file*s by using a single \file declaration. By repeating this as often as needed, any kind of distribution can be produced. It is, however, not very efficient. Suppose you have one large source file from which you want to produce many small files—for example, suppose the source for the doc package, doc.dtx, is used to generate doc.sty, shortvrb.sty, gind.ist, and gglo.ist. The file is nearly 5000 lines long, so by using four \generate declarations, DOCSTRIP would have to process 20000 lines. To speed up this process, \generate allows you to specify several \file commands within its argument. These files are processed in parallel, meaning that the *source-file*s are opened only once, and distribution of source code to *result-file*s is done in parallel.

```
\generate{\file{doc.sty}{\from{doc.dtx}{package}}
          \file{shortvrb.sty}{\from{doc.dtx}{shortvrb}}
          \usepostamble\istpost
          \file{gind.ist}{\from{doc.dtx}{gind}}
          \file{gglo.ist}{\from{doc.dtx}{gglo}}}
```

As you can see, certain other commands (\usepostamble, for example) are allowed within the argument of the \generate command. In the above example this has the effect of replacing the standard postamble with a different one (because the standard postamble adds an \endinput to the end of the generated file, something not desirable in a style file for *MakeIndex*).

Restrictions on parallel extraction
There are some restrictions with this approach. For instance, DOCSTRIP complains if the order of source files in one \file command conflicts with the order in a different one; the precise rules are discussed in the DOCSTRIP documentation [75]. If that happens, the simplest solution is to use two separate \generate declarations.

Communicating with the user

The DOCSTRIP scripting language offers some limited possibilities for user communication. Keep in mind that interactive questions, though sometimes useful, can make an installation process quite cumbersome, so these tools should be used with care.

\Msg{*message*}   \Ask{*cmd*}{*question*}

The \Msg command can be used to present a *message* on the terminal; thus, it offers a similar functionality as LATEX's \typeout command. \Ask is similar to LATEX's \typein command, with the difference that no trailing space is generated from pressing return in reply to a *question*. This way simple questions can be asked (using a bit of low-level programming). For example:

```
\Ask\answer{Should we continue? (y/n)}
\ifx\answer\y
  % code for ``y'' as answer
\else
  % otherwise
\fi
```

> `\ifToplevel{code}`

You may want to give certain information, or run certain code, only if a DOCSTRIP script is executed on its own, but not if it is called as part of a larger installation (see below). Such information or code can be placed in the argument of an `\ifToplevel` command. For example, all the individual installation scripts from the LaTeX base distribution say what to do with the generated files. However, if you use the main installation script `unpack.ins`, the messages in the subscripts are suppressed to avoid repeating the same information over and over again.

> `\askforoverwritetrue`   `\askforoverwritefalse`

Before DOCSTRIP writes its output to a file, it checks whether that operation would overwrite some existing version of this file. If so, the default behavior is to ask the user if overwriting is acceptable. This check can explicitly be turned off (or on if it was turned off) by using the command `\askforoverwritefalse` or `\askforoverwritetrue`, respectively, in the DOCSTRIP script.

> `\askonceonly`

Setting `\askforoverwritefalse` in a distribution script may not be the right thing to do, because it essentially means that it is okay to overwrite other people's files, no matter what. However, for large installations, such as the base LaTeX distribution, being asked individually about hundreds of files is not very helpful either. For this reason DOCSTRIP offers the declaration `\askonceonly`. This means that after the first time the script asks the user a question, the user is given an option to have DOCSTRIP assume that all future questions will get a "yes" as the answer. This applies to *all* future questions (manually produced by `\Ask` or generated through a file overwrite).

> `\showprogress`   `\keepsilent`

For amusement and because in the original implementation everything was so slow, there was a way to direct DOCSTRIP to show its progress when stripping comments and building new files. These days most scripts run in silent mode.

Top-level/main installation scripts

In large distributions, such as the LaTeX base distribution, it is convenient to provide separate DOCSTRIP scripts for processing individual parts. For example, `format.ins` generates the main format file `latex.ltx` and its customization files such as `fonttext.cfg`, and `classes.ins` generates the standard classes, such as the files `article.cls` and `report.cls`.

Nevertheless, you do not want to force the user to process a dozen or more installation scripts (30 in the case of the LaTeX base distribution). Therefore, DOCSTRIP offers the command `\batchinput`, which enables you to include installation scripts in some top-level installation script. Do not use `\input` for this purpose, because this command is exclusively reserved for loading the DOCSTRIP code once, as explained above, and is ignored otherwise. Except for the fact that it contains some special handcrafted code at the beginning so that it can be processed using `initex`, the file `unpack.ins` from the base LATEX distribution is a good example for such a main installation script.

Setting up preambles and postambles

As mentioned earlier, DOCSTRIP not only writes selected lines of code to the output files but also precedes them with a *preamble* and finishes each file with a *postamble*. There are default texts for both operations, but usually a DOCSTRIP script explicitly defines what should be used in these places, such as a copyright notice or your standard disclaimer (see also [57]).

```
\preamble    ⟨text lines⟩  \endpreamble
\postamble   ⟨text lines⟩  \endpostamble
```

The information that you want to add to the start of DOCSTRIP's output file should be listed between the `\preamble` and `\endpreamble` commands. Lines that you want to add at the end should be listed between the `\postamble` and `\endpostamble` commands. Everything that DOCSTRIP finds for both the preamble and postamble is written to the output file, but preceded with two % characters (or, more exactly, with the current definition of the command `\MetaPrefix`). In general, only straight text should be used, and literal command names should be of the form `\string\foo`. In addition to the user preamble, DOCSTRIP also includes some information about the current file (i.e., its name and the sources from which it was generated). This information is always added unless you use `\nopreamble` (see below) or you sidestep the standard preamble generation (explained in the DOCSTRIP package documentation [75]).

It is also possible to define a number of "named" preambles or postambles and later refer to them when generating files. In fact, this is the usual way to produce the preambles in larger projects.

```
\declarepreamble\cmd  ⟨text⟩ \endpreamble       \usepreamble\cmd
\declarepostamble\cmd ⟨text⟩ \endpostamble      \usepostamble\cmd
```

The `\declarepreamble` declaration works like `\preamble` except that it stores the preamble text for later use in `\cmd`. To activate such a preamble, `\usepreamble` is called in a DOCSTRIP script. For postambles, the declarations `\declarepostamble` and `\usepostamble` are provided. Examples of them can be found in all DOCSTRIP installation scripts in the distributions of the standard LATEX components.

```
\nopreamble    \nopostamble
```

To fully suppress the writing of a preamble or a postamble, you can use the declarations `\nopreamble` and `\nopostamble`, respectively.

17.2.3 Using docstrip with L3 programming layer code

The L3 programming layer has a few special conventions. For example, it has the concept of private commands indicated by starting a command name with two underscores, e.g., `\__para_handle_indent:`. Such commands are not supposed to be used outside of the package or the LATEX kernel. The same concept exists for variables, except that they start with `\l__` or `\g__`, for example, `\g__para_std_everypar_tl`. To ease code development and maintenance you can put a doc directive into your source, such as

```
%<@@=para>
```

after which you can write `\@@_handle_indent:` or `\g_@@_std_everypar_tl`. The `@@` is then automatically replaced with the right numbers of underscores and the module name (in this case `para`), when the source is stripped with DOCSTRIP. The same happens if you generate the source code documentation using the l3doc class, but if the source is processed with the standard doc, the `@@` are left unchanged in the source, because doc was developed for LATEX 2_ε code that uses @ in other ways.

You end the private module handling with the line `%<@@=>`. If your code uses commands that have two consecutive @ signs in their name, e.g., `\@@par`, you need to enter such names using `@@@@` while private module handling is in force.

17.2.4 Using docstrip with other languages

With some restrictions it is possible to use the DOCSTRIP mechanism to distribute and generate files not intended for a TEX installation. What you have to bear in mind is that DOCSTRIP operates on a line-by-line basis when reading source files. As a result, doing something like unpacking binary files with it is bound to produce unusable files.

Furthermore, the use of preambles and postambles is likely to conflict with the syntax requirements of the language for which the file is intended. For example, generating a shell script with a number of lines starting with `%%` is probably not a good idea. This problem can be circumvented by changing the `\MetaPrefix` (which by default produces `\DoubleperCent`). For a shell script, where you probably want a `#` sign as the comment character, this modification can be a little tricky, because TEX regards the `#` as special. Use

Changing the comment character

```
\renewcommand\MetaPrefix{\string##}
```

to produce a single hash sign as a `\MetaPrefix`. To return to the default setting, use the following definition:

```
\renewcommand\MetaPrefix{\DoubleperCent}
```

Another potential problem to watch out for is DOCSTRIP's standard behavior of stripping away all lines starting with a single percent sign. If your code contains such

Verbatim copying

lines, you may want to retain them. This can be achieved by surrounding that block with two special lines as follows:

```
%<<tag-name
    ⟨code lines to be copied verbatim⟩
%tag-name
```

You can use any *tag-name*. The important point is that this "verbatim" block ends when DOCSTRIP encounters a single line just containing a percent sign followed by *tag-name*. The other important point to note is that the *tag-name* is not used for conditional exclusion or inclusion but only for specifying the block to be copied verbatim. If such a block should be written only in some circumstances, as controlled through the second argument of \from, you have to additionally surround it by a set of conditional tags (see Section 17.1.5).

17.3 l3build — A versatile development environment

Making a package available to the LᴬTᴇX user community requires several steps: we call those *releasing* the package. Most obviously, almost all packages have PDF (Portable Document Format) documentation that needs to be compiled, including, for example, creating an index of commands. This will often be coupled with extracting code using DOCSTRIP, and to send to CTAN, creating a .zip file (see below). It is of course possible to do all of this by hand, but that tends to be error prone. To make this entire process more fluid, the LᴬTᴇX Project Team has developed l3build as a flexible tool to support development work.

The l3build program is a Lua script designed to support a range of workflows using a set of simple settings as far as possible. As such, it is quite usable without being familiar with Lua.[1]

l3build can carry out unpacking, typesetting, packaging, and uploading for release. It also features a sophisticated ability to carry out tests to probe the functionality of LᴬTᴇX code: this is an important concept and is covered in more detail in Section 17.3.2.

Because l3build is used to release all of the code authored by the LᴬTᴇX Project Team, including LᴬTᴇX itself, it has some advanced options for handling bundles of packages, nonstandard file locations, etc. In this book, the focus is on the more common situation of a single package made up of a small number of source files in one directory. This covers the needs of most package authors, but if you have more complex requirements, they are most likely covered by the more than 100 keys that can be set or altered in a configuration file; for this, take a look at the documentation [79].

l3build uses a dedicated directory (by default called build) that it creates inside the main directory holding your sources. This means that it can reliably copy *just* the files you specify into its working area, and that if you need to, you can delete all

---

[1] l3build uses Lua because this is an integral part of LuaTᴇX and therefore available on any system that has a modern TᴇX system. This means that Lua is widely used in the TᴇX ecosystem for scripting.

of the temporary material created in one go. This is also useful if you use a version control system for your package development (see Section 17.4 on page 615): there is just one location to tell it to ignore.

17.3.1 The basic interface

l3build is available in modern TeX systems as a script that can be run directly at the command line/terminal. The script understands a range of *targets*, for example doc (for typesetting package documentation). Some targets take further arguments specifying one or more names to process. There are also a number of options, with which you can tune the target behavior. For example, to run two tests, called mypkg001 and mypkg002, using the pdfTeX engine, the appropriate call is

  l3build check --engine pdftex mypkg001 mypkg002

or shorter

  l3build check -e pdftex mypkg001 mypkg002

All of the switches have a "long" name: some also have a "short" one for convenience.

Control of l3build is achieved by creating a file called build.lua in the main development directory for a package. In most cases, this will be the directory containing all your package sources, but complicated projects may structure the source files differently. Taking the very common case of a single .dtx file with a matching .ins file, all that is necessary is to inform l3build of the name to use.[1] The minimal contents of the build.lua file for a package mypkg would therefore be

Setting up a simple package

```
-- Build script for "mypkg" files

module = "mypkg"        -- Identify the package
```

Because the control file is written in Lua, line comments start with --, not %.

The standard settings in l3build specify that all of the .dtx files in the directory are taken as source files and that each .ins file is passed to DOCSTRIP for unpacking. Thus, with this minimal setup, you can already use various l3build commands.

l3build install Unpacks the code and installs it into the local TeX tree, typically ~/texmf on Linux, ~/Library/texmf on macOS, or %USERPROFILE%/texmf on Windows.

l3build uninstall Removes any code installed in the location that would be used by l3build install.

l3build check Runs all of the tests you have created for the package: this process is described in more detail in Section 17.3.2. Individual tests can be run as we have already seen by adding their names after the check target keyword.

---

[1] l3build uses the name module: this aligns with the way that for example Lua refers to loadable files providing additional functionality.

l3build doc   Typesets the documentation, which will be carried out by running a cycle of pdfTEX and *MakeIndex* runs for each file marked as a documentation target (by default all .dtx files, but see page 614). If you want to compile a single PDF, you can give its name (without the extension) after the doc target keyword.

l3build install --full   Combines l3build doc with l3build install, meaning that the PDF documentation is installed along with the code.

l3build ctan   Runs any tests available (see Section 17.3.2), then runs l3build doc, and finally builds a .zip file containing the PDFs, the .dtx and .ins files, and any .md or .txt file, suitable for upload to CTAN (see Section 17.3.3 on page 611). If any of the steps fail, the target stops: in particular, this prevents a release if there are any failing tests.

17.3.2 Creating tests

For larger projects, most notably the LᴬTEX kernel, a comprehensive test suite is essential in reducing the likelihood of problems for users. However, even for smaller packages tests are useful in helping to spot problematic changes, and we therefore encourage everyone to use them for every project. Testing is an integral part of l3build and can be carried out in a number of ways.[1]

How tests work

Testing using l3build works using the .log file[2]: TEX can be asked to write a wide range of information to file. However, TEX also writes a large amount of other material, for example, file paths, details of the engine, the output of third-part packages, etc. The approach used by l3build is therefore to manipulate the raw .log file to produce a normalized file, which should be identical between different computers and which avoids as far as possible differences between TEX engines (pdfTEX, XᴇTEX, LuaTEX, etc.). For example, dates and version numbers or low-level register numbers are masked out and spaces are normalized to avoid unnecessary failures between runs and between different engines that are unfortunately writing to the .log in slightly different ways.

For this process to produce *useful* tests, it is important that the author writes the useful information to the .log. Using \tracingall produces a lot of output but is almost always the wrong choice. The trace will always show differences whenever a code change is made, but that does not reflect at all whether the *results* are changed. For example, reworking an internal macro to be more efficient will normally not change the result, but alters the trace. Instead, you should be selective in what you write, for example the typeset result of a specific command, or the numerical value of a calculation, etc.

---

[1] The core of l3build is based on previous more focused test systems used by the LᴬTEX Project Team: l3build not only makes this functionality into a documented product but also provides the wider building environment that allows almost full automation.

[2] Testing using other files is possible, most notably using a specially modified PDF file to assess final output. However, this is a much more specialized approach, so the focus here is on the standard method.

A good practice is to write a test file for every bug report you receive and have fixed to ensure that the problem does not reappear through later modifications.[1]

Test setup

To create a set of tests for use with l3build, a directory called `testfiles` should be created inside the main directory. Inside the `testfiles` directory, one or more test sources are required: these have the extension `.lvt`. These are specially crafted LaTeX files that load the file `regression-test.tex`, which provides a small number of testing commands: these all have all-caps names.

To allow loading packages, etc., without this affecting the tests, l3build ignores anything before the command `\START`. You can also skip material using an `\OMIT` ... `\TIMO` block. The tests (and indeed the LaTeX run) can be ended using `\END` or the standard `\end{document}` command: the `\END` command attempts to stop immediately and does not produce the last page of output (which is fine if you are interested only in the content of the `.log`). Because it reduces the work TeX does, `\END` is faster than `\end{document}`. It should be preferred where possible, especially if you expect to have a large suite of tests to be executed regularly.

Constructing tests

There are two main ways to write information to the `.log` so that the results can be checked by l3build. The first is to actively write results using the command `\TYPE` (this is a specially modified version of `\typeout`). To make it easier to follow the results, tests are normally divided up into one or more `\TEST` blocks. Thus, a simple test file might read

```
\input{regression-test}
\documentclass{article}
\usepackage{mypkg} % The package to test
\START
\TEST{A first test}{%
  \mypkfunctionA{input-tokens}\outputmacro
  \TYPE{\outputmacro}
}
\TEST{A second test}{%
  \mypkfunctionB{input-tokens}{more-input-tokens}\outputmacro
  \TYPE{\outputmacro}
}
\END
```

This approach is particularly useful for code, which produces values that are stored in commands, counters, etc.: they can be written to the `.log` directly. Usefully, the `\TEST` command places the test code argument in a group: this means that local changes do not affect subsequent tests.

---

[1] It is surprising how many "harmless" changes that "surely can do no harm" have triggered test failures and in this way have saved the LaTeX Project Team from releasing faulty code.

The second approach, useful for typesetting commands, is to use TEX's ability to record the contents of a box or of the whole output page. The latter is particularly convenient, because it can simply be switched on with \showoutput, and multiple tests then appear in the output.

```
\input{regression-test}
\documentclass{article}
\usepackage{mypkg}              % The package to test
\showoutput                    % show symbolic page output in the .log
\begin{document}
\START
\mypkfunctionA{input-tokens}   % Assume this produces typeset output

\mypkfunctionB{input-tokens}{more-input-tokens}
\newpage
\OMIT
\end{document}
```

As illustrated, this type of test needs \end{document} to be present in the source, and it is usually best to force a new page and then tell l3build to ignore the remainder of the .log using \OMIT. Given that the output here is given by TEX in one block, it is usually not beneficial to use the \TEST command.

Unfortunately, the result from \showoutput can differ in different engines. While pdfTEX and XƎTEX usually (but not always) show the same symbolic output, LuaTEX often has subtle differences, e.g., a space between the command \kern and its value in some places but not in others. If you test with different engines,[1] this means that you may have to store engine-specific results and verify them individually, as explained below.

Stay vigilant

The machinery for this is available, but the danger is that one overlooks a real bug among the "expected" differences and certifies an incorrect result as the expected output — it happened to us more than once, so be careful.

Certifying and saving tests

To save a test, the l3build command is simple:

l3build save ⟨*test file without extension*⟩

This creates a single .tlg file containing the normalized results: as far as possible, system- and engine-dependent information is removed from the raw .log.

l3build itself of course does not have any insight into whether a .tlg file is showing the *correct* results, only that it is what has been produced from a LATEX run. You should therefore check new .tlg files, along perhaps with the typeset output, when you create them. Once saved, the automated system is then able to highlight

---

[1]The regression test suite with about 1 000 tests is executed with pdfTEX, XƎTEX, and LuaTEX and needs nearly 20 minutes to verify that everything is fine before we upload a new release.

changes, which may of course be deliberate because you altered the code: only the package author can check that! If a test shows differences and you verified them as being correct, you need to regenerate the .tlg file to get a new certified reference result — otherwise you must check what is wrong with the package.

With the standard settings, l3build runs each test using pdfTeX, XeTeX, and LuaTeX. You may need to save separate engine-specific .tlg files, particularly if you are testing using the typeset output. This is achieved using the -e or --engine switch, which takes a comma-separated list of engine names.

l3build save -e xetex,luatex ⟨*test file without extension*⟩

When an engine-specific .tlg file is available, this is used by l3build in preference to the engine-independent reference file. You can adjust the engines that are used by setting the checkengines table, for example to use just pdfTeX and LuaTeX add the following to build.lua:

```
checkengines = {"pdftex", "luatex"}
```

The first entry is used as the *standard engine*: the one that is used if you do not give the -e option to the save target.

Testing package loading

One area that is usually best covered by a stand-alone test file is package loading. This is a good way to pick up any errors within the code that show up only when the package is first read by LaTeX. A simple test such as the one below does that:

```
\input{regression-test}
\documentclass{article}
\START   \usepackage{mypkg}   \END
```

If your package takes options, you may want several such tests with different combinations of them. The reason why these are best handled separately from other tests is that package loading is more likely to show spurious differences in the .tlg files, because your package might load other packages that output irrelevant data, which you cannot suppress.

For the same reason it is normally best to use \START only after the preamble has ended or, if that is not possible because you want tests in the preamble, to surround \begin{document} with \OMIT and \TIMO.

17.3.3 Releasing to CTAN

CTAN, the Comprehensive TeX Archive Network, is the major distribution center for LaTeX packages. This means that releasing a LaTeX package to the wider LaTeX community actually means submitting it to CTAN; see Appendix C.4.1 on page 789.

CTAN holds a range of both LaTeX packages and support tools. The archive is not prescriptive about, for example, overlap of package functions or the way material is coded: anyone who feels that their code should be available on CTAN can upload. However, the CTAN team members ask for certain conditions to be met by the files uploaded, in particular

- that there is at least one PDF file containing documentation;

- that there is a README (plain text) or README.md (Markdown) file;

- that *derived* files (other than PDF documentation) are not uploaded: this means if a package uses a .dtx, the .sty, or other generated files, are not sent to CTAN;

- and that the uploaded files are present in a single archive: .zip or .tar.gz.

The l3build ctan target automatically arranges that the appropriate files are present in a .zip file that can be uploaded. This can be used with the web submission form (https://ctan.org/upload). Optionally, l3build can send the zip file directly to CTAN, avoiding the need to visit the website. To do this, l3build needs to know the values for various CTAN data fields. For example, for l3build itself, the relevant configuration is:

```
uploadconfig = {
   author       = "The LaTeX Team",
   license      = "lppl1.3c",
   summary      = "A testing and building system for (La)TeX",
   topic        = {"macro-supp", "package-devel"},
   ctanPath     = "/macros/latex/contrib/l3build",
   repository   = "https://github.com/latex3/l3build/",
   bugtracker   = "https://github.com/latex3/l3build/issues",
   update       = true,
   description = [[
The build system supports testing and building (La)TeX code, on
Linux, macOS, and Windows systems. The package offers:
* A unit testing system for (La)TeX code;
* A system for typesetting package documentation; and
* An automated process for creating CTAN releases.
   ]]
}
```

Notice that here we see a little Lua syntax: several strings are placed in the uploadconfig *table*, and a multiline string is created using the notation [[...]].

To actually upload using l3build, the ctan target should be run first to create a .zip file with all relevant data included. The call

l3build upload --message "⟨*announcement text*⟩" ⟨*version*⟩   or
l3build upload --file ⟨*announcement file*⟩ ⟨*version*⟩

can then be used to carry out the upload, with an optional announcement text given either as the argument to the --message switch or in a dedicated file. The ⟨*version*⟩

is optional but would normally be given, because the CTAN maintainers will otherwise query what version string to use for the release.

There are further keys that can be specified as part of the `uploadconfig` data, for example, the name of the `uploader` if it differs from the `author` and an `email` address. The latter is actually required by CTAN, but if your `build.lua` is in a publicly available repository, you may not want to record your e-mail address there to avoid it being picked up by spammers. Therefore, the l3build program asks interactively for an `email` address if none is provided.

E-mail address can be specified interactively

17.3.4 Common configurations

The standard settings in l3build are intended to mean that most package authors need to make only minor adjustments to their setup. As mentioned earlier, the only *required* value is one for `module`. Here, we cover a few common setups that can be accessed easily with l3build: for full details of all the settings, see the package documentation [79].

Adjusting the number of runs

When running tests or typesetting documentation, l3build uses a fixed set of steps (in contrast to tools such as latexmk). Depending on the exact use case, the standard values may not be appropriate.

For tests, the variable `checkruns` controls how many LaTeX cycles are executed. The standard setting is `1`, which is appropriate in many cases but does not allow for any tests that use the `.aux` file or similar. Thus, to check that cross-references are resolved, a setting such as the following is required:

```
checkruns = 2
```

When typesetting, the standard settings run 3 cycles, which includes executing *MakeIndex* and BibTeX/biber. Some more complex documents will need additional runs; e.g., the LaTeX distribution itself needs[1] this:

```
typesetruns = 4
```

Installing configuration files

Some packages provide multiple configuration files, which often are given the extension `.cfg` or `.def`. These can be included in a generic installation list

```
installfiles = {"*.cfg", "*.def", "*.sty"}
```

or can be listed with their exact file names.

Setting up a larger package with multiple sources

A larger package might also be split into multiple `.dtx` files, each covering part of the functionality. In this scenario, typesetting the programmer documentation is usually

---

[1]The real build script for LaTeX is more complex: this is an approximation to what happens.

613

achieved using a file `mypkg-code.tex`, which combines all of the `.dtx` files. The l3build setup would then exclude the `.dtx` files, thus

```
typesetfiles = {"*.tex"}
```

or

```
module = "mypkg"
typesetfiles = {module .. ".tex", module .. "-code.tex"}
```

would be appropriate (the `..` syntax joins strings in Lua).

Changing the typesetting engine

By default, l3build typesets the documentation using pdfTᴇX, which may not be appropriate, e.g., if you want to make use of features available only in Unicode engines. In that case add an appropriate setting in `build.lua`, e.g.,

```
typesetengine = "lualatex"
```

Separating user and programmer documentation

The `.dtx` format allows separation of the documentation and implementation of a package. However, for larger packages it is often useful to have a document for end users and one aimed at developers. The latter might for example expose a more formalized programmer's API than the user version. This is usually best achieved by having a file `mypkg.tex` for the user documentation, with the text in the "documentation" part of `mypkg.dtx` aimed at developers. This requires that the additional file is included for typesetting:

```
typesetfiles = {"*.dtx", "*.tex"}
```

or if you wish to be more cautious and guard against stray source files, use this:

```
module = "mypkg"
typesetfiles = {module .. ".dtx", module .. ".tex"}
```

Suppressing typesetting of the implementation part

Many package authors include the typeset implementation as part of the documentation. However, this is not always desirable. To suppress the implementation part in the automatically generated PDF, the variable `typesetcmds` is available. The exact string required depends on the document class used in the `.dtx` file. For the standard ltxdoc class, the appropriate setting is

```
typesetcmds = "\\AtBeginDocument{\\OnlyDescription}"
```

whereas for l3doc, the right setting is

```
typesetcmds = "\\AtBeginDocument{\\DisableImplementation}"
```

Notice that because Lua would interpret a single \ as an escape sequence, we require \\ in the setting here.

Creating a ready-to-install "TDS-style" `.zip` file

For simple packages comprising one `.sty` file, CTAN prefers a "flat" upload. However, when there is more complexity to a package, for example if it installs multiple files, providing a pre-extracted `.zip` file (called a TDS-style zip) is useful for end users. This can be enabled by setting

```
packtdszip = true        -- Release a TDS-style zip
```

17.4 Making use of version control tools

When developing a program or writing a large document, such as a user manual or a book (like this one), version control — the task of keeping a software system consisting of many versions and configurations well organized — is an important issue. Over time, several systems have been developed to help with this. These *version control systems* track changes in files. The oldest systems were aimed at individual users, with the idea of a central repository coming later. Even more recently, the concept of *distributed* version control systems has become the most popular: there is not one central machine, rather each user retains a "full" history of a project.

While there have been many version control systems developed since the early 1970s, a few have proved to be particularly popular, in reverse chronological order

- *Git*,[1] originally developed by Linus Torvalds (of Linux fame)

- *Subversion* (SVN)

- The *Concurrent Versions System* (CVS; see http://www.cvshome.org)

- The *Revision Control System* (RCS)

Today, Git is probably the most popular choice of version control system for new projects (certainly those that are open source). However, there are very many projects using the other systems, most notably Subversion.

If you put LaTeX documents under source control, you will often want to have access to the data about the current file or project within your document — perhaps to place the date of the last check-in and the revision number into the running header. There are LaTeX packages that can help us do that for all of the common version control systems above. Today, it is unlikely you will come across a project using CVS or RCS, so we focus here on support for Git and Subversion.

---

[1] Not a defined acronym: according to the readme file, Git stands for different things depending on your mood: three random but pronounceable letters, stupid or simple (from the slang dictionary), global information tracker (if it works for you), or g****** idiotic truckload of ... (when it breaks).

17.4.1 gitinfo2 — **Accessing metadata from Git**

Git does *not* store any revision information in the source files themselves, in contrast to Subversion, CVS, or RCS. This means that placing Git metadata into your document requires running some Git commands "behind the scenes". The gitinfo2 package written by Brent Longborough (1944–2021) provides a mechanism to extract this information and to then insert it into a LATEX document.

Setting this up needs at least a little familiarity with how Git works. Inside your development directory, there is a (hidden) directory called .git, and inside there one called hooks: this is where we need to add the necessary scripts. The gitinfo2 package is supplied with a demonstration file called post-xxx-sample.txt, which is in the *documentation* tree of your TEX installation. Perhaps the easiest way to find it is to use texdoc -l gitinfo2: this shows all of the "documentation" files for the package, including the full file path to the demonstration script.

You need to make *three* identical copies of the script inside the .git/hooks directory. These should be called post-checkout, post-commit, and post-merge, and, if you use macOS or Linux, make them executable using chmod +x. After installing the hooks, you may want to run git checkout to force them to run; otherwise, there is no metadata available until the next real commit that you make.

Loading the package with the mark option inserts a simple "watermark" footer containing key data points:

- the current branch;
- the (short) hash for the most recent commit;
- the most recent release (see below);
- the date of the most recent commit;
- any tags associated with the most recent commit.

All these data elements are available as independent commands to insert into the document (see below), and the overall structure of the watermark is customizable using the \gitMark command: this contains the various data-insertion commands and text.

All of the data made available by gitinfo2 is stored in commands with names starting with \git.. followed by a short descriptive name. For example, the data commands inserted by the standard watermark footer are

- \gitBranch
- \gitAbbrevHash
- \gitReln
- \gitAuthorDate
- \gitTags

Of these, the only one likely to be unfamiliar to a Git user is \gitReln. gitinfo2 initially assumes that a *release* is associated with a tag that starts with a number and includes a decimal point, for example, 1.4. This definition is part of the script used to extract information from Git, rather than being specified in the LaTeX code. As such, it can be adjusted by editing the three scripts installed above: this requires knowing a little shell script syntax. The standard definition is

```
RELTAG=$(git describe ... --match '[0-9]*.*' ...)
```

where ... represents parts of the standard definition that do not need our attention here. Changing the argument to --match adjusts what is captured: to accept any tag at all as a release, you would use

```
RELTAG=$(git describe ... --match '*' ...)
```

The package provides commands for most other Git metadata, for example, \gitHash (the full hash) or \gitCommitterEmail (the e-mail address given for the latest commit), etc.

17.4.2 svn-multi — Accessing Subversion keywords in multiple sources

In contrast to Git, Subversion, CVS, and RCS store revision data directly in the source file(s). This works by keyword substitution: there is a specially formatted string inside the sources that is updated by the version control system. All three systems support a common set of the most important keywords: $Author$ (account of the person doing the check-in), $Date$ (date and time of check-in in UTC), $Revision$ (revision number assigned to the check-in), $Filename$, and Id (combination field, with file name, revision, date, time, author). Initially, one simply adds one or more of these keywords (e.g., Id) to the source. Upon first check-in, they are replaced by the structure $⟨keyword⟩:␣⟨value⟩␣$, as can be seen in the next example. Later check-ins then update the ⟨value⟩ as appropriate.

As with Git-based workflows, you may want to access these keyword values from within a LaTeX document. Because of the syntax using dollar signs (which indicate formulas in LaTeX), you cannot use the keywords directly in your text, but there exist packages that provide LaTeX tags to give you access to this information in a way suitable for typesetting. Here, we cover the svn-multi package by Martin Scharrer, because it provides the most flexible and up-to-date interfaces.

There are two set of commands needed to work with SVN keyword data: those to read the information from the source and those to typeset it. In general, SVN keywords are read by the command \svnkwsave. The argument to this command *must* start and end with a dollar sign and is interpreted as described above as a keyword and a value (which can be absent). The information is then available to typset using \svnkw.

For example, a date line could be read and then typeset using

```
\svnkwsave{$Date: 2022-01-12 13:34:19 +0100 (Wed, 12 Jan 2022) $}
Date \svnkw{Date}.
```

Most commonly, files tracked by SVN use the Id keyword, which contains multiple data items. This is given therefore special handling by svn-multi, which can save the information using the command \svnid. This information is then available immediately for typesetting using \svnkw. Shortcuts for the author, date, time, and revision number are available as \svnauthor, \svndate, \svntime, and \svnrev. This (global) information is available only during a second or subsequent LᴀTᴇX run; we will see why shortly.

Information is directly available using \svnkw: the file test.tex has revision number 6, last checked in by Frank on 2022-01-12 13:34:19Z.

Global information is available during a second LᴀTᴇX run: the global revision number is 6, with the last check-in was made by Frank on 2022-01-12 13:34:19Z at 13:34:19 ᴜᴛᴄ (we might refer to it as January 12, 2022).

```
\usepackage{microtype,svn-multi}
\svnid{$Id: test.tex 6 2022-01-12 13:34:19Z Frank $}

Information is directly available using
\verb"\svnkw": the file \svnkw{Filename} has revision
number \svnkw{Revision}, last checked in by
\svnkw{Author} on \svnkw{Date}.

Global information is available during a second
\LaTeX{} run: the global revision number is \svnrev{},
with the last check-in was made by \svnauthor{} on
\svndate{} at \svntime\,\textsc{utc} (we might refer
to it as \svntoday{}).
```

17-4-1

The reason for the existence of two interfaces for typesetting SVN keyword information is that svn-multi is able to handle more complex scenarios. In particular, for a project of any scale, each file will have its own revision information when using SVN. Thus, at any point in a document you might wish to typeset the global revision information for the entire project, the specific information for the current source, or of course both. Data for the current file are available using a parallel set of typesetting commands starting with \svnfile..., so for example the revision of the current file is \svnfilerev. Normally, the main file is the first one in which \svnid occurs, but this can be adjusted using the command \svnsetmainfile. This is the reason that \svnid, etc., require two runs to print values: on the first LᴀTᴇX run, it is possible that the main file is set *after* the first typesetting calls.

The package allows further control of keyword scope by providing *grouping* of source files. Within a group of files, data items are available for the current group, so \svncgrev is the revision number of the current group. Groups are created manually, by using the \svngroup command with a *group name* as the mandatory argument. The group then continues until the next occurrence of \svngroup *or* the end of the current file: the latter restrictions ensure that parent files are not affected by a group setting in a child file.

The svn-multi package provides a number of commands for customizing the appearance of date/time values. We have seen above that \svntoday prints the value of \svndate in the format of \today. Each part of the date and time is available as a separate command, for example \svnday for the global revision day or \svnfiletimezone for the time zone of the current file.

The way that author names are printed can also be adjusted, with the command \svnRegisterAuthor, available to map the author name in the SVN data to a full name for typesetting. For example

```
\svnRegisterAuthor{Frank}{Frank Mittelbach}
```

would then allow

```
\svnFullAuthor{\svnauthor}
```

to print "Frank Mittelbach" rather than just "Frank". Notice that \svnFullAuthor expands its argument to text before looking up the name: we could have used the literal Frank or another command such as \svnfileauthor and gotten the same effect.

17.4.3 filemod — Printing or checking file modification dates

This is not exactly part of version control, but sometimes it is helpful to document the modification date (or time) of a file or compare it with some other date or time. For this Martin Scharrer produced the little package called filemod.

The example below first defines two files using the filecontents environment. The first of them is always regenerated, while the second is generated only once; thus if you run the example several times (as we do during book generation), it becomes the older of the two.

As usual, one can leave out the extension, in which case .tex is assumed. Several of the commands provided by the package are expandable, a fact we use to load the oldest and later the newest file at the end, to exhibit the mechanism:

```
\usepackage{filemod}
\begin{filecontents}[force]{trial1}
  content Trial1 % rewritten always!
\end{filecontents}
\begin{filecontents}{trial2}
  content Trial2 % written once!
\end{filecontents}
Date: \filemodprintdate{trial1.tex} \\
Time: \filemodprinttime{trial1.tex} \\[10pt]
trial1.tex: \filemodprint{trial1}    \\
% second file (written only once):
trial2.tex: \filemodprint{trial2}    \\[10pt]
Oldest: \input{\filemodoldest{trial1}{trial2}} \\
Newest: \input{\filemodnewest{trial1}{trial2}}
```

Date: 2022/12/28
Time: 13:33:47 +01'00'

trial1.tex: 2022/12/28 13:33:47 +01'00'
trial2.tex: 2022/07/17 18:13:53 +02'00'

Oldest: content Trial2
Newest: content Trial1

17-4-2

This is mainly a teaser so that you know the functionality is available. The package provides a large number of additional commands to adjust results, store them, or do more complex comparisons, e.g., compare large lists of files to select the newest or oldest, etc. For details, see the package documentation.

LaTeX Overview for Preamble, Package, and Class Writers

This appendix gives an overview of the basic programming concepts underlying the LaTeX formatter. We explain how to define new commands and environments, including those with optional arguments and other specialized input syntax. We discuss how LaTeX handles counters and their representation; we also introduce horizontal and vertical space parameters and explain how they are handled.

The third section reviews the important subject of LaTeX boxes and their use. A good understanding of this topic is very important to fully appreciate and exploit the information presented in this book.

In the fourth section we then take a deeper look at LaTeX's new hook management that was introduced in 2020. The fifth section is devoted to two package files, calc and ifthen, that make calculations and building control structures with LaTeX easier. They have been used in many examples of LaTeX code throughout this book.

Finally, we describe in detail the LaTeX interfaces that allow you to define your own packages and class files.

A.1 Linking markup and formatting

This section reviews the syntax for defining commands and environments with LaTeX. It is important that you exclusively use the LaTeX constructs described below, rather than the lower-level TeX commands. Then, not only are you able to take advantage of LaTeX's consistency checking, but your commands are also portable, (probably) without modification, to future versions of LaTeX.

LaTeX offers three major ways to define commands and environments. Simple commands can be defined with `\newcommand` and `\newenvironment` that have been available for several decades. These are discussed first.

More recently the `\NewDocumentCommand` and `\NewDocumentEnvironment` declarations were added to LaTeX. They allow you to easily define commands and environments with a richer argument structure, not only involving a single optional argument, but also those with multiple optional arguments, special argument delimiters, and much more. This is discussed in Section A.1.4 on page 632.

Finally, there are low-level methods of TeX, through `\def`, `\let`, and similar commands, and, of course, all the declarations from the L3 programming layer (formerly known as `expl3`), e.g., `\cs_new:Npn` and many more. None of that is covered in this book because these constructs should be used only for low-level programming, and their discussion would easily fill a book by itself.

A.1.1 Command and environment names

Commands

In current LaTeX, whether used with pdfTeX or with one of the Unicode engines, it is possible to enter accented characters and other non–ASCII symbols directly into the source, so it would seem reasonable to expect that such characters could also be used in command and environment names (e.g., `\größer`). However, this is not the case — LaTeX multicharacter command names should be built from basic ASCII letters (i.e., a...z and A...Z).[1] This means that `\vspace*` is actually not a command by itself; rather, it is the command `\vspace` followed by the modifier `*`. Technically, you could write `\vspace␣*` (as the space is ignored) or even put the `*` on the next line of your document.[2]

Environments

On the other hand, names of environments are different. In this case the `*` is part of the name, and spaces preceding it are not ignored. Thus, when writing something like `\begin{figure␣*}`, the space would become part of the name, and this is therefore not recognized as the start of a `figure*` environment. This is due to implementation details and seems to indicate that with environment names some additional ASCII characters work. For example:

```
\newenvironment{foo.bar:baz␣with␣space}{}{}
```

However, this is not true in general because, depending on additional packages being

---

[1] Strictly speaking this is not true, as TeX can be configured to support other configurations. There are, however, valid reasons why this is not being done for standard LaTeX. Some of these reasons are discussed in Section 9.9 describing LaTeX's encoding model.

[2] It is bad style to use this in your documents, but there is unfortunately no way to prevent it.

loaded, such environment names may no longer be recognized or may produce strange errors. Thus, it is best not to explore that implementation (mis)feature and instead to rely on officially supported names — those containing only lowercase and uppercase letters and the star character.

Strictly speaking, \cite and \label keys have (or had) the same kind of restriction. Nevertheless, it has become common practice to use keys containing colons (e.g., sec:cmds) so that most packages provided extra support to allow for at least the colon character in such keys. Around 2020, when LATEX moved to UTF-8 as its default input, that restriction was lifted as part of the necessary rewrite so that now most characters outside the ASCII range can be safely used in label keys. However, characters used in LATEX's syntax (e.g., $, _, or #) can never be used in names, whether they are keys, counters, environments, or multicharacter command names. *Citation and label keys*

With single-character command names, the situation is different again: any (single) character can be used. Symbols that are not "letters" cannot participate in multiletter command names, e.g., \foo$bar would be interpreted as the command \foo followed by the start of a math formula (signaled by $) followed by the (math) characters b, a, and r. Any following text is then also typeset in math mode. However, such symbols can appear directly after the backslash and form a so-called control symbol; e.g., \$ is perfectly valid. *Control symbols*

In contrast to multiletter commands, such control symbols do not ignore spaces after them, because that is what is normally desired in situations like 30\% or cut \& paste. Note, however, that something like \S would not be a control symbol but a multiletter command, consisting of a name with only a single letter and thus spaces are ignored after it, as shown in the following example:

A-1-1

$ 100 is different from $100. You have to write $100 to avoid the space! But §1.2 and §1.2 give the same spacing.

```
\$ 100 is different from \textdollar 100.
You have to write \$100 to avoid the space!
But \S 1.2 and \S1.2 give the same spacing.
```

Categories of LATEX commands

LATEX commands (i.e., those constructs starting with a backslash) are classified into three basic categories: document-level commands, package and class writer commands, and internal "kernel" commands.

- Document-level commands, such as \section, \emph, and \sum, usually have (reasonably) short names, by convention all in lowercase. *Document-level commands*

- Class and package writer commands, by convention, have longer mixed-case names, such as \InputIfFileExists and \RequirePackage. Some of them can be usefully applied in the document source, but many stop working after \begin{document} has been processed, producing an error message if you try. *Class and package writer commands*

- Traditionally most of the internal commands used in the LATEX implementation, such as \@tempcnta, \@ifnextchar, and \z@, contain @ in their name. This effectively prevents these names from being used in documents for user-defined commands. However, it also means that they cannot appear in a document, even in the preamble, without taking special precautions. *Internal LATEX commands*

Modern internal commands use the L3 programming layer where commands use "_" and ":" as part of their names, which makes them also (deliberately) unusable in documents.

Careful with internal commands!

As a few of the examples in this book demonstrate, it is sometimes necessary to have such bits of "internal code" in the preamble. The commands \makeatletter and \makeatother make this easy to do; the difficult bit is to remember to add them — failure to do so can result in some strange errors. For an example of their use, see page →I 210. Note that package and class files should never contain these commands: \makeatletter is not needed because this is always set up when reading such files, and the use of \makeatother would prematurely stop this behavior, causing all kinds of havoc. For modern L3 programming layer code (expl3), there are \ExplSyntaxOn and \ExplSyntaxOff that serve the same purpose.

The distinction between internal and public commands

Unfortunately, for historical reasons the distinction between these categories is often blurred. For example, \hbox is an internal command that should preferably be used only in the LATEX kernel, because it does not deal properly with color changes in its argument, whereas \m@ne is the constant -1 and would have been better named \MinusOne back then.

Nevertheless, this rule of thumb is still useful: if a command has @ in its name, then it is not part of the supported LATEX language — and its behavior may change in future releases! Any such command should be used with great care. On the other hand, mixed-case commands or those described in the *LATEX Manual* [56] are guaranteed to be supported in future releases of LATEX.

In the L3 programming layer there is much more standardization. Command names follow a predictable pattern, and what is supported and usable elsewhere is well defined: any name starting with __ is private and should not be used outside its module; all others are officially part of the programming layer. Similarly, private (local) variables start with \l__, whereas public ones have only one underscore, etc.

A.1.2 Defining simple commands

It is often advantageous to define new commands (e.g., for representing repetitive input strings or recurring combinations of commands). Here we describe how do this for simple cases, where the new commands take at most one optional argument. This is the method introduced with LATEX 2_ε in 1994. How to define commands with more complex argument structures is shown in Section A.1.4.

Complexity comes with a price tag in terms of processing speed: so for "simple" tasks we recommend simple tools, i.e., the declarations discussed here. However, already when defining commands with one optional argument, you should consider using the declarations discussed later.

> \newcommand{*cmd*}[*narg*]{*command definition*}

A new command is defined using the \newcommand declaration. The number of arguments is in the range $0 \leq narg \leq 9$. If your new command has no arguments, then the [0] can be omitted. Inside the *command definition* part, the arguments are referenced as #1 to #⟨*narg*⟩.

PostScript and its variant Encapsulated PostScript are often used for including graphics in LaTeX documents ...

```
\newcommand{\PS}{Post\-Script}
\newcommand{\EPS}{Encapsulated \PS}

\PS{} and its variant \EPS{} are often used for
including graphics in \LaTeX{} documents \ldots
```

A-1-2

The *cmd* argument always has to contain a single "token" (the name of the command to be defined), so one can omit the braces around this argument. While we do not recommend the use of this TeX syntax feature in other places, it is commonly used with \newcommand and similar declarations. In fact, we have often used this more concise syntax in this book:

Omitting argument braces

```
\newcommand\PS{Post\-Script}        \newcommand\EPS{Encapsulated \PS}
```

Note, however, that this is possible only with arguments that are single tokens to TeX (i.e., names starting with a backslash). Trying to do the same with, for instance, environment or counter names will fail. For example,

```
\setcounter mycount {5}          \newenvironment myenv{...}{...}
```

is invalid LaTeX syntax.

If a command should work both in math mode and in text mode, special care should be taken in its definition. One could, for example, use \mbox, but this has a number of drawbacks.

The series of $x_1, \ldots, x_n$ or $x_1, \ldots, x_n + G x_1, \ldots, x_n$ — but this definition does not change its size if used in the subscript position.

```
\newcommand\xvec{\mbox{$x_1,\ldots,x_n$}}

The series of \xvec\ or $\xvec+G_{\xvec}$ ---
but this definition does not change its size
if used in the subscript position.
```

A-1-3

A better solution is offered by the LaTeX 2_ε command \ensuremath. As the name implies, \ensuremath ensures that its argument is always typeset in math mode by surrounding it, if necessary, with $ signs. Thus, the definition in the above example should be replaced as follows:

The series of $x_1, \ldots, x_n$ or $x_1, \ldots, x_n + G_{x_1, \ldots, x_n}$ — both work well with the new definition.

```
\newcommand\xvec{\ensuremath{x_1,\ldots,x_n}}
The series of \xvec\ or $\xvec+G_{\xvec}$ ---
both work well with the new definition.
```

A-1-4

This has the additional advantage of producing correctly sized symbols in subscripts or superscripts, which is not the case if an \mbox is used in the definition.

Existing commands must be *redefined* with the command \renewcommand, which otherwise has the same syntax as \newcommand. Note that you can redefine a command with a different number of arguments than the original one has (though that is seldom a good idea). Therefore, you could redefine the \xvec command of the above example so that it now takes two arguments:

The series of $x_1, \ldots, x_n$ or
$x_1, \ldots, x_n + G_{x_1, \ldots, x_n}$
The series of $x_1, \ldots, x_n$ or
$y_1, \ldots, y_k + G_{z_1, \ldots, z_4}$

```
\newcommand\xvec{\ensuremath{x_1,\ldots,x_n}}
The series of \xvec\ or $\xvec+G_{\xvec}$ \par
\renewcommand\xvec[2]{\ensuremath{#1_1,\ldots,#1_{#2}}}
The series of \xvec{x}{n} or $\xvec{y}{k}+G_{\xvec{z}{4}}$
```

A-1-5

When redefining a command (or an environment — see below), you must, of course, be cautious. It is good practice to do that only to commands that you have defined yourself earlier. Overwriting commands defined by packages or the LATEX kernel may be temporarily necessary if they have bugs, but it is likely to break their usage in places you do not control, and even if the redefinition works initially, subsequent corrections or updates to LATEX or the package providing the initial definition may render your redefinition suddenly invalid.

Commands with one optional argument

With \newcommand you can also define commands so that their first argument is optional. The syntax for this is

```
\newcommand{cmd}[narg][default]{command definition}
```

An example of such a command definition is shown below:

```
\newcommand\LB[1][3]{\linebreak[#1]}
```

The default for the optional argument is given between the second pair of square brackets — the string "3" in this case. Inside the command definition, the optional argument has the number #1, while the mandatory arguments (when present) are addressed #2 to #⟨narg⟩. Thus, typing \LB is a short way of saying \linebreak[3], while \LB[2] uses the actual specified value. That is, you obtain the same effect as when typing \linebreak[2].

New commands that have only mandatory arguments are expandable, i.e., they are replaced by their definition if used in moving arguments (for example inside \section), while those that are defined with an optional first argument are automatically made robust, i.e., they do not expand in such places.

In the next example we define the command \lvec, which can be used inside or outside of formulas (due to \ensuremath). Under the assumption that the upper subscript is usually n we made it optional, while the vector variable has to be given explicitly.

For the series $x_1 + \cdots + x_n$ we have

$$x_1 + \cdots + x_n = \sum_{k=1}^{n} G_{y_1 + \cdots + y_k}$$

```
\newcommand\lvec[2][n]
    {\ensuremath{#2_1+\cdots + #2_{#1}}}
For the series \lvec{x}  we have
\[ \lvec{x} = \sum_{k=1}^{n} G_{\lvec[k]{y}} \]
```

A-1-6

In general, it is most practical to associate the case that occurs most often with the form that does not need the optional argument and to represent the cases that are used less often with longer command strings with an optional argument.

Argument restrictions for simple commands

As explained above, user-defined commands can have one optional argument and up to nine arguments in total. If defined with \newcommand, each of the arguments can receive arbitrary text with a small number of restrictions:

- Braces must be properly balanced because otherwise LaTeX is unable to determine where the argument ends.

- In an optional argument a closing bracket "]" is allowed only if hidden inside braces (e.g., \item[{a}] is allowed). Without the braces the first] would be misinterpreted as the end of the optional argument.[1]

- The \verb command, the verbatim environment, and related commands or environments are not supported within arguments of other commands.

The allowed content of arguments can be deliberately further restricted by using the \newcommand* variant of the declaration.

Disallowing \par in argument content

```
\newcommand*{cmd}[narg][default]{command definition}
```

The starred form works like \newcommand but defines a *cmd* that is not, in TeX terms, long. This means that the newly defined command does not accept empty lines or \par commands in its argument(s). This restriction can be useful for commands whose arguments are not intended to contain whole paragraphs of text.

Commands that have been defined with the low-level TeX primitive \def do not accept \par in their argument. Thus, they are equivalent to being defined with \newcommand*. The low-level TeX equivalent to \newcommand is \long\def, except that neither can be used to define a command with an optional argument.

 Relation to TeX primitives

Nesting new commands in each other

Sometimes it is necessary to nest command definitions, most commonly in the combination of commands being defined as part of the definition of some new environment. If the inner command (or environment) has arguments, there is a problem referring to them. Clearly we cannot use #1, #2, and so on, because this notation already denotes the argument(s) of the outer command or environment. The TeX solution is to double the hash marks; thus, ##1 would refer to the first argument of the inner definition, and in the case of three nested definitions we would need ####1, and so on.

---

[1] This restriction is removed if the declarations from Section A.1.4 are used instead — as long as the [...] come in matching pairs.

To make this abstract concept a bit clearer, we define a command \DEFlvec that (re)defines the \lvec command from Example A-1-6 on page 626 over and over again. As a first argument to \DEFlvec we pass the vector name that is being hardwired into the redefinition of \lvec. As the second argument we pass the upper index that becomes the default value for the optional argument of \lvec. Thus, since the vector name is now part of the definition, \lvec has only an optional argument.

Default: $x_1 + \cdots + x_n \neq x_1 + \cdots + x_k$

Now: $y_1 + \cdots + y_i \neq y_1 + \cdots + y_k$

```
\newcommand\lvec{}
\newcommand\DEFlvec[2]{\renewcommand\lvec[1][#2]%
                    {\ensuremath{#1_1+\cdots + #1_{##1}}}}
\DEFlvec{x}{n}  % initial definition
Default: $\lvec \neq \lvec[k]$ \par
\DEFlvec{y}{i} Now: $\lvec \neq \lvec[k]$
```

A-1-7

The technique used in the above example is worth studying. Try to visualize the actual definitions being carried out, for example, when the "initial definition" is executed. Also note the need for a top-level definition for \lvec: the actual definition is irrelevant, but without it we would be unable to "redefine" it inside the \DEFlvec command. The \ShowCommand described on page 767 is a good way to look at the results.

Special declarations for use in packages and classes

Besides \newcommand and \renewcommand, which were originally provided as user commands (e.g., for the document preamble), LATEX offers some extra methods of (re)defining commands that are intended for use in class and package files.

\providecommand*{*cmd*} [*narg*] [*default*] {*command definition*}

This declaration works exactly like \newcommand and \newcommand*, except that it is ignored if the command to be defined already exists. Such a feature is useful in sources that may get used in several documents, such as bibliography entries. For example, instead of using \newcommand in the @preamble of BIBTEX for logos and other constructs used in the BIBTEX entries, you can use \providecommand to avoid error messages if such commands are already defined in the document.

\DeclareRobustCommand*{*cmd*} [*narg*] [*default*] {*command definition*}

This command takes the same arguments as \newcommand and \newcommand* but declares a robust command, even if some code within the *command definition* is fragile. You can use this command to define new robust commands, or to redefine existing commands *and* make them robust. Information is placed into the transcript file if *cmd* is redefined, so it does not produce an error in this case. In the case an existing fragile command should be made robust without otherwise changing it, LATEX offers \MakeRobust\cmd, which is used in various places in the kernel.

> \CheckCommand*{*cmd*} [*narg*] [*default*] {*command definition*}

This command takes the same arguments as \newcommand and \newcommand* but, rather than defining *cmd*, checks that the current definition of *cmd* is exactly as given by *command definition*. An warning is raised if the definitions differ or if one accepts \par in its arguments and the other does not (i.e., was defined using a starred form). This command is useful for checking the state of the system before a package starts altering the definitions of commands. It allows you to check, in particular, that no other package has redefined the same command.

A.1.3 Defining simple environments

You can define and redefine an environment with the \newenvironment and \renewenvironment commands, respectively. You must specify, in each case, which actions should take place when you enter and leave an environment. For an environment called "myenv" this is signaled by the commands \begin{myenv} and \end{myenv} inside your document.

> \newenvironment{*name*} [*narg*] {*begin code*}{*end code*}
> \renewenvironment{*name*} [*narg*] {*begin code*}{*end code*}

As with the \newcommand declaration, the number of arguments is in the range $0 \le narg \le 9$. In the case of no parameters, you can omit [0]. Inside the definition part, *begin code*, these parameters are referenced as #1 to #⟨*narg*⟩. If arguments are present, then they are defined when *entering* the environment by specifying them on the command \begin{*name*}, as shown below:

> \begin{*name*}{*arg₁*}...{*arg_{narg}*}   ...*body*...   \end{*name*}

When *exiting* an environment with the command \end{*name*}, no parameters can be specified. Moreover, the parameters specified with the \begin{*name*} command when entering the environment (see above) are no longer available in the definition part *end code*, where you define the actions that should take place when leaving the environment. This means that it is your responsibility to store information needed at the end of an environment (see the Citation environment defined below).[1]

Arguments not available in end-tag

Technically, a \newenvironment declaration for the environment *name* defines a command *name* that is called during the \begin{*name*} processing and a command \end*name* that is executed (besides other things) by \end{*name*}. You may find that it is sometimes these commands rather than the environment tags that are used inside packages and classes to define related environments or commands. An example where this might be useful is given on page 131. In other situations, it is not advisable to follow this practice without a thorough understanding of LaTeX's kernel implementation and in particular its environment hooks (which are then missing).

---

[1] Again, this restriction is lifted if you use the declarations discussed in Section A.1.4 instead.

Our first example defines an environment of type "Abstract", which is often used to give a short summary of the contents of an article or a book. It starts by typesetting a boldfaced and centered title, followed by the text of the abstract inside a `quote` environment. The final `\par` command ensures that any following text starts a new paragraph with a normal paragraph indentation.

```
\newenvironment{Abstract}
  {\begin{center}\normalfont\bfseries Abstract%
   \end{center}\begin{quote}}{\end{quote}\par}
```

Abstract

This abstract explains the approach used to solve the problems at hand.

Some text following the abstract. Some text following the abstract. And some more.

```
\begin{Abstract}
 This abstract explains the approach used
 to solve the problems at hand.
\end{Abstract}
Some text following the abstract. Some text
following the abstract. And some more.
```

A-1-8

Our second example is somewhat more complex. It shows how a `Citation` environment can be defined for quoting citations by famous people. In the document it would be used as follows:

Citation 1 Man is the measure of all things.

Protagoras

This is some regular text in between two Citation environments.

Citation 2 On mourra seul. *Blaise Pascal*

More regular text ...

Citation 3 Necessity is the plea for every infringement of human freedom.

William Pitt

```
\begin{Citation}{Protagoras}
  Man is the  measure of all things.
\end{Citation}
This is some regular text in between two
Citation environments.
\begin{Citation}{Blaise Pascal}
  On mourra seul.
\end{Citation}
More regular text \ldots
\begin{Citation}{William Pitt}
  Necessity is the plea for every
  infringement of human freedom.
\end{Citation}
```

A-1-9

The LℎT∃X code for the `Citation` environment is shown on the opposite page. We start by declaring the counter `Citctr`, for numbering the citations, and a box `\Citname`, for storing the name of the person whom we are citing so that we can typeset it at the end of the citation when the `\end{Citation}` command is encountered (remember that the value of the argument specified on the `\begin{Citation}` command is no longer available at that stage).

When entering the environment, we save the value of the argument, typeset in italic, in the box `\Citname` and increment our counter. We then start a `description` environment. This environment has a single `\item` containing the counter value preceded by the word "Citation".

When exiting the `Citation` environment, we twice issue a stretchable horizontal space separated by an allowed — but discouraged — line break. It is important that this space survives if a line break happens before or after it, so `\hspace*` is used.

We also throw in a \quad of space that ensures a proper separation between the citation and the name if they appear on the same line, but vanishes if a break is taken between them. Then we typeset the contents of the box \Citname before leaving the description environment. This puts the author's name flush right and the last line of the citation flush left, regardless of whether they end up on separate lines, as you can see in the next example. Without this adjustment the text of the citation would always be fully justified, often with a lot of white space between the words. For a discussion of the counter and box commands used in this example, see Sections A.2.1 and A.3.

```
\newcounter{Citctr} \newsavebox{\Citname}
\newenvironment{Citation}[1]
   {\sbox\Citname{\emph{#1}}\stepcounter{Citctr}%
    \begin{description}\item[Citation \arabic{Citctr}]}
   {\hspace*{\fill}\nolinebreak[1]\quad\hspace*{\fill}%
%    \finalhyphendemerits=0          %  <--- see text below
    \usebox{\Citname}%
    \end{description}}
```

Surprisingly, the name in the last citation of Example A-1-9 is typeset on a line of its own, even though there is clearly enough space to place it alongside the citation. The reason is that TEX's paragraph-breaking algorithm prefers solutions that do not have the second-to-last line ending in a hyphen and therefore selects a three-line paragraph breaking at the \nolinebreak.

There are two ways to correct this behavior. First, we can discourage breaking at this point by using an optional argument of [3] instead of [1], which would work in that particular example but may not work always. Second, we can tell TEX's algorithm not to take that hyphen into account by setting the low-level TEX integer parameter \finalhyphendemerits to zero. This requires a somewhat unusual syntax, as shown in the example code above (though commented out there to display the behavior without it).

A hyphen on the second-to-last line of a paragraph

\newenvironment{*name*}[*narg*][*default*]{*begin code*}{*end code*}

As with \newcommand, one can make the first argument of an environment optional. The *default* value for the optional argument is given between the second pair of square brackets. Inside the *begin code* part, which is executed when the environment *name* is entered, the optional argument can be accessed with #1. The mandatory arguments (when present) are addressed as #2 to #⟨*narg*⟩. When the *name* environment is used without an optional parameter, #1 contains the string specified as *default*.

As an example, we implement an altDescription environment with an optional argument that is trial-typeset to determine the width of the indentation. The list labels are placed flush right if possible (by placing \hfil at the left in \makelabel). When used without an optional argument, the indentation is 1em (i.e., a \quad). By specifying the widest entry as an optional argument, you make sure that the description parts of all your entries line up nicely.

The example first shows the (default) behavior of the `altDescription` list and then displays what it looks like when using the optional argument.

```
\usepackage{calc}
\newenvironment{altDescription}[1][\quad]%
  {\begin{list}{}{%
    \renewcommand\makelabel[1]{\hfil\textsf{##1}}%
    \settowidth\labelwidth{\makelabel{#1}}%
    \setlength\leftmargin{\labelwidth+\labelsep}}}
  {\end{list}}
\begin{altDescription}
\item[First] This is a short term with text that wraps.
\item[Long term] This is a long term.
\item[Even longer term] A very long term.
\end{altDescription}
\begin{altDescription}[Even longer term]
\item[First] This is a short term with text that wraps.
\item[Long term] This is a long term.
\item[Even longer term] A very long term.
\end{altDescription}
```

First This is a short term with text that wraps.

Long term This is a long term.

Even longer term A very long term.

     First This is a short term with text that wraps.

  Long term This is a long term.

Even longer term A very long term.

A-1-10

A.1.4 Defining more complex commands and environments

With `\newcommand` and `\newenvironment` it is possible to define simple commands and environments, and in many cases this is sufficient. However, if you look at the commands offered by LATEX and the packages described in this book, you find many commands with complex argument structures, e.g., with multiple optional arguments, special argument delimiters, and much more. In the past all such commands needed to be hand-crafted with low-level methods. While one can learn how to do this, it is challenging, and it is not something an author can do in the preamble of a document.

For this reason the LATEX Project Team developed a generalized specification facility that allows you to easily set up commands with complex arguments covering all of LATEX standard syntax possibilities and several additional features that go way beyond. This was first distributed as the package xparse, and since 2020, it is part of the LATEX format. The declarations for this and the underlying concepts are discussed in this section.

First, we describe the different argument types and then move on to explain how they can be used to create both document commands and environments. Finally, more specialized features are described, which allow an even richer application of a simple interface setup.

Describing argument types

If you want to specify different kind of arguments, it is no longer enough to know the number of arguments for a function; in addition, you need to know the nature of each of the arguments. This is done by constructing an *argument specification* that defines implicitly the number of arguments and explicitly the type of each argument and any additional information needed for a parser to read the user input and properly pass it through to internal functions.

The basic form of the argument specification is a list of letters, where each letter denotes a type of argument. Some of the types need additional information, such as default values or delimiters.

The argument types can be divided into two groups, those that define arguments that are mandatory (raising an error if not found) and those that define optional arguments and thus are allowed to be missing in the input. The mandatory types are the following:

Types denoting mandatory arguments

m A standard mandatory argument, which can be either a single token alone or multiple tokens surrounded by braces {...}. Regardless of the input format, the argument is passed to the internal code without the outer braces. This is the type specifier for a normal TeX argument.

r$\langle token_1 \rangle \langle token_2 \rangle$ This denotes a delimited mandatory argument, where the delimiters are $\langle token_1 \rangle$ and $\langle token_2 \rangle$. If the opening delimiter $\langle token_1 \rangle$ is missing, an error is raised, and the special default marker -NoValue- is used as the argument value.

R$\langle token_1 \rangle \langle token_2 \rangle$ {*default*} This too is a required delimited argument. Compared to r, the *default* instead of -NoValue- is used when the argument is missing.

v This type specifies an argument that is read "verbatim". In the document it is delimited by an arbitrary character (except for %, \, #, {, }, or ␣) and its next occurrence, in the same way as the argument of the LaTeX command \verb. As an alternative, the argument can be given in a brace group {...}, which is not possible with LaTeX's \verb.

To help with error recovery, v-type arguments have to be given on a single line in the document source and raise an error if that is not the case.

A command with one or more v-type arguments produces an error when it appears within an argument of another command or environment.

b This type is suitable only in the argument specification of an environment and denotes the body of the environment, i.e., the material between \begin{*env*} and \end{*env*} in the source. If used, it has to be the last argument specified. See page 641 for details on its use.

The types that define optional arguments are:

Types denoting optional arguments

o A standard LaTeX optional argument, surrounded with square brackets, that returns the special -NoValue- marker if not given (as described later).

d$\langle token_1 \rangle \langle token_2 \rangle$ Like o, but the argument is delimited by $\langle token_1 \rangle$ and $\langle token_2 \rangle$.

O{*default*} Like o, but returns $\langle default \rangle$ if no value is given.

D$\langle token_1 \rangle \langle token_2 \rangle$ {*default*} Like d, but returns $\langle default \rangle$ if no value is given. Internally, the o, d, and O types are shortcuts to an appropriately constructed D type argument.

s Scan for an optional star, which results in a value \BooleanTrue if a star is present and \BooleanFalse otherwise. These return values can be tested with \IfBooleanTF as described later.

t⟨*token*⟩   Like s, but scans for an optional *token*; i.e., s is a shorthand for t*.

e{*token₁token₂*...}   This defines a number of optional "embellishment" arguments, one for each *tokenᵢ*. The tokens must be distinct. In the document they are given as *tokenᵢ*{*value*}, and they can appear in any order at that point in the argument list.

A premier example is subscripts and superscripts in math, which are represented by _{*value*} and ^{*value*} in the document and can be written there in any order without changing the result. They can be modeled with an e-type by specifying e{^_}. This would then define two optional arguments. If present in the document, they receive the *values* given there; if not, they return the special marker −NoValue−, which the code could then test for to execute a special action. The order in which the values accessed in the code (#⟨*number*⟩) is the order in which the *tokens* are specified, not the order in which they appear in the document. See page 640 for further details.

E{*token₁token₂*...}{{*default₁*}{*default₂*}...}   Same as the e-type but with explicit default values instead of −NoValue− if not all embellishments are present in the document. You may specify fewer defaults than tokens. See page 641 for further details.

Modifying argument types   In addition to the argument *types* discussed above, the argument specification also gives special meaning to three other characters:

+   The + character is used to make an argument long (to accept \par in the argument). In contrast to \newcommand, this applies on an argument-by-argument basis. Thus, specifying "soo+mO{*default*}" means that the mandatory argument is \long, while the optional arguments are not.

!   The ! character is used to control whether spaces are allowed before optional arguments in the source. There are some subtleties to this, because TEX itself has some restrictions on where spaces are automatically ignored: more detail is given on page 638. It can also be used with the mandatory b-type, where it has a slightly different meaning as described on page 642.

>{*processor*}   Finally, the character > is used to declare so-called "argument processors" that can be used to modify the contents of an argument before it is passed to the macro definition. The use of argument processors is a somewhat advanced topic (or at least a less commonly used feature) and is covered on page 642.

To give some first examples, \newcommand\foo[3]{...} would correspond to the argument specification "+m+m+m" (three mandatory arguments all accepting \par) and "O{bar}m" (one optional argument with default value bar followed by a mandatory one) would correspond to \newcommand*\foo[2][bar]{...}. To improve the readability of an argument specification you can put spaces between the argument specifiers, but you still need to make sure that you do not have spurious spaces in the *code* argument (unless you program using the L3 programming layer).

Creating document commands and environments

To declare commands with argument specifications as discussed above, the following family of declarations is available:

```
\NewDocumentCommand{cmd}{arg spec}{code}
\RenewDocumentCommand{cmd}{arg spec}{code}
\ProvideDocumentCommand{cmd}{arg spec}{code}
\DeclareDocumentCommand{cmd}{arg spec}{code}
```

The argument specification for the function is given by *arg spec*, and the command uses the *code* with #1, #2, etc., replaced by the arguments found by the parser. The difference between the declarations is the behavior if ⟨cmd⟩ is already defined:

- \NewDocumentCommand issues an error if *cmd* has already been defined.

- \RenewDocumentCommand in contrast issues an error if *cmd* has not previously been defined.

- \ProvideDocumentCommand creates a new definition for *cmd* only if one has not already been defined and otherwise does nothing.

- \DeclareDocumentCommand always creates the new definition, regardless of any existing *cmd* with the same name. This should be used sparingly.

As a first example consider the following declaration, which shows a way to define a \chapter command that would essentially behave like the current LaTeX command (except that it would accept an optional argument even when a * is parsed):

```
\NewDocumentCommand\chapter{s o m}
    {\IfBooleanTF{#1}{\typesetstarchapter{#3}}%
                     {\typesetnormalchapter{#2}{#3}}}
```

The \typesetnormalchapter could test its first argument for being –NoValue– to see if an optional argument was present and act accordingly. See page 639 for details on \IfBooleanTF and testing for –NoValue–.

```
\NewCommandCopy{new-cmd}{original-cmd}
\NewEnvironmentCopy{new-env}{original-env}
```

If you want to make an existing command available under a new name (and reuse the original name for something else), then in the past you had to resort to low-level TeX programming using \let. However, this does not work for commands with optional arguments or those defined with \DeclareRobustCommand, because they really consist of two commands, one of them with an internal name that is difficult to copy. To make this possible in a reliable way, \NewCommandCopy is provided. It analyzes the *original-cmd* and provides a copy of it that remains usable even after the original is redefined. Example A-4-3 on page 676 shows its usage.

There also exist \RenewCommandCopy and \DeclareCommandCopy but not \ProvideCommandCopy. For environments you can use \NewEnvironmentCopy, \RenewEnvironmentCopy, and \DeclareEnvironmentCopy in a similar fashion.

Fully expandable document commands

Document commands created using \NewDocumentCommand, etc., are set up in a way that they do not expand unexpectedly; i.e., they are robust in LATEX's terminology but use a different mechanism (provided by modern engines) that makes them work even in places where \DeclareRobustCommand or \MakeRobust would fail. Making the commands robust so that they do not expand except when doing typesetting allows for a very efficient implementation besides the fact that some constructions simply fail in an expansion context.

There are, however, *very rare* occasions when it may be useful to create functions that always expand when used. This requires a much less efficient parser that imposes a number of restrictions on the nature of the arguments accepted by a function and the code it implements.[1] For this reason, the facility should be used only when *absolutely necessary* and is typically needed only in package or class files.

\NewExpandableDocumentCommand{*cmd*}{*arg spec*}{*code*}

This command is used to create a document-level *cmd* that grabs its arguments in a fully expandable manner. The argument specification for the function is given by *arg spec*, and the function executes the *code*. In general, the *code* also needs to be fully expandable, although there are cases where this is not necessary (e.g., in the example below). As usual, the \Renew..., \Provide..., and \Declare... variants are also available.

As an example in which at least a partially expandable command is needed, consider "hiding" \multicolumn inside a definition in order to preset the font and to center the column title. To allow for headers spanning several columns, we use an optional argument to keep the column number variable, e.g.,

```
\NewDocumentCommand\header{O{1}m}{\multicolumn{#1}{c}{\bfseries #2}}
```

That definition (or the same done with \DeclareRobustCommand[2][1]{...}) would fail, because the tabular code is scanning ahead to find a \multicolumn at the start of a cell, and with the command being robust, it cannot look into it.

```
\NewExpandableDocumentCommand\header{O{1}m}
        {\multicolumn{#1}{c}{\bfseries #2}}
\begin{tabular}{lll}
   \header[2]{2-cols} & \header{1-col} \\
   -- & --- & \\ '! & '? & f ff fi ffi fl ffl
\end{tabular}
```

2-cols	1-col
— —	—
'! '?	f ff fi ffi fl ffl

A-1-11

Parsing arguments by pure expansion imposes a number of restrictions on both the type of arguments that can be read and the error checking available:

- The "verbatim" argument type v is not available.

- The last argument (if any are present) must be one of the remaining mandatory types m, r, or R.

---

[1] During expansions you cannot make assignments, and that means state information needs a lot of technical juggling, which makes the processing slow and restricts the types you can parse for.

- Argument processors (using >) are not available.

- It is impossible to differentiate between, for example, \foo[and \foo{[}: in both cases the [is interpreted as the start of an optional argument. This makes checking for arguments less robust than in the standard version.

All that plus the fact that it is much slower in processing is why the expandable commands should be avoided unless they are really needed.

```
\NewDocumentEnvironment{env}{arg spec}{begin code}{end code}
\RenewDocumentEnvironment{env}{arg spec}{begin code}{end code}
\ProvideDocumentEnvironment{env}{arg spec}{begin code}{end code}
\DeclareDocumentEnvironment{env}{arg spec}{begin code}{end code}
```

These declarations work in the same way as \NewDocumentCommand, etc., but create environments (\begin{env} ... \end{env}). In the document all arguments are given following \begin{env}.

In contrast to environments declared with \newenvironment, both the *begin code* and *end code* may access the arguments as defined by *arg spec*. Below is a reimplementation of Example A-1-9 from page 630 making use of this feature and thereby getting much simpler. This time we also set \finalhyphendemerits to zero to prove that this makes the last citation use only two lines.

```
\newcounter{Citctr}
\NewDocumentEnvironment{Citation}{ m }
   {\stepcounter{Citctr}\begin{description}\item[Citation \arabic{Citctr}]}
   {\hspace*{\fill}\nolinebreak[1]\quad\hspace*{\fill}\finalhyphendemerits=0
    \emph{#1}\end{description}}
```

Citation 1 Man is the measure of all things.

Protagoras

Citation 2 On mourra seul. *Blaise Pascal*

Citation 3 Necessity is the plea for every infringement of human freedom. *William Pitt*

```
\begin{Citation}{Protagoras} Man is the
  measure of all things.      \end{Citation}
\begin{Citation}{Blaise Pascal}
  On mourra seul.             \end{Citation}
\begin{Citation}{William Pitt} Necessity
  is the plea for every infringement of
  human freedom.              \end{Citation}
```

A-1-12

Details on optional arguments

In contrast to commands created using LaTeX's \newcommand, optional arguments created using \NewDocumentCommand and friends may safely be nested. Thus, for example, following

```
\NewDocumentCommand\foo{O{something else}m}{I grabbed '#1' and '#2'}
\NewDocumentCommand\baz{O{things}}{#1-#1}
```

using the command as \foo[\baz[stuff]]{more stuff} prints

I grabbed 'stuff-stuff' and 'more stuff'

This is particularly useful when placing a command with an optional argument *inside* the optional argument of a second command. Note, however, that all commands involved are defined using `\NewDocumentCommand` and not one of the older methods; e.g., at the moment, it would not work with `\item` or many other kernel commands, though over time this will probably change.

When an optional argument is followed by a mandatory argument using the same delimiter (not a good syntax choice but possible), the parser issues a warning because not all optional arguments in front of the mandatory one could be omitted by the user, thus becoming in effect mandatory. There are possible use cases, though, for example, "`d()sr()`". This would not allow for a single group of parentheses, but it would accept arguments of the form `(..)(..)`, `*(..)`, or `(..)*(..)`. Whether or not that is a good syntax is a different question.

The defaults for O, D, and E arguments can use the result of grabbing another argument, even of one that comes later in the input. Thus, for example

```
\NewDocumentCommand\foo{O{#2} m}
```

would use the mandatory argument as the default for the leading optional one.

Spaces before optional arguments

TEX finds the first argument after a multiletter command name irrespective of any intervening spaces. This is true for both mandatory and optional arguments, and there is no way to prevent this. Thus, `\foo[arg]` and `\foo␣[arg]` are equivalent.[1]

Spaces are also ignored when collecting arguments up to the last mandatory argument to be collected (because it must exist). After

```
\NewDocumentCommand\foo{m o m}{ ... }
```

the user input `\foo{arg1}[arg2]{arg3}` and `\foo␣{arg1}␣␣␣[arg2]␣␣{arg3}` are both parsed in the same way.

However, the behavior of trailing optional arguments *after* any mandatory arguments is selectable. The standard settings allow spaces here, and thus with

```
\NewDocumentCommand\foobar{m o}{ ... }
```

both `\foobar{arg1}[arg2]` and `\foobar{arg1}␣[arg2]` find an optional argument. This can be changed by using the modifier ! in the argument specification:

```
\NewDocumentCommand\foobar{m !o}{ ... }
```

where `\foobar{arg1}␣[arg2]` does not find an optional argument but treats `␣[arg2]` as ordinary input.

As mentioned before, there is a subtle difference in TEX's handling of control symbols where the command name is made up from a single symbol such as `\\`. Spaces are not ignored by TEX here, and thus it is possible to require an optional argument to directly follow such a command without any intervening space. The most

---

[1] In fact, even a line break is skipped over at this point, with sometimes surprising effects.

common example is the use of \\ in amsmath environments, which in the terms here would be defined as

```
\NewDocumentCommand\\{!s !o}{ ... }
```

Testing for optional argument values or optional tokens

All the tests in this section are expandable, so executing the tests is possible in situations where robust commands would simply stay put without expanding, e.g., inside moving arguments or \typeout, etc.

Optional arguments make use of dedicated variables to return information about the nature of the argument received. Those that test for the existence of a single token, i.e., s-type or t-type, return a special Boolean value that can be tested. All others that expect a value in the source (delimited in some way) return that value if found. If the optional argument is not present, they return a default value as defined in the specification of O, D, or E types, or they return the special value −NoValue− in the case of o, d, or e types.

This −NoValue− value is truly special: it prints if typeset, but it is defined with special \catcode settings so you cannot manually enter it in your document. Thus, if you type \foo[−NoValue−], that is distinguishable from \foo without any optional argument. To test for this special value the code can make use of one of the following three tests, which differ only in the branches they support:

```
\IfNoValueTF{arg}{true code}{false code}
\IfNoValueT{arg}{true code}
\IfNoValueF{arg}{false code}
```

The \IfNoValue... tests are used to check if ⟨arg⟩ (#1, #2, etc.) is the special −NoValue− marker. For example

```
\NewDocumentCommand\foo{o m}
  {\IfNoValueTF {#1}%
     {\DoSomethingWithJustTheMandatoryArgument{#2}}%
     {\DoSomethingWithBothArguments{#1}{#2}}}
```

uses a different internal function if the optional argument is given than if it is not present. If you only need to do something if the argument is present (or not present), use one of the other two tests.

```
\IfValueTF{arg}{true code}{false code}
\IfValueT{arg}{true code}
\IfValueF{arg}{false code}
```

The reverse form of the \IfNoValue... tests are also available. The context determines which logical form makes the most sense for a given code scenario.

> ```
> \IfBlankTF{arg}{true code}{false code}
> \IfBlankT{arg}{true code}                    \IfBlankF{arg}{false code}
> ```

The \IfNoValueTF command chooses the *true code* if the optional argument has not been used at all (and it returns the special –NoValue– marker), but not if it has been given an empty value. In contrast, \IfBlankTF returns true if its argument either is truly empty or contains only one or more normal blanks. Combining both gives full flexibility. As usual, the variants \IfBlankT and \IfBlankF are also provided for use when only one branch leads to some action.

```
                         \NewDocumentCommand\foo{m!o}{\par #1:
1: Real content in argument!        \IfNoValueTF{#2}{No optional}%
2: Blanks in or empty argument!              {\IfBlankTF{#2}{Blanks in or empty}%
3: Blanks in or empty argument!                             {Real content in}}%
4: Real content in argument!               \space argument!}
5: No optional argument! [x]    \foo{1}[bar] \foo{2}[ ] \foo{3}[] \foo{4}[\space] \foo{5} [x]   A-1-13
```

Note that the \space in (4) is considered real content—because it is a command and not a "space" character—even though it results in producing a space. You can also observe in (5) the effect of the ! specifier, preventing the last \foo from interpreting [x] as its optional argument.

> ```
> \IfBooleanTF{arg}{true code}{false code}
> \IfBooleanT{arg}{true code}                  \IfBooleanF{arg}{false code}
> ```

To test if a star (s-type) or some other token (t-type) is present in the input, the above three tests are available: they test if ⟨*arg*⟩ (#1, #2, etc.) is "true" or "false". This makes it easy to define conditional processing based on the existence of a star or some other token as show below:

```
\NewDocumentCommand\foo{sm}
    {\IfBooleanTF{#1}{\DoSomethingWithStar{#2}}%
                     {\DoSomethingWithoutStar{#2}}}
```

Note that the \IfBoolean... tests cannot be used to test legacy TEX or LᴬTEX switches; they are available only for testing the argument parsing results. They expect to receive either \BooleanTrue or \BooleanFalse as their argument, and these flags are set when searching for an optional character (using s or t⟨*char*⟩). The flags have user-accessible names so that you can easily define further commands whose results can be tested with \IfBooleanTF.

Using Embellishments

The optional embellishments offered through the e or E-type differ in two respects from other optional arguments: they are identified by a start token, but their value is then given in a following brace group and not by everything up to some end token. The other important difference is that the list of start tokens can appear in any order in the document and is still recognized.

To give an example, consider defining a command \xgets that produces a left arrow but allows you to add some material above and below. A possible syntax for this could be \xgets^{*above*}, \xgets_{*below*} and for material above and below \xgets^{*above*}_{*below*} (or the other way around). This is the sort of syntax that the e-types offer.

The amsmath package already has a \xleftarrow command that provides the functionality we want for \xgets, but it uses an optional and a mandatory argument for it, so you always have to specify the *above* argument even if it is empty. To exhibit the embellishment syntax, we define \xgets to simply pass its arguments to the amsmath command. We use the E-type and set up empty defaults so that if one or both of the embellishments are not present in the document, we pass empty values to the arguments of \xleftarrow. The order of tokens in the argument to E defines what is received as #1 (the value from _) and what as #2 (the value from ^) regardless of the order used in the document, where we specified ^ first. For comparison, the example shows both the embellishment syntax and the one used by amsmath.

```
\usepackage{amsmath}
\NewDocumentCommand\xgets{ E{_^}{{}{}} }{\xleftarrow[#1]{#2}}
\[ \xgets          \xgets^x        \xgets_y              \xgets^{x+y}_{x-y}       \]
\[ \xleftarrow{} \xleftarrow{x} \xleftarrow[y]{} \xleftarrow[x-y]{x+y} \]
```

A-1-14

The E-type used in the above example defines one (empty) default value per test token. However, it is allowed to make the list of default values *shorter* than the list of test tokens. For those tokens that have no default, the special −NoValue− marker is returned (as for the e-type). Thus, for example

```
E{!?}{{Bang}}
```

has default Bang for the ! test character, but returns the −NoValue− marker as a default for ?, which could then be tested for with one of the test commands. This allows mixing of explicit defaults with testing for missing values.

Using the body of an environment as an argument

While environments \begin{*env*} ... \end{*env*} are typically used in cases where the code implementing the ⟨*env*⟩ironment does not need to access the contents of the environment (its "body"), it is sometimes useful to have the body as a standard argument.

This is achieved by *ending* the argument specification with b, which is a dedicated argument type for this situation. For instance, the next example grabs the body as argument #2 and doubles it with different font settings. Environments that use this feature can be nested.

Hello world:
Lighten up!*Hello world:*
*Lighten up!?**
TT?*wicewice?*

```
\NewDocumentEnvironment{twice}{O{\ttfamily} +b}{#2#1#2?}{*}
\begin{twice}[\itshape] Hello world: \par Lighten up! \end{twice}
\par \begin{twice} T \end{twice}\begin{twice} wice \end{twice}
```

A-1-15

Special meaning of ! together with b

The + prefix is used to allow multiple paragraphs in the environment's body. By default, spaces are trimmed at both ends of the body: in the example there would otherwise be spaces coming from the ends of the lines after [\itshape] and up!. Putting the prefix ! before b suppresses space-trimming. Argument processors discussed below can also be applied to the b specifier.

When b is used in the argument specification, the last argument of the environment declaration (e.g., \NewDocumentEnvironment), which consists of the *end code* to insert at \end{*env*}, is not really needed, because one can simply put that code at the end of the *start code*. Nevertheless, this *end code* argument must be provided, even if usually empty — here we added a ? and * in these places to show that they end up one after the other.

Using argument processors

Preprocessing arguments with "argument processors" is a somewhat more advanced topic, but it offers even more flexibility for setting up new document commands. You can, for example, define commands whose arguments (mandatory or optional) consist of comma-separated lists, and the splitting of such arguments is then automatically taken care of for you.

Argument processors are applied to an argument *after* it has been grabbed by the underlying system, but *before* it is passed to *code*. An argument processor can therefore be used to regularize input at an early stage, allowing the internal functions to be completely independent of the input format used in the document. Processors are applied to user input and to default values for optional arguments, but *not* to the special −NoValue− marker.

Each argument processor is specified by the syntax >{*processor*} in the argument specification. Processors are applied from right to left, so that

```
>{\ProcessorB} >{\ProcessorA} m
```

would apply \ProcessorA followed by \ProcessorB to the tokens grabbed by the m argument. There are a number of predefined processors that we discuss below, but it is also possible to implement additional ones if the need arises. Because the latter is a rather specialized topic, we refer you to [63] for details.

\SplitArgument{*number*}{*token(s)*}

This processor splits the argument given at each occurrence of the *token(s)* up to a maximum *number* (thus dividing the input into a maximum of *number* + 1 parts). An error is given if too many *token(s)* are present in the input. The processed input is placed inside *number* + 1 sets of braces for further use, if necessary filled up by adding {−NoValue−} if there are fewer than *number* of *token(s)* in the argument. Spaces are trimmed at each end of each item parsed.

In the following example the command has one argument, which is supposed to contain two or fewer semicolons; i.e., it consists of a maximum of three parts. The result after the split is then passed for further processing to an internal command with three normal mandatory arguments:

```
\NewDocumentCommand\foo{>{\SplitArgument{2}{;}} m}
     {\InternalFunctionWithThreeArguments#1}
```

Note that even though `\InternalFunctionWithThreeArguments` expects three arguments, we have to write #1 without surrounding braces! The reason is that #1 contains three brace groups after the processor has acted, i.e., exactly the syntax that the command expects.

`\SplitList{`*token(s)*`}`

This processor splits the argument given at each occurrence of the *token(s)* where the number of items is not fixed. Each item with spaces at each end trimmed is then wrapped in braces within #1. This result can then be further processed using a mapping function of some sort. For example:

```
\NewDocumentCommand\foo{>{\SplitList{;}} m}
     {\MappingFunction#1\MappingFunctionEnd}
```

The `\MappingFunction` would then need to be a command with one mandatory argument that picks up one brace group from #1, checks if it has reached the end of the list (where it finds `\MappingFunctionEnd` instead of a brace group), and if not processes its argument and then calls itself again to pick up the next. The L3 programming layer offers a large selection of mapping functions that work in a similar way, but it is not too difficult to write them in traditional TeX either. However, even simpler is to make use of `\ProcessList` that is offered for exactly this scenario.

`\ProcessList{`*list*`}{`*function*`}`

The command `\ProcessList` applies a *function* to every entry in a *list*. The *function* should absorb one argument: the list entry. For example

```
\NewDocumentCommand\foo{>{\SplitList{;}}m}{\ProcessList{#1}{\typeout}}
```

would display each part of `\foo`'s argument on the terminal.

Two further argument processors are predefined: the first can be quite useful when dealing with arbitrary user input, while the second provides only some syntactic sugar and is mainly there because it was trivial to define it.

`\TrimSpaces`   `\ReverseBoolean`

The `\TrimSpaces` processor removes any leading and trailing spaces (tokens with character code 32 and category code 10) from either end of the argument.

In the following example we define a normal command that retains spaces and a \spaceless version that trims them off to show the difference:

```
\NewDocumentCommand\withspace{m}{\textbf{#1}}
\NewDocumentCommand\spaceless{>{\TrimSpaces}m}{\textbf{#1}}
```

Test **Hello world** lighten up!

Test **Hello world** lighten up!

```
Test \withspace{ Hello world }  lighten up!          \par
Test \spaceless{ Hello world } lighten  up!
```

A-1-16

While the user error here is obvious and probably never happens, there are many occasions where it is not and people split arguments over several lines to improve readability (and thereby introduce unwanted spaces). In such cases, trimming the argument value helps avoid subtle errors. \TrimSpaces removes even multiple spaces in a row if they happen to end up at the start or end of the argument.

Finally, the \ReverseBoolean processor reverses the logic of outcome of an s-type or t-type argument so that the example from earlier would become

```
\NewDocumentCommand\foo{>{\ReverseBoolean}s m}
    {\IfBooleanTF{#1}{\DoSomethingWithoutStar{#2}}%
                     {\DoSomethingWithStar{#2}}}
```

in other words a somewhat convoluted way of implementing \IfNotBooleanTF, which does not exist in the language.

A.1.5 Changing arguments to command names

There are a few cases when using commands or declaring new commands in which it is impossible to provide the command name as a single \... token — instead the command has to be "constructed". To facilitate this task, the L3 programming layer offers a general mechanism to manipulate arguments in various ways, but for common cases there are also two CamelCase commands for use with \NewDocumentCommand and similar constructs.

\UseName{*string*}   \ExpandArgs{*spec*} ⟨*cmd*⟩ {*arg₁*} ... {*argₙ*}

\UseName turns the *string* into a command name and then immediately executes it. The \ExpandArgs alters the arguments of *cmd* according to a *spec*. The *spec* consists of a list of letters, each of which denotes what should happen to the corresponding argument: c stands for an argument that is turned into a 'c'ommand; an n represents a 'n'ormal argument that is not altered, and N stands for a 'N'ormal argument, which is also left unchanged but one consisting only of a single token (and usually unbraced).

For example, cc stands for "turn the first two arguments into commands before passing them to *cmd*". This could then be used together with \NewCommandCopy as the *cmd* as follows

```
\NewDocumentCommand\savebyname{m}
        {\ExpandArgs{cc}\NewCommandCopy{saved#1}{#1}}
```

after which a declaration such as \savebyname{LaTeX} would copy the definition of \LaTeX to \savedLaTeX.

As a more complex example, consider the case of this book where we wanted to have a number of "copyedit" commands to add notes into the margin or for longer notes in the main galley (using the todonotes package). The copyeditors should have their notes in their own color and numbered sequentially.

For this we define[1] the command \newcopyedit, which expects as its mandatory argument the initials of the copyeditor (e.g., fmi) and as an optional argument a color name (line 1). Using the initials we define a counter (line 2), e.g., todofmi, to count the notes for that person, and we define a command to make the notes, e.g., \fmi. To be able to use \NewDocumentCommand we need to turn #2 into a command name, which is done with the help of \ExpandArgs{c} (line 3). This newly defined command scans for an optional star and one mandatory argument. It increments the counter associated with the initials (line 4) and then tests for the optional star (line 5). If there was one, it uses \todo to make an inline note (line 6) and otherwise a marginal note (line 7). In either case it shows the initials (#2) followed by the counter representation, which again needs to be constructed this time with the help of \UseName (lines 6 and 7). Finally (line 8), we apply the definition twice to get the copyedit commands \fmi and \ufi, which we then use within the text.

```
\usepackage{kantlipsum,todonotes}
\NewDocumentCommand\newcopyedit{O{blue} m}                          % 1.1
  {\newcounter{todo#2}%                                             % 1.2
   \ExpandArgs{c}\NewDocumentCommand{#2}{s m}%                      % 1.3
    {\stepcounter{todo#2}%                                          % 1.4
     \IfBooleanTF {##1}%                                            % 1.5
       {\todo[inline,color=#1!20]{#2 \UseName{thetodo#2}: ##2}}%    % 1.6
       {\todo[color=#1!20]{#2 \UseName{thetodo#2}: ##2}}}}%         % 1.7
\newcopyedit{fmi} \newcopyedit[red]{ufi}                           % 1.8
Kant:\fmi{correct} \kant*[1][1]\fmi{use a different phrase}
\kant[1][2]\ufi*{Add another paragraph!}
```

| fmi 1: correct | Kant: As any dedicated reader can clearly see, the Ideal of practical reason is a |

fmi 1: correct

Kant: As any dedicated reader can clearly see, the Ideal of practical reason is a representation of, as far as I know, the things in themselves; as I have shown elsewhere,

fmi 2: use a
different phrase

the phenomena should only be used as a canon for our understanding. The paralogisms of practical reason are what first give rise to the architectonic of practical reason.

ufi 1: Add another paragraph!

A-1-17

There are several other single letters supported in the L3 programming layer that could be used in the *spec* to manipulate arguments in other ways. If you are interested, take a look at the "Argument expansion" section in the L3 programming layer documentation [62].

---

[1]The actual definition we used in the book also added a bookmark to make navigation easy (as explained in Section 2.4.6 on page →I 103), but that is not shown here.

A.2 Counters and length expressions

A.2.1 Defining and changing counters

Every number internally generated by LaTeX has a *counter* (register) associated with it. The name of the counter is usually identical to the name of the environment or the command that generates the number except that it does not start with a \. The following is the list of all counters used in LaTeX's standard document classes:

```
part            enumi         figure       equation
chapter         enumii        table        page
section         enumiii       footnote     totalpages
subsection      enumiv        mpfootnote
subsubsection
paragraph
subparagraph
```

In addition, there are several configuration parameters that also use the counter interface for modifications. However, they normally do not change when a document is processed. These are:

```
totalnumber     bottomnumber     secnumdepth   errorcontextlines
topnumber       dbltopnumber     tocdepth
```

An environment declared by \newtheorem can also have a counter with the same name associated with it, unless the optional argument indicates that it is to be numbered together with another environment. And, of course, additional counters may get added by packages; e.g., the float package declares one counter per float type in order to number the floats of this type.

The value of a counter is a single integer. Several counters can be combined into a number, as is usually the case for numbering section headings. For example, in the book or report classes, 7.4.5 identifies the fifth subsection of the fourth section in the seventh chapter.

Below we describe all the basic LaTeX commands that define counters and modify or display their values. These commands are much more powerful if used in conjunction with the calc package, which is discussed in Section A.5.2.

`\newcounter{`*ctr*`}[`*parent-ctr*`]`

This command globally defines a new counter, *ctr*, and initializes it to zero. If a counter with the name *ctr* is already defined, an error message is printed. When you specify the name of another counter as the optional argument, *parent-ctr*, then the newly defined *ctr* is reset when the counter *parent-ctr* is incremented with the \stepcounter or \refstepcounter command. It also defines the command \the⟨*ctr*⟩ to always expand to \arabic{*ctr*} even if the optional argument is given — compare this to the behavior of the \counterwithin command described next.

\counterwithin*[*format-cmd*]{*ctr*}{*parent-ctr*}

The operation that defines that one counter is reset whenever another counter is stepped is also available as the command \counterwithin. In contrast to \newcounter, it alters \the⟨*ctr*⟩ to typeset \the⟨*parent-ctr*⟩.⟨*format-cmd*⟩{*ctr*} where ⟨*format-cmd*⟩ is a command such as \roman. If the optional argument is not present, it defaults to \arabic.

If you use the starred form, then \the⟨*ctr*⟩ is not touched, which is useful if it needs a more complex definition or is already correctly set up. Obviously, in that case the optional argument is meaningless and is ignored if given.

\counterwithout*[*format-cmd*]{*ctr*}{*parent-ctr*}

However, sometimes you need the opposite action. For example, the report class defines the footnote counter to be reset whenever a new chapter starts. If you want your footnotes nevertheless to be numbered sequentially throughout a document, then specifying

    \counterwithout{footnote}{chapter}

achieves this for you by removing it from the reset list of the chapter counter and altering \thefootnote accordingly. If you use the optional ⟨*format-cmd*⟩, then this gets applied in the definition of \the⟨*ctr*⟩; otherwise, \arabic is used. As above, the starred form does not alter \the⟨*ctr*⟩ at all.

\setcounter{*ctr*}{*val*}   \addtocounter{*ctr*}{*val*}

With \setcounter the value of counter *ctr* is globally set equal to the value *val*. With \addtocounter it is globally incremented by *val*.

\stepcounter{*ctr*}   \refstepcounter{*ctr*}

Both commands globally increment the counter *ctr* and reset all subsidiary counters — that is, those declared with ⟨*ctr*⟩ in the optional argument on the \newcounter command or in the second argument of \counterwithin.

The \refstepcounter command additionally defines the current \ref value to be the text generated by the command \the⟨*ctr*⟩. Note that whereas stepping a counter is a global operation, setting the current \ref value is done locally and thus is valid only inside the current group. As a result, Example A-2-1 on the next page does not produce the desired output but instead picks up the section number. The correct solution would be to move \refstepcounter before the \textbf command — and also precede it with \leavevmode so that it is not executed in vertical mode, which makes a difference if hyperref is used.[1]

---

[1]The hyperref package adds an anchor at the point \refstepcounter is used, and that can alter the spacing in the document if it is enountered in vertical mode.

5   A Failure

Exercise 5.a: A test.

Exercise 5.b: Another test.

Referencing exercises: 5 and 5.

```
\newcounter{ex} \renewcommand\theex{\thesection.\alph{ex}}
\newenvironment{EX}{\begin{flushleft}%
   \textbf{\refstepcounter{ex}Exercise~\theex:}}
   {\end{flushleft}}
\setcounter{section}{4} % for testing
\section{A Failure}
\begin{EX} \label{A} A test.          \end{EX}
\begin{EX} \label{B} Another test. \end{EX}
Referencing exercises: \ref{A} and \ref{B}.
```

A-2-1

\value{*ctr*}	\arabic{*ctr*}	\roman{*ctr*}	\Roman{*ctr*}
	\alph{*ctr*}	\Alph{*ctr*}	\fnsymbol{*ctr*}

The \value command produces the current value of a counter to be used in places where LATEX expects to see a number, such as in the *val* argument of the \setcounter or \addtocounter command or when comparing numbers using the command \ifthenelse from the ifthen package.

However, despite its name, the \value command cannot be used to typeset the value of the counter! For that purpose, a set of presentation commands are available, all of which take a counter name as an argument.

With \arabic the counter value is represented as an Arabic numeral. With \roman and \Roman, lowercase and uppercase roman numerals are produced, respectively. The remaining commands can be used only if the counter value is within a certain range. The \alph command displays the value as a lowercase letter: a, b, c, ..., z. Thus, the value should lie in the range 1, ..., 26; otherwise, an error is signaled. The \Alph command is similar but produces uppercase letters. Finally, \fnsymbol represents the counter value as a traditional footnote symbol (e.g., ∗, †). In that case the value must not be greater than 9, unless an extension package, like footmisc or fmtcount, is used. The next example shows all of these commands in action.

Counter presentations with restricted ranges

8, viii, VIII, h, H, ††
Anno Domini MCMXCIV

```
\newcounter{exa}\setcounter{exa}{8}
\arabic{exa}, \roman{exa}, \Roman{exa}, \alph{exa},
\Alph{exa}, \fnsymbol{exa} \par
\setcounter{exa}{1994} Anno Domini \scshape{\roman{exa}}
```

A-2-2

\the⟨*ctr*⟩

A shorthand to produce the default visual representation for a counter *ctr* is provided by the command \the⟨*ctr*⟩ (e.g., \thesection for the section counter).

As mentioned earlier, this command is initialized by the \newcounter declaration to produce \arabic{*ctr*}. However, in LATEX such a visual representation often involves more than a single number. For example, with sectioning counters one usually displays the value of the current section as well as the value of the current subsection, and so on. For this reason \the⟨*ctr*⟩ is typically (re)defined to produce a more complex representation. This practice becomes even more important when you consider that \refstepcounter not only increments a certain counter and resets lower-level counters but also defines the "current" label (as picked up by \label) to be the result of \the⟨*ctr*⟩ for the counter being stepped.

As an example, inside the standard article class, we find definitions for sectioning counters equivalent to the following:

```
\newcounter{part}                    \newcounter{section}
\newcounter{subsection}[section]  \newcounter{subsubsection}[subsection]


\renewcommand\thepart            {\Roman{part}}
\renewcommand\thesection         {\arabic{section}}
\renewcommand\thesubsection      {\thesection.\arabic{subsection}}
\renewcommand\thesubsubsection{\thesubsection.\arabic{subsubsection}}
```

You see how lower-level counters are reset when upper-level counters are stepped, as well as how the representation of the counters (the \the... commands) are constructed from the current counter and the counters at a higher level. Note how the part counter does not influence any of the lower levels.

As another example, we look at Table 4.2 on page →I 256, which shows the structure of the enumeration list counters. In fact, these counters are defined inside the file latex.ltx, which contains the kernel code for LaTeX. Only the representation, prefix, and label field commands are defined in the standard class files as follows:

```
\renewcommand\theenumi   {\arabic{enumi}}
\renewcommand\theenumii{\alph{enumii}}       \renewcommand\p@enumii{\theenumi}
\renewcommand\theenumiii{\roman{enumiii}} \renewcommand\p@enumiv{\p@enumiii\theenumiii}
\renewcommand\theenumiv{\Alph{enumiv}}       \renewcommand\p@enumiii{\theenumi(\theenumii)}

\newcommand\labelenumi   {\theenumi.}       \newcommand\labelenumii{(\theenumii)}
\newcommand\labelenumiii{\theenumiii.}       \newcommand\labelenumiv{\theenumiv.}
```

Finally, we show how the standard classes handle the equation counter. Like the enumeration counters, this counter is declared inside latex.ltx. In the article class, the counter is never reset:

```
\renewcommand\theequation{\arabic{equation}}
```

In the report and book classes, the equation number is reset for each chapter with the \counterwithin command:

```
\counterwithin{equation}{chapter}
% This automatically does:
%    \renewcommand\theequation{\thechapter.\arabic{equation}}
```

Thus, the representation also differs in both cases.[1]

---

[1] The actual definition is somewhat more complex, because some low-level code is used to suppress the chapter number if it is zero.

A.2.2 fmtcount — Specially formatted counters and numbers

We already looked at the fmtcount package in Section 3.3.1 on page →I 154 and its ability to produce ordinal numbers from counter values, allowing you to generate "Second section in 1ˢᵗ appendix" in a number of languages. In addition, it offers a set of other counter presentations not available with standard LᴬTEX.

\binary{*ctr*}   \octal{*ctr*}   \hexadecimal{*ctr*}   \Hexadecimal{*ctr*}
\aaalph{*ctr*}   \AAalph{*ctr*}   \abalph{*ctr*}   \ABalph{*ctr*}

These work like \arabic, etc., but format the counter value of *ctr* in a special format. There is also a \decimal command, which by default produces exactly the same as LᴬTEX's \arabic (but see below).

The different formats have some restrictions on the size of the value they accept, e.g., for \octal, only numbers below 32769 are allowed.[1]

Commands that produce letters (in addition to, or instead of, digits) exist in two forms: if the command name starts with an uppercase letter, then uppercase letters are typeset; otherwise lowercase letters. The \..alph commands extend the range of supported values by using several letters when we have exhausted "a, ..., z". The command \aaalph then continues with "aa, bb, ..., zz, aaa, bbb, ...", while \abalph continues with "ab, ac, ..., az, ba, bb, bc, ...".

\padzeroes [*digits*]

Sometimes you may need to typeset a set of numbers with always the same number of digits, if necessary padded with zeros. This is available for all commands that produce digits (and possible letters in addition). To specify the padding you use \padzeroes with the optional argument specifying the expected number of *digits* in the result (if the argument is not given, it defaults to 17). If the counter value is larger, then no zeros are added, and the value is typeset as is (with more digits); e.g., the binary value is not padded in the example below. To return to no padding, use 0 in the *digits* argument.

```
\usepackage{fmtcount}  \newcounter{test} \setcounter{test}{29}
\padzeroes[4]
\decimal{test} \binary{test} \octal{test} \hexadecimal{test} \par
Unpadded: \padzeroes[0]
\decimal{test} \binary{test} \octal{test} \hexadecimal{test}
```

0029 11101 0035 001d
Unpadded: 29 11101 35 1d

A-2-3

\decimalnum{*num*}   \binarynum{*num*}   \octalnum{*num*}
\hexadecimalnum{*num*}   \Hexadecimalnum{*num*}   \aaalphnum{*num*}
\AAalphnum{*num*}   \abalphnum{*num*}   \ABalphnum{*num*}

Instead of formatting the value of a counter, you can format an explicit number by using one of these commands. They too react to \padzeroes as explained above.

---

[1]There is a limit imposed by TEX for counter values, but that is much higher; thus, this is a restriction of the implementation that may get lifted one day.

A.2.3 sillypage — Page and other counting à la Monty Python

Even in a serious book there should be time for some lighthearted jokes (once in a while at least), and if you have read carefully, you may have noticed one or the other within these pages.

During the last stages of producing this book, I came across the sillypage package (by Phelype Oleinik, Paulo Cereda, samcarter, and Ulrike Fischer) that brings a masterpiece of British sketch culture to the LaTeX world: it provides Monty Python's "The Ministry of Silly Walks" in the form of a counter format, depicting the walk through twelve pictograms:

A-2-4

(repeat)

By specifying \pagenumbering{silly} the page numbers of your document loop through the above walk, while with sillynumeral, each page number is uniquely mapped to a composition of pictograms (in base 12). In either case it turns your document into a nice thumbnail book in which the page numbers perform the silly walk in a kineographic fashion. Be careful to avoid using \pageref when silly page numbering is in force, because this command would then display the references as (rather large) pictograms, which may not be what you intended.

There is also the command \silly, which requires a LaTeX counter name as its argument and can be used like \arabic or \roman. Finally, the two commands \sillystep and \sillynumeral expect an integer and turn it into the corresponding pictogram or sequence of pictograms, respectively.

A.2.4 Defining and changing space parameters

In LaTeX two kinds of space parameters (lengths) exist: "rigid" lengths (called ⟨*dimen*⟩ in *The TeXbook* [42]), which are fixed, and "rubber" lengths (called ⟨*skip*⟩ in *The TeXbook*), which have a natural length and a degree of positive and negative elasticity. New lengths in LaTeX are allocated as type ⟨*skip*⟩ so that you always have the choice of initializing them as rigid or rubber lengths (by specifying plus and minus parts). On the other hand, all standard lengths in LaTeX are of type rigid, unless specifically declared in Appendix C of the *LaTeX Manual* to be rubber. Here we discuss the commands provided by LaTeX for dealing with lengths.

```
\newlength{cmd}
```

The declaration \newlength allocates a new (rubber) length register and associates the command name *cmd* with it. If a command *cmd* already exists, you get an error message. The new length is preset to zero. Just like with \newcommand, you find that the braces around *cmd* are often omitted in actual code because the argument must consist of a single command name.

dimension	explanation	visualization
sp	Scaled point ($65536\,\mathrm{sp} = 1\,\mathrm{pt}$) TᴇX's smallest unit	
pt	Point $= \frac{1}{72.27}$ in $= 0.351\,\mathrm{mm}$	
bp	Big point $= \frac{1}{72}$ in $= 0.353\,\mathrm{mm}$, also known as PostScript point	
dd	Didot point $= \frac{1}{72}$ of a French inch $= 0.376\,\mathrm{mm}$	
mm	Millimeter $= 2.845\,\mathrm{pt}$	
pc	Pica $= 12\,\mathrm{pt} = 4.218\,\mathrm{mm}$	
cc	Cicero $= 12\,\mathrm{dd} = 4.531\,\mathrm{mm}$	
cm	Centimeter $= 10\,\mathrm{mm} = 2.371\,\mathrm{pc}$	
in	Inch $= 25.4\,\mathrm{mm} = 72.27\,\mathrm{pt} = 6.022\,\mathrm{pc}$	
ex	Height of a small "x" in the current font (approximately)	
em	Width of capital "M" in current font (approximately)	
mu	Math unit ($18\,\mathrm{mu} = 1\,\mathrm{em}$) for positioning in math mode	
fil	Infinite stretch or shrink, i.e., can be used only in plus or minus part of a rubber length and overwrites any finite stretch present	
fill	Second order infinite stretch or shrink, overwrites first order	
filll	Third order infinite stretch or shrink (for emergencies)	

Table A.1: LᴬTᴇX's units of length

```
\setlength{cmd}{length}      \addtolength{cmd}{length}
```

This sets the value of the length command *cmd* equal to the length *length* or, in the case of \addtolength, adds the specified amount to the existing value. In the examples below, the TᴇX command \the is used to typeset the actual contents of the length variable. It requires the register command name *without* braces!

```
\newlength\Mylen
\setlength \Mylen{10mm}  Mylen = \the\Mylen
\addtolength\Mylen{0pt plus 4pt minus 2pt}
\par Mylen = \the\Mylen
\addtolength\Mylen{-10mm plus 1fil}
\par Mylen = \the\Mylen
```

Mylen = 28.45274pt
Mylen = 28.45274pt plus 4.0pt minus 2.0pt
Mylen = 0.0pt plus 1.0fil minus 2.0pt

A-2-5

Lengths can be specified in various units, as shown in Table A.1. Notice the difference between the typographic point (pt), which is normally used in TᴇX, and the (big) point used by PostScript and PDF, for example. Thus, when reserving space for an EPS picture, you need to specify the bounding box dimension in bp to get the correct space.

command	explanation
\hspace{*len*}	Horizontal space of width *len* that can be a rigid or a rubber length
\enspace	Horizontal space equal to half a quad
\quad, \qquad	Horizontal space equal to the em value of the font; \qquad equals two em
\hfil	Horizontal rubber space that can stretch between 0 and ∞
\hfill	Horizontal rubber space that can stretch between 0 and ∞; overwrites \hfil
\hrulefill	Similar to \hfill, but draws a solid horizontal line
\dotfill	Similar to \hfill, but draws a dotted line

Table A.2: Predefined horizontal spaces

\settowidth{*cmd*}{*text*}
\settoheight{*cmd*}{*text*}   \settodepth{*cmd*}{*text*}

Instead of specifying a length value explicitly, three commands are available that allow you to measure a given text and assign the result. With \settowidth the value of the length command *cmd* is set equal to the natural width of the typeset version of *text*. This command is very useful for defining lengths that vary with the string contents or the type size. The other two commands work similarly but measure the height and the depth rather than the width of the typeset *text*.

width = 47.67996pt
height = 6.76pt
depth = 2.18pt
Use larger font and recalculate:
A-2-6   width = 57.21597pt

```
\newlength\Mylen
\settowidth \Mylen{Typography} width  = \the\Mylen \\
\settoheight\Mylen{Typography} height = \the\Mylen \\
\settodepth \Mylen{Typography} depth  = \the\Mylen \\
Use larger font and recalculate: \\
\settowidth\Mylen{\large Typography} width = \the\Mylen
```

\fill   \stretch{*dec-num*}

These two rubber lengths are intended to be used in the argument of \vspace and similar commands. The \fill rubber length is preset with a natural length of zero but can stretch to any positive value; in other words, it holds the value 0pt plus 1fill. Do not change its value! It is used in various places in the kernel, and a change would produce strange effects.

An often more useful rubber length is provided by the \stretch command — in fact, \fill is equivalent to \stretch{1}. More generally, \stretch{*dec-num*} has a stretchability of *dec-num* times \fill. It can be used to fine-tune the positioning of text horizontally or vertically — for instance, to provide spaces that have a certain relation to each other. Example A-2-8 demonstrates its application.

Horizontal space

Table A.2 shows horizontal space commands known to LaTeX. A flexible horizontal space of any desired width is produced by the \hspace command. The command

command	explanation
\vspace{*len*}	Vertical space of height *len* that can be a rigid or a rubber length
\smallskip	Vertical skip of \smallskipamount (default about one quarter of \baselineskip)
\medskip	Vertical skip of \medskipamount (default about one half of \baselineskip)
\bigskip	Vertical skip of \bigskipamount (default about one \baselineskip)
\vfill	Vertical rubber length that can stretch between 0 and ∞

Table A.3: Predefined vertical spaces

\hspace* is the same as \hspace, but the space is never removed — not even at a line boundary.

A space in front of or following an \hspace or \hspace* command is significant, as the following example shows:

This is a	0.5 in wide space.	`\par This is a\hspace{0.5in}0.5~in wide space.`
This is a	0.5 in wide space.	`\par This is a \hspace{0.5in}0.5~in wide space.`
This is a	0.5 in wide space.	`\par This is a \hspace{0.5in} 0.5~in wide space.` A-2-7

The next example shows how rubber lengths can be used to fine-tune the positioning of information on a line. Note that the \hfill command is, in fact, an abbreviation for \hspace{\fill}. To save typing, we also defined a command with an optional argument, \HS, which behaves like \hfill when used without an argument but can be made less or more flexible than that command by specifying the stretchability (a value of 1 has the same effect as \hfill).

```
\newcommand{\HS}[1][1.]{\hspace{\stretch{#1}}}
\begin{center}
left \hfill                                 right\\
left \HS[2]\fbox{$\frac{2}{5}$}\HS[5]        right\\
left \HS           middle \hfill             right\\
left \hrulefill\ middle \hrulefill\          right\\
left \dotfill\                               right\\
left \dotfill\ \HS[.5] \dotfill\             right\\
left \dotfill\ \HS        \dotfill\          right\\
left \dotfill\ \HS[2.] \dotfill\             right
\end{center}
```

left   right
left $\frac{2}{5}$ right
left   middle   right
left _____ middle _____   right
left .... right
left .... right
left .... right
left .... right

A-2-8

Vertical space

A vertical space is produced with the \vspace command, which works similarly to \hspace. In particular, a \vspace* command generates vertical space that is never eliminated, even when it falls on a page break where a \vspace command would be ignored at this point. Table A.3 shows vertical space commands known to LATEX that are common to all standard classes.

LATEX users are often confused about the behavior of the \vspace command. When used inside a paragraph, the vertical space is added after the end of the line containing the \vspace; between paragraphs it behaves as you would expect.

The use of a \vspace command inside a

paragraph is perhaps a bit surprising.

```
The \vspace{3mm}use of a \verb!\vspace! command
inside a paragraph is perhaps a bit surprising.

\vspace{\baselineskip}
```

Between paragraphs, adjusting the spacing is somewhat more useful, and it allows control of the white space before and after displayed material.

```
Between paragraphs, adjusting the spacing is
somewhat more useful, and it allows control
of the white space before and after displayed
material.
```

A-2-9

Stretchable space as introduced on page 653 can also be used for vertical material. The \vfill command is, in fact, an abbreviation for a blank line followed by \vspace{\fill}. More generally, you can use the \stretch command in combination with \vspace to control the layout of a complete page. This could be useful for designing a title page: if the title should be placed one third of the way down the page, one simply has to place \vspace*{\stretch{1}} before it and \vspace*{\stretch{2}} after it.

A-2-10

Geoffrey Chaucer
The Canterbury Tales

LONDON 1400

```
\newcommand\HR{\noindent\rule{\linewidth}{1.5pt}}
\begin{titlepage}
  \vspace*{\stretch{1}}
  \HR
  \begin{flushright}
    \LARGE   Geoffrey Chaucer  \\
           The Canterbury Tales
  \end{flushright}
  \HR
  \vspace*{\stretch{2}}
  \begin{center}
    \textsc{London 1400}
  \end{center}
\end{titlepage}
```

\addvspace{*space*}

While LaTeX's user command \vspace unconditionally adds a vertical space (which is removed only at page boundaries, while its starred form even suppresses this action), there exists another command for adding vertical space that is often used in the kernel and in some package files. The \addvspace command has somewhat different semantics, and although it appears to be a user-level command judging from its name, in fact it is not.

*Use with
care — if at all*

In contrast to \vspace, the command \addvspace is allowed only in vertical mode (i.e., between paragraphs). If used in horizontal mode, it issues the famous "Something's wrong–perhaps a missing \item" error, which most LATEX users know and love. Most of the time this error has nothing to do with a missing or misplaced \item but simply signals a misplaced \addvspace command. But it shows some of the history of this command: originally, it was developed and used solely for spacing items in list environments.

The other important semantic difference between \vspace and \addvspace is that the latter adds a space whose size depends on any directly preceding space. The precise rules are inherited from LATEX 2.09 and show some strange discontinuities that nobody these days seems to be able to explain fully, though for backward compatibility the command is retained in this form. If s is the space to be added by \addvspace and ℓ is the size of the vertical space (if any) before the current point, then the following rules apply:

$$
\begin{array}{llll}
\text{If} & s < 0\text{pt} < \ell & \text{do} & \text{backup by } s \\
\text{elseif} & \ell = 0\text{pt} & \text{do} & \text{add an additional space of } s \\
& & \text{else} & \text{make a space of } \max(\ell, s) \text{ out of the two}
\end{array}
$$

If we ignore for the moment the special cases in the first two lines of the rules, then the idea behind \addvspace can be described as follows: if we have two vertically oriented constructs, such as a list and a heading, and both want to surround themselves with some vertical spacing before and after, it is probably not a good idea if both such spaces are applied if the objects directly follow each other. In that case using the maximum of both spaces is usually a better solution. This is why lists, headings, and other typeset elements use \addvspace rather than \vspace.

Surprising space size changes This has some rather surprising effects. If you have two such display objects following each other, then only the maximum of the space surrounding them is used. However, if you try to enlarge that space slightly, such as by placing \vspace{4pt} between them, then suddenly the space becomes far larger. This result occurs because in a sequence like

```
\addvspace{10pt} \vspace{4pt} \addvspace{8pt}
```

the second \addvspace is unable to see the first and therefore adds all of its space (with the result that the total space is 22pt); without the \vspace in the middle you would get 10pt total. The \vspace does not interact with the following \addvspace because it actually generates a space of 4pt followed by a space of 0pt so that the second rule applies.

If you notice that your space got too large and you reduce your correction to, say, \vspace{2pt}, nothing changes substantially (you still get 20pt). Even more surprisingly, if you try to make the original space smaller by using, say, \vspace{-3pt}, you end up with 15pt total space — still more than before.

To actually get a space of 7pt in that place, you would need to back up by 11pt. Unfortunately, there is no way to determine the size of the necessary space other than by experimenting or looking into the definitions of the objects above and below, to find out what \addvspace values are used at a given point.

The same problem arises if some other invisible object separates two consecutive \addvspace commands. For example, a color-changing command or a \label effectively hides a previous \addvspace, with the result that suddenly not the maximum, but the sum of both spaces, appears.

\addpenalty{*penalty*}

Although \addpenalty is not a spacing command, it is described here because it is intended to work together with \addvspace. A penalty is TeX's way of assigning a "badness" to breakpoints. A high penalty means that this is a bad place to break, while a negative penalty indicates to TeX that this is a rather good place to start a new line or a new page. Details of this mechanism can be found in Chapters 14 and 15 of [42].

The \addpenalty command requires a TeX penalty value as an argument (useful values are between −10000 and 10000). For example, \@startsection discussed in Chapter 2 uses \addpenalty to make the space before a heading become a good place to break (default value −300). If \addpenalty and \addvspace are mixed, then this has two effects:

- LaTeX still uses the maximum of the spaces even if \addpenalty appears between two \addvspace commands.

- LaTeX moves the potential break "visually" to the beginning of the white space, even if there is an \addvspace before the \addpenalty.

The second feature is important to avoid white space remaining at the bottom of pages. See page 771 for a discussion of how this is achieved.

A.2.5. The L3 programming layer — Computation support

In 2020 (more or less thirty years after its initial conception) the L3 programming layer has become an official part of the LaTeX format and with it huge libraries for programming if you implement a package using that layer — its reference manual alone amounts to more than 300 pages [62]. These days many packages and the new parts of LaTeX core are written using this layer, and more will follow over time.

Some parts of the layer are also very useful on the document level or in packages that are otherwise implemented in traditional LaTeX 2$_\varepsilon$ style and are therefore offered also with interfaces that can be directly used in such scenarios. In this section we look at a few that deal with floating point, integer, and length calculations. Information beyond what is presented here can be found in the reference manual [62].

\fpeval{*floating point expression*}

The expandable command \fpeval takes as its argument a floating-point expression and produces a result using the normal rules of mathematics. As this command is expandable, it can be used in places where TeX requires a number and for example within a low-level \edef operation to give a purely numerical result. As a brief overview, the floating-point expressions may comprise:

- Basic arithmetic: addition $x + y$, subtraction $x - y$, multiplication $x * y$, division x / y, square root $\sqrt{x}$, and parentheses.

- Comparison operators: $x < y$, $x <= y$, $x >? y$, $x != y$, etc.

- Boolean logic: sign sign x, negation $!\,x$, conjunction x && y, disjunction x || y, ternary operator $x ? y : z$.

- Exponentials: exp x, ln x, $x\hat{\ }y$.

- Integer factorial: fact x.

- Trigonometry: sin x, cos x, tan x, cot x, sec x, csc x expecting their arguments in radians, and sind x, cosd x, tand x, cotd x, secd x, cscd x expecting their arguments in degrees.

- Inverse trigonometric functions: asin x, acos x, atan x, acot x, asec x, acsc x giving a result in radians, and asind x, acosd x, atand x, acotd x, asecd x, acscd x giving a result in degrees.

- Extrema: max$(x_1, x_2, \ldots)$, min$(x_1, x_2, \ldots)$, abs(x).

- Rounding functions, controlled by two optional values, n (number of places, 0 by default) and t (behavior on a tie, NaN by default):

    - trunc(x, n) rounds towards zero,

    - floor(x, n) rounds towards $-\infty$,

    - ceil(x, n) rounds towards $+\infty$,

    - round(x, n, t) rounds to the closest value, with ties rounded to an even value by default, towards zero if $t = 0$, towards $+\infty$ if $t > 0$ and towards $-\infty$ if $t < 0$.

- Random numbers: rand(), randint(m, n).

- Constants: pi, deg (one degree in radians).

- Dimensions, automatically expressed in points; e.g., pc is 12.

- Automatic conversion (no need for \number) of integer, dimension, and skip variables to floating-point numbers, expressing dimensions in points and ignoring the stretch and shrink components of skips.

- Tuples: $(x_1, \ldots, x_n)$ that can be added together, multiplied or divided by a floating point number, and nested.

The next example shows a computation with input on the left as a formula and output on the right (in blue) and a random number generation and a few dice rolls, so the result of that part will vary each time you rerun the example.

```
\usepackage{color}
\newcommand\dice{\fpeval{randint(1,6)}}
```

LATEX can now compute:

$$\frac{\sin(3.5)}{2} + 2 \cdot 10^{-3} = -0.1733916138448099$$

```
\LaTeX{} can now compute:
\[ \frac{\sin (3.5)}{2} + 2\cdot 10^{-3} =
    \mathcolor{blue}{\fpeval{sin(3.5)/2 + 2e-3}}
\]
```

A random number: 0.1815724000112577 and six dice rolls: 6,1,2,1,6,4.

```
A random number: $\fpeval{rand()}$ and six dice
rolls: \dice,\dice,\dice,\dice,\dice,\dice.
```

A-2-11

\inteval{*integer expression*}

The expandable command \inteval takes as its argument an integer expression and produces a result using the normal rules of mathematics with some restrictions, as explained below. The operations recognized are +, −, *, and / plus parentheses. As this command is expandable, it can be used when TeX requires a number and, for example, within a low-level \edef operation to give a purely numerical result.

This is basically a thin wrapper for the primitive \numexpr command and therefore has some syntax restrictions. These are:

- / denotes division rounded to the closest integer with ties rounded away from zero;

- there is an error, and the overall expression evaluates to zero whenever the absolute value of any intermediate result exceeds $2^{31} - 1$, except in the case of scaling operations $a*b/c$, for which $a*b$ may be arbitrarily large;

- parentheses may not appear after unary + or −; namely, placing +(or −(at the start of an expression or after +, −, *, /, or (⟨*expr*⟩) leads to an error.

In the example we calculate $1 < \frac{5}{3} < 2$ in different ways, which according the above rules is always rounded to 2. Note the need to add 0 in the last part of the equation to avoid an unary minus in front of the open parenthesis (which would fail because of the above restriction). For comparison we also do the calculation with \fpeval, which shows that the floating-point calculation does not have this issue (but of course it is much slower as it is fully programmed in TeX macros).

$$2 = 2 = 2$$

$$1 \leq 2 \approx 1.666666666666667$$

```
\[ \inteval{5/3} = \inteval{-5/-3} = \inteval{0 - (5/-3)} \]
\[ \fpeval{floor(5/3)} \leq \fpeval{ceil(-5/-3)}
                        \approx  \fpeval{-(5/-3)} \]
```

A-2-12

\dimeval{*dimen expression*}   \skipeval{*skip expression*}

Similar to \inteval but computing a length (dimen) or a rubber length (skip) value. Both are thin wrappers around the corresponding engine primitives, which makes them fast but therefore shows the same syntax peculiars as discussed above. Nevertheless, in practice they are usually sufficient. For example,

```
\newcommand\calculateheight[1]{%
  \setlength\textheight{\dimeval{\topskip+\baselineskip*\inteval{#1-1}}}}
```

sets the \textheight to the appropriate value if a page should hold a specific number of text lines. Thus, after \calculateheight{40}, it is set to 467.08005pt, given the values \topskip (10.0pt) and \baselineskip (11.72pt) in this book.

Use \dimeval if you are interested in a rigid length as a result, and use \skipeval if the calculation involves rubber lengths and the result should also be expressed with plus and minus components; e.g., above both \topskip and \baselineskip are rubber lengths (i.e., can have plus and minus parts), but we want to calculate the necessary \textheight, which is a rigid length, so \dimeval was used.

A.3 Page markup — Boxes and rules

The theory of composing pages out of boxes lies at the very heart of TeX, and several LATEX constructs are available to take advantage of this method of composition. A *box* is a rectangular object with a height, depth, and width. Its contents can be arbitrarily complex, involving other boxes, characters, spaces, and so forth. Once built it is used by LATEX as a single, fixed object that behaves much like a (potentially huge) character. A box cannot be split and broken across lines or pages. Boxes can be moved up, down, left, and right. LATEX has three types of boxes:

LR (left-right) The contents of this box are typeset from left to right. Line breaking is impossible, and commands like \\ and \newline are ignored or produce error messages.

Par (paragraphs) This kind of box can contain several lines, which are typeset in paragraph mode just like normal text. Paragraphs are put one on top of the other. Their widths are controlled by a user-specified value.

Rule A (thin or thick) line that is often used to separate various logical elements on the output page, such as table rows and columns, and running titles and the main text.

LATEX's boxes all start a paragraph (just like characters) if used in vertical mode, while TeX's primitive box commands (e.g., \hbox) behave differently depending on where they are used. There are a number of reasons to avoid using the TeX primitives directly; see the discussion in Section A.3.5. The situation with rules is slightly different; we therefore discuss TeX's primitive rule commands below.

A.3.1 LR boxes

In this section we look at horizontally oriented boxes with and without a frame.

```
\mbox{text}                      \fbox{text}
\makebox[width][pos]{text}   \framebox[width][pos]{text}
```

The first line considers the *text* inside the curly braces as a box, without or with a frame drawn around it. For example, \fbox{some words} gives some words . The two commands on the second line are a generalization of these commands. They allow the user to specify the width of the box and the positioning of the text inside.

A-3-1

```
\makebox[5cm]{some words}        \par
\framebox[5cm][r]{some words}
```

In addition to centering the text with the positional argument ([c] (the default), you can position the text flush left ([l]) or flush right ([r]). There is also an [s] specifier that stretches your *text* from the left margin to the right margin of the box provided it contains some stretchable space (e.g., some \hspace or the predefined spaces given in Table A.2 on page 653). Interword spaces are also stretchable (and shrinkable to a certain extent), as explained on page →I 745. The appearance of frameboxes can be controlled by two style parameters:

\fboxrule The width of the lines for the box produced with the command \fbox or \framebox. The default value in all standard classes is 0.4 pt.

\fboxsep The space left between the edge of the box and its contents by \fbox or \framebox. The default value in all standard classes is 3 pt.

Any changes to these parameters obey the normal scoping rules and affect all frameboxes within the scope. The change to \fboxsep in the next example, for instance, applies only to the second box.

A-3-2

```
\fbox{Boxed Text} \hfill
\setlength\fboxrule{2pt}%
{\setlength\fboxsep{2mm}\fbox{Boxed Text}}
\hfill \fbox{Boxed Text}
```

The box commands with arguments for specifying the dimensions of the box allow you to make use of four special length parameters: \width, \height, \depth, and \totalheight. They specify the natural size of the *text*, where \totalheight is the sum of \height and \depth.

A-3-3

```
\usepackage{calc}
\framebox{ A few words of advice }              \par
\framebox[\width + 8mm][s]{ A few words of advice }
\par \framebox[1.5\width]{ A few words of advice }
```

661

Zero-width boxes are very handy if you want to put a marker on the page (e.g., for placement of figures) or to allow text to be put into the margins. The principle of operation is shown below, where a zero-width box is used to tag text, without influencing the centering. Note that the optional parameter [l] ([r]) makes the material stick out to the right (left).

A sentence.[123]
Some more text in the middle.
[321]A sentence.

```
\centering
A sentence.\makebox[0pt][l]{\textsuperscript{123}}\\
Some more text in the middle.                      \\
\makebox[0cm][r]{\textsuperscript{321}}A sentence.
```

A-3-4

⟺As seen in the margin of the current line, boxes with a vanishing width can be used to make text stick out into the margin. This effect was produced by beginning the current paragraph in the following way:

```
\noindent\makebox[0cm][r]{$\Longleftrightarrow$}%
As seen in the margin ...
```

Useful, but dangerous There are also three useful but somewhat dangerous lower-level commands you often find in package code: \llap, \clap, and \rlap. Each of them takes one mandatory argument, the material to be placed. They are implemented as simple zero-sized \hboxes whose contents stick out to the left, are centered, or to the right, respectively.

They inherit the behavior of the \hbox command; i.e., they do not start a paragraph if used in vertical mode (which is sometimes what you want), but more importantly they are not color safe unless you add an extra pair of braces in their argument.

An interesting possibility is to raise or lower boxes. This can be achieved by the very powerful \raisebox command, which has two mandatory arguments and two optional arguments:

\raisebox{*lift*}[*height*][*depth*]{*contents*}

To raise or lower the box produced from the *contents*, one specifies the amount of *lift* as a dimension, with negative values lowering the box. As with other boxes, one can make use of the special commands \height, \depth, \totalheight, or even \width to refer to the natural dimensions of the box produced from *contents*. This is used in the next example to raise the word "upward" so that the descender of the "p" aligns with the baseline and to lower the word "downward" so that it is placed completely below the baseline.

x111x upward x222x downward x333x

```
x111x \raisebox{\depth}{upward} x222x
      \raisebox{-\height}{downward} x333x
```

A-3-5

Normally, LATEX takes the added height and depth into account when calculating the distance between the lines so that a raised or lowered box can result in spreading lines apart. This can be manipulated by specifying a *height* and a *depth* that the user wants LaTeX to actually use when placing its material on the page. The second pair of lines below shows that LaTeX does not realize that text has been moved upward and downward; thus, it composes the lines as though all the text was on the baseline.

```
\begin{flushleft}
x111x \raisebox{-1ex}{downward} x222x        \\
x333x \raisebox{1ex}{upward} x444x           \\[4mm]
x111x \raisebox{-1ex}[0cm][0cm]{downward} x222x\\
x333x \raisebox{1ex}[0cm]{upward} x444x
\end{flushleft}
```

A-3-6

A somewhat more useful application is discussed in Section 6.7 on page →I 476, which addresses the subject of columns spanning multiple rows in tabular material.

A.3.2 Paragraph boxes

Paragraph boxes are constructed using the \parbox command or minipage environment. The *text* material is typeset in paragraph mode inside a box of width *width*. The vertical positioning of the box with respect to the text baseline is controlled by the one-letter optional parameter *pos* ([c], [t], or [b]).

\parbox[*pos*]{*width*}{*text*}	\begin{minipage}[*pos*]{*width*} *text* \end{minipage}

The center position is the default, as shown in the next example. Note that LaTeX might produce wide interword spaces if justification is requested (default) and the measure is incredibly small.

This is the contents of the left-most parbox.   CURRENT LINE   This is the right-most parbox. Note that the typeset text looks sloppy because LaTeX cannot nicely balance the material in these narrow columns.

```
\parbox{.3\linewidth}{This is
   the contents of the left-most
   parbox.}
\hfill CURRENT LINE \hfill
\parbox{.3\linewidth}{This is
   the right-most parbox.
   Note that the typeset text
   looks sloppy because \LaTeX{}
   cannot nicely balance the
   material in these narrow
   columns.}
```

A-3-7

The minipage environment is very useful for the placement of material on the page. In effect, it is a complete miniversion of a page and can contain its own footnotes, paragraphs, and array, tabular, multicols, and other environments. Note, however, that it cannot contain floats or \marginpar commands, but it can appear inside figure or table environments, where it is often used for constructing a pleasing layout of the material inside the float. A simple example of a minipage

663

environment at work is given below. The baseline is shown with an en-dash generated by the command \HR. Note the use of the *pos* placement parameter ([c], [t], or [b]) on the three minipage environments.

```
\newcommand\HR{\rule{.5em}{0.4pt}}
\HR\begin{minipage}[b]{12mm}
           A A A A A A A A A A A A A A
\end{minipage}\HR
\begin{minipage}[c]{12mm}
           B B B B B B B B B B B B B B B B B B B B B B B B
\end{minipage}\HR
\begin{minipage}[t]{12mm}
           C C C C C C C
\end{minipage}\HR
```

```
A A A A
A A A A   B B B B
A A A A   B B B B
_A A A  _ B B B B _ C C C C_
          B B B B   C C C
          B B B B
          B B B B
```

A-3-8

If you desire more complicated alignments, then you might have to stack the different minipage environments. Compare the behavior of the next examples. Below, we try to align the two leftmost blocks at their top and align the resulting block at the bottom with a third block by adding another level of minipages.

```
\newcommand\HR{\rule{.5em}{0.4pt}}
\HR\begin{minipage}[b]{30mm}
      \begin{minipage}[t]{12mm}
            A A A A A A A A A A A A A A
      \end{minipage} xx  \begin{minipage}[t]{12mm}
            B B B B B B B B B B B B B B B B B B B B B B B B
      \end{minipage}
\end{minipage}\HR
\begin{minipage}[b]{12mm}  C C C C C C C \end{minipage}\HR
```

```
               C C C C
_A A A A xx B B B B_C C C _
A A A A   B B B B
A A A A   B B B B
A A A    B B B B
          B B B B
          B B B B
```

A-3-9

However, we do not get the expected result. Instead, the two top-aligned minipages inside the bottom-aligned minipage form a paragraph with a single line (the minipages are considered to be large units in the line containing xx). Thus, the bottom line of the outer minipage is still the one containing the xx characters. To prevent this we need to add some invisible space after the paragraph, as shown next.

```
\newcommand\HR{\rule{.5em}{0.4pt}}
\HR\begin{minipage}[b]{30mm}
      \begin{minipage}[t]{12mm}
            A A A A A A A A A A A A A A
      \end{minipage} xx  \begin{minipage}[t]{12mm}
            B B B B B B B B B B B B B B B B B B B B B B B B
      \end{minipage}
      \par\vspace{0mm}  % modification to previous example
\end{minipage}\HR
\begin{minipage}[b]{12mm}  C C C C C C C \end{minipage}\HR
```

```
A A A A xx B B B B
A A A A   B B B B
A A A A   B B B B
A A A    B B B B
          B B B B  C C C C
_         B B B B_C C C _
```

A-3-10

In the case below, the two rightmost environments are aligned at their top inside another enclosing environment, which is aligned at its bottom with the first one. If you compare it with the previous example, then you see that you obtain a quite different result, although the sequence of alignment parameters is the same. Only the stacking order of the minipage environments is different.

```
\newcommand\HR{\rule{.5em}{0.4pt}}
\HR\begin{minipage}[b]{12mm}
        A A A A A A A A A A A A A A A \end{minipage}\HR
\begin{minipage}[b]{30mm}
  \begin{minipage}[t]{12mm}
            B B B B B B B B B B B B B B B B B B B B B B B B
  \end{minipage} xx
  \begin{minipage}[t]{12mm}  C C C C C C C  \end{minipage}
  \par\vspace{0mm}
\end{minipage}\HR
```

                    B B B B xx C C C C
                    B B B B   C C C
        A A A A B B B B
        A A A A B B B B
        A A A A B B B B
A-3-11 ˍΛ A A ˍB B B B   ˍ

Again, we had to add some vertical space to achieve alignment. This does not, however, always produce the desired result. If, for instance, a letter with a descender appears in the last line of the stacked minipage, as in the example below, then the alignment of the baselines is not perfect.

```
\newcommand\HR{\rule{.5em}{0.4pt}}
\HR\begin{minipage}[b]{12mm}
        A A A A A A A A A A A A A A A \end{minipage}\HR
\begin{minipage}[b]{30mm}
  \begin{minipage}[t]{12mm}
            B B B B B B B B B B B B B B B B B B B B B B B B gg jj
  \end{minipage} xx
  \begin{minipage}[t]{12mm}  C C C C C C C  \end{minipage}
  \par\vspace{0mm}
\end{minipage}\HR
```

                    B B B B xx C C C C
                    B B B B   C C C
                    B B B B
        A A A A B B B B
        A A A A B B B B
        A A A A B B B B
A-3-12 ˍA A A ˍgg jj   ˍ

To correct this problem, you have to add (negative) vertical space that compensates for the depth of the letters.

Perhaps the easiest way (albeit the most dangerous) is to use the TeX primitive \prevdepth. This dimension register can be used only in vertical mode (i.e., after a paragraph has ended) and contains the depth of the previous line. In the next example this primitive is used to back up by this amount, thereby pretending that the bottom of the box is located at the baseline of the last line.

When using \prevdepth in this way, one has to be careful. As already mentioned, it gives an error if used outside vertical mode. Furthermore, TeX overloads this primitive by setting it to −1000pt at the beginning of a vertical box and after a horizontal rule.[1] Thus, using \vspace* instead of \vspace in the example would give a nasty surprise, because

Surprising effects of \prevdepth

---

[1] TeX uses \prevdepth to calculate the interline space needed, and −1000pt indicates that this space should be suppressed.

\vspace* actually puts in an invisible rule to ensure that the space survives at a page break. As a result, the value of \prevdepth inside would be −1000pt, and we would effectively be adding a space of 1000 points at the bottom of the box.

```
                              \newcommand\HR{\rule{.5em}{0.4pt}}
                              \HR\begin{minipage}[b]{12mm}
                                      A A A A A A A A A A A A A A A \end{minipage}\HR
        B B B B xx C C C C    \begin{minipage}[b]{30mm}
        B B B B     C C C       \begin{minipage}[t]{12mm}
        B B B B                     B B B B B B B B B B B B B B B B B B B B B B gg jj
A A A A B B B B                   \par\vspace{-\prevdepth}
A A A A B B B B                 \end{minipage} xx
A A A A B B B B                 \begin{minipage}[t]{12mm}  C C C C C C C  \end{minipage}
_A A A  _gg jj        −         \par\vspace{0pt}
                              \end{minipage}\HR
```

A-3-13

Sometimes it is helpful to predefine the vertical dimension of a paragraph box. For this purpose, today's LATEX offers additional optional arguments for \parbox and the minipage environment.

```
\parbox[pos][height][inner-pos]{width}{text}
\begin{minipage}[pos][height][inner-pos]{width}
    text
\end{minipage}
```

The *inner-pos* argument determines the position of the *text* within the box. It can be t, c, b, or s. If not specified, the value of *pos* is used. You can think of *height* and *inner-pos* as the vertical equivalent of the *width* and *pos* arguments of a \makebox. If you use the s position, the *text* is vertically stretched to fill the given *height*. Thus, in this case you are responsible for providing vertically stretchable space if necessary, using, for example, the \vspace command.

As with the other box commands you can use \height, \totalheight, and so on to refer to the natural dimensions of the box when specifying the optional argument.

```
                        \usepackage{calc}
                        xx \fbox{\parbox[b][\height+\baselineskip][s]
                                      {20mm}
                                      {Some text on top. \par\vfill
                                      And a few lines on the
                                      bottom of the box.}}
                        \fbox{\parbox[b][\height+\baselineskip][s]
                                      {20mm}
                                      {This time a few lines on the
                                      top of the box. But only one
                                      line \par\vfill down here.}} xx
```

A-3-14

| Some text on top. | This time a few lines on the top of the box. But only one line |
| And a few lines on the bottom of the box. | down here. |

A.3.3 Rule boxes

LaTeX's rule boxes are drawn with the \rule command:

> \rule[*lift*]{*width*}{*height*}

If we write \rule[4pt]{2cm}{1mm}, then we get a 2cm long rule that is 1mm thick and raised 4pt above the baseline: ▬▬▬▬▬. The \rule command can also be used to construct rule boxes with zero width, that is, invisible rules (also called *struts*). These struts are useful if you need to control the height or width of a given box (for example, to increase the height of a box framed with \fbox or \framebox or to adjust locally the distance between rows in a table). Compare the following:

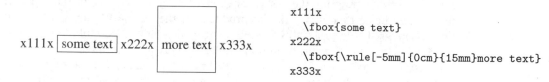

```
x111x
  \fbox{some text}
x222x
  \fbox{\rule[-5mm]{0cm}{15mm}more text}
x333x
```

A-3-15

As mentioned earlier, LaTeX makes boxes (including rules) behave like characters. For example, if used outside a paragraph, they automatically start a new paragraph. With rules this is not always the desired behavior. To get a rule between two paragraphs, for instance, we have to use \noindent to suppress a paragraph indentation; otherwise, the line would be indented and stick out to the right.

... Some text for our page that might get reused over and over again.

———————————————————————————
A following paragraph. Some text for our page that might get reused over and over again.

```
\newcommand\sample{ Some text for our page
  that might get reused over and over again.}
\ldots \sample                        \par
\noindent\rule{\linewidth}{0.4pt} \par
A following paragraph. \sample
```

A-3-16

Due to this behavior, the rule sits on the baseline of a one-line paragraph and is therefore visually much closer to the following paragraph. To place it at equal distance between the two lines, one could use the optional *lift* argument, but determining the right value (roughly 2.5pt in this particular case) remains a matter of trial and error.

One solution is to suppress the generation of interline space, using the low-level TeX command \nointerlineskip, and to add the necessary spaces explicitly as shown in the next example. This time we omit \noindent so that the rule is indented by \parindent, and we use calc to calculate the rule width such that it leaves a space of size \parindent on the right as well.

... Some text for our page that might get reused over and over again.

———————————————————————
A following paragraph. Some text for our page that might get reused over and over again.

```
\usepackage{calc}    % \sample as before
\ldots \sample                        \par
\nointerlineskip \vspace{5.8pt}
\rule{\linewidth-2\parindent}{0.4pt}\par
\nointerlineskip \vspace{5.8pt}
A following paragraph. \sample
```

A-3-17

667

	width	height	depth
\hrule	*	0.4pt	0.0pt
\vrule	0.4pt	*	*

Table A.4: Default values for TEX's rule primitives

The sum of the vertical spaces used plus the height of the rule amounts to 12 points (i.e., \baselineskip). However, this does not make the baselines of the two paragraphs 12 points apart; rather, it makes the distance from the bottom of the last line in the first paragraph (i.e., as produced by the "g" in "again") to the top of the first line in the next paragraph (i.e., as produced by the "A") be 12 points. Thus, if the text baselines should preferably fall onto a grid, a variant of Example A-3-16 on the previous page using the optional *lift* argument is more appropriate.

Instead of using \rule together with \nointerlineskip, package or class writers often use the primitive TEX rule commands. They have the advantage of automatically suppressing interline space and do not require you to specify all dimensions. On the downside, they have an unusual syntax and cannot be used if the rule needs horizontal or vertical shifting, as in the previous example.

```
\hrule height height depth depth width width \relax
\vrule height height depth depth width width \relax
```

The \hrule primitive can be used only between paragraphs, while the \vrule primitive has to appear within paragraphs. If encountered in the wrong place, the commands stop or start a paragraph as necessary. The commands can be followed by one or more of the keywords height, depth, and width together with a dimension value. Any order is allowed, and missing keywords get the defaults shown in Table A.4. An asterisk in that table means that the rule extends to the boundary of the outer box. The \relax command at the end is not required but ensures that TEX knows that the rule specification has ended and does not misinterpret words in the text as keywords.

In the next example we use the default value for \hrule, resulting in a rule of 0.4pt height running through the whole galley width (because this is effectively the next outer box).

```
% \sample as before
\ldots \sample

\vspace{6pt}\hrule\relax\vspace{6pt}
A following paragraph.
\vrule height 12pt width 2pt\relax \
\sample
```

... Some text for our page that might get reused over and over again.

A following paragraph. | Some text for our page that might get reused over and over again.

A-3-18

If you are interested in dashed rules, take a look at the dashrule package by Scott Pakin, which implements an \hdashrule command that can be used in place of

\rule. The first optional argument specifies the vertical placement, and the second handles the alignement of the dashes: by default the dashes are always in the same position on different lines, c centers the dash pattern in the available space, and x expands the pattern to fill the available space; i.e., it usually alters the spaces between the dashes. For more details see the package documentation.

```
                                       \usepackage{dashrule}
A————————————————————Z                 A\rule{5cm}{2pt}Z                          \par
A————————————————————Z                 A\hdashrule{5cm}{2pt}{}Z                    \par
A — — — — — — — Z                       A\hdashrule[.6ex]{5cm}{1pt}{10pt}Z         \par
A - - - - - - - - - - - Z               A\hdashrule[.6ex]{5cm}{1pt}{5pt 5pt}Z      \par
A ▬ ▬ ▬ ▬ ▬ ▬ Z                         A\hdashrule[-1pt]{5cm}{2pt}{5mm 1mm}Z      \par
A▬ ▬ ▬ ▬ ▬ ▬ Z                          A\hdashrule[-1pt][c]{5cm}{2pt}{5mm 1mm}Z   \par
A▬ ▬ ▬ ▬ ▬ ▬ Z                          A\hdashrule[-1pt][x]{5cm}{2pt}{5mm 1mm}Z   \par
A ·-·-·-·-·-·-·- Z                      A\hdashrule{5cm}{1pt}{2pt 4pt 6pt 4pt}Z    \par
```

A-3-19

A.3.4 Manipulating boxed material

Material can be typeset once and then stored inside a named box, whose contents can later be retrieved.

\newsavebox{*cmd*}	Declare box
\sbox{*cmd*}{*text*}	Fill box
\savebox{*cmd*}[*width*][*pos*]{*text*}	Fill box
\usebox{*cmd*}	Use contents

The command \newsavebox globally declares a command *cmd* (for example, \mybox), which can be thought of as a named bin. Typeset material can be stored there for later (multiple) retrieval.

The \sbox and \savebox commands are similar to \mbox and \makebox, except that they save the constructed box in the named bin (previously allocated with \newsavebox) instead of directly typesetting it. The \usebox command then allows the nondestructive use of the material stored inside such named bins. You can reuse the same bin (e.g., \mybox) several times within the scope of the current environment or brace group. It always contains what was last stored in it.

```
\newsavebox{\myboxa}\newsavebox{\myboxb}
\sbox{\myboxa}{inside box a}
\savebox{\myboxb}[2cm][l]{inside box b}
    x1x \usebox{\myboxa} x2x \usebox{\myboxb} x3x
\savebox{\myboxb}[2cm][r]{inside box b}
    \par
    x1x \usebox{\myboxa} x2x \usebox{\myboxb} x3x
```

x1x inside box a x2x inside box b   x3x
x1x inside box a x2x   inside box b x3x

A-3-20

Be careful not to use the command name \mybox directly, because it contains only the TeX register number of the box in question. As a consequence, \mybox on its own merely typesets the character at the position corresponding to the box number in the current font. Thus, you should manipulate boxes exclusively using the commands described above.

In addition to the above commands, there exists the `lrbox` environment with the following syntax:

```
\begin{lrbox}{cmd}
  text
\end{lrbox}
```

Here *cmd* should be a box register previously allocated with `\newsavebox`. The environment `lrbox` saves the *text* in this box for later use with `\usebox`. Leading and trailing spaces are ignored. Thus, `lrbox` is basically the environment form of `\sbox`. You can make good use of this environment if you want to save the body of some environment in a box for further processing. For example, the following code defines the environment `fcolumn`, which works like a column-wide `minipage` but surrounds its body with a frame.

```
\usepackage{calc}
\newsavebox{\fcolbox} \newlength{\fcolwidth}
\newenvironment{fcolumn}[1][\linewidth]
  {\setlength{\fcolwidth}{#1-2\fboxsep-2\fboxrule}%
    \begin{lrbox}{\fcolbox}\begin{minipage}{\fcolwidth}}
  {\end{minipage}\end{lrbox}\noindent\fbox{\usebox{\fcolbox}}}
\begin{fcolumn}    In this environment verbatim text like
    \verb=\fcolbox= can be used.                          \end{fcolumn}
```

In this environment verbatim text like \fcolbox can be used.

A-3-21

The above definition is interesting in several respects. The environment is defined with one optional argument denoting the width of the resulting box (default `\linewidth`). On the next line we calculate (using the `calc` package) the internal line length that we have to pass to the `minipage` environment. Here we have to subtract the extra space added by the `\fbox` command on both sides. Then the `lrbox` and `minipage` environments are started to typeset the body of the `fcolumn` environment into the box `\fcolbox`. When the end of the environment is reached, those environments are closed. Then the `\fcolbox` is typeset inside an `\fbox` command. The `\noindent` in front suppresses any indentation in case the environment is used at the beginning of a paragraph or forms a paragraph by itself.

A.3.5 Box commands and color

Even if you do not intend to use color in your own documents, by taking note of the points in this section you can ensure that your class or package is compatible with the color package. This may benefit people who choose to use your class or package together with the color package extensions.

The simplest way to ensure "color safety" is to always use LᴬTᴇX box commands rather than TᴇX primitives — that is, to use `\sbox` rather than `\setbox`, `\mbox` rather than \hbox, and \parbox or the minipage environment rather than \vbox. The LATEX box commands have new options that make them as powerful as the TEX primitives.

As an example of what can go wrong, consider that in {\ttfamily *text*} the font is restored just *before* the }, whereas in the similar-looking construct {\color{green} *text*} the color is restored just *after* the final }. Normally, this distinction does not matter. But consider a primitive TEX box assignment such as

```
\setbox0=\hbox{\color{green} some text}
```

Now the color-restore operation occurs after the } and so is *not* stored in the box. Exactly which bad effects this introduces depends on how color is implemented: the problems can range from getting the wrong colors in the rest of the document to causing errors in the Device Independent File Format (DVI) driver used to print the document.

Also of interest is the command \normalcolor. This is normally just \relax (i.e., does nothing), but you can use it like \normalfont to set regions of the page, such as captions or section headings, to the "main document color".

A.4 LATEX's hook management

Hooks are places in the code where packages can add code, for example, to do some initialization or to execute some final cleanup. In the past LATEX offered just a few heavily used hooks, e.g., \AtBeginDocument. Every other alteration or addition made by a package was done by overwriting existing kernel code, leading to all kinds of known issues. Furthermore, these hooks simply stored code added to them in the order it was added to the hook, which resulted in conflicts if packages were loaded in the wrong order.

Therefore, in 2020, a new hook management system and a larger number of hooks were added to LATEX, into which packages can add code in a controlled manner, avoiding the need for patching commands. The new system provides standard interfaces for declaring and using hooks, including ways to order code added to hooks by different packages in order to resolve package loading problems, and plenty more.

A.4.1 Working with existing hooks

We first discuss how you use existing hooks. Later sections then deal with adding new hooks to your own code. To add code to a hook defined by a package or by the LATEX kernel (or remove code from it) you use one of the declarations discussed below. *Adding code to* *hooks* One of the important aspects of this process is that you can do that even before the hook is officially made available. This allows you to add code to hooks defined in a package even if that package is not yet loaded. If this hook never gets defined (because the package is not loaded), then your code is dropped at \begin{document}. This solves some of the issues that made loading order of packages in the past so fragile.

> \AddToHook{*hook*}[*label*]{*code*}   \RemoveFromHook{*hook*}[*label*]

To add code to a hook you call \AddToHook with the name of the *hook* as the first mandatory argument and the *code* to add to the hook as the second. The optional *label* is normally not needed; but it can be used to identify the *code* within the *hook*. By default, this *label* is automatically determined to be the package or class name if used in a package or class or the special string top-level if used in the preamble or the body of the document.[1]

If several calls to \AddToHook use the same *label* (and the same *hook* name), their code is combined and becomes a single chunk of "labeled" code.

Code added this way to hooks is executed whenever the hook is executed, until it is again removed from it. To remove code from an hook you call \RemoveFromHook with the *hook* name as a mandatory argument. The default for the optional *label* is determined as described above; i.e., it needs to be given only if you want to remove a specific chunk, which is not the default. You can also use the special notation * in the optional argument in which case all code is removed (not recommended unless you know for sure what went into the hook).

Available hooks already provided by LATEX are discussed later. For the next example we just use one without much explanation and add some code to it. The hook cmd/quote/after is called at the beginning of the body of \begin{quote}; thus, any change we make is local to the environment. To this hook we add code to color the text blue. This is done without specifying a label, so the label used internally is top-level because we are in the preamble of the document. In addition, we add another chunk of code to specify \footnotesize as the font size. This time we use an explicit label named quotesize.[2]

Later in the document body we call \RemoveFromHook without giving a label. Thus, the code removed is the one belonging to the default label, which is top-level, and therefore the last quote appears black again. If we would have used the quotesize label instead, the quote would have been normal-sized again but still blue, and if we had used *, we would have gotten a standard quote environment again.

All quotes are in blue:

> The Quote.

and in a smaller typeface:

> Another Quote.

but this one is black:

> Final Quote!

```
\usepackage{color}
\AddToHook{cmd/quote/after}{\color{blue}}
\AddToHook{cmd/quote/after}[quotesize]{\footnotesize}

All quotes are in blue:  \begin{quote} The Quote. \end{quote}
and in a smaller typeface:
                        \begin{quote} Another Quote. \end{quote}
\RemoveFromHook{cmd/quote/after}
but this one is black: \begin{quote} Final Quote! \end{quote}
```

A-4-1

---

[1]Code labeled with top-level is special, because it is normally executed last in a hook, which means that code added in the preamble comes after code added by packages; see page 685 for details. This is even the case if the packages are loaded later in the preamble.

[2]You can think of the quotesize chunk being defined in a package with that name. Otherwise, there is little reason to make two separate declarations, unless you really want to partially retract the code you put into the hook as is done in the example.

Please do not mistake this example as the suggested way to alter the behavior of environments such as quote. It was just meant to show in a simple example how the commands \AddToHook and \RemoveFromHook work. The hook we used is one of the generic command hooks (discussed below) that exists for every command. By using it we have made use of knowledge about internal implementation details (namely, that at some point \begin{quote} calls \quote), which is seldom a good idea.

\AddToHookNext{*hook*}{*code*}   \ClearHookNext{*hook*}

Sometimes it is useful to execute code only once, i.e., just the next time a hook is called. In theory you could achieve this by including an appropriate \RemoveFromHook in the code added with \AddToHook, but the hook management offers a more convenient way. The declaration \AddToHookNext adds *code* to the *hook* that is executed only once and then automatically removed again. Because this is one-off code, it is not labeled, and it is always added to the end of all hook code so that it can overwrite code in other chunks. Typical use cases for \AddToHookNext are the hooks related to shipping out pages; e.g., you may want to use a special background on the next page.

Even though it seems logical that one adds only code for the next invocation of a hook with the intention to see it run, there are some use cases where one may need to cancel that later, and for this \ClearHookNext can be used.

Different hook flavors

Hooks can be classified in several ways. Most of them appear in code that can be used multiple times in a document, and each time this happens, the code currently associated with the hook is executed. Such hooks are called "Normal Hooks", and they make up the majority.

Normal Hooks

Some hooks, however, can be executed only once, for example, any hooks inside \begin{document}, because this environment is executed only once. It therefore makes little sense to add new hook code after such hooks have executed or to keep the code associated with the hooks after that point.

One-time Hooks

For these "One-time Hooks", LATEX applies the following strategy: the *code* in any \AddToHook for such a hook that happens during or after the hook is invoked is immediately executed, and not stored away for future invocations. For \AddToHookNext this is not done, so if this is used after the one-time hook has executed, it is simply never run.[1] In contrast, adding code with \AddToHook during the execution of normal hooks just saves the code away for use in the next invocation, which allows you to build up some chains: do this on the next invocation, do that on the one thereafter, and so forth.

\AddToHookNext *acts in a special way with one-time hooks!*

Some hooks (whether normal or one-time) come in pairs, for example, the hooks file/before and file/after, which are executed before and after the loading of every file. Typically the second of such hooks is implemented as a "Reversed Hook". This means that if you push several code chunks into both hooks, say, labeled A,

Reversed Hooks

---

[1]This gives you a choice: should your *code* always run, or should it run only exactly at the point the one-time hook is executed and, if that is not possible, then not at all?

B, and C and they get executed in one order in the first hook, then the execution order in the reversed hook is exactly the opposite. The reason for this behavior is that it allows you put environments into such hook code chunks, e.g., opening an environment in chunk A of the first hook and closing it in chunk A of the second hook. Without reversing the execution order on the second hook you would get mismatched environments, if environments are added to several chunks. Again, \AddToHookNext acts in a special way on reversed hooks, in that it remains being executed at the very end, i.e., does not participate in order reversal. This means that you cannot employ it for the use case outline above, but it gives you the opportunity to "undo" some settings made by other hook chunks just for the next invocation.

\AddToHookNext acts in a special way with reversed hooks!

There is one further category: some hooks are so called "Generic Hooks". Normally a hook has to be explicitly declared before it can be used in code. This ensures that different packages are not using the same hook name for unrelated purposes—something that would result in absolute chaos. However, there are a number of "standard" hooks where it is unreasonable to declare them beforehand; e.g., each and every command has (in theory) an associated before and after hook. In such cases, i.e., for command, environment, or file hooks, they can simply be used by adding code to them with \AddToHook. For more specialized generic hooks, e.g., those provided by babel, you have to additionally enable them with \ActivateGenericHook as explained below.

Generic Hooks

Displaying current hook status and data

To show data about a hook there are two declarations available. For developers there are also a number of conditionals that let you provide code that acts differently based on the status of a hook. Such conditionals are rather special, and if you need them, consult the hook management documentation [74].

```
\ShowHook{hook}      \LogHook{hook}
```

The \ShowHook command gives you an overview about the code chunks that have been added to a particular *hook* including information about the order they are executed. If used in interactive mode, the command stops with the usual TEX error prompt to allow you to interface with the program. The command \LogHook produces the same information but simply writes it into the transcript file so that you can look at it afterwards.

Assume we have added the following three lines to the end of the preamble of Example A-4-1 on page 672:

```
\AddToHook{cmd/quote/after}[family]{\sffamily}
\AddToHookNext{cmd/quote/after}{\itshape}
\ShowHook{cmd/quote/after}
```

then this gives us the following output:

```
-> The hook 'cmd/quote/after':
> Code chunks:
>     quotesize -> \footnotesize
```

```
>        family -> \sffamily
> Document-level (top-level) code (executed first):
>        -> \color {blue}
> Extra code for next invocation:
>        -> \itshape
> Rules:
>        ---
> Execution order (after reversal):
>        family, quotesize.
```

You can see that the hook now contains two named code chunks with the labels quotesize and family, and it also shows the code associated with them. The top-level code is \color{blue} and it is executed first, and there is \itshape as extra code for the next invocation. There are no special rules (for code chunk ordering — discussed below). At the end, the execution order of the chunks is given, in this case family followed by quotesize, i.e., in reverse of the declaration order. The reason for this is that cmd/quote/after is implemented as a reversed hook.

Important generic hooks are available out of the box

In this section we briefly discuss a number of important hooks made available by LATEX. This is not an exhaustive list, but one that is intended as an overview about those hooks that you are more likely to need occasionally. There are many more, and over time LATEX will get additional ones for special use cases.

Every environment offers a set of four generic hooks. There is the pair of hooks that are executed before and after the environment and that are therefore not restricted by the environment scope. These "outer" hooks are called env/⟨*env*⟩/before and env/⟨*env*⟩/after. You can think of them as being equivalent to placing your code before \begin{*env*} and after \end{*env*} on each occasion the environment is used. In addition, we have env/⟨*env*⟩/begin and env/⟨*env*⟩/end. They are both executed just in front of the code for the environment beginning and the code for its end; i.e., you can think of them as being the first code in the code arguments of \newenvironment or \NewDocumentEnvironment. Only the /after hook is implemented as a reversed hook; all others are normal hooks. Individual environments may offer additional hooks (e.g., the begindocument hooks discussed below), but these four are available with every environment.

Generic environment hooks:
env/⟨*env*⟩/before
env/⟨*env*⟩/after
env/⟨*env*⟩/begin
env/⟨*env*⟩/end

All tabulars are automatically centered and typeset in Sans Serif

```
\AddToHook{env/tabular/before}{\begin{center}}
\AddToHook{env/tabular/after}{\end{center}}
\AddToHook{env/tabular/begin}{\sffamily}
```

a b
c d

without explicitly adding center environments or \sffamily.

```
All tabulars are automatically centered and typeset in
Sans Serif \begin{tabular}{ll} a & b\\ c & d\end{tabular}
without explicitly adding \texttt{center} environments
or \verb=\sffamily=.
```

A-4-2

Generic environment hooks are never one-time hooks even with environments that are supposed to appear only once in a document. Thus, if one adds code to such hooks after the environment has been processed, it is executed only if the environment appears again, and if that does not happen, the code is never executed.

The hooks are executed only if `\begin{`*env*`}` and `\end{`*env*`}` are used. If the environment code is executed via low-level calls to `\`⟨*env*⟩ and `\end`⟨*env*⟩ (e.g., to avoid the environment grouping), they are not available. If you want them available in code using this method, you would need to add them yourself, i.e., write something like

```
\UseHook{env/quote/before}\quote
  ...
\endquote\UseHook{env/quote/after}
```

to add the outer hooks, etc.

Generic command hooks:
`cmd/`⟨*cmd*⟩`/before`
`cmd/`⟨*cmd*⟩`/after`

Similar to environments there are two generic hooks available for any LᴬTEX (document-level) command — in theory at least. These are `cmd/`⟨*cmd*⟩`/before` and `cmd/`⟨*cmd*⟩`/after` (the latter implemented as a reversed hook). In practice there are restrictions, and especially the `/after` hooks work only with a subset of commands. Details about these restrictions are documented in [74]. Over time more and more of them will be removed, or at least you get a suitable warning, but for now you may have to try to see if the generic hooks work for a specific command.

We give two examples. If you want all `\section` commands in your document to start a new page, then, instead of redefining this command, you could simply issue a `\newpage` in front of each, or, using the hook mechanism, specify

```
\AddToHook{cmd/section/before}{\newpage}
```

Our second example is using a `cmd/`⟨*cmd*⟩`/after` hook: remember that `\colon` in the amsmath package uses noticeably wider spacing compared to the usage in standard LᴬTEX. If you prefer less space there, you could always follow the command with `\!` (a negative thin space), or you could use a hook to insert it for you. In the example we use `\AddToHook` in the middle of the document to be able to show the difference. However, in a real document you should instead apply it in the preamble.

$f : A \to B$ in standard LᴬTEX
$f : A \to B$ in amsmath
$f : A \to B$ in our version

```
\NewCommandCopy\ltxcolon\colon  % save LaTeX's definition
\usepackage{amsmath}
$ f \ltxcolon A\to B $ \hfill in standard \LaTeX \par
$ f \colon    A\to B $ \hfill in \texttt{amsmath}\par
\AddToHook{cmd/colon/after}{\!}
$ f \colon    A\to B $ \hfill in our version
```

A-4-3

But even that could be improved upon — after all, our change should be applied only if the amsmath package was loaded or will be loaded later in the preamble of the document, but not when `\colon` retains its standard LᴬTEX meaning. To achieve this with ease you need to use two (nested) generic hooks as follows:

[Ulrike]:
Hooks are fun!

```
\AddToHook{package/amsmath/after}{\AddToHook{cmd/colon/after}{\!}}
```

Here we use a generic `package/`⟨*name*⟩`/after` hook to ensure that our cmd hook is applied only after the package was loaded, if it is loaded at all. This hook is one of a dozen hooks related to file loading that can often be useful.

For each file that is loaded by LATEX, regardless[1] of how this is done, e.g., with \input, \include, \usepackage, etc., then the following four hooks are executed. Before the file we process the general file/before hook followed by the more specific file/⟨file⟩/before hook (which is activated only if the current file to load has the name ⟨file⟩), and after the file has been read, LATEX executes the hook file/⟨file⟩/after and finally file/after. As you may have guessed, the last two are reversed hooks. The ⟨file⟩ name has to be given with its extension to be recognized, even if it is .tex, so this is different from the behavior of the \input command.

Generic file hooks:
```
file/before
file/⟨file⟩/before
file/⟨file⟩/after
file/after
```

With the above four generic hooks you are already able to specify actions to be taken before or after any package or class, e.g., by using file/array.sty/after. However, packages and classes are a special group of files (which can be loaded only once), and for that reason they have their own set of hooks. The naming scheme is the same: package/before, package/⟨name⟩/before, package/⟨name⟩/after, and package/after, but there are two important differences to the file hooks: the specific hooks that include the package name expect the ⟨name⟩ without any extension, and, more importantly, they are implemented as one-time hooks. This is essential to make our earlier example involving package/amsmath/after work: if the package was already loaded, then the code in \AddToHook is immediately applied. If we had used a file hook instead (which is a normal hook), the code would have been stored away, waiting forever for a second invocation that would never happen. A similar set of hooks exist for class files; just replace package/ by class/. You are less likely to need them, but there are a number of use cases where they can be helpful.

Generic package hooks:
```
package/before
.../⟨name⟩/before
.../⟨name⟩/after
.../after
```

Generic class hooks:
```
class/before
.../⟨name⟩/before
.../⟨name⟩/after
.../after
```

The final group of file-related hooks are those specific to files loaded with an \include command. In this case we have eight instead of the usual four hooks, due to the way this command operates. As before, there is include/before and include/⟨name⟩/before, which are executed at the beginning, but only after the \include command has issued a \clearpage to start a new page and after it has changed the .aux file to use the one for the include file.[2] When \include has finished reading the include file, but *before* it issues another \clearpage to output any deferred floats, LATEX executes two extra hooks, include/⟨name⟩/end and include/end, in that order. Then comes the \clearpage followed by the now familiar hooks: include/⟨name⟩/after and include/after. Technically we are still in include modus; i.e., the .aux has not yet switched back to the one of the main document. This means any material that is typeset by any of the hooks is excluded when the file is bypassed because of an \includeonly statement.

Generic include hooks:
```
include/before
.../⟨name⟩/before
.../⟨name⟩/end
.../end
.../⟨name⟩/after
.../after
.../excluded
.../⟨name⟩/excluded
```

All four end and after hooks are reversed hooks, and the ⟨name⟩ in the hooks has to be specified without extension. Furthermore, the specific hooks involving a ⟨name⟩ are all one-time hooks, the others normal hooks.

---

[1] This is a bit of a white lie: if a file is read using internal low-level methods, such as \@input or \openin, no hooks are executed. But these are not operations available on the document level.

[2] If you really need to place code before that, you can use the hook cmd/include/before, i.e., the generic command hook for \include.

The six hooks for `\include` we have discussed so far are executed only if the file is included (or at least an attempt is made to include it). They are bypassed if the file is explicitly excluded, i.e., if an `\includeonly` statement is given that does not contain the file ⟨*name*⟩. In that case the hooks `include/excluded` and `include/⟨name⟩/excluded` are executed instead in that order.

Special hooks available in the `document` **environment**

Until 2020 LATEX offered exactly two hooks in the `document` environment that one could use to add code to: `\AtBeginDocument` and `\AtEndDocument`.

Experiences over the years have shown that these two hooks and the place where they are executed were not enough, and as part of adding the general hook management system a number of additional hooks have been added. The places for these hooks have been chosen to provide the same support as previously offered by external packages, such as `etoolbox` and others that augmented `document` to gain better control.

Hooks inside
`\begin{`*document*`}`:
`.../before`
`begindocument`
`.../end`

Inside `\begin{document}` there are now three hooks available to the programmer: `begindocument/before` is executed at the very start of the environment and could be thought of as ending the preamble. The `begindocument` hook is executed next, after the `.aux` file has been read in and most initializations are done. They can therefore be inspected and altered by the hook code. This is the place to which `\AtBeginDocument` writes, which these days is implemented by adding to this hook. After this there are a small number of further initializations that should not be altered and are therefore coming later. Neither hook should add material for typesetting because we are still in LATEX's initialization phase and not in the document body. If such material needs to be added to the document body, use the next hook instead.

The final hook is `begindocument/end`, which is executed at the end, in other words, at the beginning of the document body. The only command that follows it is `\ignorespaces`. It can therefore be used (for example by a document class) to add typesetting material at the start of the document by placing it into this hook.

```
% Assume this to be inside the document
% class, for example, as part of a ''draft''
% option declaration:
\AddToHook{begindocument/end}
          {\begin{center}%
              \fbox{Draft material}%
           \end{center}}

\usepackage{kantlipsum}

\kant[1][1]   % the text by the author ...
```

A-4-4

| Draft material |

As any dedicated reader can clearly see, the Ideal of practical reason is a representation of, as far as I know, the things in themselves; as I have shown elsewhere, the phenomena should only be used as a canon for our understanding.

All three hooks are implemented as one-time hooks. The generic hooks executed by `\begin` also exist, i.e., `env/document/before` and `env/document/begin`, but with this special environment it is better use the dedicated one-time hooks above.

LaTeX 2_ε always provided the command \AtEndDocument to add code to the execution of \end{document} just in front of the code that is normally executed there. While this was a big improvement over the situation in LaTeX 2.09, it was not flexible enough for a number of use cases, and so packages such as etoolbox, atveryend, and others patched the kernel code to add additional points where code could be hooked into. Patching kernel code in packages is always problematical because it leads to conflicts (code availability, ordering of patches, incompatible patches, etc.). For this reason these patches have been backported to the LaTeX kernel, and a number of additional hooks have been added to allow packages to add code in various places in a controlled way without the need for overwriting or patching the core code.

Hooks inside
\end{*document*}:
enddocument
.../afterlastpage
.../afteraux
.../info
.../end

The code starts as before by adding a \par and then executing the enddocument hook (which is the hook \AtEndDocument writes to). At this point there may be still unprocessed material (e.g., floats on the deferlist or text material in the galley), and the hook may add further material to be typeset. This first hook is the only one that is allowed to add material to be typeset; all later ones are supposed to only contain code that executes certain housekeeping actions. After it, \clearpage is called to ensure that all such material gets typeset. If there is nothing waiting, this \clearpage has no effect.

The next hook is enddocument/afterlastpage. As the name indicates, this hook should not receive code that generates material for further pages. It is the right place to do some final housekeeping and possibly write out some information to the .aux file (which is still open at this point to receive data, but because there are no further pages, you need to write to it using \immediate\write). It is also the correct place to set up any testing code to be run when the .aux file is re-read next. Once this hook has been executed, the .aux file is closed for writing and then read back in to do some tests (e.g., looking for missing references or duplicate labels, etc.).

After the .aux file reprocessing has finished, the hook enddocument/afteraux is executed. It is therefore a possible place for doing final checks and displaying information to the user. However, for the latter you might prefer one of the next hooks so that your information is shown after the (possibly longish) list of files if that got requested via \listfiles.

Directly following the previous hook, the hook enddocument/info is executed. It is meant to receive code that writes final information messages to the terminal. This hook already contains some code added by the kernel (under the labels kernel/filelist and kernel/warnings), namely, the list of files when \listfiles has been used and the warnings for duplicate labels, missing references, font substitutions, etc. Instead of the two hooks in succession, there could have been just a single hook, but then going before or after the kernel material would require setting up dedicated hook rules, while with two hooks you can simply select the appropriate hook.

Near the end, just before LaTeX invokes TeX's endgame processing, there is yet another hook named enddocument/end. Whether or not this will ever be needed remains to be seen, it was mainly provided because it was already part of one of the packages that was replaced by adding the hook management to LaTeX.

679

Hooks provided for \shipout operations

Hooks inside \shipout:
shipout/before
.../background
.../foreground
shipout
.../firstpage
.../lastpage
.../after

The process that ships out the final pages also offers a number of hooks. Two are of possible interest for authors; the others are most likely needed only in packages that alter the behavior of LaTeX's output routine. The hooks that are generally useful are shipout/background and shipout/foreground. Both allow you to place some material onto each page, either in the background, i.e., behind the normal page material, or in the foreground, i.e., on top of it and thus partially hiding the text.

Both hooks add a picture environment with the (0,0) coordinate in the top-left corner of the page and locally set a \unitlength of 1pt. The hooks should therefore contain only \put commands or other commands suitable within a picture environment; see Section 8.3 on page →I 602 for possibilities.

With the starting point being the top-left corner of the page, your vertical coordinate values should be negative, which needs getting used to — if your material does not show up, it is rather too likely that you placed it outside the page by using a positive value. During the shipout the background picture is printed first, then the content of the page, and finally the foreground picture, each overwriting the other.

In the next example we use the shipout/background hook to add a logo into the background of very page. Note the absolute coordinates .5\paperwidth and −.5\paperheight to position ourselves flat in the middle of the page, and then we used a \makebox(0,0) construction to center the graphic around that point. To also exhibit the shipout/foreground hook we place a colored box at the bottom left, however, this time only on the second page by using \AddToHookNext instead of \AddToHook. Of course, you cannot seriously censor material this way. First of all the page pictures are static and the text is dynamic, but more importantly the text is still inside the PDF and only hidden through overprinting.

As any dedicated reader can clearly see, the Ideal of practical reason is a representation of, as far as I know, the things in themselves; as I have shown elsewhere, the phenomena shou only be used as a canon for our understanding. The par-

alogisms of practical reason are what first give rise to the architectonic of practical reason.

As will easily be shown in the next section, reason would thereby be made to contradict, in view of these Censor this! s, the Ideal of

```
\usepackage{kantlipsum,graphicx,color}
\AddToHook{shipout/background}
  {\put(.5\paperwidth,-.5\paperheight)
    {\makebox(0,0){\includegraphics
        [scale=.7]{latex-logo}}}}
\kant[1][1-2] % text by the author ...
\AddToHookNext{shipout/foreground}
  {\put(0,-\paperheight)
    {\colorbox{red}{Censor this!}}}
\kant[1][3]   % ... more text ...
```

A-4-5

The remaining five hooks are intended for rather specialized actions. The hook shipout/firstpage places material at the very beginning of the output file and the hook shipout/lastpage at the very end — both should contain only \special or similar commands needed for post processors handling the .dvi or .pdf output.[1]

The hook shipout/before can be used to manipulate the collected page box before it is being shipped out (or even discard it); for details, see [74]. It can also be used by packages to undo their modifications if they should not be active when the

---
[1]The shipout/firstpage hook can also be set using the command \AtBeginDvi.

page is processing during shipout. For example, some packages, noticeably those that produce verbatim text, alter the definition of active characters, and these settings should not be used while a page is built just because LaTeX decided to end the page in the middle of such an environment. If such settings remain active, this can lead to very strange errors, because during the shipout \write statements may be executed, and they would find themselves suddenly in a "verbatim" context.

The hook shipout has a similar purpose but is executed right in front of the page being shipped out, i.e., after any foreground or background material has been added. Finally, shipout/after is called after the current page has been shipped out.

Note that it is not possible (or advisable) to try to use these hooks to typeset material with the intention of returning it to the main vertical list. It will go wrong and give unexpected results in many cases — for starters it will appear after the current page, not before, and with a high likelihood the vertical spacing will be wrong! *None of these hooks should be used for typesetting*

Other hooks

LaTeX also offers other hooks, e.g., for paragraph processing[1] or font selection, but most of them are for special use cases and are of little interest to most users or even package developers. Further areas are expected to get hooks added over time. This "hookification" is under active development, and the current state and pointers to the documentation are given in [74].

A.4.2 Declaring hooks and using them in code

Up to this point we have looked at how to use existing hooks that are provided by packages or the LaTeX kernel. We now look briefly at what is necessary to define new hooks and use them in your own package code. There is more to it than we can cover here — if in doubt, refer to [74] for additional details.

Hooks have global data structures associated with them, and it is therefore essential that hooks used for different tasks are distinct, i.e., have unique names. This is why they need to be declared beforehand. If two packages declare the same name as a hook, then they cannot be used together in the same document. It is therefore important to choose a good name, preferably one that is directly related to the command or environment in which the hook is used to avoid making packages unnecessarily incompatible with each other.

```
\NewHook{hook}     \NewReversedHook{hook}
\NewMirroredHookPair{hook₁}{hook₂}
```

A new hook has to be declared with \NewHook, or, if we want to declare it as a reversed hook, then with \NewReversedHook. Given that reversed hooks are usually (but not always) paired with a normal hook, there is also \NewMirroredHookPair, which is just a shorthand for calling the other two declarations in succession.

---

[1] An example for the para/before hook is shown on page →I 429.

This covers normal and reversed hooks, but as mentioned earlier, there are also generic hooks. These are not declared beforehand because "generic" means they exist with a wide variety of names, and that makes it difficult to predeclare them. They rely on the fact that their names are structured and are therefore likely to be unique. How to provide new generic hooks is discussed later.

`\UseHook{`*hook*`}`   `\UseOneTimeHook{`*hook*`}`

In your package you execute a normal *hook* code by calling `\UseHook`. This executes all code chunks defined for the hook in a predefined order (in most cases in the order the chunks got declared), followed by the code declared with `\AddToHookNext`, if any. The latter is then automatically removed after usage.

If the hook is intended to be a one-time hook, you call it with `\UseOneTimeHook` instead. In this case the hook chunks are executed as described above, but additionally LATEX records that the hook has been executed. This has the effect that any further calls to `\UseOneTimeHook` or `\UseHook` with that *hook* name as the argument do nothing. Additionally, any future `\AddToHook` declaration for that name executes immediately instead of being stored away.[1]

If you use `\UseHook` or `\UseOneTimeHook` without declaring the hook, then the call is simply ignored — see below for when this makes sense.

Setting up additional generic hooks

The generic hooks provided by LATEX, i.e., for `cmd`, `env`, `file`, `package`, `class`, and `include`, are available out of the box. You only have to use `\AddToHook` to add code to them, but you do not have to add `\UseHook` or `\UseOneTimeHook` to your code, because this is already done for you (or, in the case of `cmd` hooks, the command is patched at `\begin{document}`, if necessary).

However, if you want to offer your own generic hooks in your code, the situation is slightly different. You provide for such a generic hook by using `\UseHook` or `\UseOneTimeHook`, but *without declaring the hook* with `\NewHook`. As mentioned earlier, a call to `\UseHook` with an undeclared hook name does nothing. So as an additional setup step, you need to explicitly activate the generic hook. Note that a generic hook produced in this way is always a normal hook.

For a truly generic hook, with a variable part in the hook name, an up-front activation would be difficult or impossible, because you typically do not know what kind of variable parts may come up in real documents. For example, babel may want to provide hooks such as `babel/`⟨*language*⟩`/afterextras`. Language support in babel is often done through external language packages. Thus, doing the activation for all languages inside the core babel code is not a viable approach. Instead, it needs to be done by such language packages (or by the user who wants to use a particular hook).

Because the hooks are not declared with `\NewHook`, their names should be carefully chosen to ensure that they are (likely to be) unique. Best practice is to

---

[1] As mentioned earlier, calls to `\AddToHookNext` have a different behavior: they are simply ignored if issued too late.

include the package or command name as was done in the babel example.

```
\ActivateGenericHook{hook}
```

Once this declaration is given, the *hook* is activated, and its use with \UseHook or \UseOneTimeHook takes effect. In contrast to \NewHook (which also activates a hook), this declaration can be used multiple times.

As an example, we color German words in blue inside an English document by adding a \color statement to the generic hook babel/ngerman/afterextras and activate the hook so that it is used. Note that such declarations can happen even before babel is loaded; thus, a class can make adjustments for babel but leave it up to the user whether babel is loaded or not.

```
\AddToHook{babel/ngerman/afterextras}{\color{blue}}
\ActivateGenericHook{babel/ngerman/afterextras}
```

Text with deutschen Worten in the middle of englischem Text.

A-4-6

```
\usepackage{color} \usepackage[ngerman,english]{babel}
Text with \foreignlanguage{ngerman}{deutschen Worten} in
the middle of \foreignlanguage{ngerman}{englischem Text}.
```

Returning to black in the previous example worked only because the German text was always limited by the scope of the \foreignlanguage command. If we had used \selectlanguage or nested commands instead, the color change would persist, because none of the other languages undo it. Thus, to work in a more complex scenario, we need similar declarations for any other language to reset the color.

The generic command hooks cmd/⟨cmd⟩/before and cmd/⟨cmd⟩/after are automatically patched into the command ⟨cmd⟩ in case code has been added to the hook, i.e., a \UseHook command is added to the beginning or end of the ⟨cmd⟩ code and the hook is activated. As mentioned, for some commands such patching is not possible, and to avoid the user getting a low-level failure, LaTeX has the declaration \DisableGenericHook. It is mainly intended for command hooks that would fail, but there may be use cases where disabling other generic hooks is useful too.

Adjusting the use of ⟨cmd⟩ hooks

Instead of disabling a nonfunctional command hook, a package developer may choose to explicitly add the \UseHook call in an appropriate place when defining the ⟨cmd⟩. If that is done, it is important to also explicitly declare the hook with either \NewHook or \NewReversedHook to make it "nongeneric", because that prevents LaTeX from later patching the ⟨cmd⟩ and incorrectly adding another \UseHook.

Reordering code chunks in hooks

The default assumption is that if several packages add data to the same hook, the order of the code execution is of no importance. Of course, in real life this is unfortunately often not true, which accounts for the many package loading issues people had in the past, for which you then got advice on the Internet such as "load package A after package B and load package C always last". In many cases the underlying reason was that different \AtBeginDocument statements had to be executed in the right order.

With the new hook management system this can now often be resolved up front. If you know that the code added to a certain hook needs to be run before or after the code added by some other package, you can declare a rule that tells the hook management to arrange for the required order. If the other package is not loaded, the rule is simply ignored, and it also does not hurt if both packages declare such a rule (as long as the rules are not in conflict with each other).

`\DeclareHookRule{`*hook*`}{`*label₁*`}{`*relation*`}{`*label₂*`}`

With this declaration you define a relation between *label₁* and *label₂* for a given *hook*. There can be only a single relation between two labels for a given hook; i.e., a later `\DeclareHookRule` overwrites any previous declaration. The supported *relation*s are the following:

before or **<** Code for *label₁* comes before code for *label₂*.

after or **>** Code for *label₁* comes after code for *label₂*.

incompatible-warning Only code for either *label₁* or *label₂* can appear for that hook (a way to say that two packages—or parts of them—are incompatible). A warning is raised if both labels appear in the same hook.

incompatible-error Like `incompatible-warning`, but instead of a warning, a LATEX error is raised, and the code for both labels is dropped from that hook until the conflict is resolved.

voids Code for *label₁* overwrites code for *label₂*. More precisely, code for *label₂* is dropped for that hook. This can be used, for example, if one package is a superset in functionality of another one and therefore wants to undo code in some hook and replace it with its own version.

unrelated The order of code for *label₁* and *label₂* is irrelevant. This rule is there to undo an incorrect rule specified earlier.

As an example we find the following declaration in the fnpct package, which ensures that inside the hook `begindocument` the code labeled fnpct runs after any code labeled hyperref if present:

```
\DeclareHookRule{begindocument}{fnpct}{after}{hyperref}
```

Remember that the default label for code chunks is the current package or class name when `\AddToHook` is used without specifying an explicit label. Thus in most cases, code chunks are labeled with the package or class name from which they originate. Therefore, this declaration really means that inside `begindocument`, the code from the hyperref should run before the code from fnpct so that the latter can make use of it, regardless of the loading order of the two packages.

The `top-level` label, which by default is used to label code added in the preamble or in the document body to a hook, is special in that it is always executed *last* in a normal hook (and first in a reversed hook). It is therefore not permitted to use this label in a hook rule. The reason is that hook declarations made in such places are typically done to overwrite code by packages to the hook, and the preamble code therefore needs to come later. If that is not the right place for code to be executed, you can give it an explicit label and then add a `\DeclareHookRule` to ensure that it is executed at the right point.

The top-level label is special

`\DeclareDefaultHookRule{`*label₁*`}{`*relation*`}{`*label₂*`}`

The `\DeclareHookRule` defines a relation between two labels for a single hook. However, if there are many hooks for which this relationship holds, then it is inefficient to be forced to declare them repeatedly for all hooks. To simplify the input, as well as to clarify the situation, there is `\DeclareDefaultHookRule` that defines a default relationship between *label₁* and *label₂* for all hooks in which these labels are used. This is useful for cases where one package has a specific relation to some other package; e.g., it is incompatible or always `voids` or needs a special ordering with `before` or `after`. If necessary, you can always overwrite that default for individual hooks by also giving a `\DeclareHookRule` for a specific hook.

A.5 Control structure extensions

This section starts with the iftex package that allows you to write code that varies based on the TeX engine it gets used with. We then describe two packages that are distributed as part of the LaTeX 2ε core distribution since its introduction in 1994. Consequently, you find them used as part of many packages and classes.

The first, calc, extends LaTeX to support infix arithmetic in many commands that expect a number or a dimension as an argument. Although there are nowadays other possibilities offered by newer TeX engines and also by LaTeX directly (see Section A.2.5 on page 657), this remains useful and is used in a number of examples in this book.

The second, ifthen, defines a number of commands for conditional processing. While this was a big step forward back then and was therefore used a lot in the past, it has a number of serious limitations and a somewhat clumsy syntax. For this reason we recommend it only for very simple tasks (if at all). A lot of its functionality can already be achieved by using the new powerful command declarations described in Section A.1.4 on page 632, and for serious coding you have a much better solution with the L3 programming layer, which offers many more sophisticated conditionals that do not exhibit the limitations of ifthen. We mainly kept it in the book because of its wide use in packages, so it helps to have some basic understanding of its functionality.

ifthen is not recommended for new package developments

A.5.1 iftex — On which TeX engine are we running on?

With different TeX engines available — each of which offering one or the other feature not available in other engines — it is sometimes necessary to ensure that a document is processed with a certain engine or one from a group of engines, i.e., one of the

Unicode engines. LATEX tries fairly hard to abstract from engine peculiarities, but even so, you may find that you want to write some commands that need different implementations for different engines.

To accomplish either task, several people have written small packages that define tests to figure out if your document is processed by a specific engine. The iftex package (by the LATEX Project Team) is a consolidation package that provides such tests for most TEX engines in use, so it has effectively many authors, because it combines ideas from Heiko Oberdiek (ifluatex, ifvtex, and ifptex), Martin Scharrer (ifetex), YATO Takayuki (ifptex), Vafa Khalighi (iftex version 0.2), and Will Robertson (ifxetex) in a single package, rendering the others (except ifptex, see below) essentially obsolete by providing all of their functionality.

All tests are constructed in the same manner and rely only on low-level constructs in order to function not only in LATEX but in any flavor of TEX, hence the slightly unusual syntax. Here is an example to test for pdfTEX:

```
\ifPDFTeX
    code to execute if the engine is pdfTeX
\else
    code to execute for all other engines
\fi
```

In the *else* part you can then make further tests to distinguish between other engines as necessary. All \if... tests exist in two forms: mixed-case as above or with a name using only lowercase characters, e.g., \ifpdftex, if you prefer that. In the listing below we give only the mixed-case names because not all of them might be obvious (the lowercase ones hopefully are).

```
\ifXeTeX    \ifLuaTeX    \ifLuaHBTeX    \ifTUTeX
```

These test if the Unicode engines XƎTEX or LuaTEX are used. \ifLuaTeX is true regardless of any extension being activated, while \ifLuaHBTeX is true only if the Harfbuzz library is available in the LuaTEX engine.

The \ifTUTeX test is not strictly testing for an engine variant: it will be true if the current engine supports the primitive \Umathchardef, which is the case for XƎTEX and LuaTEX (and possibly other engines supporting Unicode), so you could write something like

```
\ifTUTeX
    \usepackage{fontspec,unicode-math}
    \setmainfont{TeX Gyre Termes}    \setmathfont{Stix Two Math}
\else
    \usepackage{newtxtext,newtxmath}
\fi
```

to make your document work with XƎTEX, LuaTEX, and pdfTEX by selecting different font packages depending on the engine.

```
\ifpTeX      \ifeTeX      \ifupTeX      \ifpTeXng
```

\ifpTeX is true when any of the pTeX engine variants (engines that support Japanese input encodings) are used. LaTeX requires the availability of the eTeX extensions, which is not the case with all variants. For this one can could test with \ifeTeX. Similarly, \ifupTeX tests for any of the upTeX variants (engines that support Japanese but with Unicode input encoding) — again you may additionally want to check for the eTeX extensions. Finally, \ifpTeXng tests for pTeX-ng (Asiatic pTeX), \ifVTeX for the commercial VTeX engine, and \ifAlephTeX for Aleph (the successor of Omega).

Note that while the iftex package provides basic support for detecting Japanese TeX variants, it is not a full replacement for the ifptex package, which has many more detailed tests for pTeX variants and is recommended if you need granular control over the Japanese TeX system in use.

```
\RequirePDFTeX        \RequireXeTeX        \RequireLuaTeX
\RequireLuaHBTeX      \RequireTUTeX        ...
```

If your document (or package) is usable only with a specific engine, then you can use one of the \Require.. commands instead of the above tests. They test for the specific engine and stop with a suitable error message if not.

```
\ifpdf
```

Several engines can produce .pdf or .dvi output and make this configurable, for example, through \pdfoutput that can be set in the format or at the very start of the document. \ifpdf can be used to test if the output format is PDF.

A.5.2 calc — Arithmetic calculations

The package calc (by Kresten Thorup and Frank Jensen) contains a set of macros for enhanced arithmetic in LaTeX. The usual arithmetic in TeX is done by simple low-level operations like \advance and \multiply. This package defines an infix notation arithmetic for LaTeX. In fact, it reimplements the LaTeX commands \setcounter, \addtocounter, \setlength, and \addtolength so that they can accept integer and length expressions rather than simple numbers and lengths.

An integer expression can contain integer numbers, TeX's integer registers, LaTeX's counters (e.g., \value{ctr}), parentheses, and binary operators (-, +, *, /). For instance, to double a counter value and additionally advance it by five:

The value is currently "2".
The value has now changed to "9".

```
\usepackage{csquotes,calc}
\newcounter{private}
\setcounter{private}{2} % initial setting for the example
The value is currently \enquote{\theprivate}.\\
\setcounter{private}{\value{private}*2 + 5}
The value has now changed to \enquote{\theprivate}.
```

A-5-1

An example is the definition of a command to print the time (note that the TᴇX register `\time` contains the number of minutes since midnight):

```
\usepackage{calc}
\newcounter{hours}\newcounter{minutes}
\newcommand\printtime{\setcounter{hours}{\time/60}%
        \setcounter{minutes}{\time-\value{hours}*60}%
        \thehours h \theminutes min}
```

The time is 14h 16min. | The time is \printtime. | A-5-2

When dealing with lengths, the subexpressions that are added or subtracted must be of the same type. That is, you cannot have "2cm+4", but an expression like "2cm+4pt" is legal because both subexpressions have dimensions. You can only divide or multiply by integers, so "2cm*4" is a legal subexpression, but "2cm*4pt" is forbidden. Also, the length part must come first in an expression; thus, "4*2cm" is not allowed.

The commands described above allow you to calculate the width of one column in an n-column layout using the following single command (supposing that the variable n is stored as the first argument of a LᴬTᴇX macro):

```
\setlength\linewidth{(\textwidth-\columnsep*(#1-1))/#1}
```

The restriction that you can only multiply and divide by integers has been relaxed for calculations on lengths (dimensions). Those operations are allowed with real numbers.

`\real{`*decimal constant*`}`   `\ratio{`*length expression*`}{`*length expression*`}`

A real number can be represented in two forms: the first command converts the *decimal constant* into a form that can be used in a calc formula. The second form denotes the real number obtained by dividing the value of the first expression by the value of the second expression.

As an example, assume you want to scale a figure so that it occupies the full width of the page (`\textwidth`). If the original dimensions of the figure are given by the length variables `\Xsize` and `\Ysize`, then the height of the figure after scaling will be:

```
\setlength\newYsize{\Ysize*\ratio{\textwidth}{\Xsize}}
```

`\widthof{`*material*`}`   `\heightof{`*material*`}`   `\depthof{`*material*`}`   `\totalheightof{`*material*`}`

These four commands typeset *material* in a horizontal box, measure the result, and then return its width, height, depth, or totalheight (i.e., the sum of height and depth) as a length value, respectively. This can in turn be used in more complex calc expressions.

The calc package is used in a few examples in this book. If you do not want to apply it, you need to express the code given in the examples in the form of basic LaTeX commands and sometimes even primitive TeX constructs. Depending on what was used, this may be easy (these days) or still rather complicated.

For example, the setting of \fcolwidth on page 670 has to be translated from

```
\setlength\fcolwidth{#1-2\fboxsep-2\fboxrule}
```

and can today be expressed simply by using \dimeval from the L3 programming layer as follows:

```
\setlength\fcolwidth{\dimeval{#1-2\fboxsep-2\fboxrule}}
```

i.e., same syntax and only one additional command. Without \dimeval it gets worse, and we end with three fairly unreadable assignments:

```
\setlength\fcolwidth{#1}%
\addtolength\fcolwidth{-2\fboxsep}%
\addtolength\fcolwidth{-2\fboxrule}
```

Obviously the infix notation provided by calc is far more readable than the above, but today you can use in most situations \dimeval, \skipeval, \inteval, or \fpeval, which also offer infix notation and achieve similarly concise results. However, expressions involving, for example, \ratio or measurement commands such as \widthof, are not easily expressible without using calc, so it remains a useful extension.

A.5.3 ifthen — Advanced control structures

Sometimes you may want to typeset different material depending on the value of a logical expression. This is possible with the standard package ifthen (originally written by Leslie Lamport and reimplemented for LaTeX2ε by David Carlisle), which defines commands for building control structures with LaTeX. Because it is compatible with the syntax and approach used for LaTeX 2.09, it has inherited a number of limitations; in particular, it is fragile depending on the tests used and so often does not work in moving arguments.

While fine for simple cases defined in the document preamble, it is not really advisable to use it for more complex coding in packages. There we recommend using the powerful functions of the L3 programming layer [62] instead.

\ifthenelse{*test*}{*then-code*}{*else-code*}

If the condition *test* is true, the commands in the *then-code* part are executed. Otherwise, the commands in the *else-code* part are executed.

A simple form of a condition is the comparison of two integers. For example, if you want to translate a counter value into English:

```
\usepackage{ifthen}
\newcommand\toEng[1]{\arabic{#1}\textsuperscript{%
 \ifthenelse{\value{#1}=1}{st}{%
  \ifthenelse{\value{#1}=2}{nd}{%
   \ifthenelse{\value{#1}=3}{rd}{%
    \ifthenelse{\value{#1}<20}{th}}%
                        {\typeout{Value too high}}}}}}
```

This is the 5th section in the 1st appendix.

```
This is the \toEng{section} section in the \toEng{chapter}
appendix.
```

A-5-3

The following example defines a command to print the time in short form. It shows how complex operations (using the calc package) can be combined with conditional control statements.

```
\usepackage{csquotes,ifthen,calc}
\newcounter{hours}\newcounter{minutes}

\newcommand{\printtime}{\setcounter{hours}{\time/60}%
        \setcounter{minutes}{\time-\value{hours}*60}%
        \ifthenelse{\value{hours}<10}{0}{}\thehours:%
        \ifthenelse{\value{minutes}<10}{0}{}\theminutes}
```

The current time is "14:16".

```
The current time is \enquote{\printtime}.
```

A-5-4

$\boxed{\texttt{\textbackslash equal}\{string1\}\{string2\}}$

The \equal command evaluates to *true* if the two strings *string1* and *string2* are equal after they have been completely expanded. You should be careful when using fragile commands in the strings; they need protection with the \protect command.

```
\usepackage{ifthen,shortvrb}  \MakeShortVerb\|
\newcommand\BB{\CC}\newcommand\CC{\DD}
\newcommand\DD{AA} \newcommand\EE{EE}
```

\BB=\EE? False.

\BB=\CC? True.

\DD=\BB? True.

```
|\BB|=|\EE|?  \ifthenelse{\equal{\BB}{\EE}}{True}{False}.\par
|\BB|=|\CC|?  \ifthenelse{\equal{\BB}{\CC}}{True}{False}.\par
|\DD|=|\BB|?  \ifthenelse{\equal{\DD}{\BB}}{True}{False}.
```

A-5-5

$\boxed{\texttt{\textbackslash boolean}\{string\} \quad \texttt{\textbackslash newboolean}\{string\} \quad \texttt{\textbackslash setboolean}\{string\}\{value\}}$

Basic TEX knows about some switches that can have the value true or false.[1] To define your own switch, use \newboolean where *string* is a sequence of letters. This switch is initially set to false. To change its value, use \setboolean where the *value* argument is either the string true or false. You can then test the value by using \boolean in the first argument of \ifthenelse. It is also possible to test all

---

[1] In the LATEX kernel they are normally built using the more primitive \newif command.

Boolean	Description
TEX switches (can only be queried)	
`hmode`	`true`, if typesetting is done in a horizontal direction (e.g., inside a paragraph or an LR box).
`vmode`	`true`, if typesetting is done vertically (e.g., if TEX is between paragraphs).
`mmode`	`true`, if TEX is typesetting a formula.
LATEX switches (read-only)	
`@twoside`	`true`, if LATEX is typesetting for double-sided printing.
`@twocolumn`	`true`, if LATEX is typesetting in standard two-column mode (`false` inside `multicols` environments).
`@firstcolumn`	`true`, if `@twocolumn` is `true` and LATEX is typesetting the first column.
`@newlist`	`true`, if LATEX is at the beginning of a list environment (set to `false` when text *after* the first `\item` command is encountered).
`@inlabel`	`true`, after an `\item` command until the text following it is encountered.
`@noskipsec`	`true`, after a run-in heading until the text following it is encountered.
LATEX switches (read-write)	
`@afterindent`	Switch checked by command `\@afterheading` (usually used in headings) to prevent (if `false`) indentation of next paragraph.
`@tempswa`	Temporary switch used internally by many LATEX commands to communicate with each other.

Table A.5: LATEX's internal `\boolean` switches

such internal flags of LATEX with this command (the most common ones are shown in Table A.5). An example could be a test to see whether a document is using a one- or two-sided layout.

| A-5-6 | Two-sided printing. | `\usepackage{ifthen}`
`\ifthenelse{\boolean{@twoside}}{Two-sided}{One-sided}` printing. |

Note that despite the similar names there is no relationship to `\IfBooleanTF` discussed in Section A.1.4 on page 632. That command can be used only to query the parsing results of commands defined with `\NewDocumentCommand`, etc.

`\lengthtest{test}`

To compare dimensions, use `\lengthtest`. In its *test* argument you can compare two dimensions (either explicit values like 20cm or names defined by `\newlength`) using one of the operators <, =, or >.

As an example, let us consider a figure characterized by its dimensions \Xsize and \Ysize. It should be made to fit into a rectangular area with dimensions \Xarea and \Yarea, but without changing the aspect ratio of the figure. The following code calculates the new dimensions of the figure (\newX and \newY). The trick is to first calculate and compare the aspect ratios of both the rectangle and the figure and then to use the result to obtain the magnification factor.

```
\newlength{\sizetmp}\newlength{\areatmp}
\setlength\sizetmp{1pt*\ratio{\Xsize}{\Ysize}}
\setlength\areatmp{1pt*\ratio{\Xarea}{\Yarea}}
\ifthenelse{\lengthtest{\sizetmp > \areatmp}}
 {\setlength\newX{\Xarea}\setlength\newY{\newX*\ratio{\Ysize}{\Xsize}}}
 {\setlength\newY{\Yarea}\setlength\newX{\newY*\ratio{\Xsize}{\Ysize}}}
```

> \isodd{*number*}

With the \isodd command you can test whether a given *number* is odd. If, for example, the string generated by a \pageref command is a valid number (as it normally is), then you can use the command in the following way:

This is an even-numbered page.	This is an odd-numbered page.
6	7

```
\usepackage{ifthen} \newcounter{pl}
\newcommand\pcheck{\stepcounter{pl}\label{pl-\thepl}%
  \ifthenelse{\isodd{\pageref{pl-\thepl}}}{odd}{even}}
This is an \pcheck-numbered page.   \newpage
This is an \pcheck-numbered page.
```

A-5-7

The \isodd command is specially tailored to support the above application even though the result of \pageref might be undefined in the first LᴬTEX run. Note that you cannot omit the \label and \pageref and instead simply use \thepage. The reason is that pages are built asynchronously. As a consequence, your code might get evaluated while a page is being built, and afterwards LᴬTEX's output routine decides to move that bit of the text to the next page, making the evaluation invalid if \thepage were used.

> \whiledo{*test*}{*do-clause*}

The \whiledo command is valuable for executing certain repetitive command sequences. The following simple example shows how the command works:

I should not talk during seminar (1). I should not talk during seminar (2). I should not talk during seminar (3). I should not talk during seminar (4).

```
\usepackage{ifthen}  \newcounter{howoften}
\setcounter{howoften}{1}
\whiledo{\value{howoften}<5}{I should not talk
  during seminar (\thehowoften).
  \stepcounter{howoften}}
```

A-5-8

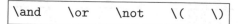

```
\and     \or     \not     \(     \)
```

Multiple conditions can be combined into logical expressions via the logical operators
(\or, \and, and \not), using the commands \(and \) as parentheses. A simple
example is seen below:

```
\usepackage{ifthen}
\newcommand{\QU}[2]{%
  \ifthenelse{\(\(\equal{#1}{ENG}\and\equal{#2}{yes}\)
    \or      \(\equal{#1}{FRE}\and\equal{#2}{oui}\)\)}%
             {''OK''}{''not OK''}}
```

You agree "OK" or don't "not OK".
D'accord "OK" ou pas "not OK"?

```
You agree \QU{ENG}{yes} or don't \QU{ENG}{no}. \par
D'accord  \QU{FRE}{oui} ou pas    \QU{FRE}{non}?
```

A-5-9

A.6 Package and class file structure

In this final section we discuss what commands are available for the authors of
package or class files. Even if you do not intend to write your own package, this
section will help you understand the structure and content of class and package files
like book or varioref and thus help you to make better use of them. Furthermore,
some of the commands for packages are sometimes also useful in the document
preamble of a document.

The general structure of class and package files is identical and consists of the
following parts:

⟨rollback information⟩
⟨identification⟩
⟨initial code⟩
⟨declaration of options⟩
⟨execution of options⟩
⟨package loading⟩
⟨main code⟩

All these parts are optional. We discuss the commands available in each of the
individual parts below. Table A.6 on the following page gives a short overview.

A number of declarations discussed below expect a *date* as one of their arguments.
Such dates can always be specified either as YYYY/MM/DD (traditional LaTeX way and
fairly readable in the author's opinion) or in ISO notation, i.e., as YYYY-MM-DD.

A.6.1 The rollback part

This first part of a package or class file provides the necessary information to roll
back the code to an earlier date or a specific release using the latexrelease package

---

Rollback part

`\DeclareRelease{`*version*`}{`*date*`}{`*file*`}`

    Declares that the *version* from a specific *date* of a package or class is stored in some *file*

`\DeclareCurrentRelease{`*version*`}{`*date*`}`

    Current version of the package or class

Identification part

`\NeedsTeXFormat{`*format*`}[`*release*`]`

    Needs to run under *format* (LaTeX2e) with a release date not older than *release*

`\ProvidesClass{`*name*`}[`*release info*`]`   or   `\ProvidesPackage{`*name*`}[`*release info*`]`

    Identifies class or package *name* and specifies *release information*

`\ProvidesFile{`*name*`}[`*release info*`]`

    Identifies other file *name* (with extension) and specifies *release information*

Declaration and processing of options (classic style)

`\DeclareOption{`*option*`}{`*code*`}`   or   `\DeclareOption*{`*code*`}`

    Declares *code* to be executed for *option*; starred form is for unknown options

`\PassOptionsToPackage{`*option-list*`}{`*package-name*`}`

    Passes *option-list* to *package-name*

`\CurrentOption`

    Refers to current option for use in `\DeclareOption*`

`\OptionNotUsed`

    For use in `\DeclareOption*` if necessary

`\ExecuteOptions{`*option-list*`}`

    Executes code for every option listed in *option-list*

`\ProcessOptions`   or   `\ProcessOptions*`

    Processes specified options for current class or package; starred form obeys the specified order

---

Declaration and processing of options (key/value style)

`\DeclareKeys[`*family*`]{`*key list with properties*`}`

    Declares *keys* and their scope

`\SetKeys[`*family*`]{`*key/value list*`}`

    Sets *keys* to values

`\ProcessKeyOptions[`*family*`]`

    Processes specified key/value options for current class/package including any global class options

`\DeclareUnknownKeyHandler[`*family*`]{`*code*`}`

    Replace the default error handler for unknown keys in *family* by executing *code* instead

---

Package loading

`\RequirePackage[`*option-list*`]{`*package*`}[`*release*`]`

    Loads *package* with given *option-list* and a release date not older than *release*

Table A.6: Commands for package and class files

or the second optional argument of \usepackage or \documentclass. See Section 2.5.5 on page →I 114 for a description of the general approach. If present, it consists of one or more \DeclareRelease declarations followed by exactly one \DeclareCurrentRelease declaration.

\DeclareRelease{*version*}{*date*}{*file*}

This declaration states that there is a release of this package or class that was made available on *date* and can be accessed as *version* (if this argument is not empty). The code for this release is stored in *file*.

If there are several declarations, then they have to be ordered by *date*, because in a rollback situation the processing stops the moment a suitable *date* is found, i.e., one that is older or equal to the requested date and the next declaration is newer than the requested date. If a search for a *version* is done, then the first line matching that is selected.

\DeclareCurrentRelease{*version*}{*date*}

This declaration describes the current release and therefore has no *file* argument. It can be given a *version* name, and it has to be given a *date*. This date should be the one when the release was first made publicly available. Because small changes and corrections are usually not tracked for use with rollback, a \ProvidesPackage line in the identification part often shows a later date.

As an example, the array package starts with the following declarations:

```
\DeclareRelease{}    {2016-10-06}{array-2016-10-06.sty}
\DeclareRelease{v2.4}{2020-02-10}{array-2020-02-10.sty}
\DeclareCurrentRelease{}{2020-10-01}

\ProvidesPackage{array}
        [2021/04/20 v2.5e Tabular extension package (FMi)]
```

This means that the newest (main) release is from 2020-10-01 and some minor fixes got added since then (so that package date is 2021/04/20), and if you roll back to a date after October 2020, you always get the latest file (no rollback). If you request an earlier date, then either array-2016-10-06.sty or array-2020-02-10.sty is loaded (based on your requested date), and the latter file is also loaded if you explicitly ask for version v2.4.

If an earlier release is selected, then processing of the current file stops, and the remainder is not looked at. This means that the files holding the earlier releases need to be complete in themselves. Typically they are just copies of the main package or class file the way it was at that point in time.

A.6.2 The identification part

This part of a class or package file is used to define the nature of the file and may also state the LATEX 2_ε distribution release minimally required.

`\ProvidesClass{`*name*`}[`*release information*`]`

A class file identifies itself with a `\ProvidesClass` command. The argument *name* corresponds to the name of the class as it is used in the mandatory argument of the `\documentclass` command (i.e., the file name without an extension). The optional argument *release information*, if present, should begin with a date in the form *YYYY/MM/DD* or *YYYY-MM-DD*, separated with a space from the version number or identification, followed optionally by some text describing the class. For example, the class report contains something like

```
\ProvidesClass{report}[2021/02/12 v1.4n Standard LaTeX document class]
```

In a document you can make use of the *release information* by specifying the date as a second optional argument to the `\documentclass` command as follows:

```
\documentclass[twocolumn]{report}[2021/02/12]
```

This enables LATEX to check that the report class used has at least a release date of 2021/02/12 or is newer. If the class file is older, a warning is issued. Thus, if you make use of a new release of a class file and send your document to another site, the people there are automatically informed if their LATEX distribution is out of date.

`\ProvidesPackage{`*name*`}[`*release information*`]`

This command identifies a package file. The structure is the same as for the `\ProvidesClass` command. Again, the date in the *release information* can be used in a second optional argument to `\usepackage` to ensure that an up-to-date version of the package file is loaded. For example:

```
\usepackage[german]{varioref}[2020/08/11]
```

`\ProvidesFile{`*file name*`}[`*release information*`]`

This command identifies any other type of file. For this reason *file name* must contain the full file name including the extension.

`\NeedsTeXFormat{`*format*`}[`*release*`]`

In addition to one of the above commands, the ⟨*identification*⟩ part usually contains a `\NeedsTeXFormat` declaration. The *format* must be the string LaTeX2e. If the optional *release* argument is specified, it should contain the release date of the required LaTeX 2_ε distribution in the form YYYY/MM/DD or YYYY-MM-DD. For example,

```
\NeedsTeXFormat{LaTeX2e}[2020/10/01]
```

would require at least the LaTeX 2_ε release distributed on October 1, 2020. If this command is present, anyone who tries to use your code together with an older LaTeX release receives a warning message that something might fail. A newer release date is accepted without a warning. For example, in 2020/10/01 the hook management was introduced in LaTeX. Thus, if your class or package makes use of this, such a line ensures that the necessary code is present.

All four declarations are optional. Nevertheless, their use in distributed class and package files eases the maintenance of these files.

A.6.3 The initial code part

You can specify any valid LaTeX code in the ⟨*initial code*⟩ part, including code that loads packages with the \RequirePackage command (see Section A.6.7) if their code is required in one of the option declarations. For example, you might want to load the calc package at this point, if you plan to use it later. However, normally this part is empty.

A.6.4 The declaration of options

In this part all options known to the package or class are declared using the \DeclareOption command. It is forbidden to load packages in this part. We describe here the standard option handling where options are simple strings that are either provided or not when the package or class is loaded but without any further structure.

Over the years a number of extension packages that provide a key/value syntax for package and class options, e.g., keyval, kvdefinekeys, kvoptions, or kvsetkeys, were developed. If any of them is used for option handling, then the commands in this part of the file are different, and you have to look at the corresponding package documentation for details.

However, these days LaTeX and the L3 programming layer also offer a general mechanism for this task and the interfaces to use that are discussed in Section A.6.6 on page 700. For new packages we recommend using the methods described there. Here we describe the traditional method with "simple" options.

\DeclareOption{*option*}{*code*}

The argument *option* is the name of the option being declared, and *code* is the code that executes if this option is requested. For example, the paper size option a4paper normally has a definition of the following form:

```
\DeclareOption{a4paper}{\setlength\paperheight{297mm}%
                       \setlength\paperwidth{210mm}}
```

In principle, any action — from setting a flag to complex programming instructions — is possible in the *code* argument of \DeclareOption.

An important function for use in \DeclareOption is the command \PassOptionsToPackage. It can pass one or more options to some other package that is loaded later.

\PassOptionsToPackage{*option-list*}{*package-name*}

The argument *option-list* is a comma-separated list of options that should be passed to the package with name *package-name* when it is loaded in the ⟨*package loading*⟩ part.[1] Suppose, for example, that you want to define a class file that makes use of two packages, say, A and B, both supporting the option infoshow. To support such an option in the class file as well, you could declare

```
\DeclareOption{infoshow}{%
    \PassOptionsToPackage{infoshow}{A}%
    \PassOptionsToPackage{infoshow}{B}%
    ⟨code to support infoshow in the class⟩}
```

If a package or class file is loaded with an option that it does not recognize, it issues an error (in the case of a package file) or silently ignores the option (in the case of a class file), assuming that it is a global option to be passed to other packages subsequently loaded with \usepackage. However, this behavior is not hardwired and can be modified using a \DeclareOption* declaration.

\DeclareOption*{*code*}

Command does not act on global options!

The argument *code* specifies the action to take if an unknown option is specified on the \usepackage or \RequirePackage command. Within this argument \CurrentOption refers to the name of the option in question. For example, to write a package that extends the functionality of some other package, you could use the following declaration:

```
\DeclareOption*{\PassOptionsToPackage{\CurrentOption}{xyz}}
```

This would pass all options not declared by your package to package xyz. If no \DeclareOption* declaration is given, the default action, described above, is used.

By combining \DeclareOption* with \InputIfFileExists (see below), you can even implement conditional option handling. For example, the following code tries to find files whose names are built up from the option name:

```
\DeclareOption*{\InputIfFileExists{g-\CurrentOption.xyz}{}%
    {\PackageWarning{somename}{Option \CurrentOption\space
                                    not recognized}}}
```

---

[1] It is the responsibility of the package writer to actually load such packages. LATEX does not check that packages receiving options via \PassOptionsToPackage are actually loaded later.

If the file g-*option*.xyz can be found, it is loaded; otherwise, the option is ignored with a warning.

> `\OptionNotUsed`

If your *code* for `\DeclareOption*` inside a class file is more complex (e.g., trying to handle some options but rejecting others as in the previous example), you might need to explicitly inform LATEX that the option was not accepted with the help of the `\OptionNotUsed` command. Otherwise, LATEX thinks that the option was used and does not produce a warning if the option is not picked up by a later package.

A.6.5 The execution of options

Two types of actions are normally carried out after all options are declared. You might want to set some defaults, such as the default paper size. Then the list of options specified needs to be examined, and the code for each such option needs to be executed.

> `\ExecuteOptions{`*option-list*`}`

The `\ExecuteOptions` command executes the code for every option listed in *option-list* in the order specified. It is just a convenient shorthand to set up defaults by executing code specified earlier with a `\DeclareOption` command. For example, the standard class book issues something similar to

```
\ExecuteOptions{letterpaper,twoside,10pt}
```

to set up the defaults. You can also use `\ExecuteOptions` when declaring other options, such as a definition of an option that automatically implies others. The `\ExecuteOptions` command can be used only prior to executing the `\ProcessOptions` command because, as one of its last actions, the latter command reclaims all of the memory taken up by the code for the declared options.

> `\ProcessOptions`

When the `\ProcessOptions` command is encountered, it examines the list of options specified for this class or package and executes the corresponding code. More precisely, when dealing with a package, the global options (as specified on the `\documentclass` command) and the directly specified options (the optional argument to the `\usepackage` or `\RequirePackage` command) are tested. For every option declared by the package, the corresponding code is executed. This execution occurs in the same order in which the options were specified by the `\DeclareOption` declarations in the package, not in the order in which they appear on the `\usepackage` command. Global options that are not recognized are

ignored. For all other unrecognized options the code specified by \DeclareOption*
is executed or, if this declaration is missing, an error is issued.

Thus, packages that use only \DeclareOption* when declaring options do
not act upon global options specified on the \documentclass, but rather accept
only those that are explicitly given on the \usepackage or \RequirePackage
declaration.

In the case of a class file, the action of \ProcessOptions is the same without
the added complexity of the global options.

There is one potential problem when using \ProcessOptions: the command
Preventing searches for a following star (even on subsequent lines) and thereby may incorrectly
unwanted expansion expand upcoming commands following it. To avoid this danger use \relax at the
end to stop the search immediately and start the execution of the options.

\ProcessOptions*

For some packages it may be more appropriate if they process their options in
the order specified on the \usepackage command rather than using the order
given through the sequence of \DeclareOption commands. For example, in the
babel package, the last language option specified is supposed to determine the main
document language. Such a package can execute the options in the order specified by
using \ProcessOptions* instead of \ProcessOptions.

A.6.6 Declaring and using options with a key/value syntax

Since 2020 the LATEX kernel offers built-in support for creating key-based options
through the L3 programming layer module l3keys for packages that are implemented
using this layer.

From the June 2022 release on, key-based options are also supported through a
small number of CamelCase commands, if the L3 programming layer is not being used.
This interface is simpler and exposes only the most common key types by default,
but these cover the vast majority of typical package option uses. Package authors
who wish to exploit the full power of l3keys to define keys using more sophisticated
key types can do so but then have to switch to L3 programming layer syntax. Details
of using l3keys are out of scope here: please refer to the L3 programming layer
documentation [62].

Please also note that this CamelCase interface is an alternative interface to the
option declarations discussed in the previous two sections — it makes little sense
to try to use both in parallel in the same package or class, even though with some
restrictions it can be made to work.

\DeclareKeys [*family*] {*key-declarations*}

Keys are created using the command \DeclareKeys, which itself takes a key–value
list of key names. Each key created will have one or more *properties*, which define

how it acts, and each of these key/property pairs has a *value*. Properties start with a period; the available ones are:

.code   executes arbitrary code when the key is used. The code can refer with #1 to the value assigned to the key;

.if   sets a TEX \if... switch, e.g., @twoside;

.notif   like .if, but sets a TEX \if... switch to its inverted value;

.store   stores a value in a macro;

.usage   defines whether the option can be given only when loading (use value load), in the preamble (value preamble), or has no limitation on scope (value general). Can be given in addition to one of the other properties.

For example, with

```
\DeclareKeys {
            draft.if      = @mypkg@draft    ,
            final.notif   = @mypkg@draft    ,
            name.store    = \@mypkg@name    ,
            address.store = \@mypkg@address ,
            debug.code    = \typeout{Debugging set to #1}
                     ...                    ,
            draft.usage   = preamble        ,
            name.usage    = load
            }
```

we create five key options for the current package: draft, final, name, address, and debug. The options draft and final are Boolean switches: they will accept only the values true or false. In the example, they have a tight relationship: specifying final=false is equivalent to draft=true (or shorter draft). The options name and address both accept any input and simply store it in the specified macros. The name can be set only when loading the package, draft can be set there or in the preamble, and address and debug can even be changed in the middle of the document. How to do that is explained below.

The .store property checks if the command used for storage exists: if not, it is defined with empty content so that it can safely be used afterwards.   .store *type options*

Similarly, .if and .notif check if the specified TEX switch exists, i.e., in our example if \if@mypkg@draft is defined; and if not, they call \newif to declare it.   .if *and* .notif *type options*

The option debug executes the code when the key is used; i.e., in the example it does a \typeout, displaying the value given to the key, and then executes some further code (indicated by ...) to set up or alter the debugging. This is similar to \DeclareOption in the classic interface, except that your code can make use of the value given to the key.   .code *type options*

Setting default values for keys If you want to set explicit default values for some or all of your keys declared with `\DeclareKeys`, use `\SetKeys` afterwards.

To ensure that keys of different packages can safely coexist, all keys declared with `\DeclareKeys` are divided up into *families*, with the requirement that the combination of *family+key* is unique across all keys ever declared. Within a package or class file, the *family* defaults to the name of the current file without extension (internally called `\@currname`), which means that every such package or class has its own name space by default.[1] If necessary, you can specify keys for other name spaces by using an explicit *family* argument, though that is seldom needed.

`\DeclareUnknownKeyHandler` [*family*] {*code*}

By default, keys unknown to the system raise an error if they are encountered during load or set with `\SetKeys`. In some situations that is not desirable, e.g., when a package wants to pass on unknown keys to some other package. In the classic interface that is handled through a `\DeclareOption*` declaration, but with key/value options there is the additional complexity of handling the given value and the fact that keys are structured by *family*.

`\DeclareUnknownKeyHandler` installs a new handler for keys of a given *family* replacing the default error handler otherwise used. The *code* receives the unknown key name as #1 and the value as #2. If no value was given, #2 is empty. These can then be processed as appropriate, e.g., by forwarding to another package.

Executing package or class options using a key/value syntax

If you use the key/value interface for options, then the processing of the options, given to the package or class, is carried out by the command `\ProcessKeyOptions` and not with the commands discussed in the previous section.

`\ProcessKeyOptions` [*family*]

The command takes the option list given to the package or class but expects it to consist of key/value pairs and processes them accordingly. In the case of a package, it also examines the global (class) options. It is normally used without the optional *family* argument, but if one was supplied to `\DeclareKeys`, then it is also needed here.

Unlike "classical" LATEX package options, key-based options remain available to be set after `\ProcessKeyOptions` has been used. In particular, any such key can be used for more general settings in the document body. The scope that keys are live in is set by the `.usage` property, which can restrict a key to load-time only, to load-time and the document preamble, or to allow general scope.

No option clash errors Unlike "classical" options, LATEX will not issue an option-clash warning when a package using `\ProcessKeyOptions` is loaded for a second time with (different) options. Instead, after the first loading, second and subsequent loading attempts

---

[1]This is not quite true: you can have a class and a package use the same base name and thus have the same default name space. In that case you may have to set the *family* explicitly.

simply pass the option list to \SetKeys. This means that it is up to the package author to decide how to handle repeated option setting. Typically, those that can be given only once will be set as .usage=load.

It is possible to use \DeclareKeys declarations after the package-supplied option list has been processed, but keys defined by it can then obviously only be altered in the preamble or in the document body, but do not act as package options. *Declaring keys that do not serve as package options*

\SetKeys [*family*] {*key/value list*}

Changing key values is achieved with the \SetKeys command: it requires a *key/value list* as its argument. For example, based on the example above

```
\SetKeys{address = {My place, My Town}}
```

would be valid within the package code after the \DeclareKeys line.

Outside the package, e.g., in the preamble or the document body, we would additionally need to provide an appropriate value for the optional *family* argument to change the key value. This is usually the package or class file name, but can be any name explicitly supplied as *family* to \DeclareKeys earlier.

Many packages offer dedicated configuration commands accepting key/value lists, e.g., \geometry, \microtypesetup, or \SetupDoc, to name a few. The naming conventions are quite diverse unfortunately. With the new interface it could be as simple as \SetKeys [*package*] {*key/value list*}. For backwards compatibility, a package switching over to the new system could still provide its old interface through a simple mapping, e.g., \newcommand\geometry{\SetKeys [geometry]}. *Standardizing the configuration interfaces*

A.6.7 The package loading part

Once the options are dealt with, it might be time to load one or more additional packages — for example, those to which you have passed options to using the command \PassOptionsToPackage.

\RequirePackage [*option-list*] {*package*} [*release*]

This command is the package/class counterpart to the document command \usepackage. If *package* was not loaded before, it is loaded now with the options specified in *option-list*, the global options from the \documentclass command, and all options passed to this package via \PassOptionsToPackage.

LaTeX loads a package only once because in many cases it is dangerous to execute the code of a package several times. Thus, if you require a package with a certain set of options, but this package was previously loaded with a different set not including all options requested at this time, then the user of your package has a problem. In this situation LaTeX may[1] issue an error message informing users of your package

---

[1]If the package uses key/value options, it depends on the properties of the keys whether a second loading attempt is possible; see the discussion on page 701.

about the conflict and suggesting that they load the package with a \usepackage command and all necessary options.

The optional *release* argument can be used to request a package version not older than a certain date. For this scheme to work, the required package must contain a \ProvidesPackage declaration specifying a release date.

It can also be used to request a specific named version [=⟨*version*⟩] or a version current at a certain date by using [=⟨*date*⟩] in the *release* argument. However, this should normally be avoided within packages or classes, because you force LATEX to always load old and possible obsolete code.[1]

\RequirePackageWithOptions{*package*} [*release*]

This command works like \RequirePackage except that the options passed to it are exactly those specified for the calling package or class. This facilitates the generation of variant packages that take exactly the same set of options as the original. See also the discussion of \LoadClassWithOptions on page 709.

A.6.8 The main code part

This final part of the file defines the characteristics and implements the functions provided by the given class or package. It can contain any valid LATEX construct and usually defines new commands and structures. It is good style to use standard LATEX commands, as described in this appendix, such as \newlength, \newcommand, \NewDocumentCommand, \NewDocumentEnvironment, and so on, rather than relying on primitive TEX commands, because the latter do not test for possible conflicts with other packages.

A.6.9 Special commands for package and class files

With a few exceptions, the commands in this section are not useful outside a package or a document class.

\AtEndOfPackage{*code*}   \AtEndOfClass{*code*}

Sometimes it is necessary to defer the execution of some code to the end of the current package or class file. The above declarations save the *code* argument and execute it when the end of the package or class is reached. If more than one such declaration is present in a file, the *code* is accumulated and finally executed in the order in which the declarations were given.

These declarations are merely for convenience and help structure the code. Instead of using them, you can certainly place the necessary code at the very end of the package or class.

---

[1]This facility is mainly intended for end users who need to reprocess an old document written when an earlier package version was the "current" one.

Special commands for package and class files

\AtEndOfPackage{*code*}   \AtEndOfClass{*code*}

    Defers execution of *code* to end of current package or class

\AtBeginDocument{*code*}   \AtEndDocument{*code*}

    Executes *code* at \begin{document} or \end{document}

\IfFileExists{*file*}{*then-code*}{*else-code*}

    Executes *then-code* if *file* exists, *else-code* otherwise

\InputIfFileExists{*file*}{*then-code*}{*else-code*}

    If *file* exists, executes *then-code* and then inputs *file*; otherwise executes *else-code*

Special class file commands

\LoadClass[*option-list*]{*class*}[*release*]

    Like \RequirePackage for class files, but does not see global options if not explicitly passed to it

\PassOptionsToClass{*option-list*}{*class*}

    Passes *option-list* to *class*

Table A.7: Special commands for package and class files

> \AtBeginDocument{*code*}   \AtEndDocument{*code*}

Other important points at which you might want to execute deferred code are the beginning and the end of the document or, more exactly, the points where the \begin{document} and \end{document} are processed. The above commands allow packages to add code to this environment without creating any conflicts with other packages trying to do the same. Note, however, that code in the \AtBeginDocument hook is part of the preamble. Thus, restrictions limit what can be put there; in particular, no typesetting can be done.

These days the commands are implemented using the hook management system of LaTeX described in Section A.4; e.g., \AtBeginDocument{*code*} is just an abbreviation for

    \AddToHook{begindocument}[*package-or-class-name*]{*code*}

and there are further hooks into \begin{document} that allow for even more granular control. For example, begindocument/after can be used to add typesetting material at the very beginning of the document body.

> \IfFileExists{*file*}{*then-code*}{*else-code*}
> \InputIfFileExists{*file*}{*then-code*}{*else-code*}

If your package or class tries to \input a file that does not exist, the user ends up in TeX's file-error loop. It can be exited only by supplying a valid file name. Your package or class can avoid this problem by using \IfFileExists. The argument *file* is the file whose existence you want to check. If this *file* is found by LATEX, the commands in *then-code* are executed; otherwise, those in *else-code* are executed. The command `\InputIfFileExists` tests not only whether *file* exists, but also inputs it immediately after executing *then-code*. The name *file* is then added to the list of files to be displayed by `\listfiles`.

`\PackageWarning{`*name*`}{`*text*`}`   `\PackageWarningNoLine{`*name*`}{`*text*`}`
`\PackageNote{`*name*`}{`*text*`}`   `\PackageNoteNoLine{`*name*`}{`*text*`}`
`\PackageInfo{`*name*`}{`*text*`}`

When a package detects a problem, it can alert the user by printing a warning message on the terminal. For example, when the multicol package detects that `multicols*` (which normally generates unbalanced columns) is used inside a box, it issues the following warning:[1]

```
\PackageWarning{multicol}{multicols* inside a box does
  not make sense.\MessageBreak  Going to balance anyway}
```

This produces a warning message, which is explicitly broken into two lines via the `\MessageBreak` command:

```
Package multicol Warning: multicols* inside a box does not make sense.
(multicol)                Going to balance anyway on input line 6.
```

The current line number is automatically appended. Sometimes it would be nice to display the current file name as well, but unfortunately this information is not available on the macro level.

Depending on the nature of the problem, it might be important to tell the user the source line on which the problem was encountered. In other cases this information is irrelevant or even misleading, such as when the problem happens while the package is being loaded. In this situation, `\PackageWarningNoLine` should be used; it produces the same result as `\PackageWarning` but omits the phrase "on input line *number*".

If the information is not really a warning, but just something you want the user to be informed about, you can use `\PackageNote` or `\PackageNoteNoLine`; both produce the same kind of output, but with `Warning` replaced by `Info`.

If this information should appear just in the transcript file, then one can use `\PackageInfo`. For example, after loading the shortvrb package and issuing the declaration `\MakeShortVerb\=`, the transcript file shows the following:

```
Package shortvrb Info: Made = a short reference for
                                  \verb on input line 3.
```

---

[1] In a box, balancing is essential because a box can grow arbitrarily in vertical direction, so all material would otherwise end up in the first column.

A \PackageInfoNoLine command is not provided. If you really want to suppress the line number in an informational message, use \@gobble as the last token in the second argument of \PackageInfo.

\PackageError{*name*}{*short-text*}{*long-text*}

If the problem detected is severe enough to require user intervention, one can signal an error instead of a warning. If the error is encountered, the *short-text* is displayed immediately and processing stops. For example, if inputenc encounters an 8-bit character it does not recognize, it produces the following error:

```
! Package inputenc Error: Keyboard character used is undefined
(inputenc)                in inputencoding 'latin1'.

See the inputenc package documentation for explanation.
Type  H <return>  for immediate help.
 ...


1.5 abc^^G
?
```

If the user then presses "h" or "H", the *long-text* is offered. In this case it is:

```
You need to provide a definition with \DeclareInputText
or \DeclareInputMath before using this key.
```

As before, you can explicitly determine the line breaks in the error and help texts by using \MessageBreak.

\ClassWarning{*name*}{*text*}   \ClassWarningNoLine{*name*}{*text*}
\ClassNote{*name*}{*text*}   \ClassNoteNoLine{*name*}{*text*}
\ClassInfo{*name*}{*text*}   \ClassError{*name*}{*short-text*}{*long-text*}

Information, warning, and error commands are not only available for packages — similar commands are provided for document classes. They differ only in the produced texts: the latter commands print "Class" instead of "Package" in the appropriate places.

\IfFormatAtLeastTF{*date*}{*true-code*}{*false-code*}
\IfPackageAtLeastTF{*package*}{*date*}{*true-code*}{*false-code*}
\IfClassAtLeastTF{*package*}{*date*}{*true-code*}{*false-code*}

Sometimes it is important to ensure that the LATEX kernel or a certain package or class is from a specific date (or later), because that decides what code to execute. For example, commands such as \NewDocumentCommand, described in Section A.1.4, were added to LATEX in 2020-10-01 and therefore cannot be used in a package running on top of an earlier distribution. That can be solved by requiring a recent enough kernel using \NeedsTeXFormat. However, as a package author you may want to support older distributions, and in that case this could be done by loading xparse, i.e.,

```
\IfFormatAtLeastTF{2020-10-01}{}{\RequirePackage{xparse}}
```

In the same way, adjustments for specific package versions (\IfPackageAtLeastTF) or class versions (\IfClassAtLeastTF) can be made.

\IfPackageLoadedTF{*package*}{*true-code*}{*false-code*}
\IfPackageLoadedWithOptionsTF{*package*}{*options*}{*true-code*}{*false-code*}

Sometimes it is useful to be able to find out if a package is already loaded, and if so, how. For this purpose, two commands are made available to class (and package) writers. To find out if a *package* has already been loaded, use \IfPackageLoadedTF. To find out if a *package* has been loaded with at least the (comma-separated) *options* list, use \IfPackageLoadedWithOptionsTF.

Note that the fontenc package cannot be tested with the above commands. That's because it pretends that it was never loaded to allow for repeated reloading with different options (see the file ltoutenc.dtx in the LATEX distribution for details).

Testing for classes can be done with the commands \IfClassLoadedTF and \IfClassLoadedWithOptionsTF. They can, for example, be used to define commands that behave differently if used with different document classes.

A.6.10 Special commands for class files

It is sometimes helpful to build a class file as a customization of a given general class. To support this concept two commands are provided.

\LoadClass [*option-list*] {*class*} [*release*]

The \LoadClass command works like the \RequirePackage command with the following three exceptions:

- The command can be used only in class files.

- There can be at most one \LoadClass command per class.

- The global options are not seen by the *class* unless explicitly passed to it via \PassOptionsToClass or specified in the *option-list*.

\PassOptionsToClass{*option-list*}{*class*}

The command \PassOptionsToClass can be used to pass options to such a general class. An example of such a class file augmentation is shown in Figure A.1 on the next page. It defines a class file myart that accepts two extra options, cropmarks (making crop marks for trimming the pages) and bind (shifting the printed pages slightly to

```
% ----------------------------- identification -----------------------
\NeedsTeXFormat{LaTeX2e}
\ProvidesClass{myart}[2021/01/01]
% ----------------------------- initial code -----------------------
\RequirePackage{ifthen}      \newboolean{cropmarks}
% ------------------------ declaration of options --
\DeclareOption{cropmarks}{\setboolean{cropmarks}{true}}
\DeclareOption{bind}      {\AtEndOfClass{\addtolength\oddsidemargin{.5in}%
                           \addtolength\evensidemargin{-.5in}}}
\DeclareOption*           {\PassOptionsToClass{\CurrentOption}{article}}
% ------------------------- execution of options -------------------
\ProcessOptions \relax                         % cf. hint on p.700!
% -----------------------------package loading ---------------------
\LoadClass{article}                            % the real code
% ----------------------------- main code ------------------------
\newenvironment{Notes}{...}{...}               % the new environment
\ifthenelse{\boolean{cropmarks}}               % support for cropmarks
   {\renewcommand{\ps@plain}{...} ...}{}
```

Figure A.1: An example of a class file extending article

the outside to get a larger binding margin), as well as one additional environment, Notes.

The cropmarks option is implemented by setting a Boolean switch and redefining various \pagestyles if this switch is true. The bind option modifies the values of \oddsidemargin and \evensidemargin. These length registers do not have their final values at the time the bind option is encountered (they are set later, when the article class is loaded by \LoadClass), so the modification is deferred until the end of the myart class file using the \AtEndOfClass command.

\LoadClassWithOptions{*class*}[*release*]

This command is similar to \LoadClass, but it always calls the *class* with exactly the same option list that is being used by the current class, rather than the options explicitly supplied or passed on by \PassOptionsToClass. It is mainly intended to allow one class to build on another. For example:

```
\LoadClassWithOptions{article}
```

This should be contrasted with the following slightly different construction:

```
\DeclareOption*{\PassOptionsToClass{\CurrentOption}{article}}
\ProcessOptions                \LoadClass{article}
```

As used here, the effects are more or less the same, but the version using the command \LoadClassWithOptions is slightly quicker (and less onerous to type). If, however, the class declares options of its own, then the two constructions are different. Compare, for example,

```
\DeclareOption{landscape}{...}
\ProcessOptions                    \LoadClassWithOptions{article}
```

with:

```
\DeclareOption{landscape}{...}
\DeclareOption*{\PassOptionsToClass{\CurrentOption}{article}}
\ProcessOptions                    \LoadClass{article}
```

In the first example, the article class is called with the option `landscape` only when the current class is called with this option. In the second example, however, the option `landscape` is never passed to the article class, because the default option handler passes only options that are *not* explicitly declared.

A.6.11 A minimal class file

Every class file *must* contain at least four things: a definition of `\normalsize`, values for `\textwidth` and `\textheight`, and a specification for page numbering. Thus, a minimal document class file[1] could look like this:

```
\NeedsTeXFormat{LaTeX2e}
\ProvidesClass{minimal}[2001/05/25 Standard LaTeX minimal class]
\renewcommand\normalsize{\fontsize{10pt}{12pt}\selectfont}
\setlength\textwidth{6.5in}
\setlength\textheight{8in}
\pagenumbering{arabic}        % needed even though this class does
                             %   not show page numbers
\pagestyle{empty}            % this is actually already in the kernel
```

This class file does not support footnotes, marginals, floats, or other features. Naturally, most classes contain more than this minimum!

---

[1]This class is in the standard distribution, as `minimal.cls`. It is not very useful, though — not even for producing bug reports; it is better use the article class for that.

Tracing and Resolving Problems

In an ideal world all documents you produced would compile without problems and give high-quality output as intended. If you are that lucky, there will be no need for you to consult this appendix, ever. However, if you run into a problem of some kind, the material in this appendix should help you to resolve your problem easily.

We start with an alphabetical list of all error messages, those after which LaTeX stops and asks for advice. "All" in this context means all LaTeX kernel errors (their text starts with LaTeX Error: or LaTeX ⟨*module*⟩ Error), practically all TeX errors (i.e., those directly produced by the underlying engine), and errors from the packages amsmath, babel, calc, color, fontenc, graphics, graphicx, and inputenc. Errors reported by other packages — those that identify themselves as

> ! Package ⟨*package*⟩ Error: ⟨*error text*⟩

where ⟨*package*⟩ is not one of the above — are not included. For such errors you should refer to the package description elsewhere in the book or consult the original package documentation.

But even if there are no real errors that stop the processing, warning and information messages might be shown on the terminal or in the transcript file. They are treated in Section B.3, where you will find all LaTeX core messages and all relevant TeX messages that may need your attention, together with an explanation of their possible causes and suggestions on how to deal with them.

The final section deals with tools for tracing problems in case the error or warning information itself is not sufficient or does not exist. We will explore ways to display command definitions and register values and then take a look at diagnosing and solving page-breaking problems. This is followed by suggestions for identifying and solving paragraph-breaking problems and includes a brief look at two LuaTeX-only packages for dealing with hyphenation issues. We finish with a description of the trace package, which helps in thoroughly tracing command execution, if your own definitions or those of others produce unexpected results.

Some of the material in this appendix can be considered "low-level" TeX, something that, to the author's knowledge, has never been described in any other LaTeX book. It is, however, often important information. Directing the reader to books like *The TeXbook* does not really help, because most of the advice given in books about plain TeX is not applicable to LaTeX or produces subtle errors when used. We therefore try to be as self-contained as possible by offering all relevant information about the underlying TeX engine as far as it makes sense within the LaTeX context.

B.1 Error messages

When LaTeX stops to display an error message, it also shows a line number indicating how far it got in the document source. However, because of memory considerations in the design of TeX itself, it does not directly show to which file this source line number belongs. For simple documents this is not a problem, but if your document is split over many files, you may have to carefully look at the terminal output or the transcript file to identify the file LaTeX is currently working on when the error occurs.[1]

Finding the source line of an error

Whenever LaTeX starts reading a file, it displays a "(" character that is immediately followed by the file name. Once LaTeX has finished reading the file, it displays the matching ")" character. In addition, whenever it starts preparing to output a page, it displays a "[" character followed by the current page number. Thus, if you see something like

```
(./trial.tex [1] (./ch-1.tex [2] [3] (./table-1.tex [4] [5]) [6]
! Undefined control sequence.
<argument> A \textss
                     {Test}
l.235 \section{A \textss{Test}}
                               \label{sec:test}

?
```

you can deduce that the error happened inside an argument of some command (<argument>) and was detected when LaTeX gathered material for page 7. It got as far as reading most of line 235 in the file ch-1.tex. In this example the error is readily

---

[1] A useful little helper for this is the structuredlog package. Once loaded, it uses the file hooks to identify the start and end of file-reading actions in the .log with lines such as "== (LEVEL 2 START) table-1.tex" and corresponding STOP lines. Thus, to find out where some error has occured you only have to search backwards for the string "(LEVEL" and if that is a START line you are done; otherwise, you have to search further for the START line with the next lower level number.

visible in the source line: \textsf was misspelled as \textss inside the argument to the \section command. In some cases, however, the relationship between error and source line is blurred or even nonexistent.

For example, if you define \renewcommand\thepart{\Alp{part}}, then the typo appears only when you use the \part command that executes your definition. In that case you get

```
! Undefined control sequence.
\thepart ->\Alp
                {part}
l.167 \part{Test}
```

In this particular case the actual error is not on line 167 and most likely not even in the current file — the \part command merely happens to call the faulty definition of \thepart.

Sometimes an error is detected by LaTeX while it is preparing a new page. Because this is an asynchronous operation, the source line listed in the error message is of no value whatsoever. So if you do not understand how the error should be related to the source line, you may well be right — there is, indeed, no relationship. Here is an example:

```
! Undefined control sequence.
\thepage ->\romen
                {page}
l.33 T
      his is a sample text to fill the page.
```

One way to obtain additional information about an error (or information about how LaTeX intends to deal with it) is to press the key h in response to the ? that follows the error message. If used with a TeX error such as the one above, we get

```
? h
The control sequence at the end of the top line
of your error message was never \def'ed. If you have
misspelled it (e.g., '\hobx'), type 'I' and the correct
spelling (e.g., 'I\hbox'). Otherwise just continue,
and I'll forget about whatever was undefined.
```

You probably already see the problem with advice coming directly from the TeX engine: you may have to translate it, because it often talks about commands that are not necessarily adequate for LaTeX documents (e.g., for \def you should read \newcommand or \NewDocumentCommand). With real LaTeX errors this is not the case, though here you sometimes get advice that is also not really helpful:

```
You're in trouble here.  Try typing  <return>  to proceed.
If that doesn't work, type  X <return>  to quit.
```

Well, thank you very much; we already knew that! Typing h ⟨return⟩ is, however, worth a try, because there are many messages with more detailed advice.

Displaying the stack of partially expanded macros

Another way to get additional information about an encountered error is to set the counter `errorcontextlines` to a large positive value. In that case LaTeX lists the stack of the current macro executions:

```
1    ! Undefined control sequence.
2    \thepage ->\romen
3                      {page}
4    \@oddfoot ->\reset@font \hfil \thepage
5                                         \hfil
6    \@outputpage ...lor \hb@xt@ \textwidth {\@thefoot
7                                          }\color@endbox }}\globa...
8
9    \@opcol ...lumn \@outputdblcol \else \@outputpage
10                                       \fi \global \@mparbotto...
11   <output> ...specialoutput \else \@makecol \@opcol
12                                       \@startcolumn \@whilesw...
13   <to be read again>
14                      T
15   l.33 T
16        his is a sample text to fill the page.
```

You read this bottom up: LaTeX has seen the T (lines 15 and 16) but wants to read it again later (<to be read again>, lines 13 and 14) because it switched to the output routine (<output>). There it got as far as executing the command `\@opcol` (lines 11 and 12), which in turn got as far as calling `\@outputpage` (lines 9 and 10), which was executing `\@thefoot` (lines 6 and 7). Line 4 is a bit curious because it refers to `\@oddfoot` rather than `\@thefoot` as one would expect (`\@thefoot` expands to `\@oddfoot`, so it is immediately fully expanded and not put onto the stack of partially expanded macros). Inside `\@oddfoot` we got as far as calling `\thepage`, which in turn expanded to `\romen` (lines 2 and 3), which is finally flagged as an undefined command (line 1).

Fortunately, in most cases it is sufficient only to display the error message and the source line. This is why LaTeX's default value for `errorcontextlines` is −1, which means not showing any intermediate context.

Error during expansion

Errors can occur when LaTeX is doing expansions rather than typesetting. This is a problematical time, because in that mode TeX is not able to do any assignments, which is a prerequisite to display LaTeX error or warning messages with useful help texts. It is also difficult to stop the expansion in time when an error condition is identified without stopping it when there is no error condition. Nevertheless, with some gymnastics it is possible to produce reasonable error messages (as long as you ignore the help text that you get by typing h in response to the error). The trick used by LaTeX is to produce a low-level TeX error, but to do this in a way that it nearly looks like a normal LaTeX error.

```
! Use of \??? doesn't match its definition.
<argument> \???
        ! LaTeX cmd Error: Required argument missing for \foo.
l. ...  }
```

The artificially generated low-level TeX error to stop the expansion is responsible for the first line of the error , i.e., "! Use of \??? doesn't match its definition". It is always the same line in such error messages — and no, nobody has defined a command with the name \???, but it is not unreasonable to think of it as a placeholder for *the current command* that has a problem.

The interesting part is the line starting with "! LaTeX ⟨*type*⟩ Error: ⟨*reason*⟩" that you can look up in this appendix. The help text, on the other hand (that you get by using h), is not helpful, because it gives an explanation of the low-level error that LaTeX had artificially produced:

```
If you say, e.g., '\def\a1{...}', then you must always
put '1' after '\a', since control sequence names are
made up of letters only. The macro here has not been
followed by the required stuff, so I'm ignoring it.
```

Thus, if you see a "! Use of \??? doesn't match ..." error and you do not understand what it means, come straight to this appendix and look up the ⟨*reason*⟩ given on the third line.

Errors can also occur when LaTeX is processing an intermediate file used to transfer information between two runs (e.g., .aux or .toc files). Data in such files can be corrupted due to an error that happened in a previous run. Even if you have corrected that error in your source, traces of it may still be present in such external files. Therefore, in some cases you may have to delete those files before running LaTeX again, although often the problem vanishes after another run. *Persistent errors*

Common sources for such nasty errors in LaTeX are so-called *fragile* commands used unprotected in *moving arguments*. Technically, a moving argument is an argument that is internally expanded by LaTeX without typesetting it directly (e.g., by using the internal LaTeX construct \protected@edef[1]). But as a rule of thumb you can think of it as an argument that is moved somewhere else before typesetting — for example, the arguments of sectioning commands, such as \section (sent to the table of contents), the argument of \caption (sent to the list of figures or tables), and the arguments of \markboth and \markright. *Errors due to fragile commands*

The best, though not very helpful, definition of a fragile command is that it is a command that produces errors if it is not preceded with a \protect command when used in a moving argument.

Commands that are not fragile either have an expansion that is harmless in a moving argument (for example, they expand to simple text characters) or they have been explicitly made *robust*, which means they do not expand at all in such arguments. Today, most common LaTeX commands have been made robust (i.e., nonexpanding) so that such protection is seldom necessary. However, if you get strange errors from a command used in a moving argument, try preceding it with \protect. *Robust commands do not expand in moving arguments*

---

[1]Some people have heard that the TeX primitive \edef exists for this purpose. It is not advisable to use it in your own commands, however, unless you know that it will never receive arbitrary document input. You should use \protected@edef instead, because that command prevents fragile commands from breaking apart if they are prefixed by \protect!

There are no precise rules defining which commands belong to which category. User-defined commands made with `\NewDocumentCommand` are generally robust, but simple commands defined with `\newcommand` and with only mandatory arguments are fragile if they contain any fragile commands in their definition. For example, the definition

```
\newcommand\frail{\ifthenelse{\value{section}<10 \and
                              \value{subsection}=1}%
                              {\typeout{Yes}}{\typeout{No}}}
```

is fragile because the comparison argument of `\ifthenelse` is fragile. If you used `\frail` in the @ expression of a `tabular` (not that this makes much sense),

```
\nonstopmode        \begin{tabular}{@{\frail}l} x \end{tabular}
```

you would see the following 101 errors before LATEX finally gives up (the left column displays the number of occurrences):

```
 1 ! Argument of \@firstoftwo has an extra }.
 1 ! Argument of \renew@command has an extra }.
 1 ! Extra \or.
83 ! Illegal parameter number in definition of \reserved@a.
 1 ! Paragraph ended before \@firstoftwo was complete.
 1 ! Paragraph ended before \renew@command was complete.
 4 ! Undefined control sequence.
 8 ! Use of \@array doesn't match its definition.
 1 !  ==> Fatal error occurred, no output PDF file produced!
```

All TeX errors can be caused by a fragile command in a moving argument!

What we can learn from this example is the following: whenever you encounter a strange TeX error that has no simple explanation (such as a misspelled command name), it is possibly due to a fragile command that got broken in a moving argument — so try protecting it with `\protect` at the point where the error occurs. Because this can be the reason behind every TeX error, we shall not repeat this possible cause for every one of them (after all, more than 60 TeX error messages are explained below).

Errors produced by cross-reference keys

As discussed in Section A.1.1, a few restrictions are placed on the characters that can be used in reference key arguments of `\label` and `\bibitem`. In a nutshell, such keys sometimes act like moving arguments and, depending on the combination characters used and the packages loaded, all kinds of dreadful TeX errors may show up. In that case protection with using the `\protect` command does *not* work; instead, you have to use a simpler key conforming to the syntax restrictions for such keys.

Alphabetical listing of TeX and LATEX errors

In the list of errors below, all TeX and all package errors are flagged with a boxed reference at the end of the error message. Newer LATEX errors originating from a specific module are flagged with the module name in parentheses, while the older

LATEX errors are unflagged. In all cases the typical prefix, e.g., "LaTeX ⟨*module*⟩ `Error:`" or "`Package` ⟨*name*⟩ `Error:`", is omitted.

* TEX

> If LATEX stops by just displaying a star, then it has reached the end of your source document without seeing a request to finish the job (i.e., `\end{document}` or `\stop`) and is now waiting for input from the terminal. While this is in itself not an error, in most circumstances it means that something went seriously wrong. If there have been no previous errors and your document finishes with `\end{document}`, then you might have forgotten to close a `verbatim` environment so that the remainder of the document was processed "verbatim".
>
> To find the source of this problem in a large document, reply `\end{foo}`, which either should give you an "Environment ... ended by..." error (indicating what environment LATEX thinks is still open) or is swallowed without any reaction, in which case you know that you are indeed in some "verbatim" context. In the latter event, try to interrupt LATEX (by pressing Control-C or whatever your installation requires) and reply with "x" to the "Interruption" error to quit the job. Looking afterwards at the last page in the typeset document usually gives some hint about where things started to go wrong.

`'⟨character⟩' invalid at this point` calc

> You loaded the calc package, and one of the expressions in `\setcounter`, `\setlength`, `\addtocounter`, or `\addtolength` used a syntax not supported by calc. See Section A.5.2 for details.

`⟨hex number⟩ too large for Unicode`

> With `\DeclareUnicodeCharacter` you can only declare Unicode characters with a ⟨*hex number*⟩ of 110FFF or less; anything larger generates this error.

`⟨command⟩ allowed only in math mode` amsmath

> This command or environment can be used only in math mode. Check carefully to see what is missing from your document.

`\< in mid line`

> The `\<`, defined within a `tabbing` environment, was encountered in the middle of a line. It can be used only at the beginning of a line (e.g., after `\\`).

`A <Box> was supposed to be here` TEX

> This error is the result of using a box command, such as `\sbox`, with an invalid first argument (i.e., one not declared with `\newsavebox`). Usually, you first get the error "Missing number, treated as zero" indicating that TEX uses box register zero.

`Argument delimiter '⟨delimiter⟩' invalid in ⟨command or environment⟩` cmd

> Some argument types available with `\NewDocumentCommand` or its siblings require you to specify delimiters. You get this error message if the specified delimiter is not a single nonblank token or if it is an implicit group token, such as `\bgroup`. Neither is supported.

`Argument of ⟨command⟩ has an extra }` TEX
> A right brace was used in place of a mandatory command argument (e.g., `\mbox}`). Fragile commands, when used without `\protect` in a moving argument, often break in a way that generates this or one of the other "extra" errors discussed below.

`Argument type 'b' must be last in ⟨environment⟩` (cmd)
> In a `\NewDocumentEnvironment` declaration you can use the type b to indicate the body of the environment. However, in this instance it is not the last argument specified, which it has to be, in order to grab the environment body.

`Bad argument specification '⟨spec⟩' of ⟨command or environment⟩` (cmd)
> The argument specification of a command defined with `\NewDocumentCommand` or an environment defined with `\NewDocumentEnvironment` has a problem. Possible causes are:
>
> - Some parts of the specification are missing required components; e.g., a D specifier needs to be followed by two delimiters and a default value;
> - The final argument of an expandable command, i.e., one defined with a `\NewExpandableDocumentCommand` declaration, cannot be optional.

`Bad \line or \vector argument`
> LaTeX issues this error if you specified a negative length or used an illegal slope with either `\line` or `\vector`. In the latter case, see Chapter 8 for alternatives.

`Bad math environment delimiter`
> This error is triggered when a `\(` or `\[` command is encountered inside a formula or when `\)` or `\]` is found in normal text. Check whether these commands are properly matched in your document.

`\begin{⟨env⟩} allowed only in paragraph mode` amsmath
> There are many places, such as within LR-mode text or math mode, where it does not make sense to have a math display. With amsmath the whole display ⟨env⟩ is simply ignored.

`\begin{⟨env⟩} on input line ⟨line number⟩ ended by \end{⟨other env⟩}`
> You receive this error when LaTeX detects that the environment ⟨env⟩ was incorrectly terminated with the end-tag for the environment ⟨other env⟩. The most likely case is that you, indeed, forgot to close the environment ⟨env⟩.
>
> Another possible source of this error is trying to use verbatim-like environments or an amsmath display environment inside the definition of your own environments, which is often impossible. See Section 4.2.4 on page →I 317 for solutions involving verbatim-like environments.
>
> If neither is the case and you are absolutely sure that all environments are properly nested, then somewhere between the start of ⟨env⟩ and the point where the error was found there must be a command that issues an `\endgroup` without a prior matching `\begingroup` so that LaTeX is fooled into believing that the

⟨*env*⟩ environment ended at this point. One way to find that problem is to move the end-tag closer to the begin-tag, until the problem disappears.

`\begin{split} won't work here` `amsmath`

Either this `split` environment is not within an equation or perhaps you need to use `aligned` here.

`Can be used only in preamble`

LaTeX has encountered a command or environment that should be used only inside a package or the preamble (i.e., before `\begin{document}`). This error can also be caused by a second `\begin{document}`.

`Cannot add code to disabled hook '⟨`*hook*`⟩'` (hooks)

Generic command hooks, e.g., `cmd/⟨`*cmd*`⟩/after`, do not work for all ⟨*cmd*⟩s (in particular the `/after` hooks). To avoid unpleasant surprises they can therefore be explicitly disabled in which case `\AddToHook` does not accept them and instead replies with this error message.

`Cannot define non-active Unicode char value < 00A0`

Unicode character values less than 00A0 (decimal 160) can normally not be used with `\DeclareUnicodeCharacter` to give them a special LICR interpretation in pdfTeX. Exceptions are a few characters that have been made active by LaTeX.

`Cannot determine size of graphic in ⟨`*file*`⟩` `graphics|graphicx`

You did not specify an explicit image size on the `\includegraphics` command, and LaTeX was unable to determine the image size from the graphics ⟨*file*⟩ directly. It usually does this automatically, for example, for `.eps` files by reading the bounding box information. However, depending on the graphics driver, it may be unable to extract this information from binary bitmap images such as `.jpg` or `.png` files.

`Cannot include graphics of type: ⟨`*ext*`⟩` `graphics|graphicx`

You get this error if you have specified a graphics type in the second argument of `\DeclareGraphicsRule` or used the `type` keyword of `\includegraphics`, for which the loaded graphics driver has no support.

`Cannot remove chunk '⟨`*label*`⟩' from hook '⟨`*hook*`⟩' because ⟨`*reason*`⟩` (hooks)

You tried to remove a chunk of code labeled ⟨*label*⟩ using `\RemoveFromHook`, but either the ⟨*hook*⟩ does not exist or there is no such chunk. You can look at the hook with `\ShowHook` to verify that there is no spelling mistake.

`Circular dependency in defaults of ⟨`*name*`⟩` (cmd)

Optional arguments in `\NewDocumentCommand` or its variants can have defaults that use the content of other arguments in their default value. If you go overboard with that approach, you may end up with a circular dependency that LaTeX is unable to resolve for you, and in that case you get this error message.

`\caption outside float`

A `\caption` command was found outside a float environment, such as a `figure` or `table`. This error message is disabled by some of the extension packages described in Chapter 7.

Command ⟨*name*⟩ already defined

You try to declare a command, an environment, a new savebox, a length, or a counter with a ⟨*name*⟩ that already has a meaning in LaTeX. Your declaration is ignored, and you have to choose a different name. This error is also triggered if you use `\newcommand` with a ⟨*name*⟩ starting in `\end...`, even if `\renewcommand` claims the ⟨*name*⟩ is unused. It is also issued if you try to define an environment ⟨*name*⟩ but the command `\end`⟨*name*⟩ already has a definition. For instance, you cannot define an environment `graf` because TeX has a low-level command called `\endgraf`.

Command ⟨*name*⟩ invalid in math mode

This is either a warning or an error message indicating that you have used a command in math mode that should be used only in normal text. In the case of an error message, use h to get further help.

Command ⟨*name*⟩ not defined as a math alphabet

This error message is issued when you attempt to use `\SetMathAlphabet` on a ⟨*name*⟩ that was not previously declared with `\DeclareMathAlphabet` or `\DeclareSymbolFontAlphabet` to be a math alphabet identifier.

Command ⟨*name*⟩ not provided in base LaTeX2e

You get this error for a handful of math symbols available in a "LaTeX symbol font" distributed with LaTeX 2.09. These fonts are no longer loaded because that wastes one of the 16 precious math symbol font families (see page 739). If you need that symbol, load either **amsfonts** or the **wasysym** package.

Command ⟨*name*⟩ unavailable in encoding ⟨*encoding*⟩

Generated by `\TextSymbolUnavailable`, which is these days very seldom used, because for most symbols suitable default mappings exist. If you get this error, it means that the symbol you attempt to typeset is not available in the current text encoding and you have to change the encoding.

Command ⟨*name*⟩ undefined

This error is triggered when you use `\renewcommand` with a ⟨*name*⟩ that is unknown to LaTeX. Either ⟨*name*⟩ was misspelled or you should have used `\newcommand` instead.

It is also issued if you try to use `\RenewDocumentCommand` or `\MakeRobust` with an undefined command ⟨*name*⟩.

Corrupted NFSS tables

LaTeX tried some font substitution and detected an inconsistency in its internal tables. This error happens if font substitution was triggered and the substitution rules contain a loop (i.e., some circular `sub` declarations exist) or when the default substitution arguments for the current encoding point to a nonexistent font shape group.

Counter too large

This error is produced if you try to display a counter value with \fnsymbol, \alph, or \Alph and the value is outside the available range for the chosen display form. See Section A.2.2 on page 650 for ways to work around this error.

Dimension too large   [TeX]

TeX can deal only with absolute sizes that are less than 16383.99998pt (about 226 inches or 7.75 meters). Even on a huge page this range should be enough.

However, the error can also be triggered by packages such as tikz or pgfplots that internally use dimension registers for calculating coordinates. Even if the coordinates and plot values themselves are small, intermediate calculation steps involving, for example, divisions by small values can exceed TeX's limits.

\displaybreak cannot be applied here   [amsmath]

An enclosing environment such as split, aligned, or gathered has created an unbreakable block.

Division by 0   [graphics|graphicx]

Usually, you get this error when you scale a graphic that has a height of zero. This can happen unintentionally — for example, if you specify angle=-90, height=3cm on \includegraphics. The rotation turns the image sideways, making the height zero, a value difficult to scale. In such a case use totalheight instead.

\DocumentMetadata should be only used before \documentclass

The \DocumentMetadata command provides data relevant to the whole document. Some of that information has to be specified at a very early stage, e.g., before the PDF (Portable Document Format) output file has been opened because it is already needed at this point. It must therefore be specified at first, and even though this is not strictly necessary for all document metadata, LaTeX prohibits its use after \documentclass has been seen, in order to ensure that all such data is stored in a single place.

Double subscript   [TeX]

Two subscripts appear in a row (e.g., x_i_2), and LaTeX does not know whether you mean x_{i2} or x_{i_2}. Add braces to indicate the subscripts: x_{i_2}.

Double superscript   [TeX]

LaTeX found two superscripts in a row. See the explanation above.

Encoding file '⟨name⟩enc.def' not found   [fontenc]

If you ask for encoding ⟨name⟩, LaTeX tries to load the definitions for this encoding from the file ⟨name⟩enc.def (after converting ⟨name⟩ to lowercase letters). If this file does not exist or cannot be found by LaTeX, you get this error message.

Encoding scheme ⟨name⟩ unknown

The encoding ⟨name⟩ you have specified in a declaration or in \fontencoding is not known to the system. Either you misspelled its name, you forgot to declare it using `\DeclareFontEncoding`, or you need to load some font support package providing it.

End of environment '⟨name⟩' already defined [cmd]

When defining a new environment with `\NewDocumentEnvironment`, it checks that neither `\⟨name⟩` nor `\end⟨name⟩` is already defined. If only the latter is defined, you get this error message, otherwise the one below. In either case your definition is not made.

Environment ⟨name⟩ already defined

You try to declare an environment with `\newenvironment` with a ⟨name⟩ that already has a meaning in LaTeX. Your declaration is ignored, and you have to choose a different name or use `\renewenvironment`. `\NewDocumentEnvironment` shows the same behavior.

Environment ⟨name⟩ undefined

You get this error if you use `\renewenvironment` on an environment name that is unknown to LaTeX. Either the ⟨name⟩ was misspelled or you should have used `\newenvironment` instead. `\RenewDocumentEnvironment` shows the same behavior. This error is also triggered if you use `\begin` with a ⟨name⟩ that is not known to LaTeX.

Erroneous nesting of equation structures; [amsmath]
  trying to recover with 'aligned'

Only certain amsmath display structures can be nested; `aligned` is one of these, so the system replaces a wrongly nested environment with it. This is probably not what you intended, so you should change the wrongly nested environment.

Extra & on this line [amsmath]

This error occurs only when you are using old amsmath environments that are not described in this book. If it does occur, then it is disastrous, and you need to check very carefully the environment where it occurred.

Extra alignment tab has been changed to \cr [TeX]

If you use an alignment structure, such as `tabular` or one of the display math environments (e.g., `eqnarray` or `split` from the amsmath package), then each row is divided into a defined number of columns separated by & signs. The error means that there are too many such characters, probably because you forgot a `\\` indicating the end of the row (`\cr` is TeX's name for the row end, but it is not a fully functional equivalent to `\\`).

Extra \endgroup [TeX]

TeX has seen an `\endgroup` without a preceding matching `\begingroup`.

Extra \middle [TeX]

Your formula contains a `\middle` that is outside of a `\left...\right` construction. Recall that `\left/\right` pairs must be part of the same "subformula". They cannot, for example, be separated by & in an alignment or appear on different grouping levels.

Extra \or ⸢TEX⸣

> TEX encountered an \or primitive that has no matching low-level \ifcase conditional. The extra \or can be the result from a bad use of \ifthenelse.

Extra \right ⸢TEX⸣

> This error is issued by TEX if it finds a \right command without a matching \left in a formula. See advice on "Extra \middle" above.

Extra }, or forgotten $ ⸢TEX⸣

> This error is triggered when math formula delimiters (e.g., $...$, \[...\]) and brace groups are not properly nested. TEX thinks it has found a superfluous }, as in $x}$, and is going to ignore it. While in this example the deletion of the closing brace is the right choice, it would be wrong in \mbox{\(a}. There a closing \) is missing, so deleting the } produces additional errors.

Extra }, or forgotten \endgroup ⸢TEX⸣

> The current group was started with \begingroup (used, for example, by \begin{..}), but TEX found a closing } character instead of the corresponding \endgroup. You get this error if you leave a stray } inside a body of an environment.

File '⟨name⟩' not found

> LATEX is trying to load the file ⟨name⟩ but cannot find it, either because it does not exist or because the underlying TEX program is looking in the wrong place. If the file exists but LATEX claims it is not available, it is possible that your TEX installation uses a hashing mechanism to speed up file access, and you may have to run a special program to make your installation aware of newly installed files (e.g., mktexlsr with the TEX Live distribution).
>
> The error is issued by commands like \input and \usepackage if they cannot find the requested file. You can suggest an alternate file in response to the error. If the new name is specified without an extension, the old extension is reused if known to LATEX. If you want to omit loading the file, press ⟨Enter⟩; to quit the run, type x or X. In some cases you might receive a similar low-level TEX error "! I can't find file '⟨name⟩'" that is slightly more difficult to quit; see the entry on page 725.
>
> If a graphics file requested with \includegraphics is missing, it may help to press h to learn which extensions have been tried when looking for the file.

File ended while scanning ⟨something⟩ ⸢TEX⸣

> This error is part of a "Runaway..." error; check the explanations on page 736.

First argument of '⟨declaration⟩' must be a command (cmd)

> The first argument to \NewDocumentCommand or its siblings has to be the command that is going to be defined or redefined. LATEX found something else instead, e.g., a character or several tokens.

Float(s) lost

> One or more floats (e.g., figure or table) or \marginpar commands have not been typeset. The most likely reason is that you placed a float environment or

marginal note inside a box by mistake — inside another float or \marginpar, or inside a minipage environment, a \parbox, or a \footnote.

LaTeX might detect this problem very late, such as when finishing the document. This can make it very difficult to find the offending place in the source. The best solution in this case is to halve your document repeatedly (for example, by using the primitive \endinput), until the fraction producing the error is small enough that you spot it.

If incorrect nesting is not the root cause, then you may have encountered a serious coding problem in the float algorithm, probably caused by some extra packages you loaded.

Font family ⟨enc⟩+⟨family⟩ unknown
    You tried to declare a font shape group with \DeclareFontShape without first declaring the font ⟨family⟩ as being available in the encoding ⟨enc⟩ using \DeclareFontFamily.

Font ⟨name⟩ not found
    LaTeX's internal font tables contain wrong information, so LaTeX was unable to find the external font ⟨name⟩. Either this font was never installed, its .tfm file cannot be found by TeX for some reason, or the \DeclareFontShape declaration referring to it contains a spelling error.

Font ⟨internal name⟩=⟨external name⟩ not loadable: ⟨reason⟩ TeX
    TeX was unable to load a font with the LaTeX name ⟨internal name⟩ having the structure \⟨encoding⟩/⟨family⟩/⟨series⟩/⟨shape⟩/⟨size⟩ in NFSS notation.[1] For example, it might say \T1/cmr/m/it/10 (Computer Modern medium italic 10 points in T1 encoding). This should give you a good hint as to which font has a problem, even if you are not able to do much about it. There are two possible ⟨reason⟩s:

    Bad metric (TFM) file TeX
        The TeX metric file for the font (i.e., ⟨external name⟩.tfm) is corrupted. Your installation may have some utility programs to check .tfm files in detail, although this usually requires expert help.

    Metric (TFM) file not found TeX
        The TeX metric file for the font (i.e., ⟨external name⟩.tfm) was not found. Your installation may have a package (e.g., cmbright) to support a certain font family but the corresponding fonts are not available or are not properly installed.

Font ⟨internal name⟩=⟨external⟩ not loaded: Not enough room left TeX
    TeX can load only a certain number of fonts, and there was no space left to load ⟨internal name⟩. To find out which fonts are loaded, use the package tracefnt described in Section 9.5.8. One possible reason for excessive loading of fonts is the use of unusual font sizes for which LaTeX has to calculate and load the corresponding math fonts; see Section 9.8.5 for details.

---

[1]This is, in fact, a single command name, but due to the slashes in the name, you cannot enter it directly in your document, unless you use \UseName{⟨encoding⟩/⟨family⟩/⟨series⟩/⟨shape⟩/⟨size⟩}.

Font ⟨*font name*⟩ not found

> This error message is issued when there is something very wrong with a \DeclareFontShape declaration—perhaps it does not contain any size specifications. Check the setup for the font shape group in question.

Generic hooks cannot be added to '⟨*command*⟩' ^(hooks)

> Generic hooks are added only to a ⟨*command*⟩ when code is added to the hook with \AddToHook. Such patching is sometimes impossible for a number of different reasons, and in that case you get this error. The precise reason is then given in the help text of the error message.

Hook '⟨*name*⟩' has already been declared ^(hooks)

> If the same hook ⟨*name*⟩ is declared by different packages or classes, disaster is guaranteed, and this action is therefore disallowed. If you get this error, then the two packages are incompatible and cannot be used together.

Key '⟨*key*⟩' may only be used during loading of package '⟨*name*⟩' ^(keys)

> The ⟨*key*⟩/value option of package ⟨*name*⟩ is allowed only while the package is loaded, but not in a \SetKeys declaration.

Key '⟨*key*⟩' may only be used in the preamble ^(keys)

> The ⟨*key*⟩ in question cannot be changed after \begin{document}, so you have to move it earlier into the preamble.

I can't find file '⟨*name*⟩' ^{TeX}

> A low-level TeX error is raised when TeX cannot find a file that was requested to load. This error can be bypassed only by providing TeX with a file that it can find or by stopping the run altogether (if your operating system allows that). To get past this error, many installations offer a file null.tex so that you can reply null in response. LaTeX normally uses the error message "File '⟨*name*⟩' not found", which supports various user actions. However, depending on the package coding, you may get the current error instead.

I can't switch '⟨*char*⟩' on or off--not a shorthand. ^{babel}

> When a user uses the command \shorthandon and passes it a ⟨*char*⟩ that is not defined to be a shorthand, this error message is displayed, and the instruction is ignored.

I can't write on file '⟨*name*⟩' ^{TeX}

> TeX is not allowed to write data to the file ⟨*name*⟩. It is probably read-only, or you may not have writing permission for its directory. On some TeX implementations (e.g., those on the TeX Live CD), the error may be preceded by a line like the following:
>
> ```
> tex: Not writing to /texmf/tex/latex/base/latex.ltx (openout_any = p).
> ```
>
> These TeX installations are by default configured to be "paranoid" (hence, "p" above) when writing to files. They allow you to write only to files below the current directory and *not* to any files specified with an absolute path name or

starting with a dot in their name. To change that behavior you have to modify the settings in the file `texmf.cnf`.

`Illegal use of \AddToHook{⟨hook⟩}[top-level]{...}` (hooks)

The code label `top-level` is reserved for use in the preamble or document body to indicate last-minute hook code added by a user. The error is issued if a package or class adds code to a ⟨hook⟩ and attempts to label the code using this name.

`Illegal character in array arg`

You get this error if the column specification for a `tabular` or `array` environment or a `\multicolumn` command contains characters that are not defined as column specifiers to LaTeX. A likely cause is that you used the extended syntax of the `array` package, described in Chapter 6, but forgot to load the package in the preamble (e.g., after you have copied a table from one document to another).

`Illegal mode change in hook 'para/⟨name⟩'. ⟨reason⟩` (hooks)

Paragraph hooks cannot contain code that changes the TeX mode (unless it is done only temporarily within the hook). For example, `para/before` is not allowed to switch to horizontal mode, because that would trigger another call to the same hook code, ending in an endless recursion. If that happens, ⟨reason⟩ says what exactly is wrong. Examine the hook code with `\ShowHook` to find the issue.

`Illegal parameter number in definition of ⟨command⟩` TeX

This error occurs when a (re)defined command or environment uses #⟨digit⟩ in the replacement text, with a digit higher than the declared number of parameters. This error can be implicitly caused by nesting declaration commands, such as `\newcommand`, and forgetting that inner commands refer to their arguments by doubling the # characters; see page 627 for details. Another possible cause is referring to environment arguments in the second mandatory argument of `\newenvironment` or `\renewenvironment`.

`Illegal unit of measure (pt inserted)` TeX

You get this error if you misspell or forget the unit when specifying the value for a length parameter; see Section A.2.4.

`Improper argument for math accent:` amsmath
  `Extra braces must be added to prevent wrong output`

The whole of the "accented subformula" must be surrounded by braces.

`Improper discretionary list` TeX

This error is produced by TeX if it encounters a `\discretionary` command whose arguments contain anything other than characters, boxes, or kerns, after expansion.

`Improper \hyphenation` TeX

If you want to specify a hyphenation exception with `\hyphenation`, then you have to ensure that the argument contains only letters and - characters to

indicate the hyphenation points.[1] The problem is that, for example, accented characters in some font encodings are individual glyphs (allowed) but in other font
encodings produce complicated constructs requiring the \accent primitive. For
example, if the T1 encoding is used, then ü or \"u refers to a single glyph. Thus,

    \usepackage[T1]{fontenc} \hyphenation{Tür-stop-per T\"ur-klin-ke}

are both valid. The same hyphenation exception used with the default OT1
encoding would produce this error. See page →I 767 for an explanation of
character differences in the major encodings.

Improper \prevdepth TEX

You used \the\prevdepth or \showthe\prevdepth outside of vertical mode,
which is not allowed. This error also shows up if you mistakenly placed a float
(e.g., a figure or table) inside a math display environment.

Improper \spacefactor TEX

You used \the\spacefactor or \showthe\spacefactor outside of horizontal mode, which is not allowed.

\include cannot be nested

LATEX encountered an \include command inside a file loaded with \include.
Because of implementation constraints, this is impossible. Either change the
inner \include into \input or rearrange your document file structure so that
all \include statements are in the main document file.

Incompatible list can't be unboxed TEX

TEX was asked to unpack a box with horizontal material while trying to build a
vertical list, or vice versa. Either you encountered a serious programming error
in a package or you used some commands in a way explicitly not supported. For
example, the commands from the soul package produce this error when they are
nested inside each other.

Incomplete ⟨conditional⟩; all text was ignored after line ⟨number⟩ TEX

A low-level TEX conditional was unfinished (no matching \fi) when LATEX reached
the end of the current input file.

Infinite glue shrinkage found ⟨somewhere⟩ TEX

To break paragraphs into lines or the galley into pages, TEX assumes that there
is no rubber length that can arbitrarily shrink, because that would mean that any
amount of material can be placed into a single line or onto a single page. Thus,
\hspace{0pt minus 1fil} in a paragraph or \vspace{0pt minus 1fil}
between paragraphs is not allowed and raises this error (⟨somewhere⟩ gives some
indication about where the offending material was found).

Infinite shrinkage found in '⟨region⟩' (marks)

The current mark region, e.g., current column or page, contains some glue that
can arbitrarily shrink. This makes it impossible to extract marks from that region.

---

[1] LuaTEX offers an extended syntax for this.

This glue should not be present and indicates a coding error in a package or the LaTeX kernel. Please report it to the appropriate maintainer.

Interruption `TeX`

You get this "error" after interrupting the LaTeX run (with Control-C or whatever your installation offers), so you should not be surprised by it. To finish the run prematurely, press x followed by ⟨*Return*⟩. Just pressing ⟨*Return*⟩ continues the run as if it was uninterrupted.

Invalid argument prefix '⟨*prefix*⟩' in ⟨*command or environment*⟩ (cmd)

The definition for ⟨*command or environment*⟩ used a ⟨*prefix*⟩ in the argument specification that is not valid at the point it is used. As explained in the help text, this can have different reasons:

- There are two identical prefixes applied to a single argument specifier — one is redundant. Perhaps an argument specifier is missing?

- A ! prefix got applied to a mandatory argument or to an optional one followed by further mandatory ones. It is supported only for trailing optional arguments;

- A command defined with \NewExpandableDocumentCommand has a mixture of long (prefix +) and short arguments. The long ones must come last in expandable commands, but this is not the case;

- The > prefix is not supported with expandable commands.

Invalid argument type '⟨*type*⟩' in ⟨*command or environment*⟩ (cmd)

A new command was defined with \NewDocumentCommand or one of its siblings, but its argument specification contains some ⟨*type*⟩ that LaTeX is not happy with. The help text gives further details; the most important reasons are:

- The specified ⟨*type*⟩ does not correspond to any defined argument type — probably a misspelling;

- The ⟨*type*⟩ is a deprecated type that is not made available by default — if you really need it, you have to load the xparse package in order to use it;

- The type b has been used with a command, but it is available only for environments;

- The specified ⟨*type*⟩ cannot be used in expandable definitions, i.e., those made with \NewExpandableDocumentCommand. For example, v (verbatim) arguments are not available in that case.

Invalid argument {⟨*arg*⟩} to \IfBoolean... (cmd)

The first argument to \IfBooleanTF or one of its variants has to be a special Boolean value, for example, the result of checking for a * in the arguments of a command defined with \NewDocumentCommand. LaTeX found something else, hence the error message. Perhaps you passed it the wrong #⟨*number*⟩ argument.

Invalid use of ⟨*command*⟩ [amsmath]

> You have used an amsmath command in a place where it does not make sense. Look up the correct use of this command.

Keyboard character used is undefined in input encoding ⟨*name*⟩ [inputenc]

> The 8-bit number encountered in the document is not mapped by the input encoding ⟨*name*⟩ to some LICR object (see Sections 9.5.4 and 9.9.3). Check whether the document is really stored in the specified encoding. These days it is usually best to store files in UTF-8 encoding and not load inputenc.

Invalid UTF-8 byte ⟨*hex number*⟩   or
Invalid UTF-8 byte sequence (⟨*sequence*⟩)

> The document does not appear to be in UTF-8 encoding. In pdfTEX, try adding \UseRawInputEncoding as the first line of the file or specify the correct encoding such as \usepackage[latin1]{inputenc} in the document preamble. Alternatively, save the file in UTF-8 using your editor or another tool.
>
> Another possible cause is the use of multibyte UTF-8 characters with packages such as listings or soul that process their input on a character by character basis, but expect the characters to be single tokens (which is not the case for multibyte characters in pdfTEX). In that case you have to either avoid or protect such characters in the input, switch to an alternative package, or use a Unicode engine. Search the Internet for advice about which option is best in your specific case.

Invalid UTF-8 byte or sequence ... replaced by U+FFFD [XƎTEX only]

> **Unicode engines**
>
> The document processed by XƎTEX does not appear to be in UTF-8 encoding. Offending bytes have been changed, but that is seldom the right corrective action. You have to make sure the input is encoded in UTF-8.

Labels '⟨*label₁*⟩' and '⟨*label₂*⟩' are incompatible in hook '⟨*hook*⟩' (hooks)

> The ⟨*hook*⟩ contains two code chunks labeled ⟨*label₁*⟩ and ⟨*label₂*⟩ that are incompatible with each other. This usually means that two packages were loaded that cannot be used together (with luck you can identify them from the label names). Depending on the severity of the issue, this message may show up only as a warning, not an error. In any case, the code for both labels is dropped.

Limit controls must follow a math operator [TEX]

> You can use \limits or \nolimits only following math operators such as \sum. See Table 11.6 for a list of common operator commands.

\LoadClass in package file

> The \LoadClass command is allowed only in class files; see Section A.6.

Lonely \item--perhaps a missing list environment

> The \item command is allowed only within list structures, but LATEX believes that this one was found outside a list. In contrast to the "Something's wrong — perhaps a missing \item" error, LATEX's diagnosis in this case is usually correct.

Mark class '⟨class⟩' already defined (marks)

You try to declare a new mark class with `\NewMarkClass`, but the ⟨class⟩ name has already been used for that purpose. Your declaration is ignored, and you have to choose a different name.

Mark region '⟨region⟩' not usable (marks)

The specified ⟨region⟩ in commands such as `\FirstMark` is not usable at this time; e.g., you cannot refer to `last-column` while LaTeX is finishing the first column of a page.

Math alphabet identifier ⟨id⟩ is undefined in math version ⟨name⟩

The math alphabet identifier ⟨id⟩ was used in a math version (⟨name⟩) for which it was not set up. An additional `\SetMathAlphabet` declaration should be added to the preamble of the document to assign a font shape group for this alphabet identifier.

Math version ⟨name⟩ is not defined

A math alphabet or a symbol font was assigned to a math version that is unknown to LaTeX. Either you misspelled its name or you forgot to declare this version (perhaps you have to add some package file). It is also possible that the math version you selected with `\mathversion` is not known to the system.

Mismatched LaTeX support files detected. ⟨reason⟩

Since 2020, LaTeX includes the L3 programming layer as part of the format. However, some parts of this layer are loaded later during document processing, and at that time LaTeX might realize that the format and these additional support files do not match. This is a fatal error, and processing stops.

Most often the reason for this nasty surprise is the use of a local format that was previously built (by mistake?) and that did not get remade after the TeX distribution was updated. To figure out which formats are available on the system, try running

```
kpsewhich -all -engine=pdftex pdflatex.fmt
```

if you are using pdfTeX. For XeTeX or LuaTeX, the engine should be `xetex` or `luahbtex` and the format `xelatex` or `lualatex`, respectively. If this returns more than one format file, remove the local one or make sure that it is properly regenerated. Further details on this can be found on the Internet.

Misplaced alignment tab character & [TeX]

LaTeX found an `&` character outside of `tabular`, `align`, or one of the other alignment environments. If you want to typeset &, use `\&` instead. A possible cause is use of the amsmath environment `cases` or `matrix` without loading the package.

Misplaced \cr or Misplaced \crcr [TeX]

A `\cr` is the TeX low-level command for ending a row in an alignment structure (`\crcr` is a variation thereof); the corresponding LaTeX command is `\\`. TeX believes it came across such a command outside of an alignment structure.

Misplaced \noalign [TeX]

 The TeX primitive \noalign is internally used to place "nonaligned" material between rows of alignment displays. It is therefore allowed only directly following the command that finishes a row. For example, you get this error when you use \hline outside of array or tabular, or not directly after \\ within these environments.

Misplaced \omit [TeX]

 The TeX primitive \omit is internally used to change the column specifications in an alignment display (e.g., to span rows with \multicolumn inside a tabular). The \omit command (and thus the commands calling it) is allowed only at the very beginning of an alignment cell (i.e., following \\ or &).

Missing \begin{document}

 This error occurs if typesetting is attempted while still within the document preamble.[1] It is most likely due to a declaration error that is misinterpreted by LaTeX. The error is also produced by text following \begin{filecontents} on the same line.

Missing control sequence inserted [TeX]

 You used \newcommand or \renewcommand without providing a command name (starting with a backslash) as the first argument.

Missing \cr inserted [TeX]

 TeX thinks it is about time to end the row in an alignment structure and inserted its low-level command for this purpose. In a LaTeX document, this guess is often wrong, so TeX's recovery attempt usually fails in such a case.

Missing delimiter (. inserted) [TeX]

 A \left, \middle, \right, or one of the \big.. commands was not followed by a delimiter. As corrective action, the empty delimiter "." was inserted. See Section 11.5.6 on page 191 for details.

Missing \endcsname inserted [TeX]

 This error can arise from using commands as part of the name of a counter or environment name (e.g., \newenvironment{Bl\"ode}).

 These days it can also show up if you use anything other than characters or very simple commands to construct a file name for use with \input and similar commands. Trying to construct a file name using a fragile command, e.g.,

 \input{test\ifthenelse{...}{a}{b}}

will fail and produce this strange error. Commands made explicitly robust (e.g., with \MakeRobust) are not executed but replaced by their name without a backslash, so that is most likely also not the desired result.

---

[1] Typesetting inside an \sbox or \savebox declaration within the preamble is allowed, but it is usually wise to move such declarations after \begin{document}, because some packages may delay their final setup until that point.

Missing number, treated as zero [TeX]

This error occurs when TeX is looking for a number or a dimension but finds something else. For example, using `\value{page}` instead of `\thepage` would produce this error, because an isolated `\value` makes TeX expect a low-level counter assignment. In general, using a length register without a proper mutator function like `\setlength` can trigger this error. You also get this message when `\usebox` is not followed by a box bin defined with `\newsavebox`, because internally such bins are represented by numbers.

One other surprising scenario is due to a limitation in TeX's implementation of integer and length expressions involving parentheses: you cannot start an expression with `+(` or `-(`. In that case add a 0 to change the + or − from an unary to a binary symbol; see Example A-2-12 on page 659.

Missing p-arg in array arg

There is a p column specifier not followed by an expression in braces (containing the width) in the argument to `tabular`, `array`, or `\multicolumn`.

Missing @-exp in array arg

There is an @ column specifier not followed by an expression in braces (containing the inter-column material) in the argument to `tabular`, `array`, or `\multicolumn`.

Missing # inserted in alignment preamble [TeX]

An alignment preamble specifies the layout of the columns in an alignment structure. Internally, TeX uses # to denote the part of the column that should receive input. In LaTeX this is unlikely to appear as a first error.

Missing = inserted for \ifnum [TeX]

TeX complains that the low-level `\ifnum` conditional is not followed by two numbers separated by `<`, `=`, or `>`. This error can occur when you forget the comparison operator in `\ifthenelse`.

Missing = inserted for \ifdim [TeX]

The low-level `\ifdim` conditional is not followed by a comparison between two lengths.

Missing $ inserted [TeX]

TeX has encountered something in normal text that is allowed only in math mode (e.g., `\sum`, `\alpha`, `^`), or something that is not allowed inside math (e.g., `\par`) while processing a formula. It has therefore inserted a $ to switch to math mode or to leave it. If, for example, you tried to get an underscore by simply using `_` instead of `\_`, LaTeX would typeset the rest of the paragraph as a formula, most likely producing more errors along the way.

Missing \endgroup inserted [TeX]

This error indicates that a grouping structure in the document is incorrectly nested. Environments internally use `\begingroup` and `\endgroup`, and for some reason TeX thinks that such a group was not properly closed. If you cannot determine why the group structure is faulty, try using the `\showgroups` or `\tracinggroups` commands, as explained on page 747.

`Missing \right. inserted` [TeX]

Your formula contains a `\left` without a matching `\right`. Recall that `\left/\right` delimiter pairs must be part of the same "subformula"; they cannot, for example, be separated by & in an alignment or appear on different grouping levels.

`Missing { inserted` [TeX]

TeX thinks there is an open brace missing and inserted one. This error is, for example, caused by a stray } inside a `tabular` cell.

`Missing } inserted` [TeX]

Something is wrong in the grouping structure of the document, and TeX tries to recover by inserting a closing brace. This attempt either gets it onto the right track again or causes you to receive more errors. Usually, the problem becomes apparent if you look at the typeset output. If you cannot determine why the group structure is faulty, try using the `\showgroups` or `\tracinggroups` commands, as explained on page 747.

`Multiple \label's: label ⟨label⟩ will be lost` [amsmath]

Within the amsmath display environments, you can have only one `\label` per equation. It is usually best to remove or replace all but the last, because it is the only one that is effective.

`Multiple \tag` [amsmath]

Within the amsmath display environments, you can have only one `\tag` command per equation. All but the first are ignored.

`No counter '⟨name⟩' defined`

The counter ⟨name⟩ referenced in either `\setcounter`, `\addtocounter`, or the optional argument of `\newcounter` or `\newtheorem` is unknown to LaTeX. It must first be declared with `\newcounter`.

`No declaration for shape ⟨font shape⟩`

The `sub` or `ssub` size function used in a `\DeclareFontShape` command refers to a substitution shape that is unknown to LaTeX's font selection scheme.

`No driver specified` [color|graphics|graphicx]

The package graphics, graphicx, color, or xcolor was loaded without specifying a target device option. On most installations this is done using the configuration files `graphics.cfg` and `color.cfg`.

`No room for a new ⟨register⟩` [TeX]

The packages loaded in your document require more internal registers (`\count`, `\dimen`, ...) than there are available in TeX. These days this error should not happen because LaTeX is using all registers available in the engine, which is a

733

huge number. So if you are getting this, then there is probably a coding issue in a package so that it allocates registers over and over again. To debug that you may need external help.

The only exception are `\write` registers: most engines have only 16 registers available, and if you run out, then you can load Bruno Le Floch's morewrites package to get additional (virtual) registers at the cost of processing speed.

No `\title` given

A LaTeX class has executed `\maketitle` without seeing a `\title` declaration. Only `\date` is optional when this command is used.

Not a letter TeX

You specified a hyphenation exception with `\hyphenation`, but the argument to this command contained some characters that TeX does not consider to be letters. For example, `\hyphenation{la-ryn-gol-o-gist's}` would produce such an error because ' is not a "letter" in TeX's categorization.

Not in outer par mode

This error is issued when a `\marginpar` or a float environment, such as `table` or `figure`, is encountered inside a box-producing command or environment. For instance, you cannot use a `\marginpar` in a footnote, a float, a `tabular`, or a similar place (because all of them produce boxes). Move the offending object to the main galley.

Not in vertical mode

Starting a paragraph with `\RawIndent` or `\RawNoindent` is allowed only if LaTeX is in vertical mode. Because these commands are intended for programmers and not for ordinary use in documents, getting this error most likely means that there is a bug in some package.

Number too big TeX

You assigned or used a number in `\setcounter` or `\addtocounter` that is larger than the largest number that TeX can handle (2147483647, hexadecimal 7FFFFFFF). This error can also happen when modifying a length register with `\setlength` or `\addtolength`.

OK TeX

You used the TeX tracing command `\showbox` or `\showlists` and the parameter `\tracingonline` is positive. After displaying the data, LaTeX stopped with this message to allow for some interaction on the command line (e.g., entering `i\show..` to view some other values). If `\tracingonline` is zero, no data is shown on the terminal and the message is slightly different; see below.

OK (see the transcript file) TeX

You used the TeX tracing command `\showbox` or `\showlists`, without also directing LaTeX to display the result on the terminal. The data is written only to the transcript (`.log`) file. Use also `\showoutput` to display it on the terminal.

`Old form ⟨command⟩ should be \begin{⟨envname⟩}` amsmath

You have used `cases`, `matrix`, or `pmatrix` in its non-amsmath command form (probably with its old internal syntax). Change to the amsmath environment form with standard internal syntax.

`Only one # is allowed per tab` TEX

This error indicates a broken alignment template. In LaTeX it should not occur, unless caused by a fragile command in a moving argument.

`Option clash for package ⟨name⟩`

The package ⟨name⟩ was requested twice with a conflicting set of options. When you press H in response to this error, LaTeX shows you the sets of conflicting options. Because LaTeX loads a package only once,[1] the best solution is to specify all options on the first occasion.

If this is not possible, because the package is already loaded as part of the class or another package, you can try to specify the required options as global options to the `\documentclass` command. In an emergency you can even load a package before `\documentclass` by using `\RequirePackage`. See Section 2.1.2 on page →I 24 for details.

Alternatively, adding a suitable `\PassOptionsToPackage` declaration before the package gets loaded might work; this is described in Section A.6.4 on page 697.

`Page height already too large`

You used `\enlargethispage` on a page whose vertical size is already larger than `8191.99998pt`, or roughly 113 inches. LaTeX thinks that this is dangerously large and does not extend the page size as requested.

`Paragraph ended before ⟨command⟩ was complete` TEX

As discussed in Section A.1.2, commands defined with `\newcommand*` or `\renewcommand*` and by default all arguments of `\NewDocumentCommand` and friends (unless their arguments are specified with a +) are not allowed to contain `\par` or an empty line. If they do, you get a `Runaway argument` together with this error. The ⟨command⟩ listed may not be the one used in your document. For example, `\emph{..\par..}` lists `\text@command` in the error message (i.e., the internal command called by `\emph`).

`pdfTeX error (font expansion): auto expansion is only` pdfTEX/LuaTEX
    `possible with scalable fonts`

This engine message is issued if you use the microtype package together with nonscalable fonts, e.g., those produced by METAFONT, and microtype tried to use font expansion. Set `expansion` to `false` in regions where such fonts are used for typesetting or switch to a different font family that is scalable.

`(Please type a command or say '\end')` TEX

You have replied with ⟨Return⟩ in response to *. See the first entry on page 717.

---

[1] The only exception is the fontenc package, which can be loaded as often as needed with different options; see Section 9.5.5 on page →I 693.

`\pushtabs` and `\poptabs` don't match

You issued a `\poptabs` command in a `tabbing` environment, but there was no previous `\pushtabs` command issued.

Requested version '⟨*version*⟩' for '⟨*package or class*⟩' is unknown

In the second optional argument of `\usepackage` or `\documentclass` you can request a specific version of the package or class using either a date or a named ⟨*version*⟩ label. The version specified, e.g., =V2, is not known to LaTeX.

Required argument missing for ⟨*command or environment*⟩   (cmd)

A command defined with `\NewDocumentCommand` or one of its siblings has an argument specification that includes a delimited mandatory argument (specified with `r` or `R`). In the document body this command is used without providing this argument, and as a result you see this error message.

`\RequirePackage` or `\LoadClass` in Options Section

A `\RequirePackage` or `\LoadClass` was found inside a package or class file between the `\DeclareOption` commands and `\ProcessOptions`. Loading packages or classes in this part is not allowed because it would clobber the data structure holding the current set of options; see Section A.6 for details. If you want to load a package when a certain option is specified, use a flag to indicate that the option was selected and load it after the `\ProcessOptions` command has done its job.

Rotation not supported   graphics|graphicx

You have requested rotation with `\rotatebox` or a similar command, but the selected graphics driver does not support the rotation of objects. LaTeX leaves the right amount of space, but the printed document might show the image in the wrong position.

Runaway ⟨*something*⟩   TeX

TeX thinks it has scanned too far while looking for the end of ⟨*something*⟩, where ⟨*something*⟩ can be either `argument`, `definition`, `preamble`, or `text`. Unless low-level TeX code is at fault, the most likely cause is `argument`. For example, if you forgot the closing brace of an argument, it might cause TeX to scan until it reaches the end of the file or until its memory is filled — whichever comes first. Incomplete definitions done with `\newcommand`, `\newenvironment`, and so forth also claim that the `argument` has run away. Only low-level definitions, involving TeX primitives like `\def`, produce a `Runaway definition`.

A `Runaway preamble` means that an alignment structure has problems (that should not occur in normal LaTeX documents), and `Runaway text` usually refers to a token register assignment (this should never happen unless there is a serious package implementation error).

In contrast to the situation with normal error messages, you do not get a line number that indicates where the error was detected (because TeX often has reached the end of the file). Instead, you see the beginning of the material that was being absorbed. For example, if you have a definition without the final closing brace,

```
\newcommand\foo{bar
\begin{document} Some text \end{document}
```

you get

```
Runaway argument?
{bar \begin {document} Some text \end {document}
! File ended while scanning use of \@argdef.
<inserted text>
                \par
<*> samplefile.tex
?
```

The fact that TEX in that case inserted `\par` as a recovery action is of little help, because the complete document was already swallowed. Instead of "`File ended while...`", you might see some other message at this point, such as "`Paragraph ended before...`".

Scaling not supported `graphics|graphicx`

You have requested scaling with `\resizebox` or a similar command, but the selected graphics driver does not support scaling of objects. LATEX leaves the right amount of space, but the printed document will show the image at the original (unscaled) size.

Something's wrong-perhaps a missing \item

This error message is produced by an `\addvspace` command when encountered in horizontal mode. The follow-up remark about "`perhaps a missing \item`" is unfortunately seldom correct. For example, forgetting the closing brace on `\mbox` as in `\mbox{...\section{..}...` would produce this error, because the `\section` command that executes `\addvspace` internally is now used in horizontal mode.

Identify which command issued the `\addvspace` causing the error, and check whether that command was used incorrectly. Refer to page 655 for an in-depth discussion of the `\addvspace` command.

Sorry, I can't find ⟨format⟩ ... `TEX`

If you get this message, then LATEX never started because TEX did not find the ⟨format⟩ containing the basic LATEX definitions. There is a problem with your TEX installation, and you have to consult the installation documentation.

Sorting rule for '⟨hook⟩' hook applied too late ... (hooks)

`\DeclareHookRule` was used to declare a sorting rule for the one-time hook ⟨hook⟩ *after* the hook was executed. Since such hooks are executed only once, the rule came too late, and you get this error message.

`Suggested extra height (⟨value⟩) dangerously large`

Using the ⟨value⟩ with \enlargethispage would make the resulting page too large (more than 113 inches or 2.87 meters) for LaTeX's liking.

`Suspicious rollback date given`

If you use the latexrelease package, you can roll back your LaTeX release (and a number of supporting packages) to an earlier point in time to process your document as if it were processed with a version current then. If this results in this error message, then the offended package has no rollback information for the date and claims it was not in existence back then.

This may just be spurious due to incomplete data but may also indicate an issue with the package. In any case LaTeX continues using the earliest version it knows about.

`Symbol font ⟨name⟩ is not defined`

You tried to make use of the symbol font ⟨name⟩ — for example, within a \DeclareMathSymbol command — without declaring it first with a suitable \DeclareSymbolFont declaration.

`Tab overflow`

LaTeX supports up to 13 tabulator positions (\=) inside a tabbing environment, and you have used a larger number. If not all of them are needed at the same time, you can try solving the problem by using \pushtabs and/or providing template lines with \kill.

`\tag not allowed here` `amsmath`

The \tag command is allowed only within the top level of a mathematical display. It is usually best to move it to the end of the logical equation in which it occurs.

`TeX capacity exceeded, ⟨explanation⟩` `TeX`

TeX ran out of some sort of memory and died. This error is discussed in detail in Section B.2 on page 744.

`Text line contains an invalid character` `TeX`

The input file contains a strange, nonprinting character that is rejected by TeX. This may happen if you used a word processor to create the file and did not save it as "text".

`The attribute ⟨attrib⟩ is unknown for language ⟨lang⟩` `babel`

You tried to activate an attribute for a language ⟨lang⟩ that is not defined in the language definition file for this language. Check the documentation of babel with respect to this language.

`The font size command \normalsize is not defined...`

A class file needs to provide a minimal setup, including a definition for \normalsize; see Section A.6.11 on page 710 for details.

`There's no line here to end`

This error is triggered if \newline or \\ is found outside a paragraph (i.e., after a \par or an empty line). If the intention was to produce extra vertical space, use \vspace or any of the other commands described on page 654.

This file needs format '⟨*format name*⟩'

> The current input file is not processed further, because it was written for a different flavor of TEX.

This may be a LaTeX bug

> This is an error message dating back to 1986, and to the author's knowledge, until now this message never actually signaled a LATEX bug. It means, however, that LATEX got thoroughly confused by previous errors and lost track of the state of its float data structure. It is best to stop and correct previous errors first.

This should not happen. ⟨*reason*⟩

> In contrast to the previous message, this message was introduced recently, and the developers are fairly confident that it signals an error in the coding of LATEX. After giving a ⟨*reason*⟩, it continues and tells you where to report the bug.

This NFSS system isn't set up properly

> This error occurs when LATEX detects a mistake while trying to verify the font substitution tables at \begin{document}. It means that either a \DeclareFontSubstitution or \DeclareErrorFont[1] declaration is corrupted. These declarations need to point to valid font shapes (declared with \DeclareFontShape). Type h for additional information and inform your system maintainer. If you are the system maintainer, read the end of Section 9.8.3.

Too deeply nested

> Standard LATEX supports a total of six levels of lists nested in each other. Those levels can include up to four lists of type itemize or enumerate. This error signals that your document has overflowed one of these limits. You probably have forgotten to end some list environments properly.
>
> If you really need additional levels and you use the enumitem package, you can increase the overall default using \setlistdepth. However, the restrictions on the number of nested itemize or enumerate environments is fixed, and if you require further levels there, you need to copy the base definitions into a private package and modify their hardwired constants.

Too many arguments for '⟨*command or environment*⟩' (cmd)

> LATEX supports command or environment definitions with a maximum of nine arguments, but your \NewDocumentCommand or \NewDocumentEnvironment declaration asks for more.

Too many columns in eqnarray environment

> The eqnarray environment supports a maximum of three columns (i.e., two & signs per row). For serious math, consider the amsmath package described in Chapter 11, which allows for more complex display structures.

Too many math alphabets used in version ⟨*name*⟩

> You used too many different math alphabet identifiers or symbol fonts in your

---

[1]The declaration \DeclareErrorFont is used during installation and points to a font (font shape + size) that should be used when everything else fails. Its default is Computer Modern Roman 10pt, which should be available with any TEX installation. See [60] for further details.

formulas. If this error occurs after adding the bm package to the preamble, define `\newcommand\bmmax{0}` before loading bm and try again; this prevents the package from preallocating math alphabets. There is also the possibility to increase the counter `localmathalphabets` to keep a higher number of alphabets flexible; see the discussion on page →I 681 for details.

Too many symbol fonts declared

This error is generated by `\DeclareSymbolFont` if it cannot install another symbol font because all available math families are already in use either by symbol fonts or by math alphabet identifiers (see previous error). It usually happens if you load too many math font packages that try to compete for the precious few math font families — a total of 16. Other than the advice on bm given above, all you can easily do is to load fewer font packages. The only other (more complicated) possibility is to define special math versions that selectively load only some of the symbol fonts and switch between them as needed. See Section 9.8.5, and especially the discussion about math versions on page →I 753, for the necessary declarations.

Too many '⟨*token(s)*⟩' separators in argument   (cmd)

LaTeX was asked to split the argument of a command or environment a number of times as a given set sequence of ⟨*token(s)*⟩ using `\SplitArgument`, but these tokens were found more often than expected. For example, with `\SplitArgument{1}{,}` you would divide an argument into two parts at a comma. If you then pass it {2,3,5}, you would get this error.

Too many unprocessed floats

Floats that cannot be placed immediately are deferred by LaTeX, possibly causing subsequent floats to be deferred as well. By default LaTeX can defer up to 18 floats before you receive this error message. This limit can be increased by using `\extrafloats{number}` in the preamble, but if there is a float that cannot be placed for some reason, this change merely delays receiving the above error. See Chapter 7 for ways to deal with this situation.

This error can also be triggered if you have too many `\marginpar` commands within a single paragraph. A `\marginpar` temporarily uses two storage bins for deferred floats as long as the current paragraph has not been typeset (this allows a maximum of nine marginal notes per paragraph, or fewer if there are already some deferred floats).

Trying to overwrite '⟨*name*⟩.tex'

The `filecontents` environment allows overwriting existing files under certain circumstances, but it always refuses to overwrite the file `\jobname.tex`, assuming that this is the file it is currently processing, because that would mean disaster. You can still shoot yourself in the foot by giving your file a different extension and then asking to overwrite it.

Two \documentclass or \documentstyle commands

Only one such command is allowed per document. Your document includes more than one, perhaps as the result of combining two originally separate documents.

Two \LoadClass commands

A class can load at most one other class to do the bulk of processing. See Section A.6 for a detailed discussion of how classes are built.

Undefined color ⟨name⟩ `color`

You have requested a color with \color or a similar command from the color or xcolor package without previously defining it with \definecolor. See [31] or the color package documentation for details.

Undefined control sequence `TEX`

This is perhaps the most common of all LaTeX errors, though it shows up as a TeX error message: you have used a command name that was not previously defined. Often you may have simply mistyped the name in your document (e.g., \bmox instead of \mbox).

To carry on in such a case, you can respond with i\mbox, inserting the correct name. You can then continue processing and correct your source document afterwards. It is also possible to get this error as a result of using a fragile command in a moving argument.

Undefined font size function ⟨name⟩

A size function used in \DeclareFontShape was misspelled. Check the entry or tell your system maintainer.

Undefined tab position

This error is raised if you try to advance in a tabbing environment with \>, \+, \-, or \< to a tabulator position that was not previously set up with \=. Either the \= is actually missing or perhaps you used \+ or \pushtabs and got confused when specifying the tabular position to which you actually want to move.

Unknown filecontents option ⟨option⟩

The filecontents environment allows a combination of overwrite (alias force), noheader, and nosearch in its optional argument. The option ⟨option⟩ is not among them; maybe it was misspelled?

Unknown float option '⟨letter⟩'

All float environments support an optional argument to specify the allowed positions. This can contain a combination of the letters !htbp in any order (and if the float or another extension package is loaded, also H). The specified ⟨letter⟩ is not among them and will be replaced by p.

Unknown graphics extension: ⟨ext⟩ `graphics|graphicx`

You get this error if you try to load a fully specified graphics file (with extension ⟨ext⟩) and the graphics driver does not know the particular extension and there is no default rule set up. The dvips program, for example, interprets every unknown extension as EPS, so with this driver you never see this error but probably others.

741

Unknown mark class '⟨class⟩' (marks)

You try to insert a mark with `\InsertMark`, but the specified ⟨class⟩ is not known to the mark mechanism. Either you misspelled the ⟨class⟩ name or you forgot to make a `\NewMarkClass` declaration for it.

Unknown option '⟨language⟩'. ⟨reason⟩ babel

When LaTeX processes the option list for babel and encounters an unknown option ⟨language⟩, it tries to load a file by the name of ⟨language⟩`.ldf`. This message is displayed when LaTeX fails to find it. This error can be caused by a simple typing mistake, or the file might not be stored on LaTeX's search path.

Unknown option '⟨option⟩' for package '⟨name⟩' (keys)

You specified an ⟨option⟩ for package ⟨name⟩ that is not declared by that package. Packages that accept key/value pairs as options produce a similar error, but prefix it with `LaTeX keys Error`. Consult the package documentation on the available options.

Unknown relationship '⟨rel⟩' between labels '⟨label₁⟩' (hooks)
    and '⟨label₂⟩' in hook '⟨hook⟩'

`\DeclareHookRule` was used to declare a relationship between two hook labels, but ⟨rel⟩ is neither `<`, `>`, `before`, `after`, `incompatible-warning`, `incompatible-error`, `voids`, nor `unrelated`. Perhaps a misspelling?

Use of \??? does not match its definition

This is a low-level TeX error, artificially generated by LaTeX to give some information about the *real* error that happened at an awkward moment. The important information comes two lines later and should be a text that can be looked up in this appendix. See page 714 for further explanation.

Use of ⟨command⟩ does not match its definition TeX

Low-level macro definitions made with `\def`, instead of `\newcommand` and friends, sometimes require special argument delimiters (e.g., the (⟨coord⟩) of the picture commands). If ⟨command⟩ is a LaTeX command, check its syntax.

Otherwise, this is most likely a spurious error due to using a fragile command in a moving argument without `\protect`. If ⟨command⟩ is `\???`, see the previous entry.

\usepackage before \documentclass

The `\usepackage` declaration can be used only after the main class was loaded with `\documentclass`. Inside a class or package file you have to use `\RequirePackage` instead.[1]

Unicode character ⟨char⟩ (U+⟨hex number⟩) not set up
    for use with LaTeX

The Unicode character denoted by the UTF-8 notation U+⟨hex number⟩ is not known to LaTeX. How the ⟨char⟩ is displayed depends on the engine setup: it may appear as a single glyph, e.g., "Δ", or as `^^e2^^88^^86`, which is of little help.

---

[1] It is technically possible to load a package before a class by using `\RequirePackage`, but this should be avoided unless you know what you are doing.

Under the precondition that the character is available in a font encoding used in the document, it has to be set up using the \DeclareUnicodeCharacter declaration; see Section 9.9.3 on page →I 758.

`\verb ended by end of line`

To better detect errors, the argument of \verb must be placed on a single line. Thus, this error signals that either you forgot the final delimiter for the argument or the argument was broken over several lines in the source. In the case of very long arguments, it may help to split them over several \verb commands and, if necessary, mask a line break between them in the source with a % sign.

`\verb illegal in argument`

Except in very special situations (explicitly documented in this book), it is not possible to use \verb (or verbatim) in the argument of other commands or environments. If you need verbatim text in such a place, use, for example, \verbdef from the newverbs package or \SaveVerb and \UseVerb from the fancyvrb package; both are described in Section 4.2.

`Verbatim-like ⟨command or environment⟩ ended by end of line` (cmd)

Commands defined with \NewDocumentCommand can have "verbatim" arguments similar to those of \verb. For them the same precaution (discussed above) is implemented; i.e., they have to appear on a single line in the source file. The same is true for environments declared with \NewDocumentEnvironment.

`Verbatim-like ⟨command or environment⟩ illegal in argument` (cmd)

With \NewDocumentCommand or \NewDocumentEnvironment you can define commands and environments that have "verbatim" arguments. Just like \verb they cannot appear in arguments of other commands or environments except in very special circumstances (see discussion above). If they cause problems, you get this error message and usually several more afterwards. See Section 4.2 for ways to deal with this issue.

`Wrong syntax for \DeclareFontSeriesDefault`

With \DeclareFontSeriesDefault one can set the series default for the md (medium) or bf (bold) series, so those are the two values allowed in the first mandatory argument. The optional argument specifies the "meta" font family. Currently supported values there are rm (Roman), sf (Sans Serif), or tt (Typewriter). Any other value generates this error message.

`You already have nine parameters` TeX

LaTeX supports command or environment definitions with a maximum of nine arguments (called parameters by TeX), but your \newcommand or \newenvironment specified 10 or more.

`You can't use 'macro parameter #' in ⟨some⟩ mode` TeX

TeX found a stray # character somewhere that does not seem to be a reference to an argument of some command. If you wanted to typeset this symbol, use \# instead.

You can't use '\spacefactor' in vertical mode [TeX]

TeX lets you refer to the \spacefactor only when you are building a horizontal list. You get this error when you use the LaTeX command \@ outside of a paragraph. Because many internal commands start with an @ in their names, you might also get this error if you use code containing such internal commands (e.g., \@startsection) without surrounding it with \makeatletter and \makeatother. In that case TeX sees \@ followed by the letters startsection, and a later use of this code then executes \@ that in turn produces this error message.

You can't use '\prevdepth' in horizontal mode [TeX]

The \prevdepth dimension can be used only while in vertical mode (i.e., between paragraphs).

You can't use '\end' in internal vertical mode [TeX]

This is one of the more misleading TeX error messages, because it refers to the TeX primitive \end (ending a TeX run) that was redefined by LaTeX to become the end-tag of environments. The error means that LaTeX's \end{document} or the \stop command was encountered while LaTeX was building a box. For example, \begin{figure}...\stop would generate it.

You can't use '⟨command⟩' in ⟨some⟩ mode [TeX]

TeX complains that ⟨command⟩ is not allowed in one of its modes. Some specific variations of this theme have already been discussed. If you have not used ⟨command⟩ directly, then the most likely cause for this error is a broken fragile command in a moving argument.

You haven't defined the language ⟨lang⟩ yet [babel]

Various user interface commands of babel check whether their argument contains a language that was specified in the option list when babel was loaded or there is at least an .ini file for it. If the ⟨lang⟩uage was *not* specified and no .ini file can be found, processing is stopped, and this error message is displayed.

B.2 Dying with memory exceeded

The TeX program contains a number of internal tables of fixed size used for storing away different kinds of information needed at run time. Whenever any of these tables overflows, LaTeX aborts with a "TeX capacity exceeded" error.

Until the mid-1990s, memory problems could, in fact, be due to the size of the document. In some cases it was impossible to process a document as a whole.[1] These days such limitations are gone or are at least less severe. For one, the average TeX implementation is already equipped with huge internal tables. In addition, most implementations allow you to modify the table sizes via configuration files instead

---

[1] The first edition of this book required a specially compiled version of the TeX program with all such tables enlarged by a factor of 10 and could be processed only on a large Unix workstation.

of requiring you to manually recompile TeX. In some cases you may have to generate a new LaTeX format; for more details, consult the documentation of your TeX distribution.[1]

Nevertheless, people experience this dreadful error once in a while, usually as the result of a faulty command definition. Below are four candidates reduced to the bare bones of the problem we want to discuss — in reality, such problems usually lurk in more complex definitions:

```
\newcommand\FAILa{.\FAILa}            \newcommand\FAILb{\FAILb x}
\newcommand\FAILc{\typeout{.}\FAILc}  \newcommand\FAILd{.\par\FAILd}
```

If you execute \FAILa as defined above, you receive the following output (the reported memory size possibly differs) after a short while:

```
! TeX capacity exceeded, sorry [main memory size=5000000].
\FAILa ->.
            \FAILa
```

The main memory is the part of TeX in which macro definitions and the material for the current page are stored. Looking at the above recursive definition, it is clear that it generates a never-ending sequence of periods. Because paragraph breaking is deferred until TeX sees a \par command or a blank line to globally optimize the line breaks, TeX waits in vain for a chance to break the paragraph material into lines.

Exceeding main memory because of too many macro definitions is less likely these days. Nevertheless, even that can happen (in theory) if the size of this memory is small and you load many packages, have a large number of huge deferred floats, or use macro packages that produce new macros on the fly.[2]

If you get this error only with larger documents and LaTeX actually produces pages before giving up, you can try to find out whether the memory is gradually filling up (which suggests a table size problem) by setting \tracingstats=2 in the preamble of your document. TeX then reports the main memory status after finishing each page, producing output like the following:

```
[765]
Memory usage before: 4262&161788; after: 1286&157691; still untouched: 1323176
[766]
Memory usage before: 3825&160983; after: 636&156520; still untouched: 1323176
[767]
Memory usage before: 3652&160222; after: 771&156307; still untouched: 1323176
```

The number reported to the left of the & is the memory devoted to large objects such as boxes; the number on the right is the amount of memory used by macro definitions

---

[1] The TeX Live distribution, for example, lets you specify the size of most tables through the configuration file texmf.cnf. See the TeX Live manual for details.

[2] For example, varioref defines two labels internally for every use of \vref, which can result in a noticeable amount of memory consumption in large documents.

and character data. Thus, one can expect a reduction in both values whenever a page has finished (i.e., the after: value). If the right-hand value is slowly increasing, however, then something is probably adding more and more definitions.

If we use \FAILb, we overflow a different table. Here the recursion happens before LaTeX actually reaches the end on the macro expansion and thus needs to store away the unprocessed part of the expansion.

```
! TeX capacity exceeded, sorry [input stack size=10000].
\FAILb ->\FAILb
                x
```

With today's size for the input stack, this message usually appears only if a recursion like the one above makes that stack grow at a frightening speed. In a normal LaTeX document you seldom find nested definitions that make this stack grow beyond a value of 50 (even for this book the maximum value was only 107).

What happens if you execute either \FAILc or \FAILd? Both are similar to \FAILa, but neither overflows any internal TeX table. Instead, both simply fill your hard disk. The only action of \FAILc is to show periods on your screen and in the transcript file, thereby very slowly filling up the disk with a huge transcript. \FAILd, on the other hand, contains a \par in its definition and therefore is able to typeset paragraphs (each consisting of a single dot); as a result it produces pages in rapid succession. Such an experiment ended on the author's machine with a document containing 22279 pages and the following message:

```
tex: fwrite: No space left on device
```

On your private machine, this is merely a nuisance, easily rectified. On systems with shared resources, however, you should be careful when letting LaTeX run unattended. This type of error once hit a student very badly; this individual processed such a document on a mainframe in batch mode without a time or size limit and was presented a bill for computer processing time of several thousand dollars.

Several other internal tables can overflow in principle. Below is the complete list of those not already discussed, along with an explanation for the most likely reason for the overflow. Some additional information can be found in [42, p. 300].

buffer size The characters in the lines being read from a file. Because the default size is usually quite large, the most likely cause for an overflow is lost line breaks due to a faulty conversion of a file during transfer from one operating system to another. A buffer overflow can also be caused by some PC word processing programs, which internally put an entire paragraph on a single line even though the text appears to be broken into several lines on the screen.

exception dictionary The number of hyphenation exceptions as specified by \hyphenation. LaTeX has some exceptions specified for the English language, and some language packages specify additional exceptions. However, if this table overflows, you must have been doing a very thorough job.

font memory The font metric data loaded by LaTeX. These days an overflow is unlikely but not impossible. If it happens, LaTeX has loaded too many fonts — probably because you used many different font sizes and LaTeX calculated and loaded math fonts for all the sizes. Increase the table size, if possible, or refer to Chapter 9 for information on how to reduce the number of fonts.[1]

`grouping levels`   The number of unfinished groups that delimit the scope for setting parameters, definitions, and other items — for instance, braces, the start of environments, or math mode delimiters. An overflow usually indicates a programming error (e.g., a definition that opens more groups than it closes). That type of error is sometimes difficult to identify. Good help is available with the command `\showgroups` to produce a listing of stacked groups starting with the innermost one. For example, placing it into the footnote on the current page yields

```
### semi simple group (level 3) entered at line 2955 (\begingroup)
### insert group (level 2) entered at line 2955 (\insert0{)
### semi simple group (level 1) entered at line 2921 (\begingroup)
### bottom level
```

The semi simple group on level 1 is due to the fact that this text is typeset in a `description` environment (the `\begin` command issues internally a `\begingroup` command). The `\footnote` command is implemented with the TeX primitive `\insert`, which contributes level 2. In fact, another semi simple group is started by `\footnote`, which ensures that color changes remain local. What we can deduce from this example is that the relationships among top-level document commands and internal groups are far from obvious or simple. However, the line numbers that show when a group was entered do help, because there are usually no long-ranging groups in normal documents.

As an alternative, use the internal tracing counter `\tracinggroups`. If it is set to a positive number, the entry and exit of groups is recorded in the transcript file; with `\tracingonline` having a positive value, this information also appears on screen.

`hash size`   The number of command names known to TeX. Most packages contribute a fixed number of new command names. Each `\label` or `\bibitem` command in the document generates one new internal command name. Thus, packages that internally use the `\label` command (e.g., varioref) may significantly contribute to filling that table in large documents.

`number of strings`   The number of strings — command names, file names, and built-in error messages — remembered by TeX. In some cases TeX is able to free unused space, but usually such strings survive even if they are used only locally. One possible reason for overflowing this table is the use of many files in an application. Each opening for reading or writing of a file contributes, even when the same file is used many times over.

---

[1]It happened during the production of this book, but only when typesetting both volumes together — this loaded more than 4000 fonts, and we had to increase the table size slightly.

For historical reasons, TeX has a somewhat unusual string-handling concept involving several tables, each of which can overflow. Thus, if you change the hash size to allow for more commands, you may need to adjust the number of strings and quite likely the pool size, and vice versa.

parameter stack size The total number of command parameters of nested commands being expanded but not yet fully processed. For example, suppose a command with 4 arguments calls a command with 5 arguments, which in turn calls a command with 3 arguments, thereby using up 12 slots in this table. The moment TeX reaches the end of a macro replacement text it frees the stack. Thus, with today's implementations it is quite difficult to hit that limit, unless you use a flaky recursive definition with arguments, for example:

```
\newcommand\FAIL[3]{\typeout{Got #1, #2, and #3 but \FAIL is a mess}\DO}
```

Do you see the problem? Because the `\typeout` contains `\FAIL` by mistake, it gets called again, before its replacement text has been fully processed (picking up the characters i, s, and a as arguments). As a result, `\DO` is never executed and we finally get

```
! TeX capacity exceeded, sorry [parameter stack size=10000].
\FAIL #1#2#3->
                \typeout {Got #1, #2, and #3 but \FAIL is a mess}\DO
l.18 \FAIL 123
```

This is similar to the `\FAILb` example from page 746, except that because of the number of arguments the parameter stack overflowed first.

pattern memory The memory available to store hyphenation patterns. This table cannot overflow during normal document processing, because such patterns are loaded only during format generation. If you receive this error during that process, reduce the number of languages for which you load hyphenation patterns into your format. Pattern loading is normally defined in the file `language.dat`.

pool size The characters in strings — command names and file names (including the full path on some implementations). If this table overflows, the most likely cause is the use of too many files, especially if they have long absolute path names. This can, for example, happen if a document includes many graphics and one uses `\graphicspath` to make LaTeX search for the images in several directories — every attempt to open a file contributes to this string pool.

save size The set of values to restore when a group ends. With today's default limits, this is again difficult to overflow. The most likely cause is the use of both local and global assignments to the same object, something that can happen only through the use of low-level TeX programming, because LaTeX assignments are either always local (for most types) or always global (e.g., counter assignments). But, of course, many packages are built using low-level methods, which means such bugs in a package are not impossible.

To avoid unnecessary growth of the save stack, the document environment has a special implementation so that it does not produce a group (as normal environments do). Without it every new definition would automatically push an unnecessary "undefined" value onto the save stack — unnecessary, because by the time that group would end, all processing would stop anyway.[1]

semantic nest size The number of token lists being worked on simultaneously. Boxes, math formulas, and other elements start a new list, suspending work on the current structure. Once they are finished, TEX has to continue constructing the suspended object, so all such unfinished objects are remembered in the semantic nest stack. With a default size of several hundred objects, it is very difficult to get even close to this limit with normal documents.[2] In an emergency, TEX offers \showlists, which displays all unfinished lists that TEX is currently working on.

text input levels The number of simultaneously open input sources (e.g., files opened with \include, \input, or \usepackage, etc.). On the author's implementation of TEX one would need to nest 1500 files to reach this limit.

B.3 Warnings and informational messages

While error messages make LaTeX stop[3] and wait for user input, warning messages are simply displayed on the terminal and in the transcript file, and processing continues. If applicable, LaTeX also shows the source line number that triggered the warning. The warnings are prefixed by "LaTeX Warning:" or "LaTeX ⟨module⟩ Warning:" if they are issued by the core LaTeX code. Otherwise, they identify the issuing package or class by starting with "Package ⟨name⟩ Warning:" or "Class ⟨name⟩ Warning:", respectively. TEX warnings, such as "Overfull...", have no standard prefix string.

In addition to warnings, LaTeX writes informational messages to the transcript file — usually without displaying this information on the terminal. To better distinguish between informational and warning messages, warnings are shown in blue and informational message in black in the following alphabetical listing.

Calculating math sizes for size ⟨text size⟩
LaTeX has to guess the correct font sizes for subscripts and superscripts because it could not find the information for the current ⟨text size⟩ in its internal tables. This message usually is followed by several font size correction warnings because LaTeX's initial guess is seldom successful. This situation can arise when you select an uncommon size using the \fontsize command; see Section 9.8.5 if the math formulas look strange.

---

[1] As a side effect it is impossible to use \begin{document} inside another environment because the grouping structure is not obeyed.

[2] The author could not think of any problematic definition that would not hit any of the other limits first.

[3] This is of course true only if you have not issued a \scrollmode or \nonstopmode command. In that case all the errors discussed earlier will also be just flush by, or, if \batchmode is used, nothing at all is shown. The only exceptions are "File not found" errors: for them LaTeX stops in \scrollmode and asks for help, or gives up in despair in the other two modes.

Cannot activate hook '⟨*hook*⟩' because it is disabled! (hooks)

> This warning is issued by \ActivateGenericHook if the ⟨*hook*⟩ has been explicitly disabled via \DisableGenericHook, because it is not functional for one or the other reason.

Cannot remove chunk '⟨*label*⟩' from hook '⟨*hook*⟩' because ⟨*reason*⟩! (hooks)

> This warning is issued by \RemoveFromHook if the code to be removed does not exist (i.e., there is no code with that ⟨*label*⟩) or if the ⟨*hook*⟩ does not exist.

Checking defaults for ⟨*enc*⟩/⟨*font shape*⟩

> This message is written in the transcript file at \begin{document} while LATEX is verifying that the substitution defaults for the encoding ⟨*enc*⟩ are sensible. It is followed either by ...okay or by an error message that is generated when the ⟨*font shape*⟩ group specified with \DeclareFontEncoding is unknown to LATEX.

Citation '⟨*key*⟩' on page ⟨*number*⟩ undefined

> The ⟨*key*⟩ specified as an argument to \cite or \nocite is not defined by a \bibitem command or you need another run of LATEX (and perhaps BIBTEX or biber) to make it known to LATEX. The latter case is indicated by an additional warning, "Label(s) may have changed...", as discussed on page 754. The page number is omitted if the warning is emitted by \nocite.

Command ⟨*name*⟩ invalid in math mode

> This is either a warning or an error message indicating that you have used a command in math mode that should be used only in normal text. A warning is generated when an obsolete, yet still valid, construction is used.

Command ⟨*name*⟩ has changed

> A test was made in some package to see if ⟨*name*⟩ has its expected meaning (usually in order to change it afterwards). This is no longer the case so that there is some likelihood that the modification is no longer adequate — hence the warning. Sometimes it does not matter, but usually it is best to contact the package developers so that they can update the package.

Defining command ⟨*name*⟩ with sig. '⟨*argument spec*⟩' (cmd)
Defining environment ⟨*name*⟩ with sig. '⟨*argument spec*⟩'

> This information is written to the transcript file if a new document-level command ⟨*name*⟩ was declared with the help of \NewDocumentCommand. For reference its signature, i.e., its argument specification, is also given. The same kind of information is recorded for environments declared with \NewDocumentEnvironment.

Document Class: ⟨*name*⟩ ⟨*date*⟩ ⟨*additional info*⟩

> This line is produced by a \ProvidesClass command in the document class code. Although not a warning, it appears both on the terminal and in the transcript file. If a document produces different output on different installations, you should compare the "Document Class:", "File:", and "Package:" messages to identify any release differences.

Empty 'thebibliography' environment

This warning is issued if a `thebibliography` environment has no `\bibitem` commands. It often indicates a problem with a BIBTEX run. For example, the BIBTEX program may have been unable to resolve a single citation.

Encoding ⟨name⟩ has changed to ⟨new name⟩ for ⟨symbol font⟩ ...

This message is issued when in the declaration of a symbol font different encoding schemes in different math versions have been used. It may mean that the `\DeclareMathSymbol` commands for this symbol font are not valid in all math versions.

(\end occurred ⟨when⟩ TEX

You receive this warning at the very end of your run whenever TEX finds the `\end{document}` or `\stop` command to be premature. As a warning the message is unfortunately misleading, because it refers to a TEX primitive `\end` that was reused by LATEX to become the environment end-tag. The ⟨when⟩ can be one of two cases:

inside a group at level ⟨number⟩) TEX

In this case the LATEX run ended while there were still some open groups. Such groups include explicit braces that are not closed (e.g., `{\itshape..`), use of `\bgroup` and `\begingroup` in macro code without their counterparts, and unclosed environments in the source. The latter normally triggers a suitable LATEX error first (i.e., "`\begin{⟨env⟩}` on...") unless you ended the run with `\stop`, because in that case no check for mismatched environments is made.

when ⟨condition⟩ on line ⟨line number⟩ was incomplete) TEX

In this case LATEX completed the run while a low-level TEX conditional remained unfinished. With LATEX documents using only standard commands, this problem should not occur unless you ended the document inside a file loaded with `\include`. In other cases it probably means there is a bug in a package. Try to identify the source of the conditional (by looking at the ⟨line number⟩) to see in which command it was used. Note that the ⟨line number⟩ may not be in the current file — unfortunately, TEX does not divulge the file name. In very difficult situations you can try to use eTEX's advanced tracing options to pinpoint the problem: if `\tracingifs` is set to 1, you get detailed trace information about nested conditionals as they are executed.

External font ⟨name⟩ loaded for size ⟨size⟩

LATEX has ignored a request to load some font shape at size ⟨size⟩ and has loaded the external font ⟨name⟩ instead. This message is generated by the size functions `fixed` (as a warning) or by the size function `sfixed` (as an informational message).

Faking ⟨command⟩ for font family ⟨name⟩ in TS1 encoding

The glyph ⟨command⟩ is not available in the TS1 encoding of the current font family. LATEX has responded by "faking" it in some way. This is, for example, done for the `\texteuro` glyph (€), if unavailable in the current font.

File '⟨*name*⟩' already exists on the system.
Not generating it from this source
This informational message is generated by a `filecontents` environment when the file ⟨*name*⟩ already exists somewhere in the search path of LaTeX, even if it would not be overwritten. If you want to unpack the file nevertheless, either delete (or rename) the version found by LaTeX or use the option `overwrite` in the optional argument of the environment.

File: ⟨*name*⟩ ⟨*date*⟩ ⟨*additional info*⟩
This line is produced from the `\ProvidesFile` command used to identify a file and its last modification date. By convention, the ⟨*additional info*⟩ starts with a version number, though it is not required. Although of the same importance as `\ProvidesClass`, this information is written only to the transcript file to avoid cluttering the terminal with messages.

If a document produces different output on different installations, you should compare the "`Document Class:`", "`File:`", and "`Package:`" messages to identify any release differences. A good way to do this is by adding `\listfiles` in the preamble of your document. This then summarizes such information for all relevant files at the end of the document.

File: ⟨*encoding*⟩⟨*family*⟩..fd ⟨*date*⟩ ⟨*additional info*⟩
This important special case of the previous informational message indicates that a font definition file for some ⟨*encoding*⟩ (usually displayed in lowercase) and ⟨*family*⟩ combination was loaded. Such files contain font shape group declarations and are described in Section 9.8.4.

First page is already shipped out, ignoring ⟨*command*⟩ (hooks)
This warning is generated by `\AtBeginDvi` or `\AtBeginShipoutFirst` if the declaration is used too late, i.e., after the first page has already been shipped out.

Float too large for page by ⟨*value*⟩
A float is too tall by ⟨*value*⟩ to fit in the current `\textheight`. It is printed on a page by itself (if permitted), thereby possibly overflowing into the bottom margin. If the float is not allowed to go on a float page, it prevents all further floats in its class from being placed.

Font shape ⟨*font shape*⟩ has incorrect series value '⟨*value*⟩'
The NFSS convention for font series names in `.fd` files is to drop the `m` if there is a second value, e.g., `c` not `mc` for medium-condensed. Obeying this convention is important, because otherwise automatic adjustments are not fully functional.

If you see this message, it usually originates from an `.fd` with incorrect data and needs to be reported to the font maintainer. It is not a warning message, because as a user you have no easy way to correct the problem other than reporting it.

Font shape ⟨*font shape*⟩ in size ⟨*size*⟩ not available
LaTeX issues this message when it tries to select a font for which the requested font attribute combination is not available and a substitution is defined in the

internal tables. Depending on the contents of these tables, one of the following additional messages is issued:

`external font` ⟨*name*⟩ `used`
> LATEX has selected the external font ⟨*name*⟩ in that particular situation and does not know to which font shape group it belongs. (This message is generated by the size function `subf`.)

`size` ⟨*size*⟩ `substituted`
> LATEX has selected the correct shape, but because the requested size is not available, LATEX has chosen the nearby size ⟨*size*⟩. This action is taken automatically if none of the simple sizes or size ranges in the ⟨*font shape*⟩ group declaration matches.

`shape` ⟨*font shape*⟩ `tried`
> LATEX has selected a different ⟨*font shape*⟩ group because the requested one is not available for the requested ⟨*size*⟩. (This message is generated by the size function `sub`.)

`Font shape` ⟨*font shape*⟩ `will be scaled to size` ⟨*size*⟩
> LATEX has loaded the requested font by scaling it to the desired size. To print a document containing scaled fonts, your printer driver must have these fonts in the correct size or must be able to scale them automatically.

`Font shape` ⟨*font shape*⟩ `undefined. Using` '⟨*other shape*⟩' `instead`
> This warning is given when a combination of font attributes is specified for which LATEX has no font shape definition.
>
> For example, requesting `\fontseries{b}\ttfamily` would normally trigger this warning, because Computer Modern fonts have neither bold typewriter nor bold extended typewriter. However, when the latter combination is requested, you do not receive this warning but only some information in the transcript file because for `\textbf{\texttt{..}}` the `.fd` files contain an explicit substitution rule.
>
> If LATEX identifies a particular symbol that it cannot typeset in the requested shape, the above warning is followed by "`for symbol` ⟨*name*⟩".

`Foreign command` ⟨*command*⟩`;` `amsmath`
`\frac or \genfrac should be used instead`
> Although the use of ⟨*command*⟩ is not an error, you are strongly discouraged from using this old form for your (generalized) fractions in LATEX. Use the amsmath commands instead.

`Form feed has been converted to Blank Line`
> The `filecontents` environment detected a "form feed" character (`^^L`) in the source and writes it as an empty line (`\par` command if interpreted by LATEX) into the external file. Because `filecontents` was designed to distribute textual data, it cannot be used for handling arbitrary binary files.

Freeze math alphabet allocation in version ⟨*version*⟩

The number of allocated math alphabets (with \DeclareMathAlphabet) and math symbol fonts (with \DeclareSymbolFont) in a given math ⟨*version*⟩ has reached the threshold defined by the counter localmathalphabets. The remaining math groups are assigned only locally (per formula) in order to allow different formulas to use the remaining slots in different ways. See page →I 681 for details.

'h' float specifier changed to 'ht'   or
'!h' float specifier changed to '!ht'

You specified h or !h as a float placement without giving any other options. LaTeX requires some alternative in case "here" leads to an impossible placement because not enough room is left on the current page. If you really want to prevent floats from floating, consider using the float package described in Section 7.3.1.

Hook 'shipout/lastpage' executed on wrong page ... ^(hooks)

LaTeX made a wrong guess and executed the shipout/last hook on a page that was not the last one. Rerun your document and the problem goes away.

Hyphen rules for '⟨*lang₁*⟩' set to \l@⟨*lang₂*⟩ (\language⟨*number*⟩) babel

Many languages explicitly request some hyphenation replacements in the corresponding .ldf files. Because not all patterns are available on all systems, these messages help when debugging problems. For additional information, use the package option showlanguages to get a list of all hyphenation patterns available in the format and the ⟨*number*⟩s that they are associated with.

Ignoring text '⟨*text*⟩' after \end{⟨*env*⟩}

This warning is issued by filecontents or filecontents* when textual material is detected following the \end tag.

Ignoring void shipout box

There was a request to produce a page (via \shipout), but the \ShipoutBox contained no material. There may be something wrong with the code producing the page or one of the output routine hooks; e.g., shipout/before voided the box. If done deliberately, then it is better to use \DiscardShipoutBox that avoids this warning.

Label '⟨*key*⟩' multiply defined

The document contains two or more \label commands with the same ⟨*key*⟩. References to this ⟨*key*⟩ always refer to the last \label defined. Ensure that all ⟨*key*⟩s are different.

Label(s) may have changed. Rerun to get cross-references right

LaTeX has detected that the label definitions, as compared to those in the previous run, have been modified and that (at least) one additional LaTeX run is necessary to resolve cross-references properly. In theory it is possible, though unlikely, that this message persists regardless of the number of processing runs.[1] If this

---

[1] For example, if the \label is near the page boundary between pages "iii" and "iv", the use of

is the case, compare the `.aux` files of different runs to determine which label alternates between different states and resolve the problem manually.

`Last declared language option is '⟨`*lang*`⟩', but the` `babel`
`   last processed one was '⟨`*other lang*`⟩'`
The main document language is set to the last declared in either the class or the package options. However, when languages are declared in *both* places, the behavior is not well defined, and this warning alerts you to this fact. The recommended setup is to request them only as class or as package options, but if for some reason you need both, you can set the main language with the package option `main=⟨`*lang*`⟩`.

`Loose \hbox (badness ⟨`*number*`⟩) ⟨`*somewhere*`⟩` `TEX`
TEX produced a horizontal box with a badness of 13 or greater (which corresponds to using 50% or more of the available stretchability). This warning can be safely ignored unless you are a perfectionist; in fact, it will not be produced unless you change the default for `\hbadness`. See the message "Underfull `\hbox`..." on page 762 for more details.

`Loose \vbox (badness ⟨`*number*`⟩) ⟨`*somewhere*`⟩` `TEX`
TEX produced a vertical box with a badness of 13 or greater (which corresponds to using 50% or more of the available stretchability). The warning is produced only if `\vbadness` was set to a value below 100. See the message "Underfull `\vbox`..." on page 763 for more details.

`Making ⟨`*char*`⟩ an active character` `babel`
For each character that is turned into a shorthand character, this informational message will be written to the transcript file. When a document shows unexpected results, this information might help if the problems are caused by inadvertent use of a shorthand character.

`Marginpar on page ⟨`*number*`⟩ moved`
A `\marginpar` could not be aligned with the text line to which it was originally attached, because a preceding `\marginpar` already occupies the space.

`Missing character: There is no ⟨`*char*`⟩ (⟨`*hex number*`⟩) in font ⟨`*name*`⟩` `TEX`
Although this message usually indicates a serious problem, it is unfortunately shown only if `\tracinglostchars` is positive. It means that somewhere in the source a request for a symbol ⟨*char*⟩ was made for which the current font (⟨*name*⟩ is the external name) has no glyph in the corresponding position. The displayed ⟨*char*⟩ may differ on different TEX installations.[1] The ⟨*hex number*⟩ is shown only on some installations. For example, using the command `\symbol`

Watch out for this message in the transcript or turn it into an error!

`\pageref` before the `\label` might result in a situation where the `\label` is moved to page "iv" if the textual reference "iii" is used, and vice versa.

[1]Sometimes you see something like `^^G` and sometimes real characters are displayed. Unfortunately, there is no guarantee that they correspond to your input: some translation that depends on the operating system may happen when the characters are written to the transcript file.

can produce this warning because you can ask for any font slot with this command. However, standard font-encoding–specific commands, as discussed in Section 9.9.4 on page →I 767, should never produce this warning.

In 2021 the engines got extended, and you can now set `\tracinglostchars` to different values: 1 (transcript only), 2 (terminal warning), or 3 (TeX error). For compatibility reasons, LaTeX sets it to 2, but because of its importance, especially with Unicode engines, we recommend using `\tracinglostchars=3` in the preamble of your documents.

No `\author` given

You used `\maketitle` without specifying an author first. In contrast to a missing `\title` this omission generates a warning.

No `auxiliary output files`

This information is displayed when you use a `\nofiles` declaration in the document preamble.

No `characters defined by input encoding change to` ⟨*name*⟩

The input encoding file ⟨*name*⟩`.def` does not seem to contain any input encoding declarations. For the `ascii` encoding, this is the expected behavior; for all other encodings, it indicates a problem.

No `file` ⟨*name*⟩

LaTeX displays this information whenever it tries to read from an auxiliary file (e.g., `.aux` or `.toc`) but cannot find the file. This is not considered an error because such files are created only after the first run. However, the same routine is also used by `\include`, so that, unfortunately, a missing "include file" triggers this unsuspicious warning too.

No `hyphenation patterns were preloaded for the language` [babel] **`'`⟨*lang*⟩`' into the format`**

All language definition files check whether hyphenation patterns for the language selected were loaded into the LaTeX format (provided the line breaking is based on this mechanism). If this is not the case, this message is displayed, and a default set of hyphenation patterns is used instead. The default patterns are those loaded into pattern register 0 (typically American English).

No `positions in optional float specifier. Default added ...`

A float environment (e.g., `figure` or `table`) was used with its optional placement argument, but it did not contain any suitable information. Hence, LaTeX used its default placement rules.

`Oldstyle digits unavailable for family` ⟨*name*⟩

You used `\oldstylenums` with a font family that does not contain oldstyle digits. As an emergency measure, LaTeX used oldstyle from a different font instead. By default this is an informational message; if you prefer a warning or error on the terminal, load the `textcomp` package with the option `warn` or `error`. Section 9.5.6 gives further details.

Optional and mandatory argument with same delimiter '⟨char⟩' (cmd)
If you define a command with mandatory and optional arguments following each other and using the same argument delimiters, e.g.,

```
\NewDocumentCommand \mycmd { d<> * r<> }{...}
```

then it is impossible to use such a command and omit all the optional arguments, simply because LATEX would interpret <X> in \mycmd<X> as the optional argument and then complain about a missing required one. You could, however, call it without problems as \mycmd*<Y>, \mycmd<X><Y>, or \mycmd<X>*<Y>. Thus, the uncommon declaration might be intentional, and therefore LATEX gives only a warning, not an error.

Optional argument of \twocolumn too tall on page ⟨number⟩
The material in the optional argument to \twocolumn was so tall that fewer than three lines remain on the page. LATEX does not start two-column mode on the current page and starts a new page instead.

\oval, \circle, or \line size unavailable
The requested size for the mentioned commands is unavailable. LATEX chooses the closest available size. See, for example, Section 8.3.2 for ways to avoid this problem.

Overfull \hbox (⟨number⟩pt too wide) ⟨somewhere⟩ TEX
TEX was forced to build a horizontal box (e.g., the line of a paragraph or a \makebox) of a certain width and was unable to squeeze the material into the given width, even after shrinking any available space as much as possible. As a result, the material sticks out to the right. In most cases this is quite noticeable, even if the total amount is small. You have to correct this problem manually, because TEX was unable to resolve it (Sections 3.1 on page →❘ 121 and B.4.3 give some advice). For a list and explanation of the possible origins (i.e., the ⟨somewhere⟩), see the warning "Underfull \hbox..." on page 762.

Overfull \vbox (⟨number⟩pt too wide) ⟨somewhere⟩ TEX
TEX was asked to build a vertical box of a fixed size (e.g., a \parbox or a minipage with a second optional argument; see Appendix A.3.2 on page 666) and found more material than it could squeeze in. The excess material sticks out at the bottom. Whether this result poses a problem depends on the circumstances. For a list and explanation of the possible origins (i.e., the ⟨somewhere⟩), see the warning "Underfull \vbox..." on page 763.

Overwriting encoding scheme ⟨something⟩ defaults
This information is written by \DeclareFontEncodingDefaults to the .log when it overwrites previously declared system-wide defaults for "text" or "math".

`Overwriting ⟨something⟩ in version ⟨name⟩ ...`

A declaration, such as `\SetSymbolFont` or `\DeclareMathAlphabet`, changed the assignment of font shapes to ⟨*something*⟩ (a symbol font or a math alphabet) in math version ⟨*name*⟩.

`Package: ⟨name⟩ ⟨date⟩ ⟨additional info⟩`

This line is produced by the `\ProvidesPackage` command, which is used to identify a package and its last modification date. By convention, the ⟨*additional info*⟩ starts with a version number, though it is not required. Although of the same importance as `\ProvidesClass`, this information is written to just the transcript file to avoid cluttering the terminal with messages. If a document produces different output on different installations, you should compare the "`Document Class:`", "`File:`", and "`Package:`" messages to identify any release differences.

`Package '⟨name⟩' has already been loaded: ignoring` (keys)
`        load-time option '⟨option⟩'`

Some packages have options that can be applied only during package loading, but not altered with `\SetKeys` afterwards. If such an ⟨*option*⟩ is found, it is ignored with a warning. You get this warning when there are several attempts to load a package (of which only the first is carried out). In that case the warning may be harmless or it may indicate a serious problem — LaTeX just does not know, and you have to check yourself.

`pdfTeX warning (dest): name{⟨name⟩} has been referenced` pdfTeX only
`        but does not exist, replaced by a fixed one`

This is a pdfTeX engine warning that indicates that the document contains an internal hyperlink to a destination that does not exist. This happens, for example, when you use `\includeonly` and you have links from your document into files not included. As a replacement, pdfTeX creates a link pointing to the first page.

> **Unicode engines**
>
> There is a similar warning when the LuaTeX engine is used, starting "`warning (pdf backend)`". It too creates an artificial destination, but one to the current page. With XeTeX, however, no warning is given, because resolving links happens in a separate program. With that program, the link is simply dead when selected.

`pdfTeX warning (ext4): destination with the same identifier` pdfTeX only
`        (name{⟨name⟩}) has been already used, duplicate ignored`

This happens if two destinations are created with the same name. A typical case is sections numbered without a chapter number. hyperref then creates the destination `section.1` in the first chapter and again in the following chapters. The remedy is to redefine `\theHsection` so that it gives an unique number, e.g.:

```
\renewcommand\theHsection{\thechapter.\thesection}
```

You also get the warning if the page numbering is reset with \pagenumbering without changing the number style, for example, after a title page. In that case hyperref creates the destination page.1 twice. The remedy here is either to use a different number style, e.g., alph, for the title page, even if the number is not visible, or to surround the title page with the NoHyper environment so that no destinations are created at all.

Redeclaring font encoding ⟨*name*⟩
> This information is recorded if \DeclareFontEncoding is used for an encoding that is already defined (thereby potentially changing its defaults).

Redeclaring math accent ⟨*name*⟩
> This information is recorded if \DeclareMathAccent is used for a math accent that was previously declared. If the command to be declared is known but not an accent, you get an error message instead.

Redeclaring math alphabet ⟨*name*⟩
> A \DeclareMathAlphabet or \DeclareSymbolFontAlphabet command was issued to declare ⟨*name*⟩, which was already defined to be a math alphabet identifier. The new declaration overrides all previous settings for ⟨*name*⟩.

Redeclaring math delimiter ⟨*name*⟩
> The command ⟨*name*⟩ was already declared as a math delimiter, and its renewed declaration with \DeclareMathDelimiter overrides the old definition. If the ⟨*name*⟩ is known but not a delimiter, you get an error instead.

Redeclaring math symbol ⟨*name*⟩
> Same as above but for math symbols redeclared with \DeclareMathSymbol.

Redeclaring math version ⟨*name*⟩
> A package or class (or you) issued a \DeclareMathVersion command for a version that was already declared. The new declaration overrides all previous settings for this version with the default values.

Redeclaring symbol font ⟨*name*⟩
> A package or class issued a \DeclareSymbolFont command for a symbol font that was previously declared. The new declaration overrides the symbol font in all known math versions.

Redefining command ⟨*name*⟩ with sig. '⟨*argument spec*⟩'   (cmd)
Redefining environment ⟨*name*⟩ with sig. '⟨*argument spec*⟩'
> An already existing command or environment ⟨*name*⟩ was redefined using \RenewDocumentCommand or \RenewDocumentEnvironment, respectively. The new (and possibly changed) argument specification is also recorded.

Reference '⟨*key*⟩' on page ⟨*number*⟩ undefined
> A reference created with \ref, \pageref, or one of the other cross-reference commands discussed in Chapter 2 used a ⟨*key*⟩ for which LaTeX has not seen a

corresponding `\label` command. If the `\label` is somewhere in the document, you simply need another LATEX run to make it known to LATEX. This situation is indicated by the additional warning "Label(s) may have changed..." discussed on page 754.

Size substitutions with differences up to ⟨*size*⟩ have occurred
This message appears at the end of the run if LATEX selected at least one significantly different font size because a requested size was not available. The ⟨*size*⟩ is the maximum deviation that was needed.

Some font shapes were not available, defaults substituted
This message appears at the end of the run if LATEX had to use automatic font substitution for some font shapes.

Suspicious rollback/min-date date given
There was a rollback request through the latexrelease package and at the same time an explicit request with a conflicting date in the second optional argument to `\usepackage` or `\documentclass`. Maybe this was intentional, but equally likely, it is the result of a leftover configuration that was not updated.

Symbol ⟨*command*⟩ not provided by font family ⟨*name*⟩
The TS1 font encoding is unfortunately implemented fully by just a minority of the font families usable with LATEX. If a symbol requested from this encoding is not available in the current font, it is instead typeset using a default family, and you get this informational message. You can turn such messages into warnings or errors by loading the `textcomp` package with the option `warn` or `error`. See Section 9.5.6 for more details.

Tab has been converted to Blank Space
The `filecontents` environment detected a "tab" character (^^I) in the source and writes it as a space into the external file. Because `filecontents` was designed to distribute textual data, it cannot generally handle arbitrary binary files.

Temporary extra page added at the end
For a number of tasks LATEX has to write configuration data to the very end of the last page. It makes an initial guess when it is about the ship out this last page, but this guess is sometimes wrong. In such cases LATEX is forced to produce an extra page just to ship out the necessary information. If that happens, it issues this warning and advises you to rerun the document. Just like with cross-references it then makes use of the knowledge from the previous run to correct the issue. The same can happen if you make extensive changes (mainly deletions) so that the information from the previous run is no longer accurate.

Text page ⟨*number*⟩ contains only floats
One or more floats processed as "top" or "bottom" floats are together so tall that very little space (less than two lines) is left for normal text on the current page. Therefore, LATEX decided to place only floats on the page in question (even if some or all of the floats do not explicitly allow for this placement). This message can

appear only when the placement parameters for floats were changed drastically from their default values; see the beginning of Chapter 7 for details.

`The following font families will use the default` `babel`
`  settings for all or some languages:` ⟨*details*⟩

> `Unicode engines`
>
> With Unicode engines, Babel automatically selects some OpenType features for the text fonts so that they are properly rendered in many languages and scripts. These default font settings may not always work. This informational message therefore shows what got selected so that you can make adjustments using `\babelfont` if that is necessary. If everything comes out fine, you can ignore this warning.

`There were multiply-defined labels`
> This warning appears at the end of a LaTeX run when LaTeX detected at least one pair of `\label` or `\bibitem` commands with the same key. Check the transcript file and make sure that all keys used are different.

`There were undefined references`
> This warning appears at the end of a LaTeX run when LaTeX detected unresolved references. If LaTeX also displays "`Label(s) may have changed. Rerun ...`" then follow its advice and rerun the document.
>
> However, if the message appears on its own, then LaTeX has concluded that rerunning the document would not resolve the references. In that case you should check the transcript file for all occurrences of "Reference ⟨*key*⟩ undefined" and "Citation ⟨*key*⟩ undefined" and correct them, either by fixing a misprint or by adding the necessary `\label` or `\bibitem` commands. In the case of missing citation ⟨*keys*⟩, all you may have to do is regenerate the bibliography with BibTeX or biber and then rerun LaTeX.

`Tight \hbox (badness ⟨number⟩) ⟨somewhere⟩` `TEX`
> TeX produced a horizontal box and had to shrink the interior spaces. You get this message only if `\hbadness` is set to a value less than 100. See the message "Underfull `\hbox`..." on the next page for more details.

`Tight \vbox (badness ⟨number⟩) ⟨somewhere⟩` `TEX`
> TeX produced a vertical box and had to shrink the interior spaces. You get this message only if `\vbadness` is set to a value less than 100. See the message "Underfull `\vbox`..." on page 763 for more details.

`Token not allowed in a PDF string (⟨⟨encoding⟩⟩): removing '⟨token⟩'` `hyperref`
> When converting input such as a section title into the format suitable for bookmarks, hyperref has to produce a simple character string and therefore removes or replaces commands as necessary. Depending on what it has to change, it may issue this warning. Commands that it does not know how to handle are removed, but their arguments will remain and may become part of the string.

In the special case of spacing commands like `\,` or `\quad`, hyperref warns about a `\kern` or a `\hskip` and either removes it (if it is small) or replaces it by a single space. If the text contains a formula, hyperref issues at least two warnings about removing a "math shift" at the beginning and the end. Superscripts and subscripts in the math will be removed with a warning. In all cases the bookmarks should be checked, and, if necessary (or to get rid of the warning), a replacement should be provided with `\texorpdfstring`.

Trying to load font information for ⟨enc⟩+⟨family⟩
You find such a message in the transcript file whenever LaTeX tries to load an `.fd` file for the encoding/family combination ⟨enc⟩/⟨family⟩.

Unable to redefine math accent ⟨accent⟩   `amsmath`
This warning is rare, but it may be issued when loading the amsmath package with nonstandard mathematical fonts.

Underfull \hbox (badness ⟨number⟩) ⟨somewhere⟩   `TeX`
TeX was forced to build a horizontal box (e.g., the line of a paragraph or a `\makebox`) of a certain width, and the white space within that box had to stretch more than it was designed to do (i.e., stretched more than 100% of the available plus parts in stretchable spaces). Internally, this situation is expressed by a badness value greater than 100; a value of 800 means that twice the total stretchability was used to produce the required width.[1]

Whether such an underfull box actually presents a noticeable problem is something that you may have to check visually in the produced output. If the badness is 10 000, the box can be arbitrarily bad. Because TeX's value for infinity is quite low, it might mean that TeX has favored one very bad line over several bad but still acceptable lines that appear in succession. In that case, using `\emergencystretch` can help you; see Section 3.1.

The limit of badness values above which such warnings are shown is controlled by the integer parameter `\hbadness`. LaTeX's default is 1000, so warnings appear only for really bad boxes. If you want to produce an important document, try a more challenging value, such as `\hbadness=10`, to find out how many lines TeX really considers imperfect.

Note that the warning always talks about `\hbox`, regardless of the actual box construct used in the source, because it is directly generated by TeX. The location where the problem occurred is indicated by ⟨somewhere⟩, which is one of the following four possibilities:

detected at line ⟨line number⟩   `TeX`
An explicitly constructed box (construction ending at line ⟨line number⟩ in the source) has the problem — for example, a `\makebox` with an explicit width argument or some other LaTeX construct that builds boxes.

---

[1] The exact formula is $\min(100r^3, 10000)$ where r is the ratio of "stretch used" to "stretch available", unless there is infinite stretch present (e.g., introduced by a command like `\hfill`), in which case the badness is zero.

`has occurred while \output is active` $\boxed{\text{TEX}}$

TEX was in the process of building a page and encountered the problem while attaching running headers and footers and the like. Because this is an asynchronous operation, no line number is given. Look at the page generated closest to where the warning was issued to determine whether it warrants manual correction.

`in alignment at lines` ⟨*line numbers*⟩ $\boxed{\text{TEX}}$

The box is part of a `tabular` or some math alignment environment. The ⟨*line numbers*⟩ give you the source position of the whole alignment structure, because by the time TEX encounters the problem, it no longer has a way to relate it back to the source in more detail.

`in paragraph at lines` ⟨*line numbers*⟩ $\boxed{\text{TEX}}$

The underfull box is due to a badly spaced line in the paragraph (source line numbers given as ⟨*line numbers*⟩). The additional symbolic display of the line in question should help you to pinpoint the problem.

`Underfull \vbox (badness` ⟨*number*⟩`)` ⟨*somewhere*⟩ $\boxed{\text{TEX}}$

TEX was forced to build a vertical box (e.g., a `\parbox` or a `minipage`) of a certain height, and the vertical space in that box had to stretch more than it was supposed to; see the discussion of badness and stretchability in the description of the "Underfull `\hbox`..." warning. You can suppress all warnings for badness values below a certain limit by setting `\vbadness=`⟨*value*⟩. Then LATEX issues warnings only for boxes with a badness larger than ⟨*value*⟩ (the default is 1000). The ⟨*somewhere*⟩ indicates the origin of the problem and can be one of the following cases:

`detected at line` ⟨*line number*⟩ $\boxed{\text{TEX}}$

The box was explicitly constructed (the ⟨*line number*⟩ points to the end of the box construction), and there is not enough stretchable space available. For example,

```
\parbox[c][2in][s]{4cm}{A test}
```

would produce this warning because the box should be 2 inches high and the contents should fill this height (argument `[s]`), but there is nothing stretchable available — for instance, something like `\par\vfill` between the two words. See Appendix A.3.2 for details on paragraph boxes.

`has occurred while \output is active` $\boxed{\text{TEX}}$

In the most frequent case, the space on the current page needed stretching beyond acceptable limits in TEX's eyes. Whether this is visually a real problem depends on many factors, such as the type of spaces on the page. For example, a large stretch in front of a heading is usually less severe than a spaced-out list. Thus, the best advice is to check such pages manually. Often, `\enlargethispage` or `\pagebreak` will help.

If the problem appears surprisingly often, then the spacing parameters for lists, paragraphs, and headings should be examined to see whether they are too rigid (see Chapters 2 to 5). Also check whether the \textheight corresponds to an integral number of text lines; see the discussion on page →I 369.

`in alignment at lines` ⟨*line numbers*⟩   TₑX

This warning should not arise with standard LATEX but can occur in some specialized applications. In such a case, use ⟨*line numbers*⟩ to identify the source lines in your document.

`Undo math alphabet allocation in version` ⟨*version*⟩

Once the number of math alphabet allocations has reached its allowed limit in a math ⟨*version*⟩, any further allocation is undone at the end of the formula so that it can be reused differently in later formulas. The message is shown when such deallocation is happening. See page →I 681 for details.

`Unused global option(s): [`⟨*option list*⟩`]`

Some of the options specified on \documentclass have been used by neither the class nor any package in the preamble. A likely reason is that the names of the options have been misspelled. Also note that some packages do not react to global options, but only to those explicitly specified when loading the package. See Appendix A.6 for details.

`warning (pdf backend): unreferenced destination with`   LuaTₑX only
`name '`⟨*name*⟩`'`

Unicode engines

A LuaTₑX engine warning that a referenced hyperlink destination is missing (the text is somewhat incorrect; the destination, not the link is missing). See the corresponding pdfTₑX warning on page 758 for more details.

`warning (pdf backend): ignoring duplicate destination`   LuaTₑX only
`with the name '`⟨*name*⟩`'`

Unicode engines

A LuaTₑX engine warning that two targets for hyperlinks ("destinations") have the same name. See the corresponding pdfTₑX warning on page 758 for more details.

`Writing file '`⟨*file*⟩`'`

This informational message is produced by both the filecontents and the filecontents* environment when they write a ⟨*file*⟩ that is definitely not yet on the system.

`Writing or overwriting file '`⟨*file*⟩`'`

In contrast to the previous informational message, the filecontents and the filecontents* environments show this message as a warning message when they write a ⟨*file*⟩ that already exists (somewhere) on the system and they are used with the `force` or `overwrite` key and therefore might overwrite it.

`Writing text '`⟨*text*⟩`' before \end{`⟨*env*⟩`} as last line of` ⟨*file*⟩
This warning is issued by the `filecontents` or `filecontents*` environment when it detects textual material directly preceding the `\end` tag.

`You have more than once selected the attribute '`⟨*attrib*⟩`'` | babel |
     `for language` ⟨*lang*⟩
This message is displayed if the same attribute is entered more than once in the second argument of `\languageattribute`; only the first occurrence triggers the activation of the attribute.

`You have requested` ⟨*package or class*⟩ `'`⟨*name*⟩`',`
    `but the` ⟨*package or class*⟩ `provides '`⟨*alternate name*⟩`'`
  You requested loading of ⟨*name*⟩ via `\usepackage` or `\RequirePackage` (in the case of a package) or via `\documentclass` or `\LoadClass` (in the case of a class), but the package or class provides a variant of the original with the internal name ⟨*alternate name*⟩. Unless this was a typo by the package or class provider, it means that your installation has a package or class variant that is likely to behave differently from the original. Thus, your document may be formatted differently when processed on another installation. Whether this is the correct behavior is something you need to investigate by looking at the package or class in question.

  Specifying a relative or absolute path name also triggers this warning as a side effect.

`You have requested release '`⟨*date*⟩`' of LaTeX,`
    `but only release '`⟨*old date*⟩`' is available`
A `\NeedsTeXFormat` command has requested a LATEX release of at least ⟨*date*⟩, but the date of your format is ⟨*old date*⟩. Usually, such a request is made to ensure that a certain feature of the LATEX format is available, so it is likely that your document will produce additional errors or strange formatting later. Update to a more recent version of LATEX.

`You have requested, on line` ⟨*num*⟩`, version '`⟨*date*⟩`' of` ⟨*name*⟩`,`
    `but only version '`⟨*old date*⟩`' is available`
A class or package was required to have a date not older than ⟨*date*⟩, but the version on your installation is from the date ⟨*old date*⟩. Update the class or package in question.

B.4 TEX and LATEX commands for tracing

In this section we discuss tools and techniques for tracing and for displaying status information — for example, finding out why something is strangely spaced on the page or why your own command definition does the wrong thing.

B.4.1 Displaying command definitions and register values

In many situations it is useful to get some information about LaTeX's current internals, the precise definitions of commands, the values of registers, and so on. For example, if the use of \newcommand reports that the command to be defined is already defined, you may want to know its current definition to ensure that you do not redefine an important command.

Displaying command definitions

For this purpose TeX offers the command \show, which displays the definition of the token following it and then stops and displays a question mark while waiting for user intervention. For example, after defining \xvec as in Example A-1-5 on page 626, we can display its definition as follows:

```
\newcommand\xvec[1]{\ensuremath{x_1,\ldots,x_{#1}}}
\show\xvec
```

This produces the following output on the terminal and in the transcript file:

```
> \xvec=\long macro:
#1->\ensuremath {x_1,\ldots ,x_{#1}}.
l.6 \show\xvec

?
```

The first line, which starts with >, shows the token being displayed (\xvec) and gives its type (\long macro), indicating that \xvec is a macro that accepts \par commands in its argument; in other words, this macro was defined with \newcommand rather than \newcommand*.

The second line shows the argument structure for the command (up to ->), revealing that the command has one argument (#1). Note that while the argument on the \newcommand declaration was indicated with [1], it is now shown differently. The rest of the line — and possibly further lines, if necessary — shows the definition part. The code is terminated with a period that is not part of the definition but helps to identify stray spaces at the end of the definition, if any.

Note that the code display is normalized. Thus, after a command that would swallow subsequent spaces, you see a space regardless of whether a space was coded in the original definition.

Following the display of the definition, the source line (including the line number in the input file) is shown. Then LaTeX stops with a question mark. To continue, you can press Enter. Alternatively, you can type h to see what other possibilities are available.

Not all commands produce such easily understandable output. Assume that you try to display a command that was defined to have an optional argument, such as \lvec as defined in Example A-1-6 on page 626:

```
\newcommand\lvec[2][n]
  {\ensuremath{#2_1+\cdots + #2_{#1}}}
\show\lvec
```

In that case you get this result:

```
> \lvec=macro:
->\@protected@testopt \lvec \\lvec {n}.
```

Apparently, the `\lvec` command has no arguments whatsoever (they are picked up later in the processing). And something else is strange in this output: what is `\\lvec`? Is it the command `\\` followed by the letters `lvec`, or is it a strange command `\\lvec` that has two backslashes as part of its name? It is actually the latter, though there is no way to determine this fact from looking at the output of the `\show` command. Such strange command names, which cannot be generated easily by the user, are sometimes used by LATEX internally to produce new command names from existing ones using `\csname` and `\endcsname` and other low-level mechanisms of TEX.

So what should you do if you want to see the definition of `\\lvec`? It should be clear that writing `\show` in front of such a command does not work, because in normal situations TEX sees `\\` and thinks that it is the command to "show". Until recently all you could do was use unwieldy low-level methods such as

Displaying internal commands with strange names

```
\expandafter\show\csname \string\lvec \endcsname
```

Technically, what happens here is that a command name is generated from the tokens between `\csname` and `\endcsname`. Inside that construct, the `\string` command turns the command `\lvec` into a sequence of characters starting with a backslash that no longer denotes the start of a command. This is why the resulting command name contains two backslashes at the beginning. The `\expandafter` command delays the evaluation of the following `\show` command so that `\csname` can perform all of its work before `\show` is allowed to look at the result.[1]

That's quite a mouthful of low-level TEX, but in an emergency it may prove helpful to know about the `\csname` trick. However, starting with the 2020 release, LATEX now offers `\ShowCommand` as an improved replacement for `\show`. If you write

```
\ShowCommand\lvec
```

then this produces the following output:

```
> \lvec=robust macro:
->\@protected@testopt \lvec \\lvec {n}.

> \\lvec=\long macro:
> default #1=n.
[#1]#2->\ensuremath {#2_1+\cdots + #2_{#1}}.
<recently read> }
```

As you can see, the first part is similar to the result from `\show`, but `\ShowCommand` recognizes that `\lvec` is a robust command and more importantly that it also needs

---

[1] Alternatively, you can use `\ExpandArgs{c}\show{\string\lvec}`, but that is not really better.

to show us its internal definition, i.e., replacement for `\\lvec`. It even tells us that #1 is an optional argument with a default of n.[1]

`\ShowCommand` can be given any command name as its argument, but it offers maximum details only with commands that have been defined with higher-level LATEX declarations such as `\newcommand`, `\NewDocumentCommand`, etc. For commands *Detecting a primitive* that are part of the TEX engine (so called primitive commands) or defined with a *command* low-level `\def`, it gives you the same result as `\show`. If the command examined is a built-in primitive command, then you get output like the following:

```
> \relax=\relax.
<argument> \relax

l.10 \ShowCommand \relax
```

i.e., a primitive command shows up as being equal to itself.

The commands `\show` and `\ShowCommand` are useful for learning about com-*Displaying* mands and their definitions or finding out if something is a primitive of TEX. However, *register values* they do not help in finding the current values of length or counter registers. For example,

```
\show\parskip \show\topmargin \show\topsep
```

gives us the following information:

```
> \parskip=\parskip.
l.5 \show\parskip
                        \show\topmargin \show\topsep

?
> \topmargin=\dimen109.
l.5 \show\parskip \show\topmargin
                                    \show\topsep

?
> \topsep=\skip29.
l.5 \show\parskip \show\topmargin \show\topsep
```

From the above we can deduce that `\parskip` is a TEX primitive (the fact that it is a rubber length is not revealed), that `\topmargin` is actually the `\dimen` register (i.e., a rigid length) with register number 109, and that `\topsep` is the `\skip` register (a rubber length) with number 29.

If we want to know the value of any such register, we need to deploy a different TEX primitive, called `\showthe` instead of `\show` or `\ShowCommand`, which gives us the following output on the terminal and also proves that `\parskip` is, indeed, a rubber length (but only because it has a nonzero plus component):

```
> 0.0pt plus 1.0pt.
l.5 \showthe\parskip
```

---

[1] `\ShowEnvironment{`*env*`}` is a comparable command for environments. It displays both the `\begin{`*env*`}` and the `\end{`*env*`}` code of the environment in the style of `\ShowCommand`.

Using `\showthe` in this way allows us to display the values of the length registers allocated with `\newlength` and of internal TₑX registers such as `\baselineskip` and `\tolerance`. What we cannot display directly with it are the values of LᴬTₑX counters allocated with `\newcounter`. For this we have to additionally deploy a `\value` command that turns a LᴬTₑX counter name into a form that is accepted by `\showthe`. For example,

LᴬTₑX counters need special handling

> `\showthe\value{footnote}`

would show the current value of the footnote counter on the terminal.

Instead of displaying the meaning of a macro or the value of a register on the terminal, you can alternatively typeset this kind of data by using `\meaning` instead of `\show` and `\the` instead of `\showthe`. The output is slightly different: the name of the token is not shown by `\meaning`; instead, only its type and "meaning" are presented. Compare the next example with the output shown earlier in this section:

Typesetting command definitions or register values

```
\long macro:#1->\ensuremath
{x_1,\ldots ,x_{#1}}
0.0pt plus 1.0pt
16.0pt
8.0pt plus 2.0pt minus 4.0pt
footnote=0
```

```
\newcommand\xvec[1]{\ensuremath{x_1,\ldots,x_{#1}}}
\ttfamily\small    % use smaller typewriter
\raggedright
\meaning\xvec    \par \the\parskip\par
\the\topmargin   \par \the\topsep \par
footnote=\the\value{footnote}
```

B-4-1

If displaying command definitions or register values is insufficient for determining a problem, you can alternatively trace the behavior of the commands in action; see Section B.4.5 on page 781.

B.4.2 Diagnosing page-breaking problems

Once in a while LᴬTₑX produces unexpected page breaks or shows some strange vertical spaces and you would like to understand where they are coming from or what precise dimensions are involved. For these tasks, TₑX offers a few low-level tracing tools.

Symbolic display of the page contents

If you specify `\showoutput` somewhere in your document, TₑX displays (starting with the current page) symbolic representations of complete pages on the terminal and the transcript file. This generates a large amount of output, of which we show some extracts that have been produced by compiling the first paragraph of this section separately.

As a side effect, the `\showoutput` command also produces symbolic displays of overfull boxes. Tracing ends at the next closing brace or environment. Thus, to see the output for full pages, you have to place the command into the preamble, or at least ensure that the page break happens before the next group ends.

Side effect of `\showoutput`

Every page output starts with the string Completed box being shipped out followed by the current page number in brackets. Then you get many lines showing the boxes that make up the page, starting with a `\vbox` (vertical box) and its sizes in pt containing the whole page. To indicate that something is the contents of a box, everything inside is recursively indented using periods instead of blanks. Spaces, even if they are rigid, are indicated by the keyword \glue (see line 3 or 6); stretchable space has some plus and/or minus components in its value, as we see later. Whether it is a horizontal or a vertical space is determined by the box in which this space is placed. For example, the \glue of 16.0pt on line 3 is a vertical space that came from \topmargin; see also Example B-4-1 on the preceding page. In the extract you also see an empty \vbox of height 12pt (lines 5 to 7), which is the empty running header, followed in line 8 by the space from \headsep (25pt), followed by the box containing the text area of the page starting at line 10. Lines 15 and following show how individual characters are displayed; here \T1/cmr/m/n/10 indicates the font for each character. The \glue in between (e.g., line 19) marks an interword space with its stretch and shrink components.

```
 1   Completed box being shipped out [1]
 2   \vbox(633.0+0.0)x407.0
 3   .\glue 16.0
 4   .\vbox(617.0+0.0)x345.0, shifted 62.0
 5   ..\vbox(12.0+0.0)x345.0, glue set 12.0fil
 6   ...\glue 0.0 plus 1.0fil
 7   ...\hbox(0.0+0.0)x345.0
 8   ..\glue 25.0
 9   ..\glue(\lineskip) 0.0
10   ..\vbox(550.0+0.0)x345.0, glue set 502.00241fil
11   ...\write-{}
12   ...\glue(\topskip) 3.1128
13   ...\hbox(6.8872+2.15225)x345.0, glue set - 0.17497
14   ....\hbox(0.0+0.0)x15.0
15   ....\T1/cmr/m/n/10 O
16   ....\T1/cmr/m/n/10 n
17   ....\T1/cmr/m/n/10 c
18   ....\T1/cmr/m/n/10 e
19   ....\glue 3.33252 plus 1.66626 minus 1.11084
20   ....\T1/cmr/m/n/10 i
21   ....\T1/cmr/m/n/10 n
22   ....\glue 3.33252 plus 1.66626 minus 1.11084
23   ....\T1/cmr/m/n/10 a
```

As a second example from a page trace, we show the symbolic display of the structures near a line break. You see the space added by TeX at the right end of a text line (\rightskip on line 5) and the box containing the line. Thus, line 6 is outdented again. It contains a symbolic representation for the costs to TeX to break after this line, indicated by the command \penalty. The actual value here is due to the value of the \clubpenalty parameter.[1] This is followed in line 7 by the vertical space

---

[1] The penalty to break after the first line in a paragraph is given by the integer parameter \clubpenalty; the cost for breaking before the last line by \widowpenalty. Both default to 150;

added between the lines, computed by TEX by taking the value of \baselineskip and subtracting the depth of the previous line box and the height of the following line box, which starts at line 8.

```
1    ....\T1/cmr/m/n/10 s
2    ....\T1/cmr/m/n/10 o
3    ....\T1/cmr/m/n/10 m
4    ....\T1/cmr/m/n/10 e
5    ....\glue(\rightskip) 0.0
6    ...\penalty 150
7    ...\glue(\baselineskip) 2.96054
8    ...\hbox(6.8872+1.94397)x345.0, glue set 0.55421
9    ....\T1/cmr/m/n/10 s
10   ....\T1/cmr/m/n/10 t
```

As a final example, we look at some part of the symbolic page output produced from a line like this:

```
\begin{itemize} \item test \end{itemize}  \section{Test}
```

The particular part of interest is the one generated from \end{itemize} and \section{Test}. What we see here (lines 1 to 7) is a curious collection of \glue statements, most of which cancel each other, intermixed with a number of \penalty points:

```
1    ...\penalty -51
2    ...\glue 10.0 plus 3.0 minus 5.0
3    ...\glue -10.0 plus -3.0 minus -5.0
4    ...\penalty -300
5    ...\glue 10.0 plus 3.0 minus 5.0
6    ...\glue -10.0 plus -3.0 minus -5.0
7    ...\glue 15.0694 plus 4.30554 minus 0.86108
8    ...\glue(\parskip) 0.0 plus 1.0
9    ...\glue(\parskip) 0.0
10   ...\glue(\baselineskip) 8.12001
11   ...\hbox(9.87999+0.0)x345.0, glue set 290.70172fil
```

These lines are generated from various \addpenalty and \addvspace commands issued; for example, lines 1 and 2 are the penalty and the rubber space added by \end{itemize}. The \section command then adds a breakpoint to indicate that the place before the section is a good place to break a page (using \@secpenalty with a value of −300). In fact, the break should be taken before the \glue from line 2, or else there would be a strange space at the bottom of that page. As it is technically impossible to remove material from the vertical galley, \addpenalty uses the trick to back up by adding a negative space (line 3), adding the penalty (line 4),

---

that is, they slightly discourage a break.

and then reissuing the \glue (line 5). In lines 6 and 7, the same method is used by \addvspace to add the vertical space before the heading.

Lines 8 to 10 are added by TeX when placing the actual heading text (line 11) into the galley. Note that technically the heading is considered a "paragraph", so \parskip is added. This is the reason why enlarging this parameter requires careful planning. The same care should be taken when adjusting other parameters (like the one added on line 7).

In fact, you see \parskip being added twice, in one case with a value of 0.0. The reason for this curiosity is that these days LaTeX trial-starts the paragraph to execute the para/before hook and then stops and restarts the paragraph again. Obviously, a real \parskip should be added only once, but because TeX always adds the current value of \parskip whenever it starts a paragraph, LaTeX locally sets it to 0pt on one of the occasions, and this is what we see.

Tracing page-break decisions

If you want to trace page-breaking decisions, TeX offers symbolic information that you can turn on by setting the internal counter \tracingpages to a positive integer value:

```
\tracingonline=1 \tracingpages=1
```

Setting \tracingonline to a positive value ensures that the tracing information appears not only in the transcript file (default), but also on the terminal.

Processing the previous paragraph starting with "If you want to..." as a separate document, we get the following lines of tracing information:

```
1   %% goal height=522.0, max depth=4.0
2   % t=10.0 g=522.0 b=10000 p=150 c=100000#
3   % t=22.0 g=522.0 b=10000 p=150 c=100000#
4   % t=55.0 plus 4.0 g=522.0 b=10000 p=-51 c=100000#
5   % t=77.0 plus 8.0 g=522.0 b=10000 p=300 c=100000#
6   % t=89.0 plus 8.0 g=522.0 b=10000 p=0 c=100000#
7   % t=90.94397 plus 8.0 plus 1.0fil g=522.0 b=0 p=-10000 c=-10000#
```

The first line starting with two percent signs shows the target height for the page (i.e., 522pt in this case), which means 43 lines at a \baselineskip of 12pt with 2pt missing, because the skip to position the first base line, \topskip, has a value of 10pt. If the goal height does not result in an integral number of lines, problems like underfull \vboxes are likely to happen.

Target size of a break   The remaining lines, starting with one percent sign, indicate a new potential page-break position that TeX has considered. You can interpret such lines as follows: t= shows the length of the galley so far and, if the galley contains vertical rubber spaces, their total amount of stretch and shrink. Line 4, for example, shows that in the layout of this book verbatim displays have an extra space of 10pt plus a stretch of 4pt (the verbatim lines are typeset in a smaller font with only 11pt of \baselineskip) and the same amount is added between lines 4 and 5.

The g= specifies the goal height at this point. This value changes only if objects *Page goal height*
like floats have reduced the available space for the galley in the meantime.

With b=, TₑX indicates the badness of the page if a break would be taken at this
point. The badness is calculated from the factor by which the available stretch or *Page badness*
shrink in t= must be multiplied to reach the goal height given in g=. In the example
the page is barely filled, so it is always 10000 (infinitely bad), except for line 7, where,
due to the added fil stretch, the page is suddenly considered optimal (b=0).

With each breakpoint TₑX associates a numerical \penalty as the cost to break *Break penalty*
at this point. Its value is given by p=. For example, it is not allowed to break directly
before the verbatim display, which is why there is a large increase in t= between
lines 3 and 4. On the other hand, a break after the display is given a bonus (p=-51).
Line 5 shows that breaking after the first line of the two-line paragraph fragment
following the verbatim text is considered bad (p=300), because it would result in both
a club and a widow line (\clubpenalty and \widowpenalty each have a value of
150, and their values are added together).

Finally, c= describes the calculated cost to break at this breakpoint, which is *Costs of*
derived from a formula taking the badness of the resulting page (b=) and the penalty *a page break*
to break here (p=) into account. TₑX looks at these cost values and eventually breaks
at the point with minimal cost. If the line ends in #, then TₑX thinks that it would be
the best place to break the page after evaluating all breakpoints seen so far. In the
example, all lines show this # — not surprising, given that TₑX considers all but the
last breakpoint to be equally bad.

If the pages would become too full if a break is taken at a particular breakpoint,
then TₑX indicates this fact with b=*. At this point TₑX stops looking for other
breakpoints and instead breaks the page at the best breakpoint seen so far.

For additional details on the output produced by these low-level display devices,
consult [42, p. 112].

B.4.3 Diagnosing and solving paragraph-breaking problems

If TₑX is unable to find a suitable set of points at which to break a paragraph into
lines, it produces, as a last resort, one or more lines that are "overfull". For each of
them you get a warning on the screen and in the transcript file, such as

```
Overfull \hbox (5.10907pt too wide) in paragraph at lines 3778--3793
\T1/hlh/m/n/10 showing you a sym-bolic dis-play of the text line and the
line num-ber(s) of the paragraph|
```

showing you a symbolic display of the text line and the line number(s) of the paragraph█
containing it. If you look at the symbolic display, you can easily diagnose that the *The black blob of*
problem is TₑX's inability[1] to hyphenate the word "paragraph". To explicitly flag *ink above is*
such lines in your document, you can set the parameter \overfullrule to a *deliberate*
positive value. For the present paragraph it was set to 5pt, producing the blob of ink

---

[1] TₑX is, in fact, perfectly capable of hyphenating "para-graph"; for the example, we explicitly
prevented it from doing so. The paragraph would have been perfect otherwise.

clearly marking the line that is overfull. The standard document classes enable this behavior with the option `draft`. On the other hand, you may not mind lines being only slightly overfull. In that case you can change the parameter `\hfuzz` (default `0.1pt`); only lines protruding by more than the value of `\hfuzz` into the margin are then reported.

If TEX is unable to break a paragraph in a satisfying manner, the reasons are often hyphenation problems (unbreakable words, as in the above example), problems with the parameter settings for the paragraph algorithm, or simply failure of the text to fit the boundary conditions posed by the column measure or other parameters, together with aesthetic requirements like the allowed looseness of individual lines. In the latter case the only remedy is usually a partial rewrite.

Dealing with hyphenation problems

With the relevant hyphenation patterns loaded, TEX is able to do a fairly good job for many languages [67]. By using microtype, described in Section 3.1.3 on page →I 126, this can be improved even further, because the font compression and expansion deployed by microtype reduce the number of hyphenations considerably.[1]

However, it usually does not find all potential hyphenation points, so sometimes one has to assist TEX in this task. To find out which hyphenation points in words like "laryngologist" are found by TEX, you can place such words or phrases in the argument of the command `\showhyphens`:

```
\showhyphens{laryngologist laryngopharyngeal}
```

Running this statement through LaTEX gives you some tracing output on the terminal and in the transcript file. The hyphenation points determined by TEX are indicated by a hyphen character:

```
[] \OT1/cmr/m/n/10 laryn-gol-o-gist laryn-gopha-ryn-geal
```

If you want to add the missing hyphenation points, you can specify all hyphenation points for one word locally in the text using `\-`, for example,

```
la\-ryn\-gol\-o\-gist  la\-ryn\-go\-pha\-ryn\-ge\-al
```

Alternatively, you can use a `\hyphenation` declaration in the preamble:

```
\hyphenation{la-ryn-gol-o-gist  la-ryn-go-pha-ryn-ge-al}
```

The latter technique is particularly useful when you detect a wrong hyphenation or often use a word for which you know that TEX misses important hyphenation points. Note that such explicit specifications tell TEX how to hyphenate words that are exactly in the form given. Thus, the plural "laryngologists" would be unaffected unless you specify its hyphenation points as well.

---

[1] This is why we generally recommend loading this package in documents that are set justified.

The \hyphenation declarations apply to the current language, so if a document uses several languages — for example, by using the methods provided by the babel system — then you need to switch to the right language before issuing the relevant declarations.

showhyphenation, lua-check-hyphen — **Display hyphenation points with LuaTEX**

> **Unicode engines**
>
> The two packages described here are unfortunately available only with LuaTEX, because they make use of features not available in any of the other engines. They interface with the paragraph building process and visualize the hyphenation points found by LuaTEX or collect all words that are finally hyphenated, respectively.
>
> The showhyphenation package by Thomas Kelkel helps you resolve cases in which TEX breaks a paragraph in a bad way, by allowing you to quickly check if TEX has missed one or the other possible hyphenation.
>
> The lua-check-hyphen package by Patrick Gundlach on the other hand writes out all words that are actually hyphenated into a file with the extension .uhy. Once your document is in final form, you can look at this file to make sure that there are not any bad hyphenations (either unfortunate ones that you may want to avoid or, worse, some wrong ones that definitely need correcting).
>
> It also offers you to maintain a list of accepted hyphenations in some external file that can be loaded with the option whitelist so that you do not have to repeatedly check the same entries over and over again. Both packages are demonstrated in the next example.

This short paragraph demonstrates the usefulness of the packages showhyphenation and check-lua-hyphens. The first automatically marks all hyphenation points found by the engine with a small triangular mark. The second package writes out all hyphenations that happened in the document into a file with the extension .uhy. You can then examine that file to find any issues with the hyphenation and correct them as necessary.

```
\usepackage{showhyphenation}
\usepackage{lua-check-hyphen}
This short paragraph demonstrates the usefulness
of the  packages \textsf{showhyphenation} and
\textsf{check-lua-hyphens}. The first
automatically marks all hyphenation points found
by the engine with a small triangular mark. The
second package writes out all hyphenations that
happened in the document into a file with the
extension \texttt{.uhy}. You can then examine
that file to find any issues with the
hyphenation and correct them as necessary.
```

B-4-2

In the example there are two lines ending in a hyphen, and the .uhy file, written by lua-check-hyphen, shows the following data:

```
automat-ically
hyphen-ations
```

If you do not like the hyphenation of "automatically", you could then turn to your document source and add an explicit \-, i.e., auto\-mati\-cally. Alternatively, you could generally disallow this hyphenation point by specifying an exception with \hyphenation{au-to-mati-cally}. Either way, our example paragraph would afterwards be broken differently.

Tracing the paragraph algorithm

Because TeX uses a global algorithm for optimizing paragraph breaking, it is not always easy to understand why a certain solution was chosen. If necessary, one can trace the paragraph-breaking decisions using the following declarations:[1]

```
\tracingparagraphs=1 \tracingonline=1
```

For readers who really want to understand the reasons behind certain decisions, we show some example data with detailed explanations below.

Paragraph tracing produces output that looks somewhat scary. For instance, one of the previous paragraphs generated data that starts like this:

```
1   @firstpass
2   @secondpass
3   []\T1/cmr/m/n/10 The [] dec-la-ra-tions ap-ply to the cur-rent lan-guage, so
4   @ via @@0 b=3219 p=0 d=10436441
```

Up to three passes over paragraph data

Line 2 says that TeX has immediately given up trying to typeset the paragraph without attempting hyphenation. This is due to the value of \pretolerance being set to 100 in the sources for the book; otherwise, TeX may have gotten further or even succeeded (in English text quite a large proportion of paragraphs can be reasonably set without hyphenating[2]). In addition to @secondpass, you sometimes see @emergencypass, which means that even with hyphenation it was impossible to find a feasible solution and another pass using \emergencystretch was tried.[3] Line 3 shows how far TeX had to read to find that first potential line ending that results in a badness of less than $\infty = 10000$. Line 4 gives details about this possible break. Such lines start with a single @; the via gives the previous breakpoint (in this case @@0, which refers to the paragraph start), the line badness (b=), the penalty to break at this point (p=), and the so-called demerits (d=) associated with taking that break (a "cost" that takes into account badness, penalty, plus context information like breaking at a hyphen or the visual compatibility with the previous line).

```
5   @@1: line 1.0 t=10436441 -> @@0
```

In line 5, TeX informs us that it would be possible to form a very loose first line ending in the breakpoint given by line 3 with a total cost (t=) equal to the demerits shown on line 4. This line would be formed by starting at breakpoint @@0. The notation line 1.0 gives the line number being made, and the suffixes .0, .1, .2, .3, respectively, stand for very loose, loose, decent, and tight interword spacing in the line. This classification is important when comparing the visual compatibility of consecutive lines.

---

[1] These parameters are also turned on by a \tracingall command, so you may get many lines of paragraph tracing data, even if you are interested in something completely different.

[2] For the *LaTeX Companion* with its many long command names in the text, this is less likely.

[3] For this to happen, \emergencystretch needs to have a positive value. See also the discussion in Section 3.1.

TₑX now finds more and more potential line breaks, such as after "if" in line 6 and after "a" in line 9. Each time TₑX tells us what kind of lines can be formed that end in the given breakpoint. If b=* appears anywhere in the trace data, it means that TₑX could not find a feasible breakpoint to form a line and had to choose an infeasible solution (i.e., one exceeding \tolerance for the particular line).

```
 6  if
 7  @ via @@0 b=1087 p=0 d=1213409
 8  @@2: line 1.0 t=1213409 -> @@0
 9  a
10  @ via @@0 b=334 p=0 d=128336
11  @@3: line 1.0 t=128336 -> @@0
12  doc-
13  @\discretionary via @@0 b=0 p=50 d=2600
14  @@4: line 1.2- t=2600 -> @@0
15  u-
16  @\discretionary via @@0 b=1 p=50 d=2621
17  @@5: line 1.2- t=2621 -> @@0
```

By hyphenating the word doc-u-ment, it finds two more breakpoints (lines 12 and 15). This time you see a penalty of 50 — the value of the parameter \hyphenpenalty (breaking after a hyphen) — being attached to these breaks. Line 15 is the last breakpoint that can be used to produce the first line of the paragraph. All other breakpoints would produce an overfull line. Hence, the next tracing line again shows more text; none of the potential breakpoints therein can be used because they would form a second line that exceeds \tolerance.

```
18  ment uses sev-eral languages\Dash for ex-am-ple, by us-ing the meth-
19  @\discretionary via @@1 b=1194 p=50 d=1452116
20  @\discretionary via @@2 b=2875 p=50 d=8325725
21  @@6: line 2.0- t=9539134 -> @@2
```

Here the breakpoint can be used to form a second line in two different ways: by starting from breakpoint @@1 (line 19) or by starting from breakpoint @@2 (line 20). If we compare just these two solutions to form the second line of the paragraph, then the first would be superior: it has a badness of 1194, whereas the second solution has a badness of 2875, which results in a factor of 5 in "costs" (d=). Nevertheless, TₑX considers the second break a better solution, because a first line ending in @@1 is so much inferior to a line ending in @@2 that the total cost for breaking is less if the second alternative is used. TₑX therefore records in line 21 that the best way to reach the breakpoint denoted by line 18 is by coming via @@2 and results in a total cost of t=9539134. For the rest of the processing, TₑX does not need to know that there were several ways to reach @@6; it just needs to record the best way to reach it.

More precisely, TₑX needs to record the best way to reach a breakpoint for any of the four types of lines (very loose, loose, decent, tight), because the algorithm attaches different demerits to a solution if adjacent lines are visually incompatible (e.g., a loose line following a tight one). Thus, later in the tracing (lines 22–40 are not shown), we get the following output:

```
41  by
42  @ via @@3 b=19 p=0 d=10841
```

```
43   @ via @@4 b=9 p=0 d=361
44   @ via @@5 b=42 p=0 d=2704
45   @@10: line 2.1 t=5325 -> @@5
46   @@11: line 2.2 t=2961 -> @@4
```

This output indicates that there are three ways to form a line ending in "by": by starting from @@3, @@4, or @@5. A line with a badness of 12 or less is considered decent (suffix .2); a line stretching, but with a badness not higher than 100, is considered loose (suffix .1). So here TeX records two feasible breakpoints for further consideration — one going through @@5 and one going through @@4.

Which path through the breakpoints is finally selected can be decided only when the very end of the paragraph is reached. Thus, any modification anywhere in the paragraph, however minor, might make TeX decide that a different set of breakpoints forms the best solution to the current line-breaking problem, because it produces the lowest total cost. Due to the complexity of the algorithm, minor modifications sometimes have surprising results. For example, the deletion of a word may make the paragraph a line longer. This may happen because TeX decides that using uniformly loose lines, or avoiding hyphenation of a word, is preferable to some other way to break the paragraph. Further details, describing all parameters that influence the line-breaking decisions, can be found in [42, p.98]. If necessary, you can force breakpoints in certain places with \linebreak or prevent them with \nolinebreak or by using ~ in place of a space. Clearly, choices in the early parts of a paragraph are rather limited, and you may have to rewrite a sentence to avoid a bad break. However, later in a paragraph nearly every potential break becomes feasible, being reachable without exceeding the specified \tolerance.

Shortening or lengthening a paragraph

Another low-level tool that can be used to help with paragraph line breaking or more often with pagination problems, is the internal counter \looseness. If you set it to a nonzero integer n, then TeX tries to make the next paragraph n lines longer (n positive) or shorter (n negative), while maintaining all other boundary conditions (e.g., the allowed \tolerance). For example on page 781, we have artificially shortened the paragraph starting in the following way:

```
\looseness=-1
Finally, you can direct \TeX{} to step through your files ... as well.
```

Without this adjustment TeX would have preferred to place the final "well." on a line by itself. Now the paragraph is set a bit too tight for TeX's taste, but the overall result is noticeably better.

Setting the value of \looseness is not guaranteed to have any effect. Shortening a paragraph is more difficult for TeX than lengthening it, because interword spaces have a limited shrinkability that is small in comparison to their normal stretchability. The best results are obtained with long paragraphs having a short last line. Consequently, extending a paragraph works best on long paragraphs with a last line that is already nearly full, though you may have to put the last words of the paragraph together in an \mbox to ensure that more than one word is placed into the last line. A more detailed discussion of this approach is given in Section 5.6.8 on page →I 427.

B.4.4 Other low-level tracing tools

TEX offers a number of other internal integer parameters and commands that can sometimes help in determining the source of a problem. They are listed here with a short explanation of their use.

We already encountered `\tracingonline`. If it is set to a positive value, all *On-line* tracing information is shown on the terminal; otherwise, most of it is written only to *tracing* the transcript file. This parameter is automatically turned on by `\tracingall`.

With `\tracingoutput`, tracing of page contents is turned on. What is shown depends on two additional parameters: `\showboxdepth` (up to which level nested boxes are displayed) and `\showboxbreadth` (the amount of material shown for each level). Anything exceeding these values is abbreviated using `etc.` or `[]` (indicating a nested box) in the symbolic display. The LATEX command `\showoutput` sets these parameters to their maximum values and `\tracingoutput` to 1 so that you get the most detailed information possible. The `\showoutput` command is automatically called by `\tracingall`.

To see the contents of a box produced with `\sbox` or `\savebox`, you can use *The contents* the TEX command `\showbox`: *of boxes*

```
\newsavebox\testbox \sbox\testbox{A test}
{\tracingonline=1 \showbox\testbox }
```

However, the result is fairly useless if you do not adjust both `\showboxdepth` and `\showboxbreadth` at the same time:

```
> \box52= []
```

```
OK.
```

Hence, a better strategy is to use LATEX's `\showoutput`:

```
{\showoutput \showbox\testbox }
```

Notice the use of braces to limit the scope of `\showoutput`. Without the braces you would see all of the following page boxes, which might not be of much interest. The same type of symbolic display as discussed in Section B.4.2 is displayed on the terminal:

```
> \box52=
\hbox(6.83331+0.0)x27.00003
.\OT1/cmr/m/n/10 A
.\glue 3.33333 plus 1.66498 minus 1.11221
.\OT1/cmr/m/n/10 t
.\OT1/cmr/m/n/10 e
.\OT1/cmr/m/n/10 s
.\OT1/cmr/m/n/10 t
```

```
OK.
```

If you add \scrollmode or \batchmode before the \showbox command, LaTeX does not stop at this point. You can then later study the trace in the transcript.

Local restores

To see what values and definitions TeX restores when a group ends, you can set \tracingrestores to a positive value. It is automatically turned on by the command \tracingall.

TeX's stack of lists

With \showlists you can direct TeX to display the stack of lists (vertical, horizontal) that it is currently working on. For instance, putting \showlists into the footnote[1] of the present paragraph, we obtain the following output in the .log file:

```
### horizontal mode entered at line 3066 []
spacefactor 1000
### internal vertical mode entered at line 3066
prevdepth ignored
### horizontal mode entered at line 3060 []
spacefactor 1000
### vertical mode entered at line 0
### current page: []
total height 514.70349 plus 26.0 minus 2.0
 goal height 522.0
prevdepth 1.70349
```

Here the text of the footnote started at line 3066, and the \spacefactor was set to 1000 at its beginning. The footnote itself was started on that same line, contributing the "internal vertical mode", and TeX correctly disregarded the outer value of \prevdepth. The footnote was part of a paragraph that started on source line 3060, which in turn was embedded in a vertical list that started on line 0, indicating that it is the main vertical galley.

Finally, the output shows some information about the current page list that is being built, including its current height, its target height, and the value of \prevdepth (i.e., the depth of the last line on the page at the moment).

Because of the default settings for \showboxbreadth and \showboxdepth, the contents of all lists are abbreviated to []. To get more detail adjust them as necessary or use \showoutput\showlists to get the full details.

Tracing the processing

Not very useful on its own, but helpful together with other tracing options, is \tracingcommands, which shows all primitives used by TeX during processing. A related internal integer command is \tracingmacros, which shows all macro expansions carried out by TeX. If set to 2, it also displays the expansion of conditionals. Both parameters are automatically turned on by \tracingall.

Tracing lost characters

When everything is set up correctly, it is unlikely that pdfTeX will ever access a font position in the current font that is not associated with a glyph. However, some commands, such as \symbol, can explicitly request any font slot, so it is not impossible.

---

[1] A footnote starts a new vertical list and, inside it, a new horizontal list for the footnote text.

> **Unicode engines**
>
> Unfortunately, the situation in the Unicode engines is worse, because these engines assume that all fonts can typeset *any* Unicode character, which is obviously false. As a result, it is rather likely that, depending on the fonts used in the document, one or the other more uncommon character is unavailable and therefore does not print when requested.

Sadly, TEX, and by extension the other engines based on it, never considered this event to be an error (which it should have). It merely traces such missing characters by writing unsuspicious transcript entries, and it takes that step only if \tracinglostchars is set to a positive value.

More recently most engines have been extended so that you now can get warnings on the terminal (\tracinglostchars set to 2) or even errors (value 3). LATEX tries to be helpful by initializing this internal integer to 2. However, especially with Unicode engines we recommend changing this to 3 in the preamble of your documents to avoid undetected missing characters in your documents.

Better use the setting \tracinglostchars = 3 in the preamble

Finally, you can direct TEX to step through your files line by line. When setting \pausing to 1, each source line is first displayed (suffixed with =>). TEX then waits for instructions regarding what to do with it. Pressing ⟨Enter⟩ instructs TEX to use the line unchanged; anything else means that TEX should use the characters entered by the user instead of the current line. TEX then executes and typesets whatever it was passed, displays the next line, and stops again. To continue normal processing you can reply with \pausing=0, but remember that this is used in place of the current source line, so you may have to repeat the material from the current source line as well.

Stepping through a document

B.4.5 trace — Selectively tracing command execution

The LATEX command \tracingall (inherited from plain TEX) is available to turn on full tracing. LATEX added \tracingnone to turn tracing off again without requiring grouping. There are, however, some problems with this kind of tracing because it turns on all tracing levels, and some parts of LATEX produce enormous amounts of tracing data that is of little or no interest for the problem at hand.

For example, if LATEX has to load a new font, it enters some internal routines of NFSS that scan font definition tables and perform other activities. And 99.9% of the time you are not at all interested in that part of the processing, but just in the two lines before and the five lines after it. Nevertheless, you have to scan through a few hundred lines of output and try to locate the lines you need (if you can find them).

Another example is a statement such as \setlength\linewidth{1cm}. With standard LATEX this gives five lines of tracing output. With the calc package loaded, however, it results in about sixty lines of tracing data — probably not what you expected and not really helpful unless you try to debug the calc parsing routines (which ideally should not need debugging).

To solve this problem, the trace package defines a pair of commands, \traceon and \traceoff, that behave like \tracingall and \tracingnone except that they selectively turn tracing on and off based on what is being processed.

Another difference between \traceon and \tracingall is that the latter always displays the tracing information on the terminal, whereas \traceon can be directed to write only to the transcript file if you specify the option logonly. This is useful when writing to the terminal is very slow (e.g., if running in a shell buffer inside emacs).

The trace package has a number of internal commands for temporarily disabling tracing. It redefines the most verbose internal LaTeX functions so that tracing is turned off while they are executing. For example, the function to load new fonts is handled in this way. If a document starts with the two formulas

```
$a \neq b$   \small  $A = \mathcal{A}$
```

then LaTeX loads 22 new fonts[1] at this point. Using standard \tracingall on that line results in roughly 7500 lines of terminal output. On the other hand, if \traceon is used, only 350 lines are produced (mainly from tracing \small).

The commands for which tracing is turned off are few and are unlikely to relate to the problem at hand. However, if you need full tracing, you can either use \tracingall or specify the full option. In the latter case, \traceon traces everything, but you can still direct its output exclusively to the transcript file.

---

[1] You can verify this with the loading option of the tracefnt package.

APPENDIX C

Going beyond

While we certainly hope that your questions have been answered in this book, we know that this cannot be the case for all questions. This appendix tries to help in that unfortunate case.

The first section deals with the fundamental problem that our book (despite being rather large) is not meant for beginners. To make good use of it, you already need some basic knowledge of LATEX. If this is missing, then there is a great online course to teach you the foundations.

For questions related to specific packages discussed in the book, it can be helpful to read the original documentation provided with the package. Appendix C.2 suggests ways to find that documentation on your system.

Appendix C.3 then shares how to find online information to research questions that you may have, and how to interact with people in the TEX community when you experience problems.

This is followed in C.4 by explaining how best to obtain LATEX packages that are missing on your installation. It also gives a brief overview of TEX distributions and LATEX services in the cloud.

The final section talks about the community itself and how you can join it to make a difference and keep the ship afloat.

C.1 Learn LaTeX — A LaTeX online course for beginners

Worry-free experimentation in a browser

If you are new to LaTeX and picked up this book hoping that it also covers the LaTeX basics (which it understandably does not, if you look at the current page number) or if you need to refresh your memory on the basics, we recommend that you take a look at the Learn LaTeX website at `https://learnlatex.org`, which offers a great online course, teaching you the fundamentals and allowing you to experiment with LaTeX online — even without installing the system locally.

Available in several languages

The Learn LaTeX project was born out of the desire to provide any easy-to-access approach for LaTeX beginners. The site has been designed and implemented by members of the LaTeX Project Team, primarily by David Carlisle and Joseph Wright, as well as a larger group of volunteers who helped shape the content and did a marvelous job of translating it to several languages so that the full course is now available in Catalan, English, Español, French, German, Marathi, Portuguese, and Vietnamese — and, who knows — soon perhaps additional languages.

18 lessons to get you going

The curriculum consists of eighteen easy-to-consume lessons with interactive examples and exercises that can be processed and modified (!) in the browser, covering the basics that you need to get started with LaTeX and that underpin all the information provided in the current book. The central idea of the site is to get people started with one of the most common LaTeX tasks: write some academic document such as an article or report. The topics start with simple LaTeX structure, cover things such as including images or building tables, and move on to longer documents and bibliographies. Typesetting mathematics is clearly a core LaTeX strength, but here the course remains deliberately lightweight and touches on only a few concepts; it is enough to get you going but certainly not enough to write a complex math paper — the thoughts being that details like those covered in Chapter 11 are better mastered in a second step.

... more on each topic

Each lesson comes with an extra "More on this topic" page that can be bypassed when working through the course for the first time but that offers additional details if you are interested in a particular topic. For example, the lesson on tables focuses on the array package as the fundamental extension to LaTeX's basic `tabular` environment and explains the main concepts such as the different kinds of column specifiers, how to add rules, and how to merge cells. The "More on this topic" page then goes into styling columns with the help of specifiers, manipulating space between columns, or producing customized rules and much more.

Recommend this to new users

Being closely linked with the LaTeX Project Team that maintains and develops LaTeX for you, the site is expected to stay up-to-date (in contrast to many other sites sprinkled across the Internet that have been set up with good intentions, but which then sadly declined in quality over the years). By offering a couple of ways to process the examples online (or off-line because the examples are plain text that is easily copied) and by presenting the course in several languages, it provides a low-barrier introduction to learning LaTeX. As it stands, it is a great resource for starting with LaTeX, and even if you personally have no need for it at your level of experience, it may be good to take a look and see how it functions. There may be a need to convince a colleague or friend to take the first steps with LaTeX, and this site may just convince them that LaTeX is not too hard to learn and worth the trouble — and for the rest there are books like the one you are currently holding in your hands.

C.2 Finding information available on your computer

When you want to use a LaTeX package, it would be nice if you could study the documentation without having to remember where the relevant files are located on your TeX system. Two important command-line tools exist to help you in your search: kpsewhich and texdoc. The first is most important if you want to study code, while the second helps you to easily find available documentation in your distribution.

C.2.1 kpsewhich — Find files the way TeX does

When TeX loads files (at least those loaded with \input or similar), it uses a special search library named kpathsea by Karl Berry that determines where to look and which file to load in case there is more than one with the same name.

The file name loaded is written into the .log file so you can find out what was loaded there, but this is not necessarily the most convenient way given that the transcript file contains a lot of other information. It also would not help if you ask yourself the question "which array.sty would LaTeX load if I use \usepackage{array}?" unless you first make a test file, run it through LaTeX, and then look at the transcript.

To help with this, the library is also available as the standalone command-line tool kpsewhich. In most cases it is enough to pass it the name of the file you are interested in, e.g., kpsewhich array.sty, and it responds with the full path for the file:

```
/usr/local/texlive/2022/texmf-dist/tex/latex/tools/array.sty
```

You can load it into your editor if you want to look at the code. You can also call kpsewhich with the option -all, in which case it returns

```
/usr/local/texlive/2022/texmf-dist/tex/latex/tools/array.sty
/usr/local/texlive/2022/texmf-dist/tex/latex-dev/tools/array.sty
```

i.e., all files with that name that it knows about.

You may wonder when (if ever) the other files are used by LaTeX. The answer is it depends on the program name used for running LaTeX. For example, if you use any of the development formats, e.g., pdflatex-dev, the array package from the latex-dev directory is used, because the search library has different search rules based on the program that is initiating the search. To mimic that with kpsewhich, pass it the option -progname=⟨prog⟩, and you get the result that would be returned to ⟨prog⟩ for the search:

```
kpsewhich -progname=pdflatex-dev array.sty
```

would return

```
/usr/local/texlive/2022/texmf-dist/tex/latex-dev/tools/array.sty
```

i.e., the package version for the next LaTeX release.

If you want to find out where the LATEX format file resides that is used by LATEX, it is not enough to just specify the name of the format file. You also have to tell kpsewhich which engine is loading it, using the option -engine=⟨engine⟩. Possible engine names are pdftex, xetex, or luahbtex. Together with the -all option, this is a great help if you receive a "Mismatched LaTeX support files" error; see page 730.

The program offers several other options; a list can be obtained with -help, but most of them are needed only for developers who set up a TEX distribution. The one that may be of interest occasionally is -debug=32. This produces detailed tracing output about how kpsewhich does its search and where it looks, which can be helpful if LATEX seems to be unable to find a file that you know is on your system. The -debug option can be given other numeric values to show other aspects of its behavior. For details on that and other features of TEX's search library, take a look at the documentation with texdoc kpathsea.

C.2.2 texdoc — A command-line interface to local TEX information

The texdoc program has a long history: it started out as a Unix shell script developed in the early nineties by Thomas Esser. The first Lua-based version was then written by Frank Küster with contributions by Reinhard Kotucha. It offered some operating system independence, because Lua, through LuaTEX, is available with any TEX (decent) distribution without the need to install separate programs.

Today's greatly enhanced version is developed and maintained by Manuel Pégourié-Gonnard and ASAKURA Takuto and the TEX Live team.

Initially you had to know the exact name of the documentation except for the file extension, so it was quite similar to kpsewhich in that regard. The current implementation, however, has a much more general search mechanism that accounts for the fact that many developers use schemes such as *package*-doc.pdf, *package*-manual.pdf, etc., for their documentation. It also has an alias mechanism through which individual documentation files can be associated with some keyword(s) people are likely to search for. For example, the file interface3.pdf (the interface documentation for the L3 programming layer) is one of the results if you search for expl3. This is managed through a configuration file that is part of the TEX distribution and regularly updated. You can also have your own configuration file as explained in the program documentation.

Opening the best result for viewing

Most of the time all you have to do is to pass texdoc the name of a package as an argument, e.g., texdoc fewerfloatpages, and it replies by opening the (what it thinks) best result in a suitable viewer for you; in this case it would open the file fewerfloatpages-doc.pdf.

Getting a list of "good" results to choose from

If this turns out not to be the documentation you have been looking for, your next possibility is to use it with the option -l. If you do that, it replies with a list of "useful" documentation files based on your input, and you can then choose one of them to be opened. For example, texdoc -l array would return five results: the official package documentation, the (possibly updated) version in the LATEX development release, as well as a French translation of the package documentation.

Getting a list of "all" results

If that is still not what you want, you can use -s instead. In that case texdoc returns all files it has found, even those that it considered to be a bad match. For example, in the case of `array`, you would then get 93 possibilities listed, among them many that have your keyword `array` as part of the name but also some that do not.

There is also the option `-m` (for mixed). It works like `-l`, but if only one result is found, then it opens that immediately for viewing instead of presenting you with a choice list with only one item. The `texdoc` program has a few more options that are helpful only in special circumstances and are not described here. If you want to learn about them, you have to read the program documentation, which you can do by — surprise — executing `texdoc texdoc`.

Using mixed mode

C.3 Accessing online information and getting help

There is a wealth of information available on the Internet, but unfortunately even with good search engines this is not always easy to find nor is it always easy to distinguish good advice from bad. To help you with both, we have selected a few different resources that we think are helpful. Obviously there are several others that are equally good — all we want to express here is that the selection forms a good and reliable starting point for getting your questions answered.

C.3.1 `texdoc.org` — searchable documentation on the Web

The website `https://texdoc.org` works similarly to the `texdoc` utility. It allows you to search for documentation just like you would do with `texdoc`'s `-l` and then choose from among the results, but instead of the command line you use a browser. This is useful if you prefer working with a GUI instead of the command line or if you have installed only a small distribution where a lot of interesting packages are excluded. By using the topic search, this enables you to find material that is not locally available. See also the CTAN catalogue that offers a similar functionality.

C.3.2 Frequently Asked Questions (FAQ) resources

Very valuable resources are the existing Frequently Asked Questions (FAQ) documents. The most important one is probably the TeX FAQ, available online at `https://texfaq.org`. It is the successor of the UK-TUG FAQ by Robin Fairbairns (1947-2022) and now curated by members of the LaTeX Project Team, with contributions from a very wide range of other TeXperts over many years, so it is likely to be reasonably current and accurate.[1]

There is also a great document named `visualFAQ.pdf` by Scott Pakin that offers a visual entry point to the TeX FAQ. It is an innovative new search interface that presents more than a hundred typeset samples of frequently requested document formatting. Any point of interest is marked with a rectangular box (green for tasks you might want to achieve and red for visual errors you might encounter), and clicking on any of them opens the corresponding FAQ entry in the TeX FAQ. Given that it is more

---

[1] If you search the Internet, you are likely to come across other FAQ documents on TeX and LaTeX in different languages. However, be aware that some of them are no longer maintained and thus are likely to give advice that is a decade or more out of date.

than thirty pages long, it covers a huge number of samples, but of course this also means that it might take you a while to locate one. The document is likely to be part of your installation; try texdoc visualFAQ. If not, you can download it from CTAN.

French version

A translation of this document into French by Jérémy Just is also available under the name visualFAQ-fr.pdf. The links it contains point to the French FAQ site (https://faq.gutenberg.eu.org), which is maintained by GUTenberg — the French-speaking TeX users group.

C.3.3 Using news groups and forums

News groups on TeX and LaTeX

If precomposed answers are not enough, then there are several news groups and, more importantly, forums that are devoted to general TeX and LaTeX questions. In the past the news groups such as news://comp.text.tex have been the premier place to go to and ask questions, but they are now less important for this. If you look at the postings in those groups, most of them are now announcements, intermixed with one or the other thread discussing a question.

Question and answer forums on TeX and LaTeX

More important therefore are the various forums devoted to TeX and LaTeX: at https://latex.net/about/ several national and international ones are listed, among them latex.org (international), TeXwelt.de (German), or TeXnique.fr (French). Another recent one is TopAnswers at https://topanswers.xyz/tex. Perhaps the most popular one right now is the StackExchange forum on TeX, which you can reach at https://tex.stackexchange.com.

In contrast to news groups that also carry announcements and other items of potential short-lived interest, such forums are meant to be a permanent record of problems and their answers. They are therefore usually easy to search and a good place to see if the problem you have has already been raised by others and already has a good answer. So please always search first to avoid asking the same question over and over again, because this wastes everybody else's time. Doing a search engine search normally works well too because the bigger forums such as StackExchange's TeX forum are regularly and often, or even instantly, indexed.

Many of the authors mentioned in this book are regular contributors on forums (or news groups) and help with answering questions and requests. Thus, there is a vast amount of helpful material on the Web that can be conveniently searched using any search engine that indexes news entries.

How to ask questions in a smart way

If you post to any of these news groups or to forums such as StackExchange, please adhere to basic netiquette. The community is friendly but sometimes direct and expects you to have done some research of your own first (e.g., read the FAQ first and search the archived news and questions) and not ask questions that have been answered several hundred times before. You should perhaps read Eric Raymond's "How To Ask Questions The Smart Way", available at http://www.catb.org/~esr/faqs/smart-questions.html, as a starter. Also, if applicable, provide a minimal *and* usable example of your problem (often referred to as an MWE[1]) that allows others

---

[1] This stands for "Minimal Working Example", and the stress is on all three words: "Minimal" means you should not just copy a huge file, just because it was the one failing, but condense it so that it contains only what is absolutely needed to show the problem; "Working" means that it should

to easily reproduce the symptoms you experience — this saves others time and might get you a faster and probably more pertinent reply.

Most of the forums allow you to mark an answer as the one that solved your problem. Be courteous and mark it as such if that is the case. It helps others having the same problem, and it always shows that you appreciate the effort somebody else has put into helping you. If there are several useful answers, upvote them all even if you can mark only one as the "correct" solution.

C.3.4 The LATEX Project's web presence

The LATEX Project Team (i.e., the people who took over from Leslie Lamport, produced LATEX 2_ε, and since then maintained and developed LATEX for you) have an official website that gives pertinent information about LATEX, lists important announcements of upcoming releases and improvements, holds the LATEX newsletters, and hosts a larger collection of the team's research papers written over the last decades. Keeping a tab on these resources, e.g., by subscribing to the news feed on the page (do not worry, it is low volume, maybe a dozen or so posts per year), helps you to learn about new developments and upcoming features that LATEX is going to offer. You can find the website at `https://latex-project.org` if you have not come across it already.

Getting news from the LATEX Project Team

The sources for LATEX are hosted on GitHub at `https://github.com/latex3/latex2e` — there releases are built (both the development releases with code for the next major release, as well as the main releases that are done about twice per year). From there they get shipped to CTAN, stored there, and then within a few days make their way into the major TeX distributions (e.g., TeX Live or MiKTeX), and if you have automatic updates enabled, they appear instantly at your desktop. If not, they appear the next time you update manually.

The ultimate home of the LATEX sources

C.4 Getting all those TeX files

In contrast to the early days of LATEX, it is nowadays rather easy to get a complete TeX distribution installed including an update service that fetches missing or changed packages from the Internet and installs them for you. This section therefore only briefly touches on the underlying foundation, the Comprehensive TeX Archive Network, and the major distributions available.

C.4.1 CTAN — The Comprehensive TeX Archive Network

The Comprehensive TeX Archive Network (CTAN for short) is a collaborative effort initiated in 1992 by the TeX Users Group Technical Working Group on TeX Archive Guidelines originally coordinated by George Greenwade (1956–2003), building on the earlier work of Peter Abbott (see [34] for the historical background). For a long

---

compile on its own, e.g., do not expect that the preamble is not important or that it is just enough to show a snippet of the part that is failing; and finally "Example" means it should really be an example of what you are asking about — surprisingly that is not always the case.

time this network of servers for hosting TEX-related software was maintained by Jim Hefferon, Robin Fairbairns (1947–2022), and Rainer Schöpf. Its services are now offered through a group of volunteers mainly based in Germany. The servers can be reached at the generic address `https://ctan.org` from which you may get redirected to a suitable mirror near to you.

Its main aim is to provide easy access to up-to-date copies of all versions of TEX, LATEX, METAFONT, and ancillary programs and their associated files. It is the authoritative source of record for most TEX distributions; i.e., what you get when installing TEX Live, MiKTEX, etc., is a copy of files stored on CTAN and update procedures of such distributions directly or indirectly obtain package updates from there. Thus, most developers submit their packages to CTAN because that is a fast easy and reliable way to get your packages distributed with all major distributions.

However, CTAN also hosts material that for one or the other reason (licensing questions usually) is not automatically part of the distributions, so it is also a place to obtain material that is available but not distributed by default.

All the data hosted on CTAN are cataloged under a larger number of topics, and there are ways to view them by topic or author as well as search them in other ways. That can be helpful if you are looking for packages addressing a certain aspect or supporting a particular language, etc.

The word "Archive" in "Comprehensive TEX Archive Network" might be a bit misleading: it is an archive in the sense that it archives the latest versions of packages and so holds, for example, also abandoned and obsolete packages only of interest for historical reasons or for reprocessing very old documents, but it is not a historical archive; i.e., you do not find older versions of software on the archive but only the latest release. It does, however, give you a link to the package author repositories if they provided CTAN with that information (where you then usually can find an older release that can be picked up in an emergency).

C.4.2 TEX distributions — past and present

There are a number of TEX distributions for installation on laptops and desktops; the most popular ones are probably TEX Live, MiKTEX, and MacTEX. The TEX Live distribution is available for different operating systems, which is rather convenient if you are a user of several ones. MiKTEX specifically targets Windows operating systems but now also supports Linux. MacTEX, as the name suggests, is for computers running macOS. All three distributions use software stored on CTAN as their point of reference, either directly or through a curated process repackaging files in the right way for the distribution.

Enable updates but also backups!   All distributions allow you to receive updates of packages and files, either automatically (if you set it up) or by initiating the update process manually. Staying current with software is often the right thing to do, but be aware that in the case of a major project being worked on (such as your thesis or a book like the one you are reading right now), you may want to stay with a stable version of all software to avoid unpleasant surprises in the last stage of production because of a change altering, say, the pagination. The distributions (except for MiKTEX) also allow you to store backups of updated packages so that it is easy to revert an update if that ever becomes necessary.[1]

The TeX Live distribution has a major update every year since 1996, and from these distribution releases, CDs and later DVDs have been produced and distributed through the TeX user groups. The original images can be found on the Internet at `https://www.tug.org/texlive/acquire.html#past` from one of the mirrors listed there. They offer you the possibility of reinstalling an older version of the TeX distribution, if that ever becomes necessary. For very important projects, such as a book production or a thesis, it may pay off to keep an image from that time next to it to have some level of assurance that you have everything available that was used at the time to reproduce the work. Of course, this gives you only the single snapshot of the distribution at a particular point in time (including the binaries). Given that throughout a year packages typically get updated, you should additionally look at the tools discussed in Section 2.5.2 on page →I 110 to get the full set of files you used in your project.

Keep images of the distribution if possible

Linux distributions

Most flavors of Linux contain TeX distributions that can be installed through the package manager of the Linux distribution you use. For a number of reasons these distributions may not use the most current TeX Live release, and if you use them to install a TeX distribution, you obtain something that is sometimes years behind a current distribution. For that reason our advice is to forget these native Linux packages, but instead take a current TeX Live distribution and use that for installation on your system. The installation is fairly straightforward, and if you know how to work the package manager of your Linux system, then following the installation procedures for TeX Live should pose no difficulties — your reward will be a current and up-to-date TeX installation.

Avoid pre-made Linux packages for TeX — or at least check that they contain a recent release

Cloud service installations

In the recent years cloud services such as Overleaf have become popular. They make LaTeX available as online installations that allow for easy collaboration between several people, because the documents are stored and processed in the cloud. This also means that everybody is using the same packages on identical release levels (i.e., no issue with one of your colleagues using a different LaTeX release than the others), nobody is forced to install a distribution on their computer before starting to collaborate, and you have or can have version control of your documents, and several other goodies. There are, of course, also some downsides, e.g., you are restricted in your editing environment because (by default) you are working in the browser, you may not be able to use cutting-edge package versions, etc., but on the whole they offer a great environment for collaborating and significantly lower the entry barrier to using LaTeX.

Under the hood, a service such as the one from Overleaf uses TeX Live distributions, so all that is described in this book is fully applicable without restriction. This

---

[1] This is seldom needed, but it provides you with a valuable safety net if some update affects your workflow in some unexpected way. Note that this is not offered by MiKTeX.

also goes for the advice given above that it is useful to keep a copy of the relevant distribution files as a DVD image together with important documentation projects because that significantly enlarges the chances that your files remain fully processable even after many years.

A simple cloud service without registration

A simpler online service, `https://texlive.net`, has been developed by David Carlisle as part of the Learn LATEX project discussed in Appendix C.1. It gives online access to a TEX Live installation without requiring any login or registration and integrates an online editor. However, it provides no mechanism to save documents, so is suitable only for small examples. By default it uses LATEX with the pdftex engine, but the engine may be changed via a comment line such as

```
% !TeX lualatex
```

at the top of the document.

C.5 Giving back to the community

Open source software lives from the volunteers who engage in its development and maintenance. In the early days of TEX, many people using TEX directly engaged with the developer community or became part of it because using TEX and LATEX meant that you had to work through many obstacles, starting from installation (which was a largely manual step) to finding packages (that were not well organized in one place or automatically showed up at your doorstep by just installing a pre-canned distribution) down to developing your own packages because your problem was not yet solved.

Over time more and more of this got streamlined, installations became simple due to distributions such as TEX Live [89], central repositories appeared and are well maintained, i.e., CTAN, and over the last decades more and more ready-to-use packages for all kind of tasks were developed — the growing size of this book from edition to edition is a living proof of that.

As a result, the continuing work of volunteers in the background to make this all happen smoothly faded more and more from people's minds, and many users now have no idea that nothing would work if there were not a handful of people spending their free time curating several dozen package updates per day, building new distributions regularly, or maintaining and developing LATEX and the many packages out there, etc.

Everything just seems to work and is at your fingertips, whether you are producing your documents on an online platform such as Overleaf or whether you download an installation for your local machine from the Internet. However, it is not quite as simple as that. Developers need resources to successfully do their work, they need a lively community through which they can exchange ideas and get feedback on work being undertaken, and they need appreciation of their work by their users.

There are many ways in which you can help to keep that ship afloat, starting from showing your appreciation after asking for help and receiving it to more substantial ways, such as contributing to one or the other project. All of them are necessary and helpful, and this final short section shows some ways through which you can make a difference.

In the *TEXbook* [42, app. J] Donald Knuth wrote an appendix called "Joining the TEX Community", which is still as relevant as it was forty years ago. Only back then, the benefits of joining a user group and paying a membership fee was obvious to many (because it was the best if not the only way to get in contact with other users and receive help), while today only a few people compared to the user base even know about such groups, let alone think that the user groups offer them any immediate benefit. Immediate — perhaps not, but in the long term most certainly yes for the reasons outlined above, so please consider becoming officially a part of the community and supporting the mission.

TEX User group(s):
TUG,
DANTE,
GUST,
GuIT,
Gutenberg,
NTG,
...

There is the international TEX Users Group (TUG) that publishes a regular journal and organizes conferences at which developers and users meet and interact. You can reach TUG at `https://tug.org`. Membership fees and/or donations to TUG or specific projects are tax-deductible in the United States. There are also several local user groups around the world, mostly based on language affinities, that are doing similar work; a current inventory is provided at `https://tug.org/lugs.html` to help you find one in your local language, but note that some are more active than others.

There is also the possibility of donating to specific projects that are of interest to you or whose work you want to specifically support either through TUG at `https://tug.org/donate` or by supporting individual developers. GitHub, for example, offers a way to sponsor developers with a recurring (smaller or larger) contribution, and besides paying for the coffee or other essentials needed to do night-long work on maintaining or developing software, this is a way of showing appreciation that is valued far higher by most than the actual monetary value.

Donations and sponsoring

Drawing by Duane Bibby,
courtesy TEX Users Group

Bibliography

[1] Adobe Systems Incorporated. Adobe Type 1 Font Format. Addison-Wesley, Reading, MA, USA, 1990. ISBN 0-201-57044-0.

The "black" book contains the specifications for Adobe's Type 1 font format and describes how to create a Type 1 font program. It explains the specifics of the Type 1 syntax (a subset of PostScript), including information on the structure of font programs, ways to specify computer outlines, and the contents of the various font dictionaries. It also covers encryption, subroutines, and hints.

https://adobe-type-tools.github.io/font-tech-notes/pdfs/T1_SPEC.pdf

[2] American Mathematical Society. User's Guide to AMSFonts Version 2.2d. Providence, Rhode Island, 2002.

This document describes AMSFonts, the American Mathematical Society's collection of fonts of symbols and several alphabets. https://www.ctan.org/pkg/amsfonts

[3] ———. AMS Author Handbook (website). Providence, Rhode Island, 2021.

Entry point to documentation and support packages for preparing articles and books for publication with the American Mathematical Society. https://www.ams.org/arc/handbook/index.html

[4] American Mathematical Society and LaTeX Project. User's Guide for the amsmath Package (Version 2.1), 2020.

The amsmath package, developed by the American Mathematical Society, provides many additional features for mathematical typesetting. It is now maintained by the LaTeX Project team.

Locally available via: texdoc amsmath

[5] American Psychological Association. Publication Manual of the American Psychological Association. APA, 7th edition, 2020.

The official style guide of the American Psychological Association (APA) for the preparation of manuscripts for publication, as well as for writing student papers, dissertations, and theses.

https://apastyle.apa.org/

[6] Apple Inc. "TrueType Reference Manual", 2019.

Apple's reference manual for the TrueType font format.

https://developer.apple.com/fonts/TrueType-Reference-Manual

[7] Michael Barr. A new diagram package, 2016.

A rewrite of Michael Barr's original diagram package to act as a front end to Rose's xypic; see [31, Chapter 7]. It offers a general arrow-drawing function; various common diagram shapes, such as squares, triangles, cubes, and 3×3 diagrams; small 2-arrows that can be placed anywhere in a diagram; and access to all of xypic's features. Locally available via: texdoc diagxy

[8] Claudio Beccari and Apostolos Syropoulos. "New Greek fonts and the `greek` option of the `babel` package". *TUGboat*, 19(4):419–425, 1998.
Describes a new complete set of Greek fonts and their use in connection with `babel`'s `greek` extension.
https://tug.org/TUGboat/tb19-4/tb61becc.pdf

[9] Nelson Beebe. "Bibliography prettyprinting and syntax checking". *TUGboat*, 14(4):395–419, 1993.
This article describes three software tools for BibTeX support: a prettyprinter, syntax checker, and lexical analyzer for BibTeX files; collectively called bibclean.
https://tug.org/TUGboat/tb14-4/tb41beebe.pdf

[10] Barbara Beeton. "Mathematical symbols and Cyrillic fonts ready for distribution". *TUGboat*, 6(2):59–63, 1985.
The announcement of the first general release by the American Mathematical Society of the Euler series fonts.
https://tug.org/TUGboat/tb06-2/tb11beet.pdf

[11] Alexander Berdnikov, Olga Lapko, Mikhail Kolodin, Andrew Janishevsky, and Alexei Burykin. "Cyrillic encodings for LaTeX 2ε multi-language documents". *TUGboat*, 19(4):403–416, 1998.
A description of four encodings designed to support Cyrillic writing systems for the multi-language mode of LaTeX 2ε. The "raw" X2 encoding is a Cyrillic glyph container that allows one to insert into LaTeX 2ε documents text fragments written in any of the languages using a modern Cyrillic writing scheme. The T2A, T2B, and T2C encodings are genuine LaTeX 2ε encodings that may be used in a multi-language setting together with other language encodings.
https://tug.org/TUGboat/tb19-4/tb61berd.pdf

[12] Jens Berger. "The `jurabib` Package", 2017.
Manual for the `jurabib` package, translated to English by Maarten Wisse.
Locally available via: `texdoc jurabib`

[13] Karl Berry. "Filenames for fonts". *TUGboat*, 11(4):517–520, 1990.
This article describes the consistent, rational scheme for font file names that was used for at least the next 15 years. Each name consists of up to eight characters (specifying the foundry, typeface name, weight, variant, expansion characteristics, and design size) that identify each font file in a unique way.
https://tug.org/TUGboat/tb11-4/tb30berry.pdf
The latest version of this scheme is available at: https://tug.org/fontname/html/

[14] Javier Bezos. The `accents` Package, 2019.
Miscellaneous tools for mathematical accents: to create faked accents from non-accent symbols, to group accents, and to place accents below glyphs.
Locally available via: `texdoc accents`

[15] Javier Bezos and Johannes Braams. Babel — Localization and internationalization — TeX, pdfTeX, XeTeX, LuaTeX, 2023.
The official user manual for Babel, describing how to use it with different flavors of TeX. A second part covers the complete source code documentation.
Locally available via: `texdoc babel`

[16] Charles Bigelow. "Oh, oh, zero!" *TUGboat*, 34(2):168–181, 2013.
A survey of attempts to make "O", "0", and similar look-alike characters distinguishable in historical and modern typography.
https://tug.org/TUGboat/tb34-2/tb107bigelow-zero.pdf

[17] ———. "About the DK versions of Lucida". *TUGboat*, 36(3):191–199, 2015.
A description of the design of the Lucida DK fonts and their history, developed as a response to [50].
https://tug.org/TUGboat/tb36-3/tb114bigelow.pdf

[18] The *Bluebook*: A Uniform System of Citation. The Harvard Law Review Association, Cambridge, MA, 21st edition, 2020. ISBN 978-0-578-66615-0.
The *Bluebook* contains three major parts: part 1 details general standards of citation and style to be used in legal writing; part 2 presents specific rules of citation for cases, statutes, books,

periodicals, foreign materials, and international materials; and part 3 consists of a series of tables showing, among other things, which authority to cite and how to abbreviate properly.

Can be ordered at: https://www.legalbluebook.com

[19] Johannes Braams. "Babel, a multilingual style-option system for use with LaTeX's standard document styles". *TUGboat*, 12(2):291–301, 1991.
The babel package was originally a collection of document-style options to support different languages. An update was published in *TUGboat*, 14(1):60–62, April 1993.
https://tug.org/TUGboat/tb12-2/tb32braa.pdf
https://tug.org/TUGboat/tb14-1/tb38braa.pdf

[20] Robert Bringhurst. Palatino — The Natural History of a Typeface. David R. Godine, Publisher, Boston, 2016. ISBN 978-1-56792-572-2.
Palatino is one of the most widely used typefaces today. Designed by Hermann Zapf (1918-2015), it has been used as a model for many other typefaces. This book discusses its evolution and history and is a fascinating read if you are interested in type design.

[21] Judith Butcher, Caroline Drake, and Maureen Leach. Butcher's Copy-editing: The Cambridge Handbook for Editors, Copy-editors and Proofreaders. Cambridge University Press, New York, forth edition, 2006. ISBN 0-521-40074-0.
A reference guide for all those involved in the process of preparing typescripts and illustrations for printing and publication. The book covers all aspects of the editorial process, from the basics of how to mark a typescript for the designer and the typesetter, through the ground rules of house style and consistency, to how to read and correct proofs.

[22] Florian Cajori. A History of Mathematical Notations. Dover Publications, New York, 1993. ISBN 978-0-486-67766-8.
This classic book on mathematical notations, originally published in two volumes in 1928-1929, devotes a full chapter to several numeral systems from antiquity, including Greek.

[23] Pehong Chen and Michael A. Harrison. "Index preparation and processing". *Software — Practice and Experience*, 19(9):897–915, 1988.
The original description of the *MakeIndex* system.
https://ctan.org/pkg/makeindex

[24] The Chicago Manual of Style. University of Chicago Press, Chicago, IL, USA, 17th edition, 2017. ISBN 978-0-226-28705-8.
The standard U.S. publishing style reference for authors and editors.
https://www.chicagomanualofstyle.org

[25] Ioannis Dimakos and Dimitrios Filippou. "Twenty-five years of Greek TeXing". *Eutypon*, 32–33:25–34, 2014.
An overview about available tools (fonts, systems, etc.) for typesetting Greek texts with TeX/LaTeX.
https://ctan.org/tex-archive/info/greek/greekinfo3

[26] Michael Downes. "Breaking equations". *TUGboat*, 18(3):182–194, 1997.
TeX is not very good at displaying equations that must be broken into multiple lines. The breqn package eliminates many of the most significant problems by supporting automatic line breaking of displayed equations.
https://tug.org/TUGboat/tb18-3/tb56down.pdf

[27] ——. "The amsrefs LaTeX package and the amsxport BibTeX style". *TUGboat*, 21(3):201–209, 2000.
Bibliography entries using the amsrefs format provide a rich internal structure and high-level markup close to that traditionally found in BibTeX database files. On top of that, using amsrefs markup lets you specify the bibliography style completely in a LaTeX document class file.
https://tug.org/TUGboat/tb21-3/tb68down.pdf

[28] Michael Downes, Høgholm, and Will Robertson. The breqn package, 2021.

A package initially developed by Michael Downes (1958–2003) for automatically breaking display equations into several lines [26]. Continued after Michael's death by Morten Høgholm and Will Robertson.   Locally available via: texdoc breqn

[29] Victor Eijkhout. TeX by Topic, A TeXnician's Reference. Lehmanns Media, Berlin, 2014. ISBN 978-3-86541-590-5. Reprint with corrections. Initially published in 1991 by Addison-Wesley. Also available free of charge from the author in PDF format.

A systematic reference manual for the experienced TeX user. The book offers a comprehensive treatment of every aspect of TeX (not LaTeX!), with detailed explanations of the mechanisms underlying TeX's working, as well as numerous examples of TeX programming techniques.
https://eijkhout.net/tex/tex-by-topic.html

[30] FUKUI Rei. "TIPA: A system for processing phonetic symbols in LaTeX". TUGboat, 17(2):102–114, 1996.

TIPA is a system for processing symbols of the International Phonetic Alphabet with LaTeX. It introduces a new encoding for phonetic symbols (T3), which includes all the symbols and diacritics found in the recent versions of IPA as well as some non-IPA symbols. It has full support for LaTeX 2_ε and offers an easy input method in the IPA environment.
https://tug.org/TUGboat/tb17-2/tb51rei.pdf

[31] Michel Goossens, Frank Mittelbach, Sebastian Rahtz, Denis Roegel, and Herbert Voß. The LaTeX Graphics Companion. Lehmanns Media, Köln, 2nd edition, 2022. ISBN 978-3-96543-303-8 (softcover), 978-3-96543-299-4 (ebook).

Reprint of the 2nd edition originally published by Addison-Wesley in the Tools and Techniques for Computer Typesetting series.

The book describes all aspects of generating and manipulating graphical material in LaTeX, including an in-depth coverage of pstricks, METAFONT and METAPOST, xcolor, xy, etc., as well as a thorough overview about applications in science, technology, medicine, gaming, and musical notation.

[32] Ronald L. Graham, Donald E. Knuth, and Oren Patashnik. Concrete Mathematics. Addison-Wesley, Reading, MA, USA, 2nd edition, 1994. ISBN 0-201-55802-5.

A mathematics textbook prepared with TeX using the Concrete Roman typeface; see also [46].

[33] George Grätzer. More Math Into LaTeX. Springer International Publishing, Cham, Switzerland, 5th edition, 2016. ISBN 3-319-23795-0.

Provides a general introduction to LaTeX as used to prepare mathematical books and articles. Covers AMS document classes and packages in addition to the basic LaTeX offerings.

[34] George D. Greenwade. "The Comprehensive TeX Archive Network (CTAN)". TUGboat, 14(3):342–351, 1993.

An outline of the conception, development, and early use of the CTAN archive, which makes all TeX-related files available on the network.   https://tug.org/TUGboat/tb14-3/tb40green.pdf

[35] Yannis Haralambous. "Typesetting old German: Fraktur, Schwabacher, Gotisch and initials". TUGboat, 12(1):129–138, 1991.

Demonstrates the use of METAFONT to re-create faithful copies of oldstyle typefaces and explains the rules for typesetting using these types, with examples.
https://tug.org/TUGboat/tb12-1/tb31hara.pdf

[36] ———. Fonts & Encodings. O'Reilly Media, Sebastopol, CA, 2007. ISBN 0-596-10242-9.

An extensive treatment of the subject in the Unicode world, including information on TeX at the time of publication; still relevant for the most part.

[37] Jean-Michel Hufflen. "Typographie: les conventions, la tradition, les goûts,..., et LaTeX". *Cahiers GUTenberg*, 35–36:169–214, 2000.

This article shows that learning typographic rules—even considering those for French and English together—is not all that difficult. It also teaches the basics of using the LaTeX packages french (for French only) and babel (allowing a homogeneous treatment of most other languages). Finally, the author shows how to build a new multilingual document class and bibliography style.

http://www.numdam.org/journals/CG

[38] Palle Jørgensen. "The LaTeX Font Catalogue", 2021.

A great online resource for fonts usable with LaTeX.   https://tug.org/FontCatalogue/

[39] Philip Kime and François Charette. biber — A backend bibliography processor for biblatex, 2022.

The official manual for biber with additional documentation not covered in this book. Original implementation by François Charette; maintained and further developed since 2009 by Philip Kime.

Locally available via: texdoc biber

[40] Philip Kime, Moritz Wemheuer, and Philipp Lehmann. The biblatex package, 2022.

The official manual for biblatex with additional documentation not covered in this book. Original implementation by Philipp Lehman; maintained and further developed since 2012 by Philip Kime and Moritz Wemheuer.   Locally available via: texdoc biblatex

[41] Donald E. Knuth. "Literate programming". Report STAN-CS-83-981, Stanford University, Department of Computer Science, Stanford, CA, USA, 1983.

A collection of papers on styles of programming and documentation.

http://www.literateprogramming.com/articles.html.

[42] ———. The TeXbook, volume A of *Computers and Typesetting*. Addison-Wesley, Reading, MA, USA, 1986. ISBN 0-201-13447-0. Jubilee 2021 edition, twenty-fifth printing with corrections.

The definitive user's guide and complete reference manual for TeX. A good secondary reading, covering the same grounds, is [29].

[43] ———. Digital Typography. CSLI Publications, Stanford, CA, USA, 1999. ISBN 1-57586-011-2 (cloth), 1-57586-010-4 (paperback).

A comprehensive collection of Knuth's writings on TeX and typography. While many articles in this collection are available separately on the Web, not all of them are, and having all in one place for studying is an additional benefit.

[44] ———. "Mathematical typography". In Knuth [43], pp. 19–65.

Based on a lecture he gave in 1978, Knuth makes the point that mathematics books and journals do not look as beautiful now as they did in the past. Because this is mainly due to the fact that high-quality typesetting has become too expensive, he proposes to use mathematics itself to solve the problem. As a first step he sees the development of a method to unambiguously mark up the math elements in a document so that they can be easily handled by machines. The second step is to use mathematics to design the shapes of letters and symbols. The article goes into the details of these two approaches.

[45] ———. "Virtual fonts: More fun for grand wizards". In Knuth [43], pp. 247–262.

An explanation of what virtual fonts are and why they are needed, plus technical details.

Originally published as: https://tug.org/TUGboat/tb11-1/tb27knut.pdf

[46] ———. "Typesetting Concrete Mathematics". In Knuth [43], pp. 367–378.

Knuth explains how he prepared the textbook *Concrete Mathematics*. He states that he wanted to make that book both mathematically and typographically "interesting", since it would be the first major use of Herman Zapf's new typeface, AMS Euler. The font parameters were tuned up to make the text look as good as that produced by the best handwriting of a mathematician. Other design decisions for the book are also described.

Originally published as: https://tug.org/TUGboat/tb10-1/tb26knut.pdf

[47] ——. "Computers and typesetting". In Knuth [43], pp. 555–562.

Remarks presented by Knuth at the Computer Museum, Boston, Massachusetts, on 21 May 1986, at the "coming-out" party to celebrate the completion of TeX.

Originally published as: https://tug.org/TUGboat/tb07-2/tb14knut.pdf

[48] ——. "The new versions of TeX and METAFONT". In Knuth [43], pp. 563–570.

Knuth explains how he was convinced at the TUG Meeting at Stanford in 1989 to make one further set of changes to TeX and METAFONT to extend these programs to support 8-bit character sets. He goes on to describe the various changes he introduced to implement this feature, as well as a few other improvements.

Originally published as: https://tug.org/TUGboat/tb10-3/tb25knut.pdf

[49] ——. "The future of TeX and METAFONT". In Knuth [43], pp. 571–572.

In this article Knuth announces that his work on TeX, METAFONT, and Computer Modern has "come to an end" and that he will make further changes only to correct extremely serious bugs.

Originally published as: https://tug.org/TUGboat/tb11-4/tb30knut.pdf

[50] ——. "A footnote about 'Oh, oh, zero'". *TUGboat*, 35(3):232–234, 2014.

Notes on early typesetting of computer programs by the ACM and Addison-Wesley as an addendum to [16] resulting in the development of a DK version of the Lucida monospaced fonts [17].

https://tug.org/TUGboat/tb35-3/tb111knut-zero.pdf

[51] Donald E. Knuth and Michael F. Plass. "Breaking paragraphs into lines". In Knuth [43], pp. 67–155.

This article, originally published in 1981, addresses the problem of dividing the text of a paragraph into lines of approximately equal length. The basic algorithm considers the paragraph as a whole and introduces the (now well-known TeX) concepts of "boxes", "glue", and "penalties" to find optimal breakpoints for the lines. The paper describes the dynamic programming technique used to implement the algorithm.

[52] Donald E. Knuth and Hermann Zapf. "AMS Euler—A new typeface for mathematics". In Knuth [43], pp. 339–366. Originally published in *Scholarly Publishing* **20** (1989), 131–157.

The two authors explain, in this article originally published in 1989, how a collaboration between scientists and artists is helping to bring beauty to the pages of mathematical journals and textbooks.

[53] Helmut Kopka and Patrick W. Daly. Guide to LaTeX. Tools and Techniques for Computer Typesetting. Addison-Wesley, Boston, MA, USA, 4th edition, 2004. ISBN 0-321-17385-6.

An introductory guide to LaTeX with a different pedagogical style than Lamport's *LaTeX Manual* [56].

[54] Klaus Lagally. "ArabTeX—Typesetting Arabic with vowels and ligatures". In "Proceedings of the 7th European TeX Conference, Prague", pp. 153–172. CsTUG, Prague, 1992. ISBN 80-210-0480-0.

A macro package, compatible with plain TeX and LaTeX, for typesetting Arabic with both partial and full vocalization.

https://www.ntg.nl/maps/20/22.pdf

[55] Leslie Lamport. "*MakeIndex*, An Index Processor For LaTeX". Technical report, Electronic Document in *MakeIndex* distribution, 1987.

This document explains the syntax that can be used inside LaTeX's \index command when using *MakeIndex* to generate your index. It also gives a list of the possible error messages.

Locally available via: texdoc makeindex

[56] ———. LaTeX: A Document Preparation System: User's Guide and Reference Manual. Addison-Wesley, Reading, MA, USA, 2nd edition, 1994. ISBN 0-201-52983-1. Reprinted with corrections in 1996.

The ultimate reference for basic user-level LaTeX by the creator of LaTeX 2.09. It complements the material presented in this book.

[57] LaTeX Project Team. "Default docstrip headers". *TUGboat*, 19(2):137–138, 1998.

This document describes the format of the header that docstrip normally adds to generated package files. This header is suitable for copyright information or distribution conditions.
                                        http://tug.org/TUGboat/tb19-2/tb59ltdocstrip.pdf

[58] ———. Configuration options for LaTeX 2_ε, 2003.

How to configure a LaTeX installation using the set of standard configuration files.
                                        Locally available via: texdoc cfgguide

[59] ———. LaTeX 2_ε for authors — historic version, 2020.

When LaTeX 2_ε was released in 1994, it was accompanied by a set of guides, e.g., [58, 60, 64, 76]. This guide describes functionality that became available with LaTeX 2_ε. Over the years it got some additions, as needed, but also kept information that is now only of historical interest. Starting in 2020, this historical version was frozen and a new guide was written in which irrelevant, old information was dropped and all new user-level functionality is documented; see [63].
                                        Locally available via: texdoc usrguide-historic

[60] ———. LaTeX 2_ε font selection, 2022.

A description of font selection in standard LaTeX intended for package writers who are already familiar with TeX fonts and LaTeX.   Locally available via: texdoc fntguide

[61] ———. Core documentation distributed with LaTeX, 2022.

The LaTeX distribution contains a number of guides, e.g., [58–60, 62–64, 76]. These, together with other useful documents, are also available from the project Web site on a couple of overview pages.   Overview at: https://latex-project.org/help/documentation

[62] ———. The LaTeX3 Interfaces, 2023.

The reference manual for the L3 programming layer, which has been part of the LaTeX format since 2020 and thus available for package development — the go-forward way for LaTeX-coding.
                                        Locally available via: texdoc interface3

[63] ———. LaTeX for authors — current version, 2023.

Starting in 2020, the core document-level functionality for LaTeX is now documented in this guide, and the original LaTeX 2_ε guide from 1994 has been moved to [59] for those who are interested in the history of LaTeX.   Locally available via: texdoc usrguide

[64] ———. LaTeX for class and package writers, 2023.

The guide to LaTeX 2_ε commands for class and package writers, but also sometimes useful in the preamble of documents. It was rewritten and extended in 2023 and the original from 2006 is available under a separate name.   Locally available via: texdoc clsguide
                                        and the historic version via: texdoc clsguide-historic

[65] Werner Lemberg. "The CJK package: Multilingual support beyond Babel". *TUGboat*, 18(3):214–224, 1997.

A description of the CJK (Chinese/Japanese/Korean) package for LaTeX and its interface to mule (multilingual emacs).   https://tug.org/TUGboat/tb18-3/cjkintro600.pdf

[66] Silvio Levy. "Using Greek fonts with TeX". *TUGboat*, 9(1):20–24, 1988.

The author tries to demonstrate that typesetting Greek in TeX with the gr family of fonts can be as easy as typesetting English text and leads to equally good results. The article is meant as a tutorial, but some technical details are given for those who have acquired greater familiarity with the font already.   https://tug.org/TUGboat/tb09-1/tb20levy.pdf

[67] Franklin Mark Liang. Word Hy-phen-a-tion by Com-pu-ter. Ph.D. thesis, Stanford University, Stanford, CA 94305, 1983. Also available as Stanford University, Department of Computer Science Report No. STAN-CS-83-977.
A detailed description of the word hyphenation algorithm used by TEX.
`https://tug.org/docs/liang/liang-thesis.pdf`

[68] Nicolas Markey. Tame the BeaST, 2009.
A lengthy tutorial about citations and bibliographical databases with tips and tricks for using a BIBTEX workflow.   Locally available via: `texdoc tamethebeast`

[69] Microsoft. "OpenType® Specification Version 1.9", 2021.
The official specification for the OpenType font format.
`https://docs.microsoft.com/en-us/typography/opentype/spec`

[70] Frank Mittelbach. "Language Information in Structured Documents: Markup and rendering—Concepts and problems". In "International Symposium on Multilingual Information Processing", pp. 93–104. Tsukuba, Japan, 1997. Invited paper. Slightly extended in *TUGboat* 18(3):199–205, 1997.
This paper discusses the structure and processing of multilingual documents, both at a general level and in relation to a proposed extension to standard LATEX.
`https://tug.org/TUGboat/tb18-3/tb56lang.pdf`

[71] ——. "A general framework for globally optimized pagination". In "Proceedings of the 2016 ACM Symposium on Document Engineering", DocEng '16, p. 11–20. Association for Computing Machinery, New York, NY, USA, 2016. ISBN 978-1-4503-4438-8.
This paper presents research results for globally optimized pagination using dynamic programming and discusses its theoretical background. It was awarded the "ACM Best Paper Award" at the DocEng 2016 conference. A greatly expanded version of this paper (37 pages) titled "A General LuaTEX Framework for Globally Optimized Pagination" was submitted to the Computational Intelligence (Wiley) in 2017 and accepted January 2018 [73].
`https://www.latex-project.org/publications/indexbyyear/2016/`

[72] ——. "Effective floating strategies". In "Proceedings of the 2017 ACM Symposium on Document Engineering", DocEng '17, p. 29–38. Association for Computing Machinery, New York, NY, USA, 2017. ISBN 978-1-4503-4689-4.
This paper presents an extension to the general framework for globally optimized pagination described [71]. The extended algorithm supports automatic placement of floats as part of the optimization using a flexible constraint model that allows for the implementation of typical typographic rules.   `https://www.latex-project.org/publications/indexbyyear/2017/`

[73] ——. "A general LuaTEX framework for globally optimized pagination". *Computational Intelligence*, 35(2):242–284, 2019.
This article is an extended version (37 pages) of the 2016 ACM article "A General Framework for Globally Optimized Pagination" [71], providing a lot more details and additional research results. The peer-reviewed publication is now freely available.
`https://www.latex-project.org/publications/indexbyyear/2020/`

[74] ——. "LATEX's hook management", 2021.
Guide to the new hook management system for LATEX introduced in 2020, including a documentation of all standard hooks in the LATEX kernel.   Locally available via: `texdoc lthooks-doc`

[75] Frank Mittelbach, Denys Duchier, Johannes Braams, Marcin Woliński, and Mark Wooding. "The docstrip program", 2022.
Describes the implementation of the docstrip program.   Locally available via: `texdoc docstrip`

[76] Frank Mittelbach, Robin Fairbairns, and Werner Lemberg. LaTeX font encodings, 2016.

An overview of all standard LaTeX font encodings and their use with 8-bit TeX engines, such as pdfTeX. *Locally available via:* `texdoc encguide`

[77] Frank Mittelbach, Michel Goossens, Johannes Braams, David Carlisle, and Chris Rowley. The LaTeX Companion. Tools and Techniques for Computer Typesetting. Addison-Wesley, Reading, MA, USA, 2nd edition, 2004. ISBN 0-201-36299-6.

The second edition of this book. The contributing authors have changed over the years.

[78] Frank Mittelbach and Joan Richmond. "R.I.P. – S.P.Q.R Sebastian Patrick Quintus Rahtz (13.2.1955–15.3.2016)". *TUGboat*, 37(2):129–130, 2016.

An obituary for my friend Sebastian. `https://tug.org/TUGboat/tb37-2/tb116rahtz-mitt.pdf`

[79] Frank Mittelbach, Will Robertson, and LaTeX3 team. "l3build — A modern Lua test suite for TeX programming". *TUGboat*, 35(3):287–293, 2014.

The workflow environment used by the LaTeX Project Team and others. Supports concepts developed over the years including regression testing methods, distribution builds, uploads to CTAN, and installation support. `https://tug.org/TUGboat/tb35-3/tb111mitt-l3build.pdf`
Locally available program documentation: `texdoc l3build`

[80] Frank Mittelbach and Chris Rowley. "The pursuit of quality: How can automated typesetting achieve the highest standards of craft typography?" In C. Vanoirbeek and G. Coray, editors, "EP92 — Proceedings of Electronic Publishing, '92, International Conference on Electronic Publishing, Document Manipulation, and Typography, Swiss Federal Institute of Technology, Lausanne, Switzerland, April 7–10, 1992", pp. 261–273. Cambridge University Press, New York, 1992. ISBN 0-521-43277-4.

This paper compares high-quality craft typography with the state of the art in automated typesetting. It explains why the current paradigms of computerized typesetting will not serve for high-quality formatting and suggests directions for the further research necessary to improve the quality of computer-generated layout.
`https://www.researchgate.net/publication/237444403_The_Pursuit_of_Quality`

[81] Scott Pakin. "The comprehensive LaTeX symbol list", 2021.

This document lists more than 18000 symbols and the corresponding LaTeX commands that produce them. Some of these symbols are guaranteed to be available in every LaTeX 2_ε system; others require fonts and packages that may not accompany a given distribution and that therefore need to be installed. All of the fonts and packages described in the document are freely available from the CTAN archives. *Locally available via:* `texdoc symbols`

[82] Oren Patashnik. BibTeXing, 1988.

Together with Appendix B of *The Manual* [56], this describes the user interface to BibTeX with useful hints for controlling its behavior. The design of BibTeX styles is described in [83].
Locally available via: `texdoc btxdoc`

[83] ——. Designing BibTeX Styles, 1988.

A detailed description for BibTeX style designers of the postfix stack language used inside BibTeX style files. After a general description of the language, all commands and built-in functions are reviewed. Finally, BibTeX name formatting is explained in detail.
Locally available via: `texdoc btxhak`

[84] Addison Phillips and Mark Davis. "Tags for identifying languages". RFC 4646, Internet Engineering Task Force (IETF), 2006.

The RTF describing the structure, content, construction, and semantics of language tags.
`https://www.rfc-editor.org/rfc/bcp/bcp47.txt`

[85] Will Robertson. A gallery of DTX files, 2007.
A gallery of sample `.dtx` files exhibiting several techniques of using DOCSTRIP.
Locally available via: `texdoc dtxgallery`

[86] Erik Spiekermann. Stop Stealing Sheep & find out how type works. TOC Publishing, p98a.berlin, Berlin, 4th edition, 2022. ISBN 978-3-949164-03-3.
A guidebook classic on how to use type most effectively. First published in 1993 by Adobe Press; the fourth edition is now also freely available under a Creative Commons license through Google Design. `https://design.google/library/catching-up-with-erik-spiekermann`

[87] Augusto Stoffel. {tikzcd} Commutative diagrams with TikZ, 2021.
User manual for creating commutative diagrams with TikZ.
Locally available via: `texdoc tikz-cd`

[88] Ellen Swanson. Mathematics into Type. American Mathematical Society, Providence, Rhode Island, updated edition, 1999. ISBN 0-8218-1961-5. Updated by Arlene O'Sean and Antoinette Schleyer.
Originally written as a manual to standardize copyediting procedures, the second edition is also intended for use by publishers and authors as a guide in preparing mathematics copy for the printer. `https://www.ams.org/publications/authors/mit-2.pdf`

[89] The *TUGboat* Team. "TeX Live CD 5 and the TeX Catalogue". *TUGboat*, 21(1):16–90, 2000.
TeX Live is a ready-to-run TeX system for the most popular operating systems; it works with all major TeX-related programs and contains a complete collection of fonts, macros, and other items with support for many languages. This article describes one of the early TeX Live CD distributions with cross-references to Graham Williams' TeX catalogue. `https://tug.org/TUGboat/tb21-1/tb66cd.pdf`
Current version for different platforms: `https://tug.org/texlive`

[90] Unicode Consortium. "International Components for Unicode (ICU)".
The International Components for Unicode (ICU) open source project is a technical committee of the Unicode Consortium providing mature C/C++ and Java libraries for Unicode support, software internationalization, and software globalization. ICU is widely portable to many operating systems and environments and provides identical results on different platforms and different programming languages. It offers various services for Unicode text handling, among them language-sensitive collation and searching, normalization, and upper and lowercase conversion. Online resources: `https://unicode-org.github.io/icu`
`https://www.unicode.org/reports/tr35/tr35-collation.html`

[91] Gabriel Valiente Feruglio. "Modern Catalan typographical conventions". *TUGboat*, 16(3):329–338, 1995.
Many languages, such as German, English, and French, have a long established typography tradition. However, despite the existence of a well-established tradition in scientific writing in Catalan, there are not yet any standards encompassing typographical conventions in this area. This paper proposes typographical rules that reflect the spirit of ancient Catalan scientific writings while conforming to modern typographical conventions. Some of these typographical rules are incorporated in Catalan extensions to TeX and LaTeX. The proposal also hopes to contribute to the development of standard rules for scientific writing in Catalan.
`https://tug.org/TUGboat/tb16-3/tb48vali.pdf`

[92] Hermann Zapf. "My collaboration with Don Knuth and my font design work". *TUGboat*, 22(1/2):26–30, 2001.
Zapf's story of collaboration with Don Knuth and some thoughts on typography.
`https://tug.org/TUGboat/tb22-1-2/tb70zapf.pdf`

[93] Justin Ziegler. "Technical report on math font encoding (version 2)". Technical report, LaTeX Project, 1994.
The groundwork for a set of 8-bit math encodings for TeX. `https://www.ctan.org/pkg/ltx3pub`

Index of Commands
and Concepts

This title somewhat hides the fact that everything (for both volumes) except for names of people is in this one long comprehensive index. To make it easier to use, the entries are distinguished by their "type", and this is often indicated by one of the following "type words" at the beginning of the main entry or a subentry:

> attribute, BIBTEX/biber command, BIBTEX entry type, BIBTEX field, BIBTEX style, boolean, counter, document class, env., file, file extension, folio style, font encoding, hook, key/option, keyword, key, language, length, library, math accent, math symbol, option, package, page style, program, rigid length, syntax, text accent, text symbol, text/math symbol, TEX counter, or value.

§ type words
used in the index

Most "type words" should be fairly self-explanatory, but a few need some explanation to help you find the entries you are looking for.

'option' and 'keyoption' Both type words indicate that the keyword can be used in the optional argument of \usepackage. If the option accepts a value, it is marked as a 'keyoption' and otherwise as a classic 'option'. Most packages with 'keyoptions' also offer configuration commands that can be used in the preamble or in the document body—see also next types.

'key' and 'value' Many modern LATEX packages implement a key/value syntax (i.e., $\langle key_1 \rangle = \langle value_1 \rangle$, $\langle key_2 \rangle = \langle value \rangle$, ...) as part of the optional argument to \usepackage, in arguments of commands or environments, or both. Keywords that can appear to the left of the equal sign are indicated by the type word 'key' (or as type 'keyoption' if allowed in \usepackage), those that can appear to the right as 'value'. Sometimes keywords can appear on either side, depending on context, in which case they are indexed according to their use on the particular page.[1]

'syntax' Keywords and strings marked with 'syntax' can appear in arguments of commands but are not part of a key/value pair.

'counter' and 'TEX counter' Names marked as 'counter' are LaTeX counters and are altered with `\setcounter`, etc., while 'TEX counters' start with a backslash and use a low-level method for modification.

'length' and 'rigid length' A 'length' register can take values with a `plus` and `minus` component, i.e., can stretch or shrink. In contrast, a 'rigid length' stores only a fixed value. Most lengths in LaTeX are flexible, i.e., not rigid.

'text symbol', 'math symbol', and 'text/math symbol' A command is classified as a 'text symbol' if it typesets a glyph for use in text, whereas a 'math symbol' can be used only in math mode and produces an error elsewhere. A few symbols are allowed everywhere and are therefore of type 'text/math symbol'.

In most cases, the actual symbol is also shown in the index entry to help you find the symbol you are looking for more easily (the command names are not always obvious). Note, however, that the glyph shown is only an approximation of reality — in your document it may come out differently depending on the fonts you use.

no type word indication The absence of an explicit "type word" means that the "type" is either a core LaTeX command or simply a concept.

Relation to packages or programs If a particular index entry is defined or used in a special way by a package, then this is indicated by adding the package name (in parentheses) to an entry or subentry. If package aaa builds upon or extends package bbb, we indicate this with (aaa/bbb). There is one "virtual" package name, tlc, which indicates commands introduced only for illustrative purposes in this book. Again, you may see (tlc/bbb), if appropriate.

Interpreting page references The index contains all entries for both volumes. To which pages the references point is indicated by →I (for part one) and →II (for part two). To save space, these indicators are given only once in each entry. An *italic* page number indicates that the command or concept is demonstrated in an example on that page. When there are several page numbers listed, **blue boldface** indicates a page containing important information about an entry, such as a definition or basic usage. However, **bold** is (normally) not used for concept entries, when all entries are of equal importance, or when there is *only one* page reference.

Sorting within the index When looking for the position of an entry in the index, you need to realize that both of the characters \ and . are ignored when they come at the start of a command or file extension. Other syntax entries starting with a period are listed in the Symbols section. Otherwise, the index entries are sorted in ASCII order, and the running header gives you an indication where you are in the index. For the rather lengthy Symbols section at the beginning of the index, this is unfortunately of little help because only a few people would know the symbol order in the ASCII encoding. We therefore show the order of symbols in the margin on those pages.

---

[1] This explains why you might find the same keyword under both type words, but given that one is usually interested only in one type of usage, this distinction is made. This distinction also exhibits the fact that different packages use the same keywords in different ways — an unfortunate side effect of the long history of LaTeX package development by independent developers.

!
"
,
(
)
*
+
,
−
.
/
:
;
<
=
>
?
@
[
#
%
&
$
_
\
^
~
{
}
␣
]
‘
|

B

C

H

Q

R

People

Biographies

Frank Mittelbach

Frank's interest in the automated formatting of complex documents in general, and in LaTeX in particular, goes back to his university days and has always been a major interest, perhaps a vocation, and throughout his IT career certainly a "second job". He studied mathematics and computer science at the Johannes Gutenberg University, Mainz, and afterwards joined EDS, Electronic Data Systems, initially working in a newly formed group for document processing using TeX and other tools and later on in the system management division.

Stanford, 1989 ...

At the TeX Users Group (TUG) conference at Stanford University in 1989, he gave a talk about the (many) problems with LaTeX 2.09, which led to him and a small team (known as the LaTeX Project Team) to take on the responsibility for the further development and maintenance of LaTeX from its original author Leslie Lamport.[1] In the capacity of technical lead of this project, he has overseen the original major release of LaTeX 2_ε in 1994 and the 36 (as of this writing) subsequent releases of this software. Right now he and the team are working on the important multi-year project to make LaTeX automatically produce tagged PDF and conform to accessibility standards.

When EDS was bought by HP he joined the global Enterprise Service Management division and eventually worked there as the European lead architect. In 2015 Frank ended his IT-industry career to fully concentrate on research in automated typesetting and Open Source software development, in particular on the future development of the LaTeX typesetting system.

---

[1] The history is briefly discussed in Section 1.1 of this edition; for a listing of all LaTeX Project team members through the years see https://latex-project.org/about/team/.

Frank is author or coauthor of many and varied LaTeX extension packages, such as $\mathcal{A}_{\mathcal{M}}S$-LaTeX, doc, multicol, and NFSS: the New Font Selection Scheme. His publication of many technical papers on LaTeX and on general research results in automated formatting brought him in contact with Peter Gordon from Addison-Wesley. Peter and Frank inaugurated the book series *Tools and Techniques for Computer Typesetting* (TTCT), with Frank as series editor. *The LaTeX Companion* (1994) was the first book of this series, which now includes titles that cover LaTeX in all its facets.

... and three decades later

He is on the board of the International Gutenberg Society, an international association for the study of the history and development of printing technology and font-oriented media, where he focuses on the more recent period. He is also involved in the print production of the society and in general enjoys designing and typesetting high-quality documents using computers but also using traditional letterpress. One of his plans after finishing TLC3 is to typeset a book on Japanese authored by Peter Gordon. When not involved with typographical questions or programming Frank enjoys reading (though the books better be of high quality in content *and* form), listening to or playing music (he is an amateur bass player), and winning or losing board games, these days often collaborative ones.

He and his wife Christel live in the Gutenberg city of Mainz; their three grown-up sons have left by now for new pastures.

Ulrike Fischer

Ulrike Fischer studied mathematics at the University of Bonn. She wrote her thesis in a rather arcane branch called model theory with an Atari text processor called Signum but did not like to have to place lots of sub and superscripts with a mouse. So when seeing an example LaTeX document, she directly ordered the floppy discs and never looked back.

Quite early she got interested in the internal handling of fonts and in chess typesetting as she wanted to print the bulletins of chess competitions she organized in her club. With the help of the first edition of the *LaTeX Companion*, she wrote the chessfss package, which allows users to choose between various chess fonts, and other chess-related packages.

After university, she moved with her husband to Siegburg and later to Mönchengladbach and worked as an assistant for a deputy of the state parliament of North Rhine-Westphalia. She found her way into the LaTeX groups on the Internet and enjoyed answering questions and debugging errors. She also helped her father who after his retirement as a professor for computer science wrote with LaTeX a number of books about Salvador Dalí's illustrations of the *Divine Comedy*. So when her job ended after a lost election, she decided to try something new and to work as a LaTeX consultant.

Her interest in fonts continued over the years and led her to accept the job of maintaining luaotfload. Talks about accessibility and tagged PDF at Dante and TUG meetings induced her to work on the tagpdf package and to present it to LaTeX team members at a workshop at the TUG meeting in Rio de Janeiro. Both together got her an invite to join the team in 2018. She had already had many online contacts with the team members in Usenet groups and chats as well as in person — she met Frank the first time at a Dante meeting in Heidelberg, where she talked about how to misuse biblatex as an address database, and he showed her how to eat some Japanese dish — and so accepted without hesitation. She now lives with her husband Gert in Bonn.

Javier Bezos

Javier Bezos is passionate about typography, science, language, and writing systems, as well as about computer programming. A curious person and self-taught by nature, his interests are broad, and he has worked in fields like book and journal publishing, design, radio, and classical music. He is an honorary member of the Unión de Correctores, the Spanish professional association of copyeditors.

As a computer programmer, he has developed systems for both LaTeX and InDesign, including tools for technical documentation, automatic typesetting and copyediting, XML, and localization. It is this last facet that he develops most actively as a member of the LaTeX Project Team.

Javier has participated as an author on several style manuals and published the book *Tipografía y notaciones científicas*. He is currently working at FundéuRAE, a foundation linked to the Royal Spanish Academy.

Hiking, reading old science books, and watching classic movies are some of his hobbies.

Johannes Braams

Johannes Braams studied electronic engineering at the Technical University in Enschede, the Netherlands. His master's thesis was on video coding, based on a model of the human visual system. During his research at the *dr. Neher Laboratories* in 1984, he came into contact with LaTeX for the first time. He was a founding board member of the Dutch-speaking TeX User Group (NTG) in 1988 and participated in developing support for typesetting Dutch documents. He started work on developing the babel system for multilingual typesetting following the Karlsruhe EuroTeX conference in 1989.

Since its inception at the EuroTeX conference in Cork in 1990, he has been a member of the LaTeX Project Team. Johannes still maintains a couple of LaTeX extension packages such as the ntgclass family of document classes and the supertabular and changebar packages.

After his studies, Johannes continued to work for the Dutch PTT, which later came to be known as KPN until 2014, mostly as an IT project manager. In 2015 he started a new career as a consultant on cybersecurity for industrial automation and control systems, first at the Software Improvement Group in Amsterdam; then in 2017 he joined Royal HaskoningDHV, a Dutch engineering firm that operates globally. He works on security by design in industrial installations. Johannes is now a board member of the Dutch chapter of (ISC)[2]. He lives with his wife in Den Ham; their two sons both graduated from the University Twente in Enschede.

Joseph Wright

Joseph Wright is a synthetic chemist who studied for his degree at the University of Leicester before moving to the University of Cambridge for his PhD. He first heard of LaTeX in about 2001 but did not start using it until writing a final report on his first research assistant position at the University of Southampton in 2004.

Joseph transitioned from being a user to a developer most obviously when he answered a "simple" question on the `comp.text.tex` newsgroup asking for a fix to the Slunits package in 2007. It soon turned out that this was the tip of a much larger task: writing a truly comprehensive units package: siunitx.

Joseph became involved with the LaTeX Project Team's work after Will Robertson asked him what he thought of the experimental ideas in expl3. Joseph liked them, so he used expl3 to develop the second version of siunitx and raised *lots* of questions about how things worked. His questions and suggestions led to an invite to join the team.

As well as writing (LA)TEX code, Joseph is one of the moderators on the TEX/LaTeX StackExchange site. He's one of two moderators who've been in place from the very start of the site, helping to ensure there's always been a welcoming approach with the aim of helping end users solve their (LA)TEX problems.

Production Notes

This book was typeset using the LaTeX document processing system (which it describes) together with substantial help from some of the extension packages covered herein, and considerable extra ad hoc LaTeX programming effort. We used the base LaTeX release dated 2022-11-01, pdfTeX as the main TeX engine, and LuaTeX for examples that involved OpenType fonts. All packages have been taken from the 2022 TeX Live distribution to ensure that the examples show what you will get when you run them yourself.[1]

The text body fonts used are Lucida Bright and Lucida Sans (Bigelow/Holmes) at 8.47pt/11.72pt. These font families can be used at rather small sizes, which can be seen by the fact that the monospaced font we matched them with is Latin Modern Typewriter (TeX Gyre foundry) at 10.36pt. This particular combination was chosen to get a reasonable amount of material on each page and to optically balance the appearance of the `typewriter font` so that it is distinguishable but without too big a contrast.

Body fonts

The text in the examples mostly uses TeX Gyre's Times Roman (`tgtermes`) with its Helvetica (`tgheros`) for sans serif. For the mathematical material in the examples we stayed with the now classic Computer Modern math fonts, so the symbols will appear familiar to the majority of mathematics users. Of course, examples intended to demonstrate the use of other fonts are exceptions.

Example fonts

Package usage in the book

If you count the examples as part of the book, then every package described in this edition has also been used in it. This is a bit of a red herring, though, because the examples are typeset as separate documents and the results are then included in the book as PDF (Portable Document Format) images. However, many of the packages

The LaTeX packages used to produce the book ...

---

[1] Well, at least initially — sometimes, though seldom, packages change in incompatible ways.

have been deployed for real to produce this edition, and for the interested reader we now list the most important ones and why they have been used.

... for the main text ...

To help in producing the explanatory text we used acro for acronyms, resetting their use count on a per-chapter basis. Thus, for most acronyms you see the first use in a chapter being displayed in its full form, e.g., as "Comprehensive TEX Archive Network (CTAN)". For quotation marks, commands from the csquotes package have been used throughout.

... for generating references ...

Heavy use was made of \vref and friends from the varioref package. We often refer to examples or sections "on the facing page", "previous", "next" or "below", etc., and in all such cases these are generated texts and not hardwired in the source. Otherwise, the layout process would have been a nightmare, requiring extensive amounts of textual adjustments whenever material moved from one page to the next and vice versa. Of course, using varioref in a book of this size is bound to produce an *impossible document* as explained on page →I 85. And indeed, it happened a handful of times that the generated text got split across two pages, rendering the wrong result in all cases. Initially, we changed the errors to warnings and ignored them, and then resolved the issues during the final pagination by adjusting the surrounding text (either rewriting parts or adding some strategic line or page breaks).

... applying optical alignment and font expansion ...

Since the second edition of *The LATEX Companion* we used "hanging punctuation" to typeset the paragraphs. In the last edition, this typographical icing was basically produced manually, but this time we have been fortunate to simply[1] apply the microtype package. This package was also used to add some light expansion/suppression using the *hz*-algorithm, which, in my opinion noticeably improved the overall look and feel of the paragraphs. For comparison, look at this paragraph and compare it with the repeat below (where both features are turned off).

... or not ... (a repeat)

2

Since the second edition of *The LATEX Companion* we used "hanging punctuation" to typeset the paragraphs. In the last edition, this typographical icing was basically produced manually, but this time we have been fortunate to simply[1] apply the microtype package. This package was also used to add some light expansion/suppression using the *hz*-algorithm, which, in my opinion noticeably improved the overall look and feel of the paragraphs. Compare this to the previous paragraph (which has both features turned on) — *which do you prefer?*

... chapter headings, lists, and running headers ...

The core design for the book dates back to the first edition and therefore chapter headings, list environments, etc., have been defined using the basic mechanisms of LATEX rather than using support packages because those were not available back then. For the running headers and the page numbers the fancyhdr package was used.

... making tables ...

To produce the various tables in the book, array and tabularx (for the extended syntax) were put to good use and on nearly every table we applied commands from the booktabs package for the formal rules. The few multipage tables have been generated with longtable and in some places we used multicol to produce a table-like appearance.

---

[1]We had to define our own configuration file, though, because the microtype package has no presets for the commercial Lucida Bright fonts and the default settings, while more or less adequate, were not totally satisfactory. Thus, we applied the advice given in Section 3.1.3.

[2]The paragraph now breaks differently and the margins are no longer optically aligned.

Graphics have been included with the help of graphicx and in a few places we used overpic to add some arrows or other data to the image. The captions have been styled with the caption package; other float-related packages were not necessary as the book requirements have been fairly light. Producing the examples, showing input and output side by side, was more elaborate and involved the use of the fancyvrb package and a fair amount of programming. The general approach we used is explained in Section 4.2.4 on page →I 315.

... showing graphics and examples ...

The boxes showing information that is only relevant for Unicode engines or that detail differences between the BibTeX and biblatex approach have been designed using tcolorbox, which in turn uses tikz.

... displaying informational boxes ...

For the bibliography we used BibTeX with a number-only style that was designed with the help of custom-bib, and natbib was used for the citations. Because this edition was split in two parts, each part got its own bibliography; this was achieved with the bibunits package.

...producing the bibliography ...

The book uses several separate indexes (even though only two are shown in the final product). To generate the raw data for them we made use of the index package and the sorting was done with *MakeIndex*. However, due to the complexity of the index (the colored page numbers, etc.) it was necessary to use pre- and post-processing by scripts to produce the final form of the index files. These were then typeset using an enhanced version of the multicol package to add the continuation lines — something that perhaps one day can be turned into a proper package. The "Commands and Concepts" index is a mixture of commands, environments, and other LaTeX elements, but also includes concept entries. The latter were produced by typesetting a version of the book with line numbers and giving that to the indexer, who produced "conceptual index entries" that were then added to the source files for the book so that pagination changes would not invalidate the index entries. This was a major testament to the quality of the lineno package, as it worked "straight out of the box".

... the different indexes ...

In anticipation of a PDF and ebook version of the third edition, we already used both the bookmark and the hyperref package. Even though this does not show in the printed form of the book it helped us tremendously during its preparation, because all internal references have been active links, allowing us to quickly jump from one place to another in the draft PDF document. Furthermore, all internal notes we made were enhanced to generate bookmarks so that the bookmark pane of the PDF reader gave us a quick overview of all the tasks still to do and text still to write.

... and interactive PDF features

Packages that should have been used for the book ...

You might be surprised that some heavily recommended packages, such as enumitem or geometry, are missing. The reason is simply that the fundamental design decisions, e.g., the page layout or the design of the headings, lists, etc., have been retained across all editions and when the first edition was typeset in 1994 those packages that can now make your life easier were not yet available, and thus the necessary code had to be handcrafted. Altering that setup was only done when improvements or changes were necessary; e.g., the titletoc package was added when we introduced the partial TOCs below the chapter headings. But in a new project such packages would have been used from the start.

... but have not

Packages supporting the production

Running out of files to write to

This book loads more than 140 `.sty` files (not counting those loaded in the examples), which is way beyond what is needed in typical documents. Several of these packages open their own write streams, and this is a rather limited resource in TeX (only 16 can be open at the same time). As a result the book died when processing the list of figures because that tried to open one stream too many. Fortunately, there is a remedy with Bruno Le Floch's morewrites package. It comes with a cost, though, because it needs additional processing time, but the important point is that it enables you to process a document of such complexity!

Color woes

The printing process for the book required two colors: black and some kind of blue as a spot color. For this, we used the packages xcolor and colorspace, but it is not a simple task to ensure that the final document does not contain color instructions in CMYK (or RGB) because some packages include hardwired color specifications using such models. As a result we had to do some patching or avoid using color in a few examples in order to not upset the final production process. This is clearly an area where LaTeX could be improved to make life easier.

Task management

To keep track of all the open tasks that needed resolving, we used the todonotes package and defined a few commands similar to those shown in Example A-1-17 on page 645, except that we also added a bookmark for each task using the bookmark package. At one point this showed several hundred entries, but now as I write this text it is thankfully down to a handful of remaining tasks.

Where are my errors?

Loading the structuredlog package enabled us to quickly identify in which source file an error occurred — not that we ever had any.[1] The footnote in Appendix B.1 on page 712 explains how to make use of this package.

Controlling the source

Using a source control approach is beneficial for nearly every project — for a complex one like this book, it is essential. It enables you and your co-authors to work without stepping on each other's toes; if something breaks, you have a history that helps you identify and resolve problems; and, last but not least, it simplifies project data synchronization across different devices and locations. For the second edition we used SVN; for this edition it was Git, and the package gitinfo2 was deployed to write source branch and date information at the bottom of every page (outside the final printing area).

Tracking file usage

Another tool we used regularly was mkjobtexmf. With its help we collected all files used during compilation in a separate tree, which was also placed under source control. This way, any updates to standard packages, font files, etc., could be easily tracked, which again helped a lot if something went awry.

The production cycle

The production of this book required a custom class and, as outlined above, many additional package files. It also needed a complex "make" process using a collection of "shell scripts" controlled by a "Makefile". One of the major tasks these accomplished

---

[1] Joke — of course, we did. All kinds of errors occurred, from simple typos to subtle package incompatibilities that resulted in talking to the developers after identifying the root cause of the problem.

was to ensure that the typeset output of each and every example really is produced by the accompanying example input. This "make" process worked as follows:

- When first processing a chapter, LaTeX generated a source document file for each example. These are the one-and-a-half-thousand "example files" you will find on CTAN at `https://ctan.org/pkg/tlc3-examples`. *Generating examples*

- The make process then ran each of these "example files" through LaTeX (also calling BibTeX, biber, or whatever else was needed) as often as was necessary to produce the final form of the typeset output.

    The resulting PDF file was post-processed with `pdfcrop` to drop all white space on the outside (making the PDF pages only as big as the visible output) and, if necessary, to split it into separate pages using `pdfseparate`.

- The next time LaTeX was run on that chapter, each of these PDF output files was automatically placed in its position in the book, next to (or near) the example input. The process was not complete even then because the horizontal positioning of some elements, in particular the examples, depends on whether they are on a verso or recto (the technique from Example A-5-7 on page 692 was used in this case). Thus, at least one or two additional runs were needed before all the cross-references were correctly resolved and LaTeX finally found the right way to place the examples correctly into the margins.

Due to the example-generating complexity — together with the use of varioref altering the generated text based on distance to the referenced object — the book required not the usual two or three but in fact six complete runs before LaTeX stopped asking for "Rerun to get cross-references right". Even on a fast iMac from 2021 with an M1 chip, that meant a half-hour wait — and this is not counting the generation of the 1540 examples. Those required another two-and-a-half hours[1] so that it took a total of three hours of computer-processing time to produce the typeset book from scratch.

The layout effort

That was about as far as automation of the process could take us. Because of the many large examples that could neither be broken nor treated as floating material, getting good page breaks turned out to be a major challenge. For this and other reasons, getting to the final layout of the book was fairly labor intensive and even required minor rewriting (on maybe 10% of the pages) in order to avoid bad line breaks or page breaks (e.g., paragraphs ending with a single-word line or a distracting hyphenation at a page break). Spreads were allowed to run one line long or one line short if necessary, and in several cases the layout and contents of the examples were manually adjusted to allow decent page breaks. *Manual labor from page 1 to 2000*

A great help in this final layout process was the package widows-and-orphans, which told us the pages that contained widows, orphans, or hyphenations across page boundaries. We then applied one of the suggestions from Section 5.6.6 on page →I 422, often adding an explicit page break in some strategic place or sometimes rewriting a *Giving widows and orphans a new home*

---

[1] The main factor here is the file I/O cost. Each example has to be run several times, and each time, TeX has to start and load all packages and fonts, over and over again.

paragraph to make it longer or shorter (after all, we are the authors and can change the text for aesthetic reasons). In a few places, no fix seemed reasonable, in which case we accepted an orphan or widow and marked the place with `\WaOignorenext`. In total, 1.5% of the pages were treated like this.

Some pagination statistics

Here are a few approximate statistics from this page layout process: 24 long spreads, 41 short spreads, 51 compressed pages (using `\enlargethispage*`) combined with forced page breaks. This is noticeably less than in the previous edition and one of the reasons is that this time we made ample use of TEX's `\looseness` functionality: we ran 125 paragraphs one line shorter than normal and 17 paragraphs one line longer than is optimal in TEX's eyes.

We added 501 forced page breaks in total, which means 25% of all pages have a forced premature ending — usually to avoid half-empty pages later due to a larger example showing up in the wrong place. While I think the results are satisfactory, getting this right was rather time consuming and difficult — here it really hurts that TEX has a global paragraph optimizer but generates its pagination with a simple greedy algorithm. While this gives reasonable results with most documents it totally breaks down in those that contain larger unbreakable parts such as this book.[1]

Searching across the final sources, there are about 1200 adjustments to the vertical spacing[2] and 100 other manual adjustments (other than rewriting or altering the examples). For the latter I do not have any reliable data, but from my recollection I would guess that about a quarter (i.e., 400) of the examples have been adjusted to better blend into the page flow.

A final word of advice

In several places in the book we have given the advice to leave any layout work until the very last minute, and on the whole we followed our advice to the letter with this book. For example, all pagination work was delayed until the copy editor had worked through all chapters and marked up all the mistakes we made (well, hopefully all) — it took me a while to convince her not to mark up ugly-looking page breaks, because they were deliberate. Given that changing a single letter in a paragraph may result in total reflow (and possibly a different number of lines) this saved me a lot of unnecessary work.

However, in one case I diverged from that principle. When I started to write this section, I realized that the chosen typewriter font seemed to be a tiny bit too large compared to the Lucida body fonts. I therefore decided to scale it down by one percent. Given that this is only used for individual words, I expected a few changes but not much. To my dismay I ended up with more than fifty pages where the pagination was totally broken, e.g., paragraphs getting shorter or longer, lines overflowing to the next page, etc. It took me a full day to repair the damage. So again, take this advice seriously and only work on pagination adjustments when you are 100% done with the text and all your other layout choices have been made — easier said than done, I know!

---

[1] I had secretly hoped that the research results outlined in [71–73] could already be applied to the production of this book, which would have saved me perhaps a month worth of effort. Unfortunately, turning the prototype into a fully working production system proved to be more complicated than I had bargained for. Thus, in the end I buried the idea and produced the layout the old-fashioned way.

[2] These adjustments are partially due to deficiencies in parameter setup for the custom class. However, by the time I realized this, several chapters had already been paginated and changing the class setup would have invalidated those. Thus, it seemed simpler to live with the imperfection.